T5-CRD-077

DIGITAL TECHNIQUES
in Simulation, Communication and Control

STEERING COMMITTEE

R. VICHNEVETSKY (IMACS President, USA)
P. VAN REMOORTERE (IMACS General Secretary, Belgium)
C. HALKIAS (IEEE-Greece Chairman, Greece)
S. TZAFESTAS (IMACS-Greece Chairman, Greece)
A. VENETSANOPOULOS (CSEE President, Canada)

SCIENTIFIC COMMITTEE

S. TZAFESTAS (Greece)
E. PROTONOTARIOS (Greece)
N. ALEXANDRIDIS (USA)
P. BORNE (France)
V. CAPPELLINI (Italy)
A. CONSTANTINIDES (UK)
T. DELIYANNIS (Greece)
C. GEORGOPOULOS (Greece)
C. HOUPIS (USA)
A. JÁVOR (Hungary)
T. KACZOREK (Poland)
R. KING (Greece)
J. NICOLIS (Greece)
G. PAPADOPOULOS (Greece)
G. SCHMIDT (FRG)
M. SINGH (UK)
A. SYDOW (DDR)
A. TITLI (France)

PLENARY SPEAKERS

M. ATHANS (USA)
A. EPHREMIDES (USA)
G. SARIDIS (USA)

DIGITAL TECHNIQUES

in Simulation, Communication and Control

Proceedings of the IMACS European Meeting on
Digital Techniques in Simulation, Communication and Control
University of Patras, Patras, Greece, July 9–12, 1984

edited by

SPYROS G. TZAFESTAS
Control Systems Laboratory
Department of Electrical Engineering
University of Patras
Patras, Greece

1985

NORTH-HOLLAND
AMSTERDAM · NEW YORK · OXFORD

ISBN: 0 444 87695 2

Published by:
ELSEVIER SCIENCE PUBLISHERS B.V.
P.O. Box 1991
1000 BZ Amsterdam
The Netherlands

Sole distributors for the U.S.A. and Canada:
ELSEVIER SCIENCE PUBLISHING COMPANY, INC.
52 Vanderbilt Avenue
New York, N.Y. 10017
U.S.A.

Library of Congress Cataloging in Publication Data

IMACS European Meeting on Digital Techniques in Simulation, Communication, and Control (1984 : University of Patras)
Digital techniques in simulation, communication, and control.

Includes index.
1. Digital computer simulation--Congresses. 2. Signal processing--Digital techniques--Congresses. 3. Automatic control--Congresses. I. Tzafestas, S. G., 1939-
II. International Association for Mathematics and Computers in Simulation. III. Title.
QA76.9.C65I38 1984 621.38 84-28684
ISBN 0-444-87695-2 (U.S.)

PRINTED IN THE NETHERLANDS

PREFACE

This work represents the proceedings of the 1984 IMACS European Meeting on "Digital Techniques in Simulation, Communication, and Control (DIGITECH '84)" held at Patras University, Greece (July 9-12, 1984). This Meeting belongs to a series of IMACS meetings in European countries with objective the exchange of the latest research and practical developments in the field of "System Simulation" and closely related areas. DIGITECH '84, which took place in parallel with the "First European Workshop on Real-Time Control of Large Scale Systems" has really provided a unique opportunity to our colleagues from seventeen countries for crossfertilizing interactions in the digital system engineering field.

The book involves 90 papers which are classified in the following five parts:

1. Modelling and simulation,
2. Digital signal processing and 2-D system design
3. Information and communication systems,
4. Control systems, and
5. Applications (robotics, industrial and miscellaneous applications).

The volume contains sufficient amount of information which reflects very well the state-of-art of the field of digital techniques.

I am grateful to the members of the scientific committee for their help in selecting the papers, the session chairmen for their assistance in running the meeting, and the authors of the papers for their high-level presentations.

Especially, I would like to thank Professor Robert Vichnevetsky, the President of IMACS, for his coming at the Meeting. His presence, together with the presence of Professor Manfred Thoma, the President of IFAC, who came for the Workshop, gave a special emphasis on the importance of the coupling between the IMACS Meeting and the EEC Workshop. Many thanks are also due to our distinguished colleagues who presented their exciting invited plenary papers.

Finally, a special word of thank should be addressed to the University of Patras for its hospitality and generous support.

In recent years, Greece has become the heart of a conference activity on systems, control and information sciences. It is hoped that this activity will steadily continue for the benefit of the whole Eastern Mediterranean and Middle East regions.

Patras, July 1984 — Spyros G. Tzafestas

CONTENTS

2.3 Image Processing and Restoration

2.4 Signal Processing Applications

3. INFORMATION AND COMMUNICATION SYSTEMS

3.1 Information Systems

5. APPLICATIONS

5.1 Robotics

5.2 Industrial Applications

5.3 Miscellaneous Applications

1. MODELLING AND SIMULATION

DIGITAL TECHNIQUES in Simulation, Communication and Control
Spyros G. Tzafestas (editor)
Elsevier Science Publishers B.V. (North-Holland) © IMACS, 1985

MODEL REDUCTION BY WALSH FUNCTION TECHNIQUES

S. Kawaji and T. Shiotsuki

Department of Electronic Engineering
Kumamoto University
Kumamoto 860, Japan

This paper discusses the application of Walsh functions expansion to reduce the order of a linear time-invariant system. First, model reduction of linear continuous systems by matching the Walsh spectra of output responses of the original and reduced models, subject to the specific inputs, is discussed. Secondly, model reduction under linear constraints on the structure of the reduced model is discussed. The latter has the advantage that the reduced model is stable and/or cause no steady-state error.

1. INTRODUCTION

Because of its importance in systems analysis and in the design of controllers, model reduction methods have received considerable attention over the past two decades [1]. The object of model reduction is to find a lower order model which preserves the dynamics of more complex, higher order system in both time and frequency domains. From this point of view, the model reduction in some aspects can be considered as a data matching process. The reduced order model may be determined by applying an identification procedure to input-output data obtained by driving the original system with a special input.

Recently, the Walsh functions have been used by many workers to analyse a wide range of systems [2]-[4]. The Walsh functions appear to be suited for digital processing of continuous time signals, and Walsh spectra characterisation of signals reduces the calculus of dynamic systems to an algebra in the approximate sense of least squares, through the so-called operational matrices.

In this paper, a new method via the Walsh function techniques is proposed for obtaining a reduced model for high order systems. First, the output data of the original and reduced models with respect to polynomial inputs are transfered into the Walsh spectra. Then by matching the two spectra, the parameters of the reduced model can thus be determined. Secondly, in order to preserve the stability requirement and/or to achieve steady state agreement between the original and reduced models, model reduction under linear constraints on the structure of the reduced model is discussed. Example for illustrative purpose is given with satisfactory result.

2. WALSH FUNCTIONS

The Walsh functions are a set of square waves and the system of Walsh functions is orthonormal and complete [5]. Fig. 1 shows the functions from ϕ_0 to ϕ_7 in the dyadic order.

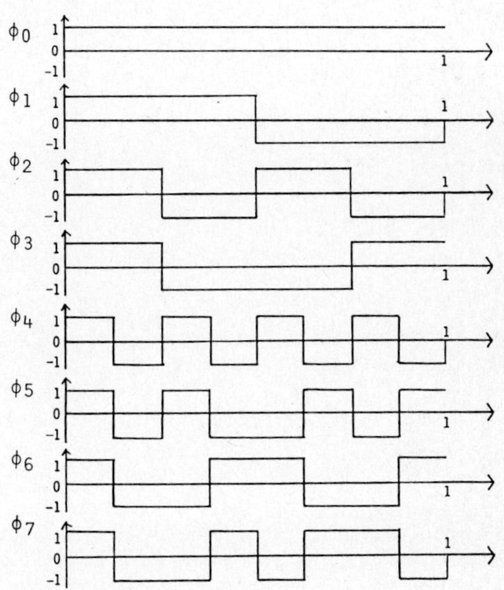

Fig. 1 Walsh functions

It is well known [6] that a square-integrable function f(t) on the interval [0,1) may be approximated in terms of the Walsh functions as

$$f(t) \simeq \sum_{i=0}^{N-1} f_i \phi_i(t) \tag{1}$$

where $N = 2^k$, k an intger. $\phi_i(t)$ is i-th Walsh function defined in [0,1), and f_i the corresponding coefficient. Eqn. (1) can be concisely written as

$$f(t) \simeq F\Phi_N(t) \tag{2}$$

where

$$F = [f_0, f_1, \cdots, f_{N-1}] \tag{3}$$

and

$$\Phi_N(t) = [\ \phi_0(t),\ \phi_1(t),\ \cdots\ ,\ \phi_{N-1}(t)]^T \quad (4)$$

The coefficient f_i are chosen to minimize

$$\varepsilon = \int_0^1 [f(t)-F\Phi_N(t)]^2\, dt \quad (5)$$

and it is uniquely given by

$$f_i = \int_0^1 f(t)\phi_i(t)\, dt \quad (6)$$

$\{f_i\}$ is also referred to as the spectrum of f(t).

The integration of Walsh function vector is related approximately to the Walsh function vector itself. That is,

$$\int_0^t \Phi_N(t)\, dt \simeq P_N\Phi_N(t) \quad (7)$$

where

$$P_N = \begin{bmatrix} P_{\frac{N}{2}} & -\frac{1}{2N} I_{\frac{N}{2}} \\ \frac{1}{2N} I_{\frac{N}{2}} & 0_{\frac{N}{2}} \end{bmatrix} \quad (8)$$

$$P_2 = \begin{bmatrix} \frac{1}{2} & -\frac{1}{4} \\ \frac{1}{4} & 0 \end{bmatrix}$$

is called the Walsh operational matrix for integration.

Repeated application of P_N for the repeated integration implies that

$$\underbrace{\int_0^t\int_0^t \cdots \int_0^t}_{j\text{-times}} \Phi_N(t)\, dt^j \simeq P_N^j\Phi_N(t) \quad (9)$$

Thus the integration is approximately achieved by premultiplying the spectral vector with the operational matrix. The result is of considerable importance to us increasing the calculus of continuous dynamical systems to an approximate (in the sense of least squares) matrix algebra.

3. MODEL REDUCTION

Consider a linear time-invariant continuous system whose transfer function is given by

$$G(s) = \frac{Y(s)}{U(s)} = \frac{b_1 s^{n-1} + b_2 s^{n-2} + \cdots + b_n}{s^n + a_1 s^{n-1} + \cdots + a_n} \quad (10)$$

where Y(s) and U(s) are respectively the Laplace transforms of the input y(t) and the output u(t). Eqn.(10) can also be represented by a differential equation

$$y^{(n)}(t) + a_1 y^{(n-1)}(t) + \cdots + a_n y(t)$$

$$= b_1 u^{(n-1)}(t) + b_2 u^{(n-2)}(t) + \cdots + b_n u(t) \quad (11)$$

with zero initial conditions. Integrating both side of (11) n times, we have

$$y(t) + a_1\int_0^t y(t)dt + \cdots + a_n\int_0^t\int_0^t \cdots \int_0^t y(t)dt^n$$

$$= b_1\int_0^t u(t)dt + \cdots + b_n\int_0^t\int_0^t \cdots \int_0^t u(t)dt^n \quad (12)$$

Both y(t) and u(t) may be approximately expressed respectively by Walsh functions of size N as

$$y(t) \simeq Y\Phi_N(t) \quad (13)$$

$$u(t) \simeq U\Phi_N(t) \quad (14)$$

We now deal with the case of input functions of the form

$$u(t) = \beta_0 + \beta_1 t + \beta_2 t^2 + \cdots + \beta_l t^l \quad (15)$$

where l is some intger. Note that for $l = 0$ we include step function, and for $l = 1$ the ramp function. The Walsh coefficient vector of u(t) in (15) is

$$U = \sum_{i=0}^{l} (i!)\beta_i \underline{e} P_N^i \quad (16)$$

where

$$\underline{e} = [1,\ 0,\ \cdots\ ,\ 0] \quad (17)$$

is the Walsh coefficient vector of the unit-step function and is derived from (6).

Substituting (13), (14) into (12) and application of (7) yields

$$Y[I + a_1 P_N + \cdots + a_n P_N^n]\cdot\Phi_N(t)$$

$$= U[b_1 P_N + b_2 P_N^2 + \cdots + b_n P_N^n]\cdot\Phi_N(t) \quad (18)$$

Since eqn.(18) must be satisfied for any value of t, equating of coefficients of $\Phi_N(t)$ gives

$$Y[I + a_1 P_N + \cdots + a_n P_N^n]$$

$$= U[b_1 P_N + b_2 P_N^2 + \cdots + b_n P_N^n] \quad (19)$$

For given values of a_i and b_i, the Walsh coefficient vector of the output is calculated as

$$Y = U\{\sum_{i=0}^{n} b_i P_N^i\}\{\sum_{i=0}^{n} a_i P_N^i\}^{-1} \quad (20)$$

$$:\ a_0 = 1,\ \ b_0 = 0$$

Assume that the transfer function of the reduced model is of order m with m < n. Then

$$\hat{G}(s) = \frac{\hat{Y}(s)}{U(s)} = \frac{\hat{b}_1 s^{m-1} + \hat{b}_2 s^{m-2} + \cdots + \hat{b}_m}{s^m + \hat{a}_1 s^{m-1} + \cdots + \hat{a}_m} \quad (21)$$

where $\hat{Y}(s)$ is the Laplace transform of output $\hat{y}(t)$ of the reduced model. The coefficient $\hat{a}_i$

and $\hat{b}_i$ are to be determined so that $\hat{G}(s)$ may be an approximate model for $G(s)$.

Letting the Walsh functions expansion of $\hat{y}(t)$ be

$$\hat{y}(t) \simeq \hat{Y}\Phi_N(t) \qquad (22)$$

where

$$\hat{Y} = [\hat{y}_0, \hat{y}_1, \cdots, \hat{y}_{N-1}] \qquad (23)$$

Similar to the case (10), we get

$$\hat{Y}(\sum_{i=0}^{m} \hat{a}_i P_N^i) = U(\sum_{i=0}^{m} \hat{b}_i P_N^i) \qquad (24)$$

$$: \hat{a}_0 = 1, \quad \hat{b}_0 = 0$$

The Walsh spectra matching means that letting $\hat{Y} = Y$ in (24). Thus

$$Y(\sum_{i=0}^{m} \hat{a}_i P_N^i) = U(\sum_{i=0}^{m} \hat{b}_i P_N^i) \qquad (25)$$

Since Y is evaluated from eqn.(20) and U is given, (25) may be used to estimate the parameters of the reduced model. For $N > 2m$, the unknown parameters $\{\hat{a}_i\}$ and $\{\hat{b}_i\}$ can be obtained by the least square estimate.

Let the equation error be

$$e = Y \sum_{i=0}^{m} \hat{a}_i P_N^i - U \sum_{i=0}^{m} \hat{b}_i P_N^i$$

$$= Y - X\Theta \qquad (26)$$

where

$$X = [-YP_N, -YP_N^2, \cdots, -YP_N^m, UP_N, \cdots, UP_N^m] \qquad (27)$$

$$\theta = [\hat{a}_1, \hat{a}_2, \cdots, \hat{a}_m, \hat{b}_1, \cdots, \hat{b}_m]^T \qquad (28)$$

It is desired to obtain the best estimate of the coefficient vector such that the cost function

$$J = e^T We \qquad (29)$$

is minimized, where W is a weighting matrix. The least square estimate of Θ is

$$\hat{\Theta} = (X^T WX)^{-1} WY \qquad (30)$$

Once $\hat{\Theta}$ is obtained, the reduced model of (21) is established.

REMARK : Recall that the Walsh functions are defined on the interval [0,1). Hence, if we evaluate the responses of the original and reduced models on the interval [0, T), we may change the time scaling for normalizing, by letting $\bar{t} = t/T$. Then, the Walsh operational matrix should be

$$\bar{P}_N = T P_N \qquad (31)$$

Further, in order to maintain accuracy, computations have to be made with increased N, the size of Walsh functions.

4. MODEL REDUCTION UNDER LINEAR CONSTRAINTS

The above model reduction method cannot guarantee to obtain a stable reduced model if the original model is stable one, and to cause no steady state response error between the original and reduced models.

For the stability requirement, combined methods may be used. That is, the conventional stable methods such as dominant pole retention, Routh approximation, Hurwitz polynomial approximation, etc. are used to determine the coefficients $\{\hat{a}_i\}$ of the denominator of transfer function of the reduced model. Then, Walsh spectra matching is used to determine the coefficients $\{\hat{b}_i\}$ of the numerator of the reduced model.

Also, the condition that the reduced model does not produce steady state error to step-input is

$$y(\infty) = \hat{y}(\infty) \qquad (32)$$

which implies that

$$b_n/a_n = \hat{b}_m/\hat{a}_m \qquad (33)$$

It follows that under the constraint (33) the Walsh spectra matching must be applied.

These constraints on the structure of the reduced model can be, in general, expressed as

$$R\Theta = \Gamma \qquad (34)$$

Therefore the cost function (29) is to be minimized under the linear constraint (34). Let $R^{\#}$ be any matrix which renders

$$R_* = \begin{bmatrix} R^{\#} \\ R \end{bmatrix}$$

nonsingular, and define as

$$\bar{\Theta} = R^{\#}\Theta \qquad (35)$$

$$XR_*^{-1} = [X_1 \quad X_2] \qquad (36)$$

then, equation error (26) can be rewritten as

$$e = (Y - X_2\Gamma) - X_1\bar{\Theta} \qquad (37)$$

Hence, the least squre estimate of $\bar{\Theta}$ is

$$\hat{\bar{\Theta}} = (X_1 W X_1)^{-1} W(Y - X_2\Gamma) \qquad (38)$$

and $\hat{\Theta}$ is given by

$$\hat{\Theta} = R_*^{-1} \begin{bmatrix} \hat{\bar{\Theta}} \\ \Gamma \end{bmatrix} \qquad (39)$$

Thus the optimal coefficients of the reduced transfer function are completely determined.

5. ILLUSTRATIVE EXAMPLE

To illustrate the method, a model representing the pich rate control system of a supersonic aircraft [8] is considered. This is one of models considered by many workers. The transfer function is given by

$$G(s) = \frac{375000(s+0.08333)}{s^7+83.64s^6+4097s^5+70342s^4+853703s^3+2814271s^2+3310875s+281250} \quad (40)$$

The input is a unit step. Then the output's Walsh coefficient vector can be obtained from eqn.(20), and this is used for the determination of systems of order two or three.

With N = 16, T = 10 sec, and weighting matrix W = I, the following reduced models are obtained.

$$\hat{G}_1(s) = \frac{0.0212s+0.2999}{s^2+2.213s+2.545} \quad (41)$$

$$\hat{G}_2(s) = \frac{-0.0474s^2+0.5887s+0.03592}{s^3+3.988s^2+5.107s+0.3302} \quad (42)$$

In Fig. 2, a comparison is made between the step responses of the original and reduced models. As can be seen from the figure, the response of $\hat{G}_2(s)$ is a good approximation to reponse of the original system over the interval [0, 10) that was considered in the derivation of $\hat{G}_2(s)$. Since true response does not reach steady state in 10 sec, some steady state error has to be expected, and amounts to 2.1%.

In the next place, the poles and zero of the original system are

zero : -0.08333

poles : -0.09193, -2.02439 ± 0.96465, -7.67437 ± 13.4461, -32.0752 ± 38.849

For the application of the second method, let the denominator polynomial of the reduced model be

$$s^2+4.04879s+5.02873$$

by retaining only the dominant complex pair. Using Walsh spectra matching to determine the coefficients of the numerator, for N = 16, T = 10, gives

$$\hat{G}_3(s) = \frac{-0.02874s+0.59797}{s^2+4.04879s+5.02873} \quad (43)$$

The comparison of the unit step responses of the original and reduced models are shown in Fig.3. The reduced systems show slight deterioration in the steady state responses, but this is overcome by applying spectra matching under constraint (33).

It is noted that the results could be improved by increasing the size of the Walsh spectra and/ or the time interval. Also only step response matching was examined, similar analysis could be used to match responses to other kinds of input.

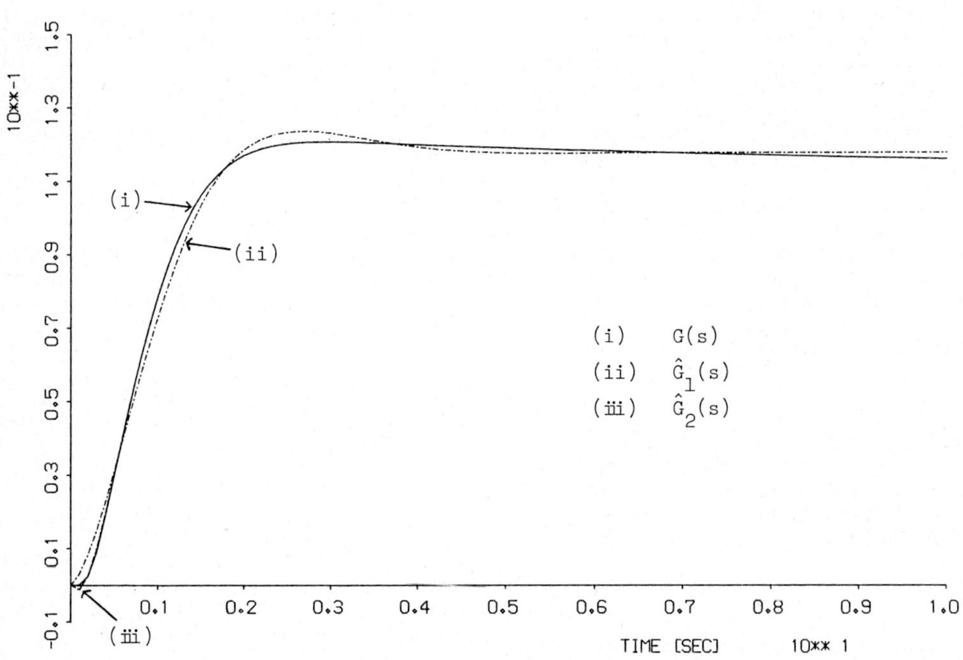

Fig.2 Step responses of the original and reduced models

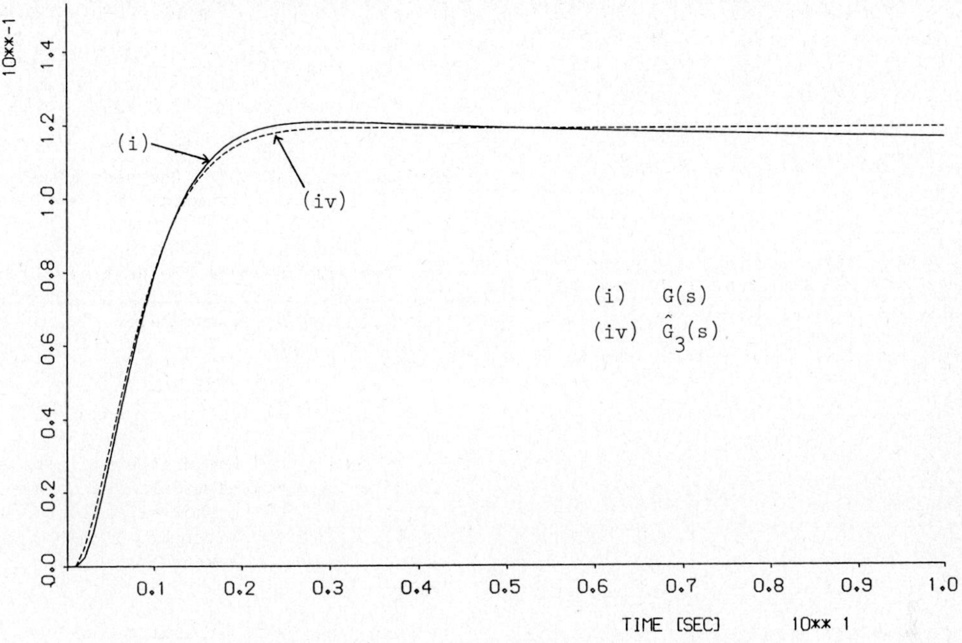

Fig.3 Step responses of the original and reduced models

6. CONCLUSION

Since information can be well kept under the Walsh transformation, the new method of using Walsh spectra matching can reserve the time-domain characteristics of the original systems satisfactory, and can be easily programmed on a digital computer. Further, by using reduction method under linear constraints, the reduced model is stable provided the original model is stable, and does not cause steady-state response error.

Other basis functions, particularly the block-pulse functions can be also used. There is no difference in the philosophy, and the format of the algorithm is the same as Walsh functions except the operational matrix for integration. Finally, it should be mentioned that the basic idea can be applied to discrete systems.

ACKNOWLEDGEMENT

The authors would like to acknowledge the continuing guidance of Prof. K. Furuta of Tokyo Institute of Technology.

REFERENCES

[1] for example,
Genesio, R, and Milanese, M., A note on the derivation and use of reduced-order models, IEEE Trans. on Autom. Contr., 21 (1976) 118-122

[2] Chen, C.F. and Hsiao, C.H., Walsh series analysis in optimal control, Int. J. Control, 21 (1975) 881-897

[3] Tzafestas, S., Walsh series approach to lumped and distributed system identification, J. of Franklin Inst., 305 (1978) 199-220

[4] Kawaji, S., Walsh series analysis in optimal control systems incorporating observers, Int. J. Control, 37 (1983) 455-462

[5] Harmuth, H.F., Transmission of Information by Orthogonal Functions (Springer, Berlin, 1971)

[6] Rao, G.P., Piecewise Constant Orthogonal Functions and Their Application to Systems and Control (Springer, Berlin, 1983)

[7] Bistritz, Y. and Langholz, G., Model reduction by Chebyshev Polynomial Techniques, IEEE Trans. on Autom. Contr., 24 (1979) 741-747

[8] Sinha, N.K. and Bereznai, G.T., Optimum approximation of higher order systems by low order models, Int. J. Control, 14 (1971) 951-959

[9] Marshall, S.A., The design og reduced-order systems, Int. J. Control, 31 (1980) 677-690

DIGITAL TECHNIQUES in Simulation, Communication and Control
Spyros G. Tzafestas (editor)
Elsevier Science Publishers B.V. (North-Holland) © IMACS, 1985

Conversion Problems of Linear Discrete-Time Systems into Linear Continuous-Time Systems

Tsutomu Mita* and Hiroshi Kaizu**

* Department of Electrical Engineering, Chiba University, Chiba, Japan
** Department of Electrical Engineering, Tokyo Metroplitan Technical College Tokyo, Japan

When the dynamics of the plant is unknown we must use the identification method to derive the structure and parameters of the plant. This identification is usually performed in the discrete time domain while the design and the analysis of control systems are frequently performed in the continuous time domain. So we sometimes want to derive the continuous time representation of the plant from its discrete time representation. This paper treats this conversion algorithm and shows the sampling theorem for the linear time-invariant finite-dimensional systems.

1. INTRODUCTION

Recently, since microprocessors are easily obtained, the modern control theory can be applied to many practical control problems.

However, when the dynamics of the plant is unknown, we must use the identification method to derive the structure and the parameters of the plant. This identification is usually performed under an assumption that the plant can be described by linear discrete-time system. While the design and the analysis of the control system are frequently performed in continuous-time systems. Therefore, we sometimes want to convert the identified discrete-time model into the continuous-time system.

In this paper, we treat such problems in detail. That is; (i) a practical conversion algorithm,and (ii) the necessary and sufficient condition under which the conversion is unique, are derived for general multi-input/output systems. The condition obtained in (ii) corresponds to a special case of well known sampling theorem.

2. A-PRIORI-INFORMATION (I)

We assume the continuous-time system which must be realized from sampled data can be described by linear time-invariant system

$$\dot{x}[t]=Ax[t]+Bu[t] \quad :A(n\times n),\ B(n\times m) \quad (1a)$$

$$y[t]=Cx[t] \quad :C(\ell\times n) \quad (1b)$$

thoughout this paper. Further we assume that we have the following conditions as a-priori-informations

A1) (A,B) is controllable, (C,A) is observable

A2) The eigenvalues r_i of A are contained strictly in the primary strip, that is

$$-\pi/T < \mathrm{Im}(r_i) < \pi/T \quad (\forall i) \quad (2)$$

where T is the sampling period.

Then we have the following conditions which are required in the sequel.

B1) Define z_i as the eigenvalue of exp[AT], then since $\det(\exp[AT])\neq 0$ ($\forall$ T), we have

$$z_i\neq 0 \quad (\forall i) \quad (3)$$

B2) Since $z_i=\exp[r_iT]$ we have the relation

$$r_i\neq r_j \quad \text{iff} \quad z_i\neq z_j$$

from A2).

B3) From A1) and A2) we have [1]

B3-1) (A,B) is controllable $\rightleftarrows$ (exp[AT], B) is controllable $\rightleftarrows$ (exp[AT], Q) is controllable, where

$$Q=\int_0^T \exp[At]dt.B \quad (5)$$

B3-2) (C,A) is observable $\rightleftarrows$ (C, exp[AT]) is observable

3. CONVERSION ALGORITHM OF DISCRETE-TIME SIGNAL

In this chapter, we realize (1) from the sampled data of the signal generated by (1).

The impulsive response matrix of (1) is written by

$$y[t]=C.\exp[At].B \quad (t\geq 0) \quad (6)$$

and its sampled data is $y(i)=C.\exp[AiT].B$ ($i\geq 0$). Then the z transform of the sequence y(i) (i=0, 1,2,...) becomes [2]

$$Y(z)=zC(zI-\exp[AT])^{-1}B \quad (7)$$

The problem is to derive the minimal realization (1) that satisfies (7) under the condition that Y(z) and T are known. For this, the following Lemma plays important roles.

<u>Lemma 1</u>. <u>(i)</u> Define $J_i(r_i)$ as the Jordan block matrix having eigenvalue r_i and N_i as the nilpotent matrix of the same size. Further define

$$A=\mathrm{diag}[J_1(r_1),..,J_p(r_p)] \quad (8)$$

where r_i's are not required to be distinct.

Then

$$\begin{aligned}\exp[AT] &=\mathrm{diag}(\exp[J_1(r_1)T],..,\exp[J_p(r_p)T]) \\ &=\mathrm{diag}(\exp[r_1T]\exp[N_1T],.., \exp[r_pT]\exp[N_pT])\end{aligned} \quad (9)$$

holds and the number of the Jordan blocks of A is the same as that of exp[AT] provided $T\neq 0$.

<u>(ii)</u> When $T\neq 0$, $\exp[N_iT]$ is a non-derogatory matrix and there is an upper triangular matrix U_i that satisfies

$$U_i^{-1} \exp[N_iT]U_i= I +N_i \quad (10)$$

(iii) There is a non-singular matrix

$$W_i = \text{diag}(z_i^k, z_i^{k-1}, \ldots, z_i) \quad (11)$$

that satisfies

$$W_i J_i(z_i) W_i^{-1} = z_i(I + N_i) \quad (12)$$

where J_i is k by k Jordan matrix and $z_i \neq 0$ is assumed.

(Proof) (i) The first statement is obvious from $r_i I$ and N_i are commute. The second statement depends on (ii). (ii) Define $N_i(k \times k)$, then $\text{rank}(\exp[N_i T]-I)=k-1$ provided $T \neq 0$ which proves $\exp[N_i T]$ is a non-derogatory matrix having eigenvalue 1. From $Xv_1=0$, $Xv_2=v_1$, ..., $Xv_k=v_{k-1}$ where $X=\exp[N_i T]$, we obtain an upper triangular matrix $U_i=(v_1, v_2, \ldots, v_k)$ which satisfies (10). (iii) Direct calculation should prove (iii).

Q.E.D.

Now, we can show the conversion algorithm. For the first step, we realize $Y(z)/z$ by the minimal realization method [3] as

$$x(i+1)=\bar{A}x(i)+\bar{B}u(i) \quad :\bar{A}(n \times n),\ \bar{B}(n \times m) \quad (13a)$$

$$y(i)=\bar{C}x(i) \quad :\bar{C}(\ell \times n) \quad (13b)$$

where $\bar{A}$ is assumed to be chosen as a Jordan block matrix. Then $Y(z)/z$ satisfies

$$Y(z)/z=\bar{C}(zI-\bar{A})^{-1}\bar{B}$$

$$=\bar{C}(zI-\text{diag}[J_1(z_1),\ldots,J_p(z_p)])^{-1}\bar{B} \quad (14)$$

where p is the number of the Jordan blocks of $\bar{A}$. Dividing $Y(z)$ by z is always possible since $Y(z)$ has the form (7) and no poles of $\bar{A}=\exp[AT]$ are zero provided $Y(z)$ is assumed to be the sampled data of the output signal of (1).

Next we make $W_i(i=1 \sim p)$ according to (11) and form

$$W=\text{diag}(W_1, W_2, \ldots, W_p) \quad (15)$$

If W is introduced to (14) as a coordinate transformation matrix, (14) becomes

$$Y(z)/z=\bar{C}W^{-1}(zI-\text{diag}[z_1(I+N_1),\ldots,z_p(I+N_p)])^{-1}W\bar{B} \quad (16)$$

On the other hand, $Y(z)/z$ equals to $C(zI-\exp[AT])^{-1}B$. Further, we know that the degrees (MacMillan degree) of (1) and (13) are the same from the condition B3), and that the number and the orders of Jordan blocks of A and $\bar{A}$ (=exp[AT]) are the same from (i) of Lemma 1. Therefore we can choose A as the form

$$A=\text{diag}[J_1(r_1),\ldots, J_p(r_p)] \quad (17)$$

where r_i's are not determined yet.

Then make U_i $(i=1 \sim p)$ and form

$$U=\text{diag}(U_1, U_2, \ldots, U_p) \quad (18)$$

This is always possible since U_i depends on T and the order of $J_i(z_i)$ rather than r_i. If U is used for the coordinate transformation matrix of $C(zI-\exp[AT])^{-1}B$, then it becomes

$$C(zI-\text{diag}[\exp[J_1(r_1)T],\ldots,\exp[J_p(r_p)T]])^{-1}B$$

$$=C(zI-\text{diag}[\exp[r_1T]\exp[N_1T],\ldots,\exp[r_pT]\exp[N_pT]])^{-1}B$$

$$=CU(zI-\text{diag}[\exp[r_1T][I+N_1],\ldots,\exp[r_pT][I+N_p]])^{-1}U^{-1}B \quad (19)$$

Since (16) must coincide with (19), we have the following relations.

$$\bar{C}W^{-1}=CU, \quad W\bar{B}=U^{-1}B, \quad z_i=\exp[r_iT] \quad (20)$$

Here we write z_i in (16) as

$$z_i=\exp[g_i+jh_i] \quad (-\pi < h_i < \pi) \quad (21)$$

using polar coordinate. Then, from (20), we have

$$C=\bar{C}W^{-1}U^{-1}, \quad B=UW\bar{B} \quad (22a)$$

$$r_i=(g_i+jh_i)/T \quad (i=1 \sim p) \quad (22b)$$

If obtained A, B and C are complex, then another coordinate transformation makes them real.

As a special case, if $Y(z)/z$ has no repeated poles, then p becomes n and $Y(z)/z$ can be written by

$$Y(z)/z=\bar{C}[zI-\text{diag}(z_1,\ldots, z_n)]^{-1}\bar{B} \quad (23)$$

and A, B and C are given by

$$A=\text{diag}(r_1,\ldots, r_n) : r_i=(g_i+jh_i)/T \quad (24a)$$

$$C=\bar{C}, \quad B=\bar{B} \quad (24b)$$

Example 1. Assume T=1 [sec] and

$$Y(z)/z=\begin{bmatrix} 1/z-e^{-1}, & e^{-1}/2(z-e^{-1})^2+e^{-2}/(z-e^{-1})^3 \\ 0 & , e^{-1}/(z-e^{-1})^2 \end{bmatrix}$$

We consider the problem on deriving (1) from $Y(z)/z$ and T under the assumptions A1) and A2).

If $Y(z)/z$ is realized by minimal realization method and an appropriate coordinate transformation is applied so that the transfer matrix becomes the Jordan form, then $\bar{A}$, $\bar{B}$ and $\bar{C}$ become

$$\bar{A}=\begin{bmatrix} e^{-1} & 1 & 0 \\ 0 & e^{-1} & 1 \\ 0 & 0 & e^{-1} \end{bmatrix}, \bar{B}=\begin{bmatrix} 1 & 0 \\ 0 & -1/2e \\ 0 & 1/e^2 \end{bmatrix}, \bar{C}=\begin{bmatrix} 1 & e & e^2/2 \\ 0 & e & e^2/2 \end{bmatrix}$$

Since p=1, n=3 and $z_1=e^{-1}$, (15) becomes

$$W=W_1=\text{diag}(e^{-3}, e^{-2}, e^{-1})$$

Further, since T=1, we have

$$\exp[N_1T]=\begin{bmatrix} 1 & 1 & 1/2 \\ 0 & 1 & 1 \\ 0 & 1 & 1 \end{bmatrix}$$

and

$$U=U_1=\begin{bmatrix} 1 & 1 & 1/2 \\ 0 & 1 & 1/2 \\ 0 & 0 & 1 \end{bmatrix}, \quad U^{-1}=\begin{bmatrix} 1 & -1 & 0 \\ 0 & 1 & -1/2 \\ 0 & 0 & 1 \end{bmatrix}$$

Therefore, from (22), we have $r_1=-1$ and

$$A=\begin{bmatrix} -1 & 1 & 0 \\ 0 & -1 & 1 \\ 0 & 0 & -1 \end{bmatrix}, B=\begin{bmatrix} e^{-3} & 0 \\ 0 & 0 \\ 0 & e^{-3} \end{bmatrix}, C=\begin{bmatrix} e^3 & 0 & 0 \\ 0 & e^3 & 0 \end{bmatrix}$$

If we apply another coordinate transformation to A, B and C, we have another representations

$$A=\begin{bmatrix}-1 & 1 & 0\\ 0 & -1 & 1\\ 0 & 0 & -1\end{bmatrix},\ B=\begin{bmatrix}1 & 0\\ 0 & 0\\ 0 & 1\end{bmatrix},\ C=\begin{bmatrix}1 & 0 & 0\\ 0 & 1 & 0\end{bmatrix}$$

4. CONVERSION OF THE PULSE TRANSFER FUNCTION MATRIX

In this chapter, we consider that (1) is the plant and the input u[t] is generated by the output of the zero th holder such that u[t]=u(i) ($iT \le t < (i+1)T$), then the pulse transfer function matrix between u(i) and y(i)=y[iT] becomes

$$G(z)=C(zI-\exp[AT])^{-1}Q \qquad (25)$$

where Q is shown in (5). We treat the problem finding the minimal realization (1) that satisfies (25) under the assumptions that we know G(z), T and a-prioi-informations A1), A2).

Firstly we realize G(z) by (13) or the right hand side of (14). Then, from (17) and (22), we obtain

$$A=\mathrm{diag}[J_1(r_1),..,J_p(r_p)] \ :r_i=(g_i+jh_i)/T \qquad (26a)$$

$$C=\bar{C}W^{-1}U^{-1} \quad ,\ Q=UW\bar{B} \qquad (26b)$$

A new problem is deriving B from Q. As the following, this is always possible which means the problem deriving (1) from Y(z) is equivalent to the problem deriving (1) from G(z).

When we derive B from Q, we must apply either the following CASE 1 or CASE 2 depending on the eigenvalues of $\bar{A}$.

<u>CASE 1</u>. [$z_i \neq 1$ ($\forall i$), i.e., $r_i \neq 0$ ($\forall i$)]:

Since expansion of exp[AT] yields

$$AQ=(AT+A^2T^2/2!\ +A^3T^3/3!+...)B \qquad (27a)$$

$$\exp[AT]B=(I+AT+A^2T^2/2!+A^3T^3/3!+..)B \qquad (27b)$$

we have

$$(\exp[AT]-I)B=AQ \qquad (28)$$

Since $\det(\exp[AT]-I)\neq 0$ iff $r_i \neq 0$ ($\forall$ i), we have

$$B=(\exp[AT]-I)^{-1}AQ \qquad (29a)$$

in this case, where

$$A=\mathrm{diag}[J_1(r_1),..,\ J_p(r_p)] \ :\ r_i=(g_i+jh_i)/T \qquad (29b)$$

$$\exp[AT]=U.\mathrm{diag}[z_1(I+N_1),..,\ z_p(I+N_p)]U^{-1} \qquad (29c)$$

<u>CASE 2.</u> [$z_1=1$, $z_i\neq 1$ ($\forall i\neq 1$), i.e., $r_1=0$, $r_i\neq 0$ ($\forall i\neq 1$)]:

Since all blocks are treated independently, we assume only z_1 is 1, i.e., $r_1=0$, for the sake of simplicity.

Then Q in (5) can be described by

$$Q=\begin{bmatrix}Q_1\\ \hline Q^*\end{bmatrix}$$

$$=\int_0^T \mathrm{diag}(\exp[J_1(0)t],..,\exp[J_p(r_p)t])dt.B$$

$$=\begin{bmatrix}\int_0^T \exp[N_1t]dt.B_1\\ \hline \int_0^T \mathrm{diag}(\exp[J_2(r_2)t],..,\exp[J_p(r_p)t])dt.B^*\end{bmatrix} \qquad (30a)$$

In this expression, B_1 and B* are defined as

$$B=\begin{bmatrix}B_1\\ \hline B^*\end{bmatrix}\begin{matrix}k\\ n-k\end{matrix} \qquad (30b)$$

where k is the order of $J_1(0)$.

Firstly, since $z_i\neq 1$ ($i=2\sim p$), the same treatment as CASE 1 yields

$$B^*=(\exp[A^*T]-I)^{-1}A^*Q^* \qquad (31a)$$

where

$$A^*=\mathrm{diag}[J_2(r_2),...,J_p(r_p)] \ :r_i=(g_i+jh_i)/T \qquad (31b)$$

$$\exp[A^*T]=U^*.\mathrm{diag}[z_2(I+N_2),..,\ z_p(I+N_p)]U^{*-1} \qquad (31c)$$

$$U^*=\mathrm{diag}(U_2,...,\ U_p) \qquad (31d)$$

Secondly, we have

$$M_1=\int_0^T \exp[N_1t]dt=\begin{bmatrix}T & T^2/2! & \cdots & T^k/k!\\ 0 & \ddots & T & \vdots\\ \vdots & & \ddots & T^2/2!\\ 0 & \cdots & 0 & T\end{bmatrix} \qquad (32a)$$

by direct integration. Therefore from (30a), B_1 is determined by the form

$$B_1=M_1^{-1}Q_1 \qquad (32b)$$

provided $T\neq 0$.

In the special case where no repeated poles exist, A, B and C are given by the following.

<u>CASE 1'</u>

$$A=\mathrm{diag}[r_1,...,r_n] \ :\ r_i=(g_i+jh_i)/T \qquad (33a)$$

$$C=\bar{C}\ ,\ B=(\bar{A}-I)^{-1}A\bar{B} \qquad (33b)$$

where

$$\bar{A}=\mathrm{diag}[z_1,...,\ z_n] \qquad (33c)$$

<u>CASE 2'</u>

$$A=\mathrm{diag}[0,r_2,...,r_n] \ :r_i=(g_i+jh_i)/T \qquad (34a)$$

$$C=\bar{C} \qquad (34b)$$

$$B=\begin{bmatrix}\bar{b}_1/T\\ \hline (\bar{A}^*-I)^{-1}A^*\bar{B}^*\end{bmatrix} \qquad (34c)$$

where

$$\bar{A}^*=\mathrm{diag}[z_2,..,\ z_n],A^*=\mathrm{diag}[r_2,..,\ r_p] \qquad (34d)$$

$$\bar{B}=\begin{bmatrix}\bar{b}_1\\ \hline \bar{B}^*\end{bmatrix}\begin{matrix}1\\ n-1\end{matrix} \qquad (34e)$$

<u>Example 2</u>. Assume that we obtain

$$G(z)=\begin{bmatrix}1/z-1, & 1/(z-1)(z-0.5)\\ 0 & ,\ 1/z-0.5\end{bmatrix}$$

from the identification method in which the sampling time is chosen as T=1 [sec]. The problem is deriving A, B and C under the assumptions A1), A2).

Firstly, we derive the minimal realization (13) of G(z), then it is given by

$$\bar{C}=\begin{bmatrix}1 & -2\\ 0 & 1\end{bmatrix},\ \bar{A}=\begin{bmatrix}1 & 0\\ 0 & 0.5\end{bmatrix},\ \bar{B}=\begin{bmatrix}1 & 2\\ 0 & 1\end{bmatrix}$$

Since $z_1=1$, $z_2=0.5$, one of the eigenvalues of $\bar{A}$ is located at 1 but they are distinct. Therefore we can use the algorithm described in (34). Then, A and C become

$$A=\begin{bmatrix}0 & 0\\ 0 & -\log 2\end{bmatrix},\ C=\begin{bmatrix}1 & -2\\ 0 & 1\end{bmatrix}$$

and $\bar{A}^*$, A*, $\bar{B}$ in (34d)-(34e) can be expressed by

$$\bar{A}^*=0.5\ ,\ A^*=-\log 2$$

$$\bar{B}=\begin{bmatrix}\bar{b}_1\\ \bar{B}^*\end{bmatrix}=\begin{bmatrix}1 & 2\\ 0 & 1\end{bmatrix}$$

Therefore B becomes

$$B=\begin{bmatrix}1 & 2\\ 0 & 2\log 2\end{bmatrix}$$

from (34c).

5. A-PRIORI-INFORMATION (II) AND RECOVERING THE DEGREE OF THE DEGENERATED SYSTEMS

In the sequel, we consider the role of a-priori-information A2). If there exists no informations like this, it is impossible to determine r_i uniquely from z_i since infinite number of poles r_i outside the primary strip produce the same $z_i=\exp[r_iT]$. Therefore r_i's must be located in the primary strip at least to assure uniqueness of the conversion. That is;

$$\text{A2')}\quad -\pi/T \leq \mathrm{Im}(r_i) \leq \pi/T \quad (\forall i) \tag{35}$$

which is somewhat different from A2). The difference is admitting the case where r_i's are on the boundary of the primary strip (BPS) such that $\mathrm{Im}(r_i)=\pm\pi/T$.

If such a case is admitted, z_i may appear as negative real pole of $Y(z)/z$ [$G(z)$]. Further, in spite of A1) and A2'), B3) may not hold, that is, the degree of (14) may be reduced from (1). But the occurrence of such reduction depends on the relative structure of A, B and C rather than the eigenvalues of A.

For example, we consider the case where A has repeated eigenvalues on the BPS such that

$$A=\left[\begin{array}{cc|cc} j\pi/T & 1 & & \\ 0 & j\pi/T & & 0 \\ \hline & & -j\pi/T & 1 \\ & 0 & 0 & -j\pi/T \end{array}\right] \tag{36}$$

then $\exp[AT]$ becomes

$$\exp[AT]=\left[\begin{array}{cc|cc} -1 & -T & & \\ 0 & -1 & & 0 \\ \hline & & -1 & -T \\ & 0 & 0 & -1 \end{array}\right] \tag{37}$$

and it has negative real eigenvalues of multiplicity 4. For this A, if B is given by

$$B=\begin{bmatrix}0 & 0\\ 1 & j\\ 0 & 0\\ 1 & -j\end{bmatrix} \tag{38}$$

then $(\exp[AT], B)$ is controllable. If C is given by

$$C=\begin{bmatrix} j & 0 & -j & 0\\ 1 & 0 & 1 & 0\end{bmatrix} \tag{39}$$

then $(C, \exp[AT])$ is observable [A, B and C can be described by real numbers if an appropriatre coordinate transformation is applied]. Therefore, the discrete -time system $(\exp[AT], B, C)$ is minimal and MacMillan degree of $Y(z)/z$ is 4.

However, when C is given by

$$C=\begin{bmatrix} 1 & 0 & 1 & 0\\ 1 & 0 & 1 & 0\end{bmatrix} \tag{40}$$

then $(C, \exp[AT])$ is not observable even though (C, A) is observable. This means the system $(\exp[AT], B, C)$ is not minimal and the MacMillan degree of $Y(z)/z$ is reduced to 2. This is because B3) does not hold in spite of A1), A2').

Even though, we can identify that $Y(z)/z$ is degenerated or not only if the eigenvalues on BPS are not repeated. Further, we can recover the degree in this case. The reason is that if r_i on BPS is not repeated, $z_i=\exp[r_iT]$ and $z_{i+1}=\exp[\bar{r}_iT]$ become the repeated poles of $Y(z)/z$ having simple eigen-structure.

To show these, we analyze the degenerated case. For the sake of simplicity, we assume that the poles which are located in the primary strip are also distinct and that only r_1 and $r_2=\bar{r}_1$ are on the BPS.

By this assumption, A, B and C can be written by

$$A=\mathrm{diag}(d+j\pi/T, d-j\pi/T, r_3, \ldots, r_n) \tag{41a}$$

$$C=(c_1, \bar{c}_1, c_3, \ldots, c_n)\ : c_i(\ell\times 1) \tag{41b}$$

$$B=\begin{bmatrix} b_1\\ \bar{b}_1\\ b_3\\ \vdots\\ b_n\end{bmatrix}\quad : b_i(1\times m) \tag{41c}$$

where $r_1=d+j\pi/T$ and $r_2=d-j\pi/T$. Then $\exp[AT]$ becomes

$$\exp[AT]=\mathrm{diag}(-\exp[dT], -\exp[dT], \exp[r_3T], \ldots\ldots, \exp[r_nT]) \tag{42}$$

where $-\exp[dT]$ is the negative real pole of $Y(z)/z$. And $Y(z)/z$ becomes

$$\frac{Y(z)}{z}=\frac{c_1b_1+\bar{c}_1\bar{b}_1}{z+\exp[dT]}+\frac{c_3b_3}{z-\exp[r_3T]}+\ldots+\frac{c_nb_n}{z-\exp[r_nT]} \tag{43}$$

We can identify that the degeneracy occurs or does not occur from the rank of $K_1=c_1b_1+\bar{c}_1\bar{b}_1$. That is, if $\mathrm{rank}(K_1)=2$, the degeneracy does not occur, and, if $\mathrm{rank}(K_1)=1$, the degeneracy occurs and the degree of the reduction is 1 [in SISO system, the degeneracy always occurs since $\mathrm{rank}(K_1)=1$].

From this preliminary considerations, we can derive the minimal realization (1) together with recovering the degree. The algorithm is the following.

We define $-a$ as the negative real poles of $Y(z)/z$ and expand $Y(z)/z$ by partial fractions as

$$\frac{Y(z)}{z}=\frac{K_1}{z+a}+\frac{K_3}{z-z_3}+\ldots+\frac{K_n}{z-z_n} \tag{44}$$

Since, we assume z_i $(i=3\sim n)$ are not repeated, $\mathrm{rank}(K_i)=1$ $(i=3\sim n)$ and K_i can be written by

$$K_i = c_i b_i \quad : c_i(\ell \times n),\ b_i(n \times m),\ i=3 \sim n \qquad (45)$$

We must treat the following two cases independently according to rank(K_1).

<u>CASE A</u> [rank(K_1)=2]:

In this case, the degeneracy does not occur, and we can choose two non-singular matrices $S(\ell \times \ell)$ and $E(m \times m)$ such that

$$SK_1E = \begin{bmatrix} I_2 & 0 \\ 0 & 0 \end{bmatrix} = \begin{bmatrix} 1 \\ -j \\ 0 \end{bmatrix} \cdot [1/2, j/2, 0] + \begin{bmatrix} 1 \\ j \\ 0 \end{bmatrix} \cdot [1/2, -j/2, 0] \qquad (46)$$

Then form the vectors c_1 and b_1 such as

$$c_1 = S^{-1} \begin{bmatrix} 1 \\ -j \\ 0 \end{bmatrix}, \quad b_1 = [1/2,\ j/2,\ 0]E^{-1} \qquad (47)$$

and determine A, B and C as

$$A = \mathrm{diag}[d + j\pi/T,\ d - j\pi/T,\ r_3, \ldots, r_n] \qquad (48a)$$

$$C = [c_1, \bar{c}_1, c_3, \ldots, c_n] \qquad (48b)$$

$$B = \begin{bmatrix} b_1 \\ \bar{b}_1 \\ b_3 \\ \vdots \\ b_n \end{bmatrix} \qquad (48c)$$

where $d = (1/T)\log a$ and $r_i = (g_i + jh_i)/T$.

<u>CASE B</u> [rank(K_1)=1]:

In this case, the degeneracy occurs, and conjugate 2 nd order mode of the continuous-time system becomes simple real negative mode of the discrete-time system. Since we have a-priori-informations A1), A2') and no repeated poles is located on the BPS, the order of the degeneracy is identified to be 1. Therefore, we can recover the order by the following method.

Choose non-singular matrices $S(\ell \times \ell)$ and $E(m \times m)$ such that

$$SK_1E = \begin{bmatrix} 1 & 0 \\ 0 & 0 \end{bmatrix} = \begin{bmatrix} 1 \\ 0 \end{bmatrix} \cdot [1/2,\ 0] + \begin{bmatrix} 1 \\ 0 \end{bmatrix} \cdot [1/2,\ 0] \qquad (49)$$

and form

$$c_1 = S^{-1} \begin{bmatrix} 1 \\ 0 \end{bmatrix}, \quad b_1 = [1/2,\ 0]E^{-1} \qquad (50)$$

Then the required A, B and C are given by (48).

The same procedure together with the method stated in Chapter 4 yields the conversion algorithm of the pulse transfer function matrix G(z). In this case, we define (48c) as Q.

<u>Example 3.</u> Assume we obtain T=1 [sec] and

$$Y(z)/z = \begin{bmatrix} 1/z+1, & 1/(z+1)(z-0.5) \\ 1/z+1, & -2/3(z+1) \end{bmatrix}$$

Here we expand Y(z)/z by partial fractions such as

$$\frac{Y(z)}{z} = \frac{\begin{bmatrix} 1 & -2/3 \\ 1 & -2/3 \end{bmatrix}}{z+1} + \frac{\begin{bmatrix} 0 & 2/3 \\ 0 & 0 \end{bmatrix}}{z-0.5}$$

Therefore, we have a negative real pole -1 with residue matrix of rank 1. This means that the degeneracy occurs and the procedure stated in CASE B will recover the order and derive the nimimal realization (1) as the following.

Reform K_3 as

$$K_3 = \begin{bmatrix} 1 \\ 0 \end{bmatrix} [0,\ 2/3] = c_3 b_3$$

and K_1 as

$$SK_1E = \begin{bmatrix} 1 & 0 \\ -1 & 1 \end{bmatrix} \begin{bmatrix} 1 & -2/3 \\ 1 & -2/3 \end{bmatrix} \begin{bmatrix} 1 & 2/3 \\ 0 & 1 \end{bmatrix} = \begin{bmatrix} 1 & 0 \\ 0 & 0 \end{bmatrix}$$

Then (50) yields

$$c_1 = S^{-1} \begin{bmatrix} 1 \\ 0 \end{bmatrix} = \begin{bmatrix} 1 \\ 1 \end{bmatrix}, \quad b_1 = [1/2,\ 0]E^{-1} = [1/2,\ -1/3]$$

Since a=1=exp[0] and 0.5=exp[-log2], d_1=0 and r_3=-log2. Then, from (48), we have

$$A = \mathrm{diag}[j\pi,\ -j\pi, -\log 2]$$

$$C = \begin{bmatrix} 1 & 1 & 1 \\ 1 & 1 & 0 \end{bmatrix}$$

$$B = \begin{bmatrix} 1/2 & -1/3 \\ 1/2 & -1/3 \\ 0 & 2/3 \end{bmatrix}$$

If some coordinate transformation is applied, another expressions of A, B and C

$$A = \begin{bmatrix} 0 & \pi & 0 \\ -\pi & 0 & 0 \\ 0 & 0 & -\log 2 \end{bmatrix}, \quad B = \begin{bmatrix} 1/2 & -1/3 \\ 0 & 0 \\ 0 & 2/3 \end{bmatrix}$$

$$C = \begin{bmatrix} 2 & 0 & 1 \\ 2 & 0 & 0 \end{bmatrix}$$

are obtained.

6. SAMPLING THEOREM FOR TIME-INVARIANT FINITE DIMENSIONAL LINEAR SYSTEM

We can conclude the contents by the following theorem.

<u>Theorem 1.</u> If and only if the eigenvalues of A satisfy

$$-\pi/T \le \mathrm{Im}(r_i) \le \pi/T \quad (\forall i) \qquad (51)$$

and all r_i's on the BPS are distinct, we can derive (1) uniquely from Y(z) or G(z).

This is the sampling theorem for the linear time-invariant finite-dimensional systems which is much milder than well known sampling theorem saying that the continuous-time signal can be reconstructed from Y[iT] iff the spectrum Y[w] is within the band $-\pi/T \le w \le \pi/T$ where $Y[w] = \mathcal{F}(y[t])$ and π/T is the Nyquist angular frequency.

Consider the signal written by Y[s]=1/s+1. Then the amplitude of the spectrum becomes $Y[w] = 1/(w^2+1)^{1/2}$ which is not bounded with respect to w. Therefore Y*(w)=Y(exp[jwT]) has the 'alias' for any choice of the sampling period T. This means y[t] can not be reconstructed from Y(z) correctly if the statement of the general sampling theorem is applied. However, from the view of Theorem 1, we can always reconstruct Y[t] from Y(z) since Y[s] has no poles outside the primary strip. This depends on the assumption that y[t] is the output of the linear continuous-time finite-dimensional systems.

More explicitly, if we use the expansion formula

$$\frac{1}{1-\exp[-sT]} = \frac{1}{T} \Big/ \sum_{k=-\infty}^{\infty} [s+j2\pi k/T] \qquad (52)$$

we obtain

$$\begin{aligned} Y^*(w) &= Y(\exp[jwT]) \\ &= \exp[jwT]C(\exp[jwT]I-\exp[AT])^{-1}B \\ &= C(I-\exp[-(jwT-A)T])^{-1}B \\ &= (1/T)\sum_{k=-\infty}^{\infty} C[j(w+2\pi k/T)-A]^{-1}B \qquad (53) \end{aligned}$$

which is usually derived using impulsive sampling. In this expression, the general sampling theorem says that the spectrum $C(jwI-A)^{-1}B$ is obtained from (53) iff the harmonic $C[j(w+2\ k/T)-A]^{-1}B$ $(k\neq 0)$ do not influence $C(jwI-A)^{-1}B$.

7. CONCLUSIONS

We consider the conversion problem of discrete-time system into continuous-time system and obtain the general algorithm of this conversion and the sampling theorem for the linear systems.

The former should be used for many practical problems together with the existing identification method. The later shows a new aspect of the linear time-invariant finite-dimensional system.

The contents can be extended to systems having input/output time delay in which the delay time is multiple of the sampling period.

REFERENCES

[1] R. E. Kalman; On the General Theory of Control Systems, Proc. of 1 st IFAC, Moscow, 1, 481/492, 1960.

[2] T. Mita; Digital Control Theory, Syokodo, Japan, 1984.

[3] H. H. Rosenbrock; State-Space and Multivariable Theory, Nelson, 1970.

[4] T. Mita and H. Kaizu; On Conversion Problems Discrete -Time Systems Into Continuous-Time Systems, 13 th SICE Control Theory Simposium, 1984

DIGITAL TECHNIQUES in Simulation, Communication and Control
Spyros G. Tzafestas (editor)
Elsevier Science Publishers B.V. (North-Holland) © IMACS, 1985

ON THE APPROXIMATION OF INVERSE SYSTEMS

Shintaro Ishijima

Department of Electrical and Electronic Engineering
The Metropolitan College of Technology, Tokyo
Japan

The approximation problem of a nonproper system by a proper system is considered. The concepts of the singular I/O transformation and the ε-singular I/O transformation are introduced for this purpose. It is shown that the singular I/O transformation is the inplicit expression of Silverman's inversion algorithm, and any system may be transformed to it's inverse system by this transformation. The approximation problem is formulated as the convergence problem of a family of ε-singular I/O transformations. A necessary and sufficient condition when an inverse system is arbitrary approximated by a proper system is derived.

1. INTRODUCTION

Let S be a linear control system with the proper transfer function matrix, G(s). Roughly speaking, the inverse system S^{-1} is the system which has $G^{-1}(s)$ as it's transfer function matrix. In general, the inverse system S^{-1} is a nonproper system. Hence, differentiators have been needed to realize inverse systems. But a differentiator is a nonproper system and we can realize it only approximately. This gives rise to the approximation problem of inverse systems by proper systems. There has been a considerable amount of literatures dealing with inversion problems,[1)-4)] but very little attention has been paid to such an approximation problem. The purpose of this paper is to derive a condition when a nonproper inverse system can be approximated by a proper system.

Through the discussion, it is shown that the inversion problem is closely related to the problem of the sigular systems. Singular systems have been paid much attention in these several years and many interesting results have been obtained. Especially, Campbell et al have derived the condition of the existence of solutions and the explicit expression of the solutions of singular systems by applying the generalized matrix inverse called the Drazin inverse (D-inverse). Most of the results about the singular systems used in this paper will be found in 6).

In section 2, the concept of the singular I/O transformation is introduced and it is shown that a linear control system is transformed to it's inverse system S^{-1}.

In section 3, the concept of the ε-singular I/O transformation is introduced and approximation problem of the nonproper inverse system by proper systems is discussed as the convergence problem of the ε-singular I/O transformations to the singular I/O transformation as $\varepsilon \to 0$. Finally, a necessary and sufficient condition when the nonproper inverse system can be approximated arbitrary by a proper system is derived.

2. The singular I/O transformation and inverse systems

Let S be a linear control system described by,

$$\dot{x}=Ax+Bu \qquad (1)$$
$$y=Cx \qquad (2)$$

where u(t), y(t) and x(t) are m-dimensional input vector, the m-dimensional output vector and the n-dimensional state vector respectively. Throughout this discussion, we assume that the number of inputs is equal to the number of outputs. The singular I/O transformation for S is defined as follows.

<u>Definition 1.</u>

The singular I/O transformation for S is the transformation defined by the equations (3), (4).

$$u(t)=Fz(t)+Gv(t) \qquad (3)$$
$$z(t)=F^{-1}u(t)+Hy(t) \qquad (4)$$

Where, v(t) and z(t) are new input and output vectors respectively and F, G and H are appropriate constant matrices.

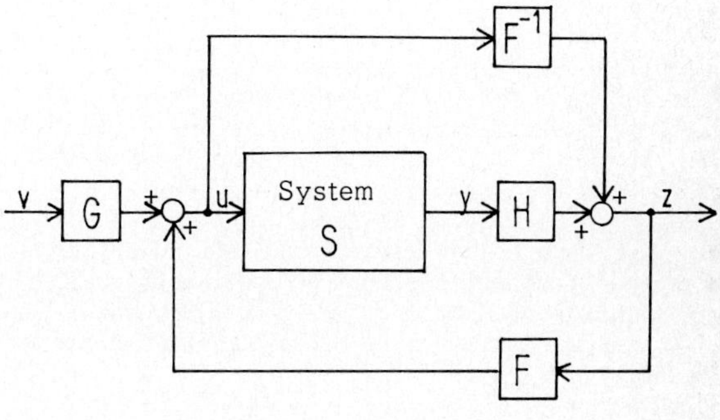

Figure 1: The singular I/O transformation for a linear system S

Let's call the resultant new system from this transformation the singularly transformed system and denote it by $\hat{S}$. From equations (3) and (4), we obtain;

$$FHy(t)+Gv(t)=0. \tag{5}$$

Tat is, the singular I/O transformation produces the constraints between the inputs and the outputs of the system. It will be clear that we can assume without loss of generality that F=-G=H=I (identity matrix) in the sequel.

Let $\tilde{S}$ be the system shown in Figure 2. We will show that the system $\tilde{S}$ is equivalent to the inverse system S^{-1}. This means that the singular I/O transformation can be interpreted to be an implicit expression of Silverman's inversion algorithm.[2)]

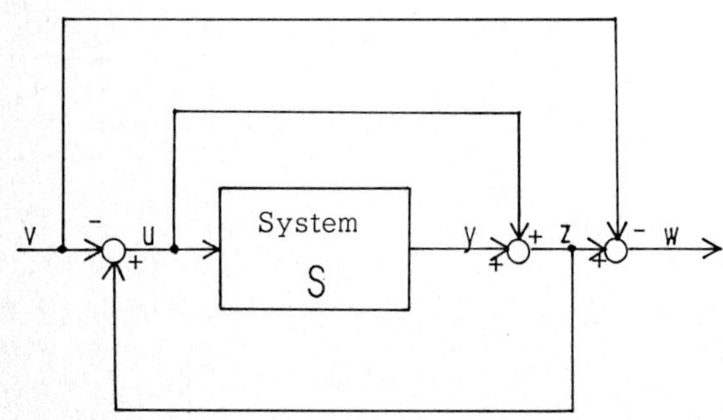

Figuare 2. Definition of System $\tilde{S}$

Lemma 1

Let v(t) be a sufficient times differentiable vector valued function. The system $\tilde{S}$ has the unique solution starting from every initial point x_0 iff the system S is invertible.

Befor proving this lemma, we summarize some results and the concepts about the singular systems[6)] in the following.

The generalized linear dynamical system

$$L\dot{x}=Ax+f \tag{6}$$

is called the singular system if L is a singular matrix, where f=f(t) is a sufficient times differentiable vector valued function. It has been shown that the singular system (6) has the unique solution starting from every "consistent" initial point iff $\det(\lambda L-A)\neq 0$ for some λ.

The index of a matrix L is defined as the least positive integer such that $\mathrm{rank}(L^k)=\mathrm{rank}(L^{k+1})$ and denoted by Ind(L). The D-inverse of L is the unique solution of the following equations and denoted by L^D.

(a) $XLX=X$
(b) $XL=LX$
(c) $L^{k+1}X=L^k$ $(k=\mathrm{Ind}(L))$

In partiqular, if Ind(L)=1 then L^D also satisfies

(d) $LL^DL=L$

and agrees with the group inverse of L.

Proof of Lemma 1

From Figure 2, we obtain ,

$$v(t)-y(t)=0$$

This equation together with the state equation (1), defines the singular system;

$$\begin{pmatrix} I & 0 \\ 0 & 0 \end{pmatrix}\begin{pmatrix} \dot{x} \\ \dot{u} \end{pmatrix} = \begin{pmatrix} A & B \\ -C & 0 \end{pmatrix}\begin{pmatrix} x \\ u \end{pmatrix} + \begin{pmatrix} 0 \\ I \end{pmatrix} v \tag{7}$$

It will be clear that the system $\tilde{S}$ has the unique solution iff the singular system (7) has the unique solution satisfying $x(0)=x_0$ for every x_0. Hence $\tilde{S}$ has the unique solution iff

$$\det\begin{pmatrix} \lambda-A & -B \\ C & 0 \end{pmatrix}\neq 0 \tag{8}$$

It is easily shown that the condition (8) is equivalent to

$$\det(C(\lambda-A)^{-1}B)\neq 0 \tag{9}$$

which is the invertibility condition of the system S. In fact, suppose that (8) dose not hold. Then there exists nonzero vectors ξ and η such that

$$(\lambda-A)\xi-B\eta=0,\ C\xi=0.$$

This means that $C(\lambda-A)^{-1}B\eta=0$ for all λ, and (9) dose not hold. Similarly it is shown that if (9) dose not hold then (8) dose not hold. This completes the proof of the lemma.

Now assume that the condition of Lemma 1 is satisfied, then applying Silverman's inversion algorithm, we obtain

$$u=-D_\alpha^{-1}C_\alpha x-D_\alpha^{-1}v \tag{10}$$

where α must be equal to the index of the matrix defined by (8). Substituting (10) into (1) yields,

$$\dot{x}=(A-BD_\alpha^{-1}C_\alpha)x-BD_\alpha^{-1}v \tag{11}$$

Equations (10) and (11) show that the system $\tilde{S}$ is equivalent to the inverse system S^{-1} of S because the output w(t) of $\tilde{S}$ coincides with u(t).

Theorem 1

Let S be invertible. Then the system $\tilde{S}$ in Figure 2 is equivqlent to the inverse system S^{-1}.

Note that the singular I/O transformation produces the inverse input output relation for any class of systems formally. Let N be a nonlinear system whose input-output relation is written as

$$y(t)=N_{x_o}(u(\cdot))$$

where x_o is an initial point. Consider the singularly transformed system $\tilde{N}$ of N.

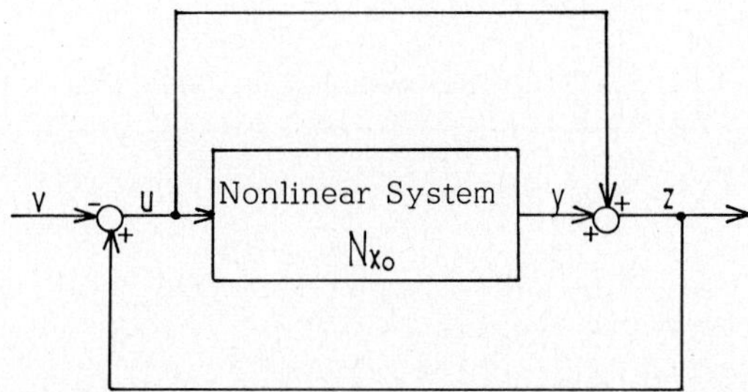

Figure 3 The singular I/O transformation for nonlinear system

From Figure 3, we obtain next equations.

$$y=N_{x_o}(u) \tag{12}$$

$$u=z-v \tag{13}$$

$$z=u+y \tag{14}$$

Hence, we get,

$$w\stackrel{\Delta}{=}z-v=N_{x_o}^{-1}(v). \tag{15}$$

This means that the input-output relation of $\tilde{N}$ is reversed by the singular I/O transformation. But it must be noted that the singularly transformed system $\tilde{N}$ may not have any solutions even if the input-output relation of N is invertible.

3.Approximation of inverse systems

In the previous section, we have pointed out that the singular I/O transformation is an implicit expression of Silverman's inversion algorithm. Here, we consider the approximation problem of the inverse system by the nearly singular I/O transformation. For this purpose, we will introduce the concept of the ε-singular I/O transformation. Let S be the system defined by (1) and (2).

Definition 2

The ε-singular I/O transformation for S is the transformation defined by,

$$u(t)=z(t)-v(t) \tag{16}$$

$$z(t)=(I+\varepsilon)u(t)+y(t) \tag{17}$$

where $\varepsilon>0$.(see Figure 4.)

Let call the system in Figure 4, the ε-singularly transformed system and denote it by $\hat{S}_\varepsilon$.

Note that the ε-singularly transformed system $\hat{S}_\varepsilon$ is a proper system if S is proper. Hence, if $\hat{S}_\varepsilon \to \hat{S}$ (= $\tilde{S}$), when $\varepsilon \to 0^+$, then we get proper systems arbitrary near to the singularly transformed system $\tilde{S}$. This means that we can approximate the nonproper inverse system S^{-1} arbitrary by proper and phisically realizable systems.

From (16) and (17), we obtain,

$$u(t)=-\frac{1}{\varepsilon}(Cx(t)-v(t)) \tag{18}$$

$$z(t)=u(t)+v(t) \tag{19}$$

Substituting (18) into (1) yields,

$$\dot{x}=(A-\frac{1}{\varepsilon}BC)x+\frac{1}{\varepsilon}Bv \tag{20}$$

Let $x_\varepsilon(t)$ be the solution of (20) then $x_\varepsilon(t)$ can be written as,

$$x_\varepsilon(t)=\exp((A-\frac{1}{\varepsilon}BC)t)x_o + \frac{1}{\varepsilon}\int_0^t \exp((A-\frac{1}{\varepsilon}BC)(t-s))Bv(s)ds \tag{21}$$

Next two lemma are necessary to discuss the asymptotic behavior of $x_\varepsilon(t)$. A matrix L is said to be semi-stable iff Ind(L)=1 and real parts of all the eigenvalues of L except zero are negative.

Lemma 2 [6)]

$\exp\,(A+\frac{1}{\varepsilon}L)$ converges as $\varepsilon \to 0^+$ iff L is semi-stable.

Lemma 3 [6)]

Suppose that L is semi-stable, then for any real number $\varepsilon>0$,

$$\exp((A+\frac{1}{\varepsilon}L)t)=\sum_{\nu=0}^{\infty}(X_\nu(t)+Y_\nu(t/\varepsilon))\varepsilon^\nu \tag{22}$$

where, $X_\varepsilon(t)$ and $Y_\varepsilon(t)$ are defined by (23)-(28).

Definition of $X_k(t)$ and $Y_k(t)$

Let Γ be a contour around zero containing no nozero eigenvalues of L inside and $(A;L)=(I-LL^D)A(I-LL^D)$.

$$X_0(t)=\exp((I-LL^D)A)(I-LL^D) \tag{23}$$

$$X_{k+1}(t)=\exp((A;L)t)\int_0^t \exp(-(A;L)s)((I;L)\cdot A(L^D\dot{X}_k-L^DAX_k))ds+L^D\dot{X}_k-L^DAX_k + \exp((A;L)t)(I;L)X_{k+1}(0) \tag{24}$$

$$X_k(0)=\frac{1}{2\pi i}\int_\Gamma ((s-L)^{-1}A)^k(s-L)ds \tag{25}$$

Let Ω be a contour around the nonzero eigenvalues of L but not including zero.

$$Y_0(t)=\exp(Lt)LL^D \tag{26}$$

$$Y_k(t)=\exp(Lt)\int_0^t \exp(-Ls)AY_{k-1}(s)ds + \exp(Lt)Y_k(0) \tag{27}$$

$$Y_k(0)=\frac{1}{2\pi i}\int_\Omega((s-L)^{-1}A)^k(s-L)ds \qquad (28)$$

See 6) for more detailed definition.

Suppose that B and C are full rank matrices (rank(B)=rank(C)=m). Then the next Lemma follows immediately.

Lemma 4

There exists a nonsingular matrix T which satisfies,

$$TB=\begin{pmatrix}B_1\\0\end{pmatrix},\quad CT^{-1}=\begin{pmatrix}C_1 & 0\end{pmatrix} \qquad (29)$$

where B_1 and C_1 are nonsingular matrices, iff

Ind(BC)=1.

Let L=-BC in the definition of $Y_k(t)$ and suppose that Ind(BC)=1. Then next Lemma follows from the above Lemma.

Lemma 5

For any positive integer k,

$$\lim_{\varepsilon\to0^+}\varepsilon^{k-1}Y_k(t/\varepsilon)B=0 \quad (t>0). \qquad (30)$$

Proof

Note that,

$$\varepsilon^{k-1}Y_k(t/\varepsilon)=\exp(-\tfrac{1}{\varepsilon}BC)\int_0^{t/\varepsilon}\exp(BCs)A\varepsilon^{k-1}\cdot Y_{k-1}(s)ds+\varepsilon^{k-1}\exp(-\tfrac{1}{\varepsilon}BC)Y_k(0)$$
$$=\int_0^t\exp((-BC)\tfrac{t-s}{\varepsilon})A\varepsilon^{k-2}Y_{k-1}(s/\varepsilon)\cdot ds+\varepsilon^{k-1}\exp(-\tfrac{1}{\varepsilon}BCt)Y_k(0) \qquad (31)$$

Hence, if for any k>1, there exists

$$P_k(t)=\lim_{\varepsilon\to0^+}\varepsilon^{k-1}Y_kB$$

we have

$$P_k(t)=\int_0^t(I-(BC)(BC)^D)AP_{k-1}(s)ds. \qquad (32)$$

Consequently if $P_1=0$ then $P_k=0$ for any k> 0, follows by induction.

From the definition of Y_1, we have,

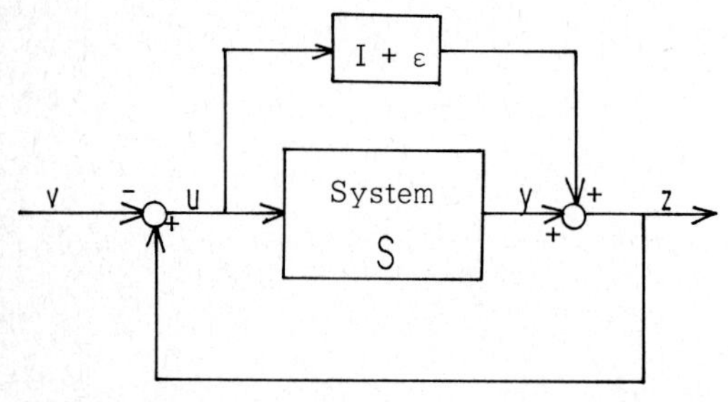

Figure 4. The ε-singular I/O transfomation

$$\lim_{\varepsilon\to0^+}Y_1(t/\varepsilon)B=\begin{pmatrix}0\\A_{21}C_1^{-1}\end{pmatrix}+\begin{pmatrix}0&0\\0&I\end{pmatrix}Y_1(0)B \qquad (33)$$

where, B_1 and C_1 are matrices defined in Lemma 4. On the other hand, we easily get that

$$\begin{pmatrix}0&0\\0&I\end{pmatrix}Y_1(0)B=\begin{pmatrix}0\\-A_{21}C_1^{-1}\end{pmatrix} \qquad (34)$$

From (33) and (34), it follows that $P_1=0$. This completes the proof.

Now, we can prove the next theorem by using these results.

Theorem 2

The ε-singular I/O transformation shown in Figure 4, converges to the singular I/O transformation iff -BC is a semi-stable matrix.

Proof

From Lemma 3 and (21), $x_\varepsilon(t)$ can be written as,

$$x_\varepsilon(t)=\exp((A-\tfrac{1}{\varepsilon}BC)t)x_0+\sum_{k=0}^{\infty}\int_0^t(X_k(t-s)+Y_k((t-s)/\varepsilon))^{k-1}Bv(s)ds \qquad (35)$$

Considering Lemma 5 and that X_k is independent of ε , it follows that

$$x_\varepsilon(t)=\int_0^t(\tfrac{1}{\varepsilon}(X_0+Y_0)+X_1)Bv(s)ds+\exp((A-\tfrac{1}{\varepsilon}BC)t)x_0+o(\varepsilon) \qquad (36)$$

From the definition, it follows that $X_0B=0$.

Now let I_ε be

$$I_\varepsilon=\int_0^t(X_1+\tfrac{1}{\varepsilon}Y_0)Bds.$$

Then after some calculations, we obtain

$$\lim_{\varepsilon\to0^+}I_\varepsilon=\begin{pmatrix}(B_1C_1)^{-1}B_1v(t)\\ \int_0^t\exp(A_{22}(t-s))A_{21}C_1^{-1}ds\end{pmatrix}. \qquad (37)$$

Let x(t) be the limit of $x_\varepsilon(t)$ as $\varepsilon\to0^+$, and divide x(t) into $x^T(t)=(x_1^T(t), x_2^T(t))$, coresponding to the partition of (37). Then,

$$x_1(t)=C_1^{-1}v(t) \qquad (38)$$

$$x_2(t)=\exp(A_{22}t)x_2(0)+\int_0^t\exp(A_{22}(t-s))A_{21}x_1(s)ds \qquad (39)$$

By differentiating both sides of (38) and (39), we get

$$\dot{x}_1(t)=C_1^{-1}\dot{v}(t) \qquad (40)$$

$$\dot{x}_2(t)=A_{22}x_2(t)+A_{21}x_1(t) \qquad (41)$$

These equations are equivalent to

$$\dot{x}=(A-B(CB)^{-1}CA)x+B(CB)^{-1}\dot{v}. \quad (42)$$

This means that the limit system is equivalent to the system S with the input u such as,

$$u=-(CB)^{-1}CAx+(CB)^{-1}\dot{v}. \quad (43)$$

That is, the ε-singular I/O transformations in Figure 4 converges to the singular I/O transformation pointwise at any $t>0$.

The necessity follows immediately from Lemma 2. This completes the proof of the theorem.

Now consider the condition that $-BC$ is semistable in the above theorem. Recall that a matrix L is called semi-stable iff i) the real parts of nonzero eigenvalues of L are negative and ii) Ind(L)=1. We can show easily that if the condition ii) is satisfied , then there always exists a matrix G such that $-BGC$ is semistable. Hence, if we take the output of the system S as $\hat{y}=Gy$ instead of y,then we can always assume the condition i).

However, next lemma shows that the condition ii) is indispensable in theorem 2.

Lemma 6

Suppose that B and C are full rank matrices. For any nonsingular matrix G, if Ind(BC)≧2, then Ind(BGC)≧2.

Proof

Since Ind(BC)≧2, there exists vectors v_1 and v_2 that are independent each other and satisfy

$$BCv_1=0, \; BCv_2=v_1.$$

Let w_1 and w_2 be vectors such that,

$$w_1=v_1, \quad Cw_2=G^{-1}(B^TB)^{-1}B^Tv_1$$

Since C has full rank, there always exists w_2, and since v_1 belongs to the range space of B, $B^Tv_1\neq0$, that is, $w_2\neq0$.

On the other hand, w_1 belongs to the null space of matrix C ,while w_2 dose not. Hence we get two linearly independent vectors which satisfy,

$$(BGC)w_1=0, \; (BGC)w_2=w_1.$$

This means that Ind(BGC)≧2.

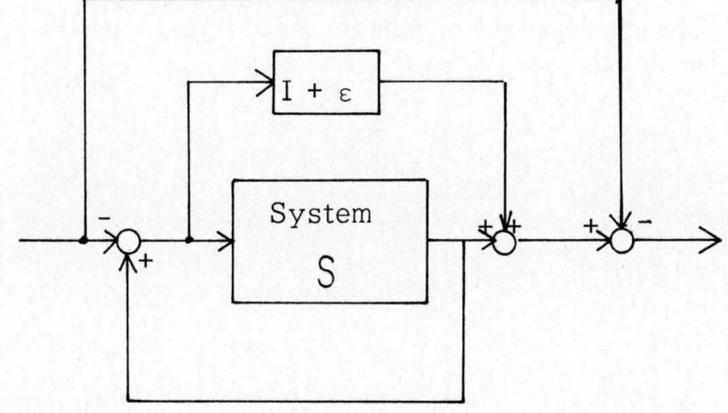

Figure 5. The ε-approximate inverse system

Let consider the system shown in Figure 5. Call this system $\tilde{S}_\varepsilon$. If $\tilde{S}_\varepsilon$ converges to the inverse system S^{-1} of S, we call $\tilde{S}_\varepsilon$the ε-approximate inverse system. From Theorem 2 and Lemma 6, next theorem follows immediately.

Theorem 3

Let S be a linear control system defined by (1) and (2) and B and C are full rank matrices. There exists the ε-approximate inverse system iff Ind(BC)=1.

4. Discrete versions of the previous results

The results obtained above cannot be directly extended to the discrete systems. The main difficulty lies in the strict causality of discrete systems.

Consider the following discrete linear system Sd.

$$x(k+1)=Ax(k)+Bu(k) \quad (44)$$
$$y(k)=Cx(k) \quad (45)$$

Now, suppose that we define the singular I/O transformation for Sd similar to the continuous case, that is,

$$u(k)=Fz(k)+Gv(k) \quad (46)$$
$$z(k)=F^{-1}u(k)+Hy(k). \quad (47)$$

Then, it follows that

$$Gv(k)+FHy(k)=0 \quad (48)$$

for every v(k). But it will be clear that this is impossible, because y(k) has already determined by v(j), j<k. In other words, the causality of the system Sd prevents from defining the singular I/O transformation by (47) and (48).

This difficulty can be avoided by introducing a "predictor" of Sd. Let $\hat{S}d$ be the system defined by,

$$p(k+1)=Ap(k)+Bu(k) \quad (49)$$
$$q(k)=Cp(k+1) \quad (50)$$

Let's call the system $\hat{S}d$ the predictor of Sd.

Definition 3

The singular I/O transformation for Sd is the I/O transformation for the predictor $\hat{S}d$ defined by,

$$u(k)=Fz(k)+Gv(k) \quad (51)$$
$$z(k)=F^{-1}u(k)+Hq(k) \quad (52)$$

Let's assume that F=-G=H=I below (see Figure 6).

Then we can derive the next theorem which is the discrete version of Theorem 1.

Theorem 4

If Ind(BC)=1 then the system shown in Figure 6 coincides with the 1 step delayed inverse system of Sd.

Proof

It is clear from the definition and Figure 6.

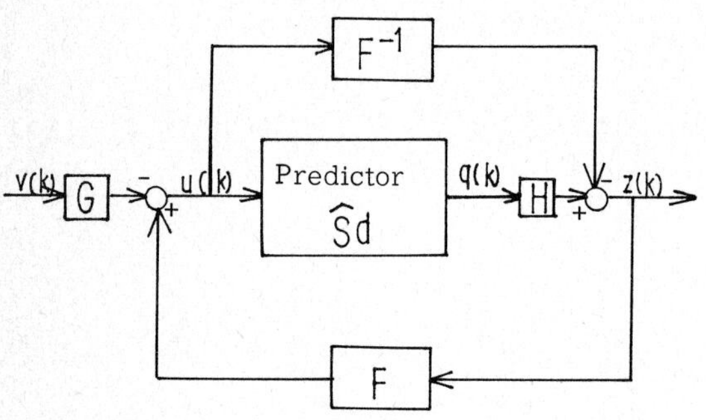

Figure 6. The singular I/O transformation for a discrete system Sd

Next we define the ε-singular I/O transformation for the system Sd as follows.

Definition 4

The I/O transformation for the predictor $\hat{S}d$ of Sd defined by

$$u(k)=z(k)+v(k) \tag{53}$$
$$z(k)=(I+\varepsilon)u(k)+q(k) \tag{54}$$

is called the ε-singular I/O transformation for the discrete system Sd (see Figure 7).

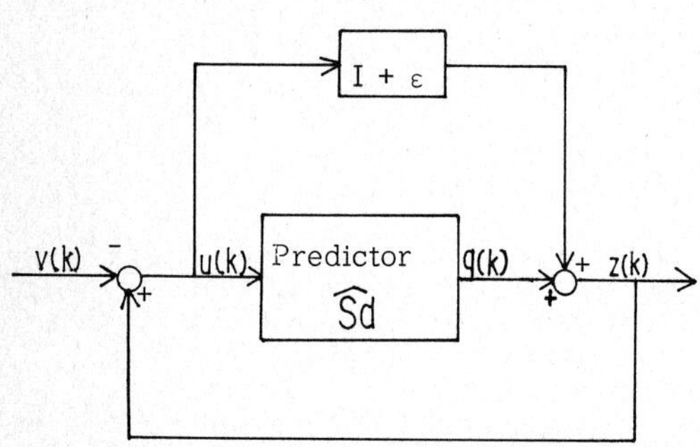

Figure 7. The ε-singular I/O transformation for a discrete system Sd

Then we can easily prove the next theorem which is the discrete version of Theorem 2.

Theorem 5

The ε-singular I/O transformation in Figure 7 converges to the singular I/O transformation as $\varepsilon \to 0$, iff Ind(BC)=1.

Note that in contrast with the continuous case, ε is not constrained to be positive. The constraint on ε in the continuous case is considered to be a penalty for the ambiguous causality of continuous systems.

6. Conclusion

We have discussed an approximation problem of a nonproper inverse system by a proper system and derived a condition when a linear proper system has an arbitrary approximated inverse system. Furthermore, we have shown that there exists the input-output transformation called the singular I/O transformation which transforms a control system to it's inverse system. The approximation problem has been formulated as the convergence problem of the ε-singular I/O transformation. In section 5, we have also shown the discrete versions of these results.

A typical example which satisfies Theorem 3 is the differentiator. In fact, a differentiator is considered to be a limit system of

$$\dot{x}= -\frac{1}{\varepsilon}x+\frac{1}{\varepsilon}v,\quad w= -\frac{1}{\varepsilon}(x-v).$$

It will be clear that the above system is the ε-singularly transformed system of an integrator.

The extension of the results obtained here to another type of inverse systems such as L-integrable inverse systems, is straightforward. An interesting problem is to extend these discussions to more general class of control systems including nonlinear systems and so on.

References:

1) T.Mori and M. Ito, On the inverse of linear systems, Trans.SICE vol-14, No.5 (1977) 494-498

2) L.M. Silverman, Inversion of multivariable linear systems, IEEE Trans. Automatic Control AC-14 (1969) 270-276

3) H.K. Sain and J.L. Massy, Invertibility of linear time invariant dynamical systems, IEEE Trans. Automatic Control AC-14 (1969) 141-149

4) S.L. Kamiyama and K. Furuta, Integral invertibility of linear time invariant systems, Int. J. Control, 25-3 (1977) 403-412

5) S.L. Campbell, C.d. Meyer Jr. and N.J. Rose, Applications of the Drazin inverse to linear systems of differential equations, SIAM J. Appl. Math., 31 (1976) 411-425

6) S.L. Campbell, Singular systems of differential equations (Pitman 1980)

7) P. Bernhard, On singular implicit linear dynamical systems, SIAM J. Control and Optimization, Vol. 20 No.5 (1982) 612-633

DIGITAL TECHNIQUES in Simulation, Communication and Control
Spyros G. Tzafestas (editor)
Elsevier Science Publishers B.V. (North-Holland) © IMACS, 1985

ON THE CONVERGENCE OF ORTHOGONAL EIGENFUNCTION SERIES

John G. Fikioris

Department of Electrical Engineering
National Technical University of Athens
Greece

The method of Watson's Transformation, well known in high frequency scattering, is applied to a two-dimensional, orthogonal eigenfunction series of rectangular harmonic functions, which provides the solution to a typical boundary value problem of Laplace's equation. A new infinite, so-called residue, series is obtained exhibiting convergence properties stronger than, in certain respects, and complementary to the original eigenfunction series. Convergence of the two series and of their derivatives is further compared and tested near points of discontinuity. Eigenfunction series of other boundary value problems are, also, discussed and similarities with the evaluation of complicated Fourier or Sommerfeld integrals via contour integration are pointed out.

1. INTRODUCTION

Many boundary value problems in Physics and Engineering can be solved in terms of infinite series of orthogonal eigenfunctions. Essential to the simple evaluation of the expansion coefficients of the series is the orthogonality of the eigenfunctions. Essential, also, is their completeness as an infinite set. Unfortunately, neither of these properties is able to insure an adequate rate of convergence of the eigenfunction series, a property crucial to the numerical evaluation of the solution or to the detection of its behavior at particular regions. In most cases the convergence of the series is not uniform in its region of validity.

A successful method to remedy the situation is the application of Watson's method: The eigenfunction series is transformed into a properly chosen contour integral in the complex plane of a variable related to the separation constant, whose infinite set of eigenvalues yielded the original series. Deforming next the path of integration and applying residue calculus transforms the contour integral into a new infinite series of different eigenfunctions, not necessarily orthogonal. The main feature of this new, so-called residue, series is its strong convergence, particulary in regions where the original series converged very slowly. One may say that the two series solutions have almost complementary convergence properties.

The method, originally developed by Watson [1,2,3,4], is well known to workers in the field of high frequency scattering and forms the basis of the geometrical theory of diffraction [1,2,4]. The initial eigenfunction series, converging rapidly at low frequencies (small scatterers), becomes useless at high frequencies (large scatterers) owing to hopelessly slow convergence. The transformed series, on the other hand, converges very rapidly at high frequencies and complements the solution at the high end of the spectrum.

Severe complications arise, however, in the evaluation of poles and residues inside the contour integral [2,4]. In this paper, a very convenient example, avoiding such complexities and related to a typical two-dimensional boundary value problem of Laplace's equation in rectangular coordinates, has been chosen to illustrate the application and all the main features of the method. Generalizations to other eigenfunction series solutions of practical boundary value problems are discussed along with convergence deterioration near points of discontinuity. Finally, similarities of the method with the evaluation of complicated Fourier or Sommerfeld integrals via contour integration are pointed out.

2. WATSON'S TRANSFORMATION

2.1 The Boundary Value Problem

A typical two-dimensional boundary value problem in rectangular coordinates requires the evaluation of a harmonic function $\psi(x,y)$ (i.e. $\nabla^2\psi(x,y)=0$) in the region $0{,}5\alpha \leq x \leq 0{,}5\alpha$, $0 \leqq y \leqq b$, which satisfies the boundary conditions:

$$\psi(0,x) = \psi(-\alpha/2,y)=\psi(\alpha/2,y)=0, \quad \psi(x,b) = V \tag{1}$$

as shown in Figure 1. $\psi(x,y)$ may represent the steady state temperature or the electrostatic potential distribution in the region etc. In the second case $\bar{E}(x,y) = -\nabla\psi(x,y)$ represents the electrostatic field distribution in the region.

Straightforward application of separation of variables yields the solution in the form of an infinite series of harmonic functions:

$$\psi(x,y)= \frac{4V}{\pi}\sum_{n=0}^{\infty}(-1)^n \frac{\cos(\frac{2n+1}{\alpha}\pi x)\sinh(\frac{2n+1}{\alpha}\pi y)}{(2n+1)\sinh(\frac{2n+1}{\alpha}\pi b)} \tag{2}$$

$$E_x(x,y) = -\frac{\partial\psi}{\partial x} = \frac{4V}{\alpha}\sum_{n=0}^{\infty}(-1)^n \frac{\sin(\frac{2n+1}{\alpha}\pi x)\sinh(\frac{2n+1}{\alpha}\pi y)}{\sinh(\frac{2n+1}{\alpha}\pi b)} \quad (3)$$

$$E_y(x,y) = -\frac{\partial\psi}{\partial y} = -\frac{4V}{\alpha}\sum_{n=0}^{\infty}(-1)^n \frac{\cos(\frac{2n+1}{\alpha}\pi x)\cosh(\frac{2n+1}{\alpha}\pi y)}{\sinh(\frac{2n+1}{\alpha}\pi b)} \quad (4)$$

The convergence of the three series will be discussed later. The only thing that needs mentioning at this point is that the convergence is not uniform in the region and that, in general, the convergence of the field expressions (the derivatives) in (3),(4) is worse than the convergence of (2), owing to the differentiation.

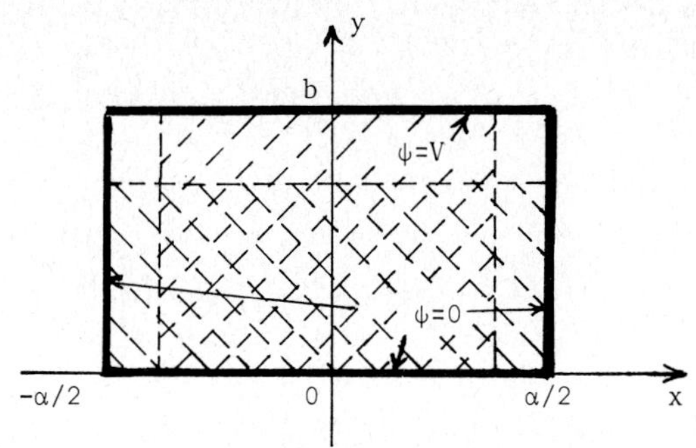

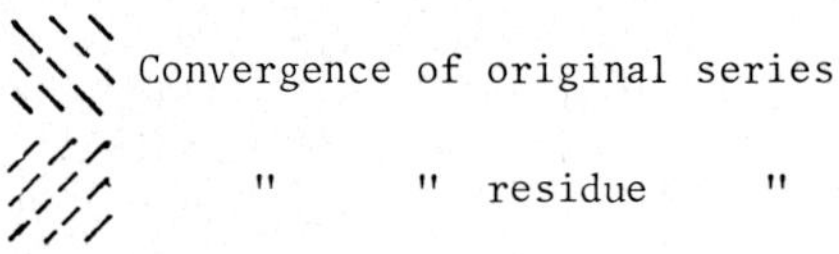

Figure 1

2.2 Transformation to a Residue Series

Following now standard steps in the application of Watson's method [3] we transform the series (2) for $\psi(x,y)$ into a contour integral in the complex v-plane:

$$\psi(x,y) = -\frac{V}{\pi i}\lim_{n\to\infty}\int_{P_n} f(v)dv \quad (5)$$

$$f(v) = \frac{\sinh(\frac{v}{\alpha}\pi y)\cos(\frac{v}{\alpha}\pi x)}{v\sinh(\frac{v}{\alpha}\pi b)\cos(v\frac{\pi}{2})} \quad (6)$$

where P_n denotes the counterclockwise travelled path $A_0A_5A_1A_0$, shown in Figure 2, with sides A_1A_0, A_5A_0 parallel and near the Real v-axis, point A_0 at $v=1/2$ and the parallel to the Imv-axis path A_5A_1 cutting the Rev-axis at $v=2n+2$. $f(v)$ is obviously an odd function of v possessing single poles at

a) $v = 2n+1$ $(n=0,1,2,\ldots)$ with residues

$$\text{Res}(v=2n+1) = -\frac{2(-1)^n\sinh(\frac{2n+1}{\alpha}\pi y)\cos(\frac{2n+1}{\alpha}\pi x)}{\pi(2n+1)\sinh(\frac{2n+1}{\alpha}\pi b)} \quad (7)$$

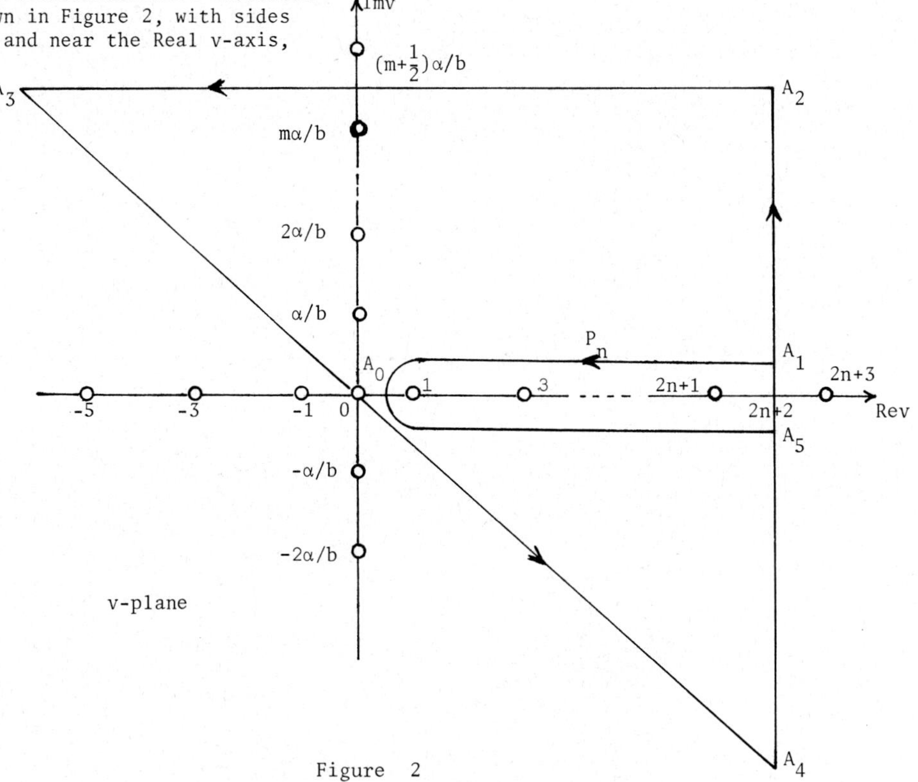

Figure 2

b) $v = 0$ with

$$\text{Res}(v=0) = y/b \tag{8}$$

c) $v = \pm im\frac{\alpha}{b}$ (m=1,2,...) with

$$\text{Res}(v=\pm im\frac{\alpha}{b}) = \frac{(-1)^m \sin(m\pi\frac{y}{b})\cosh(m\pi\frac{x}{b})}{m\pi\cosh(m\pi\frac{\alpha}{2b})} \tag{9}$$

All these poles are shown in Figure 2. Of them only the poles at $v=1,3,5,...2n+1$ (case a) are inside P_n. It can further be shown that with $v=2n+2+iv_2$

$$\lim_{\substack{n\to\infty \\ \text{or } |v_2|\to\infty}} |f(v)| = \frac{e^{-(2n+2)(b-y)\pi/\alpha} e^{-|v_2|(1-2|x|/\alpha)\pi/2}}{[(2n+2)^2+v_2^2]^{1/2}} \tag{10}$$

and, therefore, $|f(v)|$ goes to 0 exponentially with $n\to\infty$ as long as $y<b$ and with $|v_2|\to\infty$ as long as $|x|<\alpha/2$. Even at the limits $b=y$ and $|x|=\alpha/2$ the limit of $|f(v)|$ is 0 because of the denominator in (10). Comparison of (2),(5),(6) and (7) makes immediately evident the equivalence of (2) and (5), particularly in the limit $n \to \infty$, where P_n becomes a hairpin open path $A_1A_0A_5$ (with A_1, A_5 at $v = +\infty$) as indicated by the behaviour of $f(v)$ along A_5A_1 when $n \to \infty$.

We next transform this path of integration into the path $A_1A_2A_3 0 A_4A_5$, shown in Figure 2[3]. The branch A_2A_3 is parallel to the Rev-axis and cuts the Imv-axis at $v = i(m+1/2)\alpha/b$ (m=1,2,..). Owing to the odd nature of f(v) the integration along the straight-line path $A_3 0 A_4$ is 0. Also, owing to (10), the contribution of the integrals along the paths A_1A_2 and A_4A_5, where $v=2n+2\mp iv_2$, is 0 in the limit $n\to\infty$. Finally, on A_2A_3 we have $v = v_1+i(m+1/2)\alpha/b$. It is easily shown that:

$$\lim_{\substack{m\to\infty \\ \text{or } |v_1|\to\infty}} |f(v)| = \frac{e^{-|v_1|(b-y)\pi/\alpha} e^{-(m+1/2)(1-2|x|/\alpha)\pi/2b}}{[v_1^2+(m+\frac{1}{2})^2(\frac{\alpha}{b})^2]^{1/2}} = 0 \tag{11}$$

in a way similar to (10). So, as $m \to \infty$, the contribution from the integration along A_2A_3 vanishes, also. The only poles between the original and the transformed path of integration are those of case c, $v = im\alpha/b$ (m=1,2,...) and the pole at $v = 0$ which lies on the new path. As $n\to\infty$ so does m and the integral (5) is transformed into a new infinite residue series, including the full residues of equation (9) and half the residue of the pole $v = 0$. The end result is:

$$\psi(x,y)=V\frac{y}{b}+\frac{2V}{\pi}\sum_{m=1}^{\infty}(-1)^m \frac{\sin(m\pi y/b)\cosh(m\pi x/b)}{m\cosh(m\pi\alpha/2b)} \tag{12}$$

It is immediately verified that the form (12) satisfies $\nabla^2\psi(x,y) = 0$ and the boundary conditions $\psi(x,\alpha) = 0$, $\psi(x,b) = V$, whereas

$$\psi(\pm\frac{\alpha}{2},y) = V\frac{y}{b}+\frac{2V}{\pi}\sum_{m=1}^{\infty}\frac{(-1)^m}{m}\sin(m\pi y/b) = 0 \tag{13}$$

if the well known Fourier series expansion

$$y = -\frac{2b}{\pi}\sum_{m=1}^{\infty}\frac{(-1)^m}{m}\sin(m\pi y/b) \; ; \; 0 \leq y \leq b \tag{14}$$

is taken into account. Finally:

$$E_x(x,y)=-\frac{\partial\psi}{\partial x}=-\frac{2V}{b}\sum_{m=1}^{\infty}(-1)^m \frac{\sin(m\pi y/b)\sinh(m\pi x/b)}{\cosh(m\pi\alpha/2b)} \tag{15}$$

$$E_y(x,y)=-\frac{\partial\psi}{\partial y}=-\frac{V}{b}-\frac{2V}{b}\sum_{m=1}^{\infty}(-1)^m \frac{\cos(m\pi y/b)\cosh(m\pi x/b)}{\cosh(m\pi\alpha/2b)} \tag{16}$$

2.3 Convergence of the Various Series

Inspection of the series (2),(3),(4) and their counterparts (12),(15),(16) in conjuction with the asymptotic behaviour of sinz, cosz, sinhz, coshz for large positive values of z reveals the following: The original series (2),(3),(4) converge rapidly for all y not very near $y = b$. The main convergence factor arises from the ratio of the hyperbolic functions of y and is proportional to $\exp[-(2n+1)\pi(b-y)/\alpha]$. For $y = b$ the series for the derivatives E_x, E_y do not converge. So, it is not possible to evaluate $E_y(x,b)$ and the surface charge distribution on $y = b$ from (4), in the electrostatic problem. Also, $E_x(0,y) = 0$ owing to the even character of $\psi(x,y)$ with respect to x. The series (3) yields this result for $x = 0$ and for all y. This, however, does not imply that the series (3) converges for $|x| = \varepsilon << 1$ without the help of the above mentioned convergence factor. Thus:

$$E_x(\varepsilon,b) = \frac{4V}{\alpha}\sum_{n=0}^{\infty}(-1)^n \sin(\frac{2n+1}{\alpha}\pi\varepsilon) \tag{17}$$

is a series whose initial terms are small, but bunches of higher order terms are large. Such terms arise for orders n near the following values:

$$\frac{2n+1}{\alpha}\pi\varepsilon \cong \frac{\pi}{2}, \frac{3\pi}{2}, \frac{5\pi}{2}, \ldots \text{ or } 2n+1 \cong \frac{\alpha}{2\varepsilon}, \frac{3\alpha}{2\varepsilon}, \ldots$$

and the smaller the value of ε the higher the order and the number of such terms. The convergence, therefore, of $E_x(\varepsilon,y)$ is very poor, unless $b-y$ is appreciable. In particular, the convergence factor eventually leads to halving each successive term of the series for $\exp[-2\pi(b-y)/\alpha] = 0{,}5$ or for $(b-y)/\alpha = 0.1103$.

For exactly similar reasons the series (12),(15) (16) converge only for $|x| < \alpha/2$, for all y, ever $y = b$. Thus $E_x(x,b) = 0$ as required and

$$E_y(x,b) = -\frac{V}{b}-\frac{2V}{b}\sum_{m=1}^{\infty}\frac{\cosh(m\pi x/b)}{\cosh(m\pi\alpha/2b)} \tag{18}$$

a fast converging series for $|x| < \alpha/2$, useful in evaluating the surface charge distribution on the upper wall in electrostatics. The regions of convergence of the two set of series solutions are shown in Figure 1. Outside a common portion where they overlap they complement each other. Both sets fail to converse near the discontinuity points $x = \pm\alpha/2$, $y = b$.

3. GENERALIZATIONS TO OTHER EIGENFUNCTION SERIES

In high frequency scattering by cylinders and spheres Watson's method yields a residue series that converges fast at high frequencies, while the original eigenfunction series is good only at low frequencies. So, here, the complementarity is connected with the frequency behaviour of the solution. It is connected, also, with the distance from the scatterer, the residue series converging faster in the near field, in general, and the original one behaving better in the far field. The difficulties with scattering problems arise from the complicated behaviour of Hankel functions $H_\nu(x)$ (or combinations of them) with respect to their order ν. The complex ν-roots of certain transcendental equations and the behaviour of the above mentioned functions for large complex values of ν can only be obtained numerically and approximately through asymptotic evaluations, which introduce further approximations by themselves. This not only complicates the problem considerably, but limits the applicability of the method. In the example treated herein roots and residues are easily and exactly evaluated being those of sinusoidal or hyperbolic functions. This further facilitates the study of convergence of the resulting series.

The method has been applied to a number of other boundary value problems contained in [5] and [6] Similar results were obtained. In the vicinity of discontinuities or of singular points (for instance feeding points) the convergence of both series deteriorates fast. A promising effort is being made to extract out of the original series the singular term and apply Watson's method to the remaining series. In particular this effort is made in connection with the slow convergent series that evaluates the input admittance of a rectangular, cavity-backed slot antenua [6].

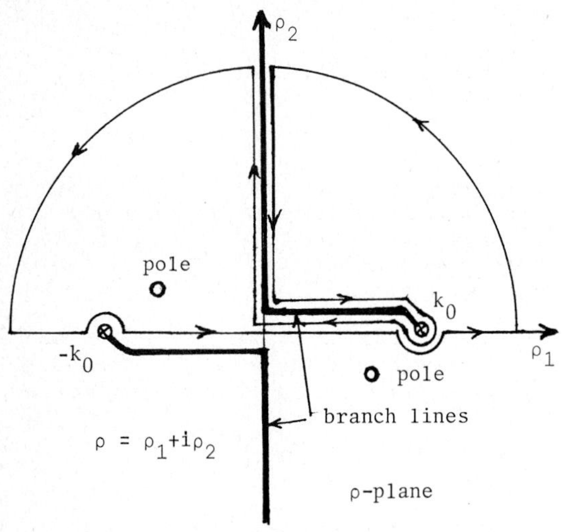

Figure 3

Finally, there exist certain similarities of Watson's method and the method of evaluating Fourier or Sommerfeld integrals by contour transformation, that are worth mentioning. Here, the governing equation is Helmholtz's equation and the integrand, beyond poles, possesses branch points and branch cuts. Thus, a recent problem being investigated, as part of a Ph.D. dissertation, refers to the evaluation of the electromagnetic field scattered by an open two-dimensional dielectric waveguide terminated at $z = 0$. We eventually come up with a Fourier cosine integral of the following form

$$I(x) = \int_{-\infty}^{\infty} (\rho^2 - k_0^2)^{1/2} f(\rho,d)\cos\rho x\,d\rho \qquad (19)$$

that measures the tangential electric field component at the interface $z = 0$. Here k_0 is real and 2d is the thickness of the guide. The function $f(\rho,d)$ may possess at most simple poles and varies as ρ^{-3} when $|\rho| \to \infty$. Then the whole integrand varies us ρ^{-2} when $|\rho| \to \infty$ and this permits a fairly good numerical evaluation of the integral by properly truncating the infinite interval of integration. For reasons well known to workers in the field the branch lines from the branch points $\rho = \pm k_0$ should be drawn along the real and the imaginary axes, as shown in Figure 3. Transforming the original path along the real ρ-axis to the semi-infinite circle and all around the branch line from k_0 (or to a corresponding path in the lower half plane, depending on the sign of x-d and on the $\exp(i\rho x)$ or $\exp(-i\rho x)$ term of $\cos\rho x$) we end up with the following integrals:

$$I(x) = \int_0^{k_0} f_1(x,\rho_1)d\rho_1 + \int_0^{\infty} f_2(x,\rho_2)\rho^{-\rho_2|x|}d\rho_2 \qquad (20)$$

where $f_1(x,\rho_1)$ is a well-behaved function in the finite interval $0 \leq \rho_1 \leq k_0$ and $f_2(x,\rho_2) \sim \rho^{-2}$ as $|\rho| \to \infty$. Thus $I(x)$ can now be evaluated through a finite integral and an infinite one whose integrand, in addition to the ρ^{-2} behaviour exhibited by the original form (19), contains the exponentially diminishing function $\exp(-\rho_2|x|)$, which allows drastic interval truncation and, therefore, quick numerical evaluation of the integral. Here, instead of the isolated set of poles along the imaginary axis of Figure 2 (for the problem of Figure 1), we have the branch line (a continuous line of discontinuities) of Figure 3 and the sum of residues becomes a line integral along the branch cut. The transformed expression (20) contains an additional exponential factor, facilitating the evaluation, just as the series (12),(15),(16) do for $|x| < \alpha/2$. Also, truncation of a convergent series to a finite sum corresponds to truncation of the infinite interval of integration.

REFERENCES:

[1] Watson, G.N., The Diffraction of Radio Waves by the Earth, Proc. Roy. Soc.London A95 (1918) 83-99; also, The Transmission of Electric Waves Around the Earth, Proc. Roy. Soc. London A95 (1919) 546-563.

[2] Jones, D.S., The Theory of Electromagnetism (Pergamon Press, Oxford, 1964).

[3] Sveshnikov, A.G. and Tikhonov, A.N., The Theory of Functions of a Complex Variable (English Translation, Mir Publishers, Moscow, 2nd Edition 1978).

[4] Tyras, G., Radiation and Propagation of Electromagnetic Waves (Academic Press, New York, 1969).

[5] Lebedev, N.N., Skalskaya, I.P. and Uflyand, Y.S., Worked Problems in Applied Mathematics (English Translation by R.A. Silverman, Dover Publ., New York, 1965).

[6] Cockrell, C.R., The Input Admittance of the Rectangular Cavity-Backed Slot Antenna,IEEE Trans. Ant. Prop. AP-24, No. 3 (May 1976) 288-294.

DIGITAL TECHNIQUES in Simulation, Communication and Control
Spyros G. Tzafestas (editor)
Elsevier Science Publishers B.V. (North-Holland) © IMACS, 1985

WALSH AND BLOCK-PULSE OPERATIONAL MATRICES IN DISTRIBUTED-PARAMETER AND DELAY SYSTEMS: AN OVERVIEW

P.Stavroulakis
ATT International (Greece)
Lekka 23-25
Athens 10562 , Greece

S.G.Tzafestas
Control Systems Laboratory
University of Patras
Patras 26500, Greece

The purpose of this paper is to provide an overview of the utilization of Walsh and block-pulse operational matrices for the study of a variety of systems theory problems, such as analysis, identification, and control for plants that are described by partial-differential or delay-differential equations. Major emphasis is placed on setting up the mathematical framework which supports this type of analysis. In all cases the use of the operational matrices results in the transformation of the system and solution equations into a computationally convenient algebraic form.

1. INTRODUCTION

Walsh and block-pulse functions constitule complete families of binary functions with interesting properties and have recently found applications in a variety of fields such as speech synthesis and analysis, sequency filtering, image processing, statistical analysis, and control theory. [1].

The foundation of the Walsh functions was established by Rademacher and Walsh [2,3]. The engineering approach to the study and utilization of these functions was originated by Harmuth [4]. Their utilization in systems and control was originated by Corrington, Chen, and Prasada Rao [5-7]. Block-pulse functions constitute another complete set of orthogonal basis functions which have a one to one relationship with Walsh functions, and naturally find applications in similar proplems.

The type of approximation is the same as with Walsh fucntions, the only difference being in the simplicity of computation. This was first shown in the case of analysis and synthesis of linear and nonlinear systems is state-space [8].

In this paper an overview is provided of the application of these sets of functions to distributed-parameter (DP) and delay systems. Similarities, differences, and relative advantages in using these functions in the study of distributed-parameter and delay systems will be pointed out as we go along. First, the interrelationship between distributed-parameter and delay systems will be shown and the major results that have been derived in studying those important areas of system theory will be discussed. Special emphasis will be placed in dynamic system analysis, synthesis, estimation, identification and control. Details of the derivations are unavoidably not included here because of space limitation, but they can be found in the references [6-30].

2. MODELING DELAY SYSTEMS AS DISTRIBUTED - PARAMETER SYSTEMS

In many situations such as linear quadratic regulator problems and observers for processes with general transportation lags, it is more convenient to convert the delay system into an equivalent distributed parameter system this technique has been successfully utilized in [19] and [20].

It is shown that a general time delay system with pure transportation delay can be analyzed by transforming the original system into a distributed parameter system the boundary conditions of which are the state and the delay form of the state of the original time delay system.

We thus observe that there exists an ultimate relationship between delay and distributed parameter systems in as far as their mathematical analysis is concerned in many control cases. This is the reason why in the following discussion we present the use of Walsh and block-pulse functions for these two systems classes in a unified way.

3. WALSH AND BLOCK-PULSE OPERATIONAL MATRICES

In order to be able to study and analyze dynamical systems, in general, the first step is to develop operational matrices for integration and differentiation by using the orthogonal sets of Walsh and /or block-pulse functions. For the cases of distributed-parameter and delay systems it is necessary to develop appropriate operational matrices for studying these types of systems. A quite general class of DP systems can be studied implementing fractional operational matrices, that have been developed and implemented for this particular class of problems.

3.1 Integration Operational matrix

For an arbitrary function f(t), we can expand it into Walsh series, if it is absolutely integrable in [0,1), in the form:

$$f(t)=\sum_{i=0}^{\infty} f_i\, w_i(t) \tag{1}$$

where $w_i(t)$ is the Walsh function and f_i the corresponding coefficient. In practice, only the first m components are considered, where m is an integral power of 2. Equation (1) can also be written as

$$f(t)=\underline{f}_w^T\, \underline{W}(t) \tag{2}$$

where

$$\underline{f}_w \equiv \begin{bmatrix} f_1 \\ f_2 \\ \vdots \\ f_m \end{bmatrix} \quad \text{and} \quad \underline{w}=\begin{bmatrix} w_1 \\ w_2 \\ \vdots \\ w_m \end{bmatrix}$$

It can be shown [6],[9] that the integral of this function, i.e. $\int_0^t f(r)dr$ can be written as

$$\int_0^t f(r)dr=\underline{f}_w^T\, \underline{E}\underline{w}(t) \tag{3}^*$$

where the operational Walsh matrix for integration $\underline{E}$ is given by

$$\underline{E}_{mxm}=\left[\begin{array}{c|c} \underline{E}_{m/2xm/2} & -\frac{1}{2m}I_{m/2xm/2} \\ \hline \frac{1}{2m}\underline{I}_{m/2xm/2} & \underline{0}_{m/2xm/2} \end{array}\right] \tag{3a}$$

---

*This is so since the integral $\int_0^t \underline{w}(r)dr$ can be approximated by

$$\int_0^t \underline{w}(r)dr=\underline{E}\,\underline{w}(t) \tag{4a}$$

Starting with $E_{1x1}=1/2$, E_{mxm} can be built from eq. (3a).

For the case where the block-pulse orthogonal set of functions is used equations (2) and (3) become [8]:

$$f(t)= \underline{f}_{\psi}^{T}\ \underline{\psi}(t) \qquad (5)$$

and

$$\int_{0}^{t} f(r)dr = \underline{f}_{\psi}^{T}\ \underline{H}\ \underline{\psi}(t) \qquad (6)$$

where

$$f_{\psi}^{T} \equiv \begin{bmatrix} f_1 \\ f_2 \\ \vdots \\ f_m \end{bmatrix}, \quad \underline{\psi} \equiv \begin{bmatrix} \psi_1(t) \\ \psi_2(t) \\ \vdots \\ \psi_m(t) \end{bmatrix}$$

and

$$H=\frac{1}{m}\begin{bmatrix} \frac{1}{2} & 1 & 1 & \dots & 1 \\ 0 & \frac{1}{2} & 1 & \dots & 1 \\ \cdot & \cdot & \cdot & \dots & \cdot \\ \cdot & \cdot & \cdot & \dots & \cdot \\ \cdot & \cdot & \cdot & \dots & \cdot \\ 0 & 0 & 0 & \dots & \frac{1}{2} \end{bmatrix} \qquad (7)$$

When we have repeated integration i.e. a multiple integral of the form $\underbrace{\int_{o}^{t}\dots\int_{o}^{t}}_{n} f(r)dr$ one can obtain a first approximation by repeated use of (3), i.e.

$$J_n(t)= \underbrace{\int_{0}^{t}\dots\int_{0}^{t}}_{n} f(r)dr^n = \underline{f}_w^T \underbrace{\int_{0}^{t}\dots\int_{0}^{t}}_{n} \underline{w}(r)dr^n$$

$$= \underline{f}_w^T \int_{0}^{t} \Big[\underbrace{\int_{0}^{t}\dots\int_{0}^{t}}_{n-1} \underline{w}(r)dr^{n-1} \Big]\ dr$$

where by (4a):

$$\int_{0}^{t}\left(\int_{0}^{t} \underline{w}(r)dr\right)dr= \int_{0}^{t} \underline{E}\ \underline{w}(r)dr$$

$$= \underline{E}^2\ \underline{w}(t),$$

and in general

$$J_n(t)= \underbrace{\int_{0}^{t}\dots\int_{0}^{t}}_{n} \underline{w}(r)dr^n \simeq \underline{E}^n \underline{w}(t) \qquad (4b)$$

Since the error of calculating the multiple integral $J_n(t)$ using (4b) is increasing with n, Prasada Rao and Palanisamy [17] have suggested a direct determination of the associated operational matrix (say $\underline{E}_n$) by minimizing the integral of the square error $J_n(t)-\underline{E}_n w(t)$. For some details on this new operational matrix , which is called "one-shot operational matrix for repeated integration (OSOMRI)" the reader is referred to [26] in this volume.

A double series approximation can be obtained for a function of two independent variables x,t if it is absolutely integrable in $x\in[0,1)$ and $t\in[0,1)$. The approximation can be written as:

$$f(x,t)= \underline{w}^T(x)\underline{F}\ \underline{w}(t) \qquad (8)$$

where the elements F_{ij} of the matrix coefficient $\underline{F}$ are given by

$$F_{ij}=\int_{0}^{1}\int_{0}^{1} f(x,t)w_i(x)w_j(t)dxdt$$

and $w_i(x)$ is the ith Walsh fuction with respect to the nariable x.
Similarly

$$\int_{0}^{t}\int_{0}^{x} f(x',t')dx'dt'=\underline{w}^T(x)\underline{E}^T\underline{F}\underline{E}\underline{w}(t) \qquad (9)$$

The same procedure applies to the case of block-pulse functions, i.e.

$$\int_{0}^{t}\int_{0}^{x} f(x',t')dx'dt'=\underline{\psi}^T(x)\underline{H}^T\underline{F}\underline{H}\underline{\psi}(t) \qquad (10)$$

This double series approximation is especially usefull in analysing single as well as simultaneous first-order differential equations [10]. A more general case for higher-order systems has been studied in [13] using multidimensional Block-pulse functions.

3.2. Fractional Operational Matrices

For many engineering problems described by partial differential equations or time-varying differential equations, when evaluated in the Laplace domain, fractional functions or transcendental functions of s result*. For example, certain problems in thermal and diffusion processes, in electromagnetic devices and transmission lines often result in mathematical models involving $\sqrt{s}$, $\sqrt{s^2+1}$, $e^{-\sqrt{s}}$ etc. The use of Laplace transform for solving these problems is not a trivial matter. Thus one must resort to some approximation techniques for deriving operational matrices that cover these important cases. The results of the previous section can be utilized to derive fractional operational matrices [11].

It is easy to show that the Walsh and block-pulse functions are related as follows

$$\underline{w}(t)=\underline{W}_{m\times m}\ \underline{\psi}(t) \tag{11}$$

for the first four functions, $W_{4\times 4}$ has the form.

$$\underline{W}_{4\times 4}=\begin{bmatrix}1 & 1 & 1 & 1\\ 1 & 1 & -1 & -1\\ 1 & -1 & 1 & -1\\ 1 & -1 & -1 & 1\end{bmatrix} \tag{12}$$

One of the properties of the $W_{m\times m}$ matrix is that [8]:

$$\underline{W}^2_{m\times m}=m\underline{I}_m \tag{13}$$

and

$$\underline{W}^{-1}_{m\times m}=\frac{1}{m}\underline{W}_{m\times m} \tag{14}$$

Substituting (11) into (3) and making use of (6) one obtains:

$$\underline{H}=\frac{1}{m}\underline{W}\ \underline{E}\ W \tag{15}$$

Inspecting $\underline{H}$ from (7) we can make the following decomposition

$$H_{m\times m}=\frac{1}{m}\left(\frac{1}{2}I_m+Q_{m\times m}+Q^2_{m\times m}+\dots+Q^{m-1}_{m\times m}\right) \tag{16}$$

where

$$\underline{Q}_{m\times m}=\left[\begin{array}{c|c}\begin{matrix}0\\ \vdots\\ 0\end{matrix} & \underline{I}_{(m-1)}\\ \hline 0 & 0\dots 0\end{array}\right] \tag{17}$$

and

$$\underline{Q}^{i}_{m\times m}=\left[\begin{array}{c|c}0 & I_{m-i}\\ \hline 0_i & 0\end{array}\right] \tag{18}$$

Equation (16) can also be written as

$$\underline{H}_{m\times m}=\frac{1}{2m}(\underline{I}_m+\underline{Q}_{m\times m})(\underline{I}_m-\underline{Q}_{m\times m})^{-1} \tag{19}$$

and

$$\underline{H}^{-1}_{m\times m}\simeq 2m\left(\frac{1}{2}I_m+\sum_{i=1}^{m-1}(-1)^i Q^i_{m\times m}\right) \tag{20}$$

If b is the eigenvalue of $\underline{H}^{-1}$ and q the eigenvalue of $\underline{Q}$, then from (20), one obtains

$$b=2m\left(\frac{1-q}{1+q}\right) \tag{21}$$

for any fractional exponent 1/n

$$b^{1/n}=(2m)^{1/n}\ h_m(q) \tag{22}$$

where $h_m(q)$ is the function $\left(\frac{1-q}{1+q}\right)^{1/n}$ expressed in a polynomial form. For example if n=2, then

$$h_2(q)=\left(\frac{1-q}{1+q}\right)^{\frac{1}{2}}=1-q+\frac{1}{2}q^2-\frac{1}{2}q^3+\dots \tag{23}$$

* s=a+jω is the complex frequency

Hence

$$\underline{H}^{-\frac{1}{2}}_{m\times m} = \sqrt{8}(\underline{I}_{4\times 4}-\underline{Q}_{4\times 4}+\frac{1}{2}\underline{Q}^2_{4\times 4}-\frac{1}{2}\underline{Q}^3_{4\times 4}+\cdots) \tag{24}$$

Equation (24) can then be used to analyse and approximate problems that involve $\sqrt{s}$. Similarly we can develop operational matrices for studying problems that involve $\frac{1}{\sqrt{s}}$, $e^{-\sqrt{s}}$, $\frac{1}{s}e^{-\sqrt{s}}$, etc.

3.3. Delay Operational Matrices

If f_i are the components of $f(t)$ in a Walsh series, then $f(t-r)$, where r is a constant less than unity, may be expressed in the form

$$f(t-\tau)\approx \sum_{i=0}^{m-1} f_i\, w_i(t-\tau) \tag{25}$$

under the assumption that the initial function $f(t)=0$, $t\in[-\tau,0)$. In particular if $\tau=a/m$, $0\leq a\leq 1$, then $w_i(t-\tau)$ can be expressed in terms of $w_i(t)$ in the form

$$\underline{w}(t-\tau)=\underline{D}^a_m\,\underline{w}(t)$$

In [12] a recursive relationship is developed to determine $\underline{D}^a_m$ from $\underline{D}^a_2$. Thus for a given $a=m\cdot\tau$ $(0\leq a\leq 1)$ one has

$$\underline{D}^a_2=\frac{1}{2}\begin{bmatrix}2-a & -a\\ a & 2-3a\end{bmatrix}$$

$$=\underline{I}_2+\frac{a}{2}\begin{bmatrix}-1 & -1\\ 1 & -3\end{bmatrix}$$

$$=\underline{I}_2+a\underline{\hat{\Delta}}_2\ ,\ \underline{\hat{\Delta}}_2=\frac{1}{2}\begin{bmatrix}-1 & -1\\ 1 & -3\end{bmatrix}$$

$$\underline{D}^a_4=\frac{1}{4}\begin{bmatrix}4-a & -a & -a & -a\\ a & 4-3a & a & -3a\\ a & a & 4-7a & a\\ -a & 3a & -a & 4-5a\end{bmatrix}$$

$$=\underline{I}_4+a\underline{\hat{\Delta}}_4$$

where

$$\underline{\hat{\Delta}}_4=\frac{1}{4}\begin{bmatrix}-1 & -1 & -1 & -1\\ 1 & -3 & 1 & -3\\ 1 & 1 & -7 & 1\\ -1 & 3 & -1 & -5\end{bmatrix}$$

and so on.

It is interesting to note that if $\tau=N/m$, then

$$\underline{D}^N_m=\frac{1}{2}\left[\begin{array}{c|c}\underline{D}^1_{m-1}+\underline{D}^o_{m-1} & \underline{D}^1_m-\underline{D}^o_m\\ \hline -\underline{D}^1_m-\underline{D}^o_m & -\underline{D}^1_m+\underline{D}^o_m\end{array}\right]N \tag{26}$$

where

$$\underline{D}^o_m=\underline{I}_m \tag{27}$$

It can also be shown [14] that this delay operational matrix can be obtained recursevily from the Walsh matrices given by eq.(12) and a new matrix $(Q_{4\times 4})$ which is obtained from the walsh matrix according to some specific rule given in [15].

The above method is more convenient especially for systems which require high accuracy because the delay operational matrix is obtained as a linear relationship between these two matrices shifted as many places to the right as the number of integer time intervals of the delay.

For example, if the delay is equal to one time interval, the shifted Walsh matrix is given by:

$$\underline{W}_{4\times 4}(1)=\begin{bmatrix}0 & 1 & 1 & 1\\ 0 & 1 & 1 & -1\\ 0 & 1 & -1 & 1\\ 0 & 1 & -1 & -1\end{bmatrix} \tag{28}$$

The shifted matrix $Q_{4\times 4}$ is given by:

$$\underline{Q}_{4\times4}(1)=\begin{bmatrix}0&1&0&0\\0&1&0&-2\\0&1&-2&2\\0&1&2&0\end{bmatrix} \qquad (29)$$

and

$$\underline{D}_{4}^{1}=\frac{1}{4}\,\underline{W}_{4\times4}(1)-\underline{Q}_{4\times4}(1)$$

$$=\frac{1}{4}\begin{bmatrix}3&-1&-1&-1\\1&1&1&-1\\1&1&-3&1\\-1&3&-1&-1\end{bmatrix} \qquad (30)$$

which is exactly the matrix obtained by (26).

One must note that the above methodology is useful when the time delay is equal to an integer number of intervals, otherwise the recursive relationship given by (20) must be used. Further results on the use of delay operational matrices in analysis, identification and control of time-delay systems may be found in [12, 17, 22, 23].

If the basis functions for the expansion of f(t) are $\psi_i(t)$ i.e., the block-pulse functions, then [14, 24]:

$$\underline{\psi}(t-\frac{N}{m})=\underline{I}(m;-N)\underline{\psi}(t)$$

where

$$\underline{I}(m;-N)=\begin{bmatrix}0&\underline{I}_{m-N}\\0&0\end{bmatrix}$$

and $\underline{I}_{m-N}$ is an (m-N)x(m-N) identity matrix.

4. CONCLUDING REMARKS

The methodology presented thus far has been used to analyze a variety of system, identification control and stochastic design applications [6-28]. The operational matrices derived constitute the basic mathematical framework for the analysis and design of distributed parameter and delay systems. In both cases it is seen that the problem is transformed into a computationally convenient algebraic form. Certain algebraic (regression) properties of these operational matrices imply enormous reduction in the computational effort associated with the algebra of these apparently large and sparse matrices.

The field has reached a high level of sophistication and maturity, but it is still expanding and the techniques are increasingly adopted in real applications Worth mentioning is the book of Prasada Rao [29] where a unified treatment of system analysis, identification and optimization using piece-wise constant orthogonal basis functions (i.e Walsh and block-pulse functions) is made,and the reprint book edited by Tzafestas [30] where a well-balanced set of papers within the whole field of Walsh and block-pulse functions (not only in control system analysis and design) is provided including Walsh-function definition and generation,Walsh transform computation, Walsh-to-Fourier conversion and various applications in image coding, E.E.G. signal processing and classification, speech coding, sequency filtering,etc.

REFERENCES

[1] S.G. Tzafestas, "*Walsh Transform Theory and its Application to Systems Analysis and Control: An Overview*",Math. Comput. Simul., vol.25, pp.214-225 (1983).

[2] H.Rademacher, *Einige Saize von Allgemeinen Orthogonal Functionen,*

Math. Ann., vol.87, pp.122-138(1922).

[3] J.L.Walsh, *A closed Set of Normal Orthogonal Functions*, Amer. J.Math; Vol.45, pp.5-24 (1923).

[4] H.F. Harmuth, *Applications of Walsh Functions in communications* IEEE Spectrum, vol.6, 82-91 (1969).

[5] M.S.Corrington, *Solution of Differential and integral Equations with Walsh Functions*, IEEE Trans. Circuit Theory, vol.CT-20, pp.470-476 (1973)

[6] C.F.Chen and C.H.Hsiao, *A State Space Approach to Walsh Series Solution of Linear Systems*, Int. J. Systems Sci., vol.6, No.9, pp. 833-858 (1975).

[7] G.Prasada Rao, L.Sivakumar, *System Identification via Walsh Functions*, Proceedings of IEE, vol.122, No.10, pp.1160-1161 (1975).

[8] P.Sannuti, *Analysis and Synthesis of Dynamic Systems via Block Pulse Functions*, Proceedings of IEE, vol.124, No,6, pp. 569-571, (1977).

[9] C.F.Chen and C.H.Hsiao, *Design of Piecewise Constant Gains for Optimal Control via Walsh Functions*, IEEE Trans. Auto. Control, AC-20, pp. 596-603 (1975).

[10] Y.P.Shih and J.Y.Han, *Double Walsh Series Solution of First-order Partial Differential Equations*, Int. J. Systems Sci., vol.9, pp.569-578(1978).

[11] C.F.Chen, Y.T.Tsay and T.T.Wu, *Walsh Operational Matrices for Fractional Calculus and Their Application to Distributed Systems*, J.Franklin Inst., vol.303, No.3, pp.267-284 (1977).

[12] K.R.Palanisamy, G.Prasada Rao, *Optimal Control of Linear Systems with Delays in State and Control via Walsh Functions*, Proceedings of IEE, vol. 130, No.6, pp.300-312 (1983).

[13] G. Prasada Rao and T.Srinivasan, *Multidimensional Block-Pulse Functions and their Use in the Study of Distributed-Parameter Systems*, Int. J.Systems Sci., vol.11, No.6, pp.689-708(1980).

[14] Y.P.Shih, C.Hwang and W.Kong Chia, *Parameter Estimation of Delay Systems via Block-Pulse Functions, Dynamic Systems, Measurement , and Control*, vol.102, pp.159-162 (1980).

[15] W.L.Chen, *Walsh Series Analysis of Multi-Delay Systems*, J.Franklin Institute, Vol. 313, pp.207-217 (1982).

[16] S.G.Tzafestas, *Walsh Series Approach to Lumped and Distributed System Identification*, J.Franklin Institute, Vol.305, No.4, pp.199-218 (1978).

[17] G.Prasada Rao and K.R.Palanisamy, *Improved Algorithms for Parameter Identification in Continuous Systems Via Walsh Functions* , Proceedings of IEE, Vol.130, Pt.D, No.1, pp.9-16 (1983).

[18] P.Stavroulakis and S.G.Tzafestas, *Distributed-Parameter Observer Based Control Implementation Using Finite Spatial Measurements*, Math.Comp.Simul. 22, pp.373-379 (1980).

[19] A.Thowsen and W.R.Perkins, *Sampled-Data Linear Quadratic Regulator for Systems with Generalized Transportation Lags*, Int.J.Control, Vol.21, No.1, pp.46-65, (1975).

[20] K.P.M.Bhat and H.N.Koivo, *An Observer Theory for Time Delay Systems*, Technical Report No.7502, University of Toronto (1975).

[21] P.Stavroulakis and S.G.Tzafestas , *Walsh Series Approach to time Delay Control Systems* , Int.J.Systems Sci.,

Vol.9, No.3, pp.287-299 (1978).

[22] G.Prasada Rao and L.Sivakumar, *Identification of Time-Lag Systems via Walsh Functions*, IEEE Trans., Vol.24, pp.806-808 (1979).

[23] G.Prasada Rao and K.R.Palanisamy, *A New Operational Matrix for Delay via Walsh Functions and Some Aspects of its Algebra and Applications*, Proc. of National Systems Conf.:NSC 78, PAU Ludbiana, pp.1/60-61 (1978).

[24] G.Prasada Rao and T.Srinivasan, *Analysis and Synthesis of Dynamic Systems Containing Time Delays via Block-Pulse Functions*, Proceedings of IEE, Vol.125(9), pp.1064-1068 (1978).

[25] G.Prasada Rao, K.R.Palanisamy and T. Srinivasan, *Extension of Computation Beyond the Initial Normal Interval in Walsh Series Analysis of Dynamical Systems*, IEEE Trans Auto Control,AC-25, pp.317-319 (1980).

[26] J.Anoussis and S.G.Tzafestas, *Coupled-Core Reactor Simulation and Identification Using One Shot Operational Walsh Matrices*, Proc. DIGITECH 84, (this volume) pp. 51-60 (1985).

[27] S.G.Tzafestas and N.Chrysochoides, *Nuclear Reactor Control Using Walsh Function Variational Synthesis, Nucl.Sci. Engrg.*, Vol.62, pp.763-770 (1977).

[28] S.G.Tzafestas and J.Anoussis, *Dynamic Reactivity Computation in Nuclear Reactors Using Block-Pulse Function Expansion*, Int. J.Modelling and Simulation, Vol.4, No.2, pp.73-76 (1984).

DIGITAL TECHNIQUES in Simulation, Communication and Control
Spyros G. Tzafestas (editor)
Elsevier Science Publishers B.V. (North-Holland) © IMACS, 1985

DIGITAL SIMULATION OF A CERAMICS TUNNEL FURNACE USING COLLOCATION METHOD

J.P. Babary and A. Hariri*

Laboratoire d'Automatique et d'Analyse des Systèmes du C.N.R.S.
7, avenue du Colonel Roche, 31077 Toulouse Cédex, France

We consider an industrial tunnel furnace for baking roof-tiles, producing 80.000 tiles a day. Because of a high energy consumption, an optimisation study has to be performed, in order to define an optimal control law of gas flowrates at each group of burners (10 groups), of the mean velocity of the charge (tiles) being carried through the tunnel, of the flowrate of countercurrent flue gas,...
A mathematical model of the thermal behaviour has been established taking into account mass and heat transfers (conduction, convection, radiation); this model is a non-linear partial derivative system of hyperbolic type.
The model has been linearized around a nominal value corresponding to the steady state of the non-linear system which is supposed to be homogeneous with respect to the distribution of the charge.
The transformation of the distributed parameter system into a lumped parameter model has been performed by means of the collocation method with actuating points as collocation points.
The purpose of this paper consists of a presentation of the modelling study, and application of the collocation method

1. INTRODUCTION

To manufacture red clay products e.g roof-tiles, bricks, it is necessary to shape the product following preparation of the clay paste. Then the product has to be dried and finally baked. The latter stage is the most delicate one as it conditions to a great extent the quality of the product. In addition the need for high temperatures leads to a high energy consumption, see [1], [2] and [3]. An optimization study was therefore required in order to obtain a control algorithm from a fine modelling of the process and to program it on a microcomputer.

2. DESCRIPTION OF THE PHYSICAL PROCESS

The tunnel furnace for baking roof-tiles (see fig. 1) is installed at Colomiers, near Toulouse (France) and is the property of GELIS Co.
This furnace mainly consists of masonry and of a heat insulation whose nature and thickness depend on the level of internal temperature. As a result, the heat flow can be more or less considered as being independent of temperature. A train of carriage transports U-shaped saggars made of refractory material (300 saggars per carriage). Each saggar is packed with 15 roof-tiles laid at right angles and parallel to the displacement direction. The train circulates intermittently by means of 1.60 meter push.
A gas blown counter currently is used to cool roof-tiles in the zone of the charge output and to pre-heat them in the zone of the charge input. In order to cool metallic parts, air is blown under the carriages.
Pressures are controlled in the air situated under the supporting frame. Hence it is possible to assume that no gas circulates between the two currents.
To free water and carbon dioxide from clay carbonates, roof-tiles have to be heated at a temperature almost reaching 1,000°C. Gas burners distributed all along the centre zone of the furnace supply the calorific energy. Given the state of the art, fuel flowrates are controlled by the temperature measured under the tunnel roof.
The different gas inlets and outlets located in the furnace consist of the following :
- one air inlet at the furnace output;
- one hot air drawing off - destined for the drier.
- three rapid coolers (cold air)
- ten groups of burners together with their supply of combustion air (50 burners).

From a qualitative viewpoint roof-tiles are therefore pre-heated first by means of the gas blown counter currently and yield their residual moisture. Then the chemical reactions occur. Finally, roof-tiles are cooled when they yield their heat to the gas. The rapid coolers ensure the proper passage of the quartz point and direct recovery is used both to cool the solid as quickly as possible and thus to recover the latter's sensitive heat.

* Engineer at the Centre of Research and Scientific Studies. Damascus (Syria)

3. ELABORATION OF THE MATHEMATICAL MODEL

Introduction

Modelling of the heat behaviour must not be too complex as a usuable system of equations must be obtained without too many difficulties at the digital level and must also be sufficiently precise as to furnish a rather accurate representation of the furnace operation.
The mathematical model presented has been established in collaboration with the researchers of the Institute of Chemical Engineering of Toulouse (France).

Basic assumptions retained

A certain number of basic assumptions have been made. It is therefore assumed that :

a - the charge consists of roof-tiles packed in U-shaped saggars subject to a temperature uniformly distributed along a cross-section;
b - conduction within the charge is negligible;
c - conduction within the gas is negligible;
d - a vertical conductive transfer occurs at the supporting frame
e - conduction within the wall is only important in the axial direction of the furnace;
f - gas thickness is thin with respect to radiation;
g - solids are grey;
h - heats resulting from the endothermal reactions involved are distributed uniformly along part of the furnace.

Modelling based upon the energy balance

The heat behaviour of the furnace has been established on the basis of the thermodynamical balance between the various furnace constituents:

First equation : Heat balance on the charge

$$\frac{\partial}{\partial t}(\rho_T S_T C_T T) + \frac{\partial}{\partial x}(U_T \rho_T S_T C_T T) = \alpha_{TG}(G-T) + \beta_{TG}(G^4-T^4)$$

$$+ \beta_{TP}(P^4-T^4) + \beta_{TS}(S^4(y=0) - T^4) + \Delta H(x) \qquad (1)$$

Second equation : Heat balance on the gas

$$\frac{\partial}{\partial t}(\rho_G S_G C_G G) - \frac{\partial}{\partial x}(U_G \rho_G S_G C_G G) = \alpha_{TG}(T-G) + \alpha_{PG}(P-G) +$$

$$+ \alpha_{GS}(S(y=0)-G) + \beta_{GT}(T^4-G^4) + \beta_{PG}(P^4-G^4) + \qquad (2)$$

$$+ \beta_{GS}(S^4(y=0) - G^4) + \sum_{i=1}^{N_B} \delta(x-x_i)\, Q_{bri}$$

Third equation : Heat balance on the wall

$$0 = \alpha_{GP}(P-G) + \beta_{GP}(P^4-G^4) + \beta_{TP}(P^4-T^4) + \alpha_{PTo}(x)$$

$$(P-T_o) + \beta_{PS}(P^4-S^4(y=0)) \qquad (3)$$

Fourth equation : Heat balance on the supporting frame

$$\frac{\partial}{\partial t}(\rho_S C_S S) = \lambda_S \frac{\partial^2 S}{\partial y^2} - \frac{\partial}{\partial x}(U_T \rho_S C_S S) \qquad (4)$$

Fifth equation : Heat balance on the gas under the supporting frame

$$\frac{\partial}{\partial t}(\rho_1 S_1 C_1 G_1) - \frac{\partial}{\partial x}(U_1 \rho_1 S_1 C_1 G_1) = \alpha_{SG1}(S-G_1) \qquad (5)$$

Sixth equation : Mass balance on the gas

$$\frac{\partial}{\partial x}(U_G \rho_G S_G) = - \sum_{i=1}^{N_B} \delta(x-x_i)\, D_{xi}\,(17.9+16.9\,q)$$

$$+ \text{REC}\ \delta(x-x_T) - \sum_{j=1}^{3} \delta(x-x_j)\, D_{RRj} \qquad (6)$$

Boundary conditions are given by

$X = 0 \qquad T(0) = T_o$

$X = L_f \qquad G(L_f) = T_o$

$\qquad\qquad G_1(L_f) = T_o$

$\forall x,\ y = 0$

$$- \lambda_S \frac{\partial S}{\partial y} L_S = \alpha_{GS}(G-S) + \beta_{GS}(G^4-S^4) + \beta_{PS}(P^4-S^4) + \beta_{TS}(T^4-S^4) \qquad (a)$$

$\forall x,\ y = L$

$$- \lambda_S \frac{\partial S}{\partial y} L_S = \alpha_{SG1}(S-G_1) \qquad (b)$$

$$\forall y,\ x = 0 \qquad S = T_o \qquad (c)$$

The mathematical model thus obtained is a non-linear partial derivative system (i.e. five partial derivative equations and one algebraic equation) with conditions at the two point boundary values :
the independent variables are time (t), and the two space variables :

- (x) distributed along the furnace lenght
- (y) distributed at right angles to the supporting frame

Model transformation and linearisation

The model obtained has two space directions which render difficult overall integration of the system. In order to have just one space direction, the derivatives in relation to (y) are replaced by a finite difference method at the level of the supporting frame equation. The supporting frame is discretised in three parts and the following approximation is established :

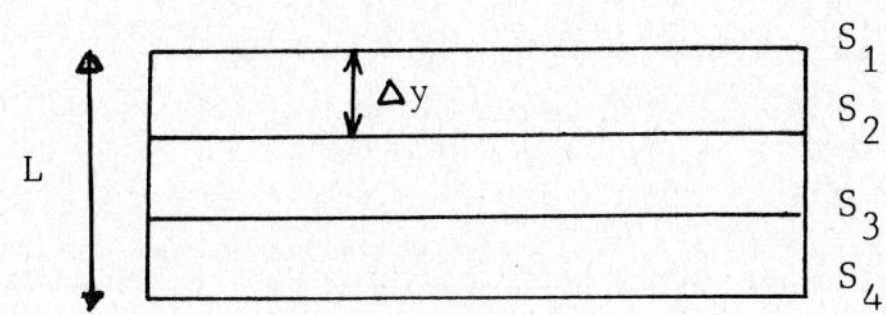

$$\frac{\partial^2 S}{\partial y^2} = \frac{S_{i+1} - 2 S_i + S_{i-1}}{\Delta y^2}$$

To determine a closed loop control law, the original model has been linearised around a nominal regime. This linearisation has been validated by simulations of both linear and non-linear models. Finally, the following model is obtained. It represents the dynamic behaviour of the furnace around its steady state.

$$\frac{\partial}{\partial t} Y(x,t) = \lambda(x) \frac{\partial}{\partial x} Y(x,t) + A(x)Y(x,t) + B(x)u(t) \qquad (7)$$

$$Y(x,t) = \left[T \; S_1 \; S_2 \; S_3 \; S_4 \; G \; G_1\right]^T$$

$$u(t) = \left[u_1 \; u_2 \; \dots \; u_{12}\right]^T$$

$\lambda(x)$: 7 x 7 diagonal matrix
$A(x)$: 7 x 7 matrix
$B(x)$: 7 x 12 matrix

The state vector $Y(x,t)$ can be partitioned as follows :

$$Y(x,t) = \text{col}\left[Y^-(x,t),\; Y^+(x,t)\right]$$

where

$$Y^-(x,t) = \left[T \quad S_1 \; S_2 \; S_3 \; S_4\right]^T \qquad \text{(solid state)}$$

$$Y^+(x,t) = \left[G \quad G_1\right]^T \qquad \text{(gas state)}$$

Thus, the matrices $A(x)$, $B(x)$, $\lambda(x)$ can be written in the following form :

$$A(x) = \begin{bmatrix} A_-^- & A_+^- \\ A_-^+ & A_+^+ \end{bmatrix}$$

$$B(x) = \begin{bmatrix} B^- \\ B^+ \end{bmatrix}$$

$$\lambda(x) = \text{diag}\left[\lambda^- \quad \lambda^+\right]$$

The linearised model meets the following conditions :

$$Y(x,0) = Yo(x) \qquad (8)$$

$$Y^-(o,t) = 0$$
$$Y^+(L_f,t) = 0 \qquad (9)$$

4. Approximated model of the partial derivative system

In order to obtain a system of ordinary differential equations the simulation of the partial derivative equations requires that the infinite dimension space be transformed into a finite space. Numerous methods make such a transformation possible. The collocation method [4] has been applied as it is well adapted to this type of method. To discretise equation (7) by means of the collocation method n+2 points are selected such that:

$$0 = x_o < x_1 < x_2 \dots < x_{n+1} = L_f$$

the Lagrange interpolation is used

$$Y(x,t) \cong \sum_{i=0}^{n+1} F_i(x)\, Y(x_i,t) \qquad (10)$$

where $F_i(x)$ is the Lagrange function :

$$F_i(x) = \prod_{\substack{j=0 \\ j\neq i}}^{n+1} \frac{x - x_j}{x_i - x_j}$$

Thus :

$$F_i(x_j) = \begin{cases} 1 & i=j \\ 0 & i\neq j \end{cases}$$

we note that :

$$Y_i(x) = Y(x_i,t)$$

$$\overset{o}{F}_{ij} = \left.\frac{d\,F_i(x)}{dx}\right|_{x=x_j}$$

with this interpolation we have the following approximations.

$$\left.\frac{\partial Y(x,t)}{\partial t}\right|_{x=x_j} = \frac{d\,Y_j}{dt} \qquad (11)$$

$$\frac{\partial Y^-(x,t)}{\partial x} \cong \sum_{i=o}^{n+1} \overset{o}{F}_{ij}\, Y_i^-(t) = \sum_{i=1}^{n+1} F_{ij}\, Y_i^-(t) \qquad (12)$$

$$\frac{\partial Y^+(x,t)}{\partial x} \cong \sum_{i=o}^{n+1} \overset{o}{F}_{ij}\, Y_i^+(t) = \sum_{i=o}^{n} F_{ij}\, Y_i^+(t) \qquad (13)$$

By taking into account the decomposition of the state vector, equation (7) can be written in the form :

$$\frac{\partial Y^-(x,t)}{\partial t} = \lambda^-(x)\frac{\partial Y^-(x,t)}{\partial x} + A^-_-(x)Y^-(x,t)+A^-_+(x)$$

$$Y^+(x,t)+B^-(x)u(t)$$

$$\frac{\partial Y^+(x,t)}{\partial t} = \lambda^+(x)\frac{\partial Y^+(x,t)}{\partial x} + A^+_-(x)Y^-(x,t)+A^+_+(x)$$

$$Y^+(x,t)+B^+(x)\,u(t)$$

By taking into account (11, 12, 13) for $x = x_1, x_2, \ldots, x_{n+1}$, for the first equation and for $x = x_o, x_1, \ldots, x_n$ for the second equation, a new state vector $\tilde{Y}$ is defined such that :

$$\tilde{Y}(t) = \text{col}\left[Y_1^-, Y_2^-, \ldots, Y_{n+1}^-, Y_o^+\, Y_1^+\, Y_n^+\right]$$

The following lumped parameter model is then obtained

$$\overset{o}{\tilde{Y}}(t) = \tilde{A}\,\tilde{Y}(t) + \tilde{B}\,u(t) \qquad (14)$$

$$\tilde{Y}(0) = \tilde{Y}0$$

where $\tilde{A}$ is a stationary matrix of dimension $[7(n+1),\ 7(n+1)]$ and $\tilde{B}$ a stationary matrix of dimension $[(7(n+1),\ 12]$. n = 11 is selected. It corresponds to 11 collocation points situated in the middle of the 11 control zones. It is then possible to obtain an 84 order lumped parameter system controlled by 12 control variables (10 burners, one set of rapid coolers, and the counter currently blown air). The derivative of the Lagrange function has been calculated by means of the algorithm presented in [5].

ANNEXE

t = time (s)
x = space variable (m)
y = space variable (m)
T = charge temperature (°K)
P = wall temperature
G = gas temperature (°K)
G_1 = gas temperature under supporting frame (°K)
S = supporting frame temperature (°K)
U_T = charge velocity (m/s)
U_G = gas velocity (m/s)
U_1 = gas velocity under S.F. (m/s)
ρ_T = bulk density of charge (Kg/m3)
ρ_G = gas density (Kg/m3)
ρ_1 = gas density under S.F. (Kg/m3)
S_T = charge volume per unit of length (m2)
S_G = gas volume per unit of length (m2)
S_1 = gas volume under S.F. per unit of length (m2)
C_T = specific heat of charge (J/Kg/°K)
C_G = specific heat of gas (J/Kg/K)
C_1 = specific heat of gas under S.F. (J/Kg/°K)
x_i = action points of burners (m)
Q_{bri} = heat supplied by burner i per unit of time (J/s)
λ_s = thermal conductivity of S.F. (w/m/°K)
D_{ri} = mass flowrate of gas at burner i (Kg/s)
D_{RR_j} = mass flowrate of rapid cooler j (Kg/s)
REC = mass flowrate of air recovered for the drier (Kg/s)
X_T = recovery point for the drier (m)
α = coefficient of convective exchange (w/m°K)
β = coefficient of radiating exchange (w/m°K^4)
T_o = ambient temperature
ΔH = decarbonatation reaction heat.

REFERENCES

[1] BABARY J.P., Thermal regulation of tunnel furnaces, 3rd Int. Symp. "Modelling, Identification and Control" - Innsbruck (Autriche), 14/17 Février 1984.

[2] EL HAJJAR H., Contrôle et Conduite numériques d'un four tunnel d'industrie céramique. Thèse de Docteur-Ingénieur n° 833, Uniersité Paul Sabatier, Toulouse, 18 Mai 1983.

[3] BARRETEAU D. et BABARY J.P., Modélisation de four-tunnel dans l'industrie céramique (à paraître dans "ENTROPIE").

[4] WYSOCKI Marian Application of orthogonal collocation To Simulation and Control of first order hyperbolic system. Mathematics and Computers in Simulation, XXV (1983) 335-345.

[5] M.L. MICHELSEN and J. VILLADSEN, A convenient computional procedure for collocation constants. Chem. Engrg. J. 4 (1972) 64-68.

FIGURES corresponding to a numerical simulation, with a nominal control, after a perturbation in the furnace.
n° 2 : Evolution of the charge temperature
n° 3 to 6 : Evolution of the supporting frame temperature in 4 points.

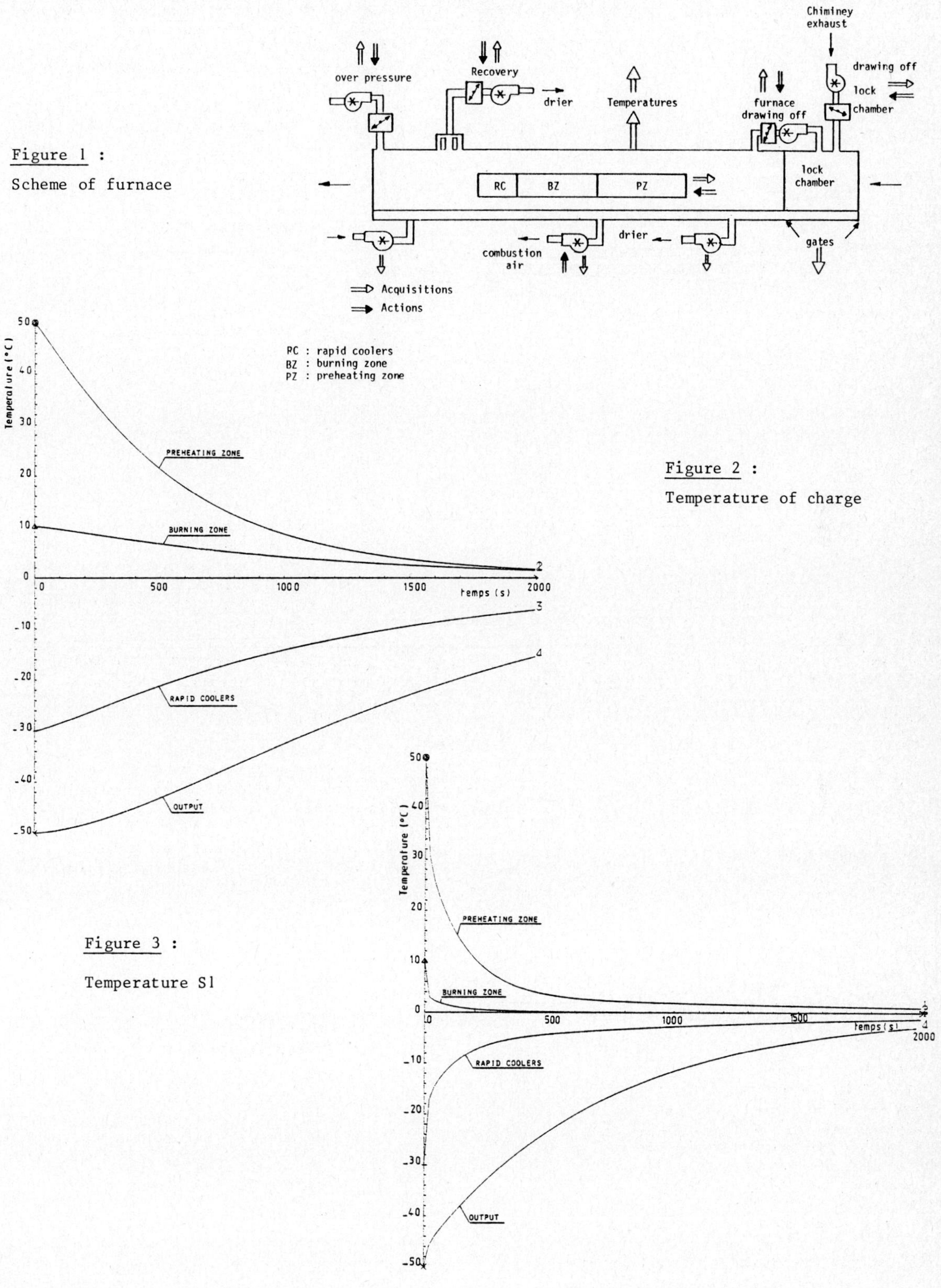

Figure 1 :

Scheme of furnace

Figure 2 :

Temperature of charge

Figure 3 :

Temperature S1

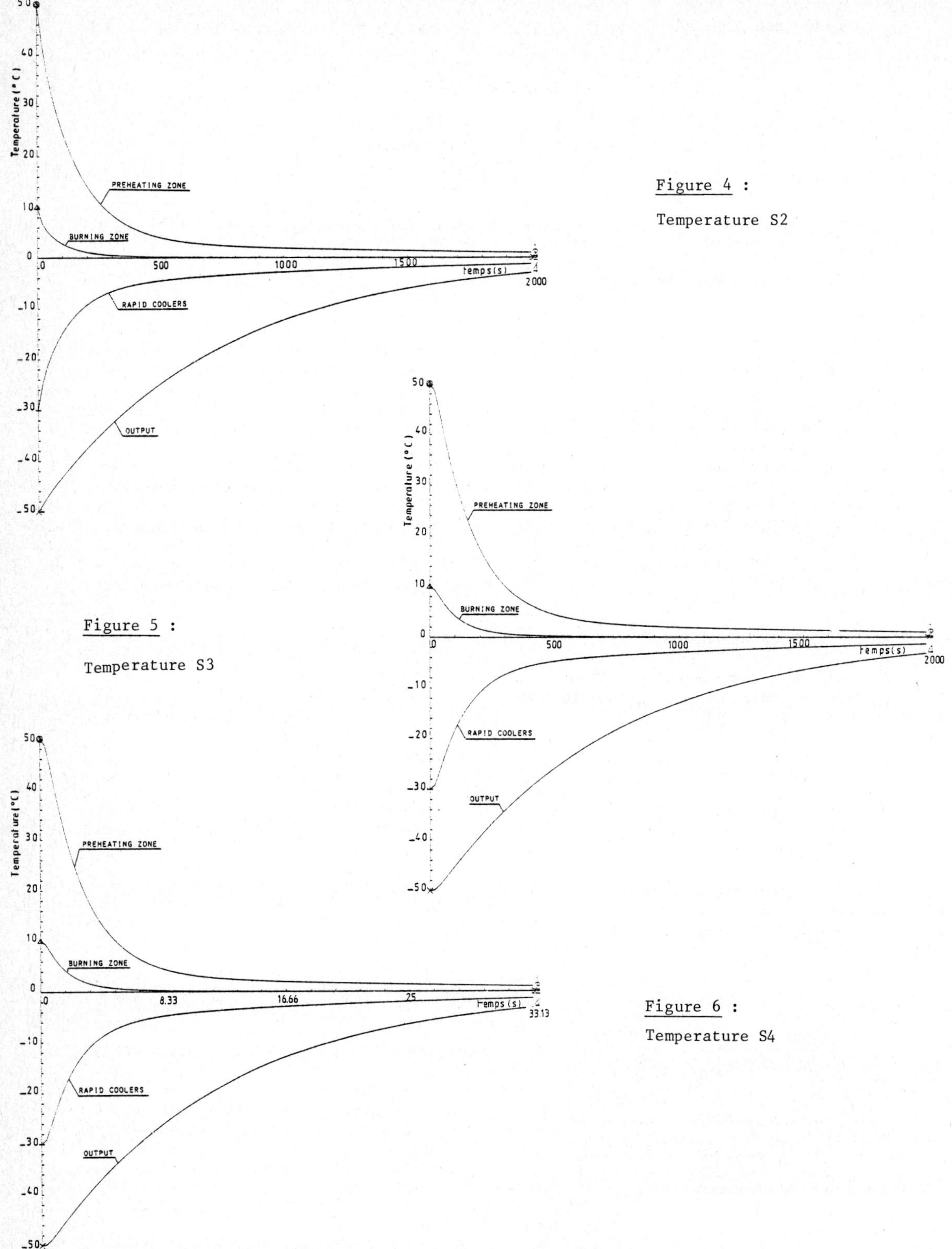

Figure 4 :

Temperature S2

Figure 5 :

Temperature S3

Figure 6 :

Temperature S4

DIGITAL TECHNIQUES in Simulation, Communication and Control
Spyros G. Tzafestas (editor)
Elsevier Science Publishers B.V. (North-Holland) © IMACS, 1985

APPROXIMATION AND SIMULATION OF SLABS REHEATING PROCESS USING SPLINE FUNCTION METHOD

Zbigniew Mrozek

Technical University Cracov
(Poland)

The spline function is used for an approximation of temperature distribution inside the slab. The method gives the possibility for approximation of any partial differential equation in space of splines. Good accurancy, small memory requirements and short computer run time are the important properities of spline function method.

1. INTRODUCTION.

Slabs reheating process has a great influence on work of rolling mill in metallurgical plant. The task of reheating furnace (Fig. 1.) is to heat slabs up to desired temperature. The main difficulty of this process is to satisfy the demand of uniform temperature in the slab cross section. Since accurate temperature measurement inside the slab is impossible, computer simulation of slabs reheating process is desired.

2.DISTRIBUTED MODEL OF REHEATING PROCESS.

A process of one-sided reheating of metal in a furnace is described by the diffusion equation

$$\frac{\partial\theta}{\partial t} = \frac{\partial^2\theta}{\partial x^2} \tag{2.1}$$

with

$$\theta(0,x) = -1 \tag{2.2}$$

$$\frac{\partial\theta}{\partial x}(t,1) = -Bi\cdot\theta(t,1) \tag{2.3a}$$

$$\frac{\partial\theta}{\partial x}(t,0) = 0 \tag{2.3b}$$

where

$\theta(t,x) \in [-1,0]$ - temperature (normalized)
$t \geq 0$ - time (normalized)
$x \in [0,1]$ - spatial coordinate (normalized)
Bi - Biot's coefficient

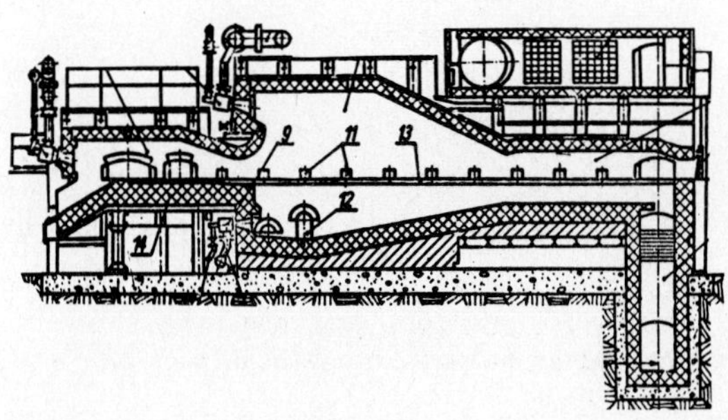

Fig 1. An example of multizone slabs reheating furnace [6].

Temperature distribution with respect to longitudal and transversal directions is assumed to be insignificant [5]. Only temperature distribution along the thickness direction is taken into consideration.

It must be underlined, that every slab keeps moving along the furnace. Since temperature depends on a place in furnace (see Fig. 2), equations (2.1) (2.4) form boundary control problem. This problem can be solved by simulation using spline function method.

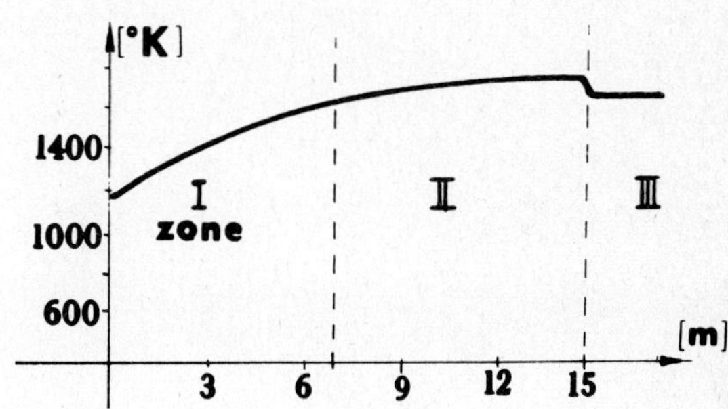

Fig 2. An example of furnace temperature versus longitudal spatial coordinate.

3. SPLINE FUNCTION AND ITS MAIN PROPERITIES

The unknown slab temperature $\theta(t,x)$ is approximated by the spline function $s(t,x)$. The spline is a piecewise polynomial satisfying certain conditions regarding continuity of the function and its derivatives. The spline can be expressed as

$$s(t,x) = \sum_i q_i(t)\cdot\Phi_i(x) \tag{3.1}$$

where

$q_i(t)$ unknown function of time — to be found
$\Phi_i(x)$ B-spline (basis function) to be described later (Fig 3.)

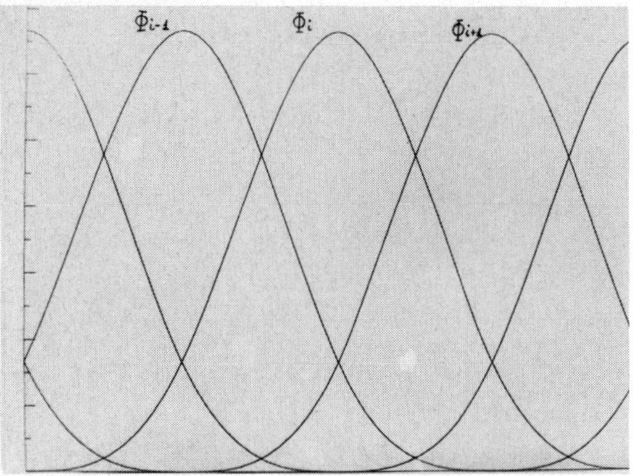

Fig 3. B-splines - basis of approximation space.

Multidimensional spline function can be determined using tensor product of one-dimensional basis functions [1]. An example of two-dimensional spline $s(x,y) = 0.1\cdot\Phi_4(x)\cdot\Phi_5(y)$ is presented on Fig. 4 [4].

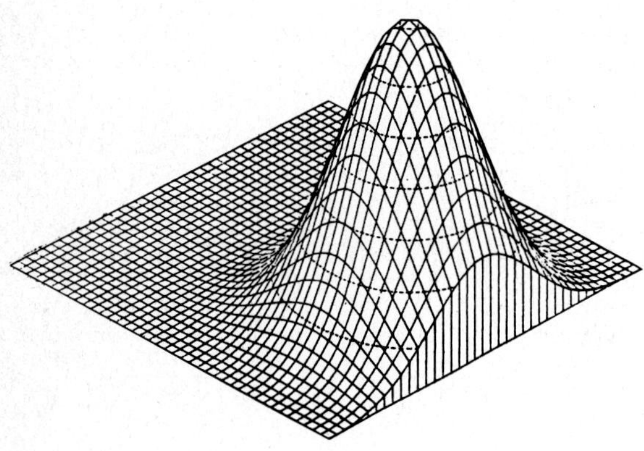

Fig 4. Two-dimensional B-spline on x-y plane.

B-spline (3.1) is expressed by polynomial of k-th degree, and its spatial derivatives can be effectively evaluated. Differentiating (3.1) one can get derivatives of spline

$$\frac{\partial}{\partial x}s(t,x) = \sum_i q_i(t)\frac{\partial}{\partial x}\Phi_i(x) \tag{3.2}$$

$$\frac{\partial^2}{\partial x^2}s(t,x) = \sum_i q_i(t)\frac{\partial^2}{\partial x^2}\Phi_i(x) \tag{3.3}$$

and so on.

Substituting (3.1),(3.2),(3.3) into partial differential equations (2.1) and its initial (2.2) and boundary conditions (2.3) yields a set of ordinary differential equations with respect to time. This set creates a finite dimensional model of distributed parameter process.

4. FINITE DIMENSIONAL MODEL OF THE PROCESS

A set of ordinary differental equatons of the first order forms the finite dimensional model of distributed parameter process. Coefficients $q(t)$ of spline are unknown functions - to be found.

4.1 SELECTION OF APPROXIMATION SPACE

It was assumed, that

(i) the normalized indepedent variable interval [0,1] is uniformly partitioned with N=3 interior knots

$$\Delta: x_0=0.<x_1=.25<x_2=.5<x_3=.75<x_4=1.$$

(ii) degree of splines k=3. This involves that the first and the second derivative, with respect to x-coordinate, is continuous. Spline space dimension is equal N+k+1=7.

(iii) following B-splines form basis of the choosen space of approximation:

$$\Phi_i(x) = \begin{cases} w(h-t)^3 & \text{for } x\in[x_{i-1},x_i] \\ w(4h^3+3t^3-6ht^2) & \text{for } x\in(x_{i-2},x_{i-1}] \\ w(h^3+3(h^2t+ht^2-t^3)) & \text{for } x\in(x_{i-3},x_{i-2}] \\ wt^3 & \text{for } x\in(x_{i-4},x_{i-3}] \\ 0 & \text{for } x\notin(x_{i-4},x_i) \end{cases} \tag{4.1}$$

where

$i=1,2,\ \ldots,N+k+1=7.$
$h=(x_i-x_{i-1}) = \text{const}$
$t=(x-x_m)<h$
x_m - first knot left from x.

4.2 GENERATION OF THE SET OF ORDINARY DIFFERENTIAL EQUATIONS

It is assumed, that temperature $\Theta(t,x)$ is approximated by spline function (2.1) with known basis function (4.1) and unknown coefficients $q_i(t), i=1,2,\ldots,7$. Substituting spline (3.1) and its derivatives into (2.1)-(2.3) yields, respectively

$$\sum_{i=1}^{7}\frac{\partial}{\partial t}q_i(t)\cdot\Phi_i(x) = \sum_{i=1}^{7}q_i(t)\frac{\partial^2}{\partial x^2}\Phi_i(x) \tag{4.2}$$

$$\sum_{i=1}^{7}q_i(0)\cdot\Phi(x) = -1 \tag{4.3}$$

$$\sum_{i=1}^{7}q_i(t)\cdot\frac{\partial}{\partial x}\Phi_i(1) = -Bi\sum_{i=1}^{7}q_i(t)\cdot\Phi_i(1) \tag{4.4a}$$

$$\sum q_i(t)\cdot\frac{\partial}{\partial x}\Phi_i(0) = 0 \tag{4.4b}$$

The following values of an x coordinate
0., .125, .25, .5, .875, 1.0
were choosen as points of collocation.

Substuting values of basis functions (4.1) (and values of its derivatives) into (4.2) yields a set of ordinary differential equations

$$2/3\ \dot{q}_1 + 8/3\ \dot{q}_2 + 2/3\ \dot{q}_3 = 64\ q_1 - 128\ q_2 + 64q \quad \text{for } x = 0.0$$

and

$$1/12\ \dot{q}_1 + 23/12\ \dot{q}_2 + 23/12\ \dot{q}_3 + 1/12\ \dot{q}_4 = = 32\ q_1 - 32\ q_2 - 32\ q_3 + 32\ q_4 \quad \text{for } x = .125$$

and so on. This collocation yields to ODE matrix equation

$$A\ \underline{\dot{q}} = B\ \underline{q} \tag{4.5}$$

where $\underline{q}$ is a vector of unknown coefficients

$$\underline{q} = [q_1, q_2, q_3, q_4, q_5, q_6, q_7]$$

and
A,B - known coefficient matrices, dim= 7 x 7

The initial values

$$\underline{q}(0)=[-.25, -.25, -.25, -.25, -.25, -.25, -.25] \tag{4.6}$$

are obtained as solution of (4.3).

An alternative of presented collocation method is a Galerkin method. But it was found, that for simulation of slabs reheating process, the Galerkin method was less accourate [4].

4.3 BOUNDARY CONDITIONS FOR FINITE DIMENSIONAL MODEL

Substituting (4.1) into (4.4a) and (4.4b) yields, assuming Bi=1.5, respectively

$$-8q_5 + 8q_7 = -1.5\ (2/3\ q_5 + 8/3\ q_6 + 2/3\ q_7) \tag{4.7}$$

$$-8q_1 + 8q_3 = 0 \tag{4.8}$$

Formulas (4.7) and (4.8) are to be used to correct q_1 and q_7 values in (4.6), to agree with boundary conditions. This yields

$$q(0)=[-.25, -.25, -.25, -.25, -.25, -.25, -1/12] \tag{4.9}$$

4.4 COMPUTATIONAL SCHEME

Matrix equation (4.5) is transformed ($A^{-1} \neq 0$) to

$$\dot{\underline{q}}(t) = A^{-1} \cdot B \cdot \underline{q}(t) \tag{4.10}$$

Solution of this ODE can be obtained by any method, e.g. 4-th order Runge-Kutta. When coefficients $\underline{q}(t)$ (as time dependent solution of ODE (4.10)) are found, the temperature distribution of slab can be calculated from (3.1) for any time t.

The following points are to be taken into account during further computation:

(i) after each time step of integration routine, it is necessary to correct some values of q(t) - to obtain agreement with boundary conditions (4.7), (4.8).

(ii) in case of distributed control , matrices A and B (4.5) may need recalculation (see paragraph 4.2) after each time step.

5. COMPUTATIONAL RESULTS

Computer program SSLAB2 [4] was prepared to test spline function method, as presented. A and B matrices (4.5) of different dimension were automaticaly generated. Fixed step, fourth order Runge-Kutta routine was used for integration of (4.10). Library programs FORSIM VI [2] and PDECOL [3] , all designed for PDE resolution, were tested too. Computational results were compared with analytical solution of problem (2.1) - (2.3).

It was found, that for both SSLAB2 and FORSIM VI, the computation errors were getting smaller, when space dimension was increased, or when time step of integration procedure was decreased. The spline program SSLAB2 was always more accurate than FORSIM VI, and needed 3.5 times less of storage than FORSIM VI. PDECOL was found to be quite useless, because of its unstability for boundary control problem (Fig 5.).

Computer running time increase was observed for the space dimension increase and for the time step decrease (Fig 6). The same computation time (50 seconds) was needed for SSLAB2 and FORSIM VI, when space dimension was equal 13, and time step was 0.001 . As results of SSLAB2 computation were more accurate, the spline function method ought to be choosen. Possible use of sparse matrix technique in SSLAB2 may result in considerable shortage of computation time, especially for large space dimension.

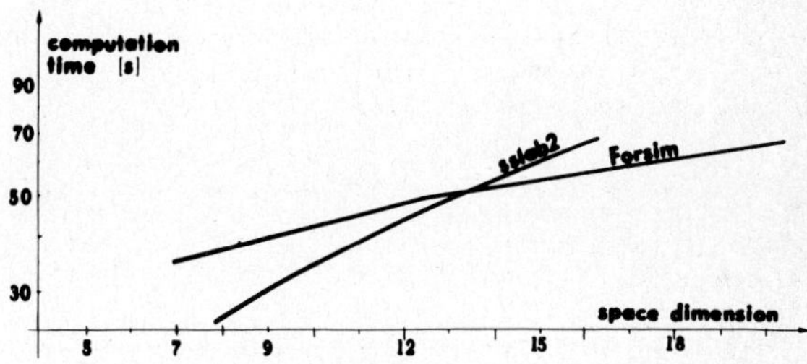

Fig 6. Computer run time versus space dimension - SSLAB2 and FORSIM VI programs only.

The extended SSLAB3 program was prepared for simulation of slabs reheating process, where the temperature profile of furnace is given and (with the exception of last furnace zone), two sided heating is performed. This involves some changes in boundary conditions. Right hand side of (2.3a) and (2.3b) are no longer constant, but the function (nonlinear) of time (see Fig 2.).

6. CONCLUSIONS

The spline function of the third degree is used for an approximation of temperature distribution inside the slab. It was shown, that good results were obtained for the spline function method programs SSLAB2 and SSLAB3 [4], prepared for the simulation of distributed parameter slabs reheating process. Library program FORSIM VI needed 3.5 times more computation memory and was less accurate. PDECOL [3] was quite useless. Good accurancy, small memory requirements and short computer run times are important properities of the spline function method.

REFERENCES

1. De Boor C. On calculating with B-splines. J. Appr. Theory, vol 6 pp 58,62 1972

2. Carver M.B. Stevard D.G. FORSIM VI, Fortran oriented system simulation package for partial and ordinary differential equations - users manual. Atomic Energy of Canada, Report AECL 5821.

3. Madsen N.K. Sincovec R.F. PDECOL, general collocation software for partial differential equations, ACM Trans. on Math. Software vol 5,3 pp 326,351 1979.

4. Mrozek Zbigniew Some methods for approximation of distributed parameter object, Ph.D. thesis, Academy of Mining and Metallurgy, Cracow - Poland 1982.
(in Polish: Wybrane, skończenie wymiarowe metody aproksymacji obiektu o parametrach rozłożonych)

5. Ogawa S. A new mathematical model for computer control of distributed parameter systems. Preprints IFAC 1975, part IIc ref 39.1

6. Senkara T. Recheating furnaces on metallurgical plants, Śląsk, Katowice 1968 (in Polish: Piece grzewcze w hutnictwie żelaza)

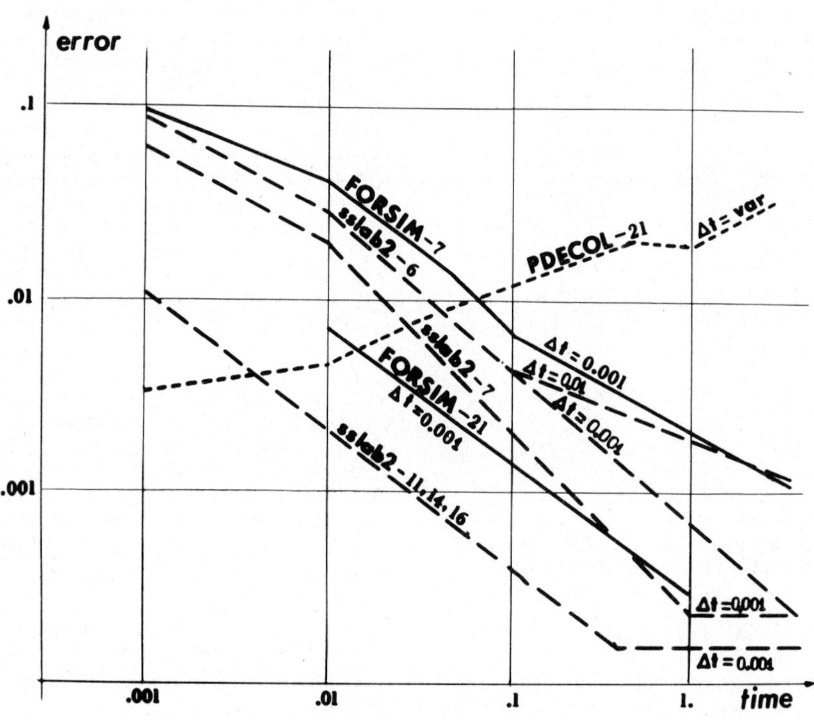

Fig 5. Absolute computation errors versus simulation time. Program name, space dimension and time step are given.

DIGITAL TECHNIQUES in Simulation, Communication and Control
Spyros G. Tzafestas (editor)
Elsevier Science Publishers B.V. (North-Holland) © IMACS, 1985

NEUTRONIC SIMULATION OF TWO-DIMENSIONAL NUCLEAR REACTORS BY AN IMPROVED SIMPLIFIED RESPONSE MATRIX TECHNIQUE

John Kollas

Nuclear Technology Department
Greek Atomic Energy Commission
Aghia Paraskevi, Attiki

An improved simplified response matrix technique is utilized in the solution of criticality problems of two dimensional nuclear reactors. The technique treats the interface partial neutron current distribution by higher order polynomials improving thus an older linear polynomial technique. Numerical results obtained by code RESPTWO implementing the present approach and compared with the corresponding results of a classical finite difference scheme indicate that the estimation of reactor criticality and of neutron leakage, absorption and production rates is successful. The economic advantage -a one order of magnitude reduction in computing time- can be further improved by editing only information of special interest, e.g. neutron fluxes at"critical" points such as hot spots.

1. INTRODUCTION

The most common methods of analyzing nuclear reactors, e.g. the classical finite difference method, the finite element method etc., deal with the solution of equations involving the neutron flux. During the last two decades alternate methods based on response matrix techniques and dealing with the solution of equations involving quantities related to the response of a region have been developed.

Selengut(1) was the first to develop a response technique based on the representation of reactor regions in terms of partial neutron currents at the boundaries of the regions. This and other response techniques have been applied extensively and usually successfully to one-dimensional problems (2), (3). However, the analysis of more realistic cases, i.e. two- and three-dimensional problems, is more difficult since the quantities connected to the response of a region depend not only on the composition and size of the region, but on other quantities too, e.g. the spatial distribution of the incoming partial neutron currents along the boundaries of the region (4), (5), (6).

In this paper a simplified response matrix technique is utilized in the solution of criticality problems of two dimensional nuclear reactors made up of symmetric but possibly heterogeneous assemblies in one energy group. The present technique improves an older one which treated the interface partial neutron current distributions by linear polynomials. (7), (8)

2. DESCRIPTION OF THE METHOD

The basic idea of the response matrix technique is to replace all assemblies constituting a reactor by black boxes which are iterconnected by their response matrices and then solve for the partial neutron current distribution along the assembly boundaries by relating outgoing and incoming partial neutron currents. The first step of the above procedure, where we calculate the response matrices of each different type of assembly we call the cell calculation and the second step where we determine partial neutron current distributions along assembly boundaries we call the reactor calculation. The second step is independent of the first.

2.1. The Cell Calculation

In order to calculate response matrices we take advantage of the linear character of group diffusion equations, which we utilize throughout this paper, and apply the principle of superposition. For a given assembly the outgoing partial neutron currents are functions of the incoming partial neutron currents at the boundaries of the assembly and by the principle of superposition the total outgoing partial neutron current is the sum of the contributions from each incoming partial neutron current. Since in two dimensions the response of an assembly depends besides its size and composition and on the spatial distribution of the incoming partial neutron currents along its boundary, we are forced to construct some approximation to this distribution.

The simplest approximation for the partial neutron current distribution is of course that of a step function. This approximation however overestimates the leakage of neutrons from the reactor and produces in general poor results (4).

The next step is to use linear functions. This approximation improves drastically the efficiency of the technique and produces in most cases acceptable results. (8) To further improve accuracy we can utilize higher order polynomials having some curvuture usually at the cost of an increase in the number of response matrices and complexity of equations. We will avoid this inconveniency in the present paper as will be shown later by taking specific forms of higher order polynomials into consideration. However, even in the most general case of increasing the number of response matrices this does not become prohibitive since the cell calculation is performed only once for each different type of assembly, and the response of each assembly is independent of the boundary conditions at its edges.

In order to calculate the response of an assembly we place it in vacuum and put in along one of its faces an isotropic in the angular direction partial neutron current distribution f(z)- the basis function-such that f(o) =1.0 at one corner and f(L)=0 at the other (Fig. 1a).

Using a simple finite difference technique we calculate the outgoing partial neutron current distributions along all four boundaries of the assembly (Fig. 1b).

We then approximate each of these distributions by a sum of two basis functions i.e. $f_l(z)=f(z), f_r(z)=f(L-z)$, where z denotes the distance along the boundaries of each assembly. For example if J_1 and J_2 denote the two values of the normalized distributions at the corners of face i of the assembly we will have:

$$J_{norm}(z) = J_1 f_l(z) + J_2 f_r(z) \tag{1}$$

where $f_l(0)=f_r(L)=1.0$ and $f_l(L)=f_r(0)=0.0$ and L is the size of the symmetric assembly.

The normalization is achieved by preserving the zeroth and first moments of each actual partial neutron current distribution $\int J^{\varepsilon}(z)dz$ and $\int zJ^{\varepsilon}(z)dz$ where ε=+ or- depending on the boundary under consideration. We will have therefore:

$$\int_{\text{boundary } i} J^{\varepsilon}(z)dz = J_1 \int_0^L f_l(z)dz + J_2 \int_0^L f_r(z)dz \tag{2}$$

and

$$\int_{\text{boundary } i} J^{\varepsilon}(z)dz = J_1 \int_0^L z f_l(z)dz + J_2 \int_0^L z f_r(z)dz \tag{3}$$

Since $f_l(z)$ and $f_r(z)$ are pretermined functions of z the integrals of the RHS of Eqs. (2) and (3) are all known.

Now let A,B,C,D,E,F,G and H denote the corresponding values of the normalized current distributions as shown in Fig. 1b. Each consecutive pair of these eight constants gives the normalized response of the assembly to the input partial neutron current f(z) and we therefore define A,B,C,D,E,F,G and H as the response matrices for the assembly under consideration (In one group analysis the response matrices are scalars but we still refer to them as matrices). By considering only symmetric assemblies one such calculation is sufficient, since in such a case the response is the same viewed from any boundary. In the most general case we must carry out in all eight such different calculations.

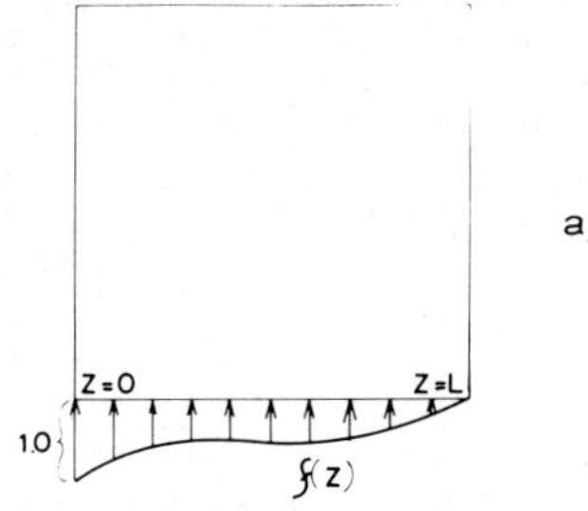

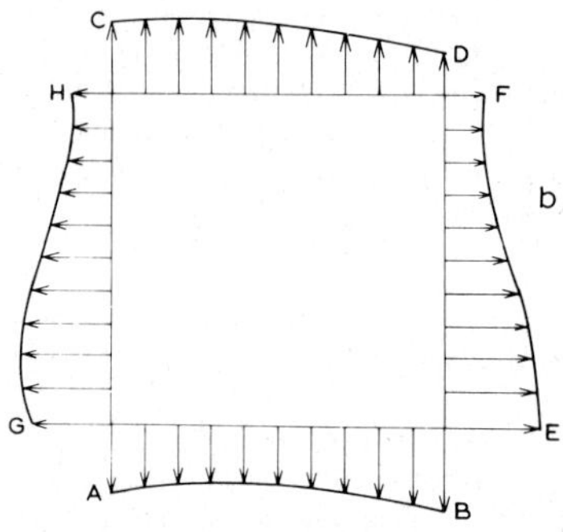

Fig. 1. Incoming and outgoing normalized neutron currents of a symmetric assembly.

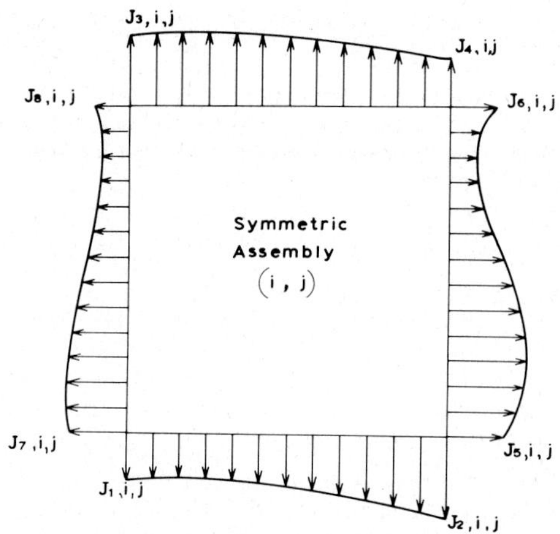

Fig. 2. Normalized partial currents associated with symmetric assembly i, j.

Since at the same time with the calculation of the partial neutron current distribution we get the flux distribution over each assembly at every mesh point we can employ it to get flux, reaction rate, and average flux response matrices for each different type of assembly.

What only remains to fix the cell calculation is the choice of the basis function f(z). In the present work we select the following third order polynomial as the basis function:

$$f(z) = 3(1 - \frac{z}{L})^2 - 2(1 - \frac{z}{L})^3, \qquad (4)$$

with zero derivatives at z =0 and L as two additional requirements, besides f(0)=1.0 and f(L)=0.0. The avantages of this choice will become apparent in the next section where we compare this scheme with three other.

2.2 The Reactor Calculation

The reactor calculation consists in determing the normalized assembly interface partial neutron currents given their response matrices. With each symmetric subassembly (i,j) we associate eight partial neutron current values $J_{k,i,j}$ (k=1,....,8) as shown in Fig. 2. Each consecutive pair of $J_{k,i,j}$ gives the approximate normalized outgoing partial neutron current distribution along the corresponding boundary of the assembly· this distribution is the response of the assembly to the four incoming partial neutron currents from the four assemblies surrounding it in the reactor configuration.

The response of assembly (i,j) in terms of the incoming partial neutron current distributions will be given in general by the following eight equations (7):

$$\begin{aligned} J_{1,i,j} = {} & A_{ij}\, J_{3,i,j-1} + B_{ij}\, J_{4,i,j-1} \\ & + C_{ij}\, J_{1,i,j+1} + D_{ij}\, J_{2,i,j+1} \\ & + G_{ij}\, J_{5,i-1,j} + E_{ij}\, J_{6,i-1,j} \\ & + H_{ij}\, J_{7,i+1,j} + F_{ij}\, J_{8,i+1,j} \end{aligned} \qquad (5)$$

$$\begin{aligned} J_{2,i,j} = {} & B_{ij}\, J_{3,i,j-1} + A_{ij}\, J_{4,i,j-1} \\ & + D_{ij}\, J_{1,i,j+1} + C_{ij}\, J_{2,i,j+1} \\ & + H_{ij}\, J_{5,i-1,j} + F_{ij}\, J_{6,i-1,j} \\ & + G_{ij}\, J_{7,i+1,j} + E_{ij}\, J_{8,i+1,j} \end{aligned} \qquad (6)$$

$$\begin{aligned} J_{3,i,j} = {} & C_{ij}\, J_{3,i,j-1} + D_{ij}\, J_{4,i,j-1} \\ & + A_{ij}\, J_{1,i,j+1} + B_{ij}\, J_{2,i,j+1} \\ & + E_{ij}\, J_{5,i-1,j} + G_{ij}\, J_{6,i-1,j} \\ & + F_{ij}\, J_{7,i+1,j} + H_{ij}\, J_{8,i+1,j} \end{aligned} \qquad (7)$$

$$\begin{aligned} J_{4,i,j} = {} & D_{ij}\, J_{3,i,j-1} + C_{ij}\, J_{4,i,j-1} \\ & + B_{ij}\, J_{1,i,j+1} + A_{ij}\, J_{2,i,j+1} \\ & + F_{ij}\, J_{5,i-1,j} + H_{ij}\, J_{6,i-1,j} \\ & + E_{ij}\, J_{7,i+1,j} + G_{ij}\, J_{8,i+1,j} \end{aligned} \qquad (8)$$

$$\begin{aligned} J_{5,i,j} = {} & E_{ij}\, J_{3,i,j-1} + G_{ij}\, J_{4,i,j-1} \\ & + F_{ij}\, J_{1,i,j+1} + H_{ij}\, J_{2,i,j+1} \\ & + C_{ij}\, J_{5,i-1,j} + D_{ij}\, J_{6,i-1,j} \\ & + A_{ij}\, J_{5,i+1,j} + B_{ij}\, J_{8,i+1,j} \end{aligned} \qquad (9)$$

$$\begin{aligned} J_{6,i,j} = {} & F_{ij}\, J_{3,i,j-1} + H_{ij}\, J_{4,i,j-1} \\ & + E_{ij}\, J_{1,i,j+1} + G_{ij}\, J_{2,i,j+1} \\ & + D_{ij}\, J_{5,i-1,j} + C_{ij}\, J_{6,i-1,j} \\ & + B_{ij}\, J_{7,i+1,j} + A_{ij}\, J_{8,i+1,j} \end{aligned} \qquad (10)$$

$$\begin{aligned} J_{7,i,j} = {} & G_{ij}\, J_{3,i,j-1} + E_{ij}\, J_{4,i,j-1} \\ & + H_{ij}\, J_{1,i,j+1} + F_{ij}\, J_{2,i,j+1} \\ & + A_{ij}\, J_{5,i-1,j} + B_{ij}\, J_{6,i-1,j} \\ & + C_{ij}\, J_{7,i+1,j} + D_{ij}\, J_{8,i+1,j} \end{aligned} \qquad (11)$$

and

$$\begin{aligned} J_{8,i,j} = {} & H_{ij}\, J_{3,i,j-1} + F_{ij}\, J_{4,i,j-1} \\ & + G_{ij}\, J_{1,i,j+1} + E_{ij}\, J_{2,i,j+1} \\ & + B_{ij}\, J_{5,i-1,j} + A_{ij}\, J_{6,i-1,j} \\ & + D_{ij}\, J_{7,i+1,j} + C_{ij}\, J_{8,i+1,j} \end{aligned} \qquad (12)$$

The above equations express the needed connection between incoming and outgoing partial neutron currents. When written for all assemblies consituting the reactor we end up with a system of linear equations $A \cdot \underline{x} = 0$, where $\underline{x}$ is the vector of $J_{k,i,j}$ and A a square matrix whose nonzero elements are either 1.0 or the response matricesof the assemblies, For a critical system we must have det(A) =0.By solving thus $A.\underline{x} = 0$ by a standard numerical procedure, we can proceed and calculate reaction rates, fluxes and average assembly fluxes by applying the principle of superposition.

3. NUMERICAL APPLICATIONS

The previous analysis has been incorporated into the computer code RESPTWO a new version of code RESPONSE (8), which calculates response matrices by one-group diffusion theory and partial neutron current distributions at each face of all assemblies making up the reactor, and reaction rates,average fluxes etc. for each assembly. The code can furthermore use a series of different basis function as input partial neutron current distribution in the cell calculation.

3.1 Comparison of Basis Functions

In the first part of this section we analyze some very simple problems of reactors made up of homogeneous assemblies, which in fact have an analytical solution, with the response matrix technique described previously when four different basis functions, those of Fig. 3, are selected as input partial neutron current distributions in the cell calculation.

All cases analyzed consist of symmetric homogeneous reactors with the geometrical and physical characteristics presented in Table 1.

Table 1. Geometrical and physical characteristics of sample problems

Case	Size L(cm)	D(cm)	v	$\Sigma_f(cm^{-1})$	$\Sigma_\alpha(cm^{-1})$
A	48	0.5	2.5	0.012	0.021
B	56	0.2	2.5	0.016	0.040
C	56	0.4	2.5	0.015	0.040
D	56	0.6	2.5	0.0113892	0.025
E	40	0.8	2.5	0.020	0.035

It is easy to show that in these simple problems and with a zero incoming partial neutron current boundary condition at the outer boundary of the reactor the criticality condition is given by:

$$2Dr \tan \frac{rL}{2} = 1.0 \tag{13}$$

and the effective multiplication factor λ_{th} by:

$$\lambda_{th} = \frac{v\Sigma_f}{2Dr^2+\Sigma_\alpha} \tag{14}$$

All five cases have been analyzed by RESPTWO and in Table 2 the results of the calculation of λ are presented.

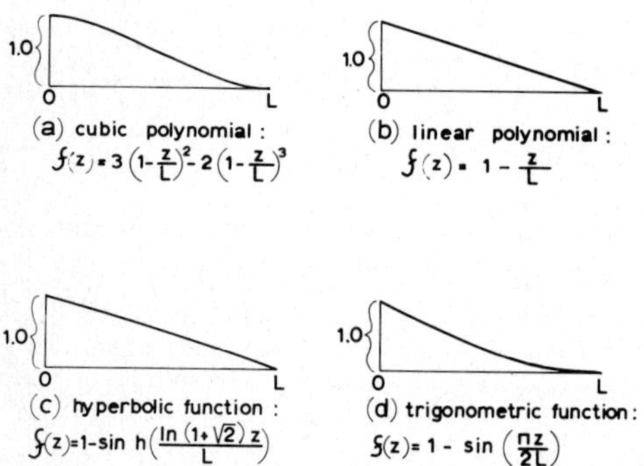

Fig. 3. Input partial neutron current distributions.

In Table 3 we present the average flux integral of certain assemblies of Case B (we consider the reactor as made up of 49 8 cm x 8cm assemblies). Similar results are obtained in Cases A,C,D and E.

From Tables 2 and 3 the superiority of the scheme using the cubic polynomial $3(1-\frac{z}{L})^2-2(1-\frac{z}{L})^3$ in the cell calculation, is apparent and we therefore select it as the more appropriate input partial neutron current approximation for the response matrix calculation in the response technique described in the previous section.

3.2 Numerical Results for a Realistic Problem

The success of the technique can be judged only when tested in realistic problems and in this section we present results of such a representative problem run also by a conventional finite difference code the results of which are considered as the "true"ones.

There is however a source of discrepancy in this comparison which stems from the different set of boundary conditions used in the two codes. Indeed RESPTWO uses the so called natural boundary conditions, i.e. a zero incoming par-

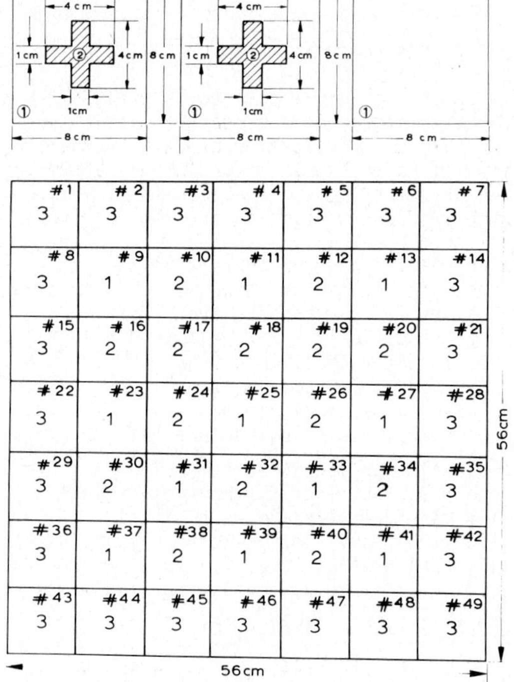

#1 3	#2 3	#3 3	#4 3	#5 3	#6 3	#7 3
#8 3	#9 1	#10 2	#11 1	#12 2	#13 1	#14 3
#15 3	#16 2	#17 2	#18 2	#19 2	#20 2	#21 3
#22 3	#23 1	#24 2	#25 1	#26 2	#27 1	#28 3
#29 3	#30 2	#31 1	#32 2	#33 1	#34 2	#35 3
#36 3	#37 1	#38 2	#39 1	#40 2	#41 1	#42 3
#43 3	#44 3	#45 3	#46 3	#47 3	#48 3	#49 3

Fig. 4. 49 assembly reactor configuration with 3 different types of assemblies

Table 2. Effective multiplication factor (% Error)

Case No	λ_{Theory}	RESPTWO			
		Cubic polynomial	Linear polynomial	Hyperbolic function	Trigonometric function
A	1.2024888	1.2020804(-0.034)	1.2016200(-0.072)	1.2039755(0.124)	1.1857945(-1.388)
B	0.97031628	0.97025432(-0.006)	0.97007256(-0.025)	0.97092058(0.062)	0.96436625(-0.613)
C	0.88485328	0.88477215(-0.009)	0.88461866(-0.027)	0.88548580(0.071)	0.87878514(-0.686)
D	1.0	0.99983476(-0.017)	0.99958816(-0.041)	1.0011631(0.116)	0.98898334(-1.102)
E	1.1502923	1.1497859(-0.044)	1.1494662 (-0.072)	1.1511811(0.077)	1.1378954(-1.078)

Table 3. Average flux integral in certain assemblies (% Error)

Assembly No	Theoretical result	REPSTWO			
		Cubic polynomial	Linear polynomial	Hyperbolic function	Trigonometric function
1,1	0.279735-02*	0.279783-02(0.02)	0.280009-02(0.10)	0.279992-02(0.09)	0.280141-02(0.15)
2,1	0.735222-02	0.735334-02(0.02)	0.735654-02(0.06)	0.735633-02(0.06)	0.735825-02(0.08)
3,1	0.104909-01	0.104922-01(0.01)	0.104959-01(0.05)	0.104957-01(0.05)	0.104979-01(0.07)
4,1	0.116090-01	0.116099-01(0.01)	0.116138-01(0.04)	0.116135-01(0.04)	0.116158-01(0.06)
2,2	0.193237-01	0.193262-01(0.01)	0.193266-01(0.02)	0.193266-01(0.02)	0.193270-01(0.02)
3,2	0.275731-01	0.275759-01(0.01)	0.275742-01(0.00)	0.275743-01(0.00)	0.275735-01(0.00)
4,2	0.305116-01	0.305135-01(0.01)	0.305110-01(0.00)	0.305112-01(0.00)	0.305099-01(-0.01)
3,3	0.393443-01	0.393470-01(0.01)	0.393413-01(-0.01)	0.393417-01(-0.01)	0.393386-01(-0.01)
4,3	0.435373-01	0.435387-01(0.00)	0.435315-01(-0.01)	0.435320-01(-0.01)	0.435279-01(-0.02)
4,4	0.481770-01	0.481769-01(0.00)	0.481681-01(-0.02)	0.481686-01(-0.02)	0.481635-01(-0.03)

* $\pm 0n \equiv 10^{\pm 0n}$

tial neutron current at the outer boundaries of the reactor, while the conventional finite difference code a zero flux boundary condition at the outer surface of the reactor. It is important to realize that the differences introduced by such different boundary conditions can be significant. For example if we were to use a zero flux boundary condition in the five problems considered previously instead of the zero incoming partial neutron current at the outer surface of the reactor, λ would take the following values (in parentheses the % difference from the values of Table 2): λ_A =1.186536(-1.327), λ_B = 0.96488(-0.085), λ_C = 0.8819845 (-0.324), λ_D =0.9894486(-1.055) and λ_E = 1.11434(-3.125) and these values indicate how significantly the boundary conditions could affect the results.

The problems we analyzed by RESPTWO and the conventional finite difference code gave more or less similar results and we present in the following the results of one of these. The reactor under consideration, Fig. 4., is a symmetrical reactor configuration consisting of 49 assemblies of three different types with the nuclear characteristics given in Table 4.

The results of the analysis are presented in Table 5. We observe that the results are in a much better agreement in the interior assemblies near the center of the reactor, which was of course expected in light of the different boundary conditions used in the two codes which affect the outer assemblies more than

Table 4. Nuclear characteristics of assemblies

	Assembly 1		Assembly 2		Assembly 3
	Mat.1	Mat.2	Mat.1	Mat.2	
D(cm)	0.4	0.4	0.4	0.4	0.8
ν	2.5	-	2.5	-	-
Σ_f (cm^{-1})	0.0225186	0.0	0.0225186	0.0	0.0
Σ_a (cm^{-1})	0.040	0.015	0.04	0.25	0.02

the inner ones. Most of the reaction rates in the interior assemblies differ by less that 1% from those of the conventional finite difference code. The difference in the effective multiplication factor is quite small.

4. CONCLUSIONS

The numerical results of the previous section suggest that the present improved response matrix technique is superior to the older scheme which used linear shapes for the partial current distribution along the boundaries of each assembly and that it can be used successfully in the neutronic simulation of two-dimensional nuclear reactors in one-group theory determining overall criticality and at least approximate reaction rates and flux distributions if needed. The ac-

Table 5. Reaction rates and effective multiplication factor.

	ABSORPTION RATE		PRODUCTION RATE	
Ass. No	Finite Difference Code	RESPTWO	Finite Difference Code	RESPTWO
1	1.9089-04*	2.6833-04		
2	6.4367-04	7.4280-04		
3	1.0435-03	1.2093-03		
4	1.4316-03	1.5773-03		
8	7.2768-04	8.5838-04		
9	6.5491-03	6.4949-03	8.4289-03	8.4183-03
10	1.5224-02	1.4875-02	1.3522-02	1.3297-02
11	1.5872-02	1.5229-02	2.0426-02	1.9738-02
15	1.5313-03	1.8361-03		
16	1.9888-02	1.9699-02	1.7658-02	1.7609-02
17	3.6717-02	3.6935-02	3.2702-02	3.3016-02
18	4.8734-02	4.7548-02	4.3281-02	4.2503-02
22	2.6655-03	3.0338-03		
23	2.8974-02	2.8832-02	3.7291-02	3.7370-02
24	7.0998-02	6.9911-02	6.3008-02	6.2493-02
25	7.0707-02	6.9082-02	9.1000-02	8.9539-02
29	2.4277-03	2.8813-03		
30	4.0014-02	3.9983-02	3.5486-02	3.5740-02
31	6.4423-02	6.3923-02	8.2914-02	8.2852-02
32	9.3448-02	9.2467-02	8.2898-02	8.2656-02
36	1.7111-03	2.0205-03		
37	1.8106-02	1.8683-02	2.3304-02	2.4216-02
38	4.4788-02	4.4925-02	3.9719-02	4.0158-02
39	4.2212-02	4.2596-02	5.4329-02	5.5209-02
43	5.0129-04	7.2351-04		
44	1.7966-03	2.1382-03		
45	2.9222-03	3.5174-03		
46	3.9111-03	4.5054-03		
λ	1.00189	1.00266 (0.077%)		

* $\pm$ 0n $\equiv 10^{\pm 0n}$

curacy of the method is probably better than the results of the previous section indicate since comparisons were made with a conventional method using zero flux boundary conditions at the outer surface of the reactor instead of zero incoming partial neutron current. It is clear also that the present scheme does not exhaust the potential of the technique since it seems possible to improve accuracy by selecting different basis functions for the partial current distributions along the boundaries of the reactor assemblies. Since the flux distribution for the cases examined are very irregular, we can conclude that the present technique can handle the situations associated with actual light water reactors.
The economic advantage of the technique -a one order of magnitude reduction in computing time- can be further improved by editing only information of special interest, e.g. neutron fluxes at "critical" points such as hot spots and by limiting information of a general nature such as the detailed spacial neutron flux distributions.

REFERENCES

1. Selengut, D.S., Partial Current Representations in Reactor Physics, in Reactor Technology KAPL-2000-20, Knolls Atomic Power Laboratory (1963).
2. Shimizu, S. et al., Application of the Response Matrix Method to Criticality Calculations of One-Dimensional Reactors, J. At. Energy Soc. Japan, 5, p.369 (1963).
3. Pfeifer, W. and Shapiro, J.L., Reflection and Transmission Functions in Reactor Physics, Nucl. Sci. Eng., 38, p. 253 (1969).
4. Shimizu, A. and Aoki, K., Application of Invariant-Embedding to Reactor Physics, Academic Press, N.Y. (1972).
5. Pryor, R.J., and Graves, W.E., Response Matrix Method for Treating Reactor Calculations, USAEC CONF-730414-P2, p. VII-179 (1973).
6. McDaniel, C.T., A Two Dimensional Few Group Response Matrix Calculation Method for Flux and Reactivity, USERDA CONF 750413, p. V-111 (1975).
7. Kollas J., The Response Matrix Method and the Solution of Reactor Criticality Problems (in Greek), Technica Chronica -Scientific Journal of the Technical Chamber of Greece, Section B, 47 (2), p. 35 (1978).
8. Kollas J., Numerical Application of the Response Matrix Method in the Solution of Criticality Problems of Two-Dimensional Reactors (in Greek),Technica Chronica-Scientific Journal of the Technical Chamber of Greece, Section B, 47(2), p.23 (1978).

DIGITAL TECHNIQUES in Simulation, Communication and Control
Spyros G. Tzafestas (editor)
Elsevier Science Publishers B.V. (North-Holland) © IMACS, 1985

COUPLED-CORE REACTOR SIMULATION AND IDENTIFICATION USING ONE-SHOT WALSH OPERATIONAL MATRICES

John Anoussis and Spyros Tzafestas
Division of Nuclear Engineering
N.R.C. "Demokritos"
Aghia Paraskevi
Attiki, Greece

For a class of coupled-core nuclear reactor systems the parameter identification problem is solved using the Walsh expansion approach. The coupled-core reactor model considered is based on the assumption that the time delay distribution function between cores has the simple lag form 1/(1+sT). Regarding the operational matrices for the successive integrations, the so-called one-shot operational matrices (OSOMRI) of Prasada Rao and co-workers are used. A simple example concerning the case of identifying the coupling time constant T is included. A full computer program for the identification of all unknown parameters involved is under preparation.

1. INTRODUCTION

Nuclear power is receiving increasing attention due to the fact that traditional energy sources are gradually being exhausted [1-3]. The power output of nuclear reactors can be increased if a number of individual reactor cores are coupled together. On the other hand almost all reactors consist or can be considered to consist of separate regions, each being a subcritical reactor with criticality being achieved through coupling between regions. When a number of nuclear cores are coupled together, there occurs a mutual exchange of neutrons between them, and so the neutron performance of one core depends upon the history of all the other cores. The successful analysis and control of any reactor requires the design of an accurate model upon which the computation of the control is to be based. In particular, since the reactor equations can be formulated using physical arguments, the problem basically reduces to that of determining some or all of the parameters involved.

Our purpose in this paper is to present one solution to the above parameter identification problem for a coupled-nuclear reactor model employing the Walsh function expansion approach [4-6]. To obtain increased accuracy the one-shot operational matrices for repeated integration (OSOMRI) suggested in [6] will be utilized for integrating the system equations. Since the coupled nuclear reactor model is actually a multivariable model, the multi-input multi-output (MIMO) theory developed in [4] will be applied. As a byproduct the Walsh expansion-based formulas which provide the solution of the reactor equations, when the model parameters and the initial conditions are known, are given. Previous work of the authors on nuclear reactor modelling identification and control includes References [7]-[13].

2. THE TWO-CORE REACTOR MODEL

The simplest reactor model is the so-called single-point lumped-parameter (i.e. space-independent) one-energy group bare reactor model, with kinetic equations

$$\frac{dn(t)}{dt}=\frac{k(1-\beta)-1}{\ell}n(t)+\sum_{i=1}^{6}\lambda_i C_i(t)$$
$$\frac{dC_i(t)}{dt}=\frac{\beta_i k}{\ell}n(t)-\lambda_i C_i(t);i=1,2,\ldots,6 \qquad (1)$$

where n(t) is the neutron level, k is the effective multiplication factor, β is the delayed neutron fraction, λ_i is the decay constant and $C_i(t)$ is the concentration of the ith delayed precursor group, and ℓ is the prompt neutron generation time.

By setting $k=k_o+\delta k, n=n_o+\delta n,\ c_i=c_{io}+\delta C_i$, introducing into (1) and eliminating steady-state terms and higher-order terms in $\delta(.)$ one obtains the model

$$\frac{d\delta n}{dt}=\frac{(1-\beta)}{\ell}(n_o\delta k+k_o\delta n)-\frac{\delta n}{\ell}+\sum_{i=1}^{6}\lambda_i\delta C_i$$
$$\frac{d\delta C_i}{dt}=\frac{n_o\beta_i\delta k}{\ell}+\frac{\beta_i k_o}{\ell}\delta n-\lambda_i\delta C_i \qquad (2)$$

which is linear in δn, δC_i and δk.

If only frequencies higher than $\omega>1$ are considered, the effects of the delayed neutrons need not be considered, and eq(2) leads to the transfer function (s is the complex frequency):

$$H(s)=(1/\ell)/(s+\alpha),\ H(s)=\delta n(s)/n_o\delta k(s) \quad (3a)$$

where the parameter α (Rossi-alpha) is equal to

$$\alpha=\frac{1-k_o(1-\beta)}{\ell} \quad (3b)$$

At criticality ($k_o=1$) we have $\alpha=\beta/\ell$ and

$$H(s)=(1/\ell)/(s+\beta/\ell) \quad (3c)$$

The magnitude and phase of $H(j\omega)$ are given by

$$M=\frac{1/\ell}{\sqrt{\omega^2+(\beta/\ell)^2}},\quad \tan\Phi=-\omega/(\beta/\ell) \quad (4)$$

The direct frequency domain identification technique is to measure experimentally M_i and Φ_i for a set of frequencies $\omega_i (i=1,2,...,N)$ and then determine the parameters $\alpha=\beta/\ell$ and $1/\ell$ so as to achieve a best fit.

A multi-region (point) reactor consists of many separate regions (cores) each being a subcritical reactor. Coupling between the regions allows the system to be critical. A 2-core linear reactor can be described as follows [14]:
(i) Each region has a dinstinct input $u_i(t)$, $i=1,2$ and output $y_i(t)=n_i(t)$, $i=1,2$.
(ii) Any perturbation in one region will be transmitted to the other, only due to its coupling to the first. Coupling is thus acting as a "feedback loop" with interaction (feedback) transfer function $K_{ij}(j\omega)$ from region i to region j ($i,j=1,2$).
(iii) Each region will have a forward transfer function similar to (3c), namely

$$H_i(s)=\frac{1/\ell_i}{s+\alpha_i} \quad (i=1,2) \quad (5)$$

but with α_i no longer being equal to β/ℓ_i since now each region is a subcritical reactor with $k_i<1$.

The block diagram of a two-coupled core reactor is a shown in Fig.1. Assuming that an input u(t) is applied to region 1 only the outputs $Y_1(s)$ and $Y_2(s)$ of the two regions are given by

$$Y_1(s)=\frac{H_1(s)}{1-K_{12}(s)K_{21}(s)H_1(s)H_2(s)}U(s)$$

$$Y_2(s)=\frac{K_{12}(s)H_1(s)H_2(s)}{1-K_{12}(s)K_{21}(s)H_1(s)H_2(s)}U(s)$$

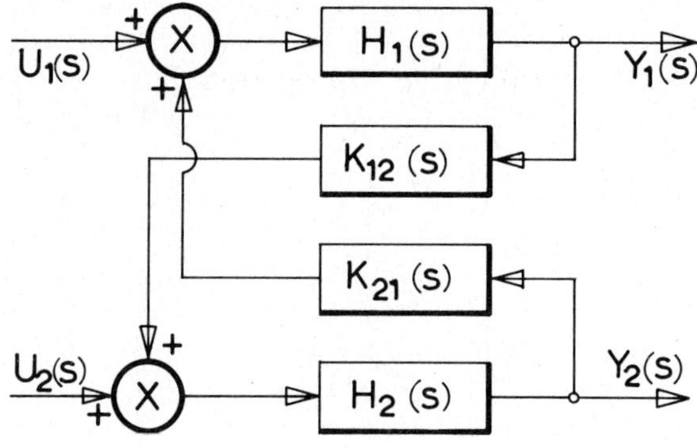

Fig.1.Structure of the 2-core reactor system

An expression for the coupling transfer function $K_{ji}(s)$ can be found as follows.

The zero-power two-region kinetic equations are

$$\frac{dy_i(t)}{dt}=\frac{k_i(1-\beta)-1}{\ell_i}y_i(t)+\sum_{m=1}^{6}\lambda_m C_{m,i}(t)+\frac{\sigma_{ji}}{\ell_i}\int_o^t f_{ji}(\tau)y_j(t-\tau)d\tau \quad (6a)$$

$$\frac{dC_{m,i}(t)}{dt}=\frac{\beta_m k_i}{\ell_i}y_i(t)-\lambda_m C_{m,i}(t) \quad (6b)$$

for $i,j=1,2 (i\neq j)$ where k_i is the effective multiplication factor for the ith core and σ_{ji} is the coupling reactivity coefficient between the jth and the ith core. Following [15,16] σ_{ji} can be defined as the probability that a neutron absorbed in, or escaping the jth zone, would be replaced by a neutron generated, or entering the ith zone. The quantity $\sigma_{ji}f_{ji}(\tau)y_j(t-\tau)d\tau$ represents the fraction of neutrons at time t in core i, which originated by fission in core j at earlier times $t-\tau$ in $d\tau$, with $f_{ji}(\tau)$ being the time delay distribution function. Thus $\sigma_{ji}\int_o^t f_{ji}(\tau)y_j(t-\tau)d\tau$ is the total quantity of neutrons originated in core j which have been absorbed in core i. The Laplace transform of this quantity gives $K_{ji}(s)Y_j(s)$. Thus

$$K_{ji}(s)=\sigma_{ji}F_{ji}(s),\ F_{ji}(s)=\mathcal{L}f_{ji}(t)$$

Any density function $f_{ji}(\tau)$ for delayed times normalized to unity (i.e. $\int f(\tau)d\tau=1$) can be used. The most usual ones are given in the following Table 1.

TABLE 1

Time Delay Density Functions

f(t)	F(s)
$\delta(t)$	1
$\delta(t-T)$	e^{-sT}
$\frac{1}{T}e^{-t/T}$	$\frac{1}{1+sT}$
$\frac{1}{T^2}te^{-t/T}$	$\frac{1}{(1+sT)^2}$

Some special cases are the following:

Case 1: Symmetric cores-Zero interaction time delay

In this case

$$\alpha_1=\alpha_2=\frac{1-k(1-\beta)}{\ell}, \quad F(s)=1$$

$$K_{21}(s)=K_{12}(s)=K(s)=\sigma F(s)=\sigma$$

$$H_1(s)=H_2(s)=H(s)=\frac{1/\ell}{s+\alpha}$$

Case II: Non-symmetric cores-Zero interaction time delay

Here

$$\alpha_1=\frac{1-k_1(1-\beta)}{\ell_1}, \quad \alpha_2=\frac{1-k_2(1-\beta)}{\ell_2}$$

$$K_{21}(s)=K_{12}(s)=K(s)=\sigma$$

$$H_i(s)=\frac{1/\ell}{s+\alpha_i} \quad i=1,2$$

Case III: Symmetric cores-Non-Zero interaction time delay

Here

$$\alpha_i=\frac{1-k\ (1-\beta)}{\ell} \quad i=1,2$$

$$K_{21}(s)=K_{12}(s)=K(s)=\sigma F(s)$$

Various types of F(s) can be assumed. In the present paper we shall consider the case where

$$F(s)=\frac{1}{1+sT}$$

The case where $F(s)=e^{-sT}$ which leads to a system with pure time delays will be considered elsewhere.

The model (6a,b) is of the integro-differential type. To obtain a differential equation model, which is switable for the identification technique to be described later, one first obtains the Laplace transforms of (6a,b) with zero initial conditions, and then replaces the complex frequency s by the derivative operator D=d/dt. The result of taking the Laplace transform of (6a,b) for the Case III above is:

$$sY_i(s)=-\alpha_i Y_i(s)+\sum_{m=1}^{6}\lambda_m C_{m,i}(s) + \frac{\sigma}{\ell_i}\left(\frac{1}{1+sT}\right)Y_j(s) \quad (7a)$$

$$sC_{m,i}(s)=\frac{\beta_m k_i}{\ell_i}Y_i(s)-\lambda_m C_{m,i}(s) \quad (7b)$$

for i,j=1,2 (i≠j).

Eliminating $C_{m,i}(s)$ in (7a) via (7b) yields

$$\left(s+\alpha_i-\frac{k_i}{\ell_i}\sum_{m=1}^{6}\frac{\lambda_m\beta_m}{s+\lambda_m}\right)Y_i(s)=\frac{\sigma}{\ell_i}\left(\frac{1}{1+sT}\right)Y_j(s) \quad (8)$$

for i,j=1,2 with i≠j where $\alpha_i=\{1-k_i(1-\beta)\}/\ell_i$. Thus the differential equation model of the reactor is

$$(1+TD)\left[D+\alpha_1-\frac{k_1}{\ell_1}\sum_{m=1}^{6}\frac{\lambda_m\beta_m}{D+\lambda_m}\right]y_1(t)=\frac{\sigma}{\ell_1}y_2(t) \quad (9a)$$

$$(1+TD)\left[D+\alpha_2-\frac{k_2}{\ell_2}\sum_{m=1}^{6}\frac{\lambda_m\beta_m}{D+\lambda_m}\right]y_2(t)=\frac{\sigma}{\ell_2}y_1(t) \quad (9b)$$

If there are external sources $c_1u_1(t)$ and $c_2u_2(t)$ ta the cores 1 and 2, then the functions $c_1(1+sT)u_1(t)$ and $c_2(1+sT)u_2(t)$ should be added on the right-hand sides of (9a) and (9b) respectively.

An alternative way to derive the model (9a,b) from (6a,b) is the following. We set

$$I_j(t)=\int_0^t f_{ji}(\tau)y_j(t-\tau)d\tau$$

$$=\int_0^t e^{-(t-\tau)/T}y_j(\tau)d\tau \quad (10a)$$

and obtain

$$\frac{dy_i(t)}{dt}=-\alpha_i y_i(t)+\sum_{m=1}^{6}\lambda_m C_{m,i}(t)+\frac{\sigma}{\ell_i T}I_j(t) \quad (10b)$$

$$\frac{dI_j(t)}{dt}=-\frac{1}{T}I_j(t)+y_j(t) \tag{10c}$$

$$\frac{dC_{m,i}(t)}{dt}=\frac{\beta_m k_i}{\ell_i}y_i(t)-\lambda_m C_{m,i}(t) \tag{10d}$$

Now, using the operator notation D=d/dt, and eliminating $I_j(t)$ and $C_{m,i}$ from (10b) via (10c) and (10d), yields again the differential model (9a,b)

3. ONE-SHOT OPERATIONAL WALSH MATRICES

The Walsh functions $\Phi_k(t), k=0,1,...,m-1$, $m=2^n$ are two-valued functions which are orthonormal in the interval $0 \leq t < 1$. Denoting the value +1 by "+" and the value -1 by "-"the functions $\Phi_k(t)$, k=0,1,2,.. ..,15 have the following form

$\Phi_o(t)$	+	+	+	+	+	+	+	+	+	+	+	+	+	+	+	+
$\Phi_1(t)$	+	+	+	+	+	+	+	+	-	-	-	-	-	-	-	-
$\Phi_2(t)$	+	+	+	+	-	-	-	-	+	+	+	+	-	-	-	-
$\Phi_3(t)$	+	+	+	+	-	-	-	-	-	-	-	-	+	+	+	+
$\Phi_4(t)$	+	+	-	-	+	+	-	-	+	+	-	-	+	+	-	-
$\Phi_5(t)$	+	+	-	-	+	+	-	-	-	-	+	+	-	-	+	+
$\Phi_6(t)$	+	+	-	-	-	-	+	+	+	+	-	-	-	-	+	+
$\Phi_7(t)$	+	+	-	-	-	-	+	+	-	-	+	+	+	+	-	-
$\Phi_8(t)$	+	-	+	-	+	-	+	-	+	-	+	-	+	-	+	-
$\Phi_9(t)$	+	-	+	-	+	-	+	-	-	+	-	+	-	+	-	+
$\Phi_{10}(t)$	+	-	+	-	-	+	-	+	+	-	+	-	-	+	-	+
$\Phi_{11}(t)$	+	-	+	-	-	+	-	+	-	+	-	+	+	-	+	-
$\Phi_{12}(t)$	+	-	-	+	+	-	-	+	+	-	-	+	+	-	-	+
$\Phi_{13}(t)$	+	-	-	+	+	-	-	+	-	+	+	-	-	+	+	-
$\Phi_{14}(t)$	+	-	-	+	+	-	-	-	+	+	+	-	-	+	+	-
$\Phi_{15}(t)$	+	-	-	+	-	+	+	-	-	+	+	-	+	-	-	+

We see that the regularity of the $\Phi_k(t)$'s is not clear. However, one way of constructing the above Walsh matrix of any order is by decomposing each Walsh function $\Phi_k(t)$ into Rademacher functions $R_s(t)$, s= 1,2,...,n which are a set of orthonormal square waves for $0 \leq t < 1$ with unit height and repetition rate (sequence) equal to 2^{s-1}.

The decomposition formula is

$$\Phi_k(t)=R_s^{d_s}(t)R_{s-1}^{d_{s-1}}(t)\ldots R_1^{d_1}(t), k=0,1,..,2^s-1$$

with initial condition $\Phi_o(t)=R_o(t)=1$, where "$d_s d_{s-1}\ldots d_1$" is the binary expression of the decimal number k.

The Walsh functions constitute a complete set of functions, and so one can expand any given function f(t), which is absolutely integrable in the interval [0,1] in a Walsh-Fourier series as

$$f(t)=\sum_{k=0}^{\infty}\xi_k\Phi_k(t), \xi_k=\int_o^1\Phi_k(t)f(t)dt \tag{11}$$

Consider the first four Walsh functions $\Phi_k(t)$, k=0,1,2,3, and integrate them from 0 up to t. The result is

$$D^{-1}\begin{bmatrix}\Phi_o(t)\\ \Phi_1(t)\\ \Phi_2(t)\\ \Phi_3(t)\end{bmatrix} \triangleq \int_o^1 \begin{bmatrix}\Phi_o(\tau)\\ \Phi_1(\tau)\\ \Phi_2(\tau)\\ \Phi_3(\tau)\end{bmatrix} d\tau =$$

$$\left[\begin{array}{cc:cc}\frac{1}{2} & -\frac{1}{4} & -\frac{1}{8} & 0\\ \frac{1}{2} & 0 & 0 & -\frac{1}{8}\\ \hdashline \frac{1}{8} & 0 & 0 & 0\\ 0 & \frac{1}{8} & 0 & 0\end{array}\right]\begin{bmatrix}\Phi_o(t)\\ \Phi_1(t)\\ \Phi_2(t)\\ \Phi_3(t)\end{bmatrix} \tag{12}$$

Equation (12) can be written in the general form

$$D^{-1}\underline{\Phi}(t)\triangleq\int_o^t\underline{\Phi}(\tau)d\tau=\underline{P}\;\underline{\Phi}(t) \tag{13a}$$

where

$$\underline{\Phi}(t)=\begin{bmatrix}\Phi_o(t)\\ \Phi_1(t)\\ \vdots\\ \Phi_{m-1}(t)\end{bmatrix}, \underline{P}=\underline{P}_m=\left[\begin{array}{c:c}\underline{P}_{m/2} & -\frac{1}{2m}\underline{I}_{m/2}\\ \hdashline \frac{1}{2m}\underline{I}_{m/2} & \underline{0}_{m/2}\end{array}\right],$$

$$P_1=\frac{1}{2} \tag{13b}$$

for $m=2^q, q=1,2,\ldots$ The operational formula (13a) was introduced by Chen [5] and shows that the integration of $\underline{\Phi}(\tau)$ over the interval [0,t] is performed approximately by simply multiplying $\underline{\Phi}(t)$ by the matrix $\underline{P}_m$.

The multiple integral

$$D^{-k}\underline{\Phi}(t)\triangleq\underbrace{\int_o^t\int_o^t\ldots\int_o^t}_{k\text{ times}}\underline{\Phi}(\tau)d\tau^k \tag{14}$$

can be approximated either as

$$D^{-k}\underline{\Phi}(t)=\underline{P}^k\underline{\Phi}(t) \tag{15}$$

where the property $D^{-(i+1)}\underline{\Phi}(t) = D^{-1}[D^{-i}\Phi(t)] = \underline{P}[D^{-i}\Phi(t)], i=0,1,2,\ldots$ is employed, or directly as

$$D^{-k}\underline{\Phi}(t) = \underline{P}_k\underline{\Phi}(t) \tag{16}$$

where the exact value $D^{-k}\underline{\Phi}(t)$ of the kth integral is expanded in Walsh series and $\underline{P}_k$ is the corresponding operational matrix of kth order (i.e. for the k-tuple integral). This operational matrix was introduced by Prasada Rao and Palanisamy [6] and is known as *one-shot operational matrix for repeated integration (OSOMRI)*. The matrix $\underline{P}_k$ is determined directly by minimizing the integral of the squared error $\underline{E}_k = D^{-k}\underline{\Phi}(t) - \underline{P}_k\underline{\Phi}(t)$, and as it was established in [6] it leads to a better approximation of the multiple integral $D^{-k}\underline{\Phi}(t)$ than the standard approximation $\underline{P}^k\underline{\Phi}(t)$, where $\underline{P}^k$ is the kth power of the single integral operational matrix defined in (13b). This was expected naturally since the approximation $\underline{P}^k\underline{\Phi}(t)$, which is algebraically simpler, gives an accumulation error which increases at each successive stage of integration, whereas the one-shot approximation $\underline{P}_k\underline{\Phi}(t)$ leads to a direct minimum error.

The OSOMRI $\underline{P}_k$ is given by

$$\underline{P}_k = \frac{1}{m}\underline{W}_m\underline{\Sigma}_k\underline{W}_m \tag{17a}$$

where $\underline{W}_m$ is the orthogonal Walsh matrix of order m with +1s and -1s as its elements ($\underline{W}_{16}$ is given at the beginning of the present section), and $\underline{\Sigma}_k$ is given by;

$$\underline{\Sigma}_k = \frac{1}{m^k}\left[\frac{1}{(k+1)!}\underline{I}_m + \sum_{r=1}^{m-1}\left\{\sum_{q=0}^{k-1}\frac{r^{q+1}-(r-1)^{q+1}}{(q+1)!(k-q)!}\right\}\nabla_m^r\right] \tag{17b}$$

where ∇_m is a square matrix with 1's on the upper diagonal and zeros all the other elements. For example.

$$\nabla_4 = \begin{bmatrix} 0&1&0&0\\0&0&1&0\\0&0&0&1\\0&0&0&0\end{bmatrix}$$

The powers ∇_4^2 and ∇_4^3 of ∇_4 are given by

$$\nabla_4^2 = \begin{bmatrix} 0&0&1&0\\0&0&0&1\\0&0&0&0\\0&0&0&0\end{bmatrix}, \quad \nabla_4^3 = \begin{bmatrix} 0&0&0&1\\0&0&0&0\\0&0&0&0\\0&0&0&0\end{bmatrix}$$

and the sum $\nabla_4 + \nabla_4^2 + \nabla_4^3$ is given by

$$\nabla_4 + \nabla_4^2 + \nabla_4^3 = \begin{bmatrix} 0&1&1&1\\0&0&1&1\\0&0&0&1\\0&0&0&0\end{bmatrix}$$

Similarly the sum $\nabla_4 + 2\nabla_4^2 + 3\nabla^3$ is given by

$$\nabla_4 + 2\nabla_4^2 + 3\nabla_4^3 = \begin{bmatrix} 0&1&2&3\\0&0&1&2\\0&0&0&1\\0&0&0&0\end{bmatrix}$$

Thus for m=4 formula (17a) and (17b) give

$$\underline{\Sigma}_1 = \frac{1}{4}\left(\frac{\underline{I}_4}{2} + \nabla + \nabla^2 + \nabla^3\right) = \frac{1}{4}\begin{bmatrix} \frac{1}{2}&1&1&1\\0&\frac{1}{2}&1&1\\0&0&\frac{1}{2}&1\\0&0&0&\frac{1}{2}\end{bmatrix}$$

$$\underline{P}_1 = \frac{1}{4}\begin{bmatrix} 1&1&1&1\\1&1&-1&-1\\1&-1&1&-1\\1&-1&-1&1\end{bmatrix}\frac{1}{4}\begin{bmatrix} \frac{1}{2}&1&1&1\\0&\frac{1}{2}&1&1\\0&0&\frac{1}{2}&1\\0&0&0&\frac{1}{2}\end{bmatrix}\begin{bmatrix} 1&1&1&1\\1&1&-1&-1\\1&-1&1&-1\\1&-1&-1&1\end{bmatrix}$$

$$= \begin{bmatrix} \frac{1}{2}&-\frac{1}{4}&-1/8&0\\ \frac{1}{4}&0&0&-1/8\\1/8&0&0&0\\0&1/8&0&0\end{bmatrix} \tag{18a}$$

In the same way one finds

$$\underline{\Sigma}_2 = \frac{1}{16}\left(\frac{\underline{I}_4}{6} + \nabla + 2\nabla^2 + 3\nabla^3\right)$$

$$= \frac{1}{16}\begin{bmatrix} 1/6&1&2&3\\0&1/6&1&2\\0&0&1/6&1\\0&0&0&1/6\end{bmatrix}$$

$$\underline{P}_2 = \frac{1}{4}\underline{W}\,\underline{\Sigma}_2\underline{W} = \frac{1}{64}\begin{bmatrix} 32/3&-3&-4&2\\8&-16/3&-2&0\\4&-2&-4/3&0\\2&0&0&-4/3\end{bmatrix} \tag{18b}$$

$$\underline{P}_3 = \frac{1}{256}\begin{bmatrix} 32/3&-28/3&-31/6&4\\28/3&-8&-4&17/6\\31/6&-4&-2&1\\4&-17/6&-1&0\end{bmatrix} \tag{18c}$$

In general

$$\underline{\Sigma}_1 = \frac{1}{m}\left[\frac{\underline{I}_m}{2} + \nabla + \nabla^2 + \ldots + \nabla^{m-1}\right] \tag{19a}$$

$$\underline{\Sigma}_2 = \frac{1}{m^2}\left[\frac{\underline{I}_m}{3!} + \nabla + 2\nabla^2 + \ldots + (m-1)\nabla^{m-1}\right] \tag{19b}$$

$$\underline{\Sigma}_3 = \frac{1}{m^3}\left[\frac{\underline{I}_m}{4!} + \sum_{r=1}^{m-1}\frac{1+6r^2}{12}\nabla^r\right] \tag{19c}$$

$$\underline{\Sigma}_4 = \frac{1}{m^4}\left[\frac{\underline{I}_m}{5!} + \sum_{r=1}^{m-1}\frac{2r^3+r}{12}\nabla^r\right] \tag{19d}$$

and so son.

4. SOLUTION OF THE REACTOR EQUATIONS

Since the reactor model is a MIMO model the technique described in [4] (Sec.III) combined with OSOMRI will be employed.

For simplicity we assume one delayed precursor group only in which case the reactor model (8) or (9a,b) gives

$$(1+TD)\left[(D+\alpha_1)(D+\lambda_1)-\frac{k_1\lambda_1\beta_1}{\ell_1}\right]y_1(t) = \frac{\sigma}{\ell_1}(D+\lambda_1)y_2(t)+c_1(1+TD)(D+\lambda_1)u_1(t) \quad (20a)$$

$$(1+TD)\left[(D+\alpha_2)(D+\lambda_1)-\frac{k_2\lambda_1\beta_1}{\ell_2}\right]y_2(t) = \frac{\sigma}{\ell_2}(D+\lambda_1)y_1(t)+c_2(1+TD)(D+\lambda_1)u_2(t) \quad (20b)$$

where $u_1(t)$ and $u_2(t)$ are the existing input sources (added on the right hand side of (6a) for i=1,2).

Carrying out the algebraic manipulation in (20a,b) one obtains

$$(D^3+a_{12}D^2+a_{11}D+a_{10})y_1(t) = (b_{11}D+b_{10})y_2(t) + (c_{12}D^2+c_{11}D+c_{10})u_1(t) \quad (21a)$$

$$(D^3+a_{22}D^2+a_{21}D+a_{20})y_2(t) = (b_{21}D+b_{20})y_1(t) + (c_{22}D^2+c_{21}D+c_{20})u_2(t) \quad (21b)$$

where the parameters a_{ij}, b_{ij} and c_{ij} are given by

$$a_{12}=\alpha_1+\lambda_1+\frac{1}{T},\ a_{11}=\alpha_1\lambda_1-\frac{k_1\beta_1\lambda_1}{\ell_1}+\frac{\alpha_1+\lambda_1}{T}$$

$$a_{10}=\frac{1}{T}(\alpha_1\lambda_1-\frac{k_1\lambda_1\beta_1}{\ell_1}),b_{11}=\frac{\sigma}{\ell_1 T},b_{10}=\frac{\sigma\lambda_1}{\ell_1 T}$$

$$c_{12}=c_1,c_{11}=c_1(\lambda_1+\frac{1}{T}),\ c_{10}=\frac{c_1\lambda_1}{T} \quad (21c)$$

$$a_{22}=\alpha_2+\lambda_1+\frac{1}{T},a_{21}=\alpha_2\lambda_1-\frac{k_2\beta_1\lambda_1}{\ell_2}+\frac{\alpha_2+\lambda_1}{T}$$

$$a_{20}=\frac{1}{T}(\alpha_2\lambda_1-\frac{k_2\lambda_1\beta_1}{\ell_2}),b_{21}=\frac{\sigma}{\ell_2 T},b_{20}=\frac{\sigma\lambda_1}{\ell_2 T}$$

$$c_{22}=c_2,c_{21}=c_2(\lambda_1+\frac{1}{T}),\ c_{20}=\frac{c_2\lambda_1}{T}$$

with

$$\alpha_i=\frac{1-k_i(1-\beta)}{\ell_i} \quad (i=1,2) \quad (21d)$$

Equations (21a,b) constitute the final model which will be utilized for both simulation and identification.

Integrating (21a,b) three times from t=0 to t=t yields

$$\begin{aligned}&y_1(t)+a_{12}D^{-1}y_1(t)+a_{11}D^{-2}y_1(t)+a_{10}D^{-3}y_1(t)\\&-y_1(0)-[a_{12}y_1(0)+Dy_1(0)]t\\&-[a_{11}y_1(0)+a_{12}Dy_1(0)+D^2y_1(0)]\frac{t^2}{2}\\&=b_{11}D^{-2}y_2(t)+b_{10}D^{-3}y_2(t)-b_{11}\frac{t^2}{2}y_2(0)\\&+c_{12}D^{-1}u_1(t)+c_{11}D^{-2}u_1(t)+c_{10}D^{-3}u_1(t)\\&-c_{12}tu_1(0)-[c_{11}u_1(0)+c_{12}Du_1(0)]\frac{t^2}{2}\end{aligned} \quad (22a)$$

$$\begin{aligned}&y_2(t)+a_{22}D^{-1}y_2(t)+a_{21}D^{-2}y_2(t)+a_{20}D^{-3}y_2(t)\\&-y_2(0)-[a_{22}y_2(0)+Dy_2(0)]t\\&-[a_{21}y_2(0)+a_{22}Dy_2(0)+D^2y_2(0)]\frac{t^2}{2}\\&=b_{21}D^{-2}y_1(t)+b_{20}D^{-3}y_1(t)-b_{21}\frac{t^2}{2}y_1(0)\\&+c_{22}D^{-1}u_2(t)+c_{21}D^{-2}u_2(t)+c_{20}D^{-3}u_2(t)\\&-c_{22}tu_2(0)-[c_{21}u_2(0)+c_{22}Du_2(0)]\frac{t^2}{2}\end{aligned} \quad (22b)$$

Now we expand $y_i(t)$ and $u_i(t)$ in Walsh series and apply the multiple integration property (16) to obtain (i=1,2):

$$y_i(t)=\underline{y}_i^T\underline{\Phi}(t),\ D^{-k}y_i(t)=\underline{y}_i^T\underline{P}_k\underline{\Phi}(t)$$
$$u_i(t)=\underline{\zeta}_i^T\underline{\Phi}(t),D^{-k}u_i(t)=\underline{\zeta}_i^T\underline{P}_k\underline{\Phi}(t) \quad (23)$$

for k=1,2,...

Similarly, we expand the functions t^o,t, and $t^2/2$ to obtain

$$t^o=1=[1,0,\dots,0]\underline{\Phi}(t)=\underline{\varepsilon}_o^T\underline{\Phi}(t)$$
$$t=\int_o^1 1dt=\underline{\varepsilon}_o^T\underline{P}_1\underline{\Phi}(t)=(\text{1st row of }\underline{P}_1)\underline{\Phi}(t) \quad (24)$$
$$t^2/2=\int_o^1\int_o^1 1dt=\underline{\varepsilon}_o^T\underline{P}_2\underline{\Phi}(t)=(\text{1st row of }\underline{P}_2)\underline{\Phi}(t)$$

Introducing the expansions (23) and (24) into (22a,b) yields:

$$\underline{\Phi}^T(t)\underline{y}_1+a_{12}\underline{\Phi}^T(t)\underline{P}_1^T\underline{y}_1+a_{11}\underline{\Phi}^T(t)\underline{P}_2^T\underline{y}_1$$

$$+a_{10}\underline{\Phi}^T(t)\underline{P}_3^T\underline{y}_1-\underline{\Phi}^T(t)b_{11}\underline{P}_2^T\underline{y}_2-\underline{\Phi}^T(t)b_{10}\underline{P}_3^T\underline{y}_2$$

$$=c_{12}\underline{\Phi}^T(t)\underline{P}_1^T\underline{\zeta}_1+c_{11}\underline{\Phi}^T(t)\underline{P}_2^T\underline{\zeta}_1+c_{10}\underline{\Phi}^T\underline{P}_3^T\underline{\zeta}_1$$

$$+\underline{\Phi}^T(t)Y_1^o\underline{\varepsilon}_o+(a_{12}Y_1^o+Y_1^1)\underline{\Phi}^T(t)\underline{P}_1^T\underline{\varepsilon}_o$$

$$+(a_{11}Y_1^o+a_{12}Y_1^1+Y_1^2)\underline{\Phi}^T(t)\underline{P}_2^T\underline{\varepsilon}_o-b_{11}Y_2^o\underline{\Phi}^T(t)\underline{P}_2^T\underline{\varepsilon}_o$$

$$-c_{12}U_1^o\underline{\Phi}^T(t)\underline{P}_1^T\underline{\varepsilon}_o-(c_{11}U_1^o+c_{12}U_1^1)\underline{\Phi}^T(t)\underline{P}_2^T\underline{\varepsilon}_o \qquad (25a)$$

$$\underline{\Phi}^T(t)\underline{y}_2+a_{22}\underline{\Phi}^T(t)\underline{P}_1^T\underline{y}_2+a_{21}\underline{\Phi}^T(t)\underline{P}_2^T\underline{y}_2$$

$$+a_{20}\underline{\Phi}^T(t)\underline{P}_3^T\underline{y}_2-b_{21}\underline{\Phi}^T(t)\underline{P}_2^T\underline{y}_1-b_{20}\underline{\Phi}^T(t)\underline{P}_3^T\underline{y}_1$$

$$=c_{22}\underline{\Phi}^T(t)\underline{P}_1^T\underline{\zeta}_2+c_{21}\underline{\Phi}^T(t)\underline{P}_2^T\underline{\zeta}_2$$

$$+c_{20}\underline{\Phi}^T(t)\underline{P}_3^T\underline{\zeta}_2+Y_2^o\underline{\Phi}^T(t)\underline{\varepsilon}_o$$

$$+(a_{22}Y_2^o+Y_2^1)\underline{\Phi}^T(t)\underline{P}_1^T\underline{\varepsilon}_o+(a_{21}Y_2^o+a_{22}Y_2^1$$

$$+Y_2^2)\underline{\Phi}^T(t)\underline{P}_2^T\underline{\varepsilon}_o-b_{21}Y_1^o\underline{\Phi}^T(t)\underline{P}_2^T\underline{\varepsilon}_o-c_{22}U_2^o\underline{P}_1^T\underline{\varepsilon}_o$$

$$-(c_{21}U_2^o+c_{22}U_2^1)\underline{\Phi}^T(t)\underline{P}_2^T\underline{\varepsilon}_o \qquad (25b)$$

where $y_i(0)=Y_i^o$, $Dy_i(0)=Y_i^1$, $D^2y_i(0)=Y_i^2$ and $u_i(0)=U_i^o$, $Du_i(0)=U_i^1$ for $i=1,2$.

Equations (25a,b) can be written in the following compact form

$$\underline{\Phi}^T(t)\left[\underline{I}+a_{12}\underline{P}_1^T+a_{11}\underline{P}_2^T+a_{10}\underline{P}_3^T \;\vdots\; -(b_{11}\underline{P}_2^T+b_{10}\underline{P}_3^T)\right]\begin{bmatrix}\underline{y}_1\\ \hdashline \underline{y}_2\end{bmatrix}$$

$$=\underline{\Phi}^T(t)\left[c_{12}\underline{P}_1^T+c_{11}\underline{P}_2^T+c_{10}\underline{P}_3^T \;\vdots\; \underline{0}^T\right]\begin{bmatrix}\underline{\zeta}_1\\ \hdashline \underline{\zeta}_2\end{bmatrix}$$

$$+\underline{\Phi}^T(t)\left[\underline{\varepsilon}_o \;\vdots\; \underline{P}_1^T\underline{\varepsilon}_o\right]\left\{\begin{bmatrix}Y_1^o\\ Y_1^1+a_{12}Y_1^o\\ Y_1^2+a_{12}Y_1^1+a_{11}Y_1^o-b_{11}Y_2^o\end{bmatrix}-\begin{bmatrix}0\\ c_{12}U_1^o\\ c_{12}U_1^1+c_{11}U_1^o\end{bmatrix}\right\} \qquad (26a)$$

$$\underline{\Phi}^T(t)\left[-(b_{21}\underline{P}_2^T+b_{20}\underline{P}_3^T) \;\vdots\; I+a_{22}\underline{P}_1^T+a_{21}\underline{P}_2^T+a_{20}\underline{P}_3^T\right]\begin{bmatrix}\underline{y}_1\\ \hdashline \underline{y}_2\end{bmatrix}$$

$$=\underline{\Phi}^T(t)\left[\underline{0}^T \;\vdots\; c_{22}\underline{P}_1^T+c_{21}\underline{P}_2^T+c_{20}\underline{P}_3^T\right]\begin{bmatrix}\underline{\zeta}_1\\ \hdashline \underline{\zeta}_2\end{bmatrix}$$

$$+\underline{\Phi}^T(t)\left[\underline{\varepsilon}_o \;\vdots\; \underline{P}_1^T\underline{\varepsilon}_o \;\vdots\; \underline{P}_2^T\underline{\varepsilon}_o\right]\left\{\begin{bmatrix}Y_2^o\\ Y_2^1+a_{22}Y_2^o\\ Y_2^2+a_{22}Y_2^1+a_{21}Y_2^o-b_{21}Y_1^o\end{bmatrix}-\begin{bmatrix}0\\ c_{22}U_2^o\\ c_{22}U_2^1+c_{21}U_2^o\end{bmatrix}\right\} \qquad (26b)$$

Equations (26a,b) can be further written as

$$\begin{bmatrix}\underline{\Phi}^T(t) & \underline{0}^T\\ \underline{0}^T & \underline{\Phi}^T(t)\end{bmatrix}\begin{bmatrix}\underline{\Sigma}_{11}^T & \underline{\Sigma}_{12}^T\\ \underline{\Sigma}_{21}^T & \underline{\Sigma}_{22}^T\end{bmatrix}\begin{bmatrix}\underline{y}_1\\ \underline{y}_2\end{bmatrix}$$

$$=\begin{bmatrix}\underline{\Phi}^T(t) & \underline{0}^T\\ \underline{0}^T & \underline{\Phi}^T(t)\end{bmatrix}\left\{\begin{bmatrix}\underline{C}_{11}^T & \underline{0}^T\\ \underline{0}^T & \underline{C}_{22}^T\end{bmatrix}\begin{bmatrix}\underline{\zeta}_1\\ \underline{\zeta}_2\end{bmatrix}+\begin{bmatrix}\underline{E}_{11}^T & \underline{0}^T\\ \underline{0}^T & \underline{E}_{22}^T\end{bmatrix}\begin{bmatrix}\underline{\eta}_1\\ \underline{\eta}_2\end{bmatrix}\right\} \qquad (27)$$

where

$$\underline{\Sigma}_{11}^T=I+a_{12}\underline{P}_1^T+a_{11}\underline{P}_2^T+a_{10}\underline{P}_3^T$$

$$\underline{\Sigma}_{12}^T=-(b_{11}\underline{P}_2^T+b_{10}\underline{P}_3^T)$$

$$\underline{\Sigma}_{21}^T=-(b_{21}\underline{P}_2^T+b_{20}\underline{P}_3^T)$$

$$\underline{\Sigma}_{22}^T=I+a_{22}\underline{P}_1^T+a_{21}\underline{P}_2^T+a_{20}\underline{P}_3^T$$

$$\underline{C}_{11}^T=c_{12}\underline{P}_1^T+c_{11}\underline{P}_2^T+c_{10}\underline{P}_3^T$$

$$\underline{C}_{22}^T=c_{22}\underline{P}_1^T+c_{21}\underline{P}_2^T+c_{20}\underline{P}_3^T$$

$$E_{11}^T=E_{22}^T=\left[\underline{\varepsilon}_o \;\vdots\; \underline{P}_1^T\underline{\varepsilon}_o \;\vdots\; \underline{P}_2^T\underline{\varepsilon}_o\right]$$

$$\underline{\eta}_1=\begin{bmatrix}Y_1^o\\ Y_1^1+a_{12}Y_1^o\\ Y_1^2+a_{12}Y_1^1+a_{11}Y_1^o-b_{11}Y_2^o\end{bmatrix}-\begin{bmatrix}0\\ c_{12}U_1^o\\ c_{12}U_1^1+c_{11}U_1^o\end{bmatrix}$$

$$\underline{\eta}_2=\begin{bmatrix} Y_2^o \\ Y_2^1+a_{22}Y_2^o \\ Y_2^2+a_{22}Y_2^1+a_{21}Y_2^o-b_{21}Y_1^o \end{bmatrix} - \begin{bmatrix} 0 \\ c_{22}U_2^o \\ c_{22}U_2^1+c_{21}U_2^o \end{bmatrix} \quad (28)$$

The matrix equations (27) involves two independent equations with 2m unknowns, namely the coefficients involved in the vectors $\underline{v}_1$ and $\underline{v}_2$. To determine 2m linearly independent equations from (27) one equates the coefficients of equal sequency terms, or equivalently applies (27) for $t=t_k=(k-1)/m$, $k=1,2,\ldots,m$.

The result is

$$\tilde{\underline{\Phi}}^T\underline{\Sigma}\;\underline{v}=\tilde{\underline{\Phi}}^T\underline{\xi},\quad \underline{v}=\begin{bmatrix}\underline{v}_1\\ \hline \underline{v}_2\end{bmatrix} \quad (29)$$

where

$$\tilde{\underline{\Phi}}^T=\begin{bmatrix} \underline{\Phi}^T(t_1) & \underline{0}^T \\ \underline{0}^T & \underline{\Phi}^T(t_1) \\ \hline \vdots & \vdots \\ \hline \underline{\Phi}^T(t_m) & \underline{0}^T \\ \underline{0}^T & \underline{\Phi}^T(t_m) \end{bmatrix},\quad \underline{\Sigma}=\begin{bmatrix} \underline{\Sigma}_{11}^T & \underline{\Sigma}_{12}^T \\ \underline{\Sigma}_{21}^T & \underline{\Sigma}_{22}^T \end{bmatrix} \quad (30)$$

$$\underline{\xi}=\begin{bmatrix} \underline{C}_{11}^T & \underline{0}^T \\ \underline{0}^T & \underline{C}_{22}^T \end{bmatrix}\begin{bmatrix}\underline{\zeta}_1\\ \underline{\zeta}_2\end{bmatrix}+\begin{bmatrix} \underline{E}_{11}^T & \underline{0}^T \\ \underline{0}^T & \underline{E}_{22}^T \end{bmatrix}\begin{bmatrix}\underline{\eta}_1\\ \underline{\eta}_2\end{bmatrix}$$

Equation (29) can now be solved for $\underline{v}$ to give

$$\underline{v}=(\tilde{\underline{\Phi}}^T\underline{\Sigma})^{-1}\tilde{\underline{\Phi}}^T\underline{\xi} \quad (31)$$

Thus the solution $y_1(t)$, $y_2(t)$ is provided by

$$\begin{bmatrix} y_1(t) \\ y_2(t) \end{bmatrix}=\begin{bmatrix} \underline{\Phi}^T(t) & \underline{0}^T \\ \underline{0}^T & \underline{\Phi}^T(t) \end{bmatrix}\underline{v} \quad (32)$$

5. REACTOR PARAMETER IDENTIFICATION

The general problem of identifying (determining) the reactor parameters reduces to solving (25a,b) for $a_{ij}, b_{ij}, c_{ij}, Y_i^j, U_i$ on the basis of the assumption that $\underline{v}_1$, $\underline{v}_2$ and $\underline{\zeta}_1,\underline{\zeta}_2$ are known (determined from the measured input u(t) and output y(t) through (23) and (11)).

Rearranging (25a,b) gives

$$\begin{aligned}\underline{\Phi}^T(t)\underline{v}_1=&\Big[-\underline{\Phi}^T(t)\underline{P}_1^T\underline{v}_1 \;\vdots\; -\underline{\Phi}^T(t)\underline{P}_2^T\underline{v}_1 \;\vdots\\ &-\underline{\Phi}^T(t)\underline{P}_3^T\underline{v}_1 \;\vdots\; \underline{\Phi}^T(t)\underline{P}_2^T\underline{v}_2 \;\; \underline{\Phi}^T(t)\underline{P}_3^T\underline{v}_2 \;\vdots\\ &\underline{\Phi}^T(t)\underline{P}_1^T\underline{\zeta}_1 \;\vdots\; \underline{\Phi}^T(t)\underline{P}_2^T\underline{\zeta}_1 \;\vdots\; \underline{\Phi}^T(t)\underline{P}_3^T\underline{\zeta}_1\Big]\underline{\theta}^1\\ &+\Big[\underline{\Phi}^T(t)\underline{\varepsilon}_o \;\vdots\; \underline{\Phi}^T(t)\underline{P}_1^T\underline{\varepsilon}_o \;\vdots\; \underline{\Phi}^T(t)\underline{P}_2^T\underline{\varepsilon}_o \;\vdots\\ &-\underline{\Phi}^T(t)\underline{P}_2^T\underline{\varepsilon}_o \;\vdots\; -\underline{P}_1^T\underline{\varepsilon}_o \;\vdots\; -\underline{\Phi}^T(t)\underline{P}_2^T\underline{\varepsilon}_o\Big]\underline{\sigma}^1\end{aligned} \quad (33a)$$

$$\begin{aligned}\underline{\Phi}^T(t)\underline{v}_2=&\Big[-\underline{\Phi}^T(t)\underline{P}_1^T\underline{v}_2 \;\vdots\; -\underline{\Phi}^T(t)\underline{P}_2^T\underline{v}_2 \;\vdots\\ &-\underline{\Phi}^T(t)\underline{P}_3^T\underline{v}_2 \;\vdots\; \underline{\Phi}^T(t)\underline{P}_2^T\underline{v}_1 \;\vdots\; \underline{\Phi}^T(t)\underline{P}_3^T\underline{v}_1\\ &\underline{\Phi}^T(t)\underline{P}_1^T\underline{\zeta}_2 \;\vdots\; \underline{\Phi}^T(t)\underline{P}_2^T\underline{\zeta}_2 \;\vdots\; \underline{\Phi}^T(t)\underline{P}_3^T\underline{\zeta}_2\Big]\underline{\theta}^2\\ &+\Big[\underline{\Phi}^T(t)\underline{\varepsilon}_o \;\vdots\; \underline{\Phi}^T(t)\underline{P}_1^T\underline{\varepsilon}_o \;\vdots\; \underline{\Phi}^T(t)\underline{P}_2^T\underline{\varepsilon}_o \;\vdots\\ &-\underline{\Phi}^T(t)\underline{P}_2^T\underline{\varepsilon}_o \;\vdots\; -\underline{P}_1^T\underline{\varepsilon}_o \;\vdots\; -\underline{\Phi}^T(t)\underline{P}_2^T\underline{\varepsilon}_o\Big]\underline{\sigma}^2\end{aligned} \quad (33b)$$

where

$$\underline{\theta}^1=\begin{bmatrix} a_{12}\\ a_{11}\\ a_{10}\\ b_{11}\\ b_{10}\\ c_{12}\\ c_{11}\\ c_{10}\end{bmatrix},\quad \underline{\theta}^2=\begin{bmatrix} a_{22}\\ a_{21}\\ a_{20}\\ b_{21}\\ b_{20}\\ c_{22}\\ c_{21}\\ c_{20}\end{bmatrix},\quad \underline{\sigma}^1=\begin{bmatrix} Y_1^o \\ a_{12}Y_1^o+Y_1^1 \\ a_{11}Y_1^o+a_{12}Y_1^1+Y_1^2 \\ b_{11}Y_2^o \\ c_{12}U_1^o \\ c_{11}U_1^o+c_{12}U_1^1 \end{bmatrix}$$

$$\underline{\sigma}^2=\begin{bmatrix} Y_2^o \\ a_{22}Y_2^o+Y_2^1 \\ a_{21}Y_2^o+a_{22}Y_2^1+Y_2^2 \\ b_{21}Y_1^o \\ c_{22}U_2^o \\ c_{21}U_2^o+c_{22}U_2^1 \end{bmatrix} \quad (33c)$$

Equations (33a,b) contain the unknown vectors $\underline{\theta}^1,\underline{\theta}^2$, $\underline{\sigma}^1$ and $\underline{\sigma}^2$ which involve a total of 28 unknown parameters and initial conditions. Hence the Walsh vector $\underline{\Phi}(t)$ needs to be at least 16-dimensional.

In compact form (33a,b) can be written as

$$\begin{bmatrix} \underline{\Phi}^T(t)\underline{y}_1 \\ \underline{\Phi}^T(t)\underline{y}_2 \end{bmatrix} = \left[\begin{array}{c|c|c|c} \underline{H}_{11}^T(t) & \underline{H}_{12}^T & \underline{0}^T & \underline{0}^T \\ \hline \underline{0}^T & \underline{0}^T & \underline{H}_{23}^T(t) & \underline{H}_{24}^T(t) \end{array}\right] \underline{\theta} \quad (34a)$$

where

$$\underline{\theta} = \begin{bmatrix} \underline{\theta}^1 \\ \underline{\sigma}^1 \\ \underline{\theta}^2 \\ \underline{\sigma}^2 \end{bmatrix} \quad (34b)$$

and the H_{ij}^T's have obvious definitions.

Hence applying (34a) for $t=t_k=(k-1)/m$ $(m\geq 16)$ $k=1,2,\ldots,14$ (or equating like sequency terms) yields

$$\underline{\tilde{\Psi}}=\underline{\tilde{H}}\ \underline{\theta} \quad (35a)$$

where

$$\underline{\tilde{\Psi}} = \begin{bmatrix} \underline{\Psi}(t_1) \\ \vdots \\ \underline{\Psi}(t_{14}) \end{bmatrix}, \underline{\Psi}(t_k) = \begin{bmatrix} \underline{\Phi}^T(t_k)\underline{y}_1 \\ \underline{\Phi}^T(t_k)\underline{y}_2 \end{bmatrix} \quad (35b)$$

$$\underline{\tilde{H}} = \begin{bmatrix} \underline{H}(t_1) \\ \vdots \\ \underline{H}(t_{14}) \end{bmatrix}, \underline{H}(t) = \left[\begin{array}{c|c|c|c} \underline{H}_{11}^T(t) & \underline{H}_{12}^T(t) & \underline{0}^T & \underline{0}^T \\ \hline \underline{0}^T & \underline{0}^T & \underline{H}_{23}^T(t) & H_{24}^T(t) \end{array}\right] \quad (35d)$$

Solving (35a) for $\underline{\theta}$ gives

$$\underline{\theta}=(\underline{\tilde{H}})^{-1}\underline{\tilde{\Psi}} \quad (36)$$

The parameters a_{ij}, b_{ij} and c_{ij} are found directly from the $\underline{\theta}^1$ and $\underline{\theta}^2$ subvectors of $\underline{\theta}$. The unknown initial conditions Y_i^j and U_i^j can be determined from the $\underline{\sigma}^1$ and $\underline{\sigma}^2$ subvectors (see (35c)) as follows.

$$\begin{array}{ll} Y_1^o=\sigma_1^1 & Y_2^o=\sigma_1^2 \\ Y_1^1=\sigma_2^1-a_{12}Y_1^o & Y_2^1=\sigma_2^2-a_{22}Y_2^o \\ Y_1^2=\sigma_3^1-a_{11}Y_1^o-a_{12}Y_1^1 & Y_2^2=\sigma_3^2 \\ Y_2^o=\sigma_4^1/b_{11} & Y_1^o=\sigma_4^2/b_{21} \\ U_1^o=\sigma_5^1/c_{12} & U_2^o=\sigma_5^2/c_{22} \\ U_1^1=(\sigma_6^1-c_{11}U_1^o)/c_{12} & U_2^1=(\sigma_6^2-c_{21}U_2^o)/c_{22} \end{array} \quad (37)$$

where σ_i^1, σ_i^2 are the ith elements of $\underline{\sigma}^1$ and $\underline{\sigma}^2$ respectively.

The original reactor parameters β,α_1,α_2, $k_1,k_2,\ell_1,\ell_2,\lambda_1,\beta_1,c_1,c_2,\sigma$, and T can be determined from the identified parameters a_{ij}'s, b_{ij}'s and c_{ij}'s by solving the algebraic system (21c,d).

It must be remarked that if in the original coupled-reactor model some of the parameters are known then it is possible either to apply the method using a Walsh vector $\underline{\Phi}(t)$ of smaller dimensionality $(m\leq 8)$, thus gaining computation time, or to use a high dimensional vector $\underline{\Phi}(t)$ combined with least squares for better accuracy.

ILLUSTRATIVE EXAMPLE

To test the method, a one delayed neutron group two-core reactor system in a symmetric configuration with nonzero interaction was considered. The realistic values:

$\beta=0.007$, $\lambda=0.1\ \text{sec}^{-1}$, $\ell_1=\ell_2=0.3\text{x}10^{-4}\text{sec}$

$\alpha_1=\alpha_2=7.43\text{x}10^2\text{sec}^{-1}$, $\delta k=-0.0154$

$\sigma=0.0021$, $T=4\text{x}10^{-3}$ sec

Under the assumption of zero external source inputs to both cores: $u_1(t)=u_2(t)=0$ for all t of interest, and initial conditions

$y_i(0)=1$, $Dy_i(0)=0$, $D^2y_i(0)=0$ $(i=1,2)$,

the outputs $y_i(t)$, $i=1,2$ were computed applying (26a,b) at four times $t_1=0, t_2=0.25$, $t_3=0.50$ and $t_4=0.75$ (i.e. the unit normalized interval $[0,1)$ was divided in four subintervals) and using a 4th-dimensional Walsh vector $\underline{\Phi}(t)$ at t_k, $k=1,2,3,4$:

$$\underline{\Phi}(0)=\begin{bmatrix}+1\\+1\\+1\\+1\end{bmatrix}, \underline{\Phi}(0.25)=\begin{bmatrix}+1\\+1\\-1\\-1\end{bmatrix}$$

$$\underline{\Phi}(0.5)=\begin{bmatrix}+1\\-1\\+1\\-1\end{bmatrix}, \underline{\Phi}(0.75)=\begin{bmatrix}+1\\-1\\-1\\+1\end{bmatrix}$$

Although only a 4-term Walsh approximation was used the step-wise approximate responses

$y_1(t)=\underline{y}_1^T\underline{\Phi}(t)$ and $y_2(t)=\underline{y}_2^T\underline{\Phi}(t)$, obtained, are quite near the exact responses computed using the available analytic solution of the model at hand.

The identification method was tested by considering all parameters involved known, except T. Using as measured data the values of $y_i(t)$, i=1,2 at t=0,0.25,0.5 and 0.75 obtained from the analytic solution, and employing (33a,b) the value of T was found to be

$\hat{T}=3.56\times10^{-3}$ sec

which is in satisfactory agreement with the true value $T=4\times10^{-3}$ sec, given that only a 4x4 Walsh operational matrix was used.

Further numerical work is in progress for finding the estimated value $\hat{T}$ with 8x8 and 16x16 Walsh operational matrices, and for developing a full general-purpose program for the identification of all reactor parameters involved.

CONCLUSION

The present paper was devoted to the realistic problem of identifying some or all of the parameters, including the coupling time lag T, of a class of coupled-core nuclear reactor systems. The Walsh function expansion approach based on the utilization of OSOMRI was adopted. Further work is in progress for studying more difficult cases such as bilinear models with time varying reactivity of the type $k(t)=k_o+\rho_1 t+\rho_2 t^2+\ldots$, coupled-core models with pure coupling-time-delay, and space-dep ndent reactor models. In these studies both the Walsh function and block-pulse function approach will be explored along the path of the present and previous papers [10-12]. Also the treatment of some control problems for the same class of models will be attempted by the same approach [8,13].

REFERENCES

1. S.G. Tzafestas, Control of Nuclear Power Plants, Auto.Control Theory and Appl., Vol.8, No.3, pp. 37-50 (1980).
2. S.G.Tzafestas and N. Chrysochoides, Canonical Decoupling Control of Multi-Core Nuclear Reactors, Nucl.Sci.and Eng.,Vol.62,pp.574-579 (1977).
3. P.B.Reddy and P.Sannuti, Optimal Control of a Coupled-Core Nuclear Reactor by a Singular Perturbation Method, IEEE Trans.Auto.Control,Vol.AC-20,pp. 766-769 (1975).
4. S.G. Tzafestas, Walsh Series Approach to Lumped and Distributed System Identification, J. Franklin Inst., Vol. 305, pp. 199-220 (1978).
5. C.F.Chen and C.H.Hsiao, Time-Domain Synthesis via Walsh Functions, Proc. IEE, Vol.122, pp.565-570 (1975).
6. G.Prasada Rao and K.R.Palanisamy, Improved Algorithms for Parameter Identification in Continuous Systems Via Walsh Functions, Proc.IEE, Vol.130, Pt.D, pp.9-16,(1983).
7. S.G.Tzafestas, On Digital-Model Design for Nuclear Reactor Computation and Control, Nucl.Instr.and Methods, Vol. 84 pp.207-210 (1970).
8. S.G.Tzafestas and N.Chrysochoides, Nuclear Reactor Control Using Walsh Function Variational Synthesis, Nucl. Science and Engrg., Vol.62,pp.763-770 (1977).
9. S.G.Tzafestas, Distributed-Parameter Nuclear Reactor Optimal Control,in "New Trends in System Analysis" (A. Bensoussan, J.L.Lions, Editors), LNICS, Springer (1977).
10. S.G.Tzafestas and N.Chrysochoides, Time-Varying Reactivity Reconstruction, IEEE Trans. Auto.Control,Vol.AC-22, pp. 886-888 (1977).
11. S.G.Tzafestas and J.Anoussis, Test Inputs for Nuclear-Reactor Identification, Auto.Control Theory and Applications, Vol.5,pp.28-40 (1977).
12. S.G.Tzafestas and J.Anoussis, Dynamic Reactivity Computation in Nuclear Reactors Using Block-Pulse Function Expansion, in "Advances in Modelling, Planning and Control of Energy, Power and Environmental Systems" (S.G.Tzafestas, Editor) ACTA Press, Calgary, Canada, pp.223-226 (1983).
13. S.G.Tzafestas, N.G.Chrysochoides and K.Rokkos, Application of an Exact Model Matching Technique to a Coupled-Core Nuclear Reactor Control, Nucl. Sci.Engrg., Vol.87,pp.454-460 (1984).
14. R.W.Albrecht and W.Seifritz, "Fundamental Properties of the Coherence Function in Symmetrical 2-node Systems", Nukleonic, II Bd.,Heff.3,pp. 143-154 (1968).
15. C.E.Cohn,Reflected Reactor Kinetics, Nucl.Sci.Engrg, Vol.13,pp.12-17 (1962).
16. U.Farinelli and N.Pacilio, The Bimodal Decay of 2-Pulsed Neutron Coupled Cores of an Organic Moderated and Reflected System, Nucl.Sci. and Engrg., Vol.36, pp.39-46 (1969).

DIGITAL TECHNIQUES in Simulation, Communication and Control
Spyros G. Tzafestas (editor)
Elsevier Science Publishers B.V. (North-Holland) © IMACS, 1985

NUMERICAL SIMULATION APPLIED TO THE CONTROL OF STEPPING-MOTORS

Daniel PINCHON and Jean-François BRUDNY

Université des Sciences et Techniques de Lille 1
Bâtiment P2
59655 VILLENEUVE D'ASCQ Cédex (FRANCE)

The behaviour of a stepping-motor driving a known load is described by a non-linear differential equation. The authors present a proposal for investigation by eliminating the dependent variables due to the non linear functions. They obtain several linear equations and a test procedure leads to the step by step solution. With this method, they can analyse the moving of the motor and determine optimal times between two successive switchings.
So, a multistep operation can be studied. It is investigated through the determination of the number of steps during each phase of the moving. The different times between successive switchings are applied to the motor which controls it in open loop; the obtained results by the experiment ratify the laws drawn out of the numerical computation . The influence of the parameters on the behaviour of the system is then studied.

1. INTRODUCTION

The authors have already studied the acceleration of a lood driven by a stepping motor [1]. They now consider a given multistep operation. A numerical method, easily implementable on a microcomputer, allow them to obtain the step by step response of the system . So, they determine the times between two successive switchings; these ones take place according to a control law which leads to a positioning without missing steps.

2. ELECTROMECHANICAL UNIT

The used testing stand which permits us to verify the results obtained by the numerical computation consists of :
- a stepping-motor STEBON 852-250-70, fed in current; it is an hybrid 200-step-per-revolution motor;
- a friction brake JAEGER CS 17 P which gives a maximum torque of 1.7 N.m;
- interchangeable inertial disks.

The observation of the position and of the speed is realized by high performance potentiometer and analog differentiator.

3. EQUATIONS OF THE SYSTEM

Given the performances of the power supply, we can consider the electrical time constant as negligible.

3.1 - General equation

The moving of the system constituted by the stepping motor driving a mechanical load is then ruled by the differential equation alone:

$$J \ddot{\theta} + F \dot{\theta} + C_R \operatorname{sgn} \theta = C \qquad (1)$$

designing by :

θ : the rotation angle
J : the moment of inertia of system referred to motor shaft
F : the viscous damping factor
C_R : the torque due to friction
C : the motor torque

3.2 - Expression of the motor torque

For an hybrid motor, we can distinguish two modes of operation :
- the mode 1 (single-phase mode) : a single winding among the four is energized at a time, and it appears four stable positions by electrical revolution.
- the mode 2 (two-phase mode) : two windings are energized and four other stable positions are then defined.

For the two modes, the motor torque C is given by :

$$C = - C_M \sin (N_R \theta + k \frac{\pi}{2}) \qquad (2)$$

where :
- k is a parameter the value of which changes at each switching
- N_R the number of rotor teeth
- C_M a quantity given by the constructor, or which can be measured. For the mode 2, this value is multiplied by the coefficient $\sqrt{2}$ compared with the mode 1.

3.3 - Expression of the different parameters

Under-mentioned, we note the parameters of the equations (1) ard (2). It should be observed that J and C_R can each one have two different values, which allow us to study the effect of these parameters on the multistep operation.

$N_R = 50$ $C_M = 1.3$ N.m $F = 6.9.10^{-3}$.N.m/rad.s^{-1}
$J_1 = 2.10^{-4}$ kg - m^2 $J_2 = 3.4.10^{-4}$ kg.m^2
$C_{R1} = 0.4$ N.m $C_{R2} = 0.2$ N.m

The step S is equal to $\frac{\pi}{100}$ rad.

4 CONTROL LAW

During the acceleration, to take advantage of the maximal available motor torque. as it is shown on the figure 1, we must generate the pulses when the rotor position reaches the values : $\frac{S}{2}, \frac{3S}{2}, \frac{5S}{2}, \ldots$ [2]

This condition which permits the determination of the successive switching times TA_i impose to the speed to be at any time monotonous increasing up to a certain limit value V_L [3] . The control times TD_i during the deceleration can be obtained by the solution of the equation (1), taking into account the position and the speed reached at the end of the acceleration. Now, for a given positioning, we don't know these values. We remove this difficulty by making the calculation in backward time : then, the initial position and speed are equal to zero and the impulses are generated when θ takes the values $\frac{-S}{2}, \frac{-3S}{2}, \frac{-5S}{2}, \ldots$

Before approaching the multistep operation, we must determine the switching times by numerical method.

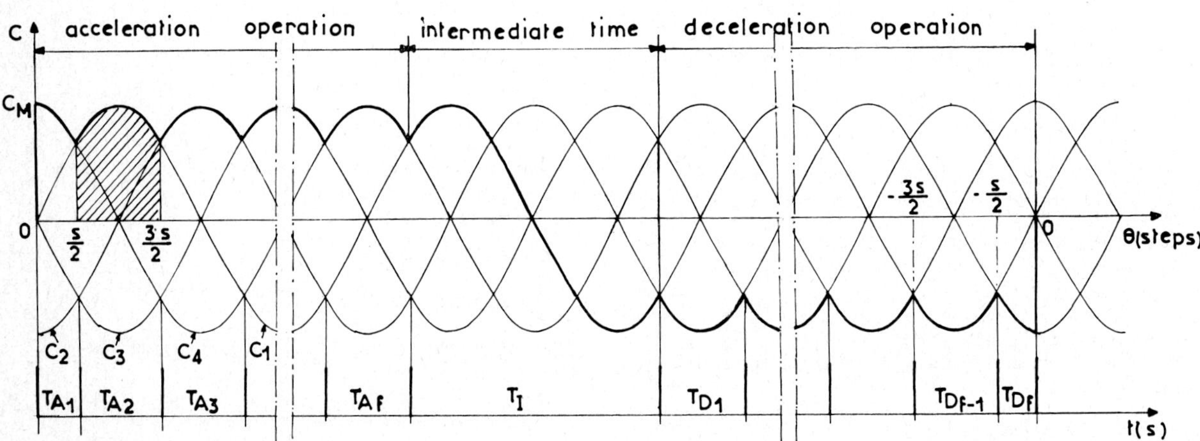

Figure 1 : Control law

5 COMPUTATION OF SWITCHING-TIMES

The used method [1] consists in obtaining the step by step response of the system. The state of this one is supposed to be known at the time t_n, by the values θ_n et $\dot{\theta}_n$. We can determine it at $t_{n+1} = t_n + \Delta t$ - Δt is the small enough resolving time -, replacing in (2) the quantity $\sin N_R \theta$ by its expansion. Using these assumptions the equation (1) becomes :

$$\ddot{\theta} + \frac{F}{J}\dot{\theta} + \frac{CM}{J}\left(B_n^1 \cos\frac{k\pi}{2} - B_n^2 \sin\frac{k\pi}{2}\right)\theta =$$

$$-\frac{CM}{J}\left(A_n^1 \cos\frac{k\pi}{2} - A_n^2 \sin\frac{k\pi}{2}\right) - K_1 \frac{C_R}{J} \qquad (3)$$

with :

$K_1 = 1$ for $\dot{\theta} > 0$

$K_1 = -1$ for $\dot{\theta} < 0$

$K_1 = 0$ for $\dot{\theta} = 0$

and :

$$A_n^1 = \sin N_R \theta_n - N_R \theta_n \cos N_R \theta_n$$

$$A_n^2 = -\cos N_R \theta_n - N_R \theta_n \sin N_R \theta_n$$

$$B_n^1 = N_R \cos N_R \theta_n$$

$$B_n^2 = N_R \sin N_R \theta_n$$

We can write :

$$\Delta = \left(\frac{F}{J}\right)^2 - 4\frac{C_M}{J}\left(B_n^1 \cos\frac{k\pi}{2} - B_n^2 \sin\frac{k\pi}{2}\right)$$

Its value depends on the parameters of the system and on the initial conditions. Therefore we must consider the sign of the speed. Moreover, the particular solution of (3) is given by

$$\theta_p = -\frac{\left(A_n^1 \cos\frac{k\pi}{2} - A_n^2 \sin\frac{k\pi}{2}\right) + \frac{K_1 C_R}{C_M}}{B_n^1 \cos\frac{k\pi}{2} - B_n^2 \sin\frac{k\pi}{2}}$$

Δ and θ_p yields the response of the system solving three linear differential equations. A test on K_1 allows us to choose the correct solution.

6 MULTISTEP OPERATION

We are in possession of two tables of switching

times corresponding with N_A et N_D steps for the acceleration and deceleration periods. For a given multistep operation, we can obtain, as it is shown on the figure 2,

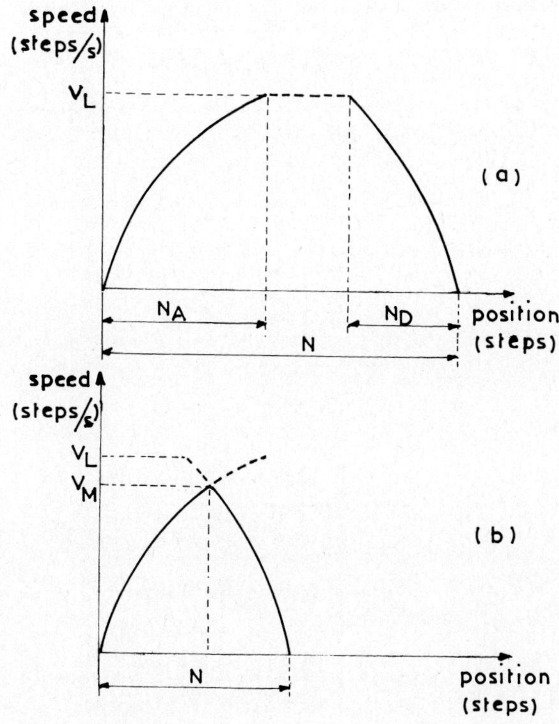

Figure 2 : Profiles of speed laws

two profiles of speed laws according to required number N of steps [4].
We have to consider the two cases :

- $N > N_A + N_D$ (figure 2a) : the two tables are completely used. Then, the limit speed V_L is reached and between the acceleration and deceleration operations, it must be intercalated a traverse at this maximum speed. As soon as the remaining steps become less than the steps necessary for deceleration, the motor will be braked to that the total steps will be equal to N.

- $N < N_A + N_D$ (figure 2b): the motor is not accelerated up to the limit speed; so, we must suspend the table of the times TA_i and use the table of deceleration.
A procedure easily implemented on microcomputer determine the number of steps during each operation.

In this paper, we only study this second case. The transition between the acceleration and deceleration is realized as it is shown on the figure 1, thanks to an intermediate time T_I during which the pulses are stopped [5].

This time corresponds to three steps; it depends on the last time of the acceleration and on the first one of deceleration, so that :

$$T_I = \frac{3}{2}\,(T_{A_F} + T_{D_1})$$

7 OBTAINED RESULTS

The profiles of acceleration and deceleration obtained by the numerical simulation are implemented in the memory of the microcomputer which, so, can drive the motor used in mode 2 (C_M = 1,3 N.m.)

7.1 - Study of a multistep operation with given parameters

We want a travelling of 40 steps with $J = J_1$ and $C_R = C_{R_1}$. The figure 3 shows the response of the motor.

We can explain the difference between the curves obtained by simulation and experiment : indeed, the torque available for the motor is inferior to that one which has been used in the computation.

7.2 - Influence of parameters

The figure 4 shows positionings on 40 pas with :

- $J = J_1$ and $C_R = C_{R_1}$
- $J = J_2$ and $C_R = C_{R_2}$
- $J = J_1$ and $C_R = C_{R_2}$

We draw the following conclusions.

a) the values of V_M at the end of the acceleration, obtained by computation and experiment are almost the same.

b) inertia for inertia, the positioning time T_P diminues with C_R, contrary to V_M.

c) friction torque for friction torque, T_P increases with J, contrary to V_M

8 CONCLUSION

The authors have studied a multistep operation of a system constituted by a variable parameter mechanical load. They have investigated not too long motion, and, now, they will work towards any positioning. They have studied the influence of each parameter on the system. The results obtained by experiment ratify these ones given by numerical computation.

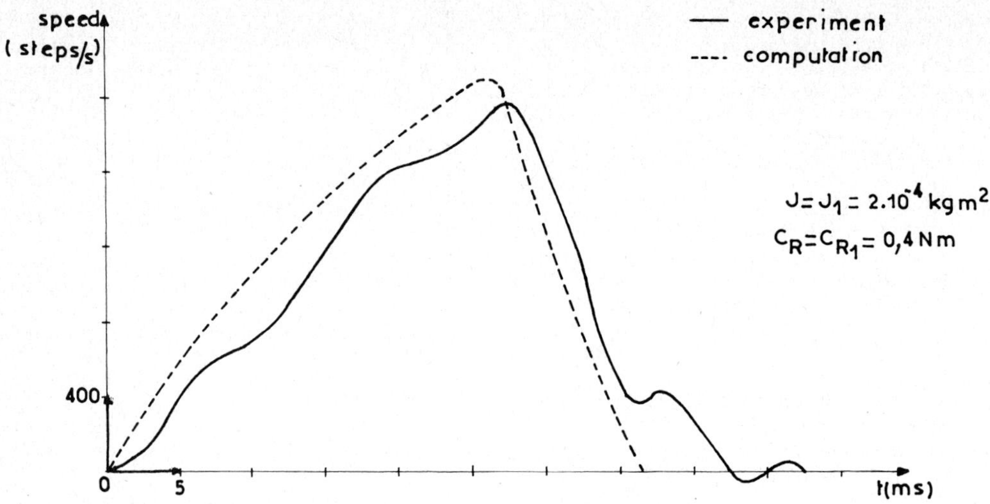

Figure 3 : Positioning on 40 steps

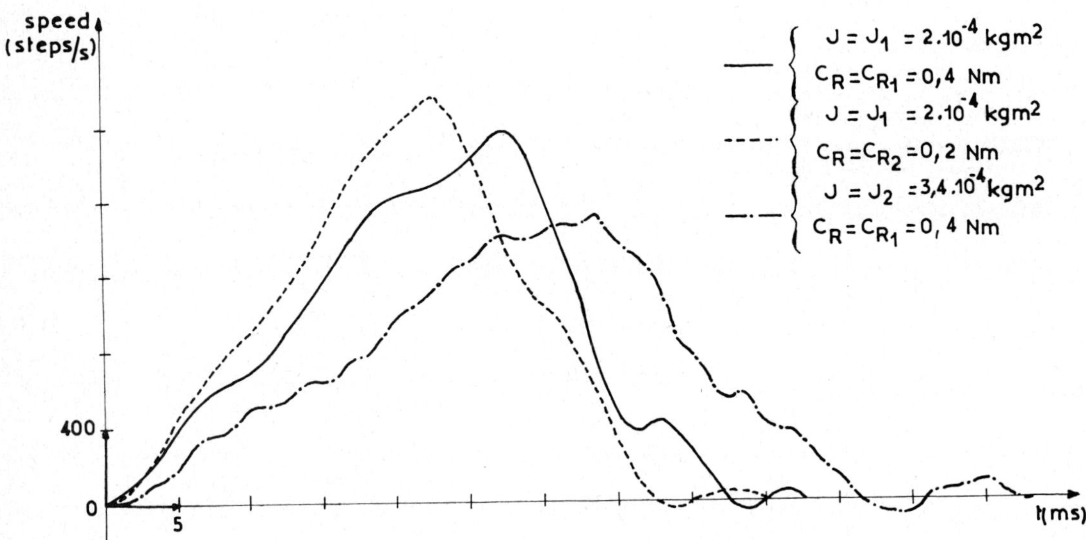

Figure 4 : Influence of parameters

REFERENCES

|1| J.F BRUDNY, D.PINCHON
" Présentation d'une procédure pour l'étude d'un moteur pas à pas sur micro-ordinateur"
I.A.S.T.E.D. International Conference :
" Computer Aided Design, Juin 1984, NICE

|2| D.PINCHON, C. GOELDEL
" Comparaison de plusieurs modes de commande d'un moteur pas à pas en accélération et décélération "
I.A.S.T.E.D. Symposium "Modelling, Identification and Control", Mars 1982, DAVOS

|3| D.PINCHON, C. GOELDEL
" Optimal acceleration of a stepping motor controlled by microprocessor "
Symposium on Electrical Machines for Special Purposes , Septembre 1981, BOLOGNE

|4| C. GOELDEL
" Contribution à la modélisation, à l'alimentation et à la commande des moteurs pas à pas "
Thèse d'Etat, Mars 1984, NANCY

|5| D.PINCHON, C.GOELDEL, P.BRUNIAUX
" Etude d'un système de positionnement à moteur pas à pas - Commandes en boucle ouverte adaptées à la charge "
Troisièmes journées d'étude sur les moteurs pas à pas, Juin 1984, NANCY.

DIGITAL TECHNIQUES in Simulation, Communication and Control
Spyros G. Tzafestas (editor)
Elsevier Science Publishers B.V. (North-Holland) © IMACS, 1985

MULTIMICROPROCESSOR SYSTEM FOR PLANT IDENTIFICATION

Jacki Caro

Laboratoire d'Automatique,
Université Claude Bernard - Lyon I
Villeurbanne, France

This paper deals with the design of multimicroprocessor system specialised for on line parameter identification of industrial processes. The purpose is to get the process transfer function in order to tune the suitable control algorithms. The designed system is intended for utilisation in an industrial context, that supposes the use of relatively transparent methods and easy man-machine communication protocoles. The proposed system is organised around three microprocessor based sub-systems. The order followed will be : the implemented identification principles, multiprocessor architecture specifications, executing procedures and system operating features.

1. IDENTIFICATION METHODOLOGY PRINCIPLE

It is based on a plant impulse response h(t) determination trough an input-output deconvolution processing (Figure 1).

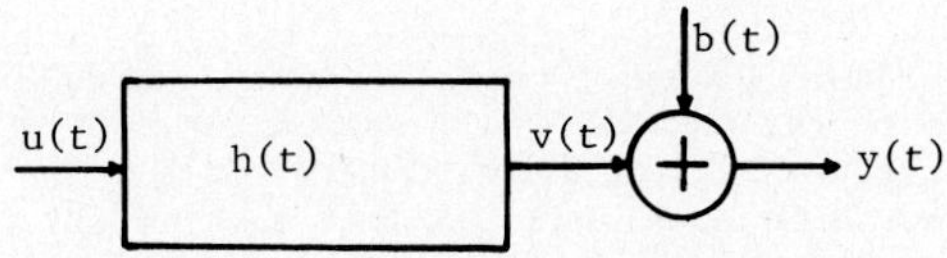

Figure 1. The open-loop system model

where $y(t) = \int_0^\infty h(\tau)u(t - \tau)d\tau + b(t)$

1.1. The deconvolution based on intercorrelation method using a PRBS excitation signal

Let us consider :

- b(t) the output reduced noise non correlated with input signal
- Cyu, Cbu, and Cuu the inter and autocorrelation functions
- $h(\tau)$ the plant impulse response to be identified.

The Wiener-Hopf relation minimises the least square state error

$$Cyu\ (\tau) = \int_0^\infty Cuu(\sigma - \tau)\ h(\sigma)\ d\sigma \qquad (1)$$

If we assume that u(t) is a gaussian noise signal, then

$$Cyu(\tau) = \int_0^\infty \delta(\sigma - \tau)\ h(\sigma)\ d\sigma = h(\tau)$$

In fact, u(t) is a PRBS sequence chosen so that its frequency spectrum is more streched than the system bandwidth. If L, $|a|$, T are respectively the length, magnitude, and sampling time period of PRBS :

$$Cuu(k) = \frac{1}{L} \sum_{0}^{L-1} u(i)u(i - k) \qquad (2)$$

has not got a Dirac shape but that of a triangle of base 2T, and presents an a/L bias value. This so as not to induce distorsion of the calculated sequence Cyu(k), implies the following choices :

- T small to approach a Dirac shape
- LT >> τ_{max} the greatest time constant of the process
- a/L small enough not to shift the initial output value.

In these conditions the intercorrelation function can be approximated by :

$$Cyu(k) = a^2 \frac{L + 1}{L} g(k) \qquad (3)$$

where g(k) is a weighting sequence.

In the case of an openloop unstable plant, the intercorrelation method can be used for the closed-loop transfer function (Figure 2) by adding a PRBS sequence to the reference input value r(t).

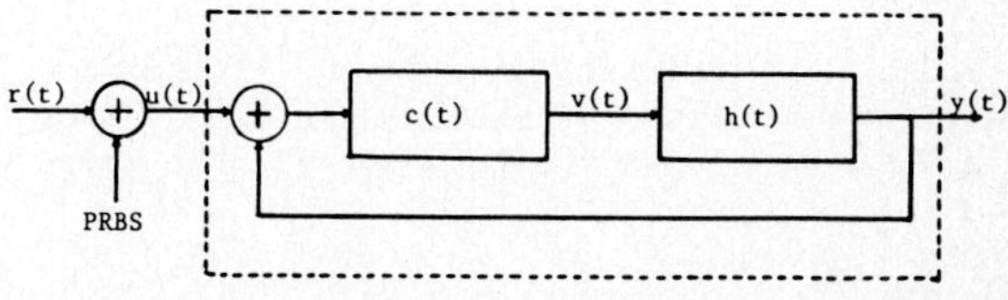

Figure 2 : Cloosed-loop transfer function determination

Another procedure is possible, by using an FFT deconvolution method.

$$y(\ell) = \sum_j v(\ell)\ h(j - \ell)$$

$$\text{or} \qquad h(k) = IFFT\left(\frac{Y(n)}{V(n)}\right) \qquad (4)$$

This methodology requires more care than the previous method does, it does not reduce the additional noise, consequently a data prefiltering and a window function processes are needed, the programmes implementation is in progress. The final goal is to obtain the weighting sequence ans step response :

$$s(k) = g_{k-1} + s_{k-1} \qquad (5)$$

We have now to determine a parameter estimation method of the transmittance and/or transfer functions.

1.2. Parameter estimation by means of the Householder orthogonal transformation

There are several estimation methods, for this apparatus design, we have eliminated the non linear programming methods because they have two drawbacks : non guarantee of convergence, non fully transparent methods. Moreover, we consider the impulse response of a linear invariant causal system of order n, assuming that all n time constants are different. Then the model

$$h(k) = \sum_{i=1}^{n} c_i \, e^{-\lambda_i kT} \qquad (6)$$

is non-linear in the parameters λ_i. The corresponding ARMA model can be written

$$h(z) = \frac{\sum_{0}^{n-1} a_i z^{-i}}{1 - \sum_{1}^{n} b_i z^{-i}} \qquad (7)$$

so from nth rank the recurrent relation can be reduced to

$$h(k) = \sum_{1}^{n} b_i \, h_{(k-i)} \qquad (8)$$

and can be viewed as a linear system in the unknown b_i parameters.

If the $\hat{b}_i$ estimation is done, then the roots of nth degree algebraic equation :

$$\sum_{1}^{n} b_i \beta^i - 1 = 0 \qquad (9)$$

provides the different λ_i by $\beta_i = e^{\lambda_i T}$. Direct analytical solutions or special efficient algorithms can be programmed to solve it. The relation (8) is of the form

$$H = C\,B \qquad (10)$$

with B the vector of the b_i
H the vector of m successive values of h_i
C the matrix such that

$$C_{k_i} = h_{k-i}$$

To solve the problem of minimisation of the norm $\|H - CB\|$, we use the triangularisation method of Householder, wich is a particularly stable non iterative algorithm. So the diagram bellow illustrates briefly the processing method :

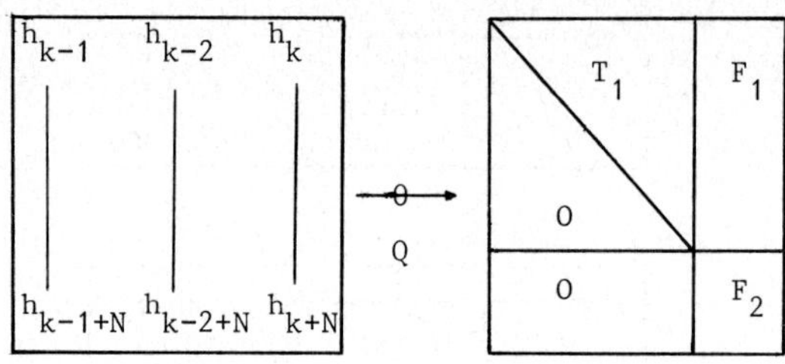

$\underline{\hat{b}_i} = T^{-1} \underline{F_1}$, Q : orthogonal transformation

2. THE MULTIMICROPROCESSOR SYSTEM STRUCTURE

To design an efficient multiprocessor system the following tasks must be met :
1 - The man-machine communication management
2 - The generation of excitation signals
3 - The measurement channels logging and processing identification methods.
On the other hand, the system configurability must be flexible to implement many other methods or control algorithms. So these points lead us to a trimicroprocessor based structure.

2.1. Architecture system

It is organised around three microprocessors based sub-systems (Figure 3) presenting two coupling degrees : a parallel bi-directional bus for the short exchanges, and two dual port memory CMGP and CMCP for the common data processing.

The three sub systems SYSG, SYSP, and SYSC are built around Intel 8085 microprocessors and their peripherals family circuits. The plant - system coupling is achivied through 12 bit resolution converters. The SYSP and SYSC sub systems involve 32 bit FPP which is AMD 9511.

A Real Time Clock is enabled by SYSG for setting the sampling time period.

2.2. The sub-systems functions

They are specialised in the following tasks :
SYSG provides the man-machine communication which is principally concerned :
- the experimental menu acquisition
- the I/O peripheral management
- the generation of exciting signals

SYSP provides :
- the mesurement channels logging handler
- the numerical data filters
- the weighting sequence and step response calculations
- the FFT Cooley-Tuckey algorithms

SYSC includes the following programmes :
- the Housholder orthogonal transformation
- the FFT algorithms
- the control strategy calculations (in progress).

Each operating sub system includes the common memory access and the bi-directional bus handlers.

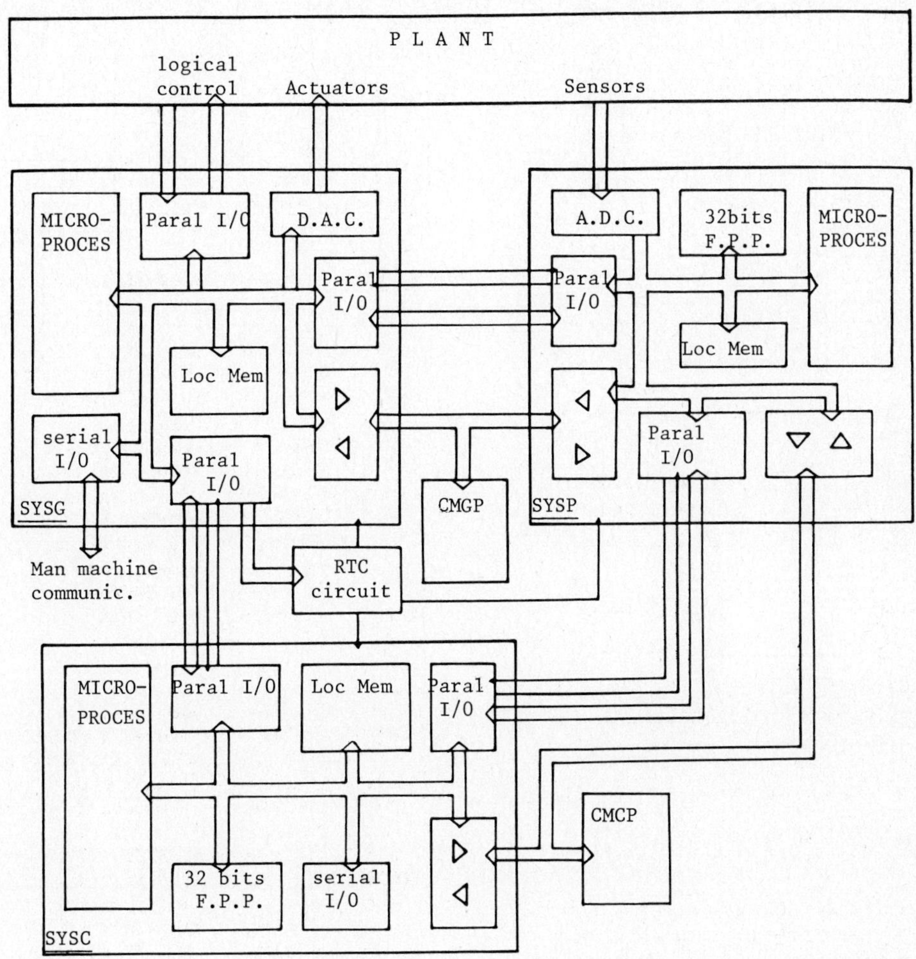

Figure 3 : The multimicroprocessor system structure

Owing to the symetrical internal structure of SYSP and SYSC, one may configure either of them in mathematical processes depending of the applications.

2.3. The interprocessors communication procedures

The parallel bi-directional bus insures the passing of parameters and the common memory allocation. The interface and timing diagram are shown Figure 4.

The dual port memory is controlled by sending a true CMA code to insure the mutual exclusive using. The principle of operation is illustrated by Figure 5.

3. THE INTERCORRELATION METHOD PROCEEDING

To satisfy this experimental type we have implemented on sub-systems the following software.

SYSG. Generation of PRBS signals with possibility to set characteristics $\{|a$, L, T, N, OF, CH$\}$ which correspond to magnitude, length, sampling time, number of sequences, offset value and measurement channel)

SYSP. The weigthing sequence and step response computations

SYSC. The recurrent matrix H triangularisation and estimation vectors $\hat{b}_i$, $\hat{\alpha}_i$ calculations.

The Figure 6 shows how the experimental procedure is executed.

It should be observed that in the first phase the man machine interactivity concerns the PRBS parameters set only. In the second phase, after the weighting sequence and step response analysis, one can choose the characterisation system parameters θ and n which are delay time and order system. In this mode, the parameters estimation and plant exciting steps can be driven in parallel. The Figure 7 shows another system software configurability concerning the FFT deconvolution method.

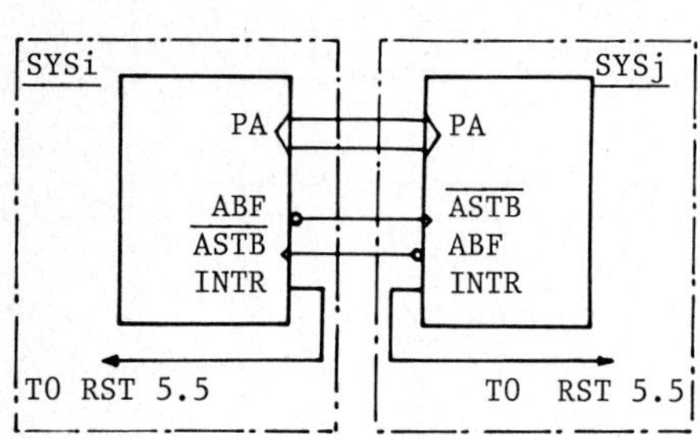

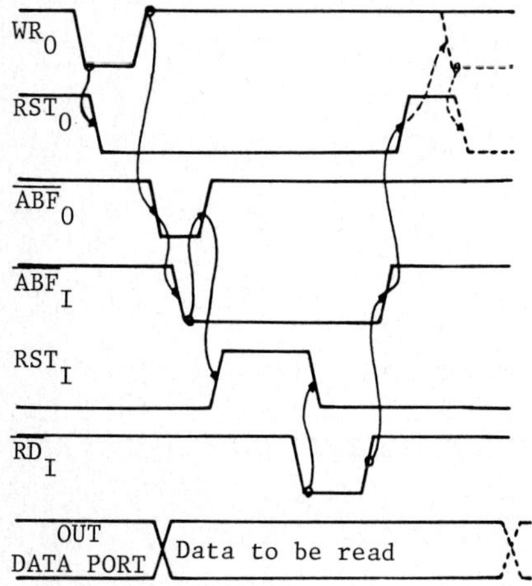

Figure 4 : Bi-directional bus
a - symetric schem using PA ports
b - strobed I/O timing an exchange takes about 12 μs.

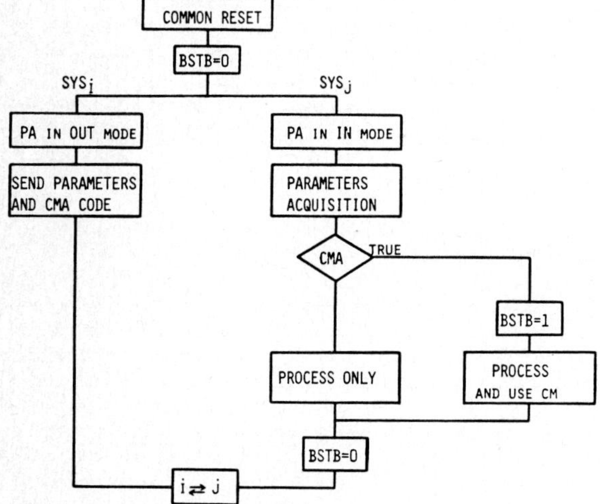

BSTB : BUFFER BUSSES STROBE SIGNAL
CM : COMMON MEMORY
CMA : COMMON MEMORY CODE

Figure 5 : Message exchange and memory allocation flowchart

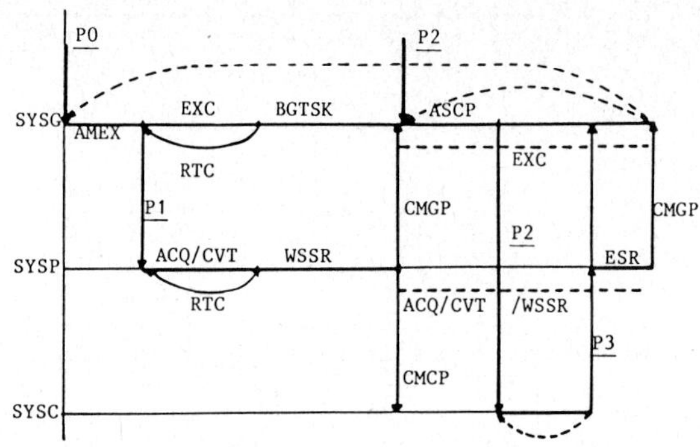

EXC : state of next PRBS calculation
AMEX : Acquisition of experimental menu from terminal or host
BGTSK : Background task
WSSR : Weighting sequence and step response computations
ASCP : System caracterisation parameters
ESR : Estimate stepe response
CMGP : Data in common memory GP
CMCP : Data in common memory CP
$\underline{P_0}$: $|T, L, N, OF, |a|, CH|$
$\underline{P_1}$: $|L, N, a, CH|$
$\underline{P_2}$: $|\theta, n|$
$\underline{P_3}$: $|\theta, \underline{\hat{b}_i}, \underline{\hat{\alpha}_i}|$

Figure 6 : Intercorrelation procedure

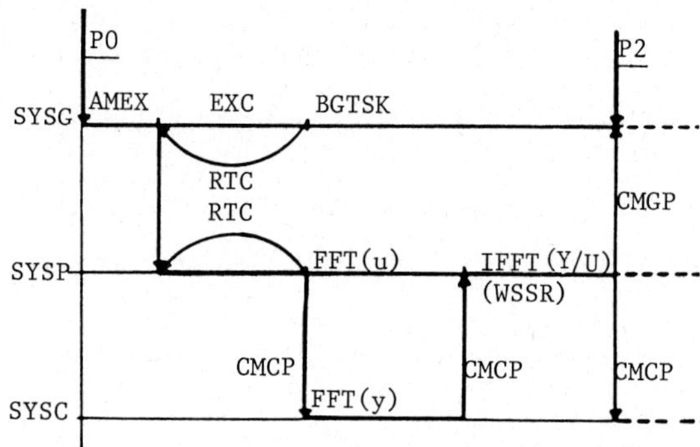

$\underline{P_1}$: |Data filter type, number of FFT points, u_k, y_k channels|

Figure 7. FFT deconvolution configuration

4. THE SYSTEM OPERATING FEATURES

All programmes are written in assembly language to provide an optimal execution time. To minimise truncature error the calculations are handled in 32 bit floating point format. Inside each sub-system the hardware interfacing provides a minimum inactive time by managing peripherals in interrupt mode. To have an idea of timing features we will note :
EXC : 150 μs WSSR : 7s for 255 points
ESTM : 1 s for 250 x 3 matrix

FFT : 130 ms for 256 points
These times are obtained with 3 MHz microprocessors and 2 MHz coprocessor, we can divide them by four with compatible better versions.

CONCLUSION

The main feature of the methods we propose is that we avoid iterative algorithms for paramater estimation. The proposed system architecture provides quite a sufficient software configuratibility for several application in the identification and control fields. The execution time performances allow to process fast plants, we may therfore start working upon self-tuning regulator implementation.

REFERENCES :

|1| De Larminat, Ph. and Thomas, Y., Automatique des systèmes linéaires (Dunod, Paris, 1977).

|2| Foulard, C., Gentil, S., Sandraz, J.P., Commande et régulation par calculateur numérique (Eyrolles, Paris, 1969).

|3| Bierman, G.J., Factorization methods for discrete sequential estimation (Academic Press, New-York)

|4| Caro,J., Biston, J., Dufour, J., Gilles, G., A further education experience in the real time digital control domain, IFAC 83 Symposium on real time digital control applications (Guadalajara, Mexico, 1983).

|5| Caro, J., Sau, J., Darmet, C., A multimicroprocessor based system applied to an on line identification methodology, Internal report, Laboratoire Automatique., Lyon Univ. (April 1984).

DIGITAL TECHNIQUES in Simulation, Communication and Control
Spyros G. Tzafestas (editor)
Elsevier Science Publishers B.V. (North-Holland) © IMACS, 1985

HANDLING INDETERMINACIES IN DISCRETE SIMULATION FOR PERFORMANCE ANALYSIS

A. Jávor

Central Research Institute for Physics
of the Hungarian Academy of Sciences
H-1525 Budapest, P.O.Box 49.
HUNGARY

The paper deals with the problem of handling indeterminacies in the simulation of discrete systems with particular respect to the simulation of information traffic and computer systems. Indeterminacies inherent in the system investigated as well as those occurring due to sequential simulation of parallel processes are discussed. A methodology for solving the posed problems is introduced. It is shown that the feedback in seemingly forward coupled entity-type networks is revealed by transformation into their level-type equivalent. Hints for the practical implementation of the methodology as a means of gaining a unified model structure, and in multimode simulation systems are given.

1. INTRODUCTION

The breakthrough in microelectronic technology enables the construction of increasingly complex, highly sophisticated multiprocessing computer system structures [1][2]. Simulation on the Processor-Memory-Switch (PMS) level [3] has proved to be a suitable tool for the evaluation and comparison of the different designs. Such simulation tools (e.g. CSS as a special purpose [4], or GPSS [5] as a general purpose tool) have already been used to investigate the performance of classical computer systems. The purpose of these investigations has been to determine the parameters (such as throughput, response time, storage utilization, etc.) characterizing the effectivity of the system. As a general rule the results of such simulation experiments are expected in the form of statistical data. Average values, distributions, standard deviations, etc. are of interest not individual events. It is however worth-while to consider certain events in more detail since they may influence the behaviour of the model significantly even if their occurrence is relatively limited. These are the cases when there is ambiguity in the model. The effect of these events may be twofold: firstly they may influence the numerical results and falsify them, secondly the operation of the model may not correctly reveal that of the simulated system.

2. NATURE OF THE PROBLEMS

Let us consider some of the types of problems that may arise. Generally the main body of such models consists of a network of interconnected elements or facilities. These model elements have a certain fixed capacity. This means that they may contain or deal with a certain number of entities at a given instant. The number of these entities may be one or more. In the case of a processor an entity may represent the program or job that it deals with and the capacity may equal 1. In the case of buffer storage the stored entities may be the data (messages, programs) stored and their number may represent their amount in given information units (bytes, characters, records, etc.). If one monitors the location and movement of these entities the statistical data needed for performance analysis can be obtained.

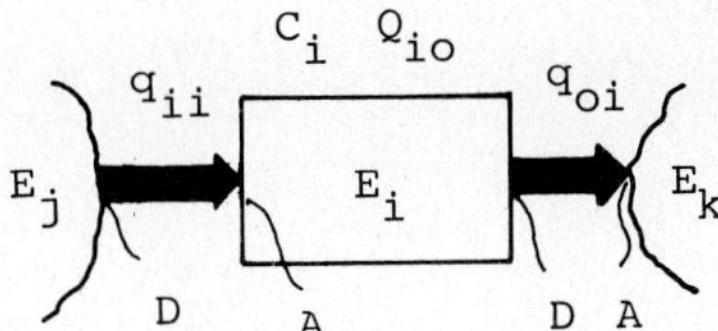

Figure 1 : Entity type model segment

If, however, the model segment shown in Figure 1 is considered, where the model element E_i with capacity C_i and stored quantity Q_{io} at a certain instant is connected to the rest of the model via element E_j that may input q_{ii}, and through element E_k to which it transfers quantities q_{oi} one at a time, with the assumption of simultaneous transfers, indeterminacies may occur.

(i) If $Q_{io} < q_{oi}$ then transfer $E_i \rightarrow E_k$ cannot take place if transfer $E_j \rightarrow E_i$ does not precede it.

(ii) If $(C_i - Q_{io}) < q_{ij}$ then transfer $E_j \rightarrow E_i$ cannot take place if transfer $E_i \rightarrow E_k$ does not precede it.

In these cases E_i is in a critical condition.

Let us now consider the examples given in Figure 2. To begin with, we assume that all model elements (E) represented by the boxes have a capacity that can store a single entity at a time and the algorithm describing their operation is such that any box aims to emit the entity contained in it at its output called "donor" into the element connected to it through its input called "acceptor". Transfer will take place at a certain donor-acceptor (D → A) connection only if the element to which the donor belongs contains an entity and the element to which the acceptor belongs is empty, i.e. is capable of accepting an entity at the time of transfer. The transfers are attempted at $t_{E_{n,m}}$ where n is the index determining the element to which the donor belongs while m is the index of the element that should accept. We should consider the case where all transfers in the model are synchronized. Nevertheless slight physical differences of timing cannot be avoided.

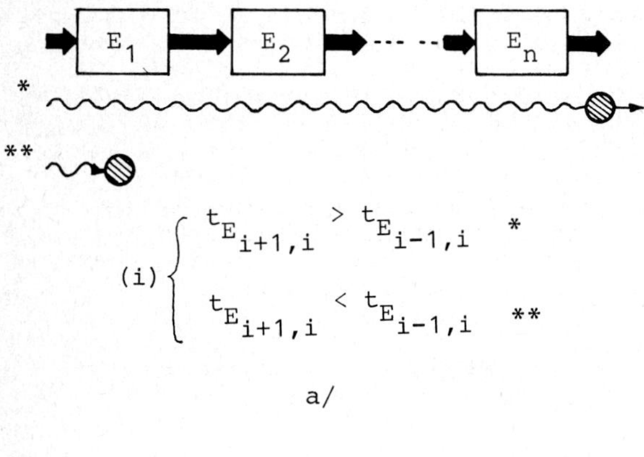

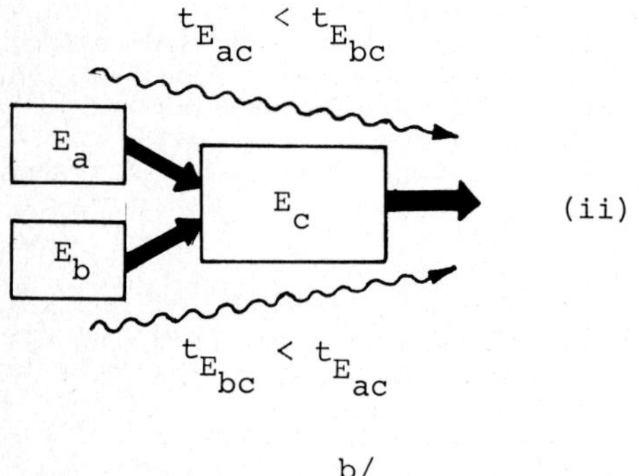

Figure 2: Examples of entity type models

In Figure 2/a, in which the precedence of transfer times is from left to right, the entity will transfer through the whole series of elements in a single tact whereas in the opposite case it will advance only one unit; Figure 2/b shows another example. Assuming simultaneous offers of quantities q_{ij} from both E_a and E_b the stream of entities will transfer via $E_a \rightarrow E_c$ if $t_{E_{ac}} < t_{E_{bc}}$ and the path $E_b \rightarrow E_c$ is blocked whereas for $t_{E_{ac}} > t_{E_{bc}}$ the open and blocked states of the paths will reverse. If however the precedence of offers or demands enabling transfers varies in time according to some random distribution, the transitions will vary in time accordingly. Such slight differences in timing or in phase synchronism may cause significant quantitative differences in performance parameters [6] (see in Figure 2/a); qualitative differences in the operation may also be caused (Figure 2/b).

These phenomena may reveal two sorts of situations: either ambiguities are present in the system being modelled or, on the other hand, we have the inadequacy of simulation which means that parallel events are mapped into serial ones. This drawback arises from the use of a sequential machine where the calling sequence of the program segments describing the elements influences the end result.

What we would need is a mechanism that simulates such cases according to a possible - if arbitrary - situation and *automatically* signalizes the presence of indeterminacies, since in a complex system their occurrence may not be obvious and if overlooked the quantitative or even the qualitative results of the simulation may be misleading. Thus if the indeterminacies are caused by the inherent properties of the simulated system, then highly valuable information is gained about it that can be used perhaps to modify or influence it thereby removing the effect (e.g. by adjusting phase synchronism properly). If however the indeterminacies are caused by the simulation model then appropriate measures can be taken to get a realistic mapping of reality (e.g. by altering or randomizing the calling sequence of element routines).

3. A SOLUTION BASED ON THE DUALITY CONCEPT

The first step towards solving the problem is to gain a clear and general view. The systems we have considered belong to the class where "entity type" event description is used meaning that the operation of the system is described by the

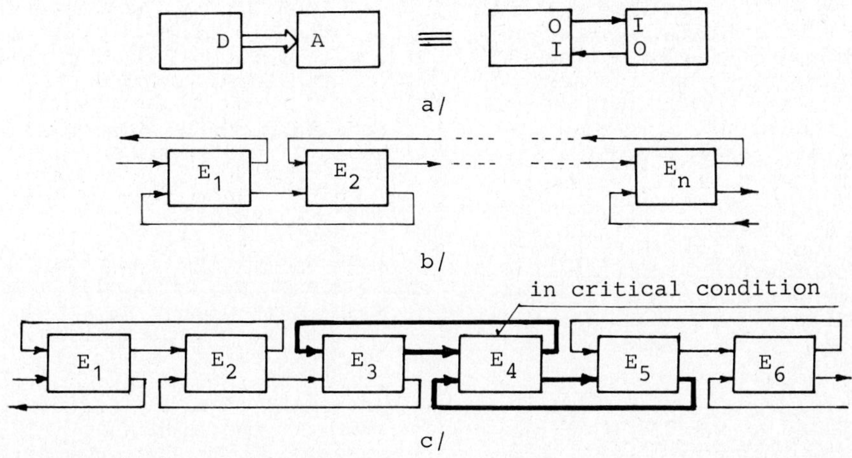

Figure 3 : Transformation from entity to level type network

movement of entities through the model network consisting of elements with entity emitting donor (D) and acceptor (A) terminals (see Figure 1).

A clear general picture of the causes and nature of the indeterminacies as well as a way to the solution can be gained by the concept of the *duality of events* in discrete simulation [7]. A D → A type connection in an entity type model can always be made equivalent to a pair of oppositely directed I → O (i.e. input → output) connections in a level type network (see Figure 3/a). A level type network is characterized by elements whose output (O) transfers values of given variables to inputs (I) of other elements.

The basic differences between the two types is that whereas the transfer in a level type network is unconditional, in an entity type network it is conditional. In the latter case, an active donor aims to emit an entity and the acceptor connected to it accepts it - should it be able to do so - and the completion of the entity transfer takes place only if the acceptor signalizes back its readiness to accept (e.g. if storage space is available). The other possibility is that the acceptor is active and sends a "demand-signal" to the entity source, and the response deciding whether entity transfer will take place depends on the response of the donor whether it can transmit (e.g. availability of the requested entity).

When making the transformation from entity to level type network description of a model it can be seen that the seemingly forward coupled networks (in entity representation) reveal the interconnected feedback loop systems causing, for example, the "significant hazards" as known in logic networks. As an example, in Figure 3/b the transformed version of the network shown in Figure 2/a is depicted.

Let us shortly overview - using the well known example of digital logic - the possible situations occurring in a level-type network containing feedback. The excitation by input signals of digital logic (i.e. level-type) networks containing feedback may have different results:

a/ the new state of the network is uniquely determined by the network, its state and the input signals.

b/ The input signal initiates a steady oscillation in the network (see e.g. Figure 4/a).

c/ The network will take a steady next state due to the change of the input signal, but due to the inherent race condition in the network structure the actual next state (chosen from a set of possible states) is not determined, and depends on the - possibly differentially small - differences of the electrical parameters (see e.g. Figure 4/b, where the values of U_3 and U_4 from time t_x will equal either those depicted with a continuous or those depicted with a dotted line).

Considering these possibilities and the purpose of investigating such systems the requirements for their modelling can be formulated as follows. The model should reveal the dynamic behaviour of the system realistically for all cases (i.e. a/, b/ and c/). For case c/ it is desirable that it should also provide for the detection of the "significant hazard" i.e. the fact that the next state of the system is not uniquely determined. It should be noted that the simulation of all possible continuations of model behaviour - taking into consideration the spreading of this phenomenon in topological "space" as well as in time - taking into account all possible next state combinations, would increase the complexity of the program to such extent that its execution would not be feasible.

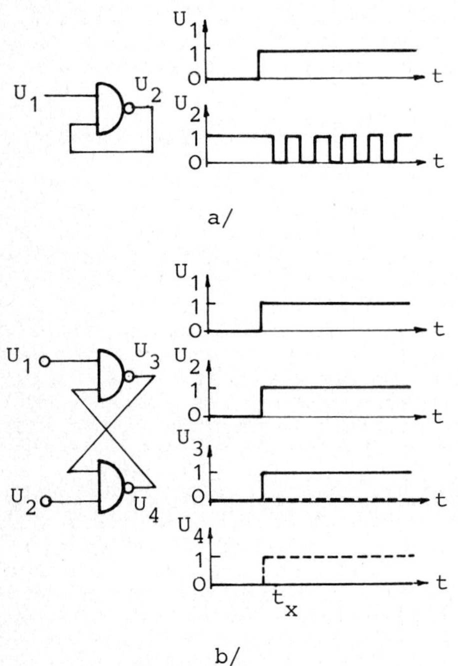

Figure 4 : Examples of the operation of digital logic networks containing feedback

The handling of the - transformed - level type network can be accomplished by the *quasideterministic state description* [8]. We shall use a three component vector description for describing states ($\bar{q}$), inputs ($\bar{x}$), and outputs ($\bar{y}$) of the elements:

$$\bar{q} = \{q_S, q_{IFO}, q_{ISO}\} \quad (1)$$

$$\bar{x} = \{x_S, x_{IFO}, x_{ISO}\} \quad (2)$$

$$\bar{y} = \{y_S, y_{IFO}, y_{ISO}\} \quad (3)$$

the indexes designating:

S value of (assumed) deterministic parameter,

IFO indeterminacy of first order (i.e. transient state between deterministic values),

ISO indeterminacy of second order (i.e. signalizing that the value of the parameter is in a given subset of all possible values that contain that of the first component).

Modelling can be described by the equations

$$\bar{q}(t+\tau) = \Psi[\bar{q}_r(t), \bar{x}_r(t)] \quad (4)$$

$$\bar{y}(t) = \Phi[\bar{q}(t), \bar{x}_r(t)] \quad (5)$$

with next state function Ψ, output function Φ, and index r meaning a reduced form of the vector description taking the third component for zero. Thus, if during simulation an ISO occurs it will be signalized but it will not propagate in time (i.e. to the next state of the element), nor in model space (i.e. to the other element(s) whose input(s) is connected to the output of the element where the ISO appeared). Simultaneously the first vector component will take one possible value.

Implementation of the method can be achieved in a way that the model topology has to be analysed and the connected loop systems have to be detected and analysed to see whether they have a single stable state (i.e. no ISO) or more (ISO present and one state chosen). This can be undertaken by investigating the model segments containing feedback loops (see Figure 5) and searching whether there is a single stable state or not (i.e. zero or more):

IF < $\bar{L}=\bar{l}$ > THEN < stable > ELSE < unstable >

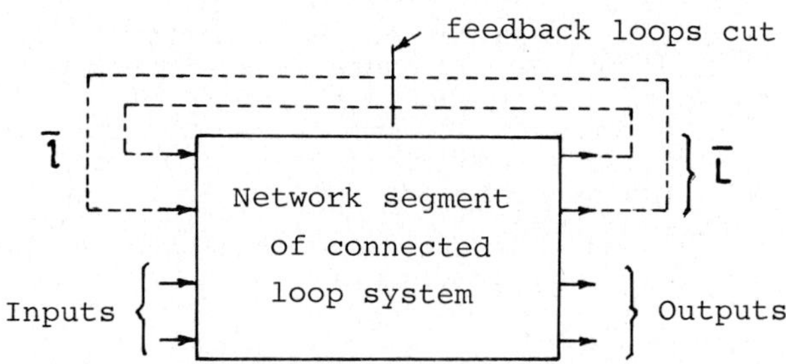

Figure 5 : Model segment containing feedback loops

This method of determining ISO's has already been successfully applied in the LOBSTER system [9] for digital logic simulation where the starting assumption for practical implementation is that in logic networks such segments are rare. In such cases they were determined prior to the dynamic run and the special routine called if such a segment was effected by a signal propagating to it. As this was a valid assumption the implementation was effective.

In our case of PMS modelling another approach seems to be more appropriate. A simple topological search in our case does not seem to give enough information for effective implementation of the methods since practically the whole dually transformed model would in many cases be a single interconnected loop system and the special handling routine might be called more often than necessary. It seems to be more effective only if those loop segments were to be investigated that are in a critical situation - as has been determined above ((i) and (ii)). Thus if elements take the critical condition then the search for ISO's is undertaken only in the model segments affected by them, so the dynamic allocation of the investigated "loop systems" during a simulation run will reduce the number and size of the model segments that have to be treated specially and in this way the effectivity of the simulator can be increased. In Figure 3/c, element E_k is in a critical condition and the connected loop system that has to be investigated for an ISO is indicated by thick lines.

Concerning the indeterminacies of first order (IFO's); their significance has to be stressed in cases when a fine model description in time is necessary. The transfer of entities from one block to another takes a certain time and during the transfer time the location of the entity is either partially in the transmitting and partially in the receiving block, or there is a transient ambiguity in whichever of the two blocks the entity can be found during the transfer time. Such phenomena may cause indeterminacies of second order should the state of the entity during that time be sampled for some reason. Such events can be simulated using asynchronous representation of events in time.

4. CONNECTION WITH OTHER LEVELS AND FIELDS OF MODELLING

Regarding the design of computer systems in the past it can be seen that there were very sharp borders between the different stages. Looking at the trend of VLSI it seems that a more integrated view will be desired, i.e. more integrated models and simulation systems that are able to deal with a mixture of levels [10]. This trend was marked first by the appearance of *mixed mode simulators* aimed at closing the gap between logic simulators and circuit analysis programs [11][12][13], and *multimode* [14] simulators that are able to handle the whole verticality of levels are demanded.

For the effective solution of this problem it seems advantageous to map the different levels of model descriptions into a single unified inner core of the simulator [15]. One important aspect is a universal handling and connection description. The transformation from an entity-type model (e.g. PMS segments) to a level-type model (e.g. logic network segments) promotes this. It is interesting to note that the entity-type description with its relationship to level-type description can also be of interest at the "other end" of multimode simulator building. In MOS integrated logic circuits, conventional logic simulation does not seem to be sufficient because of their bidirectional transfer of signals and dynamic storage. Therefore several methods were proposed to overcome this problem [11][12].

A possibility for including this level of simulation in the universal internal structure of a multimode simulator can be undertaken [7] realizing that in such systems the primary effect is the transport of charges stored in the capacitors of the nodes (see Figure 6) that are transferred through - controlled (linearly or nonlinearly modelled) - resistances. Using a charge quantum adequately chosen for our purposes we get an entity type discrete model instead of a continuous one. This results in an overall discrete simulation system where starting from internal state representation to time scheduling everything can be accomplished with discrete simulation methods. In this way, the need to synchronize the simulation of discrete and continuous processes can be avoided. It should be added that the method in itself does not limit the accuracy of the approximation of the continuous processes and this can - obviously - be adjusted by using a proper quantum size. This solution also shows that discrete simulation of continuous processes may have certain advantages in electronics similarly to micro and macro mechanics, as shown by Greenspan [16].

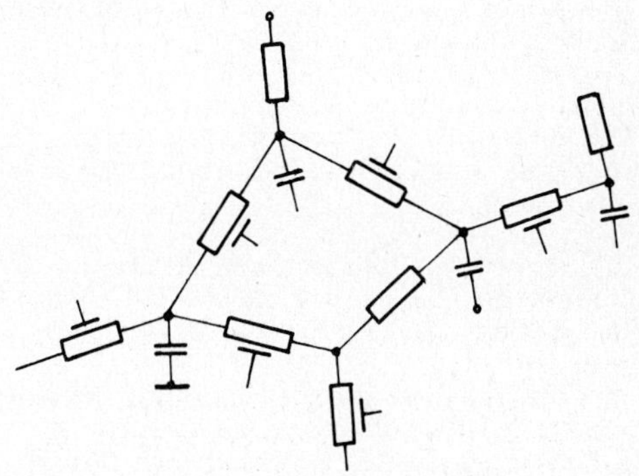

Figure 6 : MOS switched capacitor network

There is also another aspect that is worth mentioning. There is a wide variety of different simulation models apart from computer system models, e.g. urban traffic; transportation by lorries, ships, rail; mass service in supermarkets; distribution of goods in overall stock; etc. which are described by basically similar entity-type discrete simulation models. The problems that may arise can also be very similar. In urban traffic, simultaneous arrivals at crossings from all directions may cause roadblocks the resolving of which is indeterminate (causing really hazardous situations!). As our method for handling such situations is not specific and is applicable to entity-type networks in general it can be applied in these fields as well [7].

5. CONCLUSIONS

Using the above methods, automatic signalization of hazards or indeterminacies in entity-type networks can be achieved. This enables the detection of possibly falsified statistics for performance parameters or the eventually occurring discrepancies in model operation that can be overcome by adjusting the simulation model or the simulated system. The application of these methods enable the unified treatment of models in multimode simulation. Besides the field of computer system modelling they can be applied to discrete simulation models in other fields as well.

6. REFERENCES

[1] Moto-oka, T. (ed.), Fifth Generation Computer Systems (North-Holland, Amsterdam, 1982).

[2] Ameling, W., Simulation Using Multiprocessor Systems, in Jávor, A. (ed.), Discrete Simulation and Related Fields (North-Holland, Amsterdam, 1982).

[3] Siewiorek, D., Introducing PMS, Computer, December (1974)

[4] Computer System Simulator/360 (360A-SE-29T), Program Description and Operations Manual, IBM Application Program

[5] Gordon, G., System Simulation (Prentice Hall, Englewood Cliffs, New Jersey, 1969)

[6] Csákány, A., Jávor, A., Investigation of Throughput Efficiency of Multilevel Data Networks by Means of Simulation, XIX Rassegna Internazionale Elettronica Nucleare ed Aerospaziale, Rome, March (1972) B-12, 253-258.

[7] Jávor, A., Dual Nature of Events in Discrete Simulation, Mathematics and Computers in Simulation XXV (1983) 66-69.

[8] Jávor, A., An Approach to the Modelling of Uncertainties in the Simulation of Quasideterministic Discrete Event Systems, Problems of Control and Information Theory 4(3) (1975) 219-229.

[9] Jávor A., Benkő T.né, Simulation of Discrete Systems (Müszaki Könyvkiadó, Budapest, 1979) (in Hungarian)

[10] Moore, G., VLSI: Some Fundamental Challenges, IEEE Spectrum (April 1979) 30-37.

[11] Chawla, B.R., Gummel, H.K., Kozak, P., MOTIS - An MOS Timing Simulator, IEEE Trans. on Circuits and Systems CAS-22 No. 12 (Dec. 1975) 901-910.

[12] Lightner, M.R., Hachtel, G.D., MOS Switch Level Simulation Macromodelling and Testing, ISCAS'82 Rome, 63-67.

[13] DeMan, H., Mixed-mode Analysis and Simulation Techniques for Top-down MOSVLSI Design, Proc. 1981 European Conf. on Circuit Theory and Design, The Hague (25-28 August 1981) 5-10.

[14] Ruehli, A.E., New Aspects of Large-Scale Circuit Analysis and Simulation, Proc. 1981 European Conf. on Circuit Theory and Design, The Hague (25-28 August 1981) 151-155.

[15] Jávor, A., Proposals on the Structure of Simulation Systems, in Jávor, A. (ed.), Discrete Simulation and Related Fields (North-Holland, Amsterdam, 1982).

[16] Greenspan, D., Discrete Numerical Method in Physics and Engineering (Academic Press Inc., 1974).

DIGITAL TECHNIQUES in Simulation, Communication and Control
Spyros G. Tzafestas (editor)
Elsevier Science Publishers B.V. (North-Holland) © IMACS, 1985

AN INTERACTIVE COMPUTER AIDED ALGORITHM FOR DESIGN SCALING

Romane MEZENCEV

Process Control Laboratory (ERA 134)-Mechanical Engineering School
E.N.S.M. 1 Rue de la Noë 44072 Nantes Cédex France

The parametric optimization of some components of a process seems to be performed in a similar way to the scaling of an analog simulation : a static constrained optimization is followed by iterations on a simulation which modifies the static constraints in order to satisfy the dynamic constraints.

This paper concerns the great similarity which exists between the task of an engineer preparing some design and the investigation of a scientist working on some analog simulation :

- the first gentleman must solve a size problem before drawing any line of his blue-print,
- the second gentleman has to choose the possible maximum value of every variable before any run of his analog simulation.

Even if, from now on, the analog or hybrid simulation seems to be out dated and is usually replaced by a digital simulation, some tools and some attitudes of the analog scientist may be fruitfully preserved :

- The decomposition of the mathematical model of some process in elementary integrators and time delays, is quite similar to the state space representation. Let us insist upon the fact that these two components, the integrator and the time delay, may be considered as the only self-living cells of the simulation : they are the only dynamic operators.

In physical models, all other operators, including non linear operators, appear as static operators.

- The model with per-unit variables is the second tool of any analog scientist, which is widely used by any engineer.

Why should we leave, both tools, even if we are convinced by the digital simulation supremacy ?

THE SCALING PROBLEM

Let us take first, a linear model, without any delay, written under the usual state form (1) :

$$\underline{\dot{x}} = A\underline{x} + B\underline{u} \quad \dim \underline{x} = n \tag{1}$$

$$\underline{y} = C\underline{x} \quad \dim \underline{y} = m \quad \dim \underline{u} = r$$

The model (1) is not a dynamic model ! It only gives the flow graph between n living cells, the equations of which are usually implied, and which consist in the following system (2) :

$$\underline{x} = \underline{x}_o + \int_o^t \underline{\dot{x}}\, dt \tag{2}$$

$\underline{x}_o$ being the initial value of the state $\underline{x}$. The first equation (1) needs some work, with the help of equation (2), in order to obtain the maximum value which is reached by the state $\underline{x}$ when the time t evoluates from 0 to TF.

On the contrary, the maximum value of the output $\underline{y}$, given by the second equation of the system (1), is straightforward obtained when the state maximum values are known.

So let us say that, in some aspect, and mainly when system (1) becomes non linear, the state maximum values, obtained by means of the dynamic system (2), which is always a linear system, are somewhat unpredictable contrarily to all other variables of system (1).

Let us write the following diagonal scaling matrices :

$$M = \text{diag}(xi_m) \; ; P = \text{diag}(yi_m) \; ; Q = \text{diag}(ui_m)$$

where xi_m, yi_m, ui_m are respectively the maximum values of the components xi, yi, ui of $\underline{x}$, $\underline{y}$, $\underline{u}$.

For the user some ones of these maximum values are unknown at the beginning of his investigation.

Performing on system (2) the change of variable $\underline{x} = M\underline{X}$, and taking into account some accelerated or idled simulation time τ = BET.t, we obtain the classical per-unit equation, or scaled equation (3) :

$$\underline{X} = \int_o^{BET.t} M^{-1}\underline{\dot{x}}/(BET)\, d\tau + \underline{X}_o \tag{3}$$

where $\underline{X}$ is the per-unit state or, better said, the scaled state : every component Xi of the scaled state is such that $Xi \leqslant 1$ if $t \in]0,TF]$

The simulation is accelerated respectively to the real time t, if BET < 1. System (1) gives the integrand of equation (3) and the scaled output $\underline{Y}$ under the form (4) :

$$M^{-1}\dot{x}/(BET) = M^{-1}A M\underline{X}/(BET) + M^{-1}BQU/(BET)$$
$$\underline{Y} = P^{-1}CM\underline{X} \qquad (4)$$

In the analog technology, the integrators have usually some gain possibilities DI, upon each one of their inputs. For example DI ∈ [1,2,10,20]. In the same manner, the engineer preparing a design, has to select for every king of component, the right class among various possible classes : we may imagine that class number two has more capacity than class number one and therefore, is more expensive.

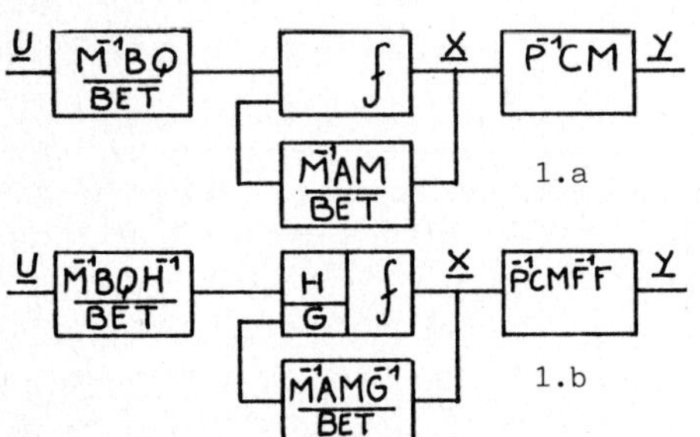

Fig. 1

It is the author's feeling that in the simulation the input gains may be compared with the classes. Of course the per-unit values of the variables have the same meaning as the load ratio for the real components.

Figure 1a represents the equation (4) and figure 1b takes into account, for the same equation, the various classes by means of some gain-matrices H, G, F.

The engineer task consists in :

- anticiping the values of the diagonal scale matrices M, P, Q,
- deducing the class matrices H, G, F taking into account a lot of external constraints which limits and orients his choice for the xi_m. Indeed some xi_m remain unknown or it exists many possibilities so the engineer is obliged to call for some optimization technique.

If the process model (1) is non linear, the matrix form is not always possible and it becomes necessary to calibrate every equation separately.

In the following, we name CXI, I = 1,2 ..., NC the elements of the matrices $M^{-1}BQ/(BET)$; $M^{-1}AM/(BET)$; $P^{-1}CM$ (5)
and CI, I = 1,2...,NC the elements of the matrices $M^{-1}BQH^{-1}/(BET)$;$M^{-1}AMG^{-1}/(BET)$;$P^{-1}CMF^{-1}$:
CI = CXI/DI with DI = 1,2...,NC the inputs gains; NC is the number of non zero coefficients of the matrices (5).

Before proposing any optimization strategy let us apply the described method to a simple second order system :

$$\begin{cases}\dot{x}_1 = x_2\\ \dot{x}_2 = -\omega_n^2 x_1 - 2\zeta\omega_n x_2 + K\omega_n^2 u\\ y = x_1\end{cases} \qquad \begin{cases}\underline{\dot{x}} = A\underline{x} + \underline{b}u\\ y = \underline{c}^T\underline{x}\end{cases}$$

with $A = \begin{bmatrix}0 & 1\\ A_{21} & A_{22}\end{bmatrix}$; $\underline{b} = \begin{bmatrix}0\\ B\end{bmatrix}$; $\underline{c}^T = [1 \quad 0]$

and $M = \begin{bmatrix}x1_m & 0\\ 0 & x2_m\end{bmatrix}$; $P = x1_m = y_m$; $Q = u_m$

The formula (4) gives

$$\frac{M^{-1}\dot{x}}{BET} = \frac{1}{BET}\begin{bmatrix}0 & x2_m/x1_m\\ A_{21}\;x1_m/x2_m & A_{22}\end{bmatrix}\underline{X} + \frac{1}{BET}\begin{bmatrix}0\\ Bu_m/x2_m\end{bmatrix}U \qquad (6)$$

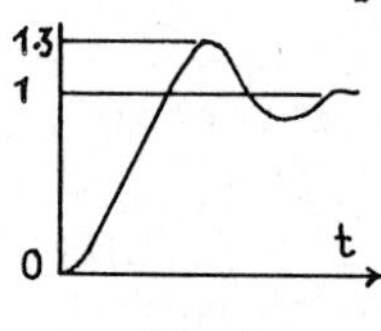

Fig.2

For some given input, say u = 1, and for some given initial conditions, for instance $\underline{x} = [^0_0]$, it is well known that with a damping coefficient such as ζ = 0.4 (fig.2) the state will remain less that 1.5. Let us also suppose that K = 10 and $\omega_n = 6.28$ then $A_{21} = -39.438$; $A_{22} = -5.024$; $B = 394.38$ and we can take $x1_m = 1.5$; $u_m = 1$. Moreover we know that x2 remains less than 10 for $0 < t \leq \infty$. In case of a more complicated model, it would not be so easy to anticipate the maximum value $x2_m$. So let us suppose that we have to optimize the unknown value of $x2_m$, which induces the choice of some physical component among various classes of the same type. The straightforward way to prove that some choice is the right choice, is to make a simulation such as in fig. 3, with :

$CX1 = B.u_m/(BET.x2_m)$; $CX2 = A_{22}/BET$
$CX3 = A_{21}.x1_m/(BET.x2_m)$; $CX4 = x2_m/(BET.x1_m)$
CI = CXI/DI , I = 1,2,3,4.

$$H = \begin{vmatrix}0\\ D1\end{vmatrix} ; \quad G = \begin{vmatrix}0 & D3\\ D4 & D2\end{vmatrix} ; \quad F = [1 \quad 0]$$

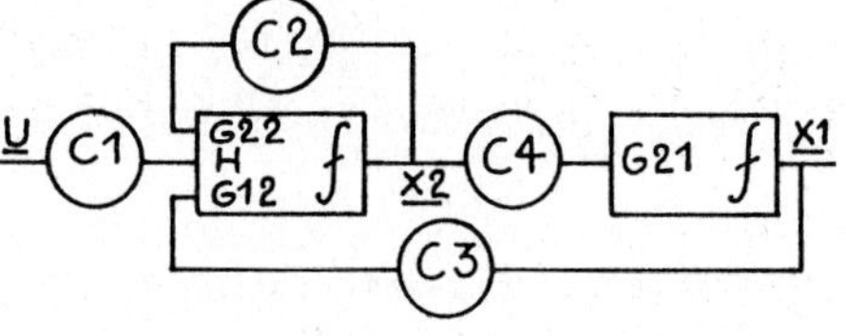

Fig. 3

So the only coefficients which take part in the optimization process are CX1, CX3 and CX4.

HOW TO CHOOSE AN OPTIMIZATION CRITERION ?

In its class, every component must be used at, let us say, 80 % of its maximum possibility and the class must be chosen in order not to be dynamically overload the component. For the simulation this means that the per-unit variables must evoluate not too far from 0.8. Let us suppose that in order to save money, the engineer tries to use the most reduced class number. That means, for the simulation that he has to anticipate the scales xi_m in such a way that the DI's be minimized. In the analog simulation the CI are represented by potentiometers whose values can only be in the domain]0,1[. The nearer to one are these values, the more precise becomes the simulation. These CI's are homogenization coefficients for the per-unit model.

So we can make the following suggestion for the real system :

Choose the scales in order that the DI's be minimized and that the homogenization coefficients be less than - and near to 1 : that will give the better signal transfer between two successive cells.

We can also tell that the cost of some kind of equipment goes up with its class and that this class is bound with its adjustment possibilities, evaluated, between 0 and 1, by the homogenization coefficient CI.

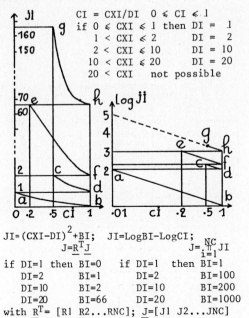

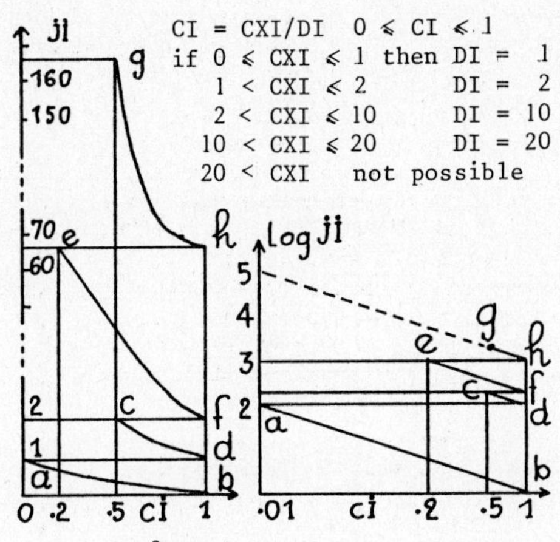

$JI=(CXI-DI)^2+BI$; $\quad JI=\text{Log}BI-\text{Log}CI$;

$J=\underline{R}^T\underline{J}$ $\quad J=\prod_{i=1}^{NC} JI$

if DI=1	then BI=0	if DI=1	then BI=1
DI=2	BI=1	DI=2	BI=100
DI=10	BI=2	DI=10	BI=200
DI=20	BI=66	DI=20	BI=1000

with $\underline{R}^T=$ [R1 R2...RNC]; $\underline{J}$=[J1 J2...JNC]

Fig. 4

Now fig. 4 suggests two optimization criterions J built from individual criterions JI for each coefficient CXI :

$$\dot{J} = \underline{R}^T \dot{\underline{J}} \text{ for the parabolic case} \qquad (7)$$

$$\dot{J} = \prod_{i=1}^{NC} R_i J_i \text{ for the logarithmic case}$$

with $\underline{J} = [J_1 J_2 \dots J_{NC}]^T$; $R = [R_1 R_2 \dots R_{NC}]^T$

As an example, if no constraint were present and if during some experimentation on some scale, CXI should increase from 0^+ to 20, the value of CI would change between 0^+,1 ; 0.5,1 ; 0.1,1 ; 0.5,1 while DI would take successively the values 1,2,10,20 and the criterion JI would follow the curve abcdefgh.

At the beginning of his design, the engineer has no idea about the weighting coefficients RI, I = 1,2 ..., NC, so he may take the same value for everyone : 1.

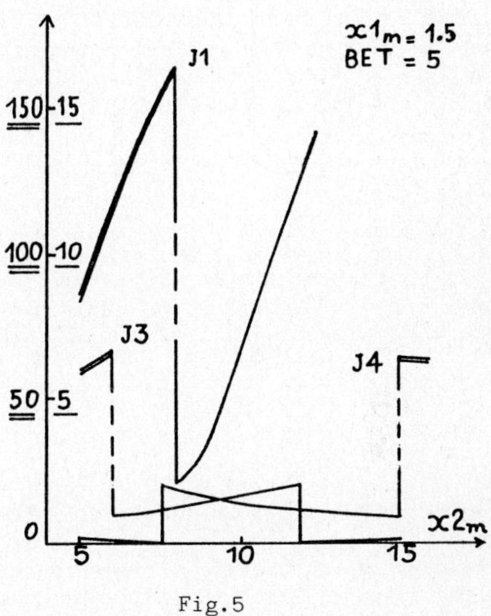

Fig.5

Fig. 5 and fig. 6 give for the simple example of our second order system, and with BET = 5, the curves of J_1, J_3, J_4 and the resulting global criterion J with the following assumptions :

$x1_m = 1.5$; $u_m = 1$; $5 \leqslant x2_m \leqslant 15$.

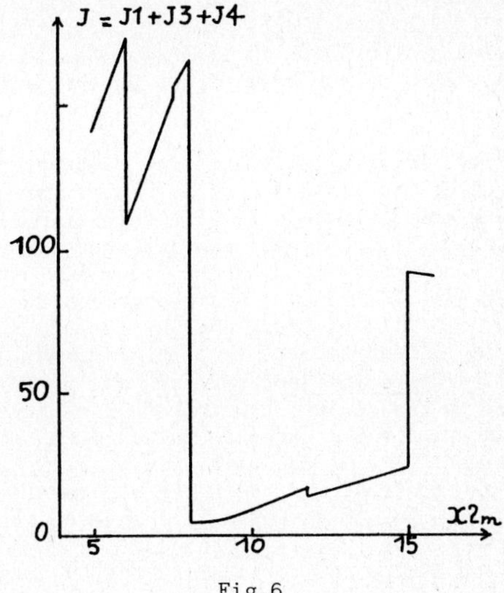

Fig.6

Fig. 7 gives the curve of the global logarithmic criterion.

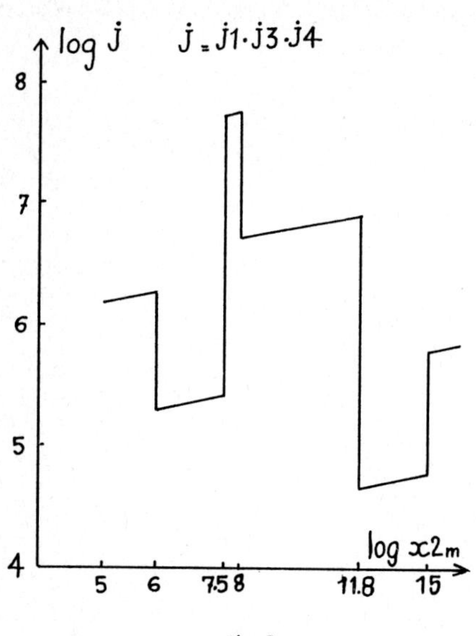

Fig. 7

It is quite evident that these global criterions are not convex, but it is not yet possible to conclude very easily because various constraints, static and dynamic, limit the admissible domain of variations of each scale xi_m.

INFLUENCE OF STATIC CONSTRAINTS

They represent some external conditions carried by the user such as :

$$xi_{mmn} \leqslant xi_m \leqslant xi_{mmx}$$

Especially the initial condition on the state is clearly a lower constraint $xi_m \geqslant xi_o$: in the example proposed in this text, with $x_o = [^o_o]$ and $u(t) = \delta(t)$ (a step signal) $x2_m \simeq 9.5$ so that the choice of the value 10 is very close to the optimum value, in the case of the parabolic criterion (7).

The various existing softwares for calculating the vapor balance on board of a ship or for obtaining the nominal point of a rolling mill prove that, for non linear complex processes, computing coherent initial conditions all along the process, is already a heavy problem. Due to the non convexity of the global criterion, there is no simple general optimization software. So a modified Hooke and Jeeves method was prepared in order to respect the absolute constraints xi_{mmx} and xi_{mmn}. For each new value of xi_m the coefficients CXI, CI and DI are calculated, so it is easy to remain in the convexity domain of the starting point, where no DI change occurs. It is the responsibility of the user to decide to cross a limite and to enter in the adjacent domain : this must be an interactive part of the software.

INFLUENCE OF DYNAMIC CONSTRAINTS

It is more difficult to take into account these constraints because, with complex and non linear systems, they are impredictable, except by a simulation.

Returning to our example, let us suppose that during a first run of simulation, the state X2 reaches its limit ± 1 : the scale $x2_m$ must increase. As a consequence of this overflow, the simulation must stop and we are obliged to multiply the lower constraint by some coefficient $KA > 1$: $x2_{mmn}$ becomes $KA.x2_{mmn}$. Now if no convexity domain limit is crossed, we can start a new run of the simulation. If some DI changes, it is useful, first to renew the static optimization.

In a symetric way, every state which poorly uses its domain of variation, is underloaded. In that case we must change its maximum constraint such that xi_{mmx} becomes xi_{mmx}/KA. Here again, we may start a new run or in case of any change in the DI's values, we must first renew a static optimization.

In order to see wether an acceptable use of the domain $[xi_{mmn}, xi_{mmx}]$ is performed during a run, we suggest to sample each state and to calculate the mean values $\overline{XI}$ and the mean square deviations $\tilde{XI}$: the domain is properly used if

either $|\overline{XI}| \geqslant .5$ or either $\tilde{XI} \geqslant .3$

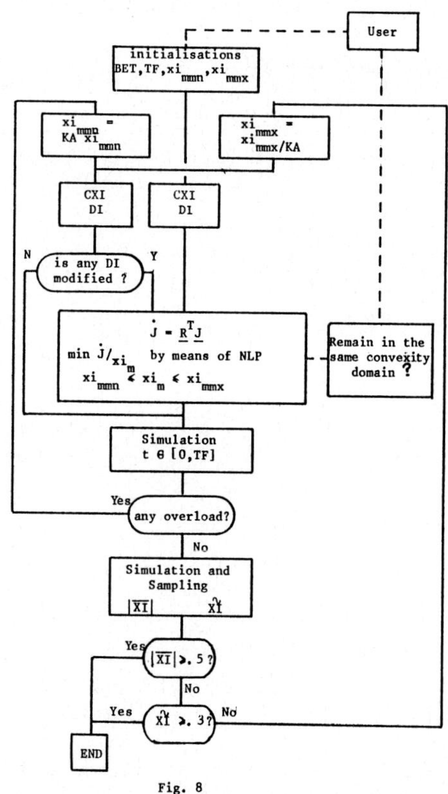

Fig. 8

CONCLUSION

The choice of the class of some component, among various classes and the scaling of some analog simulation seem to derive from the same optimization strategy : a static constrained optimization gives a starting point and dynamic simulations modify iteratively the constraints as shown in fig. 8.

This investigation, not yet concluded, is supported by the National French Research Center (CNRS)[1]

REFERENCES

Interface Hybridrechenanlage des EDV-Zentrum des Technisches Universität Wien Nr 15/16 juni 1980

Analog and analog/hybrid computer programming Arthur Hausner, Prentice Hall Englewood Cliffs 1971

(1) Realised in collaboration with J. Szymanowski, visiting professor in the Universitary Center of Tlemcen.

DIGITAL TECHNIQUES in Simulation, Communication and Control
Spyros G. Tzafestas (editor)
Elsevier Science Publishers B.V. (North-Holland) © IMACS, 1985

ANALOG INPUT/OUTPUT INTERACTIVE STATION FOR PROCESS COMPUTER SIMULATION

J. Martínez Ayuso, L. Fernández González, A. Lara Villen
Centro de Investigación y Estudios - C.T.N.E.
Madrid

In this paper software and hardware architecture used for implementing an interactive workstation with analog I/O on a MDS system is presented; moreover the system appears as a VAX-11/780 computer terminal. The system is opened to the addition of new commands or hardware resources, showing a STATION/VAX joint feature as a single entity for the user when performing process simulation and signal processing.

1. INTRODUCTION

The communication complexity of a minicomputer (VAX-11/780) with analog world is known. Dedicated equipments are necessary and many software problems arise for data adquisition in real time. In this paper a standard development system (MDS) is used to obtain an intelligent workstation with many facilities for the user.

The idea behind this project is to obtain a remote station of a VAX minicomputer wherein analog data acquisition or reconstruction is performed making use of the development resources (disk, ports, prom programmer, etc); at the same time the calculation power of the minicomputer can be used for the mathematical operations to be performed with the samples of the stored signals. In this manner, the development system is converted into an intelligent terminal with the calculation power of VAX and this can make use of the hardware flexibility of the MDS.

2. SYSTEM CONFIGURATION

The system configuration is shown in figure 1. MDS system is connected by a RS-232 line at 9600 bauds and XON/XOFF protocol. The station operates as master setting the communication cadence from the minicomputer; moreover it scans the VAX availability for receive information. The system has two working modes chosen by the user at any moment: as a standard terminal (non-intelligent) or as an intelligent terminal that continously settles the operation to be achieved including the service request to the mini.

3. SYSTEM INPUT/OUTPUT

The system has analog input/output with sample frequency user selectable through commands. There are two sample and reconstruction speeds: 10 KHz and 30 KHz. The analog signal is converted with 8 bits resolution; this samples are introduced/extracted into/out of the MDS through digital ports. The transferences are supervised by the main program.

Data buffer has a maximun size of 30.000 samples per operation due to the memory limitation of the MDS. With respect to the system input/output, we indicate that MDS has a MULTIBUS structure that can be used for increasing I/O capabilities with standard MULTIBUS boards. This enlargemeny is easily inclused in software structure.

4. SOFTWARE STRUCTURE

Software structure is wholly structured; every module is described in this section.

4.1. COMMUNICATION MODULE

This module performs communications control between systema at the lowest level. It drives the XON/XOFF protocol in transmition as well as in reception. In the reception case, this take place at intervals defined by windows during which the minicomputer can send information. The window beguinning and end are controlled by XON/XOFF commands. This reception is carried out by a circular buffer, data are logged into the buffer by interrupt procedures at the same time they are being received. Other procedures take the data out of the buffer and take them to display, disk or memory.

4.2. COMMAND INTEPRETER

The nucleus is the intelligent part of the terminal; it receives and interpretes every line typed by the user. If the line is a terminal command it is executed, if it is not the terminal remains transparent to it. In the last case, the line is transmitted to the minicomputer. In this manner the user sees only one system where he can use the minicomputer resources as well as the workstation resources through commands.

The modular structure of this interpreter allows to increase easily the software capabilities; to do this it suffices to add the command and its execution procedures.

4.3. FILES MANAGEMENT MODULE

All the necessary procedures for file management are included in this module to open files, close them, read them, read them, etc over disk units.

5. AVAILABLE FACILITIES

In this section we present the terminal commands actually available.

5.1. STATION CONFIGURATION COMMAND

This command allows to define the station as an intelligent terminal or a standard one. In the first case the command interpreter is activated and all the resources are available; in the latter, only the minicomputer resources can be used.

5.2. INPUT/OUTPUT COMMANDS

These commands allow the performance of the following operations: –Analog data acquisition of 30.000 samples at 30 KHz rate. –The same but at 10 KHz rate. –Digital/analog conversion over any signal segment at 30 KHz rate. –The same but at 10 KHz rate.

5.3. SIGNAL SEGMENT SELECTION COMMAND

Two pointers can be set by the user at any address over the data memory, selecting the initial and end points of the segment. This segment is now available for the other commands.

5.4. STORE/RECOVER SAMPLES COMMANDS

There are the following posibilities: –Disk storage of any data memory segment; there are two recording formats: binary (samples are recorded as they were in memory) and decimal ASCII (every sample is converted into four ASCII characteres). This last recording format helps the sample reading by means a display or printer. –Data file reading (binary or decimal ASCII formats).

In any case, file name and file format is asked to the user.

5.5. FILE TRANSFERENCE COMMANDS

The system allows file transferences between station and minicomputer: this files must be in memory or disk. The format of the data to be transfered can be ASCII or binary; in the last case data must be converted to hexadecimal due to the lack of transparency of the communication channel. When the user chooses format data transmision, deconversion is automatically performed in the respective protocol.

The program interactivelly request the user the file source name (in MDS or VAX), format and the file destination name (in VAX or MDS). In the case of MDS destination, the program request data allocation: disk for storage or memory for data reconstruction.

5.6. PROM PROGRAMMER FILES COMMAND

This command allows the target file (generally obtained in VAX) to be converted into INTEL hexadecimal format and recorded in disk. This file can be used directly by a PROM PROGRAMMER.

5.7. HELP COMMAND

The command ensamble and the instruction set form system utilization are supplied through this command.

5.8. EXIT COMMAND

With the exit command the user can return to the ISIS operating system; in this case, the workstation is only a development system.

6. CONCLUSIONS

This structure allows the user to have available the high level resources of a minicomputer and the low level resources of a development system. The workstation above mentioned is at this time being used in the Research Center of Spanish Telephone Company for voice and signal acquisition, signal processing or process simulation and EPROM generation for voice synthesizers.

7. REFERENCES

[1] Intellec MDS Hardware Reference Manual.

[2] VAX/VMS User Manual.

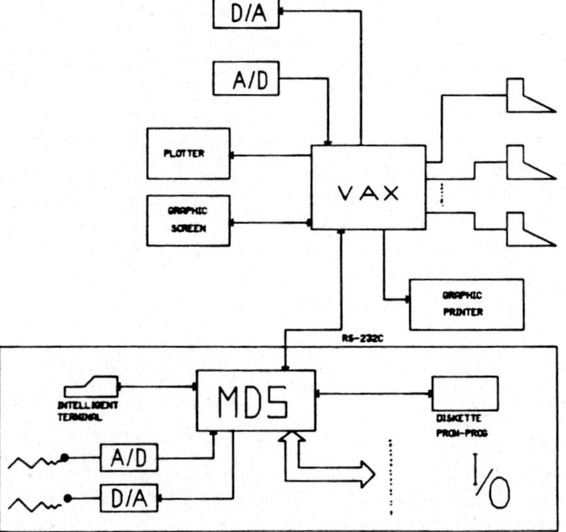

Fig. 1 System Configuration

DIGITAL TECHNIQUES in Simulation, Communication and Control
Spyros G. Tzafestas (editor)
Elsevier Science Publishers B.V. (North-Holland) © IMACS, 1985

HIGH LEVEL HYBRID SOFTWARE APPLIED TO PROCESS/EXPERIMENT CONTROL SYSTEM EVALUATION

Rajko Milovanovic (x,xx), Miodrag Askrabic (xx), Emir Humo (x)

(x) Faculty of Electrical Engineering, Toplicka bb
(xx) Energoinvest-Iris, Stup
Sarajevo, Yugoslavia

Following a brief introduction to the organization of the hybrid system, we establish a hybrid computing methodology and present the integrated support for systems simulation in the high level language. We examine its two fundamental aspects: simulation of the object system, that is controlled or supervised by the computer system whose design is being evaluated, and simulation of the events flow within the computer system attached to such an object system. Simulation results are used as a confirmation for initial design validity or they indicate its faults and bottlenecks. Finally, comparative advanta es of such evaluation are stressed, as well as the limitations for its use.

1. INTRODUCTION

The synthesis of the process (as well as the experiment) control and supervision system (PECS) is seriously influenced by the technology-dependant details of the system being automated. On the other hand, in order to facilitate efficient synthesis of such systems, it is highly desirable to have unified design, evaluation and testing methodology.

A PECS is usually supported by the event driven multitasking operating system machine (or machines) with a variety of process oriented devices. The architecture of such systems is rather heterogenous, depending on many conflicting factors. Real time constraints normally impose non-standard solutions for each problem, due to the peculiarities of the occasional bursts of traffic of process data (particularly in the case of experiments, wide ranges of aggregate data rates during different plant states (start-up or operation close to the nominal values), specific high-priority communication and control lo ps within the system, etc.

In this paper we examine the possibility of using relativelu inexpensive resource - a hybrid computer - for at least a portion of this process. Section 2. presents basic structural properties of the general purpose PECS and outlines specific classes within it. We consider possibilities and experiences in testing and tuning the system in the standard manner - first at the production platforms, later on the object itself. Section 3. presents a configuration of the hybrid computing system that is used to expediate a part of simulation, verification and performance evaluation process. On such basis, section 4. contains an analysis of the possibilities of using such an utility for final testing and evaluation of parts as well as the whole of PECS.

2. TESTING AND TUNING

PECS usually contains several functions with subsets being used on specific objects. All these functions can be separated into three main groups: functions dealing with the procees, functions orientated towares human operators and/or higher order personnel, and functions dealing with data storage in the general sense. It should be kept in mind that PECS class we are considering here marginally includes systems that are basically multiloop digital controllers.

The first group of functions gathers all forms of process information, periodically or at certain events, commands and controls the process. Each of process input or output points is supported by its analog or digital channel within the PECS. Consequently, this group of functions poses most serious constraints with the reseect to the duration of computation. The second group of functions supports the supervision of events flow in the process or its parts, registration of the process variables, reporting at the end of each production cycle, allarms and warnings in the case of significant events, change of process parameters and the PECS itself (as well as some parts of the process), and commanding and control of the process via the closed loops including the operator. The third group of functions, besides its taks of providing informational support for the first two groups via the process data base, supports long-term reporting, computation of quality/performance indices, magtape archieving, and creation of the cyclic events history. In this sense, the third group of functions is starting point for extensions of real-time PECS with extended real-time support (optimization, long- and short-range estimation and planning).

These functions are normally carried out with one or more processors, each of them with a set of human-oriented peripheral devices, suitable peripheral storage, and basically two options for interaction with the process: either via process interface connected to the CPU's (parallel) input/output bus (with typical data rates of up to 10 Mbit/s and efficient use of interrupts and DMA), or via process interface contained in stand-alone remote microprocessor based subsystems performing direct data acquisition and/or control functions. In the second case, the master machine is linked with the remote station via communication interfaces with a wide performance range - from several uundred bit/s for miliampere loops, to several Mbit/s for local nets. The choice of transmission technique is largely determined by the distances, cabling considerations, noise, etc. Two typical configurations are depicted on Fig.1.

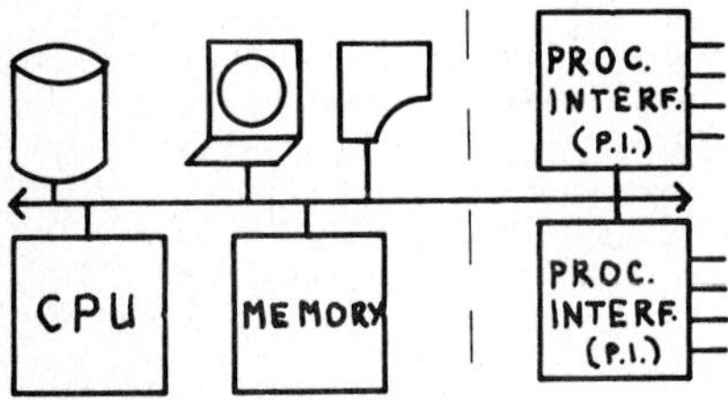

(a) centralized

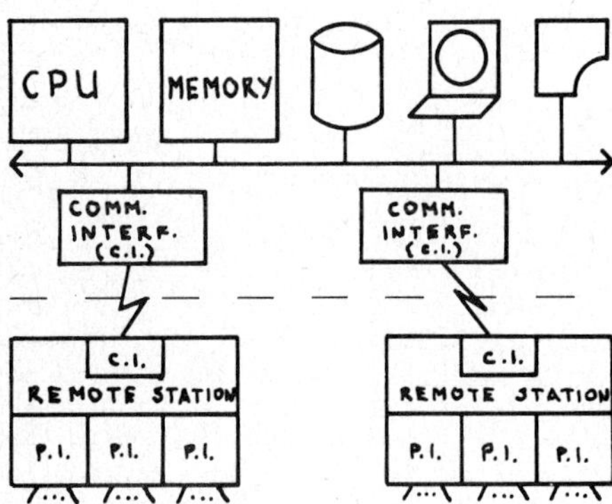

(b) distributed

Figure 1 - Typical PECS configurations

The choice of hardware is often determined by different factors, with economical ones often taking the prominent place (dependance on product range of the organizations designing, developing and assembling PECS). Software offers much wider space for variations, and it is a standard practice to use it as a resource for adapting the PECS to the object specific details and requirements. With all these variabions in mind, it is still possible to outline a general model of programs (or processes) structure within the PECS, a model of the process data base, process activation/deactivation and communication mechanisms. The general PECS software structure on Fig.2. does not contain explicit division into separate programs; in principle, each element consists of several programs. Their communication mechanisms are statis event indicators and statis shared data regions, dynamic message lists etc.; process activation and deactivation

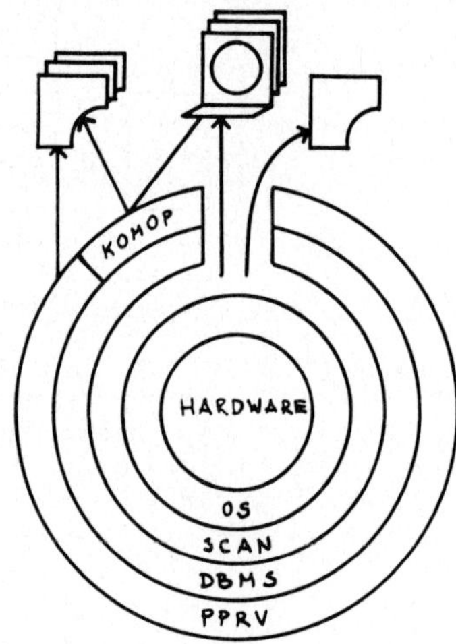

igure 2 - General structure of the PCCS software (OS: operating system, SCAN: detection of process states, allarming, event chronology, identification, DBMS: process data base, programs for control of data, KOMOP: operator supervision and command programs, PPRV: extended real-time programs)

is determined by events in the process, time intervals, or via explicit operator command.

The testing process is usually performed on the production platforms, with additional hardware being represented by signal generators, communication line monitors, switching devices, etc. Fine tuning is mostly based on the designer's estimates, and its second stage takes place in the field, after the system installation. Such approach is inevitably costly as well.

3. HYBRID COMPUTER CONFIGURATION

We will consider a hybrid machine IMP-6000 with the hybrid software developed at the Faculty of Electrical Engineering in Sarajevo. It is a medium capacity machine with high degree of functionality. It is particularly suitable for our purpose since its digital portion is PDP-11/34, a member of the family that is extensively used in PECS systems manufactured by Energoinvest-Iris.

Continuous systems are simulated with the aid of 38 integrators - with individual IC-OP-HC cycling, 80 manual and 20 elpots, 10 multipliers, 14 function generators and 16 comparators, switches and relays each. Logic patchboard contains 16-bit counter/shift register, 4 digit BCD counter, 16x16 bit memory, a number of flip-flops and gates. Block structure of the system is given on the Fig.3.

Besides modelling continuous systems with changes of system structure with the aid of

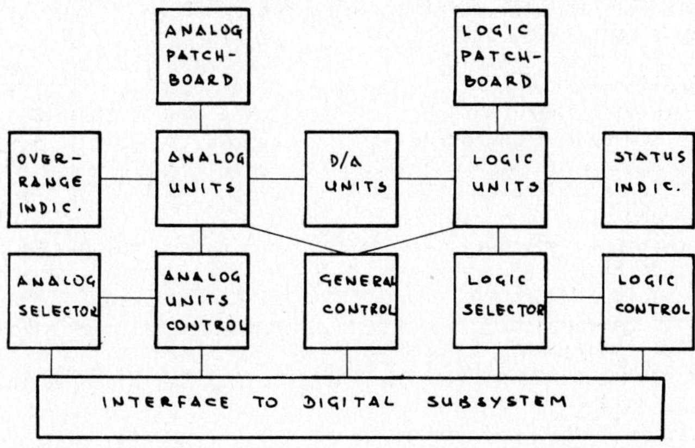

Figure 3 - Block structure of the analog portion of IMP-6000

of comparators and switches/relays, complex forms of decision making can be accomplished with the memory control mechanism, Fig.4. The most complex form of desision making is naturally made by the digital computer. Its interface towards the analog subsystems is totally transparent to the FORTRAN (or other high level language) programmer. This is possible with the use of hybrid systems software that includes the functions equivalent to analog computer's operator actions (reading or setting the state of the analog subsystem, analog or logic computing elements), functions supporting all interrupts (general purpose, real-time clock interrupts, A/D and D/A conversion system interrupts, end-of-DMA, error, etc.). High level hybrid programmer simply writes calls that initiate sequences of conversions, ignoring all the ireelevent details.

4. SIMULATION AND PERFORMANCE EVALUATION

Configurations of systems presented on Fig.1(a) and Fig.1(b) are equivalent in the sense that input/output process data streams are multiplexed on the point of contact with the SCAN ring, Fig.2.; in such context, evaluation of the PECS software prrtions on the hybrid computer might also reveal shortcomings of the proposed hardware structure. This is not usually done, simply because initial estimation of hardware forms and parameters is performed with sufficient ammount of spare resources (time, memory, communication effectivness). We are thus left with the problem of software evaluation, with a fixed hardware configuration.

Simulation has two basic aspects: simulation of the object system, and simulation of events within the PECS itself. Due to the nature of the analog modelling, the first problem is solved much easier on the hybrid computer than on the production platform; instead of signal generators and similar devices, we are able to set up the whole dynamical model of the object system. Continuous variables are easily scanned with actual rate of 1 KHz, that is more than sufficient for industrial processes, but often requires time-scaling for fast experiments. Digital signals are read-out from the memory in the logic patchboard, from registers, counters, etc., based on program requests or via general purpose interrupt. Each of these interrups may represent several distinct causes.

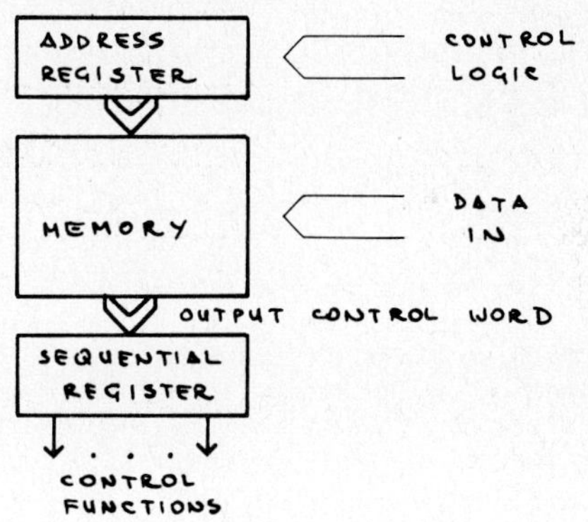

Figure 4 - Memory control mechanism

The second aspect of simulation can be portioned into three phases: simulation of events pertaining to a single process variable, simulation of events linked to statistics of program interaction, and simulation of events dealing with aggregate indicators - the output of PPRV group of programs, Fig.2. Among these, program interaction statistics stand out in the sense that hybrid modelling offers no advantage to it.

One of the most significant PECS quality

indicators is response time, for example from the moment of process variable braaking the limit to the memont of allarm given to the operator, or from issuance of the command to its actual fullfilment. This time sometimes streaches up to several seconds, with its distribution being basically determined by the frequency of such events. Appropriate model on the analog subsystem models this frequency, and PECS response is measured; possibility of time-scale change in the analog model is particularly suitable here. Generation of series of digital-type events is most easily done with the memory in logic patchboard.

Control of the quality of chronological events recording is implemented via counters, with a single event causing several "consequences". The resulting information produced for the operator will have the same sequence ordering if the process synchronization within the PECS is properly designed. Closely connected with this is the issue of time resolution of PECS: how closely the events processed by PECS may be spaced, before we are faced with the overflow of, say, alarm lists. This sort of testing is most easily done with different periodical signals generated on the analog subsystem.

Simulation of events dealing with aggregate process indicators confirms usability of PECS output not only for operators. The production cycle normally lasting hours or days is easily time-scaled. Its output values like quality of operation, sums, averages, optimal states, etc., are visually verified on the process model itself. On the other hand, PECS computes equivalents of these values. Comparison of those two sete reveals possible inconsistencies and faults.

5. CONCLUSIONS

Quoted examples of use of the hybrid computer fully justify employing it for evaluation of PECS software through simulation. Testing and evaluation on the production platform and in the field are not eliminated, but they are significantly reduced in size and complexity.

Widely differeng specific software solutions prevent the creation of universal hybrid programs for this purpose; instead of that, on the basis of principles outlined above, each specific csse should be dealt with separately. Full evaluation procedure implies the availability of the dynamic model of the plant, or some sort of its approximation; otherwise the greatest portion of comparative advantages of hybrid simulation and evaluation is lost. This restriction, though a serious one at a first glance, is usually satisfied anyway: the practice has proved taht a high quality PECS cannot be designed without previous detailed insight into the technology of the plant being automated.

6. REFERENCES:

/1/ M.Askrabic, Data structures in data-acquisition systems, ETF Belgrade, 1983.

/2/ R.Milovanovic, Hybrid computer software, ETF Zagreb, 1981.

/3/ Manuals of PECS systems manufactured by Energoinvest-Iris, Sarajevo, 1983/4

/4/ M.Zelkovic, Software design principles, Fizmatgiz, Moscow, 1979

/5/ V.Tassel, Stil, razrabotka, efektivnost, otkladka i ispitanije program, Nauka, Moscow, 1981 (in Russian).

2. DIGITAL SIGNAL PROCESSING AND 2-D SYSTEM DESIGN

DIGITAL TECHNIQUES in Simulation, Communication and Control
Spyros G. Tzafestas (editor)
Elsevier Science Publishers B.V. (North-Holland) © IMACS, 1985

THREE METHODS FOR 16-BIT MICROPROCESSOR IMPLEMENTATION OF DIGITAL FILTERS

A.N. Skodras and T. Deliyannis

Electronics Laboratory
University of Patras
Patras, Greece

A 16-bit microprocessor, MC68000, is used in the implementation of a second-order IIR digital filter by three different methods with regard to the way of calculating the product of two fixed-point numbers in two's complement form. These three methods are applied purely by means of software and are compared in terms of time and ammount of memory necessary for running their corresponding programs.

1. INTRODUCTION

It is clear to every one working in the field that multiplication is the operation that takes most of the time in the digital filter algorithm. The usual method of multiplying (shifts and additions) two fixed point numbers, which is most time consuming,is replaced, when using 8-bit microprocessor implementation of digital filters, by one of the following methods: a) Use of an external multiplier [1], b) Use of Look-up-Tables [2] and c) Use of Distributed Arithmetic (Vector Multiplier) [3,4,5]. With the advent of 16-bit microprocessors the implementation of digital filters in real time can be improved , provided that the facilities offered by these microprocessors are advantageously exploited. In fact all 16-bit microprocessor units have vastly improved memory space, the ability to handle various types of data, improved instruction set including more powerful arithmetic capabilities, symmetry, and completeness in instruction set as far as addressing modes are concerned. Their facilities for calculating the product of two numbers using the "multiply instruction" makes things easier in the realization of digital filters in real time [6].

In this paper a comparative study is presented with regard to the required time and memory space for the realization of digital filters purely by means of software (without the use of additional circuitry) using the system MEX68 KECB with MPU the MC68000 of Motorola. Some details for connecting the ADC and DAC to the microcomputer board are given in section 2. In section 3 three methods of implementing a 2nd-order recursive digital filter using this system are explained and results are discussed in the final section. All programs written in assembly language corresponding to these methods are given in Appendices I to III.

2. HARDWARE DESCRIPTION

System MEX68KECB/D2 of Motorola (the MC68000 Educational Computer Board) was used in the realization of digital filters in this work. This includes MPU MC68000 at 4 MHz, a 32K RAM, a 16K ROM and offers the possibility for assembly/disassembly functions [9]. MC68000 has a 16-bit data bus. The following are also available from it [8]: a) Eight 32-bit data registers, which can be used for byte, word and long word operations. b) Seven 32-bit address registers, which can be used for work and long word address operations. c) Two 32-bit stack pointers (user and supervisor) d) A 32-bit program counter. e) A 16-bit status register.

All seventeen registers may be used as index registers. An additional circuit was constructed for the input and output of samples to the system. Its main parts are as follows: a) A Sample-and-Hold (S/H) circuit. b) A 12-bit Analog-to-Digital Converter (ADC). c) A 12-bit Digital-to-Analog Converter (DAC). d) Four sets of octal edge-triggered D-type registers. e) Buffers, flip-flops and gates.

This circuit and its connection to the Computer Board are shown in detail in Figure 1. It is directly connected to the Data-Bus of the μP and not through the Parallel Interface/Timer i.e. the i/o registers are memory mapped. More specifically, the registers for the input samples are mapped in the address $ 40000 and those for the output in the address $ 50000. These addresses have been selected for simplicity reasons, because the Educational Computer Board has available two outputs E_2, E_3, which can become active for the above addresses.

It should be pointed out that the analog to digital conversion of each new sample is performed automatically after the reading in of the preceding sample. This is achieved using a monostable, which is triggered each time the contents are read from the registers that store the values of the input samples. The output from the monostable is connected to input Start Conversion (SC) of the ADC.

3. SOFTWARE DESCRIPTION

In this section three-methods are examined for the realization of a second order recursive digital filter with the following difference

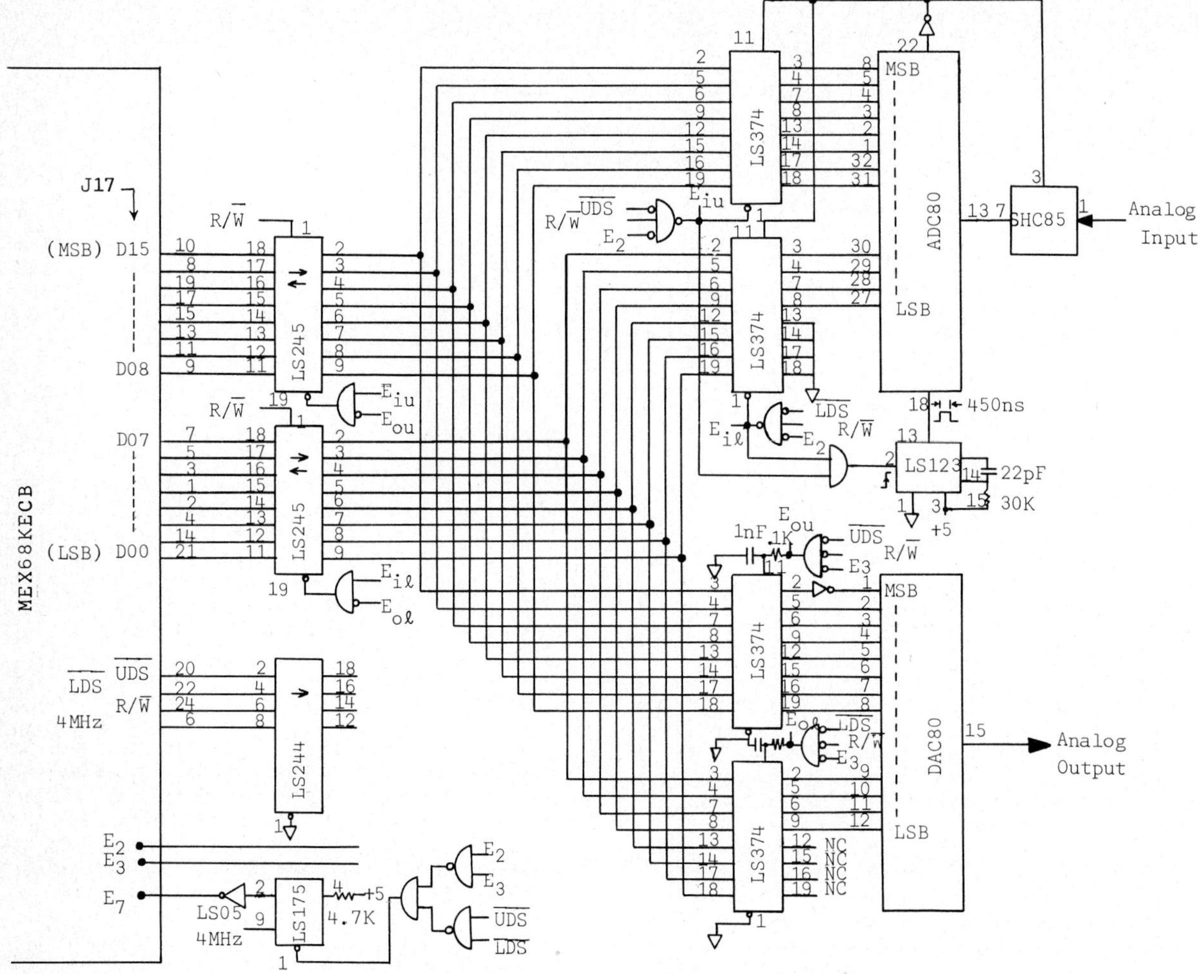

Figure 1: Details of system hardware.

equation:

$$y_n = a_0x_n + a_1x_{n-1} + a_2x_{n-2} - b_1y_{n-1} - b_2y_{n-2} \qquad (1)$$

The reason for selecting a second-order function is because this is the basic structure, in one important method, for building high-order digital filters. The realization is achieved by means of the system, which was described in the previous section, and all three methods of realization described below are applied using purely software. That is no additional external circuitry is used. In all three methods 2's complement arithmetic is used.

3.1 Implementation using Look-up Tables

In accordance with this method all values of the five products which are required in the realization of eqn (1) have been precalculated and stored in consecutive memory locations, thus forming the so called Look-up-Tables (LUT). One LUT is needed for each product [2]. So for the implementation of eqn (1) five LUTs are needed to be formed in the general case. As it was mensioned in section 2 each sample is quantised using 12 binary digits. Therefore all possible values of each product a_jx_{n-j} or b_ky_{n-k}, j=0,1,2, k=1,2 are 2^{12}=4096. And since the value of each product is 16-bit or 2 bytes long (as a MPU with 16-bit data bus is available), each LUT will occupy 8192 bytes i.e. 8Kbytes. Thus for the five products in eqn (1) 40Kbytes of memory will be occupied.

The memory address, where a specific product is stored e.g. a_0x_i, x_i is the value of the ith sample, is A0+2*x_i, where A0 is the address of the first value of the corresponding LUT. The value x_i has been multiplied by 2 because each product occupies two bytes.

The program in assembly language and the corresponding clock periods for the implementation of eqn (1) according to this method are given in Appendix I.

3.2 Implementation using the "Vector Multiplier" mechanisation

Eqn (1) can be written in the following form [3,4]

$$y_n = \sum_{j=1}^{B-1} 2^{-j} \rho(x_n^j, x_{n-1}^j, x_{n-2}^j, y_{n-1}^j, y_{n-2}^j) - \rho(x_n^o, x_{n-1}^o, x_{n-2}^o, y_{n-1}^o, y_{n-2}^o) \quad (2)$$

where

$$\rho(x_n^j, x_{n-1}^j, x_{n-2}^j, y_{n-1}^j, y_{n-2}^j) = a_0 x_n^j + a_1 x_{n-1}^j + a_2 x_{n-2}^j + (-b_1) y_{n-1}^j + (-b_2) y_{n-2}^j$$

and B the wordlength including the sign bit. Function ρ has five binary arguments giving it 2^5=32 distinct values. Each value however of ρ is two bytes long. Therefore a LUT for all possible values of ρ would occupy 64 bytes. The values of ρ are calculated and stored in memory before running the main program of the filter. A particular value of ρ is obtained as the sum of those coefficients $a_o, a_1, a_2, (-b_1), (-b_2)$ for which the corresponding bits $x_n^j, x_{n-1}^j, x_{n-2}^j, y_{n-1}^j, y_{n-2}^j$ are set [4].

In Appendix II the assembly listing of the program and the corresponding clock periods are given when implementing eqn (2). Bit positions 4 up to 15 in data registers D0 to D4 contain the values of $x_n, x_{n-1}, x_{n-2}, y_{n-1}, y_{n-2}$ respectively. The value of each ρ is held in data register D6 (bits 0 to 4). The test of the value of each bit for each sample is achieved using the instruction Bit Test (BTST), thus avoiding sample shifting. It has been taken care that the time required for testing the value of one bit and for the corresponding change or not in the value of D6 is constant and independent of the bit values. This way, the sampling frequency will always be the same.

3.3 Implementation using the "Multiplication Instruction"

MC68000 in accordance with all 16-bit μPs has available instructions for the multiplication of 16-bit signed or unsigned numbers. The product is a number 32-bit long.

In Appendix III the program listing is given in assembly language together with the corresponding clock periods when implementing eqn (1) using multiplication instructions in the system under consideration here. It is clear that for the multiplying operation 74 clock periods are necessary at maximum. This means that the processing time of each sample will varry depending on the coefficient sets. That the multiplication time is not constant is a result of the fact that the multiplication operation in MC68000 is performed using a sequence of micro instructions [7] and not extra circuitry.

4. COMMENTS AND CONCLUSIONS

Three different methods for realizing a 2nd-order IIR digital filter by means of the 16-bit MEX68 KECB/D2 system have been presented above. No external harware has been added to the system. The required clock periods and memory space for each method are given in Table I. It can be seen that the method of LUT leads to the shortest sampling period but the required memory space is excessively high. In the method of Vector Multiplier the required memory space is small but the sampling period is very long. Finally when using the Multiply instruction the memory space required is the smallest for the three methods, whereas the sampling period takes a maximum value between the corresponding sampling periods in the other two methods. This period can be reduced by up to 17% depending on the values of the filter coefficients.

From the above it appears that the method using the Multiply instuctions for calculating the products is superior. It requires minimal memory space and offers flexibility in the realization of digital filters with a logical value of sampling period. This conclusion is further substantiated by the fact that this method leads to better noise performance, because the value of each sample y_n is the result of adding products of double precision. In the other two methods examined here the sum-of-rounded products is performed, although the sum-of-double-precision-product approach could also be applied in these. However in this case the required memory space would be double and there would also be need for additional clock periods.

TABLE I

	Look-Up Tables	Multiplication Instruction	Vector Multiplier
Sampling Period (in clock periods)	153	507 max	2283
Required Memory (in Bytes)	40960+53+0 (* ** ***)	0+59 +9 (* ** ***)	64+109+0 (* ** ***)

* Refers to memory locations occupied by the LUTs.

** Refers to memory locations occupied by the main filter program.

*** Refers to memory locations occupied by the coefficients and samples.

REFERENCES

[1] Allen, P.J. and Holt, A.G.J., Alternative multiplication configuration in microprocessor-based digital filters, Electron. Lett., 15, 481-482 (1979).

[2] Skodras, A.N., On the use of look-up tables in the microprocessor implementation of digital filters, Int. J. of Electronics, Vol. 55, No. 4, 675-679 (1983).

[3] Farhang-Boroujeny, B. and Hawkins, G.J., Study of the use of microprocessors in digital filtering, Computers and Digital Techniques, Vol. 2, No. 4 (Aug. 1979).

[4] Allen, P.J. and Holt, A.G.J., Controlling a vector-multiplier-based digital filter by using a microprocessor, Computers and Digital Techniques, Vol. 2, No. 4 (Aug. 1979).

[5] Arjmand, M. and Roberts, R.A., On comparing hardware implementations of fixed point digital filters IEEE Circuits and Systems Magazine, Vol. 3, No. 2 (1981).

[6] Nagle, H.T. and Nelson, V.P., Digital filter implementation on 16-bit microcomputers, IEEE Micro (Feb. 1981).

[7] Stritter, S. and Tredennick, N., Microprogrammed implementation of a single chip microprocessor, SIGMICRO NEWSLETTER, Vol. 9, No. 4, (Dec. 1978).

[8] Motorola Inc., MC68000UM(AD2), 16-bit Microprocessor User's Manual (1980).

[9] Motorola Inc., MEX68KECB/D2, MC68000 Educational Computer Board User's Manual (1982).

APPENDIX I

*** MC68000 ***
- IMPLEMENTATION OF EQUATION (1) USING LOOK-UP TABLES.
- DATA REGISTERS D0,D1,D2,D3,D4 HOLD THE VALUES OF THE SAMPLES $x_n, x_{n-1}, x_{n-2}, y_{n-1}, y_{n-2}$ RESPECTIVELY.
- ADDRESS REGISTERS A0,A1,A2,A3,A4 HOLD THE ADDRESSES OF THE FIRST CONTENT OF EACH LOOK-UP TABLE.

CURRENT LOCATION	MACHINE OPERATION CODE	OPERATION FIELD	OPERAND FIELD	COMMENT FIELD	CLOCK PERIODS
000B30	4BF900040000	LEA.L	$00040000,A5		
000B36	4DF900050000	LEA.L	$00050000,A6		
000B3C	3015	MOVE.W	(A5),D0	INPUT XN	8
000B3E	E648	LSR.W	≠3,D0	D0 [12:1]←D0 [15:4]	12
000B40	3E300000	MOVE.W	0(A0,D0.W),D7	D7←A0*XN	14
000B44	DE711000	ADD.W	0(A1,D1.W),D7	D7←D7+A1*XN-1	14
000B48	DE722000	ADD.W	0(A2,D2.W),D7	D7←D7+A2*XN-2	14
000B4C	9E733000	SUB.W	0(A3,D3.W),D7	D7←D7-B1*YN-1	14
000B50	9E744000	SUB.W	0(A4,D4.W),D7	D7←D7-B2*YN-2	14
000B54	3C87	MOVE.W	D7,(A6)	OUTPUT YN	9
000B56	E64F	LSR.W	≠3,D7	D7 [12:1]←D7 [15:4]	12
000B58	0247FFFE	AND.W	≠-2,D7	D7 [1]←0	8
000B5C	C342	EXG	D1,D2	XN-2←XN-1	6
000B5E	C141	EXG	D0,D1	XN-1←XN	6
000B60	C744	EXG	D3,D4	YN-2←YN-1	6
000B62	CF43	EXG	D7,D3	YN-1←YN	6
000B64	60D6	BRA.S	$000B3C	BRANCH FILTER LOOP	10
					153

APPENDIX II

*** MC68000 ***
- IMPLEMENTATION OF EQUATION (2) USING DISTRIBUTED ARITHMETIC.
- DATA REGISTERS D0,D1,D2,D3,D4 HOLD THE VALUES OF THE SAMPLES $x_n, x_{n-1}, x_{n-2}, y_{n-1}, y_{n-2}$ RESPECTIVELY.
- ADDRESS REGISTER A0 HOLDS THE ADDRESS OF THE FIRST CONTENT OF THE LOOK-UP TABLE.
- TO AVOID OVERFLOW THE COEFFICIENTS HAVE BEEN SCALED DOWN BY A FACTOR OF 2.

```
000F30   41F80C00       LEA.L    $00000C00,A0
000F34   43F900040000   LEA.L    $00040000,A1
000F3A   45F900050000   LEA.L    $00050000,A2
000F40   3011           MOVE.W   (A1),D0          INPUT XN                          8
000F42   7A04           MOVE.L   #4,D5            D5←4                              4
000F44   4247           CLR.W    D7               D7←0                              4
000F46   4246           CLR.W    D6               D6←0                              4
000F48   0B00           BTST     D5,D0            TEST THAT BIT OF DO WHICH         T
000F4A   6602           BNE.S    $000F4A          IS POINTED BY D5. IF IT           |
000F4C   6004           BRA.S    $000F52          EQUALS TO ONE, THEN SET THE      24
000F4E   00460001       OR.W     #1,D6            FIRST BIT OF D6.                  |
000F52   0B01           BTST     D5,D1                                              T
000F54   6602           BNE.S    $000F58                                            |
000F56   6004           BRA.S    $000F5C                                           24
000F58   00460002       OR.W     #2,D6                                              |
000F5C   0B02           BTST     D5,D2                                              T
000F5E   6602           BNE.S    $000F62                                            |
000F60   6004           BRA.S    $000F66                                           24
000F62   00460004       OR.W     #4,D6                                              |
000F66   0B03           BTST     D5,D3                                              T
000F68   6602           BNE.S    $000F6C                                            |
000F6A   6004           BRA.S    $000F70                                           24
000F6C   00460008       OR.W     #8,D6                                              |
000F70   0B04           BTST     D5,D4                                              T
000F72   6602           BNE.S    $000F76                                            |
000F74   6004           BRA.S    $000F7A                                           24
000F76   00460010       OR.W     #16,D6                                             |
000F7A   E346           ASL.W    #1,D6            D6←D6*2                           8
000F7C   E247           ASR.W    #1,D7            D7←D7/2                           8
000F7E   0C05000F       CMP.B    #15,D5                                             8
000F82   6612           BNE.S    $000F96          IF D5=15 THEN                    10
000F84   9E706000       SUB.W    0(A0,D6.W),D7    D7←D7-(A0+D6)                    14
000F88   E547           ASL.W    #1,D7            D7←D7*2                           8
000F8A   3487           MOVE.W   D7,(A2)          OUTPUT YN                         9
000F8C   C744           EXG      D3,D4            YN-2←YN-1                         6
000F8E   C342           EXG      D1,D2            XN-2←XN-1                         6
000F90   C141           EXG      D0,D1            XN-1←XN                           6
000F92   C747           EXG      D3,D7            YN-1←YN                           6
000F94   60AA           BRA.S    $000F40          BRANCH FILTER LOOP               10
000F96   DE706000       ADD.W    0(A0,D6.W),D7    D7←D7+(A0+D6)                    14
000F9A   5205           ADDQ.B   #1,D5            D5←D5+1                           4
000F9C   60A8           BRA.S    $000F46          CONTINUE WITH NEXT SET OF BITS   10
                                                                                 ----
                                                                                 2283
```

APPENDIX III

*** MC68000 ***

- IMPLEMENTATION OF EQUATION (1) USING THE MULTIPLICATION INSTRUCTION
- ADDRESS REGISTER A0 POINTS AT THE LOCATIONS WHERE THE COEFFICIENTS ARE STORED. THESE ARE TWO BYTES LONG AND STORED IN THE FOLLOWING SEQUENCE: a_0,a_1,a_2,b_2,b_1.
- ADDRESS REGISTER A1 POINTS AT THE LOCATIONS WHERE THE SAMPLES ARE STORED. THESE ARE TWO BYTES LONG AND STORED IN THE FOLLOWING SEQUENCE: $y_{n-1},y_{n-2},x_{n-2},x_{n-1}$.

```
000A00   49F80900       LEA.L    $00000900,A4
000A04   47F900050000   LEA.L    $00050000,A3
000A0A   45F900040000   LEA.L.   $00040000,A2
000A10   43F80910       LEA.L    $00000910,A1
000A14   204C           MOVE.L   A4,A0            A0 POINTS AT COEF. A0                          4
000A16   4C99000F       MOVEM.W  (A1)+,D0-D3      D0←YN-1,D1←YN-2,D2←XN-2,D3←XN-1               28
000A1A   3812           MOVE.W   (A2),D4          INPUT XN                                       8
000A1C   48A19800       MOVEM.W  D0/D3-D4,-(A1)   UNIT DELAYS                                   23
000A20   C9D8           MULS.W   (A0)+,D4         D4←A0*XN                                      74 MAX
```

```
000A22    C7D8    MULS.W    (A0)+,D3    D3←A1*XN-1                74 MAX
000A24    C5D8    MULS.W    (A0)+,D2    D2←A2*XN-2                74 MAX
000A26    C3D8    MULS.W    (A0)+,D1    D1←B2*YN-2                74 MAX
000A28    C1D0    MULS.W    (A0),D0     D0←B1*YN-1                74 MAX
000A2A    D883    ADD.L     D3,D4       D4←D4+D3                   8
000A2C    D882    ADD.L     D2,D4       D4←D4+D2                   8
000A2E    9881    SUB.L     D1,D4       D4←D4-D1                   8
000A30    9880    SUB.L     D0,D4       D4←D4-D0                   8
000A32    E384    ASL.L     ≠1,D4       D4←D4*2                   10
000A34    4844    SWAP.W    D4          D4[31:16] D4[15:0]         4
000A36    3304    MOVE.W    D4,-(A1)    YN-1←YN                    9
000A38    3684    MOVE.W    D4,(A3)     OUTPUT YN                  9
000A3A    60D8    BRA.S     $000A14     BRANCH FILTER LOOP        10
                                                                 ---
                                                                 507 MAX
```

DIGITAL TECHNIQUES in Simulation, Communication and Control
Spyros G. Tzafestas (editor)
Elsevier Science Publishers B.V. (North-Holland) © IMACS, 1985

DIGITAL FILTER IMPLEMENTATION USING AN ENHANCED 16- BIT μC

Evan Zigouris[*], Keping Chen[**]

[*] Electronics Laboratory, Patras University, Patras, Greece
[**] Department of Electrical Engineering
Linköping University, Linköping, Sweden

This paper outlines how an enhanced, by a co-processor, 16-bit μC, can be effectively used to implement digital filters. This 16-bit unit performs a 50th order bandpass FIR filter at a sample rate of 22 kHz and a 6th order lowpass state-space filter at a rate up to 5 kHz. The μC does the effective handling and transfer of data and the co-processor takes care of the most time consuming operation, which is the sum-of-products one.

1. INTRODUCTION

It is well known that general purpose microprocessors are not suitable for implementing digital filters. And for the case of 8-bit μPs, this is because either they lack multiplication instructions or even when they have them, still remain time consuming. Therefore the possible to be processed signal bandwidth is limited to the low frequencies range. To increase this banwidth some techniques have already been reported /1/. In the case of 16-bit microprocessors, even if they include multiplication instructions, they are still time consuming, so they can handle bandwidths of up to a few kHz /2/. To the question, how these 16-bit CPUs can improve their ability to handle broader bandwidths, different alternatives have been proposed /3/. In our case an enhanced 16-bit μC, which is built around MC68000, and which makes use of a co-processor, has been extensively exploited /4/. Actually this system includes a "vector-multiplier", to take care of the most time consuming operation, the sum-of-products, quite often appearing in many other algorithms besides digital filtering.

2. SYSTEM OVERVIEW

The system is organized according to the block diagram shown in Figure 1. The μC is built around a 16-bit microprocessor, the MC68000. The co-processor, a PROM control store microprogrammable machine, is centered around the TRW 16*16 TDC 1010J MAC. Both, μC and co-processor are using an 8 MHz clock. The synchronization of both, the I/O data transfer and the algorithm execution, are based on the exploitation of the privileged states of the CPU.

2.1 Co-processor Architecture

The machine is a 16-bit microprogrammable processor which uses two's complement (fractional) arithmetic. It is composed of two main functional elements, the "data-unit" which performs the arithmetic processing and a "control-unit", which controls system operation under the direction of firmware, Figure 2. In supporting this machine, some memory both for the data and for the microprogram is provided. The PROM based control store, is a 64*32 PROM. On the other hand the data and coefficients memory consists of an 1K*16-bit fast RAM.

2.2 Data Unit

The heart of the Data Unit is a Multiplier-Accumulator, the TRW TDC 1010J. This device accepts two 16-bit data inputs and produces a 35-bit result including a 3-bit integer field. Today this device could be substituted by a CMOS version for lower power consumption, almost as fast as its predecessor and pin to pin compatible to it /6/, /7/. In our case in order to route both data and coefficients to the MAC inputs from the fast RAM, we use a single bus only, Figure 3.

This fast RAM in fact accepts data from different sources, from the Host processor, the MC68000 μC, from the I/O FIFO and from the MAC output. On the other hand, it supplies data, to the Host, to the MAC inputs, to the I/O FIFO and loads the pointers. It is actually addressed either from the Host or from the data pointers, or from the Control Unit directly. By using 2-bits of the microinstruction, the four possible addresses can be multiplexed to access this memory.

2.3 Control Unit

The control of the Data Unit outlined above is provided by the Control Unit, Figure 4. A bipolar microprogram controller (the Am2910 microsequencer) governs the access to the control store and thereby provides the correct sequence of control words for the Data Unit. The sequencer permits 5-levels of subroutining and also includes a 12-bit microprogram loop counter permitting up to 4096 program loops, /8/, /9/. The Am2910 receives the branch address (D-input) from one of the two sources:

- The Pipeline Register, or
- The Instruction Register

The control architecture is fully pipelined. Therefore, while the current control word residing in the pipeline register, governs the execution of a particular operation within the Data Unit, additional information, also in the current control word, instructs simultaneously the microprogram sequencer to begin fetching the next control word from the control store. In this way instruction execution and fetching is completely overlapped. The program sequencing can be modified by conditional instructions which depend on the status of particular flag. An additional 1*16 memory is used, partially to store a flag which can be tested by the Host and partially to accept from the Host the microroutine starting address (two-level migroprogramming).

2.4 Instruction Format and microroutines

Each microword, which is 32-bit wide, has been segmented into the various control fields. These fields are formed by clustering all bits that perform related functions. Actually the microprogram consists of a combination of the three following microinstruction types.

- Conditional jump
- Load "Address generator"
- Arithmetic instruction

The address generator is controlled by the microinstructions and supplies indirectly the coefficient and data addresses required for the arithmetic operations, and for the data transfer to/and from the FIFOs to memory, and to/and from the Host to the memory. The addressing mode which is actually used here, is the "Vector addressing". This mode is suitable for the realization of the digital filter algorithms. The coefficients and the state variables of the filters are stored as vectors in areas of the coefficients and data memory, and their elements must be accessed sequentially. Two control store resident microroutines, are used in realizing the chosen digital filter structures. The instruction cycle for the co-processor is 125 ns. The DOT microroutine requires therefore only (9+2*(N-1))* 125 ns, where N is the number of the vector elements. To this time we must add also, the overhead time to supply, under the Host control, the needed by the co-processor vectors, with which the pointers are loaded. At runtime when a microword is fetched from the control store, it is loaded into the pipeline register and from there the bits contained in that microword perform the intended control function. It is apparent therefore that the link between hardware and software is provided by the microword and its organization.

2.5 Input-Output

The I/O circuitry actually consists of a 10-bit A/D and a 12-bit D/A converter, plus a S/H. The In and Out of data to the system, are buffered accordingly using two 64*12 FIFOs. These are connected to the common data bus, through a tristate buffer. The control of the transfer of the data to and out the fast memory (double buffering) is due to the I/O microroutine, which takes care of it, by activating the corresponding control lines of the microinstruction.

3. LOW NOISE STATE-SPACE FILTER IMPLEMENTATION

In recent years low-noise state-space realizations of digital filters have become popular, especially in narrow-band cases. Optimum design of state-space filters, with short coefficient wordlengths, limit-cycle free, and low roundoff noise performance, have been proposed /10/. A disadvantage in implementing such filters, is that the number of multiplications which are needed, is much higher than in other approaches. A Nth order state-space filter can be described by the following state-space equations:

$$\underline{v}(k+1) = \underline{\underline{A}}\underline{v}(k) + \underline{B}x(k) \qquad (1.a)$$

$$y(k) = \underline{\underline{C}}\underline{v}(k) + Dx(k) \qquad (1.b)$$

Where v(k) is the N-element state vector, x(k) is the input signal, y(k) is the output signal. A is the NxN coefficient matrix, B, C are N-element coefficient vectors, D is a coefficient. Equations (1.a) and (1.b) can be written compactly as

NEW = G*OLD

where

NEW = (y,v1(k+1),v2(k+1)...vn(k+1))

OLD = (x,v1(k),v2(k)...vn(k))

G is N+1 order matrix.

It is clear that this structure can be realized by N+1 sum-of-products operations, with N+1 element length for each operation. The speed of implementing a state-space filter in a microcomputer is depended on two factors. One factor is the time to compute the sum-of-products, the second factor is the coefficient and data addressing (manipulation). The fundamental operation for a state-space filter is the sum-of-products. The co-processor is designed mainly to perform this operation. By giving the vector address of the multiplicand, the address of the multiplier, that of the result and the length of the sum-of-products, the co-processor can produce the result of the sum-of-products.

After every step of sum-of-products, the addresses should be adjusted accordingly for the next step. At the end of the frame, the address pointer points back to the beginning. The addressing of the results of the sum-of-products is done simply, just by increasing the pointer by one for every step of sum-of-products. The addressing of coefficients can be realized by increasing the addressing pointer by the length of N+1. N represents the order of the state-space filter. The address of the old vector remains unchanged. At the end of one frame, the first data in the results memory is sent to the output buffer. By interchanging the addresses the latest results vector becomes the old vector. Then the next data is fetched and the calculation of the next frame starts. As an example a 6th order elliptic LP state space filter has been implemented.

4. FIR FILTER IMPLEMENTATION

Because FIR digital filters can have exactly linear phase, they are of considerable interest in many applications /11/. In recent years, many approaches have been proposed for implementing FIR filters /5/, /12/, /13/. A Nth-order finite impulse response (FIR) digital filter is characterized by an input-output relationship of the form

$$y(n) = \sum_{m=0}^{N-1} h(m)x(n-m)$$

where $x(n)$ is the input, $y(n)$ the output and $h(n)$, $0 \leq n \leq N-1$, the impulse response. A direct-form realization of such a filter is shown in Figure 5. Basically, the implementation of FIR filters has two stages:
The sum-of-products operation and the performance of delays. The co-processor is very capable to do the sum-of-products operation. The delay can be realized, generally speaking, in two ways: In the most straightfoward implementation the data is shifted from memory location to memory location. This requires N-1 additional shifts (each involving a load and store) per sample for a Nth-order FIR filter. On the other hand, instead of shifting the data physically from memory to memory, the delay is realized by introducing an additional memory and making effective use of the addressing pointers. In this paper, the second approach of implementing the delay is adopted. By using N extra storage locations, as it is shown in Figure 6, the whole operation is sped up. M1 and M2 are the two memory sections, each one having the same length, M. This length is equal to the order N of the FIR filter /14/. The M1 and M2 are located in such a way that the first address of M2 is the next address of the last memory of M1. Instead of performing the delay in a straightforward manner by moving the content of the memory, it can be realized by moving the addressing pointers. Let A1 be the vector addressing data memory M1, and A2 the addressing pointer to the additional data memory M2. At the beginning, both addressing pointers are pointing to the bottom of each section of the memory. The input datum is fed into each one memory. Then the sum-of-products operation of length N is performed, starting from the address memory location pointed by A2. After one step of sum-of-products, the A1 and A2 are decreased by a word length. When A1 and A2 reach the top of each memory location, they should return to the bottom. It must be pointed out, that this delay could be also realized by running a microroutine. This would mean a further reduction in time and consequently an important increase in the signal bandwidth. As an example a 50th order bandpass FIR filter has been implemented /15/. The result is considered quite satisfactory. The sampling frequency can reach up to 22kHz.

5. CONCLUSIONS

By incorporating a microprogrammable co-processor to a general 16-bit microprocessor, it is possible to extent its capabilities to process broader signal bandwidths. If on the other hand this co-processor is designed to be digital filter algorithm oriented, this capability can be improved further.

ACKNOWLEDGEMENT

The authors wish to thank J.Arvidson and L. Dahlberg, the first of them for designing the hardware and both of them for the fruitful and creative discussions they had with them during the period this work was carried out.

REFERENCES

[1] Zigouris, E.and Deliyannis,T., "An Augmented microprocessor system for digital filter Implementation", Proc. of the 1980 European Conference on circuit theory and design, ECCTD' 80, Vol. 2, pp 539-544, Warsaw, Sept. 1980.

[2] Nagle,Jr, H.T. and Nelson, V.P., "Digital filter implementation on 16-bit microcomputers", IEEE Micro. Feb. 1981, pp 23-41.

[3] Larsson, B.O. and Johansson, A., "A microprogrammable microprocessor system for real-time signal processing", Dept. of Telecom. Theory, Royal Institute of Technology, Stockholm, Sweden, TRITTA-TTT, Dec. 1980.

[4] Chen, K. and Zigouris, E.,"Digital filter implementation using an extented 16-bit μC". Internal Report LiTH-ISY-I-0651, Linköping University, Sweden, February 1984.

[5] Roethe, N., "Architecture and programming of a multirate digital filter", Proc. of IEEE ICASSP 83, Boston, Apr. 1983, pp 427-430.

[6] TRW, LSI Multiplier-Accumulator, TRW LSI Products, Redondo Beach, CA., 90278.

[7] Analog Devices., "Cook-book Approach to Digital Filtering and DSP Applications", Norwood MA. 02062.

[8] Mick, J. and Brick, J., Bit-Slice microprocessor design, McGraw-Hill, New York 1980.

[9] Microprogram controller Am2910, AMD Sunnyvale, CA., 94026.

[10] Renfors, M., "On the design of efficient Digital Filters using Graph Theoretic Equivalence Transformations", Ph.D.diss., Tampere University of Technology, Publications No. 15, Tampere, Finland, April 1982.

[11] Oppenheim, A.V. and Schafer, R.W., Digital signal processing, Prentice-Hall Inc., Englewood Cliffs, New Jersey, USA 1975.

[12] Lim, Y.C. and Parker, S.R., "Efficient FIR implementation using microprocessor", Proc. of IEEE ICASSP 83, Boston, Apr. 1983, pp 443-446

[13] Zigouris, E.,"Digital filter implementation using the μPD 7720", Internal Report LiTH-ISY-I-0613, Linköping University, June 1983.

[14] Rabiner, L.R., "A Simplified Computational Algorithm for Implementing FIR Digital Filters", IEEE Trans. on ASSP, June 1977, pp 259-261.

[15] McClellan, J.H. Parks, T.W. and Rabiner, L.R., "A computer program for designing Optimum FIR Linear Phase Digital Filters", IEEE Trans. Audio Electroacoustic., Vol. AU-21, pp 506-526, Dec. 1973.

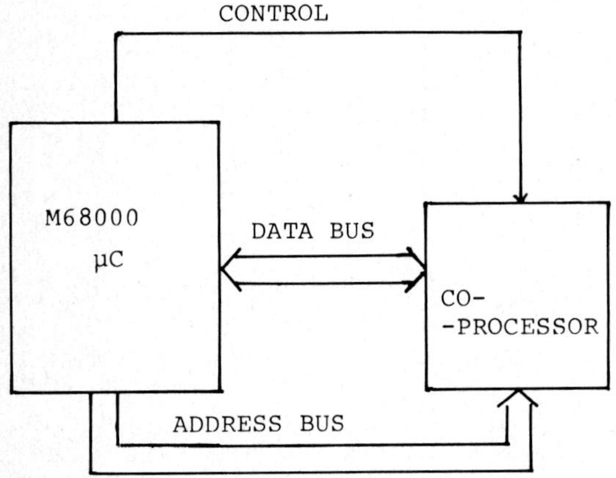

Figure 1: Block diagram of a 16-bit μC, enhanced by a co-processor

Figure 2: Block diagram architecture of the co-processor

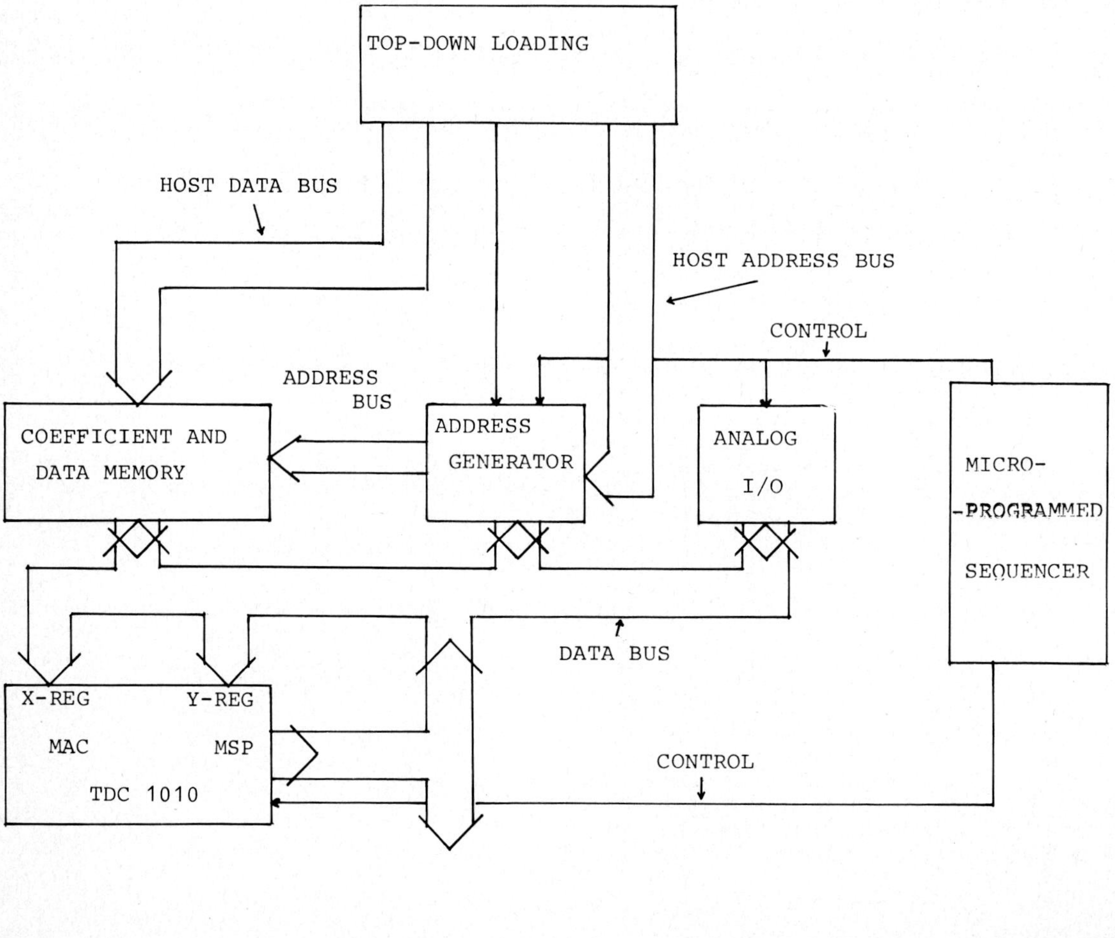

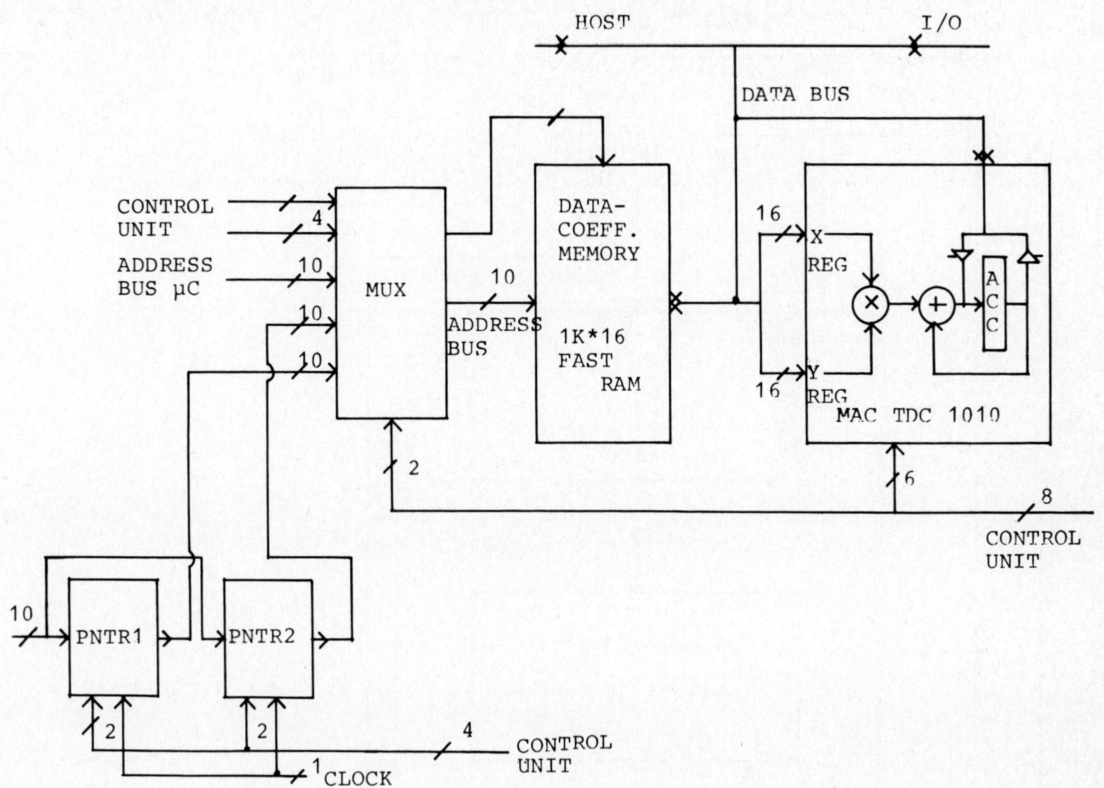

Figure 3: Data unit architecture

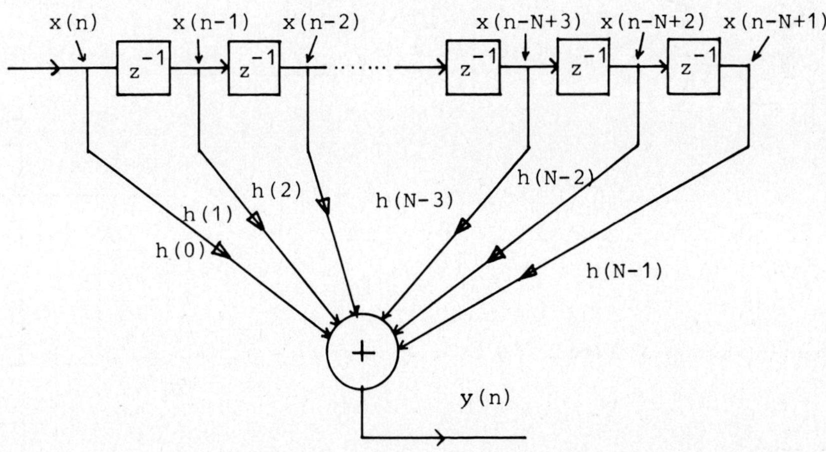

Figure 5: Direct-form realization for FIR filter

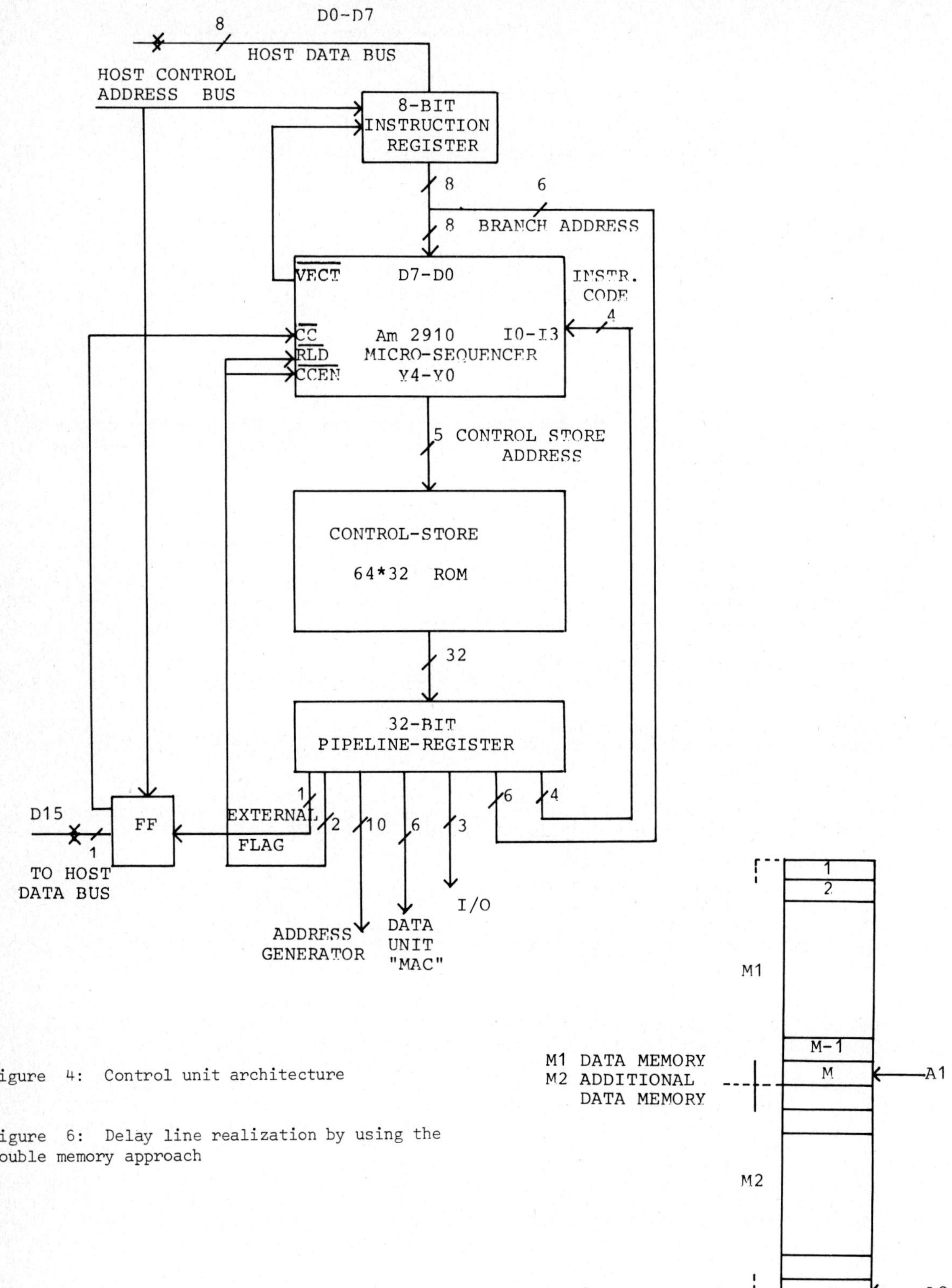

Figure 4: Control unit architecture

Figure 6: Delay line realization by using the double memory approach

DIGITAL TECHNIQUES in Simulation, Communication and Control
Spyros G. Tzafestas (editor)
Elsevier Science Publishers B.V. (North-Holland) © IMACS, 1985

NTH-BAND FIR FILTERS WITH SIMPLE COEFFICIENT RELATIONSHIPS

V. Anastassopoulos and T. Deliyannis

University of Patras, Electronics Laboratory,
Patras, Greece

Groups of Nth-band FIR filters are derived, in which most of the coefficients (in each filter) are simply related to each-other. These filters can be economically realized in the case of filtering delta-modulated signals. This is demonstrated by designing a third-band FIR filter of those derived and actually building it using general purpose integrated circuits. Experimental results are included.

1. INTRODUCTION

The main characteristics of the FIR filters, namely linear phase and absolute stability, make these filters preferable to IIR filters in some cases of signal processing, in spite of the necessity for a much higher-order FIR filter than an IIR filter for a prescribed frequency response. To improve the FIR filters with regard to this main drawback, which accordingly makes them quite demanding in terms of hardware, various methods have been developed towards either economical realizations or finding more suitable functions for these filters. The latter alternative includes the integer programming techniques and particularly the powers of two technique [1-2].

In the present paper this latter approach is exploited towards obtaining suitable functions for FIR filters by combining the Hamming window [3], properly modified, and the impulse response of the ideal lowpass filter. This way groups of FIR filter functions are obtained, in which a simple relationship (1:2) exists among most of their coefficients. The filters thus obtained are most suitable for economical realization as FIR filters for delta-modulated (d.m.) signals and this is explained by actually designing a third-band FIR filter and building it using general purpose integrated circuits (i.cs). Experimental results are also included.

2. NTH-BAND FIR FILTER GROUPS WITH SIMPLE RELATIONSHIPS AMONG THE COEFFICIENTS

In a Nth-band FIR filter, N represents the number of taps in each side lobe of the impulse response each tap corresponding to a coefficient in the filter transfer function. For N=2 the filter is called half-band, for N=3 the filter is a third-band and so on. For reasons of economy in the realization we are interested in Nth-band filters with simple relationships among most of their coefficients.

We classify here the Nth-band FIR filters in groups, each group comprising all Nth-band filters, which correspond to the same number of side-lobes in the impulse response. Thus all filters in each group correspond to the same finite impulse response, but differ in the number of coefficients in their transfer function, since their coefficients correspond to different numbers of taps in each lobe.

Nth-band FIR filters, with simple relationships among most of their coefficients, can be obtained by multiplying the impulse response of the ideal lowpass filter by a proper window function, which is suitably terminated through a computer program. The procedure is similar for all groups of this type of filters; for this reason we describe it below only for the first group.

A suitable window function for this type of application is the Hamming window given as follows:

$$w(n)=\begin{cases} 0.54+0.46\cos\frac{2\pi n}{2NK} & \text{for } |n|\leq NK \\ 0 & \text{elsewhere} \end{cases} \qquad (1)$$

On multiplying the impulse response of the ideal Nth-band filter $h'(n)$, where

$$h'(n)=\frac{1}{N}\;\frac{\sin(n\pi/N)}{n\pi/N} \qquad (2)$$

by the Hamming window w(n) the Nth-band FIR filter impulse response h(n) is obtained, i.e.

$$h(n)=h'(n)w(n) \qquad (3)$$

On calculating h(n) from(3)for various values of K we have determined that the first group of Nth-band FIR filters with a simple relationship among most of their coefficients is obtained for K=7 in (1). In this case for the right-of-the-centre lobes

$$h(n+N)\simeq-\frac{h(n)}{2}\;,\quad n>N \qquad (4)$$

and for the left-of-the-centre lobes

$$h(n-N)\simeq-\frac{h(n)}{2}\;,\quad |n|>N \qquad (5)$$

The interpretation of eqns (4) and (5) is that

coefficients of the filter obtained from a certain lobe of the impulse response are, to a very good approximation, one-half the corresponding coefficients, which are obtained from the lobe adjacent to it on the side of the centre lobe.

Other groups of Nth-band FIR filters are obtained by selecting suitable values of K in eqn.(1) greater than 7. Such values of K, which determine the termination of the Hamming window and thus the impulse response of the FIR filters, are found through computer minimization of the sum

$$\sum_{n=-\frac{M-1}{2}}^{\frac{M-1}{2}} |h(n)-a_n|$$

where h(n) is as given by eqn (3) and a_n is the value of the corresponding coefficient as it is calculated from eqns (4) or (5) in the regions of their validity. In the above sum M is the number of coefficients in the filter given by

$$M=2(SL+1)N+1 \tag{6}$$

where SL is the number of lobes on each side of the main lobe in the impulse response.

It has thus been determined that the other groups of Nth-band FIR filters with the required property are obtained for values of SL which are multiples of six. It should be pointed out that in these cases the value of K is not the one corresponding to the Hamming window, but it has been adjusted to result in the simple (1:2) relationship among most of the coefficients of the filter. Fortunately this adjustment of K does not reduce the minimum attenuation appreciably; it remains around 45dB.

3. REALIZATION OF DERIVED FILTERS FOR DELTA-MODULATED SIGNALS

The FIR filters, which were developed in the previous section, can be very economically realized in the case of filtering delta-modulated (d.m) signals. [4]. As in the case of digital filtering, certain circuits are required for perfoming the arithmetic operations implied by the filter transfer function. The required circuits here are delta-adders, delta-multipliers and delays. These circuits have, in fact, been developed in recent years and can be realized using general purpose integrated circuits.

The circuit of delta-adder [5] is shown in Figure 1. It consists of a conventional full-adder (FA) and a D. flip-flop. The sum (S_n) and carry (C_n) outputs of the delta-addition are obtained from the carry and sum outputs of the FA respectively, but with the observation that in actual fact half-sums are obtained rather than full sums of the under addition delta sequences. However this turns out to be an advantage rather than a disadvantage in bulding multipliers for delta signals by numbers smaller than unity. Such a delta-multiplier can be realized [5] using delta-adders only, as it is shown in Figure 2

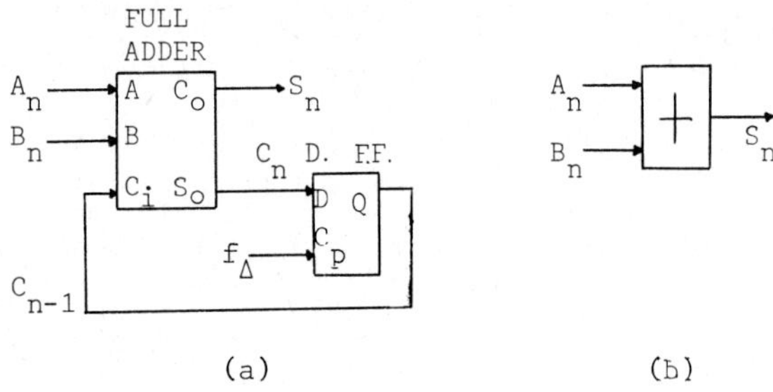

Figure 1: a) Delta-adder, and b) its symbol.

in the case of multiplying the delta-sequence X_n by the constant $(0.1011)_2$ or $(0.6875)_{10}$. Multiplication is carried-out in levels, for all bits of the constant starting with the LSB. When a bit is 1 the delta sequence is entering the adder corresponding to the weight of the bit in the multiplying constant, whereas, when it is 0, the idling pattern sequence $\{I_n\}$ is used instead.

However, it is possible on realizing a FIR d.m. filter all necessary multiplications to be carried out in a combined manner using one multiplier circuit only, which is then called the interconnected multiplier [6] (perhaps the term combined-multiplier would have been more suitable). The method of designing such a multiplier is similar to that in Figure 2, it is based on the same principle described above and the circuit is built also out of adders only. The realization of the FIR d.m filter is thus becoming more economical compared to the realization using separate multipliers.

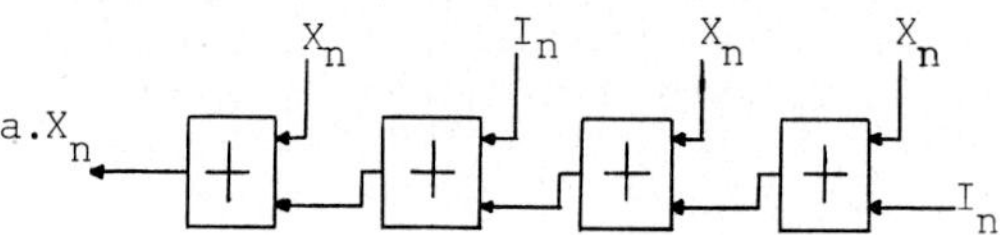

Figure 2: A circuit for multiplying delta samples X_n times the constant $a=(0.1011)_2$

Finally the delays are easily implemented using shift-registers, which are available as general purpose integrated circuits. Thus the realization of a Nth-band FIR filter for d.m. signals is possible and this is demonstrated by means of a third-band FIR filter.

3.1 Third-band FIR d.m. filter with M=43

The d.m. sequence at the filter output is given in terms of the input d.m. sequence as follows:

$$Y_n = \sum_{-\frac{M-1}{2}}^{\frac{M-1}{2}} a_i X_{n-im} \qquad (7)$$

where a_i, $i = -\frac{M-1}{2}, \ldots 0, \ldots \frac{M-1}{2}$ are the coefficients of the filter as obtained from the filter impulse response by taping each lobe at three points for the third-band filter case. Since M=43, there are six lobes on each side of the main lobe in the impulse response, as it is shown in Figure 3. This response has been obtained according to the method suggested in Section 2. Because of the approximate relationship among the coefficients, the required coefficients, obtained by tapping the central lobe and the two adjacent to it side lobes, are as given in Table I. Also in Table I the non-zero coefficients related to each-other are given. The zero coefficients are included in the table too.

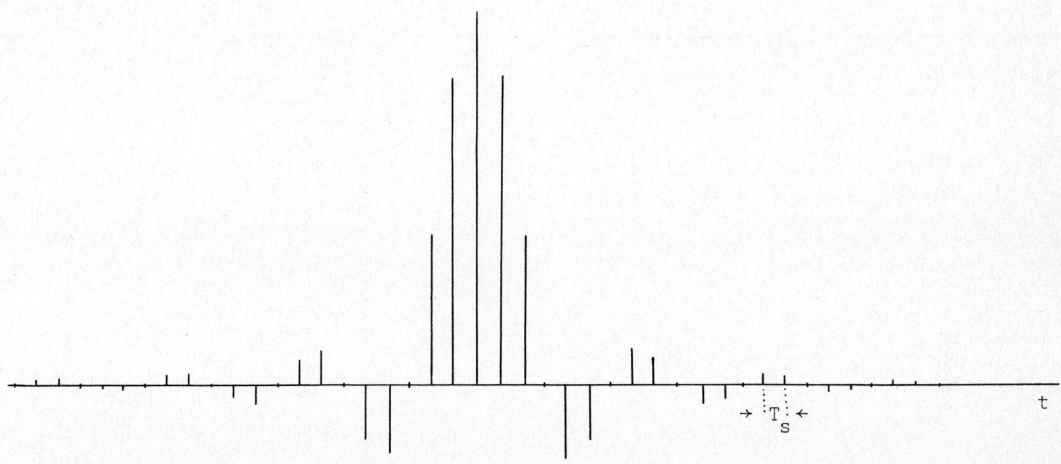

Figure 3. Impulse response of a third-band FIR filter with M = 43.

TABLE I

coefficient	decimal	binary
a_o	.3330078	.0101010101
$a_{\pm1}$	.2734375	.0100011
$a_{\pm2}$	.1347656	.001000101
$a_{\pm4}$	-.0625	-.0001
$a_{\pm5}$	-.046875	-.000011
$a_{\pm19} = -\frac{1}{2} a_{\pm16} = \frac{1}{4} a_{\pm13} = -\frac{1}{8} a_{\pm10} = \frac{1}{16} a_{\pm7} = -\frac{1}{32} a_{\pm4}$		
$a_{\pm20} = -\frac{1}{2} a_{\pm17} = \frac{1}{4} a_{\pm14} = -\frac{1}{8} a_{\pm11} = \frac{1}{16} a_{\pm8} = -\frac{1}{32} a_{\pm5}$		
$a_{\pm21} = a_{\pm18} = a_{\pm15} = a_{\pm12} = a_{\pm9} = a_{\pm6} = a_{\pm3} = 0$		

In eqn. (7) m is the ratio of the sampling frequency f_Δ in the delta-encoder to the sampling frequency f_s of the FIR filter. For low noise m must be as high as possible. Here it is selected to be 128, which, for f_s=1kHz, makes the required sampling frequency in the delta-encoder equal to $f_\Delta = 128$ kHz.

In order to take advantage of the possibility to use the interconnected multiplier in the realization of the filter we pursue the following procedure: We first form the following sums:

$$V_n = -\frac{1}{2} X_{n+5m} + \frac{1}{4} X_{n+8m} - \frac{1}{8} X_{n+11m} + \frac{1}{16} X_{n+14m} - \frac{1}{32} X_{n+17m} + \frac{1}{64} X_{n+20m}$$

$$V'_n = -\frac{1}{2} X_{n-4m} + \frac{1}{4} X_{n-7m} - \frac{1}{8} X_{n-10m} + \frac{1}{16} X_{n-13m} - \frac{1}{32} X_{n-16m} + \frac{1}{64} X_{n-19m}$$

These signals are next delayed by T_s giving

$$V''_n = -\frac{1}{2} X_{n+4m} + \frac{1}{4} X_{n+7m} - \frac{1}{8} X_{n+10m} + \frac{1}{16} X_{n+13m} - \frac{1}{32} X_{n+16m} + \frac{1}{64} X_{n+19m}$$

$$V'''_n = -\frac{1}{2} X_{n-5m} + \frac{1}{4} X_{n-8m} - \frac{1}{8} X_{n-11m} + \frac{1}{16} X_{n-14m} - \frac{1}{32} X_{n-17m} + \frac{1}{64} X_{n-20m}$$

Finally the following sums are formed:

$$Z_n = \frac{V_n + V'''_n}{2}$$

$$Z'_n = \frac{V'_n + V''_n}{2}$$

All these operations are performed by means of the circuit shown in Figure 4. Also in a side circuit the following sums are obtained:

$$Q_n = \frac{1}{2}(X_{n-2m} + X_{n+2m})$$

$$Q'_n = \frac{1}{2}(X_{n-m} + X_{n+m})$$

All signals Z_n, Z'_n, Q_n, Q'_n and X_n are fed to the interconnected multiplier as shown in Figure 5. In this they are multiplied respectively by $4a_5$, $4a_4$, $2a_2$, $2a_1$ and a_o, the modified coefficients a_5, a_4, a_2, a_1 and a_o, in order to take care of the division by 2 in some of the adders, when these signals are formed that has not been taken care-of already in the same corresponding circuits. For this same purpose a doubler [7] may be included in the circuit of the interconnected multiplier, as is shown also in Figure 5, to compensate, for the result of the last addition in this multiplier if this is considered necessary.

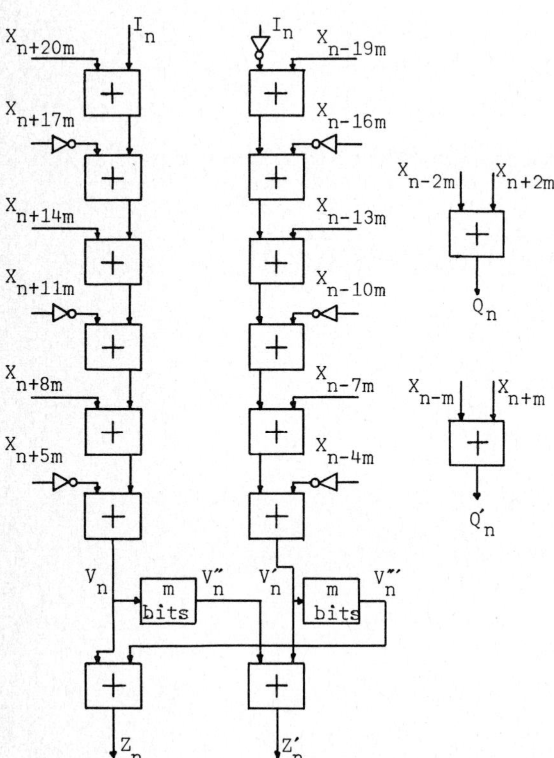

Figure 4: Circuits performing required additions of delta samples for effective use of interconnected multiplier in the step of filter implementation that follows this step.

The overall circuit was actually built using available general purpose integrated circuits (MC 14008 FAs, MC 14013 DFF, MC 14517 Shift Registers) and tested. Its frequency response is as shown in Figure 6 which is considered satisfactory.

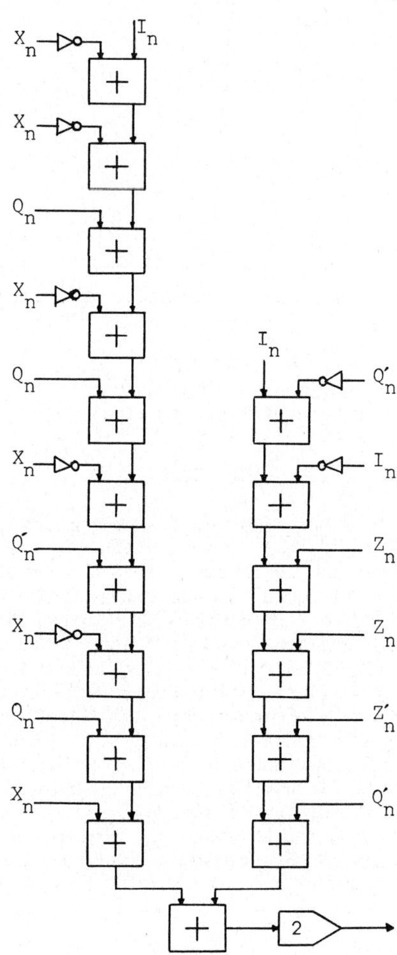

Figure 5: Circuit of the interconnected multiplier.

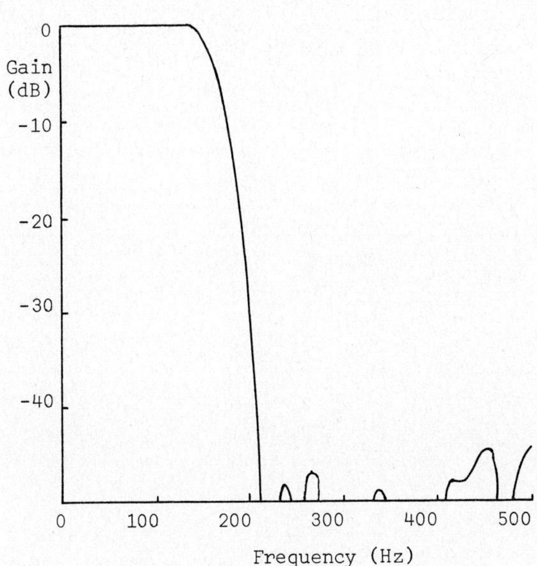

Figure 6: Frequency response of the third-band d.m. FIR filter with M = 43.

4. COMMENTS AND CONCLUSIONS

In Section 2 it was shown that by properly adjusting the Hamming window, useful Nth-band FIR filters can be obtained from the impulse response of the ideal lowpass filter. These filters can be economically realized as d.m. filters, and this was demonstrated by building a third-band FIR filter belonging to the first group. A half-band and a fourth-band filters belonging to the same group with the third-band filter were also realized as d.m. filters by the method explained in Section 3.1, and subsequently built using the same types of integrated circuits. These were then tested and found to work satisfactorily. Since only general purpose i.cs are used in the implementation of these filters, it is clear that they can be produced as custom made i.cs.

REFERENCES

[1] Kodek, D.M: "Design of Optimal Finite Wordlength FIR Digital Filters using Integer Programming Techniques", IEEE Trans. on Acoustics, Speech, and Signal Processing, Vol. ASSP-28, No. 3, pp 304-307, June 1980.

[2] Lim, Y.C., Parker S.R., Constantinides, A.G: "Finite Word Length FIR Filter Design using Integer Programming over a discrete Coefficient Space" IEEE Trans. on Acoustics, Speech, and Signal Processing, Vol. ASSP-30, No 4, pp 661-664, August 1982.

[3] Antoniou, A: "Digital filter analysis and design" McGrqw-Hill Inc. 1979.

[4] Steele, R: "Delta modulation systems" Pentech Press, London 1975.

[5] Kouvaras, N.: "Operations on Delta-modulated signals and their application in the realization of digital filters" The Radio and Elect. Eng., Vol. 48, No 9, pp 431-438, Sept 1978.

[6] Kouvaras, N.: "Some rovel elements for Delta-modulated signal processing". The Radio and Elect. Eng., Vol. 51, No 5, pp 241-249, May 1981.

[7] Kouvaras, N.: "A special purpose delta multiplier" The Radio and Elect. Eng., Vol. 51, No 5, pp 241-249, May 1981.

DIGITAL TECHNIQUES in Simulation, Communication and Control
Spyros G. Tzafestas (editor)
Elsevier Science Publishers B.V. (North-Holland) © IMACS, 1985

USE OF THE BILINEAR TRANSFORM TO OBTAIN SC FILTERS FROM ANALOG CBR FILTERS

S. Fotopoulos and T. Deliyannis

University of Patras,
Electronics Laboratory
Patras, Greece

Two prospective methods for designing Switched-Capacitor (SC) Cascade of Biquartic Sections (CBR) filters using the bilinear transform are examined. The method of transforming the whole continuous Biquartic Section (BR) to its corresponding SC one is preferable to the method of replacing all resistors in the continuous circuit by switched-capacitors through the application of bilinear-transform. A design example is given for the former method. The pertinent circuit was examined using the SWITCAP program. Results seem promising.

1. INTRODUCTION

An active RC network can be converted to a SC active network by substituting each resistor with a combination of switches and a capacitor [1]. But to get good results the frequency of changing the states of the switches f_s should be much higher than the highest frequency of interest f in the signal i.e. $f_s \gg f$. Even then however the results cannot be considered satisfactory, because of the effect of parasitics on the circuit performance [2].

When the frequency of switching cannot be much higher than the highest frequency of interest f in the signal, the direct substitution of the resistors in the active RC network with combinations of switches and capacitors can be effected through the use of the bilinear transformation [3].

However better results are obtained if the active RC filter is transformed to a SC one as a whole by means of the bilinear transformation of its transfer function.

The purpose of this paper is to give the guidelines for designing cascade of biquartic sections filters [4] as SC networks. In what follows the design of CBR filters is reviewed briefly and then the procedure for deriving CBR SC filters using the bilinear z-transform is explained.

2. CBR ACTIVE RC FILTERS

High-order filter functions can be realized by cascading fourth-order sections and depending on the order, a second and / or a first-order sections. Each fourth-order section is called a biquartic section (BR) and, for low sensitivity reasons, is realized in the form of the block diagram shown in Figure 1. Suitable low sensitivity one-, two- or three- operational amplifier biquads are used in the corresponding blocks in Figure 1.

In the case of bandpass filters, which have been obtained by the application of the usual lowpass-to-bandpass transformation to all pole lowpass filters, the present authors have optimized the

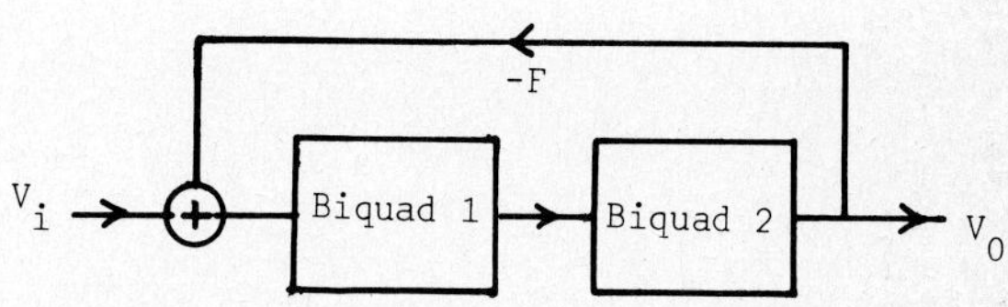

Figure 1: Block diagram of a BR stage.

design with respect to sensitivity and noise created inside the filter [4]-[6]. Their optimization procedure leads also to near minimum distortion of the signal passing through the filter.

Very briefly this procedure is as follows: Once the bandpass function has been obtained by the lowpass-to-bandpass trasformation to an all-pole filter function, the pairs of poles with equal Q factors are grouped together to form the denomimator polynomial of the birquartic functions. To each such function two zeros at the origin and two at infinity are assigned to form the biquartic function. Each biquartic function is then realized as the biquartic section in Figure 1, in which the negative feedback is selected in such a way that the two biquads inside the loop are identical. If Q is the common Q factor of the two pairs of poles in the biquartic function and ω_1, ω_2 the corresponding pole-frequencies, the necessary feedback to result in identical biquads is given by

$$F = \frac{1}{h'_1 h'_2}(\omega_1-\omega_2)^2 \left(1-\frac{1}{4Q^2}\right) \qquad (1)$$

where h'_1, h'_2 are the gain constants of the two

biquads. The overall filter is optimized with respect to minimum distortion of the signal by assigning suitable gain factors to each biquartic section and consequently to each biquadratic section. Then according to the value of the Q factors of the biquadratic functions in Figure 1, one-, two-or three- operational amplifier biquads are used in the realization of biquartic functions. An economical but practical BR section suitable for biquads with Q<30 is shown in Figure 2.

In terms of Laplace Transform we may write for the charge

$$Q_m(s) = \frac{G_m}{s} V_m(s) = \frac{R_m}{s} I_m(s) \tag{2}$$

If resistor R_m is substituted by a SC C_m, Figure 3.b, we may write in terms of z - transform for the charge

$$Q_m(z) = C_m \frac{b_1 z + b_o}{a_1 z + a_o} V_m(z) \tag{3}$$

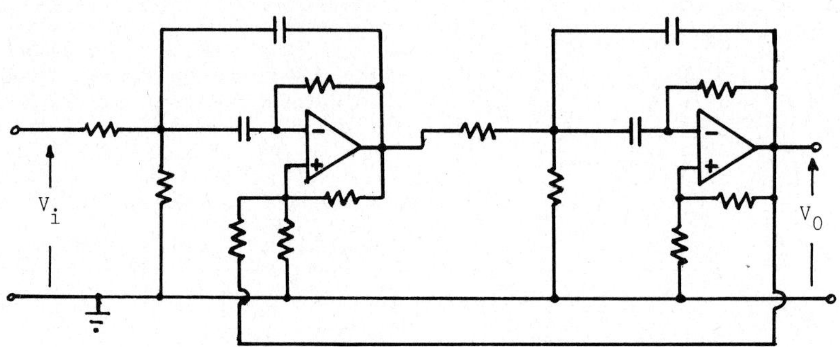

Figure 2: A practical BR section for Q<30 in each biquad.

3. CBR SC FILTERS

A CBR SC filter can be obtained from the correspondig active RC CBR filter using the bilinear transform in the following ways according to the indirect method of designing SC networks:

a. Each resistor in the prototype active RC network is substituted by a bilinear resistor [3], [7] i.e. a SC equivalent resistor obtained through the use of bilinear transform.
b. Each BR stage in the prototype block diagram is bilinearly transformed to a SC block diagram and the biquadratic sections in the new diagram are realized using known SC biquads [8], [9].

These two methods are explained to some detail below.

3.1 Resistor substitution in a BR stage by Switched-Capacitors

Consider resistor R_m in a BR stage in an active RC filter as it is shown in Figure 3a.

For the two charges to be equivalent we may write

$$Q_m(z) = \frac{G_m}{F(z)} . V_m(z) \tag{4}$$

when

$$\frac{G_m}{F(z)} = C_m \frac{b_1 z + b_o}{a_1 z + a_o} \tag{5}$$

Now for simplicity let

$$C_m b_1 = C_m b_o = \frac{G_m T}{2}, \qquad a_1 = - a_2 = 1 \tag{6}$$

where T is half the switching period T_s, i.e. T is the time within which switches change position once. Substituting values in eqn (5) gives

$$F(z) = \frac{2}{T} \frac{z-1}{z+1}$$

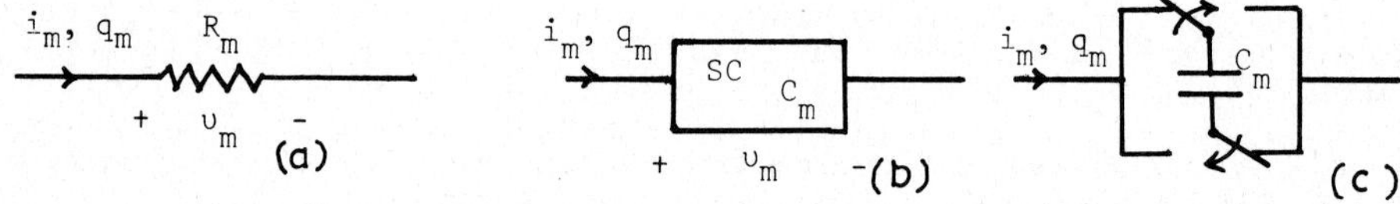

Figure 3: a) A conventional resistor b) its SC equivalent and c) practical SC arrangement.

which is the bilinear z-transform.

But within the switching period T_S all switches change potition twice. Then the value of the equivalent switched-capacitor C_m will be from eqn (6).

$$C_m = \frac{G_m T}{2} = \frac{G_m T_s}{4} = \frac{1}{4 f_s R_m} \qquad (7)$$

The switched-capacitor arrangement is in practice as shown in Figure 3.c.

Then the proceduce for designing a SC CBR filter by the resistor substitution method is as follows:

a. Given the SC filter specifications, passband and stopband characteristic frequencies ω_{pi}, ω_{si}, i=1,2,...are translated to the corresponding frequencies Ω_{pi}, Ω_{si}, i=1,2,.... of the continuous time CBR filter through the formula

$$\Omega = \frac{2}{T} \tan \left(\frac{\omega T}{2}\right) \qquad (8)$$

b. The CBR active RC filter is then designed according to the procedure explained in section 2.
c. Next each resistor R_m in the CBR filter is substituted by a switched-capacitor C_m as shown in Figure 3.c, the value of which is given by eqn (7).
d. A sample-and-hold circuit may be required to precede the SC CBR filter. Usually a continuous time smoothing filter (e.g. a simple RC) is added at the output of the filter.

The following points should be noted on the above procedure: If the switching frequency is selected much higher (>100 times) than the highest frequency of interest in the filter response then the first step in the procedure is unecessary.

An undesired charge leakage, due to the fact that the switches do not remain in their positions at the sampling instances only, may lead to unsatisfactory operation of the SC filter. This can be avoided by cascading the filter by a sample-and-hold circuit, the response of which, however, has to be considered in the design procedure. Obviously the described procedure is general and does not apply only to SC CBR filters.

There are some disadvantages in this method of designing SC CBR filters namely:

a. It may require the realization of floating capacitors, which creates manufacturing problems in MOS technology and sensitivity to parasitics.
b. Biquads with operational amplifiers having ungrounded input terminals should be avoided in the realization of the BR stages and this may lead to uneconomical designs, increased power consumption etc.

These disadvantages are not present in the method of designing SC CBR circuits which is described next.

3.2 BR stage transformation as a whole

The second method using the bilinear transform to obtain a SC BR stage is as follows: Once the biquartic function is known in the analog domain, it is realized as usual in block diagram form. Then the bilinear transform is applied to the function of each biquadratic block, which is thus transformed to a biquadratic function in the z-domain. Each of these functions is then realized using one of the known biquadratic SC circuits. Because of the overall negative feedback applied to each BR section one of the two biquadratic sections inside the loop must have negative gain and the other positive gain. The negative feedback is then applied in the same manner the input signal is applied to the first biquad. Depending on the type of biquad which is first in the cascade a sample-and-hold circuit may be required between the signal source and the BR section.

This procedure is applied similarly to the design of the other BR sections of the overall filter, all the BR sections are then cascaded as in the case of cascading SC biquads.

If the SC biquads used in the realization of the biquartic sections are parasiticsinsensitive the overall CBR filter will be paraciticsinsensitive also.

As an example consider that the transfer function of a BR section is the continuous 4th-order bandpass function, which has been obtained by applying the lowpass to-bandpass transformation

$s_n \to 10\left(\frac{s^2+1}{s}\right)$ to the second-order Butterworth lowpass function. Following the usual procedure for the realization of this function as a BR stage [4] the continuous filter in block-diagram

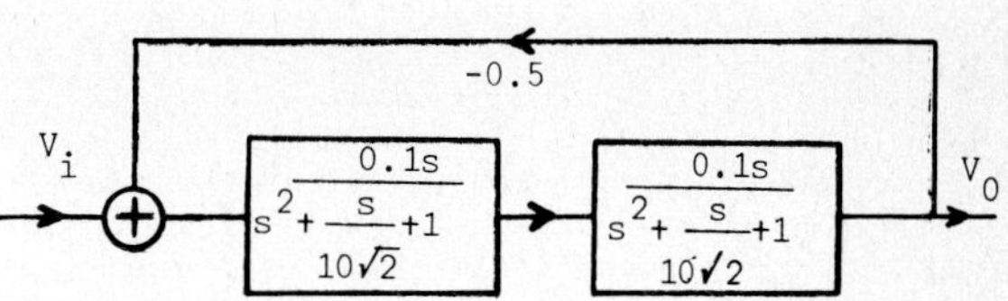

Figure 4: The BR stage in block diagram realizing a 4th-order Butterworth bandpass filter.

form is as shown in Figure 4. Applying the bilinear z-transform

$$s \to \frac{2}{T}\,\frac{z-1}{z+1}$$

to the transfer function of each biquad the following biquadratic function in the z-domain is obtained:

$$F(z) = \frac{k\,(z^2-1)}{z^2 - b_1 z + b_0} \qquad (9)$$

where

$$k = \frac{0.1(T/2)}{1+a(T/2)+(T/2)^2}$$

$$b_1 = 2\frac{1-(T/2)^2}{1+\alpha(T/2)+(T/2)^2}$$

$$b_o = \frac{1-\alpha(T/2)+(T/2)^2}{1+\alpha(T/2)+(T/2)^2}$$

$$a = 1/10\sqrt{2}$$

A SC biquad [9],[10] that can realize this transfer function is shown in Figure 5. If the output is obtained from node (5) the gain is negative, whereas positive gain is obtained from node (3). It is clear that a S/H circuit

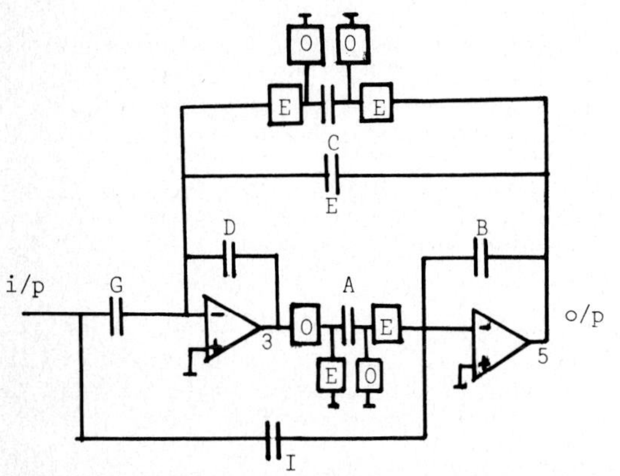

Figure 5: A SC biquad useful in practice

should precede this biquad. The boxes labelled E or O in the figure signify switches, which are closed during the (E) or the odd (O) phase respectively.

The design of the two biquads required in the realization of the biquartic stage is effected by matching the coefficients of the network T.Fs (positive and negative gain) with the coefficients of the function in eqn (9) provided the values of sampling frequency and the filter center frequency are known. Selecting the centre frequency at 1kHz and the sampling frequency at 100kHz the coefficients of the function in eqn (9) are calculated and, on matching these with the coefficients of the biquad transfer function, the capacitor values for each biquad corresponding to the overall SC filter shown in Figure 6 are given in Table I. It should be said that from this coefficient matching only capacitor ratios are calculated. From these capacitor ratios and assuming that the values of capacitors $B_1 = D_1 = 100$pF, $i = 1,2$ the capacitor values in Table I have been calculated. Also because the number of unknown capacitor ratios in each biguad is higher than the number of equations obtained from the coefficient matching, some "arbitrary" assumptions are innevitable, but they have to be made carefully to avoid excessive ranges of capacitor ratios.

TABLE I Capacitances in pf

Capacitor	Biquad 1	Biquad 2
A_i	6.26897	6.26897
B_i	100	100
C_i	6.26897	6.26897
D_i	100	100
E_i	7.06655	7.06655
G_{01}	9.98569	
I_{01}	0.313	
I_{12}		9.98569
G_{12}		1.01864
G_{21}	4.99285	
I_{21}	0.1565	

The overall network was tested using the program SWITCAP and its frequency response is shown in Figure 7 together with the frequency response of the corresponding ideal continuous filter.

It is clear from Figure 6 that there are no floating capacitors in the circuit, whereas all operational amplifiers used are single-input (the non-inverting input is grounded). Therefore the overall circuit is parasitics insensitive.

4. COMMENTS AND CONCLUSIONS

A CBR active RC filter can be transformed to a SC filter using the bilinear transform. The method of transforming the block diagram of each BR stage seems preferable because it leads to parasitics insensitive SC filters provided that parasitics insensitive biquads are used in the realization. It may also result to more economical filters with regard to the number of switches required in the realization.

The results presented here should be regarded as preliminary and the authors are aware that a lot is needed to be done to establish the SC CBR filters as useful filters in practice. Since the method is based on the bilinear z-transform it is expected, that there will be no inherent distortion or higher sensitivity to element variations resulting from imperfect modeling of the continuous time CBR filter. It is to the authors's intentions though to examine in detail the SC CBR filter. Sensitivity to capacitor ratios, noise performance, optimization with

with respect to the range of capacitor values, minimization of total capacitance, dynamic range etc are to be studied in detail.

ACHNOWLEDGEMENTS

The authors are indebted to Dr. D.Haigh and

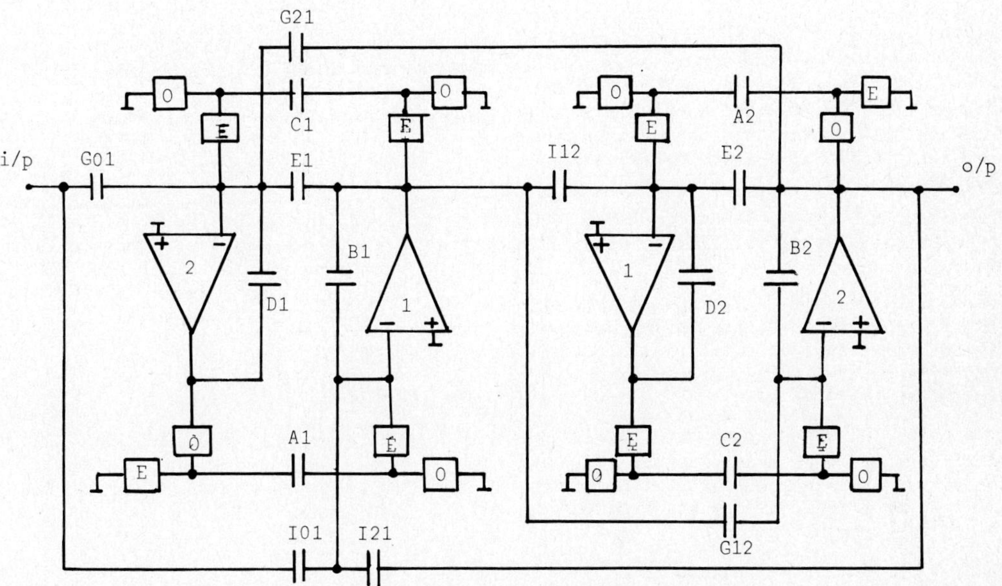

Figure 6: A SC realization of the BR stage in Figure 4

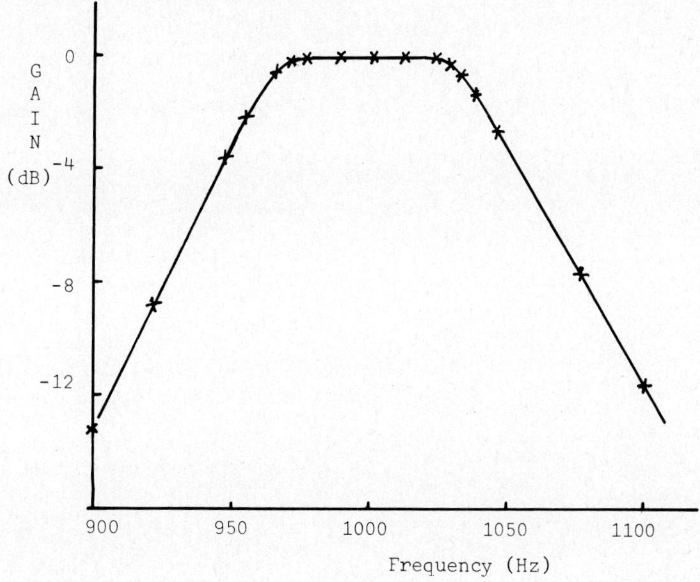

Figure 7: Frequency responses of the SC filter in Figure 6 (crosses) obtained using the SWITCAP program and of the corresponding continuous time ideal filter

Mr. J. Franca for many useful discussions on SC filters. They also thank J. Franka for designing the two SC biquads and for checking the circuit in Figure 6 using the SWITCAP program at Imperial College, London.

REFERENCES

[1] Caves, J.T, Copeland, M.A. Rahim, C.F and Rosenbaum, S.D., "Sampled analog filtering using Switched Capacitors as switched resistors" IEEE Jrnl. Solid-State Circuits SC-12 592-599, Dec. 1977.

[2] Brodersen, R.W. Gray, P.R and Holges, D.A., "MOS Switched Capacitor filters" Proc. IEEE, 67, 61-75 Jan. 1979.

[3] Temes, G.C. Orchard, H.J. and Jahanbegloo, M. "Switched-Capacitor Filter Design using the bilinear z-tranform" IEEE Trans. on Circuits and Systems, Vol. CAS 25, No 12, pp 1039-1044, Dec. 1978.

[4] Fotopoulos, S. and Deliyannis, T., "Active-RC realization of high order bandpass filter functions by cascading biquartic sections" Intl. J. on Circuit Theory and Applications (accepted for publication).

[5] Deliyannis, T. and Fotopoulos, S., "High order filter realization by cascading biquartic sections" Proc. ELLTD 81, Hague, 25-28 Aug. 1981, pp 962-966.

[6] Deliyannis, T. and Fotopoulos, S., "Noise in the cascade of biquartic section filter" IEE Proc. Vol. 128, Pt G, No 4, pp 192-194, Aug. 1981.

[7] Temes, G., "The derivation of switched capacitor filters from active-RC prototypes" Elect. letters Vol. 14, No 12, pp 361-362 8th June 1978.

[8] Martin, K. and Sedra, A.S., "Exact design of switched capacitor bandpass filters using coupled biquad structures" IEEE Trans. on circuits and systems CAS-27, 469-475 June 1980.

[9] Ghausi, M.S. and Laker, K.R., "Modern filter design" Englewood Cliffs, N.J. Prentice Hall, 1981.

[10] Fleischer, P.E. and Laker, K.R., "A family of active switched-capacitor biquad building blocks" Bell Syst. Tech. J. 58, pp 2235-2269 December 1979.

DIGITAL TECHNIQUES in Simulation, Communication and Control
Spyros G. Tzafestas (editor)
Elsevier Science Publishers B.V. (North-Holland) © IMACS, 1985

BINARY LOGARITHM-BASED COMPUTING SYSTEMS:APPLICATION TO DIGITAL FILTER IMPLEMENTATION

S. G. Tzafestas
Control Systems Laboratory
University of Patras
Patras, Greece

G. P. Frangakis
Computer Department
NRC "Demokritos"
Aghia Paraskevi, Attiki, Greece

This paper is devoted to the study of the binary logarithmic coding of binary numbers, and reviews the various available approximation methods for the fast computation of the logarithm and antilogarithm of a given number. Error considerations for the log-antilog conversion, as well as for the multiplication, division, addition and power/root calculation by means of it are included. From among the various digital hardware set-ups for log-antilog operation, the most recent one [7] is discussed, which is fast and needs a small amount of logic circuitry. Finally, the application of log-based computation (log-antilog conversion and logarithmic number systems) to digital filtering is considered and a number of important conclusions are presented.

1. INTRODUCTION

The two principal factors influencing the complexity and cost of digital filters are *accuracy* and *speed*. In a filter where standard linear fixed-point arithmetic is used the accuracy of a number depends on its magnitude and so the dynamic range of the filter is strongly limited, if a high S/N ratio is desirable. As it is known, in linear arithmetic the numbers in registers are directly proportional to the amplitudes of the variables (signals) that are stored in them.

The present paper is concerned with the logarithmic representation of numbers (i. e. the numbers in registers are proportional to the logarithm of the signal amplitude) which offers a considerable increase in the dynamic range of digital computation and filtering [1-9]. Of course, using floating-point arithmetic one can increase accuracy at the expense of speed, but it was shown in [9] that using logarithmic arithmetic algorithms one can have accuracy with speed as required in most real-time digital signal processing applications. Actually Lee and Edgar [9] have developed appropriate software algorithms for implementing 8-bit and 16-bit logarithmic processing on Intel MDS-800 8-bit microcomputer.

For those situations where the speed of computation is much more important than the accuracy (e.g. in real time digital filtering of radar video for moving target detection, synthetic aperture processing, and pulse compression), a number of approximation techniques have been proposed for the fast computation of the binary logarithms and antilogarithms [1-7]. These techniques, together with the available hardware implementations, will be presented here in a review form, along with their error considerations. In particular the use logarithm-based computing units to digital filtering is studied and the resulting accumulated roundoff errors are discussed.

To appreciate right from the beginning the large increase of the dynamic range (i.e. of the largest positive number divided by the smallest positive number) of logarithm-based calculations, let us consider a filter implemented with 16-bit words, with desired accuracy 0.1% [2]. If the maximum number of the calculations must not exceed ±32768, for accuracy 0.1% =0.001 the maximum dynamic range using linear arithmetic is 32:1 under the condition of perfect scaling throughout the filter. To obtain an accuracy of 0.1% in logarithm-based calculations one needs 10 bits for the mantissa of the logarithm (since $1.001 \simeq \exp(2^{-10})) = \exp(1/1024))$, while one bit is needed for the sign of the signal and another bit is (usually) required to indicate whether or not the signal has zero value (to avoid the calculation of $\log 0 = -\infty$). Thus four bits are available for the characteristic of the logarithm which implies that a maximum dynamic range of signals equal to $\exp(2^4) \simeq 9.000.000$ can be achieved. In practice, in order to ensure that the discontinuity near zero is less than 0.1% of a signal the dynamic range is reduced to 9000:1. If the zero/nonzero bit is used in the characteristic the total range becomes $\exp(2^5) \simeq (9.000.000)^2 = 8.1 \times 10^{13}$. The discontinuity near zero is twice the smallest value and so the dynamic range becomes $8 \times 10^{13} : 2 \times 10^3 = 4 \times 10^{10}$.

2. LOGARITHM-BASED APPROXIMATE BINARY CODING

2.1. Logarithmic Binary Coding

Let N be a nonzero finite length binary number of the form

$$N=\sum_{i=j}^{r} J_i 2^i \qquad (r\geq j) \tag{1}$$

where $J_i=0$ or 1 (J_i is the ith bit of N), J_j is the least significant bit (LSB) and J_r is the most significant bit (MSB). Clearly

$$2^j\leq N\leq 2^{r+1}$$

If J_k is the most significant "1" of N ($r\geq k\geq j$) then

$$N=2^k+\sum_{i=j}^{k-1} J_i 2^i \tag{2}$$

which can be written as

$$N=2^k(1+\sum_{i=j}^{k-1} J_i 2^{i-k})=2^k(1+x) \tag{3}$$

where

$$0\leq x=\sum_{i=j}^{k-1} J_i 2^{i-k}<1 \text{ since } j\leq k \tag{4}$$

The exact binary logarithm $\log_2 N\triangleq \lg N$ of N is given by

$$\lg N=k+\lg(1+x) \tag{5}$$

where k is the logarithm characteristic and the mantissa is only a function of x.

In the following we briefly outline four methods of approximating lgN of eqn. (5) by a linear or piece-wise-linear function of x.

Method 1 (Mitchell [4])

This is based on the approximation

$$\lg(1+x)\simeq x, \quad 0\leq x<1 \tag{6a}$$

which yields the following approximate value $\hat{\lg}N$ of lgN:

$$\hat{\lg}N=k+x,\ k=0,1,2,\ldots\ (0\leq x<1) \tag{6b}$$

The error $E=\lg N-\hat{\lg}N$ is equal to

$$E=\lg(1+x)-x \tag{6c}$$

Thus for x=0 we have E=0, and the maximum error occurs at the value of x which is the solution of $dE/dx=0$, i.e. at $x=1/\ln 2-1=0.44269$ where $\ln x\triangleq\log_e x$. The maximum error (absolute value, not percentage) is $E_{max}=\lg(1+0.44269)-0.44269=0.08639$. Hence the range of the error is

$$0\leq E\leq 0.08639 \tag{6d}$$

Method 2 (Taylor series expansion [1])

In this approximation use is made of the linear terms of a Taylor series expansion of $\ln(1+x)$ about $x=x_o$, $0\leq x_o<1$ to obtain

$$\hat{\ln}(1+x)=\ln(1+x_o)+(x-x_o)/(1+x_o)$$

or

$$\hat{\lg}(1+x)=\frac{\lg e}{1+x_o}x+\lg(1+x_o)-\frac{x_o \lg e}{1+x_o} \tag{7a}$$

i.e. $\hat{\lg}N=k+\hat{\lg}(1+x)$

The error of this approximation is

$$E=\lg N-\hat{\lg}N$$

$$=\lg\frac{1+x}{1+x_o}-\frac{x-x_o}{1+x_o}\lg e \tag{7b}$$

Method 3 (Combet et al. [5])

This is a piece-wise linear approximation of $\lg(1+x)$ based on a division of [0,1] into four subintervals. The general expression in each subinterval is $\hat{\lg}(1+x)=x+a\sigma(x)+b$ where $\sigma(x)=x$ if in this subinterval the slope of $\lg(1+x)$ is greater than 1 and $\sigma(x)=1-x$ if the slope is less than 1. For easy logic circuitry implementation instead of $\sigma(x)=1-x$ we use $\sigma(x)=\bar{x}$ where $\bar{x}$ is the bit-by-bit binary complement of x, and the coefficients a and b are fractions with integer numerator and a power of two as denominator. The values of a and b can be selected by trial and error to make the deviations of $\lg(1+x)$ and $\hat{\lg}(1+x)$ small . The resulting piece-wise linear approximation is

$$\hat{\lg}(1+x)=\begin{cases} x+(5/16)x & \text{for } x\varepsilon[0,1/4) \\ x+5/64 & \text{for } x\varepsilon[1/4,1/2) \\ x+(1/8)\bar{x}+3/128 & \text{for } x\varepsilon[1/2,3/4) \\ x+(1/4)\bar{x} & \text{for } x\varepsilon[3/4,1) \end{cases} \tag{8}$$

The maximum positive absolute error of this approximation is 0.008 and the maximum negative is -0.006. Thus the error range is 0.014 i.e. less than one sixth of the error range 0.08639 obtained by the single interval approximation of Mitchell [4]. The realized absolute error range through simulation using

128 values of x in the interval (0,1) is 0.019.

Method 4 (Hall et.al. [1])

This is also a piece-wise approximation where the coefficients of the linear expression are chosen so as to minimize the mean square error.
Consider the linear expression

$$\hat{lg}(1+x)=ax+b \tag{9a}$$

The mean-squared error is

$$\overline{E}^2=\frac{1}{x_2-x_1}\int_{x_1}^{x_2}[lg(1+x)-ax-b]^2dx \tag{9b}$$

where $[x_1,x_2]:0\leqslant x_1\leqslant x\leqslant x_2<1$ is the subinterval over which the approximation is used. Setting $\partial\overline{E}^2/\partial a=0$, $\partial\overline{E}^2/\partial b=0$ and solving for a and b gives the expressions

$$a=\{B-(x_1+x_2)\frac{A}{2}\}\,/\,\{\frac{x_2^3-x_1^3}{3}-\frac{(x_2-x_1)(x_1+x_2)^2}{4}\} \tag{9c}$$

$$b=\frac{A}{x_2-x_1}-a\frac{x_1+x_2}{2} \tag{9d}$$

where

$$A=\int_{x_1}^{x_2} lg(1+x)dx,\quad B=\int_{x_1}^{x_2}x\,lg(1+x)dx \tag{9e}$$

Using the above values one can, for any partition of the interval [0,1], find the optimum coefficients, the minimum, and the maximum absolute error.

The expression $\hat{lg}(1+x)=ax+b=x+a'x+b$ for a four subdivision realization, where for simple logic circuitry the coefficients a' and b have been quantized to seven bits, is as follows

$$\hat{lg}(1+x)\simeq\begin{cases} x+\frac{37}{128}x+\frac{1}{128} & \text{for } x\varepsilon[0,1/4) \\ x+\frac{3}{64}x+\frac{1}{16} & \text{for } x\varepsilon[1/4,1/2) \\ x+\frac{7}{64}\bar{x}+\frac{1}{32} & \text{for } x\varepsilon[1/2,3/4) \\ x+\frac{29}{128}\bar{x} & \text{for } x\varepsilon[3/4,1) \end{cases} \tag{10}$$

where $\bar{x}=(1-x)$.

The range of the theoretical maximum error in this case is

$$-0.0782<E_{max}<0.00994 \tag{11a}$$

and the realized maximum mean-squared error is

$$\overline{E}^2_{max}=3.33x10^{-6} \tag{11b}$$

Method 5 (Kingsbury and Rayner [2])

The accuracy of this method is $\pm2^{-11}$.
The number N is written as

$$N=2^k(1+2^{-n})^{\ell}(1+\eta) \tag{12a}$$

where n is a constant positive integer, k is the integral part of lgN and ℓ is the largest integer for which $\eta\geqslant0$. From the above expression it follows that

$$0\leqslant\eta<2^{-n}$$

Now, one can write $N/2^k$ in the form

$$N/2^k=2^{lgN-k}=(1+2^{-n})^{\gamma\delta x} \tag{12b}$$

where $\delta x=lgN-k$ is the fractional part of lgN, and $\gamma=1/lg(1+2^{-n})$. From (12a) and (12b) one gets

$$1+\eta=(1+2^{-n})^{\gamma\delta x-\ell}$$

which by using the binomial law expansion yields

$$\eta\simeq2^{-n}(\gamma\delta x-\ell) \tag{12c}$$

with a maximum error $(1/8)2^{-2n}=2^{-2n-3}$

For an accuracy within 2^{-11} one must select $n\geqslant4$, and for minimum ℓ, n must be as small as possible.

Thus

$$n=4 \text{ and } \gamma=1/lg(1+2^{-4})=11.42 \tag{12d}$$

for $0\leqslant\ell\leqslant11$.

From (12a), (12c) and (12d) one obtains the final approximate representation

$$\hat{N}=2^{\hat{lg}N}\simeq2^k(1+2^{-4})^{\ell}[1+2^{-4}(\gamma\delta x-\ell)] \tag{13}$$

where ℓ is the largest integer $\ell=1,2,\ldots,11$ for which $\gamma\delta x-\ell$ is positive.

2.2. Antilogarithm Conversion

Mitchell [4] has suggested the following method for computing the binary antilogarithm (binary exponent) 2^M of a binary number

$$M=lgN=k+x,\quad 0\leqslant x<1 \tag{14a}$$

where k is an integer .
From (14a) it follows that

$$\mathrm{AlgM}=2^M=2^k 2^x \quad (14b)$$

which is approximated by

$$\hat{\mathrm{Alg}}M=2^k(1+x) \quad (14c)$$

The approximation (14c) is the inverse of (6a).

Hall et.al. [1] proposed a minimum mean-square error piece wise linear approximation similar to the one used for the logarithmic coding. Suppose that the interval $x\varepsilon[0,1]$ is divided into a number of subintervals $[x_1,x_2]$ where $0\leqslant x_1\leqslant x\leqslant x_2<1$.

The linear mean squared error is

$$\bar{E}^2=\frac{1}{x_2-x_1}\int_{x_1}^{x_2}\{2^x-(ax+b)\}^2dx \quad (15)$$

which if minimized with respect to a and b gives the values

$$a=\left[B-\frac{(x_1+x_2)}{2}A\right]/\left[\frac{(x_2^3-x_1^3)}{3}-\frac{(x_2-x_1)(x_1+x_2)^2}{4}\right] \quad (16a)$$

$$b=\left[A-a\frac{(x_2^2-x_1^2)}{2}\right]/(x_2-x_1) \quad (16b)$$

$$A=\int_{x_1}^{x_2}2^x dx,\quad B=\int_{x_1}^{x_2}x2^x dx \quad (16c)$$

Using the above expressions for a four subinterval realization and quantizing the coefficients to seven bits one finds that

$$\hat{2}^x=\begin{cases}x+(1/4)\bar{x}+3/4 & \text{for } x\varepsilon[0,1/4)\\ x+(13/128)\bar{x}+55/64 & \text{for } x\varepsilon[1/4,1/2)\\ x+(9/128)x+7/8 & \text{for } x\varepsilon[1/2,3/4)\\ x+(35/128)x+23/32 & \text{for } x\varepsilon[3/4,1)\end{cases} \quad (17a)$$

The maximum error ranges over

$$-0.00327<E_{max}<0.00796 \quad (17b)$$

and the realized maximum mean squared error is

$$\bar{E}^2_{max}=1.475\times10^{-6} \quad (17c)$$

We close our discussion on antilogarithm computation by recalling that the formula (13) of Kingsbury and Rayner [2] gives actually the antilogarithm of $x=\mathrm{lg}N$ i.e.

$$\hat{2}^x=2^k(1+2^{-4})^{\ell}[1+2^{-4}(\gamma\delta x-\ell)] \quad (18)$$

where $\delta x=x-k$ is the fractional part of x, with an error of $\pm 2^{-11}$.

3. BINARY LOGARITHM-BASED NUMERICAL OPERATIONS

Using the preceding logarithmic codings of digital number there have been developed corresponding methods for multiplication, division and addition accompanied with the relevant error analysis theory.

3.1. Multiplication and Division

The logarithm of a product is equal to the sum of the logarithms of the multiplier N_1 and the multiplicant N_2.

We have

$$N_1=2^{k_1}(1+x_1),\quad N_2=2^{k_2}(1+x_2) \quad (19a)$$

$$P=N_1N_2=2^{k_1+k_2}(1+x_1)(1+x_2) \quad (19b)$$

$$\mathrm{lg}P=k_1+k_2+\mathrm{lg}(1+x_1)+\mathrm{lg}(1+x_2) \quad (19c)$$

$$\hat{\mathrm{lg}}P=k_1+k_2+x_1+x_2 \quad (19d)$$

Equation (19d) is splitted in two separate expressions according to whether x_1+x_2 gives a carry to k_1+k_2 or not, i.e.

$$\hat{\mathrm{lg}}P=\begin{cases}(k_1+k_2+1)+(x_1+x_2-1), & x_1+x_2\geqslant1\\ k_1+k_2+(x_1+x_2), & x_1+x_2<1\end{cases} \quad (19e)$$

Thus, taking the antilogarithm gives

$$\hat{P}=\begin{cases}2^{k_1+k_2+1}(x_1+x_2), & x_1+x_2\geqslant1\\ 2^{k_1+k_2}(1+x_1+x_2), & x_1+x_2<1\end{cases} \quad (19f)$$

The error in the multiplication is given by

$$E_p=(\hat{P}-P)/P=\hat{P}/P-1 \quad (20)$$

which by (19b) and (19f) gives

$$E_p=\begin{cases}\dfrac{2(x_1+x_2)}{(1+x_1)(1+x_2)}-1, & x_1+x_2\geqslant1\\[2ex] \dfrac{1+x_1+x_2}{(1+x_1)(1+x_2)}-1, & x_1+x_2<1\end{cases} \quad (21a)$$

Working in an analogous way one can find that the division error E_d is given by

$$E_d=\begin{cases}\frac{(1+x_1-x_2)(1+x_2)}{(1+x_1)}-1, x_1-x_2\geq 0 \\ \frac{1}{2}\,\frac{(2+x_1-x_2)(1+x_2)}{(1+x_1)}-1, x_1-x_2<0\end{cases} \quad (21b)$$

Mitchell has studied the error expressions (21a,b) for maximum and minimum values and found that:

$$E_{p,max}=-11.1\% \text{ (at } x_1=x_2=\tfrac{1}{2}),\quad E_{p,min}=0 \ (x_1=x_2=0) \quad (22a)$$

$$E_{d,max}=12.5\% \text{ at } x_1=1, x_2=\tfrac{1}{2} \text{(no borrow case)}$$
$$\text{at } x_1=0, x_2=\tfrac{1}{2} \text{ (borrow case)} \quad (22b)$$
$$E_{d,min}=0 \text{ (at } x_2=0 \text{ or when } x_1=x_2) \quad (22c)$$

From (19b) and (19f) one finds that the product error is:

$$P-\hat{P}=\begin{cases}2^{k_1+k_2}(x_1x_2), & x_1+x_2<1 \text{ (no carry)} \\ 2^{k_1+k_2}(x_1'x_2'), & x_1+x_2\geq 1 \text{ (carry case)}\end{cases} \quad (23)$$

where x_1' and x_2' are the 2's complements of x_1 and x_2. Thus to reduce the multiplication error the correction term (23) should be added to the multiplication result obtained using the formula (19f). The maximum error obtained using this correction reduces to -2.8%.

Regarding the division operation there is not such simple way of reducing the error since the error expression is a series which does not converge fast enough to allow the utilization of its first term. However one can use prestored correction terms for the various intervals of x.

A similar error analysis for the multiplication and division operations was made for the least squares approximations of Hall et.al. [1]. Quantization, truncation and coefficient errors depend on the actual hardware used and are not included in this analysis.

The binary numbers N_1 and N_2 in (19a) are encoded as approximate binary logarithms of the form $(0\leq x_1,x_2<1)$:

$$\hat{lg}N_1=k_1+x_1+y_1,\quad y_1=a_1'x_1+b_1$$
$$\hat{lg}N_2=k_2+x_2+y_2,\quad y_2=a_2'x_2+b_2 \quad (24)$$

where the values of a_i' and b_2 are as in (10) for the case of four subdivisions.

The approximate logarithm of the product $P=N_1N_2$ is given by

$$\hat{lg}P=\hat{lg}N_1+\hat{lg}N_2 = k_1+k_2+x_1+y_1+x_2+y_2 \quad (25)$$

where we have again the two dinstinct cases

$$x_1+y_1+x_2+y_2<1 \text{ (no carry case)}$$
$$x_1+y_1+x_2+y_2\geq 1 \text{ (carry case)} \quad (26)$$

The approximate product (binary antilogarithm of $\hat{lg}P$) is given by

$$\hat{Alg}P=\begin{cases}2^{k_1+k_2+1}(x_1+x_2+y_1+y_2+z_{12}), & \text{carry case} \\ 2^{k_1+k_2}(1+x_1+x_2+y_1+y_2+z_{12}'), & \text{No carry case}\end{cases} \quad (27)$$

where the linear correction terms are given by

$$z_{12}=a_3(x_1+y_1+x_2+y_2-1)+b_3$$
$$z_{12}'=a_3(x_1+y_1+x_2+y_2)+b_3 \quad (28)$$

where again the coefficients a_3 and b_3 are as shown in (10).

The error $E=P-\hat{Alg}P=N_1N_2-\hat{Alg}P$ is a hyperbolic paraboloid and is a monotonic function over the subintervals of interest, and takes its maxima and minima at the boundary of the region. For the present 4-region subdivision we have the following errors in the 16 (x_1,x_2)-regions:

x_2 \ x_1	[0,1/4)	[1/4,1/2)	[1/2,3/4)	[3/4,1)
[0,1/4)	0.01907	0.01280	0.1059	0.01270
[1/4,1/2)	0.01280	0.01758	0.01163	0.00838
[1/2,3/4)	0.01059	0.01163	0.00773	0.00994
[3/4,1)	0.01277	0.00838	0.00994	0.01531

The maximum error occurs at $x_1=x_2=1/4$ and is $E_{max}=0.01907$ and is one fourth of the maximum error obtained by Mitchell's approximation (see (22a)).

In the special case where N_2 is a constant number C known exactly (i.e. $lgN_2=lgC=k_2+lg(1+x_2)$) the error of the product $P=N_1C$ takes the largest value 0.01321 which occurs at $x_1=25/64$ and

$x_2=14/32$.

When the approximate logarithms $\hat{lg}N_1$ and $\hat{lg}N_2$ in (24) are used, the error of the quotient

$$Q=\frac{N_1}{N_2}=\frac{2^{k_1}(1+x_1)}{2^{k_2}(1+x_2)} \tag{29a}$$

has the form

$$E_d=\begin{cases} 2^{k_1-k_2}\left[\frac{(1+x_1)}{(1+x_2)}-(1+x_1+y_1-x_2-y_2-z_{12})\right], & \text{no borrow} \\ 2^{k_1-k_2}\left[\frac{(1+x_1)}{(1+x_2)}-\frac{1}{2}(1+x_1+y_1-x_2-y_2-z'_{12})\right], & \text{borrow} \end{cases} \tag{29b}$$

where

$$z_{12}=a_3(x_1+y_1-x_2-y_2)+b_3, x_1+y_1>x_2+y_2 \quad \text{(no borrow)} \tag{29c}$$

$$z'_{12}=a_3(1+x_1+y_1-x_2-y_2)+b_3, x_1+y_1<x_2+y_2 \quad \text{(borrow)}$$

The quotient error E_d in the 16 (x_1,x_2)-regions is as follows:

x_2 \ x_1	[0,1/4)	[1/4,1/2)	[1/2,3/4)	[3/4,1)
[0,1/4)	0.00985	0.00741	0.00692	0.00590
[1/4,1/2)	0.00724	0.00490	0.00490	0.00364
[1/2,3/4)	0.01779	0.00724	0.00657	0.00497
[3/4,1)	0.01776	0.00779	0.00612	0.00594

The maximum error $E_{d,max}$ is about 1/5 of the corresponding error obtained using Mitchell's approximation.

3.2. Addition and subtraction

The addition and subtraction of numbers represented as logarithms (i.e. represented in a logarithmic number system) was studied by Kingsbury and Rayner [2], Lee and Edgar [9], and Kurokawa, Rayne and Lee [3]. A logarithmic number is expressed in binary form as

$$Ya_0a_1\ldots a_\alpha\cdot b_1b_2\ldots b_\beta \quad (=\pm 2^{\text{a-part.b-part}})$$

where Y is the sign of the number, and α_i, β_j are 0 or 1. The a-part and b-part combined represent the exponent. The base can be any positive constant but here we are restricted to the base 2. The dot "•" denotes the binary point of the exponent which has 2's complement form.

Some examples of logarithmic binary numbers of this form are

$2^{(2+1/4)} \rightarrow$ 00010.010

$2^{-(1+1/2)} \rightarrow$ 01110.100

$-2^{-(2+\frac{1}{2}+\frac{1}{4}+\frac{1}{8})} \rightarrow$ 11101.001

Some examples of arithmetic using this logarithmic representation are |2,3|:

i) Multiplication: 00010.010 $(2^{9/4})$
 01110.100 $(2^{-3/2})$

Result 00000.110 $(2^{3/4})$

ii) Addition: 00010.010 $(2^{9/4})$
 00001.101 $(2^{3/2})$

The machine representation of

$$2^{9/4}+2^{3/2}=2^{9/4}(1+2^{-3/4})=2^{9/4+lg(1+2^{-3/4})}$$

is $lg(1+2^{-3/4})$. Thus, the logarithmic addition can be done by a fixed-point addition. The value of $lg(1+2^{-3/4})$ can be be obtained by a precomputed look-up table as the function G(3/4), i.e G(3/4)=G(0000.110)=0000.101
Thus

 0010.010
 +0000.101 (from look-up table)
sign→00010.111 (result in machine representation)

The value of the result is $2^{(2+1/2+1/4+1/8)}$.

The general theory of addition and subtraction is as follows [2]. The numbers to be added are N_x and N_y, and are represented as

$a=lg|N_x|$, $b=lg|N_y|$ with their sign bits

$s_a=sgn|N_x|$, $s_b=sgn|N_y|$. Their sum is represented as

$c=lg|N_x+N_y|$, $s_c=sgn(N_x+N_y)$

If $s_a=s_b$ then

$$c=lg(2^a+2^b)=a+lg(1+2^{b-a}) \tag{30a}$$

$$=b+lg(1+2^{a-b}) \tag{30b}$$

where (30a) or (30b) is used such that the exponent b-a or a-b is negative. Thus the problem is to compute $lg(1+2^{-d})$ where $d=|a-b|$, as shown in the above example.

If $s_a=-s_b$ then for $|N_x|>|N_y|$ we have,

$s_c=s_a$, and

$$c = \lg(2^a - 2^b) = a + \lg(1 - 2^{b-a})$$
$$= a + \lg(1 - 2^{-d}), d = |a-b| \qquad (30c)$$

Thus the problem is to compute $\lg(1-2^{-d})$, $d>0$.

Using (30a-c) one needs not very long registers (as in the case of first calculating 2^a and 2^b and then taking the lg of their sum or difference) since $0<2^{-d}<1$. For example for a 0.1% system 2^{-d} needs an accuracy to within 0.001.

The value of $\lg(1+\omega), 0 \leqslant \omega = 2^{-d} < 1$ can be approximately found by any one of the methods presented in Sec.2.1. One has to first compute 2^{-d}, add or subtract from 1 and then take the lg of the result. This is the direct approach. A faster, but slightly more complex, way is to store the function $G_{\pm}(d) = \lg(1 \pm 2^{-d})$ for a discrete set of values of d. This needs a storage equal to the number of values of d multiplied by the maximum number of bits required for $G_{\pm}(d)$. One way of reducing the storage requirements is to store d at address $G_{\pm}(d)$ instead of $G_{\pm}(d)$ at addres d. Another way is to store $G_{\pm}(d)$ every kth (say k=8) value of d and use linear interpolation for the intermediate values.

An other binary representation is the floating-point one for normalized numbers for which $0.5 \leqslant |\text{fractional part}| < 1$ [3,9,15, 16]. A floating-point number in this system is represented as

$$c_0 c_1 \ldots c_f g_0 . g_1 g_2 \ldots g_h \quad (= \text{g-part} \times 2^{\text{c-part}})$$

where c_i, g_i are 1 or 0, $g_0 . g_1 g_2 \ldots g_h$ = g-part is the fractional part and $c_0 c_1 \ldots c_f$ = c-part is the exponent. The exponent is an integer and both parts are in 2's complement representation.

4. HARDWARE IMPLEMENTATION

The first attempt for implementing the approximation $\hat{\lg} N = k + x$ (see (6a,b)) was reported by Mitchell for $N \geqslant 1$ and was based on the principle of shifting and counting [4]. This method was extended in [6] to hold for the case $0<N<1$. A new fast system for computing lgN using Mitchell's approximation $\hat{\lg} N = k + x$, which does not require any shifting or counting was proposed in [7]. A system for implementing the heuristic piece-wise linear approximation of Combet et.al.for the case of dividing [0,1] into four subintervals was presented in [5].

Our purpose here is to show how one can implement the operations of multiplication and division,and the computation of powers and roots, using the system given in [7]. Some other results on calculating roots and powers can be found in [14].

Here the following assumptions are made.
(1) The binary numbers are represented in fixed-point form with a sign bit. For example the number $N = (-0.9375)_{10}$ is represented in a 13-bit register as 1000000.111100.

(2) The circuit BLU of [7] which is shown in Fig. 1 is available.

This system computes $\hat{\lg}|N|$, i.e. the (approximate) binary logarithm of the absolute value of N, and gives the result in 1's complement form. Here it is represented in block-diagram form as shown in Fig. 2.

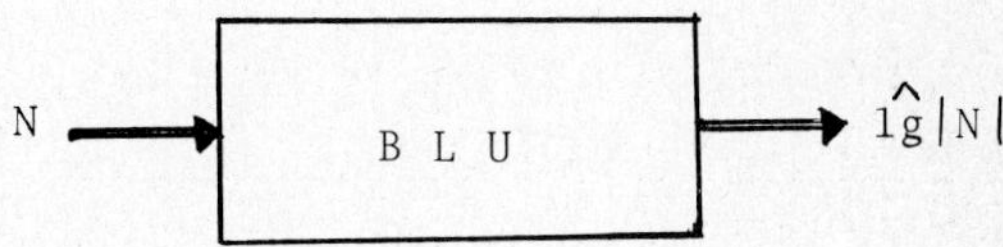

Fig. 2. Block diagram of binary logarighm unit.

The outputs of the priority units I and II (in Fig.1) can also be used to check whether $N \neq 0$ or $N=0$ (to avoid the computation of log 0).
(3) The circuit ABLU of [7] (see Fig.3) which accepts $\hat{\lg}|N|$ in 1's complement form and gives at its output $|\hat{N}|$ is available.

This unit is represented here by the block diagram of Fig. 4.

Fig.4.:Block diagram of binary antilogarithm unit.

Multiplication and Division

The operations of multiplication and division of two numbers N_1 and N_2 using the above circuits BLU and ABLU can be done easily. Namely

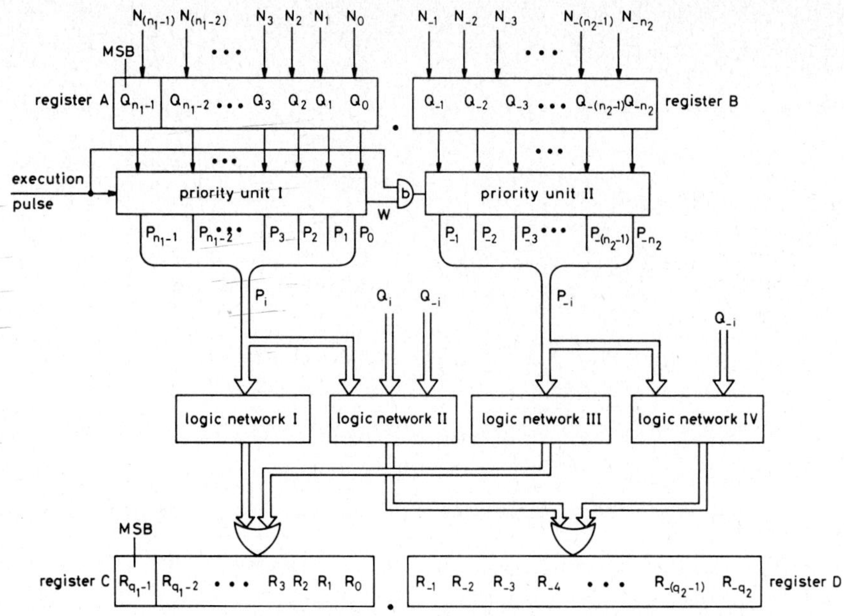

Fig. 1: Set up of fast binary logarithm computing unit (BLU).

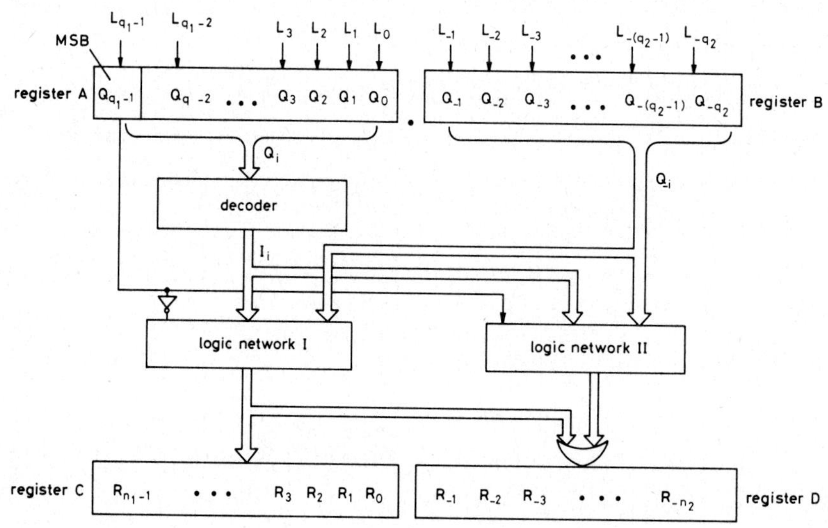

Fig. 3.: The binary antilogarithm computing unit.

$\hat{\lg}|P| = \hat{\lg}|N_1| + \hat{\lg}|N_2|$ for $|P| = |N_1||N_2|$

$\hat{\lg}|Q| = \hat{\lg}|N_1| - \hat{\lg}|N_2|$ for $|Q| = |N_1|/|N_2|$

$|\hat{P}| = \lg^{-1}(\hat{\lg}|P|), |\hat{Q}| = \lg^{-1}(\hat{\lg}|Q|)$

The sign bit Y of the result is computed by

$Y = Y_1 \oplus Y_2$

where Y_1 and Y_2 are the sign bits of N_1

and N_2, respectively. The block diagram of the circuit implementing multiplication and division is shown in Fig. 5.

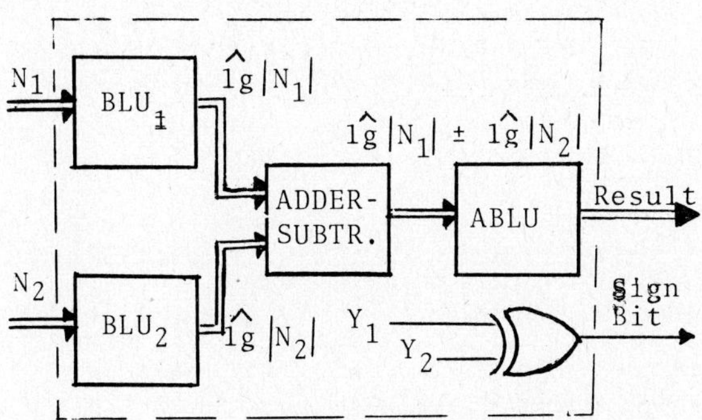

Fig.5.:Block diagram of log-based multiplication and division.

To compute the product P=K.N where K is a constant number and N a variable one can use the circuit of Fig.5 with only one BLU, since lg|K| can be precomputed and stored, and then added to lg|N| as many times as required.

Examples

Ex.1:Let $N_1=(-0.9375)_{10}$=1000000.111000

$N_2=(+5.125)_{10}$ =0000101.001000

where the first bit on the left is the sign bit. The exact value is $P=N_1.N_2$ = $(-4.8046)_{10}$.

From Fig. 5 one obtains

$\hat{lg}|N_1|$=111111.111000 (Output of BLU_1 in 1's complement)

$\hat{lg}|N_2|$=000010.010010 (Output of BLU_2 in 1's complement)

$\hat{lg}|N_1|+\hat{lg}|N_2|$= 000010.001011 (Output of adder)

$|\hat{P}|=lg^{-1}(\hat{lg}|N_1|+\hat{lg}|N_2|)$=000100.101100 (Output of ABLU)

Since $Y=Y_1 \oplus Y_2=1 \oplus 0$ =1, the final result is

$\hat{P}$=1000100.101100=$(-4.6875)_{10}$

↑ sign bit

$$\text{Error}=\frac{-4.8046+4.6875}{-4.8046}=2.4\%$$

Ex.2:$N_1=125_{10}$=01111101,$N_2=15_{10}$=00001111

Output of BLU_1:$\hat{lg}|N_1|$=110.111101

Output of BLU_2:$\hat{lg}|N_2|$=011.111000

Output of adder:1010.110101

Output of ABLU:11101010000=1872

Exact value:125x125=1875

Error=(1875-1872)/1875=0.016 (0.16%)

Ex.3:Let $Q=N_1/N_2=1534/25=61.36_{10}$

N_1=10111111110, N_2=00000011001

BLU_1:$\hat{lg}|N_1|$=1010.0111111110

BLU_2:$\hat{lg}|N_2|$=0100.1001000000

SUBTRACTOR:0101.1110111110

ABLU:111011.11100=59.85_{10}

Error:(61.36-59.85)/61.36=2,4%

Ex.4.: Let $P=N_1.N_2=64x16=1024_{10}$

BLU_1:$\hat{lg}$64=0110.000

BLU_2:$\hat{lg}$16=0100.000

ADDER:$\hat{lg}$64+$\hat{lg}$16=1010.000

ABLU:$\hat{P}=\hat{lg}^{-1}$1010.000

=10000000000

=1024_{10}

Error:Zero (since N_1 and N_2 are integer powers of 2).

Powers and Roots

$$\text{Let } P=N^{u/v} \tag{31}$$

where N,u and v are binary numbers in fixed-point representation. Taking the logarithm of P gives

$\hat{lg}|P|=\frac{u}{v}\hat{lg}|N|$

Thus

$$\hat{lg}(\hat{lg}|P|)=\hat{lg}|u|-\hat{lg}|v|+\hat{lg}(\hat{lg}|N|)=K \tag{32a}$$

and

$$|\hat{P}|=\hat{lg}^{-1}(\hat{lg}^{-1} K) \tag{32b}$$

To implement (32a,b) we can use the circuit of Fig.5 with an auxiliary register R. The calculation steps are:

Step 1: Take $\hat{lg}|N|$ from BLU_1 and store it in R. Also take $\hat{lg}|u|$ from BLU_2 and ADD to the Accumulator.

Step 2: Take the lg of the content of register R (i.e. $\hat{lg}(\hat{lg}|N|)$) from BLU_1 and store in R. Also take the $\hat{lg}|v|$ from BLU_2 and subtract from the Accumulator.

Step 3: Add the contents of register R to the Accumulator.

Step 4: Take the antilog of ACC using ABLU and transfer the result in register R.
Step 5: Take the antilog of the content of register R. This gives the final result.

Example

Let $P=N^{u/v}$ where $N=(1024)_{10}$, $u=5_{10}$, $v=7_{10}$

Using the above procedure one obtains

Step 1: $\hat{lg}|N|=001010.000000$ (BLU_1). Store in R.
$\hat{lg}|u|=00010.010000$ (BLU_2).
Add to Acc.i.e. 00010.010000.

Step 2: $\hat{lg}|R|=000011.010000$. Store in R.
$\hat{lg}|v|=000010.110$.
$\hat{lg}|u|-\hat{lg}|v|=-(000000.100000)$
Accumulator.

Step 3: Add to Acc the contents of R.Acc= 000010.110000.
Step 4: From ABLU, $\hat{lg}^{-1}(Acc)=000111.000$.
Store in R.

Step 5: From ABLU, $\hat{lg}^{-1}R=10000000.00000=128_{10}$.

The exact value is $P=1024^{5/7}=141.32$.

The absolute error is 141.32-128=13.32, and the percenteege error is 13.32/141.32 =9.42% . This is large since we take the approximate logarithm ($\hat{lg}$) twice.

5. DIGITAL FILTERING USING LOG-BASED COMPUTATION

The primary limiting factor in the hardware or software implementation of digital filters is generally the time taken to perform multiplication. This limitation is strongly reduced if log-based computation is used since multiplication and division is reduced to addition and subtraction. However as we have already seen the use of any logarithmic representation implies some approximation error in addition to the existing input quantization, coefficient quantization and accumulated round off errors of successive arithmetic operations [10-12].

Actually, there are two ways of implementing using log-based arithmetic. In the first one computes the binary logarithms of the signals to be processed (using a LOG unit such as the BLU of Fig.1), performs the computations using the logarithms, and then go back into the original representation using an antilogarithm unit (e.g. the ABLU of Fig.3).

Suppose that we want to implement the following nonrecursive digital filter

$$y_k=\sum_{i=0}^{k-1} a_i u_{k-i}$$

Using the log-antilog method one has to perform the computation

$$y_k=\sum_{i=0}^{k-1} lg^{-1}\{lg(a_i)+lg(u_{k-i})\}$$

If the filter is implemented by direct multiplication using a cobweb array multiplier, for six-bit numbers, one needs a total of 30 full adders if all product bits are retained and 21 full adders if truncation of the result up to six bits is done. Now suppose that the log approximation of Hall et al. is used [1] (see (10)). Since two adders are needed for each bit, a total of 12 adders are required for the log conversion, 8 adders for the log addition and 10 for the antilog conversion. Thus again 30 adders are needed for the overall operation. Hence in this case the log antilog approach has no hardware saving over the cobweb approach.

However if a parallel filter is to be implemented with n parallel sub filters, then the cobweb multiplication needs 21n adders, and the log-antilog operation (where a common input log device is used) needs 12+18n. Thus in order to have a hardware saving with the log-antilog calculation the following inequality must hold: 21n>12+18n, whence n>4, i.e. the number of parallel filters should be greater than four.

If the log and antilog circuits BLU and ABLU of Figs.1 and 3 are used then we need only 6 adders to perform the log addition as shown in Fig.5. No adders are needed in the BLU and ABLU units, but a number registers, priority units and logic units. Direct comparison is not possible in this case, but it is likely that the log-antilog circuits are superior.

A class of applications where the log antilog computation is a necessity is in the implementation of multiplicative filters [13] where the input signals are products of two or more components. This class of filters as well as the class of filters with convolved signals needs sophisticated treatment if linear arithmetic is used, but it is very easily handled by means of log-based arithmetic. Work is in progress to built some parallel-bank and multiplicative filters using our BLU and ABLU units.

In the above log-antilog approach, if the actual input and output signals of the filter are analog, one must use appropriate A/D and D/A converters, which obviously reduce the dynamic range of the overall filter.

The second approach is to convert the digital logarithmic signal directly into analog form. This can be done by feeding a reference voltage to an amplifier chain, and causing each bit of the logarithm to switch the overall gain by a factor 2^{2^p} where p is the significance of that bit ($p<0$ is the mantissa, and $p\geq 0$ is the characteristic). The input A/D conversion can be obtained by employing a high gain comparator with the D/A converter to approximate successively the converter output to the signal input.

We close our discussion with a brief review of the log-based-filter error analysis results derived by Kurokawa, Payne and Lee [3].

If x is the true number and x_r is the machine representation of x, the absolute error ε_1 is $\varepsilon_1 = x_r - x = x(x_r/x-1)$ and the relative error is $\varepsilon = \varepsilon_1/x = x_r/x-1$. It is assumed that x is uniformly distributed over $[x_1, x_2)$, $0<x_1<x_2$ with

$$x_1 = x_r 2^{-(2^{-\beta-1})}, \quad x_2 = x_r 2^{(2^{-\beta-1})}$$

The mean value and variance (m and σ^2) of ε are given by

$$m = E[\varepsilon] = \frac{1}{2}(2^{2^{-\beta-1}} + 2^{-2^{-\beta-1}} - 2),$$

$$\sigma^2 = E[\varepsilon^2] = \frac{1}{12}(2^{2^{-\beta-1}} - 2^{-2^{-\beta-1}})^2$$

Since multiplication is exact in the logarithmic system, the error was considered only for addition. A general recursive digital filter of the form

$$y_k = \sum_{i=0}^{M} b_i x_{k-i} - \sum_{i=1}^{L} a_i y_{k-i}$$

was considered and found that the theoretical accumulated roundoff error to output signal ratio $E[\varepsilon_k^2]/E[y_k^2]$, $\varepsilon_k = y_k - \hat{y}_k$ (y_k is the true output sequence, and $\hat{y}_k$ is its machine representation) is less (at least 2.89 times) using the logarithmic number system as compared to using floating-point number systems. In other words, for a fixed number of bits per data word, the accumulated roundoff error of the digital filter is less when using the binary (or any other) logarithmic number system. This theoretical conclusion was actually verified experimentally through simulated filtering, which was extended to include quantization in both input signal and filter coefficients. An other conclusion from these experiments is that the limitation in implementing digital filters using logarithmic number systems is a function of the range of the numbers which may be represented [3,9]. Finally, it is worth mentioning that procedures are available for carrying out logarithmic arithmetic operations on microprocessors such as the 8-bit Intel MDS-800 system, etc.

6. CONCLUSIONS

In many real life signal processing applications such as the radar video for moving target etc, the accuracy of a single computation has less importance than the mean and variance of a signal over a certain single ensemble, whereas the broad bandwidth and associated high data flow rates make real time multiplication with conventional linear computation circuits very difficult. For this type of applications where the speed of processing is more critical than the accuracy of single computations, a number of digital circuits have been developed which multiply and divide signals in logarithmic coded form. The present paper has provided an overview of this field, also including the class of logarithmic number systems. Besides the increased speed of processing, the logarithmic coding and logarithmic number systems offer a considerable increase of the range of signals that can be handled.

Work is in progress by the present authors towards the end of designing simple and fast digital circuits which will perform the log-antilog conversion on the basis of refined approximations such as the least squares approximation of Hall et. al. [1] (see (10)) and the approximation of Kingsbury and Rayner [2] (see (13)). Also digital filters will be implemented and checked for practical accuracy and speed.

In general, digital log-antilog units can be used in applications where one needs to multiply or divide quickly varying variables. Such an application is the optimal control of dynamic systems, where the multiplication of a time varying gain matrix with the state vector variable is needed for implementing the optimal state feedback law in real-time.

REFERENCES

1. Hall, E.L.,Lynch, D.D.and Dwyer,S.J., Generation of products and quotients using approximate binary logarithms for digital filtering applications, IEEE Trans. Computers, C-19, 2 (1970) 97-105.
2. Kingsbury, N.G. and Rayner, P.J.W., Digital filtering using logarithmic arithmetic, Electronics Letters, 7, 2 (1971) 56-58.
3. Kurokawa, T., Payne, J.A. and Lee S.C., Error analysis of recursive digital filters implemented with logarithmic number systems, IEEE Trans. Acoustics, Speech and Signal Processing, ASSP-28, (1980) 706-715.
4. Mitchell, J., Computer multiplication and division using binary logarithms, IRE Trans. Electronic Computers (August, 1962) 512-517.
5. Combet, M.,Van Zonneveld, H. and Verbeek, L., Computation of the base two logarithm of binary numbers, IEEE Trans. Electron. Computers, EC-14, 6 (1965) 863-867.
6. Frangakis, G.P.,Fast binary logarithm computing circuit for binary numbers less than one, Electronics Letters,16, 15 (1980) 574-575.
7. Frangakis, G.P.,A new binary logarithm-based computing system, Proc.IEE,130-Pt.E, 5 (1983) 169-173.
8. Swartzlander, E.E.Jr.and A.G.Alexopoulos, The sign/logarithm number system, IEEE Trans. Computers, C-24 (1975) 1238-1242.
9. Lee. S.C.and Edgar, A.D., The focus number system, IEEE Trans. Computers, C-26 (1977) 1167-1170.
10. Gold, B. and Rader, C.M., Digital Processing of Signals (McGraw-Hill, New York, 1969).
11. Tzafestas, S.G.(Ed.), Microprocessors in Signal Processing, Measurement and Control (D. Reidel, Dordrecht-Boston, 1983.
12. Tzafestas,S.G., Digital Signal Processing:Lecture Notes (Control Systems Lab., Patras Univ., 1980).
13. Oppenheim, A.V., Schafer, R.W. and Stockham, T.G. Nonlinear filtering of multiplied and convolved signals, Proc. IEEE, 56, 8 (1968) 1264-1291.
14. Lo,Y.Y.,Binary logarithms for computing integral and non-integral roots and powers, Int.J.Electronics, 40, 4 (1976) 357-364.
15. Samberg, I.W.,Floating-point-roundoff accumulation in digital filter realizations, Bell Syst.Tech.J., 46 (1967) 1775-1791.
16. Kan,E.P.F. and Aggarival,J.K., Error analysis of digital filter employing floating-point arithmetic IEEE Trans. Circuit Theory,CT-18,(1971) 678-685.

DIGITAL TECHNIQUES in Simulation, Communication and Control
Spyros G. Tzafestas (editor)
Elsevier Science Publishers B.V. (North-Holland) © IMACS, 1985

MIN-MAX DESIGN OF 2-D RECURSIVE DIGITAL FILTERS SATISFYING PRESCRIBED MAGNITUDE AND GROUP DELAY SPECIFICATIONS

V. Ramachandran*, M. Ahmadi and S. Golikeri

Department of Electrical Engineering, University of Windsor
Windsor, Ontario N9B 3P4, Canada

* Department of Electrical Engineering, Concordia University
Montreal, Quebec H3G 1M8, Canada

In this paper generation of the 2-variable very strictly Hurwitz polynomial (VSHP) using properties of derivatives of even or odd parts of Hurwitz polynomials and their applications in designing 2-D recursive digital filters satisfying prescribed magnitude and constant group delay response is described.

1. INTRODUCTION

In this paper a method is presented for generating a 2-variable VSHP using the properties of derivatives of even or odd parts of Hurwitz polynomials.

Then the derived 2-variable VSHP will be assigned to the denominator of a 2-D analogue reference filter, which is

$$H_a(s_1,s_2)=\frac{A(s_1,s_2)}{B(s_1,s_2)}=\frac{\sum_{i_1=0}^{M_1}\sum_{i_2=0}^{M_2} a(i_1,i_2)\, s_1^{i_1} s_2^{i_2}}{\sum_{i_1=0}^{M_1}\sum_{i_2=0}^{M_2} b(i_1,i_2)\, s_1^{i_1} s_2^{i_2}} \tag{1}$$

Bilinear transformation is then applied to eqn. (1) to obtain the discrete version of the filter which is

$$H_a(z_1,z_2)=\frac{N(z_1,z_2)}{D(z_1,z_2)}=\frac{\sum_{i_1=0}^{M_1}\sum_{i_2=0}^{M_2} n(i_1,i_2)\, z_1^{i_1} z_2^{i_2}}{\sum_{i_1=0}^{M_1}\sum_{i_2=0}^{M_2} d(i_1,i_2)\, z_1^{i_1} z_2^{i_2}} \tag{2}$$

Parameters of eqn. (2) will then be used as the variables of optimization in a Min-max norm so as to minimize the maximum of error of the desired and designed magnitude and group delay response of the filter.

2. GENERATION OF 2-VARIABLE VSHP

A 2-variable VSHP can be generated using the following steps [1]: i) A suitable even or odd part of a 2n-variable Hurwitz polynomial is generated. ii) The corresponding derivatives giving the odd or even part are associated with it. iii) The resulting 2n-variable Hurwitz polynomial is converted to a 2-variable VSHP.

For example, consider the polynomial M_{2n} given by

$$M_{2n} = \det |\mu I_{2n} + B_{2n}| \tag{3}$$

where μ is a diagonal matrix of order 2n given by

$$\mu = \operatorname{diag}\, [\mu_1,\ \mu_2,\ \mu_3,\ \ldots,\ \mu_{2n}] \tag{4}$$

and B_{2n} is a skew-symmetric matrix of order 2n given by

$$B_{2n} = \begin{bmatrix} 0 & b_{12} & b_{13} & \cdots & b_{1,2n} \\ -b_{12} & 0 & b_{23} & \cdots & b_{2,2n} \\ -b_{13} & -b_{23} & 0 & \cdots & b_{3,2n} \\ \cdot & & & & \cdot \\ \cdot & & & & \cdot \\ \cdot & & & & \cdot \\ -b_{1,2n} & -b_{2,2n} & & \cdots & 0 \end{bmatrix} \tag{5}$$

From the diagonal expansion of the determinant of a matrix [2] M_{2n} can be written as

$$M_{2n} = \det B_{2n} + \sum_{1\le i_1<i_2\le 2n} \mu_{i1}\,\mu_{i2}\, |B_{i1\,i2}| + \sum_{1<i_1<i_2<i_3<i_4<2n} \mu_{i1}\mu_{i2}\mu_{i3}\mu_{i4}\, |B_{i1i2i3i4}| + \ldots + \mu_1\,\mu_2\,\mu_3 \cdots \mu_{2n} \tag{6}$$

where $|B_{i1\ i2}|$ is the determinant of the submatrix of B_{2n} obtained by deleting both the i_1th and the i_2th rows and columns, and is of order

$(2n-2)$, $|B_{i1\ i2\ i3\ i4}|$ is the determinant of the sub-matrix of B_{2n} obtained by deleting the i_1th, i_2th, i_3th, i_4th rows and columns, and is of order $(2n-4)$ and so on.

The following properties should be noted: i) All odd-order terms of the type μ_{i1}, $\mu_{i1}\mu_{i2}\mu_{i3}$ etc. are absent, since the determinant of an odd-order skew-symmetric matrix is zero. ii) The degree of any μ_i $(i = 1, 2, \ldots, 2n)$ is unity. iii) The quantity det B_{2n}, $B_{i1\ i2}$, $B_{i1\ i2\ i3\ i4}$ etc. are non-negative numbers, since the determinant of an an even-order skew symmetric matrix is a perfect square. Since the matrix $[\mu I_{2n} + B_{2n}]$ is always physically realizable, μ_{2n} represents the even part of a 2n-variable Hurwitz polynomial. Therefore, $(\partial M2n/\partial \mu_i)/M_{2n}$ is a reactance function [3]. As a consequence

$$M'_{2n} = M_{2n} + \sum_{j=1}^{2n} k_j \frac{\partial M2n}{\partial \mu i} \qquad (7)$$

is a 2n-variable VSHP.

From eqn. (7), a 2-variable VSHP can be generated by putting some of the μ's equal to s_1 and the rest of the μ's equal to s_2 with the condition that det $B_2 \neq 0$.

3. FORMULATION OF THE DESIGN PROBLEM

In this method a 2-variable VSHP is assigned to the denominator of eqn. (1) using eqns. (3) and (7), and the numerator is left unchanged. Then bilinear transformations are applied to the derived 2-D analogue transfer function to obtain the discrete version of the filter.

The error between the ideal and designed magnitude response is calculated using the relationship

$$E_M(\omega_{1m}, \omega_{2n}) = |H_I(\omega_{1m}, \omega_{2n})| - |H_D(\omega_{1m}, \omega_{2n})| \qquad (8)$$

where E_M is the error of the magnitude response calculated at discrete frequency points in ω_1-ω_2 plane as the difference between $|H_I|$ and $|H_D|$, which are the amplitude responses of the ideal and designed filters, respectively.

The error between the ideal and designed group delay response can be calculated using the following relationship:

$$E_{\tau_{\omega i}}(\omega_{1m}, \omega_{2n}) = \tau_I T - \tau_{\omega_i}\left|e^{j\omega_{1m}T}, e^{j\omega_{2nT}}\right|$$

$$i = 1, 2 \qquad (9)$$

where τ_I is a constant representing the ideal group delay of the filter, and its value is chosen equal to the order of the filter [4] and $\tau_{\omega i}$, $i = 1, 2$, is the group delay response of the designed filter.

Using eqns. (8) and (9) we can generate our cost function using the following relationship

$$E_G = \text{Max}\left\{ \underset{m,n\,\epsilon I_{pS}}{E_M(\omega_{1m}, \omega_{2n})},\ \underset{m,n\epsilon\, I_p}{E_{\tau_{\omega 1}}(\omega_{1m}, \omega_{2n})},\ \underset{m,n\,\epsilon\, I_p}{E_{\tau_{\omega 2}}(\omega_{1m}, \omega_{2n})} \right\} \qquad (10)$$

where I_{pS} is a set of all discrete frequency points in the passband and stopband of the filter and I_p is a set of all discrete frequency points in the passband of the filter only.

Now any suitable non-linear optimization technique can be used to calculate parameters a and b of the filter transfer function so as to minimize the E_G in eqn. (10).

4. DESIGN EXAMPLE

To illustrate the usefulness of the method we design a fan filter with the following specifications

$$|H_I(\omega_{1m}, \omega_{2n})| = \begin{cases} 1.0 & \text{for } \omega_2 < 0.8\,\omega_1 \\ 0 & \text{for } \omega_2 > 1.2\,\omega_1 \end{cases}$$

And constant group delay response which is equal to the order of the filter. In this example, matrix B_{2n} in Eqn. (5) is chosen to be of order 4 x 4, and K's in Eqn. (7) are set to unity. Obviously in this example the order of the filter will be 2 so τ_I in Eqn. (9) will be two. The optimization technique used in this method is that of Hooks and Jeevs [5]. Table (1) shows values of the parameters of the designed filter, Fig. (1) shows the amplitude and Figs. (2a) and (2b) show the group delay characteristics of the designed filter.

5. CONCLUSIONS

In this paper a method is presented for the design of 2-D filters with specified magnitude and constant group delay characteristics using Min-max norm. This method is based on the properties of the derivatives of a 2n-variable Hurwitz polynomial and their use in generating a two-variable VSHP. This method can be used by adapting any unconstrained non-linear optimization method, and can be easily extended to N-D, including the 1-D case.

REFERENCES

[1] Ramachandran, V., and Ahmadi, M., "Design

of 2-D stable analog and recursive digital filters using properties of the derivative of even or odd parts of Hurowitz polynomials". The Franklin Institute Journal, Vol. 315, No. 4, pp. 259-267, April 1983.

[2] Hohn, F.E., "Elementary matrix algebra", (McMillan Company, pp. 87-88) 1966.

[3] Koga, T., "Synthesis of finite passive n-port with prescribed two variable reactance matrices". IEEE Trans., 1966, CT-13, No. 1.

[4] Chottera, A., Jullien, G.A., "Designing near linear phase recursive filters using linear programming". Proc. 1977 ICASSP, pp. 88-92.

[5] Kueston, J.L., and Mize, J.H., "Optimization techniques with Fortran". (McGraw Hill) pp. 309-319.

TABLE 1 Value of the Coefficients of the Designed Fan Filter.

NUMERATOR COEFFICIENTS	DENOMINATOR COEFFICIENTS
$a_{00} = -37.84$	$b_{12} = 2.30$
$a_{01} = -2.180$	$b_{13} = -4.25$
$a_{02} = -12.66$	$b_{14} = -2.489$
$a_{10} = -55.83$	$b_{23} = -5.28$
$a_{11} = 21.39$	$b_{24} = -7.22$
$a_{12} = -24.40$	$b_{34} = 3.45$
$a_{20} = 66.14$	
$a_{21} = -33.92$	
$a_{22} = 7.28$	

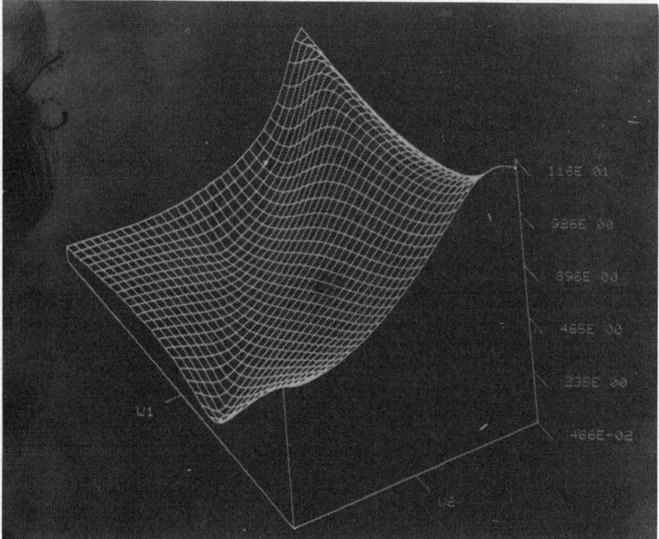

Fig. (1) Magnitude Response of a Fan Filter.

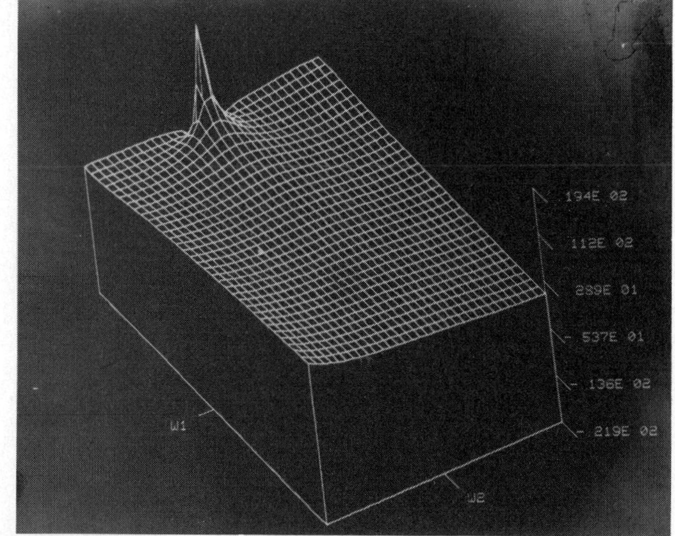

Fig. (2a) Group Delay Response w.r.t.w_1.

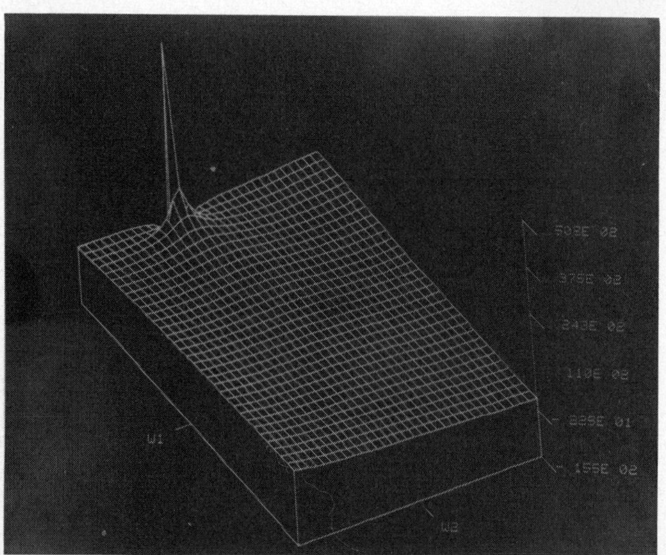

Fig. (2b) Group Delay Response w.r.t.w_2.

DIGITAL TECHNIQUES in Simulation, Communication and Control
Spyros G. Tzafestas (editor)
Elsevier Science Publishers B.V. (North-Holland) © IMACS, 1985

A UNIFIED PRESENTATION OF SYMMETRY RELATIONS FOR DISCRETE DOMAIN SIGNALS AND THEIR TRANSFORMS

P. Karivaratha Rajan
Dept. Electrical Engineering
Tennessee Technological University
Cookeville, Tennessee 38505 USA

M.N.S. Swamy
Dept. Electrical Engineering
Concordia University
Montreal, Canada H391M8

A relation between the types of symmetries that exist in signal and Fourier transform domain representations is derived for discrete domain signals and their transforms. The symmetry is expressed by a set of parameters and the relations derived in this paper will help to find the parameters of a symmetry in signal or transform domain resulting from a given symmetry respectively in transform or signal domain. A duality among the relations governing the conversion of the parameters of symmetry in the two domains is also brought to light. The application of the relations is illustrated by a number of two-dimensional examples.

I. INTRODUCTION

Multi-dimensional (M-D, M>2) Fourier transform plays an important role in the analysis and design of M-D linear continuous and discrete domain systems. The transform uniquely relates the impulse or unit sample response of a linear system with its frequency response. Hence, symmetry in one response (either impulse or frequency response) may be expected to induce some form of symmetry in the other response. The existence of such symmetries can be utilized to simplify the analysis and design of these systems. Such utilization and the resulting simplification have been reported in the design and analysis of two-dimensional digital filters [1-10]. This was done in references [2-6] by identifying the nature of transfer functions that possess the various types of symmetries in their magnitude responses. In references [7-9] the various symmetries were expressed in a general framework and the interrelationships in the inverse Fourier transform samples in discrete domain as a result of various symmetries in the frequency response functions of two dimensional digital filters were derived and used. The results were extended to multi-dimensional systems in [9]. In this paper we report in a unified manner the type of symmetry induced in one function (Fourier transform or inverse Fourier transform) as a result of a particular symmetry in the other function. The results as applicable to continuous domain signals were presented in [11]. Here, the results are presented for multi-dimensional discrete domain case and the relations for two-dimensional functions can be easily obtained from the m-dimensional relations.

The main contributions of this paper are i) to modify the symmetry parameters so that they present a similar form in both the domains, and ii) to establish the duality in both the domains. It is also shown how different sampling strategies affect the symmetry parameters.

Section 2 lists the notations to be used in this paper. In Section 3, we present the definition of symmetry in a general framework and describe some of the commonly occurring symmetries. Symmetry interrelationships for discrete domain Fourier transform pair are derived in section 4.

II. NOTATIONS

R = the set of real numbers

R^m = RxRx . . .xR m-dimensional real vector space

ω = m-dimensional frequency vector

W = $\{\omega | -\infty \leq \omega_i \leq \infty\ ,\ i=1,1,\ldots,m\}$

Ω = m-dimensional normalized frequency vector

Ωp = $\{\Omega | -\pi \leq \Omega_i \leq \pi\ \ i=1,2,\ldots,m\}$

λ = $(A, b, \delta, \beta, \phi)$ parameters of T-Ψ symmetry

N = the set of integers

N^m = N x N x . . . x N m-dimensional integer vector space. m-dimensional lattice.

$h(n)$ = $h(n_1,..,n_m)$ discrete domain signal

$\hat{H}(\Omega)$ = $H(\Omega_1,..,\Omega_m) = H(e^{-j\Omega 1}, e^{-j\Omega 2}, \ldots, e^{-j\Omega m})$ = Fourier transform of h(n)

$v_1, v_2, \ldots, v_m$ = m sample-direction and interval vectors

This work was supported in part by Natural Sciences and Engineering Research Council of Canada under Grant A-7739 to M.N.S. Swamy and in part by Tennessee Technological University under its Faculty Research support program to P.K. Rajan.

$V = (v_1 v_2 \dots v_m)$ sampling basis matrix
$[x]^*$ = complex conjugate of x
det A = determinant of A
$X = \{x \mid -\infty \leq x_i \leq \infty, i = 1,2,\dots,m\}$
$A^{-t} = [A^{-1}]^t$, t stands for transpose

III. DEFINITION AND TYPES OF SYMMETRY

We say that a function f(x) possesses a symmetry if a pair of operations, performed simultaneously one on the variable x and other on the function value, leaves the function unchanged. Stated in another way, existence of symmetry in a function implies that the value of the function at x in a region is related in some way to the value of the function at x_T where x_T is obtained by some operation on x, this condition being satisfied for all the points in the region. Along these lines, Aly and Fahmy [7] proposed a general definition for symmetry. Modifying this definition slightly we propose the following definition to describe the different types of symmetries.

<u>Definition</u>: A function f(x) is said to possess a T-Ψ symmetry over a region D if

$$\Psi[f(T[x])]=f(x) \text{ for all } x \in D, \qquad (1)$$

where Ψ is an operation on the value of f(x) and T is an operation on x that maps D onto itself on a one-to-one basis.

If in the T-Ψ symmetry definition given above, the region D consists of all the points in the whole x space, i.e., D=X, then the function is said to possess a global T-Ψ symmetry. In this paper we will restrict our attention only to global T-Ψ symmetries and the adjective "global" will be omitted in their descriptions.

The above definition for a T-Ψ symmetry differs from that for a T-P symmetry of Aly and Fahmy [7] in the following two ways. (i) The Ψ operations are applied on f(T[x]) rather than on f(x). This is done so that the definition resembles the conventional notion of symmetry more closely. It is easily seen that $\Psi[.]=P^{-1}[.]$. Further, as will be shown later, the Ψ operation is chosen in a more general form than the P operation. (ii) The region D has been constrained such that all the points generated by the application of T on the points of D are in D on a one-to-one basis. This is necessary for the function obtained after the operations are performed to remain identical to the original function. We next discuss the nature of Ψ and T operations.

3.1 Nature of Ψ-Operations

Of the many possible complex scalar operations, the following definition for Ψ covers many useful ones:

$$\Psi[f(x)]=|f(x)|\, e^{j(\delta \measuredangle f(x)+\beta^t x+\phi)} \qquad (2)$$

where $\delta = \pm 1$, $\measuredangle f(x)$ denotes the argument of f(x), β is a (mx1) real constant vector and ϕ is a real constant. The term $\beta^t x$ was not present in the P operation suggested in [7]. This has been included in the Ψ operation to account for some of the delay type symmetries that may be present in some functions. We list in Table 1 four specific Ψ-operations used in various symmetry descriptions along with the commonly used names and the proposed symbols.

3.2 Nature of T-operations

Simple T-operations that find applications in symmetry studies can be represented by the transformation (known as affine transformation in geometry):

$$T[x]=Ax+b \qquad (3)$$

where A is an (mxm) real nonsingular matrix and b is a real mx1 vector. T is said to be an equiaffine transformation if det A=$\pm$1 in which case corresponding regions in the transformed and original spaces have the same (hyper) volume. Cyclic transformations and congruent transformations are special classes of equi-affine transformations. Displacement, rotation and reflection are the widely used transformations. For a description of these transformations and their parameters, references [7], [9], and [12] may be consulted.

3.3 Composite Symmetry Operation and Symmetry Parameters:

Combining the T and Ψ operations together, we define a composite symmetry operation λ as $\lambda=(T,\Psi)=(A,b,\delta,\beta,\phi)$ where Ψ and T are defined as in (2) and (3). In terms of λ, the symmetry definition can be given as

$$\lambda[f(x)]=f(x) \qquad \forall x \in D. \qquad (4)$$

As the five parameters (A,b,δ,β,ϕ) describe the symmetry operation completely, they will hereafter be called symmetry parameters and be used to specify the various symmetries. When a function possesses two types of symmetries λ_1 and λ_2, then it can easily be verified that it also possesses a symmetry which is a combination of the above two. For example, in the 2-D case,

if $\quad f(x_1,x_2)=f(-x_1,x_2)=\lambda_1[f(x)]$

and $\quad f(x_1,x_2)=f(x_1,-x_2)=\lambda_2[f(x)]$

then we also have $f(x_1,x_2)=f(-x_1,-x_2)=\lambda\,[f(x)]$

We can obtain the parameters of λ_3 in terms of λ_1 and λ_2 as shown next.

<u>Theorem 1</u>: Let f(x) possess $\lambda_1=(T_1,\Psi_1)$ and $\lambda_2=(T_2,\Psi_2)$ symmetries. Then it possesses a $\lambda_3=(T_3,\Psi_3)$ symmetry where $T_3=(A_2A_1, A_2b_1+b_2)$ and $\Psi_3=(\delta_1\delta_2, (\delta_1\beta_2+A_2^{-t}\beta_1), \delta_1\phi_2+\phi_1-b_2^t A_2^{-t}\beta_1)$

<u>Proof</u>: Let $x_1=A_1x+b_1$ for some $x \in X$. (5)

Then, from the definition of λ_1-symmetry, we

have $|f(x)| = |f(x_1)|$ and

$$\measuredangle f(x) = \delta_1 \measuredangle f(x_1) + \beta_1{}^t x_1 + \phi_1. \quad (6)$$

Let $x_2 = T_2[x_1] = A_2 x_1 + b_2$.

Then $|f(x_1)| = |f(x_2)|$ and (7)

$$\measuredangle f(x_1) = \delta_2 \measuredangle f(x_2) + \beta_2{}^t x_2 + \phi_2. \quad (8)$$

Substituting for $|f(x_1)|$ and $\measuredangle f(x_1)$ from (7) into (8), we get $|f(x)| = |f(x_2)|$ and

$$\measuredangle f(x) = \delta_1\delta_2 \measuredangle f(x_2) + \delta_1\beta_2{}^t x_2 + \delta_1\phi_2 + \beta_1{}^t x_1 + \phi_1. \quad (9)$$

Now, $x_2 = T_2[x_1] = T_2[T_1[x_1]] = A_2A_1x + A_2b_1 + b_2 = T_3[x]$ where $T_3 = (A_2A_1, A_2b_1 + b_2)$ (10)

From (7) $x_1 = T_2^{-1}[x_2] = A_2^{-1}x_2 - A_2^{-1}b_2$ Substituting for x_1 in (9), we get

$$\measuredangle f(x) = \delta_1\delta_2 \measuredangle f(x_2) + (\delta_1\beta_2{}^t + \beta_1 A_2^{-1})x_2 + \delta_1\phi_2 + \phi_1 - \beta_1{}^t A_2^{-1} b_2) \text{ i.e.,}$$

$$\Psi_3 = (\delta_1\delta_2, (\delta_1\beta_2{}^t + \beta_1{}^t A_2^{-1})^t, \delta_1\phi_2 + \phi_1 - \beta_1{}^t A_2^{-1} b_2). \quad (11)$$

Combining T_3 and Ψ_3, we get the λ_3 symmetry operator. In other words a valid compounding rule for λ_2 and λ_1 is given by

$$\lambda_2 \circ \lambda_1 = (A_2A_1, A_2b_1 + b_2, \delta_1\delta_2, (\delta_1\beta_2 + A_2^{-t}\beta_1), \delta_1\phi_2 + \phi_1 - \beta_1{}^t A_2^{-1} b_2) \quad (12)$$

It may be verified that the above compounding operation is in general not commutative. However, it may be verified that the compounding rule obeys associative property, namely $\lambda_3 \circ (\lambda_2 \circ \lambda_1) = (\lambda_3 \circ \lambda_2) \circ \lambda_1$. We may define the identity operator as $\lambda_I = (I, 0, 1, 0, 0)$ where I is the identity matrix. Next we state the λ^{-1} symmetry operation.

<u>Theorem 2</u>: If a function f(x) possesses a $\lambda = (A, b, \delta, \beta, \phi)$ symmetry, then it also possesses a symmetry defined by the operation

$$\lambda^{-1} = (A^{-1}, -A^{-1}b, \delta, -\delta A^t\beta, -\delta\phi - \delta b^t\beta) \quad (13)$$

The proof of this theorem follows along the same lines as that of Theorem 1. It may also be verified that $\lambda^{-1} \circ \lambda = \lambda \circ \lambda^{-1} = \lambda_I$. Based on Theorem 1, we can define

$$\lambda^2 = \lambda \circ \lambda = (A^2, (A+I)b, 1, (\delta I + A^{-t})\beta, (\delta+1)\phi - b^t A^{-t}\beta). \quad (14)$$

In a similar manner λ^k, for any integer k, can be obtained. We next discuss an important property of λ based on the definitions given above.

<u>Property</u>: If a function possesses symmetry with respect to a composite symmetry operator λ, then it also possesses symmetries with respect to λ^k, k being any interger. Further, the set of all distinct λ^k, where $\lambda^0 \triangleq \lambda_I$, forms a symmetry group. If for some $K \neq 0$, $\lambda^K = \lambda_I$, then the group will contain K elements $\{\lambda_I, \lambda, \lambda^2, \ldots, \lambda^{K-1}\}$ and λ is called a K-cyclic symmetry operator and the function is said to possess a K-cyclic symmetry. It is easy to verify that the symmetry group generated by the operator $\lambda = (I, d, 1, 0, 0)$, where d is a constant vector, will contain an infinite number of elements.

If a function possesses symmetry with respect to symmetry operators λ_1 and λ_2, then one can generate the symmetry group by employing the compounding rule discussed above. This will enable one to determine the various symmetries that are generated by a given set of symmetries.

IV. SYMMETRY RELATIONS

Let $\hat{H}(\Omega)$ be the m-dimensional Fourier transform of h(n). In general, we assume h(n) and $\hat{H}(\Omega)$ to be complex functions of the real variables n and Ω respectively and h(n) is such that its m-dimensional Fourier transform $\hat{H}(\Omega)$ exists. The Fourier transform pair connecting h(n) and $\hat{H}(\Omega)$ are given by [14].

$$\hat{H}(\Omega) = \sum_{n \in N} h(n) e^{-j\Omega^t n} \quad (15)$$

and

$$h(n) = \frac{1}{(2\pi)^m} \int_{\Omega \in \Omega_p} \hat{H}(\Omega) e^{+jn^t\Omega} d\Omega \quad (16)$$

where $\Omega_p = \{\Omega \mid -\pi \leq \Omega_i \leq \pi,\ i = 1, 2, \ldots, m\}$ and $d\Omega = d\Omega_1 \cdot d\Omega_2 \cdot \ldots \cdot d\Omega_m$.

As may be easily verified from (15), $H(\Omega)$ is a periodic function of Ω with periods of 2π in Ω_1- Ω_m-directions. If h(n) has been derived from a continuous domain signal by employing periodic sampling with intervals and directions given by $v_1 \ldots v_m$ vectors in a Cartesian co-ordinate system, the actual co-ordinates of the sample points are given by

$$\ell_s = V n, \ n \in N^m \quad (17)$$

where ℓ_s is a real m x 1 vector and $V = (v_1 v_2 \ldots v_m)$ is a m x m matrix whose columns are the sampling basis vectors. Then the actual frequency ω (in rad/unit length) will be related to the normalized frequency Ω (in radians) by the relation [9,13].

$$\Omega = V^t \omega. \quad (18)$$

The following theorem relates the symmetry parameters in the two-domains.

Theorem 3: Let $\lambda_\omega = (\tilde{A},\tilde{b},\tilde{\delta},\tilde{\beta},\tilde{\phi})$ be the parameters of a T-Ψ symmetry of $\tilde{H}(\omega)$, the response of a periodically sampled system in the actual frequency ω domain and $\Psi_\Omega = (A,b,\delta,\beta,\phi)$ be that of $\hat{H}(\Omega)$, in the normalized frequency domain. Then λ_ω and λ_Ω are related as follows:

From λ_ω to λ_Ω	From λ_Ω to λ_ω
$A=V^t\tilde{A}V^{-t}$	$\tilde{A}=V^{-t}AV^t$
$b=V^t\tilde{b}$	$\tilde{b}=V^{-t}b$
$\delta=\tilde{\delta}$	$\tilde{\delta}=\delta$
$\beta=V^{-1}\tilde{\beta}$	$\tilde{\beta}=V\beta$
and $\phi=\tilde{\phi}$	and $\tilde{\phi}=\phi$

Proof: From the definition of a T-Ψ symmetry, we have

$$|\tilde{H}(\omega_T)|e^{j(\delta\} \tilde{H}(\omega_T)+\tilde{\beta}^t\omega+\tilde{\phi})}=\tilde{H}(\omega) \qquad (19)$$

where $\omega_T = T_\omega[\omega] = \tilde{A}\omega + \tilde{b}$.

let Ω_T be the normalized frequency corresponding to ω_T.

Substituting from (27) $\omega=V^{-t}\Omega$ and $\omega_T = V^{-t}\Omega_T$ into (19) we get

$$\Omega_T = V^t\tilde{A}V^{-t}\Omega + V^t\tilde{b},$$

i.e., $T_\Omega[\Omega] = A\Omega + b$

where $A=V^t\tilde{A}V^{-t}$ and $b=V^t\tilde{b}$.

Replacing $\tilde{H}(\omega)$ by $\hat{H}(\Omega)$ in (19) we get

$$|\hat{H}(\Omega_T)|\, e^{j(\tilde{\delta}\} \hat{H}(\Omega_T)+\tilde{\beta}^t V^{-t}\Omega_T + \tilde{\phi})}=\hat{H}(\Omega).$$

Then from the definition of T-Ψ symmetry we identify $\delta = \tilde{\delta}$, $\beta=V^{-1}\tilde{\beta}$ and $\phi=\tilde{\phi}$. Hence the proof.

Using the above relations and Theorem 4 to be discussed next, one can directly relate the symmetry parameters of $\tilde{H}(\omega)$ and h(n). Because of the periodic nature of $\hat{H}(\Omega)$ displacement symmetries in $\Omega_1 \ldots \Omega_m$ directions are always present. This is due to the discrete nature of h(n). We will consider the effects of remaining symmetries in $\hat{H}(\Omega)$ on h(n) and vice versa. The results are presented in Theorem 4.

Theorem 4: Let h(n) and $\hat{H}(\Omega)$ be a m-dimensional Fourier transform pair. Then $\hat{H}(\Omega)$ possesses a T-Ψ symmetry with parameters (A,b,δ,β,ϕ), det $A=\pm 1$ if and only if h(n) possesses a T-Ψ symmetry with parameters $(\delta A^{-t}, \delta\beta, \delta, -\delta b, b^t\delta + \phi)$ where A,b,δ,β,ϕ are as discussed in section III, and h(.) is assumed to have zero values for noninteger arguments.

Proof: As $\hat{H}(\Omega)$ possesses a T-Ψ symmetry with parameters (A,b,δ,β,ϕ), it satisfies the following equation for all $\Omega \in R^m$

$$|\hat{H}(A\Omega+b)|\exp(j\delta\}\hat{H}(A\Omega+b) + \beta^t(A\Omega+b)+\phi)=H(\Omega) \qquad (20)$$

Substituting for $\hat{H}(\Omega)$ from (15) we get

$$\Big|\sum_{n\in N^m} h(n)\ \exp(-j\, n^t(A\Omega+b))\Big|\exp[j(\delta\}\sum_{n\in N^m} h(n)\exp(-j\, n^t(A\Omega+b))+\beta^t(A\Omega+b)+\phi)] = \sum_{n\in N^m} h(n)\exp(-j\, n^t\Omega). \qquad (21)$$

$\delta = -1$ corresponds to taking the conjugate of the function and the conjugate of a sum is equal to the sum of the conjugates; hence, equation (21) can be rewritten as:

$$\sum_{n\in N^m} |h(n)|\, \exp\,[j(\delta(\} h(n) - n^t(A\Omega+b)) + \beta^t(A\Omega+b)+\phi)] = \sum_{n\in N^m} h(n)\, e^{-j\Omega^t n}. \qquad (22)$$

Let $n = \delta A^{-t}n' + \delta\beta$. Substituting for n in terms of n′ in LHS expression of (22) and then replacing n′ with n, we get

$$\sum_{n\in N_c} |h(\delta A^{-t}n+\delta\beta)|\, \exp[j(\delta\}h(\delta A^{-t}n+\delta\beta) - (\delta A^{-t}n+\delta\beta)^t\delta b + b^t\beta+\phi\}]\, e^{-j\Omega^t n} = \sum_{n\in N^m} h(n)e^{-j\Omega^t n}, \qquad (23)$$

where $N_c = \{n \mid (\delta A^{-t}n+\delta\beta) \in N^m$. The above equation will be satisfied for all Ω only if

$h(n) = 0$, $\forall$ n such that $\delta A^{-t}n+\delta\beta \notin N^m$ and

$$h(n)=|h(\delta A^{-t}n+\delta\beta)|\, \exp[j(\delta\}h(\delta A^{-t}n+\delta\beta) - (\delta A^{-t}n+\delta\beta)^t\delta b+b^t\beta+\phi)],\ \forall\ n \text{ such that } \delta A^{-t}n+\delta\beta \in N^m. \qquad (24)$$

In other words defining $h(\delta A^{-t}n + \delta\beta) = 0$ for $A^{-t}n+\delta\beta \notin N^m$, the impulse response condition can be written as

$$h(n)=|h(\delta A^{-t}n+\delta\beta)|\exp[j(\delta< h(\delta A^{-t}n+\delta\beta) - (\delta A^{-t}n+\delta\beta)^t\delta b+b^t\beta+\phi)],\ \forall\ n \in N^m. \qquad (25)$$

Comparing equation (25) with the definition for T-Ψ symmetry we find h(n) possesses a T-Ψ symmetry with the parameters $(\delta A^{-t}, \delta\beta, \delta, -\delta b, b^t\beta + \beta)$ as in the continuous case. Hence the necessity part of the theorem is proved. Sufficiency part of the theorem can be proved either by noting that h(n) and $\hat{H}(\Omega)$ are uniquely related on a one-to-one basis by the Fourier transformation, or by following the above steps starting with h(n) domain symmetry.

Observations: Next we make the following observations based on Theorem 4.

i) If $(A,b,\delta,\beta,\phi)_\Omega$ and $(A,b,\delta,\beta,\phi)_n$ are respectively the Ω-domain and the n-domain symmetry parameters, the corresponding n and Ω parameters are obtained by the following relations.

$$(A,b,\delta,\beta,\phi)_\Omega \Rightarrow (\delta A^{-t}, \delta\beta, \delta, -\delta b, b^t\beta+\phi)_n \qquad (26)$$

and

$(A,b,\delta,\beta,\phi)\underset{n}{\Rightarrow}(\delta A^{-t},-\delta\beta,\ \delta,\ \delta b,\ b^t\beta+\phi)_{\Omega}$. (27)

One can easily verify the compatibility of the two relations by noting that one relation is the inverse of the other relation. The reason for the appearance of the negative sign in front of δb in (26) while it is in front of $\delta\beta$ in (27) may be attributed to the differing signs $\exp[\pm j\Omega^t n]$ in the definitions of Fourier and inverse Fourier transforms (15) and (16).

ii) Theorem 4 and the observation (i) also illustrate the duality present in Ω and n domain symmetries.

iii) Further, it may be noted that the nature of symmetry transformation, such as rotation, reflection, etc., as identified by the A-matrix remains the same in both Ω and n domains.

iv) Identical symmetries result in both Ω and n domains if $\delta=1$, b=0 and $\beta=0$.

We next illustrate the application of Theorem 4 using an example.

Example: Let $\hat{H}(\Omega)$ of a hexagonally sampled 2-D system possess 6-fold rotational conjugate symmetry. Determine the interrelationships among impulse response samples. For the hexagonal sampling, the sampling basis matrix

$$V = \begin{bmatrix} 2/\sqrt{3} & 1/\sqrt{3} \\ 0 & 1 \end{bmatrix}.$$

For 6-fold rotation $T[\omega]$ is given by

$$\tilde{A} = \begin{bmatrix} 1/2 & -\sqrt{3}/2 \\ \sqrt{3}/2 & 1/2 \end{bmatrix},\ \tilde{b} = 0$$

Then $\lambda_\omega=(\tilde{A},\tilde{b},-1,0,0)$. Applying Theorem 3 we find λ_Ω as

$$\lambda_\Omega=(\begin{smallmatrix} 0 & -1 \\ 1 & 1 \end{smallmatrix}),0,-1,0,0).$$

Applying Theorem 4 we find λ_n as

$$\lambda_n=((\begin{smallmatrix} -1 & 1 \\ -1 & 0 \end{smallmatrix}),\ 0,\ -1,\ 0,\ 0).$$

Then from the definition of λ operation we have $h(n_1,n_2)=[h(-n_1+n_2,-n_1)]^*$. It may be easily verified that λ_n is a 6-cyclic symmetry operator, i.e., $\lambda_n,\lambda_n^2,\lambda_n^3,\lambda_n^4$, and λ_n^5 are also symmetry operators for the above function. Corresponding to each one of them, we have a symmetry condition as

$h(n_1,n_2)=[h(-n_1+n_2,-n_1)]^*=h(-n_2,n_1-n_2)=$
$[h(n_1,n_2)]^*=[h(-n_1+n_2,-n_1)]^*=[h(-n_2,n_1-n_2)]^*$.

Remarks: One may wonder that the operation could have been defined in a more general form as $\Psi[f(x)]=r\,|f(x)|\,e^{j(\delta\angle f(x)+\beta^t x+\phi)}$ where r is a real number. We will show that this is not suitable for Fourier transform pairs. As discussed in Section III, if λ is a symmetry operation for f(x), λ^k, k being any integer, will also be a symmetry operation. This will mean $|f(T_k[x])| = r^k |f(x)|$, $-\infty< k <\infty$, where T_k is the transformation part of λ^k. It is easily verified that if $r\neq 1$, f(x) will be an unbounded function that is not Fourier transformable. A similar situation occurs if T[x] is not an equiaffine transformation, i.e., det $A\neq\pm 1$.

VI SUMMARY

The relation between the symmetries of a function in signal and Fourier transform domain representations is investigated. It is established that symmetry in one domain induces a similar symmetry in the other domain and a duality exists with respect to the symmetries in both the domains. The symmetry relations among the Fourier transform pairs have been established for discrete domain signals. The results are obtained for m-dimensional signals and an example have been given to illustrate the application of the results in the 2-D case.

REFERENCES

[1] J. G. Fiasconaro, Two-Dimensional Non-recursive Filters: Picture Processing and Digital Filtering, (Topics in Applied Physics, Vol. 6, T. S. Huang, Ed., New York, Springer-Verlag, 1975, Ch.3, pp. 69-129).

[2] P. K. Rajan and M. N. S. Swamy, Quadrantal Symmetry Associated with Two-Dimensional Digital Filter Transfer Function: IEEE Trans. Circuits Sys., (Vol. CAS-25, pp. 340-343, 1978).

[3] ____________, Some Results on the Nature of a Two-Dimensional Filter Function Possessing Certain Symmetry in its Magnitude Response: IEE J. Electron. Circuits Syst., (Vol. 2, pp. 147-153, 1978).

[4] ____________, Symmetry Constraints on Two-Dimensional Half-Plane Digital Transfer Functions: IEEE Trans. Acoust., Speech, Signal Processing, (Vol. ASSP-27, pp. 5067-511, 1979).

[5] D. M. Goodman, Quadrantal Symmetry Calculations for Non Symmetric Half-Plane Filters, in Proc. 14th Asilomore Conf., Vol. 14, (1980).

[6] P. K. Rajan, H. C. Reddy and M. N. S. Swamy: Four Fold Rotational Symmetry in Two-Dimensional Functions: IEEE Trans Acoust., Speech, Signal Processing,(Vol. ASSP-30, pp. 488-499, 1982).

[7] S. A. H. Aly and M. M. Fahmy: Symmetry in Two-Dimensional Rectangularly Sampled Digital Filters, IEEE Trans. Acoust., Speech, Signal Processing, (Vol. ASSP-29, pp. 794-805, 1981).

[8] ____________: Symmetry Exploitation in the Design and Implementation of 2-D Rectangularly Sampled Digital Filters, IEEE Trans. Acoust., Speech, Signal Processing, (ASSP-29, pp. 973-982, 1981).

[9] J. H. Lodge and M. M. Fahmy: K-Cyclic Symmetries in Multi-Dimensional Sampled Signals, IEEE Trans. Acoust., Speech, Signal Processing, (Vol. ASSP-31, 1983.)
[10] B. P. George and A. N. Venetsanopoulos: Design of Two-Dimensional Recursive Digital Filters on the Basis of Quadrantal and Octagonal Symmetry, Circuits, Systems and Signals Processing, (Vol. 3, No. 1, 1984).
[11] P. K. Rajan, H. C. Reddy and M. N. S. Swamy: Symmetry Relations in Two-Dimensional Fourier Transforms, Proc. 1984 International Symposium on Circuits and Systems, (Montreal, Canada, 1984).
[12] D. Gaus, Transformations and Geometries, Appleton-Century-Crofts, New York, (1969).
[13] D. P. Petersen and Middleton: Sampling and Reconstruction of Wave number Limited Functions in n-Dimensional Euclidean Spaces, Information and Control, (vol.5, pp. 279-323, 1962).
[14] R. M. Bracewell: The Fourier Transform and Its Application, McGraw Hill Book Co., New York, (1965), pp. 241-245.
[15] D. E. Dudgeon and R. M. Mersereau, Multi-Dimensional Digital Signal Processing, Prentice Hall, Inc., Englewood Cliffs, New Jersey, (1984).

Table 1: Ψ-operations and the names of the resulting symmetries

δ	$\underline{\beta}$	ϕ	Ψ-operation	Symmetry name	Symbol
1	$\underline{0}$	0	$\Psi[f(x)] = f(x)$	Identity symmetry	Ψ_I
1	$\underline{0}$	π	$\Psi[f(x)] = -f(x)$	Anti-symmetry	Ψ_A
-1	$\underline{0}$	0	$\Psi[f(x)] = [f(x)]^*$	Conjugate symmetry	Ψ_C
-1	$\underline{0}$	π	$\Psi[f(x)] = -[f(x)]^*$	Conjugate anti-symmetry	Ψ_{CA}

DIGITAL TECHNIQUES in Simulation, Communication and Control
Spyros G. Tzafestas (editor)
Elsevier Science Publishers B.V. (North-Holland) © IMACS, 1985

2-D HALF-PLANE CEPSTRUM IN DIGITAL FILTER ANALYSIS AND DESIGN

G. Garibotto

3M Italia Ricerche S.p.A. - 17016 Ferrania (Savona) - Italy

The paper describes a 2-D recursive filter design with stability and vector block-processing constraints. The analysis of stability as well as minimum -phase spectral factorization are performed in the cepstrum domain. The selected support for the filter coefficients is a causal symmetric half-plane mask to take advantage of pipeline vector-processing through an array-processor. The method can be applied to general digital filtering applications and an example of image restoration is referred, using power spectrum equalization.

1. INTRODUCTION

Two dimensional digital filtering has proved to be a valuable tool in signal processing, whenever the problem can be efficiently modelled as a 2-D partial differential equation. In particular, linear filtering has found important applications in geophisics, for velocity selection [1] with fan-like frequency specifications, and for 2-D wave migration [2] , with amplitude and phase constraints. On the other hand in most picture processing problems, as in adaptive contrast equalization, it is necessary to refer to non-linear, space-variant digital systems. Anyway, also in this field, linear space invariant filtering can be useful to achieve image restoration based on the power spectrum characteristic of the ideal and distorted pictures. An example of application will be referred in section 4, to demonstrate the usefulness of this approach. The choice of a 2-D half-plane recursive structure is motivated by the higher flexibility with respect to finite-impulse response filtering, as well as by remarkable saving in the processing computation and data memory. The additional stability problems with respect to FIR filtering, are solved in the cepstrum domain. In section 3 the properties of 2-D cepstrum and the required computational techniques are briefly recalled. A generalization of this method is presented to achieve at the same time a control of stability as well as the filter stabilization, if requested.

2. HALF-PLANE RECURSIVE FILTERING

The general transfer function of a 2-D recursive filter is expressed in its direct form as a ratio of polynomials :

$$H(z_1, z_2) = G\cdot A(z_1, z_2) / B(z_1, z_2) \qquad 1)$$

with $A(z_1, z_2) = \sum_{S_A} a(n_1, n_2) z_1^{n_1} z_2^{n_2}$

$$B(z_1, z_2) = \sum_{S_B} b(n_1, n_2) z_1^{n_1} z_2^{n_2}$$

the coefficient supports S_A and S_B have to satisfy some different constraints. For instance the mask of the denominator in the most general case should be the asymmetric half-plane S_H, which, for a filter degree $N_\emptyset$ is given by :

$$S_H = (n_1 = 0 \cap 1 \leq n_2 \leq N_\emptyset) \cup (1 \leq n_1 \leq N_\emptyset \cap |n_2| \leq N_\emptyset) \qquad 2)$$

as depicted in Fig. 1a). Unfortunately this solution is not suitable for vector block-processing, due to the inherent recursive computation for $n_1 = 0$. In fact let us consider the following canonical realization, row by row :

$$v(N_\emptyset, n) = x(n) - \sum_{S_H} b(k_1, k_2)\, v(N_\emptyset - k_1, n-k_2) \qquad 3)$$

$$y(n) = G \cdot \sum_{S_A} a(k_1, k_2)\, v(N_\emptyset - k_1, n-k_2) \qquad 4)$$

In this case the updating of the state matrix $v(m_1, m_2)$ in (3) can be written as :

$$v(N_\emptyset, n) = x(n) - \sum_{S_S} b(k_1, k_2)\, v(N_\emptyset - k_1, n-k_2) - \sum_{k_2=1}^{N_\emptyset} b(0, k_2)\, v(N_\emptyset, n-k_2) \quad 5)$$

where the only recursion involved is due to the last term and $S_s \equiv (1 \leq n_1 \leq N_\emptyset) \cap (|n_2| \leq N_\emptyset)$ represents the casual symmetric support, shown in Fig. 1b). In the following, a suboptimal solution is used, consisting in a causal symmetric support S_s for the denominator coefficients and a fully symmetric mask (as in Fig 1c) for the numerator . In this way equations 4), 5) are efficiently implemented in vector order through an array processor.

- Filter design

The example of application considered in the paper, as shown in section 5, requires the approximation of a magnitude squared function $P(\ _1, \ _2)$ This task is accomplished according to a recently proposed non-linear optimization technique [3] , to minimize the frequency error :

$$J(G, \underline{a}, \underline{b}) = \sum_{(\omega_1,\omega_2)\in\Omega} W(\omega_1,\omega_2)\cdot\left[|H(\omega_1,\omega_2)|^2 - P(\omega_1,\omega_2)\right]^P \quad 6)$$

This algorithm allows a convergence to a local minimum of the function, but no stability constraints are included, even if, in most simple situations, the designed denominator turns out to be already a minimum-phase sequence. In fact, with reference to the extensive literature on 2-D stability [4] , the main stability property, which will be used in the paper, is the following general definition :

A 2-D recursive filter, with a transfer function as in (1), is stable if its denominator polynomial is a minimum-phase sequence.

The 2-D cepstrum function, described in section 3, will be used to achieve two major goals : test of stability for the designed filter and stabilization of those sequences which are eventually found unstable.

3. TWO-DIMENSIONAL CEPSTRUM ESTIMATION

The definition of the 2-D complex cepstrum $c(n_1, n_2)$ of a given sequence $b(n_1, n_2)$ is usually given in the Z-transform domain as :

$$C(z_1, z_2) = \log B(z_1, z_2) \quad (7)$$

according to the Z-transform pairs :

$$C(z_1, z_2) = Z\left[c(n_1, n_2)\right]$$

$$B(z_1, z_2) = Z\left[b(z_1, z_2)\right]$$

The spatial relations between the sequence $b(\cdot)$ and its cepstrum $c(\cdot)$ are obtained by equating the function derivatives of (7), with respect to the complex variables (z_1, z_2) :

$$\frac{\partial C(z_1, z_2)}{\partial z_i} = \frac{1}{B(z_1\ z_2)}\ \frac{\partial B(z_1, z_2)}{\partial z_i} \quad (8)$$

$$i = 1, 2$$

which corresponds to the 2-D convolution :

$$n_1\ c(n_1, n_2) ** b(n_1, n_2) = n_i b(n_1, n_2)$$

$$i = 1, 2 \quad (9)$$

Of course equations (8) and (9) can be used to estimate the cepstrum $c(\cdot)$ only is the original sequence $b(\cdot)$ is a minimum-phase function; otherwise the corresponding recursive equation would produce divergence, due to instability :

$$c(n_1, n_2) = b(n_1, n_2) - \sum_{S_B} \frac{n_i - k_i}{n_i}\, b(k_1, k_2)\, c(n_1-k_1, n_2-k_2) \quad (10)$$

$$i = 1, 2$$

with initial conditions $c(n_1, n_2) = 0$ for $(n_1 < 0) \cup (n_1 = 0 \cap n_2 < 0)$ and $c(0, 0) = \log b(0, 0)$.

In a stable situation the inverse relation (11) can be used to estimate a minimum-phase sequence $b(n_1, n_2)$, from its cepstrum, as :

$$b(n_1, n_2) = \sum_{S_c} \frac{k_i}{n_i}\, c(k_i, k_2)\, b(n_1-k_1, n_2-k_2) \quad (11)$$

$$i = 1, 2$$

Since we are using a causal symmetric mask for the coefficients $S_B = S_S$, the corresponding spatial support of the cepstrum, S_C is the triangular sector shown in Fig. 2. Because of this choice both sequence $b(\cdot)$ and $c(\cdot)$ are zero for $n_1 = 0$, unless for the initial conditions at (0, 0). As a consequence, the two equations (10) and (11) have to be computed only for $n_1 > 0$ and $i = 1$.

4. STABILITY CONSTRAINTS IN THE CEPSTRUM DOMAIN.

The 2-D cepstrum has been profitably used for stability analysis of 2-D half-plane recursive filters [5], [6]. Of course these methods are also suitable for a causal symmetric mask S_S which represents a sub-class of the general half-plane S_H. In the paper, the previously discussed cepstrum properties are efficiently used in a single process, to perform both a stability test on the designed filter as well as a stabilization procedure in the hypothesis of an unstable condition. In fact the denominator sequence obtained with the optimization technique described in section 2 is analysed in the following way :

I. An estimate of the cepstrum function, corresponding to the denominator sequence, is computed according to equation (10) on a finite region S_c, wide enough to avoid significant truncation errors. A threshold value T_c is selected so that IF $|c(n_1, n_2)| > T_c$, at any index pair (n_1, n_2), go to step III.

II. Otherwise, the inverse relation (11) is evaluated, to obtain a sequence $b'(n_1, n_2)$ and the two approximation errors are computed :

$$D_B = \sum_{(n_1, n_2) \in S_S} \left| b(n_1, n_2) - b'(n_1, n_2) \right|$$

$$\overline{D} = \sum_{(n_1, n_2) \notin S_S} \left| b'(n_1, n_2) \right| \qquad (12)$$

Again a threshold control is performed so that if $D_B \leq T_B$ and $\overline{D} \leq \overline{T}$, the procedure is stopped, and the filter is considered computationally stable. The threshold values $\overline{T}$ and T_B are conditioned by the choice of the cepstrum support S_c.

III. Since the filter is found unstable, a cepstrum estimate is computed as the inverse Fourier transform :

$$c'(n_1, n_2) = \mathrm{IDFT}\left[\log |B(\omega_1, \omega_2)|\right] \text{ for } (n_1, n_2) \in S_c$$

$$c'(0, 0) = c'(0, 0) / 2 \qquad (13)$$

$$c'(n_1, n_2) = 0 \quad \text{for} \quad (n_1, n_2) \notin S_c$$

and a stable sequence $b'(n_1, n_2)$ is obtained, using equation (11). It is worthwhile to remark that the spatial support of $c'(n_1, n_2)$ has to be the symmetric region S_c; otherwise additional errors could produce an unstable estimate $b'(n_1, n_2)$.

5. EXAMPLE OF RESTORATION FILTER.

A typical problem of digital picture processing is the restoration of linearly distorted images. Unfortunately, in most practical situations, it is quite difficult to have reliable models of the blurring function as well as of the noise. A very promising blind-deconvolution technique, based on power spectrum equalization, has been suggested a few years ago in [7]. In this case the frequency specifications of the restoration filter are given by :

$$P(\omega_1, \omega_2) = P_I(\omega_1, \omega_2)/P_D(\omega_1, \omega_2) \qquad (14)$$

where $P_I(\cdot)$ represents the power spectrum of the ideal image field and $P_D(\cdot)$ is the power spectrum of the distorted observations, through the blurring function $D(\omega_1, \omega_2)$, as :

$$P_D(\omega_1, \omega_2) = |D(\omega_1, \omega_2)|^2 \cdot P_I(\omega_1, \omega_2) + P_N(\omega_1, \omega_2) \qquad (15)$$

$P_N(\cdot)$ being the noise power spectrum of the current image. In this approach an a-priori estimate of $P_I(\cdot)$ is requested, to describe the ideal energy distribution in the frequency domain. The actual filtering constraints are determined by the power spectrum estimate $P_D(\cdot)$ of the current distorted image, through average of 2-D finite periodograms.

Henceforth, the function (14) represents the magnitude squared function in (6) to be approximated by a symmetric half-plane filter. In the following example the selected ideal power spectrum $P_I(\cdot)$ was a circularly simmetric gaussian function with $\sigma = 0.25\ \omega$, ω being the sampling frequency,

$$P_I(\omega_1, \omega_2) = K \cdot \exp\left\{-(\omega_1^2 + \omega_2^2)/2\sigma^2\right\} \qquad (16)$$

$P_D(\ )$ has been estimated for the X-ray image shown in Fig. 3 as follows. The image has been divided into half-width overlapped blocks of size (32x32) pixels; Hanning windowing was used for each block followed by FFT's and average of the squared transforms. The corresponding frequency function (14) to be approximated is shown in Fig. 4 together with the obtained magnitude squared frequency response of the designed half-plane recursive filter. The filter degree was $N_\emptyset = 2$ with a symmetric mask for the 14 numerator coefficients (Fig. 1c) and for the 10 samples denominator sequence (Fig. 1b). Using this filtering function the result of Fig. 5 has been obtained, where the emphasis of intermediate frequencies is balanced by a reasonable control of high frequency noise. Due to the symmetric support of the coefficients, block-parallel processing can be used for the filter implementation. Using a DEC-LSI 11/23 microcomputer and a 1 MFlops SKYMNK-Q-array processor the input 512x512 pixel image has been processed in $\approx$ 80 seconds.

CONCLUSIONS

The paper describes a recursive filtering technique with applications to digital image restoration. A stability test and, if requested, a filter stabilization are performed using the minimum-phase properties of the 2-D complex cepstrum. Block-processing implementation is possible with additional symmetric constraints on the spatial support of the filter coefficients. An example of X-ray image restoration is referred, to demonstrate the potential effectiveness of this approach. Further significant improvements are possible, by selecting more appropriate power spectrum estimates for the ideal input image field.

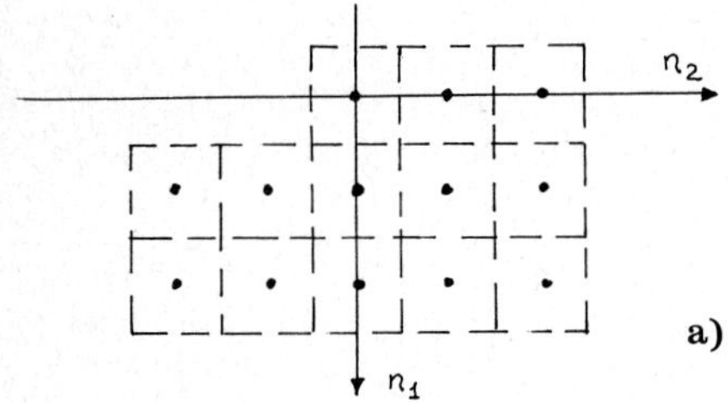

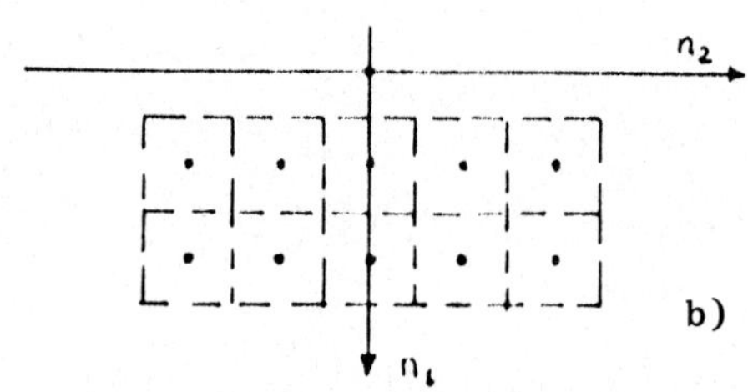

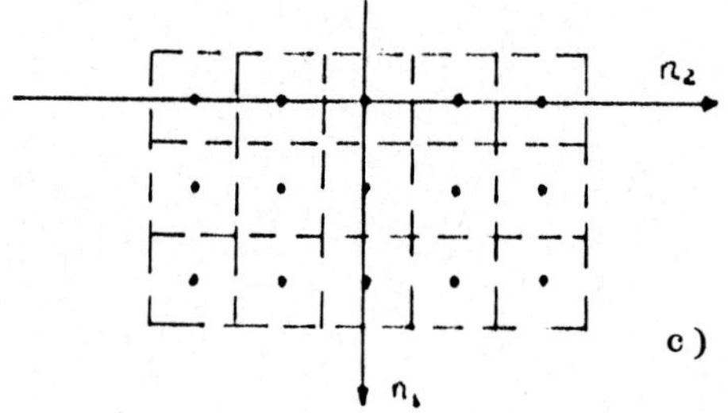

Fig. 1 - Coefficient support of 2-D half-plane filter. a) asymmetric mask. b) causal symmetric mask. c) fully-symmetric mask.

REFERENCES :

[1] Garibotto G., Molpen R., A New Approach to Half-Plane Recursive Filter Design, IEEE Trans. on Acoust. Speech and Signal Proc. vol. ASSP-29, n. 1, (1981), 111-115.

[2] Garibotto G., 2-D Recursive Phase Filters for the Solution of Two-Dimensional Wave Equations, IEEE Trans. on Acoust. Speech and Signal Proc., vol. ASSP-27, n. 4,(1979), 367-373.

[3] Lodge J.H., Fahmy M.M., An Optimization Technique for the Design of Half-Plane 2-D Recursive Digital Filters, IEEE Trans. on Circuits and Systems, Vol. CAS-27, n.8, (1980), 721-724.

[4] Jury E.I., Stability of Multidimensional Scalar and Matrix Polynomials, Proceedings of the IEEE, vol. 66, n. 9, (1978), 1018-1047.

[5] Garibotto G., Two-Dimensional Stability Analysis using the Complex Cepstrum, Proceedings of ISCAS' 82, Rome, (1982), 868-871.

[6] Garibotto G., Ghisio G., 2-D Recursive Filter Stabilization, Proceedings of the ECCTD'81, The Hague, (1981), 681-685.

[7] Cole E.R., The Removal of Unknown Image Blurs by Homomorphic Filtering, University of Utah, Computer Science Dep., Report UTEC-CSc-74-029, (June 1973).

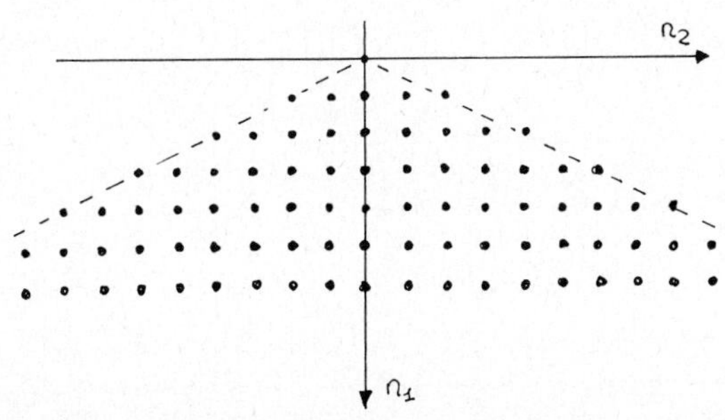

Fig. 2 - Spatial support of the 2-D half-plane symmetric cepstrum.

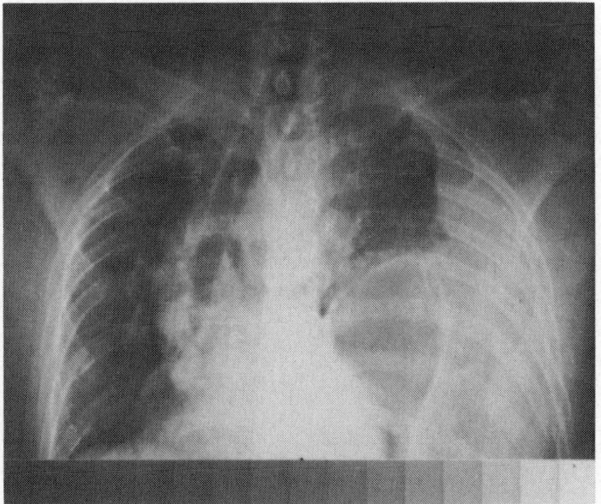

Fig. 3 - Original digitized X-ray image : 400x512 pixels with 9 bits of quantization.

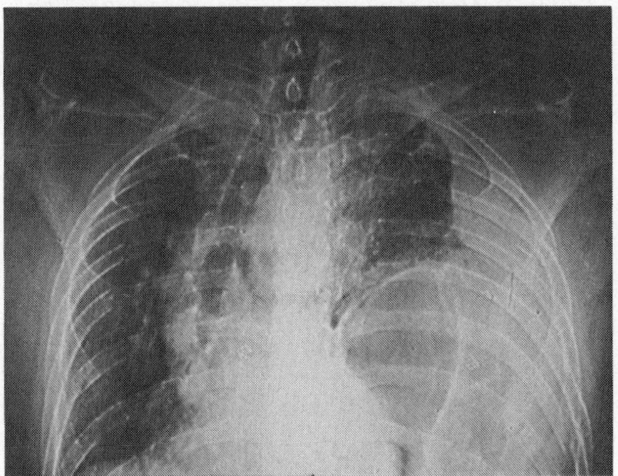

Fig. 5 - Results of blind deconvolution by power spectrum equalization.

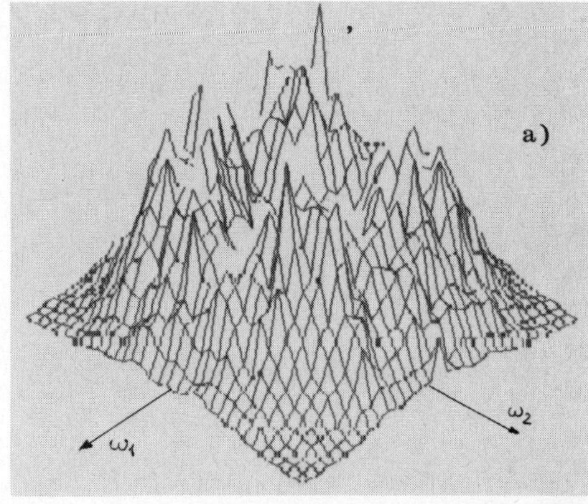

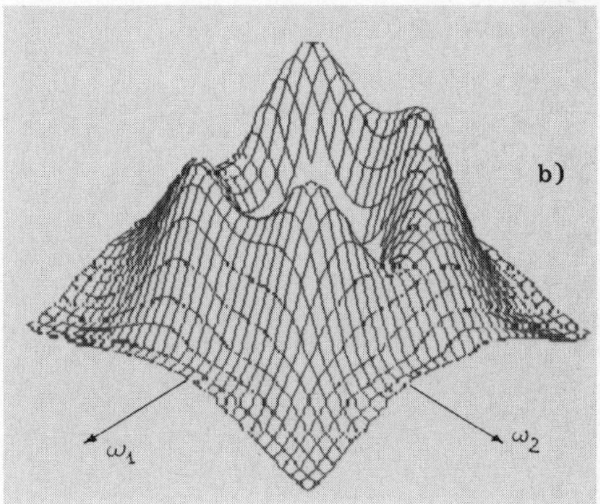

Fig. 4 - a) : frequency specifications for the restoration filter; b) : magnitude squared function of the 2-D designed filter.

DIGITAL TECHNIQUES in Simulation, Communication and Control
Spyros G. Tzafestas (editor)
Elsevier Science Publishers B.V. (North-Holland) © IMACS, 1985

STABILITY OF HALF-PLANE TWO-DIMENSIONAL DIGITAL SYSTEMS

H. C. Reddy, P. K. Rajan and M. N. S. Swamy

Dept. of Electrical Engrg.
Tennessee Tech. University
Cookeville, TN 38505, USA

Dept. of Electrical. Engrg.
Concordia University
Montreal, P.Q., Canada

Two-variable (2-V) semi-Hurwitz polynomials find application in the testing of the stability two-dimensional (2-D) half-plane digital filters. In this paper, a classification of these polynomials into very strict, principal, narrow sense and broad sense semi-Hurwitz polynomials is presented, and their properties studied. As in the case of regular 2-V Hurwitz polynomials this classification is carried out on the basis of the absence or presence and the nature of the zeros on the imaginary axes of the (s_1, s_2)-biplane. Application of these semi-Hurwitz polynomials in testing the stability of 2-D half-plane digital filters is discussed. A sufficiency condition on the coefficients of the denominator polynomials of 2-D half-plane digital filter transfer functions that ensures their stability is also presented.

I. INTRODUCTION

There is a growing interest in 2-D digital filters due to their application in several practical areas such as image processing and processing of biomedical, pictorial, sonar and radar data. Half-plane 2-D digital filters have been shown to be a more general class of filters capable of possessing a wider range of frequency responses. Similar to the quarter-plane filter design, the stability analysis is an important aspect of the design of half-plane filters. This analysis is often carried out by testing for the absence of zeros of the denominator polynomials of system transfer functions in certain specified regions of the variable domains. To aid in the testing of 1-D continuous and discrete systems, axis (analog) Hurwitz polynomials and circle (discrete) Hurwitz polynomials have been defined, their properties studied and testing procedures developed [1-5]. From the point of view of applications, two and multivariable (analog) very strict Hurwitz polynomials (VSHP) were introduced [6, 7]. It has been shown that the transfer function of a structurally stable 2-D quarter plane discrete (z_1, z_2) domain system function when transformed to analog (s_1, s_2) domain function using double bilinear transformation (DBT) will possess a VSHP denominator. We can study the stability of half-plane 2-D digital systems by developing the theory of special types of Hurwitz polynomials. The properties of presently known Hurwitz polynomials cannot be used in the design of 2-D half-plane digital filters. Thus, a new type of Hurwitz polynomial called semi-Hurwitz polynomial has been defined for this purpose [8]. The properties of this polynomial can directly be related to the stability analysis and design of 2-D half-plane filters.

In Section II, some notations and preliminaries are discussed. The definitions and properties of various types of semi-Hurwitz polynomials are given in the following section. Based on the semi-Hurwitz concept, some results on the stability of 2-D half-plane systems are presented. A sufficiency condition on the coefficients of the denominator polynomials of 2-D half-plane digital system transfer functions that ensures their stability is also presented.

II. NOTATIONS AND SOME PRELIMINARIES

Extended Complex Plane S: By an 'extended plane,' we denote the plane that includes the infinite distant points. In this extension, the infinite distant points are assumed to converge to a point called the point at infinity. The behaviour of a function at this point can be studied by mapping this point to any arbitrary point c by a transformation

$$s' = \frac{as + b}{s - c}$$

where a, b and c are arbitrary complex constants. The neighborhood of the point at infinity will be mapped to the neighborhood of c. A convenient transformation is obtained if c is chosen as the origin, a = 0 and b = 1.

In a similar manner, the extended biplane S^2 is defined as $S^2 = S_1 \times S_2$ where S_1, S_2 are extended complex planes. For further discussion of this extension one may see [9].

The following symbols are used to denote the various regions in S_1, S_2 and S^2. For $i = 1, 2$

$$S_{i+} = \{s_i | R_e s_i > 0, \ s_i < \infty\} =$$
The open right half-plane.

$S_{i-} = \{s_i | R_e s_i < 0, \ s_i < \infty\} =$
The open left half-plane.

$S_{io} = \{s_i | R_e s_i = 0\} =$
The imaginary axis including the point at infinity.

$S_{i\oplus} = S_{io} \cup S_{i+} =$
The closed right half of s_i-plane.

$S_{i\theta} = S_{io} \cup S_{i-} =$
The closed left half of s_i-plane.

$S^2_{\alpha,\beta} = S_{1\alpha} \times S_{2\beta}$ where $\alpha,\beta \in \{+, -, 0, \oplus, \theta\}$

where X denotes the Cartesian product of two sets.

In Z-domain, the notation used is the following:
$\bar{U}^2 = \{(z_1, z_2) | \ |z_1| \le 1, |z_2| \le 1\} =$
closed unit bidisc.

$T^2 = \{(z_1, z_2) | \ |z_1| = 1, |z_2| = 1\} =$
The distinguished boundary of the unit bidisc.

III. VARIOUS TYPES OF SEMI-HURWITZ POLYNOMIALS

Following are the definitions of various types of semi-Hurwitz polynomials:

<u>Definition 1</u>: $P(s_1, s_2)$ is a broad sense semi-Hurwitz polynomial weak in s_1(BSSHP - 1) if it has no zero sets in the region $\{(s_1, s_2) | R_e(s_1) = 0, R_e s_2 > 0, |s_1| \le \infty$, and $|s_2| \le \infty\}$.

In terms of previously developed notation $P(s_1, s_2)$ has no zero sets in S^2_{0+}.

$P(s_1, s_2)$ is a broad sense semi-Hurwitz polynomial weak in s_2(BSSHP - 2) if $P(s_1, s_2) \ne 0$ in S^2_{+0}.

<u>Definition 2</u>: $P(s_1, s_2)$ is a narrow sense semi-Hurwitz polynomial weak in s_1(NSSHP - 1) if it has no zero sets in the region $\{(s_1, s_2) | R_e s_1 = 0, R_e s_2 > 0, |s_1| < \infty$ and $|s_2| < \infty\} \cup \{(s_1, s_2) | R_e s_2 = 0, |s_2| < \infty\}$ i.e. $P(s_1, s_2) \ne 0$ in $S^2_{0+} \cup S_{2o}$.

$P(s_1, s_2)$ is a narrow sense semi-Hurwitz polynomial weak in s_2(NSSHP - 2) if $P(s_1, s_2) \ne 0$ in $S^2_{+0} \cup S_{1o}$.

<u>Definition 3</u>: $P(s_1, s_2)$ is a principal semi-Hurwitz polynomial weak in s_1(PSHP - 1) if it has no zero sets in $S^2_{0\oplus}$ except at isolated points on S^2_{oo} and $P(s_1, s_2)$ is a principal semi-Hurwitz polynomial weak in s_2(PSHP - 2) if it has no zero sets in $S^2_{\oplus o}$ except at isolated points on S^2_{oo}.

<u>Definition 4</u>: $P(s_1, s_2)$ is a very strict semi-Hurwitz polynomial weak in s_1(VSSHP - 1) if it has no zero sets in the region $\{(s_1, s_2) | R_e s_1 = 0, R_e s_2 \ge 0, |s_1| \le \infty, |s_2| \le \infty\}$ i.e., $P(s_1, s_2) \ne 0$ or 0/0 in $S^2_{o\oplus}$.

$P(s_1, s_2)$ is a very strict semi-Hurwitz polynomial weak in s_2(VSSHP - 2) if $P(s_1, s_2) \ne 0$ or o/o in $S^2_{\oplus o}$.

It may be noted that conditions in the definition of each successive semi-Hurwitz polynomial include the conditions in the previous definitions and so each successive class of semi-Hurwitz polynomial is a sub-class of earlier classes.

The following are examples for the above four types of semi-Hurwitz polynomials.

<u>Example 1</u>: $P(s_1, s_2) = (s_2^2 + 1)(s_1^2 - 1)(s_1 s_2 + s_1 + 1)$ is a BSSHP weak in s_1. Note that under the definition 1, $P(s_1, s_2)$ can have a zero for $R_e s_2 = 0$ independent of s_1-variable.

<u>Example 2</u>: $P(s_1, s_2) = (s_1 s_2 + 1)(s_2^2 - 1)(s_1 s_2 + s_1 + s_2)$ is a NSSHP weak in s_2. If the distinguished boundary zeros are isolated points, we can call $P(s_1, s_2)$ as PSHP.

<u>Example 3</u>: $P(s_1, s_2) = s_1 s_2 - s_2 - 1$ is a PSHP weak in s_1.

<u>Example 4</u>: $P(s_1, s_2) = (s_1^2 + s_1 - 2)s_2 + (s_1^2 + s_1 - 1)$ is a VSHP weak in s_1.

It can be seen that the adjective 'very strict' is applied if the polynomial does not have any zero or second kind singularities in S^2_{oo} which includes infinite distant points. The other types can have zeros in S^2_{oo}. It will be shown in the next section that VSSHPs will find applications in testing the stability of 2-D semi-casual digital filters. The other types of Hurwitz polynomials find application in the study of 2-V analog networks that may contain positive as well as negative elements in one of the variables. In this paper, we will discuss the properties and applications of VSSHP. First, we will list some of the important properties of VSSHPs (proofs are omitted).

Property 1: Let $P(s_1, s_2) = \sum_{m=0}^{M} \sum_{n=0}^{N} p_{mn} s_1^m s_2^n$ be a VSSHP weak in s_1. Then for all $s_2 \varepsilon S_{2\oplus}$, the number of zeros in s_{1+} is a constant M_1, $(M_1 < M)$ and the number of zeros in s_{1-} is $M - M_1$.

Property 2: If $P(s_1, s_2)$ is a VSSHP weak in s_1, then $\partial^k P(s_1, s_2)/\partial s_2^k$, $k = 1, 2, \ldots, n-1$ are also VSHHPs weak in s_1. In a similar way, if $P(s_1, s_2)$ is a VSSHP weak in s_2, $\partial^k P(s_1, s_2)/\partial s_1^k$, $k = 1, 2, \ldots, M-1$ are also VSSHPs weak in s_2.

Property 3: Let $P(s_1, s_2) = \sum_{n=0}^{N} A_n(s_1) s_2^n$ be a VSSHP weak in s_1. Also let, for some $s_2 \varepsilon S_{2\oplus}$, $P(s_1, \hat{s}_2)$ have M_1 zeros in S_{1+} and M_2 zeros in S_{1-}. Then each $A_n(s_1)$, $n = 0, 1, \ldots, N$ has M_1 zeros in S_{1+} and M_2 zeros in S_{1-} and no zeros in S_{1o}.

Property 4: Let $P(s_1, s_2) = \sum_{n=0}^{N} A_n(s_1) s_2^n$ be a VSSHP weak in s_1. Then $A_i(s_1)/A_{i-1}(s_1)$, $i = 1, 2, \ldots, N$ are minimum reactive susceptive strict pseudo positive real functions [10].

The following theorem gives a testing procedure for a VSSH polynomial.

Theorem 1: Let $P(s_1, s_2) = \sum_{m=0}^{M} \sum_{n=0}^{N} p_{mn} s_1^m s_2^n =$

$$\sum_{m=0}^{M} B_m(s_2) s_1^m = \sum_{n=0}^{N} A_n(s_1) s_2^n .$$

Then, $P(s_1, s_2)$ is a VSSHP weak in s_1 if the following conditions are satisfied:

i) $p_{MN} \neq 0$

ii) $B_M(s_2) \neq 0 \quad \forall\, s_2 \varepsilon S_{2\oplus}$

iii) $A_N(s_1) \neq 0 \quad \forall\, s_1 \varepsilon S_{1o}$

and iv) $P(j\omega_1, j\omega_2) \neq 0 \quad -\infty < \omega_i < \infty$ $(i=1,2)$.

IV. RESULTS ON THE STABILITY OF 2-D HALF-PLANE DIGITAL FILTERS

As indicated at the beginning of this paper, there exists a strong relation between the VSSHP's and the denominator polynomials of half-plane digital filters. The next theorem brings out this relationship and in so doing, paves the way for the application of VSSHP's in testing the stability of half-plane filters. Further, this relationship will also become useful in the generation of stable half-plane filters.

Among the various half-plane filters, we will consider the half-plane filters which are causal in z_2-direction and semi-causal in the z_1-direction. These are referred to as $(*\oplus)$ type.

The transfer function of such half-plane filters can be written as $H(z_1, z_2) = C(z_1, z_2)/D(z_1, z_2)$ where

$$D(z_1, z_2) = \sum_{m=0}^{M_2} d_{mo} z_1^m + \sum_{m=-M_1}^{M_2} \sum_{n=1}^{N} d_{mn} z_1^m z_2^n \qquad \ldots(1)$$

and $C(z_1, z_2)$ is an arbitrary polynomial in z_1 and z_2.

This half-plane filter $H(z_1, z_2)$ is stable if the following conditions are satisfied [11].

Let $D_1(z_1, z_2) = z_1^{M_1} D(z_1, z_2)$.

Then i) $D_1(z_1, z_2) \neq 0$ for $|z_1| = 1$, $|z_2| \leq 1$

and ii) $D(z_1, 0) \neq 0$ for $|z_1| \leq 1$ $\ldots(2)$

We next state the theorem relating $D_1(z_1, z_2)$ to a VSSHP.

Theorem 2: Let $D_1(z_1, z_2) = z_1^{M_1} D(z_1, z_2)$ be the denominator polynomial of $(*\oplus)$ half-plane filter. Let

$$P(s_1, s_2) = (1 + s_1)^{M_1 + M_2} (1 + s_2)^N [D_1(z_1, z_2)] \Big|_{z_i = (1 - s_i)(1 + s_i),\ i = 1, 2}$$

If $D(z_1, z_2)$ satisfy the conditions for the stability of a $(*\oplus)$ half-plane filter, then $P(s_1, s_2)$ is a VSSHP weak in s_1 and $P(s_1, 1)$ has exactly M_1 zeros at $s_1 = 1$ and no more zeros in S_{1+}.

Proof: The stability conditions on $D(z_1, z_2)$ are given by (2). The bilinear transformation $z_i = (1 - s_i)/(1 + s_i)$ maps $|z_i| = 1$ onto S_{io} and $|z_i| \leq 1$ onto $S_{i\oplus}$. In other words, the region $Z^2_{o\theta} = \{(z_1, z_2) \mid |z_1| = 1, |z_2| \le 1\}$ is mapped onto the region $\{(s_1, s_2) \mid s_1 \varepsilon S_{1o}, s_2 \varepsilon S_{2\theta}\} = S^2_{o\theta}$. Therefore, if $D_1(z_1, z_2)$ does not have any zeros in the region $Z^2_{o\theta}$, then $P(s_1, s_2)$ obtained by bilinear transformation of $D_1(z_1, z_2)$ does not have any zeros in $S^2_{o\theta}$. Hence by definition, $P(s_1, s_2)$ is a semi-Hurwitz polynomial weak in s_1.

The stability condition (ii) states that $D(z_1, 0) \neq 0$ for $|z_1| \le 1$ or $D_1(z_1, 0) = z_1^{M_1}$ $D(z_1, 0)$ has exactly M_1 zeros at $z_1 = 0$ and no more zeros in $|z_1| \le 1$. As bilinear transformation maps $z_i = 0$ point to $s_i = 1$, we get $P(s_1, 1)$ has exactly M_1 zeros at $z_1 = 1$ and no more zeros in $S_{1\theta}$. In other words, $P(s_1, 1)$ has M_2 zeros in S_{1-} and M_1 zeros in S_{1+}. Hence the proof.

As a result of the above correspondence between the denominator polynomial $D_1(z_1, z_2)$ of half-plane filters and VSSHP's and the property 3 of VSSHP's, we can establish the following property of $D_1(z_1, z_2)$.

Theorem 3: Let $D_1(z_1, z_2)$ be as defined in (2). Then for any $\hat{z}_2$, $|\hat{z}_2| \le 1$, $D_1(z_1, \hat{z}_2)$ has exactly M_1 zeros inside the unit circle and M_2 zeros outside the unit circle in the z_1-plane.

Based on this theorem, we can state an alternate test for the stability of half-plane filters.

Theorem 4: The half-plane filter defined in (1) is stable if and only if

i) $D_1(z_1, z_2) \neq 0 \quad |z_1| = 1, |z_2| = 1$

ii) $D(1, z_2) \neq 0 \quad |z_2| \le 1$

and iii) $D(z_1, 1)$ has exactly M_1 zeros in $\{z_1 \mid |z_1| < 1\}$.

In z-domain, this may not have any advantage. However, if the test is carried out in s-domain, the modified test becomes

i) $P(s_1, s_2) \neq 0 \quad \forall (s_1, s_2) \varepsilon S^2_{oo}$

ii) $P(0, s_2) \neq 0 \quad \forall s_2 \varepsilon S_{2+}$

and iii) $P(s_1, 0)$ has exactly M_1 zeros in S_{1+}.

This has a slight advantage over the previous s-domain test in that we can get $P(0, s_2)$ as $B_0(s_2)$ without any effort.

V. A SUFFICIENT CONDITION FOR THE STABILITY OF HALF-PLANE DIGITAL FILTERS

So far we discussed the relationship between VSSHP's and the testing for the stability of half-plane digital filters. In the following, we give a result which establishes a sufficiency condition for the stability of 2-D half-plane digital filters based on the coefficient relationship. First, we will consider the following general result.

Theorem 5: A sufficient condition that a 2-D digital polynomial $D(z_1, z_2) = \sum_{p=0}^{m} \sum_{q=0}^{n} b_{pq} z_1^p z_2^q = 0$ in $\bar{U}^2 - T^2$ is that for some$(k, \ell) \neq (0, 0)$

$$|b_{k\ell}| > \sum_{\substack{p=0 \\ p \neq k}}^{m} \sum_{\substack{q=0 \\ q \neq \ell}}^{n} |b_{pq}|$$

We observe the following points from the above theorem.

(1) It was shown in [12] if

$$b_{oo} > \sum_{p=0}^{m} \sum_{q=0}^{n} |b_{pq}| \quad , (p, q) \neq (0, 0),$$

$B(z_1, z_2) \neq 0$ in $\bar{U}^2$

(2) If condition (1) is satisfied, we get the following zero set pattern for $B(z_1, z_2)$:

For any z_2 on the unit circle, $|z_2| = 1$,

(a) $B(z_1, z_2)$ has k zeros in the region $|z_1| < 1$ and (m-k) zeros in the region $|z_1| > 1$.

For any z_1 on the unit circle, $|z_1| = 1$,

(b) $B(z_1, z_2)$ has ℓ zeros in the region $|z_2| < 1$ and $(n-\ell)$ zeros in the region $|z_2| > 1$.

Based on the above, the result relating to the stability of half-plane filters is the following:

Theorem 6: The sufficiency condition that

$D(z_1, z_2) = \sum_{i=0}^{m} \sum_{j=0}^{n} b_{ij} z_1^i z_2^j$ has no zero sets in

$\{(z_1, z_2) \mid |z_1| = 1, |z_2| \le 1\}$ is

(i) $b_{ko} > \sum_{i=0}^{m} \sum_{j=0}^{n} |b_{ij}|, \{(i,j) \neq (k,o)\}$

for some $k \varepsilon [o,m]$

(ii) $D(1, z_2) \neq 0$ for $|z_2| < 1$.

It is to be noted that under the above conditions, $B(z_1, z_2)$ has k zeros in $|z_1| < 1$ for any fixed $z_2 = z_{20}$ where $|z_{20}| = 1$.

VI. CONCLUSIONS

In this paper, various types of two-variable semi-Hurwitz polynomials were defined. The relationship between the structural stability of 2-D half-plane digital filters and very strict semi-Hurwitz polynomials has been established. Finally, a sufficiency condition for stability based on the coefficients of the denominator polynomial of a 2-D half-plane digital system is presented.

ACKNOWLEDGEMENTS

This work was supported by the National Science Foundation under the grant ECS-8307541 and the Department of Electrical Engineering, Tennessee Technological University, Cookeville, TN 38505, USA.

REFERENCES

[1] H. G. Ansell, "On certain two-variable generalizations of circuit theory in the application of the networks of transmission lines and lumped reactances," IEEE Trans. Circuit Theory, vol. CT-11, pp. 214-223, June 1964.

[2] M. Saito, "Synthesis of transmission line networks by multivariable techniques," Proc. of the Symposium on Generalized Networks, Polytechnic Institute of Brooklyn, New York, pp. 353-392, 1966.

[3] T. Koga, "Synthesis of resistively terminated cascade of uniform lossless transmission lines and lumped passive lossless two-ports," IEEE Trans. on Circuit Theory, vol. CT-18, No. 4, pp. 444-455, July 1971.

[4] A. Fettweis, "On the scattering matrix and the scattering transfer matrix of multidimensional lossless two-ports," Arch. Elektr. Ubertr., vol. 36, pp. 374-381, Sept. 1982.

[5] E. I. Jury, "Stability of multidimensional scalar and matrix polynomials," Proceedings of the IEEE, vol. 66, pp. 1018-1047, Sept. 1978.

[6] P. K. Rajan, H. C. Reddy, M. N. S. Swamy and V. Ramachandran, "Generalization of two-dimensional digital functions without the nonessential singularities of the second kind," IEEE Trans. on Acoustic, Speech, Signal Processing, vol. ASSP-28, pp. 216-223, April 1980.

[7] H. C. Reddy, P. K. Rajan and M. N. S. Swamy, "Studies on n-dimensional filter transfer functions without second kind singularities," Proc. of the IEEE International Conference on Acoustic, Speech, Signal Processing, pp. 753-757, April 1980.

[8] P. K. Rajan, H. C. Reddy and M. N. S. Swamy, "Semi-Hurwitz polynomials and half-plane filters," Proceesings of 25th Midwest Symposium on Circuits and Systems, August 30-31, 1982, pp. 38-41.

[9] V. S. Vladimirov, "Methods of the theory of functions of many complex variables," The MIT Press, 1966, pp. 36-38 (book).

[10] H. C. Reddy, B. C. Sun and L. F. Lin, "Theory and applications of pseudo-positive real functions in one and two-variables," Proc. of 1983 Intl. Symp. on Circuits and Systems, Newport Beach, California, May 1983.

[11] M. P. Ekstrom and J. W. Woods, "Two-dimensional spectral factorization with applications in recursive digital filtering," IEEE Trans. Acoustic, Speech, Signal Processing, vol. ASSP-24, pp. 115-128, Apr. 1976.

[12] H. C. Reddy, P. K. Rajan and M. N. S. Swamy, "Simple sufficient criterion for the stability of multidimensional digital filters," Proc. IEEE, pp. 301-303, March 1982.

DIGITAL TECHNIQUES in Simulation, Communication and Control
Spyros G. Tzafestas (editor)
Elsevier Science Publishers B.V. (North-Holland) © IMACS, 1985

INPUT / OUTPUT PROCESSING IN 2D SYSTEMS SIMULATION

Dr. Eugenia Kalisz

Polytechnical Institute of Bucharest, Computer dpt.
Bucharest, Romania

The principles of input/output processing in the analysis via simulation of bidimensional (2D) discrete systems are introduced.
This processing consists of nontrivial matrix-to-sequence and sequence-to-matrix conversions.
Both simulation models and conversion algorithms designed for efficient input/output processing in 2D systems simulation are presented.

1. INTRODUCTION

The unidimensional models [1, 2] used for the simulation, on monoprocessor digital computers, of bidimensional (2D) discrete systems operate with sequential inputs and outputs.

Since the 2D systems inputs and outputs are matrices, it follows that the analysis via simulation of 2D systems (fig. 1) requires specific input/output processing, which consists of nontrivial matrix-to-sequence (2D/1D) and sequence-to-matrix (1D/2D) conversions.

The input/output processing implied by the 2D systems simulation can be performed in two modes:

- on-line, using simulation models designed for both 2D system simulation and input/output conversions ;
- off-line , via simulation or by means of adequate conversion programs.

The paper presents simulation models and conversion algorithms designed for efficient input / output processing in 2D systems simulation.

2. MATRIX-TO-SEQUENCE AND SEQUENCE-TO-MATRIX CONVERSIONS

Let us consider an $N * M$ matrix, $\|u\|$, processed by a 2D system. In this case the matrix element $u_{i,j}$, $i \in [\emptyset, N-1]$, $j \in [\emptyset, M-1]$ is processed only after the processing of all elements in the set $\{u_{r,k} \mid r \in [\emptyset, i-1] \text{ , } k \in [\emptyset, j-1]\}$.
It follows that two vertically/horizontally adjacent elements of the matrix will not be adjacent in the equivalent sequence -i.e., if the sequence indices of matrix elements $u_{i,o}$ and $u_{o,j}$ are io and jo , then the sequence indices of matrix elements $u_{i+1,o}$ and $u_{o,j+1}$ are (io + M) and (jo + N).

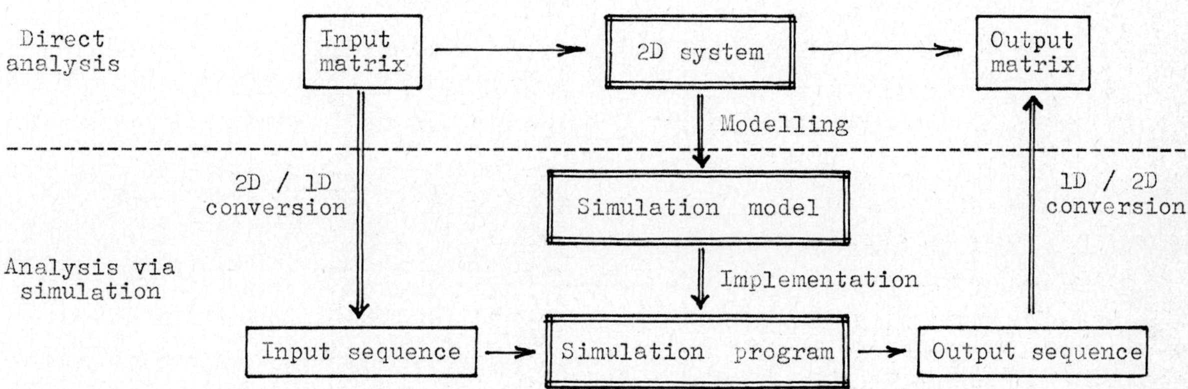

Figure 1 : Analysis of 2D discrete systems.

By induction, the sequence index **k** of a matrix element $u_{i,j}$, $i=\emptyset,N-1$, $j=\emptyset,M-1$ is given by the formula

$$k = q + i * M + j * N$$

where **q** is the sequence index of the matrix element $u_{o,o}$. Usually $q=\emptyset$ or $q=1$. Figure 2.a.presents the case of a 3 * 4 matrix, indicating the sequence indices for each matrix element.

It is obvious that, in order to insure a distinct sequence index for each matrix element, the matrix dimensions (N and M) must be relative prime integers.

$u_{o,o}$ (1)	$u_{o,1}$ (4)	$u_{o,2}$ (7)	$u_{o,3}$ (1o)
$u_{1,o}$ (5)	$u_{1,1}$ (8)	$u_{1,2}$ (11)	$u_{1,3}$ (14)
$u_{2,o}$ (9)	$u_{2,1}$ (12)	$u_{2,2}$ (15)	$u_{2,3}$ (18)

a. the matrix

index	value
1	$u_{o,o}$
2	∅
3	∅
4	$u_{o,1}$
5	∅
6	$u_{1,o}$
7	$u_{o,2}$
8	$u_{1,1}$
9	$u_{2,o}$
1o	$u_{o,3}$
11	$u_{1,2}$
12	$u_{2,1}$
13	∅
14	$u_{1,3}$
15	$u_{2,2}$
16	∅
17	∅
18	$u_{2,3}$

b. the sequence (q = 1)

Figure 2 : A 3 * 4 matrix and the equivalent sequence

The sequence equivalent to an N * M matrix includes (N-1)*M + (M-1)*N + 1 elements. Only N*M of those elements, corresponding to the matrix elements, are significant for the simulation process. To the other (N * M - N - M + 1) sequence elements the implicit value zero is assigned (see figure 2.b.).

3. SIMULATION MODELS FOR 2D/1D AND 1D/2D CONVERSIONS

Let us consider the case of 2D systems analysis performed by a specialized simulator, which operates on simulation models represented as sets of interconnected primitive blocks.

The 2D/1D and 1D/2D conversions can be performed (on-line or off-line) by appropriate simulation models, if the 2D simulator in use provides the following types of primitive blocks:

(a) READ and WRITE blocks with three parameters:

p1 - the identifier of the input / output sequential file ;

p2 - the input / output interval - a value is transferred from/in the p1 file at every p2 simulation step; at the intermediate simulation steps the READ block outputs a zero value ;

p3 - the input / output starting moment (i.e. the simulation step at which the first input / output transfer is performed) ;

(b) DELAY blocks, performing the delay specified by the block parameter p , $p \in \mathbf{N}$ (a DELAY block outputs the current input value after p simulation steps) ;

(c) summer blocks , with two or more inputs.

In order to generate the equivalent sequence, an N * M matrix can be processed by rows or by columns. In both cases, the vertically adjacent elements must be relatively delayed by the number of columns - M - and the horizontally adjacent elements must be delayed by the number of rows - N .

If distinct sequential files are used to store the matrix rows,then the delay between the elements of the same row is insured by a READ block , with an appropriate value for its second parameter: p2 = N . The delay between the matrix rows will be insured by DELAY blocks with parameter p = M .

The simulation model for the 2D/1D (matrix-to-sequence) conversion, presented in figure 3, includes:

- k READ blocks, with p2 = k
  p3 = Ø ;
- (k-1) DELAY blocks, with p = d ;
- (k-1) summer blocks.

The values of **k** and **d** are determined by the matrix elements recording mode:

- by rows, in which case k = N
  d = M
- by columns; in this case k = M
  d = N

In an analoguous way, the 1D / 2D (sequence-to-matrix) conversion can be performed by the simulation model presented in figure 4.

Note that if the N matrix rows are recorded in N sequential files, then at each of the M input/output steps the READ/WRITE blocks transfer the N values of a matrix column.

It is obvious that, in order to minimize the number of blocks in the simulation models in figures 3 and 4, the processing mode must be chosen as a function of the matrix dimensions - by rows if N < M and by columns otherwise.

The number of READ and WRITE blocks in the simulation model, as well as the total number of unit delays implied by the DELAY chain, are limited (more severly if the simulator is implemented on a mini or microcomputer). Therefore, the 2D/1D and 1D/2D conversions cannot always be implemented on-line. In such cases, besides the simulation phase, additional pre and postprocessing (conversion) phases are required. The interface between the simulation phase and the conversion phases is insured by sequential files in which the simulation model 1D input and output are recorded. It is obvious that for the efficiency of the conversion phases it is suitable to use specialized conversion programs.

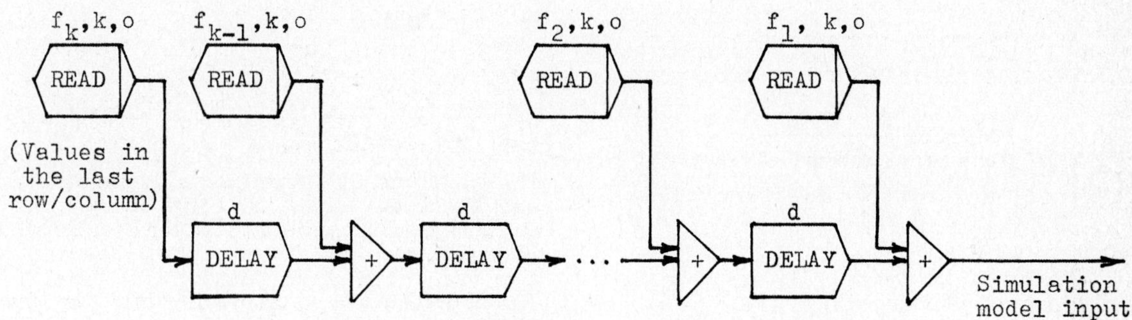

Figure 3 : Simulation model for 2D / 1D (matrix-to-sequence) conversion.

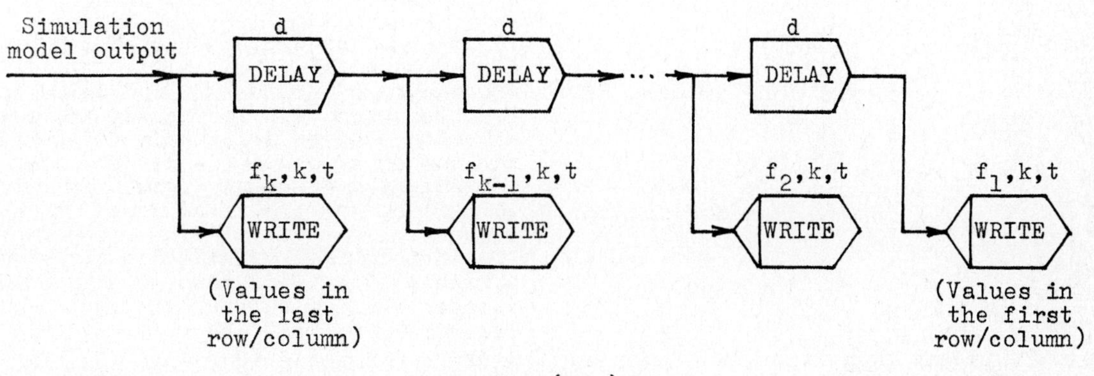

$$t = d * (k-1) + 1$$

Figure 4 : Simulation model for 1D/2D (sequence-to-matrix) conversion.

4. ALGORITHMS FOR 2D/1D AND 1D/2D CONVERSIONS

The conversion algorithms presented in what follows operate on matrices and their equivalent sequences the same way as the simulation models presented in the previous section. The values stored at a given simulation step by the DELAY chain in the simulation models and the output of the last summer are stored in a vector **v** , with **nt** elements , nt = (k-1) * d + 1 .

Both algorithms operate on two sequential files:

- the pseudo 2D file, in which the following informations are recorded:
- N and M - the matrix dimensions ;
- **rmf** - a flag indicating the matrix recording mode - if the matrix elements are recorded by rows , then **rmf** = 1 ; otherwise **rmf** = 2 ;
- the matrix elements, by rows or by columns, as **rmf** specifies ;

- the 1D file, in which the matrix dimensions and the equivalent sequence elements are recorded.

For the 2D/1D and 1D/2D conversions the following algorithms are proposed:

ALGORITHM C2D1D

INPUT : **mfile** - a pseudo 2D file ;

OUTPUT: **sfile** - the 1D file equivalent to mfile.

METHOD:

```
read(N,M,rmf); (* from mfile *)
write(N,M) ;   (* in sfile *)
if rmf=1 then begin k:=M ; d:=N end
         else begin k:=N ; d:=M end ;
iw := 1 ;
nt := (k-1) * d + 1 ;
for i:=1 to nt do  v[i] := Ø ;
for i:=1 to d do
 begin ir := iw ;
       for j:=1 to k do
        begin read( v[ir] ) ;
              ir := ir + d ;
              if ir > nt then ir:=ir-nt;
       end ;
       for j:=1 to k do
        begin write( v[iw] ) ;
              iw := iw + 1 ;
              if iw > nt then iw:=iw-nt;
       end
 end ;
for i:=1 to k * d - k - d + 1 do
 begin write( v[iw] ) ;
       iw := iw + 1 ;
       if iw > nt then iw := iw - nt ;
 end.
```

ALGORITHM C1D2D

INPUT : **sfile** - the 1D file to be converted ;
rmf - the matrix recording mode **flag** ;

OUTPUT: **mfile** - the pseudo 2D file resulting from the sfile conversion.

METHOD:

```
read(N,M) ;        (* from sfile *)
write(N,M,rmf); (* in mfile *)
if rmf=1 then begin k:=M ; d:=N end
         else begin k:=N ; d:=M end ;
nt := (k-1) * d + 1 ;
for i:=1 to nt-k do read( v[i] ) ;
ir := nt -k + 1 ;
for i:=1 to d do
 begin for j:=1 to k do
       begin read( v[ir] ) ;
             ir := ir + 1 ;
             if ir > nt then ir:=ir-nt;
       end ;
      iw := ir ;
      for j:=1 to k do
       begin write( v[iw] ) ;
             iw := iw + d ;
             if ir > nt then iw:=iw-nt;
       end
 end.
```

Note that the vector **v** used by the conversion algorithms is processed as a circular queue.

The conversion algorithms presented above were used to implement the input/output processor included in the 2D systems simulation medium developed for the Intel 8080-based FELIX M-18 / FELIX M-118 microcomputers and for the PDP 11-compatible CORAL 4011 minicomputers.

REFERENCES

1 Necula,M.A. and Kalisz,E., SADASIM - 1D and 2D systems simulators , Proc. ICD'82 Symposium (Tunis, 1982)

2 Necula,M.A., Kalisz,E., Droaşcă,B. and Stănescu,D., Sisteme discrete bidimensionale - Analiza asistată de calculator, in AMC 35 (Editura Tehnică, Bucureşti, 1983).

DIGITAL TECHNIQUES in Simulation, Communication and Control
Spyros G. Tzafestas (editor)
Elsevier Science Publishers B.V. (North-Holland) © IMACS, 1985

MODEL REDUCTION TECHNIQUES FOR 2-D DISCRETE SYSTEMS

P.N. PARASKEVOPOULOS

Department of Electrical Engineering, School of Engineering,
Democritus University of Thrace,
XANTHI, GREECE

A survey is presented of the recently developed techniques for model reduction of two-dimensional (2-D) systems. These techniques may be grouped into the following three categories: Padē-type, continued-fraction expansion and optimal model reduction.

1. INTRODUCTION

It is usually desirable (for realization, con trol, computation and other purposes) to be able to represent "adequately" a high order system by a lower order model. To this end, several methods have been developed for systems having one dimension [1] - [10] .

This paper refers to the model reduction of two-dimensional (2-D)systems. This type of systems have been recently developed in relation to several modern engineering fields, such as 2-D digital filtering, multivariable network realisability, 2-D system synthesis, digital picture processing, seismic data processing, X-ray enhancement, image deblurring, etc. Up-to-data reviews of most of the reported results on 2-D systems and signals are given in [11] - [16].

The problem of model reduction of 2-D systems has been under investigation only the last few years. The reported results are very few and they may grouped into three approaches as follows: The Padē-type [17] - [22] , the continued-fraction expansion type [23] and the optimum model reduction type [24] . The present paper is devoted in reviewing these three approaches. It is mentioned that the material of this paper has been previously reported in [31] .

2. PADE-TYPE MODEL REDUCTION

Let $H(w,z)$ and $G(w,z)$ be the transfer functions of the given system and the desired reduced order model, respectively, where

$$H(w,z) = \frac{a(w,z)}{b(w,z)} = \frac{\sum\limits_{i=0}^{\bar{m}} \sum\limits_{j=0}^{\bar{n}} a_{ij} w^i z^j}{\sum\limits_{i=0}^{m} \sum\limits_{j=0}^{n} b_{ij} w^i z^j}$$

and

$$G(w,z) = \frac{c(w,z)}{d(w,z)} \quad \frac{\sum\limits_{i=0}^{\bar{q}} \sum\limits_{j=0}^{\bar{p}} c_{ij} w^i z^j}{\sum\limits_{i=0}^{q} \sum\limits_{j=0}^{p} d_{ij} w^i z^j} \qquad (1)$$

where $d_{00}=1$ and $m+n\leq q+p$. Also let the double power series expansion of $H(w,z)$ and $G(w,z)$ be given by

$$H(w,z) = \sum_{i=0}^{\infty} \sum_{j=0}^{\infty} h_{ij} w^i z^j \text{ and } G(w,z) = \sum_{i=0}^{\infty} \sum_{j=0}^{\infty} g_{ij} w^i z^j \qquad (2)$$

Simply speaking, the Padē-type model reduction of 1-D systems consists of matching the first σ power series coefficients of the given system and the model, where σ is the number of the unknown parameters of the model. The Padē type model reduction for 2-D systems consists, as well, of matching the first σ power series coefficients h_{ij} of the given system $H(w,z)$ and the correspoding power series coefficients g_{ij} of the model $G(w,z)$, where $\sigma = (\bar{q}+1)(\bar{p}+1)+(q+1)(p+1)-1$ is the number of the unknown parameters of $G(w,z)$. Clearly, in both 1-D and 2-D systems, the Padē-type model reduction will lead to a linear algebraic system of σ equations with σ unknowns whose solution will yield the parameters of the reduced-order model sought.

In the sequel, let $(\hat{i},\hat{j})$ denote the set of pairs of indices i and j of the chosen "first" σ terms of the power series (2). For example, for the set of power series terms $(1,w,z,wz,w^2)$ the corresponding set of the pairs $(\hat{i},\hat{j})$ will be: (0,0), (1,0),(0,1),(1,1),(2,0). The general form of $(\hat{i},\hat{j})$ is as follows: $(\hat{i},\hat{j}) = \{(0,0),\ldots,(i,j),(i',j'),\ldots,(k,\ell)\}$, where $k\leq q+\bar{q}$, $\ell\leq p+\bar{p}$, and the degree difference $(i'+j')-(i+j)$ of any two consecutive terms must be either zero or one.

Definition: The transfer function $G(w,z)$ is a Padē-approximant of $H(w,z)$ if and only if

$$h_{ij} = g_{ij}, \quad \forall (i,j) \in (\hat{i},\hat{j}) \qquad (3)$$

where the set of pairs of indices $(\hat{i},\hat{j})$ is preassigned and involves σ pairs of indices.

The problem considered in this paper, therefore, consists of determining the σ free parameters of $G(w,z)$ such that condition (3) is satisfied.

Define the following transfer function error

$$e(w,z)=g(w,z)-h(w,z)=\frac{c(w,z)-h(w,z)d(w,z)}{d(w,z)}=\frac{k(w,z)}{d(w,z)} \quad (4)$$

$$=\frac{b(w,z)c(w,z)-a(w,z)d(w,z)}{b(w,z)d(w,z)}=\frac{\ell(w,z)}{b(w,z)d(w,z)} \quad (5)$$

where use was made of (1) and (2). Let the power series of e(w,z) be given by

$$e(w,z)=\sum_{i=0}^{\infty}\sum_{j=0}^{\infty} e_{ij}w^i z^j \quad (6)$$

Since $e_{ij}=g_{ij}-h_{ij}$, it follows that an equivalent expression for condition (3) is

$$e_{ij}=h_{ij}-g_{ij}=0,\ \forall\ (i,j)\in(\hat{i},\hat{j}) \quad (7)$$

Now, consider the following transfer function

$$y(w,z)=\frac{\gamma(w,z)}{\beta(w,z)}=\frac{\sum_{i=0}^{\tau_1}\sum_{j=0}^{\tau_2}\gamma_{ij}w^i z^j}{\sum_{i=0}^{v_1}\sum_{j=0}^{v_2}\beta_{ij}w^i z^j},\ \beta_{00}\neq 0 \quad (8)$$

where $\gamma_{ij}=0\ \forall(i,j)\in(\hat{i},\hat{j})$, that is, the function $\gamma(w,z)$ has its "first" σ terms missing. Then, it can readily be shown that the power series expansion of (8) has also its correspoding σ "first" terms missing, that is

$$y(w,z)=\sum_{\forall(i,j)\notin(\hat{i},\hat{j})}\sum y_{ij}w^i z^j \quad (9)$$

where, whenever $(i,j)\in(\hat{i},\hat{j})$, then $\{(s,t);\ 0\leq s\leq i,\ 0\leq t\leq j\}$ is also contained in $(\hat{i},\hat{j})$, while

$$y_{ij}=0,\ \forall(i,j)\in(\hat{i},\hat{j}) \quad (10)$$

Application of the relation (10) to (4) yields that if

$$k_{ij}=0,\ \forall(i,j)\in(\hat{i},\hat{j}) \quad (11)$$

where k_{ij} are the power series coefficients of k(w,z), then relation (7) holds. That is, in order to secure Padé-type approximation as expressed by (7), it suffices to guarantee (11).

To proceed, let $a(w,z)=\mathbf{w}_{\bar{m}}^T\mathbf{A}\mathbf{z}_{\bar{n}}$, $b(w,z)=\mathbf{w}_m^T\mathbf{B}\mathbf{z}_n$, $c(w,z)=\mathbf{w}_{\bar{q}}^T\mathbf{C}\mathbf{z}_{\bar{p}}$, and $d(w,z)=\mathbf{w}_q^T\mathbf{D}\mathbf{z}_p$. Equating the numerators in the transfer function error (4) and letting h(w,z) be approximated by its truncated series $h_\sigma(w,z)$, where

$$h_\sigma(w,z)=\sum_{(i,j)\in(\hat{i},\hat{j})}\sum h_{ij}w^i z^j=\mathbf{w}_{q+\bar{q}}^T\mathbf{H}\mathbf{z}_{p+\bar{p}} \quad (12)$$

we have the relationship

$$k(w,z)=c(w,z)-h_\sigma(w,z)d(w,z) \quad (13)$$

or

$$\mathbf{w}_{2q+\bar{q}}^T\mathbf{K}\mathbf{z}_{2p+\bar{p}}=\mathbf{w}_{2q+\bar{q}}^T\tilde{\mathbf{C}}\mathbf{z}_{2p+\bar{p}}-\mathbf{w}_{2q+\bar{q}}^T(\mathbf{H}^*\mathbf{D})\mathbf{z}_{2p+\bar{p}} \quad (14)$$

or

$$\mathbf{w}_{2q+\bar{q}}^T\left[\mathbf{K}-\tilde{\mathbf{C}}+(\mathbf{H}^*\mathbf{D})\right]\mathbf{z}_{2p+\bar{p}}=\mathbf{0} \quad (15)$$

where $\tilde{\mathbf{C}}$ has the form

$$\tilde{\mathbf{C}}=\left[\begin{array}{c|c}\mathbf{C} & \mathbf{0}\\ \hline \mathbf{0} & \mathbf{0}\end{array}\right]$$

and the matrix $(\mathbf{H}^*\mathbf{D})$ is the coefficient matrix of the polynomial which results from the product $h_\sigma(w,z)d(w,z)$, where $*$ denotes convolution. This matrix can readily be determined, for example, by extending the results reported in [25] for 1-D polynomials to cover the present 2-D polynomial case.

Relation (15) holds true if and only if $\mathbf{K}=\tilde{\mathbf{C}}-(\mathbf{H}^*\mathbf{D})$, or

$$\mathbf{k}_{ij}=\tilde{c}_{ij}-(\mathbf{H}^*\mathbf{D})_{ij},\ \forall(i,j)\in(\hat{i},\hat{j}) \quad (16)$$

where $\mathbf{k}_{ij}$, $\mathbf{c}_{ij}$ and $(\mathbf{H}^*\mathbf{D})_{ij}$ are the (i,j)th elements of $\mathbf{K}$, $\tilde{\mathbf{C}}$, and $(\mathbf{H}^*\mathbf{D})$, respectively. Making use of (11), condition (16) takes on the form

$$c_{ij}=(\mathbf{H}^*\mathbf{D})_{ij},\ \forall(i,j)\in(\hat{i},\hat{j}) \quad (17)$$

Ralation (17) is the relation sought, since it is an algebraic system of equations with σ equations and σ unknowns and it may readily be solved to yield the parameters of the reduced order model G(w,z) [21], [22].

3. MODEL REDUCTION BY CONTINUED-FRACTION EXPANSION

Without loss of generality, assume that the initial system transfer function is of order (2,2) in which case

$$H(w,z)=\frac{a_{00}+a_{01}z+a_{02}z^2+a_{10}w+a_{11}wz+a_{12}wz^2+a_{20}w^2+a_{21}w^2z+a_{22}w^2z^2}{b_{00}+b_{01}z+b_{02}z^2+b_{10}w+b_{11}wz+b_{12}wz^2+b_{20}w^2+b_{21}w^2z+b_{22}w^2z^2} \quad (18)$$

Then, the partial fraction expansion of the **IA** type [26] of the above transfer function is given by

$$H(w,z)=C_1+\cfrac{1}{A_1w+\cfrac{1}{C_2+\cfrac{1}{B_1z+\cfrac{1}{C_3+\cfrac{1}{A_2w+\cfrac{1}{C_4+\cfrac{1}{B_2z+\cfrac{1}{C_5}}}}}}}} \quad (19)$$

To obtain a reduced order model, say of order (1,1), one may truncate (19) starting from A_2 and downwards. This yields the reduced order model transfer function G(w,z) which is the truncated continued-fraction

$$G(w,z)=C_1+\cfrac{1}{A_1w+\cfrac{1}{C_2+\cfrac{1}{B_1z+\cfrac{1}{C_3}}}} \quad \text{or}$$

$$G(w,z) = \frac{c_{00}+c_{01}z+c_{10}w+c_{11}wz}{1+d_{01}z+d_{10}w+d_{11}wz} \quad (20)$$

where, by application of the algorithm given in [27], we get: $c_{00} = C_1+C_2+C_3$, $c_{10} = A_1(C_2+C_3)C_1$, $c_{01} = B_1(C_1+C_2)C_3$, $c_{11} = A_1B_1C_1C_2C_3$, $d_{00} = 1$, $d_{10} = A_1(C_2+C_3)$, $d_{01} = B_1C_3$ and $d_{11} = A_1B_1C_2C_3$.

Clearly, the aim of the approximation is to obtain a model with a lower degree and the highest possible accuracy. To this end, in the evaluation of the c_{ij}'s and d_{ij}'s, the remaining constant coefficients C_4 and C_5 may be maintained without affecting the order of the reduced model, while at the same time increasing the accuracy of the model. This is the approach taken in this paper. In general, if we represent by R the sum of all the C_i terms in the expansion (19), then the coefficients of the transfer function G(w,z) will then be: $c_{00} = C_1+C_2+R$, $c_{10} = A_1(C_2+R)C_1$, $c_{01} = B_1(C_1+C_2)R$, $c_{11} = A_1B_1C_1C_2R$, $d_{00} = 1$, $d_{10} = A_1(C_2+R)$, $d_{01} = B_1R$ and $d_{11} = A_1B_1C_2R$. This set of coefficients give better results than the previous set [23].

Example 1. The initial transfer function is given by [26]

$$H(w,z) = \frac{7+30z+16z^2+60w+78wz+24wz^2+72w^2+48w^2z}{1+7z+4z^2+24w+54wz+24wz^2+72w^2+48w^2z} \quad (21)$$

The Padé approximation method yields

$$P(w,z) = \frac{7+27.5641z+44.5378w+48.2638wz}{1+6.6520z+21.7911w+38.3875wz} \quad (22)$$

and the continued-fraction expansion yields

$$G(w,z) = \frac{7+24z+12w+36wz}{1+6z+16w+36wz} \quad (23)$$

In Fig. 1 one may observe the difference in the implementation of the initial (21) and the reduced (23) transfer function. In Fig. 2, the plots of magnitude responses of the transfer functions of the initial system (21), the Padé-approximant (22) and the continued-fraction expansion approximant (23) are given. From these figures it is clear that the curves of (21) and (23) are very close to each other, whereas the curve of (22) is quite different.

Example 2. The initial transfer function is given by [27]

$$H(w,z) = \frac{3+8z+21w+12wz+24w^2}{0.5+2z+9w+12wz+24w^2} \quad (24)$$

The Padé approximation method yields

$$P(w,z) = \frac{6+17.4178z+30.41379w+28.5714wz}{1+4.23645z+16.06897w+24.78818wz} \quad (25)$$

and the continued-fraction expansion method yields

$$G(w,z) = \frac{6+16z+10w+24wz}{1+4z+10w+24wz} \quad (26)$$

Fig. 3 gives the implementation of the initial system transfer function (24) and the reduced order model (26). Fig. 4 gives the magnitude responses of the initial transfer function (24), the Padé-approximant (25) and the continued-fraction approximant (26) which gives better results than that of the Padé-type.

4. OPTIMAL MODEL REDUCTION

The present method is in the time domain and starts by deriving an expression for the output $y(k_1,k_2)$ in terms of its previous values, as well as in terms of the input $u(k_1,k_2)$ and its previous values. This expression is then used to construct an error function. This error function is subsequently minimized by the least squares technique to yield an estimate of the parameters sought.

The present method starts by using the relationship $Y(w,z) = G(w,z)U(w,z)$, where $Y(w,z)$ and $U(w,z)$ are the input and output 2-D signals. Upon introducing the explicit form of G(w,z) and after some algebraic manipulations, we arrive at the following reduced order model 2-D difference equation

$$\begin{aligned} y(k_1,k_2) = & -d_{10}y(k_1-1,k_2)-d_{01}y(k_1,k_2-1)- \\ & -d_{11}y(k_1-1,k_2-1)-\ldots-d_{pq}y(k_1-p,k_2-q) \\ & +c_{00}u(k_1,k_2)+c_{10}u(k_1-1,k_2)+c_{01}u(k_1,k_2-1) \\ & +c_{11}u(k_1-1,k_2-1)+\ldots+c_{\bar{p}\bar{q}}u(k_1-\bar{p},k_2-\bar{q}) \end{aligned} \quad (27)$$

Equation (27) can be written more compactly as follows

$$y(k_1,k_2) = \mathbf{p}^T(k_1,k_2)\boldsymbol{\vartheta} \quad (28)$$

where

$$\begin{aligned} \mathbf{p}^T(k_1,k_2) = [& y(k_1-1,k_2),\ y(k_1,k_1-1),\ y(k_1-1,k_2-1), \\ & \ldots,\ y(k_1-p,k_2-q), u(k_1,k_2), u(k_1-1,k_2), \\ & u(k_1,k_2-1),\ldots,u(k_1-\bar{p},k_2-\bar{q})] \end{aligned}$$

and

$$\boldsymbol{\vartheta}^T = (-d_{10},-d_{01},-d_{11},\ldots,-d_{pq},c_{00},c_{10},c_{01},\ldots,c_{\bar{p}\bar{q}})$$

Now let (k_1,k_2) in (28) range from (0,0) to (δ_1, δ_2) and suppose that the total number of pairs of points (k_1,k_2) taken, are N. Then we get a set of N equations which may be written compactly as follows

$$\mathbf{P}(\delta_1,\delta_2)\boldsymbol{\vartheta} = \mathbf{y}(\delta_1,\delta_2) \quad (29)$$

where

$$\mathbf{P}(\delta_1,\delta_2) = \begin{bmatrix} \mathbf{p}^T(0,0) \\ \mathbf{p}^T(1,0) \\ \mathbf{p}^T(0,1) \\ \vdots \\ \mathbf{p}^T(\delta_1,\delta_2) \end{bmatrix} \quad \text{and} \quad \mathbf{y}(\delta_1,\delta_2) = \begin{bmatrix} y(0,0) \\ y(1,0) \\ y(0,1) \\ \vdots \\ y(\delta_1,\delta_2) \end{bmatrix}$$

The optimal model reduction problem may now be stated as follows: Given the input data u(0,0), u(1,0), u(0,1),... and the output data y(0,0), y(1,0), y(0,1),..., find the parameter vector $\boldsymbol{\vartheta}$ of the low order model such that the least squares error in (29) is minimized.

To solve the present problem, one may directly extend the minimization technique for 1-D systems [28], to the present case. This approach yields the optimum parameter vector $\boldsymbol{\vartheta}$, denoted as $\boldsymbol{\vartheta}^*(\delta_1,\delta_2)$, given by

$$\boldsymbol{\vartheta}^*(\delta_1,\delta_2)=\left[\mathbf{P}^T(\delta_1,\delta_2)\mathbf{P}(\delta_1,\delta_2)\right]^{-1}\mathbf{P}^T(\delta_1,\delta_2)\mathbf{y}(\delta_1,\delta_2) \tag{30}$$

Expression (30) is quite suitable for computer computation. The only problem is that a large amount of data must be stored, especially when the sampling rate is very high. This problem is also met in the 1-D case, but for the 2-D case, the data storage problem becomes more severe. This difficulty may be overcome by using an appropriate recursive algorithm analogous to the one used for 1-D systems. For notational convenience, relation (29) is written as

$$\mathbf{P}(N)\boldsymbol{\vartheta}(N)=\mathbf{y}(N) \tag{31}$$

where $\mathbf{P}(N) = \mathbf{P}(\delta_1,\delta_2)$, $\mathbf{y}(N) = \mathbf{y}(\delta_1,\delta_2)$ and the point (δ_1,δ_2) corresponds to the Nth equation in (31). Next consider having an additional pair of input-output data. Then (31) becomes

$$\mathbf{P}(N+1)\boldsymbol{\vartheta}(N+1) = \mathbf{y}(N+1) \tag{32}$$

where

$$\mathbf{P}(N+1) = \begin{bmatrix}\mathbf{P}(N)\\ \hline \mathbf{p}^T(N+1)\end{bmatrix} \quad \text{and} \quad \mathbf{y}(N+1) = \begin{bmatrix}\mathbf{y}(N)\\ \hline y(N+1)\end{bmatrix}$$

where $\mathbf{p}^T(N+1) = \mathbf{p}^T(\ell_1,\ell_2)$ and $y(N+1) = y(\ell_1,\ell_2)$, where the point (ℓ_1,ℓ_2) is the point "next" to (δ_1,δ_1).

Using the notation in (32), the recursive algorithm sought may now be stated as follows: The new estimate of $\boldsymbol{\vartheta}$ for the N+1 measurement is denoted by $\boldsymbol{\vartheta}(N+1)$ and is given by [28], [29]

$$\boldsymbol{\vartheta}(N+1) = \boldsymbol{\vartheta}(N)+\boldsymbol{\gamma}(N)\left[y(N+1)-\mathbf{p}^T(N+1)\boldsymbol{\vartheta}(N)\right] \tag{33}$$

where $\boldsymbol{\gamma}(N)$ is a weighting factor given by

$$\boldsymbol{\gamma}(N) = \frac{\mathbf{R}(N)\mathbf{p}(N+1)}{1+\mathbf{p}^T(N+1)\mathbf{R}(N)\mathbf{p}(N+1)} \tag{34}$$

where the matrix $\mathbf{R}(N)$ is recursively computed from the following relationship

$$\mathbf{R}(N+1) = \mathbf{R}(N)-\frac{\mathbf{R}(N)\mathbf{p}(N+1)\left[\mathbf{R}(N)\mathbf{p}(N+1)\right]^T}{1+\mathbf{p}^T(N+1)\mathbf{R}(N)\mathbf{p}(N+1)} \tag{35}$$

To start the algorithm, one matrix inversion is required. Let the starting point N_0 for N, be equal to the number of the unknown elements in $\boldsymbol{\vartheta}$. Then

$$\boldsymbol{\vartheta}(N)=\left[\mathbf{P}(N_0)\right]^{-1}\mathbf{y}(N_0) \quad \text{and} \quad \mathbf{R}(N_0)=\left[\mathbf{P}^T(N_0)\mathbf{P}(N_0)\right]^{-1} = \left[\mathbf{P}(N_0)\right]^{-1}\left[\mathbf{P}^T(N_0)\right]^{-1}$$

Example 3. Consider a 2-D transfer function of a stable rotated digital filter having the form

$$H(w,z) = F(w,z)F(w,z), \quad \text{where}$$

$$F(w,z) = \frac{f_{00}+f_{10}w^{-1}+f_{01}z^{-1}+f_{11}w^{-1}z^{-1}}{e_{00}-e_{10}w^{-1}-e_{01}z^{-1}+e_{11}w^{-1}z^{-1}}$$

The coefficients of F(w,z) are selected from Ref. [30], table I and for an angle of rotation $\beta=315^0$. Application of the proposed algorithm yields a reduced order model of order (1,1) whose coefficients are given below.

Initial system coefficients	
d_{00} = 1.48189	c_{01} = -0.434666
d_{01} = 1.058261	c_{02} = -0.047234
d_{02} = 0.188933	c_{10} = -0.434661
d_{10} = 1.058255	c_{11} = 1.036208
d_{11} = 0.469412	c_{12} = 0.245733
d_{12} =-0.302531	c_{20} = -0.047233
d_{20} = 0.188931	c_{21} = 0.245730
d_{21} =-0.302530	c_{22} = -0.319606
d_{22} = 0.121108	
Reduced order model coefficients	
a_{00} = 1.48189	b_{01} = -0.147468
a_{01} = 0.63266	b_{10} = -0.147465
a_{10} = 0.632660	b_{11} = 0.657767
a_{11} =-0.146478	

Fig. 5 and Fig. 6 give the magnitute and impulse response, respectively, of the initial system and Fig. 7 and Fig. 8 give the corresponding responses for the reduced order model.

REFERENCES

1. Davison E.J.: *IEEE Trans. Autom. Contr.*, vol. 11, pp. 93-101, 1966.
2. Hutton M.F. and Friedland B.: *IEEE Trans. Autom. Contr.*, vol. 20, pp. 329-337, 1975.
3. Aoki M.: *IEEE Trans. Autom. Contr.*, vol. 23, pp. 173-182, 1978.
4. Kokotovic P.V., O'Malley R.E. and Sannuti P.: *Automatica*, vol. 12, pp. 123-132, 1976.
5. Wilson D.A.: *Proc. IEE*, vol. 117, pp. 1161-1165, 1970.
6. Varoufakis S.J. and Paraskevopoulos P.N.: *Electronics Letters*, vol. 15, pp. 789-790, 1979.
7. Genesio R. and Milanese M.: *IEEE Trans. Autom. Contr.*, vol. 21, pp. 118-122, 1976.
8. Sandell N.R., Varaiya Jr.P., Athans M. and Savanov M.G.: *IEEE Trans. Autom. Contr.*, vol. 23, pp. 108-128, 1978.
9. Varoufakis S.J. and Paraskevopoulos P.N.: *Int. J. of Modelling and Simulation*, vol. 2, pp. 171-178, 1982.
10. Paraskevopoulos P.N.: "Techniques in model reduction for large scale systems", a Chapter in vol. XX of Control and Dynamic Systems: Advances in Theory and Application, Academic

Press, Edited by C.T. Leondes (to appear).
11. Special issue on digital filters, *Proc. IEEE,* vol. 63, 1975.
12. Special issue on multidimensional systems, *Proc. IEEE,* vol. 65, 1977.
13. Bose N.K.: Multidimensional Systems: Theory and Application, IEEE Press, New York, 1978.
14. Mitra S.K. and Ekstrom M.P.: Two-Dimensional Digital Signal Processing, Dowden, Hutchinson and Ross Inc, Pennsylvania, 1978.
15. Paraskevopoulos P.N.: *Proc. Fourth International Conference on Analysis and Optimization of System,* Versailles, France, pp. 763-780, 1980.
16. Tzafestas S.G., Paraskevopoulos P.N. and Pimenides T.: *Proc. Appliced and Informatics Conference,* University of Lille, March 1983, France.
17. Chisholm J.S.R. and McWan J.: *Proc. R. Soc. Lond.* A 336, pp.421-452, 1974.
18. Hughes Jones R.: *J. of Approximation Theory,* vol. 16, pp. 201-233, 1976.
19. Levin D.: *J. Inst. Math. App.,* vol. 18, pp. 1-8, 1976.

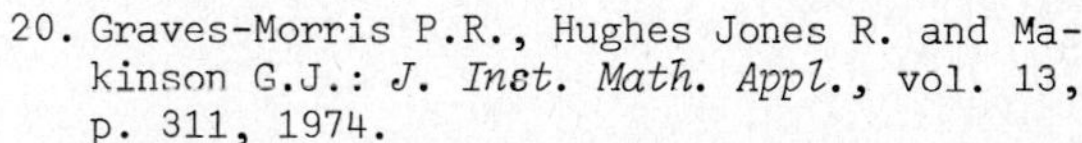

20. Graves-Morris P.R., Hughes Jones R. and Makinson G.J.: *J. Inst. Math. Appl.,* vol. 13, p. 311, 1974.
21. Bose N.K. and Basu S.: *IEEE Trans. Autom. Contr.,* vol. 25, pp. 509-514, 1980.
22. Paraskevopoulos P.N.: *IEEE Trans. Autom. Contr.,* vol. 25, pp. 321-324, 1980.
23. Varoufakis S.J. and Paraskevopoulos P.N.: *International conference on Applied Modelling and Simulation,* Paris, France, 1982.
24. Varoufakis S.J. and Paraskevopoulos P.N.: *Proc. of the MELECON'83 Conference,* May 1983, Athens, Greece.
25. Paraskevopoulos P.N.: *Proc. Inst. Electr. Eng.,* vol. 123, pp. 831-834, 1976.
26. Mitra S.K., Sagar A.D. and Pendegrass N.A.: *IEEE Trans. on Circuits and Systems,* vol. 22, No. 3, pp. 177-184, 1975.
27. Garg K. and Singh H.: *Int. J. Control,* 1981, vol. 34, No. 1, pp. 191-196, 1981.
28. Sinha N.K. and Pille W.: *Int. J. Control,* vol. 14, pp. 111-118, 1971.
29. Aström J.K. and Eykhoff P.: *Automatica,* vol. 7, pp. 123-162, 1971.
30. Mnemey S.H., Venetsanopoulos A.N. and Costa J.M.: *IEEE Trans. on Circuits and Systems,* vol. 28, pp. 995-1003, 1981.
31. Paraskevopoulos P.N.: *Proc. IV Polish-English Seminar on Real Time Process Control,* Jablonna, Poland, pp. 270-282, 1983.

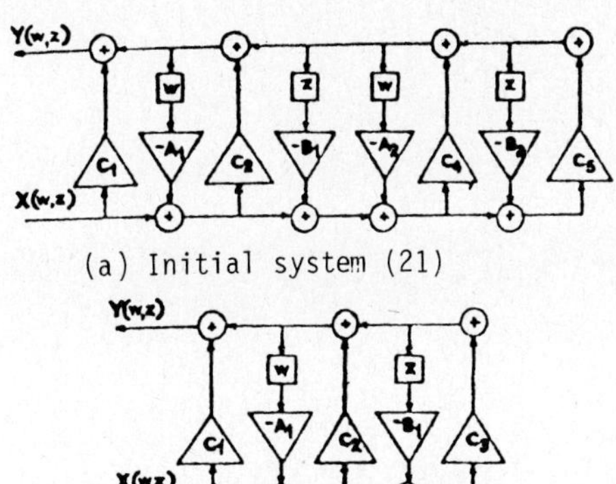

(a) Initial system (21)

(b) Readuced order model (23)

Fig,1. Realization of the system(21)and of the reduced order model (23) of example 1.

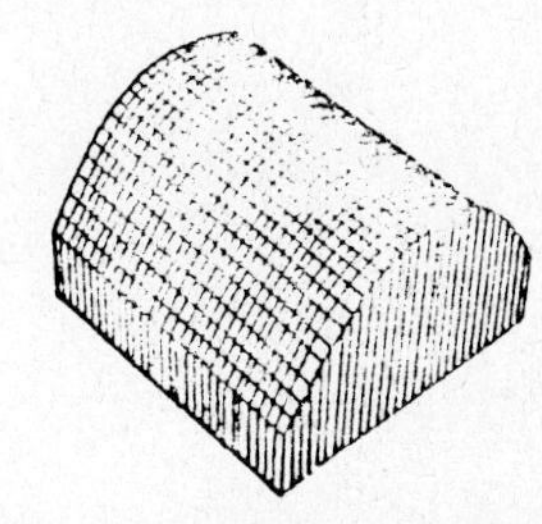

(a) Initial system (21)

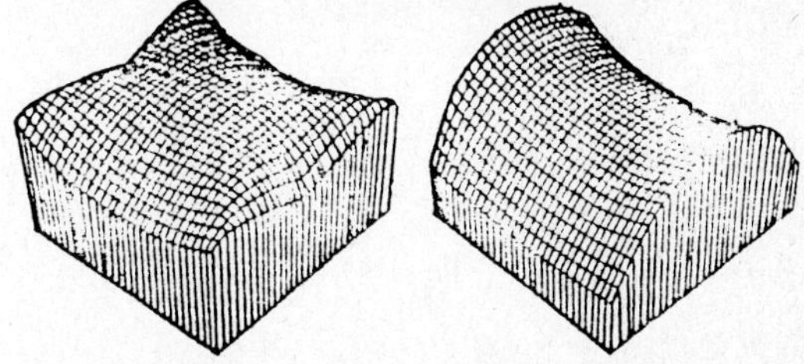

(b)Padė-approximant(22) (c)Continued-fraction approximant (23)

Fig.2. Magnitude response of the initial system (21), the Padė-approximant (22) and the continued-fraction approximant (23) of example 1.

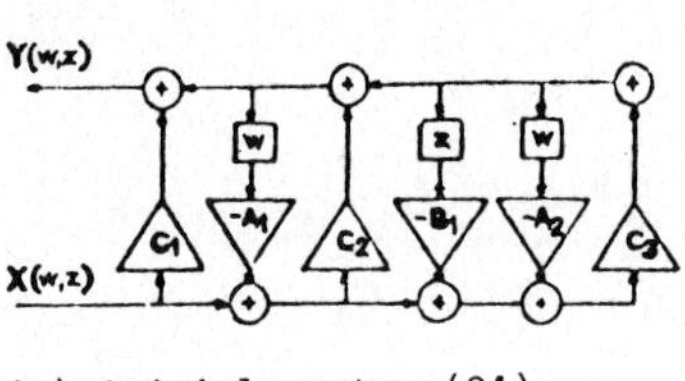

(a) Initial system (24)

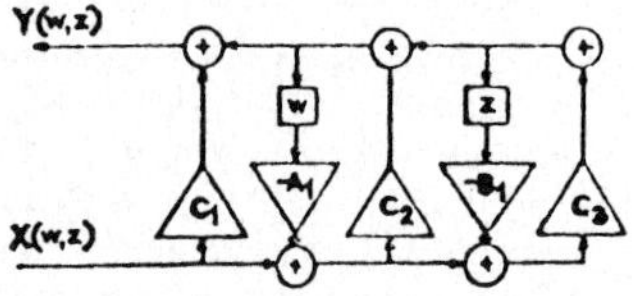

(b) Reduced order model (26)

Fig.3. Realization of the system (24) and of the reduced order model (26) of example 2.

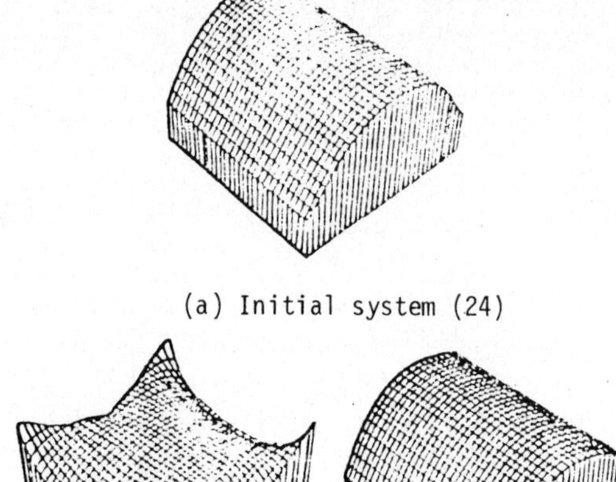

(a) Initial system (24)

(b) Padé-approximant (25) (c) Continued-fraction approximant (26)

Fig.4. Magnitude response of the initial system (24), the Padé-approximant (25) and the continued-fraction approximant (26) of example 2.

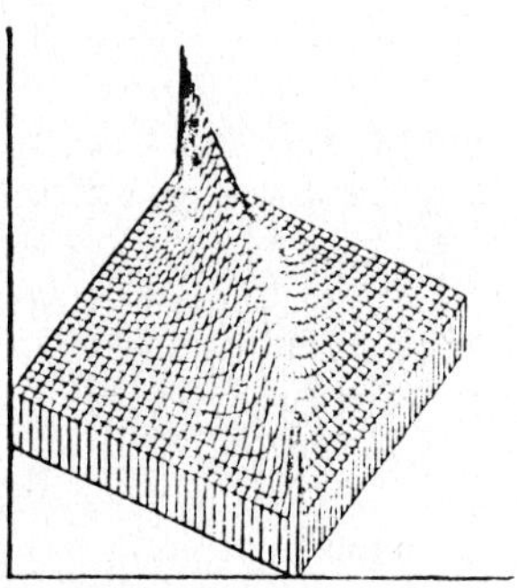

Fig. 5. Initial system magnitude response of example 3.

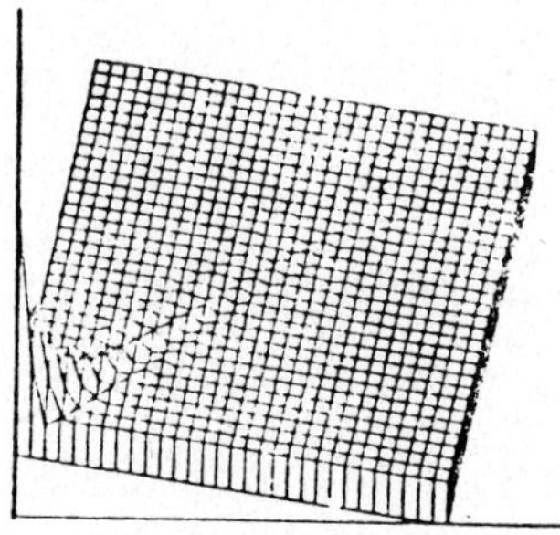

Fig. 6. Initial system impulse response of example 3.

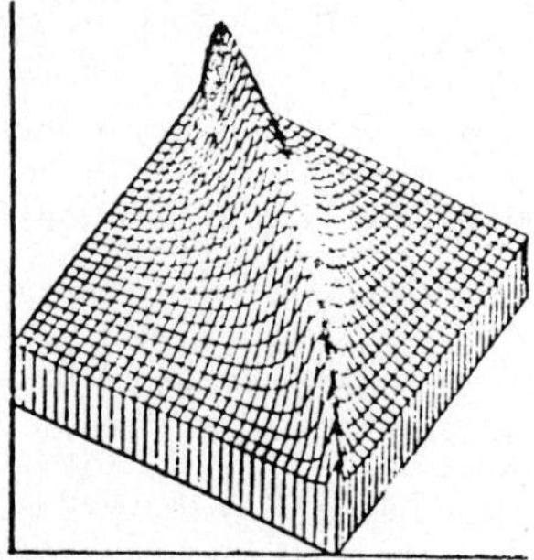

Fig. 7. Reduced order model magnitude response of example 3.

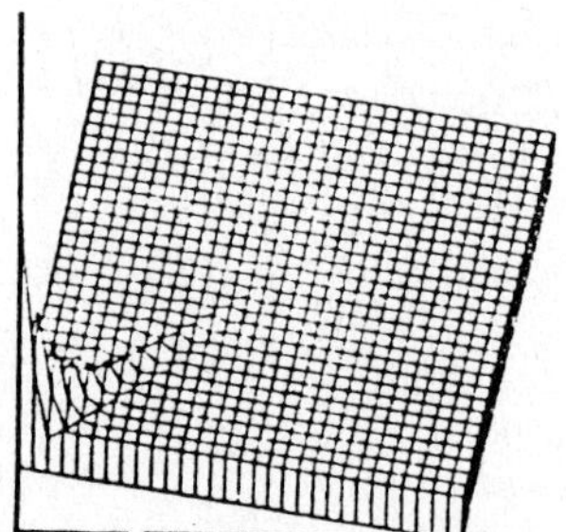

Fig. 8. Reduced order model impulse response of example 3.

DIGITAL TECHNIQUES in Simulation, Communication and Control
Spyros G. Tzafestas (editor)

NEW RESULTS IN THE 2-D SYSTEM SYNTHESIS

A.M.Necula, B.Droaşcă, D.Stănescu

Polytechnical Institute of Bucharest
Department of Control and Computer

In this paper several new results concerning the 2-D digital linear system synthesis are presented. It was pointed out that without increasing the complexity of the system and by an appropiate selection of the system parameter values it is possible to obtain special transformations of the output sequence - so called "special-effects". This "special effects" can represent an interesting way to approach the image digital processing techniques. Some interesting aspects of 2-D system realization were releaved. In order to ilustrate the theoretical results, experimental work was done by using a specialized simulation instrument.

1. INTRODUCTION

During the last years an increasing interest was paid to the 2-D system theory due to its impact on some major research domains as: digital image processing, digital filtering, and so on.

In this paper some theoretical and practical results regarding 2-D system analysis and synthesis obtained by the authors are presented. We consider these results very useful for 2-D system designers as well as for researchers in domains such as image digital processing.

2. MATHEMATICAL MODELS OF 2-D LINEAR SYSTEMS

It is known that 2-D discrete systems accept as input a 2-D sequence and produce as output a 2-D sequence as well (fig. 1). The dimensions of the input and output sequence can be equal or different.

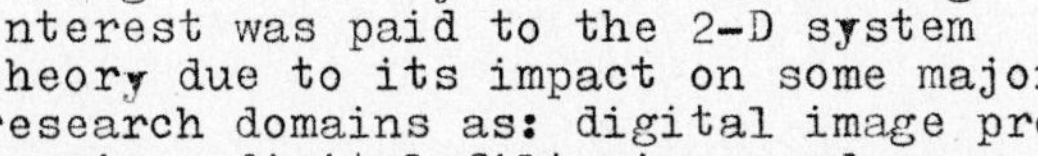

$\{u_{m,n}\}$ → [ ] → $\{y_{k,p}\}$

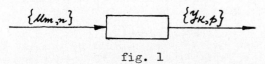

fig. 1

In this paper we are concerned with 2-D linear discrete systems, which means that the output sequence $\{y_{k,p}\}$ is obtained by linear operations applied to the input sequence $\{u_{m,n}\}$. If the input-output transfer is expressed by an operator $T[\cdot]$, such that

$$T[\{x_{1m,n}\}+c\{x_{2m,n}\}]=T[\{x_{1m,n}\}]+cT[\{x_{2m,n}\}] \tag{1}$$

where: $\{x_{1_{m,n}}\}$ and $\{x_{2_{m,n}}\}$ are sequences in the class of inputs accepted by the system;

If, besides (1) the following equations hold , c an arbitrary constant,

$$T[\{u_{m,n}\}]=\{y_{m,n}\} \tag{2}$$

$$\{y_{m-m_o,n-n_o}\}=T[\{u_{m-m_o,n-n_o}\}]$$

where m_o,n_o arbitrar integers, then the system is invariant too.

Let us consider the input sequence

$$\{\delta_{m,n}\}=\begin{cases}1 & m=n=0\\ 0 & m\neq 0;\ n\neq 0\end{cases} \tag{3}$$

defined as 2-D unity impulse. For a system satisfying (1) and (2)

$$T[\{\delta_{m,n}\}]=\{h_{m,n}\} \tag{4}$$

and $\{h_{m,n}\}$ is called the weight sequence of the system.

As in the unidimensional (1-D) case, the 2-D linear invariant systems can be characterized by weight and respectively input sequences convolution.

It is known that 1-D system analysis and synthesis are easier done if some adequate mathematical transformations are used (such as Laplace transformation for the continuous case and Z-transformation for the discrete one).

Since the systems represented in fig.1 are discrete ones, the Z-2-D transformation is useful in their case too [1].

There are 2 types of Z-2-D transformations defined in the literature. In this paper we define the standard Z-2-D transform of a sequence by the eq. (5)

$$Z[\{u_{m,n}\}]=U(z_1,z_2)=\sum_{i=0}^{\infty}\sum_{j=0}^{\infty} u_{i,j}z_1^{-i}z_2^{-j} \quad (5)$$

and since we consider only finite dimensional input sequence, i.e $0 \leq m \leq M$; $0 \leq n \leq N$, it follows that upper limits of sums in (5) are M, respectively N.

By applying Z-2-D transformation to the input and output sequences of a system (fig. 1) and assuming that the initial conditions are zero, it follows that a 2-D discrete linear invariant system admits a transfer function of the form:

$$H(z_1,z_2) = \frac{Y(z_1,z_2)}{U(z_1,z_2)} \quad (6)$$

We shall consider that eq. (6) is a rational irreductible function of the form

$$H(z_1,z_2) = \frac{A(z_1,z_2)}{B(z_1,z_2)} \quad (7)$$

where

$$A(z_1,z_2)=\sum_{m=0}^{M_a}\sum_{n=0}^{N_a} a_{m,n}\, z_1^{-m}z_2^{-n} \quad (8)$$

$$B(z_1,z_2)=\sum_{i=0}^{M_b}\sum_{j=0}^{N_b} b_{i,j}\, z_1^{-i}z_2^{-j}; b_{0,0}=1 \quad (9)$$

From (6) and (7), the following reccurence formula can be obtained in order to compute the elements the output sequence elements [2]

$$y_{k,t}=\sum_{m=0}^{M_a}\sum_{n=0}^{N_a} a'_{m,n}u_{k-m,t-n} - \sum_{i=0}^{M_b}\sum_{j=0}^{N_b} b'_{i,j}y_{k-i,t-j} \quad (10)$$

(i,j not simultaneously 0)

where

$$a'_{m,n} = a_{m,n}/b_{0,0} \quad (11)$$

$$b'_{i,j} = b_{i,j}/b_{0,0} \quad (11)$$

$u_{k-m,t-n}$ - input sequence elements,

$y_{k-i,t-j}$ - precomputed elements of the output sequence.

Eqs. (6) and (10) represent the types of input/output oriented models used for 2-D discrete linear invariant systems.

Another type of 2-D linear invariant discrete systems frequently used in 2-D system specification is a state model Roesser type, as it is given by (12)

$$p\in[1,k] \; r\in[1,q] \quad \begin{bmatrix} x_{vp}(i+1,j) \\ x_{hr}(i,j+1) \end{bmatrix} = A \begin{bmatrix} x_{vp}(i,j) \\ x_{hr}(i,j) \end{bmatrix} + b\,u(i,j) \quad (12)$$

$$y(i,j) = cx(i,j)$$

where x_{vi}, x_{hr} represent the vector of vertical and, respectively, horizontal states of the system and A, b, c are matrices of appropiate dimensions.

3. SPECIAL EFFECTS OBTAINED WITH 2-D DISCRETE LINEAR SYSTEMS

Given a 2-D system by its Z-2-D transfer function H we have established parametric synthesis procedures such that the output sequence of the sythetized system to be in a certain type of relationship with the output sequence of H, providing both systems have the same input.

We have developed a sythesis procedure by which one can produce an output sequence (matrix) preserving the original output matrix of H, but containing also additional intertwined lines and/or columns; we call this the "magnifying lens" effect.

We have established also a systhesis procedure by which the new element values in the new output sequence (matrix) can be preferentially amplified/attenuated or even eliminated (replaced by zero); we call this the "contrast" effect.

3.1. MAGNIFYING LENS EFFECT

<u>Definition</u>: A "k-order vertical magnifying lens effect" (MVE_k) consists of:

Consider a 2-D system specified by its transfer function $H(z_1,z_2)$ and let

$\{u_{m,n}\}$ and $\{y_{i,j}\}$ be its input, respectively, output finite rectangular 2-D sequences (matrices).

A new 2-D system is synthetized - its $H^*(z_1,z_2)$ transfer function being obtained by modifying the $H(z_1,z_2)$ coefficients such that if to the new system the same $\{u_{m,n}\}$ input matrix is applied, its $\{y^*_{i,j}\}$ output satisfies the following rules:

$$\text{a) } C^*_o = C_o \tag{13}$$

b) $C^*_{ki} = C_i$; k - any positive integer
$i = 1, \ldots, N$

where C^* - the columns of Y^* matrix
C - the columns of Y matrix
N - the horizontal dimension of Y.

In the same manner a "k-order horizontal magnifying lens effect" (MHE_k) and a "k-order total magnifying lens effect" (MTE_k), can be defined.

Proposition 1

Consider the transfer function

$$H(z_1,z_2) = \frac{1}{\sum_{i=0}^{1}\sum_{j=0}^{1} b_{i,j} z_1^{-i} z_2^{-j}} \tag{14}$$

and let the system input be of the unity impulse type (3).

The necessary conditions for obtaining the magnifying lens effect are:

$$MHE_k \begin{cases} b_{0,1} = -b'_2 & b'_2 > 0 \\ b_{1,1} = b_{1,0} \cdot b_{0,1} \end{cases} \tag{15}$$

$$MVE_k \begin{cases} b_{1,0} = -b'_1 & b'_1 > 0 \\ b_{1,1} = b_{1,0} \cdot b_{0,1} \end{cases} \tag{16}$$

$$MTE_k \begin{cases} b_{0,1} = -b'_2 & b'_2 > 0 \\ b_{1,0} = -b'_1 & b'_1 > 0 \\ b_{1,1} = b_{1,0} \cdot b_{0,1} \end{cases} \tag{17}$$

The new synthetized transfer function

$$H^*(z_1,z_2) = \frac{1}{\sum_{i=0}^{1}\sum_{j=0}^{1} b^*_{i,j} z_1^{-i} z_2^{-j}} \tag{18}$$

is obtained as follows

$$MHE_k \begin{cases} b^*_{0,1} = \sqrt[k]{b'_2} \\ b^*_{1,1} = -b_{1,0}\sqrt[k]{b'_2} \end{cases} \tag{19}$$

$$MVE_k \begin{cases} b^*_{1,0} = \sqrt[k]{b'_1} \\ b^*_{1,1} = -b_{0,1} \cdot \sqrt[k]{b'_1} \end{cases} \tag{20}$$

$$MTE_k \begin{cases} b^*_{1,0} = \sqrt[k]{b'_1} \\ b^*_{0,1} = \sqrt[k]{b'_2} \\ b^*_{1,1} = \sqrt{b'_1\, b'_2} \end{cases} \tag{21}$$

There are several posibilities of proving the proposition, one of them consisting of computing the elements of matrices $\{y_{i,j}\}$ and $\{y^*_{i,j}\}$ by using (10) and the comparing the results [3], [4].

Proposition 2

Consider a 2-D system given by its transfer function

$$H(z_1,z_2) = \frac{1}{\sum_{i=0}^{m}\sum_{j=0}^{1} b_{i,j} z_1^{-i} z_2^{-j}}; \quad b_{0,0}=1 \tag{22}$$

and with an unity impuls as input.

The necessary conditions for a MHE_k are:

$$\begin{aligned} & b_{0,1} = -b'_2 \qquad b'_2 > 0 \\ & b_{i,1} = b_{i,0} \cdot b_{0,1}; \; i = 1, \ldots, m \end{aligned} \tag{23}$$

One obtains a new transfer function

$$H^*(z_1,z_2) = \frac{1}{\sum_{i=0}^{m}\sum_{j=0}^{1} b^*_{i,j} z_1^{-i} z_2^{-j}} \tag{24}$$

$$\text{where: } \begin{aligned} & b^*_{0,1} = \sqrt[k]{b'_2} \\ & b^*_{i,1} = -b_{i,0}\sqrt[k]{b'_2}; \; i=1,\ldots,m \end{aligned} \tag{25}$$

Proposition 3

Let us consider a 2-D system given by

$$H(z_1,z_2) = \frac{1 + a_{1,0}z_1^{-1}}{1+b_{1,0}z_1^{-1}+b_{0,1}z_2^{-1}+b_{1,1}z_1^{-1}z_2^{-1}} \tag{26}$$

with an unity impulse unit.

The necessary conditions for obtaining the magnifying lens effect [4] are:

$$MHE_k \begin{cases} b_{0,1} = -b'_2 ; \; b'_2 > 0 \\ b_{1,1} = b_{1,0} \cdot b_{0,1} \end{cases} \tag{27}$$

$$MOE_k \begin{cases} b_{1,0} = -b'_1 ; \; b'_1 > 0 \\ b_{1,1} = b_{1,0} \cdot b_{0,1} \\ a_{1,0} = k^o \cdot b'_1 ; \; k^o = ct. \end{cases} \tag{28}$$

The effects are obtained if a new transfer function $H^{*})z_1,z_2)$ is synthetized, of the same form as (26), where the new coefficients $b^{*}_{i,j}$ are given by

$$MHE_k \begin{cases} b^{*}_{0,1} = \sqrt[k]{b'_2} \\ b^{*}_{1,1} = -b_{1,0}\cdot\sqrt[k]{b'_2} \end{cases} \quad (29)$$

$$MOE_k \begin{cases} b^{*}_{1,o} = \sqrt[k]{b'_1} \\ b^{*}_{1,1} = -b_{0,1}\cdot\sqrt[k]{b'_1} \\ a^{*}_{1,0} = k^{o}\cdot\sqrt[k]{b'_1} \end{cases} \quad (30)$$

Proposition 4

Consider a 2-D system given by

$$H(z_1,z_2)= \frac{1+a_{1,0}z^{-1}_1+a_{0,1}z^{-1}_2+a_{1,1}z^{-1}_1z^{-1}_2}{1+b_{1,0}z^{-1}_1+b_{0,1}z^{-1}_2+b_{1,1}z^{-1}_1z^{-1}_2} \quad (31)$$

with an unity impulse input.

The necessary conditions for obtaining the magnifying lens effects are:

$$MHE_k \begin{cases} b_{0,1} = -b'_2 \qquad b'_2 > 0 \\ b_{1,1} = b_{1,0}\cdot b_{0,1} \\ a_{0,1} = k^{o}_1\cdot b'_2 \ ; \ k^{o}_1 = ct. \\ a_{1,1} = k^{o}_2\cdot b'_2 \ ; \ k^{o}_2 = ct. \end{cases} \quad (32)$$

$$MVE_k \begin{cases} b_{1,0} = -b'_1 \qquad b'_1 > 0 \\ b_{1,1} = b_{1,0}\cdot b_{0,1} \\ a_{1,0} = k^{o}_3\cdot b'_1 \ ; \ k^{o}_3 = ct. \\ a_{1,1} = k^{o}_4\cdot b'_1 \ ; \ k^{o}_4 = ct. \end{cases} \quad (33)$$

The synthesis of the new $H^{*}(z_1,z_2)$ can be done similarly as in the Propositions 3 and 4.

The MTE_k, for case of propositions 2, 3 and 4, can be obtained by cumulating the conditions and the rules given for MHE_k and MVE_k.

The above results can be easily extended to the general case, where

$$H(z_1,z_2)= \frac{\sum_{k=0}^{p}\sum_{r=0}^{s} a_{k,r}z^{-k}_1z^{-r}_2}{\sum_{i=0}^{m}\sum_{j=0}^{n} b_{i,j}z^{-i}_1z^{-j}_2} \quad (34)$$

Based on the results obtained in [4] and in this paper, the following theorems are in order:

a) Consider a transfer function $H(z_1,z_2) = P(z_1,z_2)/Q(z_1,z_2)$ where $P(z_1,z_2)$ and $Q(z_1,z_2)$ are 2-D polynomials in z^{-1}_1 and z^{-2}_2 and an unity impulse unit.
If $\max.\text{order}_{z_1}(P)=0$ then the coefficients of P do not affect the conditions for obtaining MHE effect. Similarly, if $\max.\text{order}_{z_2}(P)=0$, the conditions for MVE_k are not affected by P coefficients.

b) Let $\max.\text{order}_{z_1}(P) = \lambda$ and $\max.\text{order}_{z_2}(P) = \beta$. The coefficients of P are always satisfying the necessary conditions for obtaining the magnifying lens effects.

3.2. CONTRAST EFFECTS

We mention that the contrast effects can be obtained in a great variety and therefore, we shall restraint here only to several representative situations.

We call

a) a vertical contrast effect (CE_V) - the effect produced on the column of Y;

b) a horizontal contrast effect (CE_H) - the effect produced on the rows of Y;

c) a zero contrast effect ($CE_{\emptyset}$) - the effect consisting of supressing certain values (or columns/rows) in Y.

In order to obtain a CE_V at a system given by $H(z_1,z_2)$ of the form (14) it is necessary to synthetize a new transfer function

$$H^{*}(z_1,z_2)= \frac{P(z_1)}{\sum_{i=0}^{1}\sum_{j=0}^{1} b_{i,j}z^{-i}_1z^{-j}_2} \quad (35)$$

where $P(z_1)$ is a polynomial of the arbitrary order m, in z_1.

Proposition 5

The necessary condition for obtaining a (CE_V) is that the coefficients a_i of $P(z_1)$ satisfy the eqs:

$$a_0 = 1 \quad (36)$$
$$a_i = (-b_{1,0})^{i}\cdot\lambda_i, \ _i=ct., \ ; \ i=1,\dots,m$$

where λ_i is an arbitrary constant and $i = 1,\ldots,m$.

Example

Let $P(z_1) = 1 + a_1z_1^{-1} + a_2z_1^{-2}+a_3z_1^{-3}$. It follows that $\lambda_1 = a_1/-b_{1,0}$; $\lambda_2 = a_2/b_{1,0}^2$; $\lambda_3 = a_3/(-b_{1,0})^3$. If we take $P(z_1)$ such that:

a) $\lambda_1\neq 0$; $\lambda_2=0$; $\lambda_3=0$ - one obtains a CE_V, namely the columns $C_1,C_2,\ldots$, are amplified or attenuated by the factor $(1+\lambda_1)$;

b) $\lambda_1=-1$; $\lambda_2=0$; $\lambda_3=0$ - one obtains a $EC_\emptyset$, namely all the columns, except the column C_0, become zero;

c) $\lambda_1=-1$; $\lambda_2=0$; $\lambda_3=1$ - one obtains a $EC_\emptyset$ namely the columns C_1,C_2 in Y are zeroed and the rest are unmodified. And so on.

It is obvious that by increasing the order of P, new contrast effects can be obtained, the most spectacular ones corresponding to a polynomial P of the 2-D type - $P(z_1,z_2)$ [3].

4. CONSIDERATIONS ON THE HARDWARE REALIZATION OF A 2-D SYSTEM

4.1. ON THE 2-D SYSTEM ANALYSIS USING A SPECIALIZED SIMULATOR

The digital simulation represents a currently used technique in computer assisted system analysis. In many cases this technique is more efficient than the analitic approach.

The simulation of any system is based on a system model and implies the existence of an adequate software tool - a simulator - which can process the informations contained in the system model in order to generate informations about its behaviour.

Taking into account the characteristics of 2-D system models, a specialised simulator was designed and implemented. This simulator proved itself a very useful tool for 2-D system analysis, as well as for some synthesis problems solving.

A characteristic of the 2-D systemsis the matricial form of their inputs and outputs. Since the simulation process is a sequential one, in order to analise in a simulation the behaviour of 2-D systems, intermediate 1-D sequential forms of the matricial inputs and outputs have to be used. Therefore, the main phases of the 2-D system analysis via simulation are the follwing(fig.2):

- simulation model specification on the basis of the system mathematical model;
- matricial-to-sequential (2-D/1-D) input conversion;
- digital simulation, which generates a sequential output for a given simulation model and input sequence;
- sequential-to-matricial (1-D/2-D) output form conversion.

All phases are implemented, as distinct modules, in the SADASIM simulation system, whose structure is presented in fig. 3.

The SADASIM modules interface is represented by disk sequential files, containing the 1-D input-output sequences.

This simulation system is implemented on the Romanian Felix M-18/118 microcomputers, but due to the use of Fortran as implementation language, it is highly portable.

SADASIM operates in a conversational mode, using a set of concise and yet suggestive messages, easily understood and answered even by the unexperienced user.

The SADASIM simulation models are represented by sets of interconected blocks. Each block implements a specific input-output function, which defines the block type, and has up to 3 parameters and up

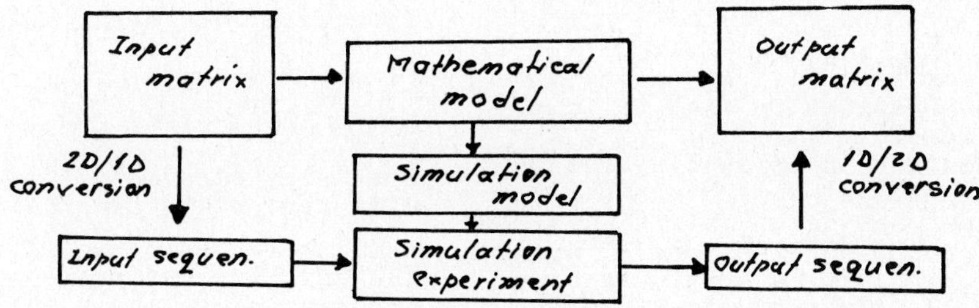

fig. 2.

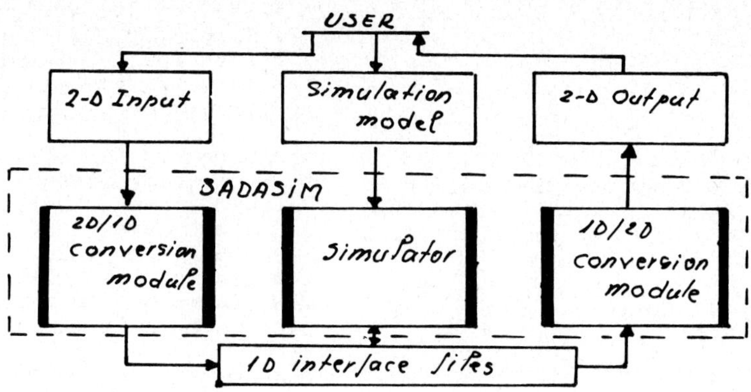

fig. 3.

to 3 inputs.

Each block in a SADASIM simulator model is identified by a distinct integer and its type is specified by means of an alphanumeric symbol.

The basic block types in the discrete simulation are the variable delay and weighted summer (fig. 4).

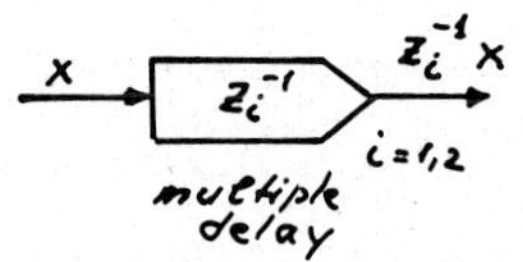

fig. 4.

horizontal and vertical sampling intervals. In the simulation process this distance is represented by the delay with which the value in the matrix point is applied to the simulation model input (The value in the matrix origin is applied with a null delay).

From the sequential point of view the input matrix can be regarded as a sequence of "vertically" - delayed "horizontal" sequences and, in the same time, as sequence of "horizontally" - delayed "vertical" sequences.

Some other additional types of blocks can be equally used in the SADASIM simulation models specification.

The most important ones are the input/output blocks (C/E) which allow the access to the sequential files used as interface between the simulator and the conversion modules.

Once generated the simulation model for a given 2-D system, the user has to prepare the input sequences for the intended simulation experiments. In this phase he is assisted by the 2-D/1-D conversion module.

The Theoretical bases of the conversion algorithm is presented in what follows.

Since a simulation experiment proceeds in a finite number of simulation steps, it follows that the input matrix must be a finite one, with NL lines and NC columns (NL, NC $\in \mathbb{N}$). The matrix origin is considered as the (0,0) point. The distance between any matrix point and the origin depends on the point coordinates and the

By the same reasoning, the relative delay, betwwen two-horizontally or vertically adjacent points is a function of the matrix dimensions - NL, NC - and the sampling intervals - δx, δy -:

$$\Delta z_1^{-1} = NL \times \delta y \tag{37}$$

$$\Delta z_2^{-1} = NC \times \delta x \tag{38}$$

Therefore, the delay between any matrix point $u_{i,j}$ and the matrix origin is given by the following relation:

$$K = i \times NC \times \delta x + j \times NL \times \delta y \tag{39}$$

The delay associated to a matrix point $u_{i,j}$ represents its index in the corresponding 1-D sequence. It follows, that the sampling intervals δx, δy must be integers or suitably scaled to integer values.

In most cases the uniform unitar sampling $\delta x = \delta y = 1$ is used.

In order to generate a sequence including as distinct elements all the values in the input matrix, the horizontal and vertical delays(37, 38) must be relative prime integers. Otherwise, there will be matrix points with the same index k (39) and the generation of a correct 1-D sequence becomes impossible.

The 1-D sequence length is given by the following formula:

$$NT = (NL-1)\times NC\times\delta x + (NC-1)\times NL\times\delta y + 1 \tag{40}$$

In such a sequence there are more elements than in the original matrix. It can be shown that the intermediate elements values in the 1-D sequence are irrelevant for the matricial output, but they might create simulation numerical stability problems. Therefore, it is suitable to assign zero values to all intermediate elements.

For the example in fig. 5.

the 1-D/2-D conversion module will be used, this module accepts as input a user specified interface file and generates as output the 2-D form of the sequence in this file.

4.2. ON THE HARDWARE IMPLEMENTATION OF 2-D SYSTEMS

It is known that a hardware realization of a 2-D transfer function requires a number of total delay elements (horizontal and vertical) greater than function denominator order.

Thus, considering

$$H(z_1,z_2)=\frac{\sum_{i=0}^{m}\sum_{j=0}^{n} a_{i,j} z^{-i} z^{-j}}{\sum_{i=0}^{m}\sum_{j=0}^{n} b_{i,j} z_1^{-i} z_2^{-j}} \tag{41}$$

its hardware realization requires either 2m vertical delay elements and n horizontal ones or 2n horizontal delay elements and m vertical ones [6].

$u_{0,0}$ (0)	$u_{0,1}$ (5)	$u_{0,2}$ (10)	$u_{0,3}$ (15)	$u_{0,4}$ (20)	$u_{0,5}$ (25)
$u_{1,0}$ (6)	$u_{1,1}$ (11)	$u_{1,2}$ (16)	$u_{1,3}$ (21)	$u_{1,4}$ (26)	$u_{1,5}$ (31)
$u_{2,0}$ (12)	$u_{2,1}$ (17)	$u_{2,2}$ (22)	$u_{2,3}$ (27)	$u_{2,4}$ (32)	$u_{2,5}$ (37)
$u_{3,0}$ (18)	$u_{3,1}$ (23)	$u_{3,2}$ (28)	$u_{3,3}$ (33)	$u_{3,4}$ (38)	$u_{3,5}$ (43)
$u_{4,0}$ (24)	$u_{4,1}$ (29)	$u_{4,2}$ (34)	$u_{4,3}$ (39)	$u_{4,4}$ (44)	$u_{4,5}$ (49)

$u_{i,j}$ - matrix element ; (·) corresponding delay

fig. 5.

The 2-D/1-D conversion module generates a 50 elements sequence:

$$u_{0,0}\,0\,0\,0\,0\;u_{1,0}\;u_{0,1}\;0\;0\;0\;u_{0,2}\;u_{1,1}\;u_{2,0}$$
$$u_{1,2}\;u_{2,1}\;u_{3,0}\;0\;u_{0,4}\;u_{1,3}\cdots\;0\;0\;u_{4,5}$$

which is stored in a sequential interface file.

The 2-D/1-D conversion module requires as input, for each matrix to be converted, its dimensions (NL,NC) and the matrix values, in row order. The resulting 1-D sequence is stored in an user specified disk file. From this file, the sequence can be applied, by means for a type C block, to the simulation model input.

The simulation generated 1-D sequences can be stored, using E blocks, in interface files. For the conversion of the output sequences to the matricial form,

An example:

$$H(z_1,z_2)=\frac{Az_1^{-1}+Bz_2^{-1}+Cz_1^{-1}z_2^{-1}}{1+\alpha z_1^{-1}+\beta z_2^{-1}+\gamma z_1^{-1}z_2^{-1}} \tag{42}$$

requires for examples 2 vertical delay elements and 1 horizontal delay element.

Let a 2-D system be represented by a state model Roesser type (12):

$$\begin{bmatrix} x_v(i+1,j) \\ x_h(i,j+1) \end{bmatrix} = \begin{bmatrix} a_1 & a_2 \\ a_3 & a_4 \end{bmatrix}\begin{bmatrix} x_v(i,j) \\ x_h(i,j) \end{bmatrix} + \begin{bmatrix} b_1 \\ b_2 \end{bmatrix} u(i,j) \tag{43}$$

$$y(i,j) = \begin{bmatrix} c_1 & c_2 \end{bmatrix}\begin{bmatrix} x_v(i,j) \\ x_h(i,j) \end{bmatrix}$$

The hardware implementation of this

system is presented in Fig. 6.

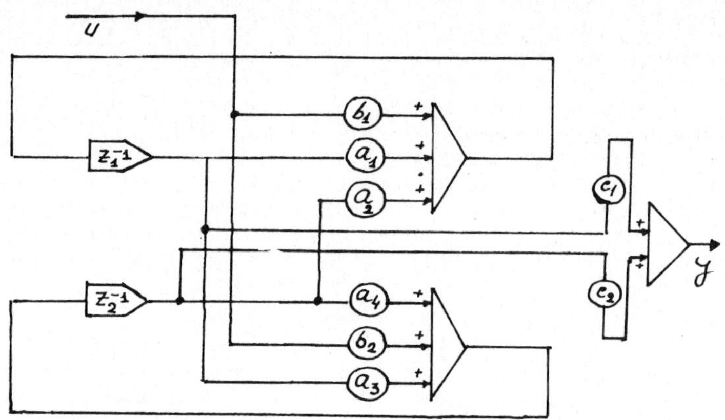

Fig. 6

It can be noticed that this transfer function is in the same class as (1), but its implementation requires the minimal number of delay elements (1 + 1).

Therefore, it is obvious that the 2-D system simulation (hardware implementation) using the state-model will always lead to the minimal number of horizontal plus vertical delay elements.

In order to express the dependence between the transfer function and state model parameters we have established the appropiate formulae [7].

Based on a system representation as in (4) a simulation model can be obtained in which the vertical and horizontal evolutions are decoupled [7] as in fig. 7.

CONCLUSIONS

In this paper, several new results concerning the 2-D digital linear system synthesis are presented.

It was pointed out that without increasing the complexity of the system and by an appropiate selection of the system parameter values it is possible to obtain special transformations of the output sequence - so called "special-effects". This "special effects" could represent an interesting way to approach the image digital processing techniques. Some interesting aspects of 2-D system realization were revealed.

In order to illustrate the theoretical results, experimental work was done by using a specialized simulation instrument.

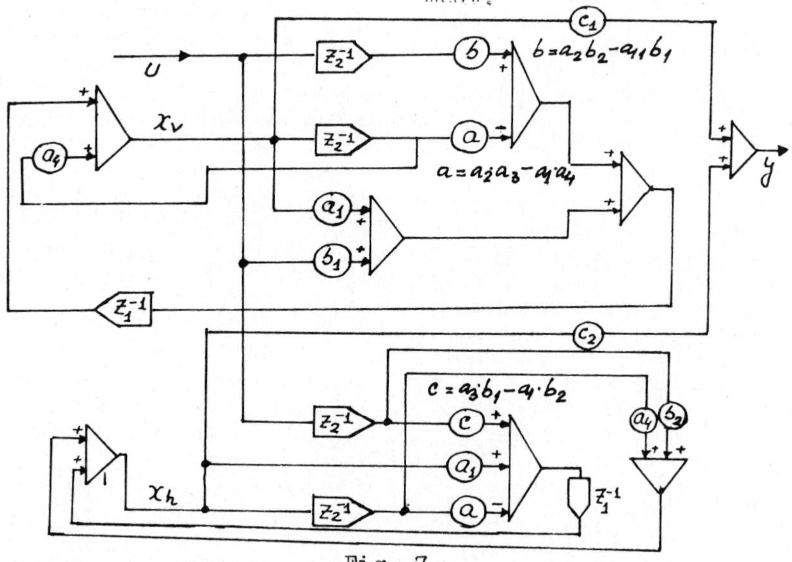

Fig. 7.

REFERENCES

[1] - R.Mersereau, D.Dudgeon
Two-dimensional Digital Filtering
Proceedings of IEEE/apr.1975.

[2] - J.L.Schauks, J.H.Justice
Stability and Synthesis of Two-Dimensional Recursive Filters.
IEEE Trans.on Audio and Electroac.
vol. AU-20/2/1972.

[3] - A.M.Necula, B.Droaşcă
Computer Assisted Analysis of 2-D Digital Systems
1-st International Symposium of ICD, Tunis, 1982.

[4] - B.Droaşcă, A.M.Necula, Doina Stănescu
Special Effects Obtained with 2-D Digital Systems.
Part 2. (in Romanian).

[5] - A.M.Necula, E.Kalisz, B.Droaşcă, D.Stănescu
Bidimensional Discrete Systems.
Computer Aided Analysis (in Romanian).

[6] - M.Morf et al.
New results in 2-D System Theory.
Part. II.
IEEE Proceedings, March, 1977.

[7] - B.Droaşcă, A.M.Necula, D.Stănescu
On the hardware implementation of 2-D Systems 5-th Conference international on control systems and computer science.

DIGITAL TECHNIQUES in Simulation, Communication and Control
Spyros G. Tzafestas (editor)
Elsevier Science Publishers B.V. (North-Holland) © IMACS, 1985

INFORMATION-THEORETIC IMAGE RESTORATION METHODS

R.C. Papademetriou*, T.J. Ketseoglou** and N.S. Tzannes*

* Department of Electrical Engineering, University of Patras, Patras, Greece

** Hellenic Navy Supply Center, Skaramagas, Greece

In this paper the Mutual Information Principle (MIP) is applied to the image restoration problem with the adoption of Hershel's modelling approach of an object as a probability density function. It is easily demonstrated that this method is more general than the Maximum Information (MI) method proposed by Frieden and includes Frieden's method as one of its subcases.

1. INTRODUCTION

The first part of this introductory section reviews the Mutual Information Principle (MIP) as a method of assigning a prior probability mass (or density) function to a random variable in the presence of some prior information.

In the second part, the image restoration problem is outlined as an inverse source problem with insufficient data for yielding a unique solution.

1.1 The Mutual Information Principle (MIP)

In 1973, N.S. Tzannes and J.P. Noonan [1] proposed a new approach to the general problem of assigning a prior probability density function for a random variable, based on Rate Distortion Theory (RDT) [2]. This approach, using the informational theory concept of mutual information with a fidelity criterion, was named MIP. It is applicable in finding the prior $p(x_n)$ of a continuous or discrete r.v. X, when one has prior information not about X, but about another discrete r.v. Y, related to X by a known error (or distortion) criterion of the form

$$E\{d(X, Y)\} \leq \varepsilon \tag{1}$$

This distortion function d(X, Y) models the "error" or "noise" introduced by the system between X and Y. Assuming that one can set an upper bound ($\varepsilon > 0$) to the expected value of this distortion, he can then extremize the mutual information I(X;Y)

$$I(X;Y) = \sum_{m,n} p(x_n)p(y_m|x_n)\ln\frac{p(y_m|x_n)}{p(y_m)} = \text{extremum} \tag{2}$$

between input X and output Y (they are both assumed discrete here) subject to this and any other constraint, in order to obtain the optimum $p(x_n)$.

This is the philosophy of the MIP that we will be confronted with in what follows.

1.2 The Image Restoration Problem

The ultimate goal of image restoration is to obtain the best estimate of an image which has been degraded.

Before defining any solution, it must be known how the data image was formed. To proceed, we must have a mathematical model of the image formation system. For this work, the standard linear model will be used, which may be written as

$$d_m = \sum_{n=1}^{N} o_n s_{mn} + n_m \quad , \quad m = 1,2,\ldots,N \tag{3}$$

where $\{d_m\}$, m = 1,2,.., N are the given data about the unknown image, called the objective $\{o_n\}$, n = 1,2,...,N; $\{n_m\}$ is random noise and s_{mn} is the point spread function (psf) of image formation (i.e., the image of a point). The estimate of the objective function will be called $\hat{o}_n$.

Since the random noise can never be precisely known, there is no unique solution to system (3) of N equations in the 2N unknowns $\hat{o}_n$ and $\hat{n}_m$. Therefore, the particular choice of solution is arbitrary and depends on the choice of a restoration criterion, made by the user, which defines what is meant by the term restoration. There are many restoration criteria which have proven useful. Maximum likelihood [3], minimum-mean-square error (mmse) [4], maximum a posteriori probability (MAP) [5] and maximum entropy (ME) [6] are a few of them.

This paper will discuss the MIP restoration criterion. After the modelling procedure of our system under study, we will be able to see how it applies to our case.

2. MODELLING THE SYSTEM AS AN INFORMATION CHANNEL

Adopting Hershel's [7] approach to modelling an object as a probability density function, we start our image formation analysis by considering the general information channel (Fig. 1) with input and output signals x_n (the position

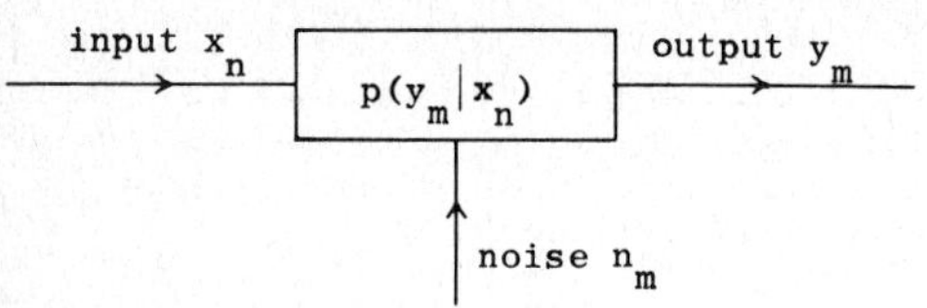

Fig. 1

of a photon in the object plane) and y_m (the position of a photon as it strikes the image plane), respectively. An object value o_n representing the intensity at position x_n of the object plane (Fig. 2), also represents, by the law of large numbers, the probability $p(x_n)$ that a photon radiates from position x_n. So we can write

$$p(x_n) = o(x_n) \equiv o_n \quad , \quad o_n \geq 0 \tag{4}$$

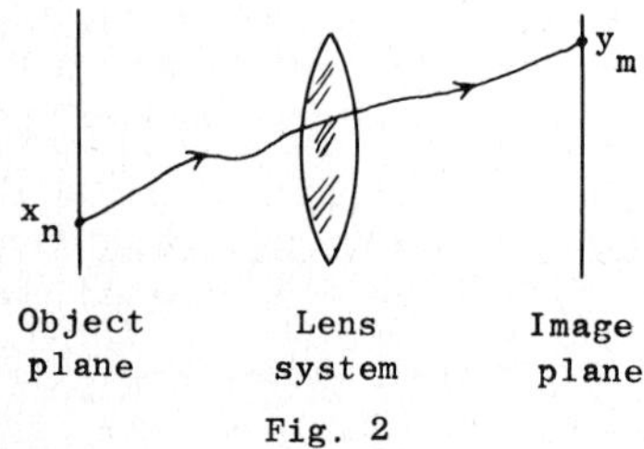

Fig. 2

By identical reasoning, an image value d_m representing the intensity at position y_m in the image plane, also represents the probability $p(y_m)$ that a photon will strike the image plane at position y_m, that is

$$p(y_m) = d(y_m) \equiv d_m \tag{5}$$

Note that for the satisfaction of the law of large numbers, a large number of photons must radiate from the object and reach the image. Hence, we are considering only high-light-level cases.

Coming,now, to the probability $p(y_m|x_n)$, we can find, after a little thought, that for signal photons only

$$p(y_m|x_n) = s(y_m;x_n) \equiv s_{mn} \tag{6}$$

which is the point spread function (psf), while for noise photons

$$p(y_m|x_n) = n(y_m) \equiv n_m \quad , \quad n_m \geq 0 \tag{7}$$

Supposing that fraction f of all photons in the image are source-dependent photons and the remaining fraction $\bar{f} \equiv 1 - f$ are noise photons, we can find that the net probability $p(y_m|x_n)$ obeys

$$p(y_m|x_n) = fs_{mn} + \bar{f}n_m \tag{8}$$

Substitution, now, of Eqs. (4), (5) and (8) into

$$p(y_m) = \sum_n p(x_n)p(y_m|x_n) \tag{9}$$

leads to

$$d_m = f\sum_n o_n s_{mn} + \bar{f}n_m \quad , \quad m = 1,2,\ldots,N \tag{10}$$

which may be interpreted as the ordinary imaging equation [8], but where the signal part is attenuated by fraction f and the noise part is modified by (1 - f).

More about the above modelling procedure can be found in [9] and [10].

3. THE MIP RESTORATION CRITERION

Having modelled the physical problem at hand, we can proceed, now, to lifting the redundancy of the image restoration problem by using the above explained MIP as a norm, or criterion of quality, for the restoration $\{\hat{o}_n\}$.

Following the philosophy of MIP, we are trying to find the object $\{o_n\}$ by extremizing the Mutual Information functional I(X;Y), using as constraints the known values of the data $\{d_m\}$ together with the quite general error criterion (1).

But since H(Y) in the established equality

$$I(X;Y) = H(Y) - H(Y|X) \tag{11}$$

is known - it represents the entropy of the data -

$$H(Y) = H(D) = -\sum_m d_m \ln d_m \tag{12}$$

we reach the conclusion that equation

$$H(Y|X) = -\sum_{m,n} p(y_m|x_n)p(x_n)\ln p(y_m|x_n)$$

$$= \text{extremum} \tag{13}$$

can be finally used as the actual implementor of Eq. (2), which is the basic criterion.

This last equation, with the help of Eqs. (4) and (8), becomes

$$H(Y|X) = -\sum_n \hat{o}_n \sum_m (fs_{mn} + \bar{f}n_m)\ln(fs_{mn} + \bar{f}n_m)$$

$$= \text{extremum} \tag{14}$$

Of course, this extremum must also be constrained by the data, through the N constraints (10), which, written as

$$n_m = \bar{f}^{-1}(d_m - f\sum_n \hat{o}_n s_{mn}) \tag{15}$$

eliminate the unknown set $\{n_m\}$ from the problem.

The solution $\{\hat{o}_n\}$ to Eqs. (14) and (15) must also obey the equality constraint

$$\sum_n \hat{o}_n = 1 \tag{16}$$

(normalization for the probability o_n) and the inequality constraints (4) and (7).

But which is the role of the average-error constraint (1) in our problem?

If we choose $d(x_n, y_m)$ to be

$$d(x_n, y_m) = |\bar{f}^{-1}(d_m - f\sum_n \hat{o}_n s_{mn})|^2 = |n_m|^2 \tag{17}$$

the final form of the constraint (with equality for simplicity) becomes

$$E\{n_m^2\} = \varepsilon \tag{18}$$

implying some knowledge of the noise statistics (specifically of the noise power), which may be known a priori or measurable a posteriori from the image [11].

This last equation is important in actually performing the extremization in a practical problem. Knowledge of ε enables the investigator to constraint the values of the noise to a region around the mean of the noise of the form $(-\sigma_n, +\sigma_n)$. The necessity of constraining the values of n_m is discussed in [9], [10] and [12] and the MIP constraint leads naturally to a such capability.

Bypassing for the moment the quite challenging problem of extremizing $H(Y|X)$ subject to the inequality constraints, we would like to point out that, with this particular distortion measure (17) given above, the MIP image restoration reduces mathematically to the Maximum Information (MI) image restoration proposed by Frieden [12].

Of course, Frieden maintains [9] that the extremization procedure leads to a maximum of $I(X;Y)$ - philosophically optimistic - while the MIP was originally thought to lead to a minimum - philosophically pessimistic. The solution, however, is the same.

It should also be pointed out that Frieden appears to add the noise constraint as part of his numerical solution attempts, although he does mention that it is an integral part of the overall procedure. The MIP has this condition as part of the basic formulation, and being so, it can be easily seen to handle any $d(X, Y)$ of practical interest; not just the one mentioned above for comparison with Frieden's work.

Finally, we must say, that, as far as the relationship between MIP and MEP is concerned, it can be easily shown (the proof is identical with that for MI) [12], that for an impulsive object whose pulses are spaced farther apart from one another than the support of s_{mn} and with no noise present the MIP norm goes into the well-known Maximum-Entropy (ME) norm

$$H(X) = -\sum_n \hat{o}_n \ln \hat{o}_n \tag{19}$$

4. CONCLUSIONS

The Mutual Information Principle (MIP) is applied to the image restoration problem with the adoption of Hershel's model of an object as a probability density function.

The MIP is also compared with Frieden's Maximum Information (MI) method and shown to be more general and more inclusive of all prior data available to the investigator.

5. REFERENCES

[1] Tzannes, N.S. and Noonan, J.P., The Mutual Information Principle and Applications, Information and Control, Vol. 22, No. 1 (Feb. 1973).

[2] Berger, T., Rate Distortion Theory, A Mathematical Basis for Data Compression (Prentice-Hall, 1971).

[3] Harris, J.L., Resolving Power and Decision Theory, J. Opt. Soc. Am. 54 (1964), 606-611.

[4] Helstrom, C.W., Image Restoration by the Method of Least Squares, J. Opt. Soc. Am. 57 (1967), 297-303.

[5] Hunt, B.R., Bayesian Methods in Digital Image Restoration, IEEE Trans. Comp., Vol. C-26 (Mar. 1977), 219-229.

[6] Frieden, B.R., Restoring with Maximum Likelihood and Maximum Entropy, J. Opt. Soc. Am. 62 (1972), 511-518.

[7] Hershel, R.S., Unified Approach to Restoring Degraded Images in the Presence of Noise, Techn. Rep. 71, Optical Sciences Center, Univ. of Arizona, Tuscon (Dec. 1971).

[8] Goodman, J.W., Introduction to Fourier Optics (McGraw-Hill, 1968).

[9] Frieden, B.R., Image Restoration Using a Norm of Maximum Information, Opt. Eng., Vol. 19, No. 3 (May/June 1980).

[10] Frieden, B.R., Statistical Models for the Image Restoration Problem, Computer Graphics and Image Processing 12 (1980), 40-59.

[11] Andrews, H.C. and Hunt, B.R., Digital Image Restoration (Prentice-Hall, 1977).

[12] Frieden, B.R., Maximum-Information Data Processing: Application to Optical Signals, J. Opt. Soc. Am., Vol. 71, No. 3 (Mar. 1981).

DIGITAL TECHNIQUES in Simulation, Communication and Control
Spyros G. Tzafestas (editor)
Elsevier Science Publishers B.V. (North-Holland) © IMACS, 1985

USING FUNCTIONAL PROGRAMMING FOR HIERARCHICAL STRUCTURES IN IMAGE PROCESSING

N.A.Alexandridis

Dept. of Electrical and Computer Engineering - Ohio University
Athens,Ohio,USA

N.A.Bilalis P.D.Tsanakas

Computer Science Division
National Technical University
Athens-Greece

A quadtree is a form of picture encoding which is compact and easily handled. It is based on a description of the recursive subdivision of those parts of the image where there is detail until some desired resolution is reached. Functional Programming is a radical departure from the von Neumann style programs, and deal with hierarchically constructed data.This paper proposes a method of storing quadtrees and operating on images by using a Functional Programming Language.

1. INTRODUCTION

Current trends in technology are such that the cost of hardware is diminishing dramatically.In the same period neither the architecture of computers nor the programming languages used to control them have changed significantly.It is becoming clear that software is the limiting factor in putting raw computer to use.It is time therefore to look again at our programming languages and ask what higher level features we can now afford to incorporate in order to ease the task of building certain kinds of programs.Otherwise software may now cost more than the machines they run on.We can anticipate therefore, that the trend in high-level languages will be to provide features that are progressively more user-oriented and at higher levels.An alternative functional style of programming is founded, by J.Backus [1,2] , on the use of combining forms for creating programs.Functional programs are hierarchically constructed, do not name their arguments, and do not require the complex machinery of procedure declarations to become generally applicable.

Quadtrees are compact hierarchical representations of images.In this paper, we define the efficiency of functional programming in representing image by using a quadtree.This technique is best used when the picture is a square matrix whose dimensions is a power of 2. The creation process of the quadtree has been described by an Algorithm, which uses functional programming language.In general, a quadtree is a more compact representation of an image. If we use a processor for each node of the quadtree and connect the processors according to the structure of the quadtree then we have an active quadtree network of processors. On the other hand, functional programming is an approach which allows parallel operations to be expressed easily, it suggests hardware designs built from large numbers of identical units than can achieve highly parallel operation, designs well suited to VLSI technology [13].

II. QUADTREE CONSTRUCTION

Quadtrees are receiving increasing attention from researchers in computer graphics,image processing,cartography and related fields. Let A be a rectagular array with K nodes (where $K=2^n \times 2^n$, and n is an integer) in which a picture P is stored.The quadtree representation is based on successive subdivisions of the array into quadrants.The root node represents the whole image and stores the average gray level.The image is divided into four subimages, and four children of the root are constructed.As long as the variance in gray level in any quadrant is higher than a threshold,the process is recursively applied.The result is a tree that represents the image to a degree of accuracy dependent on the threshold.A uniform quadrant of the image is represented by a leaf in the tree; a nonuniform quadrant is represented by an internal node.By changing the threshold on the variance,a whole class of quadtrees can be constructed.Two major disadvantages are related with a quadtree representation of an image.The arbitrariness of thresholding values and the arbitrariness of the dividing lines.Arbitrariness of thresholds is related to the problem of what kinds of information should be discarded and of whether this elemination of data could lead to significant loss of information .Arbitrariness of the dividing lines, which is related to the problem of whether dividing the picture into subpictures,implies some sort of loss of important informations.Algorithms have been developed for the efficient over passing of these disadvantages [3,4].

The quadtree representation reduces one large image to a hierarchically related series of smaller images; those at the beginning of the hierarchy are coarser.With proper parameter selection, subpictures can be of sizes that can fit into fast memory.Even when this is not the case, quadtree representation stores picture regions as neighboring data elements in secondary storage,minimizing input/output transfers.Furthermore, hierarchical representation of an image allows parallel operations [13].

By using a processor for each node of the quadtree, we have an active quadtree network of processors.While computing-power and hardware costs get cheaper every year, parallel processing of indentical units,are architectures that make much better use of the power of VLSI.Multiple processor hardware systems yield benefits in the analysis of large digitized picture arrays.

III. PICTURE SYMMETRIES

Algorithms have been developed for conversion from other representations of regions, such as boundary codes, binary arrays, and rasters to quadtrees, and vice versa [5,6,7] .Alexandridis and Klinger [8] used symmetries as a global coarse-picture parameter (i.e. a subregion characteristic) for pictures regularly decomposed to a lower dimensional dataset and presented algorithms for determining picture symmetries.Also, symmetry detection algorithms have been proposed to reduce the amount of storage that a picture representation requires [9,10,11] .Reducing the large amount of data we have a more manageable dataset that usually fits into fast memory.In this paper we describe a feature-independent algorithm, using functional programming language, to identify picture symmetries.Feature-independent symmetry algorithms produce global characterizations of images, that are useful for digital picture archives.

Two quadrants, lying symmetricaly opposite with respect to a given line constitute a set $S_i^k(d)$ where i is the set number and d denotes the direction along which the quadrants lie.

The classes $S_{i,j}^k$ (d) , j = 1,2,..........(1)

(which denote the pair of quadrants which are symmetric) are the elements of the set S_i^k (d) (2)

The quadtree can be defined as a tree whose nodes are either leaves or have four sons.The NW quadrant is encoded with 0, the NE with 1, the SW with 2, and the SE with 3. Each pixel is then encoded in a weighted quaternary code, i.e. with digits 0,1,2,3 in base 4, where each succesive digit represents the quadrant subdivision from which is originates.Thus, the digit of weight 4^{n-h} , $1 \leq h \leq n$ (where 2^n X 2^n

the picture array) identifies the quadrant to which the picture belongs at the hth subdivision.

As an example, in the case of horizontal symmeties there are 2^k sets $S_i^k(h)$.At level 2 (Fig. 1) the sets are

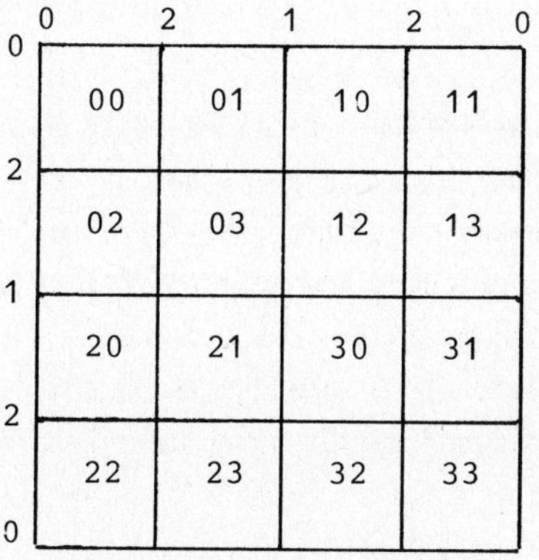

00	01	10	11
02	03	12	13
20	21	30	31
22	23	32	33

(Border labels: top 0 2 1 2 0; left 0 2 1 2 0)

Fig. 1: Picture at level 2

$$S^2_1(h)=\{S^2_{1,1}(h),\ S^2_{1,2}(h)\}$$

$$S^2_2(h)=\{S^2_{2,1}(h),\ S^2_{2,2}(h)\}$$

$$S^2_3(h)=\{S^2_{3,1}(h),\ S^2_{3,2}(h)\}$$

$$S^2_4(h)=\{S^2_{4,1}(h),\ S^2_{4,2}(h)\}$$

where

$$S^2_{1,1}(h)=\{00,11\}$$

$$S^2_{1,2}(h)=\{01,10\}$$

$$S^2_{2,1}(h)=\{02,13\}\quad \text{etc.}$$

In section VI we shall give an algorithm in Functional Programming Language to determine the quadrants which belong to the sets $S_i^k(h)$ at any level of the quadtree.

IV. FUNCTIONAL PROGRAMMING

In its simplest form a von Newmann computer has three parts a Central Processing Unit, a Store and a connecting tube that can transmit a single word between the CPU and the store.This von Neumann bottleneck blocks parallel operation and the effective use of VLSI circuits.Programs in present languages use variables to imitate the computer's storage cells,control statements elaborate its jump, and assignment statements imitate its fetching, storing, and arithmetic.If programming is to be really simplified, it is crucial to be able to build high-level programs from existing programs, and one must be able to do this knowing only the purpose of each constituent program without a lot of other details.A functional programming language has been proposed by J. Backus on the use of combining forms for creating programs.Functional programs deal with structured data, are often nonrepetitive and nonrecursive, are hierarchically constructed and do not name their arguments.This approach allows parallel operations to be expressed easily.The function-level style constructs the program directly by applying program-forming operations to existing programs,instead of describing how to form the result object for a program by applying object-forming operations to objects.

For example, the function-level discription of average is

Def average half @+

Two simple programs (half, +) built average.The Program-Forming Operations (PFO) @ denotes do the right operation (+) first, then do the left one (half) to the result.Thus "average" applied to a pair of numbers is simply the half of their sum.

It is the ability to build up meaningful programs from either simple of complex ones that is the principal strength of the function-level style.The program *P @ Q* means to apply *P* to the things that *Q* produces.If one starts with three given programs *P* ,*Q* and *R* and builds the program *P @ [Q, R]* the meaning is first do *[Q,R]* to form a pair of objects, the first the result of applying *Q* , the second the result of applying *R* . Then do *P* to that pair. When the program *[Q,R]* is executed, it makes no difference whether *Q* or *R* is done first or whether both are done together .This potential for parallelism in function-level programming, if incorporated into new computer architectures would lead to a better use of VLSI.

System Description

Function level programs consist:

a. a set of objects.

Objects are, numbers,words,sequences,or symbols.A sequence of objects $<y_1, y_2, \ldots\ldots, y_n>$ consists of y's which are either words, numbers,symbols or sequences. The object $\emptyset$ is used to denote the empty sequence. The objects T and F are used to denote "true" and "false" . Also ? is an object and means undefined or bottom .Bottom denotes the value returned as the result of an undefined operation, e.g. division by zero.

b. a set of functions that map objects into objects.

Every function is either primitive, that is supplied with the system,or it is defined or it is functional form.

To formally characterize the primitive functions, we use a modification of Mc Carthy's conditional expressions

$p_1 \to u_1 ; \ldots\ldots\ldots ; p_n \to u_n ; u_{n+1}$

This statement is interpreted as follows: return function u_1 if the predicate p_1 is true, ..., u_n if p_n is true.If none of the predicates are satisfied then default to u_{n+1}

We give as an example, the definitions of some primitive functions.

Null

$null: x \equiv x = ? \to T ; x \neq ? \to F ; ?$

Tail

$tl: x \equiv x = <x_1> \to ? \; x = <x_1, \ldots\ldots, x_n> \wedge n \geq 2 \to <x_2, \ldots\ldots\ldots, x_n> ; ?$

Selector function

$1: x \equiv x = <x_1, \ldots\ldots, x_n> \to x_1 ; ?$

and for any positive integer S

$S: x \equiv x = <x_1, \ldots\ldots, x_n> \wedge n \geq s \to x_s ; ?$

c. an operation called "application"and is designated by the colon " ; ". "Application" is the operation of applying a function (x) to the object <4,5> we write

X: <4,5> = 20

d. a set of functional forms

Functional forms are expressions that combine existing functions to form new ones. If *f* and *g* are any functions, then *f@g* is a functional form.

e. a set of definitions that define some functions and assign a name to each

As an example, we define the function "last " that produces the last element of a sequence.

Def $last \equiv null @ tl \to 1 ; last @ tl$

To see this definition in action, lets compute $last : <1,2>$

$last: <1,2> \equiv (null @ tl \to 1 ; \quad last @ tl): <1,2>$

(by the definition of last)

$\Rightarrow last @ tl: <1,2>$

(because $null @ tl: <1,2> =$
$= null : <2> = F$)

$\Rightarrow last : (tl <1,2>)$

$\Rightarrow last: <2>$

(by the definition of tail)

$\Rightarrow (null @ tl \to 1 ; \quad last @ tl): <2>$

(by the definition of last)

$\Rightarrow 1: <2>$

(because $null @ tl: <2> =$
$= null : \emptyset = T$) $\Rightarrow 2$

(by the definition of selector 1)

Definitions of primitive functions

Transpose

$trans : X \equiv X = <\emptyset, \ldots, \emptyset> \to \emptyset ; x = <x_1, \ldots, x_n> \to <y_1, \ldots\ldots\ldots, y_m> ; ?$

where

$x_i = <x_{i1}, \ldots\ldots, x_{im}>$ and $y_j = <x_{1j}, \ldots, x_{nj}>$,

$1 \leq i \leq n \quad , \quad 1 \leq j \leq m$

Example:

$trans : <<1,2>, <3,4>> = <<1,3> <2,4>>$

Split

$split : x \equiv x < x_1 > \to <x_1> ;$

$x = <x_1, x_2, \ldots\ldots\ldots, x_k> \wedge K > 1 \to$
$<<x_1, \ldots\ldots\ldots, x_n>, <x_{n+1}, \ldots\ldots\ldots, x_k>> ; \quad ?$

where $n=[K/2]$

Apply to all (&)

$\&f : X \equiv X = \emptyset \rightarrow \emptyset$;

$X = \langle X_1, \ldots\ldots\ldots, X_k \rangle \rightarrow \langle f{:}X_1, \ldots, f{:}X_K \rangle$; ?

Equals

$eq{:}X \equiv X = \langle y,z \rangle \wedge y=z \rightarrow T$; $X = \langle y,z \rangle \wedge y \neq z \rightarrow F$;?

Length

$length : X \equiv X = \langle X_1, X_2, \ldots\ldots, X_k \rangle \rightarrow K; X = \emptyset \rightarrow 0$;?

Identity

$id : \quad X \equiv X$

Pair

$pair : X$

$X = \langle X_1, \ldots\ldots X_k \rangle \wedge K > 0 \wedge K$ is even $\rightarrow$

$\rightarrow \langle \langle X_1, X_2 \rangle, \ldots\ldots, \langle X_{k-1}, X_k \rangle \rangle$;

$X = \langle X_1, \ldots\ldots X_k \rangle \wedge K > 0 \wedge K$ is odd $\rightarrow$

$\rightarrow \langle \langle X_1, X_2 \rangle, \ldots\ldots, \langle X_k \rangle \rangle$;?

Reverse

$Reverse : \quad X \equiv X = \emptyset \rightarrow \emptyset$;

$X = \langle X_1, \ldots\ldots X_k \rangle \rightarrow \langle X_k, \ldots\ldots, X_1 \rangle$; ?

Constant

$\overline{X} : Y \equiv Y = ? \rightarrow ?; X$

V. CREATING A QUADTREE USING FUNCTIONAL PROGRAMMING.

We assume that we start with an image that can be accessed row by row. This is the case when it is stored on a tape or disk, or when it is digitized by a drum-scan divice or one based on a television camera. The given image is a 2^n X 2^n array of unit square "pixels " To form the tree we use a bottom-up approach. We create quadruples of pixels in the order shown in figure 2.

Then we create a new array of the image whose elements are the quadruples. We repeat this procedure until the image array be consisted of four subarrays.

$$\begin{bmatrix} \begin{bmatrix} X_{11} & X_{12} \\ X_{21} & X_{22} \end{bmatrix} & \cdots & \begin{bmatrix} X_{1(n-1)} & X_{1n} \\ X_{2(n-1)} & X_{2n} \end{bmatrix} \\ \vdots & & \vdots \\ \begin{bmatrix} X_{(n-1)1} & X_{(n-1)2} \\ X_{n1} & X_{n2} \end{bmatrix} & \cdots & \begin{bmatrix} X_{(n-1)(n-1)} & X_{(n-1)n} \\ X_{n(n-1)} & X_{nn} \end{bmatrix} \end{bmatrix}$$

Figure 2. The array of the image

Algorithm A.

Creating a Quad tree using Functional Programming.

Def QT $eq \,@\, [length \,@\, 1, \bar{2}] \rightarrow id \,;\, QT \,@\, T$

where T is defined

Def T =&& trans @ & pair @&trans@pair

To see the Algorithm A in action , lets use the table of figure 2.

$T : \langle\langle X_{11}, \ldots\ldots, X_{1n} \rangle, \ldots\ldots\ldots, \langle X_{n1}, \ldots X_{nn} \rangle\rangle \equiv$

$\equiv$ *&&trans @&pair @&trans @pair:*

$\langle\langle X_{11}, \ldots\ldots, X_{1n} \rangle, \ldots\ldots, \langle X_{n1}, \ldots, X_{nn} \rangle\rangle \equiv$

$\equiv$ *&& trans @& pair & trans :*

$\langle\langle\langle X_{11}, \ldots\ldots, X_{1n} \rangle, \langle X_{21}, \ldots\ldots, X_{2n} \rangle\rangle, \ldots,$

$\langle\langle X_{(n-1)1}, \ldots\ldots, X_{(n-1)n} \rangle, \langle X_{n1}, \ldots\ldots, X_{nn} \rangle\rangle\rangle \equiv$

$\equiv$ *&& trans :*

$\langle\langle\langle\langle X_{11}, X_{21} \rangle, \langle X_{12}, X_{22} \rangle\rangle, \ldots, \langle\langle X_{1(n-1)},$

$X_{2(n-1)} \rangle, \langle X_{1n}, X_{2n} \rangle\rangle\rangle, \ldots\ldots, \langle\langle\langle X_{(n-1)1},$

$X_{n1} \rangle, \langle X_{(n-1)2}, X_{n2} \rangle\rangle, \ldots, \langle\langle X_{(n-1)(n-1)}, X_{n(n-1)} \rangle,$

$\langle X_{(n-1)n}, X_{nn} \rangle\rangle\rangle\rangle \equiv$

$\equiv \langle\langle\langle\langle x_{11}, x_{12}\rangle, \langle x_{21}, x_{22}\rangle\rangle, \ldots,$

$\langle\langle x_{1(n-1)}, x_{1n}\rangle, \langle x_{2(n-1)},$

$x_{2n}\rangle\rangle\rangle, \ldots, \langle\langle\langle x_{(n-1)1},$

$x_{(n-1)2}\rangle, \langle x_{n1}, x_{n2}\rangle\rangle, \ldots,$

$\langle\langle x_{(n-1)(n-1)}, x_{(n-1)n}\rangle,$

$\langle x_{n(n-1)}, x_{nn}\rangle\rangle\rangle\rangle \equiv \mu$

The result from applying *QT* to μ is the Quad Tree representation.

$QT : \mu \equiv \langle \cdots \langle\langle\langle x_{11}, x_{12}\rangle,$

$\langle x_{21}, x_{22}\rangle\rangle, \langle\langle x_{13}, x_{14}\rangle, \langle x_{23},$

$x_{24}\rangle\rangle, \langle\langle x_{31}, x_{32}\rangle,$

$\langle x_{41}, x_{42}\rangle\rangle, \langle\langle x_{33}, x_{34}\rangle,$

$\langle x_{43}, x_{44}\rangle\rangle\rangle \ldots\rangle.$

VI. LOOKING FOR SYMMETRIES IN AN IMAGE

We give four algorithms to determine symmetries in an image. The algorithms determine the quadrants which belong to the sets S_i^k (d) at any level of the quadtree. Our investigation is restricted to examining classes only along the following principal directions;

(1) d = h along a horizontal direction (0^0 or 180^0) where we are examining grid-pointslying symmetricaly opposite a vertical line.

(2) d = v along a vertical direction (90^0 or 270^0) where we are examining grid-points lying symmetrically opposite a horizontal line

(3) d = r along the direction of a right diagonal line (45^0 or 225^0) where we examine grid-points lying symmetrically opposite a left diagonal line.

(4) d = l along the direction of a left-diagonal line (135^0 or 315^0) where we are examining grid-poids lying symmetrically opposite a right diagonal line

Horizontal Symmetry Classes (d = h)

Def HOR ≡ *H @ QT*

where H is defined

Def H &1@ & split @& trans @& [id,reverse]

Vertical Symmetry Class (d=u)

Def VER ≡ V@ QT

where*V* is defined

Def V ≡ H @ trans

Right-Diagonal Symmetry Classes (d = r)

Def RDIAG ≡ RD @ QT

where *RD* is defined

Def RD≡ &trans@ trans @ [id, &reverse@ reverse@ trans]

Left-diagonal Symmetry Classes (d = l)

Def LDIAG LD @ QT

where *LD* is defined

Def LD≡ &trans @ trans @ [id, trans]

VII. CONCLUDING REMARKS

Image processing involving many parallel computations, with functional programming could become much easier.Programming time could be reduced, also repetitive programming of similar problems could be simplified so that each one of potential users could write programs for his own needs without the help of a professional programmer. Combined with the increased speed that would be possible with new computer architectures and VLSI design, a vast expansion of computer applications in visual recognition and computer graphics is entirely conceivable.

REFERENCES

1. J.Backus, "Can programming be liberated from the von Neumann style ?A functional style and its algebra of programms "Commun. of ACM Vol 21, 1978.

2. J.Backus, "Function-level computing" IEEE spectrum, August 1982

3. N.Alexandridis,J.Kalogeras,N.Bilalis "Adaptive thresholding in regular decomposition with regard to picture content and transmission time restrictions"Proceedings of the 6th International I.A.S.T.E.D. Symposium MECO 83, Athens Greece, Vol 1, 1983

4. A.Klinger,C.Dyer "Experiments on picture representations, using regular decomposition "Comput. Graphics and Image Proces 5, 1976

5. C.Dyer,A.Rosenfeld,H.Samet "Region representation: Boundary codes from quadtrees " Commun.of ACM Vol 23, no 3, 1980

6. H.Samet "Region representation Quadtrees from binary arrays "Comput.Graphics Image Proces , Vol 13, 1980

7. I.Pavlidis, "Algorithms for graphics and image processing "Springer-Verlag, 1982

8. N.Alexandridis, A.Klinger "Picture decomposition, Tree data-structures, and identifying directional symmetries as node combinations "Comput Graphics Image Proces, Vol 8, 1978.

9. N.Alexandridis, N.Bilalis "Obtaining a minimum quadtree representation of a 2-D binary pictorial data by examining symmetries in images "Proceedings of the 1st I.A.S.T.E.D. symosium on Appled Informatics, Lille-France, Vol 1, 1983

10. N.Bilalis,N.Alexandridis,J.Kollias "An algorithm for converting rasters to minimal quadtrees by looking at symmetries in images" Proceedings of Mediterranean Electrotechnical Conference, Athens-Greece, Vol 2, 1983

11. N.Alexandridis,N.Bilalis,S.Mohlulis, "A feature- independent procedure in restructuring an image as a minimal quadtree" International AMSE Conference, Athens,Greece 1984

12. P.Henderson,"Functional Programming," Prentice-Hall,1980.

13. G.Mago,"A net work of microprocessors to execute reduction languages, "Int. J. Comp.Inform. Sci. 8,5,1979; 349-385 , 8,6 1979,435-471.

DIGITAL TECHNIQUES in Simulation, Communication and Control
Spyros G. Tzafestas (editor)
Elsevier Science Publishers B.V. (North-Holland) © IMACS, 1985

A PROPOSAL FOR AN EFFICIENT AEROPHOTOGRAPHIES PROCESSING SYSTEM

Nikolaos G.Bourbakis

University of Patras, School of Engineering

Dept. of Computer Engineering

26500 Patras, Greece

This paper discusses the hardware-software development of an efficient aerophotographies processing system (APS).The APS has the ability to speed up the process of a number of aerophotographies at the same time. The processes applied at the aerophotographies are;input, storing,reduction,recognition etc.
The APS system consists of an optical scanning system (i.e. vidicon tube) which accepts the original photography, an A/D converter which produces the digital version of the photography elements, a host computer in which the main processes take place, and a terminal from which the user communicates with the host computer to choose or affect the picture processing. The whole picture processing is protected by a proper software security package.

1- INTRODUCTION

The usefulness of the picture processing system increases day-to-day by covering new application areas. The aerophotography is a research area with significant interest and many authors have presented various methods and systems[1,2, 3,4,5,...] for its processing, such as geographic analysis,petroleum searching, etc.

In this paper an efficient aerophotographies processing system is presented which speed up the photography processing such as proper storing and retrival by using hierarchical pyramid structures [6,7,14] and reduction of the pictures information by using the Regular Decomposition method [8,9] . All external commands from the user are controlled by the security package. The whole software pictures processing is realized under a proper data base system. A significant point of this APS system is the usage of data structures for the multireconstruction of $l x l$ pictures at the same frame by giving a more global or local view of the desired area.

This work is divided in three main sections. Section 2 gives the hardware description of the APS in brief. Section 3 develops the software components and the manner in which they are used. Section 4 presents the APS operations and some advantages-disadvantages of the APS system with proposals for extention and further development.

2- APS HARDWARE COMPONENTS

The aerophotographies processing system (APS) consists of four main hardware components:(i) an optical scanning system (ii) an A/D converter,(iii) a host computer and (iv) a terminal, see Fig. 1.

2.1- Optical Scanning System (OSS)

The OSS of the proposed system could be a vidicon camera. The choice of the vidicon camera is based on two significant reasons [10] :(i) the high resolution of the vidicon tube and (ii) the satisfactory time duration of the photography at the photosensive vidicon tube surface. The above reasons provide the APS with ability to scan the image elements and to feed them into the A/D converter.

2.2-A/D converter

The A/D converter accepts as inputs the currents of the image elements and converts them to digital numbers of 1-bit binary picture or k-bits gray level picture,(i.e. k=8).The outputs of the A/D device are sets of 8,16 or 32 bits depending on the word length of the host computer The words preparation is materialized by an I/Ointerface package.

2.3- Host Computer

The host computer must have available an enough memory capacity to support the demanded pictures processing. The computer accepts as inputs the digitized version of the pictures. Each digital picture enters the proper memory location under the data base control, where at an appropriate time its pyramid data structure will be realized. The computer output is directed into a terminal display and a plotter device

2.4- Terminal

The terminal device(not necessary intelligent) is used for the proper pictures retrival and for further picture operations. The user communicates from the terminal with the host computer by asking a proper local or global picture view,

Fig.5. Finally, a plotter for a picture representation could be used.

3- APS SOFTWARE COMPONENTS

The most usefull software components of the APS are:(i) Scanning Algorithms (SA), (ii) Pyramid Data Structures(PDS), (iii) Regular Decomposition Method(RDM), (iv) Recognition or Matching Algorithms (RMA) and (v) Picture Security (PS).

3.1- Scanning Algorithms (SA)

The scanning algorithms have been presented in enough detail by [1]. The SA are used to access image data in various forms, and to feed the data into the processing machine. An efficient application of the SA such as the fast creation of pyramid data structure has been referred in [12], while another important application has been referred in [11,13]. The SA provide the advantages of the fast picture data entry, pyramid data structure and the picture reconstruction from the various pyramid levels,see section 4.

3.2- Pyramid Data Structure (PDS)

The pyramid data structure (bottom up method) is described in brief, and its importance and usefulness have been discussed by Tanimoto-Pavlidis [6,7].

Definition [6,7]:"A pyramid consists of L+1 arrays of $2^m \times 2^m$ dimensions stacked one upon the other, with the original highest resolution picture of $2^L \times 2^L$ at the base and the single pixel image at the top", see Fig. 2a.

Figure 2b shows an arbitrary set of four pixels (2x2), at the level k, mapped into the one pixel labelled P_0 at the level k+1.

Here, it is assumed that $E_k(i,j)$ represents the gray level of a pixel at position (i,j) at level k. Then $E_{k+1}(i,j)$ is defined as [6] :

$$E_{k+1}(i,j) = f\ E_k(P_1),E_k(P_2),E_k(P_3),E_k(P_4) \qquad (1)$$

where f is a particular tranformation such as:

$$f_{average}=1/4 \sum_{m=1}^{4} E_k(P_m) \qquad (2)$$

and replaces $E_{k+1}(P_0)$ by the average of its four predecessors at level k.

3.3- Regular Decomposition Method(RDM)

The regular decomposition is an hierarchical data structure (top down method) that has been developed enough by 8,9 . The main features of the RDM are briefly discussed in this paper.

Definition [8]:"The RDM defines successive quadrants of either the entire picture or a previous picture quadrant and a four successor zree results", see Fig. 3.

The RDM compresses the original amount of picture data since the resultant will contain only informative areas of picture.

A picture description function $\alpha(d)$ is defined as the importance of quadrant P_x in its father quadrant P_y, by using threshold values r_1,r_2 arbitrarly [8]:

$$\alpha(d)= \begin{array}{lll} \text{"informative"} & \text{if} & r_2\ d \\ \text{"not-sure"} & \text{if} & r_1\ d\ r_2 \\ \text{"non-informative} & & 0\ d\ r_1 \end{array} \qquad (3)$$

where d is a norm:

$$d(P_x,P_y)= \frac{\text{Average Intensity of } P_x}{\text{Average Intensity of } P_y} \qquad (4)$$

3.4- Recognition or Matching Algorithms (RMA)

The recognition(or matching) algorithms are not discussed here because many authors have proposed different methodologies which present advantages or disadvantages on memory requirements and computing time.

3.5- Picture Security (PS)

The APS has a software package which rovides security during the picture entry, pictures processing and pictures reconstruction. The security system is based on key-words. Some key-words allow to the user to access part(or parts) of the stored pictures, some other give the ability to affect some pictures data, while some others provide the printing facilities. The whole security support is based on a proper data base system. The security procedures are activated at the the APS system start.Also, the key-words provide the protection of the pictures data from any unauthorized usage.

4- APS OPERATIONS

The APS system accepts as inputs aero photographies, by using a proper OSS. The input of each photography into the APS is controlled from the user by using the proper entry key-words. The digitized version of the photographies are stored in a suitable memory space.

When the user desires to retrieve pictures at the terminal screen, by using their specific code expressions, key-words and the allowable operations can realize it. The APS supports some useful operations to the user which facilitate the APS usage. Some of these operations are [16]:

PYRAMID :means the pyramid creation of the picture data.
LEVEL :choice of the desired pyramid level
DISPLAY :displaying of the chosen picture levels
RETRIEVE:retrieving of the pictures

etc.

4.1- An Example

The user by choosing the above operations has the ability to "see" on his screen a global or local view of the around area. This feature is shown in the Fig. 4, 5.The Figure 4 shows an original photography (level l_0) and its pyramid level. Figure 5a shows the terminal screen at which a global view has been displayed. Each small quadrant is at l_2 pyramid level of the represented pictures. If the user wishes a focus on the upper left four quadrants of the whole area can do it by using the proper operations. The Figure 5b gives a focus of the upper left area at the l_1 level. This focusing provides to the user more details about the contents of the quadrants. A more detailed level (l_0) is the original image, on which the user has the possibility to affect (under the security control) the picture data. A picture enchancement technique could give more detail for picture elements by realizing a proper elements approach [15].

An efficient picture information reduction will be realized by using the known RD methodology. The RDM rejects the non-informative areas and gives to the user the benefit to save memory space and keep the picture in spatial manner, that is seful for picture portion representation [9]. The specific operations to realize a RDM are:PYRAMID,LEVEL,REDUCTION,...

Finally, a "window area"with variable size (2^kx 2^k), where k=0,1,2,... exists, which provides to the user the possibility of new picture (or picture parts) recreation by using the existing pictures.

4.2-Advantages-Disadvantages

The discussed APS system presents some advantages which are:(i) a global view of the various levels of the neighboring image areas, (ii) a local view of the picture parts in original picture level, (iii) a possible usage of picture enchancement for further picture approach. However a significant disadvantage of the APS is the large amount of memory requirements.

5- CONCLUSIONS

In this paper a discussion of an aerophotographies processing system has been done. The realization of the APS system could provide significant facilities to the users,on protection, reconstruction, control, retrieval,... of geographical areas. The APS development is in progress at the University of Patras, Dept. of Computer Engineering. Also, a proposal of the APS system has been submitted to the Ministry of Planning, Housing and Enviroment of Greece.

REFERENCES

1 - Chang S.K. and Kunii T.L."PICTORIAL DATA BASE SYSTEMS", IEEE COMPUTER Nov. 1981, Vol.14, No.11, pp.13-21.

2 - Chang N.S. and Fu K.S."PICTURE QUERY LANGUAGES FOR PICTORIAL DATA BASE SYSTEMS", IEEE COMPUTER Nov. 1981, Vol. 14, No.11, pp. 23-33.

3 - Zobrist A.L. and Nagy G."PICTORIAL INFORMATION PROCESSING OF LANDSAT DATA FOR GEOGRAPHIC ANALYSIS", IEEE COMPUTER Nov. 1981, Vol.14, No.11, pp.34-41.

4 - Chock M., Cardenas A.E. and Klinger A. "MANIPULATING DATA STRUCTURES IN PICTORIAL INFORMATION SYSTEMS", IEEE COMPUTER Nov. 1981, Vol.14, No.11, pp. 43-50.

5 - Nevatia R. and Price E.K."LOCATING STRUCTURES IN AERIAL IMAGES", IEEE Trans. on PAMI, Vol.4, No.5, Sept. 1982.

6 - Tanimoto S. and Pavlidis T."A HIERARCHICAL DATA STRUCTURES FOR PICTURE PROCESSING", Int. Journal on CGIP, Vol 4, 1975, pp. 104-119.

7 - Tanimoto S."IMAGE TRANSMISSION WITH CROSS INFORMATION FIRST", Int. Journal on CGIP, Vol. 9, 1979, pp. 72-76.

8 - Klinger A. and Dyer C."EXPERIMENTS ON PICTURE REPRESENTATION USING REGULAR DOCOMPOSITION", Int. Journal on CGIP, Vol.5, No.1, March 1976, pp. 68-105.

9 - Klinger A. and Rhodes L.M."ORGANIZATION AND ACCESS OF IMAGE DATA BY AREAS", IEEE Trans. on PAMI, Vol.1, No.1, 1979, pp. 50-60.

10- Freedman D."OPTICAL CHARACTER RECOGNITION", IEEE SPECTRUM March 1974, pp. 44-52.

11- Bourbakis N."NEW, REAL-TIME PROCESSING METHODS OF STRUCTURED IMAGES", PhD. thesis 1982, Patras Univ., Dept. of Computer Engineering, Patras, Greece.

12- Bourbakis N."A SCANNING SYSTEM, and A Z IMAGE SCANNING TECHNIQUE FOR FAST PYRAMID DATA STRUCTURE", Proc. Int. Symp. on MIC, March 2-5,1982, Davos, Switzerland, pp. 156-159.

13- Bourbakis N., Alexopoulos C. and Serpanos D."EFFICIENT ALGORITHMS FOR FAST FEATURES DETECTION IN BINARY PICTURES",Proc. of Int. Symp. on Automation and Robotics, June 22-24,1983, Lugano Switzerland, pp.77-80.

14- Levine M.D."REGION ANALYSIS USING A PYRAMID DATA STRUCTURE", Academic Press ed. Tanimoto/Klinger, Structured Computer Vision, 1980, pp.57-100.

15- Habibi A. and Robinson G."A SERVEY OF DIGITAL PICTURE CODING", IEEE Computer Magazine 1974, pp. 22-34.

16- Economopoulos P. and Lochousky F.H."A SYSTEM FOR MANAGING IMAGE DATA",Proc. of the 9th World Computer Congress, IFIP-83, Paris, France, Sept. 1983.

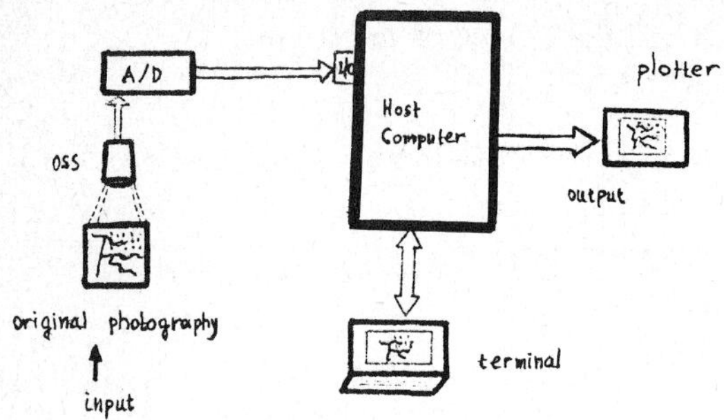

Fig. 1:It shows the APS system

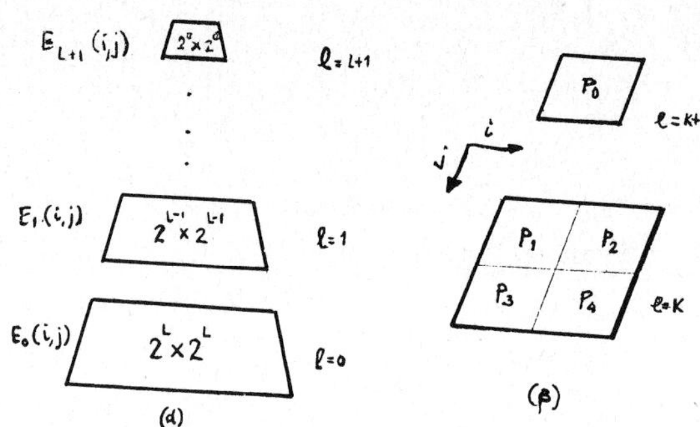

Fig. 2:It shows a) the schematical representation of the pyramid L+1 levels, b) the smple transition from the level k to level k+1.

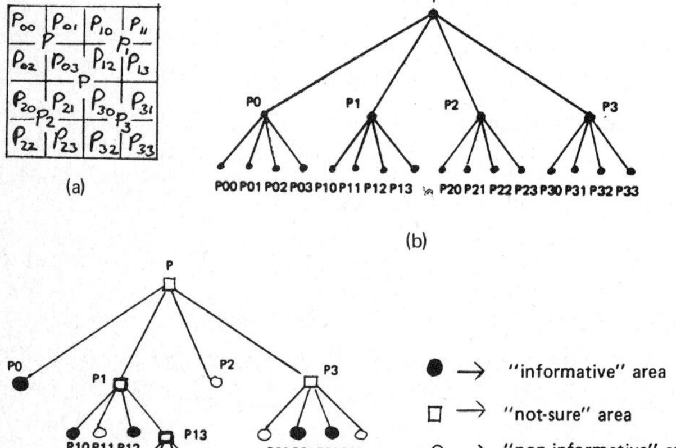

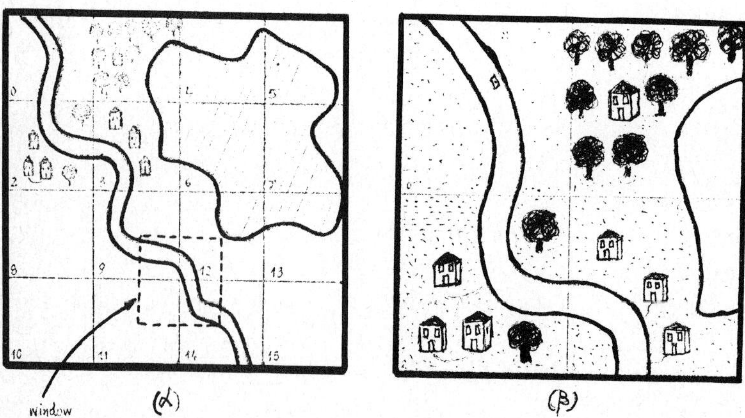

Fig. 3:It shows a) the original picture P partitioned into 16 subquadrants, b) its equivalent quad-tree and c) the creation of the minimum informative picture tree.

Figure 4

Figure 5

DIGITAL TECHNIQUES in Simulation, Communication and Control
Spyros G. Tzafestas (editor)
Elsevier Science Publishers B.V. (North-Holland) © IMACS, 1985

ON A DATA-DRIVEN MULTIPROCESSOR ARCHITECTURE FOR THE IMPLEMENTATION OF THE WALSH-HADAMARD TRANSFORM OF REGULARLY DECOMPOSED DIGITAL IMAGES

N.A.Alexandridis
Dept. of Electrical and Computer Engineering,
Ohio University,
Athens,Ohio,USA

P.D.Tsanakas S.V.Konstantinidou
Computer Science Division
Electrical Engineering Dept.
National Technical University
Athens-15773,Greece

An architecture for the parallel implementation of the Walsh-Hadamard transform of images is presented.The transformation procedure is performed progressively by adjusting to the various hierarchies of nodes of the quad-tree which is associated with the processed picture,according to the Regular Decomposition procedure.
The architecture of the proposed machine is based on the data-driven model of computation in which an operation is executed when its operands are available.The specific requirements of the image processing algorithms have been taken into account, principally the efficient handling of array data-structures.The tagged-token method supports recursive operations and helps for better exploiting the inherent parallelism of the transformation algorithm.

1.INTRODUCTION

This paper is concerned with the parallel implementation of a typical orthogonal transformation, the 2-D Walsh-Hadamard (W-H) transformation, [1]. Since the amount of computations involved in the W-H transformation procedure is extremely large, conventional computer architectures have been proved very slow and inefficient [7]. Some parallel architectures have been proposed [2,3,4] for better exploiting the inherent parallelism of the transformation procedure.
The architecture proposed in this paper is based on the concept of data-driven computation, which is a fundamentally different way of looking at instruction execution in machine -level programs, an alternative to sequential instruction execution.In a data-driven computer, an instruction is ready for execution when its operants are available [14,16] There is no concept of control flow, and no need for program counters. A consequence of data-activated instruction execution is that many instructions of a program may be available for execution at once.Thus, highly concurrent computation is a natural consequence of the data-driven concept.The idea of data-driven computation is old [11].Many researchers have recently made notable contributions to the development of data-driven (data-flow) systems either as general purpose computer systems [13,15] or for dedicated applications [8].
We first present the basic features of the method of Regular Decomposition and we give a brief introduction to the W-H transform along with the presentation of an alternative implementation scheme.Then, the notation of the dataflow graphs is presented and the transformation procedure is expressed by using this notation.Finally we give a general description of the proposed architecture and we provide the specifications of the required data packets.

2. REGULAR DECOMPOSITION

Presented here are the basic features of the Regular Decomposition procedure.Details can be found in [6] .Regular Decomposition (R-D) is a picture information compression scheme,associating a digital image with a hierarchical quad-tree which preserves the descriptive characteristics of the picture patterns and geometric features.This procedure examines the digital image,defines successive subquadrants and forms a quad-tree (4-successor tree), which serves for the hierarchical description of the picture contents.Each node of the tree corresponds to a picture subquadrant of area inversely related to the node level on the tree.The next subdivision step proceeds as follows:

(a). A node is *eliminated* from the tree-structure if the respective subquadrant is non-informative, according to a metric.

(b). A node is *saved* if the respective subquadrant is very-informative.

(c). A node is *retained and further analyzed* by dividing into the four subquadrants if the information content in it is between the "save " and "eliminate "thresholds.This node is regarded as "not sure "element.

Many information-content metrics can be applied, measuring the various picture attributes for the decision process of the R-D.We apply here the one proposed in [5],

$$d(P_i, P_{i,j}) = \frac{\text{Average intensity in subquadrant } P_{i,j}}{\text{Average intensity in Parental Subquadrant } P_i}$$

where:

P_i is the ith level subquadrant

$P_{i,j}$ is the jth subquadrant of the four into which P_i is subdivided

P_o is the whole picture

If ϑ_1 and ϑ_2 are the threshold values set for the acceptance or rejection of the respective subquadrant, the quad-tree formation algorithm goes as follows:

$$P_{i,j} \text{ is } \begin{cases} \text{(a). "non informative " if } 0 \leq d(P_i,P_{i,j}) \leq \vartheta_1 \\ \text{(b). "very informative " if } \vartheta_2 \leq d(P_i,P_{i,j}) \leq 1 \\ \text{(c). "not sure " if } \vartheta_1 \leq d(P_i,P_{i,j}) \leq \vartheta_2 \end{cases}$$

The net result of the R-D procedure is the minimal quad-tree, in which higher level tree nodes contain gross, global picture information, which becomes finer at the lower-level nodes of the tree.

3. WALSH-HADAMARD TRANSFORM

If a picture is to be digitally transmitted, it will be advantageous to transform it first through the Walsh-Hadamard (W-H) transformation. This transformation has been used to reduce the image transmition bandwidth and provide noise immune communications [1].

The W-H transform of an image represented as a matrix P of size n X n is an n X n picture F given by the formula :

$$F = \frac{1}{n^2} \cdot H \cdot P \cdot H \qquad (1)$$

where H is the n X n Hadamard matrix, a symmetric matrix which is defined by the recursion :

$$H \equiv H_n = \begin{bmatrix} H_{n/2} & H_{n/2} \\ H_{n/2} & -H_{n/2} \end{bmatrix} \qquad n \geq 2 \quad (2)$$

$$H_1 = \begin{bmatrix} 1 & 1 \\ 1 & -1 \end{bmatrix}$$

The W-H transform is the simplest to implement, since the Hadamard matrix is composed of only ones and minus ones.In the case of a 4 X 4 picture, the respective Hadamard matrix H_2 is :

$$H_2 = \begin{bmatrix} 1 & 1 & 1 & 1 \\ 1 & -1 & 1 & -1 \\ 1 & 1 & -1 & -1 \\ 1 & -1 & -1 & 1 \end{bmatrix}$$

In the case of regularly decomposed image we deal with a quad-tree instead of a usual array structure.Thus, the W-H transform should be performed on a tree data-structure.This fact leads to a hierarchical transformation procedure, which conists of successive transforms of all the tree levels,begining from the lowest one. Each tree level represents the original image in a detail that increases with the tree level. From now on, in order to simplify the evaluation procedure, we omit the factor $1/n^2$ from Eq.(1), yielding to a new expression :

$$W = H \cdot P \cdot H \qquad (3)$$

The picture P can be written in terms of its four subquadrants P_1, P_2, P_3 and P_4 as:

$$P = \left[\begin{array}{c:c} P_1 & P_2 \\ \hdashline P_3 & P_4 \end{array}\right] \qquad (4)$$

Applying (2) and (4) into (3) we obtain :

$$W = \left[\begin{array}{c:c} W_1+W_2+W_3+W_4 & W_1-W_2+W_3-W_4 \\ \hdashline W_1+W_2-W_3-W_4 & W_1-W_2-W_3+W_4 \end{array}\right] \qquad (5)$$

where $W_i = H_{n/2} \cdot P_i \cdot H_{n/2}$, i=1,2,3,4

W_1, W_2, W_3 and W_4 correspond to the W-H transforms of the four subquadrants P_1, P_2, P_3 and P_4. The above formula clearly implies that the transform matrix W would be evaluated recursively.

4. DATAFLOW GRAPHS AND W-H TRANSFORMATION

We proceed now with a brief introduction to the concept of dataflow graphs and then,using this notation,we present an algorithm for the evaluation of the W-H transform of a given image.

The data-driven model of computation has been proposed as an attractive alternative to the conventional (von Neumann) computer architecture. The basic features of this approach include :

i. Asynchronous execution of operations,based on the availability of data.

ii. Applicative semantics, which do not allow side-effects to operations.

It is well known that data-driven machines are programmed through directed graphs, data-flow programs, instead of assembly language programs. The attractive properties of the data-flow languages and data-flow program graphs are well documented [9,10] .

For the purpose of describing the W-H transform as expressed in (5) we use a dataflow graph notation which allows the use of recursive operations.The nodes of such graphs represent functions, whereas the arcs represent data dependencies between functions.Values are represented as tokens on the arcs of the graph.

In Figure 1 is shown the transformation procedure for an image of arbitrary size.The input of the procedure is an image A of size n X n, whereas the output is an array W of size n X n, which represents the W-H transform of the input image.When an image is put on the input arc of the procedure, it is first determined its size (n) through the operation FIND-SIZE.If the input image is of size 2 X 2, then it is transfered to the TWO-HADAMARD operation, which is analyzed in Fig.2.The TWO-HADAMARD procedure produces the W-H transform of an image of size 2 X 2.If the initial image is of greater size, it is transfered in parallel to the procedures FIND-P1, FIND- P2, FIND-P3 , and FIND-P4.Each of these operations produce two outputs.The first output is the array P_i, i=1,2,3,4 which corresponds to the i-th subquadrant of the input image.The second output is the boolean HOMOGENEOUS.If the respective subquadrant is consisted of identical elements,the HOMOGENEOUS output is set TRUE otherwise it remains FALSE.If a subquadrant is homogeneous, i.e. $a_{ij} = a_{11} \ \forall\, i,j$, its W-H transform is an array B for which $b_{11} = a_{11}$ and $b_{ij} = 0$, $i \cdot j \neq 1$. If a subquadrant is not homogeneous, it is transfered recursively to the HADAMARD procedure. Eventually, the results of these invocations are fed to the RESULT procedure.This procedure, which is analyzed in Fig.3, constructs the W-H transform of an image after receiving the W-H transforms of its subimages. It must be noted that, if N X N is the size of the initial image, the maximum number of the recursive invocations of the procedure HADAMARD is MNI =4·(logN-1)

This formula gives a measure of the effectiveness of the proposed algorithm, e.g. in the case of an 1024 X 1024 image, procedure HADAMARD should be invoked no more than 36 times.This number may be reduced dramatically if there exist any homogeneous areas in the original image.

It must be noted that the previously described procedure is repeated for every level of the picture's quad-tree.This is necessary in order to achieve a progressive transformation scheme.

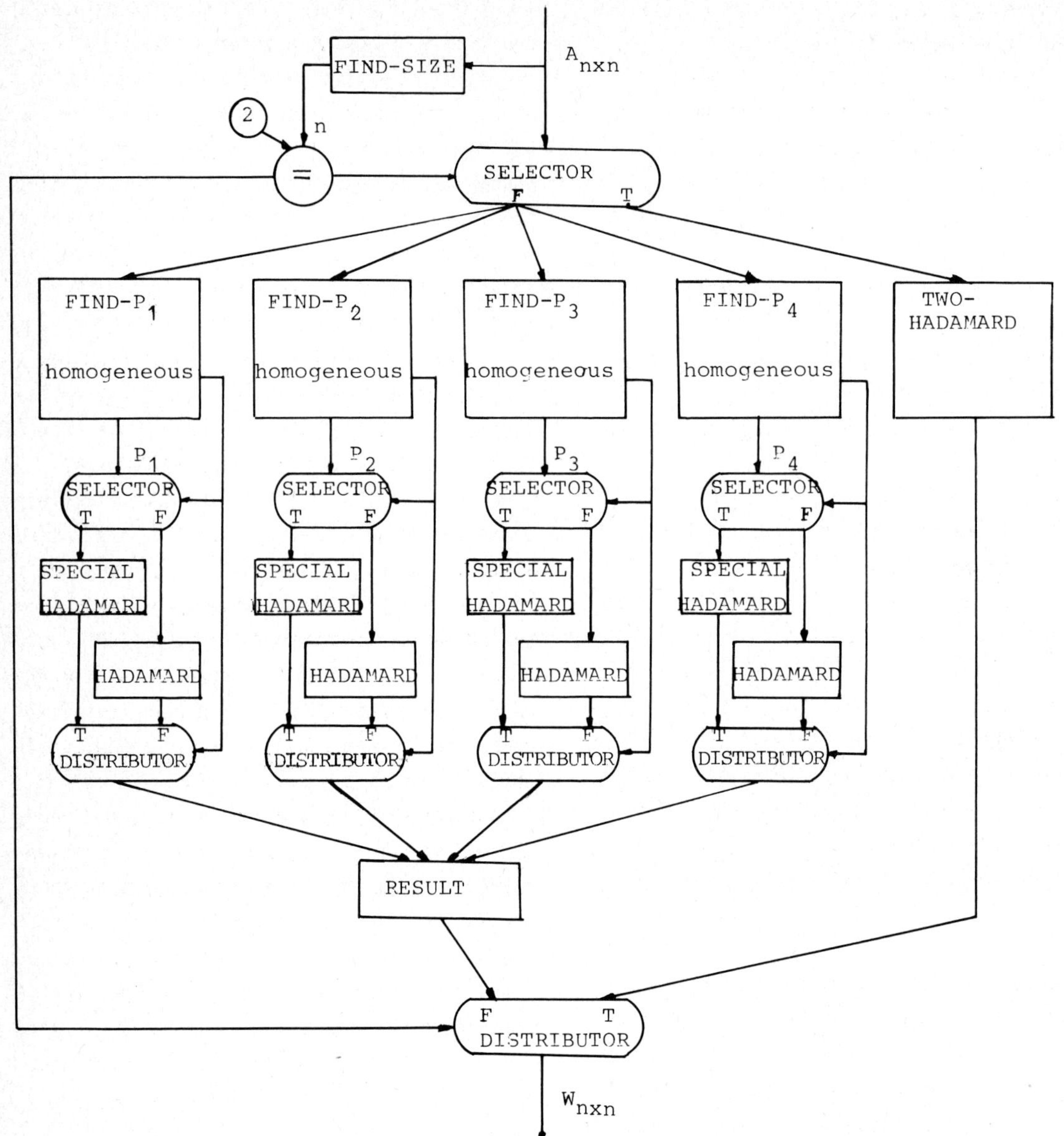

Figure 1:The recursive data-flow graph of procedure HADAMARD.

5. ARCHITECTURAL CONSIDERATIONS

In this chapter we propose an implementation scheme of the previously discussed algorithm for the W-H transformation.This scheme follows the principles of data-driven systems.The advantages offered by these systems are well documented [12,13,14] .Data driven systems constitute an attractive alternative to the conventional Von Neumann (control-driven) systems [5].

The basic characteristics of the presented W-H transformation algorithm (Fig. 1) are :

1. It is recursive
2. Every new invokation of the HADAMARD operation results in a division of the graph into four similar subgraphs, which can be executed in parallel since no data dependencies exist

among them.

A data driven machine which provides tools for the implementation of both recursion and parallel execution is the one designed at MIT [15]. We adopt here the basic notions of this model in order to construct a special purpose architecture for the implementation of the W-H transformation.

The proposed machine comprises a number of identical Processing Elements (PE's) which are connected toghether by an n-cube network,like the one shown in Fig.4.In Fig. 5 is shown the block diagram of a PE.Every PE comprises the following basic sections :

i. *Waiting-matching section* :When an activity template carrying a value enters the PE, it is inspected for a possible partner.If it needs a partner-in order to "fire"an instruction- it is passed to this section, where its tag is associatively matched against the tags of the activity templates -also called tokens- already stored in the waiting-matching section. If a match is not found,the token is placed in the associative store,else the pair proceeds to the next section.

ii. *Instruction-fetch section:*This section fetches the instruction indicated by a field named *instruction address* in the tag of the tokens.If a constant is needed as an input to an instruction,this section fetches it and passes the opcode and the operands to ALU for execution.

iii. *ALU:*The ALU section receives the operation packets and performs the operation on the accompanying operands.

iv. *Output section:* It generates the result tokens,which consists of a data value computed by the ALU and a tag.

From the point of view of the machine, a data-flow program is a set of code-blocks.A code-block is a set of data-flow instructions like a procedure or a loop. A code-block may have within it instructions that invoke the same code-block (recursion or loop) or other codeblocks (nested loops).When a program enters to the system,it is assigned to a set of consecutively addressed PE's, called Physical Domain,in such a way that no instruction code is split across two PE's. During the execution, the Physical Domain is divided into Physical Sybdomains which are assigned a different code-block.When the same

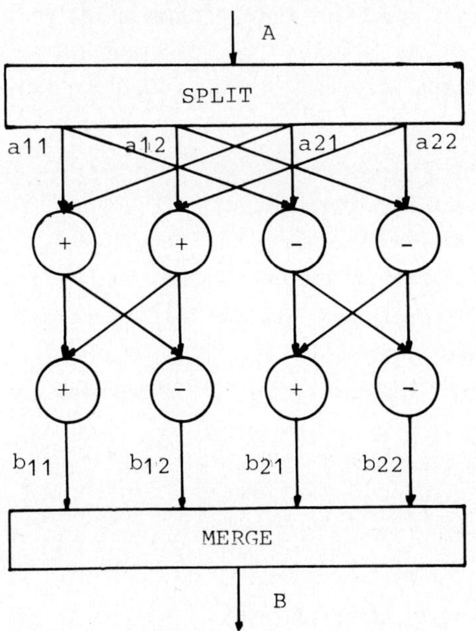

Figure 2:The data-flow graph of the TWO-HADAMARD procedure.

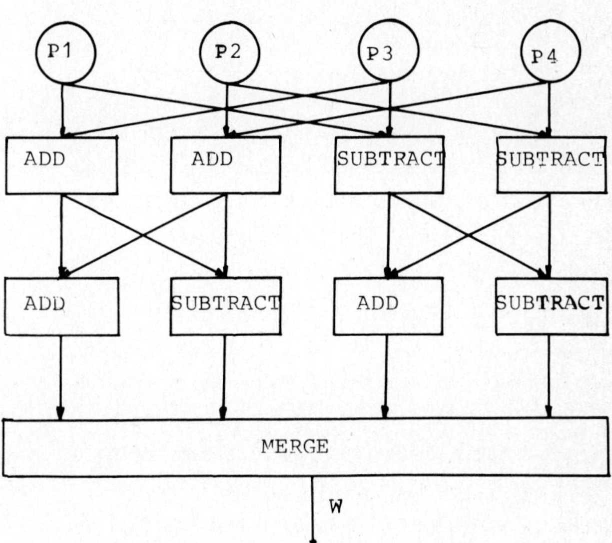

Figure 3:The data-flow graph of the RESULT procedure.

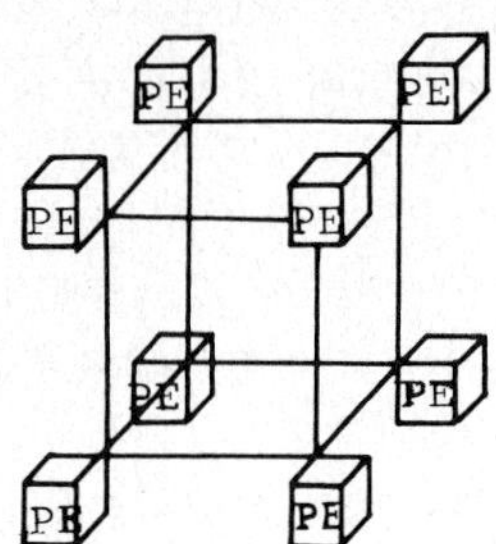

Figure 4: A special case of the n-cube network.

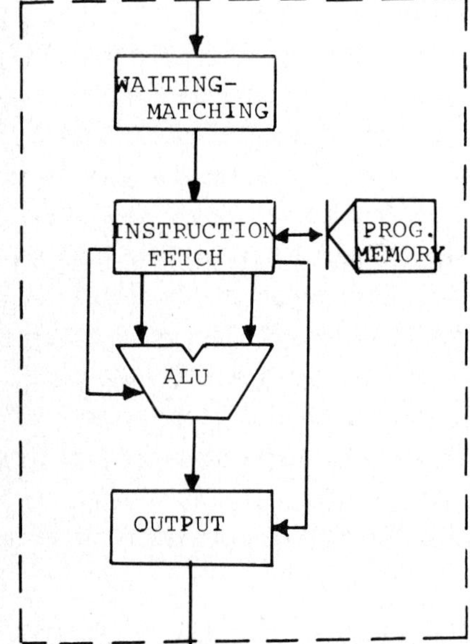

Figure 5: The block-diagram of a PE

code-block is invoked from an instruction within it, it is assigned to the same Physical Subdomain. If another code-block is invoked, it is assigned to another Physical Subdomain.

Each Physical Subdomain is identified by its *color*, while the same code-blocks within a Physical Subdomain are identified by an *initiation number*. A part of the systems memory has the role of System's Manager. The System's Manager Knows exactly which PE's have the same color and which PE's are not used. Thus, when a Physical Subdomain needs more PE's or a new Physical Subdomain must be created, the System's Manager handles the cases.

The distribution of activities over many PE's by spliting and distributing the program code, need not be done a priori. This is done during the execution, exploiting the parallelism of the machine.

If a token is addressed to an instruction in the same PE, all it has to know is the identity of the PE and the absolute address of the instruction. However, a token produced within a code-block might have as destination an instruction within another invokation of the same code-block or an instruction of another code-block. In cases like these, the tag of the token must contain the following informations:

i. identity of the PE
ii. instruction's address
iii. color of the Physical Subdomain
iv. initation number of the destination code-block.

The instructions format is given below:

<Header>
<Opcode>
<Token 1 disposition> (Declares if this token is the first or second operand)
<Token 2 disposition>
<Constant disposition> (If one of the operands is constant)
<Constant specification> (Contains the constant value)

<Destination>
<Number of tokens to enable instruction>
<Destination instruction port-number>
<Destination virtual address>
<Destination list flag>

The <Destination> item may be repeated as often as required, with all but the last <Destination list flag> set to 1.

The tokens that can "fire "an instruction are of the type:

<Token type> =0
<PE number>
<Tag>
<Color>
<Instruction address>
<Initiation number>
<Number of tokens to enable instruction>
<Port number>

<Data>

<Data value>

Let us see now, how the W-H transformation algorithm is implemented.Once the HADAMARD procedure is initially invoked,it is assigned to a Physical Domain.Then, as the four similar procedures FIND-Pi are invoked, they are assigned to different Physical Subdomains (different colors) and are executed in parallel.The same happens when procedures TWO-HADAMARD,SPECIAL-HADAMARD and RESULT are invoked.

It is interesting to see how this machine executes procedure RESULT (Fig.3) which handles a large amount of data.The operations ADD and SUBTRACT, which can be executed in parallel, are assigned to different Physical Subdomains, since each new cycle of the loops of ADD and SUBTRACT is a new code-block with the same color and different initiation number,it is assigned to a different PE.This means that simple operations such as addition and subtraction of two matrices can be executed totally in parallel.

6. CONCLUDING REMARKS

The proposed architecture seems to have attractive properties for the efficient handling of digital image structures.Even though the analysis was focused on the hierarchical W-H transform,it can be easily shown that the system's concepts can be applied to any other orthogonal transformation.The asynchronous execution and the lack of central control in the proposed architecture, characterize it as an efficient massively-parallel image processing machine.

REFERENCES

1. W.Pratt, J.Kane,H.Andrews, "Hadamard Transform Image Coding ", Proceedings of IEEE, Vol 57, (Jan 1969) 58-68.
2. N.Bourbakis,N.A.Alexandridis, "An Efficient Real-time Method for Computing W-H transformed Images ", IEEE International Conference on ASSP,Paris,France,May 3-5,1982.
3. N.Alexandridis,N.Bourbakis,B.Dimitriadis, "A Pipelined Configuration for Computing the W-H Transform of Regularly Decomposed Picture" International Journal of Mini and Microcomputers, Vol.4, No 2,1982,24-47.
4. B.Dimitriadis,N.Alexandridis,N.Bourbakis, "A C-MOVE Architecture Based Multiprocessor System for Encoding Walsh-Hadamard Transformed Images,"Microprocessing and Microprogramming,North Holland,Amsterdam,No 11,1983.
5. P.C.Treleaven et.al. "Data-driven and Demand-driven Computer Architecture ", Computing Surveys, 14,1,March 1982, 93-143
6. A.Klinger,C.R.Dyer, "Experiments on Picture Representation Using Regular Decomposition " UCLA-ENG 7494, School of Engineering and Applied Science, UCLA,Los Angeles,1974;Computer Graphics and Image Processing 5, 1976,68-105
7. N.Alexandridis, "Walsh-Hadamard Transformations in Image Proccessing ", UCLA-ENG 7108, School of Engineering and Applied Science, UCLA,Los Angeles,1971.
8. K.Krönlöf, "Execution Control and Memory Management of a Data-Flow Signal Processor," 10th Annual International Symposium on Computer Architecture,1983,230-235.
9. W.B.Ackerman, "Data Flow Languages,"Computer (IEEE) Feb. 1982, 15-24.
10. A.L.Davis,R.M.Keller, "Data-Flow Program Graphs," Computer (IEEE), Feb. 1982, 26-40
11. D.A.Adams, "A Computation Model with Data Flow Sequencing,"CS 117, Comp.Science Dept, Stanford University,Palo Alto,Calif., 1968.
12. Arvind,K.P.Gostelow, "The U-Interpreter," Computer (IEEE) Feb. 1982, 42-48.
13. I.Watson,J.Gurd, "A Practical Data-Flow Computer,"Computer (IEEE) Feb. 1982, 51-57
14. J.Dennis, "Data flow Supercomputers,"Computer (IEEE) Nov. 1980, 48-56
15. Arvind et.al. "The Tagged Token Data Flow Architecture ", MIT lab. for Comp. Science,1983

DIGITAL TECHNIQUES in Simulation, Communication and Control
Spyros G. Tzafestas (editor)
Elsevier Science Publishers B.V. (North-Holland) © IMACS, 1985

AN IMPROVED OBJECT BOUNDARY REPRESENTATION BY INVESTIGATING NEIGHBOR QUADRANTS IN A QUADTREE STRUCTURE OF AN IMAGE

N.A.Alexandridis
Dept of Electrical and Computer Engineering,
Ohio University-Athens,Ohio,USA

N.A.Bilalis, S.Ziavras
Computer Science Division,
National Technical University
Athens-Greece

A quadtree representation of an image enables efficient storage and approximate structural description of constituent patterns.A disadvantage of the method is the arbitrariness of dividing lines.Picture areas and the dividing lines imposed may combine to slice single objects into fragments which could be "non informative"
As a result objects present in the original image are unrecognizable or completely absent in the reduced picture.Search of neighbor areas of a quadrant should yield improved reduced pictures.A preprocessing predictive-correcting method is proposed. This decision procedure examines neighbor quadrants at any level of a quadtree and judges whether it is worth saving a quadrant or not by testing the surrounding area.The procedure is recursive based on three-level front-end algorithm for any pair of tree levels.A set of neighbor subquadrant templates are suggested for a better object boundary representation by determining neighbor subguadrant importance defined relative to parts of the examining quadrant.Other sets of templates could be used to detect Specific Shapes.
Segmentation errors caused by the top-down recursive partitioning of picture area into successively finer quadrants can be overcome by the proposed procedure.The method effects a more informative representation of an image.It is possible to pay a penalty at the cost of increased processing time but the percentage of intensity of the picture kept after decomposition using the neighbor procedure is strongly improved.

Introduction

Our basic intention is the overpassing of the disadvantages of regular decomposition |1|,|4|.
The two main disadvantages of regular decomposition are:
i) The arbitrariness of thresholds: This problem is related to the problem of what kinds of information should be discarded and of whether this elimination of data could lead to significant loss of information.
ii) Arbitrariness of the dividing lines: this problem is related to the problem of whether the union of subproblems into which the general problem is divided is equivalent to the general problem, i.e. whether dividing the picture into subpictures implies some sort of loss of important information.
We divide our work into three sections.In section I we present the regular decomposition method and the advantages and disadvantages of this aspect.In section II we present our proposals for overpassing the disadvantages of regular decomposition.In section III we present our conclusions.

Section I

Regular Decomposition

We assume that we have succeded the digitization and quantization of intensity of the picture which we want to process.Every picture can be represented by an N X N array of numbers, called picture matrix.Each element of this matrix corresponds to a unit area picture element, called a pixel, its value, which is an 8-bit digital number, denotes the quantized intensity value,which is also called gray level's value of that area of the picture and its position in the array benotes the position of the corresponding pixel in the picture.We denote a region of the picture as an ordered 4-tuple (Xmin, Xmax,Y min, Ymax) where X and Y are the coordinate variables of a coordinate system set at the upper left vertex of the picture matrix (fig.1).

Now we are ready to compute the region's total intensity.If we denote this region as R then we have:

$$\text{total intensity of R}: \Phi_R = \sum_{i=X\min}^{X\max} \sum_{j=Y\min}^{Y\max} P_{ij}$$

where Pij is the element of the i-th row and the j-th column of the picture matrix.The presented procedure is a top-down approach to the segmentation problem.This approach permits large non-informative areas of the picture to be deleted.That is, after partitioning the total picture into four subquadrants we denote the four subquadrants as informative or non-informative or not-sure.This task is executed by examining three possibilities when looking at a quadrant:

a. No features are visible indicating nothing informative is contained there, so we can eliminate this part of the picture without loss of information.This quadrant is called non-informative.

b. We can "see"a lot of features in the quadrant,so we can decide that this quadrant contains information that we must use.This quadrant is called informative.

c. Only a few features appear in the quadrant, so there is a small amount of information in this quadrant.In this case we can not make a final decision, that is, if we must save this quadrant.Now, we must subdivide this quadrant into four subquadrants and go to the first step of the recusrive algorithm of this method.In this way we ask the same questions about the son-quadrants:

Is the ith subquadrant informative ?

Is the ith subquadrant non-informative?

Is the ith subquadrant not-sure?

where $i = P_a, P_b, P_c, P_d$ is a son-quadrant and P is the father quadrant. For succeeding this classification we use four ratios.For every sybquadrant we form the ratio:

$$d(P,P_*) = \frac{\text{total intesity of } P_*}{\text{total intesity of } P} \quad \text{, where}$$

$* = a,b,c$ or d.

This ratio is called relative importance of P_* with regard to its father P and is denoted by $d(P,P_*)$.The above mentioned classification can be done by the following inequalities:

P_* is non-informative if $0 \le d(P,P_*) < \vartheta_1$

P_* is informative if $\vartheta_2 \le d(P,P_*) \le 1.0$

P_* is not-sure if $\vartheta_1 \le d(P,P_*) < \vartheta_2$

where ϑ_1, ϑ_2 are numbers that satisfy the following: $0 \le \vartheta_1, \vartheta_2 < 1$

As we mentioned before the non-informative subquadrants are discarded, the informative ones are saved in the data-structure and the not-sure ones are further partitioned into four and we begin a new cycle of the procedure.This procedure constructs a quadtree (Fig. 2), where the informative and the non-informative quadrants are located at the leaves of the quadtree and the not-sure quadrants are located at the branch nodes of this quadtree.We stop this process when no more not-sure subquadrants appear |1|,|4|,|5|-|12|.

One of the disadvantages of regular decomposition is the arbitrariness of the dividing lines. For softening this disadvantage (slicing of single objects into parts which may finally be judged separately as unimportant) we describe regular decomposition as a three-level process. Up to now, we have described regular decomposition as a two-level process.Now we'll describe the third level of this process.The third level is composed of the neighborhood of the informative and not- sure quadrants.In order to avoid the image degradation we "activate " some level-three subquadrants inside the non-informative subquadrants produced in the current cycle of the procedure, which are neighboring to either the informative or the not-sure subquadrants of the same father.These neighbor subquadrants contain at best fragmentary, yet important, linkage information between quadrants. Fig 3 shows quadrant configurations (i.e. the informative or "not - sure " quadrants and the neighborhood subquadrants).These level-three subquadrants (neighborhood) are subjected to a revised importance test.They are classified either informative or not-sure or non-informative,the feature being relative importance of level three subquadrant K with respect to the informative or not-sure level-two subquadrants,denoted by $d(\{b_1,\ldots,b_n\},K)$ and is equal to:

$$\frac{\text{total intensity of } K}{\frac{1}{n}\sum_{i=1}^{n} \text{total intensity of } b_i}$$

Now we also use a nonnegative number ε,that satisfies the inequality: $\varepsilon < \vartheta_1$.

We classify the level-three subquadrants as informative,non-informative or not-sure by using the following discrimintation function:

K is informative if $\vartheta_2-\varepsilon \le d(\{b_1,\ldots,b_n\},K) \le 1$

K is not-sure if $\vartheta_1-\varepsilon \le d(\{b_1,\ldots,b_n\},K) < \vartheta_2-\varepsilon$

K is non-informative if $0 \le d(\{b_1,\ldots,b_n\},K) < \vartheta_1-\varepsilon$.

Now, as when we classify the level-two subquadrants,the informative level-three subquadrants are saved, the non-informative ones are discarded and the not-sure ones are partitioned into four new subquadrants and a new cycle of the procedure begins.

Advantages of Regular Decomposition

The advantages of regular decomposition in image processing are:

1. Via unconditional partitioning,pictures which are physically too big to store in fast memory at one time can be processed as a sequence of subpictures extracted during processing.
2. Representations permit recursive analysis of subpictures.
3. We can address for rapid access to any geographical part of the total image.
4. The procedure treats all picture points alike.
5. Regular decomposition retains explicitly in thedata-structure a hierarchical description of the picture patterns,elements and their relation ships.Hence this scheme may also be used with syntactic pattern recognition.
6. The resultant tree-structure distinguishes object from non-object.
7. The decomposition algorithm contains major routines(traversal,tree-creation) which are independent of image class.Small changes can adapt regular decomposition to widely different types of pictures.
8. The transformation of the two-dimensional picture to a series of one dimensional pictures used in regular decomposition reflects area coherence,thus leaving topological interrelations between pixels intact.

Disadvantages of Regular Decomposition

1. The use of neighbor subquadrants "softens " the effect of the dividing lines.However the templates appearing in fig. 3 favor objects with diagonal orientation.
2. The arbitrariness of the thresholding values $\vartheta_1,\vartheta_2,\varepsilon$ where suboptimal selected values can lead to significant image degradation.
3. The discrimination function for the neighbor subquadrants relates them with the either informative or not-sure part of the level-one initial quadrant whereas they should be related with their neighborhood only.

Section II

As we know, regular decomposition is a three-level process.Now, we'll also propose a three -

level process, but on the third level we'll also have subquadrants of the informative and not-sure quadrants. That is, we propose the informative quadrants to be partitioned into four subquadrants, which we'll call "*temporary subquadrants*". We use this abjective (temporary) because these subquadrants are really temporary subquadrants. That is, if P is the informative quadrant then the four temporary subquadrants are the subquadrants named P_a, P_b, P_c and P_d. In fig 4 we present the proposed templates for the examination of the neighborhood of the informative (and not-sure) quadrants. There, we can see that we examine the neighbor subquadrants with regard to a part of the informative (or not-sure) quadrants and specifically the part of the quadrants that is closest to the neighborhood. The basic idea derives from a law that exists in the nature and we also use in the everyday activities. This law is:

"We succeed the most optimal comparison between two things, if the things that are compared are of equal size". In the task which we present now, we succeed to satisfy the previous law by comparing quadrants of the third level. If x_i is the total intensity of that part of the informative or not-sure quadrant which is presented in fig 4 and y is the total intensity of the corresponding neighborhood presented in the same figure, then the relative importance of the neighborhood with regard to the above mentioned part of the informative (or not sure) quadrants is the ratio

$$d(x,y) \quad \frac{y}{\frac{1}{n}\sum_{i=1}^{n} Xi}$$

, where n is the number of informative and not sure quadrants. We classify the level-three subquadrants (neighbor subquadrants) as informative, non informative or not-sure by using the discrimination function presented before for regular decomposition, i.e.

neighborhood is informative if $\vartheta_2 - \varepsilon \leq d(x,y) \leq 1.0$, neighborhood is not-sure if $\vartheta_1 - \varepsilon \leq d(x,y) < \vartheta_2 - \varepsilon$,

neighborhood is non-informantive if $0.0. \leq d(x,y) < \vartheta_1 - \varepsilon$.

Our main intention is to reduce, as much as possible, the influence of the thresholding values $\vartheta_1, \vartheta_2, \varepsilon$, the arbitrariness of dividing lines, and to get better results from the neighborhood. That is, we generally want to erase the main disadvantages of regular decomposition. It is possible to pay a penalty at the cost of increased processing time but the percentage of intesity of the picture kept after decomposition using the neighbor proce dure is strongly improved. The proposed procedure "softens "the neighborhood of the informative (and not-sure) quadrants every time; since the algorithm of regular decomposition is recursive the previous mentioned improvement occurs every time we follow the main part of the algorithm. It is obvious that this step-by-step improvement implies the improvement of the entire picture processing, that is we maintain a technique of "recursive improvement".

The proposed algorithm is:

STEP 1. In put of the entire picture.

STEP 2. Find total intensity.

STEP 3. Partition into four subquadrants. This has been done before for quadrants labeled by z, so we have the subquadrants labeled by Y.

STEP 4. Definition of the informative, not-sure and non-informative subquadrants of the second level. We label the not-sure ones by z.

STEP 5. Partition of the informative (not-sure) quadrants of the second level into four subquadrants and characterization of the four subquadrants by the label X(y).

STEP 6. Activation of the corresponding level-three subquadrants as defined in fig 4.

STEP 7. Definition of all the informative, not-sure and non-informative subquadrants of the third level.

STEP 8. Decharacterization of the subquadrants

labeled by X, that is we discard all subquadrants labeled by x.

STEP 9. Save all informative subquadrants of the second and third level.

STEP 10. Discard all non-informative subquadrants of the second and third level.

STEP 11. If neither one subquadrant of the second or third level appears then continue (go to step 12), else consider each not-sure subquadrant of the second (labeled by z) or third level as input to this procedure and go to step 1.

STEP 12. End.

Section III

We have suggested a set of neighbor subquadrant templates for a better object boundary representation by determining neighbor subquadrant importance defined relative to parts of the examining quadrant. The proposed method was used in a number of examples and we have taken good results. It is obvious that the processing time is longer than before, but the percentage of information in the picture kept after decomposition using the neighbor procedure is strongly improved.

If we assume that A is the intensity of neighbor subquadrants and B is the intensity of the not-sure and informative quadrants, then the relative importance will be:

$$d(A,B) = \frac{A}{B}.$$

If we now use the proposed method, then the denominator of d(A,•) will be a number C, where $C \leq B$ (we consider a part of the not-sure and informative quadrants, so we will have $C \leq B$) That is, by the proposed method we have greater value for d(A,.) ($d(A,C) \geq d(A,B)$), which means that the probability of considering the neighborhood as informative is greater now. The previous discussion is a theoritical proof of the worth of the proposed method.

This algorithm is also used for the analysis of images using difference of intensity [3].

References

1. A.Klinger and C .R. Dyer "Experiments on picture Representation using Regular Decomposition "Computer Science Department,UCLA, Los Angeles,California,July 1974
2. N.A.Alexandridis, J.K.Kaloyeras,N.A.Bilalis "Adaptive thresholding in Regular Decomposition with regard to picture content and transmission time restrictions " Athens, Greece,1983.
3. S.Ziavras, "Image analysis using intensity difference (and entropy) and dynamic definition of the discrimination function depending on the intensity differencies of its content "Graduate thesis,National Technical University of Athens,Greece,June 1984.
4. N.Alexandridis and A.Klinger, "Picture Decomposition, Tree Data-Structure and Identifying Directional Symmetries as Node Combinations,"Computer Graphics and Image Processing 8, pp. 43-77,1979.
5. N.Bilalis, "Digital Image Analysis and Tree Data-Structure to Image Pattern Recognition," NTU - DSUC, Athens,March 1980.
6. G.M. Hunter and K.Steiglitz, "Operations on images using quadtrees " IEEE trans.Pattern Anal.Machine Intell,Vol. PAMI-1, pp 145-153 1979.
7. C.R.Dyer,A.Rosenfeld,and H.Samet, "Region representation: Boundary codes from quadtrees " Commun.Ass.Comput.Mach., Vol 23,pp. 171-179,1980.
8. H.Samet, "Region representation: Quadtrees from boundary codes,"Commun.Ass.Comput.Mach, Vol. 23,pp 163-170,1980.
9. H.Samet, "A distance transform for images represented by quadtrees,"Comput.Science Center,University Maryland,College Park, Tech.Rep. 780, July 1979.
10. C.R. Dyer, "Computing the Euler number of an image from its quadtree,"Computer graphics

Image Proccessing,Vol. 13,pp. 270-276,1980.

11. I.Gargantini, "Detection of Connectivity for Regions Represented by linear quadtrees," Comp. and Maths with Appls, Vol. 8, No 4, pp. 319-327,1982.

12. W.I.Grosky,R.Jain,"Optimal Quadtrees for Image Segments,"IEEE Trans.on pattern Analysis and Machine Intelligence, Vol.PAMI-5, No 1, January 1983.

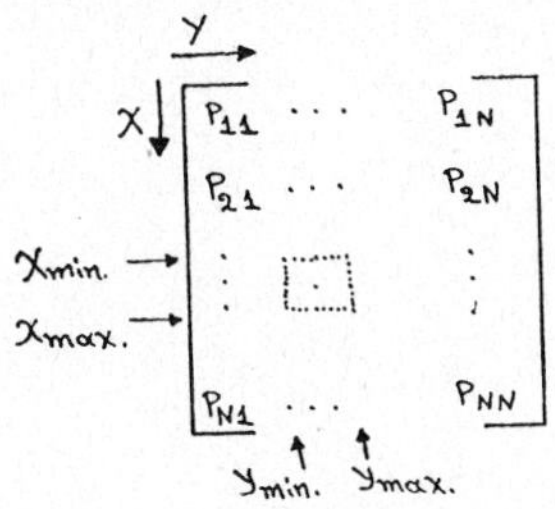

Fig. 1. Picture Matrix

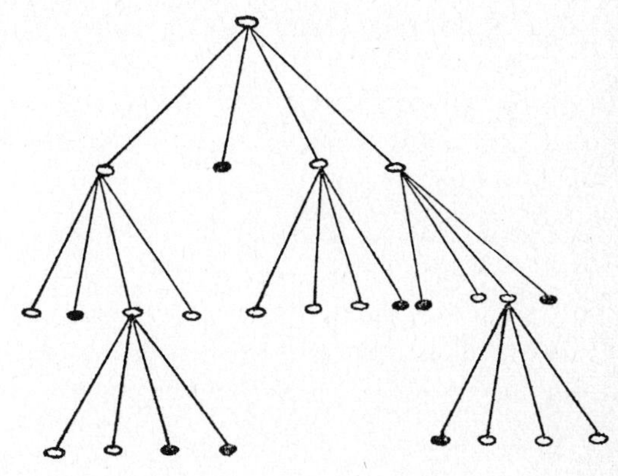

Fig. 2.a. A quadtree of Regular Decomposition method

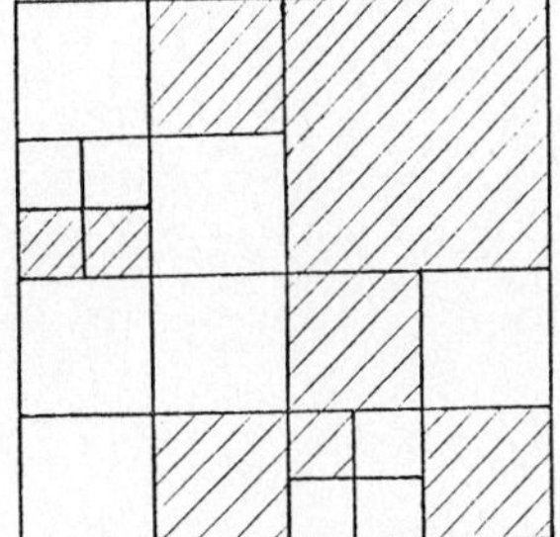

Fig. 2.b. The corresponding picture.

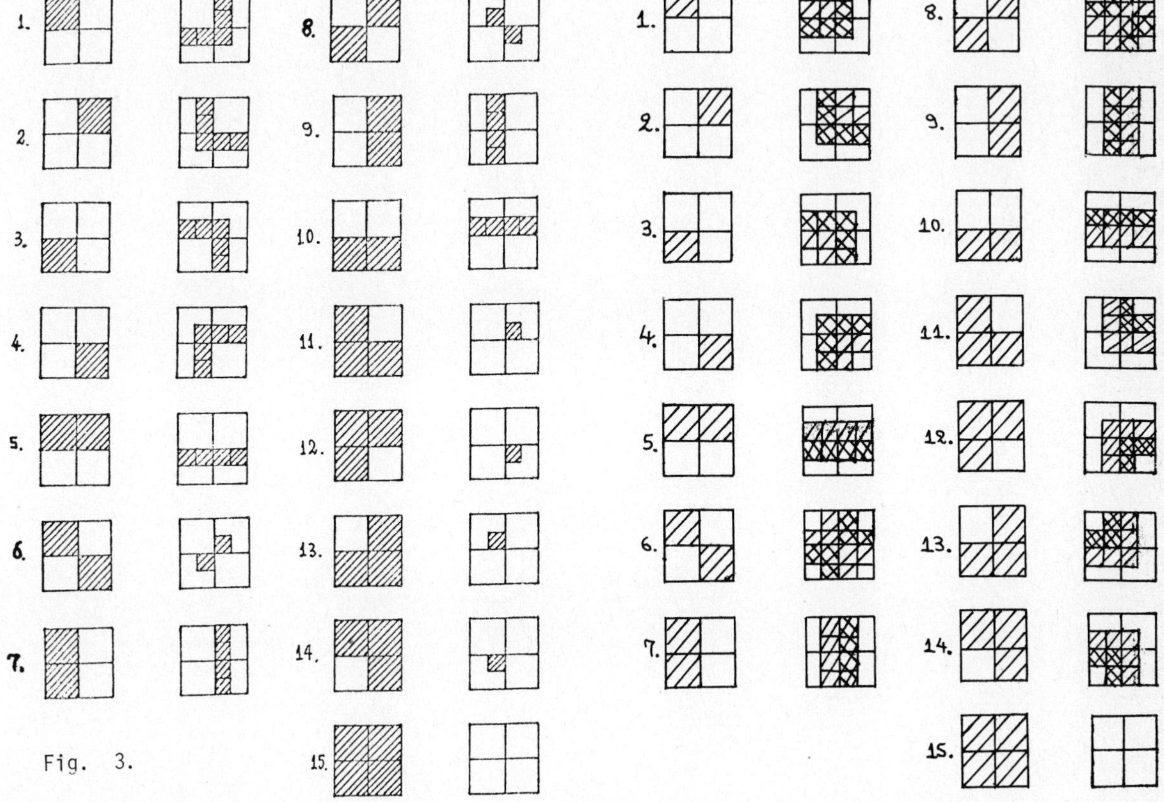

Fig. 3.

DIGITAL TECHNIQUES in Simulation, Communication and Control
Spyros G. Tzafestas (editor)
Elsevier Science Publishers B.V. (North-Holland) © IMACS, 1985

REAL-TIME QUADTREE TO RASTER CONVERSION ALGORITHM

Vassiliki J. Kollias
Laboratory of Soils
Athens Faculty of Agriculture
Votanicos, Athens, Greece.

F. Warren Burton
Dept.of Comp. Engineering
Univ. of Colorado at Denver
Denver, CO 80202, USA.

J.(Yiannis) Kollias
Dept.of Computer Science
National Technical Univ.
Zografou, Athens, Greece.

ABSTRACT

The problem of transforming an image representation to another is one of the debated problems in pattern recognition. An algorithm - coded in PASCAL - is developed for sequentially displaying (i.e a row at a time) an arbitrary image defined by a quadtree. The algorithm offers two main advantages over other algorithms which convert quadtrees to rasters: (a) it has modest storage requirements (because only one line of the raster needs to be in core), and (b) it can be performed at real-time (because processing and output may overlap).

1. INTRODUCTION

The problem of transforming an image representation to another is one of the debated problems in pattern recognition (See for example, (1) (2) and (3)). The derived algorithms are very important because one representation might be more efficient than another for a specific set of operations.

Samet has considered the following two problems: First, the construction of a quadtree for a binary image given its row-by-row description (4). Second, the sequential output (i.e. a row at a time) of an image given its quadtree (5). The restriction that the raster representation of the image must be input or output by rows complicates the algorithms but it offers them the following two main advantages over other algorithms (e.g.(1)): First, they require less memory space (because only the row currently processed need to exist in core) and second, the constructions may be performed at real-time (because the scanning and the processing of data may overlap).

In a previous paper Kollias et al (6) implemented in PASCAL the raster to quadtree construction algorithm by developing a variation of Samet's algorithm (4).
In this study we develop an algorithm - coded in PASCAL - for sequentially displaying an image defined by a quadtree. The present algorithm offers the following three advantages over the algorithm developed by Samet (5) (see above): (a) it is coded in PASCAL and not in an non existing language (Algol like), (b) it makes a better utilisation of storage when storing the nodes of the quadtree, and (c) it operates for arbitrary images (and not only for binary ones).

Section 2 introduces to raster and quadtree representations of images. The algorithm is presented in Section 3 while Section 4 concludes the study.

2. RASTER AND QUADTREE REPRESENTATION

In picture processing an image may be partitioned into a large number of pixels by a grid (7). Associated with each pixel is a value giving the average intensity of that part of the picture within the pixel. Binary images may be viewed as black and white pictures, where pixel values are either 0 (white) or 1 (black).

Binary images may be used to represent regions, where a pixel value 0(1) denotes that the pixel lies outside (inside) the region (Figure 1a). The pixel array representation of a binary image can be transformed to a block form by performing the following process. The pixel array is divided into four square subarrays. If a subarray is constant (i.e. has all 0 valued pixels or 1 valued pixels) then the subarray can be represented by a single value. Otherwise, the subarray is again quartered into four smaller subarrays, in a recursive fashion. The quartering may continue down to the level of individual pixels, which of course are constant (Figure 1b).

The process described above may also be applied to non binary images. For example, consider the case where the image represents an area partitioned into a number of districts. The pixel values may then well be assigned the number of the district they belong. If this is the case then it is also possible to perform the block decomposition process described above (Figures 2a and 2b). For the rest of this presentation we consider pixel arrays which may take any integer value.

As in (4) we restrict our attention to pixel arrays which contain $2^k \times 2^k$ elements for some integer k. (Any array can be embedded in such an array. The cost of using an overly large array as the basis for the structure defined below is usually not significant).

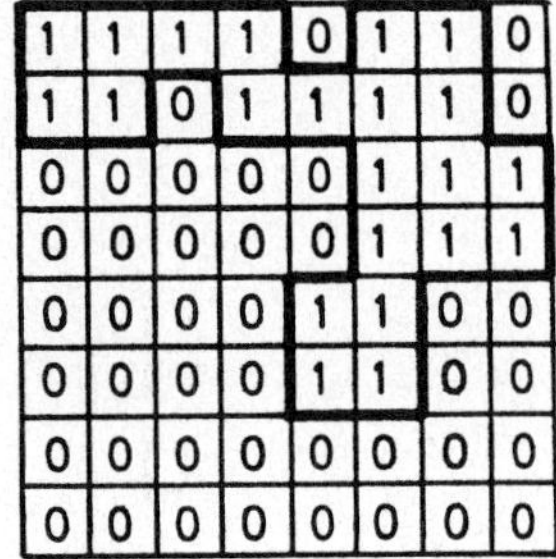

(a)

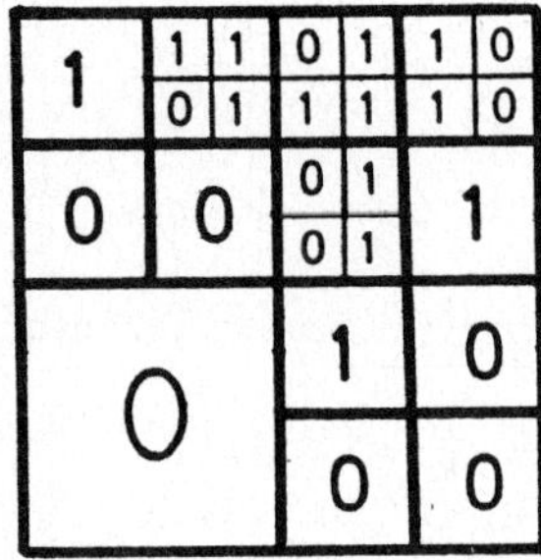

(b)

Figure 1: A region.(a) Pixel array of the region. (b) A compact representation of the region.

1	1	1	1	1	1	1	1	2	2	2	2	2	2	2	2
1	1	1	1	1	1	1	1	2	2	2	2	2	2	2	2
1	1	1	1	1	1	1	1	2	2	2	2	2	2	2	2
1	1	1	1	1	1	1	1	2	2	2	2	2	2	2	2
1	1	1	1	1	1	3	3	2	2	2	2	2	2	2	2
1	1	1	1	1	3	3	3	2	2	2	2	2	2	2	2
1	1	1	1	3	3	3	3	2	2	2	2	2	2	2	2
3	3	3	3	3	3	3	5	5	5	5	2	2	2	2	2
3	3	3	3	3	3	3	5	5	5	5	5	5	5	5	5
3	3	3	3	3	3	3	5	5	5	5	5	5	5	5	5
3	3	3	3	3	4	4	4	5	5	5	5	5	5	5	5
3	3	3	3	3	3	4	4	5	5	5	5	5	5	5	5
3	3	3	3	4	4	4	4	5	5	5	5	5	5	5	5
4	4	4	4	4	4	4	4	5	5	5	5	5	5	5	5
4	4	4	4	4	4	4	4	4	5	5	5	5	5	5	5
4	4	4	4	4	4	4	4	4	5	5	5	5	5	5	5

(a)

(b)

Figure 2: A map.(a) Pixel array approximating a map.(b) A compact representation for a map.

The quartering of the image process described above may be represented by the quadtree data structure which may be defined as the following PASCAL record type:

```
type pointer = ↑descendants;
     quadrec = record
               case constant: Boolean of
                    true: (val: integer);
                    false: (detail: pointer)
               end;

   descendants = array [1..2, 1..2] of quadrec;
```

A quadree is a degree four tree of height $\underline{k}$ or less. We will use the term quadree to denote a tree or subtree and the term node to denote quadtree exclusive of its descendants. The term leaf may be used for a node where the value of the tag field, constant is true. Each node of a quadtree corresponds to a square array or subarray of pixels. If all of the pixels in the subarray have the same value, then the node is a leaf (constant is true) and the val field contains the common value. Otherwise (constant is false) the array is partitioned into four subarrays. Each subarray is represented by one of the four quadtrees to which the pointer in the detail field points. The subarrays correspond to the elements of descendants as follows: [1,2]=upper left; [2,2]= upper right; [1,1]= lower left; [2,1]= lower right. Figure 3 is the quadtree representation of the pixel arrays in Figures 2a and 2b.

The quadtree implicitly defines a hierarchy of grids, with one grid per level of the tree. We will use G_i to denote the grid where each grid cell contains 4^i pixels, so that G_o is the grid where each cell contains one pixel and G_k is the grid with a single cell containing the entire image. Clearly G_i corresponds

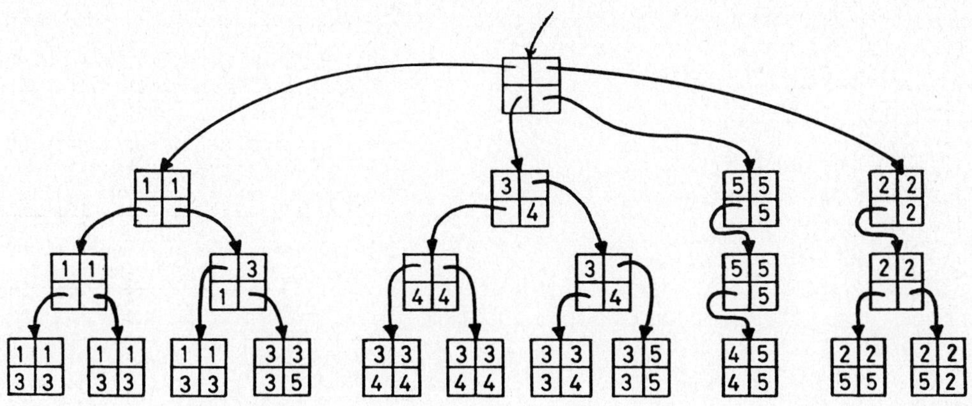

Figure 3: The quadtree representation of the blocks in Figure 2b.

to level k-i of the quadtree.

Algorithm in the following section requires some additional types and global values, defined as follows:

```
const k = ?;
      w = ? {2 to the k};
type raster = array [0..w-1, 0..w-1] of integer;
    point = record x, y: 0..w-1 end;
    cell = record xmin, ymin, width: integer
                                        end;
    var  top: cell;
       {top.xmin:= 0; top.ymin :=0; top.
                                width = w;}
```

A raster is a pixel array. The constant w is equal to 2^k. A point is an x, y pair. We will assume that the point (0,0) is in the lower left, and that raster [0,0] is in the upper left and corresponds to point (0, w-1). In general, raster [i,j] corresponds to point (j, w-1-i) or equivalently point (x,y) corresponds to raster [w-1-y, x].

A cell identifies a cell of one of the grids in the hierarchy. The value of the width field will always be a power of 2, equal to 2^i for a cell of G_i. The values of the xmin and ymin fields will always be a multiple of the width field. A cell c contains the pixel for which:

c.xmin ≤ x < c.xmin + c.width, and

c.ymin ≤ y < c.ymin + c.width

Finally, top is a global variable which always denotes the single cell of G_k, which contains the entire image.

3. THE QUADTREE TO RASTER ALGORITHM

The algorithm consists of two procedures: getraster and getstring. The getraster procedure builds a raster from quadtree. The raster elements are created by rows from left to right. Each call to procedure getstring from the procedure getraster causes one row of the raster to be filled.

The getstring procedure considers two basic cases. First, the node currently processed is a leaf. The constant value of this node fills the pixels of the current row which correspond to that node. (The parameters ypos and xpos denote the exact pixels of the raster which are to be filled). Second, the node is not a leaf. The getstring processes the left and right subtrees of the node.

```
procedure getraster(var data: raster;
                    var image: quadrec);
 var row: integer;
 begin
  for row : =  0 to top.width - 1 do
  getstring(image, top, data, row)
 end;
```

```
procedure getstring(var block: quadrec;
 window: cell; var data: raster; row: integer);
 var xpos, ypos: integer;
    level: 1..2;
 begin
  ypos :=  top.width - 1 - row;
  if block.constant then
   for xpos := window.xmin to window.xmin +
      window.width - 1 do
      data[ypos,xpos] := block.val;
   else
    begin
     window.width := window.width / 2
     if ypos < window.ymin + window.width then
       level := 1
     else
      begin
       level := 2;
       window.ymin := window.ymin + window.width
      end;
     getstring(block.detail↑[1,level], window.
       data, row);
     window.xmin := window.xmin + window.width;
     getstring(block.detail↑[2,level], window,
       data, row)
    end
 end;
```

4. CONCLUSION

The study presented a PASCAL implementation of an algorithm for converting raster to quadtree representation of images. In addition to presenting the specific algorithm , the paper illustrated general coding techniques for processing quadtrees. We envisage that the techniques may be applied to the following two contexts. First, to produce efficient PASCAL implementations of other image processing algorithms presented in the literature either verbally or/and using ALGOL type languages ((1),(2),(3),(4) and (8)). Second, to implement other possible transformation algorithms between image representation, e.g. exponential pyramids (9) to quadtrees.

REFERENCES

[1] Samet, H., Region representation: Quadtrees from binary arrays, Computer Graphics and Image Processing 13 (1980) 88-93.

[2] Samet, H., Region representation: Quadtrees from boundary codes, Comm. ACM 23 (1980) 163-170.

[3] Dyer, C.R., Rosenfeld, A. and Samet, H., Region representation: Boundary codes from quadtrees, Comm. ACM 23 (1980) 171-179.

[4] Samet, H., An algorithm for converting rasters to quadtrees, IEEE Trans. Patt. Anal. and Mach. Intell. 3 (1981) 93-95.

[5] Samet, H., Algorithms for the conversion of quadtrees to rasters, Computer Vision, Graphics and Image Processing (1984) (in press).

[6] Kollias, J.G., Burton, F.W. and Kollias, V. J., An algorithm for constructing a quadtree from the pixel array representation of a region, in Tzafestas, S.G. and Hamza, M.H. (eds), Advances in Modelling, Planning Decision and Control of Energy, Power and Environmental Systems (Acta Press, Zurich, 1983).

[7] Rosenfeld, A. and Kak, A.C., Digital Picture Processing (Academic Press, New York, 1977).

[8] Hunter, G.M. and Steiglitz, K., Operations on images using quadtrees, IEEE Trans. Patt. Anal. and Mach. Intell. 1 (1979) 145-153.

[9] Burton, F.W., Kollias, J.G. and Alexandridis, N.A., An indexing scheme to implement the exponential pyramid data structure with application to determination of symmetries in pictures, Computer Vision, Graphics and Image Processing 25 (1983) 218-225.

DIGITAL TECHNIQUES in Simulation, Communication and Control
Spyros G. Tzafestas (editor)
Elsevier Science Publishers B.V. (North-Holland) © IMACS, 1985

SPECIAL PURPOSE PROCESSOR FOR BLOCK CIRCULANT SPARSE MATRICES WITH ELLIPTICAL STRUCTURE

C.E. Goutis

Department of Electrical and Electronic Engineering
The Merz Laboratories
The University of Newcastle upon Tyne, NE1 7RU
England

A new architecture for a special purpose processor is introduced, which implements an image reconstruction algorithm consisting of the solution of a linear system having a very large sparse matrix, and the back projection. The difference block circulant matrix derived from the above matrix has all no zero elements within an elliptical strip. Each processor unit includes RAM and each row of the array processor stores one submatrix which is partitioned accordingly. The data flow for the current estimate of the solution, is such that the elliptical strip is split into two curved strips which are converted into straight ones to produce strip diagonal matrices. The product of each sub-row with the current sub-vector is computed in parallel and added to those of the corresponding sub-rows in a pipeline configuration. An architecture for the back projection of the solution of the linear system to give the image reconstruction was also produced. It includes a one dimensional array which stores each sub-vector for back projection in the local RAM and employs a simple address generator and a linear interpolation circuit. Two VLSI chips for this machine have been designed.

1. INTRODUCTION

In many applications special purpose processors result in much higher faster algorithm implementations than those of the general purpose processors, as they exploit the specific structure of the system involved. Existing CAD tools allow the design of simple processor units with minimal effort, a number of which can be included in a single chip using current CMOS VLSI technology.

General purpose array processors avoid the drawback of conventional computers where all operations are channelled through the single Arithmetic Logic Unit forming a bottleneck; however they are frequently limited by the data flow in that the operands are not available when required and a very large percentage of the processor units are idle at each time period. To overcome this, the architecture of the array processor should be tailored to suit the data flow requirements of the application.

Solutions of linear systems with large sparse matrices require special architectures. An algorithm and hardware for MIMD is given in [1] and the computational bounds of sparse matrix triangulation using fixed number of processor units was studied in [2]. The structure of the matrix of this paper is more specific and is exploited to introduce a new architecture.

The algorithm introduced in [3] and briefly outlined in section 2 produces image reconstruction for both parallel and divergent-ray projections. Its performance is higher than that of the convolution algorithm used in most current commercial scanners. The special purpose processor below was designed to implement the algorithm in [3] with very high speed. In section 3 an architecture is introduced which exploits the fact that all non zero matrix elements lie on an elliptical strip and an architecture for the Tomographic back projection is given in section 4.

2. SPARSE MATRIX STRUCTURE

In divergent-ray Tomography a large number of detectors lie on a circumference which encloses the object for reconstruction and the x-ray source is rotated around the object. For each position of the source, the detector measurements form a projection. A large number of projections is usually taken to reconstruct the image of the corresponding slice. Similarly in parallel-ray scanning the x-ray source and the detectors are moved in parallel to obtain a projection and then rotated to take the

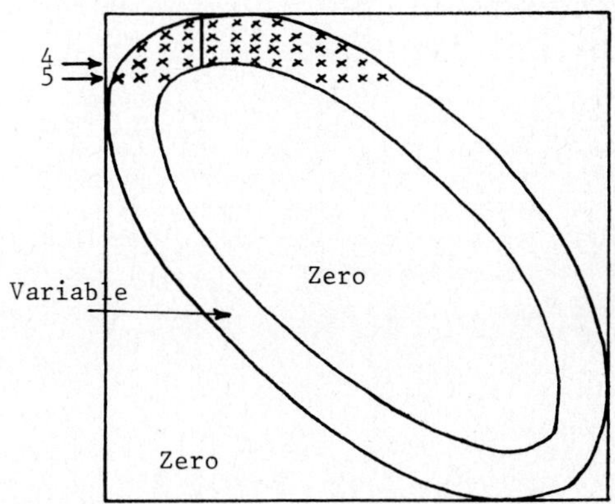

Fig. 1 Elliptical sparse matrix B' structure

projections at other orientations.

Let

$g_k^T = [g_{k1}, g_{k2}, \ldots g_{kP}]$, k=1,2,..N

where g_{ki} denote the ith measurement of the kth projection. If the domain of image definition is a circle, the Lagrange multipliers $\{\lambda_{ki}\}$ introduced in the dual optimisation are related with the projections as [3].

$$g = B\lambda \qquad (1)$$

or as

$$\begin{bmatrix} g_1 \\ g_2 \\ \cdot \\ \cdot \\ g_N \end{bmatrix} = \begin{bmatrix} B_0 & B_1 & \cdot\cdot & B_{N-1} \\ B_{N-1} & B_0 & \cdot\cdot & B_{N-2} \\ \cdot & \cdot & \cdot\cdot & \cdot \\ & & & \\ B_1 & B_2 & \cdot\cdot & B_0 \end{bmatrix} \begin{bmatrix} \lambda_1 \\ \lambda_2 \\ \cdot \\ \cdot \\ \lambda_N \end{bmatrix}$$

where

$\lambda_k^T = [\lambda_{k1}, \lambda_{k2}, \ldots \lambda_{kP}]$, k=1,2,..N

and the size of matrix B is NP x NP. As the values of N=256 and P=512 may be used, matrix B has a very large size, usually $10^5 \times 10^5$ approximately which leads to excessive computational requirements when solving system (1) above to obtain λ.

The excessive computation is drastically reduced by exploiting the structure of the submatrices $\{B_k\}$ where there are, in general, two areas of equal elements separated by an elliptical strip. The submatrix elements outside the strip are all zero, those inside have a constant value for each submatrix and the ones on the elliptical strip vary from zero to the constant value above.

For each submatrix $\{B_k\}$ a difference submatrix is generated (Fig. 1) by replacing the ith subrow by the difference of the $(i-1)^{th}$ subrow from the ith subrow for i=2,3,..P and leaving the first subrow unchanged. Having computed and stored the non zero elements of all difference submatrices once only for all future uses, the steps of the algorithm are

(i) Compute the initial estimate using $\lambda^o_{ki} = g_{ki}/B_0(i,i)$ for all ki.

(ii) Estimate $\hat{g}^n_{ki}$, i=1,..P from λ^n and system (1). Note that the product of a subvector and the ith subrow is equal to the sum of its product with the $(i-1)^{th}$ subrow and the ith difference subrow respectively.

(iii) Update λ_k as

$$\lambda^{n+1}_{ki} = \lambda^n_{ki} + \frac{\gamma}{B_0(i,i)} [g_{ki} - \hat{g}^n_{ki}]$$

$$i = 1, 2 \ldots P$$

where γ is the relaxation factor. Repeat steps (ii) and (iii) until the noise variance is matched.

(iv) Back project λ to obtain the image of the slice.

The back projection procedure is explained in section 4.

3. ARRAY PROCESSOR ARCHITECTURE

3.1 The Processor Unit

The array processor in Fig. 2 solves steps (ii) and (iii) of the successive relaxation algorithm given in the previous section. Step 2 which is the most time consuming section as it requires the product of the difference matrix B and the subvector λ, is computed by

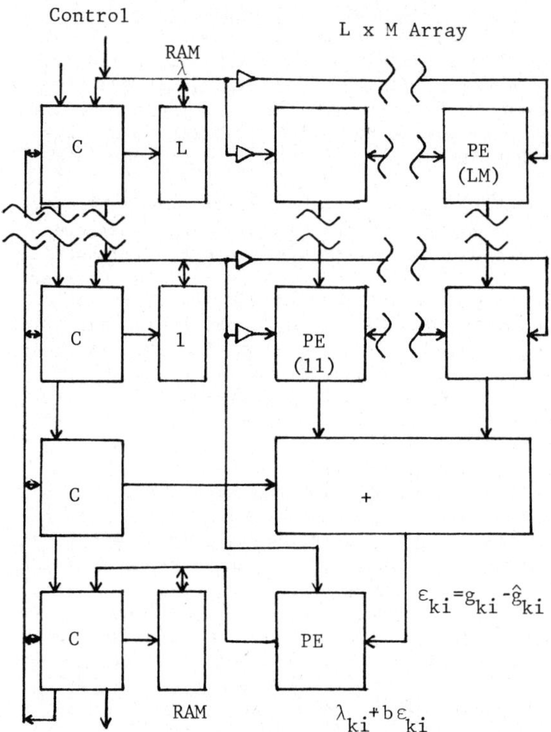

Fig. 2. 2-D array processor. Each subrow products are computed in parallels

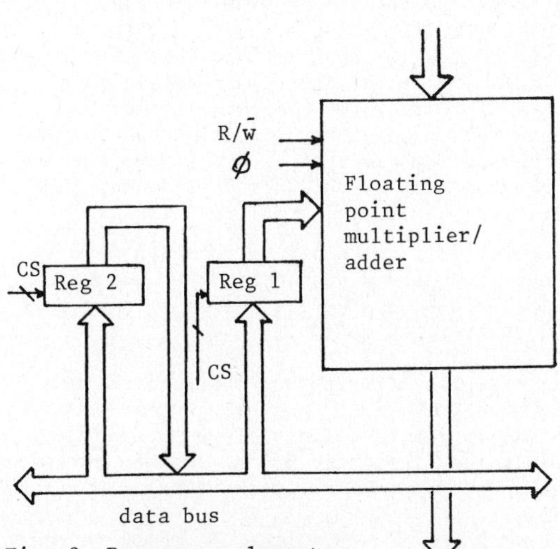

Fig. 3 Processor element. Registers facilitate shifting operations.

the L x M processor elements and Step 3 is executed by the processor at the bottom.

Each processor has a RAM where parts of a submatrix are stored permanently and the elements of each subvector $\{\lambda_k\}$ stored in RAM as shown, can flow along the corresponding processor row in both directions by shifting appropriately. The control signals for each processor row are provided by the control unit on the left, all control units being identical except that the contents of their local RAMs differ.

This two-dimensional (2-D) array L x M may be considered as an extension of the 1-D array given in [4]; they differ in that the array of Fig. 2 stores the matrix locally and allows bi-directional flow in each processor row. By keeping the matrix stored permanently and by bi-directionally moving the subvector elements as required, the elliptical strip is split into two half elliptical strips and also each half is converted into a straight strip to produce two strip diagonal matrices which can then be readily multiplied with the subvectors.

Each row of processors computes the product of a submatrix stored permanently in the local RAMs with all subvectors as required and therefore the number of rows is equal to the number of submatrices viz L = N, however, the architecture is applicable for L < N where a row of processors corresponds to more than one submatrix. The subvectors $\{\lambda_k\}$ are stored in the RAM as shown, if L < N special RAM should be provided to store the subvectors not currently used.

The estimated projections $\{\hat{g}_{ki}\}$ - index n is omitted for convenience - required in step (iii) of the algorithm are computed in a parallel and pipeline configuration. As an example the computation of $\hat{g}_{1i}$ will be considered by taking L = N. First the products associated with the ith subrow of B'_{N-1} and subvector λ_N is computed by the top row of processors (Fig. 2) in parallel, and are transferred to the second row of processors where they added to the products associated with the ith subrow of B'_{N-2} and λ_{N-1}; the bottom processor row computes the products associated with B'_0 and λ_1 and all products and received sums are added to give $\hat{g}_{1i}$. As B'_0 is a diagonal matrix, one processor only is required in the bottom processor row.

By permanently storing the constant array $\gamma/B(i,i), i=1,..P$ in the local RAM of the processor at the bottom of Fig. 2, the element λ_{1i} is updated using the error $(g_{1i}-\hat{g}_{1i})$ produced by the adder/subtractor, and the current value of λ_{1i} stored in RAM 1. After the complete subvector has been updated the subvectors $\{\lambda_k\}$ stored in RAM 1 to N are circulated using DMA, as the block circulant property requires.

The processor element shown in Fig. 3 consists of Reg 1 and 2 and the inner product step processor [5] which is a floating point multiplier/adder performing the operation $x_0 = x_i + b_n y_i$ where x_i and y_i are the inputs, x_0 is the output and $\{b_n\}$ denotes the matrix element stored in the RAM included in the processor. The multiplier/adder circuit was implemented using an optimal algorithm, which is

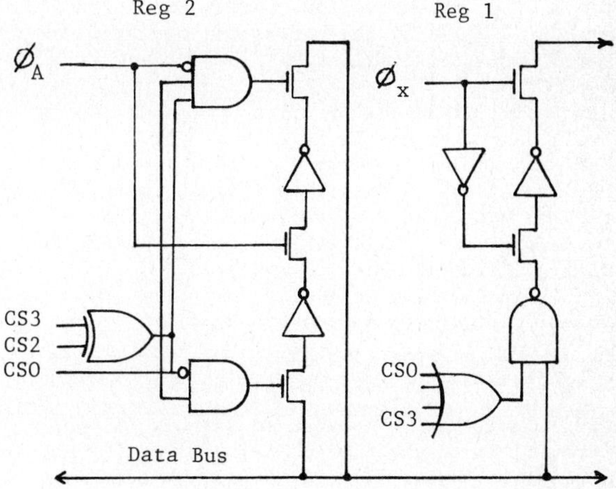

Fig. 4 Logic of registers in the processor element. The Control unit provides CSO-3 and clocks.

Code CS3..CS0	Mnemonic	Operations
0 0 0 0	NOP	No operation
0 0 0 1	NS	No shift
0 0 1 0	LS	Left shift
0 0 1 1	RS	Right shift
0 1 0 0	LSLR	LS + load Reg 2
0 1 0 1	LSSR	LS + store Reg 2
0 1 1 0	RSLR	RS + load Reg 2
0 1 1 1	RSSR	RS + store Reg 2
1 0 0 0	NSLR	NS + load Reg 2
1 0 0 1	NSSR	NS + store Reg 2

Table 1 Shift instructions of processor element. Loading/storing is required whenever more than three elements exist in the subrow. Multiplication is performed during one cycle which includes three subcycles.

regular, fast and recursive in that the size of the mantissa and exponent can be increased by a straightforward recursive procedure. It also has an optimal area-time complexity product.

It is interesting to note here that only two additional simple registers are used with the multiplier/adder and the local RAM to produce the processing element of the array which demonstrates that the use of a conventional processor would have introduced a complexity not justified in this application.

Reg 1 of Fig. 3 one bit of which is shown in Fig. 4, holds the subvector element which is being multiplied by the corresponding matrix element or zero in situations where there is no contribution from the local product and the sum received from the previous processor row is simply passed on to the next row. Reg 2 (Fig 4) holds the subvector element in situations where the current row of the strip diagonal matrix contains more than M elements and therefore the M processors in the corresponding row repeat the multiplication/addition as required.

During one cycle specified by the clock Φ_x in Fig. 5 a multiplication/addition is performed. The period t_0t_1 is used to read into Reg 1 the subvector element presented on the bus (if no operation is required, Reg 1 is cleared), read the matrix element from the local RAM and transfer the sum vertically to the next processor row; the multiplication/addition takes place during t_1t_0'.

The important requirements that the correct subvector element is presented on the bus at each cycle, is met by having a number of horizontal shift instructions shown in Table 1, which are executed during one subcycle; a cycle includes three subcycles. Therefore three shifts on either direction can be performed during one cycle. The instructions are presented to the processor unit during the positive pulses of Φ_A in Fig. 5 and are executed during the period which follows as shown; the period until the first positive pulse is used by the control unit to produce the instruction code.

Two examples of using the instructions are given below. If M=3 and the current and next submatrix row have three elements each and the latter is shifted by one to the left (e.g. lines 4 and 5 in Fig. 1) the three instructions will be: RS, NS, NS. If line 4 above had nine elements and the current cycle computes the products associated with the first group of three elements, then the three shift instructions would have been: LSLR, LS and LS. During the next cycle which computes the product associated with the second group, RS, RS and RS would have been sent. The last cycle of this row would have used RSSR, NS and NS.

Each submatrix including half elliptical strip, is partitioned and stored in the RAM of the row of the processors to which it corresponds. For M=3 the partitioning is achieved as follows: In each submatrix row, the elements are partitioned into groups of three, if the number of elements is not an integer multiple, zeros are added. The first element of all these groups is stored in the local RAM of the first processor on the left in order, i.e., an element of a row should proceed any element of the same row, which is on its right, and also

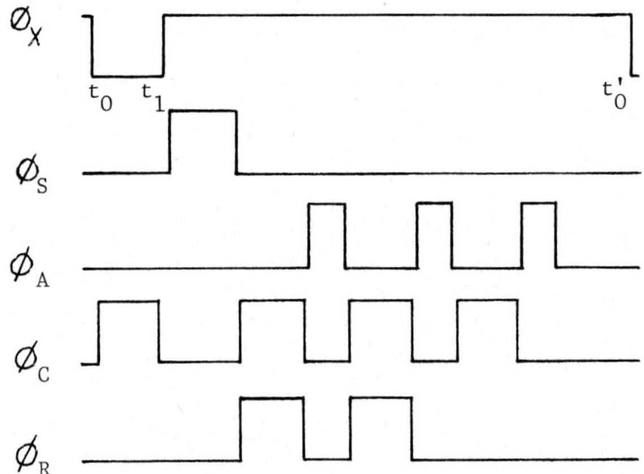

Fig. 5 Clock waveform produced by the control unit

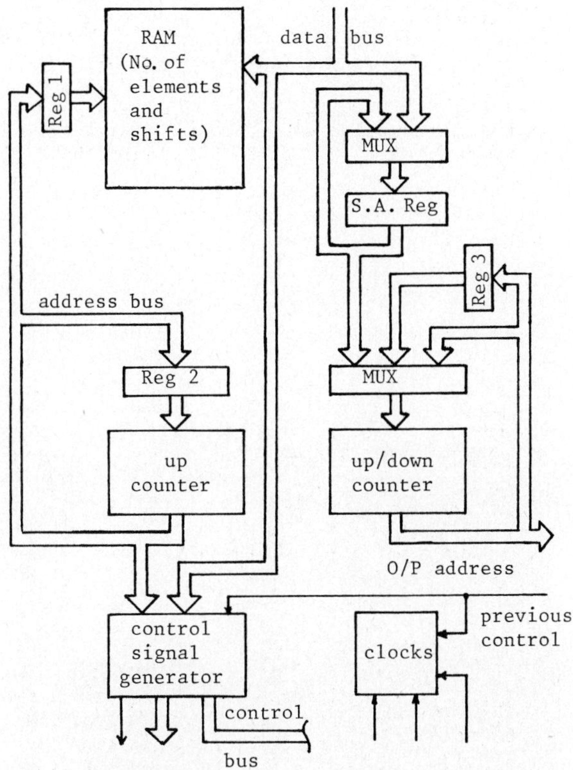

Fig. 6 Control unit for one row of processor. It incorporates DMA for circulating subvector data

the elements of all subsequent rows. Similarly, the second/third element of all these groups of three elements, are stored in the RAM of the second/third processor.

3.2 The Control Unit

This unit provides the control signals CS0-CS3 which form the shift instructions for the processors, the address for the RAM storing subvectors $\{\lambda_k\}$, the DMA control for circulating the subvectors, the necessary interrupts for the control of the flow of the products, and the clocks.

Each row of processors has its own control unit shown in Fig. 6. The RAM consists of 2P bytes and stores information which, in effect, enables the derivation of the indices corresponding to each matrix element stored in the local RAM of the processors. This is necessary as the non zero elements of the elliptical strip are partitioned and stored sequentially, and is achieved by storing in each byte (i) the difference of the column index for the first non zero element in present subrow from that of the previous subrow and (ii) the number of non zero elements in the present row.

During each cycle two bytes are read from this RAM. The first corresponds to the current sub-row and the second is used for generating the necessary interrupts which ensure that a processor will wait if the one below it has not completed the product computation so that inappropriate products are not summed.

The up/down counter generates the address for the RAM of the subvectors $\{\lambda_k\}$ and is preset at its output, the contents of the Reg 3 or the starting address (SA) register. It generates three addresses per cycle for the corresponding three shift instructions. Reg 3 stores the output of the counter in situations where the number of non zero elements in the subrow is more than M in order to facilitate the addressing for the next subrow. As the two half elliptical strips are used separately, two starting addresses are required; one for each first subrow. They are stored in the S.A. register of Fig. 6 which is a two stage register circulating its contents at the first and P^{th} cycle. The up counter produces the address for the RAM, which is stored in the two stage registers 1 and 2 (Fig. 6).

4. BACK PROJECTION ARRAY PROCESSOR

The parallel back projection of a 1-D continuous function f(x) along the y-axis generates a 2-D functions $f'(x,y) = f(x)$ which represents a surface produced by shifting f(x) along the y-axis; the projection angle is zero as f(x) lies on the x-axis. Back projection at angle θ is achieved by rotating f(x) at angle θ and then back projecting it along y_θ; (x_θ, y_θ) denote the Cartesian co-ordinates rotated at angle θ. Each subvector $\{\lambda_k\}$ found in the previous section by solving system (1), corresponds to angle θ which specifies the orientation of the associated projection $\{g_k\}$, is linearly interpolated and back projected accordingly to give a 2-D function which is sampled to produce a 2-D image. By summing the image produced by all the subvectors $\{\lambda_k\}$, the reconstructed image is obtained.

The computation of the contribution of a back projected $\{\lambda_k\}$ into an image pixel requires (i) the addresses of the two, in general, samples of the discrete $\{\lambda_k\}$ which are to be interpolated and (ii) the linear interpolation. The back projection is achieved by an array of N interpolators with equal number of RAMs and address generators; a complete subvector being stored in each RAM. The address generator produces the address of the two subvector elements which contribute to the pixel considered and the linear interpolator consists of a subtractor and fixed point multiplier/adder which compute $\lambda_{ki} + a(\lambda_{k(i+1)} - \lambda_{ki})$. Fig. 7 shows the interpolator which forms a section of a chip.

The address generator is based on an algorithm which (i) exploits the fact that the geometrical projection of any straight line section joining two adjacent pixel on the same column, is a straight line section whose length depend only on θ (ii) the address is an integer number from zero to P.

5. CONCLUSIONS

A data flow VLSI architecture was presented for the recursive solution of linear systems with very large block circulant matrices of elliptical structure, namely, all the non zero elements lie within an elliptical strip or the elements outside the strip are zero, and inside are equal to a constant value for each submatrix. This form of system arises in Tomographic image processing.

Each row of processors of the 2-D array computes the products associated with a subrow in parallel and the results are added to those of other subrows computed in pipeline. The elements within the elliptical strip of each submatrix are appropriately partitioned and stored in the local RAM of each processor element. As these elements are read sequentially, the horizontal flow of the present estimate of the solution is controlled to obtain the correct products.

An array architecture was also introduced for fast implementation of the back projection - a fundamental procedure generating images from 1-D functions. Two chips have been designed for this procedure.

6. ACKNOWLEDGEMENTS

The author would like to express his appreciation to Mr. Jaffer Sheblee and Dr. Charles Allen for their discussions on aspects of this paper and help in the VLSI implementations.

7. REFERENCES

1. Arnold, C.P., Parr, M.I. and Dewe, M.B., An efficient parallel algorithm for the solution of large sparse linear matrix equations, IEEE Trans., Computers, Vol. C-32, No. 3, (1983) 265-273.

2. Huang, J.W. and Wing. O., Optimal triangulation of a sparse matrix, IEEE Trans. Circuits Syst., Vol CAS-26, No. 9 (1979) 726-733.

3. Goutis, C.E. and Drossos, S.N., Fast iterative algorithm for reconstruction from divergent-ray projections, IEE Proc., Vol. 131, Pt. E, No. 3 (1984) 89-96.

4. Mead, C.A. and Conway, L.A., Introduction to VLSI systems (Addison-Wesley, Reading, 1980).

5. Yung, H.C. and Allen, C.R., Optimal floating point multiplication processor for signal processing, Image and Vision Computing Jrnl. Vol. 1, No. 3 (1983) 151-156.

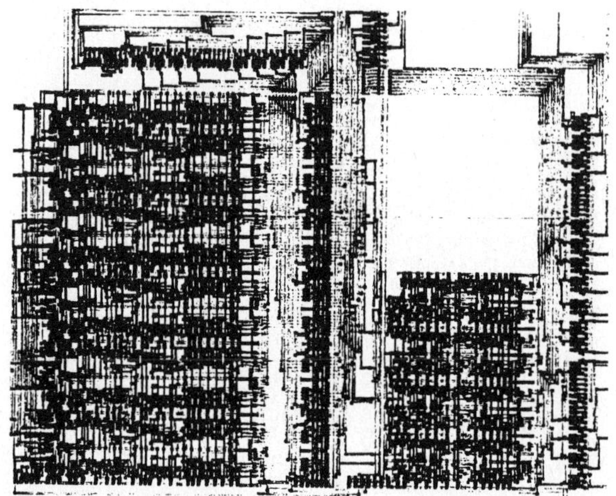

multiplier/adder $x = x_1 + ay$ subtractor $y = x_2 - x_1$

Fig. 7 Layout of the interpolator $x = x_1 + a(x_2 - x_1)$

DIGITAL TECHNIQUES in Simulation, Communication and Control
Spyros G. Tzafestas (editor)
Elsevier Science Publishers B.V. (North-Holland) © IMACS, 1985

Wiener Filtering for the Tomographic Reconstruction of Radiographs

George Mitsiadis[†] and Anastasios Venetsanopoulos[‡]

[†]Department of Computer Science, University of Toronto
[‡]Department of Electrical Engineering, University of Toronto
Toronto, Canada

ABSTRACT

In this paper a recent approach for the digital restoration of radiographs is presented. A signal processing model for the radiologic process is introduced and the optimal filter, in the minimum mean square error sense, to retrieve depth information is derived by considering the contribution from the other layers of the exposed object as additive noise. The performance of this method is demonstrated with simulated radiographs.

1. Introduction

Conventional radiographs are two-dimensional displays of three-dimensional objects. The X-ray image on the film plane is formed by a superposition of the images from the individual layers of the exposed object.

The main features of the radiologic process are the following :

1) The X-ray source, the focal spot, emits radiation which penetrates the objects and, therefore, information from all the layers is displayed.
2) The size of the focal spot is not infinitesimal and, thus, contributes to the *penumbra effect* ;
3) The whole process is non-linear following an exponential law.

The problem of X-ray image enhancement for a layer located at a specific depth of the exposed object was addressed in [1,2]. A linear model of the radiologic model was introduced, which took advantage of the penumbra effect. In [3] an extended model was introduced, which took into account the divergence of the X-ray beam.

In this paper, the application of the optimal filter, in the minimum mean square error sense (Wiener), to extract depth information from a single radiograph is described.

2. Description of the Radiologic Model

The radiologic process is characterized, in general, by the following quantities :

(a) The focal spot X-ray intensity distribution ;
(b) the absorption coefficient function of the exposed body, and
(c) the received image on the film plane.

The focal spot has finite dimensions and, therefore, there is an associated spatial intensity distribution. This is usually modelled by a Gaussian or a twin-peaked Gaussian distribution.

Let $i_0(x_0, y_0; x, y)$ denote the X-ray intensity distribution of the focal spot, where x_0, y_0 are the coordinates on the focal-spot plane ; and let $\mu'(x_s, y_s, z)$ be the absorption coefficient of the exposed body at depth z measured from the focal spot with x_s, y_s being the coordinates on the *sth* layer (see figure 1). Finally let $i'(x, y)$ be the X-ray intensity of the received image at the point (x, y) on the film plane. Then, the equation that governs the system is given by [1] :

$$i'(x, y) = \iint_D i_0(x_0, y_0; x, y)\, e^{-\int_L \mu'(x_s, y_s, z)\, dl}\, dx_0\, dy_0 \tag{1}$$

where D is the focal spot area, L is the straight line connecting the points (x_0, y_0) and (x, y), and dl is the differential length along this line at the point (x_s, y_s).

The system described by (1) is non-linear and space-varying. The analysis of the radiologic process will be carried out in this paper based upon the following assumptions [1,2] :

1) The focal spot plane and the film plane are assumed parallel.

$$i_0(x_0, y_0; x, y) = i_0(x_0, y_0)$$

2) The variations of μ' around its mean value $\bar{\mu}$ are small.

$$\mu'(x_s, y_s, z) = \bar{\mu} - \mu(x_s, y_s, z)$$

where $\bar{\mu}$ is the mean value and $\mu(\cdot)$ is the variation around the mean.

3) The dimensions of the film are much smaller than the distance between the focal spot and the film plane.

The first of these assumptions renders the system spatially invariant, while 2) and 3) permit the linearization of the exponential factor of (1), thus, yielding :

$$i'(x, y) = e^{-\bar{\mu} d} \left[\bar{i} + i(x, y) \right] \tag{2}$$

where

$$\bar{i} = \iint_D i_0(x_0, y_0)\, dx_0\, dy_0 \qquad (2a)$$

is a constant independent of $\mu(\cdot)$ and

$$i(x,y) = \int_0^l \iint_D i_0(x_0, y_0)\, \mu(x_s, y_s, z)\, dx_0\, dy_0\, dz \qquad (3)$$

The term described by (2a) is the mean value of the image, $\bar{i}$, and can be subtracted before processing. (3) expresses the variations of $i'(\cdot)$ around $\bar{i}$.

Figure 1 shows the coordinates in the space-invariant model.

Equation (3), which amounts to a linearization of (1) can be transformed in the frequency domain. The two-dimensional Fourier transform of (3) is given by :

$$I(f_x, f_y) = \int_0^d \left(\frac{d}{z}\right)^2 I_0\left[\frac{z-d}{z} f_x, \frac{z-d}{z} f_y\right] M\left[\frac{d}{z} f_x, \frac{d}{z} f_y, z\right] dz \qquad (4)$$

where (f_x, f_y) is the spatial frequency pair and the capital letters denote the two-dimensional Fourier transforms of the respective quantities in (3).

For the particular case of the image of a very thin layer of the exposed body located at depth z_s and thickness Δz, (4) can be approximated by :

$$I_s(f_x, f_y) = (\Delta z)\left[\frac{d}{z_s}\right]^2 I_0\left[\frac{z_s-d}{z_s} f_x, \frac{z_s-d}{z_s} f_y\right] \cdot M\left[\frac{d}{z_s} f_x, \frac{d}{z_s} f_y, z\right] \qquad (5)$$

Since the image $i(x,y)$ is the superposition of the images $i_s(x,y)$ of the various layers, it is clear that

$$i(x,y) = \sum_{s=1}^{N} i_s(x,y)$$

where N is the number of layers. From this equation the equivalent model of the radiologic system can be obtained. This model is shown in figure 2 . In this model C_s is a nonlinear transformation caused by the divergence of the X-ray beam, such that :

$$C_s\left[\mu(x, y, z_s)\right] = \mu\left[\frac{z_s}{d} x, \frac{z_s}{d} y, z_s\right]$$

$u_s(\cdot)$ is the output of this transformation and the filters H_s, are uniquely determined by the focal-spot intensity distribution and the corresponding depth with transfer function given by :

$$H_s(f_x, f_y) = (\Delta z)\, I_0\left[\frac{d-z_s}{z_s} f_x, \frac{d-z_s}{z_s} f_y\right]$$

The outputs of these filters are combined to give $i(x,y)$.

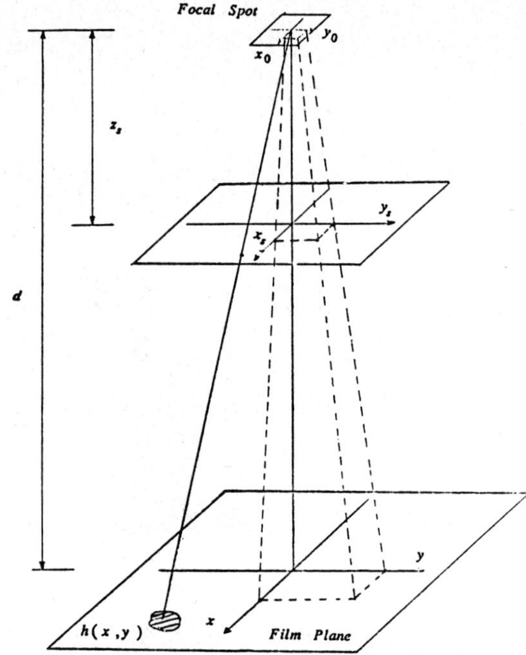

Figure 1

3. Tomographic Filters

The problem of digital restoration of radiographs can be formulated as follows: Given a single X-ray image $i(x,y)$ design a filter whose transfer function is $V_s(f_x, f_y)$ such that the output image approximates the image $u_s(x,y)$ of the layer located at depth z_s .

Our approach to retrieve depth information is the following : We make the best estimate, in the mean square error sense, of the image i_s , and then obtain an estimate for u_s of figure 2 by inverse filtering [4]. This is equivalent to finding a filter $V_s(\cdot)$ such that :

$$E[u_s(x,y) - \hat{u}_s(x,y)]^2 = \text{minimum}$$

where $\hat{u}(\cdot)$, is the estimate of the desired signal and E denotes the expected value operator.

The optimal filter for i_s is given by [5] :

$$W_s(f_x, f_y) = \frac{S_{i_s i}(f_x, f_y)}{S_{ii}(f_x, f_y)}$$

where $S_{ii}(\cdot)$ and $S_{i_s i}(\cdot)$ denote the autocorrelation of the image and the cross-correlation of the radiograph and the desired image respectively. Therefore, the optimal filter for $u_s(\cdot)$ is given by :

$$V_s(f_x, f_y) = W_s(f_x, f_y) \cdot H_s^{-1}(f_x, f_y) \qquad (6)$$

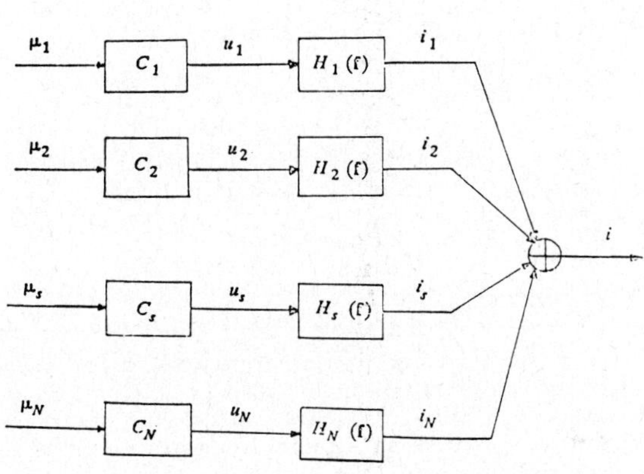

$$u_s = C_s\left[\mu_s(x,y,z_s)\right] = \mu_s\left[\frac{d}{z_s}x, \frac{d}{z_s}y, z_s\right]$$

Signal Processing Model of the Radiologic Process.

Figure 2

The calculation of the correlation function was performed under the assumption that the statistics of the exposed object are wide-sense stationary and its layers are not correlated. Thus, defining :

$$R_{\mu\mu}(x,y,z_1,z_2) = E[\mu(x'+x,y'+y,z_1)\cdot\mu(x',y',z_2)]$$

the autocorrelation of $\mu(\cdot)$, the following relation is satisfied :

$$R_{\mu\mu}(x,y,z_1,z_2) = R_p(x,y)\cdot\delta(z_1-z_2)$$

where $R_p(\cdot)$ is the autocorrelation of the object with respect to the variables x and y and $\delta(\cdot)$ denotes Dirac's delta function.

Under the foregoing assumptions, calculation of the power spectral density of the X-ray image gives [3] :

$$S_{ii}(f_x,f_y) = \int_0^d \left| I_0\left[\frac{z-d}{z}f_x, \frac{z-d}{z}f_y\right]\right|^2 \cdot S_p\left[\frac{d}{z}f_x, \frac{d}{z}f_y\right]\left[\frac{d}{z}\right]^2 dz$$

where $S_p(\cdot)$ is the two-dimensional Fourier transform of $R_p(\cdot)$.

Similarly, the following expression for the cross-spectral density can be obtained :

$$S_{i_s i}(f_x,f_y) = (\Delta z)\left| I_0\left[\frac{z_s-d}{z_s}f_x, \frac{z_s-d}{z_s}f_y\right]\right|^2 \cdot S_p\left[\frac{d}{z_s}f_x, \frac{d}{z_s}f_y\right]\left[\frac{d}{z_s}\right]^2$$

Therefore, the optimal filter is given by :

$$V_s(\mathbf{f}) = \frac{I_0^*\left[\frac{z_s-d}{z_s}\mathbf{f}\right] S_p\left[\frac{d}{z_s}\mathbf{f}\right]\left[\frac{d}{z_s}\right]^2}{\int_0^d \left|I_0\left[\frac{z-d}{z}\mathbf{f}\right]\right|^2 S_p\left[\frac{d}{z}\mathbf{f}\right]\left[\frac{d}{z}\right]^2 dz} \qquad (7)$$

where,for brevity,we have used $\mathbf{f} \triangleq [f_x\ f_y]^T$ and $*$ signifies complex conjugation.

An interesting observation can be made regarding the previous equation. If the focal spot is assumed to be a point source, then $I_0(f_x,f_y) = 1$ for all (f_x,f_y), and the optimal filter is reduced to :

$$V_s(\mathbf{f}) = \frac{S_p\left[\frac{d}{z_s}\mathbf{f}\right]\left[\frac{d}{z_s}\right]^2}{\int_0^d S_p\left[\frac{d}{z_s}\mathbf{f}\right]\left[\frac{d}{z}\right]^2 dz} \qquad (8)$$

Since the numerator of (8) is depth dependent, an optimal restoring filter can be determined, even though the focal spot intensity distribution is an impulse. This fact can be attributed to the divergence of the X-rays or in terms of the system model presented here to the nonlinear transformation C_s of figure 3. Note that this phenomenon can not be obtained on the basis of previous models [1,2], which were deterministic.

Expressions (7) and (8) can be calculated analytically in certain cases. When the focal spot has a Gaussian distribution and the exposed object is not correlated (i.e. it is a white noise process), the following transfer function of the filter for depth z_s can be obtained :

$$V_s(f) = A\cdot f\,\exp\left\{-2\pi^2\sigma^2\left[\frac{d-z_s}{z_s}\right]^2 f^2\right\} \qquad (9)$$

where $f = \sqrt{f_x^2+f_y^2}$ and σ is the parameter of the Gaussian distribution. Figure 3 depicts the normalized transfer function $V_s(f)$ for $\eta = \frac{z_s}{d} = \{0.3, 0.4, 0.5, 0.6, 0.7\}$.

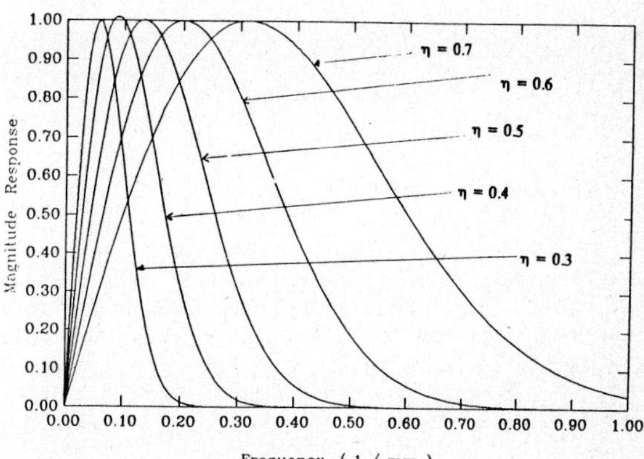

Wiener Filter for a White Noise Process

Figure 3

In contrast, the inverse filter is high-pass with transfer function [1,2] :

$$J_s(f) = B \cdot \exp\left\{2\pi^2\sigma^2\left[\frac{d - z_s}{z_s}\right]^2 f^2\right\} \qquad (10)$$

This filter restores the image $i_s(x, y)$ from its blur, but ignores the contribution of the other layers and has the disadvantage of enhancing high frequency noise.

Similarly, if the exposed object is modelled as a second order Markov process, possessing circular symmetry and power spectral density given by :

$$S_p(f) = \frac{6\pi\beta^3}{\left[4\pi^2 f^2 + \beta^2\right]^{5/2}}$$

and the focal spot is assumed to be a point source, then, the calculation of the transfer function of the optimal filter yields [3] :

$$V_s(f) = \frac{A\, f\left\{8\pi^2 f^2 + 2\beta^2 + \pi f\sqrt{\beta^2 + 4\pi^2 f^2}\right\}}{\left\{4\pi^2\left[\frac{d}{z_s}\right]^2 f^2 + \beta^2\right\}^{5/2}} \qquad (11)$$

where β is the parameter of the Markov process.

Figure 4 shows a family of curves derived from (11) for $\eta = \frac{z}{d} = \{0.4, 0.5, 0.6, 0.7\}$.

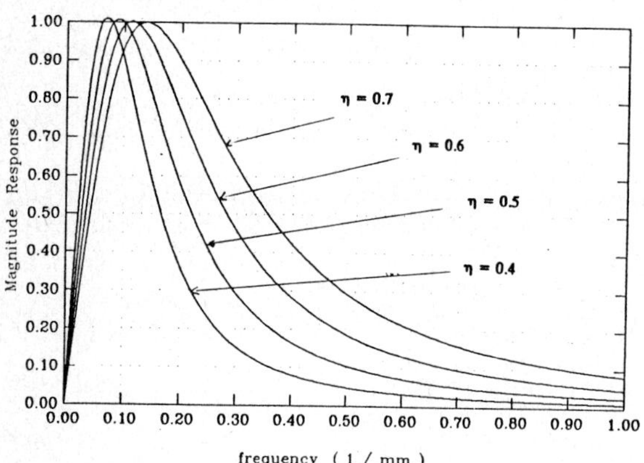

Wiener Filter for a Markov Process

Figure 4

It should be emphasized that (11) has no counterpart corresponding to the inverse filter, because the focal spot was assumed to consist of a single point.

4. Simulation Results

To demonstrate the performance of the optimal filter a number of simulations were performed. Figure 5 depicts a simulated phantom consisting of an "X" and a "+" of approximately equal size located at respective depths $z_1 = 300mm$ and $z_2 = 700mm$ measured from the focal spot. The focal spot to film distance was $1m = 1000mm$. The X-ray intensity distribution was Gaussian with $\sigma = 2$.

$$i_0(x_0, y_0) = \frac{1}{2\pi\sigma^2} \cdot \exp\left[-\frac{x_0^2 + y_0^2}{2\sigma^2}\right]$$

A Hamming window [6] was applied to the image of figure 5, to reduce the effect of the edges. Figure 6 is the result after processing the windowed image with the filter of equation (11).

5. Conclusions

The optimal, in the mean square error sense, filter for information extraction from a specific layer located at a given depth of an exposed object has been presented. The problem was formulated as signal extraction from noisy data. The observation that a filter can be determined even when the focal spot is a point source facilitates its design. The simulations have demonstrated that it performs better than previously published techniques.

6. References

[1] **J. Costa, A.N. Venetsanopoulos, M. Trefler,** "Digital Tomographic Filtering of Radiographs." *IEEE Trans. Med. Imaging*, vol. 2, pp. 76-88, June 1983.

[2] **J. Costa, A.N. Venetsanopoulos, M. Trefler,** "Design and Implementation of Digital Tomographic Filters." *IEEE Trans. Med. Imaging*, vol. 2, pp.89-100, June 1983.

[3] **G. Mitsiadis,** "Optimal Filters for Radiographs", M.A.Sc Thesis, Dept. of Elec. Engin., Univ. of Toronto, 1983.

[4] **Lim, J.S.,** "Image Restoration by Short Space Spectral Subtraction." *IEEE Trans. on Acoustics Speech and Signal Processing*, vol. 28, pp. 191-197, April 1980.

[5] **Papoulis, A.,** "*Signal Analysis*", McGraw Hill, 1977.

[6] **F.J. Harris,** "On the Use of Windows for Harmonic Analysis with the Discrete Fourier Transform." *Proc. IEEE*, vol. 66, pp. 51-83, January 1978.

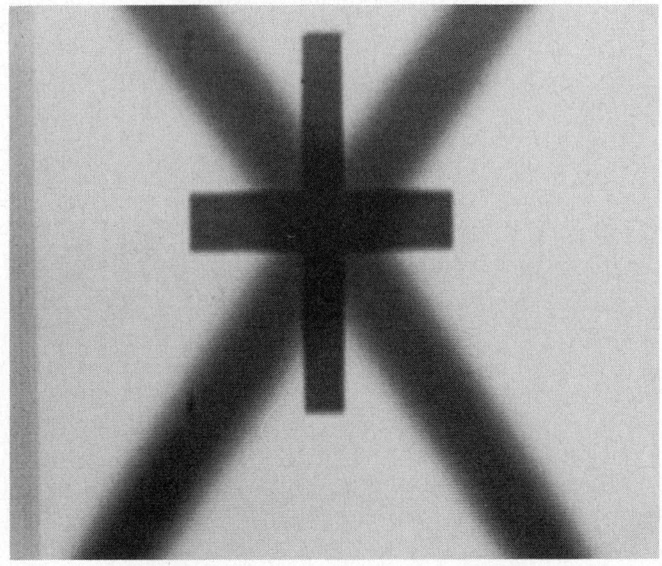

Figure 5 : Original Image

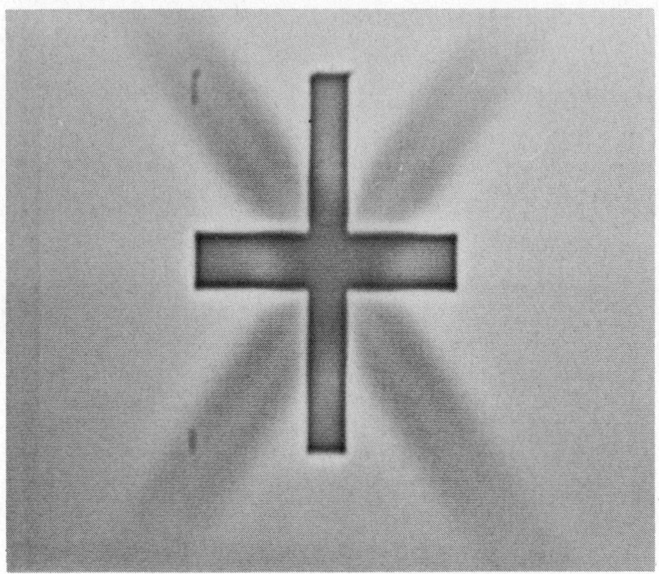

Figure 6 : Output of the Optimal Filter

DIGITAL TECHNIQUES in Simulation, Communication and Control
Spyros G. Tzafestas (editor)
Elsevier Science Publishers B.V. (North-Holland) © IMACS, 1985

A DISTRIBUTED MICROPROCESSOR BASED DATA COMPRESSION SYSTEM USING FAST WALSH TRANSFORM

G.P.Frangakis

Computers Department
N.R.C."DEMOCRITOS"
Aghia Paraskevi Attikis
Athens - GREECE

G.Papakonstantinou

Nat.Techn.Univ.of Athens
Electrical Eng. Dept.,
Computer Science Div.,
Athens 15773 - GREECE

A distributed microcomputer system which implements a data compression and transmission system, using Fast Walsh Transform is presented. This configuration increases the accuracy and the speed of operation.
The system was tested using real ECG waveforms.

1. INTRODUCTION

In communications, biomedical signal processing systems, etc., a large amount of input data must be processed and transmitted.

Many methods and algorithms have been proposed to perform data compression operations [1]. One of the methods for data compression consists of encoding the input digital signal by means of a linear orthogonal transformation. A well known transformation of this type is the Walsh-Hadamard transform.
Microprocessor (μP) based systems can be used for the implementation of such transformation algorithms, since they have great flexibility and can replace hardwired circuits, increasing the capability and lowering the cost. On the other hand, the speed of operation is not so high while the accuracy is low. To overcome these disadvantages, parallel or distributed processing can be applied, especially in real-time applications.

In this paper, a real-time compression system for Electrocardiogram signals (ECG's), using Walsh functions for the transformation, and its implementation using distributed microcomputers (μC's), working in parallel, is proposed.

2. THE WALSH TRANSFORM

The Walsh functions constitute a family of binary orthogonal functions $W(k,t)$, $k=0,1,\dots,n-1$ $n=2^m$ in the interval $t \in [0,1)$.

There are several types of ordering for the Walsh functions, but in digital signal processing applications, the sequency-ordered Walsh functions (Fig.1) are the most usual. The Walsh functions can be generated by hardware [2] or software means.

A continuous-time signal $x(t)$, which is absolutely integrable in the time interval $[0,1)$, has the Walsh series expansion:

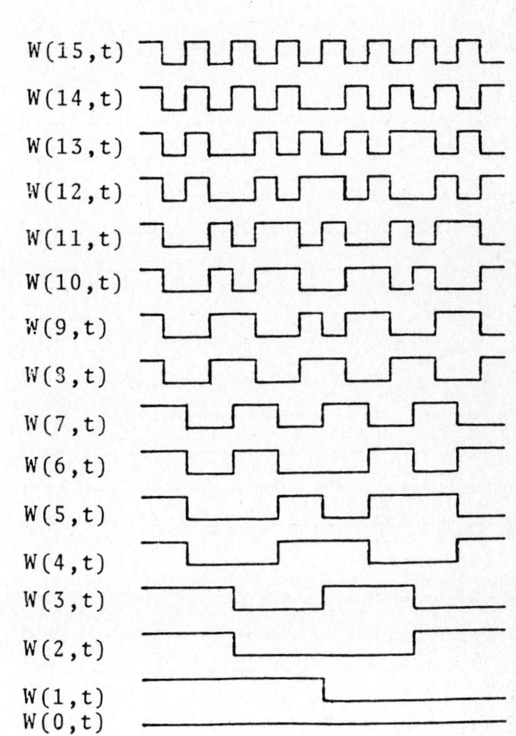

Fig.1. Walsh Functions in sequency order

$$x(t) = \sum_{n=0}^{\infty} a_n W(n,t) \tag{1}$$

where a_n is the coefficient of Walsh function $W(n,t)$, and can be determined by

$$a_n = \int_0^1 x(t)W(n,t)dt \tag{2}$$

Equations (1) and (2) form the "Walsh Transform pair". For digital applications, in discrete time, eqn.(2) can be approximated as:

$$a_n = \frac{1}{N} \sum_{i=0}^{n-1} x(i)W(n,i) \ , \quad n=0,1,2,..,N-1 \qquad (3)$$

while the related inverse Walsh transform, is:

$$x(i) = \sum_{n=0}^{N-1} a_n W(n,i) \ , \quad i=0,1,2,\ldots,N-1 \qquad (4)$$

A direct computation of the Walsh transform, given by eqn (3), requires N^2 operations. A number of algorithms have been developed that can compute a N-point Walsh transform in $N\log_2 N$ rather than N^2 operations. The flow diagram of such a Fast Walsh Transform (FWT) algorithm is shown in Fig.2, with normal input and sequency ordered output [3]. This algorithm offers, in certain applications, considerable advantages and carrying out in-place computation, it requires about half the memory of other algorithms.

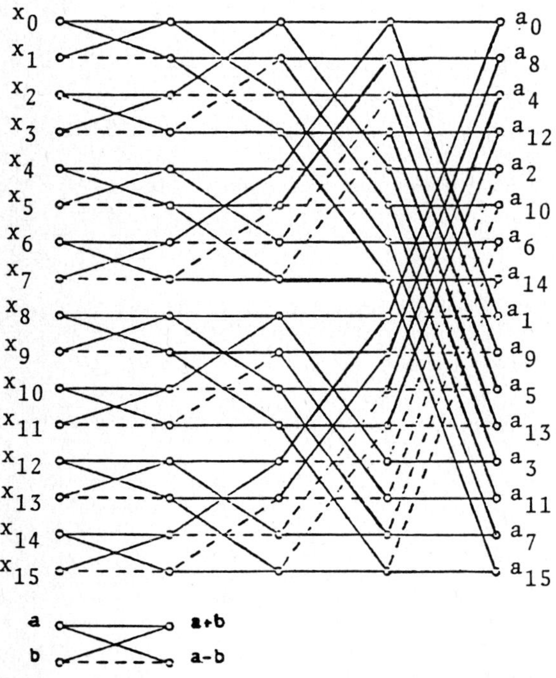

Fig.2. Flow graph of FWT. The input data is in normal order. The Walsh Coefficients are in bit-reserved sequency order.

It has also been shown [4] [5] that only a set of M most dominant terms (in absolute value order) among the complete set of N terms (M<N), is sufficient for synthesizing a waveform if reasonable errors can be accepted, and in this sense a data-compression scheme can be achieved.

The block diagram of a data compression-transmission and retrieval system for Electrocardiogram input signal (ECG), which uses the algorithm of Fig.2 for the FWTransformation, selects and transmits the M-dominant terms rather than N terms, is shown in Fig.3.

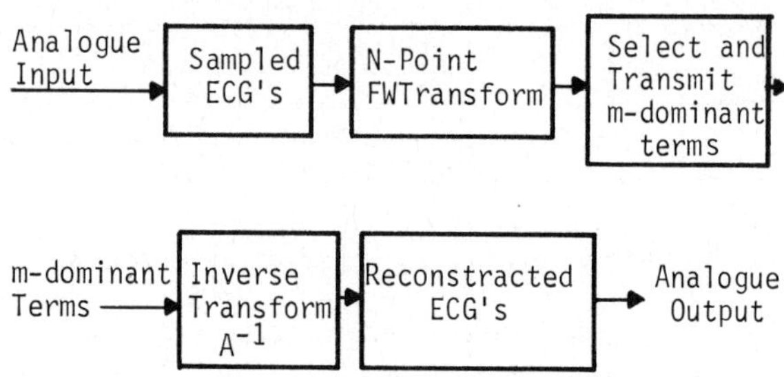

Fig.3. A data compression-transmission and retrieval system.

3. SYSTEM IMPLEMENTATION

For the implementation of the transmitter section of Fig.3, a distributed μP system using two μC's working in parallel was used (Fig.4). It functions as follows:

At the beginning the μC-1 samples and converts into digital form the first group (in our case 64 points) of the input points. At the end of this sampling period, it informs the μC-2 to start sampling the next input points of the second group while μC-1 continuous with the application of FWT for the determination of the Walsh coefficients, the calculation of the most dominant terms and the transmition of them. When the sampling by μC-2 is completed, the μC-1 is informed by the μC-2 to continue with the sampling of the 3rd group while μC-2 determines the Walsh coefficients of the already obtained points, calculates the most dominant terms and transmits them. This changing of roles between μC-1 and μC-2 is continued, until all the input points have been processed.

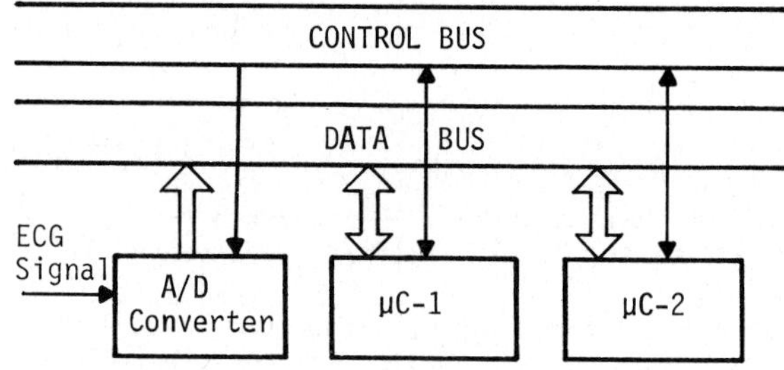

Fig.4. Block diagram of the system

In Fig.5, the timing function of the operation of μC-1 and μC-2 is given.

The reconstruction of the original signal at the

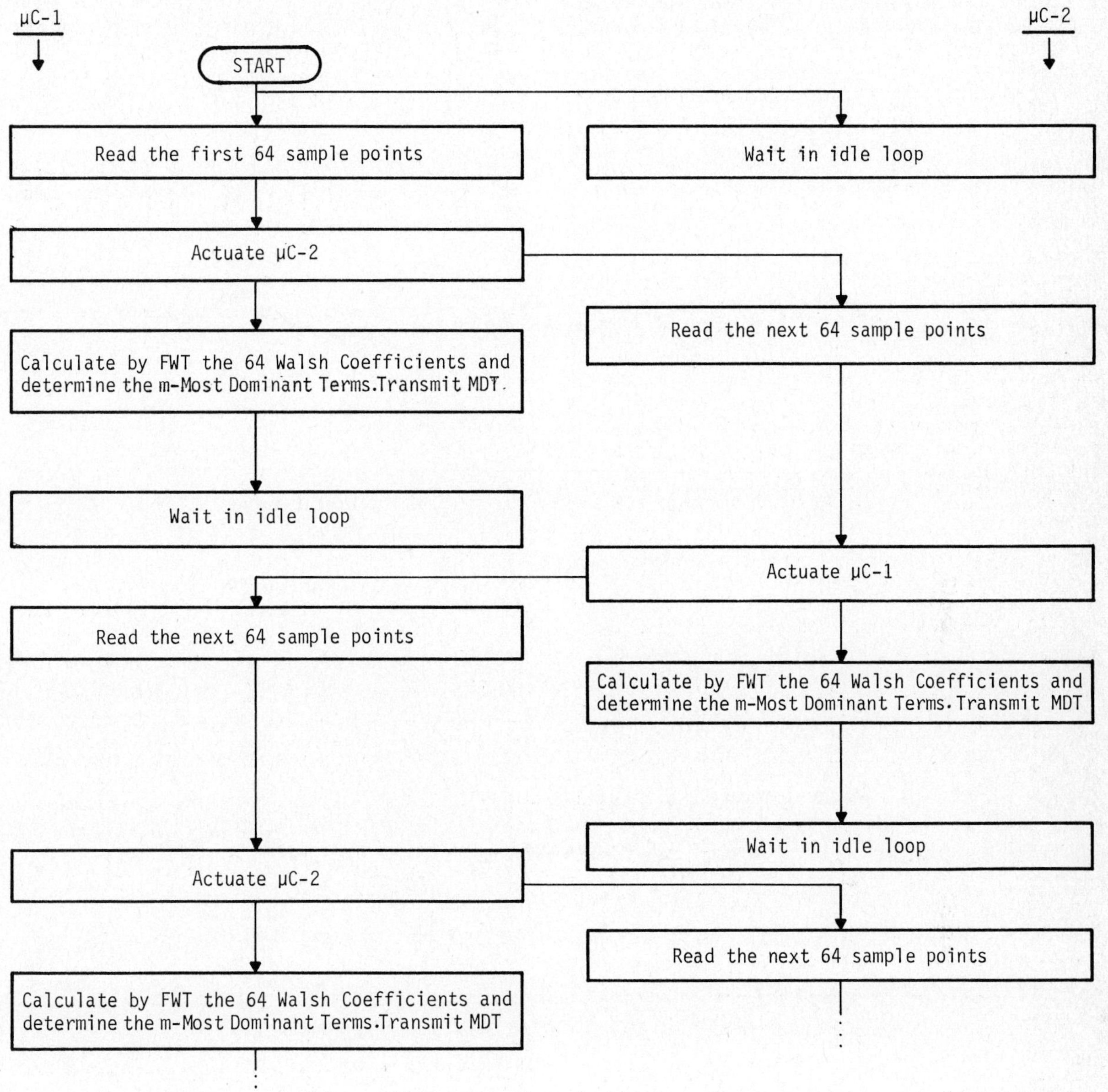

Fig.5. Timing diagram of the system

receiver section applying the reverse fast Walsh transform, can be accomplished by hardware [6] or software methods.

The analogue ECG input signal was obtained by the Hittman CDC-70 system, while the SDM-853 Burr-Brown data aquisition module was used for the convertion of this analogue signal into digital form.

Each μC is based on the 8080A μP, and the required memory was about 3K-ROM and 0.5K-RAM memory for each μC.

The sampling rate which can be achieved by the system was at least 500 samples/sec, without optimization.

In Figs 6 and 7 the reconstructed ECG signal is shown on the original signal, using 8 and 16 most dominant terms.

We can see that the reconstruction is not so accurate in the QRS complex but this is not so important in the case of arrythmia analysis in contrast to the complete analysis of the ECG, where accurate measurements are required.

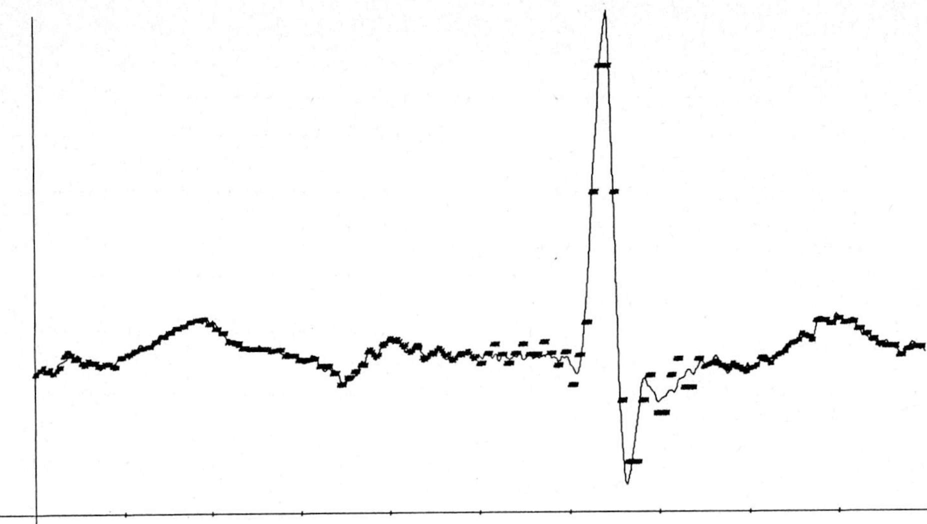

Fig.6. Reconstruction of ECG signal, using 8 most dominant terms

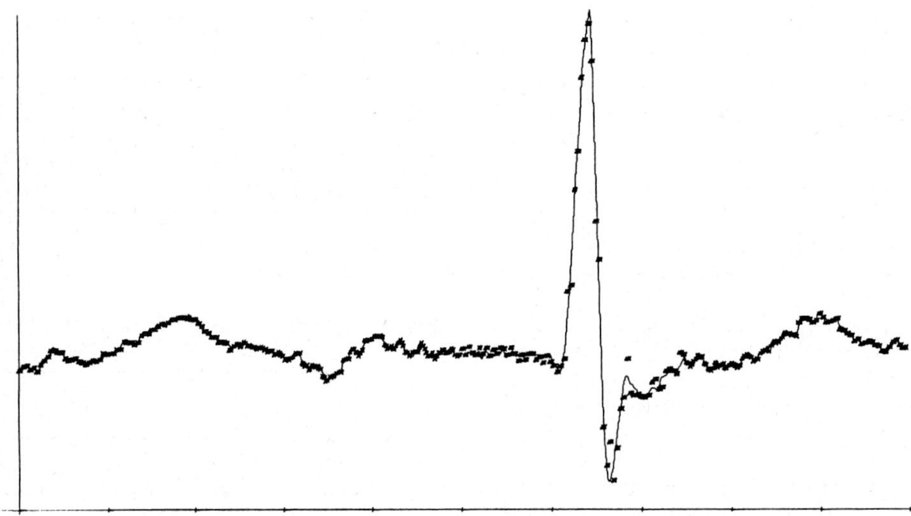

Fig.7. Reconstruction of ECG signal, using 16 most dominant terms

The "quickshort" algorithm, for sorting the Walsh coefficients can be used which is very fast. The system can be easily extended by using more μC's. Additional data compression can also be achieved by using a limited number of bits in order to represent the Walsh coefficients [7].

REFERENCES

[1] Benelli,G.,Cappellini,V.,and Lotti,F.,Data compression techniques and applications, The Radio and Electr.Eng.,50 (1980) 29-53.

[2] Tzafestas,S.,Frangakis,G.,and Pimenidis,T., Global Walsh function generators, Electronic Engineering,(1976) 45-49.

[3] Larsen,H., An algorithm to compute the sequency ordered Walsh transform,IEEE Trans. Acoust.,Speech & Signal Proc.,24(1976) 335-336.

[4] Kitai,R.,Synthesis of Periodic sinusoids from Walsh waves, IEEE Trans.on Instr. and Measur.,IM24(1975) 313-317.

[5] Brown,W.O.,and Elliott,A.R.,IEEE Proc.Symp. Applications of Walsh funstions,Washington, D.C.,AD744650.

[6] Tzafestas,S.,Frangakis,G., A fast Walsh Hadamard signal processing system, Mathematics and Computers in Simulation XXIII (1981) 163-169.

[7] Kuklinski,W.S., Fast Walsh transform data-compression algorithm:e.c.g. applications, Med.& Biol.Eng.& Comput., 21 (1983) 465-472.

DIGITAL TECHNIQUES in Simulation, Communication and Control
Spyros G. Tzafestas (editor)
Elsevier Science Publishers B.V. (North-Holland) © IMACS, 1985

SYNTHESIS OF GREEK VOWELS USING AN IMPROVED FORMANT-SYNTHESIZER AND REDUCED MEMORY

N. Yiourgalis, G. Kokkinakis

Laboratory of Wire Communications, School of Engineering
University of Patras, Patras, Greece

As a first step towards synthesizing Greek speech with formant coded speech segments, the Greek vowels have been synthesized, using a software cascade/parallel formant synthesizer given by Dennis Klatt[2]. In order to get a more acceptable speech quality, two improvements have been introduced to the synthesizer:

i. A polynomial has been used as a shaping filter for the simulation of the glottal excitation waveform
ii. Two different values have been used for the first formant, corresponding to the cases the glottis is open and closed during a period.

Acoustic tests with listeners have proved the improvement of the speech segments quality. Another main concern has been the reduction of the necessary memory for the parameter storage. To this end, a special algorithm has been used, which has drastically reduced the memory.
As the results up to now are very encouraging, the work is continued with the goal to code all 134 speech segments, with which Greek speech can be synthesized.

I. INTRODUCTION

In a previous project, computer text-to-speech synthesis of the Greek language has been achieved by using 134 elementary speech segments extracted from natural speech and standardized appropriately. The speech segments which represent single vowels (V) and combinations of consonants and vowels (CV,CCV,etc), are LP-coded and stored in files. The text to be converted to speech is segmented by a program, in characters corresponding to speech segments. Then, these segments are called from the memory and concatenated in such a way that an acceptable speech quality is produced[1].

In a project under way now, we are proceeding to produce the 134 elementary speech segments and synthesize speech with these segments, using an improved version of the cascade/parallel formant synthesizer given by Dennis Klatt[2]. With formant synthesis and the cascade/parallel synthesizer which combines the advantages of both kinds of synthesizers, we hope that speech quality will be highly improved while the memory needed for segment storage will be substantially reduced. The results achieved up to now with the synthesis of the Greek vowels |a|,|e|,|i|,|o|,|u| which are presented here, have justified our hopes.

The synthesizer of Dennis Klatt is shown in (Fig. 1) with continuous lines. The upper part includes an impulse generator for pitch simulation, a LP-filter (FGP), two types of pulse shaping filters (an antiresonator FGZ, to simulate a particular glottal waveform, and a LP-filter FGS, to produce a quasi-sinusoidal waveform), two types of glottal waveform sample amplitudes (AV,AVS) and the cascaded resonators (F1,F2,...etc). The lower part includes a random number generator as noise source, a LP-filter, two types of amplitudes (AH,AF) and the resonators in parallel.The upper path with source AV (Amplitude of Voicing) and the cascaded resonators is used for the simulation of vowels, nasals and sonorant consonants (glides, semivowels). To produce the remaining voiced consonants the output of the AVS (quasi-sinusoidal voicing source) is sent through the cascade vocal tract model and the noise source excites the parallel branch. The unvoiced consonants (fricatives, affricates etc.) are produced using the noise source and the resonators in parallel. Aspiration (letter h) is produced by the noice source and the cascaded resonators.

This synthesizer has been modified in two points in order to meet the goal for improved speech quality (dashed-lines in Fig.1):

a. The glottal waveform in the upper voicing path is replaced with a pulse shape which according to experiments carried out by Rosenberg, ranks the highest scores in synthetic speech quality[3]. Furthermore, the slope of this waveform is made dependent on intensity values, to simulate the dependence of glottal pulse shape on vocal effort.
b. Two different frequency values for the first formant are introduced to simulate the effect produced by the glottis when it is open and closed.

The goal of reducing memory has been approached as follows:

For the production of any speech segment a number of parameters particular to each segment are used. The latter include some time varying parameters. In a storage scheme where memory size does not play a significant role, as in the Dennis Klatt paper, all parameters values are stored separately for each segment and then expanded by a program to cover the whole segment

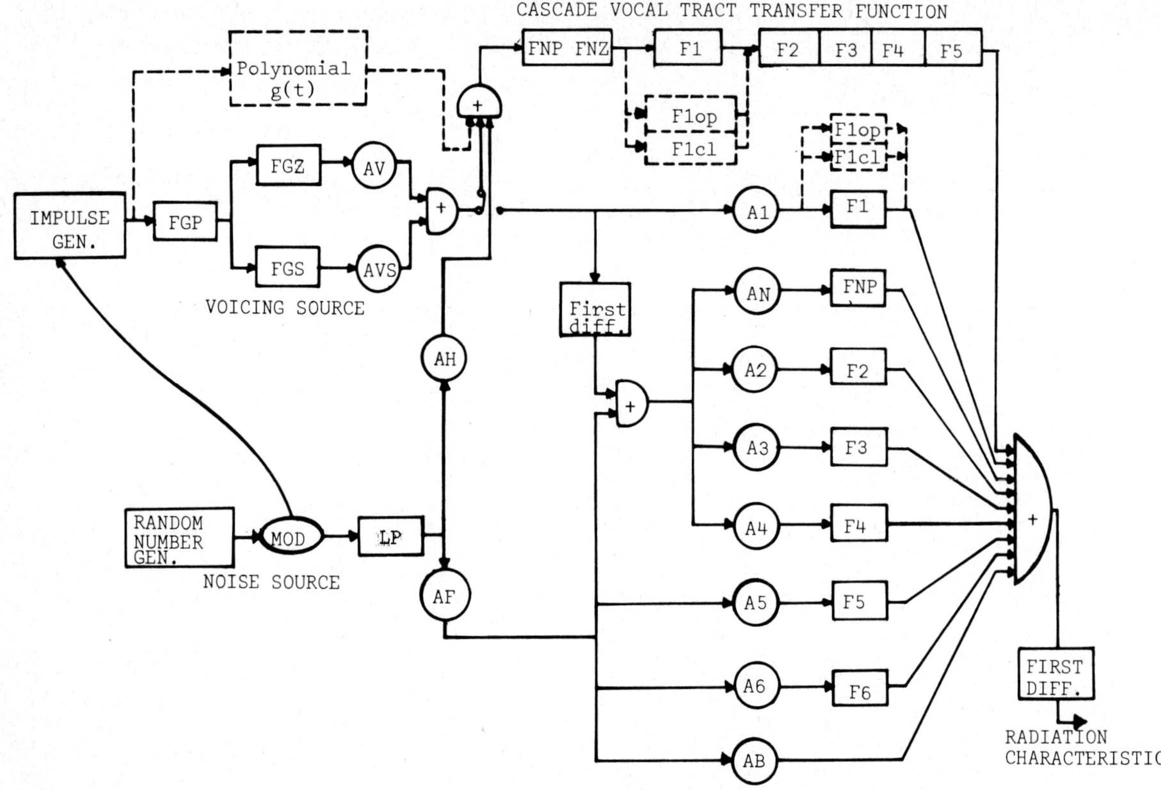

FIG. 1. Block diagram of the cascade/parallel formant synthesizer. Digital resonators are indicated by the prefix F and amplitude controls by the prefix A.

duration.

In the memory reducing scheme we have used, all common parameters are stored only once, while time varying parameters are calculated when needed from a few stored values and common, to all segments, formulas. This, in combination with the algorithm used to store the above data, has substantially reduced the necessary memory.

In the following sections the mentioned techniques for speech quality improvement and memory reduction are presented in detail.

II. GLOTTAL PULSE SHAPE FOR HIGH QUALITY SPEECH

Figure 2. shows the waveforms produced by the voicing part of the Dennis Klatt synthesizer. The lower path with source AVS and the cascaded resonators gives an almost sinusoidal glottal waveform (Fig.2(a)). It is simulating the case where the vocal folds may vibrate without meeting in the midline as in the case of voiced fricatives. The filtered impulses have a spectrum that falls off smoothly at approximately -24db/octave, i.e. higher harmonics of the voicing source above 50Hz, are significantly reduced and the waveform looks nearly sinusoidal.

The upper path with source AV and the cascaded resonators produces the waveform shown in Fig. 2(b). Certainly this is not the best to use in voiced speech (vowels, nasals etc). Klatt[2] says: "This waveform does not have the same phase spectrum as a typical glottal pulse, nor does it contain spectral zeros[4] of the kind that often appear in natural voicing".

The most important conditions which an acceptable glottal excitation waveform should fulfil are as follows[3]:

a. It should not have very small opening or closing times
b. Examination of source spectra of natural speech has shown that decays of the order of -12db/octave are typical. Thus a good

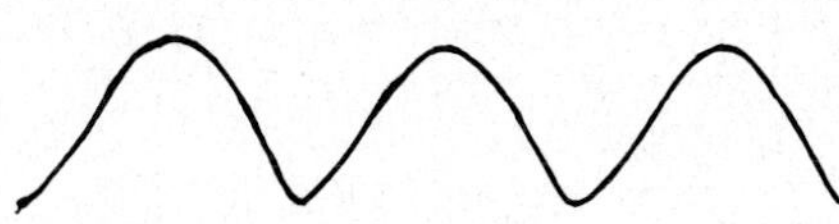

(a) SMOOTHED VOICING WAVEFORM

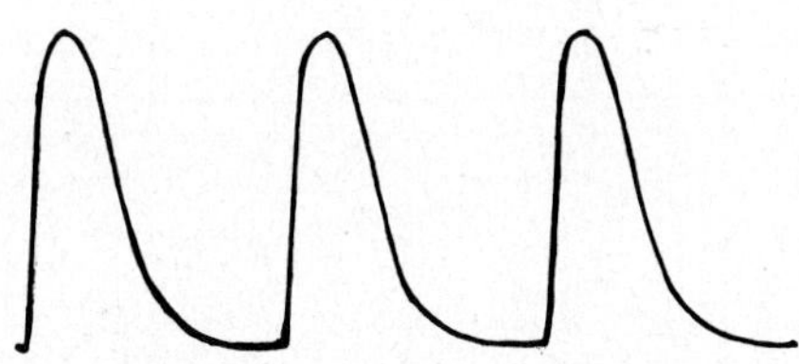

(b) NORMAL VOICING WAVEFORM

FIG. 2. Three periods from the synthetic waveforms of (a) quasi-sinusoidal voicing and (b) normal voicing.

glottal waveform should have a single slope discontinuity at closure

c. In natural source excitation, dips are non-existent. Such dips are associated with complex zeros of the Laplace transform of the source pulses, that is the complex frequencies $s=\sigma+j\omega$, for which the source's Laplace transform G(s) is equal to zero. For small σ, the dips in the spectrum are quite sharp. Since the speech spectrum is the product of source spectrum with vocal-tract spectrum, it is possible that this sharp minimum due to a source zero, cancels a maximum due to a vocal-tract formant. Hence the speech output will be altered.
Thus a good glottal waveform should avoid symmetric shapes which produce pronounced spectral dips. This is so, since symmetric pulses have zeros lying on the jω axis, i.e. zero value of σ.

d. Zeros of glottal waveforms should show approximately uniform frequent spacing, particularly at high frequency[4].
A pulse shape satisfying all four conditions mentioned above is shown in Fig. 3. This is used as the upper voicing excitation waveform (Fig.1 dushed lines) in our version of Klatt's synthesizer.

This waveform has been simulated using the following simple polynomial:

$$g(t) = (AV)\left[3\left(\frac{t}{T_p}\right)^2 - 2\left(\frac{t}{T_p}\right)^3\right] \qquad 0<t\leq T_p$$

$$g(t) = (AV)\left[1-\left(\frac{t-T_p}{T_N}\right)^2\right] \qquad T_p\leq t<T_p+T_N$$

The period T of the glottal excitation wave is given by

$$T = \frac{f_o}{F_o}$$

Where f_o the sampling rate of the speech waveform
F_o the fundamental frequency of the speech produced

To satisfy condition (a) the following times have been experimentally defined[3]:

Opening time: $T_p = 0.4T$
Closing time: $T_N = 0.16T$

Every 0.1 ms, a new value of g(t) is calculated and inputed to the cascade resonators of the synthesizer (Fig.1). The AV-Parameter multiplies the function g(t), to simulate the effect of vocal folds effort on the slope at closure of the glottal waveform. The slope at closure increases with increasing AV and vice-versa.

Finally, care has been taken not to use any updated value of AV (all variables are updated every 10 ms), until the end of the glottal period, in order to avoid unwanted clicks at the output.

III. FIRST FORMANT DURING OPEN AND CLOSED GLOTTIS

Formant frequencies depend on the open or closed condition of the glottis. This influences speech quality, especially by the first formant. When the glottis is open, the first formant frequency rises to a value larger than that during closing time[5]. To simulate this, F1 parameter has been split into two parameters: F1op and F1cl (Fig.1 dashed lines). The program decides whether the source excitation sample corresponds to a time smaller than T_p (glottal opening time). If it does, then this sample excites F1op resonator. Otherwise it excites F1cl.

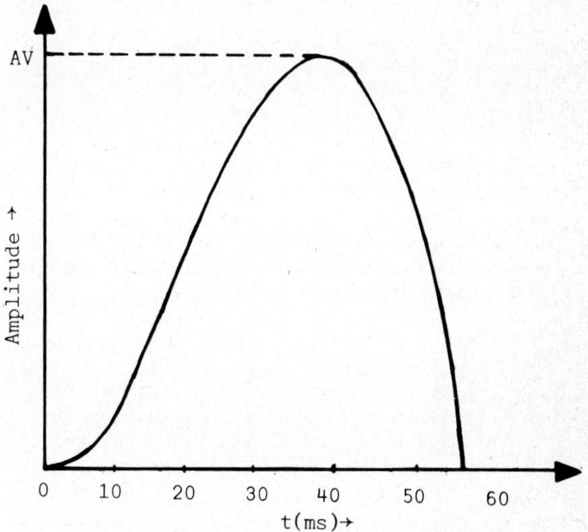

FIG.3. Pulse shape for voicing excitation

IV. EXPERIMENTS AND THEIR RESULTS

The Greek vowels |a|,|e|,|i|,|o|,|u|, have been synthesized in our Lab. using the system shown in Fig.4. It consists of a desktop calculator (HP 9845B) on which the formant synthesizer is simulated, an interface, a D/A converter, a LP-filter and a loudspeaker.

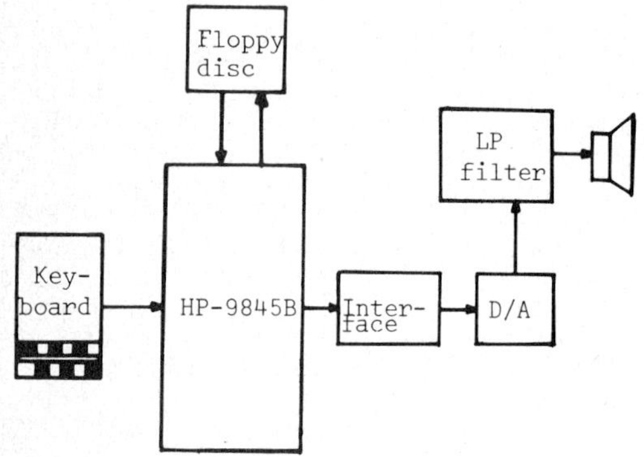

FIG. 4. Block diagram of the system for text-to-speech synthesis.

The parameter values listed in table I.are finally accepted for the synthesis, after consideration of theoretical aspects[2], measurements already performed in other works[6] and long experimentation.

TABLE I. Parameter values for the synthesis of Greek vowels. Amplitude AV and fundamental Fϕ should be given appropriate contours.

Vowel	F1op	F1cl	F2	F3	B1	B2	B3
|a|	860	720	1230	2340	80	75	120
|e|	610	480	1820	2500	65	85	120
|i|	350	270	1900	2800	50	60	140
|o|	660	450	870	2435	95	65	75
|u|	440	300	770	2280	55	65	70

Listening tests performed with many listeners using both Dennis Klatt synthesizer and the modified version previously described, proved that speech quality in the latter case is much better and more than acceptable. Vowels are not only inteligible, but sound also naturally, lacking the characteristic machine quality of synthetic speech.

V. MEMORY REDUCTION ALGORITHM

To reduce the memory needed to store the data used to produce the elementary speech segments, the algorithm given by Dennis Klatt which processes the data and inputs them into the synthesizer should be changed.

TABLE II.* List of control parameters for the software memory reduced formant synthesizer.

CONSTANT** Parameters

Parameter code	Parameter symbol	Name
1	SW	Cascade/parallel switch
2	FGP	Glottal resonator 1 frequen.
3	BGP	Glottal resonator 1 bandwid.
4	B4	Fourth formant bandwidth
5	F5	Fifth formant frequency
6	B5	Fifth formant bandwidth
7	F6	Sixth formant frequency
8	B6	Sixth formant bandwidth
9	BGS	Glottal resonator 2 bandwid.
10	SR	Sampling rate
11	NWS	Number of samples per chunk
12	GO	Overall gain control
13	NFC	Number of cascaded formants

VARIABLE Parameters

Parameter code	Parameter symbol	Name
14	AV	Amplitude of voicing
15	AH	Amplitude of aspiration
16	AF	Amplitude of frication
17	AVS	Amplitude of sinusoidal voic.
18	Fϕ	Fundamental freq. of voicing
19	A2	Second formant amplitude
20	A3	Third formant amplitude
21	A4	Fourth formant amplitude
22	A5	Fifth formant amplitude
23	A6	Sixth formant amplitude
24	AB	Bypass path amplitude
25	BNP	Nasal pole bandwidth
26	BNZ	Nasal zero bandwidth
27	B1	First formant bandwidth
28	B2	Second formant bandwidth
29	B3	Third formant bandwidth
30	F1op	First formant frequ.(open)
31	F1cl	First formant frequ.(closed)
32	F2	Second formant frequency
33	F3	Third formant frequency
34	FNZ	Nasal zero frequency
35	FNP	Nasal pole frequency
36	F4	Fourth formant frequency

* Names as given in reference 2.
** Values for Constant parameters as given in reference 2.

Table II. gives the necessary parameters for the production of any elementary speech segment.

There are 13 constant parameters and 23 variable ones. The former have the same value for all speech segments. There are stored in file no 1, which is common to all segments.

The latter vary from segment to segment. For example F2 parameter has the value 1680 for segment |e| and 1200 for segment |a|. Amongst these 23 variable parameters there are some which have different values every 10 ms (update rate). We call these parameters actual variables. Their values follow a contour depending on the segment. For example, Fϕ varies linearly from 120 to 95 for a vowel.

The memory reduction comes from a reduction of the data which must be stored and from the way these data are stored into RAM. In particular, from the data defining the contour of actual variables only some values are suitably stored, with the aid of which the rest is calculated.

The variables, actual variables and their countours, all representing each particular speech segment, are stored in file no 2. An example of storage is shown in table III.for the segment representing the vowel |e| of duration 160 ms.

TABLE III. Variables and contour of actual variables

|←—— 23 Variables ——→| Actual Variables |
AV AH AF F2 F3 FNP F4 | AV AH Fϕ
0,0,0,0,0,...,1680,2500,...,300,3300,14,15,18,

-1*,0,42,80,42,120,33,0,15,80,15,120,6,0,120,120,95
|← AV Contour →|← AH Contour →|Fϕ Contour|

* -1 is used to separate contours from actual variables. The contour, given above for letter |e|, has been used for the synthesis of the other vowels as well.

There are three storage sections: The first one is given to the 23 variables. The value of each variable is stored in the corresponding place. The second section contains the code numbers of the actual variables of the segment. The third section contains the values of the contours corresponding to the actual variables of the second section. These two sections are separated by the number -1. The values of two adjacent contours are separated by timing comparison. The meaning of the values of a contour is explained on the example of the AV contour: 0,42,80,42,120,33.

From 0 ms to 80 ms the value of AV is 42.
From 90 ms to 120 ms the value of AV is linearly interpolated from 42 to 33 and from 130 to 160 ms the value of AV is zero. This is the value of the AV variable in the first section.

To synthesize a speech segment file no 1 and the corresponding to this segment file no 2 are stuck into an array. (In a future hardware version of the synthesizer, these data would be kept in ROM for permanent storage). From this array using linear interpolation for amplitudes and Fϕ variables and half-cosine interpolation for the rest of the actual variables, their intermediate values are obtained[7]. These are used to calculate the different resonator coefficients and other parameters necessary to simulate the formant-synthesizer. All these interpolated parameters are stored in a 2D matrix, whose number of rows is the number of parameters the synthesizer needs to operate, and number of columus, the number of update frames the particular speech segment needs (Table IV). Hence each column represents the data used to produce 10 ms of speech.

To realize the extent of ROM memory saving, we need 36 bytes for the production of any vowel and 13 bytes for the constant common variables. Hence for the vowels |a|,|e|,|i|,|o|,|u|, a memory of 36x5+13=193 bytes is necessary no matter what their duration is, since only a few values of the contour of variables is needed, leaving the calculation of intermediate values to interpolation. In LPC for a vowel of 256 ms duration, 600 parameters are needed (40 frames covering the whole segment with 15 parameters for a frame). Hence for the 5 vowels 3000 bytes should be stored[1]. Although contiguous frames with the same

TABLE III 2D-Matrix storage of parameters used in synthesis of any phoneme

1	AV						
2	AH						
3	AF	2nd	3rd	→	→		
4	AVS	frame	frame				
5	Fϕ						
6	A2						
7	A3						
8	A4						
9	A5						
10	A6	↓	↓				
11	AB						
12	BNP						
13	BNZ						
14	B1	↓	↓				
15	B2						
16	B3						
17*	F1op	↓	↓		↓		
18	F1op						
19	F1op						
20	F1cl						
21	F1cl	↓	↓				
22	F1cl						
23	F2						
24	F2	↓	↓				
25	F2						
26	F3						
27	F3						
28	F3	↓	↓				
29	FNZ						
30	FNZ						
31	FNZ	↓	↓				
32	FNP						
33	FNP						
34	FNP						
35**	Naflas						
36	F4	F5	F6	FGS			
37	F4	F5	F6	FGS			
38	F4	F5	F6	FGS			
39**	C(47)						
40	FGP						
41	FGP						
42	FGP						

* To simulate a digital resonator, three coefficients are needed[2]

** Names of parameters are those used in ref. 2

values can be grouped, thus reducing the memory, the necessary memory for all 134 segments is still by far larger than in our case.

VI. FURTHER WORK

Our further work being under way concentrates on producing the CV-segments. By concatenating corresponding segments using spectral derivative, segment duration modification and merging of isolated segments, techniques already applied to concatenation of words[8], Greek words will be synthesized. An overall pitch contour is applied to the words in order to produce continous speech[9]. As a first step, segment "ma" has been synthesized using the modified version of the cascade/ parallel synthesizer. The segment concatenation techniques mentioned above are currently examined on the synthetic word "mama".

Aiming at further RAM memory reduction as well (not important in a hardware version though),we are going to update the parameters every 20 ms well within the limits set by Rosenberg[10].

VI. CONCLUSION

Synthesis of the Greek vowels has been performed using a modified cascade/parallel formant synthesizer. The results achieved in speech quality and computer memory reduction are so encouraging that work is continued towards synthesizing consonant-vowel combinations and whole words by concatenating elementary speech segments.

REFERENCES

1. P. Stathopoulou, G. Kokkinakis, A.G. Mian, "Synthesis of Greek Speech with Elementary Speech Segments" International Conference on Inform. Sciences and Systems, University of Patras, Greece, July 1979, Vol.1, p.p. 506-515

2. Dennis H. Klatt, "Software for a Cascade/ Parallel Formant Synthesizer", JASA Vol.67, No 3, March 1980

3. A.E. Rosenberg, "Effect of glottal pulse shape on the quality of natural vowels", JASA Vol. 49, No 2, Part 2, 1971

4. M.V. Mathews, J.E. Miller, E.E. David, "Pitch Synchronous Analysis of Voiced Sounds", JASA Vol.33, No 2, Feb. 1961

5. Thomas H. Tarnoczy, "Vowel Formant Bandwidths and Synthetic Vowels", JASA, March 1962, p.p. 859-860

6. P. Stathopoulou, G. Kokkinakis, "Measurement of the Formants of the Greek Vowels", IASTED MECO, Tunis 1982, Vol. 1

7. Dennis H. Klatt, "Structure of Phonological Rule Component for Synthesis-by-Rule-Program", IEEE Transactions ASSP, Vol. ASSP-24, No 5, October 1976, p. 393

8. L.R. Rabiner, R.W. Schafer, J.L. Flanagan, "Computer Synthesis of Speech by Concatenation of Formant-Coded-Words, Bell System Tech. J. 50, 1541-1558 (1971)

9. L. Rabiner, "Speech Synthesis by Rule, an Acoustic Domain Approach", Bell System Tech. J. 47 17-37 (1968)

10. A.E. Rosenberg, R.W. Schapper, L.R. Rabiner, "Effects of Smoothing and Quantizing the Parameters of Formant-Coded Voiced Speech", JASA Vol. 50, No 6, Part 2, 1971

DIGITAL TECHNIQUES in Simulation, Communication and Control
Spyros G. Tzafestas (editor)
Elsevier Science Publishers B.V. (North-Holland) © IMACS, 1985

EFFICIENT METHODS FOR PREPROCESSING GREEK LETTERS

Bourbakis N., Pintelas P., Alexiou G. and Zeinis S.
Dept. of Computer Engineering
University of Patras
Patras 26500, Greece

This paper presents three different methods for automatic input of Greek characters in a computer for further processing such as storage, recognition and retrieval of typewritten text.
A particular scanning system which consists of an electromechanical array of 11x7 photocells, moving in raster form over the scanned text characters is used for this purpose. The system scans one character at a time. The character is introduced to the computer in three different methods. The first method is called FBA (Full Bit Array). In this method every cell of the scanning system corresponds to a single bit. In the second UITI (Useful Information with Two Indeces) method, only the useful information of the character is introduced to the computer, using a pair of two indeces (i,j) per cell. In the third method UIOI (Useful Information with One Index), a single index i is used for every information cell. Memory requirements for the computer storage of each character are given for all these methods. Finally some proposals for extention are given.

1- INTRODUCTION

Several types of text processing systems have been proposed in the past[1,2]. Some of these systems are based on Optical Character Readers (OCRs) to introduce the characters to the computer for recognition, classification and processing in general, while some other systems introduce the characters through some keyboard [3,4] . All these systems presented advantages and dis advantages depending on the kind of application they have been used for [4] .

The present work does not attempt to give an efficient text processing system, instead the efficient preprocessing of text characters is examined. This preprocessing is based on the category of systems that make use of optical character or text scanners [1,4] .

The optical character scanning system consists of an electromechanical array of 11x7 photocells scanning the text in a raster form [4]. Three different methods of presenting the scanned characters to the computer are examined and a memory requirements comparison is made.

The present work is split into three major parts. The first part describes in detail the optical character scanner and the representation of the Greek characters (the method, of course, can be used for any kind of characters). The second part presents the three different methods of introducing the characters to the computer and gives a comparison of memory requirements for characters. In the third and final part some conclusions and suggestions for extending the present work are given.

2- OPTICAL SYSTEM FOR SCANNING TEXT CHARACTERS (OSSTC).

The OSSTC presented here is one of the three proposed Optical Text Scanning Systems(OSTS) discussed in [4]. More precisely, it is the electromechanical 11x7 array of photocells (SEAP), which has been purposely chosen since it is the basic element for a complete covering-scanning of a character.

2.1 System of Electromechanical Array of Photocells (SEAP)

SEAP consists of 11X7 photocells put together in a two dimensional array form as in figure 1, to fully cover any text character.

Every cell of SEAP is a photodiode which accepts a light intensity and converts it into an electric current. This current is amplified and introduced to a corresponding A/D converter which in turn delivers a binary number corresponding to the one of the two allowable light intensities, that is, black and white (and eventually 1 and 0).

It was decided that the form of the array cells should be rectangular since it was needed to have a faithful representation of the original picture (text) in its mosaic form. Other forms such as pentagon and circle were not chosen because they would have left blank areas in the picture mosaic.

The photoarray consists of two parts. The cells along the edges form the circumference (i.e. the cells of first and seventh column and those of first and eleventh row) while the other cells form the 9X5 array, which we call the useful area (Figure 1). It is the useful area which is used for the representation of each character. The reason for using the circumference is for controling whether SEAP is focussing its useful area over the scanned character or not. Furthermore, during the move of SEAP towards the next character, the cells of seventh column (of the previous character) become the cells of the first column for the next character. It is therefore obvious that the space between the characters is also represented (see figure 2).

It should be mentioned that the cells on the circumference are scanned in a different way than those of the useful area. The Spiral Scanning (SS) has been chosen for the circumference cells, and the Horizontal Raster (H.R.) for the useful area cells. These two scanning modes are shown in figure 1, [6].

SEAP is moving electromechanically in a raster form over the scanned page as in figure 3, in order to locate and scan the existing characters.

For every scanned character a binary sequence is created which is intercepted by an I/O package. This package is responsible for the recreation of the read in character and it's delivery to another package (program) which stores the character in a buffer for further processing such as word recreation.

2.2. Representation of the Greek characters with SEAP.

As mentioned earlier the character under examination is represented within the 9X5 useful area. In an attempt to represent the characters as faithfully as possible, the maximum length and width of each character was measured. For this purpose the SCRIBE writing form of Greek characters on an IBM typewriter was used. The results of the measurements are given in table 1. The total surface taken up by each character and it's total number of cells is also shown in the same table. As a result of the measurements, table 2 was created giving the 11X7 arrays of all characters.

3. METHODS OF INTRODUCING THE CHARACTERS TO THE COMPUTER.

This section presents in detail the three methods of introducing the scanned characters to the computer. Some other methods have been ruled out due to their similarity with the ones given here, as shall be seen soon.

3.1. Full Bit Array (FBA)

In this method each character is introduced as a sequence of bits scanned in a raster form as shown by the numbering of figure 4. Each cell number in this figure is a single bit. This implies that each character is represented in memory by a total of 45 bits or 6 bytes of 8 bits each (if expressed in bytes). The number 45 comes from the fact that out of the 11X7 photocells only the 9X5 are used as the useful area. The circumference P is not part of the useful information and used only to focus SEAP over the character under examination. The useful area U, that is the cell surface covered by the 45 cells which are left after subtracting the cells of P from the total 11X7 cells of SEAP, is given by the formula (2). The circumference P is given by the formula (1).

(1) $P=\{C_{ij} \mid 1\leq i\leq 11 \text{ and } j\in\{1,7\}$
$\cup\{C_{ij} \mid 2\leq j\leq 6 \text{ and } i\in\{1,11\}\}$

(2) $U=\{C_{ij} \mid 2\leq i\leq 10 \text{ and } 2\leq j\leq 6\}$

The I/O package responsible for the creation of the character makes use of U and the way the character was scanned, to recreate the character as a string of bits or bytes. This string is subsequently compared against the table of memory stored character set(in the same representation i.e. string of bits or bytes) for correctness checking. The package returns the ASCII code of the recognized (matched) character or an indication of faulty character if no match took place. Subsequent packages may attempt to recognize the character taking into account possible misstypings. This last package is part of our further research and shall not be discussed in this paper. Figure 5 is the icon of the Greek letter "Φ" in it's FBA representation.

3.2. Useful Information of Two Indecies (UITI).

In this method the scanned character is introduced to the computer in the form of packed coordinates. In UITI each pair of indices (i,j) which contains a section of the examined character is expressed by one byte. It should be mentioned here that only pairs of coordinates that contain some section of the character under examination are extracted by SEAP and introduced to the computer. For the extraction of these pairs (SEAP) the extra hardware needed for the packing of coordinates i and j into a byte. In this method the amount of cells per character's useful information is variable and depends on the character. Figure 6 shows characters "Φ" and "," which take up 17 and 5 cells respectively.

3.3. Useful Information with One Index (UIOI).

Similar to UITI is the behavior of UIOI which uses a single index per useful information cell of the character under the SEAP. In UIOI the extracted index takes the form of one byte and corresponds to some cell which contains a section of the character. Figure 7 shows the character "Φ" in UIOI representation. Some similarity on the amount of memory taken up by both UITI and UIOI representations, as indicated by figures 6 and 7 will be discussed in the next section.

3.4. Comparison of Memory Requirements.

According to the amount of cells taken up by each character of the previously discussed methods, diagrams 1 to 5 have been built describing the occupied memory in bytes. At first glance methods UITI and UIOI appear to occupy the same amount of memory. In a closer examination of their structure in bits we see that they differ, while both are inferior to FBA in memory requirements (table - 3). This however, does not imply that FBA is the best. The justification is found in [7], where the character recognition algorithms are different. After the indroduction of a character to the computer by the FBA method the algorithms search all the memory stored prototypes (entire character set) one by one until a match is found or not found. On the other hand, for characters introduced by UITI or UIOI, the algorithms are more efficient (in time) because they attempt a match with the stored characters of the same length (i.e. same number of bytes).

4- CONCLUSIONS

In this paper three efficient methods for the input of text characters into a computerized document processing and retrieval system have been presented. Furthermore, a memory requirements comparison of the methods has been given. The FBA method presents an advantage in memory space over the other two methods. The UITI and UIOI methods, on the other hand, have the advantage of using a more efficient representation of the introduced text characters to the system for the next processing step (i.e. the matching algorithms).

REFERENCES

1 - Freedman D."OPTICAL CHARACTER REC/TION" IEEE Spectrum March 1974, pp. 44-52.

2 - Throssell W.R. and P.R. "THE MEASURMENT OF PRINT QUALITY FOR OPTICAL CHARACTER RECOGNITION SYSTEMS", Int. Journal of Pattern Recognition, Pergamon Press 1974, Vol. 6, pp. 141-147.

3 - Scan Data Co. "SCAN DATA PAGE READER SYSTEM", Equipment Description, 800 East Main Street Norristown, Pen/nia.

4 - Bourbakis N., Pintelas P., Alexiou G. and Christodoulakis D. "PROPOSALS FOR AN AUTOMATIC TEXT PROCESSING SYSTEM", Int. IMACS Meeting ,DIGITECH-84, July 9-12, Patras Univ., Patras, Greece.

5 - Zeinis S."EFFICIENT METHODS FOR PREPROCESSING GREEK LETTERS", Technical Report, Dept. of Computer Engineering, Patras Univ., Patras , Greece.

6 - Bourbakis N. "NEW, REAL-TIME PROCESING METHODS OF STRUCTURED IMAGES", PhD thesis 1982, Dept. of Computer Engineering Patras, Greece.

7 - Bourbakis N., Zeinis S., Pintelas P. and Alexiou G. "EFFICIENT MATCHING ALGORITHMS OF GREEK CHARACTERS", to be submitted.

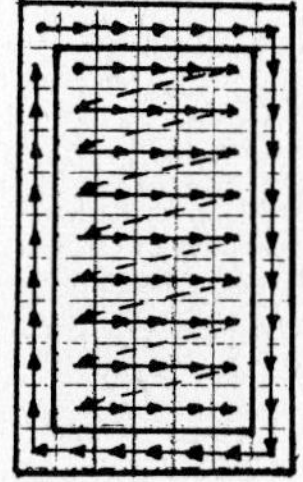

Fig. 1: Schematical representation of the SEAP cursor

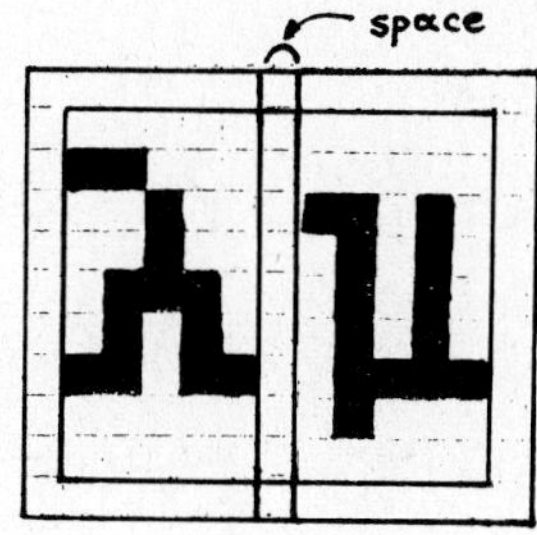

Fig. 2: Schematical representation of the cursor motion.

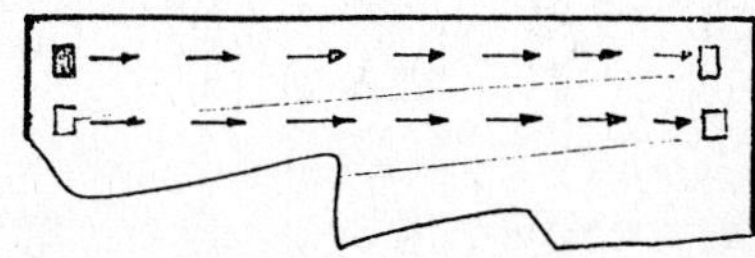

Fig. 3: Raster Scanning of a page by the SEAP

TABLE -1-

Characters	Length	Width	Area	Cells	Characters	Length	Width	Area	Cells
Α	0.253	0.212	6×5	15	ψ	0.323	0.187	8×5	16
Β	-//-	0.197	-//-	18	ω	0.187	0.192	4×5	15
Γ	-//-	0.167	6×4	12	ς	0.227	0.152	5×4	13
Δ	-//-	0.187	6×5	17	ά			6×5	19
Ε	-//-	0.192	-//-	17	έ			7×5	16
Ζ	-//-	0.187	-//-	16	ή			-//-	17
Η	-//-	0.202	-//-	17	ί			-//-	14
Θ	-//-	0.182	-//-	19	ό			-//-	15
Ι	-//-	0.167	-//-	14	ύ			-//-	16
Κ	-//-	0.212	-//-	16	ώ			6×5	20
Λ	-//-	0.202	-//-	12	ϊ			7×5	17
Μ	-//-	0.207	-//-	17	ϋ			7×5	19
Ν	-//-	0.207	-//-	19	Ø	0.253	0.162	6×4	12
Ξ	-//-	0.177	6×4	13	1	-//-	0.177	6×5	11
Ο	-//-	0.187	6×5	18	2	-//-	0.162	6×4	11
Π	-//-	0.197	-//-	17	3	-//-	0.162	6×4	13
Ρ	-//-	0.192	-//-	16	4	-//-	0.192	6×5	13
Σ	-//-	0.162	6×4	16	5	-//-	0.162	6×4	14
Τ	-//-	0.192	6×5	14	6	-//-	0.162	-//-	13
Υ	-//-	0.207	-//-	14	7	-//-	0.157	-//-	10
Φ	-//-	0.167	6×4	17	8	-//-	0.162	-//-	18
Χ	-//-	0.202	6×5	14	9	-//-	0.162	-//-	14
Ψ	-//-	0.192	-//-	16	(	0.338	0.106	8×3	12
Ω	-//-	0.197	-//-	18	)	0.338	0.106	8×3	12
α	0.187	0.182	4×5	14	&	0.253	0.157	6×4	18
β	0.298	0.162	7×4	17	*	0.212	0.192	5×5	12
γ	0.258	0.192	6×5	10	;	0.268	0.096	6×2	9
δ	0.263	0.157	6×4	15	:	0.182	0.071	5×2	8
ε	0.197	0.157	5×4	11	·	0.152	0.066	3×1	3
ζ	0.283	0.146	6×4	14	/	0.323	0.172	8×4	10
η	0.227	0.162	5×5	12	?	0.253	0.182	6×4	14
θ	0.258	0.187	6×5	16	£	0.263	0.187	6×5	16
ι	0.202	0.146	5×4	9	$	0.338	0.162	8×4	20
κ	0.187	0.162	5×4	13	%	0.303	0.177	7×5	20
λ	0.263	0.172	6×5	13	"	0.141	0.192	3×3	6
μ	0.247	0.177	6×5	14	+	0.207	0.192	5×5	9
ν	0.197	0.177	5×4	10	.	0.071	0.071	2×2	4
ξ	0.313	0.146	7×4	18	,	0.131	0.096	3×2	5
ο	0.197	0.162	5×4	10	=	0.136	0.162	3×4	8
π	0.187	0.167	4×4	11	−	0.037	0.172	1×4	4
ρ	0.247	0.157	6×4	13	´	0.091	0.121	2×3	5
σ	0.202	0.177	5×4	13	’	0.131	0.096	2×2	4
τ	0.212	0.167	4×5	9	blank				0
υ	0.197	0.172	5×4	11					
φ	0.258	0.162	6×4	15					
χ	0.258	0.177	6×4	13					

Table -1- shows the dimensions each Greek character in cm.

TABLE - 2 -

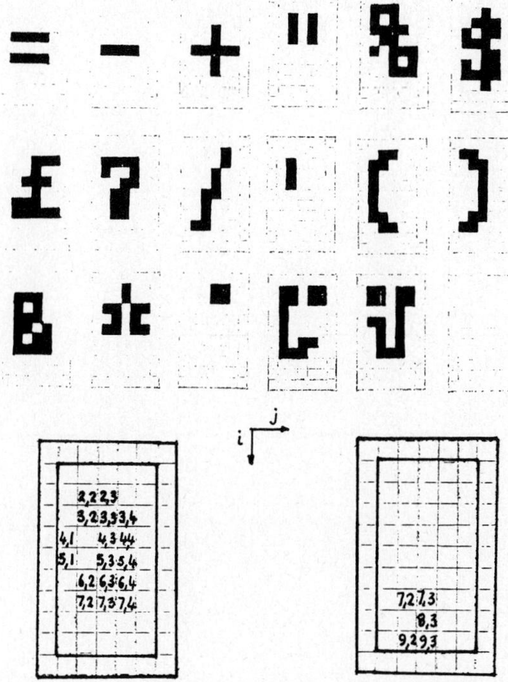

Fig.4:Schematic (numbered) scanning in FBA.

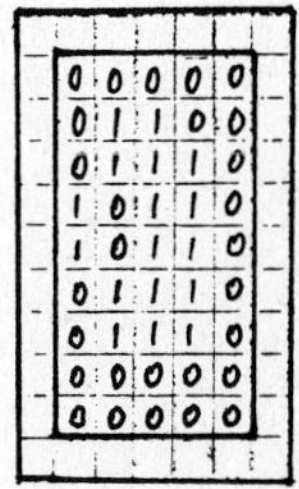

Fig.5:Representation of character" Φ " in FBA using 45 bits or 6 bytes.

Fig. 6 : Representation of characters " Φ " and "," (SEAP) where "Φ" occupies 17 cells and "," only 4.

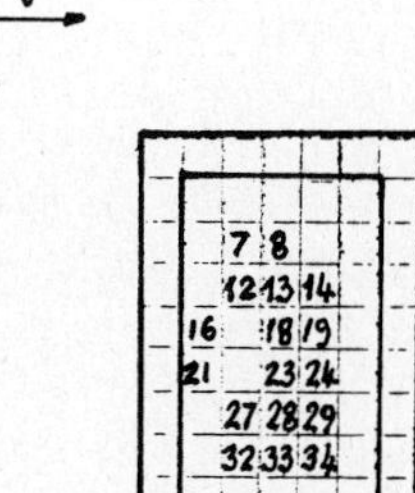

Fig. 7 : Representation of character "Φ" in UIOI . The character occupies 17 cells.

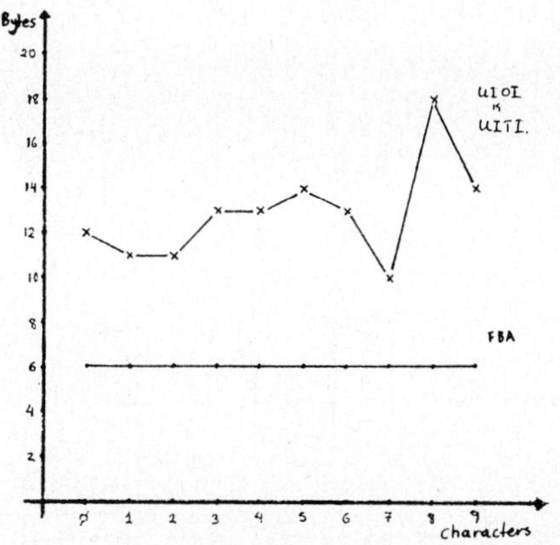

(1)

CHARACTERS (in total)	FBA	UITI or UIOI
24 Capital Letters	192 bytes	382 bytes
25 Lower Letters	200 "	325 "
7 Toned Vowels	56 "	117 "
2 Special Vowels	16 "	36 "
10 Digits	80 "	129 "
21 Special Characters	168 "	199 "
Total: 89 Characters	712 "	1187 "

Table-3-: Total memory required for FBA, UITI and UIOI.The used 1byte corresponds to 6bits here.

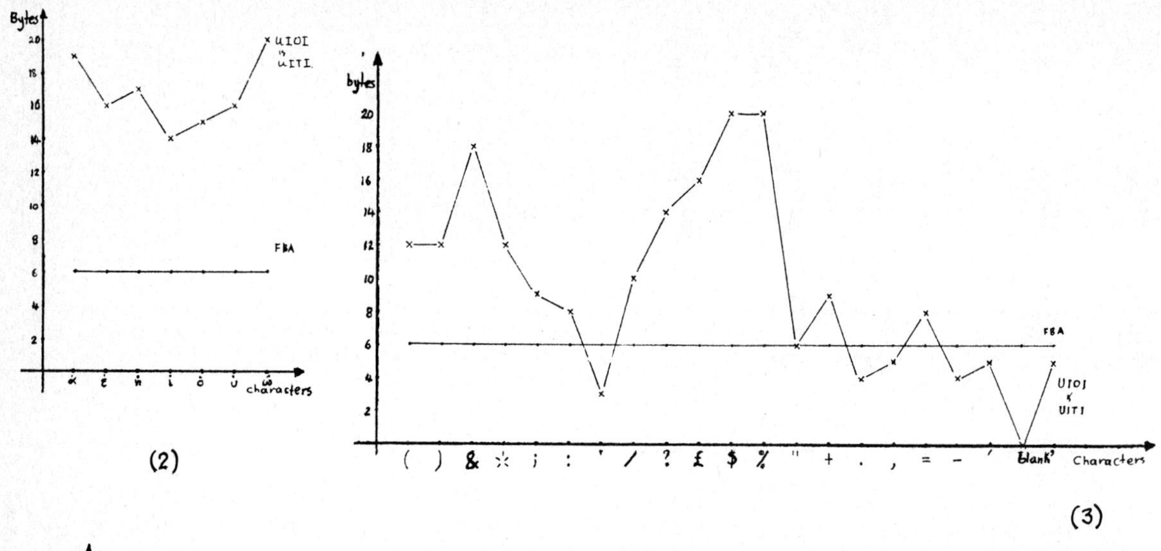
Bytes
UIOI
&
UITI
FBA
characters
bytes
Characters
blank'

(2)

(3)

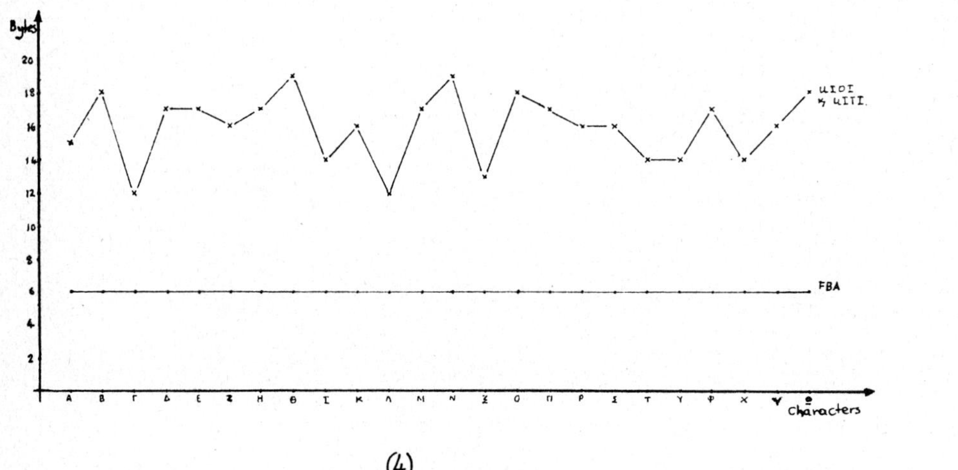
Bytes
UIOI
&
UITI
FBA
Characters

(4)

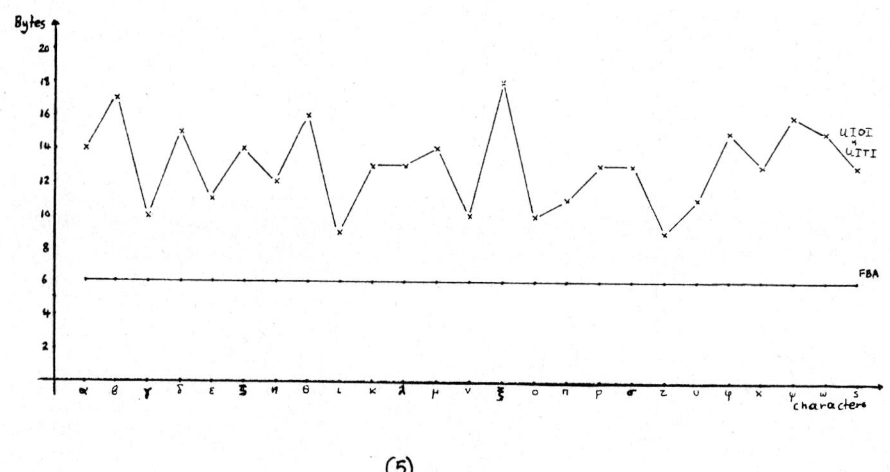
Bytes
UIOI
&
UITI
FBA
characters

(5)

DIGITAL TECHNIQUES in Simulation, Communication and Control
Spyros G. Tzafestas (editor)
Elsevier Science Publishers B.V. (North-Holland) © IMACS, 1985

PROPOSALS FOR AN AUTOMATIC TEXT PROCESSING SYSTEM (ATPS)

BOURBAKIS N., PINTELAS P., ALEXIOU G., CHRISTODOULAKIS D.
and ZEINIS S.

DEPT. OF COMPUTERS AND INFORMATION SCIENCE
UNIVERSITY OF PATRAS
PATRAS 26500, GREECE

The hardware-software description of three types of text processing systems (ATPSs) is presented in this paper. The ATPS's consist of an optical text scanning system (OSTS) which scans the text pages in order to extract the characters, an A/D converter and a terminal. The A/D converter passes to the host computer the digital form of the characters for processing. The terminal which is also connected to the host computer is used to control the ATPS and the kind of text processing requested by the terminal user. The three types of text processing are compared with regard to (a) scanning speed, (b) implementation cost, (c) percentage of character loss, (d) scanned character stability and (e) memory requirements for character storage.
The digital form of the text inside the host is subjected to several kinds of processing on user request, which may be expressed by menu selections on the windowed terminal screen. Requests for processing may include text recognition, classification, storage and retrieval/recostruction. A multi-level security system is suggested to ensure that only authorized accesses to the system are permitted.

1. INTRODUCTION

Lately, the interest in the development of expert systems has been significantly increased targeting at the world market [1,7,9]. The Automatic Text Processing Systems (ATPS), of which a prerious form was termed OCR [3], belong to the category of expert Systems.
The OCR systems appeared in several types [2,3,4]. The "mechanical" type (popular in 1960) consisted of a mirror, a system of lences, a Cathod Ray Tube (CRT) and a photocell. The mechanical system scanned one by one the text points in a raster form.
The "vidicon" consisted of a vidicon CRT on the photosensitive surface of which the text is focussed and scanned in raster form point-by-point.
The "moving spot" system consisted of a CRT, a lense system and a multiplier phototube. This system too scanned the text in a point-by-point raster form.
One other OCR type is the "hybrid" which consisted of a mirror, a lense system and a photocell array and scanned the text points in raster form again.
The above systems, as well as several others not mentioned here [3,9], scan the text characters point-by-point and produce as output a time changing waveform (see figure 11).
This characteristic property, shown in figure 11, introduces a significant disadrantage to these systems. The disadrantage is due to the fact that the algorithm for the recreation and recognition of the characters is complicated and the stored amount of information is large [9].
One recent ATPS, "Alphaword" [7], with keyboard, 16 character liquid crystal screen and RS232C interface has demonstrated significant results, but is also following the same principle as the systems mentioned earlier.
The present paper is a proposal for three new ATPS systems based on a different principle than that of the previous systems. This principle is a grid of cells (cursor) with dimensions 11X7 able to cover any text character.
The cells of the grid are photodiodes, whose exits are introduced to corresponding hardware circuitry to create the binary representation of the characters.
The proposed systems automaticaly introduce to a host computer text form IBM typewriters in courier, scribe, gothic and italic form.
The presented types of ATPS's are .

(i) Electromechanical array of 11X7 photocells which scans the text characters one-by-one creating a "reading" scan,
(ii) Electromechanical row of 64 cursors in a row to scan the text line-by-line and
(iii) Page photoarray which consists of a compact two dimensional page size array of cursors.

In the first part of this paper the proposed Optical Systems for Text Scanning (OSTS) which constitute the basic part of the ATPS systems are presented and a brief comparison between them is given. The second part is a description of three different methods of introducing the scanned text to the host computer [5]. The third and final part discusses some proposals and ideas on the subsequent processing of the text within the host computer and suggests some software ergonomic [12] issuses such as multiwindowing and menu driven software for the ATPS.

2. OPTICAL SYSTEMS FOR TEXT SCANNING(OSTS)

In this paragraph the following four types of optical systems for text scanning are briefly described. These are :

- . Electromechanical array of 11X7 photocells,
- . Electromechanical row of 11X448 photocells,
- . Page photo-array,and
- . Vidicon camera.

The first three are systems proposed in this paper, while the fourth (Vidicon, representing a generation of OCR systems) is only used for comparison purposes.

2.1. System of Electromechanical Array 11X7 photocells (SEAP).

The SEAP consists of 11X7 photocells put together as depicted in figure 1, to fully cover any text character. Every single cell of SEAP is a photodiode which accepts an illumination intensity and converts it to an electric current. This current is amplified and introduced to a corresponding A/D converter in order to create a binary number which corresponds to one of two allowable illumination intensities (black or white 1 or 0).
The SEAP is moving over the scanned text page in raster form,as shown in figure 2, attempting to discover the characters of the text under examination.
For every scanned character a sequence of binary digits is created and this sequence is intercepted by an I/O package. This package is responsible for the creation (recreation) of the character that was read in. The I/O package delivers the character to another package (program) which stores the character into a buffer for further processing (e.g. correctness check and word formation) by other packages.

2.2. System of Electromechanical Row of 11X448 Photocells (SERP).

SERP consists of a set of 11X448 photocells put together as shown on figure 3.
The number 448 is indicative and represents a maximum number of 64 characters per line (row).
The arrangement of photocells in rows and columus is predetermined in such a way so that a line of text is fully covered and scanned at a time.
The length of SERP extends over all the characters of the text line by corresponding a small array 11X7 photocells to every character.
With the above explanation in mind it is immediately understood that a SERP is a multiple serial form of a SEAP.

The SERP operates in a manner similar to that of SEAP, with the extra capability of parallel character processing, that is,a whole line of text at a time.
The electromechanical movement of SERP over the scanned page of text is vertical (see figure 4).

2.3. System of Page Photoarray (SPP).

SPP is a two dimentional version of the previous systems, which covers and "scans" an entire text page at a time. SPP's width is 64 SEAP whilst its length is determined by the manufacturer who has taken into account some specific page size (e.g. A4). Here again the operation of SPP is similar to that of SEAP and SERP except that there is no electromechanical movement and the system has the capability of processing one page of text at a time.

2.4. System of Vidicon Camera (SVC).

SVC is a well known system of text processing which makes use of a vidicon Camera [3].
The main part of SVC is a cathodic tube with its photosensitive surface.
Its operation is based on the sufficiently long time of representation of the text characters on the photosensitive surface [3] and the raster scanning of this surface afterwards. The scanned points on the photosensitive surface create electric currents which after amplification and A/D conversion deliver a sequence of digitaly equivalent points is bits or bytes.

2.5. Comparison of Optical Systems for Text Scanning.

The previously proposed OSTS systems present advantages and disadvantages if we examine them within a set of basic parameters of efficiency such as the following :

- Text scanning speed
- System implementation cost
- Percentage of character loss
- Stability of scanned character and
- Memory requirements of character storage.

2.5.1. Text scanning speed.

Of the above four OSTS the slowest is SEAP because it scans electromechanically the text characters one by one. SPP appears to be the fastest of all. A justification of this is the fact that SPP scans only the useful part of a page (i.e. excluding the margins) whilst SVC represents the entire page (margins included) on its photosensitive surface and scans this surface afterwards [9].

2.5.2. Implementation Cost.

Taking in to account the capabilities and developments in technology, it has been worked out that SEAP has the lowest implementation cost, while SPP is the one with the highest cost based on the complexity of its construction [9].

2.5.3. Character loss percentage.

Assuming that a correct scanning of the text page took place, it has been proven that SEAP, SERP and SPP present the same character loss percentage which is higher than the one for SVC [9,10]. An off hand justification for this is that SVC has a bigger mapping resolution [3].

2.5.4. Stability of scanned character.

Out of all four systems SPP presents the highest scanned character stability. This is due to the fact if the same characters of a page are scanned twice, SPP will deliver the same bit string in both cases while with SEAP and SERP the result depends on the accuracy of the electromechanical movement [9]. SVC, finally, will give the lowest stability because of the problems of overlaping or moving apart of the scanned points [10]. The reason for this is that the electromagnetic beam used for the scanning of the photosensitive surface declines after each scan, as shown on figure 5.

2.5.5. Memory requirements for character storage.

SEAP has the smallest memory storage requirements. This is due to the fact that it transmits to the host computer only existing (non blank) characters [5]. If the other systems are also to avoid transmiting blank characters (or blank lines) they have to be equiped with special preprocessing which will slow them down slightly.

3. EFFICIENT METHODS FOR CHARACTER RECOGNITION

This section reports the basic Input/Output methodology, creation and recognition of characters. For a full discussion on these see [6].
Three basic methods of introducing characters into the host computer [5] making use of SEAP are mentioned.
The first method is the Full Bit Array (FBA) in which each character is introduced as a sequence of bits which are scanned in a raster form as can be seen by the numbering of the cells of figure 6.
Each cell number in figure 6 represents a single bit. This implies that each character is represented in memory by a sequence of 45 bits or 6 (8-bit) bytes if expressed in bytes.
The determination of the number 45 is due to the fact that out of the 11X7 cells of the array the cells on the circumference constitute the Perigram P, formula (1), which is not part of the useful information. P plays the role of the character adjustor within the cursor and is only used for the focussing-allignment of SEAP over the character [5]. It's cells should be blank (0).

$$P=\{C_{ij} \mid 1\le i\le 11 \text{ and } j\in\{1,7\}\} \cup \{C_{ij} \mid 2\le j\le 6 \text{ and } i\in\{1,11\}\} \quad (1)$$

where C_{ij} is the array cell on row i and column j.
The useful cell area U, the number of cells which may convey useful information about the character, consists of 45 cells which are left by subtracting the perigram from the total 11X7 cells of SEAP.
U is given from the formula (2).

$$U=\{C_{ij} \mid 2\le i\le 10 \text{ and } 2\le j\le 6\} \quad (2)$$

The I/O package which is responsible for the character creation makes use of U and taking into account the scanning method, recreates the character as a sequence of bits or bytes and compares it against a stored (in the same representation) character set for correctness checking. The package returns the ASCII or EBCDIC code of the recognized character or a fault (not recognized character) indication. In the latter case it is possible to activate other programs/subprograms which attempt to recognize the character taking into account that the original character was mistyped, or force SEAP to reread the character a predefined number of times.
We shall not refer any further to these programs since they are part of our continued research and will be reported on [6]. Further more, the amount of work and intelligence involved in these programs are a good excuse for not discussing them in the present paper.
The second method is the Useful Information with two indices (UITI) in which the scanned character is introduced to the computer in the form of packed coordinates (indices). In UITI each pair of indices (i,j) which represents a portion of the useful information of a character is expressed as one byte of information. It should be mentioned here that only pairs of indices (coordinates) expressing some

portion of the character are produced by the corresponding System (SEAP,SERP,SPP). For this purpose each one of the above systems is equiped with the extra hardware (see figure 7) needed to materialize the packing of the coordinates (i,j) in the form of a byte.
In this case the I/O package receives from the A/D device the useful information U'

$$U' = \{C_{ij} \mid 2 \le i \le 10 \text{ and } 2 \le j \le 6, \text{ where } C_{ij} \in U \text{ and } C_{ij} = 1\}$$

as a sequence of bytes. This sequence, representing the character, is compared against a subset of the stored characters for correctness purposes, in a manner similar to that of FBA [5].
In this case as well, the I/O package returns the ASCII or EBCDIC code of the character for further processing.
It is obvious that in this method the information introduced to the I/O package for every character depends on the number of cells that the character occupies, see figure 8.
The third method of Useful Information with One Index (UIOI) has a similar behavior. In UIOI a single index is used for the extraction of the useful information of each character.
The index passed to the I/O package is in the form of one byte of information and corresponds to a cell which contains a portion of the character under examination, see figure 9.
It should be mentioned that the systems SEAP, SERP and SPP must posess the corresponding hardware (see figure 10), which delivers as output a proper index for every single cell that contains a portion of the character ($\forall C: C \in U'' \to i$). The useful information U'' ,

$$U'' = \{C_i \mid 1 \le i \le 45, C_i \in U \text{ with } C_i = 1\}$$

in the form of a sequence of bytes is undergone a treatment similar to the one mentioned earlier for the previous methods.

4. EFFICIENT ALGORITHMS FOR TEXT RECOGNITION

Following the recognition of a character with the help of the efficient algorithms described in [6], the ASCII or EBCDIC equivalent that is returned is stored in a buffer of a "page" size. In this page buffer the ASCII characters are accumulated properly recreating the text under examination.
After the text of the page under examination is placed in the buffer or the buffer is filled up, special word recognition programs are activated. These programs search the buffer text to descover certain key-words. The key-words either pre exist in the ATPS or are requested by the system from the terminal user.
The ATPS employes special windows on the terminal for the interaction with the user. The windows contain menus with the operations available to the user.
For example, rearrangement, deletion and addition of keywords.
It must be mentioned here that the ATPS is under the control of a security system for protection against intentional missuse.
The main purpose of the key-words, in a first phase is to assist in the classificaion and storage of the text within the Data Base area where it physically belongs and the retrieval of the text from the data base.
In a second phase the key-words, under special processing, shall play a significant part in a user requested whole text reproduction, partial reproduction or summary reproduction (Heuristic text processing Algorithms [13]).
It is mentioned that the key-words exhibit a varying hierarchy between them and have weights of significant attached to themselves either as plain words or words within a sentence or whole paragraphs.
More detail on the subject of text meaning creation is not given here since it is part of the current research of the authors and represents the main part of the inteligent system for document processing they propose.

5. CONCLUSIONS

In this paper three types of automatic input of text into a computer have been proposed, as part of an ATPS. These types of systems were based on a scanning mechanism of the examined characters which is different than that of the known ATPS's. The scanning mechanism is a 11X7 grid of cells. The proposed systems exhibit significant advantages in speed and accuracy which make them suitable candidates for future implementations of ATPS's. Their implementation is also expected to contribute significantly to the EUROTRA project. [11] .

REFERENCES

1 - ESPRIT: Proc. of Commision of EUROPEAN COMMUNITIES, Final COM (82), 486, Brussel, Belgium, Nov. 5, 1982.

2 - IEEE Proceedings Vol.68 No.7 , 1980, pp.

3 - Freedman D."OPTICAL CHARACTER RECOGNITION ", IEEE Spectrum, March 1974, pp. 44-52.

4 - Throssell W.R. and Fryer P.R."THE MEASURMENT OF PRINT QUALITY FOR OPTICAL CHARACTER RECOGNITION SYSTEMS Int.

Jurnal of Pattern Recognition, Pergamon Press 1974, vol.6, pp. 141-147.

5 - Bourbakis N., Pintelas P., Alexiou G. and Zeinis S "EFFICIENT METHODS FOR PREPROCESSING GREEK LETTERS"Int. IMACS Meeting DIGITECH 84, July 9-12 1984, Univ. of Patras, Patras, Greece

6 - Bourbakis N., Zeinis S., Pintelas P. Alexiou G. "EFFICIENT MATCHING ALCORITHMS OF GREEK LETTERS"to be submitted.

7 - Alphaword III, Compuscan INC., 81 TWO Bridges Road, Bidg 2, Fair-field N.J. 07006, USA.

8 - Scan Data Co. "Scan DATA PACE READER SYSTEM", Equipment Description, 800 East Main street Norristown, Pen/ nia, USA.

9 - Bourbakis N. "NEW, REAL-TIME PROCESSING METHODS OF STRUCTURED IMAGES" PhD. thesis 1982, Patras Univ. Dept. of Computer Engineering, Patras, Greece.

10- Klinger A. "REGULAR DECOMPOSITION AND PICTURE STRUCTURE", Proc. 1974 Int. IEEE Conf. on SMC, Dallas Texas, N.Y. 1974, pp. 307-310.

11- king. M. "EUROTRA: Technical specification", Geneva, July 30, 1980

12- Pintelas P. "Day-to-Day Problems in Software Product Development or the lack of software Ergonomics: A Practitioners view" submitted

13- Bourbakis N."HEURISTIC TEXT PROCESSING ALGORITHMS" in preparation.

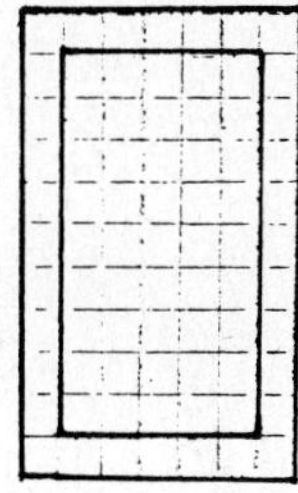

Fig. 1: Schematical representation of the SEAP cursor.

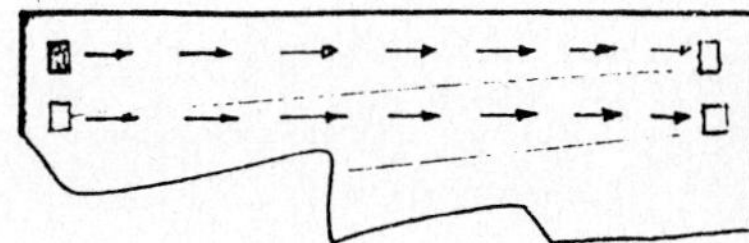

Fig. 2: Raster scanning of a paga from the SEAP.

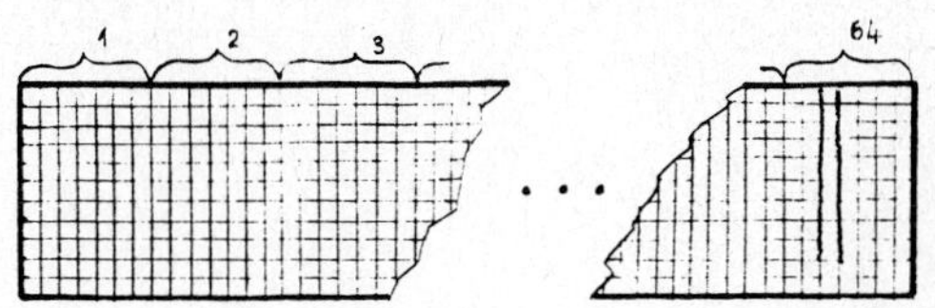

Fig. 3: Schematical Representation of the SERP.

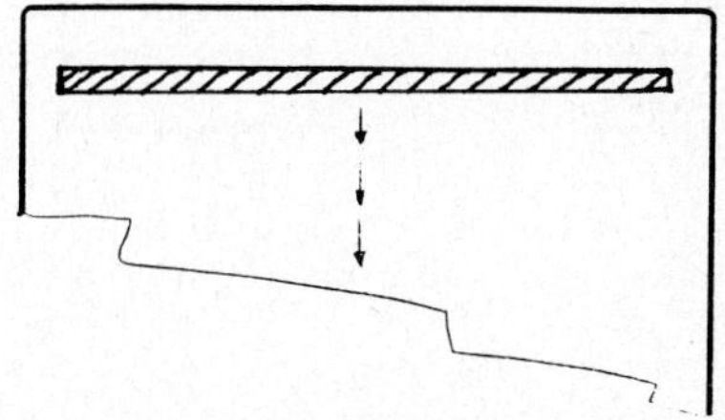

Fig. 4: Page scanning from SERP.

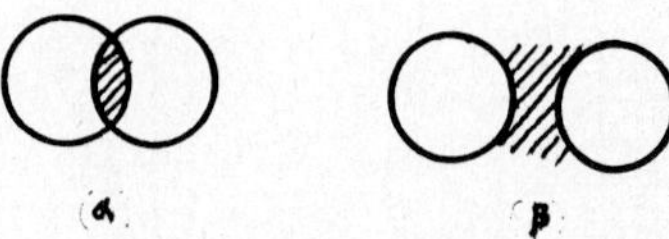

Fig. 5: Schematical representation a) Overlapping, b)Distance of the scanning points. The cycles indicate the scanned points of the photosensitive surface.

Fig. 6: Schematic (numbered) scanning of the cells that overlap the characters area. The perigram of (1-32) cells is used as the character adjustor

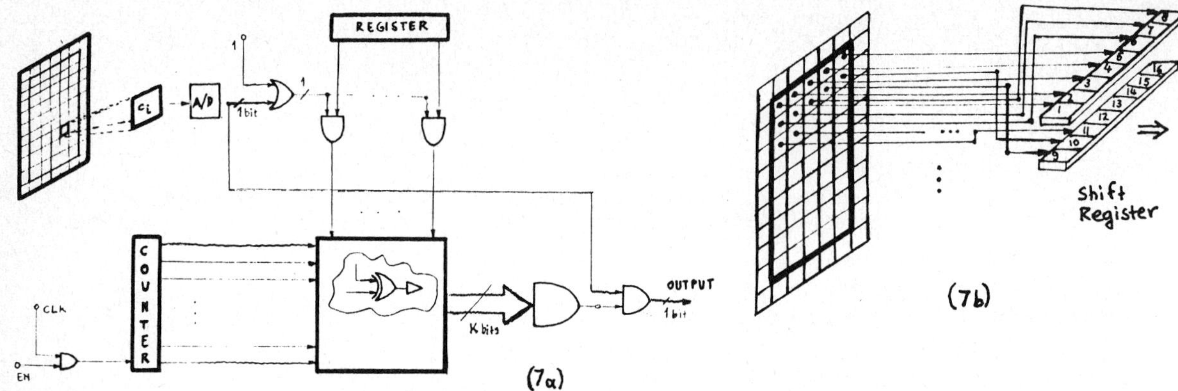

Fig.7:a)It shows the hardware that completes the 11x7 photodrid for the proper cells output and the preparation of the computer words. The above hardware corresponds to the FBA method. b) It shows another hardware that completes the cursor for the FBA method. This hardware has parallel mode.

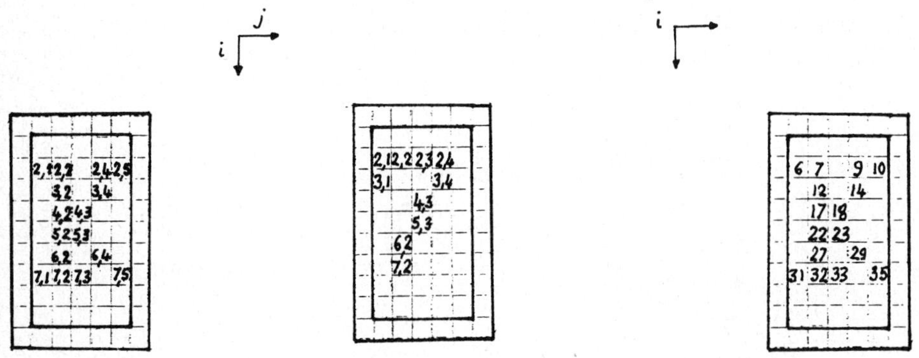

Fig. 8:Representation of characters "K" and "7" (SEAP) where "K" occupies 16 cells and "7" only 10.

Fig. 9: Representation of character "K" (SEAP) in UIOI. The character occupies 16 cells.

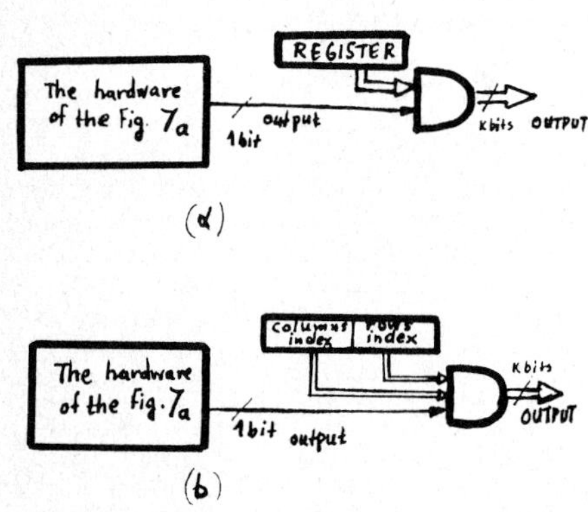

Fig. 10: It shows the complement hardware for the UITI and UIOI methods.

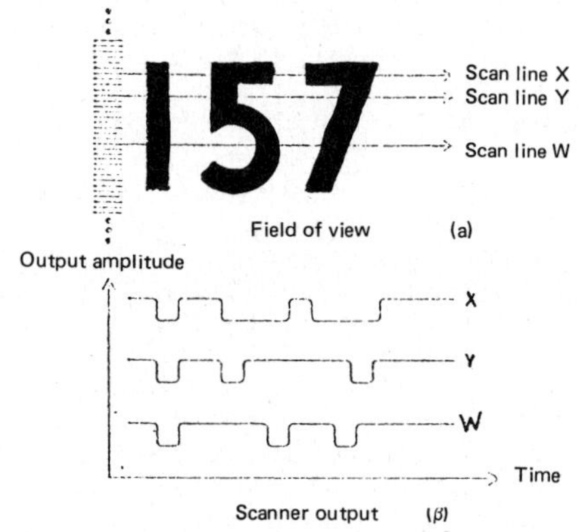

Fig. 11: It shows the output of three scanning lines X,Y,W, when the elements 1 5 7 of a binary picture are scanned from a Raster scanning system.

DIGITAL TECHNIQUES in Simulation, Communication and Control
Spyros G. Tzafestas (editor)
Elsevier Science Publishers B.V. (North-Holland) © IMACS, 1985

COMPUTER BASED CARDIAC STATE DIAGNOSIS USING FOURIER ANALYSIS

E. A. Giakoumakis

Computer Science and Information Div.,Electr. Eng. Dept.
National Technical University, Athens - Greece

The most widely used method for diagnosizing the state of the heart is the interpretation of the 12-lead ECG. Nevertheless, this interpretation is done without commonly acceptable criteria and involves an elaborate procedure.
In this work we are trying to make a classification between a physiological cardiac state and a non-phisiological one, by appropriately processing the signal of the II-lead of ECG. In particular after transforming by FFT the II-lead signal we obtain the power spectrum of it. By considering only two features of this spectrum, we have proved that very satisfactory results are derived as for as the classification of this cardiac state is concerned in the above two categories. The classification is done with the help of Bayes decision theory. The above processing was entirely done with the help of computer fasilities.

1. INTRODUCTION

Nowadays , it is commonplace that computers are invaluable tools to support research and clinical practice in electrocardiology. Numerous papers on the processing of electrocardiogram (ECG) signals have been published. Most of these papers study the cardiac signals in the time domain . Five major ploblems have been isolated and extensively treated in this domain|3|. These are : a) The QRS detection b) artifact detection and correction (Baseline wandering, Line interference, Muscle artifacts, spikes, sudden baseline) c) QRS typification and alignment d) ST-T typification e) P-wave detection.
There are, however, a few papers, which use transformed versions of the ECG. Apart from the well known Fourier transform, the Walsh-Hadamard transform has also been tested. The noise added to the cardiac signal by the electrocardiographer has been studied in the frequency domain. The effect of the finite electrocariographer bandwith on the cardiac signal has also been considered. An amplidude decrease of the frequency components of the QRS wave of people suffering from myocardial infraction has been observed. In our contribution we propose a new criterion for the healthy-non healthy classification. This criterion may briefly be described as follows : The energy stored in two frequency bands of the ECG signal is measured. Let X_1 and X_2 be the corresponding energies. Then the position of the point (X_1, X_2) in the two dimensional space R_2 is considered. We have observed, that the position of this point gives information about the cardiac state corresponding to the signal. Therefore it can be used for the classification mentioned before.

2. THE PROCESSING OF THE ECG SIGNAL

We record the electrical activity of the heart using a system of 12-leads. The position on the body for each lead is determined once for all and is constant during the ECG. The ECG is consisted of various waves each one corresponding to the electrical and mechanical activity of a particular part of the heart. The ECG diagnosis for the patient is based on the analysis of specific features of the 12-leads ECG signal.
The automated processing of ECG by the computer requires first of all the digitazation of the signal.
Working, at the begining, with one-chanell signal we chose ammong the 12-lead, the so called lead-II, because it exhibits more clearly some features taken under consideration for the diagnosis, (such as, greater signal amplitude, more acute QRS wave). They had to digitize the lead-II signal. We gathered a sample of healthy and non-healthy patients, and with the help of specialist we selected the most representative (most ferquently occuring) beats. With the help of a digitizer we sampled the heart beat on 512 points per beat and the sampling rate would always allow a frequency band of at least 150 Hz. As the electrocardiographer had a 3db point at 120Hz, and as it is well known that the interesting frequency band for the cardiologist lies below 80 Hz, we had achieved the necessary sampling rate using 512 samples per beat.
We sampled the value of the signal with 8 bit resolution.
For each signal we obtained a sequence of real

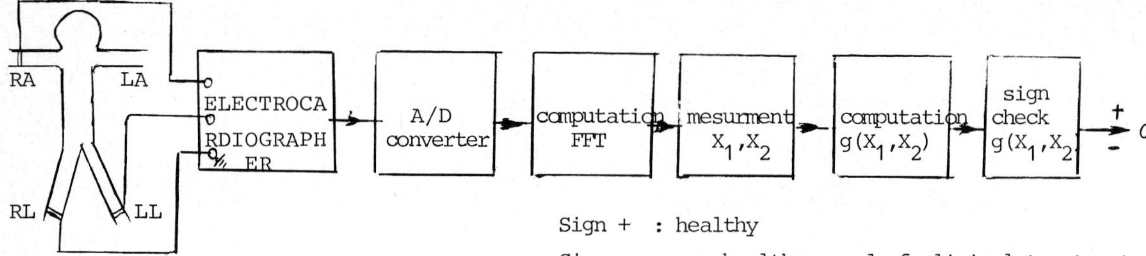

Figure 1 : The ECG processing

number X(m), m=0, 511. Figure 1. We applied the FFT algorithm in order to compute the $C_x(k)$ sequence given by the definition of the Discrete Fourier Transform :

$$C_x(k) = \frac{1}{N}\sum_{0}^{N-1} X(m)\,e^{-j2\pi km/N} \qquad N = 512,\ k = 0,1,\ldots 511$$

Since X(m) is a real sequence we know that we will have :

$$\bar{C}_x\left(\frac{N}{2} - l\right) = C_x\left(\frac{N}{2} + l\right) \qquad l=0,1,\ldots,N/2$$

and $\bar{C}_x(k)$ the complex conjugate of $C_x(k)$.
The power spectrum of the ECG signal (lead II) is given by the p(k), k=o,...256 where $p(k)=|C_x(k)|$.
Note that the distance between two successive components of the power spectrum are f_o the apart, with $1/f_o$ being the time period of the heart beat. We also note that the p(0) component reflects the DC component the signal and has a close relation to the respiration/breathing movements of the person examined, and also to the bad contact of the electrical probes of the electrocardiographer. A good contact of the probes on the body (for example), reduces this component.
To the following figures (2-) we see selected characteristic cases of plotted ECG signal, in both the time and frequency domain.

3. THE MODEL (Bayes decision theory)

Let $\Omega = \{\omega_1, \omega_2\}$ be two elements set, where ω_1 denotes the healthy state and ω_2 denotes the non-healthy state. Suppose we have an algorithm which enables us to decide between ω_1 and ω_2. Let a_1 denote the decision healthy and a_2 denote the decision non-healthy. Let $A=\{a_1,a_2\}$. It should be clear that a perfect algorithm would give a_1 whenever ω_1 is true and a_2 whenever ω_2 is true. According to the standard terminology a_1 and a_2 are called "actions". So far, we have not given the data of the algorithm. It is obvious that certain characteristics of ECG signal should be used for this purpose. In fact we use a 2-dimensional vector usually known as feature vector.
Let $\lambda(a_i/\omega_j)$ be the loss incurred for taking action a_i when the cardiac state is ω_j. Let the feature vector $\bar{x}$ be a 2 - component vector valued randon variable and let $p(\bar{x}/\omega_j)$ be the state -conditional probability density function for $\bar{x}$. Finally let $P(\omega_j)$ be the apriori probability of the state ω_j. Then the a posteriori probability $P(\omega_j/\bar{x})$ can be computed from $p(\bar{x}/\omega_j)$ by Bayes rule :

$$P(\omega_j/\bar{x}) = \frac{p(\bar{x}/\omega_j)P(\omega_j)}{p(\bar{x}/\omega_1)P(\omega_1)+p(\bar{x}/\omega_2)P(\omega_2)}$$

Suppose that we observe a particular $\bar{x}$ and that we contemplate taking action a_i, if the true state is ω_j, we will incure the loss $\lambda(a_i/\omega_j)$. Since $P(\omega_j/\bar{x})$ is the probability that the true state is ω_j, the expected loss associated with taking action a_i is merely :

$$R(a_i/\bar{x})=\lambda(a_i/\omega_1)P(\omega_1/\bar{x})+\lambda(a_i/\omega_2)P(\omega_2/\bar{x})$$

the $R(a_i/\bar{x})$ is known as conditioned risk. Whenever we encounter a particular observation $\bar{x}$ we can minimize the expected loss by selecting the action that minimizes the conditional risk. If $\lambda_{ij}=\lambda(a_i/\omega_j)$ we obtain :

$$R(a_1/\bar{x})=\lambda_{11}P(\omega_1/\bar{x})+\lambda_{12}P(\omega_2/\bar{x})$$
$$R(a_2/\bar{x})=\lambda_{21}P(\omega_1/\bar{x})+\lambda_{22}P(\omega_2/\bar{x})$$

We take action a_1, that is we decide ω_1, if $R(a_1/\bar{x})<R(a_2/\bar{x})$ or if

$$(\lambda_{21}-\lambda_{11})P(\omega_1/\bar{x}) > (\lambda_{12}-\lambda_{22})P(\omega_2/\bar{x})$$

or if

$$(\lambda_{21}-\lambda_{11})p(\bar{x}/\omega_1)P(\omega_1) > (\lambda_{12}-\lambda_{22})p(\bar{x}/\omega_2)P(\omega_2)$$

These conditions are equivalent to the following one :
Decide ω_1 if

$$\frac{p(\bar{x}/\omega_1)}{p(\bar{x}/\omega_2)} > \frac{\lambda_{12}-\lambda_{22}}{\lambda_{21}-\lambda_{11}}\ \frac{P(\omega_2)}{P(\omega_1)}$$

We define a loss function of particular interest

for this case, the so-called symmetrical or zero -one loss function

$$\lambda(a_i/\omega_j) = \begin{cases} 0 & i=j \\ 1 & i\neq j \end{cases}$$

And we obtain the following rule :
We decide ω_1 if $R(a_1/\bar{x}) < R(a_2/\bar{x})$ or

$$P(\omega_2/\bar{x}) < P(\omega_1/\bar{x}) \quad \text{or}$$

$$P(\omega_1/\bar{x}) - P(\omega_2/\bar{x}) > 0$$ otherwise we decide ω_2. So if we define a function, $g(\bar{x})$ known as discriminant function by

$$g(\bar{x}) = P(\omega_1/\bar{x}) - P(\omega_2/\bar{x}) \quad \text{or by}$$

$$g(\bar{x}) = \log P(\omega_1/\bar{x}) - \log P(\omega_2/\bar{x})$$

We get the following decision rule :
Decision ω_1 if $g(x)>0$ otherwise decide ω_2. The structure of a Bayes classier is determined primarily by the conditional densities $P(x/\omega_j)$. Assume our population follows the normal density that is approximately 95% of the samples fall in the internal $|x-\mu| \leq 2\sigma$. In this case the normal density is completely specified by two parameters the mean μ and the variance σ^2. For simplicity we write $p(x) \sim N(\mu,\sigma^2)$.
For our case the normal density is written as

$$p(\bar{x}) = \frac{1}{2\pi|\Sigma|^{1/2}} \exp\left(-\frac{1}{2}(\bar{x}-\bar{\mu})^T\Sigma^{-1}(\bar{x}-\bar{\mu})\right)$$

where $\bar{x} = \begin{pmatrix} x_1 \\ x_2 \end{pmatrix}$, $\bar{\mu} = \begin{pmatrix} \mu_1 \\ \mu_2 \end{pmatrix}$ the mean vector, Σ is the 2-by-2 covariance matrix $(\bar{x}-\bar{\mu})^T$ is the transpose of $\bar{x}-\bar{\mu}$, Σ^{-1} is the inverse of Σ and $|\Sigma|$ is the determinant of Σ. Formally $\bar{\mu}=E[\bar{x}]$ and $\Sigma=E[(\bar{x}-\bar{\mu})(\bar{x}-\bar{\mu})^T]$.
The loci of points of constant density are hyperrellipsoids on which the quadratic form $(\bar{x}-\bar{\mu})^T\Sigma^{-1}(\bar{x}-\bar{\mu})$ remains constant. The principal axes of these hyperrellipsoids are given by the eigenvectors of Σ, the eingenvalues determining the lengths of these axes. In this case, where the density is normal, the discriminant function of minimum-error classification is written :

$$g(\bar{x}) = -\frac{1}{2}(\bar{x}-\bar{\mu}_1)^T\Sigma_1^{-1}(\bar{x}-\bar{\mu}_1) - \frac{1}{2}\log|\Sigma_1| + \log P(\omega_1) +$$

$$+\frac{1}{2}(\bar{x}-\bar{\mu}_2)^T\Sigma_2^{-1}(\bar{x}-\bar{\mu}_2) + \frac{1}{2}\log|\Sigma_2| - \log P(\omega_2)$$

where the index 1 means the healthy-population and index 2 means the non-healthy one.

If $W_i = -\frac{1}{2}\Sigma_i^{-1}$

$$\bar{w}_i = \Sigma_i^{-1}\bar{\mu}_i$$

$$w_{io} = -\frac{1}{2}\bar{\mu}_i^T\Sigma_i^{-1}\bar{\mu}_i - \frac{1}{2}\log|\Sigma_i| + \log P(\omega_i)$$

we have :

$$g(\bar{x}) = \bar{x}^T W_1\bar{x} + \bar{w}_1^T\bar{x} + w_{10} - \bar{x}^T W_2\bar{x} - \bar{w}_2^T\bar{x} - w_{20}$$

4. EXAMPLE

We observed that if we define X_1 as the energy of ECG in the area (o,12] Hz and X_2 as the energy of ECG in the area (12,36]Hz (formally $X_1 = \sum_{k=1}^{N} p(k)$ where $|Nf_o - 12| = \min$ and $X_2 = \sum_{N+1}^{\lambda} p(k)$ where $|\lambda f_o - 36| = \min$).

ECG	X_1	X_2	$g(\bar{x})$
N1	74.974	43.430	71.46
N13	45.107	20.902	11.81
N18	73.415	17.408	7.20
N29	55.931	15.158	3.98
N17	55.255	15.400	4.24
N22	125.140	33.824	41.18
N4	42.249	20.776	11.62
N7	61.036	17.763	7.27
N10	108.845	35.998	46.60
N26	31.993	24.580	18.90
U1	5.918	2.406	-4.34
U2	37.030	7.376	-2.48
U3	7.261	6.068	-3.49
U7	36.343	4.129	-3.40
U10	26.294	5.913	-3.32
U11	16.543	5.101	-3.75
U12	4.487	2.333	-4.36
U14	73.282	8.404	-0.31
U4	36.810	16.850	5.78
U9	17.839	9.587	-1.54

Table 1 : The values of X_1, X_2 and $g(\bar{x})$ for deferent samples.

The values of X_1,X_2 for samples are shown in table 1. We use letter N_{xx} (Normal) whenever the patient is considered to be healthy according to the actual diagnose made by the cardiologists, who took under consideration every other possible source of medical information. Similarly we use U_{xx}, for the non-healthy cases. Computing $\bar{\mu}_1$, $\bar{\mu}_2$, Σ_1, Σ_2 we have :

$$\bar{\mu}_1 = \begin{bmatrix} 67,194 \\ 24,524 \end{bmatrix} \qquad \bar{\mu}_2 = \begin{bmatrix} 26,181 \\ 6,807 \end{bmatrix}$$

$$\Sigma_1 = \begin{bmatrix} 768,57 & 152,43 \\ 152,43 & 87,01 \end{bmatrix} \qquad \Sigma_2 = \begin{bmatrix} 395,41 & 34,96 \\ 34,96 & 16,20 \end{bmatrix}$$

By solving the equations $|\Sigma_i - \lambda I| = 0$ we take the eigenvalues $\lambda_{1a}=801,11$, $\lambda_{1b}=54,47$ and $\lambda_{2a}=398,61$, $\lambda_{2b}=13,00$.
From equations $\Sigma_i\bar{x}_{ij} = \lambda_{ij}\bar{x}_{ij}$, $i=1,2$ $j=a,b$ we take the eigenvectors

$$\bar{x}_{1a} = \begin{bmatrix} 4,68 \\ 1 \end{bmatrix}, \quad \bar{x}_{1b} = \begin{bmatrix} 1 \\ -4,68 \end{bmatrix}$$

$$\bar{x}_{2a} = \begin{bmatrix} 10,94 \\ 1 \end{bmatrix} \quad \bar{x}_{2b} = \begin{bmatrix} 1 \\ -10,94 \end{bmatrix}$$

and the following discriminant function :

$$g(X_1,X_2) = 10^{-3}|0,57X_1^2 + 46,94X_2^2 - 3,25X_1X_2 + 12,11X_1 - 144,87X_2| - 3,46 + \log\left|\frac{P(\omega 1)}{P(\omega_2)}\right|$$

We use for our sample the probabilities $P(\omega_1)=0,3$, $P(\omega_2)=0,7$ being obtained from the statistics of the hospital which provided the data.
Calculating the discriminant function $g(X_1,X_2)$

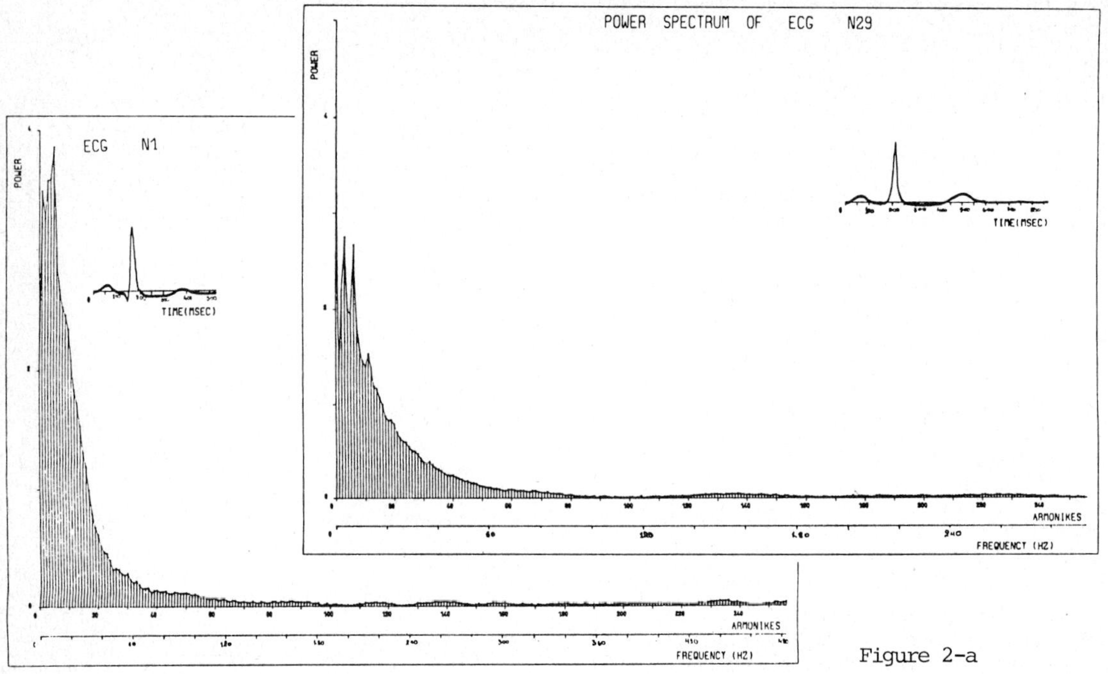

Figure 2-a

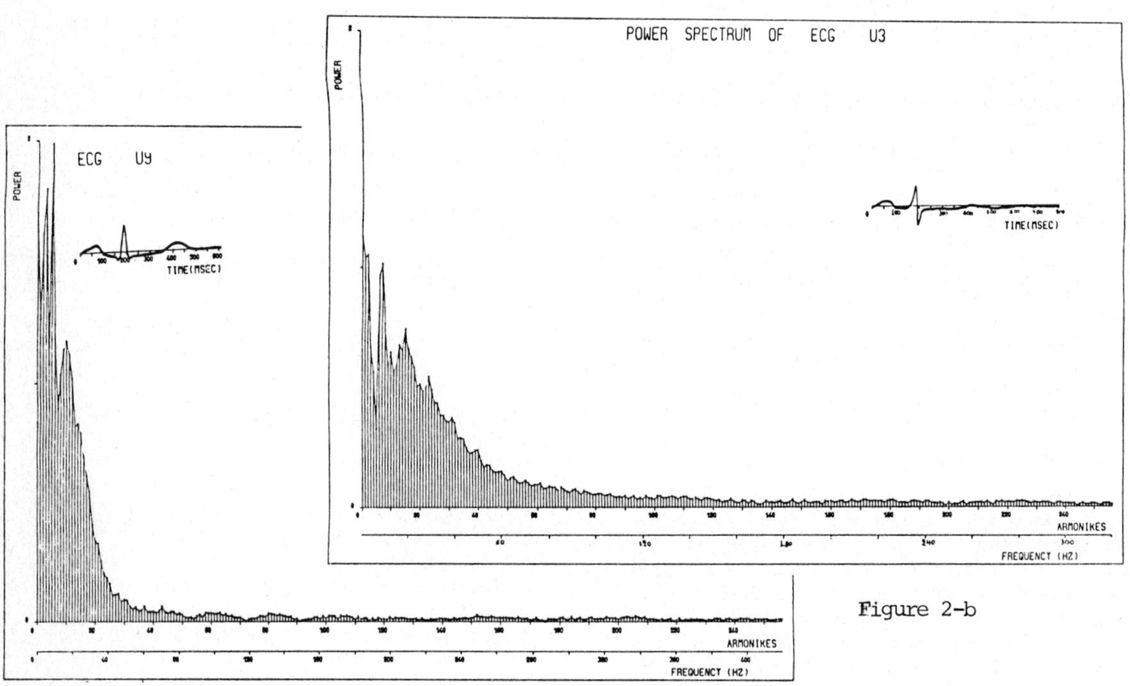

Figure 2-b

Figure 2 : Charasteristic cases of signal (in the time and frequency domain) a.healthy persons, b.non-healthy

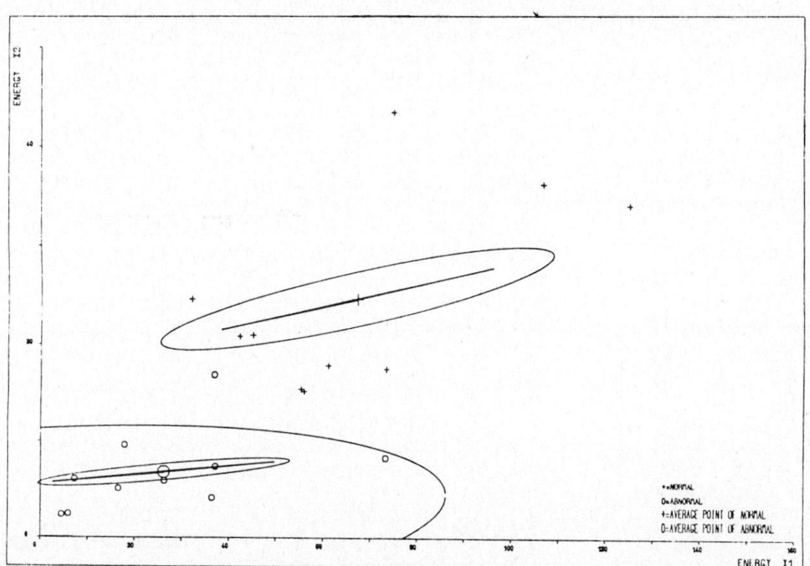

Figure 3 :The distirbution Healthy and non-Healthy population in the (X_1-X_2)-plane.

corresponding to our sample we take the values are shown in the table 1. We observe that the positive values correspond to the healthy population, the negative values of $g(X_1,X_2)$ correspond to non-healthy population. We observe also that our algorithm is inefficien only in the case of U4 ECG. The only excuse for it is that the patient of this case really didn't need any clinical treatment.
The distirbution of our sample in the (X_1,X_2)-plane, the discriminant curve and the hyperellipsoids of constand density can be seen in figure 3.
These curves are obtained from the data of table -1. We tested this result against a random sample of 2 patients considered clinically to be healthy and against another 2 patients considered to be non-healthy and we found the values are shown in the table 2.
We observe that the test based on the data of table 2, produces results in accordance with the clinical diagnose.

ECG	X_1	X_2	$g(X_1,X_2)$
N2	60.146	11.501	1.77
N6	57.866	11.340	1.16
U8	17.792	1.901	-4.13
U13	31.377	9.600	-1.41

Table 2 : The test data

5. CONCLUSIONS

The algorithm that is developed here based on the information being obtained from the power spectrum of leed II signal, for the classification of a papulation according to their cardiac state (healthy , non-healthy) is proved to give very good results as compared with the initial diagnosis of the cardiologists. This algorithm however has not as yet a medical explenation. Its application on larger sample of patients would increase its reliability and would be an impetus examining its medical meaning.

ACKNOWLEDGMENTS. The author would like to thank Drs B. Dimitriades, D. Sideris, E.N. Protonotarios for the fruitful discussions he had with them. The necessary data were collected by cooperation of the cardiological department of Alexandre's Hospital in Athens.

REFERENCES.

1) R. O. Duda -P.E. Hart: Pattern classi fication and scene Analysis (J. Willey & Sons 1973).

2) A.V. Oppenheim - R.W. Schafer : Digital Signal processing (Prentice-Hall 1975).

3) J.L. Talmon : Pattern recognition of the ECG (PHD thesis).

4)Hengeveld, S.J. and J.H.Van Belmmel computer detection of P-waves comp. and Biomed. Res.,9,125-132,1976

5) S.A. Arbelt - I.L. Rubin - H. Gross: Differencial Diagnosis of the electroca-rdiogram (F.A. Davis company 1975)

6) B.s.Lipman - E.Massie - R.E.Kleiger: Clinical Scalar elecardiography (Year book Medical publishers incorporated)

7)T.Y. Young-T.W.Calvert : classification estimation and pattern recognition (American elsevier publishing Company INC).

8)Willems, at all : Protocol for the EEC concerted action project : Common standards for quantitative Electrocardiography .CSE Working document, 1984

9)P.W. Macfarlane-D.I. Melvicce -M.R. Horton-J.J. Bailey:"Comparative evaluation of the IBM (12-leads) and Royal infirmary (orthogonal three-lead) ECG Computer programs";Circulation 63,No.2, 1981.

10)V.Bhargava-A. Goldberger:"Myocardial infraction diminishes both low and high frequency QRS potentials, Power spectrum analysis of lead II" ; J. electrocardiology 14(1),1981,57-60.

11) A. Oberg-R.G.Samuelsson:"Fourier analysis of cardiac action potentials"; J.electrocardiology 14(2),1981,139-142

12)D. Liu-A.Peled : "A new hardware realization on high-speed FFT"IEEE trans. on acoustics, speech and signal processing, Vol ASSP-23,No 6, December 1975.

13)A.F. Shackil:"Microprocessors and the M.D. ". IEEE spectrum April 1981.

14)M. Okada :A digital filter for the QRS complex detection"; IEEE trans. on Biom. Eng. BME -26 December 1979.

15)G.D.Meier - M.C. Ziskin- W. P. Santamore - A.A.Bove: "Kinematics of the beating heart"; IEEE trans. on Biom. eng. BME-27 June 1980.

16)R. F. Santopietro:"The origin and characterization of the primary signal noise, and interference sources in the high frequency electrocardiogram"; Proceedings of the IEEE vol 65,No 5 May 1977.

17) M. Bertrand- R. Guardo-F.A. Roberge -P. Blondeau: "Microprocessor application for numerical ECG encording and transmission"; Preceeding of the IEEE, vol 65,No 5, May 1977.

18) D.E.Gustafson - A.S.Willsky - et.al. :A statistical approach to rhythm diagnosis of cardiograms ; Proceedings of IEEE May 1977

19) Ahmed N. - Rao K.R.:Orthogonal transforms for digital signal processing"; Springer-Verlag 1975.

3. INFORMATION AND COMMUNICATION SYSTEMS

DIGITAL TECHNIQUES in Simulation, Communication and Control
Spyros G. Tzafestas (editor)
Elsevier Science Publishers B.V. (North-Holland) © IMACS, 1985

Chaotic Dynamics of Information Processing: The "Magic Number Seven Plus - Minus Two" revisited.

John S.Nicolis
Dpt of Electrical Engineering
University of Patras, Greece

Ichiro Tsuda
"Bioholonics",Nissho Bldg.5F
Koishikawa 4-14-24
Bunkyo-Ku Tokyo 112,Japan

In a well known collection of his essays in Cognitive Psychology (1974) George A. Miller describes in detail a number of experiments aiming at a determination of the limits (if any) of the human brain in processing information. He concludes that the "channel capacity" of human subjects does not exceed a few bits or that the number of categories of(one dimensional) stimuli from which unambiguous judgement can be made are of the order of "Seven Plus or Minus Two". This "magic number" holds also, Miller found, for the number of random digits a person can correctly recall on a row and also the number of "Self-embeddings" of a recursive linguistic subroutine (that is the number of sentences that can be inserted inside a sentence in a natural language) a human can read throughout without confusion. The above attributes of human performance are not necessarily related; they may be coincidental.

In this paper we propose a dynamical model of information processing by a self-organizing system which is based on the possible use of strange attractors as cognitive devices. It comes as a surprise to find that such a model can, among other things, reproduce the "magic number seven plus-minus two" and also its variance in a number of cases and provide a theoretical justification for them; This justification is based on the optimum length of a code which maximizes the dynamic storing capacity for the strings of digits constituting the set of external stimuli.

We are not however really interested in "explaining away" Millers's numbers per se.Rather our aim is to suggest a mechanism for the following fact: How come that the "human channel" which is so narrow and so noisy(of the order of just few bits per second or few bits per category) possesses the ability of squeezing or "compressing" practically an unlimited number of bits per symbol-thereby giving rise to phenomenal memory.

The issue then is to look after a model which determines the optimum resolution or precision of (dynamically) storing information under the maximum possible capacity. The compressibility of the stored information is also investigated.

1. Possible role of dissipative chaotic dynamics in information processing-Generalities.

Reliable information processing rests upon the existence of a "good" code(or map) or language: namely a set of non-linear recursive rules which generate and store variety (strings of symbols or"templates")at a given hierarchical level and subsequently compress it thereby revealing information at a higher level. To accomplish this task a language-like good music-should strike at every moment an optimum ratio of variety(stochasticity) versus the ability to detect and correct errors (memory). Is there any dynamics available today which might model this dual objective in state space? The answer is: in Principle, Yes (see for example Nicolis 1982,a,b,1983 a,b,c,) we have been investigating recently dynamical systems described by at least three coupled first order ordinary non-linear differential equations whose repertoire include (for different sets of values of the control parameters) multiple steady states, stable periodic orbits (limit cycles) tori and strange chaotic attractors.

We may consider (subscribing to the scientist's credo that events are deduced only by observation and measurement)that variety is generated when the volume in state space expands along certain directions through the dynamical evolution of our system (thereby decreasing resolution) and gets compressed (dissipated) when the volume in state space occupied by the flow contracts (increases resolution) along other directions towards a "compact" ergodic set-the attractor.

A three-dimensional strange attractor for example creates variety along the direction of his positive Lyapounov exponent λ_+ and constrains variety (thereby revealing information) along the direction of his negative Lyapounov exponent λ_-. Since $|\lambda_-| > \lambda_+$ the atractor is acting literally as a "compressor"-on the average that is * . (see next section below).

For values of the control parameters outside those associated with chaos variety (and complexity) is generated by a dynamical system via cascading bifurcations giving rise to broken symmetry**; within the values of the control parameters which trigger aperiodic trajectories variety is generated (or dissipated) via cascading iterations of the (e.g one-dimensional) map on the interval which is constructed as a "poincaré return map" of the attractor. This type of "analog to-digital conversion" is accomplished by parametrizing the attractor along a one-dimensional cut and plotting the position a trajectory crosses the cut versus the position it crosses the next time around the attractor.
This stands for a "stroboscopic" pursuit of the (three dimensional) state space flow and gives rise to a Markov chain whose number of states depend on the partition of the interval.
The change in observable information is generally given by the $\log_2$ of the ratio of states $\Sigma(t)$ distinguishable before and after some time interval.

$$\Delta I = \log_2 \frac{\Sigma_f}{\Sigma_i} \text{ or} \sim \log_2 \frac{V_f}{V_i}$$ where V_f, V_i

are the final and initial volumes in state space. The rate of information creation or dissipation is given as

$$\frac{dI}{dt} = \frac{1}{V}\frac{dV}{dt} \sim \frac{1}{\Sigma}\frac{d\Sigma}{dt}$$

In non-chaotic systems the sensitivity of the flow on the initial conditions grows with time at most polynomially say as $\Sigma(t) \sim t^n$; then $\frac{dI}{dt} \simeq \frac{n}{t}$. The variety creation rate from such a system converges to zero as time passes so the system's behavior is predictable; the set of generated strings form rational numbers.

In chaotis systems the sensitivity of the flow on the initial conditions grows with time exponentially, say as

$\Sigma(t) \sim e^{nt}$ and $\frac{dI}{dt} \sim n$; such a system is a continouous information source; this information is not implicit in the whatever initial conditions but is generated by the flow itself in state space: A chaotic dynamics creates strings of digits which constitute aperiodic oscillations or segments of irrational, non-computable numbers. If such a chaotic system is observed by another cognitive system at a sampling rate less than n, no prediction of the system is possible. We are interested here in cognitive systems characterised by non conservative compact flows where the phenomenon of attraction that is of dimensionality compression (see next section) is possible.

Now for any given typical one-dimensional map in the interval y=F(x) the probability density P(x) for finding the orbit at x can be estimated via successive iterations, from the recursive relation.

$$P_n(x) = \sum_{i=1}^{2^{n-1}} \frac{P_1(x_i)}{\left|\frac{dF^{(n-1)}}{dx}\right|_{x_i}}$$

where $x_i = (F^{n-1})^{-1}(y)$
$x(n+1) = F(x(n)),\ (n,=2,3,....),$

and the first p.d.f $P_1(x)$ can be taken arbitrarily and the resulting P(y)-corresponding to the initial $P_1(x)$ transformed by the action of the map-is the first approximation. Successive iterations of the map will produce closer and closer approximations to the correct asymptotic function of P(x). If the map possesses a stable steady state or a number of stable periodic orbits P(x) will converge to a sharp "δ" function spike or a series of "δ" -like functions on the periodic points. In the chaotic regime of the control parameters the map will possess a continouous P(x) with interspersed spikes.
The information change ΔI per iteration of the particular initial point x on the interval will be determined as

$\Delta I = \log_2 \left|\frac{dF}{dx}\right|$ and will amount to variety

* The Lyapounov exponents determine the average amount of information production ($\lambda>0$) or dissipation ($\lambda<0$) per iteration.
** For example this is the case of Hopf bifurcation leading from a destabilized steady state to a stable limit cycle.

creation for slopes >1 and information (dissipation) for slopes <1.
The average information change over the whole interval $0<x<1$ will be given by

$$\langle I\rangle = \int_0^1 P(x)\log_2 \left|\frac{dF(x)}{dx}\right| dx \text{ bits};$$

If $t(x)$ stands for the time between successive passes through the return map, the average information production (or dissipation) rate will be

$$\left\langle\frac{dI}{dt}\right\rangle = \int_0^1 \frac{P(x)}{t(x)} \log\left|\frac{dF(x)}{dx}\right| \cdot dx \ \frac{\text{bits}}{\text{sec}}$$

Finally if the initial condition from which the process starts is not known exactly (which is always the case)* i.e it is determined by a apriori probability density distribution $P_0(x)$, one gets for the informational value of this initial condition the expression

$$S = \int_0^1 P_0(x)\log_2\left\{\frac{P_0(x)}{P(x)}\right\} dx \text{ bits within the}$$

interval; then the "memory" of the processor measured as the time elapsing until the flow gets completely disconnected from the initial conditions is given

as $$T = \frac{S}{\left\langle\frac{dI}{dt}\right\rangle} = \frac{\int_0^1 P_0(x)\log_2\left\{\frac{P_0(x)}{P(x)}\right\}dx}{\int_0^1 \frac{P(x)}{t(x)} \log_2\left|\frac{dF(x)}{dx}\right| dx} \text{sec}$$

Beyond this limit, the iterative process becomes so fine that the processor amplifies essentially intrinsic microscopic noise; due to the great resolution created by the cascade of iterations this noise cannot be "smeared out" any longer and declares itself on the cognitive level thereby rendering any further measurement or observation unreliable.
Computing simulation (Shaw, 1981) shows that in specific cases the number of iterations under which T is achieved may be rather small. (∿20÷30).

II. Information dimension, compressibility and non-uniform processing.

The information dimension D_1 of a strange attractor (see for example Farmer. 1982, Farmer et al. 1983) is the number of bits one requires for the unambiguous determination of any point on the attractor; in turn it represents the maximum number of bits we can reliably store in such a self sustained dynamics - under a given resolution.
The "average degree of compressibility" ensured by the attractor is defined (Nicolis et al 1983$_c$) as $n = \frac{N-D_1}{N}$ % where N is the dimensionality of state space in which the attractor is embedded as a compact subset.

Formally in order to calculated D_1 one proceeds as follows:
One partitions the N-dimensional state space in $n(\varepsilon)$ hypercubes of size (degree of resolution) ε from each of which the flow (or "the trace of the scanning path" of the processor) passes at least once. Let $P_i(\varepsilon)$ be a number proportional to the relative frequency with which the scanner visits the specific square i. Then the "entropy" of the digitized pattern can be calculated as:

$$-\sum_{i=1}^{n(\varepsilon)} P_i(\varepsilon)\log_2 P_i(\varepsilon) \text{ bits,}$$

and as the resolution becomes finer and finer one may be interested in calculating how the distribution $P_i(\varepsilon)$ scales with resolution. One could obtain the "information dimension" or the bits required for the determination of any point on the "scanning curve" of the processor as:

$$D_1 = \lim_{\varepsilon\to 0} \frac{-\sum_{i=0}^{n(\varepsilon)} P_i(\varepsilon)\log_2 P_i(\varepsilon)}{\left|\log_2 \frac{1}{\varepsilon}\right|}$$

i.e the asymptotic value of the slope of entropy versus resolution.
To make calculations feasible one should not start from the above expression however, but rather from a relationship between the information dimensionality and the spectrum of the Lyapounov-exponents of the flow (or the discrete map) and calculate not only D_I but also the standard deviation ΔD_I from the second moments of the distribution of local divergence rate of trajectories whose first moments are the Lyapounov exponents; ΔD_I would indicate how much fuzziness enters in the average degree of compressibility:

$$\eta = \frac{N-D_I}{N}$$ of information realized by the attractor in N-dimensional space.

Since compressibility of a string of digits is the necessary prerequisite for

---

*This initial condition is a point x_0 on the unit interval. It can be expressed as a digital number.0110011100111...; with overwhelming probability this number is incompressible.

the subsequent simulation of the time series involved, the importance of strange attractors as information processing models cannot be overlooked.
Indeed for an attractor simulating some aspects of a cognitive, system one has two basic requirements: Big storage capacity and good compressibility.

Let us turn first to the simplest attractors (in any N-dimensional state space) namely stable steady states and stable limit cycles: They have information dimensionality of zero and one respectively. *Consequently they are very poor as information storage units but since they possess only non-positive Lyapounov exponents are ideal as information compressing devices.
Strange attractors on the other hand, via an harmonious combination of positive and negative Lyapounov exponents λ_+, λ_- can in principle comply somewhat with both requirements:
Strange attractors may possess a considerable information dimension and this idiom makes them suitable for information storage; On the other hand, being "attractors" i.e possessing also negative Lyapounov exponents λ_- such that $|\lambda_-|>\lambda_+$ they can serve at the same time as information compressors.
The type of the strange attractor however we intend to employ as a model here must be rather "loose" in order to comply with the preceding experimental results.
It must, in other words, possess a large information dimensionality in order to allow for maximum dynamical storage of variety.
We are going to investigate the optimum resolution ε under which this information dimensionality becomes maximum; the ensuing compressibility factor $C_I=N-D_1$ will be also investigated. So in case where our primary aim is compessibility the best attractors around are steady states and limit cycles.
In case however our data (this case) ask for a model which can ensure first of all large storage ability-without jeopardizing compressibility-a "loose" strange attractor is the preferred model.
In cognition usually one needs both types of attractors-working in "tandem" perhaps. But in some cases (Nicolis and Tsuda 1984) we can do better. Namely we can have just one attractor which under the action of external noise switches from the one model to the other, thereby complying with both requirements for maximum compressibility and maximum storage capacity.

----
* In the limit $\varepsilon\to 0$; For ε finite, the dimensionality of a limit cycle $D_1<<1$.

III. Specific examples and Relevance of the Model to Cognitive Psychology-experimental results.

What is the relevance (if any) of the dynamical theory given in sections I and II vis-a-vis the experimental results reported in the introduction-which results essentially refer to empirical limitations of human attributes in information processing? To answer this question let us try to see if there exists in various specific cases of dynamical models of processors an optimum resolution ε (different for each model) or an optimum codeword length for which the cardinal parameter in our theory, the information dimension of the attractor becomes maximum-without jeopardizing the average "compressibility factor"

$$\eta=\frac{N-D_I}{N}\ \%$$

Let us consider the expression $C_I=N-D_I$ for the degree of average compression realized by the particular attractor and try to calculate the critical resolution ε^* for which D_I becomes maximum or,

$\frac{\partial C_I}{\partial \varepsilon}=0$. To take into accout the best case let us perform the above calculation for the maximum value of

$$D_I=\frac{-\sum_{i=1}^{n(\varepsilon)} P_i(\varepsilon)\log_2 P_i(\varepsilon)}{\log 1/\varepsilon},\ (\varepsilon \text{ finite})$$

The maximum value of the information dimension under given finite resolution ε is the "fractal dimension" of the attractor and is realized for

$$P_i(\varepsilon)=\text{const}=\frac{1}{n(\varepsilon)}\ \text{so,}$$

$$D_I=-\frac{\ln[n(\varepsilon)]}{\ln\varepsilon}\ \text{and}$$

$$C_I=N+\frac{\ln[n(\varepsilon)]}{\ln\varepsilon}=\frac{N\ln\varepsilon+\ln[n(\varepsilon)]}{\ln\varepsilon}=$$

$$=\frac{\ln[\varepsilon^N n(\varepsilon)]}{\ln\varepsilon}$$

We intent now to express $n(\varepsilon)$ in terms of the Lyapounov exponents of the attractor and the resolution length ε.
To this end, we proceed as follows:
Let the number of points on a (one-dimensional) poincaré return map of the attractor concerned be M; this means that we determine the orbit with strings of M digits long. The number of points-"boxes" representing the attractor, on the other hand, with a degree of coars-

ness ε is just n(ε).

The number of points representing the attractor per cycle is therefore

$\frac{n(\varepsilon)}{M} \sim t_c$ where t_c is the time between successive striongs of M bits long. The degree of resolution ε has to do with the precision with which we can determine any one of 2^M strings of 0's and 1's that is the Mth refinement of a Markov partition: we have then,

$$\varepsilon \sim \frac{1}{2^M} \text{ and } M = \frac{\ln\frac{1}{\varepsilon}}{\ln 2}\text{ ; So } n(\varepsilon) = t_c \frac{\ln(\frac{1}{\varepsilon})}{\ln 2}$$

During the time t_c, $\frac{n(\varepsilon)}{M}$ sampling have occurred with say sampling time period $\Delta\tau \sim 1$.

But after $\frac{n(\varepsilon)}{M}$ iterations in the map the system is completely disengaged from the initial conditions which means that the time t_c can be estimated from the relation:

$\varepsilon e^{\lambda_+ . t_c} \sim 1$ where λ_+ is the positive Lyapounov exponent. So,

$$t_c \sim \frac{\ln(\frac{1}{\varepsilon})}{\lambda_+} \text{ and finally } n(\varepsilon) = \frac{\left\{\ln(\frac{1}{\varepsilon})\right\}^2}{\lambda_+ . \ln 2};$$

Substituting in the expression of C_I we get:

$$C_I = \frac{N\ln\varepsilon + 2\ln(\ln\frac{1}{\varepsilon}) + \ln(\frac{1}{\lambda_+ . \ln 2})}{\ln\varepsilon} \text{ or}$$

$$C_I = N + \frac{\gamma + 2\ln(\ln\frac{1}{\varepsilon})}{\ln\varepsilon} \text{ where } \gamma = \ln(\frac{1}{\lambda_+ . \ln 2})$$

The requirement for maximum fractal dimension $\frac{\partial C_I}{\partial \varepsilon} = 0$ gives for the optimum resoloution $\varepsilon^* = \exp\left[-e^{\frac{2-\gamma}{2}}\right]$ or the optimum code length $M^* = \frac{\ln(\frac{1}{\varepsilon^*})}{\ln 2}$ (1) from which,

$$C_I(\varepsilon^*) = N - 2e^{-\frac{2-\gamma}{2}} \text{ bits} \quad (2)$$

These are our final formulas, for the minimum average compressibility i.e the maximum fractal dimensionality of the attractor concerned and the corresponding optimum code length M*. It remains to make sure that the extremum of the function:

$$f(\varepsilon) = -D_i(\varepsilon) = \frac{\gamma + 2\ln(\ln\frac{1}{\varepsilon})}{\ln\varepsilon}, \varepsilon \neq 0$$

is indeed a minimum or $D_I(\varepsilon)$ is maximum.

In fact we have:

$$\frac{\partial f(\varepsilon)}{\partial \varepsilon} = \frac{2 - \left[\gamma + 2\ln(\ln\frac{1}{\varepsilon})\right]}{\varepsilon(\ln\varepsilon)^2} \text{ and}$$

$$\frac{\partial^2 f(\varepsilon)}{\partial \varepsilon^2} = \frac{-6 + 2\gamma + 4\ln(\ln\frac{1}{\varepsilon}) + (\ln\varepsilon)\left[\gamma - 2 + 2\ln(\ln\frac{1}{\varepsilon})\right]}{\varepsilon^2(\ln\varepsilon)^3};$$

for $\varepsilon = \varepsilon^* = \exp\left[-\exp(\frac{2-\gamma}{2})\right]$ we get

$$\left(\frac{\partial^2 f(\varepsilon)}{\partial \varepsilon^2}\right)_{\varepsilon=\varepsilon^*} = \frac{2}{\exp\left[-2\exp(\frac{2-\gamma}{2})\right]\exp(\frac{3}{2}(2-\gamma))}$$

which is always positive. So f(ε) possesses a minimum at ε* and consequently $D_I(\varepsilon) = -f(\varepsilon)$ becomes maximum.

$D_I(\varepsilon)$ becomes zero for $\varepsilon_0 = \exp\left\{-e^{-\gamma/2}\right\}$.

Negative values of D_I do not possess of course any physical meaning.

Let us now apply formulas (1) and (2) to a number of simple case.

a) The Lorenz attractor, $\dot{x} = \sigma(y-x)$, $\dot{y} = -y + rx - xz$, $\dot{z} = xy - bz$ (for b=4, σ=16 and r= 45.92)

we calculate with the computer $\lambda_+ \cong 1{,}5$ $\gamma \sim -0.03895$,

$C_I(\varepsilon^*) \sim 3 - 0{,}72157 \sim 2{,}28$ $\varepsilon^* \sim 0.062$ and $M^* \sim 4$.

That is, the optimum code which maximizes storing capacity by the Lorenz attractor is 4 bits long; Nevertheless the resulting compressibility is impressive too-much larger of what one calculates from the information dimensionality with ε→0. ($C_I(0) \cong 3 - 2.06 = 0.94$)

b) The Bernoulli map: $x' = \mathrm{Mod}_1(2x)$.

In this case of one-dimensional map-assumed here to be uniform-the number of covering segments of resolution ε is

$n(\varepsilon) \sim \frac{\ln(1/\varepsilon)}{\lambda_+}$ from which we get,

$$C_I \sim N + \frac{\ln(\ln \frac{1}{\varepsilon}) - \ln\lambda_+}{\ln\varepsilon}$$ The requirement

$$\frac{\partial C_I}{\partial \varepsilon} = 0$$ gives for the optimum resolution

$$\varepsilon^* \sim \exp\left\{-e^{1+\ln\lambda_+}\right\}$$ from which

$$C_I(\varepsilon^*) = N - e^{-(1+\ln\lambda_+)}$$

The numerical calculation for $\lambda_+ = 2$ in this case, give $C_I(\varepsilon^*)=0,81606$, $\varepsilon^* = 0,004354$. and $M^*\sim 7\div 8$ bits.

The second case above corresponds to a map with uniform p.d.f P(x). So the NUF(1) here is zero. In other cases however (the assymetric tent map the logistic map, the Henon map, the Rössler attractor, Nicolis et al 1983c) the NUF may, for certain intervals of the control parameters greatly exceed the Lyapounov exponent.

In such cases the maximization of the average storing capacity does not provide the optimum code length: One expects a great variance ΔM^*-which is in conformity with most of Miller's experiments about the limitinglength of errorless recall of strings of items or digits.

----

(1) Non-uniformity-factor. Describes the variance of the local divergence rate of a chaotic trajectory.

References

1) G.A. Miller "The psychology of communication",Penquin (1974)

2) J.S.Nicolis "The role of chaos in Reliable information processing" J.of the Franklin Inst. In press. Also in "Synergetics"(Ed.H.Haken) Proceeding of the Elmau Conference 1-8 May (1983)a

3) J.S.Nicolis "Sketch for a dynamical theory of Language" Kybernetes (1982a) April, 11 pp 123-132.

4) J.S.Nicolis "Should a reliable information processor be chaotic"? Kybernetes (1982b) Oct. 11 pp.269-274

5) J.S.Nicolis "Dynamics of Hierarchical Systems. An evolutionary approach" To appear in Springer series of Synergetics (H.Haken Ed) (1983)b.

6) J.Doyne Farmer, E.Ott, J.A Yorke "The Dimension of chaotic attractors" Physica 7D 1983 p153.

7) J.S.Nicolis, G Mayer-Kress, G Haubs "Non uniform chaotic dynamics with implications to information processing" Z.Naturforsch (1983c) 38a pp1157-1169.

8) Robert Shaw "Strange Attractors, Chaotic Behavior, and Information Flow" Z.Naturforsch. 36a, pp 80-112 (1981)

9) J.Doyne Farmer "Information Dimension a-d the probabilistic structure of chaos" Z.Zaturforsch 37a 1304 (1982)

10) J.S.Nicolis, I.Tsuda Submitted to: Bulletin of Mathematical Biology (1984)

DIGITAL TECHNIQUES in Simulation, Communication and Control
Spyros G. Tzafestas (editor)
Elsevier Science Publishers B.V. (North-Holland) © IMACS, 1985

FREQUENCY RESOLUTION: A COMPARATIVE STUDY OF FOUR ENTROPY METHODS

N.A. Katsakos-Mavromichalis, M.A. Tzannes and N.S. Tzannes

Electrical Engineering Department
University of Patras, Greece

Four entropy methods (MESA, SMESA, MCESA and SMCESA) are used in the problem of resolving two sinusoids, in the presence of additive white and 1/f noise. SMCESA appears to have the overall edge in this study.

1. THE FOUR ENTROPY METHODS

The four entropy methods considered in this paper are outlined below. Details of each method can be found in the reference given for each method.

A. Maximum Entropy Spectral Analysis (MESA): The estimation of the spectrum $S(\omega)$ in this case is based on maximizing the functional

$$\int_{-\infty}^{+\infty} \log S(\omega)\, d\omega \qquad (1)$$

subject to costraints of the form

$$R(n) = \frac{1}{2\pi} \int_{-\infty}^{+\infty} S(\omega)\, e^{jn\omega} d\omega \qquad (2)$$

which reflect the a priori calculated values of the correlation function $R(\tau)$ of the data. The method was introduced by Burg [1].

B. Minimum Cross-Entropy Spectral Analysis (MCESA) : In this case $S(\omega)$ is estimated by minimizing the functional

$$\int_{-\infty}^{+\infty} q(x) \log \frac{q(x)}{p(x)}\, dx \qquad (3)$$

where $q(x)$ denotes a probability density function of the data and $p(x)$ an a priori guess of $q(x)$. Details of the method can be found in Shore [2]. Under certain conditions the functional (3) reduces to minimizing an expression involving $S(\omega)$ and a prior guess of $S(\omega)$ denoted by $P(\omega)$. The minimization is also subject to constraints of the form (2). The method reduces to MESA when $P(\omega)$ is taken to be flat (white noise).

C. Spectral MESA (SMESA): Here the maximized functional has the form

$$\int_{-\infty}^{+\infty} S(\omega) \log S(\omega)\, d\omega \qquad (4)$$

and again, the maximization is subject to constraints like (2). The method is due to Tzannes and Argeris [3] and others.

D. Spectral MCESA (SMCESA): This method is based on estimating $S(\omega)$ by minimizing the functional

$$\int_{-\infty}^{+\infty} S(\omega) \log \frac{S(\omega)}{P(\omega)}\, d\omega \qquad (5)$$

under constraints of the form (2). $P(\omega)$ is a prior guess of the desired $S(\omega)$. The method is due to Tzannes, Politis and Tzannes [4].

2. FREQUENCY RESOLUTION APPLICATIONS

The above methods were used in trying to resolve two sinusoids in the presence of additive noise. In both of the applications described below, the two sinusoids were brought closer together until resolution was lost. The performance of each method and comparisons between them are given for each application. When a prior guess of the spectrum was necessary, it was taken to be that of the noise. All the calculations were based on the Discrete Fourier Transform and simple Newton-Raphson algorithms were used for the determination of the estimated spectra.

A. Two sinusoids in white noise: In this application the true data is assumed to have a spectrum of the form

$$G_{\pm K} = \begin{cases} 1.05 & (f_x = 0.165) \\ 1.05 & (f_n = \text{movable points}) \\ 0.05 & \text{elsewhere} \end{cases}$$

as shown below in Fig.1.

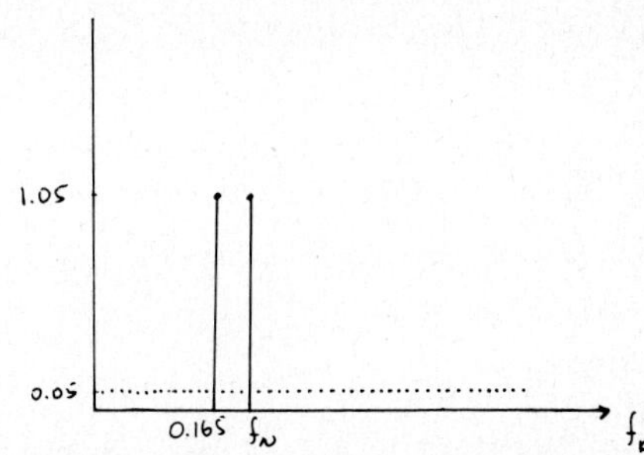

Fig. 1. Application A. The true Spectrum

The frequency range was 50 equally spaced points 0.005, 0.015....0.50. One of the two sinusoids was kept at f_k=0.165 and the other was moved - from an initial location which provided resolution (if it existed) - closer and closer to f_k=0.165, until resolution was not certain. The estimated spectra for each f_n were found by using six values of the R(τ) of the assumed spectrum. Since the noise was assumed white, only two methods are applicable here, MESA and (SMCESA becomes SMESA).

Figures 2,3 and 4 show the results for MESA. In Figure 2 f_n=0.315 and the two sinusoids are clearly resolvable. When f_n=0.255, the appearance of the two is still indicated, as shown in Fig.3. For f_n=0.245, the existence of the second sinusoid becomes uncertain, as shown in Figure 4.

Figures 5,6 and 7 show the results for SMESA, Resolution is lost here at f_n=0.255. MESA appeas to have a small edge in the presence of additive white noise.

B. Two Sinusoids in 1/f noise: In this application the true spectrum was taken to be

$$G_{\pm k} = \begin{cases} 2.0 \; (f_k = 0.165) \\ 2.0 \; (f_n = f_n \text{ movable}) \\ 1/f_k \text{ elsewhere} \end{cases}$$

whose form is shown in Fig. 2 below

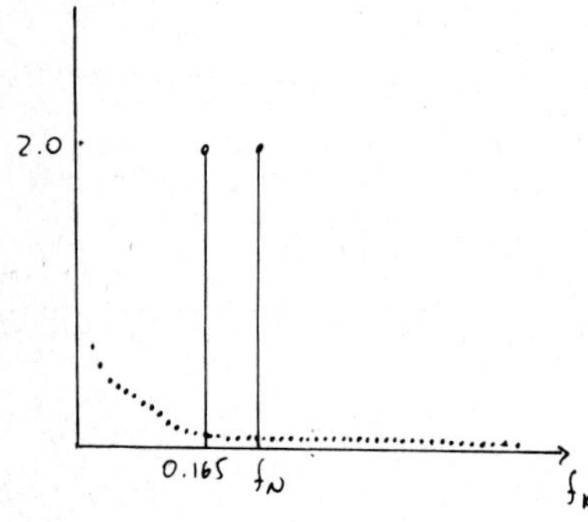

Fig. 2. Application B. True Spectrum

The rest were exactly the same as in application A.

The results of the application of the four methods are given in Figs. 9-20. It is obvious that SMCESA has the big edge here. MESA and MCESA follow with approximately equal performance, the least effective is SMESA.

3. CONCLUSION

The method suggested by our research group SMCESA, appears to be best in the presence of 1/f noise. In the presence of white noise, its equivalent, SMESA, performs somewhat worse, a fact suggested by the results in [5]. What is interesting, however, is that SMCESA - largely ignored due to the results in [5]- jumps to first place in the resolution problem when the noise is 1/f. We suspect that such a performance is maintained for other non-white additive noises.

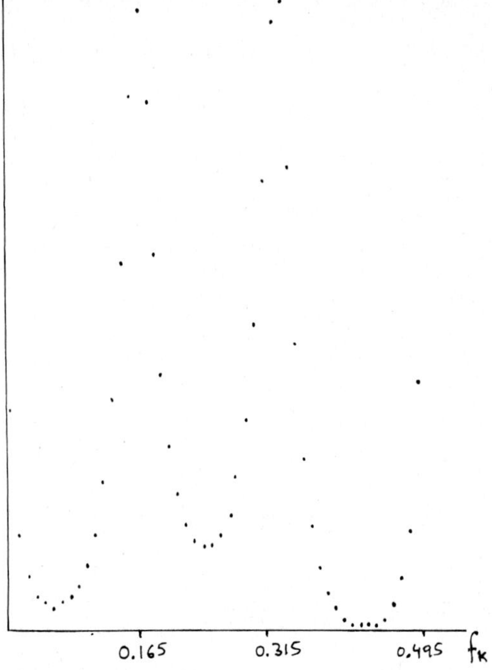

Fig. 3 Application A. MESA:f_n = 0.315

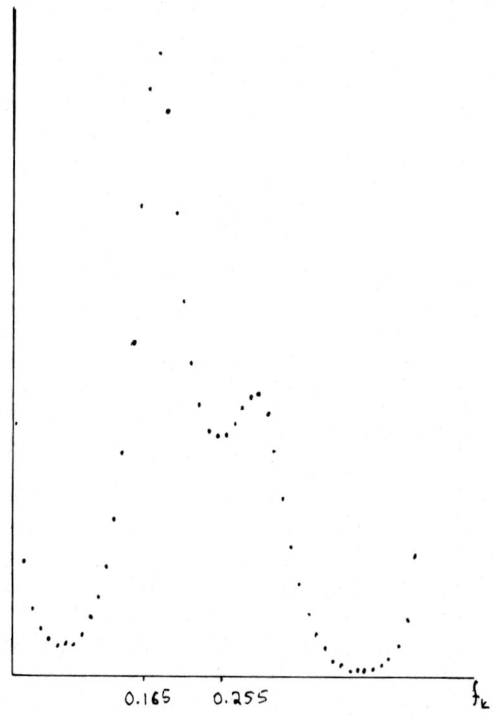

Fig. 4 Application A. MESA: f_n = 0.255

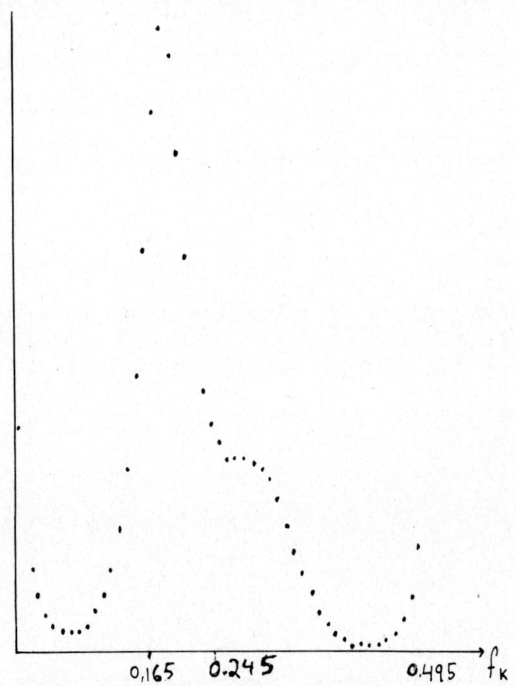

Fig. 5 Application A. MESA: f_n=0.315

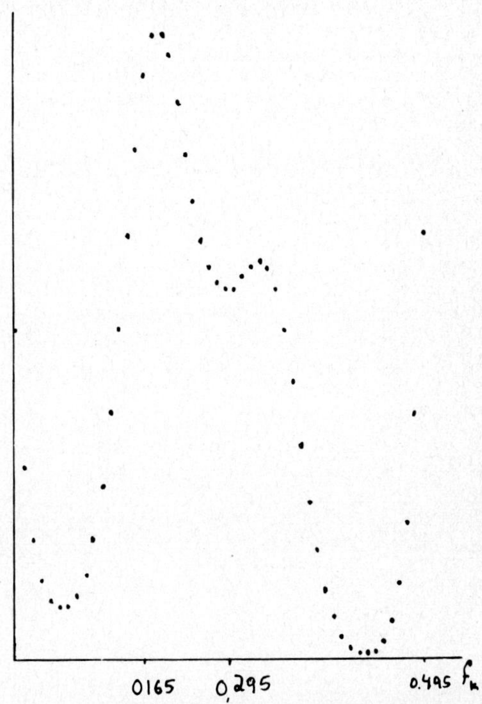

Fig. 7 Application A. SMESA: f_n=0.265

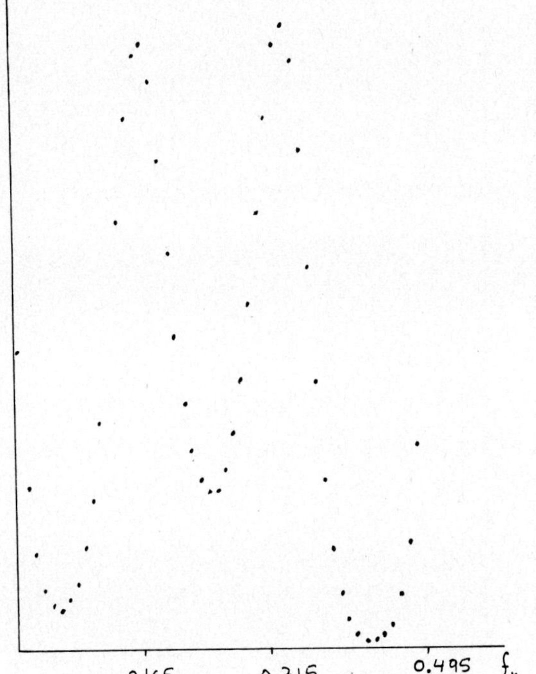

Fig. 6 Application A. SMESA: f_n=0.315

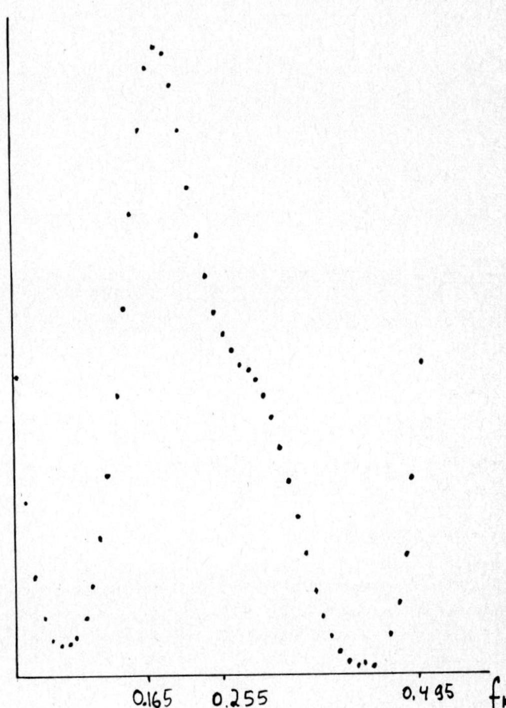

Fig. 8 Application A: SMESA: f_n=0.245

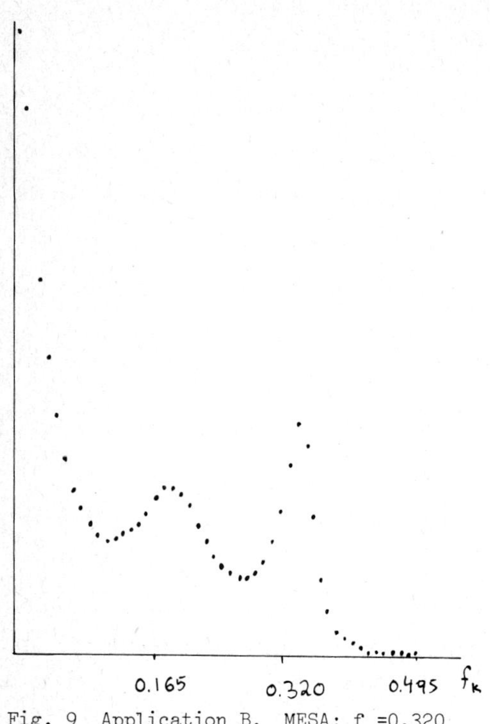

Fig. 9 Application B. MESA: f_n=0.320

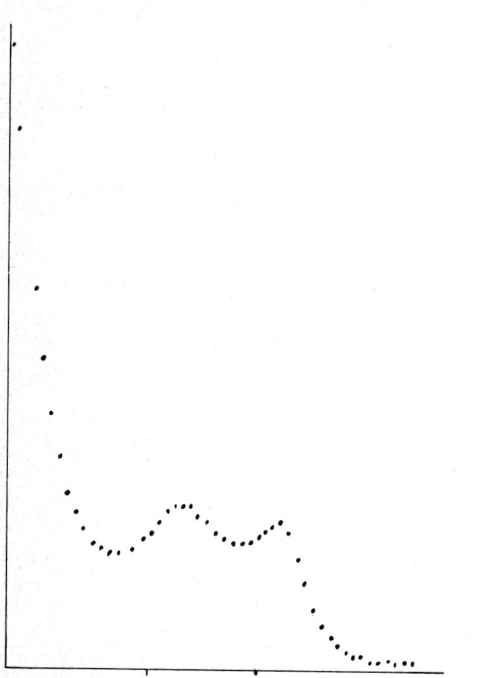

Fig. 10 Application B. MESA: f_n=0.305

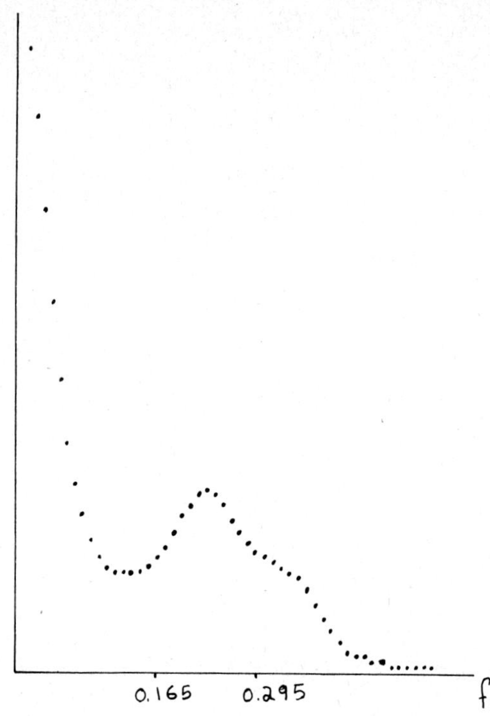

Fig. 11 Application B. MESA: f_n=0.295

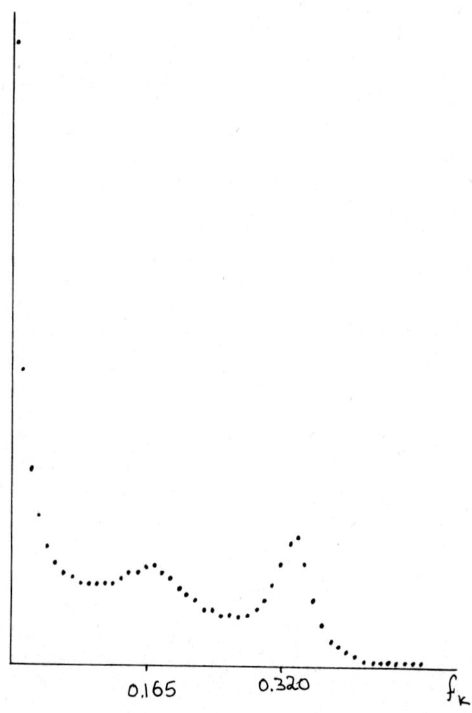

Fig. 12 Application B. MCESA: f_n=0.320

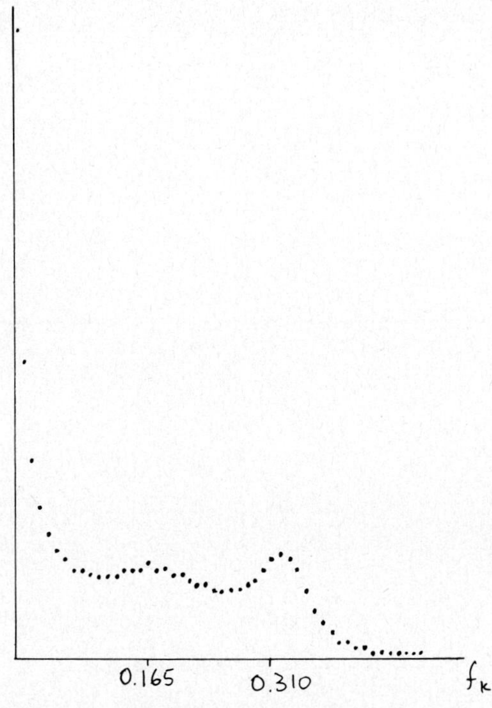

Fig. 13 Application B. MCESA: f_n=0.310

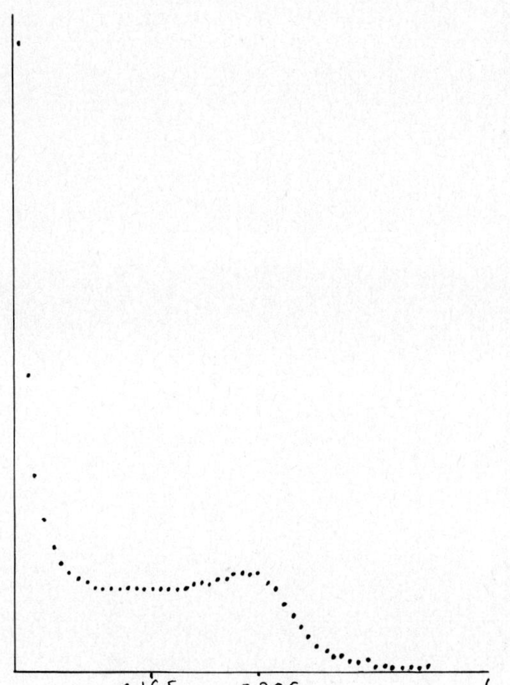

Fig. 14 Application B. MCESA: f_n=0.295

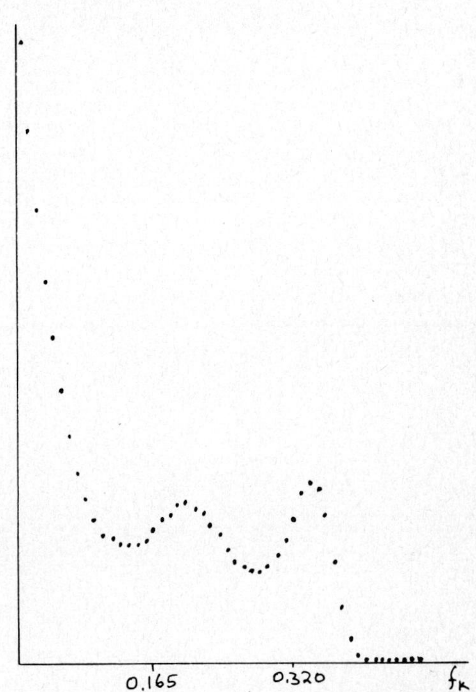

Fig. 15 Application B. SMESA: f_n=0.320

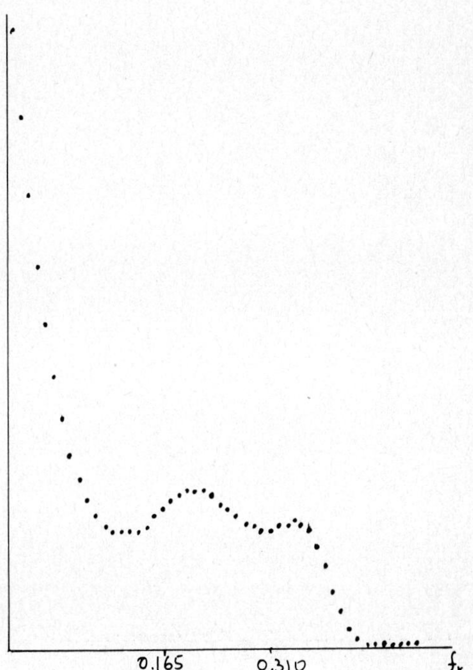

Fig. 16 Application B. SMESA: f_n=0.310

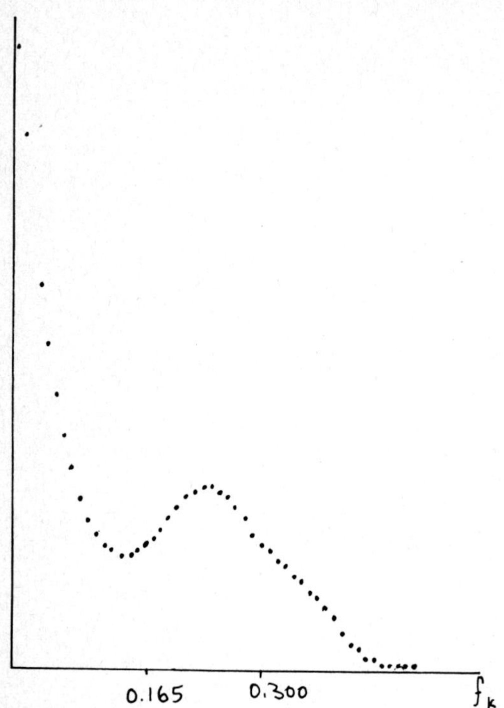

Fig. 17 Application B. SMESA: f_n=0.300

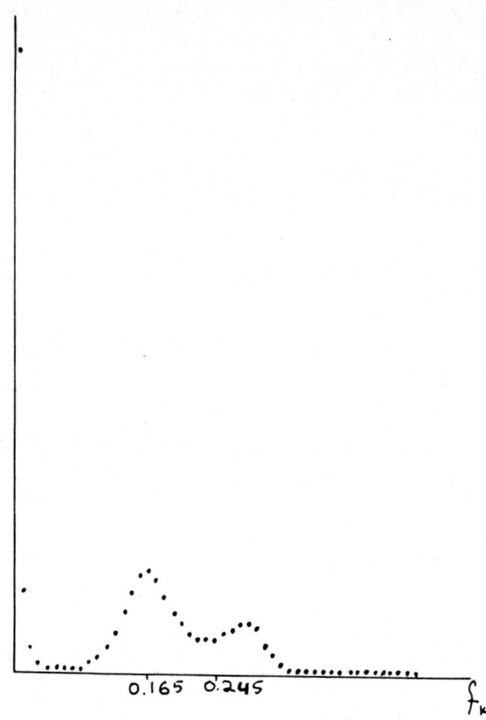

Fig. 19 Application B. SMCESA: f_n=0.245

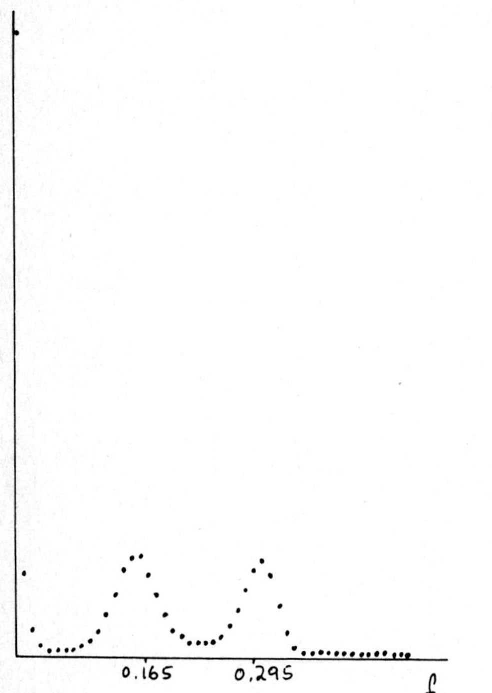

Fig. 18 Application B. SMCESA: f_n=0.295

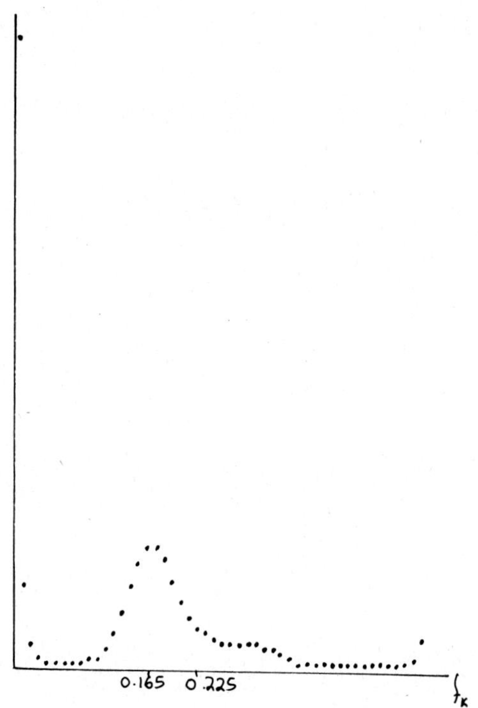

Fig. 20 Application B. SMCESA: f_n=0.225

REFERENCES:

[1] J.P. Burg, "Maximum Entropy Spectral Analysis", Proc. 37th Meeting Society of Exploration Geophysics (Oklahoma City) Oct. 31 1967.

[2] J.E. Shore,"Minimum Cross-Entropy Spectral Analysis" IEEE Trans. ASSP, Vol. ASSP-29, No. 2, April 1981.

[3] N.S. Tzannes and T.G. Argeris, "A New Approach to the Estimation of Continuous Spectra" Kybernetes, Vol. 10, pp. 123-133, 1981.

[4] M.A. Tzannes, D. Politis and N.S. Tzannes, "A General Method of Minimum Cross-Entropy Spectral Estimation" to appear in IEEE ASSP transactions.

[5] R. Johnson and J.E. Shore, "Which is the Better Entropy Expression for Speech Processing: - SlogS or logS?" IEEE Trans. ASSP, February 1984.

DIGITAL TECHNIQUES in Simulation, Communication and Control
Spyros G. Tzafestas (editor)
Elsevier Science Publishers B.V. (North-Holland) © IMACS, 1985

CONSIDERATIONS ON LOW COMPLEXITY CODES CONCERNING SYMMETRY AND CYCLICITY

F. Afrati and M. Dendrinos

Electrical Engineering Department
National Technical University
Athens, Greece

The binary error correcting codes that are examined in this paper are codes, which are constructed out of shorter subcodes. The method of construction is well described by a bipartite graph. The one set of nodes of this graph represents the single bits of a codeword of the new code, while the other set of nodes represents the subcodes; there are edges only between subcode-nodes and bit-nodes, having the interpretation that the set of bits that are connected to a specific subcode must be a codeword of this subcode.
Cyclically symmetrical structures of such code constructing graphs are studied here and the positive effect of cyclic codes (when used as subcodes on such structures) on the error-correcting capability of the resulting code is demostrated. A class of codes with error-correcting capability t=3 is extensively studied in a rigorous theoretical way.

I. INTRODUCTION

The construction of longer error correcting codes out of shorter subcodes is an often used method for the derivation of long codes with relatively simple decoding algorithms. Such an example consist the product codes. The following structure can be considered to be a generalisation of the product codes [1].

We construct a long code by defining a number of subsets (not necessarily disjoint) of the set of bits that constitute its codewords and demanding that each subset (with its elements-bits in a certain order) should satisfy the parity-check equations of a certain subcode. In other words each such subset of bits must form a codeword of its corresponding subcode ; the length of the subcode is of course equal to the cardinality of the corresponding subset. This structure is better illustrated by the use of a bipartite graph. A bipartite graph is a graph, the nodes of which consist of two disjoint sets and edges are allowed only between nodes of different sets. In our structure one of the sets of nodes represents the subcodes used and each node of the other set represents each single bit of a codeword of the code that we are constructing. There is an edge between a subcode-node and a bit-node if the particular bit is amongst the bits that must form a codeword of that subcode. See fig.1 for an example. The constructed code C is of length 12 and a sequence of bits $d_1 d_2 \ldots d_{12}$ is a codeword of C if and only if for every subcode C_i, the set of bits connected with that subcode and in the order indicated by the labels in the connecting edges constitute a codeword of C_i, e.g. $d_1 d_3 d_2 d_4 d_5$ must be a codeword of C_1, etc.
This code constructing technique is a very general one and it does not give any particular properties of the new code except of the obscure indication that the decoding algorithm of the subcodes can be used in the decoding procedure of the resulting code, which, it seems, is made much simpler by this way. In that context, certain classes of such code constructions are studied in this paper.

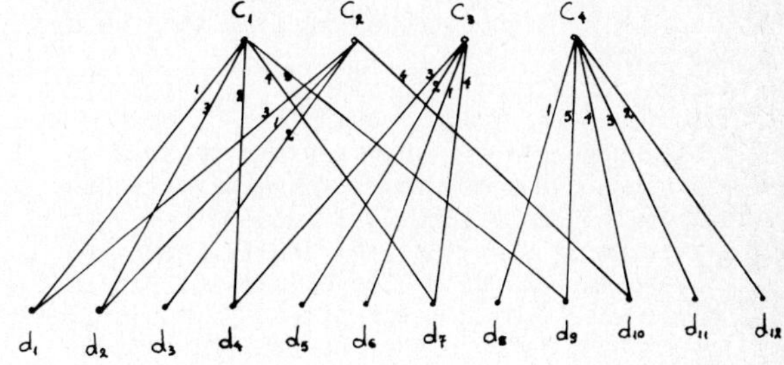

Fig.1 Example for the illustration of the constructing method; a code of length 12 is created out of four subcodes

In particular, in section II, four structures are examined. In all of them the bipartite graph that supports the construction is cyclically symmetrical. In these structures, by using as subcodes mostly the Hamming codes (7,4,3) or simple cyclic codes as the (9,6,2) etc., a number of certain good codes are found (as compared to the ones referred in the table in ref. [3]). It is observed that when cyclic codes are used as subcodes the resulting codes exhibit greater error correcting capability and it is conjectured that for bipartite graphs which are cyclically symmetrical the use of cyclic codes

as subcodes gives the best results as far as error correcting capability of the new code is concerned.
In section III, the construction of a whole class of codes is demonstrated, namely the codes $(2(2^r-1),\ 2^r-1-r,\ d)$ which are constructed from a cyclically symmetrical bipartite graph by using the Hamming code $(2^r-1,\ 2^r-1-r,\ 3)$ as the center subcode and the simple code(3,2,2)(a simple parity check equation)as the outer subcodes;d is shown to be equal to 6 and it is shown that when the Hamming code used is cyclic then the minimum distance of these codes is 7. Also in the latter case a simple decoding algorithm is given which corrects all the 3 errors that the code is able to correct; the complexity of this algorithm equals (up to a constant factor) the complexity of the decoding algorithm of the Hamming code, i.e., it grows linearly with the length of the code.

II. DERIVATION OF CODES FROM CYCLICALLY SYMMETRICAL STRUCTURES

In this section we shall examine four different structures,on which if we apply proper subcodes we end up with a new code. In each of these structures we are searching for the best derived code, under all possible permutations of the edge-labeling (which gives the order in which the bits appear in each subcode) keeping the subcodes the same.
An equivalent but more convenient technique of doing this is the following:instead of permuting the edge-labeling, we keep it unchanged and we permute the columns of the parity-check matrix of the corresponding subcode.
Also instead of studying the results under all possible permutations of the columns of the check matrices (which is practically impossible) we use (in the 1st and the 2nd structure) a "half-exhaustive" search following a criterion according to which certain permutations are equivalent(i.e they end up with equivalent codes); this reduces the number of cases that must be examined considerably (by a factor of nearly 55000 for the 1st structure and 28,000 for the 2nd one).

1st structure

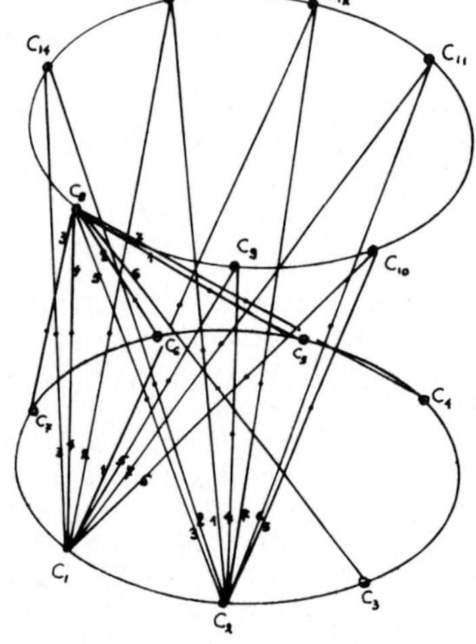

Fig.2

We consider the bipartite graph with 14 subcode-nodes being placed on two rings-7 nodes each ring (see fig. 2). There are 49 bit -nodes, each bit-node being connected with a subcode on the first and a subcode on the second ring, in such a way that each pair of subcodes-one belonging to the first and the other to the second ring-to have one and only one bit in common. Thus the subcodes should be of length 7. We use the Hamming code (7,4,3) for all the subcodes. The edge-labeling is cyclic and we can see it in fig.2. It is reasonable to retain the cyclic symmetry of the graph in the labeling too. By cyclic symmetry we mean, here,that rotating the graph around the axis that connects the centres of the two rings,so that subcode-node i is superimposed to subcode-node j then the edge-labeling of i (in its new position) remains the same as the edge-labeling of j (in its original position). Additionally the relation of the labeling for the subcodes of the upper ring to the labeling of the subcodes of the lower ring is such that the graph retains symmetry-in the above sense-as to the plane that is perpendicular in the middle to the above axis.
We use identical parity-check matrices for the subcodes of the same ring, having thus two parity check-matrices on which we try several combinations of permutations of their columns.It is easy to show that the only structures of the parity-check matrix H of the Hamming code that give different (not equivalent)codes when used in the code-contruction indicated in fig.2 are the following.First remember that the columns of H (3X7)consist of all the vectors (except the zero one)of the vector space of 3 dimensions on the finite field $\{0,1\}$.Thus in any matrix H a basis of that vector space appears necessarily either in the first 3 columns or in the 1st,2nd & 4th columns.This is so because a)$h_1+h_2\neq 0$ & b)either $h_3\neq h_2+h_1$ or $h_3=h_1+h_2$ respectively. (Where h_i the i-th column of H).
All the matrix structures that come up from different such bases but from the same setting of the rest ofthe columns, if these columns are seen as linear combinations of the specific basis vectors,have the same effect on the code-construction. (The number of these equivalent parity check-matrices are $4\times 7!/5!=168$). Thus, independently of which the vectors b_1, b_2, b_3, are,the matrix (the 1st case considered) $[b_1,b_2,b_3,b_1+b_2,\ b_1+b_3,\ b_2+b_3,\ b_1+b_2+b_3]$ will always have the same effect, while the matrix $[b_1,b_2,b_3,b_2+b_3,b_1+b_2,b_1+b_3,b_1+b_2+b_3]$ will have a different effect.Concludingly,we can use a specific vector basis (the $[0,0,1]$, $[0,1,0]$, $[1,0,0]$) and derive all the structures of H that result to non-equivalent codes by considering all the permutations of the rest 7-3=4 columns of H in the first case (these columns being the 4th-7th) or of the rest 3 columns of H (the 3rd is defined) in the 2nd case (being the 5th-7th) .

In the first case matrix H= $[h_1,h_2\ldots h_7]$ will

have the form $\begin{bmatrix} 0 & 0 & 1 & \\ 0 & 1 & 0 & \cdots \\ 1 & 0 & 0 & \end{bmatrix}$, while in the 2nd case it will have the form $\begin{bmatrix} 0&0&0&1& \\ 0&1&1&0&\cdots \\ 1&0&1&0& \end{bmatrix}$

So we end up with 4!+3!=30 different combinations to be examined while in the first place we had 7!=5040 combinations ($30=\frac{5040}{168}$). Thus we must examine each of the 30 case of the check matrix of the top subcode with the 30 cases of H of the bottom subcode, i.e. 30X30=900 cases. But because of the reflexive symmetry of the labeling in the graph the 900 cases are reduced to 30+29+...+2+1=465. Therefore instead of trying 7!X7! cases we try only 465 cases.
The 4 best codes being derived by this graph in addition with the corresponding check matrices HT and HB of the top and bottom subcodes are the following :i) HT= $(b_1,b_2,b_1+b_2,b_3,b_1+b_3,b_2+b_3,b_1+b_2+b_3)$ HB=$(b_1,b_2,b_3,b_1+b_3,b_2+b_3,b_1+b_2,b_1+b_2+b_3)\Longrightarrow(49,7,21)$,

ii) HT=$(b_1,b_2,b_1+b_2, b_3, b_1+b_3, b_1+b_2+b_3,b_2+b_3)$, HB as above $\Longrightarrow(49,8,20)$,

iii) HT=$(b_1,b_2,b_3,b_1+b_2,b_1+b_3,b_2+b_3,b_1+b_2+b_3)$, HB=$(b_1,b_2,b_3, b_1+b_2+b_3,b_2+b_3,b_1+b_3,b_1+b_2)\Longrightarrow(49, 12,16)$,

iv) HT=$(b_1,b_2,b_3,b_1+b_2,b_2+b_3,b_1+b_2+b_3,b_1+b_3)$HB as in case (i)$\Longrightarrow(49,16,9)$.

2nd structure

We consider the bipartite graph with $\ell+1$ subcode-nodes forming a spoked-wheel. One of these nodes is placed in the center (center subcode-node) and the rest ℓ in the circumference (outer subcode-nodes). There are $\frac{\ell(\ell+1)}{2}$ bit-nodes, corresponding to all possible pairs of subcode-nodes and being connected to them. We examine 2 cased of ℓ.1st case: For $\ell=7$ (see Fig.3) the code has length 28 and the subcodes have length 7. So we use Hamming codes as the center subcode and as the outer one as well (common for all the outer subcode nodes).We put cyclic edge-labeling with cyclical symmetry too.

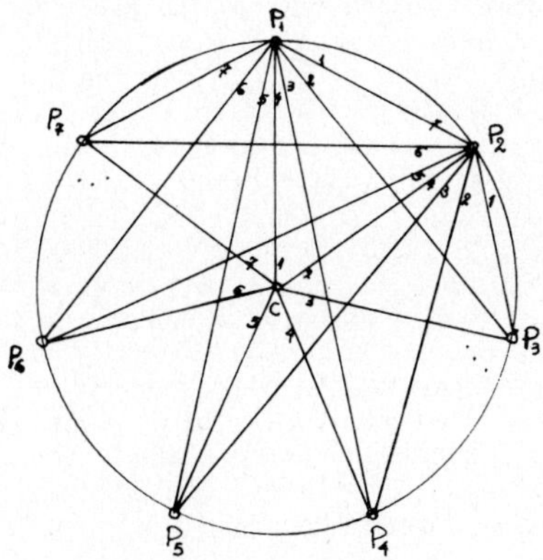

Fig.3

After examining all possible combinations of HC and HO (the check matrices of the center and the outer subcodes correspondingly) it is noticed that the best codes result when the center subcode is cyclic, that being an effect obviously of the cyclic symmetry of the graph. If HC= $(b_1,b_2,b_3,b_1+b_2,b_2+b_3,b_1+b_2+ b_3,b_1+b_3)$ and HO=$(b_1,b_2,b_1+b_2,b_3,b_1+b_2+b_3,b_2+b_3,b_1+b_3)\Longrightarrow(28,9,10)$.
Other good codes found by the use of this graph are (28,5,12) and (28,10,6).
2nd case: For $\ell=9$ the code has length 45 and the subcodes have length 9. As the center subcode we use the cyclic code(9,6,2) with generator polynomial $g(x)=x^3+1$. The parity check matrix HC of this code is made from the check polynonial

$$h(x)=\frac{x^9+1}{g(x)}=x^6+x^3+1.$$

A code (9,5,3) is used as the outer subcode whose check matrix HO can be made by 9 distinct and non zero columns of 4 bits, in random order. Trying such codes in place of the outer subcode we find some codes (45,k,d). The best found codes are (45,7,20) and (45,9,17)

$$HO=\begin{bmatrix} 0&1&0&1&0&0&0&1&1 \\ 1&0&0&0&1&0&1&0&0 \\ 1&0&1&1&0&1&1&1&0 \\ 0&1&1&1&0&0&1&0&0 \end{bmatrix}\Longrightarrow(45,7,20)$$

$$HC=\begin{bmatrix} 0&0&1&0&0&1&0&0&1 \\ 0&1&0&0&1&0&0&1&0 \\ 1&0&0&1&0&0&1&0&0 \end{bmatrix}$$

$$HO=\begin{bmatrix} 1&1&0&0&1&0&1&1&1 \\ 1&1&1&0&1&1&0&0&1 \\ 1&1&0&1&0&1&0&0&0 \\ 0&1&0&0&1&1&1&0&0 \end{bmatrix}\Longrightarrow(45,9,17)$$

These codes are very good and we can find them in Mac Williams' table (1976) of the best known codes [3].

3rd structure

We consider the bipartite graph with ℓ subcode-nodes being places on a ring. There are $\frac{\ell(\ell-1)}{2}$ bit-nodes corresponding to all possible pairs of subcode-nodes and being connected to them. For $\ell=8$ we are directed to the code (28,4,13), for $\ell=10$ the best resulted codes are (45,10,15) and (45,11,13) and for $\ell=11$ the best codes are (55,11,20), (55,12,18), (55,13,16).

4th structure

We consider the bipartite graph with $\ell+2$ subcode-nodes, the ℓ of them on a ring and the other 2 (the center nodes) above and below the plane of the ring. There are $\frac{(\ell+2)(\ell+1)}{2}-1$ bit-nodes corresponding to all possible pairs of subcode-nodes and being connected to them except the pair of two center nodes. For $\ell=7$,& $\ell=9$, using cyclic centre subcodes (the 7,4,3) and the (9,6,2) respectively), the best resulted codes are (35,4,17), (35,10,9), (35,8,11) and the (54,14,16), (54,15,14), (54,16,12).

III. THEORETICAL STUDY OF THE CLASS OF CODES $(2(2^r-1),2^r-1-r)$

The graph used here is a simpler form of the one in Fig.3.

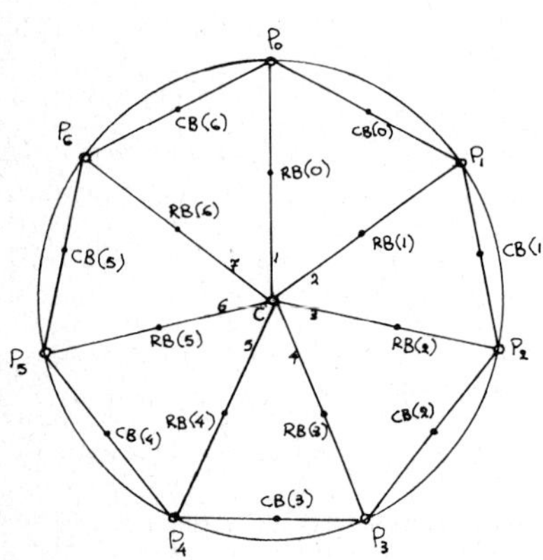

Fig.4

This form of spoked wheel is made as follows : we connect the center subcode-node with all the outer ones and we do the same for every pair of neighbouring outer subcodes-nodes; then we replace each edge by a bit-node and two edges (see Fig.4). If the number of the outer subcode-nodes is 2^r-1 the number of bits-nodes is $2(2^r-1)$.

Fig.4 can be generalised for 2^r-1 outer subcodes-nodes. Let C be the center and $P_0,P_1,P_2...,P_{2^r-2}$ the outer suboce-nodes, RB(i) the radius-bit between C and P_i and CB(i) the chord-bit between P_i and P_{i+1}.

Since the center subcode-node has degree $s=2^r-1$ we associate it with a $(2^r-1, 2^r-1-r,3)$ Hamming code. Every outer subcode-node represents a simple parity check between the 3 bits connected to it. Let s be the length of the center subcode. Then the code being built by the graph has length 2s. Such a construction results to doubling the length of the code adding only parity bits. This is so, because the outer subcodes consitute s parity checks or s equations in GF(2) with s unknown variables (the chord-bits). Thus the added s bits (chord-bits) are dependent on the original ones (radius-bits), i.e. they are parity bits. Therefore the number of information bits remains the same.

The null space of the new code results from the rows of a matrix M which can be easily formed from the graph. M has the r rows of the center subcode's check matrix HC and 2^r-1 rows in addition, which represent the parity checks of the 2^r-1 outer subcodes. Since $n=2(2^r-1)$ and $k=2^r-1-r$ it implies that the number of the redundant bits equals to $r+2^r-1$. So all the rows of M are linearly indepedent. Thus M is a check matrix (let us call it H hereafter) of the code. H has a special form that leads us to find the minimum distance of the code.

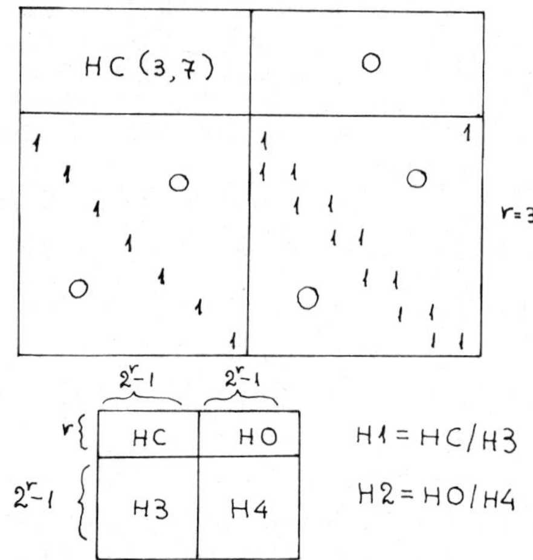

Fig. 5

<u>Theorem-1:</u> A lower bound for the minimum distance of the code $(2(2^r-1),2^r-1-r)$, being built as above, is 6.

Proof: We break the matrix H in 2 parts. Let H_1 be the $(r+2^r-1)\mathrm{x}(2^r-1)$ submatrix (i.e. the left half) and H_2 be the remaining submatrix (i.e. the right half). See Fig.5 for illustration. We shall prove that all the linear combinations of 5 or less columns of H are nonzero and there is, in general, a linear combination of 6 columns equal to zero. [4].

It is easily seen that for a linear combination of columns of H to be zero it is necessary to involve both columns from the H_1 matrix and from the H_2 matrix. Especially at least 3 of H_1's columns must be involved in the sum in order to make its first r components equal to zero. Since any sum of H_2's columns has even weight we must add to it an even number of H_1's columns in order to derive a zero vector. Therefore 4 H_1's columns at least must be added to 2 H_2's columns to have probably a zero vector. Since we can choose freely the order of the columns of the matrix HC, it is certain that there would be some ordering which will result in 6 columns of H being added to zero

We think that by choosing properly matrix HC, it is possible to construct a matrix H such that no linear combination of 6 columns of H can be zero. Let H_3 be the $(2^r-1)\mathrm{x}(2^r-1)$ unity submatrix and H_4 be the neighbouring $(2^r-1)\mathrm{x}(2^r-1)$ sumbatrix (see Fig.5). Consider a vector V of weight 4 that results as the sum of 2 H_4's columns. Its 'ones' are always located at 2 pairs of neighbouring positions,

and especially cyclically neighbouring. The term "cyclically" means that the first and last positions are considered also as neighbouring. E.g. See in fig.5 the special case of H for r=3. The sum of the 2nd and 7th columns of H_4 is V=(1,1,1,0,0,0,1).
Vector V equals also to the sum of 4 H_3's columns and especially of those columns corresponding to the nonzero positions of V. Therefore the only way to make a linear combination of 4 H_3's columns and 2 H_4's columns to be equal to zero is to take care that the 4 columns of H_3 to be 2 pairs of neighbouring columns. Consequently if matrix HC has such a structure that no sum of 4 such columns equals to zero then it is impossible to exist 6 columns of H that sum up to zero. So we conclude that the minimum distance of such a code would be 7.
What kind of code has a check matrix HC with the previous properties?
We prove in Lemma-1 that the check matrix of a cyclic Hamming code has this proper structure.

Lemma-1 :The vector resulting as the sum of 4 columns of the check matrix of a cyclic Hamming code such that 2 of these columns be neighbouring and the other 2 be also neighbouring (2 pairs of neighbouring columns) is always nonzero. (We mean cyclically neighbouring).
Proof: A cyclic Hamming code of length 2^r-1 has a check matrix
$H=(1,\alpha,\alpha^2,\dots,\alpha^{2^r-2})$ where α is a primitive element of GF (2^r), a root of a primitive polynomial of degree r(e.g. x^3+x+1 for r=3).
Let see the sum of the 2 neighbouring columns α^n, α^{n+1} and the 2 also neighbouring α^m,α^{m+1}, where n,m aren't succesive (let n>m).
$\alpha^{n+1}+\alpha^n+\alpha^{m+1}+\alpha^m=\alpha^n(\alpha+1)+\alpha^m(\alpha+1)=\alpha^m(\alpha+1)$.
$.(\alpha^{n-m}+1)\neq 0$ because $\alpha\neq 0,\alpha^{n-m}\neq 1$ (α is a primitive element of GF (2^r))
Therefore the following theorem has been proved.

Theorem-2 . The minimum distance of the $(2(2^r-1),2^r-1-r)$ code equals 7 if the center subcode is cyclic.

The decoding algorithm of the code $(2(2^r-1),\ 2^r-1-r,7)$

For some received vector v=(RB(0),RB(1),..., ,RB(2^r-2)) we construct a vector (called characteristic) $V_{CH}=(C,\ P_0,\ P_1,P_2,\dots,P_{2^r-2})$.

C=1 if the syndrome of the center subcode is nonzero, otherwise C=0. P_i is equal to XOR{CB (i-1),RB(i),CB(i)}. P_i=0 implies that either there is no error in the 3 bits being connected to subcode-node P_i or there are 2 errors; P_i=1 implies that either 1 of the 3 or all of them are in error. Notice that additions involving indices are meant modulo (2^r-1).
The following lemma relevant to the structure of the check matrix of a cyclic Hamming code is used in the algorithm. Let CN_i the i_{th} column of the matrix.

Lemma-2 . Every column of the check matrix H of a cyclic Hamming code (say the CN_j) results as the sum of one and only one pair of neighbouring columns. It means that there are no 2 other neighbouring columns which sum up to CN_j .

Proof:$H=(1,\alpha,\alpha^2,\dots,\alpha^{2^r-2})$. Suppose that $CN_i+CN_{i+1}=\alpha^n$. Then $CN_{i+1}+CN_{i+2}=\alpha^{n+1}$
$CN_{i+2}+CN_{i+3}=\alpha^{n+2}$, etc. Since the order of α is 2^r-1, these 2^r-1 sums are all distinct.
This simple property of cyclic codes helps us in locating the positions of 2 neighbouring errors.
This couldn't have been possible if the center subcode was not cyclic in which case we could not have corrected every combination of 3 errors. In any way the use of both lemmas 1 and 2 will be made more clear in the exposition of the decoding algorithm of this code.
Below we state the decoding algorithm of the code $(2(2^r-1),2^r-1-r,7)$ consisted of 9 cases. See for illustration the special case of Fig.5. The name of a case represents the number of errors made in radius or chord-bits . E.g. R_2C_1 means 2 errors in radius-bits and 1 error in a chord-bit. Also we define as features of each case those of the variables of the characteristic vector which are equal to 1.

I) CASE R_1

Features:C,P_i. They appear in R_1C_1 too. Thus we need for the decoding more information. This is taken from the syndrome s of the central subcodeword. Here s=CN_i ⟹ RB(i) false.

II) CASE C_1

Features :P_i,P_{i+1} ⟹ CB(i) false

III) CASE R_1C_1

Features:C,P_i (as in R_1). If s=CN_{i-1} ⟹

⟹ RB(i-1),CB(i-1) false; if s=CN_{i+1} ⟹

⟹ RB(i+1), CB(i) false

IV) CASE R_2

Features:C,P_i,P_j (they appear in R_2C_1-α and R_2C_1-b too). Here s=CN_i+CN_j ⟹ RB(i),RB(j) false.

V) CASE C_2

SUBCASE C_2-α

Features:P_i,P_{i+2} ⟹CB(i), CB(i+1) false

SUBCASE C_2-b

Features: $P_i, P_{i+1}, P_j, P_{j+1}$ with i,j not successive $\Longrightarrow$ CB(i), CB(j) false

VI) CASE R_3

Features: C(0 or 1), P_i, P_j, P_k (they appear in R_1C_2-α and R_1C_2-b too). Here $s=CN_i+CN_j+CN_k \Longrightarrow$ $\Longrightarrow$ RB(i), RB(j), RB(k) false.

VII) CASE R_1C_2

SUBCASE R_1C_2-α

Features: C, P_i, P_{i+1}, P_k and k not succesive to i or i+1 (as in a special case of R_3). If $s=CN_{k-1} \Rightarrow$ $\Longrightarrow$ CB(i), RB(k-1), CB(k-1) false, if $s=CN_{k+1} \Rightarrow$ $\Longrightarrow$ CB(i),RB(k+1), CB(k) false.

Here notice that if the syndrome could have been equal to $CN_i+CN_{i+1}+CN_k(R_3)$ and to CN_{k-1} (R_1C_2-α) at the same time, then we woudn't have the ability to recognize which of the 2 combinations of errors had occured. But this assumption contradicts lemma-1.

So using a not cyclic center subcode the correction of every combination of 3 errors wouldn't have been possible. For the same reason s cannot be equal to $CN_i+CN_{i+1}+CN_k$(R3) and to $CN_{k+1}(R_1C_2$-α) at the same time.

SUBCASE R_1C_2-b

Features: C, P_i, P_{i+1}, P_{i+2} (as in a special case of R_3). Here $s=CN_{i+1} \Longrightarrow$ CB(i), RB(i+1),CB(i+1) false.

VIII) CASE R_2C_1

SUBCASE R_2C_1 -α

Features: C, P_i, P_j (they appear in R2 and R_2C_1-b too). If $s=CN_{i-1}+CN_j$(1) $\Longrightarrow$ RB(i-1), CB(i-1),RB(j) false; if $s=CN_i+CN_{j+1}$ (2) $\Longrightarrow$ $\Longrightarrow$ RB(i), RB(j+1), CB(j) false

SUBCASE R_2C_1-b

Features: C, P_i, P_j with i,j not successive (as in special cases of R_2 and R_2C_1-α).

If $s=CN_i+CN_{j-1}$(3) $\Longrightarrow$ RB(i),CB(j-1), RB(j-1) false; if $S=CN_{i+1}+CN_j$(4) $\Longrightarrow$ RB(i+1),CB(i),RB(j) (4) false.

(1) and (2) cannot hold at the same time because of lemma-1 . Neither can the following pairs of equations:{(1),(3)}, {(2),(4) },{(3),(4) }.

SUBCASE R_2C_1-c

Feature: C. The corresponding combination of errors is the triangular combination. It means, 1 chord-bit & 2 radius-bits of a triangle, i.e. RB(i),RB(i+1),CB(i). The outer subcodes don't help us to find this i. Since the false radius-bits are neighbouring the syndrome has to be equal to the sum of 2 neighbouring columns. Because of lemma-2 there is a unique pair of neighbouring columns with the same sum. Thus i has been recognized.

IV) CASE C_3

SUBCASE C_3-α

Features: $P_i, P_{i+3} \Longrightarrow$ CB(i),CB(i+1),CB(i+2) false

SUBCASE C_3-b

Features: $P_i, P_{i+2}, P_j, P_{j+1}$ with i,j not successive and $j \neq i+2 \Longrightarrow$ CB(i),CB(i+1),CB(j) false

SUBCASE C_3-C

Features: $P_i, P_{i+1}, P_j, P_{j+1}, P_k, P_{k+1}$, with i,j and j,k & k,i not successive CB(i),CB(j),CB(k) false. It is easy to see that, the complexity of the above algorithm grows linearly with the length of the code [2]. By the use of the characteristic vector (in addition with the syndrome, if C=1) we find easily, using the above algorithm the occured errors. Some examples are given below for greater illustration:

1) V_{CH}= (0,0,1,0,0,0,1,0) $\Longrightarrow C_3$ with i=5 $\Longrightarrow$ CB(5), CB(6),CB(0) false.

2) V_{CH}=(1,0,0,1,0,0,0,0,) $\Longrightarrow R_1$ or R_1C_1. If $s=CN_3 \Longrightarrow$ R1 with RB(2) false; if $s=CN_2 \Longrightarrow R_1C_1$ with RB(1),CB(1) false; if $s=CN_4 \Longrightarrow R_1C_1$ with RB(3), CB(2) false.

3) V_{CH}=(1,1,0,1,0,0,0,0) $\Longrightarrow R_2$ or R_2C_1-α or R_2C_1-b. If $s=CN_1+CN_3 \Longrightarrow R_2$ with RB(0),RB(2) false; if $s=CN_7+CN_3 \Longrightarrow R_2C_1$-α with RB(6),CB(6),RB(2) false;
if $s=CN_1+CN_4 \Longrightarrow R_2C_1$-α with RB(0), RB(3),CB(2) false; if $s=CN_2+CN_3 \Longrightarrow R_2C_1$-b with RB(1), CB(0), RB(2), false; if $s=CN_1+CN_2 \Longrightarrow R_2C_1$-b with RB(0), RB(1),CB(1) false.

V. REFERENCES

[1] Tanner, M., A recursive appoach to low complexity codes, IEEE Transaction on Info.T., Vol. IT-27,No.5. (Sep.1981).

[2] Aho, Hopcroft and Ullman, The design and analysis of computer algorithms (1974).

[3] MacWilliams and Sloane, The theory of error-correcting codes (North Holland Pub.C., N.Y.1977)

[4] Peterson and Weldon, Error correcting codes (Cambridge, MA:MIT Press, 1972).

DIGITAL TECHNIQUES in Simulation, Communication and Control
Spyros G. Tzafestas (editor)
Elsevier Science Publishers B.V. (North-Holland) © IMACS, 1985

IMPLEMENTING Q.B.E.

F.Afrati, C.Papadimitriou, G.Papageorgiou, E.Paschos

National Technical University
Athens

Q.B.E is a user-friendly Data Manipulation Language (D.M.L) for a Data Base system. It is referred to the relational model and it exhibits features that make it very powrful. It is proved that it is more powerful than the relational algebra.

In this paper we describe the structure of Q.B.E. and we report the problems that arose at implementing Q.B.E. in the computer using PASCAL.

1. INTRODUCTION

In handling a large collection of data (i.e. a data base-D.B), the D.M.L plays a basic role; The D.M.L is the most important part of the Data Base Management System (D.B.M.S) and it is used for the communication of the user with the D.B. The ever growing need of manipulating a large number of data rises the interest for the development of efficient D.M.L's. By the term manipulation we mean the execution of operations such as retrieval, insertion, deletion or update of the stored in the D.B. information; for obtaining correct results after the execution of these operations and for reassuring the integrity of the D.B., a number of constraints are necessary, such as, which attribute will be the key, on which domain are the attributes defined, e.t.c.

Qyery languages (Q.L.) for the relational model break down into two broad classes:the relational algebra based languages and the relational calculus (R), based ones, the latter class being further divided into two classes corresponding to the two forms of relational calculus, namely the tuple R.C (T.R.C) and the domain R.C (D.R.C). The equivalence of the expressive power of these three abstract languages is proved [1].

A language that can (at least) simulate tuple calculus or equivalently relational algebra or domain calculus is said to be complete.

Real Q.L. usually provide the capabilities of the abstract languages and additional capabilities as well,such as insertion, deletion, modification of tuples; some additional features frequently available, are arithmetic capability, assignment and print commands, aggregate functions.

For these reasons, the well known query languages are really "more than complete", that is they can compute functions, that have no counterpart in relational algebra or calculus. Many, but not all become equivalent to relational calculus when we throw away arithmetic and aggregate operators.

Languages directly equivalent to the one of the two calculus are called nonprocedural, while languages directly equivalent to the R.A are called procedural languages. The language in which we are interested here is the Query-by-Example (Q.B.E) and it is a nonprccedural language, directly equivalent to D.R.C. It was developed by Zloof [2,3,4,5]. The basic principle of this language is the formulation of logical expressions equivalent to the D.R.C.; this is done with the use of symbols and operators in proper places on the tables that describe the several relations of the D.B. and which are displayed by the computer terminal for convenience. It is noted that Q.B.E remains "more than complete" even after eliminating arithmetic and aggregates; in particular Q.B.E allows also computation of the transitive closure of a relation.

The main symbols used are:
P. (print) for retrieval
I. (insert) for data insertion
D. (update) for data update
KEY for key definition
DOMAIN for domain definition
c.e.(constant element):numbers or words of the domain of an attribute.
<u>e.e.</u> (example element):underlined strings not usually in the domain of an attribute.

We give here some examples which show the quere formulation in Q.B.E [2].

<u>Simple retrieval</u>: Print out all colours.

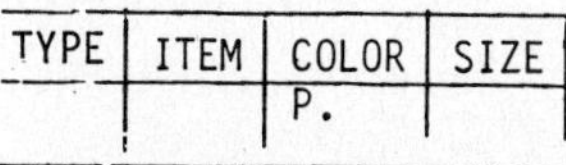

TYPE	ITEM	COLOR	SIZE
		P.	

Fig. 1

<u>Qualified retrieval</u>: Print the names of the employees who work in the toy department and

earn more than $10.000

EMP	NAME	SAL	MGR	DEPT
	P.	> 10.000		TOY

Fig. 2

Qualified retrieval using links: Print all the green items sold by the toy department

TYPE	ITEM	COLOR	SIZE
	P.NUT	GREEN	

SALES	DEPT	ITEM
	TOY	NUT

Fig. 3

Example elements linked in the same table: Find the names and salaries of the employees who earn more than Lewis.

EMP	NAME	SAL	MGR	DEPT
	P.	P.>S1		
	LEWIS	S1		

Fig.4

Simple insertion: Insert into the employee table a new employee of the Toy Department named Jones, whose salary is $10.000 and whose manager is Henry.

EMP	NAME	SAL	MGR	DEPT
I.	JONES	10000	HENRY	TOY

Fig.5

Simple deletion: Delete all information about employees in the Toy Department.

EMP	NAME	SAL	MGR	DEPT
D.				TOY

Fig.6

Simple update Update Henry's salary to $50.000

EMP	NAME	SAL	MGR	DEPT
U.	HENRY	50.000		

Fig.7

Operators of the Q.B.E are all the commonly known arithmetic and relational operators.

There is also a number of built-in functions like CNT.(count), SUM., AVG. (average),MAX.(maximum), MIN.(minimum), UN.(unique),two ordering functions A.O (ascending order), D.O(descending order) [zℓo2].
The special expression ALL ee represents a multiset (that is a set with duplications of its elements).

2. THE CONVERSION OF THE QUERY FROM THE NON-PROCEDURAL FORM TO A PROCEDURAL ONE

A Q.B.E interpreter which translates Q.B.E into PASCAL is constructed.

The most important feature of our Q.B.E interpreter is that it works parametrically.

The Query answering is not based on the given relational scheme but on the language characteristic elements (operators, example elements-e.e, constant elements-c.e.,e.t.c.). This parametrical form of Q.B.E is useful for any use into any relational D.B.
i.e.
The answering procedure of a question like: "Find the employees who earn $10.000" is the same with the corresponding one of the question "Find the books which have one author named Marx". Indeed the anwering procedure of both queries contains a selection referred to the value $10.000 or Marx of the corresponding columns and finally a projection on the column Employee or Booktitle.

The general idea of the answering procedure is the following.If there are in the question c.e (or relational operators followed by a c.e) we make a selection (or restriction generally).

After this operation,we are left with one or more smaller relations than the initial ones. We work further with them and/or some of the initial relations, of course (if needed).

Subsequently if there are identical e.e in some places of the tables (in the same or in different relations) we make a natural (or θ-) join.

In this way we have constructed hyper-relations of two or more of the initial relations. (This step is optional and is applied only if there are e.e.).

The final step is projection. It's applied after all the answering procedure operations (selections, restrictions, joins) have been done. It's applied on the attribute where there is a P. operator (stand for print).

Other optional operations applied before the projection are all the operations referred to the build-in function, to the secondary operators, e.t.c.

In an attempt to illustrate schematically the query answering procedure we show a bottom-up tree.

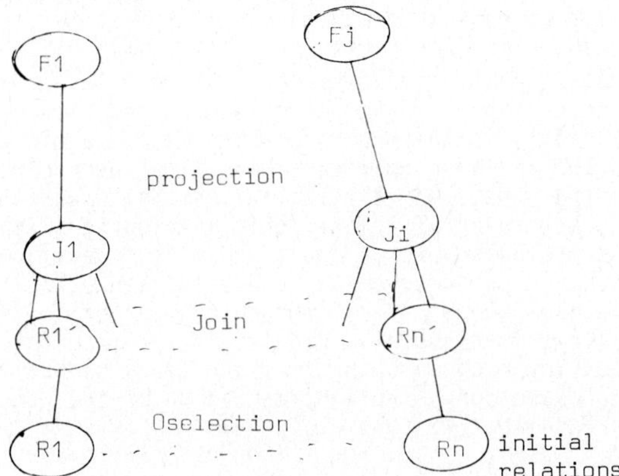

Oselection means selection or no operation at all.

Fig. 8

We give an example of the query answering procedure.
Sapose we have a relational scheme:
EMP (NAME,SAL,MGR,DEPT)
TYP (ITEM, COLOUR, SIZE)
SALES (DEPT, ITEM)
SUPPLY (ITEM, SUPPLIER)

Where:
EMP, TYP, SALES, SUPPLY and NAME, SAL, MGR,DEPT, ITEM, COLUR SIZE, SUPPLIER are relation names and attribute names respectively.

The query:
"Print all the green items sold by the toy department".
The question is expressed in Q.B.E. as follows:

TYP	ITEM	COLOUR
	P.x	GREEN

SALES	DEPT	ITEM
	TOYS	x

in D.R.C.

$$\{r:(r,\text{GREEN}) \varepsilon \text{ TYP } \wedge (\text{TOYS},r) \varepsilon \text{ SALES}\}$$

in R.A

$$\Pi_{\text{ITEM}} (\sigma_{\text{GREEN}} \text{ TYP } |X| \sigma_{\text{TOYS}} \text{ SALES})$$

where:

Π :stands for projection
$|X|$:stands for natural join
σ :stands for selection

The three forms of the question mentioned above are equivalent (Codd).

The query answering procedure mentioned above solves another problem as well, i.e the conversion from the non-porcedural form (since Q.B.E is a non-procedural language) to procedural (R. A's expressions equivalent to Q.B.E).

The above procedure is the main part of the code generator of our interpreter, since it transforms Q.B.E expressions into R.A expressions expressible in PASCAL(a strongly structured language).

Our interpreter wasn't extended to include other query-like operations as well, such as insertion, deletion, update (although they can be done in the same framework as the rest processing) since these operations are closely related to the design and implementation of the Data Definition Language.

3. THE DETAILS OF THE IMPLEMENTATION

Our Q.B.E interpreter has been designed and implemented into Pascal.

It can translate queries referred to anyone Relational scheme consisted of up to thirty relations with thirty attributes each. Relations were files-of-records of Pascal. Each record represented a tupple of a relation.

Firstly the user's interface has been designed as follows. In the terminal screen the tables that represent the relations are displayed. These are of the form:

R.N	A.N1	A.N2 ....

Where:R.N is the relation name A.N1,A.N2,...are the atribute names.

The space below is to be used for stating our query.

For the design of the Lexical-box a compiler-design technique has been used.

The Lexical analyzer recognises the strings and returns the information concerning them.
It recognises if the string is key-word (P.,I., D., U.), if it is a constant element, an example element (of the form WORD , where WORD may be every string), a built-in function, an ALL-operator, G-operator, e.t.c.
In the design of the Lexical-box, the finite-automata theory technique has been used.

The design of grammar-box has been ommited since every expression in Q.B.E is legal, except possibly some trivial faults.

The information coming out of the Lexical-box is further processed into the code generation

box, which has been already described in the previous section.
The algorithm of the code generation box can be described as follows:

```
begin
if "string" is a C.E then SELECT;
if "string1" is an E.E. then
                    begin
                      VAR:="string1"
                     SEARCH RELS;
if "string2" is an E.E and VAR="string2" then
                                        JOIN
                 end;
if a P. has been recognised then PROJECT;
end
```

This algorithm is an $O(n^2)$ algorithm since the most time consuming procedure (JOIN) has an $O(n^2)$ processing time.

The operations of R.A are Pascal's procedures.

The procedure SELECT makes the selection on any constant element appearing in the tables and fills the rejected tuples with nulls.

The procedure JOIN makes the natural join of two or more relations and writes the resulted relation in a new file (obviously larger that the initial one).

Two procedures SPROJECT, CPROJECT were necessary for the projection operation, being used respectively on initial files or files resulting from selection operation only and on files resulting from join operation.

Several control and secondary procedures were also included in the code generation box.

The greater problem we were confronted with was the files of Pascal whose manipulation was hard and parametrical.
This problem was solved with the strict and literal reference to the filenames in the program a cost being payed in program length and execution time.

Another important problem was that Pascal has not variable length records and record length had to be strictly declared in the program declaration part.
For its solution a number of files of several lengths were available and we modulated in accordance the procedures JOIN and CPROJECT.

CONCLUSION

The work that was described here consitutes a first approach to the problem of implementing QBE, which seems to be a very advantageous query language, since it does not require from the user particular familiarity with the computer. The implementation was done in Pascal. The main problems that arose from that job, that we had undertaken, were dealt with while some problems that were not considered crucial were left for a next stage. Thus, we focused on the parametricality of the program, where we had against us the Pascal compiler; it was also taken care, so that the algorithm that gives the answer to a query to be efficient, this meaning that it was preferred, for example, a select operation to be executed before a join operation. Not special care was taken for several other refinements that could be done to the program for reducing even more the time and space needed for its execution. The implementation of the conditional box was also left out.

REFERENCES

[1]. Ullman J.D., Principles of Database systems (Pitman, London, 1980).

[2]. Zloof M.M., Query-by-example:a data base language IBM SYST. J, No 4 (1947) 324-343.

[3]. Zloof M.M., Query-by-example, AFIPS conference Proceedings, National Computer Conference 44, (1975) 431-438.

[4]. Zloof M.M., Query-by-example, The Invocation and Definition of Tables and Forms, Proceedings of the International Conference on Very Large Data Bases, (1975) 1-24.

[5]. Zloof M.M., Query-by-example:Operations on the Transitive Closure, Research Report RC5526, IBM Thomas J.Watson Research Center, Yorktown Heights, New York, 1975.

DIGITAL TECHNIQUES in Simulation, Communication and Control
Spyros G. Tzafestas (editor)
Elsevier Science Publishers B.V. (North-Holland) © IMACS, 1985

CHAINED INDEXES: A DATA STRUCTURE FOR EFFICIENT PROCESSING OF CONJUCTIVE QUERIES ON MULTIPLE ATTRIBUTES

G. (Yiorgos) Famelis and J. (Yiannis) Kollias

National Technical University of Athens
Department of Electrical Engineering
Division of Computer Science
9, Heroon Polytechniou Avenue,
Zografou, Athens (624), Greece

A common characteristic of simple indexing techniques is that each technique might be better than others for some type of usage but concurrently the same technique might be worse than others for some other type of usage.
A data structure, called chained indexes, is proposed in an attempt to combine what is considered to be efficient simple indexing techniques for some usage into a new multiattribute index. The structure is defined in terms of a logical description, its physical implementation and a number of processing algorithms. The study suggests promising directions for further study.

1. INTRODUCTION

We consider a file consisting of a number, NREC, of normalized records (1) with each record comprising values for each of n+1 attributes A_o, $A_1,\dots,A_n$. Each attribute, A_i, may take d_i distinct values, i=0,1,...,n. We assume that the attribute A_n is the primary key for purposes of storage and retrieval (i.e. d_n=NREC). The other attributes A_i (i=0,1,...,n-1) are the secondary attributes.

The database system is to support queries-based on the values of secondary attributes-of the form "Given $A_o \varepsilon V_o$ and $A_1 \varepsilon V_1$ and ... and $A_{n-1} \varepsilon V_{n-1}$ retrieve records" (*) where each V_i may be one of the following (i=0,1,...,n-1):

(a) A single value for the attribute A_i,

(b) a range of consecutive values for the attribute A_i, and

(c) a list of numbers sampled from the d_i distinct values of the A_i attribute.

It is worth noting that queries of the form (*) (as defined above) are very general because (i) they contain simpler queries as a case (i.e. simple and range queries (2)), and (ii) more complex queries (e.g. containing the logical operator or as well) may be decomposed to others of the form (*). Queries of the form (*) are regularly termed conjuctive queries (on multiple attributes) (3).

To circumvent the problem of reading the entire file when satisfying a query of the form (*) (and its variants) a large number of secondary file organization schemes has been proposed. To limit the scope of searching the majority of organizations utilize indexes which establish the relation between attribute values and the records in the file which contain the value concerned. Below we present some of the most commonly used secondary indexing schemes grouped into three categories:

1. Single indexes

The inverted and the multilist file organizations are the two most typical (and in fact the most commonly used) indexing schemes in this category (2,4). The organizations utilize some form of directory to structure one secondary attribute. Such an approach is very satisfactory when the queries (*) qualify values just for one of the secondary attributes (i.e. simple or range queries). If more than one attributes are involved in (*) then it is very likely that a large number of records will be retrieved which do not satisfy the query. When the inverted file organizations have been employed then the problem can be (partially) solved by performing an (in core) intersection of the values which appear in the qualification part of the query. However, such an approach complicates the software required and what is more it may slow down the performance significantly particularly if more than, say, 3 indexes are involved in (*).

The next two categories may be viewed as an attempt to improve the system performance when asked to satisfy queries of the form (*).

2. Combined indexes

The organizations create (inverted) directories which correspond to more than one attribute, i.e. combined indexes. The number of attributes contained in a directory vary from 1 (i.e. single index) to n. Lum observed that if only the 3 secondary attributes A_1, A_2 and A_3 are involved in (*) then the three combined indexes using the concatenated keys $A_1A_2A_3$, $A_2A_3A_1$ and $A_3A_1A_2$ suffice for answering any subset of queries of the form (*) without performing any intersection. It is worth noting that it has been reported that Lum's approach has never been applied in practice basically because it requires an excessively large storage and maintenance cost (6). Schneiderman observed that it is advantageous to maintain the combined indexes $A_1A_2A_3$, A_1A_3, A_2A_3 and A_3 instead of the three combined indexes suggested by Lum (3). This is due to the fact that the new set of combined indexes requires less storage and maintenance cost. Nevertheless such approaches become impractical for large values of n in (*). For example, when n=5 then 16 combined indexes are required (3).

3. Multidimensional indexes

The approach utilizes a single directory, structured as a tree, to index all the secondary attributes which may be involved in query (*). The attribute concerned depends on the level of the tree examined. In particular (7) employes a binary tree while (8) a quintary tree. However, the approaches have the following drawbacks when used for large volatile databases (i) if the values V_i in (*) define a range or a list of values taken by the attribute A_i then the searching process may become a prohibitive task, and (ii) the structures are not only (relatively) expensive to maintain but what is more their performance deteriorates (due to insertions, deletions and changes) very fast over time. This may require very often costly reorganization process (9,10).

From the above discussion it follows that a common characteristic of single indexing techniques is that each technique might be better than others for some type of usage but concurrently the same technique might be worse than others for some other type of usage. In this study we propose a data structure, called chained indexes, in an attempt to combine what is considered to be efficient simple indexing techniques for s me usage into a new multiattribute index. The hope is that this new structure will offer better overall performance for a variety of usages.

In particular the new structure aims at satisfying conjuctive queries on multiple attributes in an efficient manner. The structure is based on the following two main objectives:

1. No record will be accessed, which do not satisfy a query (*), for inspection in the memory. In other words all the work will be done within the indexes themselves.
2. The amount of storage required by the structure will not be excessively large. The structure will not impose a provibitevely large overhead for maintenance due to record insertions, updates and deletions.

In the next section we present a logical description of the chained indexes data structure using data structure diagrams (11). The description allows us to keep as a variable to the presentation certain possible physical implementation. By considering a particular physical implementation in Section 3 a number of queries to be processed by the structuce are given. Finally Section 4 discusses alternative implementations and suggests directions for further research.

2. CHAINED INDEXES

Fig. 1 illustrates the structure of the chained indexes data structure using data structure diagrams (11). The symbol → signifies either 1:n or 1:1 relationships between record types.

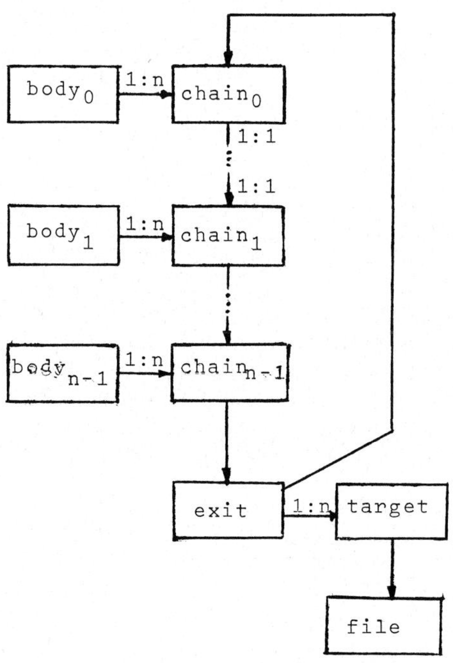

Fig. 1: Data structure diagram of chained indexes.

As Fig. 1 suggests to describe the structure we need first define the logical content of the record types involved. In the next five subsections we describe in turn the five different record types which appear in Fig. 1.

2.1 Record type "file"

This record type refers to the NREC records of the primary file. Each record consists from n+1 attributes A_0, A_1,..., A_n (Section 1). The structure of the primary file (e.g. indexed sequential, random, etc) is assumed to be known but our study can cope with any primary file organization (e.g. indexed sequential, random, etc).

2.2 Record type "body"

This record type corresponds normally to a single index for the secondary attribute A_i (i=0,1, ...,n-1). There are d_i entries to each record type $body_i$ (where d_i is the number of distinct values taken by the i-th attribute). Each entry contains the following fields:

value: A distinct value taken by the attribute A_i.

count: The number of records in the primary file which contain that particular key value, V_i.

list: Pointer at the head of the record type $chain_i$. (In fact-using the CODASYL terminology-this is a link between the OWNER record $body_i$ and the MEMBER record type $chain_i$ (4)).

It is worth noting that the record type defined above can easily cover the case where each index entry corresponds to a combine index instead of a single index.

2.3 Record type "chain"

From the previous subsection it follows that for each $body_i$ there are also d_i entries of this record type. Each entry consists now from a list of elements indicated through the 1:n relationship between the record types $body_i$ and $chain_i$ (Fig. 1). The list can be implemented by various methods (table, linked list, etc). A node of the list must contain the following fields quite irrespective from its physical implementation (see also Section 3).

value: The value taken by the A_{i+1} attribute of the record being indexed through the record type $body_i$ (i=0,1,...,n-1). As far as the attribute A_{n-1} is concerned it contains as a value of that field the V_o value, i.e. the next values are taken modulo n.

same: Pointer at that particular list. (Using standard database terminology this field establishes a 1:1 correspondance between the record types $chain_i$ and $chain_{i+1}$).

last: With reference to Fig. 1 we note that the last index points to another record type, the exit one. The current field establishes the pointer next either to the record type exit or to the record type chain.

2.4 Record type "exit"

This record type serves two main objectives. The first objective is to close the record types $chain_o$ to $chain_{n-1}$ to a circular list. This is achieved through the field next which exists on this record type.

The second objective is to contain a pointer to the last record type target. This is achieved through the second field named list.

2.5 Record type "target"

The last record type contains so many entries as the number of distinct combinations (of the attributes) that exist in the file being indexed through the chained indexes. Each entry contains a list of the records in the primary file which have all their V_i values the same.

We finish this section by presenting the definitions described in Subsections 2.2 to 2.5 using the PASCAL notation:

```
body = record
       value : values;
       list : ↑ chain;
       count : integer
       end;

chain = record
        value : values;
        same : ↑ chain
        case last : boolean of
        true : (next : ↑ exit);
        false : (next :↑ chain)
        end;

exit = record
       next : ↑ chain;
       list : ↑ target
       end;

target = file of integer;
```

3. APPLICATION OF THE STRUCTURE

Fig. 2 demonstrates an application of the chained indexes to structure a file described in (6). The file contains 4 attributes. The A_o, A_1 and A_2 attributes are the secondary attributes while the A_4 attribute serves as the primary key.

For the rest of this section we make certain clarifications for the performance of the structure by considering the following 3 types of queries of the form (*).

"Given A_1=E and A_2<D retrieve records" (1)

"Given A_2=D retrieve records" (2) and

"Given A_1=E retrieve records" (3)

With reference to the (1) query we note that our method finds extremely fast that no record in

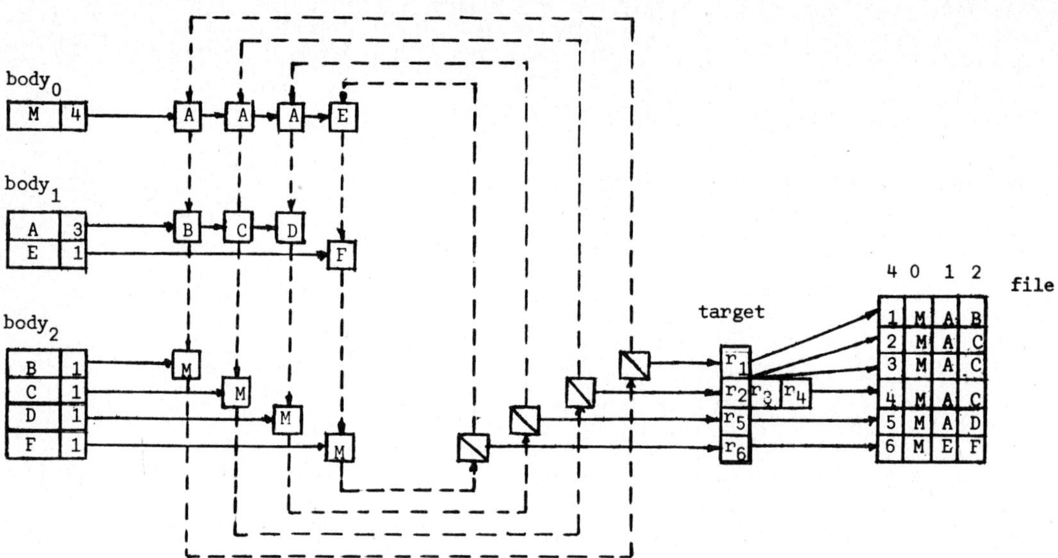

Fig. 2: The chained indexes data structure.

the primary file satisfies this particular query. This is because the searching starts from the $body_1$ where it is immediately discovered that the only record in the primary file which has the value A_1=E it turns out that it has A_2= =F. This performance of the chained indexes is the best possibly achieved by utilizing other existing indexing techniques.

The type of query (2) is satisfied by the structure in Fig. 2 with (almost) the same cost with the cost expended by the most popular single indexing structures, i.e. inverted, multilist. However, the satisfaction of the (3) query requires slightly more time to be satisfied by our structure. This is because it is impossible to branch to the exit type of record unless we are prepared to visit the $chain_2$ type of record.

However, such an inefficiency can be removed by applying alternative physical implementations of Fig. 1. One alternative physical implementation may permute the $body_1$ and $body_2$ if it is known in advance that $query_1$ (3) $occurs_2$ more frequently from query (2). Another possibility is to have the exit record type to be pointed by the second (or any other) attribute.

Nevertheless, from the above discussion it follows that there are practical instances where the new structure performs the same, better or worse than previous structure. In the next section we suggest directions for further research which might result to more efficient implementation of the chained indexes.

4. CONCLUDING REMARKS

We envisage that the chained indexes data structure introduced may be further studied in the following contexts:

1. To consider the case that each body does not refer to a single attribute but to 2 or more attributes.

2. To try to develop different optimization models which decides about (i) which attributes to be indexed, (ii) the optimal permutation of the record types body, and (iii) when to reorganize the structure.

3. To investigate the possibility of eliminating either the entire or part of the primary file since (most of) the attribute values exist within the structure.

4. To consider that the structure is a mechanism for storing relations (1). If the structure is viewed this way then it is very sensible to study its suitability to perform relational algebra operations, i.e. project and join.

5. To try to exploit what opportunities of parallelism the structure offers when it is stored on special purpose multiprocessing devices.

REFERENCES

[1] Codd, E.F., A relational model of data for large shared data banks, CACM, Vol.13(1970) No. 6, pp. 337-347.

[2] Knuth, D.E., The art of computer programming. Sorting and searching, Vol. 3, 1973, Addison-Wesley, Reading, Mass.

[3] Shneiderman, B., Reduced combined Indexes for efficient multiple attribute retrieval, Inform. Systems, Vol. 2 (1977), No. 2,pp. 149-154.

[4] Date, C.J., An introduction to database systems, 1981 (3rd Edition), Addison-Wesley, Reading, Mass.

[5] Lum, V.Y., Multiattribute retrieval with combined indexes, CACM, Vol. 13 (1970), No. 11, pp. 660-665.

[6] Cardenas, A.F., Analysis and performance of inverted database structures, Comm. ACM, Vol 18 (1975), No. 5, pp. 253-263.

[7] Bentley, J.L., Multidimentional binary search trees used for associative searching Comm. ACM 18(1975), 509-517.

[8] Lee, D.T. and Wong, C.K., Quintary Trees: A file structure for multidimensional data - base systems, ACM Transaction Database Systems 5,3 (Sept. 1980), 339-353.

[9] Sockut G.H. and Golbberg R.P., Database reorganization-principles and practice. Computing Surveys, Vol. 11 (1979), No. 4, pp. 371-391.

[10] Hatzopoulos M., and Kollias, J.G., The determination of the optimum database maintenance points. Computer Journal, Vol. 25 , (1982), No. 1, pp. 126-129.

[11] Bachman, C.W., The evolution of storage structures, CACM, Vol. 15 (1972), No. 7, pp. 628-634.

DIGITAL TECHNIQUES in Simulation, Communication and Control
Spyros G. Tzafestas (editor)
Elsevier Science Publishers B.V. (North-Holland) © IMACS, 1985

PERFORMANCE EVALUATION OF A GI/D/1 PRIORITY QUEUE

M.E. Anagnostou, E.N. Protonotarios

National Technical University
Athens, Greece

The performance of a GI/D/1 discrete time queueing system is studied. Arriving customers belong to one of a set of P different priority classes. Customers of the same class have equal service times, and follow an FCFS discipline. The queueing system is a preemptive priority system. The preemptive resume case is considered.

1. INTRODUCTION

Discrete time queueing models have recently come into prominence because of the widespread use of computers |1| ,|2|. Exotic protocols |3| stimulate scientists to investigate the properties of brand-new queueing systems. Discrete time models are more appropriate than continuous time models, because computer systems usually operate on a discrete time basis. The cycle time of a processor, the packet duration (in a packet switching network) are examples, which show the existence of discrete structures of intrinsic nature. However, discrete time models have not been adequately studied, as compared with continuous time models.

Throughout this paper time will be considered discrete. The time axis is segmented into intervals of fixed length, often called slots |1|. The time unit equals(by definition) the slot duration. Customers, who arrive in a slot are considered to arrive at its beginning.

Arriving customers belong to one of a set of P different priority classes. Customers of the i'th class are serviced before customers of the jth class if $1 \le i < j \le P$. The top priority class is the P'th class. Customers of the same class obey the FCFS (First-Come-First-Served) queueing discipline. The system is preemptive, that is, a customer in the process of being served is ejected from service and returned to the queue whenever a customer of higher priority appears in the queue. The ejected customer picks up from where he left off.

The service time of an i'th class customer equals n_i, where n_i is a constant, that is, customers of the same class have equal service times.

It is obvious that one can ignore the existence of the classes 1,2,...,i-1 if one wishes to study the delay experienced by customers of the i'th class. Therefore, it is sufficient to examine only the quality of service offered by the system to 1'st class customers.

We assume that the interarrival time distribution corresponding to 1'st class customers is arbitrary, but known. Therefore the probabilities $Pr\{X_n=m\}$ are also known, where $X_n=t_n-t_{n-1}$, and t_n is the (integer) arrival time of the n'th customer of the first class. To complete the description of the arrival process, one should model the arrivals of customers belonging to other classes in the same way. Let $X_n^{(i)}$ be the interarrival time corresponding to the customers n-1, n of the i'th class. Clearly $X_n^{(1)}= X_n$. For reasons of mathematical tractability we do not allow $X_n^{(i)}$ $(i \ge 2)$ be arbitrarily distributed, as we did with $X_n^{(1)}$. Instead, we assume that the random variables $X_n^{(i)}$ are geometrically distributed for $i \ge 2$, that is

$$Pr\{X_n^{(i)}=m\}=p_i(1-p_i)^{m-1} \quad (1 \le m, 2 \le i \le P) \qquad (1)$$

Let also

$$Pr\{X_n^{(1)}=m\} = x_m \qquad (2)$$

It should be clear that one might use this model
(a) to analyze the performance of all the classes of a queueing system, where only the lowest priority customers follow an arbitrary interarrival time distribution, or
(b) to analyze the performance of the system corresponding to the classes i,i+1,...,P if the arrivals of customers belonging to the classes i+1,i 2,...,P are geometrically distributed, whereas the class i arrivals are arbitrarily distributed. The way the arrival process of classes 1,...,i-1 is decribed does not affect the analysis, or
(c) to approximately analyze the performance of a queueing system, where all the arrival are described by independent arbitrarily distributed random variables $X_n^{(i)}$ $(1 \le i \le P)$. In this case the model is used as follows: When the

performance measures for the i'th class are computed, the correct $X_n^{(i)}$ ($j\neq i$, $1\leq j<P$) are assumed to follow geometrical distributions (with properly adjusted mean values). This application is based on the observation that the performance measures of the class i mainly depend on its own arrival process, and only on the arrival rates of higher priority classes (the influence of the higher moments of their interarrival times being negligible).

2. DELAY ANALYSIS

Let t_n' denote the time at which the service required by the n'th customer of the i'th priority class is brought to its end. Recall that t_n is the arrival time of this customer. Then his total delay is given by

$$D_n^{(i)}= t_n' - t_n \tag{3}$$

We shall also define the random variable $S_n^{(i)}$ as follows

$$S_n^{(i)} = t_n' - b_n \tag{4}$$

where b_n is the time, at which the first service slot of the n'th customer begins. Therefore the random variable defined by (3) equals the length of the time interval, which begins at the beginning of the n'th customers service, and ends at its completion. Note also that this variable is quite important in applications, in which the beginning and the end of a customer's service should not be too far apart from each other.

2.1 Delay of top priority class customers

In case of a P'th class customer the solution of the performance problem is trivial: $S_n=n_P$ (we have omitted the class indicator P in order to simplify the notation), because nobody has the right to ask the ejection from service of a top priority customer. It is only a bit more difficult to find expression for the delay. It is easy to see that the total delay $D_n^{(P)}$ of the n'th priority class customer is related to $D_{n-1}^{(P)}$ as follows

$$D_n^{(P)} = (D_{n-1}^{(P)} - X_n^{(P)})^+ + n_P \tag{5}$$

where $a^+=\max(a,0)$. From (5) immediately follows that

$$\Pr\{D_n^{(P)}=k+n_P\}= \sum_{m=0}^{\infty} \Pr\{D_{n-1}^{(P)}=m+k\}\Pr\{X_n^{(P)}=m\}+ +\delta_{k0}\sum_{m=0}^{\infty} \Pr\{D_{n-1}^{(P)}=m\}\Pr\{X_n^{(P)}=m+1\} \tag{6}$$

where δ_{ij} is Kronecker's delta function. Eq. (6) must be iteratively used for n= 1,2,... (with $\Pr\{D_0=0\}=1$) for the computation of the i'th customer delay distribution. If (1) holds, then the generating function of the delay in the steady state, defined by

$$D^{(P)}(z)= \sum_{m=0}^{\infty} z^m \lim_{n\to\infty} \Pr\{D_n^{(P)}=m\} \tag{7}$$

is given by

$$D^{(P)}(z)= \frac{(1-p_P)(z-1)n_P z^{n_P}}{(z-1+p_P)-p_P z^{n_P}} \tag{8}$$

Expression (8) is easily obtained from (5) and (7). By differentiating and setting z=1, one can show that the mean delay is given by the following expression (in the steady state)

$$E\{D^{(P)}\}=n_P+p_P \frac{n_P(n_P-1)}{2(1-p_P n_P)} \tag{9}$$

Of course a steady state exists for the top priority class iff the job arrival rate $n_P p_P$ does not exceed the maximum service rate, which equals 1. Observe that (9) is consistent with our expectations:

(a) If the arrival rate p_P is close to 0, then the delay is just the service time n_P, since the customers do not find in the queue other customers of the same (top) priority class.

(b) If the service time n_P equals 1, then E{D}=1 that is, top priority customers immediately enter service.

2.2 Computation of the delay due to preemptions.

According to previously presented arguments, it is sufficient to obtain expressions only for the performance measures corresponding to lowest priority customers. In order to simplify the notation we set $S_n^{(1)}=S_n$, and $D_n^{(1)}=D_n$. In this section we shall obtain expressions for the statistics of S_n.

Let us begin our analysis with a listing of the arrivals, which probably occur at time m. From eq. (1) it it obvious that p_i is the probability that an i'th class customer arrives at m, and $1-p_i$ is the probability that no such customer arrives. Define the variable N_m , which equals the total work (measured in slots), which is brought to the system at time m by higher priority customers. Then

$$\Pr\{N_m= \sum_{i=2}^{P} \delta_i n_i\}= \prod_{i=2}^{P} (\delta_i p_i+(1-\delta_i)(1-p_i)) \tag{10}$$

$$\delta_i= \begin{cases} 1, & \text{if an i'th pr. cust. arrives at m} \\ 0, & \text{otherwise} \end{cases} \tag{11}$$

There are $M=2^P-1$ possible non-zero values N_m can assume. Let them be denoted by m_k (k=0,1,2,...) where $m_0=0$, and let

$$q_k= \Pr\{N_m=m_k\} \qquad (k=1,\dots,M)$$
$$q_0= 1-q_1-q_2-q_3-\dots \tag{12}$$

From (10), (11), and (12) follows that q_i is

expressed in terms of p_i as follows:

$$q_k = \prod_{i=2}^{P} (\delta_i p_i + (1-\delta_i)(1-p_i)) \iff m_k = \sum_{i=2}^{P} \delta_i n_i \quad (13)$$

If no higher priority customers arrive at b_n+1, $b_n+2,\ldots,b_n+n_1-1$, then $S_n=n_1$. If, however, such arrivals occur at the time instants given above, suppose that they bring to the system a total work equal to G_1 slots. We shall name them "the first generation slots". At the beginning of every first generation slot new arrivals possibly occur. Therefore G_2 additional slot will be added to the delay of the n'th (lowest priority) customer. These G_2 slots are the"second generation slots". Each of the second generation slots may generate several third generation slots, and so on. The process stops whenever no new arrivals occur in all the slots of a generation. Therefore

$$S_n = n_1 + G_1 + G_2 + \ldots + G_K \quad (14)$$

where K+1 is the smallest natural number, with the property $G_{K+1}=0$. However, since $G_i=0$ implies $G_{i+1}=0$, it is possible to express S_n as follows:

$$S_n = G_0 + G_1 + G_2 + \ldots + G_K + G_{K+1} + \ldots \quad (15)$$

where $G_0=n_1-1$. Then it is easy to compute the average S_n as follows:

$$E\{G_i/G_{i-1}=k\}=kd \quad (16)$$

where

$$d = q_1 m_1 + q_2 m_2 + \ldots + q_M m_M \quad (17)$$

Obviously d is the average number of additional slots generated by each slot of G_{i-1}. Then

$$E\{G_i\} = \sum_{k=0}^{\infty} Pr\{G_{i-1}=k\} E\{G_i/G_{i-1}=k\} = \sum_{k=0}^{\infty} kd\ Pr\{G_{i-1}=k\} = d\ E\{G_{i-1}\} \quad (18)$$

Since $G_0=n_1-1$, from (16) follows that $E\{G_1\} = (n_1-1)d$. Then from (18) $E\{G_2\}=(n_1-1)d^2$, and finally:

$$E\{G_m\} = (n_1-1)\ d^m \quad (19)$$

Then from (15) and (19) follows that :

$$E\{S_n\} = \frac{n_1-1}{1-d} \quad (20)$$

Recall that d is given by (17).

The generating function of G_i is obtained as follows:Let Y_j be the number of slots generated by the j'th (j=1,...,m) slot of the i'th generation. Then

$$E\{z^{G_{i+1}}/G_i=m\} = E\{z^{Y_1+\ldots+Y_m}/G_i=m\} = \prod_{i=1}^{m} E\{z^{Y_i}\} \quad (21)$$

because the variables Y_i are mutually independent , and also independent of G_i. But Y_i follows the same distribution as N_m does (see eqs. (10) and (11)). Therefore

$$E\{z^{Y_i}\} = \sum_{j=0}^{M} q_j z^{m_j} \quad (22)$$

and from (21)

$$E\{z^{G_{i+1}}\} = \sum_{m=0}^{\infty} Pr\{G_i=m\} \left(\sum q_j z^{m_j} \right)^m = E\{\left(\sum q_j z^{m_j} \right)^{G_i}\} \quad (23)$$

Recall that $G_0=n_1-1$, which implies that $E\{z^{G_0}\} = z^{n_1-1}$.

Suppose that K=k. Then, the generating function of S_n, as given by (14) is

$$E\{z^{G_0+G_1+\ldots+G_k}\} = \sum_{k_0=0}^{\infty} z^{k_0} Pr\{G_0=k_0\} \sum_{k_1=0}^{\infty} z^{k_1} Pr\{G_1=k_1/G_0=k_0\} \ldots \sum_{k_k=0}^{\infty} z^{k_k} Pr\{G_k=k_k/G_{k-1}=k_{k-1}\} \quad (24)$$

because G_i depends only on G_{i-1}. It can be shown that

$$E\{z^{G_0+G_1+\ldots+G_k}\} = E\{(zz_0)^{G_0}\} = (zz_0)^{n_1-1} \quad (25)$$

where

$$z_j = \sum_{i=0}^{M} q_i \,(z\, z_{j+1})^{m_i} \quad (j=0,\ldots,k-1) \quad (26)$$

and

$$z_k = 1 \quad (27)$$

By using (25) and letting $k\to\infty$ it is possible to show that

$$E\{S_n(S_n-1)\} = (n_1-2)(n_1-1)\left(\frac{d}{1-d}\right)^2 + (n_1-1)\cdot \left(\frac{2d}{1-d} + \frac{2d^2}{(1-d)^2} + \frac{2}{(1-d)^3} \left(\sum_{j=1} m_j(m_j-1)q_j \right) \right) \quad (28)$$

The standard deviation σ_S of the random variable S_n is calculated by using

$$\sigma_S^2 = E\{S_n(S_n-1)\} + E\{S_n\} - E^2\{S_n\} \quad (29)$$

where the mean value of S_n is given by (20)

2.3 Delay of lowest priority class customers

The total delay of the n'th customer (of the 1'st class) is expressed in terms of the previous (same class) customer delay as follows

$$D_n = (D_n - X_n)^+ + R_n \qquad (30)$$

Eq. (30) is similar to eq. (5), where $R_n = n_p$. For first class customers, however, R_n is greater than n_1, because R_n includes not only the service time of the n'th customer, but also the service time of higher priority customers. From (30) follows that

$$\Pr\{D_n=k\} = \sum_{m=1}^{\infty} \Pr\{R_n=k/X_n-D_{n-1}=m\} \sum_{r=1}^{\infty} x_{m+r} \Pr\{D_{n-1}=r\} + \sum_{r=1}^{\infty} \Pr\{D_{n-1}=r\} \sum_{m=0}^{r} \Pr\{R_n=k-r+m/D_{n-1}-X_n = r-m\}\, x_m \qquad (31)$$

The probability distribution of D_n can be computed by using (31) iteratively. However, the conditional probabilities appearing in (31) shouls be computed first:

(I) If $X_n \leq D_{n-1}$, then $t_n - t_{n-1} \leq t'_{n-1} - t_{n-1}$, which gives $t_n \leq t'_{n-1}$. The last inequality means that the n'th customer arrived at the system before or at the end of the service of the (n-1)'th customer. This fact gives us the information that no higher class customers were present in the system at $t'_{n-1}-1$, because were they present, the (n-1)'th customer's service completion would have been postponed. If higher priority customers do not arrive at t'_{n-1}, the n'th customer enters service at t'_{n-1}. Otherwise a time period used by one or more higher priority customers begins, and the service of the n'th customer begins after the end of this period.

Suppose that at time m the system needs time Q_m in order to be able to satisfy all the uncompleted service demands of customers, who arrived at t, where $t \leq m$. Therefore Q_m is the unfinished work at time m |2|. Consider now the modified system, which results after applying the following modifications to the original one:
(a) Cancel all arrivals of lowest priority customers, which occur at t , for $t > t_n$.
(b) Cancel all arrivals of higher priority customers, which occur at t, for $t \geq t'_n$.

These modifications have no influence on the delay of the n'th customer. They are useful, however for the derivation of the conditional distribution of the random variable R_n. Let Q'_m denote the unfinished work in the modified system. Let us put the origin of the m-axis at t'_{n-1}, that is m=0 at t'_{n-1}. Since t'_{n-1} is the time, at which the service of the (n-1)'th customer comes to its end, no higher priority arrival occured at t'_{n-1}, and all the service demands of previously arrived customers have been satisfied. However, at t'_{n-1} the n'th customer doesnot enter service always. If higher priority customers arrive at t'_{n-1}, then Q'_0 becomes equal to $n_1 + A_0$, where A_0 denotes their service demands and n_1 is the service time needed by the n'th customer. Then Q'_m is given by

$$Q'_m = \begin{cases} Q'_{m-1} - 1 + A_m & , \text{ if } Q'_{m-1} > 1. \\ 0 & , \text{ otherwise} \end{cases} \qquad (32)$$

where A_m is the work demanded by customers of priority >1, who arrive at the system at m. Observe that Q'_m is non-negative.

The meaning of the first row of eq. (32) is obvious. The second row states that Q'_m becomes equal to 0, whenever its previous value equals either 1 or 0. This statement is based on the observation that (r-1,r) is the last service slot of the n'th customer if and only if $Q'_{r-1}=1$. If this is true, then $A_r=0$ according to modification (b), and Q'_r becomes 0, and remains there because of both (a) and (b). Observe that since $Q_r = Q_{r+1} = \ldots = 0$, there is only one r, which satisfies the condition $Q_r=1$. Let us now see why (r-1,r) is the last service slot of the n'th customer, on the assumption that $Q_{r-1}=1$. Since $Q_{r-1}=1$, the n'th customer has either completed his service or needs one slot. Suppose he has completed his service at m, where m<r. Then at m-1 there is no unfinished work due to higher priority customers at the system. Moreover $A_m=0$, otherwise the n'th customer would not have access to the slot (m-1,m). Therefore $Q_{m-1}'=1$. From this fact,however, follows that $Q'_m=0$, $Q'_{m+1}=0$, and so on, because of (a) and (b). These results contradict the assumption that $Q'_{r-1}=1$ for m less than r.

From (32) follows that

$$\Pr\{Q'=k\} = \sum_{i=0}^{k} \Pr\{A_m=i\} \Pr\{Q'_{m-1}=k-i+1\} + \Pr\{Q'_{m-1}=0\}\delta_{k0} \qquad (33)$$

where

$$\Pr\{A_m=m_j\} = q_j \qquad (j=0,1,\ldots,M) \qquad (34)$$

and

$$\Pr\{Q'_0=n_1+m_j\} = q_j \qquad (35)$$

Observe now that the events $\{R_n \leq r\}$ and $\{Q'_r=0\}$ are equivalent. Therefore, for $k \geq 0$

$$\Pr\{R_n \leq r/D_{n-1}-X_n \geq k\} = \sum_{j=1}^{M} \Pr\{Q'_r=0/Q'_0=n_1+m_j\}\, q_j \qquad (36)$$

An alternative way to derive expressions of the statistics of R_n is to use the analysis for S_n of section 2.2. One should make the following change: $G_0=n_1+m_j$ with probability q_j. This implies that

$$E\{z^{G_0}\} = \sum_{j=0}^{M} z^{n_1+m_j} q_j \tag{37}$$

This modification affects the second part of eq. (25). Then

$$R_n = G_0+G_1+G_2+\ldots \tag{38}$$

The mean value of R_n is

$$E\{R_n/D_{n-1}-X_n \geq 0\} = \frac{n_1+d}{1-d} \tag{39}$$

(II) If $X_n-D_{n-1}=r\geq 1$, then $t_n-t_{n-1}-(t'_{n-1}-t_{n-1})=r$ or $t_n-t_{n-1}=r$. This means that the n'th customer arrives at the queue after the departure of the (n-1)'th customer. The analysis would be the same as in (I) if we knew the state of the system at t_n. What we actually know, however, is (again) that the unfinished work at $t'_{n-1}-1$ equals 1. If we set $\mu=0$ at t'_n, then

$$Q_\mu=(Q_{\mu-1}-1)^+ + A_\mu \qquad (1\leq\mu\leq r-1) \tag{40}$$

where $Q_0=n_1+m_j$ with probability q_j. From (40) the following formula for the corresponding probabilities is obtained:

$$\Pr\{Q_\mu=k\} = \sum_{i=0}^{k} \Pr\{A_\mu=i\}\Pr\{Q_{\mu-1}=k-i+1\}+$$
$$+\Pr\{A_\mu=k\}\Pr\{Q_{\mu-1}=0\} \quad (1\leq\mu\leq r-1) \tag{41}$$

Let us define m=0 at t_n. Then for m>0 eqs. (32), (33), and (34) can be used for the derivation of the distribution of R_n. At t_n: $\mu=r$, m=0, and $Q_r=Q'_0$. Then $R_n\leq k$ iff $Q_k=0$. Therefore:

$$\Pr\{R_n\leq k/X_n-D_{n-1}=r\} = \sum_{j=0}^{\infty} \Pr\{Q'_k=0/Q'_0=j\}\cdot$$
$$\cdot\sum_{i=0}^{M} \Pr\{Q_r=j/Q_0=n_1+m_i\}q_i \tag{42}$$

We have already seen what happens before and after t_n. Let us now see what happens at t_n. At t_n the n'th customer arrives and

$$Q_r=(Q_{r-1}-1)^+ + A_r + n_1 \tag{43}$$

From (43) :

$$\Pr\{Q_r=k+n_1\} = \sum_{i=0}^{k} \Pr\{A_r=i\}\Pr\{Q_{r-1}=k-i+1\}+$$
$$+\Pr\{A_r=k\}\Pr\{Q_{r-1}=0\} \tag{44}$$

Let us now summarize how eq. (42) is used: The conditional prob. in the first (upper) summation of eq. (42) is computed by using r-1 times eq. (40) in order to find the distribution of Q_{r-1} from the distribution of Q_0. Then eq. (44) is used for the derivation of the distribution of Q_r. Recall that $Q_r=Q'_0$. Finally eq. (33) is used k-1 times for the computation of the distribution of Q'_k from the distribution of Q'_0. This result is put in place of the conditional prob. in the second summation.

3. CONCLUSIONS

A queueing model for the delay analysis of a discrete time preemptive priority queue has been presented. Analytical closed form results for the time, which lapses from the beginning to the end of the service of customers have been obtained. Expressions for the evaluation of the delay distribution have been presented. The usefulness of the latter performance measure is well-known, whereas the former one is extremely important in time critical applications (such as packetized voice transmission), where the beginning of the service should not be too far apart from its end.

REFERENCES

|1| Kobayashi, H. and Konheim, A.G., Queueing Models for Computer Communications System Analysis, IEEE Trans. on Commun., Vol. COM-25, No. 1, (Jan. 1977) 2-29.

|2| Kleinrock, L., Queueing Systems, Vols. I and II (Wiley, New York, 1975).

|3| Tanenbaum, A.S., Computer Networks,(Prentice Hall, Englewood Cliffs, 1981).

APPENDIX

Derivation of the $E\{z^{G_0+G_1+\ldots+G_N}\}$ (see eq.(25)):

$$A_{i-1} = \sum_{k_N=0}^{\infty} z^{k_i}\Pr\{G_i=k_i/G_{i-1}=k_{i-1}\}A_i$$

and

$$A_{N-1} = \sum_{k_N} z^{k_N}\Pr\{G_N=k_N/G_{N-1}=k_{N-1}\}$$

Then

$$A_{N-1} = (\sum_{j=0}^{M} q_j z^{m_j})^{k_{N-1}} = z_{N-1}^{k_{N-1}}$$

$$A_{N-2} = \sum_{k_{N-1}} z^{k_{N-1}}\Pr\{G_{N-1}=k_{N-1}/G_{N-2}=k_{N-2}\}z_{N-1}^{k_{N-1}} =$$

$$= E\{(z\, z_{N-1})^{G_{N-1}}/G_{N-2}=k_{N-2}\} =$$

$$= (\sum_{j=0}^{M} q_j (z\, z_{N-1})^{m_i})^{k_{N-2}} = z_{N-2}^{k_{N-2}}$$

where

$$z_{N-2} = \sum_{j=0}^{M} q_j (z\, z_{N-1})^{m_j}$$

Since $A_0=z_0^{k_0}$, the last sum is

$$\sum_{k_0} z^{k_0}\Pr\{G_0=k_0\}A_0 = E\{(zz_0)^{G_0}\}$$

DIGITAL TECHNIQUES in Simulation, Communication and Control
Spyros G. Tzafestas (editor)
Elsevier Science Publishers B.V. (North-Holland) © IMACS, 1985

ADAPTIVE ROUTING IN RADIO COMMUNICATION NETWORKS

Anthony Ephremides
Department of Electrical Engineering
University of Maryland
College Park, Maryland 20742

After a brief review of the field of routing algorithms for communication networks this paper focuses on adaptive routing for radio networks of mobile nodes. Two algorithms are proposed and their performance is evaluated and compared to that of flooding.

1. INTRODUCTION

Few problems in the field of computer communication networks have received as early and extensive attention as the routing numerous studies of flow problems in network theory that provide a basis for modeling the routing problem in a mathematically tractable way and, second, routing has proved to be a necessary and fundamental design choice for the operation of message or packet switched networks.

In its simplest form the statement of the routing problem is as follows. Consider a node that receives messages from an incoming link and has a choice of forwarding them via one of two outgoing links. Let λ be the average rate of the arrival message stream. By implementing a specific routing decision the node produces two outgoing streams the average rates of which are λ_1 and λ_2. Of course in order to maintain equilibrium and finite delays it is necessary that

$$\lambda_1+\lambda_2=\lambda$$

and thus λ_1 and λ_2 can be represented as

$$\lambda_1=\Phi\lambda, \quad \lambda_2=(1-\Phi)1$$

where $0\leqslant\Phi\leqslant1$. The routing problem consists of choosing Φ to maximize a given performance measure which is usually related to the average delay per message in the network. A variety of constraints usually accompany this optimization problem. A more detailed formulation will follow later. Now we provide an early view of the classification of routing algorithms according to various solution philosophies. These philosophies emerge according to the answere chosen for the following questions:

1) *How* is Φ chosen (i.e. *by whom* and on the basis of *what* information)?
2) *How often* is Φ updated?
3) Are there any limitations in the *range of values* Φ can take?

The first question leads to a distinction between *centralized* and *distributed* routing algorithms.

The second question distinguishes *static* from *dynamic* algorithms.

Finally the third question separates *fixed* from *alternate* routing algoritms.

2. EARLY ANALYTICAL APPROACHES

Unlike other communication network design problems, such as topological design or error and flow control, the routing problem is amenable to analytical formulation, if certain assumptions are made. We will describe here a few of the most notable analytical approaches.

In [1] the first mathematical model was proposed to accomplish centralized, static, alternate routing. To apprepriate the degree of difficulty associated with the analytical treatment of the routing problem, we must emphasize that even though the centralized, static alternate problem is the least complex of the routing problems, the model proposed in [1] falls short of obtaining a true solution even in the presence of strong, idealized assumptions.

Consider a network of N nodes and M links. Let $r_i(j)$ represent the average rate of exogenous message traffic entering the network at node i and destined for node j for i,j=1,...,N. These quantitites represent the traffic load matrix. Each entry represents the value of one commodity; that is each source destination pair corresponds to a separate commodity. Let C_i represent the capacity of link i,i=1,..,M in bits/s.

Assume that the average length of each message is $\frac{1}{\mu}$ bits. Suppose that the routing variables are chosen so as to induce traffic of average rate λ_i on link i, $i=1,\ldots,M$. Obviously the value of λ_i is determined by the $r_i(j)$'s and by the routing variables. If the assumption is made that link i behaves like an M/M/1 queueing system independently of all other links and with customer arrival rate λ_i and service rate μC_i, then it is possible to express the average delay per message for traversing that link as

$$T_i=\frac{1}{\mu C_i-\lambda_i}$$

for $\lambda_i<\mu C_i$. The preceding assumption is a very strong one and requires some discussion. It was observed early by Kleinrock [2] that packet-switched or, more generally, store-and-forward communication networks can be modeled as queueing networks. Each link can be thought of as an autonomous service system with service time composed of three components: propagation time (which is independent of message length and is negligible for short distance), transmission time (which depends on link capacity and message length), and processing time (often quite small and partly dependent on message length). Messages arriving at a node are stored in a buffer of sufficiently large capacity, so that overflows are rare. Thus each link has all the attributes of a queueing system. Unfortunately only a very specialized class of interconnected queueing systems is amenable to analysis. This is the class of Jacksonian networks, so termed because of the pioneering study of them by Jackson [3]. Recently a great deal of attention has been paid to non-Jacksonian networks for the purpose of extending to them the analytical treatment techniques that were successful in the case of Jacksonian networks. A Jacksonian network consists of *independent* exponential servers that are interconnected so that a customer may visit several of them in succession. The exogenous customer arrival streams are assumed to be Poisson processes. In order for a communication network to be usefully modeled by a Jacksonian network it is therefore necessary to assume the following:

a) the exogenous message arrival streams are Poisson processes.

b) the service time for each message on each link is exponentially distributed with rate μC_i.

c) the service times at different links for the same message are independent.

The last assumption is the truly problematic one since each message retains its length as it traverses successive links. Thus the "service" times it encounters on different links are strongly correlated. Making the crucial *independence* assumption permits the use of Jacksonian models for communication networks. For certain types of, so called, "large-and-balanced" networks experimental results have shown that the independence assumption can be tolerable if used with care and applied judiciously [4].

In any event, with the indepedence assumption the routing problem becomes

$$\min_{\{\lambda_i\}} T$$

where $T=\sum_{i=1}^{M}\lambda_i\frac{1}{\mu C_i-\lambda_i}$; that is, minimize the weighted total average delay subject to the constraint $0\leq\lambda_i<\mu C_i$. The optimization can be carried out by a variety of classical methods since T is a convex function of the λ_i's. The flow deviation method (a form of steepest descent algorithm) was used in [1] to produce a set of optimizing link flow rate values. For this reason the approach was called the flow assignment procedure. Note that just by obtaining a set of optimal flows we have not yet solved the routing problem. The next step is to find the values of the routing variables (the Φ's) which when applied to the given input variables (the $r_i(j)$'s) will produce the desired link flows (the λ_i's). It is clear that for certain topologies of the network and for certain regions of values of the input variables it is not possible to meet the "λ" values obtained by solving the minimization problem. In those cases the already complicated mathematical programming problem of matching the inputs to the induced flows by means of the appropriate splitting fractions "Φ" becomes an approximation problem in which the objective becomes not to find exactly, but simply to come "close" to the desired values.

The next major breakthrough in the routing problem was Galleger's algorithm [5] which appeared in the literature in 1977. In that algorithm a solution was obtained for a distributed, alternate, quasi-static routing problem that minimized weighted average delay, that guaranteed the absence of loops, and that did not explicitly require the independence assumption.

Using the notation introduced above and defining the following additional quantities we can briefly state the nature of the algorithm's result. Let

$r_i(j) \triangleq$ average rate of exogenous traffic entering at i for j as before

$t_i(j) \triangleq$ average rate of total traffic entering i for j,

$\lambda_{ik} \triangleq$ average rate of combined traffic of all commodities on link (i,k), i.e. on the link that connects nodes i and k (replacing what was called λ_i before); this quantity is zero if there is no link (i,k), and $\Phi_{ik}(j) \triangleq$ the routing variable of node i for link (i,k) and for commodity (destination) j; equivalently, the percentage of the commodity j that node i routes to neighbor k (if there is no link (i,k), then $\Phi_{ik}(j)=0$).

Clearly the following are true:

$$t_i(j)=r_i(j)+\sum_{k=1}^{N}\Phi_{ki}(j)t_k(j), \forall\ i,j$$

$$\lambda_{ik}=\sum_{j=1}^{N}t_i(j)\Phi_{ik}(j) \qquad ,\forall\ i,k$$

$$\Phi_{ik}(j)\geq 0 \qquad ,\forall\ i,k,j$$

$$\sum_{k=1}^{N}\Phi_{i,k}(j)=1 \qquad ,\forall\ i,j$$

Instead of assuming that the average delay T_{ik} per message on link (i,k) is given by the M/M/1 formula used before, which would be tantamount to making the independence assumption, it is simply assumed that the delay is an increasing, convex function of the link flow f_{ik} only*. Then the routing problem becomes

$$\min_{\{\Phi's\}} T$$

$T \triangleq \sum\sum_{i,k} f_{ik}T_{ik}$; that is minimizing the average weighted total delay as before. So the problem looks like the earlier one except that it attempts minimization directly with respect to the routing variables rather than indirectly by means of the link flows, and that it does not make the independence assumption;that is, it still looks like a *static, centralized, alternate* routing problem, but in a less restricted framework. It is during the attempt to solve this problem that it became clear that a *distributed* and *quasi-static* implementation of the solution was feasible, thus transforming the algorithm into a distributed, quasi-static, alternate routing scheme. Convergence of that implementation was shown and a scheme to avoid loops at all stages of the algorithm was incorporated in the solution. A major difficulty that had to be resolved was the non-convex dependence of the objective function on the routing variables. Another non-trivial complication associated with this algorithm is the need to find an initial feasible and loop-free set of flows by other means. There exist algorithms and methods to achieve this goal, however, and thus it is possible to establish the initial conditions the algorithm needs. The nature of the algorithm is briefly the following. Each node, between periodic updates, measures a local "distance measure"to his neighbors. It then passes to, and receives from, his neighbors information about those measurements. This exchange of information must follow specific rules of order in order to avoid loops and to guarantee convergence. Then each node alters the previous values of the Φ_{ik}'s by appropriate step sizes so that more traffic is sent towards those neighbors that promise less delay, and less traffic is routed via the neighbors that exhibit tardiness. If the rate of change in the input variables is less than the convergence rate of the algorithm, it becomes possible to "track" the shifting optimum set of values of the routing variables.

An important drawback of this algorithm is that it cannot be implemented in its pure form because of the difficulty in obtaining well-behaved estimates of the quantities that each node must measure and because of the problems associated with its convergence. Its chief value lies in the fact that it showed how ana lytical treatment can "drive" the choices of practical routing algorithms, thus making total reliance on heuristics unnecessary. It also inspired subsequent work on routing that evetually led to very practical and robust schemes that

---

*it can be argued that this assumption is equivalent to assuming independence because only for a network of interconnected *exponential* servers is it true that the average delay in each stage depends on the average flow in that stage only and not on the average flows in the other stages. However, Gallager's algorithm has been generalized to allow arbitrary convex increasing dependence of link delay on all of the flows [6].

can be, and have been, implemented.

It was later shown by Bertsekas [7,8] that Gallager's algorithm can be viewed as a special case of a much more general class of optimization techniques known as projected Newton methods and Goldstein-Levitin-Poljak gradient projection methods . These methods have been adequately described in the literature but have failed so far to be translated into useful routing algorithms. It is noteworthy that the end-to-end flow control problem which was previously unanalyzed and unmodeled, was reduced to a routing problem in the context of the Gallager-Bertsekas class of models by means of a simple ingeneous observation explained in [9].

3. THE RADIO-NETWORK CASE

The discussion so far has implicitly assumed that the networks considered are of the store-and-forward type with land-links. An equally important class of networks consists of the so called radio-networks. The links in these network are radio-based. The key difference in this case is that a radio link is a multiple access and broadcast channel; that is a node's transmission is subject to interference from the transmissions of other nodes and it can be also received by nodes other than the destination node. These properties of the radio links give new dimensions to the routing problem. Furthermore in a radio network a node is not necessarily stationary. Mobility of the nodes may induce frequent topological changes that make the routing problem much more difficult and challenging.

In this section we will describe two routing algorithms that designed for a special type of a radio network and we will compare several attributes of their performance to those of their chief competitor, namely flooding [10].

Consider the case of N mobile nodes that wish to remain interconnected via radio links. Suppose that the communication range is variable and cannot cover the entire geographical area of node dispersion. Many factors may account for such circumstances: limited power, interference, variable antenna orientation, node motion, physical objects, etc. In such an environment the first question is how these nodes can organize themselves into a reliable network by means of a distributed algorithm. This question corresponds to the physical layer design according to the OSI architecture model. The second question is how the discovered links can be activated by each node, again in a distributed way, and without interference. This question addresses the multiple access aspect of the radio environment and corresponds to the link layer of the OSI model. These questions can be handled in a variety of ways. In reference [11-14] some solutions and algorithms are described that can take care of these fundamental issues.

Next comes the questions of routing that resides naturally in the third (or network) layer of the OSI architecture. How should a node send a message to a remote destination? Clearly due to the assumed volatility of the connectivities in the network it is not possible to employ any of the existing methods of routing. In other words we cannot assume that a node may know the location of the destination node or his distance from that node. The only exception is flooding which can still be used. It must be noted, however, that in a radio environment, flooding has additional disadvantages since it generates unnecessary interfering and bandwidth consuming traffic. Nevertheless flooding will ensure the delivery of the message to its destination. The question is at what cost relative to that of other candidate algorithms. Let us consider one alternative.

Suppose that note i wishes to send a message to node j. There is no prior knowledge about the location of j nor of his distance from i in terms of any specific distance measure. A natural thing to do is to send a short query to all neighbors of i. Instead of uncontrollably flooding this query message further out, i's neighbors perform the steps of a structured process. Each neighbor of i passes on the received query to every neighbor of his except to doesn't pass on that query to anyone received the query. Furthermore he doesn't pass on that query to anyone if he had originated a query about the same destination node himself (and to which query he hasn't received a response yet). In this manner the query will start propagating in all directions away from the originating node. The first node who, on receipt of the query, finds that he has knowledge of the whereabouts of the destination node currently under search, either because that node is a direct neighbor or because he has already found out by means of a response to an earlier query, immediately generates a response which he transmits to all nodes from which he has received a query about that destination node. Each node who receives a response to a query passes it on to all those neighbors from which he has received queries. In this manner the response propagates back toward the inquiring node in a controlled fashion without unnecessary flooding. Clearly care must be taken in specifying the precise rules of order in such a process of propagation in order to avoid cycles and deadlocks under any possible relative ordering of the steps of this basically asynchronous process of transmissions and retransmissions of the same query. The procedure described above succeeds in avoiding cycles and deadlocks and terminates with the response to the query received by the originating node. It is possible however that there will be redundant responses since the response message may propagate along different parallel paths back to the origin.

The reason that a query, rather than the main message itself, is forwarded in this manner to the destination is twofold. First, it is a much shorter message since it consists merely of a flag and of the source destination identity. Secondly, and most importantly, all nodes that participate in this search process gain knowledge of the whereabouts of that particular destination node, eliminating thus the need for future queries of their own should they later desire to send a message to that node themselves. The path actually selected for routing the message after receipt of the response to the query is not important here. It could be simply the one via the neighbor through whom the response was received first, or a selection process can be implemented that is based on some distance measure. It is assumed that an acknowledgement message mechanism exists so that a node can detect a change of connectivities that destroys the previously sought and established path and can reinitiate a query. It is clear that the number of steps involved in a second search will be in general less than in the original one, since nodes with valid existing paths to the destination are likely to be encountered in the close vicinity of the inquiring node.

A simple modification to the algorithm just described may generate additional knowledge about the connectivities in the network at a rather negligible additional overhead cost that may eventually save in total overhead. It was assumed that the query message consisted only of a flag and of the identity of the destination node. Suppose it is enlarged to include the identity of the inquiring node as well. Furthermore, as an additional option, it may include a field for updating a "distance" value that could be simply the number of "hops". Each intermediate node augments the distance field entry before passing it on (if the distance measure is simply the number of hops, the entry is augmented by one). In this manner, as the query propagates outward, several nodes gain knowledge of the whereabouts of the *source* node, plus of its distance from them. This information can be stored at each intermediate node for future use. Thus many future queries become unnecessary. As far as the response message is concerned, it, too, may be enlarged to include an entry for distance. Thus, as it propagates back toward the source node, the distance entry is appropriately augmented to provide knowledge to all nodes that can be used to choose amonget alternate paths. In all other respects the algorithm remains unchanged.

In order to evaluate the performance of these algorithms it was necessary to utilize simulation techniques. It is impossible to analyze mathematically the performance, no matter what idealized assumptions are made, simply because there is strong dependence on topological layouts and on mobility scenarios neither of which can be analytically modeled. These simulation results were reported in [10].

REFERENCES

1. L. Fratta, M.Gerla, L. Kleinrock. "The Flow Deviation Method-An Approach to Store-and-Forward Communication Network Design", Networks, Vol.3, pp. 97-133, 1973.
2. L. Kleinrock, Communication Nets-Stochastic Message Flow and Delay, McGraw-Hill, New York, 1964.
3. J.R.Jackson, "Networks of Waiting Lines", Operations Research, Vol.5,pp. 518-521, 1957.
4. L. Kleinrock, Queueing Systems, Vol. II, Wiley-Interscience, New York,1976.
5. R.G.Gallager, "A Minimum Delay Routing Algorithm Using Distributed Computation", IEEE Trans.on Communications, Vol.COM-25, pp. 73-85, 1978.
6. A.Ephremides, "Extension of an Adaptive Distributed Routing Algorithm to Mixed Media Networks", IEEE Trans.on Communications, Vol.26, No.8, August 1978.
7. D.P.Bertsekas, "A Class of Optimal Routing Algorithms for Communication Networks", Proc.5th International Conference on Computer Communications, Atlanta, GA, October 1980, pp.71-76.
8. D.P.Bertsekas, "Projected Newton Methods for Optimization Problems with Simple Constraints", SIAM Journal on Control and Optimization,Vol.20,pp.

221-246, 1982.

9. R.G. Gallager, S.J. Golestaani, "Flow Control and Routing Algorithms for Data Networks", Proc. 5th International Conference on Computer Communications, Atlanta, GA, October 1980, pp.779-784.
10. M.Weber, A. Ephremides, "A Simulated Performance Study of Some Distributed Routing Algorithms for Mobile Radio Networks", Proc.of Johns Hopking Conference, Baltimore, MD, March, 1983.
11. J.E. Wieselthier, D.J.Baker, A. Ephremides, D.N.McGregor, "Preliminary System Concept for an HF Intra-Taska Force Communication Network", NRL Report 8637, August, 1983.
12. D.J.Baker, A. Ephremides, "The Architectural Organization of a Mobile Radio Network via a Distributed Algorithm", IEEE Trans. on Communications, Vol.COM-29, pp. 1694-1701, November, 1981.
13. D.J.Baker, A. Ephremides, J.E.Wieselthier, "A Distributed Algorithm for Scheduling the activation of Links in a Self-Organizing, Mobile, Radio Network", Proc.of the ICC, Philadelphia, PA, June 1982.
14. A. Ephremides, "Distributed Protocols for Mobile Radio Networks", Proc.of NATO Advanced Study Institute on the Impact of Processing Techniques to Communications, Chateau Bonas, France, July, 1983.

DIGITAL TECHNIQUES in Simulation, Communication and Control
Spyros G. Tzafestas (editor)
Elsevier Science Publishers B.V. (North-Holland) © IMACS, 1985

ADAPTIVE ALGORITHMS FOR LOAD SHARING BETWEEN PROCESSORS WITH APPLICATIONS TO ROUTING SCHEMES

E.D.Sykas, D.P.Markovitch and E.N.Protonotarios

National Technical University of Athens
Department of Electrical Engineering
Patission 42, Athens 106 82, Greece

A simple queueing system exhibiting features that make it appropriate for the study of load sharing problems or adaptive routing algorithms is examined. The system consists of m parallel servers with different, in general, processing rates. Arrivals are classified into two types: jobs that require service from a particular server and jobs that can be served by any one server. The latter are assigned to a server according to the decisions of a dispatcher. The dispatcher bases its decisions on information about the queue lengths in all servers and the assignment policy is deterministic and state dependent. Heuristic assignment policies can be constructed as follows: The dispatcher assigns a job to the server characterized, at the time of its arrival, by the largest value of a certain decision function. Several decision functions are proposed and the performance of the corresponding system is determined for the case where there are two servers. In this case, an efficient numerical solution method can be developed.

1. INTRODUCTION

Queueing systems which are used extensively for modelling computer systems are not adequate for the study of dynamic routing schemes or load sharing policies in such systems. It is the standard assumption in these models [1,2] that routing decisions are static, that is, the routing policy does not change as time proceeds, but it may be of probabilistic nature. On the other hand, dynamic policies base their decisions upon the available information about the system state. Although their performance is generally better than the corresponding one of probabilistic strategies [3-6], little is known about decision rules that lead to optimal dynamic policies [7,8]. In this paper we consider a simple queueing system that can be used for the study of load sharing problems in multi-processor systems and for the study of dynamic routing algorithms in packet-switching networks. We will start with a description of the examined system and later we will discuss its possible applications in more details. The examined system may be considered as a queueing system consisting of m parallel queues and a dispatcher as in Fig.1. There are two types of arrivals at the system: jobs that require service from a particular server and jobs that can be served by any one server. Arrivals form Poisson processes with rates λ_i, i=1,2, 3,...,m and λ, respectively. Jobs from stream λ_i are served by server-i exclusively, while the jobs belonging to stream λ are routed by the dispatcher upon their arrival to one of the m servers. The decisions of the dispatcher follow a rule which will be referred to as the assignment policy. Jobs that are destined for server-i or are assigned to it by the dispatcher are served in order of arrival, FCFS rule, and their service time follows a negative exponential distribution with mean $1/\mu_i$ (s), that is, its probability density function is $\mu_i \exp(-\mu_i t)$, i=1,2,..., m. We assume that jobs which are assigned to a particular server, belonging either to stream λ_i or λ, remain there until they are served. Moreover, preemption of a job in service is not allowed. Because of the previous assumptions the vector $\mathbf{n} = (n_1, n_2, \ldots, n_m)$ having as components the lengths n_i of the queues (job in service included) describes the state of the system completely.

Assignment policies may be of a probabilistic or deterministic nature and may depend on the state of the system or not. In the following, we will consider only deterministic state-dependent assignment policies. Such policies can be described by a dispatching function d(•), where, given the state $\mathbf{n}$ of the system upon the arrival of a stream λ job at the dispatcher, the server to which this particular job is assigned is $i^* = d(\mathbf{n})$. The just-described system is closely related to applications, such as, routing algorithms in computer networks or load balancing policies in multi-processor computer systems. In the case of a packet-switching computer network, the previous system may model the function of an isolated node. That is, stream λ_i represents packet arrivals which must be routed to the i-th outgoing link (the server in this case), while for the packets of stream λ there is a freedom in the selection of an appropriate outgoing link, as it happens when bifurcation is permitted. Another interpretation is to consider the examined system as the model of a multi-processor computer. Then, stream λ_i consists of the tasks that must be serviced by the i-th processor, while tasks from stream λ may be executed to any one processor. A similar interpretation is to think of the servers as separate computer systems supporting a distributed application. In all cases, it can be assumed that streams λ_i, i=1,2,...,m do not bypass the dispatcher, but they result from the probabilistic splitting of a common stream γ into sub-streams. Then one can say that the examined assignment policy is a mixed one, that is, it shares features of both probabilistic and deterministic ones.

It should be noticed that the examined assignment policies are quite different from scheduling algorithms used by operating systems for the efficient utilization of a processor(s), since preemption and/or reassignment of tasks are not allowed here, the last two properties being the main features of such scheduling algorithms. Moreover, the examined system differs from the systems studied in [4-8] in one or more points. For example, in [4,7] equal processing rates are assumed, in [5-7] there are no arrivals bypassing the dispatcher and in [8] only a single queue is formed in front of the dispatcher, there are no arrivals at all, but a given collection of jobs is to be served.

In the next section we will show how efficient deterministic state-dependent assignment policies can be defined. The approach which will be used is heuristic and it is based on the idea that sending a job to the server where a given performance criterion is maximized(minimized) is near-optimal. The previously described system can be studied with the help of an m-dimensional Markov chain. The case of two servers is simpler and amenable to numerical solution. In fact, for this case an efficient numerical solution method can be developed, as it will be shown in Section 3.

2. ASSIGNMENT POLICIES

A good way to determine assignment policies is the following heuristic method: Find appropriate decision functions $f_i(\mathbf{n})$, i=1,2,...,m, one for each server. Then, define the dispatching function $d(\mathbf{n})$ as follows

$$d(\mathbf{n}) = i^* = \max_i [i: f_i(\mathbf{n}) = f^*] \quad (1)$$

$$\text{where } f^* = \min(\max) [f_1(\mathbf{n}), f_2(\mathbf{n}), \ldots, f_m(\mathbf{n})] \quad (2)$$

That is, when a stream λ job arrives at the dispatcher, it is assigned to the server for which the decision function $f_i(\mathbf{n})$ is minimized(maximized). In case there is no one unique such server, the tie is resolved by assigning the job to the server with the largest index i. An increasing ordering of the servers with respect to their capacities is assumed, that is, $\mu_1 \leq \mu_2 \leq \ldots \leq \mu_m$. Then, the criterion in Eq.(1) is equivalent to saying that jobs are assigned to the fastest server exhibiting the minimum(maximum) decision function.

Some remarks about the appropriate choice of decision functions follow.

. Their definition must be related to quantities characterizing the effectiveness of the examined system. Then, it can be reasonably expected that the performance of the system will be satisfactory.

. It is possible to assume that the decision function $f_i(\mathbf{n})$ depends only on the number n_i of jobs in queue at server-i. Then, the decision functions can be computed separately at each server. Otherwise, the dispatcher is responsible for collecting the necessary information and then computing the decision functions. Both alternatives are possible, but as we will see soon all the examined decision functions can be reduced to the form $f_i(n_i)$, i = 1,2,...,m.

. It seems reasonable that the decision functions must exhibit the property that joining large queues is inefficient. A simple way to express this is the choice of monotonic decision functions. The dissatisfaction at joining large queues, if $f_i(n_i)$ is selected to be increasing(decreasing) in n_i, is expressed by an assignment policy that dispatches to the server characterized by the minimum(maximum) value of the decision function.

Let us for the moment ignore the job arrivals and assume that the system is in state $\mathbf{n} = (n_1, n_2, \ldots, n_m)$. Then we have only job departures and the corresponding processes evolve independently in each server. Since the time required for the completion of service of the first job in queue, residual time, remains exponentially distributed with the same pdf as every job in server-i, the departure process can be viewed as a Poisson process with rate λ_i that stops at the n_i-th event. Because of the FCFS rule, the n-th job in queue at server-i has an Erlang-n waiting time distribution. That is, the time until the completion of service of the n-th job has the following pdf

$$g_{i,n}(t) = \mu_i(\mu_i t)^{n-1}\exp(-\mu_i t)/(n-1)! \ , \quad t>0, \ 1\leq n\leq n_i$$
$$= \mu_i P_{i,n-1}(t) \quad (3)$$

where

$$P_{i,n}(t) = (\mu_i t)^n \exp(-\mu_i t)/n! \ , \qquad n<n_i \quad (4)$$

is the probability that after t seconds n jobs will have been served at server-i. Obviously, for the last job in server-i it holds

$$P_{i,n_i}(t) = 1 - P_{i,0}(t) - P_{i,1}(t) - \ldots - P_{i,n_i-1}(t)$$
$$= G_{i,n_i}(t) \quad (5)$$

where $G_{i,n}(t)$ is the probability distribution function corresponding to $g_{i,n}(t)$. Let also $G^*_{i,n}(s)$ be the corresponding probability generation function, that is

$$G^*_{i,n}(s) = [\mu_i/(s+\mu_i)]^n \quad (6)$$

We can use the previous results for the analysis of the behaviour of the system for an interval between successive arrivals. The idea is, from these results, to calculate quantities characterizing the effectiveness of the system, which can be used as decision functions and, in this way, construct heuristic assignment policies. Some candidate for this purpose quantities are: the response time, the throughput, the completion probability, e.t.c. Their definition and the way in which the can be used in dispatching rules are presented in the following.

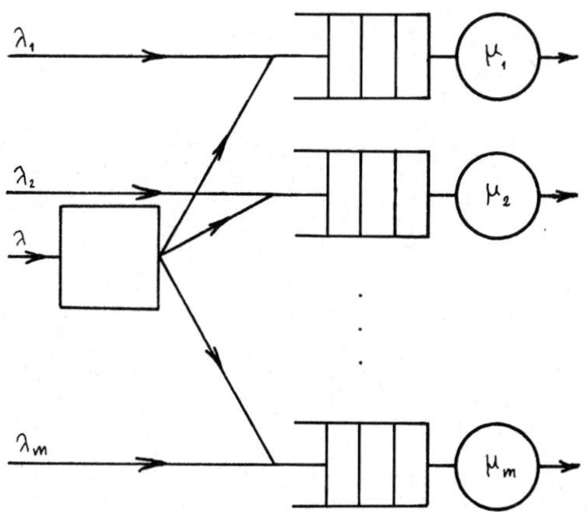

Fig. 1 The examined system

Policy-R

Response time is the expected waiting time for the completion of service of a job. According to Policy-R, an arriving job is dispatched to the server where its response time is the lowest. That is, when a stream λ job arrives at the dispatcher and finds the system in state **n**, then, its response times at each server are

$$f_i^R(n_i) = (n_i+1)/\mu_i \ , \quad i = 1,2,...,m \tag{7}$$

respectively. Thus, the job is dispatched, as Eqs.(1), (2) indicate, to the fastest server exhibiting the smallest service time.

Policy-C

Completion probability is the probability that an arriving stream λ job at the dispatcher will be served in a prescribed time interval. This interval can be chosen arbitrarily. A first possibility is to define it as the time until the next stream λ arrival. Thus, if a job is assigned to server-i, its completion probability is

$$f_i^C(n_i) = \int_0^\infty G_{i,n_i+1}(t) \ \exp(-\lambda t)\,\lambda\, dt = G^*_{i,n_i+1}(\lambda)$$
$$= [\mu_i/(\mu_i+\lambda)]^{n_i+1}, \ i = 1,2,...,m \tag{8}$$

Similarly, we can calculate the completion probability for the interval until the next arrival at the system. Since the next job arrives at the system following an exponentially distributed time with rate $\gamma = \lambda+\lambda_1 + \lambda_2 + ... + \lambda_m$ we have

$$f_i^C(n_i) = [\mu_i/(\gamma+\mu_i)]^{n_i+1} \ , \ i = 1,2,...,m \tag{9}$$

Another possibility is to use the interval until the next stream λ or stream λ_i arrival. Then

$$f_i^C(n_i) = [\mu_i/(\mu_i+\lambda+\lambda_i)]^{n_i+1} \ , \ i = 1,2,...,m \tag{10}$$

Using any of these decision functions, Policy-C dispatches to the fastest server with the maximum completion probability.

Policy-N

Policy-N consists in dispatching an arriving job at the dispatcher so that the expected number of departures from the system will be maximized. The number of departures are counted during an interval which is defined like the corresponding one for the completion probability. Policy-N and Policy-C are closely related, in fact, theyare identical. We can avoid computation of the relevant decision functions if we reason as follows: we only have to determine the difference in the expected number of departures due to the assignment of the arriving job to a certain server instead of another one. That is, the expected number of departures from the system increases because of the assignment of a job to server-i, with respect to its value before the assignment, by the probability of completion of this particular job. Therefore, the largest expected number of departures from the system appears when an arriving job is assigned to the server exhibiting the largest completion probability.

Policy-D

Another possibility is to dispatch an arriving job to the server in which the total waiting time (sum of finishing times for all jobs in queue) is minimum. Thus, Policy-D assigns an arriving job at the fastest server having the lowest value of the following decision function

$$f_i^D(n_i) = (1+n_i)(1+n_i/2)/\mu_i \ , \quad i = 1,2,...,m \tag{11}$$

It is noteworthy that the expected value of the above function in an M/M/1 queue is the marginal delay [9]. In case of static probabilistic routing [10] policies the optimal decision is to route jobs so that the marginal delays in the used paths will be equal.

Policy-T

Throughput is the expected rate of departures from the system. At equilibrium, its value is equal to the sum of all arrival rates and it does not carry any useful routing information. Therefore, in order to be able to use it in assignment policies we have to compute its expected values for short intervals. The most reasonable such computation of "instantaneous" throughput values is to divide the expected number of departures in a prescribed time interval by its expected length. An appropriate definition of such an interval is the time between two successive job arrivals at the system. It is easy to see that this approach leads to a policy that is identical to Policies C and N. A slight change in the above computation is to calculate the expected value of the ratio of the number of departures from the system by the time interval in which they occur. This definition, although it is not theoretically justified, was used in [5]. Reasoning in the same way as for Policy-N, we conclude that we have to compute only the increase in throughput that an assignment to server-i causes, that is, the difference in the values of the expected throughput for states $(n_1, n_2,...,n_i+1,...,n_m)$ and $(n_1,n_2,...,n_i,...,n_m)$. This difference is the expected value of the ratio of the completion probability divided by the time interval for its calculation, that is

$$f_i^T(n_i) = \int_0^\infty G_{i,n_i+1}(t) \ a(t)/t \ dt \tag{12}$$

where a(t) is the pdf of the time interval until the next arrival at the system. Taking into account that a(t) is, in fact, the negative exponential distribution with rate $\gamma = \lambda + \lambda_1 + \lambda_2 + ... + \lambda_m$ we find that the integral in Eq.(12), finally, yields

$$f_i^T(n_i) = -\gamma[\ Q_i/1+Q_i^2/2+...+Q_i^k/k + \ln(1-Q_i)] \tag{13}$$

where $Q_i = \mu_i/(\gamma+\mu_i)$. Thus, Policy-T consists in assigning an arriving job at the dispatcher to the fastest server in which the above function is minimized.

3. ANALYSIS OF A TWO-SERVER SYSTEM

In this section we will present a solution technique appropriate for the analysis of a special case of the previously described system, namely, the case when there are only two servers. For such a system we present an efficient method for the numerical computation of the steady state probabilities. Is is clear that in the general case, m>2, the examined system can be modelled as an m-dimensional Markov chain with state variable the vector $\mathbf{n} = (n_1,n_2,..,n_m)$. Although it is not difficult to write the steady state equations (we only have to equate flows in and out of a given state) there is no closed form solution. The method of local balance equations [1] does not seem to work here even in the simplest case m=2.

Nevertheless, when m=2 there is a significant simpification in the corresponding state transition diagram, which is a result of the fact that we assumed monotonic decision functions. It should be obvious that in this case the state space is divided into two areas as shown in Fig.2. In one area, the common traffic (formed by the jobs belonging in stream λ) is always sent to the first server. In the other area, it is always sent to the second server. The border line between these two areas is called the policy line and it is uniquely defined from the corresponding decision functions. The reason is easy to understand. If the number of jobs in queue at server-1 is n_1 and $f_1(n_1)$ is the value of the decision function, then as long as $f_2(n_2) \leq f_1(n_1)$ ($f_2(n_2) \geq f_1(n_1)$) the common traffic is routed to the second server. Otherwise, if $f_2(n_2) > f_1(n_1)$ ($f_2(n_2) < f_1(n_1)$) the common traffic is sent to the first server. Because of the monotonic nature of the decision functions there is a unique change-over point.

The method which will be described later can be used for all decision functions presented in the previous section or whenever a policy line partitioning the space state into two areas as in Fig.2 can be defined. Since closed form solutions do not seem to exist, a numerical solution can be found if we assume that buffer space in each server is finite. That is, if we truncate the state space diagram so that the largest number of jobs in queue at server-1 (2) will be $N_1(N_2)$. If $N_1(N_2)$ are large enough and the point (N_1,N_2) lies on the policy line, then the steady state probabilities of the truncated system will be a very satisfactory approximation of the correct values.

Let $p(i,j) = \Pr[n_1=i,\ n_2=j]$ be the steady state probabilities. They can be computed by writting the global balance equations for all states (n_1,n_2), $0 \leq n_1 \leq N_1$, $0 \leq n_2 \leq N_2$, the normalizing equation

$$\sum_{i=0}^{N_1} \sum_{j=0}^{N_2} p(i,j) = 1 \qquad (14)$$

and solving the resulting system of linear equations in $(N_1+1)(N_2+1)$ unknowns, the probabilities $p(i,j)$.

An equivalent, but more elegant, method of writting the global balance equations (GBEs), which finally leads to the solution of a smaller system of linear equations, N_1 or N_2 unknowns, will be described in the following. This method results from the particular form that the state transition diagram assumes when m=2 and monotonic decision functions are used. Before we proceed, let us define the following quantities:

$e(i,j)$ = the total outward transition rate from state (i,j)

$r_1(i,j)$ = the transition rate from state (i,j) to state $(i+1,j)$

$r_2(i,j)$ = the transition rate from state (i,j) to state $(i,j+1)$

Then, it is not difficult to see that for transition diagrams like the one in Fig.2, we have

$$e(i,j) = \lambda I((i,j)\neq(N_1,N_2)) + \lambda_1 I(i\neq N_1) + \lambda_2 I(j\neq N_2) + \mu_1 I(i\neq 0) + \mu_2 I(j\neq 0) \qquad (15)$$

where $I(\cdot)$ is the indicator function, that is

$$I(A) = \begin{cases} 1 & \text{if } A \text{ holds} \\ 0 & \text{otherwise} \end{cases} \qquad (16)$$

Similarly, if $f_i(n_i)$ are increasing functions in n_i we find that

$$r_1(i,j) = \lambda I(f_1(i) < f_2(j))\, I((i,j)\neq(N_1,N_2)) + \lambda_1 I(i\neq N_1) \qquad (17)$$

and

$$r_2(i,j) = \lambda I(f_1(i) \geq f_2(j))\, I((i,j)\neq(N_1,N_2)) + \lambda_2 I(j\neq N_2) \qquad (18)$$

The inequalities in Eqs.(17),(18) are inversed if $f_i(n_i)$ are decreasing functions in n_i. The GBE for state (i,j) can be written now as follows

$$p(i,j)e(i,j) = p(i+1,j)\mu_1 I(i\neq N_1) + p(i-1,j)\, r_1(i-1,j)\, I(i\neq 0) + p(i,j-1)\, r_2(i,j-1)\, I(j\neq 0) \qquad (19)$$

In vector form the previous equation can be written as follows

$$\mathbf{p}_{i+1} = \mathbf{D}_{i-1}\mathbf{p}_{i-1} + \mathbf{A}_i \mathbf{p}_i \qquad (20)$$

where $\mathbf{p}_i$ is a column vector with elements the steady state probabilities $p(i,j)$, $j=0,1,\ldots,N_2$, of the states in the i-th column of the transition diagram, that is

$$\mathbf{p}_i = [p(i,N_2),\ p(i,N_2-1),\ldots,\ p(i,0)]^T \qquad (21)$$

Eq. (20) holds for all $i=0,1,\ldots,N_1$ if we set

$$\mathbf{p}_{N_1+1} = \mathbf{0} \qquad (22)$$

and define the matrices $\mathbf{D}_i$ and $\mathbf{A}_i$ as follows

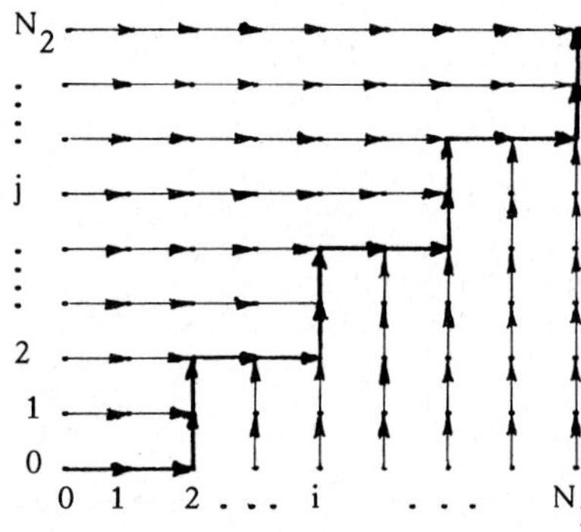

Fig. 2 Simplified state transition diagram. Only rate λ is shown. The omitted rates μ_1,μ_2,λ_1 and λ_2 cause transitions of the form: state (i,j) to state $(i-1,j)$, $(i,j-1)$, $(i+1,j)$ and $(i,j+1)$, respectively.

$$\mathbf{D}_{-1} = \mathbf{0} \tag{23}$$

$$\mathbf{D}_i = (-1/\mu_1)\,\mathrm{diag}[\,r_1(i,N_2),\ r_1(i,N_2-1),\ldots,\ r_1(i,0)],\quad i = 0,1,\ldots,N_2-1 \tag{24}$$

and

$$\mathbf{A}_i = (1/\mu_1)\begin{bmatrix} e(i,N_2) & -r_2(i,N_2-1) & \cdots & 0 & 0 \\ -\mu_2 & e(i,N_2-1) & \cdots & 0 & 0 \\ 0 & -\mu_2 & \cdots & 0 & 0 \\ \vdots & \vdots & & \vdots & \vdots \\ 0 & 0 & \cdots & 0 & -r_2(i,0) \\ 0 & 0 & \cdots & -\mu_2 & e(i,0) \end{bmatrix},\quad i = 0,1,\ldots,N_2 \tag{25}$$

Because of Eq.(23) we can write Eq.(20) as follows when i=0

$$\mathbf{p}_1 = \mathbf{A}_0\,\mathbf{p}_0 = \mathbf{B}_0\,\mathbf{p}_0 \tag{26}$$

Then writting Eq.(20) for i=1 and substituting $\mathbf{p}_1$ from Eq.(26) we get

$$\mathbf{p}_2 = \mathbf{D}_0\,\mathbf{p}_0 + \mathbf{A}_1\,\mathbf{p}_1 = (\mathbf{D}_0 + \mathbf{A}_1\,\mathbf{A}_0)\,\mathbf{p}_0 = \mathbf{B}_2\mathbf{p}_2 \tag{27}$$

and so on. In general, it holds

$$\mathbf{p}_i = \mathbf{B}_i\,\mathbf{p}_0\ ,\quad i = 0,1,\ldots,N_2 \tag{28}$$

Substituting Eq.(28) into the last of Eq.(20), we have

$$\mathbf{p}_{N_1+1} = (\mathbf{D}_{N_1-1}\mathbf{B}_{N_1-1} + \mathbf{A}_{N_1}\mathbf{B}_{N_1})\mathbf{p}_0 = \mathbf{B}\,\mathbf{p}_0 = \mathbf{0} \tag{29}$$

Eq.(29) is a homogeneous system of (N_2+1) linear equations. Setting p(0,0)=1 we can solve it with respect to the remaining unknowns p(0,j), j=1,2,..., N_2. Then, using Eqs.(28) we finally find all p(i,j), i=0,1,...,N_1, j=0,1,...,N_2. The previous computation method does not yield the exact values of the probabilities p(i,j), but scaled versions of them, since the normalizing Eq.(14) has not been taken into account. Their correct values are easily calculated since we only have to add their present values and then divide all of them by the resulting sum. Similar results can be obtained if we write the GBEs for the states in the j-th row of the state transition diagram. Then, a system of linear equations results as in Eq.(29), but now there are N_1+1 unknowns. Experimentation has shown that its better to apply the first approach when $N_1>N_2$, since then round-off errors arising from the matrix multiplications in Eqs.(28) are smaller.

We close this section giving formulas for the calculation of performance measures. First, the mean queue lengths are

$$q_i = \sum_{n_1=0}^{N_1}\sum_{n_2=0}^{N_2} n_i\,p(n_1,n_2)\ ,\ i=1,2 \tag{30}$$

The arrival rates at each server are

$$r_i = \sum_{n_1=0}^{N_1}\sum_{n_2=0}^{N_2} r_i(n_1,n_2)\,p(n_1,n_2)\ ,\ i=1,2 \tag{31}$$

Therefore, by Little's Law [1] we get the average system delay as

$$TS = (q_1+q_2)/(r_1+r_2) \tag{32}$$

The average delay for jobs belonging in stream λ is

$$TL = \sum_{n_1=0}^{N_1}\sum_{n_2=0}^{N_2} [(n_1/\mu_1)\,I(f_1(n_1)<f_2(n_2)) + (n_2/\mu_2)\,I(f_1(n_1)\geq f_2(n_2))]\,p(n_1,n_2) \tag{33}$$

when $f_i(n_i)$ are increasing functions, otherwise, the inequilitities in Eq.(33) should be inversed.

REFERENCES

[1] L. Kleinrock, Queueing Systems, Vol. 1, Theory, New York: Wiley, 1975.

[2] L. Kleinrock, Queueing Systems, Vol. 2, Computer Applications, New York: Wiley, 1976.

[3] T.P. Yum, "The Design and Analysis of a Semi-dynamic Deterministic Routing Rule," IEEE Trans. on Comm., Vol. COM-29, pp. 498-504, Apr. 1981.

[4] T.P. Yum and M. Schwartz, "The Join-Biased-Queue Rule and Its Applications to Routing in Computer Communication Networks," IEEE Trans. on Comm., Vol. COM-29, pp. 505-511, Apr. 1981.

[5] Y.-C. Chow and W.H. Kohler, "Models for Dynamic Load Balancing in a Heterogeneous Multiple Processor System," IEEE Trans. on Comp., Vol. C-28, pp. 354-361, May 1979.

[6] E.N. Protonotarios, E.D. Sykas and D.I. Giannopoulos, "Load Sharing in Parallel Processor Systems," Proc. of MELECON'81, pp. 3.1.3-3.1.4, Tel-Aviv, May 1981.

[7] A. Ephremides, P. Varaiya and J. Walrand, "A Simple Dynamic Routing Problem," IEEE Trans. on Autom. Control, Vol. AC-25, pp. 690-693, Aug. 1980.

[8] A. Agrawala, E.G. Coffman, Jr., M.R. Garey and S.K. Tripathi, "A Stochastic Optimization Algorithm Minimizing Expected Flow Times on Uniform Processors," IEEE Trans. on Comp., Vol. C-33, pp. 351-356, Apr. 1984.

[9] C.E. Agnew, "On Quadratic Adaptive Routing Algorithms," Comm. of the ACM, Vol. 19, pp. 18-22, Jan. 1976.

[10] R.G. Gallager, "A Minimum Delay Routing Algorithm Using Distributed Computation," IEEE Trans. on Comm., Vol. COM-25, pp. 73-85, Jan. 1979.

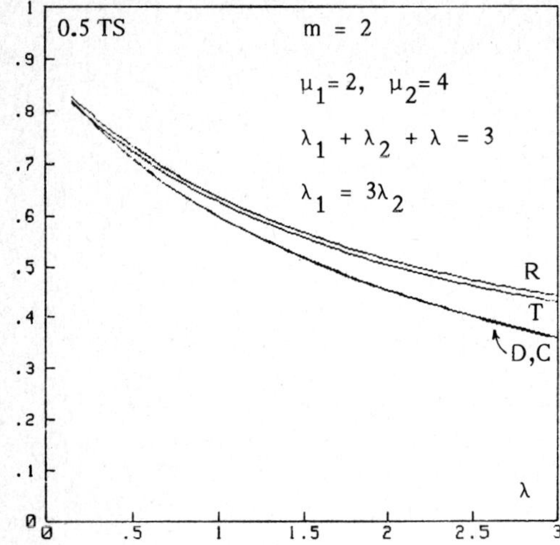

Fig. 3 Mean delay TS versus arrival rate λ for (R) Policy-R, (D) Policy-D, (C) Policy-C and (T) Policy-T.

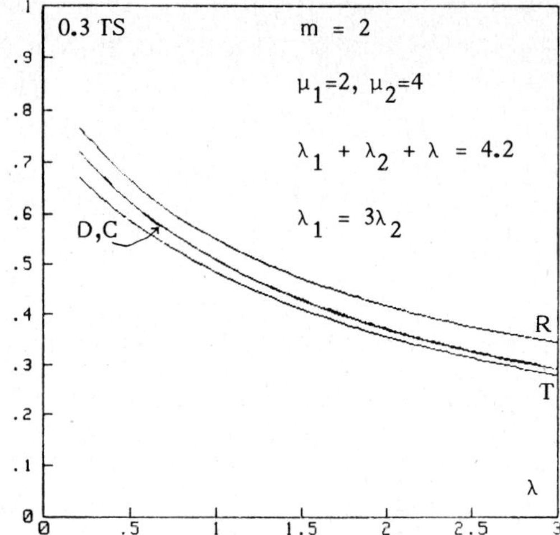

Fig. 4 Mean delay TS versus arrival rate λ for (R) Policy-R, (D) Policy-D, (C) Policy-C and (T) Policy-T.

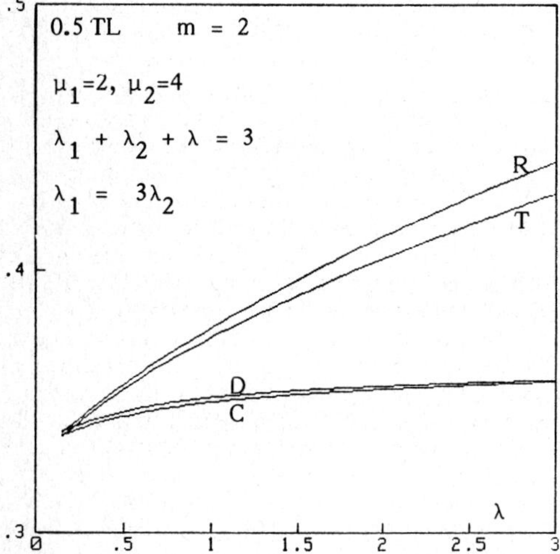

Fig. 5 Mean delay TL versus arrival rate λ for (R) Policy-R, (D) Policy-D, (C) Policy-C and (T) Policy-T.

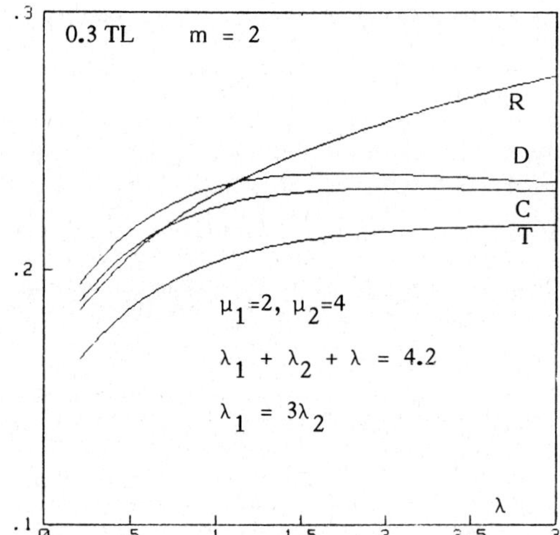

Fig. 6 Mean delay TL versus arrival rate λ for (R) Policy-R, (D) Policy-D, (C) Policy-C and (T) Policy-T.

DIGITAL TECHNIQUES in Simulation, Communication and Control
Spyros G. Tzafestas (editor)
Elsevier Science Publishers B.V. (North-Holland) © IMACS, 1985

BIFURCATED SHORTEST PATH ROUTING IN COMMUNICATION NETWORKS

G.I. Stassinopoulos , N. Bambos

National Technical University of Athens
42, Patission str. , 10682 Athens
Greece

The routing problem in data communication networks is examined. We propose a bifurcated routing following a shortest path rule , so that each node does not use exclusively one single path towards the destination , as happens in current shortest path implementations. Properties of the proposed routing are examined and a corresponding algorithm is given.

1. INTRODUCTION

The development of data communication networks has made necessary 'intelligent' routing strategies with a view in improved system performance and utilization of resources. The increasing scale and complexity of computer networks calls for specialized, highly efficient computational schemes,which should also guarantee stability and adaptability to changing operation parameters.

Routing procedures can be classified in dynamic,static and quasistatic. Static routing presupposes constant input flows of information messages entering the network, resulting to constant link flows. Its implementation is the simplest one but optimality will not hold if the network parameters deviate from their assumed values. On the other extreme, dynamic routing takes into account transient changes in network parameters and can react fast, leading the network to the new optimal operation point. However, a detailed implementation for the general problem is prohibitive due to theoretical difficulties and excessive computational requirements. It has been observed (see [4]), that average values of traffic change little in the case of large scale computer networks. Hence the need to distinguish the dynamic behaviour decreases here and an appropriate approach is the quasistatic modelling. In quasistatic models we do not get down to detailed queuetheoretic analysis of the interconnected network facilities (as links,nodes,etc) but consider macroscopically, slowly time varying rates of inputs, flows on liks, etc. These changes are slow enough to allow settling on different 'static' operation points but on the other hand adequately describe changing network conditions, so that the algorithms become inherently adaptive. These arguments are particularily valid for medium to large network loads.

The routing problem in data communication networks consists in finding appropriate rules to send messages to their destination over selected paths, so that a general performance criterion associated with time delay can be minimized. Under medium to heavy load conditions, traffic can be regarded as a stationary flow on links of limited capacity. It is well known, both theoretically and experimentally, that the mean time delay on each link is an increasing function of link utilization and hence by suitably manipulating link flows, one can reach an overall optimal performance. Routing is ultimately effected locally at node level. However the necessary computations of the routing scheme can be realized either centrally or in a distributed manner. In the first case a central computational unit based on measurements of parameters throughout the network, decides the overall routing strategy and informs all nodes to act accordingly. In the distributed case every node , based on local or global information disseminating through the network, decides its own part of routing policy,i.e. determines the flow on outgoing links. Reliability of centralized routing is inferior when compared with the decentralized one ([6]), since failure of the central computational unit leads to a complete breakdown. In the decentralized case failure of links or even nodes disturbs the network operation only in the vicinity of the anomaly.

This paper considers quasistatic adaptive decentralized routing schemes, which share the advantages stated above. Taking as performance criterion the mean delay encountered per message, it has been shown that the optimal routing follows an 'equal marginal delay' law for each outgoing path (see [7],[4],[8], [9],Section III). A salient feature of routing of this type is bifurcation, i.e. the use of more that one outgoing links for forewarding traffic to a particular destination. However, practical data networks (i.e. ARPANET, see [1],[2]) have not shown preference to the above strategy and use instead shortest path policies. These do not use bifurcation, in order to maintain implementation simplicity. However, technological developments leading to increased computational power on the node processors, combined with encouraging simulation results ([5]), require a fresh examination of the possibility of bifurcated routing.

The question of stability even under static inputs needs special care and relevant problems have been long occupying designers of large networks, like ARPANET. It is worhty to note, that even in the case of constant inputs ARPANET may remain in a bounded region of possible oscillations, rather than settle to a stable equillibrium point. Moreover particular examples exist, where without a special bias term, the ARPANET routing can demonstratively show violent oscillations (see [3]).

After introducing in Section 2 the optimal routing policy, we prove some fundamental properties of shortest path routing using bifurcation and draw attention to their practical consequences. In Section 4 a illustrative example provides intuition to the properties of bifurcated shortest path routing. In Section 5, we present an appropriate algorithm and the paper closes with suggestions for further research and possible implementations in this area.

2. BIFURCATED SHORTEST PATH ROUTING

We examine data communication networks of the 'store and foreward' type. Accumulation of messages is not considered to happen on nodes, but upon reception of a message, the node immediately assigns it to one of its outgoing links. There, the message waits to be transmitted, suffering queueing delay and giving rise to the development of queues belonging to links. We suppose network operation under medium to heavy load, a fact that permits us to macroscopically model the network by input and link message flows.

Let N denote the set of nodes and L the set of links of the network under discussion. We regard links as being directed and $(i,k) \in L$ is the link from node i to node k. We define as I_i and O_i the sets

$$I_i = \{ k \in N / (k,i) \in L \} \quad \text{and} \quad O_i = \{ k \in N / (i,k) \in L \},$$

i.e. the set of incoming and outgoing links from node $i \in N$. Each message has a source and a destination and we denote the source-destination pair i,j as $s=[i,j]$. There are $n(n-1)$ possible source-destination pairs in a network of n nodes, but we restrict attention to those $s=[i,j]$, $i,j \in N$, $i \neq j$ for which a strictly positive flow r_s entering node i with j as destination exists. Let S denote the set of all those pairs and $S^j = \{[i,j] / i \in N\}$ the set of all pairs with common destination j. In general several directed paths p(s) exist, joining the source i to the destination j of pair $s \in S$. For each $s \in S$ let P(s) be the set of all those possible paths, which we always assume nonempty. Further $P = \cup\{P(s)/s \in S\}$. The set of all links belonging to the path $p \in P$ is denoted by $L_p \subset L$ and $\chi_p(i,k)$, $p \in P$ is a fuction on the set of links taking the value 1 if $(i,k) \in L_p$ and 0 otherwise. The chain of nodes N_p includes all nodes, which belong to the path $p \in P$. For a particular source-destination pair s the set of all paths passing through link (i,k) is denoted by $P_s(i,k)$. With $f_{p(s)}$ we denote the portion of the total flow r_s following path $p(s) \in P(s)$. A particular routing consists of the collection $\mathcal{B}$ of nonnegative real numbers

$$\mathcal{B} = \{ \beta_{p(s)} / \beta_{p(s)} = \frac{f_{p(s)}}{r_s},\ p(s) \in P(s),\ s \in S \}$$

i.e. each $\beta_{p(s)}$ is the fraction of r_s flowing on path $p(s) \in P(s)$. We must have

$$\sum_{p(s) \in P(s)} \beta_{p(s)} = 1 \qquad \text{for all } s \in S \tag{1}$$

It is clear that the total flow on each link can be immediately obtained by the following formulas. Thus we have

$$f_{ik}^j = \sum_{s \in S^j \& p(s) \in P(s)} r_s\, \chi_{p(s)}(i,k)\, \beta_{p(s)} \tag{2}$$

for the flow on link (i,k) with destination j, while for the total flow on the same link we obtain

$$f_{ik} = \sum_{s \in S \& p(s) \in P(s)} r_s\, \chi_{p(s)}(i,k)\, \beta_{p(s)} \tag{3}$$

We have chosen to employ the arc-chain instead of the node-arc formulation for describing flows (see also [10], Section I.2 for this terminology and appropriate comments). While the $\beta_{p(s)}$'s uniquely define the link flows according to (3), the converse is not true in general. We now define the mean delay per message on the link $(i,k) \in L$ as D_{ik}. Under the conditions considered above (i.e. stationarity of flows, medium to heavy network load), this delay is a function of the total flow f_{ik} on the link. In accordance to theoretical and experimental findings, we consider the function $D_{ik}(f_{ik})$ to be positive, convex, continuously differentiable and strictly increasing in the interval $[0, C_{ik})$, with C_{ik} representing the link capacity. Under Kleinrock's simplifying assumption [11], the expression given for the mean delay per message is $D_{ik} = (C_{ik} - f_{ik})^{-1}$, which satisfies all previous requirements. For each path $p \in P$, the mean delay per message for transvesing this path is given by

$$D_p = \sum_{(i,k) \in L_p} D_{ik}(f_{ik}) \tag{4}$$

We remark that for a particular network operation point, each source-destination pair $s=[i,j]$ has available a variety of paths P(s) and for each one of those a cost (4) is associated.

<u>Definition.</u> The routing

$$\mathcal{B}^* = \{ \beta^*_{p(s)} / \beta^*_{p(s)} = \frac{f^*_{p(s)}}{r_s},\ p(s) \in P(s),\ s \in S \} \tag{5}$$

is a <u>bifurcated shortest path routing</u> iff

$$\beta^*_{p(s)} > 0 \Rightarrow D_{p(s)} = \min_{\tau(s) \in P(s)} \{ D_{\tau(s)} \} = D^*_s \tag{6}$$

for all $p(s) \in P(s)$, all $s \in S$.

Thus the bifurcated shortest path routing has the property that for every source-destination pair s, all paths carrying flow from the particular source to the particular destination have the same length, while there exists no other strictly shorter path p(s) with zero flow $f_{p(s)}$. We denote by D^*_s the common shortest lenght for all paths carrying flow for the particular pair s. The bifurcated shortest path routing minimizes via the expression (3) the global cost

$$\sum_{(i,k)\in L} \int_0^{f_{ik}} D_{ik}(f_{ik})\,df_{ik} \tag{7}$$

Notice that whenever $D_{ik}(\cdot)$ satisfies our assumption for link cost, so does its integral appearing in (7). Conversely, for any minimizing set of link flows f^*_{ik} there corresponds at least one routing $\mathcal{B}^*$ being a bifurcated shortest path routing. To see this notice that [8] arrives at the 'equal marginal delay' law for optimal paths, which in our framework reduces to the case of bifurcated shortest path routing.

3. PROPERTIES OF BIFURCATED SHORTEST PATH ROUTING

The first property of bifurcated shortest path routing given below is essential for the development of decentralized related algorithms. It shows that a routing can be identified as one satisfying definition (6) only by local criteria. We let P_i^j be the set of all directed paths from node i to destination j. Notice that in P_i^j, node i is not neccessarily an input node for traffic with destination j, as is the case with $P([i,j])$.

Theorem 1. $\mathcal{B}^*$ is a bifurcated shortest path routing iff,
for all $i,j \in N$ such that $i \neq j$,
all $p \in P_i^j$ with $f_{ik}^j>0$ for all $(i,k)\in L_p$,
it satisfies the relation

$$D_p = \min_{\tau\in P_i^j} \{D_\tau\} = D_i^j \tag{8}$$

Since all paths on which flow with destination j exists and originate from node i, have equal length, while all others have greater, the quantity D_i^j in (8) represents the minimal delay per message from node i to destination j. Moreover if node i is adjacent to node k and a link (i,k) exists, than

$$D_i^j \leq D_{ik}^j + D_k^j \tag{9}$$

Equality holds if $f_{ik}^j > 0$.

Proof of theorem 1. By taking i as an entry node of some source-destination pair $s=[i,j]$, we easily find that (8) is sufficient for $\mathcal{B}^*$ to be a bifurcated shortest path routing. For the converse refer to Fig. 1 below and assume that through node i, traffic flows to node j.

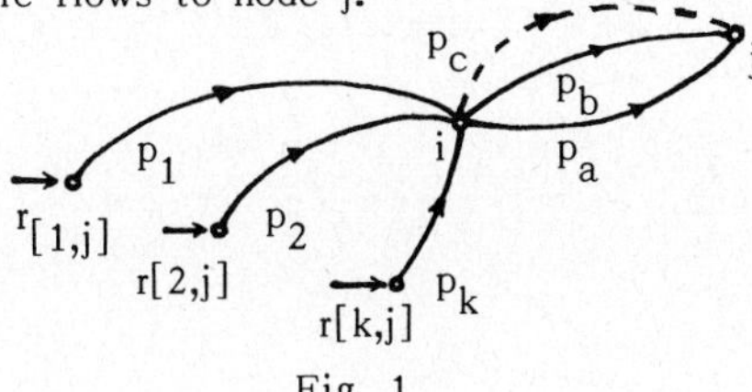

Fig. 1

Paths $p_a,p_b \in P_i^j$ are such that $f_{mn}^j>0$ for every $(m,n) \in L_{p_a}$, L_{p_b} respectively.

Path $p_c \in P_i^j$ and carries no traffic to j, i.e. there is at least one $(m,n)\in L_{p_c}$ with $f_{mn}^j=0$. Among some possible paths $p_1,\dots\dots,p_k \in P$ at least one carries flow to node i with destination j. First suppose without loss of generality that i receives traffic for j only through p_1. Since p_1,p_a,p_b carry traffic with source 1 and destination j, we have with p_{1a} the union of paths p_1,p_a, etc.

$$\beta^*_{p_{1a}} > 0\ ,\ \beta^*_{p_{1b}} > 0\ ,\ \beta^*_{p_{1c}} = 0 \tag{10}$$

From definition (6), we have

$$D_{p_{1a}} = D_{p_{1b}} \leq D_{p_{1c}} \tag{11}$$

This, by (4) is equivalent to

$$D_{p_a} = D_{p_b} \leq D_{p_c} \tag{12}$$

and the theorem holds in this case.
Next consider that

$$\beta^*_{p_{1a}} = 0\ ,\ \beta^*_{p_{1b}} > 0\ ,\ \beta^*_{p_{1c}} = 0 \tag{13}$$

hence flow on path p_a must come from some path other than p_1 and let it be p_2 without loss of generality. We now can define some other set $\tilde{\mathcal{B}}^*$ as follows

$$\begin{aligned}
\tilde{\beta}^*_{p_{1b}} &= \beta^*_{p_{1b}} - \Delta\beta > 0\\
\tilde{\beta}^*_{p_{1a}} &= \Delta\beta > 0\\
\tilde{\beta}^*_{p_{2a}} &= \beta^*_{p_{2a}} - \Delta\beta > 0\\
\tilde{\beta}^*_{p_{2b}} &= \beta^*_{p_{2b}} + \Delta\beta > 0
\end{aligned} \tag{14}$$

where $\Delta\beta \in (0,\min\{\beta^*_{p_{1b}}, \beta^*_{p_{2a}}\})$ and all other elements of $\tilde{\mathcal{B}}^*$ remaining unaltered. The new routing can be easily verified to satisfy (1) without changing any flow f_{ik} on any network link. Since (6) involves only link flows f_{ik}^j through (4) and since $\mathcal{B}^*$ fulfills (6), the same happens with $\tilde{\mathcal{B}}^*$ since $f^{*j}_{ik} = \tilde{f}^{*j}_{ik}$ for all $i,j \in N$, $(i,k) \in L$. Thus $\tilde{\mathcal{B}}^*$ is also a bifurcated shortest path routing. Additionally by construction of $\tilde{\mathcal{B}}^*$, we have

$$\tilde{\beta}^*_{p_{1a}} > 0\ ,\ \tilde{\beta}^*_{p_{1b}} > 0\ ,\ \tilde{\beta}^*_{p_{1c}} = 0$$

The conclusion of the proof follows by analogous arguments as (10),(11),(12). The two cases examined are exhaustive and so, the theorem is fully proved.

We now state the next essential property, proving that the bifurcated shortest path routing is loop free.

Theorem2 If $\mathcal{B}^*$ is a bifurcated shortest path routing, then for every destination j there exists no $p \in P$ such that N_p contains some node twice and $f^{*j}_{ik} > 0$ on every element of L_p.

Proof. Suppose in contradiction that a loop exists as given in Fig. 2, where traffic through node i

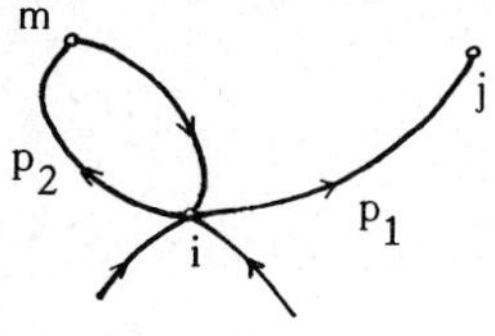

Fig. 2

flows to node j. By assumption and Theorem 1 we have that $D_{p_{231}} = D_{p_1}$. From (4) follows that

$D_{p_3} + D_{p_2} = 0$, which is impossible by the strict positivity of the costs D_{p_3}, D_{p_2}. So the theorem is proved.

4. EXAMPLE

We examine analytically a simple example on which all pertinent properties of bifurcated shortest path routing can be demonstrated. In Fig. 3 node 3 is the destination and r_1, r_2 represent the input flow. For simplicity of notation we write i instead of [i,3] in this single destination case. All links have capacity C=10.

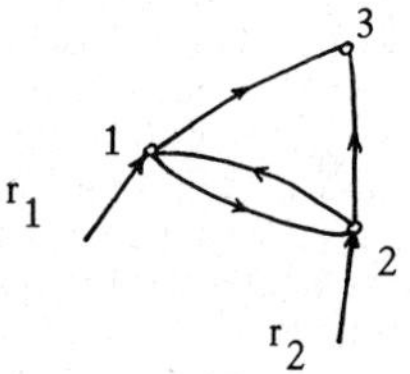

Fig. 3

A constant input flow of $r_1=7$ is assumed for node 1. In node 2 we increase the input flow from 0 to the maximal value $r_2= 13$, as determined by the Max Flow - Min Cut theorem ([11]). Kleinrock's simplifying assumption is invoked and we take $D_{ik} = (10-f_{ik})^{-1}$. In Fig. 4(a), we plot $\beta_{13}r_1$, $\beta_{123}r_1$, while in Fig 4(b), the equivalent quantities $\beta_{23}r_2$, $\beta_{213}r_2$ appear.

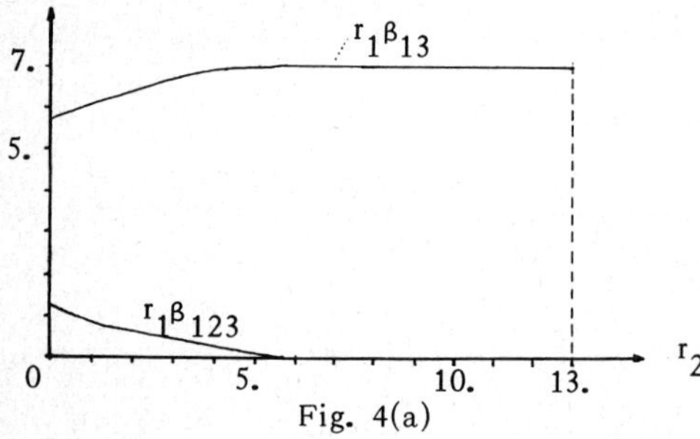

Fig. 4(a)

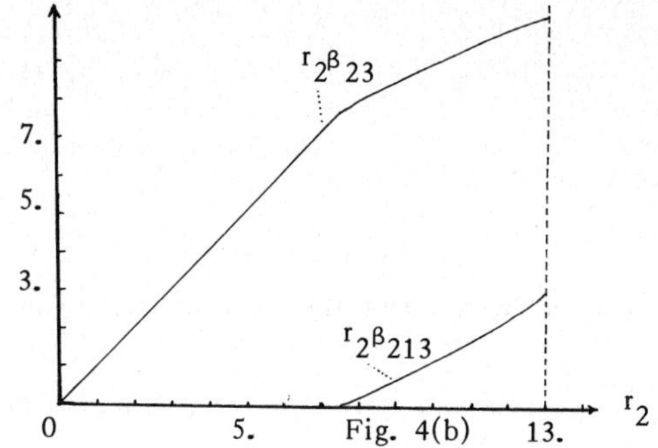

Fig. 4(b)

Initially r_1 flows through both available paths 1-3 and 1-2-3 fulfilling the condition $D_{13}=D_{123}$. The reader may verify that for $r_2=0$ and $r_1< 5.$ only path 1-2 would be used. However we take $r_1=7$ and thus have by (6) that both paths must be used, making the interplay between 1 and 2 interesting. For $r_2< 5.71$ flow r_2 can only use 2-3 in order that (6) is satisfied. For $5.71< r_2< 7.69$ flow r_2 pushes out flow r_1 from link 2-3 and 1-2, 2-1 remain unused. In this case $D_{12}+D_{23}> D_{13}$ and $D_{21}+D_{13}> D_{23}$. Finally for $r_2> 7.69$, r_2 penetrates also through 2-1-3 fulfilling the condition $D_{21}+D_{13}=D_{23}$.

Corresponding costs are given in Fig.5. We give the delay suffered per unit time by all messages of r_1 and r_2 seperately, as well as the total delay suffered by r_1+r_2:

$$\mathcal{D}_1=\frac{\beta_{13}r_1}{10-\beta_{213}r_2-\beta_{13}r_1}+\frac{\beta_{123}r_1}{10-\beta_{123}r_1}+\frac{\beta_{123}r_1}{10-\beta_{23}r_2-\beta_{123}r_1}$$

$$\mathcal{D}_2=\frac{\beta_{23}r_2}{10-\beta_{123}r_1-\beta_{23}r_1}+\frac{\beta_{213}r_2}{10-\beta_{213}r_2}+\frac{\beta_{213}r_2}{10-\beta_{13}r_1-\beta_{213}r_2}$$

$$\mathcal{D}=\mathcal{D}_1+\mathcal{D}_2$$

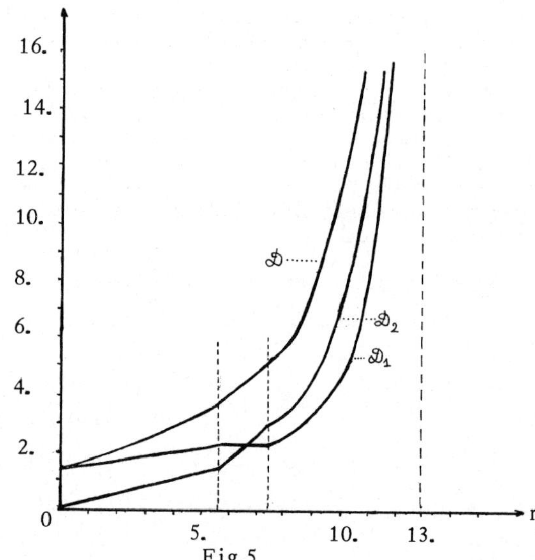

Fig.5

As r_2 increases from small values within the interval [0,5.71) it pushes out flow of r_1 and thus gains the whole capacity of link (2,3) for its own servicing. This effect does not happen in the next interval [5.71,7.69) and correspondingly an increased slope of the curve $\mathcal{D}_2$ is observed. At r_2=7.69 a new path (i.e. 2-1-3) becomes available for r_2 , which results in a sudden drop of the slope of $\mathcal{D}_2$. From here on , the flow of r_2 through (1,3) benefits in cost at the expense of flow r_1. Notice that although r_1 is constant, it suffers now more and more delay. Notice also the drop of the rate of increase of the total delay curve at the characteristic values of r_1 given above.

The example above clearly illustrates the following remarks regarding the properties of the bifurcated shortest path routing. Each source-destination pair tries to find as many paths of equal length as possible for distributing its input flow, so that the time delay per message for this pair is reduced. This can be expressed by the 'cost' for pair s

$$D_s = \min_{\beta_{p(s)}} \max \{D_{p(s)} / p(s) \in P(s), \beta_{p(s)} > 0\}$$

The bifurcated shortest path routing reflects the state of equillibrium or the competing demands with respect to the cost D_s for each pair. At this equillibrium $D_s = D_s^*$ as in (6). Pairs with large demand from the network, push out flow of pairs with lesser demand and thus reduce their mean delay per message at their expense . This trend can reach the point where paths are blocked for pairs of lesser demand and/or more paths for pairs of large demand come into being.

5. ALGORITHM

Every algorithm for the realization of the bifurcated shortest path routing must contain the following features: a) Measurement of mean delay per message on every link, b) Dissemination of measured values through the network , and computation on each node i of the quantities D_i^j (shortest length from node i to every destination j) and c) Calculation of the new routing based on current deviations from the shortest path values and with an aim to enforce a situation where definition (6) is approached. The following proposed algorithm falls into the above framework.

Algorithm For every destination $j \in N$, every node $i \in N$ computes the quantities at t+1 based on the ones at t

1. $D_i^j(t)$, the mean delay per message on the shortest path joining i to j. Let k_{min} be the next node on the shortest path.
2. $\delta D_i^j(t) = D_{ik}^j(t) + D_k^j(t) - D_i^j(t)$, for all $k \in O_i$
3. If $\delta D_{ik}^j(t) < \zeta$ then $k \in A_i^j(t)$ otherwise $k \in B_i^j(t)$
4. For each $k \in B_i^j(t)$,
$$\Delta f_{ik}^j(t) = f_{ik}^j(t)$$
5. For each $k \in A_i^j(t)$
$$\Delta f_{ik}^j(t) = \min \{f_{ik}^j(t), \xi\, \delta D_{ik}^j(t)\}$$
6. $$f_{ik}^j(t+1) = \begin{cases} f_{ik}^j(t) - \Delta f_{ik}^j(t) & \text{for } k \in O_i ,\ k \neq k_{min} \\ f_{ik}^j(t) + \sum_{k \in O_i} \Delta f_{ik}^j(t) & \text{for } k = k_{min} \end{cases}$$

The above algorithm uses the idea of [7], where the fraction sent out on the best link equals the fraction of traffic reduced on nonoptimal links. However here we employ the algorithm for mean delay per message rather than for 'marginal delay'. Another difference is the introduction of the threshold ζ and the associated set $B_i(t)$. Thus expensive paths are cut off and no flow is sent through them according to the new routing. Experimental evidence exists for the advantages of bifurcating the flow by a simple threshold rule (see [5]) . As opposed to ARPANET our algorithm (as well as the one in [7]) allows flow to remain on nonshortest paths and thus prevents an oscillatory behaviour. It is clear that with some predefined accuracy on the computation of $D_i^j(t)$, the algorithm once posed on a situation where we have a bifurcated shortest path routing , will remain there. The reason for this is that every $\delta D_{ik}(t) = 0$ for every $i,j \in N$, $k \in O_i$. In case that more than one equal shortest paths exist , we take additional provision in Step 6 to distribute the increment equally among them. Notice also the threshold in Step 3, which will not be effective when only small differences in the input rates at node i occur. On the contrary, a large network disturbance (as for example loss of a link) will result in a drastic increase of the cost of all paths containing it. These will be automatically eliminated by the algorithm. Simulation results on simple cases have shown all above features and will be published elsewhere.

A lot of work remains to be done on the theoretical proof of convergence and the dynamic performance of the above algorithm. Also, the possibility of refinements to include a more appropriate distribution of the differential flow on each outgoing link must be examined. A possible way is to take a priori into account the increase in cost on each path by incorporating first order approximates with derivatives.

REFERENCES

[1] J.M.McQuillan,G.Falk,I.Richer,"A Review of the Development and Performance of the ARPANET Routing Algorithm", IEEE Trans.Commun.,Vol.COM-26, No 12,Dec.1978.

[2] J.M.McQuillan,I.Richer,E.C.Rosen,"The New Routing Algorithm for the ARPANET", IEEE Trans.Commun.,Vol. COM-28,No. 5,May 1980.

[3] D.P.Bertsekas,"Dynamic Behaviour of Shortest

Path Routing Algorithms for Communication Networks", IEEE Trans. Autom. Contr.,Vol. AC-27,No.1,Dec. 1979.
[4]D.P.Bertsekas,"Optimal Routing and Flow Control Methods for Communication Networks",Proc. 5th Int. Conf. on Analysis and Optimization of Systems, Versailles,France,Springer,Berlin & New York, 1982.
[5] A.N.Venetsanopoulos,W.Waung,"Adaptive Bifurcation Routing Algorithms for Computer-Communication Networks", to appear in Kybernetika.
[6] M.Schwartz,T.E.Stern,"Routing Techniques Used in Computer Communication Networks" , IEEE Trans. Commun.,Vol. COM-28,No. 4, April 1980.
[7] R.G.Gallager,"A Minimum Delay Routing Algorithm Using Distributed Computation", IEEE Trans. Commun., Vol. COM-25. No. 1, Jan. 1977.
[8] T.E.Stern," A Class of Decentralized Routing Algorithms Using Relaxation", IEEE Trans. Commun., Vol. COM-25, No. 10, Oct. 1977.
[9] A.Segall ,"The Modeling of Adaptive Routing in Data Communication Networks",IEEE Trans. Commun., Vol. COM-25.No. 1, Jan.1977.
[10] L.R.Ford,D.R.Furkerson,"Flows in Networks", Princeton University Press, Princeton NJ, 1962.
[11] L.Kleinrock,"Communication Nets: Stochastic Message Flow and Delay", New York, McGraw-Hill , 1964.

DIGITAL TECHNIQUES in Simulation, Communication and Control
Spyros G. Tzafestas (editor)
Elsevier Science Publishers B.V. (North-Holland) © IMACS, 1985

ANALYSIS OF A RESERVATION MULTIPLE ACCESS PROTOCOL FOR A LOCAL COMPUTER NETWORK

S. A. Koubias and G. D. Papadopoulos

Applied Electronics Laboratory
School of Engineering, University of Patras

In this paper we give the analysis of a Multiple Access Protocol, named ATP-2, based on analytical and simulation results. This protocol belongs in the catagory of the Self-Adaptive Reservation Multiple Access Protocols and it uses the channel splitting idea. Thus, there are two subchannels, the Request channel and the Information channel. The first operates with a TDMA (Round Robin or Random) protocol, while the second is partly a TDMA channel which, with the proposed accessing rules, combines dynamically the advantages of the two basic accessing methods, the Random (S-ALOHA) and the Fixed (TDMA) Access methods. Thus, the ATP-2, through the information contained in the Reservation subchannel minislots, can be reconfigured according to the instantaneous service needs of the users. Because of this dynamic behavior the whole system performance is very high and under some operation condition it approaches the ideal system (M/D/1 queue) performance.

1. INTRODUCTION

Recent developments in the area of Packet Computer Communication Networks have resulted in the proposition of several communication protocols. For the special case, where a single communication channel is available to a population of users, a large number of Multiple Access Protocols (MAPs) have been developed trying to optimize the channel assignment to the users (18,24).

There are several categories of MAPs, according to the methods used for the channel accessing (16,24). The Fixed Access Protocols (FAPs), like TDMA (7,17), FDMA and CTDMA, have the disadvantage of the poor channel bandwidth exploitation at low channel loads, because of the predetermined assignment of the channel time or frequency slots to the users, regardless of their activity. On the other hand, the main disadvantage of the Random Access Protocols (RAPs) (S-ALOHA, CSMA), is their inherent instability at the high values of the channel traffic due to the packet collisions (1,11).

Starting from these basic considerations, other more sophisticated MAPs have been proposed to give good performance for all values of channel traffic (6,13). Furthermore the Reservation Protocols, by making into consideration the users' requests provide some very efficient ways for the optimum assignment of the channel bandwidth (23, 25). However, this category has the problems of the reservation subchannel implementation, as well as the implementation of a distributed global queue.

In this paper we give the analytical and simulation results for a new Reservation MAP (16), named ATP-2, that combines the advantages of the two classic well known protocols S-ALOHA (RAP) and TDMA (FAP) using a simple, but effective, accessing algorithm. The system status monitoring is made through the users' requests transmitted in a collision free Request subChannel (RC). The Information subChannel (IC) is time slotted like a TDMA channel, but there is a dynamic assignment of its slots to the users. The above mentioned subchannels are implemented by frequency division of the available channel bandwidth (25).

In analyzing the new protocol, named ATP-2, we exploit the Markov chain properties of the events by examining the system at the beginnings of the IC slots. Numerical and simulation results are presented and compared, so that the dynamic behaviour of the ATP-2 protocol is studied in detail.

2. THE ATP-2 PROTOCOL

As it is mentioned before, in the ATP-2 protocol there are two sbchannels, the RC for the users' Request Packets (RPs) and the IC for the transmission of the Information Packets (IPs). The format of these frequency separated subchannels is shown in Fiq.1. It is evident from this figure that there are N RC minislots during an IC slot, so that N is defined as,

$$N=T_{ip}/T_{rp} \tag{1}$$

where T_{ip} and T_{rp} are the time durations of the IPs and RPs, respectively. The identity of the user that can use the mth RC minislot during the k-1th IC slot is symbolised as $U^{k-1}_{r,m}$, while the user to whom the k-1th IC slot is assigned (like the TDMA protocol) is the U^{k-1}_{i}. Also, u^k is the number of active users at the beginning of the kth IC slot.

The selection of the users' identities for the

RC minislot accessing determine the kind of the TDMA protocol (Round Robin or Random) for the IC because we impose the following initial condition: Every Last (Nth) RC miniSlot (LRCS) is related to the following IC slot according to the following relationship,

$$U_i^k = U_{r,N}^{k-1} \quad (2)$$

Thus, if $U_{r,N}^k = U_{r,N}^{k-1}+1$, for all k, the Round Robin TDMA is used for the IC, while if the $U_{r,m}^k$, for all k and m, is randomly selected, the IC slots are assigned to the users as in the Random TDMA. For the purpose of analysis we use here the Random TDMA, which is a stationary process and thus leads to fairly simple analytical solutions.

The access of the IC slots by the users is based on the following rules:

a) Only the u^k active users existed at the beginning of the kth IC slot may use the following N RC minislots during this IC slot.
b) If in the LRCS defore an IC slot there is an RP, then only the corresponding user transmitts his IP in this IC slot, as in the TDMA protocol.
c) If the LRCS before an IC slot is empty, but there are RPs in some of the previous N-1 RC minislots, then only the first user, who transmitted an RP, uses this IC slot for an IP transmission.
d) If all the N RC minislots are empty then the next IC slot is characterized as a Free IC Slot (FICS). In this case, any active user may transmit his IP in this FICS, according to an accessing probability, p_a, like the S-ALOHA protocol.

From the above description of the ATP-2 the following advantages are evident. First, this protocol guarantees at least TDMA service quality, because an active user may always use his TDMA slot. Second, it has the capability of dynamic assignment procedures by means of the FICS, which would remain unused in the TDMA protocol. Third, there is an inherent flexibility that offers more channel capacity to the users with larger service demands. Finally, the ATP-2 is always stable, because at high channel traffic conditions it moves toward to the TDMA protocol.

We next proceed to give the analysis of the ATP-2 protocol, using a Markov chain observed at the beginnings of the IC slots. Through this analysis the effect of the critical system parameters, N and p_a, is examined with the objective to approach the optimal system performane.

3. SYSTEM ANALYSIS

The following assumptions about the queueing model are commonly used:

1) There is a population of M users, each having a local source of information, a data buffer and a transmitter/receiver interface.
2) The source of information is Bernoulli with blocked calls lost (22). This means that the buffer can contain only one information message. The information source generates messages with probability p per IC slot.
3) The information messages consist of one IP.
4) The channel propagation delay is negligible.
5) Every user is characterized as busy or active if his data buffer contains an IP and idle if this buffer is empty.

Let us denote by u^k (Fig.1) the random sequence that represents the number of active users at the beginning of the kth IC slot. It is evident that knowing u^k one can predict the state of the system at the beginning of the following k+1th IC slot, without requiring to know the system history prior the kth IC slot. Thus, the behavior of the chain u^k is completely describable as a Markov process (12).

Generally, the one step transition probabilities, q_{ij}, for a given protocol (26,27) may be expressed as,

$$q_{ij} = B(M-i, j-i+1, p)n(i) + B(M-i, j-i, p)(1-n(i)) \quad (3)$$

where n(i) is the conditional throughput, that is the probability of a succesfull packet transmission, given i contending users, p is the already mentioned probability for a new IP arrival per IC slot and B(a,b,c) is the binomial distribution, that is,

$$B(a,b,c) = \binom{a}{b} c^b (1-c)^{a-b}, \quad b=0,\ldots,M \quad (4)$$

For the conditional throughput of the ATP-2 protocol, $n_{atp-2}(i)$, the following relation holds,

$$n_{atp-2}(i) = (1-p_{nr}(i)) + (p_{nr}(i)p_{st}(i)) = \quad (5)$$

=Prob(IP transmission due to a reservation)+
+Prob(IP transmission due to the accessing probability)

where,

$p_{nr}(i)$=Prob(no RPs into the N RC minislots during an IC slot, given i active users at the beginning of this IC slot)=
$=(1-p_{rp}(i))^N$, i=0,...,M (6a)

$p_{rp}(i)$=Prob(transmission of a RP during an IC slot, given i users at the beginning of this IC slot)=
=i/M, i=0,...,M (22) (6b)

$p_{st}(i)$=Prob(succesfull IP transmission into an IC slot, given that this IC slot is a FICS and i active users at the beginning of the preceding IC slot)=

$$= \begin{cases} \bar{A}(i)p_a(1-p_a)^{(\bar{A}(i)-1)}, \text{ if } \bar{A}(i)>=1 \\ 0, \text{ if } \bar{A}(i)<1 \end{cases} \quad (7a)$$

$\bar{A}(i)$=Mean number of active users at the beginning of an IC slot, given i active users at the beginning of the preceding IC slot=

$$= \sum_{k=i}^{M} B(M-i,k-i,p)k \quad (7b)$$

Thus, using Equs.4-7 the one step transition probability matrix, $Q=\langle q_{ij}\rangle$, for the ATP-2 protocol may be found. The Markov chain for this protocol is irreducible, aperiodic, homogeneous and recurrent non-null with finite state space. Therefore, the stationary probability distribution, g_k, for the number of the busy users at the beginnings of the IC slots is uniquely determined by means of the following well known equations (12)

$$\sum_{l=0}^{M} g_l=1 \quad (8a)$$

$$g_l=\sum_{u=0}^{M} g_u q_{ul}, \; l=0,\ldots,M \quad (8b)$$

It is evident that the system throughput, S, may be found from the following relationship,

$$S=\sum_{l=0}^{M} g_l n_{atp-2}(l) \quad (9)$$

while the mean number of busy users at the beginnings of the IC slots is,

$$\bar{u}=\sum_{l=0}^{M} l g_l \quad (10)$$

Thus, the average IP normalized delay, D, can be found by using Little's formula (20),

$$D=\bar{u}/S \quad (11)$$

The mean probabilities for a slot to be a FICS and for a succesfull IP transmission into a FICS, p_{fics} and p_{succ}, respectively, are,

$$p_{fics}=\sum_{l=0}^{M} g_l p_{nr}(l) \quad (12a)$$

$$p_{succ}=\sum_{l=0}^{M} g_l p_{nr}(l) p_{st}(l) \quad (12b)$$

From the above analysis the influence of the system parameters N and p_a may be examined. The numerical and simulation results that describe the system performance under the various operating conditions are presented in the next section.

4. NUMERICAL AND SIMULATION RESULTS

The derived analytical formulas were applied for several values of the system parameters N and p_a, given a user population M=10. For comparison purposes corresponding results for the optimal S-ALOHA (21), Random TDMA and the M/D/1 system (perfect scheduling) are also included. Figs.2-4 depict the characteristic curves for three values of the parameter N (1,3,6). For each value of N four curves are plotted corresponding to four values of p_a (.2,.4,.6,.99).

From these figures it is seen that the influence of the FICS accessing is evident mainly for small values of N in relation with M, because in these cases a large number of IC slots are FICSs. Thus, the curves for various values of p_a are highly sepapated for small N, as it can be seen from Fig.2. For low throughput values, the system performance increases as p_a increases (p_a->1), because the mean number of active users at the beginnings of the IC slots is small (Equ.10), so that the probability, p_{succ}, (Equ.12b) is high. On the other hand, the system performance improves, as p_a decreases at high channel loads (S->1), because u->M and p_{succ}->0. For the middle range values of the throughput, S, there is a value of p_a that gives the optimum system performance, for a given N. This optimal value of p_a, that maximizes the throughput and minimizes the delay simultaneously (Equ.11), may be found by using Howard's policy iteration method (dynamic programming formulation) (9), for a given value of N.

By increasing the values of N we obtain better results for the system performance, because in these cases the users have a better chance to declare their service demands, during the RC slots (Equ.6a), thus rendering the dynamic assignment of the IC slots more effective. However, as the value of N increases, the bandwidth used for the IC, W_{ic}, decreases because of the following equations,

$$W=W_{ic}+W_{rc} \quad (13a)$$

$$W/W_{ic}=1+N(b_{rp}/b_{ip}) \quad (13b)$$

where b_{rp} and b_{ip} are the numbers of bits into the RPs and IPs, respectively, W_{rc} is the RC bandwidth and W is the available channel bandwidth (Bandwidth=Packet Bits/Packet Time Duration). The quantity $N(b_{rp}/b_{ip})$ is the system overhead, that is the bandwidth wasted for the RC implementation and it must be taken into account for the S and D computation. Here the value of this ratio is assumed to be negligible for simplicity.

In Figs.5-7 we give the comparison between the analytical and simulation results for the following three sets of N and p_a parameters (1,0.6) (3,0.4) (6,0.2). Also, in these figures the corresponding curves for the p_{fics} and p_{succ} probabilities are plotted. It is seen that there is a maximum value for the p_{succ}, because in low throughputs (S->0) many FICSs remain unused, while as S->1 the FICS number decreases (p_{fics} curves) in addition to the fact that packet collisions occur frequently into the existing FICSs. The discrepancy between the analytical and simulation curves in Fig.5 is due to the approximation that has been done in Equ.7a, where we assumed that $p_{st}(i)=0$ for $\bar{A}(i)<1$. The influence of this approximation becomes apparent mainly for small values of N, because in these cases the FICS number is large.

From the above analysis it is shown that the ATP-2 protocol is a simple, self-adaptive MAP that efficiently becomes a RAP or a FAP according to the instantaneous system status. The ATP-2 performance is strongly dependent on values of N and the selection of p_a and in some cases (mainly for N->M) approximates the M/D/1 system performance.

5. CONCLUSIONS

In this work an analysis of a new Reservation Multiple Access Protocol, named ATP-2, was presented. This protocol uses two subchannels (Request and Information) and operates with a simple, easily constructed algorithm, that combines the advantages of a RAP and a FAP. The ATP-2 is self-adaptive, so that it approaches the S-ALOHA protocol as the throughput decreases, while it becomes a TDMA scheme when the channel load is heavy.

The analysis was based on a Markov chain process observed at the beginnings of the Information subChannel slots. By means of this analysis the influence of the critical system parameters N and p_a was examined in detail.

REFERENCES

(1) Abramson, N.,"The ALOHA System-Another Alternative for Computer Communications," AFIPS Conference Proceedings 1970 Fall Joint Conference, 37, 281-285.

(2) Abramson, N.,"Packet Switching with Satellites," 1973 NTC, AFIPS Conference Proceedings, 42, 695-702.

(3) Binder, R.,"A Dynamic Packet-Switching System for Satellite Broadcast Channels," Proceedings of the IEEE ICC, San Francisco, California, 41-1 to 41-5, June 16-18,1975.

(4) Chu, W.W.,"A Study of the Technique of Asynchronous Time Division Multiplexing for Time-Sharing Computer Communications," Proceedings of the 2nd HICSS, University of Hawaii, Honolulu, Hawaii, 607-610, Jan. 1969.

(5) Chu, W.W. and A. G. Konheim,"On the Analysis and Modeling of a Class of Computer-Communications System,"IEEE Transactions on Communications, COM-20, No.3, part II, June 1972, 645-660.

(6) Crowther, W. etal.,"A System for Broadcast Communication: Reservation-ALOHA,"Proceedings of the 6th HICSS, University of Hawaii, Honolulu, Hawaii, Jan. 1973.

(7) Hayes, J.F.,"Performance Models of an Experimental Computer Communication Network,"BSTJ, 53, No.2, Feb. 1974, 225-259.

(8) Hayes, J.F. and D.M. Sherman,"A Study of Data Multiplexing Techniques and Delay Performance," BSTJ, 51, No.9, Nov. 1972, 1983-2011.

(9) Howard, R.A.,"Dynamic Programming and Marcov Processes," Cambridge, MA: MIT Press, 1960.

(10) Kleinrock, L. and S.S. Lam."Packet-Switching in a Multi-Access Broadcast Channel :Performance Evaluation," IEEE Transactions on Communications, COM-23, No.4, April 1975, 410-423.

(11) Kleinrock, L. and F.A. Tobagi,"Packet Switching in Radio Channels: Part I-Carrier Sense Multiple-Access Modes and Their Throughput-Delay Characteristics," IEEE Transactions on Communications, COM-23, 1975, 1400-1416.

(12) Kleinrock, L., Queueing Systems, Vol. 1, 1975; Vol. 2, 1976, Wiley-Interscience, New York.

(13) Kleinrock, L. and Yemini,"An Optimal Adaptive Scheme for Multiple Access Broadcast Communications," Proceedings of IEEE ICC, 1978, 7.2.1-7.2.5.

(14) Koubias, S., G. Papadopoulos and S. Leventis,"A New Multiple Access Protocol," Proceedings of IEEE Region 8 28th International Congress on Electronics, Rome, March 23-25, 1981.

(15) Koubias, S., G. Papadopoulos and S. Leventis,"A New Multiple Access Protocol and its Simulated Performance," Proceedings of the 15th HICSS, University of Hawaii, Honolulu, Hawaii, 423-429, Jan. 6-8, 1982.

(16) Koubias, S.,"Development of Self Adaptive Multiple Access Protocols for Computer Networks," Ph.D. Thesis, University of Patras, 1982.

(17) Lam, S.S.,"Delay Analysis of a Time Division Multiple Access (TDMA) Channel," IEEE Transactions on Communications, COM-25, No.12, Dec. 1977, 1489-1494.

(18) Lam, S.S.,"Satellite Packet Communication-Multiple Access Protocols and Performance," IEEE Transactions on Communications, COM-27, No.10, Oct. 1979, 1456-1466.

(19) Lam, S.S. and L. Kleinrock,"Packet Switching in a Multi-Access Broadcast Channel: Dynamic Control Procedures," IEEE Transactions on Communications, COM-23, No.9, Sept. 1975, 891-904.

(20) Little, D.C.,"A Proof of Queueing Formula: L= W," Operation Research, 9, 1961, 383-387.

(21) Metcalfe, R.M.,"Packet Communication," MIT, Project MAC TR-114, Cambridge, Dec. 1973.

(22) Mittal, K.K. and A.N. Venetsanopoulos,"On the Dynamic Control of the URN Scheme for Multiple Access Broadcast Communication Systems," IEEE Transactions on Communications, COM-29, No.7, Jul. 1981, 962-970.

(23) Roberts, L.G.,"Dynamic Allocation of Satellite Capacity through Packet Reservation," AFIPS Conference Proceedings, 1973 NCC, 42, 711-716.

(24) Tobagi, F.A.,"Protocols in Packet Communication Systems," IEEE Transactions on Communications, COM-23, No.4, April 1980.

(25) Tobagi, F.A. and L. Kleinrock,"Packet Switching in Radio Channels: Part III:

Split Channel Reservation Multiple Access," IEEE Transactions on Communications, COM-24, No.8, Aug.1976.

(26) Sykas, E.D., D.E. Karvelas and E.N. Protonotarios,"A Combined URN and TDMA Scheme for Multiple-Access Protocols in Local Area Networks,"Proceedings of MELECON'83, A1.04-A1.05, Athens, 24-26 May, 1983.

(27) Koubias, S. and G. Papadopoulos,"Analysis of a New Self-Adaptive MAP With Mixed Structure,"prepared for publication.

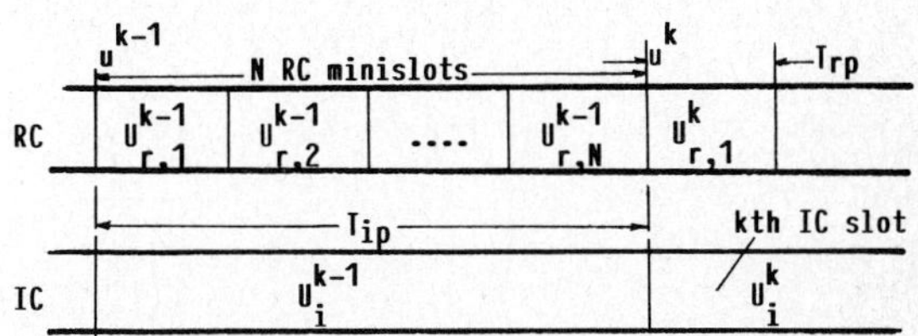

Fig.1. The Format of the RC and IC for the ATP-2.

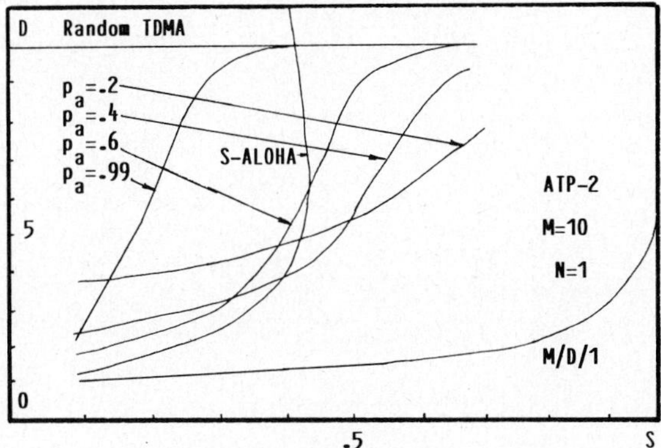

Fig.2. The Characteristic Curves of the ATP-2 for N=1.

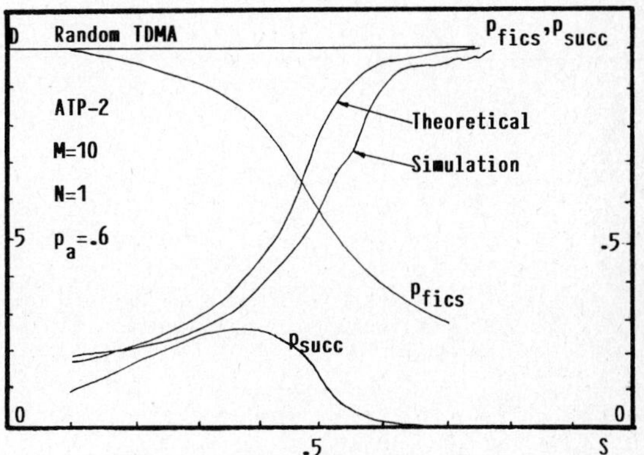

Fig.5. Analytical and Simulation Curves for N=1, p_a=.6.

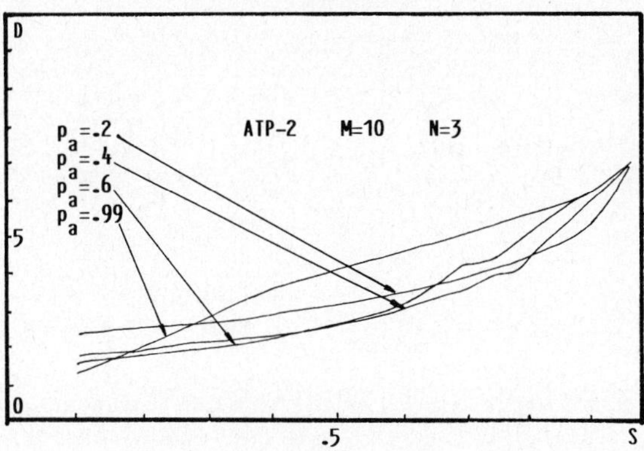

Fig.3. The Characteristic Curves of the ATP-2 for N=3.

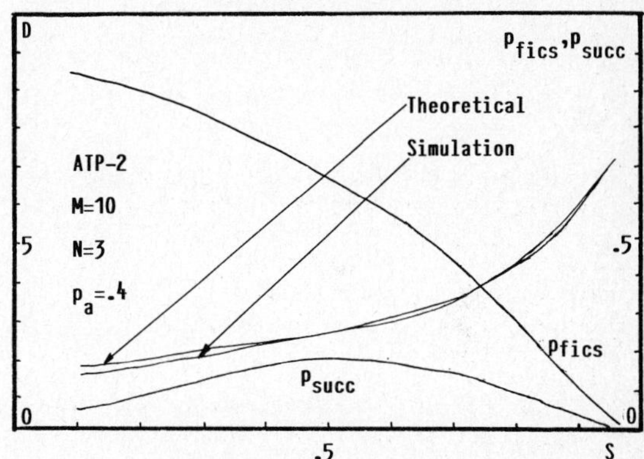

Fig.6. Analytical and Simulation Curves for N=3, p_a=.4.

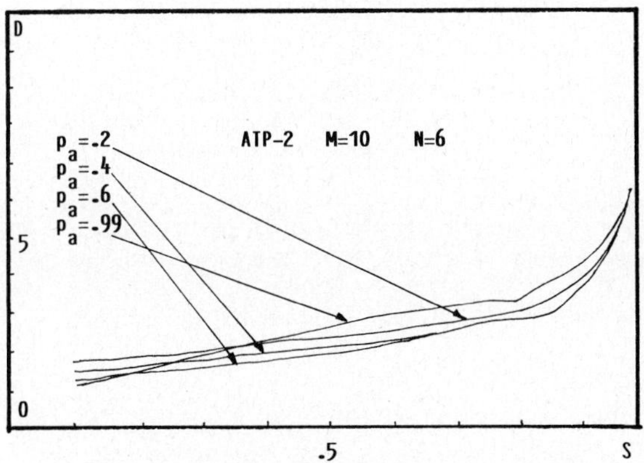

Fig.4. The Characteristic Curves for the ATP-2 for N=6.

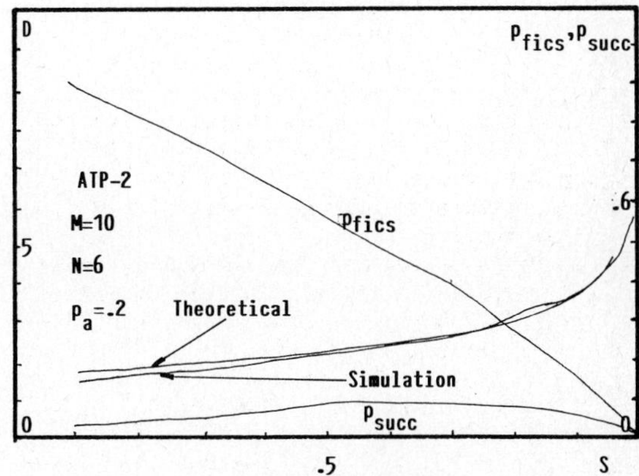

Fig.7. Analytical and Simulation Curves for N=6, p_a=.2.

DIGITAL TECHNIQUES in Simulation, Communication and Control
Spyros G. Tzafestas (editor)
Elsevier Science Publishers B.V. (North-Holland) © IMACS, 1985

ON THE USE OF A LOCAL AREA NETWORK IN A DECENTRALIZED CONTROL STRUCTURE

Michel MARITON, Gabriel DIB, Michel DROUIN

Laboratoire des Signaux et Systèmes
C.N.R.S. - E.S.E.
Plateau du Moulon
91190 Gif-sur-Yvette, France.

ABSTRACT : Distributed microprocessor structures provide the natural support for control of systems with a wide geographical repartition . Methods were developed to design local control laws associated with each subsystem. On the basis of one of these methods, it is shown how the introduction of a new and more power full communication medium, the Local Area Network, modifies the usual approach of such problems.

INTRODUCTION

A large scale geographical distribution associated with an interconnected structure is often encountered for industrial processes. A typical example may be a steel plantwhere local production units are coupled through the tie-lines. For such processes partially decentralized control laws are desired, since one would like to associate a local controller to each production unit, while transferring the necessary coordinating task to a centralized upper level. On the eve of decomposition-coordination techniques [1,2], it was thought that they could solve these problems. However mainly off-line calculus applications were reported, and it is only recently that a new approach has been proposed [3] to solve the on-line problem.

This communication studies the interplay between the design of structurally constrained controls by this method, and the use of a Local Area Network (LAN). Since it is clear that the different control units have to exchange informations to compute an overall efficient control law, communication requirements are specified. The necessity of a LAN will be explained from a critic of a previous realization where the media were several point to point RS232 lines. A part from increasing the speed of communications, the LAN allows wider data exchanges because a unique shared medium replaces the point to point lines.

After recalling the method in section 1, with special interest on how it handles structural constraints, the second section presents general concepts about LAN and justifies the choice of a particular technology. Finally the last section gives indications on the selection of information and the use of supplementary measures in a decoupling strategy.

I. DESIGN OF STRUCTURALLY CONSTRAINED CONTROLS

Consider a given large scale system with N interconnected subsystems. These subsystems will be described by their usual state space discrete time equation :

$$ss_i \begin{cases} x_{ik+1} = A_{ii}\, x_{ik} + z_{ik} + B_{ii}\, u_{ik} \\ z_{ik} = \sum_{j \neq i} A_{ij}\, x_{jk} \end{cases} \qquad (1)$$

The vector z_{ik} corresponds to coupling effects from other subsystems. The design of a regulator for this system is sought through the minimization of a quadratic criterion

$$J = 1/2 \sum_{k=o}^{K} x_{k+1}^T\, Q x_{k+1} + u_k^T\, R u_k \qquad (2)$$

In this section, we shall focus attention on the first level of the hierarchical structure that can be used to solve

$$u^* = \text{Arg} \min_u J \qquad (3)$$

The interested reader will find a complete description of the method in [4]. The first level task, when the upper level is off, will assure a feedback, so that the process will remain controled even if the supervisor fails or communications are interrupted. For this purpose, only the instantaneous local part of the cost function (2) is considered

$$J_{ik} = 1/2\, x_{ik+1}^T\, Q_i\, x_{ik+1} + 1/2\, u_{ik}^T\, R_i u_{ik} \qquad (4)$$

with $Q = \text{diag}(Q_i)$ and $R = \text{diag}(R_i)$, a direct derivation yields, for the control agent number i

$$u_{ik} = \Gamma_i\, x_{ik} + \Lambda_i\, z_{ik} \qquad (5)$$

The gain matrices Γ_i and Λ_i are given by

$$\begin{cases} \Gamma_i = -(R_i + B_{ii}^T\, Q_i\, B_{ii})^{-1}\, B_{ii}^T\, Q_i\, A_{ii} \\ \Lambda_i = -(R_i + B_{ii}^T\, Q_i\, B_{ii})^{-1}\, B_{ii}^T\, Q_i \end{cases}$$

The spatial decomposition (index i) in (4) is made on the pattern of the system structure (1), so that u_i feedbacks through Γ_i the subsystem state x_i. From (5) it is clear however that the control is not decentralized : it is required either to measure the interaction z_{ik}, either to compute it from the knowledge of A_{ij}, $j \neq i$, and the measures of x_j, $j \neq i$. This is in contradiction with our initial purpose of a decentralized local level.

To satisfy the decentralization constraint, the instantaneous local criterion is slightly modified in

$$J_{ik} = 1/2\ x_{ik+1}^T\ Q_i\ x_{ik} + 1/2\ u_{ik}^T\ R_i\ u_{ik} \qquad (6)$$

Moreover the initial weighting matrix Q_i is replaced by a matrix of free parameters S_i

$$J_{ik} = 1/2\ x_{ik+1}^T\ S_i\ x_{ik} + 1/2\ u_{ik}^T\ R_i\ u_{ik} \qquad (7)$$

This free matrix is used simultaneously to minize the importance of the upper level in the overall optimality (we shall not discuss this step here, see [4]) and to satisfy the constraints on the structure of the feedback. Applying to (7) the same derivations as to (4), one gets the control

$$u_{ik} = \Gamma_i\ x_{ik} \qquad (8)$$

with $\Gamma_i = -\ R_i^{-1}\ B_{ii}^T\ S_i$

The law (8) is now independant from the other subsystems measures. Different choicesof J_{ik} can improve this law while maintaining its decentralized structure (see [5]).

With

$$y_{ik} = C_{ii}\ x_{ik} \qquad (9)$$

the observation equation, a choice $S_i = C_{ii}^T Q_i'\ C_{ii}$, will give an output decentralized feedback ($u_{ik} = -\ R_i^{-1}\ B_{ii}^T\ C_{ii}^T\ Q_i'\ y_{ik}$), thus avoiding the reconstruction of the local state x_{ik}.

It was the initial idea to constrain the feedback to be decentralized. This approach was justified by the communication techniques state of the art ten years ago, when the standard media were asynchronous point to point lines. The emergence of Local Area Networks as the medium of the future in distributed control processingmodifies this picture.

II. LOCAL AREA NETWORKS IN PROCESS CONTROL.

The concept of local area networks can be originated to the mid-seventies, when its necessity was first formulated by major business companies for their decentralized data processing needs. Since then the trend was greatly accentuated, and several commercial products are by now available. In this section, it is intented to give a few basic ideas on local area networks, with process control applications in mind. Detailed information can be found in [6].

2.1. General presentation

To briefly introduce the need of a LAN in a process control application, one can picture a typical situation, where three decision makers have to exchange information. Figure 1 shows the media requirements for the classical point to point solution

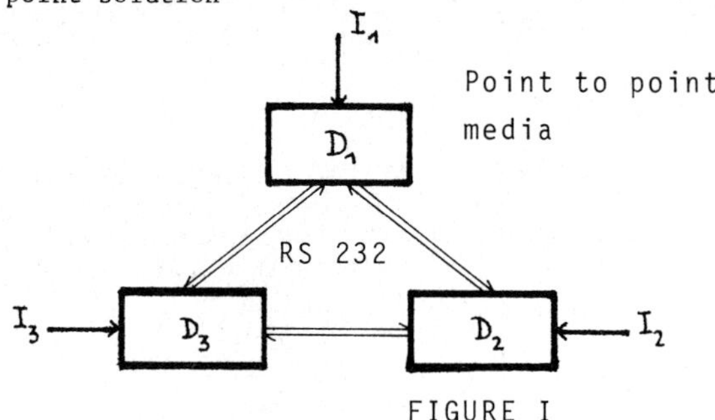

FIGURE I

Six lines are necessary, six lines that are to be managed, that can fail .... The idea behind the LAN concept is to notice the high redundancy in Figure 1, and to prefer the solution of a shared medium. Figure 2 gives the corresponding picture

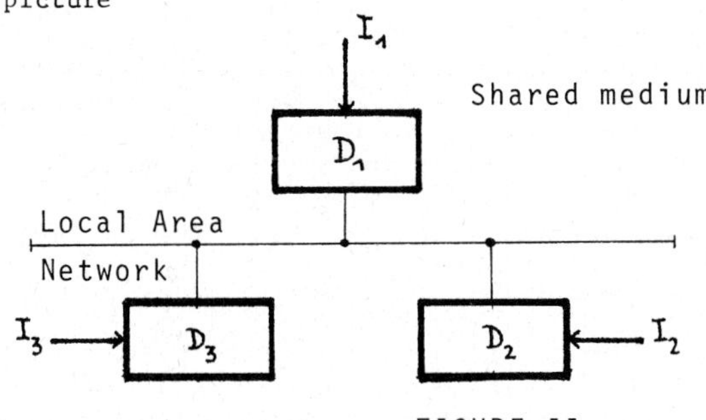

FIGURE II

The specifity of a LAN can be illustrated by comparing its privileged range of applications to that of a microprocessor bus and a network (Figure 3)

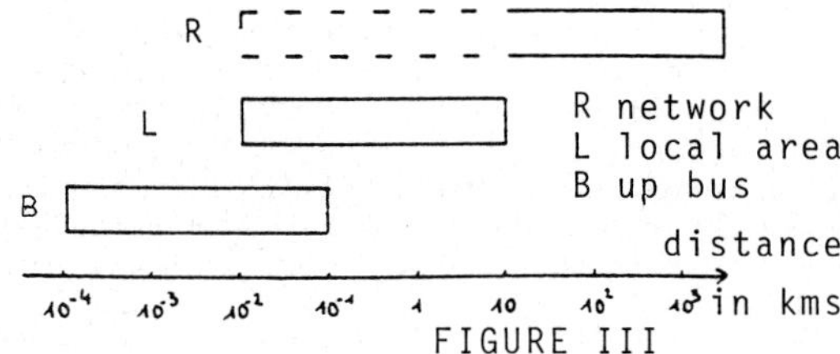

FIGURE III

The doted part for the network corresponds to distances for which networks will be replaced by LAN in a near future.

From a user point of view, the main characteristic of a LAN is its protocol.

By this it is usually meant the software modules that organize the access to the medium, prepare the messages ... The conception of efficient protocols is a subject of research on its own, and this field is quickly changing. To make it short,one can distinguish two main types of access. The first type is based on the CSMA-CD principle (Carrier Sense Multiple Access - Collision Detection). Random effects are accepted. Whenever a station has a message, it passes it to the LAN. Collisions between messages from different stations are bound to happen. In such a case, collision must be detected, and try-again procedures engaged. This technology was choosen by Intel, Xerox and Dec for Ethernet. The other solution is to avoid randomicity. The principle here is called Token Passing (TP). A station must wait its turn to send its message on the LAN. Stations are scrutinized deterministically as a token circulates. Texas and IBM choosed this technology.

2.2. Choice of a technology.

Local Area Networks were first conceived for business applications. The probiem here is to exchange many data, organized in large files,without crucial time constraints. A bank clerk will not be anoyed if the count situation, he asked to the computer of another bank, is delivered after a time interval, that may vary randomly from one to a few seconds. Process control applications are very different. Here the messages are most often short (coding of a sensor measure) but must be delivered immediatly. The time constraint is essential, it is typically the control interval. An instable process has to be controlled at the next sample period lest it should diverge. Table 1 gives the caracteristics of the main process control messages

MESSAGE	RESPONSE TIME	FIABILITY	FREQUENCY	LENGTH (bits-K)
Control	Short	High	Very high	Medium (64)
Alarm	Very short	High	Medium	Short (10)
File	Long	High	Low	Long (100)

Table I

This difference guides the choice between CSMA-CD or TP technologies. If collisions may occur, one cannot guarentee the transmission of a message in a specified time. The try-again procedure can be long. With Token Passing the maximal delay is the time needed for an all round scrutation of stations. It can be specified. This is why a TP protocol network was prefered for our pilot realisation.

One would like to stress here that this picture, though up-to-date, will certainly evolve. CSMA-CD could be adapted to process control requirements by sophistications such as station priorities, emergency protocols ...

The next question is to define the services that are asked to the LAN. International classifications have been defined by the International Standards Organization (ISO), to caracterize the different functions. It appears that many levels are not needed for process control applications (Figure 4)

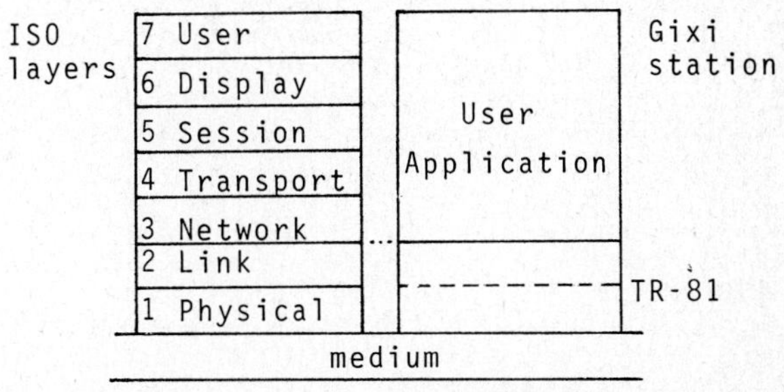

FIGURE IV

Presentation, session, transport and network are not necessary, the application level is of course taken in charge by the user host computer.

Finally after contacts with different constructors, Gixinet, built by the french firm Gixi, was selected, its Token Passing strategy is a direct circling scrutation called Round Table (Trade Mark).

2.3. How was the LAN hosted ?

The first section introduced the two levels. The first one, said local, is a feedback on the subsystem outputs. It will be designed to stabilize the process. It is clear then that it must be computed and applied at each command interval, to keep the process under control. The second level is implemented in a different computer called the supervisor. Its control can be added to improve the trajectories.

The protocol was built to meet these control constraints. The local tasks were activated by the command real time interrupt. A time diagram will briefly explain the main features of this protocol.

The following notations are introduced :

- E : Analog-Digital conversion, scale adjusment
  These programs enter the system measurements in the controler and prepare them for the control computation
- C : This program is the control algorithm itself. It is charged on a specialized fast arithmetic unit.
- S : Digital Analog conversion, scale adjusment
  These programs exit the computed controls and apply them to the process
- G_i: Emission of the ith subsystem via the LAN
- D_i: Reception of the ith subsystem measures
- TP: Token Passing

For the application with three stations described in the next section, the supervisor was set number 0 in the round table, when local controlers were respectively set number 1 and 2.

With two time lines for each station, one for the station central processor, the other for the station network processor, the activities during one control period are summed up by the following diagram, when communications are needed from local units to the supervisor (central) only, for example in a monitoring and alarm mode.

Protocol diagram for a Local→Central communication

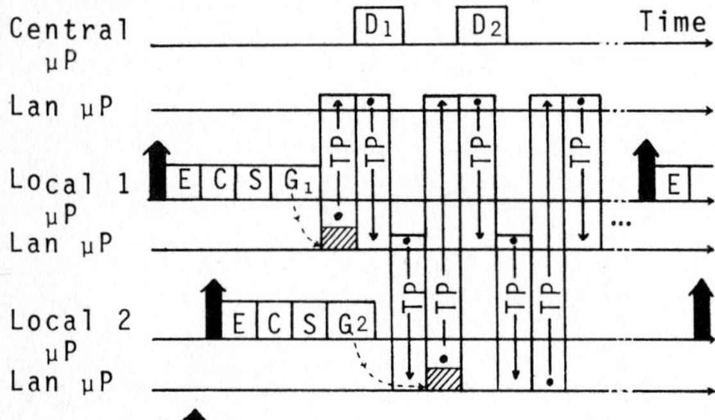

The sign ⬆ notes the real time clock interrupt

III. INFLUENCE OF THE LAN ON CONTROL SYNTHESIS

Attention is now turned again on specific control problem, and it will be shown how the control synthesis is influenced by the LAN capacities.

3.1. Information selection

Compared to the point to point asynchronous lines, the LAN allows much wider exchanges.Before it was necessary to physically connect a line between two controllers when an exchange between them was needed, it is now only a software connection that is programmed through the shared medium.

This facility could,in a first move, encourage the designer to select an "open-world" information strategy. That is to give all the measures to all the controllers. However, at the local level, these controllers are implemented on cheap calculators, most often microprocessors. Their computing power is therefore limited and the everything to everyone strategy is not realistic, should it be preferable from a regulation point of view. The use of a LAN consequently sets up a new question : how to select the most efficient information with respect to the control problem ?

This very basic question has remained unanswered so far. Information structure problems have been considered in a stochastic game framework [7].

Two approaches were developped with the idea to measure the influence of an extra measurement on a cost function. The bigger this influence was, the most efficient was rated this measure. This yields an ordering of the measure with respect to their efficiency in the control problem. The two approches differ on how the influence is measured. A first solution is to simulate the process and numerically estimate the criterion decrease when a specific loop is added to the control structure. Numerical results along this path will be find in [8].

The other approach is based on a sensitivity measure.

For a feedback $u = \Gamma x$, the suboptimal criterion is

$$J_{so} = 1/2\, x_o^T H x_o \tag{10}$$

where H satisfies a Ljapunov equation

$$\tilde{A}^T H + H \tilde{A} = - Q - \Gamma^T R \Gamma \tag{11}$$

with $\tilde{A} = A + B\Gamma$

In section 1, a feedback $\Gamma = - R^{-1} B^T S$ was derived. The structure of S was imposed by the decentralization constraint. That is certain coefficients of S were fixed to zero. Now, thanks to the LAN, non zero values are authorized and it is desired to decide which coefficients will be let non zero values. To do this, a small variation ε is made on s_{ij} the coefficient of S that corresponds to feeding back the jth measure in the ith control. The resulting suboptimal cost variation measures the efficiency of this extra-loop. It is found to be, with obvious notations, at the first order in ε

$$\frac{\Delta J_{ij}}{\varepsilon} = 1/2\, x_o^T M_{ij}\, x_o \tag{12}$$

where M_{ij} satisfies a Ljapunov equation

$$\tilde{A}^T M_{ij} + M_{ij} \tilde{A} = - \hat{Q}_{ij} \tag{13}$$

The quotient $\Delta J_{ij}/\varepsilon$ is used to order the j measure for a given i control. Details can be found in [9].

3.2. Non-interacting control

With point to point lines, control laws were constrained to the decentralized structure :

$$u_i = U_i(y_i) \tag{14}$$

The LAN allows the more general form

$$u_i = U_i(y_i,\ y_j) \text{ with } j \neq i \tag{15}$$

That is information from the jth subsystem is fed back into the control of the ith subsystem. A potential application of this possibility is to design a decoupling effect that would counterback the interaction that come, inside the system, from the jth element to the ith. The general scheme of non interacting control (Figure 5) become therefore applicable in large scale problems

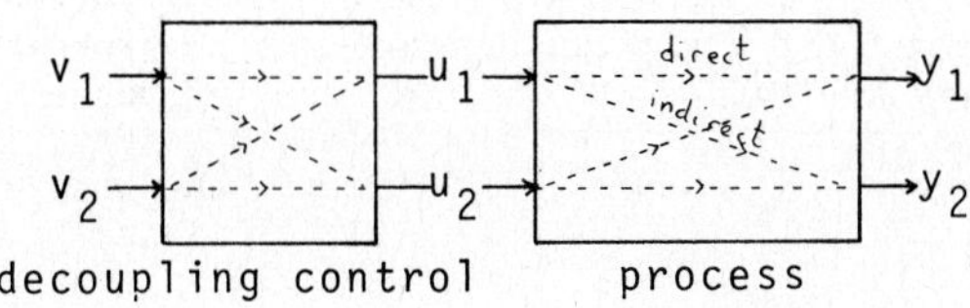

FIGURE V

3.3. Example

To test these ideas, the following distributed control structure was assembled in our laboratory (Figure 6)

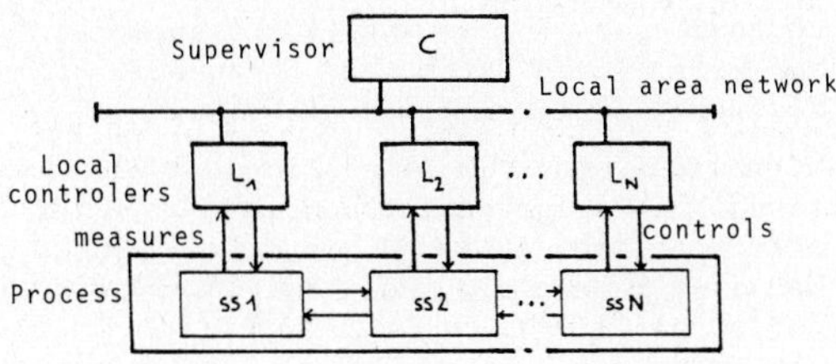

FIGURE VI

The upper level task was not described in this communication (see [9]). The controlled process consisted of two connected third order subsystems

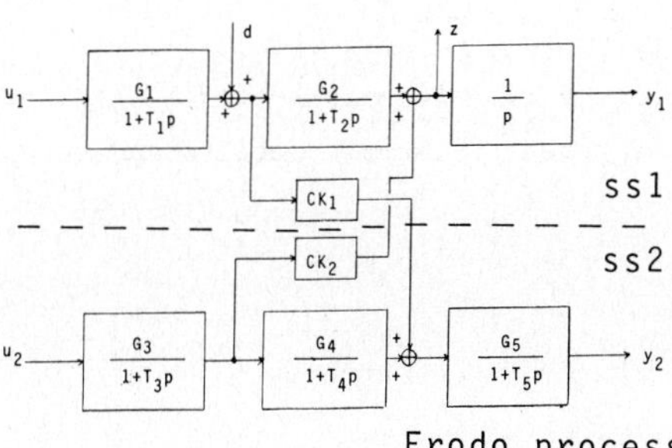

Set-points were given to the outputs y_1 and y_2, and the control was designed to improve the trajectories towards these final values.

Since the set-point on the second subsystem was zero ($y_{2d}=0$), a decoupling control was needed through u_2 to counterback the disturbance coming from the first subsystem. Available variables for this purpose are y_1 and u_1. They were first compared by the information selection procedure. It indicated that u_1 was to be choosen preferably to y_1. To validate this procedure, both feedbacks were however optimized to check whether the a posteriori result would corroborate the a priori selection scheme. Figure 7 presents the second output trajectories for the three cases, without decoupling, with decoupling by y_1 and with decoupling by u_1.

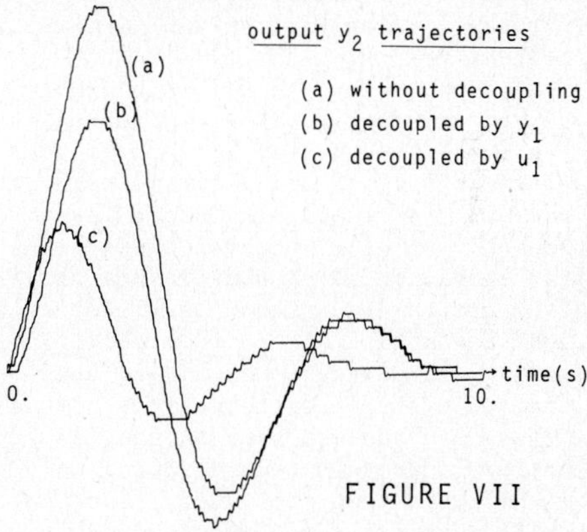

FIGURE VII

The feedback on u_1 is a posteriori found to be better than that on y_1, as indicated the information selection procedure. Figure 8 gives the control on the second subsystem

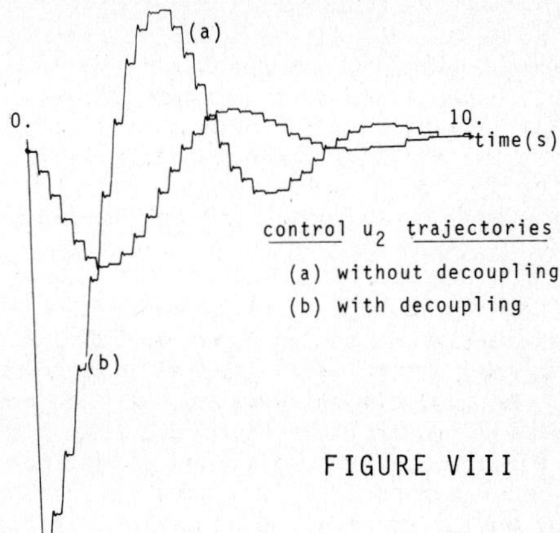

FIGURE VIII

CONCLUSION

The extension of microprocessors allowed, at a low cost, the construction of distributed control structures. These structures are very well suited for large scale systems where process units are often distant. Moreover they closely imitate the concepts of decentralized and hierarchical control methods. Base on one of this method, oriented towards on-line problems, an experimental realization was built up in our laboratory, to validate the algorithm in a real context.

Communication between local units were especially studied here. It was shown why Local Aera Networks surely represent the solution of the future. This new medium allows much wider data exchanges. An improvement of the control can then be obtained by decoupling units. Due to computing limits of local stations, one must however select the measures that will be used. Finally a simple example was given to illustrate these ideas.

In a more general context, the conclusion is that the use of a Local Area Network reduces the gap between Large Scale distributed systems and compact multivariable processes. Thus a very good behavior will be obtained with the sole first level. It is no longer necessary to rely on the centralized second level for such purposes as decoupling. Freed from this task, the supervisor computing power can be used for other jobs, as disturbance rejection, adaptation... These are consequences of the LAN implementation form a process control point of view. But it is believed that other very important changes will result in the process conception itself. So far coupled process units were difficult to handle, and it was very often decided to avoid it in the conception itself. A classical technique, in chemical industry for example, was to insert large buffers between units. This often resulted in an overall sluggish performance. The ability to cope with coupling effects by means of control actions, will certainly allow more accurate constructions of the process itself. Economic benefits are then obvious.

REFERENCES

[1] M.D. MESAROVIC, D. MACKO, Y. TAKAHARA, Theory of hierarchical multilevel systems, Academic Press, New York, 1970.

[2] M.G. SINGH, A. TITLI, Systems : decomposition, optimization and control, Pergamon Press, London, 1978.

[3] M. DROUIN, P. BERTRAND, A new coordination structure for on-line control of complex processes, Large Scale System 3, 1982, pp. 147-157.

[4] M. DROUIN, H. ABOU-KANDIL, P. BERTRAND, On a practical approach to real time control, Proc. IFAC Symposium LSSTA, Warsaw, 1983, pp. 125-129.

[5] G. DUC, M. DROUIN, P. BERTRAND, On the design of simple control laws for complex processes, Proc. 22 nd CDC, San Diego,1983.

[6] G. DIB, Systèmes informatiques répartis temps réel pour environnements automatisés, Rapport interne LSS, Gif, 1983.

[7] H.S. WITSENHAUSEN, On information structures feedback and causality, SIAM J. Control, Vol. 9, N° 2, pp. 149-160.

[8] G. DIB, Impact des réseaux locaux sur la commande des processus géographiquement répartis, Thèse de Docteur-Ingénieur, Université de Paris-Sud, Orsay, 1984.

[9] M. MARITON, Contribution à la commande hiérarchisée des processus complexes. Coordination et contraintes de structure, Thèse Doctorat 3ème cycle, Université de Paris-Sud, Orsay, 1984.

DIGITAL TECHNIQUES in Simulation, Communication and Control
Spyros G. Tzafestas (editor)
Elsevier Science Publishers B.V. (North-Holland) © IMACS, 1985

PERFORMANCE EVALUATION OF THE H-NETWORK THROUGH SIMULATION

N. Dimopoulos and C.W. Wong

Electrical Engineering Department
Concordia University
Montreal, Quebec, Canada

This work presents an analytical method for obtaining the average utilization factor for a local area network employing CSMA-CD and backoff. Simulation results for three back-off strategies are also presented, and a comparison between them is made.

Introduction

The H-Network is a high-speed distributed packet switching local computer network designed for very short haul computer communication. Its primary application is to facilitate user interaction and control of the Homogeneous Multiprocessor [2,3].

The H-Network [4]is an additional fast pathway of the Homogeneous Multiprocessor architecture and it is designed to facilitate user interaction, control and file transfer to/from the Homogeneous Multiprocessor, as well as information exchange between distant processors.

The H-Network is a baseband local area network with a structure which resembles that of the Ethernet [5]; yet, by providing separate pathways for data transmission, network acquisition and collision detection, and due to the fact that the total length of the network is of the order of 10m, we were able to achieve higher data rates (~7Mbytes/sec) in comparison with those of the classical architectures.

As it may be seen in Figs. 1 and 2, the H-Network consists of a group of four pathways plus network stations which interface the network with the Homogeneous Multiprocessor. The four pathways are: (a) The H-bus. This is the data highway which consists in the present implementation, of 16 data lines. (b) The Access line. This is a single control line and it is used to ensure the mastership of the network by a single station with high probability. A fast (T & S) module is provided to each of the station controllers. This module, upon request from the station controller, can sense the condition of the Access line, and if free set it within a window of vulnerability of 100 ns. This short window of vulnerability, increases the probability that only one station will become master of the network of any given time. (c) The ID line. This is a single line and it is used by the station controllers to detect possible collisions. (d) Timing and control. This group of lines, facilitates the actual transmission of data through the H-bus.

Footnote This research is supported by the Natural Sciences and Engineering Research Council, Canada under grant # A1337 and by Fonds FCAC pour l'aide et la soutien a la recherche under grant # EQ 2007.

The H-Network protocol is divided into four phases. Network acquisition, packet transmission, collision detection and retransmission. Upon the arrival of a packet, the station attempts (through the T & S module) to obtain the network. The network can be obtained within a window of vulnerability a by the T & S Module, which informs the station within a recycle time of T secs. The recycle time T is defined as the time interval needed by the network station to read the results of the Test and Set operation performed by the T & S module and respond accordingly.

If the network was found busy, then the station tries again.

If the network was obtained, then the station initiates a packet transmission and in parallel it checks for collisions.

If a collision is detected, then the current transmission is aborted, and the station performs a backoff algorithm. Otherwise, the current transmission is allowed to proceed and finish.

In this work, we present a theoretical analysis of a network of N stations where it is assumed that ready packets exist in all the stations all the time.

We also present the utilization factor obtained through simulation of a similar network of N stations.

Performance Analysis of the H-Network With Back-Off

We present here a worst case analysis of the performance of the H-Network. We assume that there are N stations on the network ready to transmit all the time. Our objective is to determine the average utilization factor (defined as the percentage of time the network is successfully transmitting). Due to the structure of the network, there is always a finite recycle time T between successive attempts of an idle station to capture the network. Denote also by a the window of vulnerability and by τ and δ the transmission and collision detection periods. The network alternates between idle and busy (transmission or collision) states.

In this analysis we consider the case of back-off. Thus, at the end of the current busy period, all the stations will try to obtain mastership of the network. If a station was not involved in a collision during the current busy period it will try to gain mastership immediately after the end of the busy period with probability of one. If on the other hand, the station was involved in a collision, then it will delay d_n seconds before trying to obtain the channel again within one recycle period. The magnitude of delay d_n depends of the number of the previous collisions n this station has been involved since its last successful transmission, usually in a linear or geometric fashion.

The next busy period will be a successful transmission if the first and second requesting stations (after the current busy period) make requests at points of time that differ more than a (the window of vulnerability). Otherwise a collision will result.

The average utilization factor is defined as

$$\bar{S} = \frac{\bar{U}}{\bar{I} + \bar{B}}$$

where $\bar{u}$ is the average successful transmission period given as:

$\bar{U} = \tau P$ [successful transmission]

$\bar{I}$ is the average idle period and

$\bar{B}$ is the average busy period given as $\bar{B} = \tau P$ [successful transmission] + δ (1-P[successful transmission]).

In order to calculate the probability of successful transmission, used in the derivation of $\bar{S}$, we need to know the state of the network at the end of the current busy period.

The state of the network determines the number of stations which were involved in collisions at the end of the current busy period, and therefore must be delayed in their attempts to acquire the network.

Denote by $N=\{n_0,n_1,\ldots,n_k,x_0,x_1,\ldots,x_k\}$ the state of the network where $n_i;i=0,1,\ldots,k$ is the number of stations that collided at the end of the current busy period and this was their i^{th} collision since their last successful transmission. $x_i;i = 1,2,\ldots,k$ is the number of stations which did not collide at the end of the current busy period but they have already collided i times since their previous successful transmission.

$$x_0 = 0$$

Denote now by

$M = \{m_0,m_1,\ldots,m_k, y_0,y_1,\ldots,y_k\}$ the state of the network at the end of the next busy period and by $P_{N,M}$ the probability of transition between states N and M.

There exist three cases.

Case a This is a case of successful transmission by a station which has not collided since its previous successful transmission. That is the transmitting station comes from the population n_0. Since the next busy period is a successful transmission no station collided and therefore $m_1 = m_2 = \ldots m_k = 0$. Also since the transmitted packet came from the population n_0, and since we assumed that all the stations are ready to transmit all the time then $n_0 = m_0 \neq 0$.

Also, $y_i = x_i + n_i$; $i = 1,2,\ldots,k$, this signifies that all the delayed stations (which did not collide in the previous period) will not be delayed again.

Denote now by t_j; $j = 1,2,\ldots,N$ the network request times of the N stations. Then if the first station arrived at time t, then a successful transmission is achieved in the case where all the other stations arrive at least a seconds afterwards.

That is

$$dP^a_{N,M}(t) = \sum_{j=1}^{n_0} P\{t_j\varepsilon[t,t+dt]\ ;\ t_i > t+a,\ t_i\varepsilon[0,T],$$

$$i\ \varepsilon\ [1,n_0],\ i \neq j;\ t_{q_r}\ \varepsilon\ [d_r,T+d_r],\ q_r\varepsilon[1,n_r],$$

$$r = 1,2,\ldots,k\}$$

$$= n_0 \frac{dt}{T} \left[\frac{T-t-a}{T}\right]^{n_0+x-1} \cdot \prod_{r=1}^{k} \left\{\frac{T+d_r-\max(t+a,d_r)}{T}\right\}^{n_r}$$

where $x = \sum_{i=1}^{k} x_i$

and it is assumed that t_{q_r} are random variables uniformly distributed in the interval $[d_r,T+d_r]$. Therefore the transition probability between states N and M is given as

$$P^a_{N,M} = \int_0^{T-a} dP_{N,M} \qquad \text{if } n_0 + x > 1$$

$$P^a_{N,M} = \int_0^{T} dP_{N,M} \qquad \text{if } n_0 + x = 1$$

Case b   This is also a case of successful transmission. The packet transmitted had q previous collisions, (i.e. it came from the population n_q+x_q. Therefore, one extra station becomes ready with a packet having no previous collisions.

Therefore,

$$m_0 = n_0+1, \quad y_q = x_q+n_q-1, \quad y_i = x_i+n_i; \; i \neq q$$

and $m_1 = m_2 = \ldots = m_k = 0$.

Then

$$dP^b_{N,M}(t) = \sum_{j=1}^{n_q} P\{t_j \in [t,t+dt];\; t_i \in [d_q, T+d_q],$$

$$t_i > t+a,\; i \neq j,\; i \in [1,n_q] \;;\; t_{p_s} > t+a,$$

$$t_{p_s} \in [d_s, T+d_s],\; P_s \in [1,v_s],\; s=0,1,2,\ldots,k,\; s \neq q\}$$

$$+ \sum_{j=1}^{x_q} P\{t_j \in [t,t+dt];\; t_i > t+a,\; t_i \in [0,T],\; i \neq j,$$

$$i \in [1,x_\lambda];\; t_{p_s} > t+a,\; t_{p_s} \in [d_s, T+d_s],$$

$$p_s \in [1,u_s],\quad s=0,1,2,\ldots,k\}$$

with $v_0 = n_0 + \sum_{i=1}^{k} x_i \qquad d_0 = 0$

$$v_i = n_i \;;\quad i \neq q$$

$$u_0 = n_0 + \sum_{\substack{i=1 \\ i \neq q}}^{k} x_i,$$

$$u_i = n_i; \quad i = 1,2,\ldots,k$$

Thus

$$dP^b_{N,M} = n_q \frac{dt}{T}\left[\frac{T+d_q-t-a}{T}\right]^{n_q-1} \cdot \left(H_{d_q}^{T+d_q-a}(t)\right)^{n_q-1}$$

$$\cdot \left(H_{d_q}^{T+d_q}(t)\right)^{n_q}$$

$$\cdot \prod_{\substack{j=0 \\ j \neq q}}^{k} \left\{\frac{T+d_j-\max(t+a,d_j)}{T}\right\}^{v_j}$$

$$\cdot \left(H_0^{T+d_j-a}(t)\right)^{v_j}$$

$$+ x_q \frac{dt}{T}\left[\frac{T-t-a}{T}\right]^{x_q-1} \cdot \left(H_0^{T-a}(t)\right)^{x_q-1} \cdot \left(H_0^{T}(t)\right)^{x_q}$$

$$\cdot \prod_{j=0}^{k} \left\{\frac{T+d_j-\max(t+a,d_j)}{T}\right\}^{u_j}$$

$$\cdot \left(H_0^{T+d_j-a}(t)\right)^{u_j}$$

with
$$H_a^b(t) = \begin{cases} 0 \text{ if } t < a \\ 1 \text{ if } a \leq t \leq b \\ 0 \text{ if } t > b \end{cases}$$

Then
$$P^b_{N,M} = \int_0^{T+d_q} dP_{NM}.$$

Case c   This is a collision case where m_i; $i = 1,2,\ldots,k$ packets collided during the current busy period. The conditions for this case to happen are as follows:

$n_0 - m_0 = m_1$; m_1 ready packets from the population n_0, collided and therefore they must delay d_1 units of time before they try to acquire the network.

Similarly, $\quad n_i + x_i = m_{i+1} + y_i \quad i = 1,2, \; k-2$

i.e. m_{i+1} packets from the pool of $n_i + x_i$ packets with i previous collisions, collided and therefore must delay d_{i+1} units of time before they attempt to acquire the network. Also, $n_{k-1} + n_k + x_{k-1} + x_k = m_k + y_{k-1} + y_k$. That is from the population of $n_{k-1} + n_k + x_{k-1} + x_k$ packets with k or k-1 previous collisions, m_k collided while y_{k-1} and y_k did not. Thus,

$$y_{k-1} \leq n_{k-1} + x_{k-1} \quad \text{and}$$

$$y_k \leq n_k + x_k.$$

Assume that the set of the m_{i+1} packets that collided is composed from δn_i packets from the population of n_i and δx_i packets from the population of x_i. Then,

$$P^c_{N,M} = \sum_{\text{permutation}} \prod_{j=0}^{k} \binom{n_j}{\delta n_j}\binom{x_j}{\delta x_j} \int_0^{T+\max(d_q)} dP_c$$

{the first packet attempt was at time t, $\Sigma\delta n_j + \Sigma\delta x_j$ packets attempted to acquire the network during the interval [t,t+a] while all others attempted the acquisition at times greater than t+ a} .

Thus,

$$dP^c = \sum_j P\{t_j \in [t,t+dt];\ t_j \in [d_j,T+d_j],$$

$$t_{\lambda_j} \in [t,\min(t+a,T+d_j)],\ \lambda_j \in [1,\delta n_j-1];$$

$$t_{\delta_j} > t+a,\ \delta_j \in [1,n_j-\delta n_j];\ t_{u_i} \in [t,\min(t+a,T+d_i)]$$

$$t \in [d_i,T+d_i],\ u_i \in [1,\delta n_i];\ t_{v_i} > t+a,$$

$$v_i \in [1,n_i-\delta n_i];\ i \neq j,\ i=0,1,2,\ldots,k;$$

$$t_{s_i} \in [t,\min(t+a,T)],\ t \in [0,T],$$

$$s_i \in [1,\sum_{q=0}^{k}\delta x_q];\ t_{x_i} > t+a,\ x_i \in [1,\sum_{q=0}^{k}(x_q-\delta x_q)]\}$$

$$+\sum_j P\{t_j \in [t,t+dt],\ t \in [0,T], t_{\lambda_j} \in [t,\min(t+a,T)],$$

$$\lambda_j \in [1,\delta x_j-1];\ t_{q_j} > t+a,\ q_j \in [1,x_j-\delta x_j];$$

$$t_{u_i} \in [t,\min(t+a,T+d_i)],\ t \in [d_i,T+d_i],$$

$$u_i \in [1,\delta n_i]\ ;\ t_{v_i} > t+a,\ v_i \in [1,n_i-\delta n_i],$$

$$i=0,1,2,\ldots,k;\ t_{\sigma_i} \in [t,\min(t+a,T)],$$

$$t \in [0,T],\ \sigma_i \in [1,\sum_{i\neq j}^{k}\delta x_i];$$

$$tx_i > t+a,\ x_i \in [1,\sum_{i=0}^{k}(x_i-\delta x_i)]\}$$

Thus,

$$dP_c = \sum_{j=0}^{k} \delta n_j \frac{dt}{T}\left\{\frac{\min(a,T+d_j-t)}{T}\right\}^{\delta n_j-1} \cdot \left\{\frac{T+d_j-\min[T+d_j,\max(t+a,d_j)]}{T}\right\}^{n_j-\delta n_j} \cdot \left(H_{d_j}^{T+d_j}(t)\right)^{\delta n_j}.$$

$$\prod_{i\neq j}\left\{\frac{\min(a,T+d_i-t,a-d_i+t)}{T}\right\}^{\delta n_i} \cdot \left\{\frac{T+d_i-\min[T+d_i,\ \max(t+a,d_i)]}{T}\right\}^{n_i-\delta n_i} \cdot \left(H_{d_i-a}^{T+d_i}(t)\right)^{\delta n_i}$$

$$\cdot\left\{\frac{\min(a,T-t)}{T}\right\}^{\Sigma\delta x_i} \cdot\left\{\frac{T-\min(T,t+a)}{T}\right\}^{\Sigma(x_i-\delta x_i)} \cdot\left(H_0^T(t)\right)^{\Sigma\delta x_i}$$

$$+\frac{dt}{T}(\Sigma\delta x_j)\cdot\left\{\frac{\min(a,T-t)}{T}\right\}^{(\Sigma\delta x_i)-1} \cdot\left\{\frac{T-\min(T,t+a)}{T}\right\}^{\Sigma(x_i-\delta x_i)} \cdot\left(H_0^T(t)\right)^{\Sigma\delta x_i}$$

$$\cdot\prod_{i=0}^{k}\left\{\frac{\min(a,T+d_i-t,a-d_i+t)}{T}\right\}^{\delta n_i} \cdot\left\{\frac{T+d_i-\min[T+d_i,\max(t+a,d_i)]}{T}\right\}^{n_i-\delta n_i} \cdot\left(H_{d_i-a}^{T+d_i}(t)\right)^{\delta n_i}$$

For any other case the transition probability $P_{N,M} = 0$.

From the transition matrix $\Pi = [P_{N,M}]$ we can find the stationary probabilities P_N for the states N, as the eigenvector corresponding to eigenvalue $\lambda=1$ of the transition matrix Π. [5]

We are now in a position to calculate the probabilities for successful transmission, collision and the average idle time, which are needed for the calculation of the utilization factor S.

$$P_s = \sum_N P_N \cdot P\,[\text{successful}/N]$$

But the probability of successful transmission between two states of N and M has been considered in cases a and b. Thus

$$P[\text{successful}/N] = \sum_N (P_{NM}^a + P_{NM}^b)$$

The probability of collision is given as

$$P_c = 1-P_s$$

while the average idle interval can be calculated as follows.

$$\bar{I} = \sum_N P_N \cdot \bar{I}_N$$

where $\bar{I}_N$ is the average idle interval given that the current busy period has a state N.

$$\bar{I}_N = \int_0^{T+\max_j(d_j)} t \cdot dP[t_j \varepsilon (t,t+dt),\ t_i > t,\ i \neq j]$$

$$= \int_0^{T+\max_j(d_j)} t \cdot \frac{dt}{T} \sum_{j=0}^{k} v_j \cdot$$

$$\cdot \left(\frac{T+d_j-\min[T+d_j,\ \max_j\ (t+d_j)]}{T}\right)^{v_j-1}$$

$$\cdot \left(H_{d_j}^{T+d_j}(t)\right)^{v_j}$$

$$\cdot \prod_{i \neq j}^{k} \left(\frac{T+d_i-\min[T+d_i, \max_i(t+d_i)]}{T}\right)^{v_i}$$

$$\cdot \left(H_{d_i}^{T+d_i}(t)\right)^{v_i}$$

with $v_0 = n_0 + \sum_j xj$

$v_i = n_i,\ i = 1,2,\ldots,k$

Simulation

The H-Network was also simulated under PAWS [1]. Three types of backoff algorithm were used. Quadratic, linear and a combination of quadratic and linear, where the collided station follows a quadratic backoff for the first three collisions and a linear backoff for the rest. The average utilization factor for the various backoff strategies and for varying number of stations and traffic are presented in Figs.3,4,5

Discussion

In this work we presented an analytical method for obtaining the average utilization factor for a local area network employing CSMA-CD and Backoff. This analysis was performed under the worst case assumption where all the stations in the network are ready all the time.

We also presented simulation results for three backoff strategies namely linear, quadratic and a combination of the above. As it can be seen, the quadratic strategy presents the best performance, for high traffic, while all of them coincide for diminishing traffic.

References

[1] Berry R. et al., "PAWS 2.0 Performance Analyst's Workbench System", Information Research Associates, Austin, Texas (1982).

[2] Dimopoulos, N.,"On the Structure of the Homogeneous Multiprocessor" to appear in IEEE Trans. on Computers.

[3] Dimopoulos, N., "The Homogeneous Multiprocessor Architecture - Structure and Performance Analysis", Proceedings of the 1983 Int'l Conference on Parallel Processing, August 1983, pp. 520-523.

[4] Dimopoulos, N. and Kehayas, D.,"The H-Network A High Speed Distributed Packet Switching Local Computer Network", Proceedings of MELECON '83. Mediterraneal Electrotechnical Conference, Athens, Greece, May 24-26, 1983, pp. A1.02.

[5] Metcalfe, R.M. et al.,"Ethernet: Distributed Packet Switching for Local Computer Networks", Comm. ACM.19, pp. 395-404, July 1976.

[6] Papoulis, A., "Probability, Random Variables and Stochastic Processes", McGraw Hill (1965).

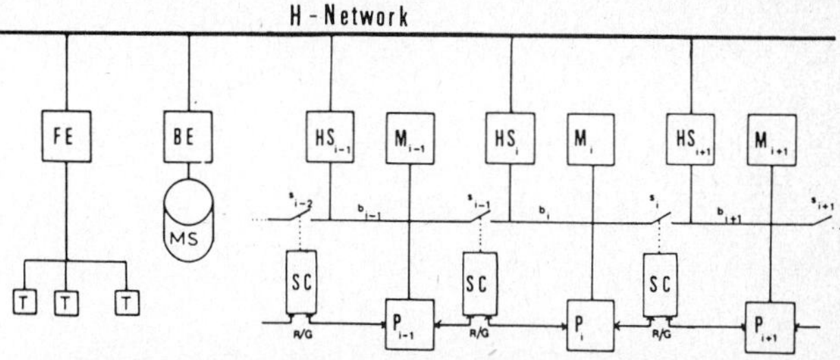

Figure 1. The Homogeneous Multiprocessor

P: Processor M: Memory s: Bus switch

FE: Front End BE: Back End SC: Switch Controller

b: Local Bus T: Terminal MS: Mass Storage

HS: H-Network Station R/G: Bus Request/Grant

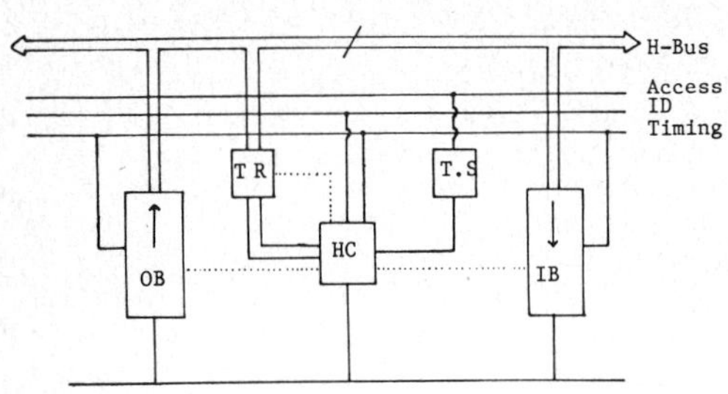

Figure 2. A Network Station.
OB: Output Buffer IB: Input Buffer
HC: Station Controller ID: Collision Detection
TR: Temporary Register T.S:Test and Set module

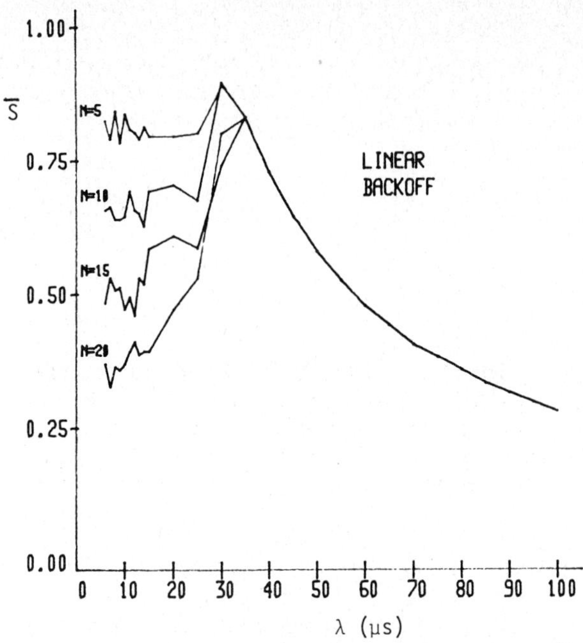

Figure 4. The average Utilization Factor $\bar{S}$ vs. the average packet interarrival interval λ for N stations and a linear backoff strategy.

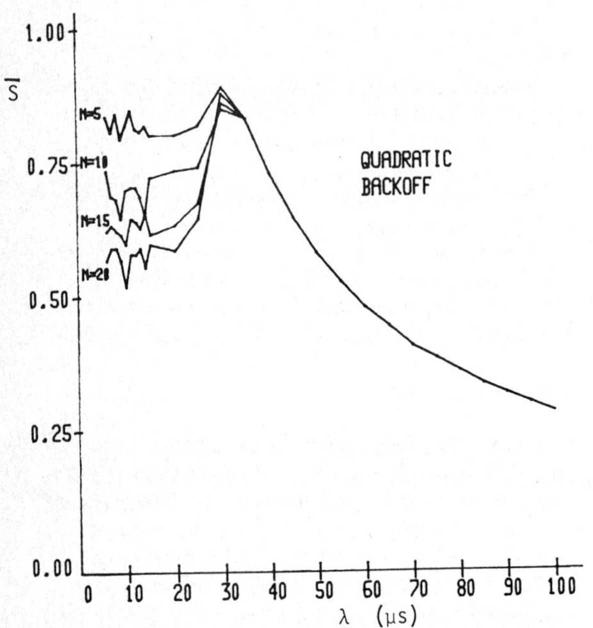

Figure 3. The average Utilization Factor $\bar{S}$ vs. the average packet interarrival interval for N stations and a quadratic backoff strategy.

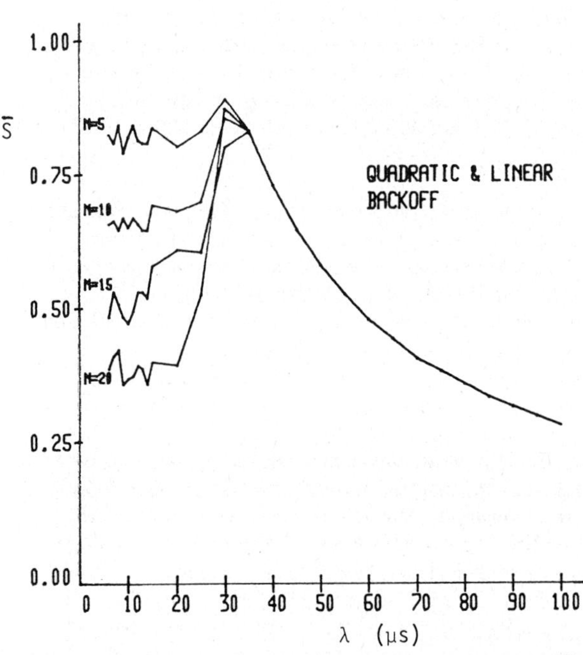

Figure 5. The average Utilization Factor $\bar{S}$ vs. the average packet interarrival interval λ for N stations and a quadratic & linear backoff strategy

DIGITAL TECHNIQUES in Simulation, Communication and Control
Spyros G. Tzafestas (editor)
Elsevier Science Publishers B.V. (North-Holland) © IMACS, 1985

THE ROLE OF THE DIGITAL PABX IN A GENERALISED NETWORK ENVIRONMENT

A J Kingsmill
Plessey Office Systems Limited
United Kingdom

ABSTRACT

Digital PABXs interconnected in private networks, or in consort with the emerging publicly provided integrated services digital network (ISDN), and invoking a new range of message based signalling protocols, are becoming a serious contender to effect the transport of all manner of digitally encoded information. This paper summarises this circumstance, summarises the interfaces presented to the user, comments on protocol enhancements to effect a generalised network service, and relates it to highway based local area networks.

1. OVERVIEW

The core attribute of telecommunications is to achieve interconnection. The characteristics of the services and devices which wish to invoke this interconnection have expanded very considerably in recent years. Dominated by the needs of telephony and telegraphy for many years, this interconnection function now has to serve the needs of not only dissimilar terminal devices with a wide range of presentation attributes - voice, data, image etc., - but also has itself to provide communication between other (perhaps proprietary) networks of widely different characteristics operating to widely different protocols.

On a local site, the analogue PABX was initially dragooned into performing this interconnection function. However, the general characteristics of the analogue PABX when confronted with digital information (relatively high error rates, long call set-up times, limited bandwidth, the need for modulation), were inadequate for the characteristics being generated by the data processing types of applications. In response to this need (and technological advances that made it possible), new network topologies, aimed primarily at digital data, were spawned - the era of the local area network (LAN). These LANs are typically characterised by high bandwidth, low error rates, low delays and full connectivity at the logical level. However, they generally have fairly limited geographical coverage and have to, or would like to, resort to public or private wide area networks to achieve dispersed interconnection.

Meanwhile, the PABX technology has evolved (particularly, the processor controlled digital devices), redressing many of the inadequacies of the earlier PABXs as they sought this more generalised networking role. This progress in PABX design is matched by developments in the public networks and a new era of advanced signalling and networking protocols shared between PABXs and public networks is leading to a composite end-to-end connection facility for all manner of devices and (sub)networks. The foreseeable environment in both the public and private domain is that of a service to subscribers affording a 64Kbit/s + 64Kbit/s plus some element of a 16Kbit/s service, separately switchable, presented to the subscriber interface, in a time division (digital) fashion on a single twisted pair. These services cater for full duplex working. In the most general case, one, (if not two) of the 64Kbit/s channels will be employed by the subscriber for voice traffic. Additionally, consideration is being given to the submultiplexing of the 64Kbit/s channels. Multiplexed 64Kbit/s channels are also available for inter-node trunks, and a switched 2.048 Mbit/s capability, (again, in both the local private and wide area public, domain) will follow in the future.

The networked PABX, in conjunction with publicly available wide band digital trunks (such as the British Telecom 'Kilostream' and 'Megastream' services), therefore, afford the setting up of a medium/high speed end-to-end digital physical network link. However, to make claim to a generalised role within the concept of open systems interconnection (OSI), functionality in the network gateways, termination points or in the end-user systems themselves, should implement the services defined in the (emerging) specification for the OSI Network Service. Upon this, can then rest the higher layer protocols that would be meaningful to end-user applications.

The invocation of the OSI Network Service would facilitate the PABX/ISDN network acting as an internetwork network for end-user systems that may themselves be proprietory networks of dissimilar performance and characteristics - typically local area networks. These matters are covered in the paper.

2. THE ISPBX/ISDN ENVIRONMENT

2.1 General

The realities of a generalised networking solution are predicated by the characteristics of the publicly provided wide area networks, or private networks which aim to serve the same ends. Solutions which do not countenance this need have a very limited span of relevance. By far the most geographically pervasive networks in this context are those that see telephony as their primary service.

With the progress of technology, the cost effective transmission and switching of voice information and the needs of data transmission have found common ground in digital networking. The initial concept of integrating digital transmission and digital switching for voice has lead to the concept of the IDN (integrated digital network). The further intent to carry other services, particularly of a non-voice nature, on the same infrastructure has lead to the more generalised intent of the ISDN - the integrated services digital network. At its outset (save in a United Kingdom pilot system) the ISDN will afford a 64Kbit/s + 64Kbit/s + 16Kbit/s service to a subscriber, part of the 16Kbit/s channel being used for signalling. Additionally, groups of thirty two 64Kbit/s channels can be catered for by a 2.048 Mbit/s trunk service. The basic parameters of this service should be ratified at the CCITT plenary in November 1984.

In parallel with this, and in many cases somewhat ahead of it, developments in PABX design have followed a similar strategy leading to the concept of the ISPBX -the integrated services private (automatic) branch exchange. Neither of these concepts have yet reached full implementation fruition, but this paper will be set in an environment which pre-judges their emergence. Certainly the core 64 Kbit/s public services will be available on a pilot system in the United Kingdom, in 1984, and a fairly rapid build-up will follow. Private networked PABXs employing the new switching protocols will be available in a similar time scale.

2.2 Signalling Protocols

Commensurate with these new composite services is a new era of signalling protocols. These protocols take advantage of the time division multiplexing strategy employed in the ISDN regime and congregate the switching information for a group of 30 channels in one time slot - the so-called common channelling signalling architecture. For subscriber loops, the signalling information is carried as a component of the 16Kbit/s channel. Thus, the signalling information is carried in a logical channel time separately from the voice or data channels, but typically in the same wideband trunk (or cable pair).

Modern digital PABXs will employ this signalling strategy along with the wider area networks, and already a number of complementary signalling protocols, to cater for the various interconnections, have reached a level of maturity. These are depicted in Fig 1.0.

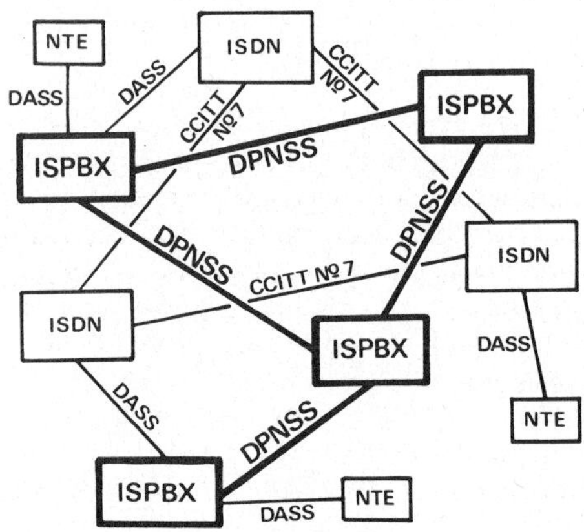

Fig 1.0 Signalling Protocols

The principle signalling protocols relevant to this topology are:-

CCITT No.7	the signalling protocol to be employed between main exchanges on an IDN/ISDN network.
DASS	(digital access signalling system) which describes the signalling protocol to be employed between Network Terminating Equipment (NTE), including PABXs, and an IDN/ISDN exchange.
and	
DPNSS	(digital private network signalling system), a new signalling protocol to be employed between ISPBX's in order that they may interwork in private networks.

CCITT No.7 is described in the CCITT 'Yellow books', whilst the latest version of DASS is detailed in British Telecom Network Requirement (BTNR) 190. DPNSS is a new British Telecom promoted private network switching protocol and in the context of the PABX networking role, it is apposite to dwell on that.

2.3 DPNSS - Digital Private Network Signalling System

Like CCITT No.7 and DASS, DPNSS is a message based, common channel signalling system normally carried via TS16 of a 32 channel (2.048 Mbits/s) circuit. DPNSS has many protocol elements identical to CCITT No.7, but it is enhanced to give the full cross-network functionality that private networks can offer. This is particularly true of services that cannot be invoked on the public network because of unresolved tariff implications (e.g. ring back when free).

DPNSS facilitates a fully distributed network implementation affording full functionality to and between all users, irrespective of their point of connection to the network. In the data (non-voice) environment it means that servers (resources) can be positioned anywhere in the network without prejudice to the subscribers' perception of the service that they afford.

DPNSS works on a link-by-link basis with each message being passed to the adjacent PABX, which either acts upon it or repeats it to the next PABX dependant upon the message content. The principle of DPNSS is to gain maximum utilization of the inter PABX channels by holding a connection for the shortest possible time. To this end simple calls encountering busy, etc, and certain supplementary service requests are immediately released by a backward clear request.

The layering of the protocol clearly facilitates enhancements. Should new requirements be identified, the protocol data unit repetoire (i.e. the scope of the signalling messages) can be augmented without impact on the method of their transmission. The initial message repetoire caters for all manner of telephony and data requirements amongst the basic of which are such protocol elements as 'initial service request message' (ISRM), 'number acknowledge message' (NAM), 'call connected message' (CCM) and 'clear request/indication message' (CRM/CIM).

Above the level 3 protocol resides the switching and routing application programs. It is quite evident that these programs could be enhanced (and the signalling repetoire extended, to cater for) such user requests as least cost delivery or expedited delivery (etc). Given the widespread range of services and disparate tariffs, the procedure for choosing the most cost effective transmission for a non-real time communication (e.g. document transfer) may probably be beyond the understanding, or will, of the user. The ISPBX network, invoking public services (e.g. telex, telematic and message handling systems) could invoke the routing algorithms, to facilitate these decisions.

2.4 The User Interface

The services made available by an ISPBX and the ISDN will normally be presented to a user's Network Terminating Equipment (NTE) as part of a 64Kbit/s + 64Kbit/s + 16Kbit/s basic access service, over a two wire local line. Alternatively, it may be part of a multi-line service affording thirty two 64Kbit/s channels (thirty of which are available for voice/data) carried by a 2.048 Mbit/s circuit. These are the basic attributes of the future ISPBX/ISDN.

However, functionality in the NTE will normally cater for the connection of data devices of incremental data rates up to 64Kbit/s synchronous or a 9.6Kbit/s asynchronous, besides, or in addition to, voice. The matching of these data rates with the core 64Kbit/s service requires adherence to a uniform rate adaption technique which features as part of the system implementation definition. (In these circumstances the lower rates nevertheless occupy a full 64Kbit/s channel.) Similar concepts will apply to that part of the 16Kbit/s signalling channel available for customer data.

These intentions are built into the draft recommendations seeking approval at the November 84 plenary of CCITT. 'Channels' is employed here in the sense that it represents the specified portion of the information carrying capacity of an interface, which may, in certain circumstances, be greater than the 'access capability', which details the data rate capacity actually available for communication purposes.

CCITT recognises, and future ISPBX and ISDN will provide, a number of channel types, of which type B and type D predominate. B channels are the primary information channels, affording a 64Kbit/s service for voice or data. The signalling function is not carried by these channels. It is the D channels that are primarily intended to carry signalling information, typically at 16Kbit/s for the basic access service, and 64Kbit/s for the primary rate (32 channel) access. However, the date rate occupancy of the signalling component is sufficiently modest that it is envisaged that the D channels may also encompass telemetry, messaging, and (relatively) low speed data. These culminate in proposed CCITT channel structures of

Basic access	2B+ D	(144Kbit/s)
Primary rate access	30B+ D	(2.048 Mbit/s including synchronisation channel)

The initial facilities afforded by ISPBXs and ISDN will involve the individual switching of the 64Kbit/s channels. The future intention is to switch a complete 'channel structure' -normally the 2.048 Mbit/s service - although considerations of frame sequencing and synchronisation will inhibit this intention on a wide scale for the immediate future. However, private networked ISPBXs will afford this capability considerably ahead of its general availability leading to considerations of teleconferencing and other high information rate services.

Interest in the B channel extends to its possible submultiplexing and super-multiplexing

1) Sub-multiplexing

The basic B channel bandwidth quantum of 64Kbit/s is considered by some as a wasteful allocation of bandwidth resource for many 'data' applications, and even for voice traffic derived from compression algorithms. As a result, a consensus has evolved that requires the possibility of sub-multiplexing the B channel. However, the signalling complexity that arises from this intent has not yet been resolved. Competing approaches involve the modification of the DPNSS/DASS fields, so that the additional signalling information is carried in the common signal channel or, alternatively, for additional signalling information to be carried in the sub-multiplexed fields. The latter erodes the sub-channels 'access capability'. These concepts lead to a possible additional complexity of higher level protocols that will enable would-be communicating devices to negotiate the optimum data rate for the particular transaction. All this leads to a third view, which believes that, in this circumstance at least, the conservation of bandwidth is an historical throwback, which does not merit the additional complexity.

2) Super-multiplexing

A contrary pressure, is for the B channels to be super-multiplexed to afford even wider-band services. Although video-phones do not appear to create any short term need, teleconferencing services are beginning to create a demand and there is more general need for bulk information transfer -typically, of computer-held files. The signalling requirements in this circumstance are less onerous than sub-multiplexing, but the technical complexity of retaining frame sequence and synchronisation over a number of channels does not yet benefit from an agreed solution. However, and as already mentioned, the new generation of integrated service PABXs networked over private wideband trunks are likely to offer a solution within a very short time scale.

3. NETWORKING

The overall goal in respect of present attitudes to networking is to achieve open systems interconnection - that is, devices and components of applications should be able to interconnect without concern to the characteristics of the underlying tele-communication services and functions. This is embodied in the scope and intent of the International Standards Organisation (ISO) open systems interconnection (OSI) basic reference model. Through joint discussions with ISO, CCITT are also actively involved with the OSI concept. OSI acknowledges a hierarchy of seven layers -physical, data link, network, transport, session, presentation and application to achieve this end. It is not intended here to attempt a rigorous treatment of the ISDN/ISPBX environment, in terms of the OSI basic reference model, but the discipline that the model imposes is an attractive vehicle for considering the various characteristics and attributes of the ISDN/ISPBX architecture.

3.1 Physical level

The physical level 'provides mechanical, electrical, functional and procedural means to activate, maintain and deactivate physical connections .....' It is thus couched in terms of V24 and X21 and the transmission techniques employed in the physical transfer of the (digitally encoded) information. Devices of the ISDN/ISPBX era will conform to a series of agreed reference points which in various combinations will enable a number of functional interfaces to be defined. These reference points are embodied in Fig. 2.0, which as a

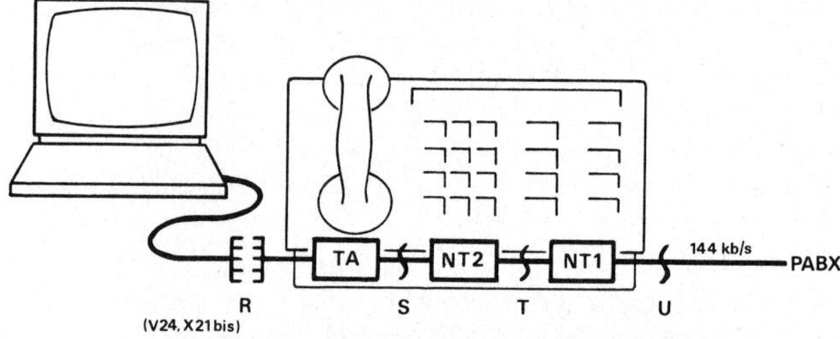

Fig 2.0 Network termination reference points with a possible first level implementation

background, depicts a possible first level physical implementation.

The device NT1 will normally be the line termination unit and many administrations may deem this as part of the administration (or network provider) monopoly supply. NT2 may or may not be present, but would normally represent some multiplexing/concentration function - a PABX would be an ultimate example. TA is a terminal adaptor and serves to match the interfaces of prevailing terminals (X21, V24, etc) to the transmission and signalling characteristics of the main (ISDN or ISPBX) network.

The commercial opportunities that follow from the reference point concept is the design flexibility that it permits. Proprietory devices can encompass different measures of the functionality embodied at the different reference points, thus providing a range of network terminating equipment (NTE). This can range from a fully featured telephony terminal with an integral data port (as in Fig 2.0), through to a sophisticated voice, graphics, messaging workstation. The physical arrangements and access protocols permit simultaneous employment of voice and data channels to separate destinations, whilst the layered structure makes no judgement as to the services that may be accessed from such a terminal device.

The transmission technique involved in the physical transfer of the bit stream will be dependant upon the local administration, or at the network providers prerogative. In the United Kingdom two methods - burst mode or echo cancellation are candidates. In burst mode the information is transmitted in high data rate blocks, with blocks time-interleaved in each direction. With echo cancellation a subtraction process segregates outbound and inbound data. Both methods permit full duplex working (64 + 64 + 16 Kbit/s) over twisted copper pairs, with burst mode catering for cable lengths of 1.5KM (or so) and echo-cancellation up to 5KM. Thus no special wiring is necessary to enable devices to be connected to the network, and the architectures have relevance to the commercial, industrial and domestic environment.

3.2 Link level and network level

The link level and network level, in hierachical manner, serve to provide the OSI Network Service. This enables any physical network to meet the intent of open systems interconnection and to be party to a general strategy for network interworking schemes. Although not a basic pre-requisite of the link level, some measure of error detection and correction, is normally included in that level, leading to an HDLC-like transmission protocol involving content framing or blocking. In this circumstance these two levels provide a reliable (in the error detection sense) cross-network routing and switching function independant of the characteristics of the communications media, in all things other than quality of service (which lies with the transport level). It has been recognised that the network level has (at least) two sublayers, one relating to the network protocols of the physical network with which it is associated (the communications service or sub-network sublayer) and the other supporting enhancement functions which support inter network protocols. These culminate in the OSI Network Service in the open systems environment.

The connection oriented (CO) Network Service is undergoing parallel development in ISO and CCITT. Although there are differences in the draft, the large extent of that which is common, has enabled a United Kingdom intercept recommendation* to be published. The role of would-be implementators is to determine what functions are needed above that offered by the real communications media to provide the OSI Network Services. These real networks are 'sub-networks' in the terminology of OSI. In the case of circuit switched regime without previous precedence the OSI network service could be implemented directly, but the most likely resolution is to enhance already defined protocols.

As the basic ISDN/ISPBX infrastructure only affords the physical level for the data channels, end-user systems, or gateways or the network terminating devices, will have to invoke link level and network layer protocols.

Contenders for the sub-network transport service implementation on an ISPBX/ISDN network could be X25 used as an enhancement protocol to the physical level entities, or X21, supplemented by HDLC to provide a data link service - as defined in recommendation S.70. To implement the OSI transport service above the sub-network sublayer, some elements of X25 may be restricted or extended (these provisions are detailed in the UK intercept recommendations). Similarly extension mechanisms

---

* an intercept recommendation represents the judgement of the Information Technology Standards Unit of the United Kingdom Department of Trade and Industry that an emerging national or international standard has reached sufficient maturity for it (or some subset of it) to be considered for use by manufacturers and implementators. It also makes judgement on preferred implementations where options or alternatives exist in the standard.

will be necessary to X21, particularly in the call establishment phase, in the X21/S.70 type of solution. Either route culminates in the provision, by the physical network entities of the OSI Network Service. The circumstance is depicted in Fig 3.0

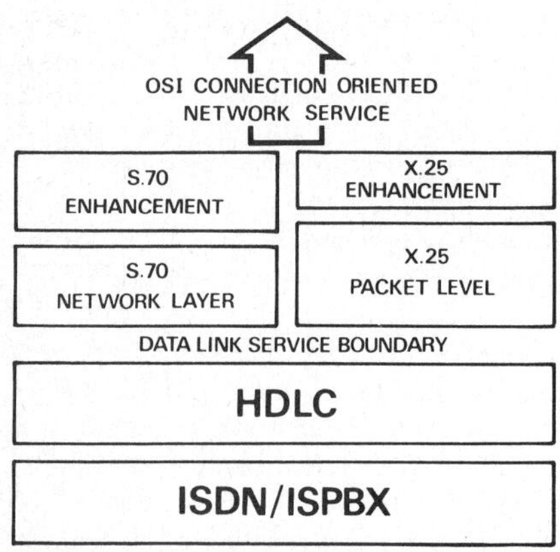

Fig 3.0 The OSI Network Service

3.3 Transport, Session and Presentation layers

Discussion on these network-independant higher layers of the OSI basic reference model are not within the scope of this paper. However, draft ISO international standards do exist, for two of these layers giving addional credence to the goal of comprehensive open system interconnection specifications. These ISO draft international standards which are included in the United Kingdom intercept recommendations, are:

Transport service	DIS 8072	Session service	DIS 8326
Transport protocol	DIS 8073	Session protocol	DIS 8327

The role of the presentation layer is currently the subject of discussion. However, the bit transparent service afforded by an ISPBX/ISDN network will require agreed protocols to interpret and present, the transmitted information in a manner meaningful to the application layer.

Application Layer

Although the network service provided by the physical entities should be entirely application independant, a number of applications may have more general relevance (in an end-user system sense) to an integrated networked service. One such topic is messaging. Discussions in CCITT SGVII have culminated in a series of recommendations for inter-personal message handling and these are in the throes of being adopted by ISO. These recommendations embrace a layered protocol in the application layer, comprising two sublayers - a message transfer sublayer and a user-agent sublayer above it. The message transfer sublayer provides a general message transfer service invoking the lower layers of the model whilst the higher sublayer invokes the protocol for an inter personal messaging service. The networking capabilities provided by DPNSS for a widespread inter connected PABX based network, particularly the desk-to-desk connection facility and the geographical independance of the connect point of services such as message handling facilities, may considerably facilitate the provision of the functional entities that will implement these application level protocols.

4. LOCAL AREA NETWORKS (LAN)

Baseband local area networks employ various contention control strategies in their architectures which make their suitability for interactive voice traffic, problematical. Broadband LANs can allocate channels and employ strategies amenable to voice traffic and could implement the functions of an ISPBX and invoke the network services featured in this paper. However, the cost effectiveness of installing a wideband physical media and the cost of interfacing to it, to implement a geographically embracing voice service, as yet, seems far from proven. Nevertheless, the basic tenet of this paper is technology independant (consistent with the OSI concept).

However, for the purpose of this paper, the emphasis in respect of LANs, relates to their predominant role of catering for anisochronous data.

These highway based local area networks have grown on the back of emerging technology and have been characterised by protocols and control strategies driven more by entrepreneurial flair, than by standards. Their success however has led to a need to achieve inter connection of these isolated (local area) networks, whose domain may be no greater than a suite of offices or laboratories.

Inter connection may be required within the confines of a site or campus, or between such geographical entities. The general environment is one in which some form of wide area network is likely to be involved. The case for the ISDN/ISPBX combination, or a privately networked ISPBX configuration to perform this role, is substantial.

The basic considerations of connecting LANs and ISPBX together relate to the disparity normally existing between the data rates of the two architectures, and the connection oriented circuit switched regime of the ISPBX and the connectionless datagram type of control strategy of the LAN. In any one particular circumstance some type of gateway solution can, at a cost, afford some measure of interconnection between them. However, commercial demand, and the goal of open systems interconnection, requires a more general solution.

This general solution can be expected to be based on the enhancement of the individual sub-system (PABX and LAN) protocols to the level of the OSI Network Service. However, the network service has two invocations - connection (circuit switched) oriented and connectionless (datagram) oriented. The general view prevails that where the sub network service is not of the same type as the overlaying Transport Service, conversion of the mode of operation should be performed within the network layer. As the pervading Transport Service afforded by public networks is a connection-oriented service, the foregoing considerations lead to the requirement that the LAN (in turn) should invoke a connection-oriented service (and not a connectionless service, which appears more basic to most LAN architecture). To this end, IEEE Project 802 acknowledges a Logical Link Control Class 2 (LLC-2) which combines the connectionless LLC-1 service with a connection-oriented Data-Link Service very similar to that provided by point-to-point HDLC. This is tantamount to a virtual circuit service over the LAN. Thus the two would-be-connected networks (LAN and PABX) can work in a connection-oriented environment. Their individual implementations of the data link service, or at least the implementation afforded by their associated gateways, termination points or in the end-user systems themselves, can then be augmented to the level of the OSI Network Service. Fig 4.0 shows candidates for this strategy. The network independent higher levels would rest on this common implementation of the Network Service, as shown in the figure.

Signalling is an additional component of the PABX-LAN interface. So far this has received fairly modest attention, although discussions are now underway in contemplating the extension of the DPNSS protocol elements to cater for the service requirements of such a link. The European view is that the DPNSS repertoire, and its relevance to modern wide area networks, is far richer than the CPI (Computer to PABX interface) protocol based on the 1.544Mbit/s T1 carrier system, proposed in North America.

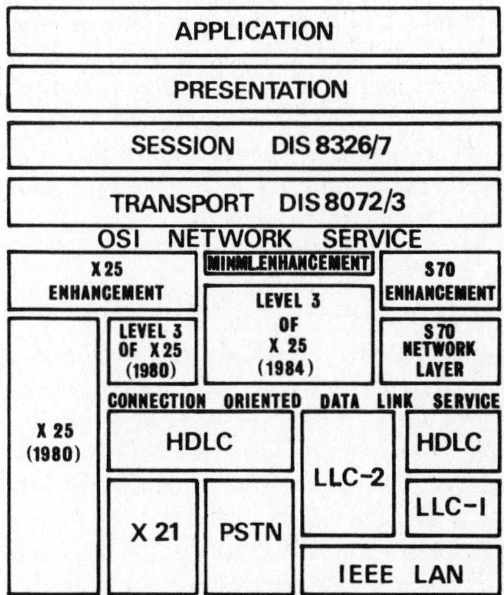

Fig 4.0 Internetwork layered model

Overall, the most general definition of the physical interface between a LAN and a PABX would be couched in terms of a data rate of 2.048Mbit/s, with signalling based on some derivative of the CCITT 'D' channel architecture, and with rate adaption consistent with CCITT Recommendation X.30.

The ISPBX/ISDN with its wide geographical pervasiveness not only offers the possibility of limited resort to successive frame fragmentation and re-combination (as would happen in a concatenation of dissimiliar networks) but might also serve to dictate the nature of a preferred LAN virtual circuit service.

5. ADDRESSING

The ISPBX/ISDN environment has the advantage of an internationally administered numbering plan. The CCITT Recommendation X.121 identifies a unique point of interface to public networks for all end user systems. In OSI parlance, however, it is a subnetwork address and needs to be augmented if this recommendation is to be considered as the basis of an OSI Network Address (which identifies a Network Service access point at the Network/Transport boundary). In fact, there is purpose in constructing Network Addresses from X.121 numbers, and the intent has general sympathy. In this circumstance, the Network Address will have to cater for the possibility of a layer of nested subnetworks. However, at the moment there is no international consensus on the addressing strategy to be employed. There is no agreement on the maximum length, structure or degree of flexibility to be incorporated into the address plan. However, the topic is uppermost in the minds of the various standardisation authorities - notably CCITT and ISO, and some strategy based on a prefix + X.121 number (or ISDN number) + further sub address component, appears most likely.

In the absence of additional, concatenated, subnetworks beyond the PABX (e.g. LAN's) the addressing regime is much simpler (although yet to be incorporated into an overall internationally agreed plan). End users, connected directly to a PABX/ISDN port, will already have a unique address. Additionally a number of the ISPBX 'voice' features would have direct relevance - such as cross network 'follow-me', 'diversion' and 'ring back when free'. All these attributes would be available to resource suppliers (e.g. applications) and resource users (e.g. human beings) irrespective of their connection point to the network. In particular the re-routing attributes such as 'follow me' and 'diversion' could retain mapping between naming (who) and addressing (where) in a wholly dynamic fashion.

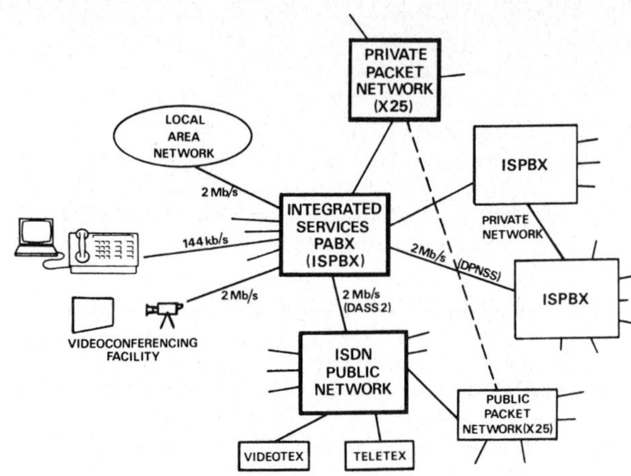

Fig 5.0 An integrated generalised network

6. COMMENT

In the commonality of the emerging ISDN (integrated services digital network) and the digital ISPBXs (integrated services private branch exchange) one is seeing a very powerful architecture developing, for the transport of all manner of digitally encoded information. With certain enhancements, such networks can offer the full functionality of the OSI Network Service. The substantially shared signalling protocols and procedures and the common topology and architecture, provide a geographically and facilities pervasive, generalised network. Equally so, similar protocols applied to dispersed ISPBXs connected by high bandwidth private digital circuits afford a private integrated communication system of very high utility - to which at best, highway-based local area networks are periphery to the core network. A schematic of the concept is depicted in Fig 5.0.

7. ACKNOWLEDGEMENTS

This paper augments the author's earlier paper 'PABX Networks - revisited', presented at the ITU 4th World Telecommunications FORUM (Geneva 1983), and acknowledgement is given to that occasion.

The author gratefully acknowledges the contribution of his colleagues at Plessey Office Systems Limited, and to the work of the Information Technology Standards Unit of the UK Government's Department of Trade and Industry.

The author is also grateful to the directors of Plessey Telecommunications and Office Systems Limited for permission to publish this paper.

A.J. Kingsmill is Product Line Manager - Data for Plessey Office Systems Ltd. He has a special interest in wide area and local area networks and is actively involved with ISO and BSI committees on text preparation and interchange.

DIGITAL TECHNIQUES in Simulation, Communication and Control
Spyros G. Tzafestas (editor)
Elsevier Science Publishers B.V. (North-Holland) © IMACS, 1985

A SIMULATION SYSTEM OF ANALOG AND DIGITAL TRANSMISSIONS

G. Benelli, V. Cappellini and E. Del Re

Dipartimento di Ingegneria Elettronica, Florence University and IROE-C.N.R.
Florence, Italy

A complete simulation package for communication systems is presented, including digital as well as analog operations to be performed on the signal to be transmitted. The transmitter, the communication channel and the receiver are simulated.
The digital transmission simulation considers data communication systems with digital filtering and source-channel coding. The analog transmission simulation includes the modulator, the transmitter pulse shaping filter, the communication channel, the receiving filter and the demodulator.
Digital simulation results are presented regarding some combination of the following techniques: digital filtering, predictive source coding, block codes able to correct random and burst errors, modulation techniques as AM, M-level PSK, FSK and MSK.

1. INTRODUCTION

The design and performance evaluation of a complete communication system is in practice very difficult, due to the great number of different parameters and subsystems that can be used and chosen. Some powerful methods are available for a theoretical analysis, but in many cases the computer simulation of a complete communication system as well as some of its parts is a convenient practical approach - and sometimes the only practical solution.

In this paper a complete communication-system simulation-package is described for both analog and digital transmissions. The package simulates the transmitter, the communication channel and the receiver. The input signal can be either analog or digitized analog or digital data. The simulation of data communication systems includes the operations of digital filtering, source and channel coding and decoding. The package includes also the simulation of the modulator, the transmitter pulse shaping filter, the physical transmission channel, the receiving filter and the demodulator. This part is very general, so that it allows the simulation of both analog and digital transmissions. It operates both in the time domain and in the frequency domain (through the suitable use of the fast Fourier transform - FFT algorithm).

Digital simulation results are given regarding some of the above operations and techniques, in particular considering modulation techniques such as AM, M-level PSK, FSK and MSK.

2. GENERAL ORGANIZATION OF THE SIMULATION SYSTEM

The general structure of the simulation system is shown in Figure 1. The system consists of an input section, a processing section and an output section [1].

The input section can deal with both analog signals and digital data. Analog signals are first sampled and quantized. The sampling frequency, the number of quantization bits and the quantization law (as linear or non-linear quantization) can be arbitrarily chosen according to the characteristics of the signal and the transmission system to be analyzed. The digital signal is stored in an intermediate memory (as the computer magnetic tape or disk).

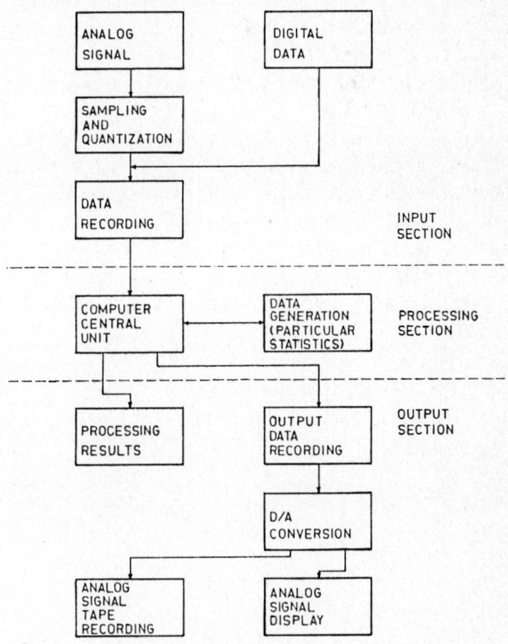

Figure 1 : General structure of the simulation system

The processing section includes the computer central unit, that reads and processes in a suitable way the stored digital information in order to simulate the transmission system to be analyzed. The computer may also generate particular data patterns with specified statistics and variable length in order to simulate some desired random data or signals (as for the modeling of noise in the analog communication channel and of random and burst errors in digital transmission).

The results of the computer processing are supplied to the output section. Here the results can be directly presented in output, as those concerning the overall performance (as the error statistics and/or the signal-to-noise ratios) of transmission systems, or can be stored in an intermediate memory. After an appropriate digital--to-analog conversion, the output section can supply the analog signal suitable for a tape recording and for a direct display.

3. PROCESSING SECTION

The block-diagram of the whole processing section is shown in Figure 2. From the input section, the stored version of the input signal is read first.

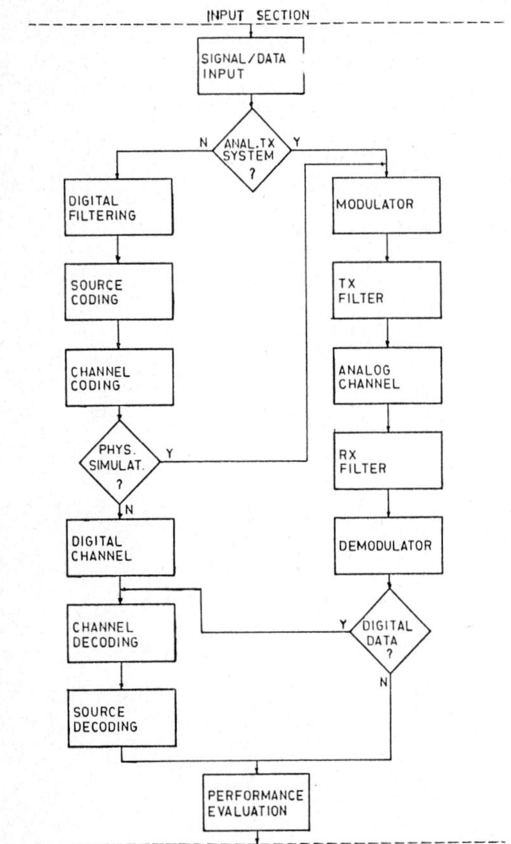

Figure 2 : Processing section block-diagram

In the case of digital transmission simulation, the processing section can perform the operations of digital filtering, source coding and channel coding. Hence two possible alternatives can occur and be simulated. In the first one (logical simulation) only the two-state (0 and 1) digital stream of data is of interest in any point of the transmission system (in other words only the logic value of the digital data has to be considered and simulated). In this case the simulation system requires a pure digital channel. After the digital channel simulation, the channel and source decoding operations at the digital receiver are performed. In the second alternative (physical simulation) the waveform of the transmitted digital signal is of interest and therefore must be simulated (this is the case, for instance, when baseband or modulated digital transmission must be analyzed). Therefore, the simulation system requires the modulator to shape the digital data, the transmission filter, the analog channel, the receiver filter and the demodulator. At this point digital data are again obtained at the receiver and must be decoded as in the previous case.

When analog transmission systems must be analyzed, after having received the digitized input signal, the processing section simulates the transmitter-channel-receiver chain by means of the same processing blocks as shown in Figure 2. Of course, after the demodulator, in this case, no channel and source decoding operations have to be performed.

At the end of this simulation procedure, the recovered digital data or digitized analog signal at the receiver output are processed to obtain meaningful parameters for system performance evaluation, and can be compared with the system input data or signal to obtain, for instance, the statistics of the error rate of digital transmission systems and the signal-to-noise ratios for analog transmission systems.

Each block of Figure 2 corresponds to a program package with standardized input and output interfaces to communicate with other blocks. This allows a great flexibility in the actual system configuration and use.

Further the structure shown in Figure 2 is able to simulate the most general transmission systems of interest. Of course, it can be easily adapted to particular systems having a simpler structure: any block but the decision blocks can be bypassed without affecting the operations of the other blocks.

In the following the blocks performing the simulation of digital and analog transmission systems are described.

3.1 Digital Transmission simulation

The simulation of a digital transmission system includes the operations of digital filtering, source coding and decoding (data compression), channel coding and decoding, and the effects of the digital transmission channel when the simulation of the physical channel is not of interest.

For what regards the digital filtering, both finite-impulse-response (FIR) and infinite-impulse-response (IIR) digital filters can be simulated [2] . From an implementation point of view, several structures can be simulated: the direct form, the cascade form, the frequency-sampling structure. Once the filter structure has been chosen, the program reads the structure parameters as external data.

As source coding and decoding, many methods can be simulated: algorithms using prediction or interpolation, in particular adaptive linear prediction (ALP); differential pulse code modulation (DPCM), delta modulation (DM); methods using digital transformations (FFT or fast Walsh transform - FWT) [3] .

For what concerns channel coding and decoding, block codes (in particular cyclic codes) and convolutional codes (with threshold or sequential decoding) can be simulated. It is of particular interest, in connection with channel coding-decoding, to consider the characteristics of the noise introduced by the communication channel: binary symmetric channel (BSC) as memory-less channel or Gilbert channel as channel with memory (described using a Markov chain with two states).

Integrated forms of data compression and channel coding can also be simulated. An interesting form of this type is represented by a special technique in which the time information added to compressed data is used in reception for error control [4] .

3.2 Analog Transmission Simulation

In the simulation of modulated signals, it is often convenient to deal with an equivalent baseband model to reduce computation time and sample number.

Different modulation methods can be simulated, such as PSK and MSK modulation. A PSK modulated signal can be written in the form

$$s(t)=\sqrt{2E}\cos(\omega_0 t+\phi_k), \qquad kT \le t \le (k+1)T \tag{1}$$

where E is the average power of the signal, ϕ_k is 0 or π if the kth data d_k to be transmitted is 0 or 1, respectively, and T is the symbol interval. An MSK modulated signal can be written as

$$s(t)=\sqrt{2E}\cos(\omega_0 t+\frac{\pi}{2T}d_k t+\alpha_k) \tag{2}$$

where the constants α_k are determined in such a way as to obtain a phase continuity at the end of the signaling intervals

$$\alpha_k=\alpha_{k-1}+(d_{k-1}-d_k)\frac{k\pi}{2} \tag{3}$$

$$\alpha_0=0$$

Other modulations considered are quaternary PSK (QPSK) and FSK for data transmission and amplitude modulation for the transmission of analog signals.

In the simulation chain of Figure 2, including the modulator, the transmission filter, the analog channel, the receiving filter and the demodulator, the signals are generally represented by their equivalent baseband model (baseband representation). An exception to this computationally efficient approach for the signal representation is when dealing with non-linear operations.

The block-diagram of the program package usually employed in the simulation of analog transmission systems is shown in Figure 3. The simulation of the transmission filter, the analog channel and the receiving filter is carried out in the frequency domain through the appropriate use of the FFT algorithm. The software organization of Figure 3 is able to simulate linear transmission systems and channels with additive-type noise. This is by far the most frequent case. In the few cases where non-linear operations are involved in some part of the signal path (for example, in the presence of a non-li-

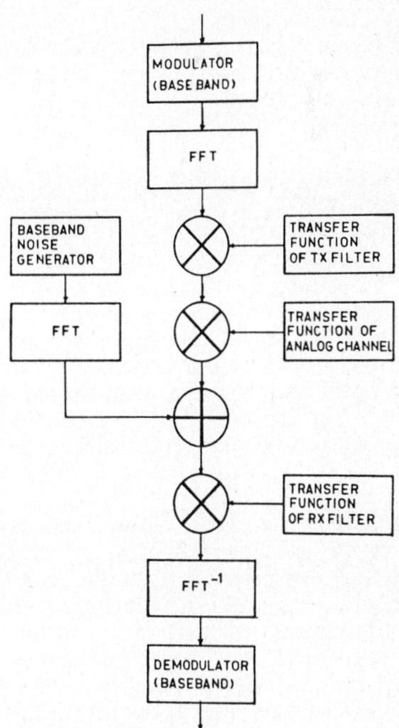

Figure 3 : Block-diagram of the analog transmission simulation

near channel), the corresponding simulation package operates in the time domain: this is easily obtained including an inverse FFT transformation at the package input and a direct FFT transformation at the package output, after the time domain non-linear simulation. Generally, in this case, the simulation operations cannot be performed on the baseband signal representation and require the recovery of the signal in the correct modulated form.

3.3 Performance Evaluation

The performance evaluation of analog or digital transmission systems is carried out in the corresponding block of Figure 2, after the analog signal has been demodulated or the digital data have been decoded.

For analog transmission the following parameters are generally computed:
- received signal mean power, evaluated without the addition of the channel noise;
- received noise mean power, evaluated without transmission signal;
- mean and peak error signals, where the error signal is defined as the difference between the received and transmitted signals (as preferred, the system output signal in the presence or in absence of channel noise can be considered as the received signal).

For digital transmission the following parameters are evaluated:
- probability of error of the received data;
- compression ratio C_a, defined as the ratio of the number of bits of the input signal to the number of the received bits (when source coding is included);
- mean and peak error signals (defined as before), when the transmission of digitized analog signals is simulated.

4. EXAMPLES OF APPLICATION OF THE SIMULATION SYSTEM

In this section we present some results obtained from the simulation package previously described. In particular the results refer to two different communication schemes. The first scheme simulates the digital part of a communication system, including data compression operations and channel coding. The second scheme simulates a complete communication chain, including the analog section.

The first scheme was considered to evaluate the performance of data compression in noisy conditions and its integration with the channel coding operation [4] . To characterize the performance of systems of this type, four structures were simulated: uncompressed-uncoded (UU), compressed-uncoded (CU), uncompressed-coded (UC) and compressed-coded (CC). For all these cases, the compression ratio C_a and the rms error ε (as percentage of the full scale signal) were obtained. In the CU and CC systems, ε includes the distortion introduced by the compression error and the channel noise. To show the different influence of these two error types, the rms error due only to the channel noise was also computed. The results considering only the distortion introduced by the channel noise are denoted with asterisk.

The algorithm utilized for data compression is the zero-order-predictor (ZOP). The code of burst error correction is a Samoylenko binoid code (90,80) defined in a Galois field GF(31). In the binary transmission the code is of the type (450,400) and is able to correct all the bursts of length 21 bits or less. The communication channel is simulated using the Gilbert model, which describes approximately the behaviour of some channels with memory, as telephone channels. The transmitted signal, which is an electrocardiogram (ECG), is first processed using a third-order low-pass digital filter. The resulting rms error ε versus the channel error probability P_e is shown in Figure 4. Data compression using time information representing the number of non-transmitted samples is denoted with the index 1, while data compression with time information identifying the absolute position in the frame of the transmitted samples is denoted with the index 2. For high P_e the error ε is mainly determined by the channel noise while the influence of the compression distortion is negligible. By reducing P_e, the importance of the compression errors becomes higher and higher.

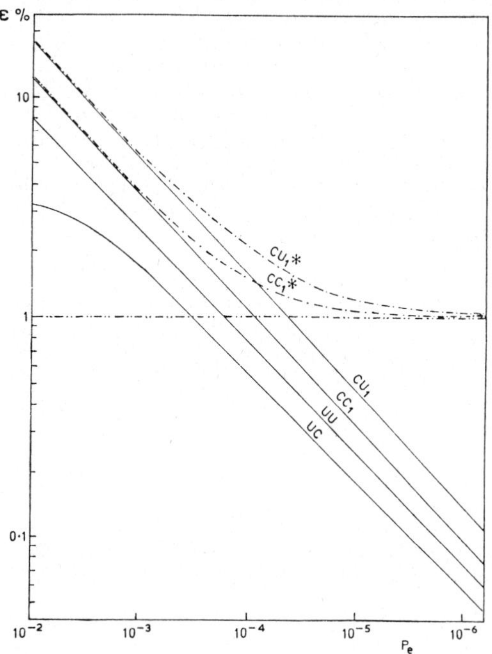

Figure 4 : The rms error ε versus P_e

The following compression ratio values were obtained for the different structures

UU	UC	CU_1	CU_2	CC_1	CC_2
1	0.89	3.07	2.6	2.73	2.16

The second scheme is a communication system for the simultaneous transmission of voice and data using the same carrier. The voice signal is transmitted by modulating the carrier amplitude, while the data signal modulates the phase of the same carrier [5] . This scheme was studied for the introduction of a data link between aircraft and ground stations through a simple and economical implementation. The digital modulations utilized for data transmission are binary PSK (BPSK), quaternary PSK (QPSK), FSK and MSK. The band-pass filters in the communication chain are modeled as Butterworth filters with the following characteristics:

- transmit filter: fourth order, with -3 dB single-side bandwidth 7.5 kHz;
- receive filter: eighth order, with -3 dB single-side bandwidth 5 kHz.

They are implemented in the frequency domain. The signal is processed in blocks of 2048 samples, the sampling frequency being 19200 Hz.

Figure 5 shows some obtained results, regarding the signal-to-noise ratio (dB) versus the bit rate v_s for the cases in which the signal, modulating the carrier amplitude, is a tone at 937.5 Hz (curves (a)), at 1875 Hz (curves (b)) and the sum of five tones from 468.75 to 2343.75 Hz (curves (c)). Further the modulation index is assumed equal to 0.8. These results confirm the actual capability of the hybrid modulation system of transmitting both the analog voice and the data on the same carrier with a negligible interference, especially at low bit rate (300-600 bits/s). This communication solution appears therefore practically attractive, especially for small aircrafts, due to the minimal modifications required for the on-board equipments (only the addition of the data modulator) and ground stations.

In conclusion, the performed tests confirm the good performance of the developed simulation system.

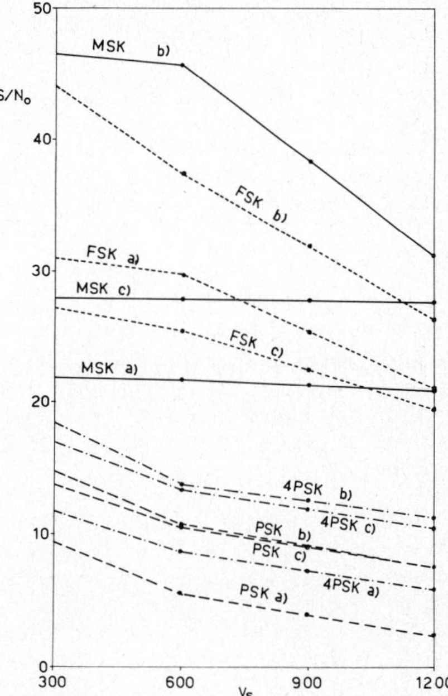

Figure 5 : Signal-to-noise ratio (dB) versus v_s

REFERENCES

[1] Benelli, G., Cappellini, V. and Del Re, E., Simulation system for analog and digital transmissions, IEEE J. on Selec. Areas in Communications, vol. SAC-2, n. 1 (1984) 77-88.

[2] Cappellini, V., Constantinides, A.G. and Emiliani, P., Digital Filters and Their Applications (Academic Press, London-New York, 1978).

[3] Benelli, G., Cappellini, V. and Lotti, F., Data compression techniques and applications, Proc. IERE, vol. 50 (1980) 29-53.

[4] Benelli, G., Cappellini, V. and Del Re, E., Integrated data communication systems with data compression and error correcting codes, in Skwirzynski, J.K. (ed.), Communication Systems and Random Process Theory (Sijthoff & Noordhoff, Alphen aan den Rijn, 1978).

[5] Benelli, G. and Fantacci, R., An integrated voice-data communication system for VHF links, IEEE Trans. Comm., vol. COM-31 (1983) 1304-1308.

DIGITAL TECHNIQUES in Simulation, Communication and Control
Spyros G. Tzafestas (editor)
Elsevier Science Publishers B.V. (North-Holland) © IMACS, 1985

A µP-CONTROLLED SYSTEM FOR TRAFFIC DATA ACQUISITION AND PROCESSING IN ELECTROMECHANICAL TELEPHONE EXCHANGES

D.Lymberopoulos, G.Kokkinakis

Laboratory of Wire Communications, School of Engineering,
University of Patras, Patras, Greece

This paper presents a µP-controlled system which can cost-effectively upgrade conventional electromechanical exchanges in the areas of circuits supervision, traffic data acquisition and traffic data processing. The system is capable of monitoring a big number of individual circuits (up to 2000 in a full capacity design), of acquiring detailed traffic data and processing these data automatically.
A version of the system already constructed, monitors 200 subscriber lines. This will soon be connected in exchanges of the local network of Patras to collect traffic data from different subscriber groups.

I. INTRODUCTION

Modern stored program controlled (SPC) exchanges possess automatic acquisition and processing of the data concerning the usage of individual circuits. As a result, detailed information on the statistics of the traffic carried out by each circuit is obtained, which is valuable for the appropriate use of existing equipment,the design of new equipment, etc. Furthermore defective circuits not carrying traffic, the so called "killer trunks" are easily detected [1].

On the contrary, conventional electromechanical exchanges are equipped with traffic recording apparatus which provides only limited and global traffic data. Also, there is no automatic acquisition and processing of these data.

This paper presents a µP-controlled system which can cost-effectively upgrade electromechanical exchanges in the areas of circuit supervision, traffic data acquisition and traffic data processing. The system is capable of monitoring a big number of individual circuits through scanning (up to 2000 in a full capacity design) and collects the data defining the separate seizures of each circuit in the measuring period. The system can be connected to any incoming or outgoing trunks of an exchange, to trunks between selector stages or to subscriber trunks [2,3].

A version of the system which we have constructed in the Lab. of Wire Communications, monitors 200 subscriber lines by scanning the status (busy or idle) of the a-wires and records for each line:

i. the time of the beginning and the end of successive seizures
ii. the duration of each seizure and the duration between seizures
iii. the two first dialled digits in outgoing local calls and the four first digits in outgoing DDD-calls.

Recording of the called number has been restricted to two or four digits, although the whole number could be recorded as well, since these digits are sufficient for the purpose to which the system is designed, i.e. the investigation of subscribers´traffic. Also, only the a-wire is scanned although both the a-and-c-wires could be scanned, due to some dificulties in accessing the c-wires in the exchanges in which the system will be used. Thus, a subscriber´s incoming traffic must be indirectly distinguished from the outgoing traffic, a fact that causes a small error in the calculated values.

The recorded data are transferred every 15 min. from the processor´s RAM to a floppy disc and later to a desk-top calculator for processing. A transfer to a printer is also provided. From the data processing, the following information is taken:

a. The distribution of incoming and outgoing traffic of each line in the measuring period and the distributions of the whole subscriber trunk
b. The busy hour of the trunk
c. The mean duration of seizures
d. The number of successful and unsuccessful outgoing calls
e. The number of a subscriber´s repeat attempts
f. The outgoing traffic to each direction of the local and DDD-network.

The system has already been tested in the laboratory and will soon be connected in exchanges of the local network of Patras, to collect data from different subscriber groups.

In the following,the system´s hardware architecture and operation, the packaging, the software and the further development are described.

II. HARDWARE ARCHITECTURE AND OPERATION OF THE SYSTEM

The system consists of three functional blocks, as it is seen in its block diagram (fig.1):
The control, containing two microprocessors the subscriber interfaces, which are common to both processors and the peripheral equipment for data storage and processing.

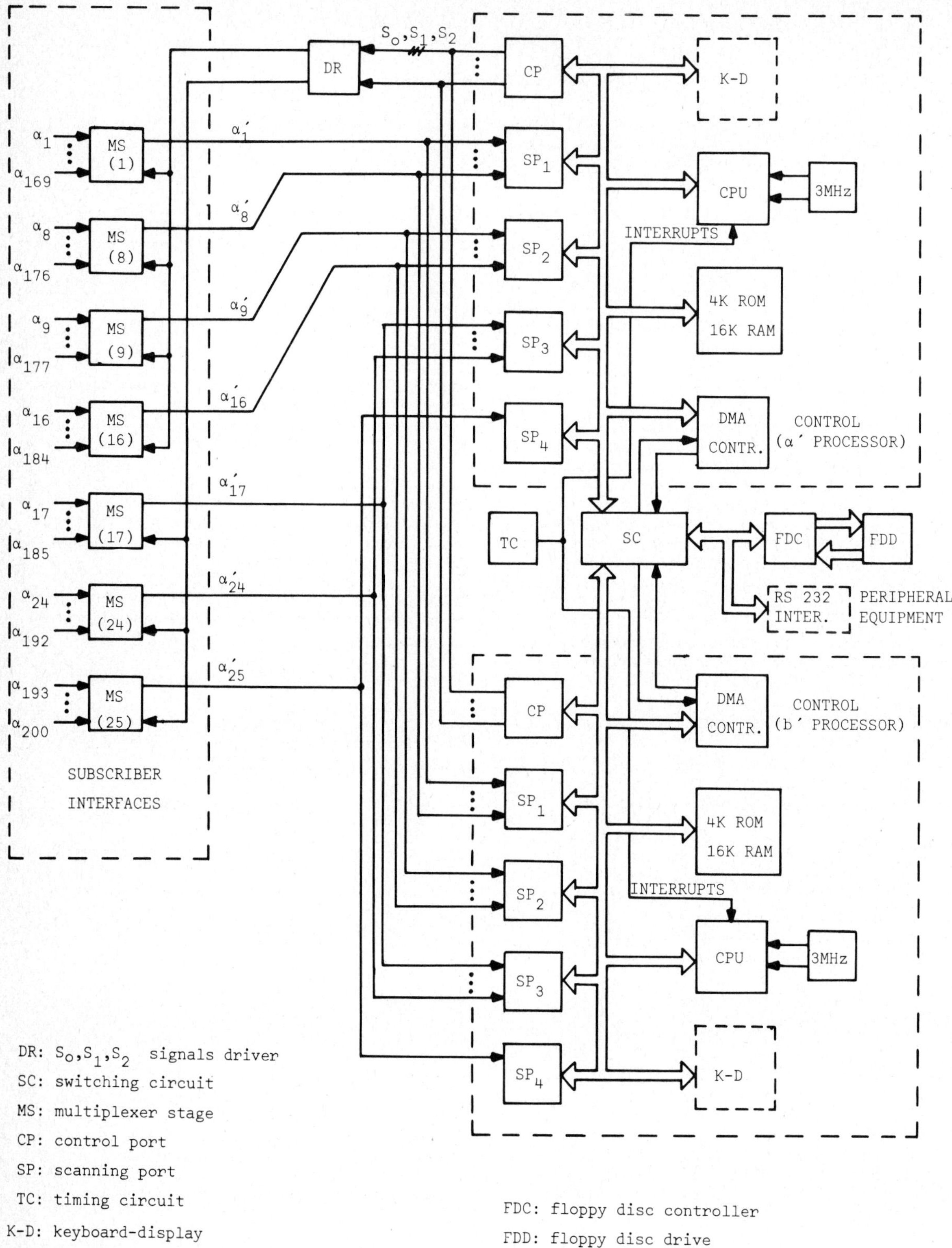

Figure 1: System block diagram

The interfaces between every subscriber´s a-wire and the control are performing the necessary voltage and current adaptation between the electromechanic and the electronic equipment. The interface (fig.2) is designed for minimal current consumption from the a-wire in order to avoid any disturbance of the exchange. As it is seen, there are two independent power supplies with independent grounds (-6V for the exchange side and +5V for the control) and in connection with the opto-

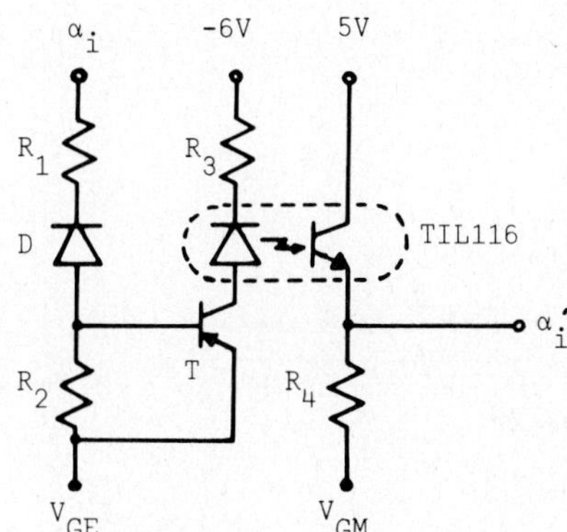

α_i: subscriber´s loop potential

α_i': subscriber´s interface output

V_{GE}: exchange ground

V_{GM}: microcomputer ground

Figure 2: Subscriber´s interface (SI)

coupler a full separation between the interface´s input and output is achieved. Moreover, the whole design ensures a reliable functioning of the interface, eliminating the effects of pulse distorions, spikes, etc. Nevertheless, if during the scanning of dial pulses a pulse gets lost, this is recognized and corrected by an appropriate software [4].

Eight subscriber interfaces are connected to a multiplexer, (fig.3), eight multiplexers are connected to a port (fig.1). The signals S_o,S_1,S_2 to a multiplexer are delivered from a control port and define which input α_1' to α_8' is read as output α''.

Each processor consists of a CPU 8085A of Intel Co., 4K ROM, 16K RAM, a DMA controller to achieve the necessary speed by the data transfer to the floppy disc, a switching circuit which connects the bus of each processor to the interface of the floppy disc controller (FDC) during the data transfer and, finally, a special connector for the connection of a keyboard with display.

The peripheral equipment consists of a floppy disk drive (FDD), a keyboard-display and a desktop calculator. As floppy disc drive the model 848 of TANDON Co, has been used, which possesses

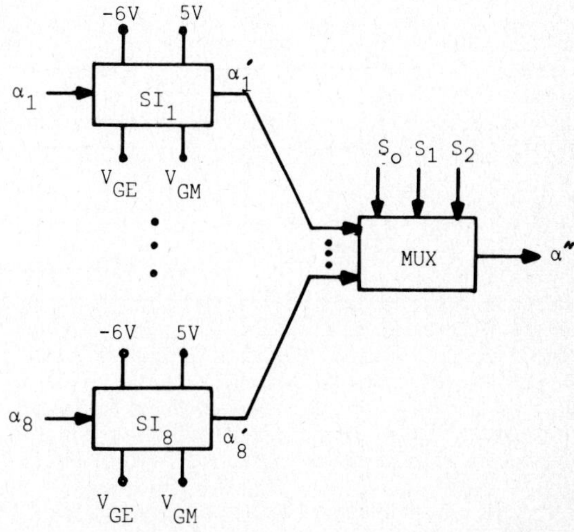

MUX: multiplexer

α': multiplexer output

S_o,S_1,S_2: multiplexer control signals

Figure 3: Multiplexer stage connection

double density recording capability on an 8´ discette and 1.2 Mb informated memory. As floppy disc controller the 8272 of Intel Co. is used and as DMA controller the 8257 of the same company, which is using the µP´s clock. The FDC-interface includes a 2K ROM, containing the programs of the chips 8272 and 8275 [5].

The floppy disc data are processed on desk-top calculator HP9845B.

The system has a power supply: 220V /+5,-6,+24, ±12V.

The scanning is controlled successively by the two microprocessors. A µP is active during 15 min. controlling the scanning, while the other is performing some tasks and then stands by. The tasks are compression of the data stored in the previous 15 min in its RAM and transfer of these data to the floppy disc. This takes less than 5 min. In the remaining 10 min. the processor executes the scanning programs without writting in its 16K RAM. So, it is ready to assume the scanning from the other processor when 15 min. are reached. In case that dialling falls in the change over, the second processor continuous the recording of pulses in its memory. The whole number is later reconstructed from all data written in the two processor memories.

Scanning of the a-wires is performed every 30ms. Thus, the minimum duration of dial pulses (40ms) is covered. The samples are guided through the multiplexers and the ports to the active processor and are stored in memory places provided for each subscriber.

Two times are stored between two successive line seizures: The occupation time of the line and the time till the next seizure. For the recording of these times 4 bytes are given to any subscriber (2 bytes for each time).

For the recording of the 2 or 4 digits of the dialled number in case of an outgoing call, two more bytes are provided to each subscriber. Thus, 6 bytes are maximally needed for the recording of a call. To each subscriber 60 bytes are provided, which are sufficient for up to 10 call recordings per 15 min. For the 200 subscribers 12K RAM is occupied. If a subscriber exceeds the limit of 10 calls he is given another 60 bytes for 10 more calls. But this possibility can be given only to a limited number of subscribers.

The place of each subscriber´s memory in the 12K RAM block is indicated by an appropriate address. These addresses are stored in a memory, with 8 bytes per subscriber or 1.6K RAM for all subscribers. It must be noted that the subscribers´ addresses are changed during scanning, depending on the calls each subscriber is dialling and receiving. This memory is used by the scanning programs. The status of each line (busy or idle) is held there in special places.

Another RAM of 1.2K (6 bytes per subscriber) is used by the time measuring program, which scans the lines every 1 sec. and records the times of seizures, etc. This memory receives the status of the lines from the 1.6K RAM, before each running of the time measuring program.

III. PACKAGING

The above mentioned components are mounted on 36 double sided cards, as follows:

- One intefaces of 8 subscribers and their multiplexer on a (18x9 cm) card. There are 25 such cards for the 200 subscribers.
- One CPU 8085A with 4K ROM and 3 Ports on a (18x11 cm) card. Two such cards are serving the two CPU´s.
- The 16Kb RAM on a (18x11 cm) card. There are two such cards.
- One DMA controller and 6 ports on one (18x11 cm) card. There are two such cards.
- On single cards
  - . the floppy disc inteface with 2K ROM (18x15 cm)
  - . the timer and drivers (18x10 cm)
  - . the keyboard and display (20x15 cm)
  - . the RS 232 bus interface (18x10 cm)

There are 8 different card types. All cards are mounted on a 40x60x42 cm rack, together with the floppy disc drive and the power supply. A fan is also incorporated, to ensure the appropriate cooling of the system during high environment temperatures (figures 4, 5, 6).

IV. THE SOFTWARE

The programs executed by each processor are divided into three categories:

i. Initialization programs
ii. Data acquiring programs
iii. Data compression and floppy disc storage programs.

a. Initialization Programs

These programs perform all the operations which are necessary to start data acquirement from the subscriber lines. There are three main programs performing:

i. The writting of each subscriber´s address in the 1.6K address RAM.
ii. The writting of the addresses in the 1.2K RAM used by the time measuring program.
iii. The formatting of the discette by the floppy disc interface in order to be ready for data storage.

b. Data acquiring programs

These programs perform the operations of collecting the data from the subscriber lines and storing them in the processor´s RAM. There are three programs:

i. The basic operation program is supervising and coordinating the operation of the two processors.

Figure 4: Front side Figure 5: Front side (open) Figure 6: Rear side (open)

ii. The scanning program scans the lines every 30 ms and records their status and the digits of the dialled number. It consists of two independent subroutines A_0 and A_1, which are called when the line´s potential is 0 Volts and -60 Volts respectively.

iii. The time measuring program is executed every 1 sec. and records the occupation times and the times between occupations. To this purpose it requires the current status of the lines. This is taken, by a small status updading subroutine, from the 1.6 address RAM, immediately before the time measuring program´s execution.

The scanning and time measuring programs are initiated by interrupts. While these programs are executed, the execution of the basic operation program is interrupted. The time measuring program is executed in the period of 30 ms between two successive scannings, immediately after the execution of the scanning program and the status updating subroutine.

c. Data compression and storage program

These programs perform a data compression and then the transfer of the data to the floppy disc:

i. The compression program arranges the calls of the subscribers realized in a period of 15 min. one after another, eliminating the memory places not used. Special coded numbers are designating the beginning and the end of each subscriber´s calls, so that they can be distinguished during processing. This compression is necessary in order to save recording place in the discette.

ii. The storage program transfers the data from a processor´s RAM to the floppy disc.

The above three categories of programs are executed during the measurements in the electromechanical exchange. The data stored on the floppy disc are then transferred to the peripheral memory of HP-9845B calculator by another program, using the keyboard, the display and the RS232 interface. The processing of the data is performed on the HP-9845B.

V. FURTHER DEVELOPMENT

In the previous sections a system was presented which records in detail the traffic of 200 subscriber lines. Preserving the basic design and using similar hardware, this system can be modified to serve more or fewer lines and other purposes. Some applications which we are considering for development are:

i. Monitoring of up to 2000 individual lines in junction trunks both for maintenance purposes and traffic recordings.

ii. Monitoring of up to 2000 individual subscriber lines for traffic recordings.

iii. Monitoring of up to 1000 subscriber lines for detailed ticketing.

These systems can costeffectively upgrade electromechanical exchanges in the area of data acquiring and processing, since both functions are performed automatically by electronic equipment assembled with off-the shelf components.

CONCLUSION

Conventional electromechanical exchanges can be costeffectively upgraded in the areas of circuits supervision, traffic measurement and detailed ticketing with μP controlled equipment, as the one presented above. This equipment can be tailored to cover specific needs in respect to capacity and functions performed.

ACKNOWLEDGMENT

The authors wish to thank Mr. Constantin Falangaras, OTE-Engineer, for his contribution in the design of the subscriber´s interface.

REFERENCES

1. Georg Daisenberger, Joseph Reger und Gerhard Wegmann, "Verkehrsmessung und- überwachung ein Hilfs mittel für Planung und Betrieb von Fernsprech-Vermittlungsstellen und - netzen", Telcom report 4 (1981), Heft 3, s.222-232

2. "Data Capture and Control for Network Management", Telecommunications, Sept.1980, p.66-69

3. Rudolf Baumann und Bernd-Uwe Langnickel, "Verkehrsregistrier-und-analyseeinrichtung VERAN, ein neues Fernsprech-Verkehrsmeßsystem bei der Deutschen Bundespost",Telcom report 4 (1981) Heft 1. s.50-57

4. M. Koukias, D. Lymberopoulos, G. Kokkinakis, "Microprocessor applications to telephone traffic measurements", IASTED, ICD 82, TUNIS Conf. Proc. vol. 1, p.p. 19.1-19.4

5. "An Intelligent Data Base System Using the 8272", Application Note AP-116, INTEL Co.

DIGITAL TECHNIQUES in Simulation, Communication and Control
Spyros G. Tzafestas (editor)
Elsevier Science Publishers B.V. (North-Holland) © IMACS, 1985

IMPLEMENTATION OF A 2400 BIT/S DATA MODEM ON DIGITAL SIGNAL MICROPROCESSOR

J.Y. FORET, E. CARMES, J.P. VORSANGER, J.P. LE BARON

LABORATOIRE D'AUTOMATIQUE
INSTITUT NATIONAL DES SCIENCES APPLIQUEES
35043 RENNES CEDEX

Keywords : Application of Digital Signal Processing, Telecommunications, Filtering.

This paper describes the implementation of a 2400 bit/s data modem on the NEC 7720 signal microprocessor. The modem is fully compatible with the CCITT recommendations V 26 bis. This implementation is not possible on a classical microprocessor because of the too long cycle time of these devices. The arrival of microprocessors specialized in digital signal processing has allowed the study of such implementations. The performances of the new processors are obtained by a multi-bus structure. A parallel processing of several operations decreasing the cycle time to about 250 ns is made possible by the integration of memories, a 16 bit arithmetic and logic unit, a separated 16 x 16 bit fully parallel multiplier and specialized functions on the same chip. The characteristics of the 2400 bit/s modem have been defined, for the first time, in simulation with the Computer Aided Design SIRENA on a 16 bits Hewlett-Packard computer. The results of these simulations have been the starting point of the implementation on a microprocessor NEC 7720.

The use of only one processor for the transmitter and the receiver compelled us to manage judicious by the different inputs and outputs of the chip so as to require no additional hardware. We fixed ourselves two essential aims for the software : a modular realization of the programs and a minimal execution time. The two ends can be reached by making a good choice of memory data address implementation and by writing a subroutine for each primary function in the modem. In emission, the modem includes a four state differential modulator allowing the generation of a signal modulated by the binary input. A 12 bits digital-analog converter, followed by a low-pass filter limiting the modulated signal spectrum are used before transmitting the signal on a telephone line. After going through the telephone line, the received signal is treated by an unoverlap filter before being applied to an analog-digital converter. Then, the signal spectrum is limited to the transmission channel band by a band-pass filter and corrected by a linear equalizer which suppresses the amplitude and phase distorsions. The signal variations in the time domain are corrected by an automatic digital gain control. After these corrections, the signal is demodulated in a differential way, then filtered by a low-pass filter to obtain the detected signal. The decision is taken on this signal and the corresponding data is extracted synchronously with the received baud rate clock.

INTRODUCTION

Until now, the numerical modem realization came up against semiconductor technology difficulties (speed limitations, precision of numerical calculations, memory capacity, etc...). The advent of LSI processors for digital signal processing bring in interesting solutions for communication equipments and we have developed new methods to design and implement a 2400 bit/s data modem. The modem functions have been defined with the Computer Aided Design SIRENA on a 16 bits Hewlett-Packard computer. This CAD system allows the study of binary data communication equipments [1],[2]. The results of the 2400 bit/s data modem simulation (respecting international V 26 bis CCITT normalisation) with the transmission channel (modelled by a transfer function) have been the starting point of the implementation on the NEC 7720 microprocessor. Besides the compatibility with the CCITT recommendations, the major design objective is to have both transmitter and receiver functions realized by a NEC 7720 unit only. In this paper, the results of the implementation of a 2400 bit/s modem will be discussed in terms of hardware, software, speed, and so on, after a short presentation of the NEC 7720 microprocessor and the modem structure.

DESCRIPTION OF THE NEC 7720 SIGNAL PROCESSOR

1. Hardware

The general architecture of the NEC 7720 signal processor in composed of three different blocks :
- program and data memories,
- calculating unit,
- inputs and outputs.

A multi-bus structure allows to obtain simultaneously two data from various sources (either two from RAM or one from RAM and the other from data ROM, etc...).

2. Program Memory

The program memory (ROM or EPROM) has a capacity of 512 words. The word length is of 23 bits to store the microinstruction. The address of the instruction to be executed is given by a 9 bits program counter associated with a stack of 4 words.

3. Data Memory

The data memory is divided into two independent parts :

- a data ROM (512 words of 13 bits),
- a RAM (128 words of 16 bits).

The word length of the data ROM satisfies almost every possible coefficient accuracy requirement.

4. Calculating Unit

The calculating unit is composed of an arithmetic and logical unit (ALU) and a multiplier. In fact to exploit the high speed parallel multiplier, horizontal microprogramming technique is employed. Microinstructions can control in parallel, the multiplier and the ALU or the RAM. The multiplier executes a single 16 x 16 bits multiplication in 250 ns. The ALU can perform 16 different operations on two data of 16 bits.

5. Inputs and Outputs

The NEC 7720 processor has a 8 bits parallel input/output port and serial input/output ports.

2400 BIT/S MODEM STRUCTURE

The modem is fully compatible with the CCITT recommendations V 26 bis [3]. The modulation technique is the four phase PSK (phase shift keying) with 1800 Hz carrier frequency and baud rate of 1200 Hz. The transmitter treats incoming data bits by groups of two bits and used each group to determine one of the four basic waveforms. The receiver includes a fixed equalizer to compensate for the effects of channel distorsion and a differential demodulator. The block diagram of the modem is shown on figure 1.

2400 BIT/S MODEM IMPLEMENTATION

Figure 2 shows a block diagram of the realized 2400 bit/s modem. The hardware developed allows to manage the inputs/outputs of the modem and the clocks and signals necessary for the NEC 7720 microprocessor. The block diagram of the implementation can be divided into five parts :

- the NEC 7720 signal processor,
- the clock system,
- the serial input of the analog signal before demodulation,
- the serial output of the analog signal after modulation,
- the 8 bits parallel input/output port for the binary data and the control signals.

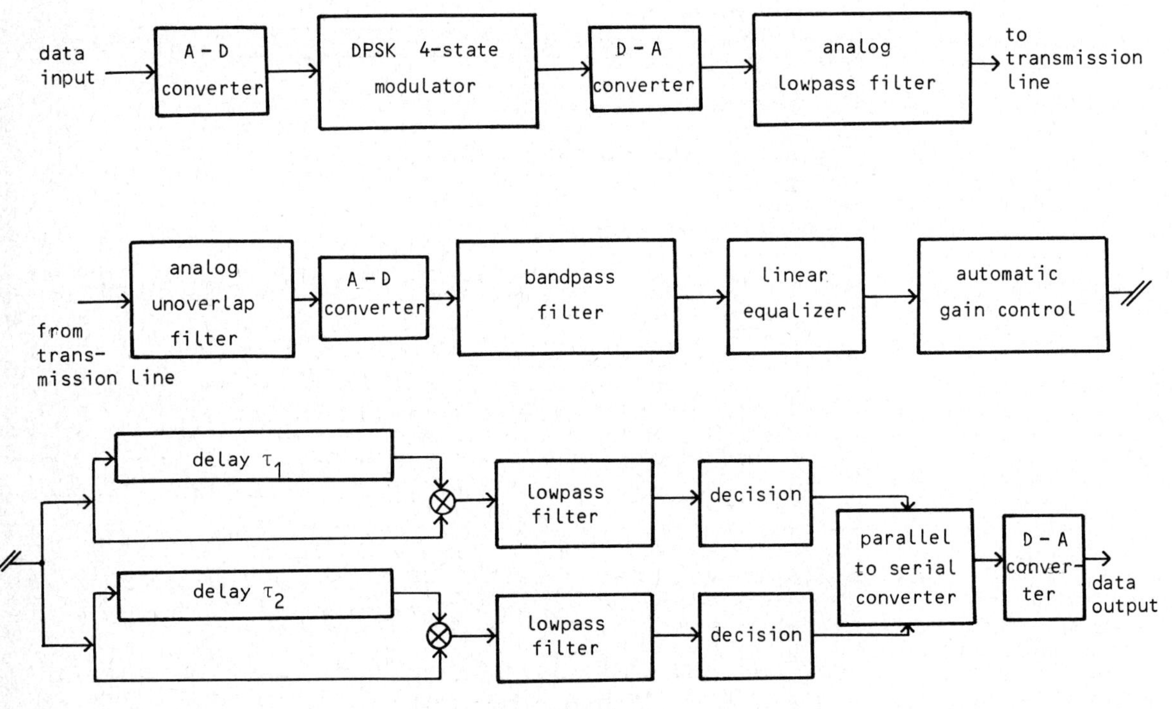

FIGURE 1

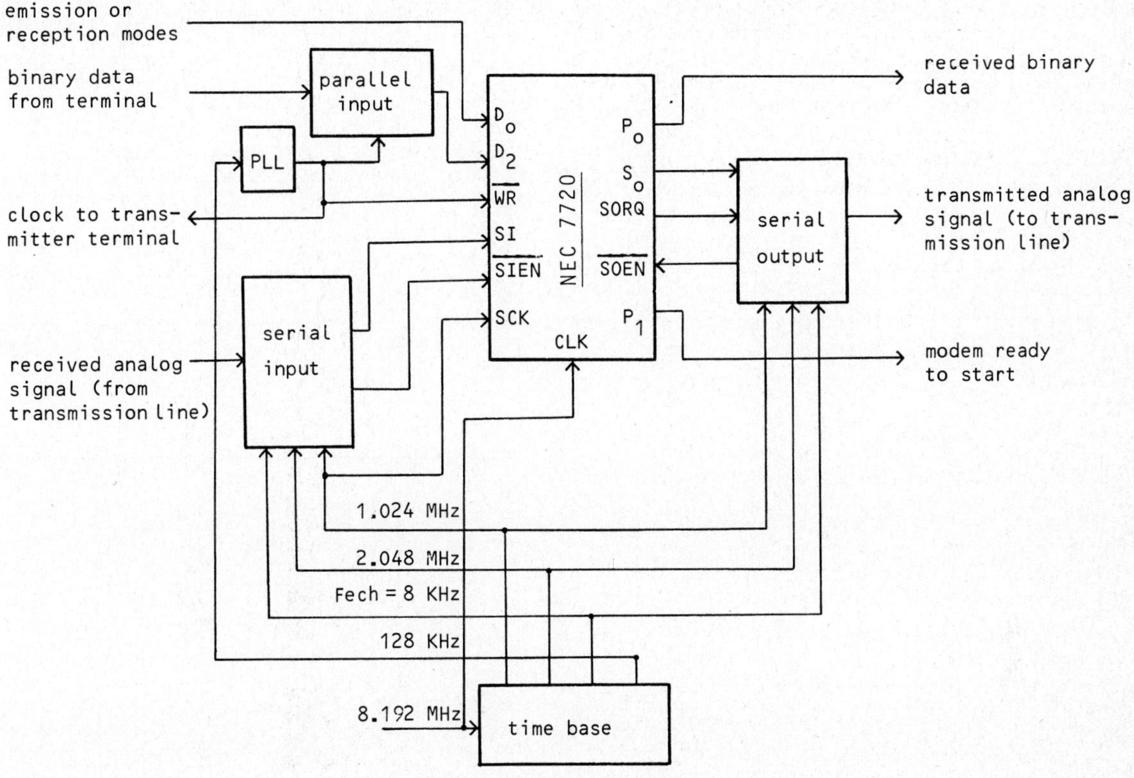

FIGURE 2

1. The Clock System

The clock system generates various clocks from a 8.129 MHz crystal oscillator. This system allows to obtain the sampling rate (8 KHz), the reference frequency (128 KHz) for the phase-locked loop (PLL) and the frequencies for serial/ parallel conversion (1.024 MHz) and for parallel/ serial conversion (2.048 MHz).

2. The Serial input of the Analog Signal before Demodulation

The analog signal coming from the telephone line is treated by an unoverlap filter (INTEL 2912 chip). The filtering signal is numerically converted by an analog-digital converter (word length of 12 bits, conversion time of 25 µs), then sent to the microprocessor after a parallel/ serial conversion. The transfert of serial data in the shift register of the microprocessor is performed at the rate of the SCK clock after validation by the $\overline{\text{SIEN}}$ signal.

3. The Serial output of the Analog Signal after Modulation

The output of the data is also performed at the rate of the SCK clock. The dialogue between the microprocessor and the serial output interface is controlled by SORQ and $\overline{\text{SOEN}}$ signals. A serial/parallel conversion is performed before the digital-analog conversion on 12 bits. The signal is sent to the telephone line after being filtered by a specialized circuit (INTEL 2912 chip).

4. The 8 bits Parallel input/output

The microprocessor receives on the DØ line, the configuration order for emission or reception. After the necessary initialisations to the chosen mode, an high logic level on the P1 port shows that the microprocessor is ready.

In emission, the microprocessor receives the binary data on the D2 line at the rate of the 2400 bit/s clock. This clock is synchronised with the sampling rate through the phase-locked loop system (PLL). In reception, the microprocessor emits the binary data at the frequency of 2400 bit/s on the PØ port.

REALIZATION OF THE MAIN FUNCTIONS OF THE MODEM

When conceiving the software, we fixed ourselves the following objectives :

- a modular realization of the programs,
- a minimal executing time.

These two objectives can be reached by making the proper choice of memory data address implementation and by writing a subroutine for each elementary function met in the modem. The association of these various modules allows to realise the complete modem afterwards.

1. The Four Phase PSK Modulator

The modulator is shown on figure 3.

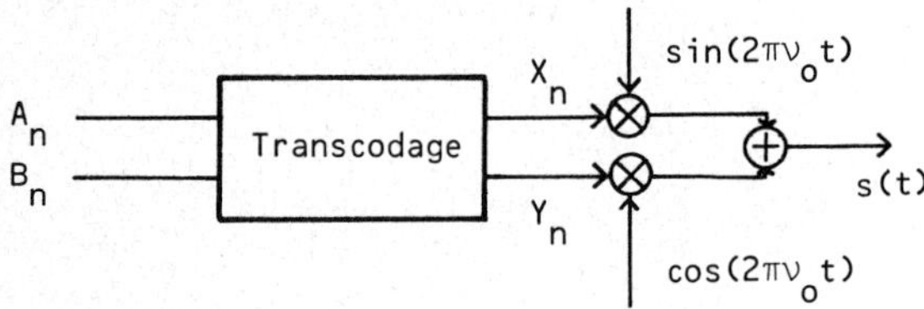

FIGURE 3

The modulated signal is given by :

$$s(t) = X_n \cdot \sin(2\pi\nu_o t) + Y_n \cos(2\pi\nu_o t)$$

The $\sin(2\pi\nu_o t)$ and $\cos(2\pi\nu_o t)$ signals can be generated in two different ways :

- either with samples computed off time and stored in memory
- or by programming the trigonometrical equations [4].

The second method allows an important saving of memory words and generates the carrier frequency by the following equations

$$x(kT) = \sin(2\pi\nu_o kT) = \cos(2\pi\nu_o T) \cdot x[(k-1)T] + \sin(2\pi\nu_o T) \cdot y[(k-1)T]$$

$$y(kT) = \cos(2\pi\nu_o kT) = \cos(2\pi\nu_o T) \cdot y[(k-1)T] - \sin(2\pi\nu_o T) \cdot x[(k-1)T]$$

These equations are computed at every sampling period ($\Delta T = 125$ µs). At every baud period, we must determine the phase rotation of the carrier in function of a group of two bits received. This operation is realized by the two following equations :

$$X_n = a \cdot X_{n-1} + b \cdot Y_{n-1}$$

$$Y_n = c \cdot X_{n-1} + d \cdot Y_{n-1}$$

The a,b,c and d values characterize the phase rotation of the carrier. The program which realizes the four phase PSK modulator uses 72 microinstructions, 18 data ROM words and 7 RAM words. The execution time of the modulator is 18 µs.

2. The Second Order Filter

A digital filter can be obtained as an interconnection of second order filters. Consider the following second order filter transfer function in the Z form :

$$H(z) = g \cdot \frac{b_2 + b_1 \cdot z^{-1} + b_o \cdot z^{-2}}{1 - c_1 \cdot z^{-1} - c_o \cdot z^{-2}}$$

The b_1 and c_1 coefficients can be higher than one and the chosen structure is shown on figure 4. The implemented equations are the following :

$$W_n = g \cdot x_n + \frac{c_1}{2} \cdot W_{n-1} + \frac{c_1}{2} \cdot W_{n-1} + c_o \cdot W_{n-2}$$

$$Y_n = b_2 \cdot W_n + \frac{b_1}{2} \cdot W_{n-1} + \frac{b_1}{2} \cdot W_{n-1} + b_o \cdot W_{n-2}$$

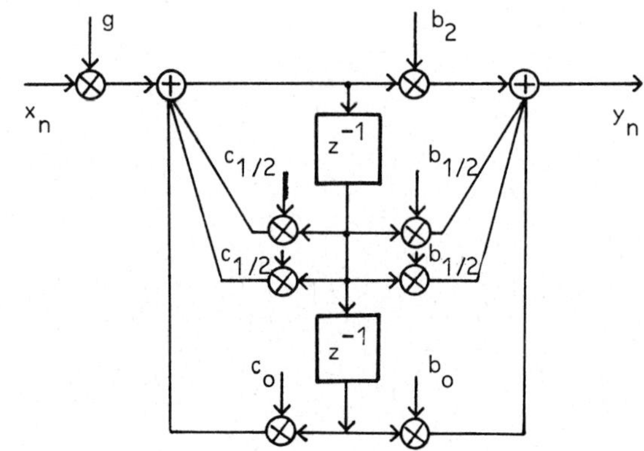

FIGURE 4

One second order filter is realized by 12 microinstructions with 2 data ROM words and 6 RAM words and computes in 3 µs.

3. Automatic Gain Control (AGC)

This function allows to bring the input signal to a constant reference value. Figure 5 shows the block diagram of the AGC.

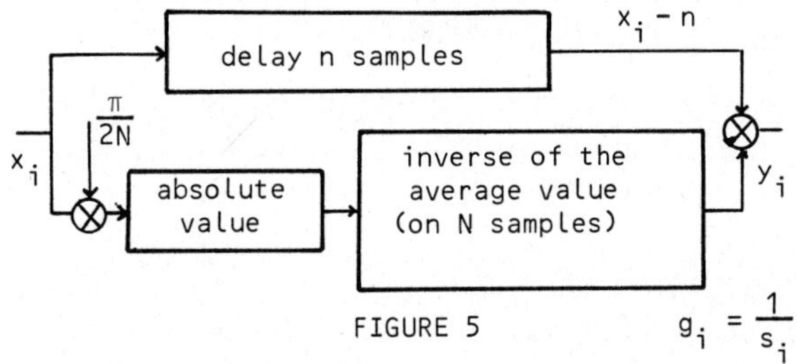

FIGURE 5 $g_i = \frac{1}{s_i}$

The implementation of the AGC is totally digital. The output signal is the result of the multiplication between the input signal delayed of n samples and a gain factor. This gain factor, computed at every sampling, is in fact the inverse of the mean value of the signal on a N window. The output signal can be written under the following form :

$$y_i = g_i \cdot x_{i-n}$$

with $g_i = \frac{1}{s_i}$

where

$$s_i = \sum_{j=i-N+1}^{i} \left|\frac{\pi}{2N} \cdot x_j\right|$$

For the digital realization, all x_j signals are such that $-1 \leqslant x_j < +1$. Then, on this condition it is possible to write :

$$s_i = 2^{-m} \cdot z$$

where m is an integer $\geqslant 0$ ans z a real such as $0{,}5 \leqslant z < +1$.

Whence we infer that the corresponding values for g_i and y_i :

$$g_i = 2^m \cdot \frac{1}{z}$$

$$y_i = 2^m \cdot \frac{1}{z} \cdot x_{i-n}$$

The major problem is to compute the inverse of z. The result of this operation can be approached by using k levels on the curve $f(z) = \frac{1}{z}$ like on figure 6. Then, if $c_j \leqslant z \leqslant c_{j+1}$, the gain factor is constant and equal to G_j.

$$y_i = 2^m \cdot G_j \cdot x_{i-n}$$

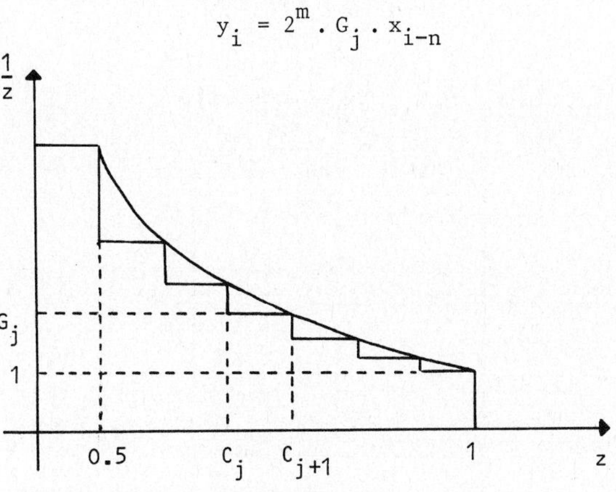

FIGURE 6

The AGC subroutine uses 32 microinstructions, 19 data ROM words and (N + n + 5) RAM words. The computation time is 13,75 μs.

EXPERIMENTAL RESULTS

1. The Transmitter

Figure 7 shows the measured spectrum of the signal generated by the modulation subroutine for the carrier frequency of 1800 Hz.

The side lobes (3600 and 6200 Hz) are about 50 dB down and the carrier frequency derives in the worst case in the order of 1/1000.

Figure 8 shows the spectrum of the modulated signal at the output of the transmitter. The spectrum is rapidly reduced after the frequency of 3400 Hz by the filtering of the unoverlap analog filter.

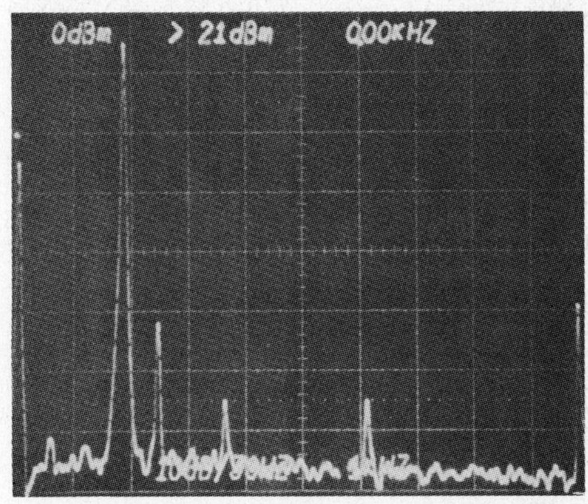

FIGURE 7

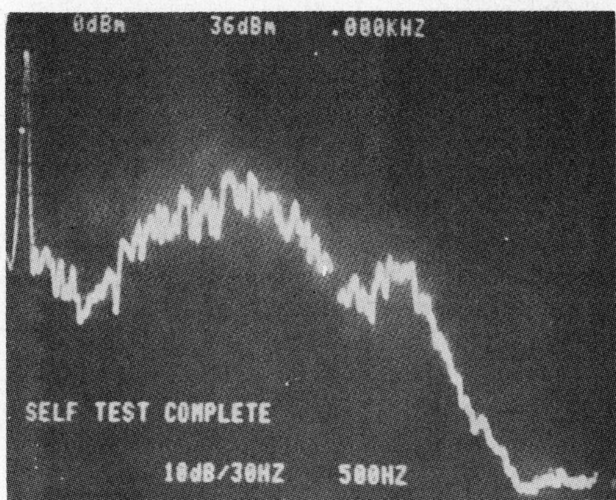

FIGURE 8

2. The Band-Pass Filter of the Receiver

The design of this filter (order 6) has been carried out by SIRENA and the wordlengh coefficients have been optimised at 13 bits by application of the DOREDI program edited by IEEE Press [5]. The magnitude response is shown on figure 9.

Generally speaking, it can be established that the implementation of recursive digital filters with coefficients truncated at 13 bits causes no particular problem. It does not show any notable differences between the magnitude responses obtained, on the one hand, with a filter whose coefficients have an infinite wordlengh, on the other hand, with a filter whose coefficients have a wordlengh of 13 bits.

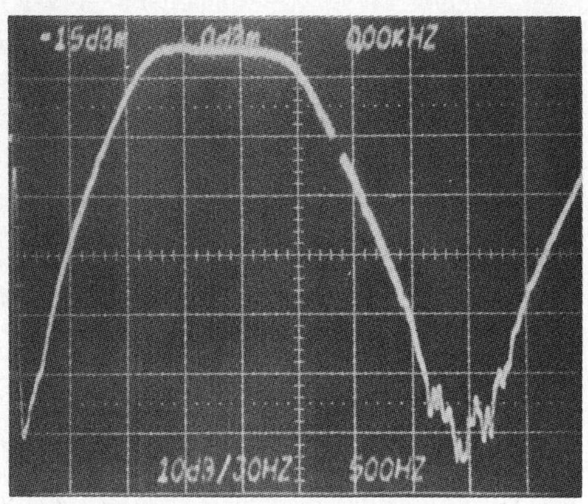

FIGURE 9

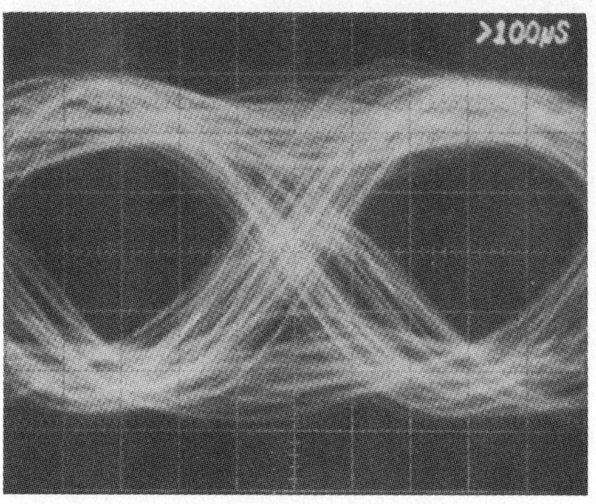

FIGURE 10

3. Visualisation in Time Domain (eye pattern)

Figure 10 shows an eye pattern from the demodulated signal, filtered and synchronised with the bit frequency. The detection of the emitted signal is fairly easy. The restitution of the emitted symbols can be made correctly by comparing the demodulated signal with the value of the decision threshold of an open eye.

4. Memory Capacity and Computation Time

The following table (1) sums up the necessary memory capacity and the computation time of each subroutine for the transmitter, the receiver and the modem.

FUNCTION	SOFTWARE (NUMBER OF INSTRUCTIONS)	DATA ROM	DATA RAM	TIME MAX (µs)
Generation of a sinusoïdal signal	16	2	2	3,5
Transcodage	53	16	5	13,25
EMITTER	72	18	7	18
Second order filter	12	6	2	3
Delay (n)	9	-	(n + 2)	1,75
Automatic gain control	32	19	14	13,75
Clock recovery	46	12	7	18
Decision	19	1	7	4,75
RECEIVER	168	80	59	80,75
MODEM (The Whole)	240	98	66	98,75
Available space of time	512	510	128	125

TABLE 1

CONCLUSION

This paper has shown how to realize with a digital signal processor the various functions necessary for the implementation of a totally digital modem. The implementation of a 2400 bit/s modem is possible on the NEC 7720 microprocessor.

Besides, we think that the advent -in the near future- of the "second generation" of digital signal processors will allow the integration of high speed modems (from 4800 bit/s up). The reduction of the cycle time and the increase of memory capacity will allow the implementation of very fast adaptive algorithms which are now an obstacle to the integration of high speed modems.

ACKNOWLEDGMENT

The authors wish to thank Professor C. BRIE of the Automatic Control Laboratory of INSA - RENNES for his constant support and continual encouragements throughout the course of this work.

This work has been supported by the French DGT (Direction Générale des Télécommunications) and realized with the collaboration of the CCETT (Centre Commun de Télévision et de Télécommunications de RENNES-FRANCE).

REFERENCES

[1] FORET J.Y., TOURBAH A., LE BARON J.P., BRIE C. Simulation de chaînes de transmission de données binaires. MIMI Symposium, DAVOS, March 1982.

[2] FORET J.Y. Conception d'un modem 2400 bit/s à l'aide du système de CAO SIRENA. IASTED Symposium, TUNIS, September 1982.

[3] C.C.I.T.T orange book volume VIII.1, 1977.

[4] TOURBAH A. Conception assistée par ordinateur d'un modem numérique en modulation de fréquence. IASTED Symposium, TUNIS, September 1982.

[5] DEHNER G. Programs for digital signal processing.
Digital signal processing comittee, IEEE Press, 1979.

DIGITAL TECHNIQUES in Simulation, Communication and Control
Spyros G. Tzafestas (editor)
Elsevier Science Publishers B.V. (North-Holland) © IMACS, 1985

SIGNALLING TONES ON PCM CHANNELS

L. C. FERNANDEZ GONZALEZ Y J. A. MARTINEZ AYUSO

CENTRO DE INVESTIGACION Y DESARROLLOS C.T.N.E.
MADRID - SPAIN

An efective method to detect signalling tones between switching centers on P. C. M. channels is presented in this paper; signalling techniques are in accordance to - C.C.I.T.T. Rec 5-Bis.
Instantaneous power estimation of each toneis FFT techniques based which profit from equal tone spacing and free interference points in the spectrum in order to make an optimal estimation.
In addition, the impact of finite operating arithmetics machine is shown; in order - to perform it, specifical software tools for this simulation which include trunca - tion and rounding, when implementing the method on finite precidion machine, are - used.
The presented system alows the simultaneous detection of all the 2.048 Mbits/s link channels using only 40 signal samples per channel.
The achieved level for cost, consumption and volume is competitive with other alter- native approaches.

1. INTRODUCTION

The detection of the multifrecuency tones used in the spanish inter-central signalling (Rec. N-5 Bis CCITT, (1)) implies that the detection system must fulfill the following specification:

a.- The system must detect the following frequencies: 700, 900, 1200, 1400, 1800 and 1900 Hz.

b.- The digitalized samples correspond to tones with power levels between -5,5 dBm and -30,5dBm.

c.- The system must evaluate the power of all - the tones present in the channel.

In accordance with these specifications a wholly digital detection method has been chosen. This method makes use of the properties of the sig - nals to be analysed.

2. DETECTION ALGORITHM

It is possible to build a null variance unbiased estimator based on the equal frecuency spacing properties of the signal.

It is well know (2) that, with N samples of a fo frecuency tone its Discrete Fourier Trans - form is:

$$X(K) = \sum_{n=0}^{N-1} x(n)\, W_K^n \qquad (1)$$

where

$$W_K^h = \exp\,(-j\,2\;\;K\,n/N) \qquad (2)$$

The implicit use a rectangular window polutes the espectral estimation with a continuous interference give by the expresion:

$$X(f) = (\sin\,(\pi(f-fo) - N/fm))/\pi.(f-fo) \qquad (3)$$

where

fm = sample frequency
fo = tone frecuency

This function presents zeroes at the frecuencies:

$$f_K = (K \cdot fm/N) + fo \qquad K = \pm 1, 2, \ldots \qquad (4)$$

The zeroes of the function are points where the espectral estimation polution is null. In our case the tones to be detected are equally spaced with a 200 Hz spacing.

Thus the frecuencies to be detected can be expresed as:

$$fi = i.\Delta f + f1 \qquad i = 0, 1, \ldots 6 \qquad (5)$$

where

Δf = 200 Hz and f1 = 700 H

if

$$fi + 1 - fi = \Delta f \text{ and } \Delta f = fm/N \qquad (6)$$

the signal does not interfere another one. In our case, with 200 Hz inter-tone spacing, the sampling frecuency is 8 KHz and the tones are not exact multiples of the sampling frecuency.

This compels to use non-integer Ks, with:

$$N = j.40 \qquad j = 1,2,.. \qquad (7)$$

if

$$N = 40$$
$$K_i = 3.5 + i \qquad i = \emptyset,1, ...6 \qquad (8)$$

The tone power estimation is given by the expression:

$$P(F_K) = 10 \log \ (A^2 + B^2)/N \qquad (9)$$

$$A = \sum x(n).\cos \ (2\pi Kn)/N \qquad (10)$$

$$B = \sum x(n).\sin \ (2\pi Kn)/N \qquad (11)$$

3. SIMULATIONS

The simulation results of the proposed algorithm are presented. The simulation has been carried out on a VAX-11/780 computer with, and without the limitation of the used arithmetic length.

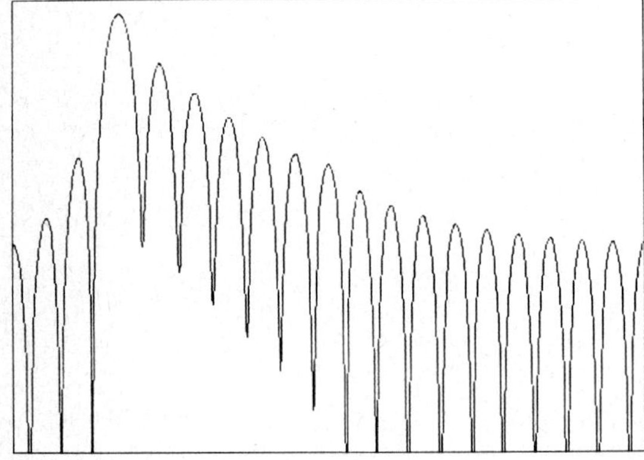

figure 1

In figure 1 the spectrum of a test signal is presented. The signal is composed of 40 samples corresponding to the 7 tónes with power levels between -5,5dBm and -30,5 dBm. The power decreases linearly with frequency.

In table 1 the results of the algorithm without word length limitation are presented throughout three 40 samples analysis cycles. There is no error in this estimation.

CICLE	F1	F2	F3	F4
1	-.5500E+01	-.9667E+01	-.1383E+02	-.1800E+02
2	-.5500E+01	-.9667E+01	-.1383E+02	-.1800E+02
3	-.5500E+01	-.9667E+01	-.1383E+02	-.1800E+02
CICLE	**F5**	**F6**	**F7**	
1	-.2217E+02	-.2633E+02	-.3050E+02	
2	-.2217E+02	-.2633E+02	-.3050E+02	
3	-.2217E+02	-.2633E+02	-.3050E+02	

table 1

Table 2 presents the results of the algoritm for a test signal with three tones at the frequencies F5, F6 and F7. The power of the tones is -22, 17, -26, 33 and -30,5 dBm. The estimation power at the other frequencies is less then --130 dBm.

CICLE	F1	F2	F3	F4
1	-.1404E+03	-.1440E+03	-.1373E+03	-.1329E+03
2	-.1409E+03	-.1363E+03	-.1387E+03	-.1352E+03
3	-.1482E+03	-.1468E+03	-.1352E+03	-.1305E+03
CICLE	**F5**	**F6**	**F7**	
1	-.2217E+02	-.2633E+02	-.3050E+02	
2	-.2217E+02	-.2633E+02	-.3050E+02	
3	-.2217E+02	-.2633E+02	-.3050E+02	

Table 2

Table 3 shows the results of a simulation of the algorithm on a machine with the folowing characteristics:

CICLE	F1	F2	F3	F4
1	-.6528E+02	-.6769E+02	-.6225E+02	-.5802E+02
2	-.6528E+02	-.6769E+02	-.6225E+02	-.5802E+02
3	-.6528E+02	-.6769E+02	-.6225E+02	-.5802E+02
CICLE	**F5**	**F6**	**F7**	
1	-.2261E+02	-.2638E+02	-.3056E+02	
2	-.2261E+02	-.2638E+02	-.3056E+02	
3	-.2261E+02	-.2638E+02	-.3056E+02	

Table 3

a.- 32 bit point multiplier/adder, with one sign bit for the integer part and the remmant for the decimal part.

b.- 8 bit (7 decimal plus 1 signum) samples.

c.- 16 bit (15 decimal plus 1 signum) sine/cosine soefficients.

It can be seen that the power estimation at the frecuencies F5, F6 and F7 is affected by an error due to the word length limitation of the different parameters and to quantization noise; the power in the remmnant tones is basically quantization noise.

A machine with these characteristics is enough to fulfill the proposed specifications.

4. HARWARE SOLUTION

According to the above mentioned results the following structure, based on high multiplier/adder is proposed (3).

The basic cell, that we will name estimator is presented in figure 2. The 2N coefficients need to independently estimate every frequency will be stored in ROM; in all 7.2.N memory locations will be needed (560-12 bit words).

The values of these coefficients answer to the following expressions:

$$AK(n) = \cos((2\pi K/N).n) \quad 0 \leq n \leq N-1 \qquad (12)$$

$$BK(n) = \sin((2\pi K/N).n) \quad 0 \leq n \leq N-1 \qquad (13)$$

for

K = 3.5, 4.5, 5.5, 6.5, 7.5, 8.5, 9.5

The values of K define the coefs. which correspond to the power estimation of every tone from F1 to F7.

The working of the cell is as follows:

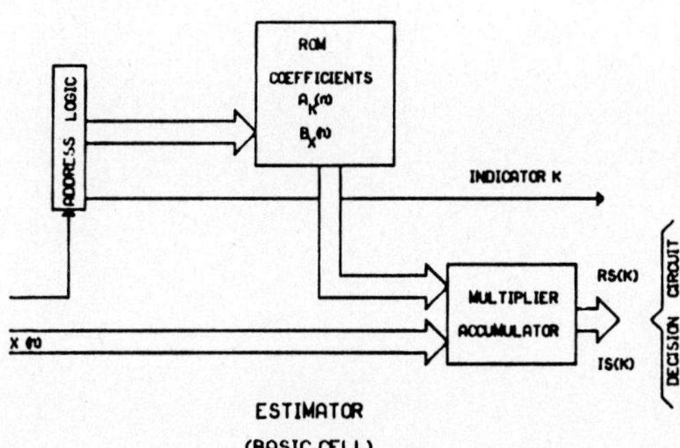

FIG 2 ESTIMATION CELL

I.- After the N consecutive samples belonging to one of PCM channels have been acquired and stored in RAM (40 samples) they are partialy multiplied by their corresponding coefficients AK (n) and added accumulatively according to the equation:

$$RS(K) = \sum x(n).\ AK(n) \qquad (14)$$

This process is repeated for every K.

2.- A similar process is performed with the BK(n) coefficients according to equation:

$$IS(K) = \sum x(n).\ BK(n) \qquad (15)$$

This process is repeated for every K.

3.- In this way the estimations of the real and imaginary parts of the spectrum have been obtained in every point of interest in a given channel. With these calues an intelligent processor will able to estimate the power spectral densyty of every point of the spectrum in the analyzed chanel.

4.- The repetition of the point 1, 2, and 3 for every one of the 32 channels will allow the - implementation of the whole system.

The basic cell takes 400ns (typical) for every multiplicating and adding operation, including the flow of data. Thus the complete time for the analysis of the channel is 2.7.40.400ns = =200µs.

If a double buffering system is used (16 channels being treated while the 40 samples of the 16 chanels are being updated), one of them can be analyzed while the other is being filled, provided that the duration of the analysis be samaller than the during of the filling.

The filling time will be 16.200µs=3,2ms aproximately, while the filling time will be 40.1/8000 =5ms.

Thus, the implementation of the whole tone detection system will be feasible using a single multiplier/accumulator chip following the structure show in figure 3.

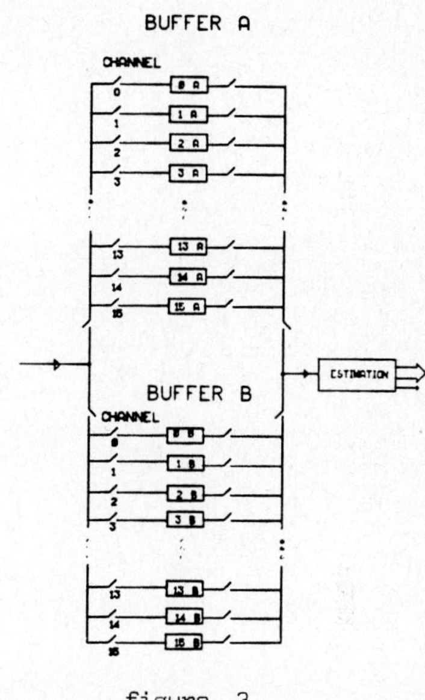

figure 3

5.- CONCLUSIONS

The system presented proves that in certain circunstancies, basic estimation methods can yield optimum and eficient solutions.

The cost, consumption and size of the hardware is very favourable with respect to other alternative solutions.

We have restricted our attention to the signalling tones detection system, without dealing with the hardware necessary for the complete implementation of the system.

REFERENCES

(1) Manual de señalización C.I.E./C.T.N.E. 1975

(2) A.V. Oppenheim and R.W. Schafer, "Digital Signal Processing", Prentice Hall, New Jersey 1975.

(3) L. Schirm. "Multiplier-Accumulator application notes", TRW LSI Products January 1980.

DIGITAL TECHNIQUES in Simulation, Communication and Control
Spyros G. Tzafestas (editor)
Elsevier Science Publishers B.V. (North-Holland) © IMACS, 1985

ANALYSIS AND DESIGN OF A 10-20 MHz DOUBLE LOOP PLL SYNTHESIZER

Vasilios Pallios and Vasilios Makios

Laboratory of Electromagnetics
School of Engineering, University of Patras
Patras, Greece

Analysis design and experimental verification of the performance of a 10-20 MHz double loop Phase Locked Loop (PLL) synthesizer is presented in this paper, which is the driving unit for a X-band microwave synthesizer. In the design procedure there is a compromise between the dynamic range, the noise performance and the suppression of spurious outputs of the double loop PLL.
The final design was reached after a trial and error procedure in order to obtain the appropriate compromise between the predetermined requirements. The reference frequency of the main loop is 100 KHz and that of the secondary loop is 1 KHz. The 100 KHz reference frequency at the main loop is used in order to get a small multiplication factor and therefore a large pull-in range and a small cut-off frequency for the loop which produces a fast aquisition time. A sharp Band-Pass Filter (BPF) is used after the mixer of the secondary loop to suppress in-band intermodulation products and three stages video preamplifier for the driving of the main loop counters.

1. INTRODUCTION

The purpose of this paper is to study experimentally the performance of a 10-20 MHz PLL synthesizer which is the driving unit for a X-band microwave synthesizer. The design parameters of the synthesizer are determined from the requirements of the microwave system. Theoretical design its implementation and experimental results are presented and compared for the 10-20 MHz unit.

The indirect synthesis technique is used here, which represents better suppression of the spurious signals at frequencies far offset from the carrier frequency, higher resolution, larger system bandwidth, better phase noise performance and adequate switching time as compared with direct synthesis. (1)

Table 1 represents a comparison of the two basic techniques of the coherent method, the direct (using double-mix-divide) and the indirect (using a digital PLL). A double loop PLL is designed which obtains improved switching times and noise characteristics as compared to a simple loop. In this way we have a low cost and low power driving unit that retains better noise and stability performance for the microwave synthesizer.

The required basic characteristics of the driving unit are:
1) Large bandwidth (1 octave)
2) High quality output spectrum (spurious outputs lower than 60 dB, phase noise better than 80 dB/Hz).
3) High resolution (a standard value in communications in 1 KHz).
4) Moderate switching time (less than 0.1 sec).

2. BASIC THEORY

A. Second order PLL using perfect integrator

Figure 1 represents the linearized equivalent of a PLL. The open loop gain is given by: (2)

$$G_{op.loop} = \frac{a_{\varphi} a_{VCO} (R_2/R_1) [S+1/T_2]}{S^2} \quad (1)$$

where $\pi K_{\varphi} = a_{\varphi}$, $\frac{K_{VCO}}{N N_2} = a_{VCO}$

TABLE 1

		Double-mix-divide (direct)	Digital PLL (indirect)
1	Switching time	of the order of μsec	up to 10 μsec
2	Resolution	of the order of 10^2 Hz	less than 10^{-3} Hz
3	Spurious outputs	of the order of 60-100 dB	better than 100 dB
4	Phase noise	near the reference signal	of the order of 80 dB
5	Bandwidth	hundrends of MHz	of the order of GHz

and K_φ = phase comparator sensitivity
K_{VCO} = VCO sensitivity.
The transfer function is given by:

$$\left|\frac{\theta_o(s)}{\theta_r(s)}\right|_{\text{perfect integrator}} =$$

$$= \frac{K_\varphi K_{VCO}(R_2/R_1)\left[S+{}^1/T_2\right]}{S^2+a_\varphi a_{VCO}(R_2/R_1)S+(a_\varphi a_{VCO}/T_2)(R_2/R_1)} \quad (2)$$

where $$F(s) = \frac{R_2}{R_1}\left[\frac{S+1/T_2}{S}\right] \quad (3)$$

denotes the filter transfer function

and $$T_2 = R_2C$$

or $$\left|\frac{\theta_o(s)}{\theta_r(s)}\right|_{\text{perfect integrator}} = \frac{2\zeta\omega_n S+\omega_n^2}{S^2+2\zeta\omega_n S+\omega_n^2} \quad (4)$$

where $$\omega_n = \left[\frac{a_\varphi a_{VCO}}{T_2}\left(\frac{R_2}{R_1}\right)\right]^{\frac{1}{2}} \text{ rad/sec} \quad (5)$$

and $$\zeta = \frac{1}{2}\left[a_\varphi a_{VCO}T_2(R_2/R_1)\right]^{\frac{1}{2}} \quad (6)$$

The 3dB bandwidth is:

$$B_{3dB} = \frac{\omega}{2\pi}\; 2\zeta^2+1+\sqrt{(2\zeta^2+1)+1} \quad (7)$$

The 3dB noise bandwidth is:

$$B_n = \frac{a_\varphi a_{VCO}(R_2/R_1)+1/T_2}{4} \text{ Hz} \quad (8)$$

The pull-in range is theoretically infinite, and the switching time is given by:

$$\text{tacq,total} = \text{tacq,freq}+\text{tacq,phase} \cong$$

$$\cong T_2\left[\frac{\Delta\omega_\varphi}{a_\varphi a_{VCO}(R_2/R_1)}-\sin\theta_o\right]+$$

$$+\frac{2}{a_\varphi a_{VCO}}\,\omega_n\left(\frac{2}{\gamma_{lock}}\right)\text{sec} \quad (9)$$

B. Basic characteristics of a 2nd order PLL in the design of frequency synthesizers

In a frequency synthesizer the main objective is how to reduce the phase noise of the output. From Figure 2 we have that:
i) The PLL operates as a low-pass for the noise of the reference signal and as a high-pass filter for the phase noise of the VCO; the cut off frequency where the open loop gain is equal to unity (2).
ii) A second order PLL with a perfect integrator has:
a) for a step change in the input frequency, zero steady state error, and
b) for a ramp change in the input frequency, $\theta_r(s) = \frac{d\Delta\omega}{dt}/S^3$, a steady state error of the form (2),(3):

$$\varepsilon_{ss} = \left(\frac{R_1}{R_2}\right)\frac{T_2 d\Delta\omega/dt}{a_\varphi a_{VCO}} \quad (10)$$

3. CIRCUIT AND NOISE DESIGN OF THE 10-20 MHz, FREQUENCY SYNTHESIZER

The design of the 10-20 MHz driving unit is based on the requirements of the x-band synthesizer set in the introduction.

A. CIRCUIT DESIGN

Following, the basic design procedure will be presented and the final design which was reached after a trial and error procedure in order to obtain the appropriate compromise between the predetermined requirements (see Figure 1).

From 2,4 it is apparent that the bandwidth of the loop can not be greater than the reference frequency. Since the reference frequency is usually the resolution step of the loop, the double loop approach is selected. The reference frequency of the main loop is 100 KHz and that of the secondary loop is 1 KHz. The 100 KHz reference frequency at the main loop is used in order to get a small multiplication factor and therefore a large pull-in range and a small cutoff frequency for the loop which produces a fast aquisition time. The 1 KHz reference frequency of the secondary loop is the resolution step; the large multiplication factor produced is not critical since small pull-in range is required for the secondary loop. The cutoff frequencies for the loops are:
i) main loop less than 10 KHz, and
ii) secondary loop less than 500 Hz.
In this way:
i) the secondary loop has a swithcing time less than 50 msec
ii) the noise filter behavior of the system is optimum. In 2 it is demonstrated that a PLL is effectively a Low-Pass Filter (LPF) with respect to the noise associated with the reference signal and a High-Pass Filter (HPF) with respect to the VCO noise (see eq.(1),(2)). Since the main concern is the low-level far-out noise for a low-cost reference signal, low cutoff frequencies for the two loops and adequate attenuation from the LPF´s of the feedback loops of the system are selected.
iii) Since the cutoff frequencies of the system LPF´s are of the order or greater than by an order of magnitude the reference frequencies,

enough suppression of the spurious outputs is obtained.

The output of the secondary loop is 8-15 MHz, in order to get optimum mixer operation (Fig.1) with respect to the intermodulation products (IM). The in-band IM products of the mixer (inputs 8-15 MHz and 10-20 MHz) were measured to be at levels lower than -70 dB. The nearband IM products were found to be either at the input frequencies of the signal, f_s=8-15 MHz, with a signal level of -13 dB, or at the carrier frequencies, f_c=10-20 MHz, with a signal level of -28 dB. A sharp Band-pass Filter (BPF) was used after the mixer with a pass-band from 2 to 5 MHz. Since the mixer output was at approximately 1mV and it had to drive the counters, an amplifier consisting of three preamplifying stages of video differential amplifiers, was used. Finally the main loop VCO consists of two VCO´s one with alinear range at 10-15 MHz and another one at 15-20 MHz, using an external digital control circuit.

B. NOISE DESIGN

Figure 2 shows the phase noise diagrams of the VCO and the reference signal curves a and b respectively. The reference signal is obtained by a VCO chip used as a crystal controlled oscillator (VCXO). Curve b is the VCXO phase noise diagram improved by 20 dB, due to the ÷ 100 divider. This improvement is permitted by the noise figure of the phase detector (PD)(5).From Figure 2 it is observed that a PLL of cutoff frequency less than 1 KHz is concerned only with the phase-noise of the reference signal. A PLL with a cutoff frequency of 800 Hz has a phase noise within our requirements and that is why this cutoff frequency, was chosen for the main loop. In this case the multiplication factor for the main loop is in the required range of 100-200 (40 to 43 dB). At this stage the phase noise of the VCO of the secondary loop was ignored in the noise analysis. The results show that it does not affect the resulting phase noise of the system (Figure 2, curve c).

The circuit analysis has shown that the mixer IM products are significant only out-of-band of interest. The BPF of the loop provides attenuation for these signals before the phase detector. Since the cutoff frequency of the loop is at 800 Hz any contribution from the above signals to the spurious outputs of the system produced by the mixing of the IM products and the reference frequency of 100 KHz at the phase detector is adequately attenuated.

4. EXPERIMENTAL RESULTS

The measured spectral characteristics of the main loop output at 20 MHz is shown in Figure 3. The switching time of the secondary loop is less than 45 msec. The phase noise diagram of the system output is shown in Figure 2 as curve c, (2, eq.2-60).

From the above figures we can derive the following characteristics for the 10-20 MHz synthesizer.

i) The phase noise is 80 dB/Hz for offset frequencies higher than 800 Hz, for offset frequencies lower than 800 Hz the worst case phase noise is 60 dB/Hz, which is in good agreement to our requirements.
ii) The spurious output levels is better than -55 dB also in good agreement to our requirements. The spurious outputs are at the same frequencies with the spurious signals at the spectrum of the reference signal.
iii) The system switching time is less than 45 msec.
iv) The resolution step is 1 KHz.

5. CONCLUSIONS

The design and experimental verification of a 10-20 MHz synthesizer that can serve as the driving unit of a microwave synthesizer has been presented. The indirect coherent technique of a double loop PLL is used. The main concern is the optimum noise filter performance of the PLL in order to achieve good noise performance of the system at far offset from carrier frequencies. The experimental results show that using better components (especially the mixer and the reference source) a high quality low cost unit can be obtained.

REFERENCES

1. Tipon, P., "New Microwave-Frequency synthesizers that Exhibit Broader Bandwidths and Increased Spectral Purity" IEEE Trans. 1974, MTT-22, pp.1246-1254.
2. Manassewitch, V., "Frequency Synthesizers Theory and Design", John Wiley and Sons.1976.
3. Blancard, A., "Phase Locked Loops", John Wiley and Sons 1976.
4. Gardner, F., "Phase Lock Techniques", John Wiley and Sons 1966.
5. "MC4044 Phase detector" Motorola Semiconductor Products.

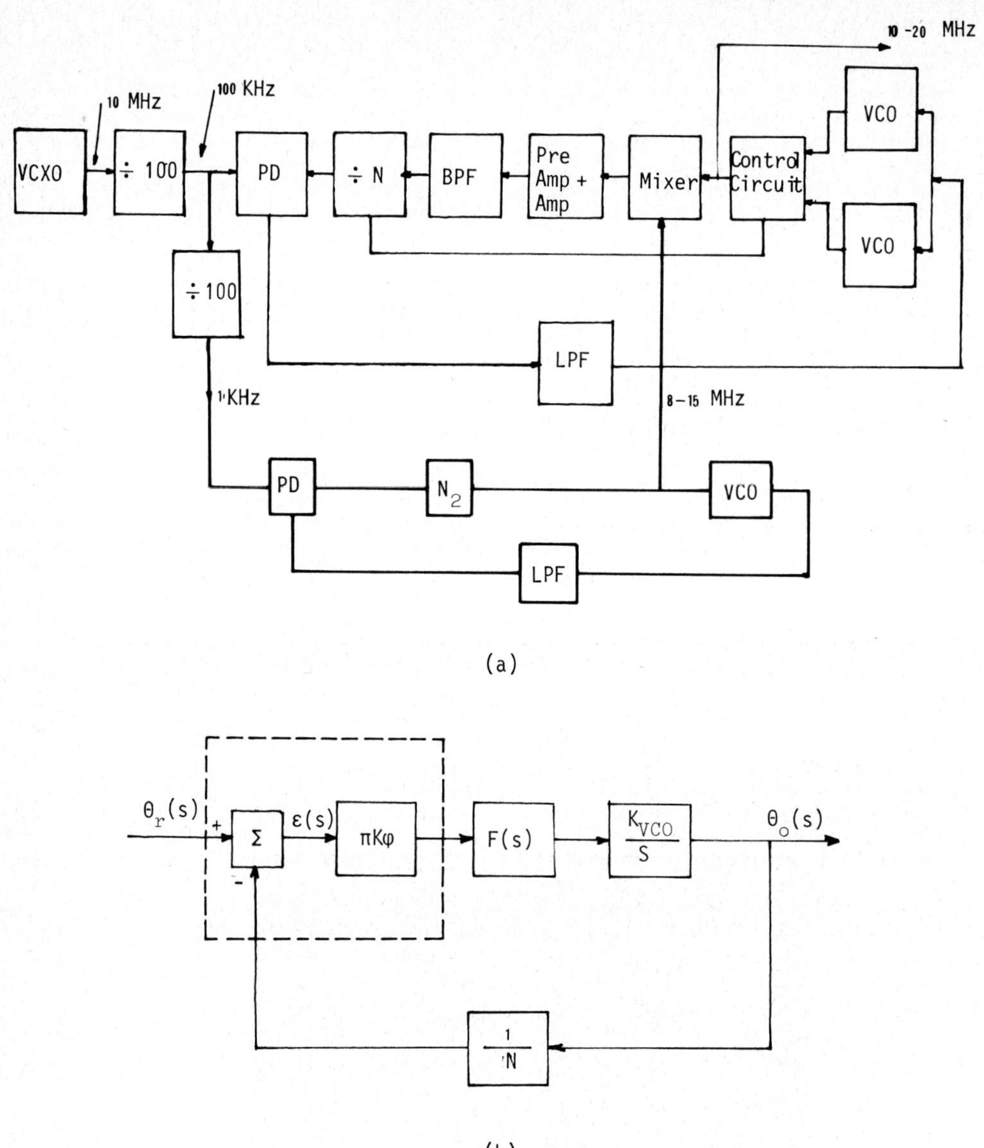

Figure 1: a) The double loop PLL and
b) its linearized model block diagrams.

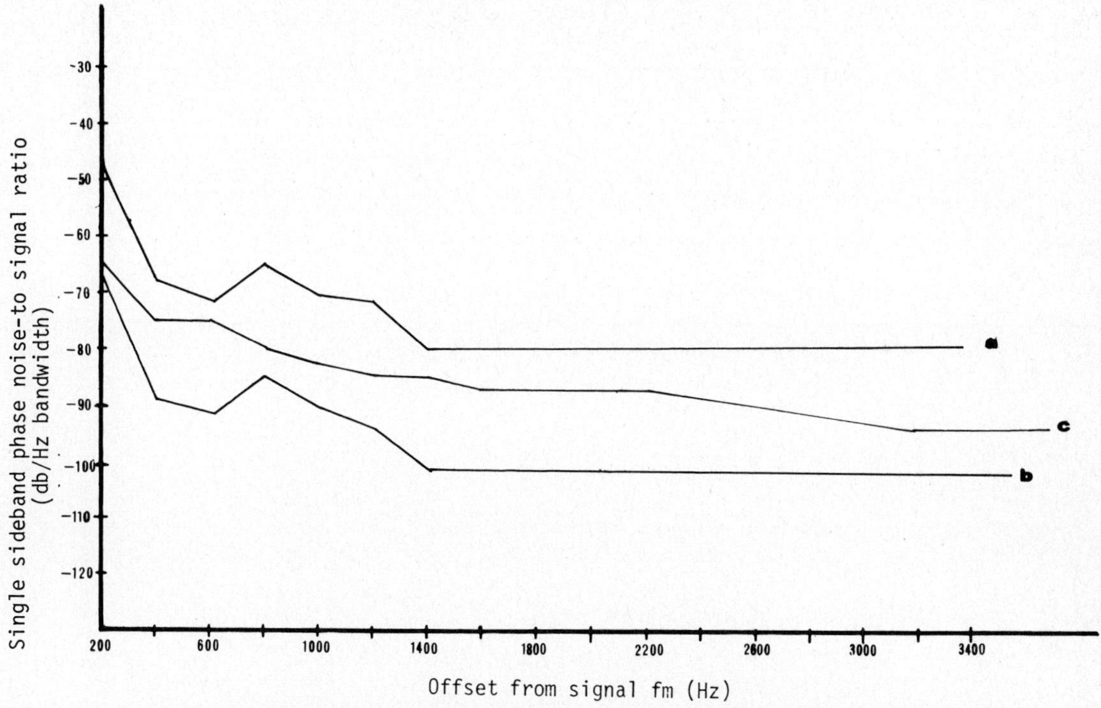

Figure 2: The phase noise diagrams of a) Input b) Input after divider c) output.

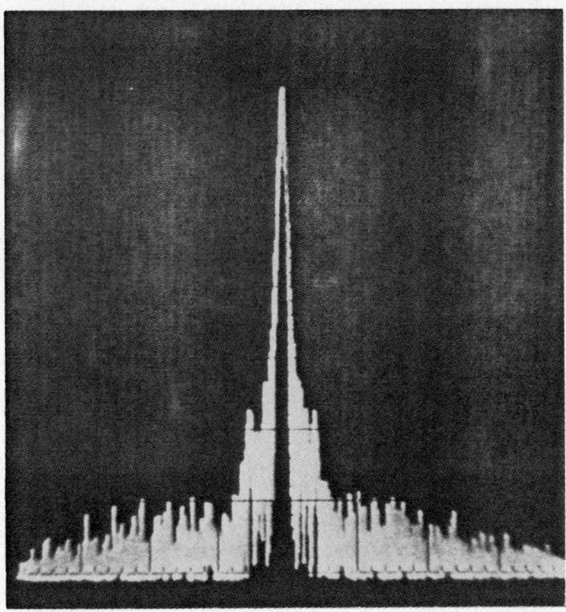

Figure 3: The output spectrum at 20 MHz with bandwidth and scan width 1 KHz.

DIGITAL TECHNIQUES in Simulation, Communication and Control
Spyros G. Tzafestas (editor)
Elsevier Science Publishers B.V. (North-Holland) © IMACS, 1985

COMPUTER SIMULATION RESULTS OF A DESIGNED ERROR CORRECTION CODE FOR A LINEAR DELTA MODULATION SYSTEM

Nicos C. David and Vasilios Makios

Laboratory of Electromagnetics
School of Engineering, University of Patras
Patras, Greece

The purpose of this paper is to examine briefly the step response of a linear delta modulator system, in the presence of transmission errors, indicate a method for improving the performance of the system whenever an error has been detected and finally present computer based simulation results which prove the efficiency of the eror correction algorithm.

1. INTRODUCTION

Techniques for correcting transmission errors in digitally encoded signals have been reported in the literature in the past by N. Scheinberg and D.L.Schilling (1), D.J. Connors (2) and others (3),(4),(5). Especially Scheinberg and Schilling have developed cute and efficient algorithms for correcting transmission errors for digital delta modulation systems. In this paper we examine the performance of a linear delta modulation system (in terms of signal-to-noise ratio) in the presence of transmission errors with the aid of a specific correction code. Computer based simulation results are presented and the demodulated signals for errorless transmission, transmission in the presence of an error and error corrected transmission are compared.

2. ERROR CORRECTION ALGORITHM

The block diagram of a linear digital Delta Modulation system is shown in Figure 1.

When C_i is at a high state (logical "one") y increases by one step Δ (which is fixed) and when C_i at a low state (logical "zero") y decreases by one step Δ, in a manner such that y(t) always approximates the input signal x(t). Figure 2 shows the response of the delta modulation system to an arbitrary waveform in an errorless transmission (solid line) and in the presence of one transmission error (dotted line).

From Figure 2 we observe that in the presence of a transmission error there is a permanent dc shift in the demodulated signal equal to twice the step size, 2Δ. Thus, if an error has been detected the demodulator should increase (decrease) the dc level by 2Δ when the number of zeros received is larger (less) than the number of zeros sent.

This correction is accomplished with the aid of two additional bits sent by the transmitter at the end of every n-bit sequence (in this paper n=14) which indicate the following:

1. The first bit (DB) indicates the parity of the sequence, or

$$n^t \text{ even} \quad : \text{FB} = 0$$

$$n^t \text{ odd} \quad : \text{FB} = 1$$

where n^t is the number of zeros in the n-bit sequence.

Equivalently the above statement may be expressed as follows:

FB is such that the n+1 bit (n represents data and the (n+1)th is the FB) contains an odd number of zeros.

2. The second bit (SB) indicates the order of zeros of the n digit word in a manner such that

$$\text{SB} = 0 \text{ if } n^t = 4K \text{ or } 4K+1$$

$$\text{SB} = 1 \text{ if } n^t = 4K+2 \text{ or } 4K+3$$

The above two assumptions are summarized in Table 1.

n^t	FB	SB	n^t_{all}
4K	0	0	4K+2
4K+1	1	0	4K+2
4K+2	0	1	4K+3
4K+3	1	1	4K+3

Table 1

In the above Table n^t_{all} represents the number of zeros in the n-bit sequence of data plus the two control bits.

At the receiver the error correction process functions as follows:

a. If the number of zeros in the (n+1)bit sequence (state + FB) is odd, then, no error has been detected and no correction process is activated. Note that in this case SB is not considered at all.
b. If the number of zeros in the (n+1)bit sequence is even then an error has been detected.

Case	s/n → db	Improvement → db
Errorless Transmission (Fig. 4)	12.39	—
Transmission with error (Fig.5)	9.77	1.80
Transmission with error (Fig. 6)	4.74	6.83
Error corrected transmission (Fig.7)	11.57	—

Table 2

Assuming that only error may occur in every (n+2) bit sequence we conclude that SB is correct and the error lies in the data sequence. The probability that the error be the FB (parity bit) is 1/(n+1) which is considered to be negligible compared to the probability that an error occur within the data bits (n/n+1).

Thus the control bits with reference to Table 1 specify the correct data stream sent.

For example if n^t=4K+1 then FB=1 and SB=0. If an error occurs during the transmission the number of zeros received will be:

$$\text{either } n_1^r = 4K$$

$$\text{or } n_1^r = 4K+2$$

$$\text{If } n^r = n_1^r = 4K < 4K+1 = n^t$$

the demodulator decreases the dc level by 2Δ.

$$\text{If } n^r = n_2^r = 4K+2 > 4K+1 = n^t$$

the demodulator increases the dc level by 2Δ.

3. COMPUTER SIMULATION RESULTS

A mini computer HP 9845 A was used in the study of the performance of the system. The number of samples was equal to 512. The process signal was a square waveform as shown in Figure 3a. This signal was low pass filtered to form the input signal to the coder (modulator) as shown in Figure 3b (frequency domain) and 3c (time domain). The sampling ratio was taken T_s/T_i=1/128 where T_s in the sampling period and T_i the period and T_s the period of the square waveform.
The filter was assumed to be ideal (Figure 3b) with cut-off frequency $f_c = 8f_i$ ($f_i = 1/T_i$).

The signal-to-noise ratio is defined as:

$$s/n = \frac{\sum_{i=1}^{512} x_i^2}{\sum_{i=1}^{512} (x_i - y_i)^2}$$

where x_i are the samples entering the modulator and y_i are the samples coming out from the LPF of the demodulator.

Figure 4 shows the digital sequence coming out from the modulator (to be transmitted) as well as the tracking signal, its Fourier Spectrum and the signal after the low pass filter of the demodulator (errorless transmission).

In Figure 5 the response of the demodulator is shown in the presence of a transmission error. This is the case that the errors cancel out each other so that the dc shift appears to be zero.

A worse case is shown in Figure 6 where the errors are added and a permanent dc shift results.

Figure 7 shows the improvement that is achieved with the use of the correction algorithm. The visible improvement is obvious while the improvement in terms of signal-to-noise ratio is presented in Table 2.

4. CONCLUSIONS

In this paper we have presented computer-based simulation results for an error correction code used to improve the performance of a linear delta modulation system in the presence of transmission errors. The introduction of two additional bits results in a significant improvement of the signal-to-noise ratio i.e. 1.8 db for the case of Figure 5 and 6.8 db for the case of Figure 6 for the step response of the system. It is also noted that the signal-to-noise ratio of the correcting system is less only by 0.81 db than that of the ideal system.

ACKNOWLEDGEMENTS

The authors wish to thank Mr. S. Boucouris for his great help with the computer simulation.

REFERENCES

1. Scheinberg N., and Schilling D.L., IEEE Trans. Commun., Vol.COM-24, pp.1064-1069, Sept.1976.
2. Connor D.J., IEEE Trans. Commun., Vol. COM-21, p.p.695-706, June 1973.
3. Rydbeck N., and Sundberg C.E.W., IEEE Trans. Commun., Vol. COM-24, pp.59-65, Jan. 1976.
4. Yan H., and Donaldson R.W., IEEE Trans., Commun., Vol. COM-20, pp.281-290, June 1972.
5. Dostis I., Bell Syst. Tech. J., Vol.44, pp. 2227-2243, Dec. 1965.

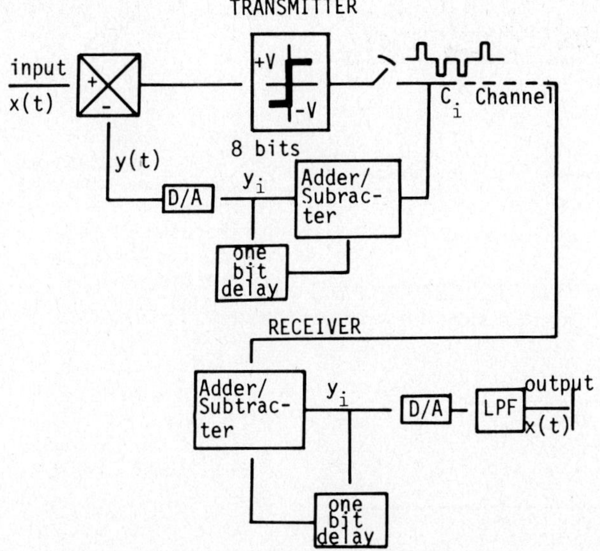

Figure 1. Linear Digital Delta Modulation System.

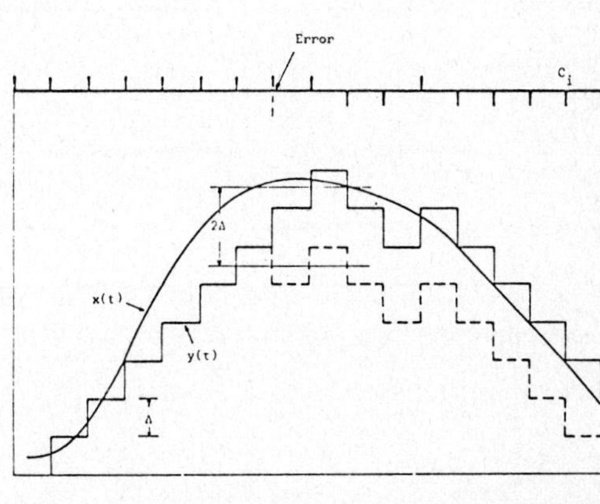

Figure 2. Response of the Linear DM System to an Arbitrary Input Signal.

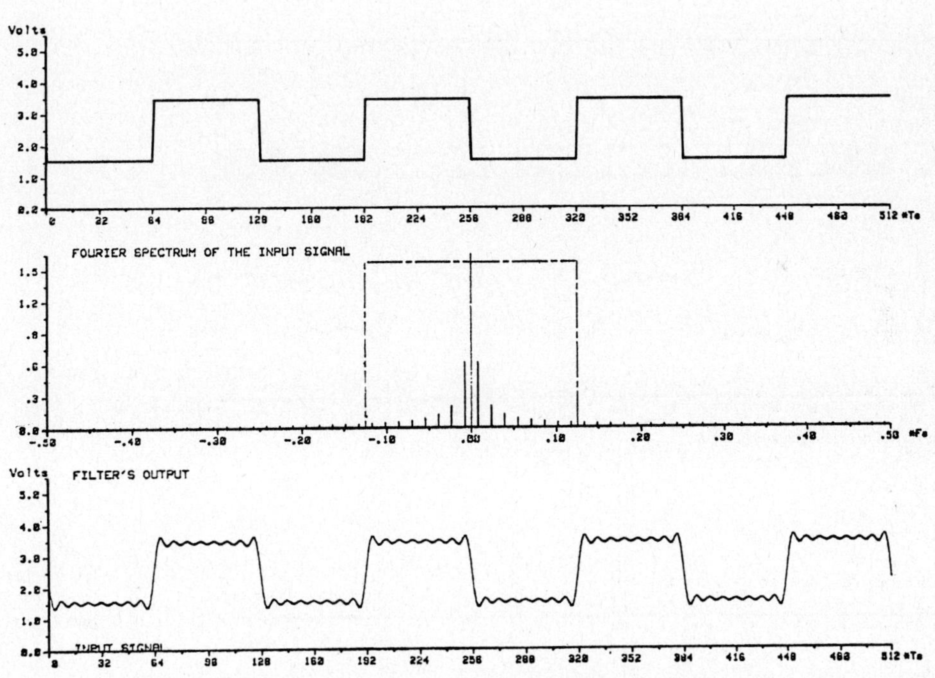

Figure 3. Input Signal
a. Input to the Filter
b. Input to the Modulator (Frequency Domain)
c. Input to the Modulator (Time Domain).

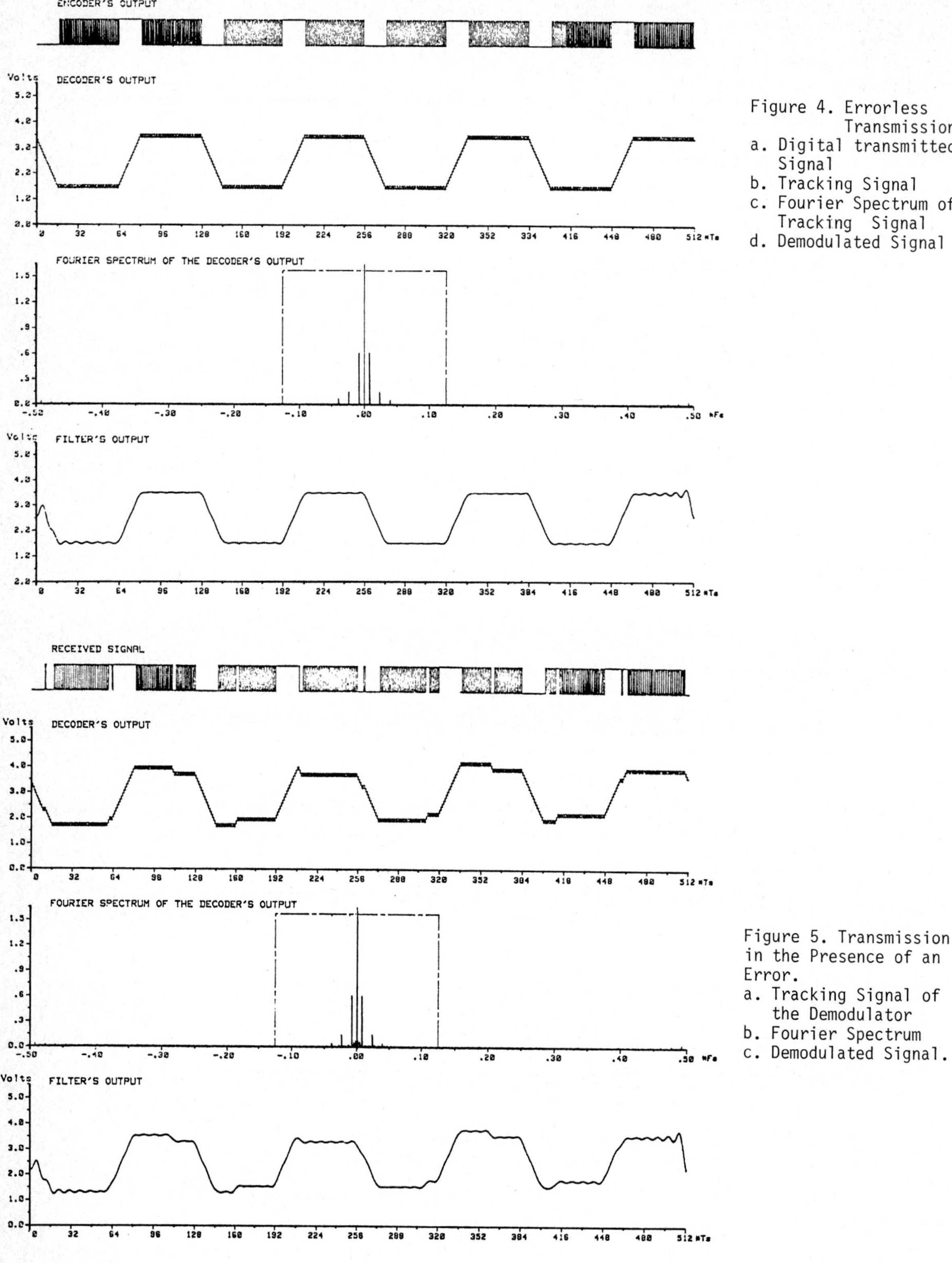

Figure 4. Errorless Transmission
a. Digital transmitted Signal
b. Tracking Signal
c. Fourier Spectrum of Tracking Signal
d. Demodulated Signal

Figure 5. Transmission in the Presence of an Error.
a. Tracking Signal of the Demodulator
b. Fourier Spectrum
c. Demodulated Signal.

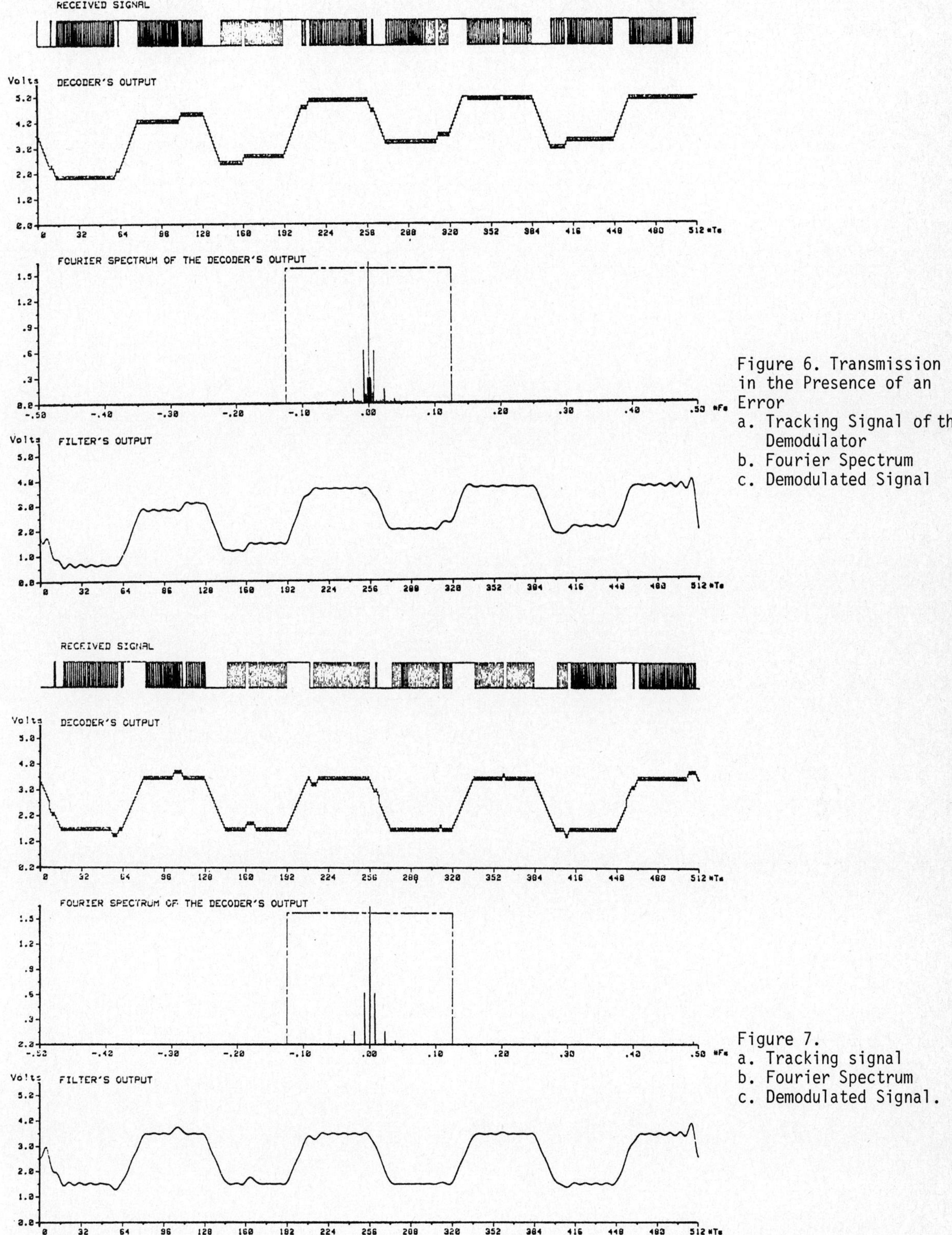

Figure 6. Transmission in the Presence of an Error
a. Tracking Signal of the Demodulator
b. Fourier Spectrum
c. Demodulated Signal

Figure 7.
a. Tracking signal
b. Fourier Spectrum
c. Demodulated Signal.

DIGITAL TECHNIQUES in Simulation, Communication and Control
Spyros G. Tzafestas (editor)
Elsevier Science Publishers B.V. (North-Holland) © IMACS, 1985

OPTIMUM PERFORMANCE OF AN ADAPTIVE DELTA MODULATION CODER

Spyros Boucouris, Nicos C.David and Vasilios Makios

Laboratory of Electromagnetics
School of Engineering, University of Patras
Patras, Greece

The purpose of this paper is to examine the step response of an "one bit" memory delta modulation system. More specifically the algorithm adopted here is such, that the ratio of the step size at a certain time instant to the step size of the previous time instant is P or Q depending on the relative polarity of the last two output states of the coder.
Using computer-based simulation results, this algorithm has been designed to be optimum for signals with step variations.
Because of the strong non-linearity of the delta coder we could not come up with useful conclusions considering only a few step levels of the input signal. For this reason we used as input, step functions of various amplitudes; we then found the signal-to-noise ratios for each amplitude separately, after that we calculated the average and the deviation of the values of the signal-to-noise ratios and finally we ended up with an algorithm with a maximum average and minimum deviation. Based on the simulation results we implemented a delta coder and compared the experimental results with the computer simulation results.

1. INTRODUCTION

In this paper computer simulation as well as experimental results of the step response of an adaptive delta modulation system are presented.

The step size is an exponential function of two constant values P and Q. In other words the step size at a certain instant is equal to the step size at the previous time instant multiplied by either P or Q depending on the polarity of the present and previous output states (bits). We have chosen the exponential variation of he step because it gives the best response for step signals.

In the past a lot of others have dealt with the same subject. (1),(2),(3)

Jayant (1) made the first analysis for the specification of the optimum values of P and Q but his analysis was limited to the case P·Q=1.

Song et al (2) presented a wider theoretical analysis but he also examined only a few pairs of P,Q (Song´s et al algorithm differs a little from Janyant´s and is equivalent to that in overload regions for P=1.15, Q=0.5).

Finally Cutler (3) studied the optimum limitations of the step size using Jayant´s algorithm (P=1.5, Q=1/P).

In this paper we are seeking for the optimum values of P and Q and the limitations of the step size for step-like input signals.

2. DESCRIPTION OF THE ALGORITHM

Figure 1 shows the block diagram of the delta coder under examination. The step varies exponentially, i.e. the step size (Δ_i) at the time instant (i) equals the step size (Δ_{i-1}) at the time instant (i-1) multiplied by P if $C_i=C_{i-1}$ or by Q if $C_i \neq C_{i-1}$.

This value (Δ_i) is then added to or subtracted from the approximation of x_i (which is y_{i-1}) to form the new approximation y_i which is then compared to x_i (see Figure 1).

Expressing the above mathematically we may write:

$$C_i = \mathrm{sgn}(x_i - y_i)$$

$$\Delta_i = \begin{cases} P\Delta_{i-1} & \text{if } C_i = C_{i-1} \\ Q\Delta_{i-1} & \text{if } C_i \neq C_{i-1} \end{cases}$$

$$\Delta_i = \begin{cases} \Delta_i' & \text{if } \Delta_{min} \leq \Delta_i' \leq \Delta_{max} \\ \Delta_{max} & \text{if } \Delta_i' > \Delta_{max} \\ \Delta_{min} & \text{if } \Delta_i' < \Delta_{min} \end{cases}$$

$$y_i' = y_{i-1} + C_i \Delta_i$$

$$y_i = \begin{cases} y_i & \text{if } 0 \leq y_i' \leq y_{max} \\ y_{max} & \text{if } y_i \geq y_{max} \\ 0 & \text{if } y_i' \leq 0 \end{cases}$$

The value of the y_{max} depends on the digital integrator.

3. LIMITATIONS OF THE PARAMETERS

The main parameters of the proposed modulator are the constants P and Q and the limits of the step size Δ_{min} and Δ_{max}. Some apparent limitations of these parameters are:

1. In order for the step size to increase for increasing signals, it should be:

$$P > 1$$

2. In order for the step size to decrease for decreasing signals, it should be:

$$Q < 1$$

Beyond the above two constraints that are stated by Jayant (1) we may add also the following ones:

3. Right after a step change of the input signal there is an overload resulting in a continous increase of the step size. When y 'catches' the input signal, the response of the modulator will have one of the forms of Figures 2,3 or 4 depending on the value of the product P·Q. Thus for PQ>1 the system is unstable (Figure 2), while for PQ=1 the system is not unstable but the step does not always get its minimum value and it retains a bigger value resulting in oscillations with period $2k\,T_s$ (Figure 3). (T_s is the sampling period). Finally for PQ<1 the oscillations, that might occur, are decaying (Figure 4).

4. As it was mentioned before after a step change of the input signal the modulator oscillates with a period $2k\,T_s$ where k satisfies the following relationships:

$$Q \sum_{n=0}^{k-1} P^n > 1$$

$$k \geq 2$$

The oscillations with a period $4T_s$ cannot be cancelled out. However we are able to cancell the oscillations with period greater than $4T_s$ by selecting P and Q in a manner such, that,

$$Q(1+P) \geq 1$$

5. Finally we limited the value of P so that,

$$1.375 \leq P \leq 3$$

In the case that P<1.375 the increase of the step size was too slow resulting in a long time of the overload condition.

Jayant showed that the optimum P should be less than two. The results we took for $P > 2$ well confirmed the above.

Another important parameter is the limits of the step size. In our simulation Δ_{min}=1, where Δ_{max} does not exceed 64.

4. SIMULATION

On the basis of the previous discussion we wrote a program that ran in a CDC 6600 Cyber Computer. The values of P varied from 11/8 to 24/8 with a step 1/8 and the values of Q varied from 4/16 to 11/16 with a step 1/16. The values of Δ_{max} varied from 20 to 64 with a step 4. Another important parameter of the optimum algorithm should be the dynamic range (i.e. the region where the signal-to-noise-ratio is held relatively constant over a wide variation of the input signal level). Because of the strong non-linearity of the system a 50 mV change of the input signal amplitude results in 5 dB change of the signal-to-noise ratio. It is noted that the signal-to-noise ratio has been defined as:

$$S/N = \frac{\sum_{n=1}^{256} x_n^2}{\sum_{n=1}^{256} (x_n - x_n')^2}$$

where x_n' is the filtered output of the local decoder (y_i).

Using as input signal a square waveform of period $T_i=64T_s$, we found the signal-to-noise ratio for any three values P,Q,Δ_{max} and for a 100 levels of the input signal (i.e. from 0.048 V_{pp} to 4.8 V_{pp} and step 0.048V). From these values we found the average signal-to-noise ratio and its deviation that corresponded to each three values of P,Q,Δ_{max} (Figure 5).
Finally we selected a small number of the three values P,Q,Δ_{max} that gave the greatest average and the smallest deviation and formed diagrams of the signal-to-noise ratio vs. the input amplitude level. On the basis of these diagrams we concluded in the following three values,

$$P_{opt} = 7/4$$

$$Q_{opt} = 7/16$$

$$\Delta_{maxopt} = 52$$

These value also give a maximum dynamic range (Figure 5). Figure 6 shows the waveforms we get with the aid of the simulation i.e. the decoder output its Fourier Spectrum and the filtered output of the local decoder.

The obtained signal-to-noise ratio is around 19.5 dB for input levels from 50mV to 5V which corresponds to a dynamic range of 40 dB. Besides we may observe the limited numbers of the intermodulation products (Figure 6). It is also worthwhile to note that $Q_{opt}=R_{opt}/4$ which eases the circuit realization, using digital circuits, immensely.

5. CIRCUIT IMPLEMENTATION OF THE PROPOSED CODER AND EXPERIMENTAL RESULTS

Figure 7, shows the detailed block diagram of the coder we built in the laboratory. The demodulator is the same as the local decoder plus a low pass filter.

The experimental results as well as the computer simulation results (obtained with the aid of an HP9845B Computer) are shown in Figures 8, 9, 10 and 11.

From these Figures we observe the complete similarity of the experimental and the computer simulation results.

This similarity makes us sure about the validity of the computer simulation results and the optimallity of the proposed algorithm.

Another observation from Figures 8,9,10,11 is the strong dependence of the overshoot on the step amplitude. We also see that during tracking the step size ends up at its minimum value. After the filtering the oscillations disappear and the output signal is a very satisfactory replica of the input signal.

6. CONCLUSIONS

In this paper we presented a specific algorithm for a non-linear (adaptive) delta modulation system where the step size varies exponentially. Using computer simulation methods we found the optimum parameters of the system and we then implemented the whole system.

Finally we presented and compared computer simulation results and experimental results. The comparison confirmed the validity of our method.

REFERENCES

1. Jayant, N.S., "Adaptive delta modulation with a one bit memory", Bell Systems Tech.J., 49, No.3, 321-342, March 1970.
2. Song C.L., Garodnick, J., and Shilling, D.L., "A Variable Step-Size Robust Delta Modulator" IEEE Trans. on Communications, Vol.19, No.12, p.1033-1044, Dec. 1971.
3. Culter, C.C., "Delayed encoding stabilizer for adaptive coders", IEEE Trans. on Communications, Vol. COM.19, No.12, p.898-906, Dec. 1971.
4. Steele, R., "Delta modulation systems", Pentech Press, London, 1975.

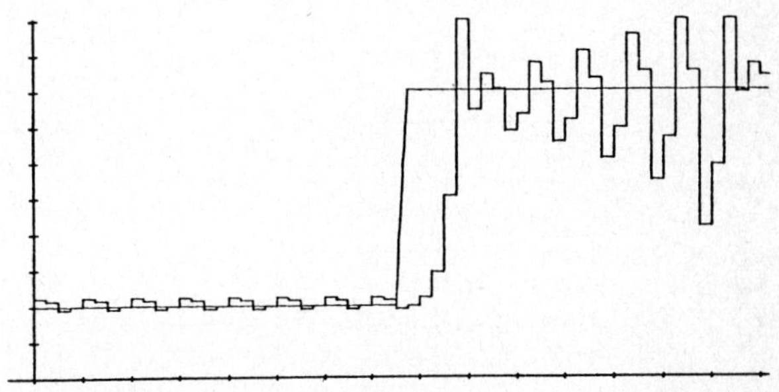

Figure 2. Step response with PQ>1 (P=3,Q=0.4).

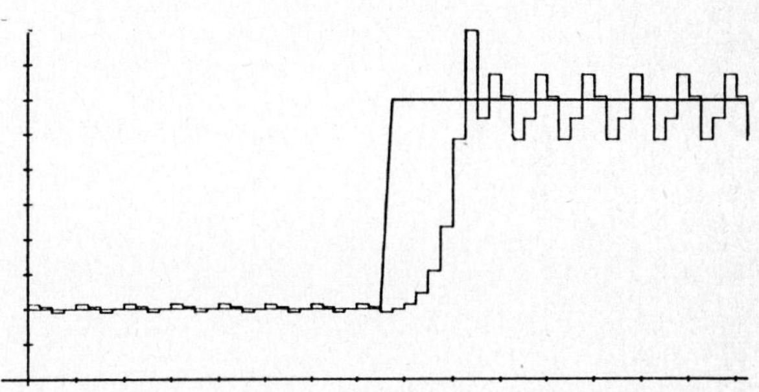

Figure 3. Step response with PQ=1 (P=2,Q=0.5).

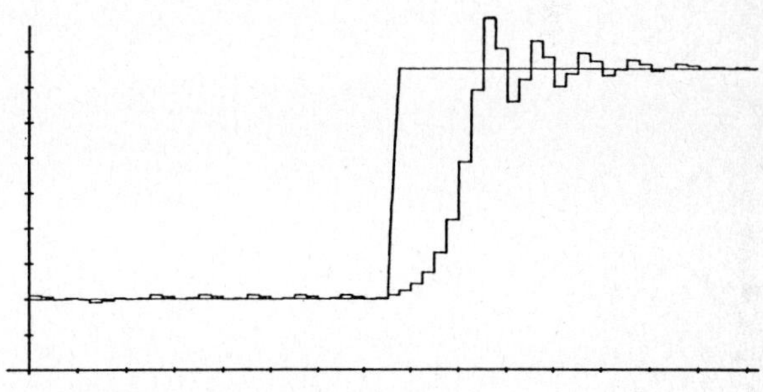

Figure 4. Step response with PQ<1 (P=1.75, Q=0.438).

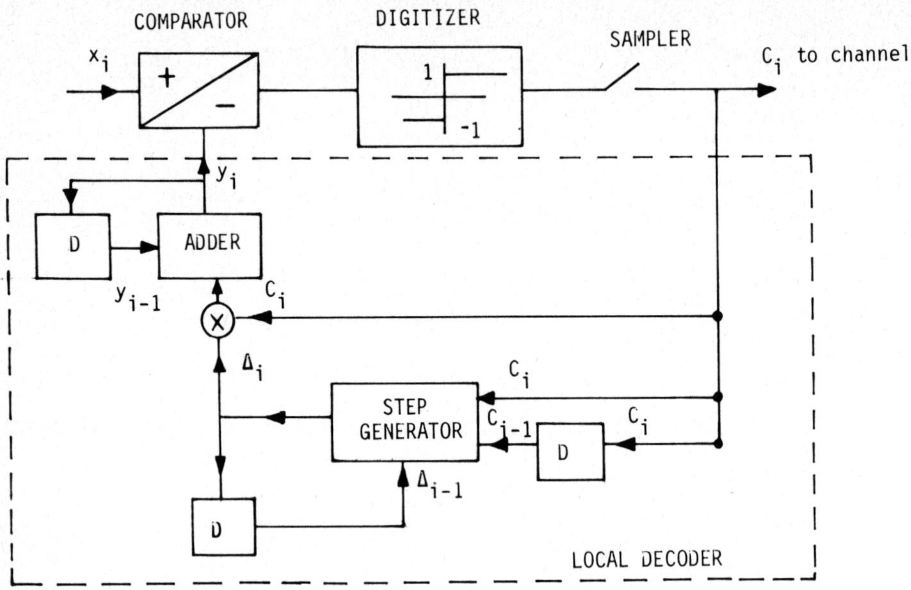

Figure 1. Block diagram of the delta coder.

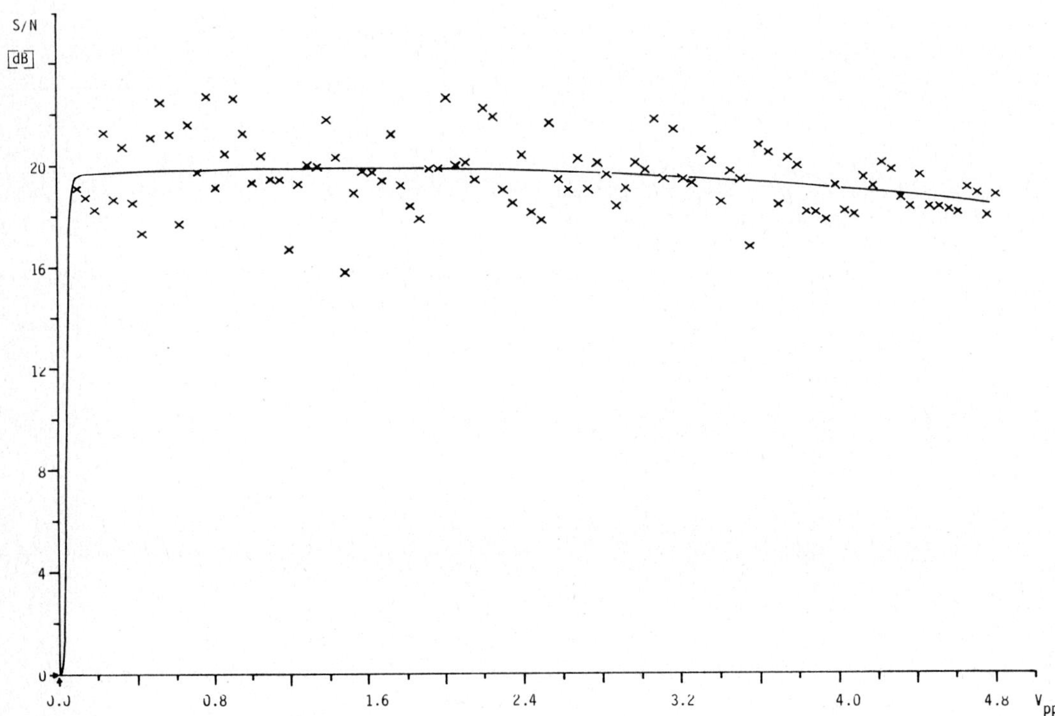

Figure 5. S/N vs. the input amplitude level for P=7/4, Q=7/16 and Δ_{max}=52.

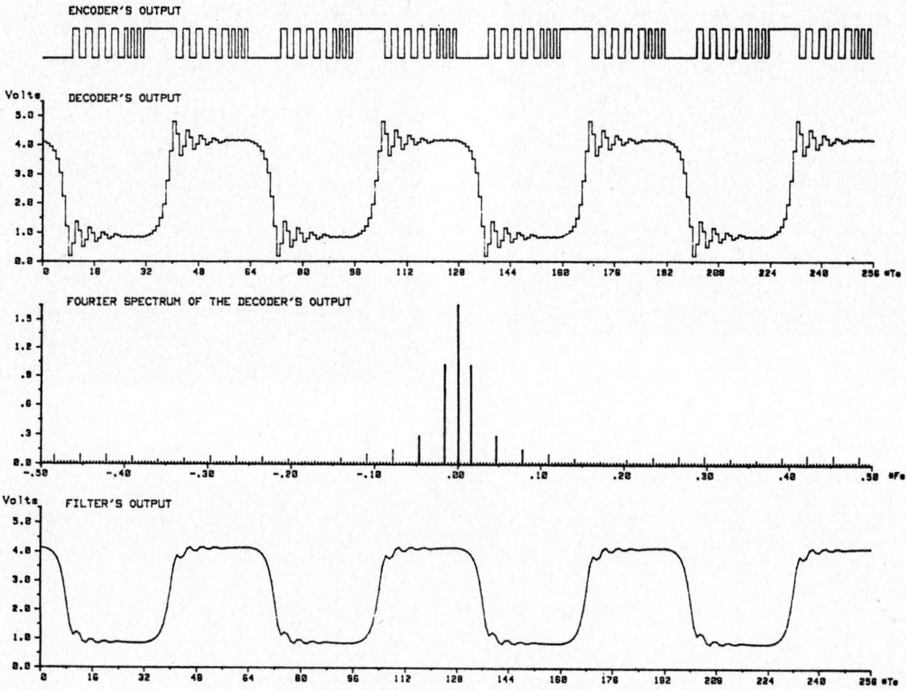

Figure 6. Computer simulation results.

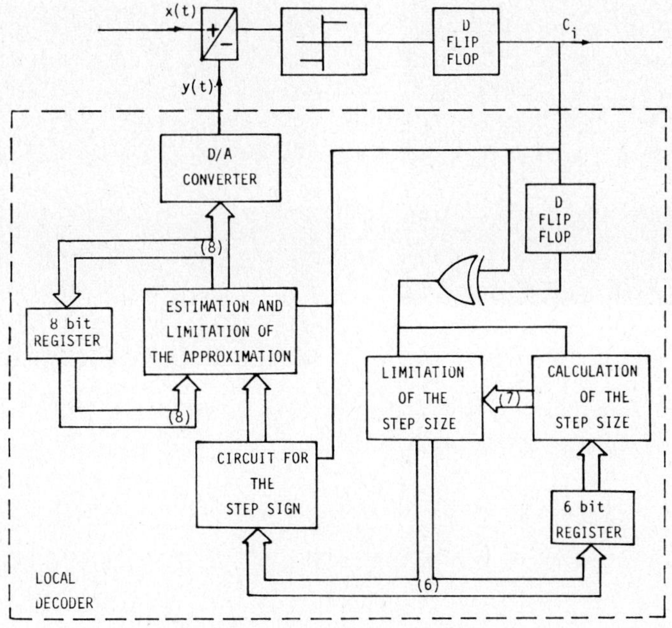

Figure 7. Detailed block diagram of the delta coder.

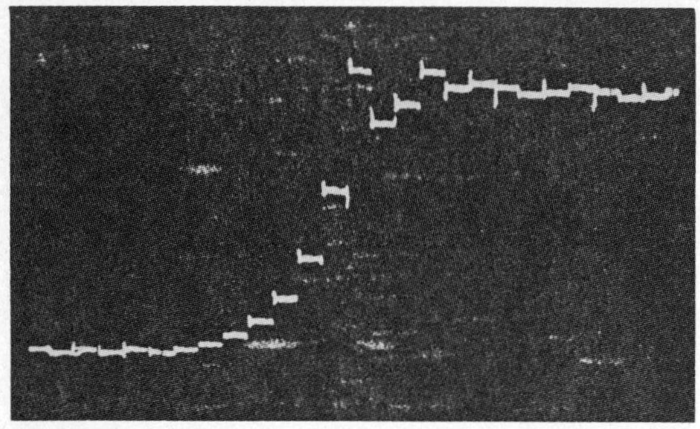

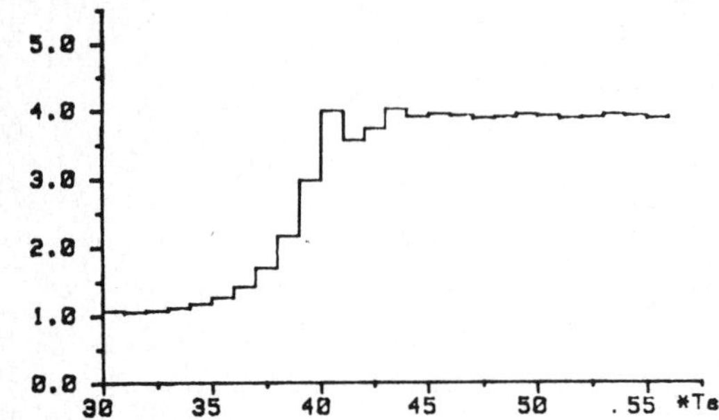

Figure 8. Step response of the coder (Amplitude level 4).

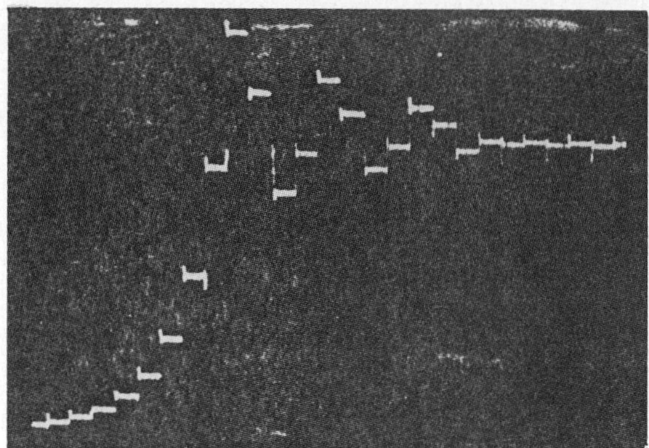

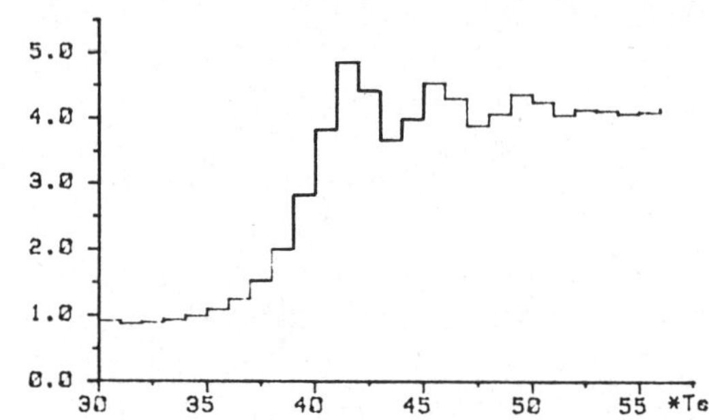

Figure 10. Step response of the coder (Amplitude level 5).

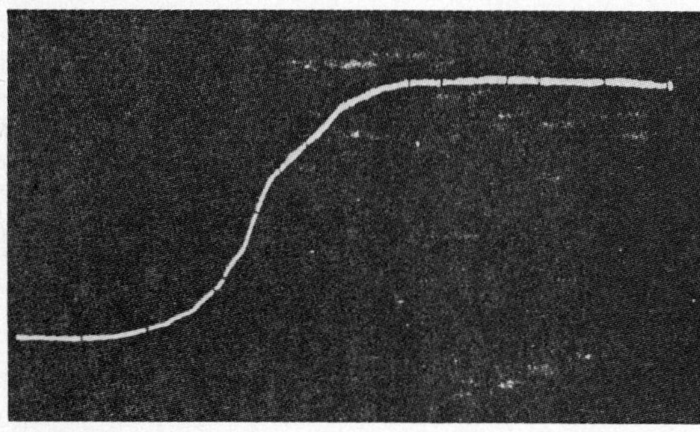

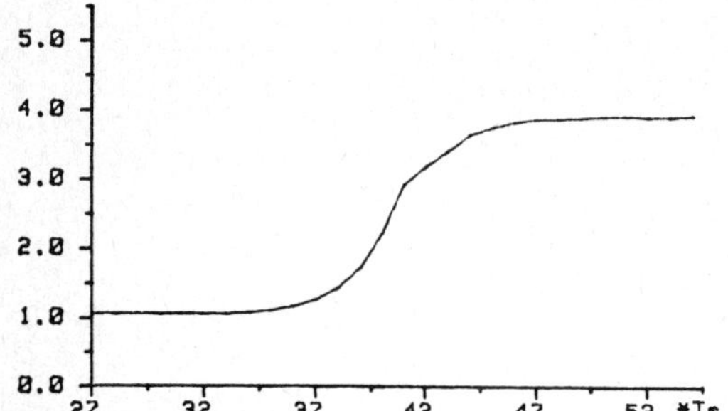

Figure 9. Filtered output of the local decoder (Amplitude level 4).

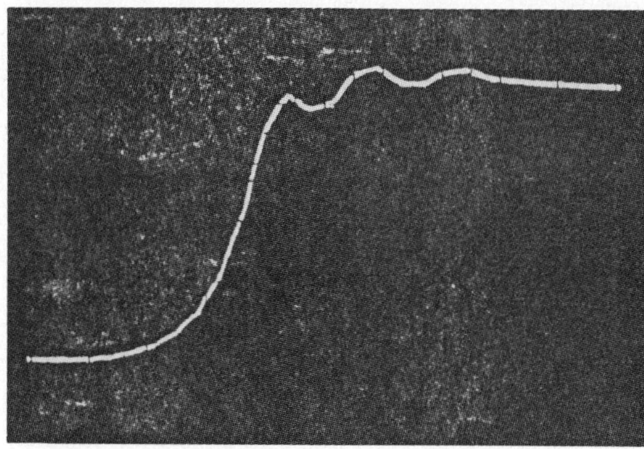

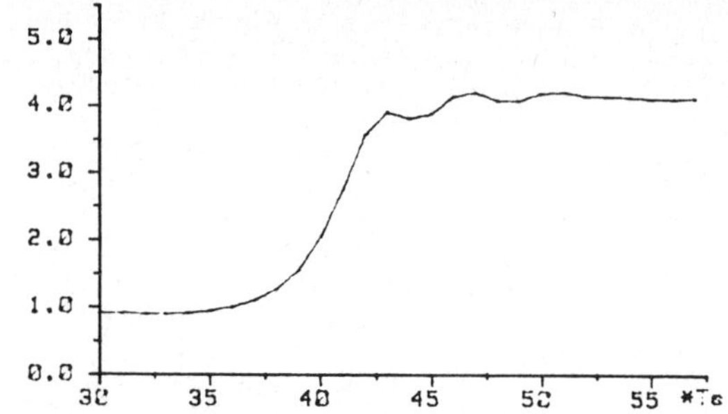

Figure 11. Filtered output of the coder (Amplitude level 5).

DIGITAL TECHNIQUES in Simulation, Communication and Control
Spyros G. Tzafestas (editor)
Elsevier Science Publishers B.V. (North-Holland) © IMACS, 1985

SPREAD-SPECTRUM TECHNIQUES FOR RELIABLE AND PRIVATE COMMUNICATIONS IN THE OFFICE OF THE FUTURE.

Chris J. Georgopoulos

Dept. of Electrical Engineering
University of Thrace
Xanthi, Greece

This paper discusses applicable RF and IR spread-spectrum techniques as they apply to the office communications environment for reducing interference and facilitating the communication of simultaneous users of common channel(s). In applying spread-spectrum techniques to an optical (IR) system, it is important to keep in mind, among other things, that there are important differences between an optical and a conventional electronic system regarding the strategy of suppressing interference and noise.

1. INTRODUCTION

Two advanced transmission techniques for communications in an office environment are : radio frequency (RF) and infrared (IR) radiation.(1) Most commercial wireless telephones operate with radio carrier frequencies around 50MHz using FM modulation. But when more users are using the network the 862-960 MHz band allocated to mobile radio is more appropriate. In either case, certain interference regulations should be observed. On the other hand, IR radiation is essentially restricted to the room in which it is generated, cannot be detected outside the office, and will not interfere with similar systems in adjacent offices.

Spread spectrum communication systems offer a number of advantages in multiple access situations, compared with alternative approaches.(2) They have the advantage that there is no absolute limit to the number of channel assignments, as there is with both TDMA and FDMA.(3)

Spread spectrum will reduce both the interference of the RF signal with any existing system and decrease the detectability of the signal outside the office building. Spread spectrum technology can also be employed in IR communication channels to provide a multiple access capability or reductions in transmitted power spectral density. It can also be used to provide anti-interference (or antijamming).(4) This means that it can equally be applied to PABX - infrared telsets and terminal environment, that is in an office, to take care of the noise effects due to background light and especially of those transient phenomena that occur during the ignition phase of fluorescent lamps. It can also be used for voice/data security purposes.

2. SPREAD-SPECTRUM CONSIDERATIONS

2.1. A Brief Review

According to C.E. Shannon' s relationship,(2)

$$C=W\log_2\left(1+\frac{S}{N}\right) \Rightarrow \frac{N}{S}=\frac{1.44W}{C}, \qquad (1)$$

where C = capacity in bits per second
W = bandwidth in Hertz
N = noise power
S = signal power

Under certain assumptions and approximations we obtain :

$$\frac{N}{S}=\frac{1.44W}{C}\approx\frac{W}{C} \qquad (2)$$

which shows that for any given noise to signal ratio we can have a low information-error rate by increasing the bandwidth used to transfer information.

A signal lasting T seconds needs not to occupy more than the order of $W\approx(1/T)$Hz of bandwidth, that is $TW\approx 1$. Systems using more than this bandwidth, that is $TW\gg 1$, are identified as spread spectrum systems. Some properties and signal characteristics of modern spread spectrum systems are as follows :(2,4)

a) The carrier is an unpredictable, or "pseudorandom", wide-band signal.
b) The bandwidth of the carrier is much wider than the bandwidth of the data modulation.
c) Reception is accomplished by cross correlation of the received wide-band signal with a synchronously generated replica of the wideband carrier.
d) Selective addressing capability.
e) Code division multiplexing is possible for multiple access.
f) Message screening from eavesdroppers.
g) High resolution ranging.
h) Interference rejection.

These properties and characteristics permit a receiver or cluster of receivers to be addressed by assigning a given reference code to them, whereas others are given a different code. Selective addressing can then be as simple as transmitting the proper code sequence as modulation.

The term "pseudorandom" is used specifically to mean random in appearance but reproducible by

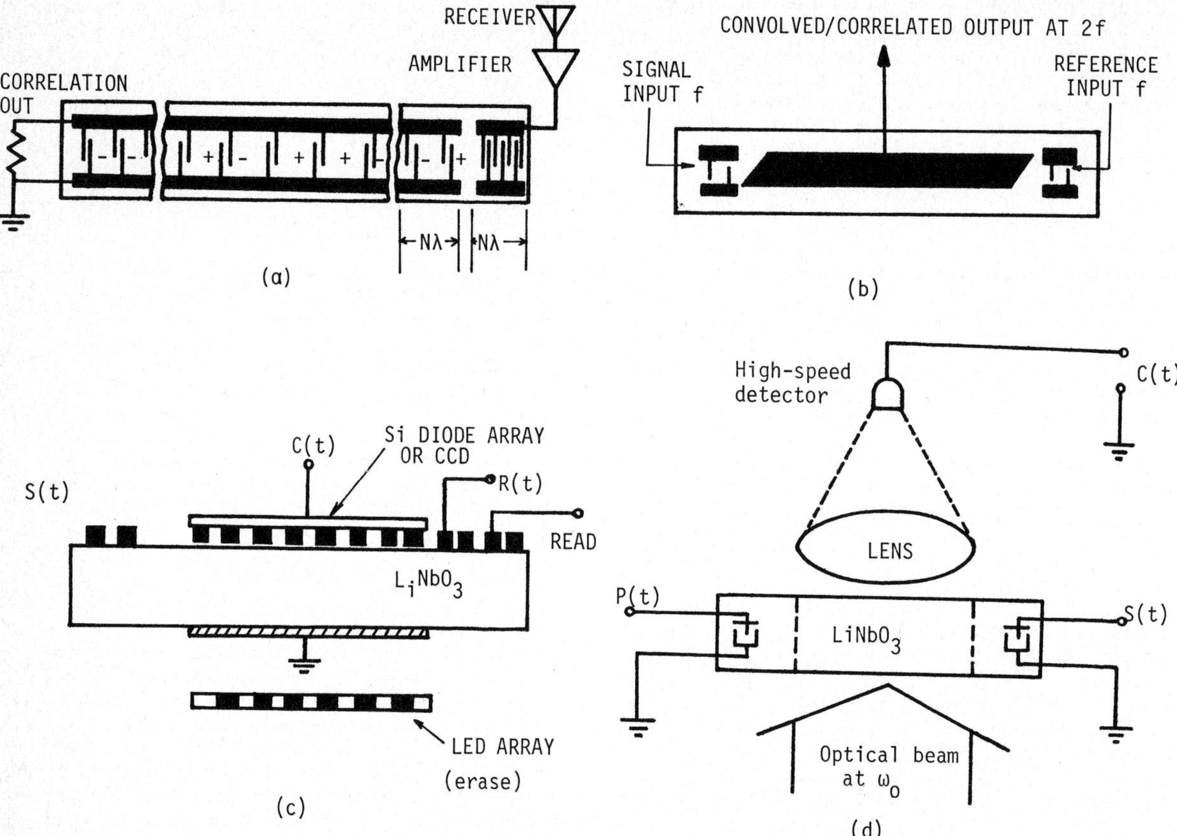

Figure 1 : For spread spectrum communications in which matched-filter devices are used, SAW correlators (a) and convolvers (b) are often used. Other devices include acoustoelectric correlators (c) and acousto-optic convolvers (d).

deterministic means. A key parameter of spread spectrum systems is the number of essentially orthogonal signaling formats which are used to communicate a data symbol. Here, two signaling formats are orthogonal in the sense that the signals employed in one format for communication would not be detected by a processor for the other format, and vice versa. The number of possible orthogonal signaling formats is called the multiplicity factor of the communication link. While conventional communication systems other than wide-band frequency modulation (FM) have a multiplicity factor near unity, spread spectrum systems typically have multiplicity factors in the thousands.

Spread spectrum systems, because of the nature of their signal characteristics, have among other performance attributes the following :

1) High time resolution is attained by the correlation detection of wide-band signals. Differences in the time of arrival of the wide-band signal, on the order of the reciprocal of the signal bandwidth, are detectable. This property can be used to suppress multipath and, by the same token, to make disturbances ineffective.

2) Transmitter-receiver pairs using independent random carriers can operate in the same bandwidth with minimal cochannel interference. These systems are called spread-spectrum code-division multiple access (CDMA) systems.

3) Cryptographic capabilities result when data modulation cannot be distinguished from the carrier modulation, and the carrier modulation is effectively random to an unwanted observer. In this case the spread spectrum modulation takes on the role of a key in a cipher system. A system using indistinguishable data and spread spectrum carrier modulations is a form of privacy system.

2.2. Direct Sequence and Filter Systems.

Direct sequence systems employ pseudorandom sequences, phase-shift-keyed (PSK) into the carrier, for spreading. The time spent in transmitting a single carrier symbol from this sequence is called the chip time of the system. With binary PSK data antipodally modulated on this spread spectrum carrier, the resultant system's multiplicity factor is given by :

multiplicity factor (m.f.)=(data bit time)/(chip time) (3)

Direct-sequence spreading in conjuction with PSK data modulation is perhaps the most common spread spectrum approach used in practice. This technique is general and its use is not limited to any particular modulation technique. Altought NRZ coding of both data and direct sequence codes is assumed, any other compatible combination of possible formats can be be used in practice.

The receiver in a direct sequence system must acquire and track the direct code, generally before carrier tracking and data demodulation take place. It is assumed that acquisition has been accomplished and the direct sequence receiver is operating in the track mode. The performance results of such a system can be extended in a straightforward manner to other modulation techniques, data formats and code formats.

Filter systems generate a wide-band transmitted signal by pulsing a matched filter (MF) having a long, wide-band, pseudorandomly controlled impulse response. Signal detection at the receiver is accomplished by an identically pseudorandom, synchronously controlled matched filter which performs the correlation computation. Rapid pseudorandom variation of the transmitter's impulse ensures the unpredictability of the wideband carrier. Such filters can be implemented using a variety of devices as shown in Fig.1.(5)

3. INTERFERENCE PROBLEMS

3.1. Types of Interference in the Office Environment

Considering the direct spread spectrum performance without coding in the presence of a variety of types of interference, we can list the following types of interference pertinent to direct systems, under two categories : narrowband and wideband (Table I).

As narrowband (or equivalently, partial band) is characterized any interference signal whose bandwidth occupies only a small part of that occupied by the direct sequence signal. Similarly, as wideband (or fullband) is characterized any interference signal that occupies most or all of the bandwidth occupied by the direct sequence signal.

3.2. Stressing the Differences Between RF and IR channels

In the case of RF channels, if two signals at the same frequency are added, the result is a single signal of the same frequency (with altered amplitude and phase) that is the vector sum of the two signals (Fig.2a). On the other hand, two light pulse trains at the same pulse repetition interval (PRI), will sum into a combined light pulse train without a well-defined PRI (fig.2b). When two sinusoids at the same frequency have a 180-degree difference in phase, they cancel out(Fig. 2c). If two light pulse trains at the same PRI have a 180-degree difference in phase, the sum will be a single light pulse train with one-half the PRI (Fig.2d).

In an IR system an important factor is the existing ambient light conditions in a given room. Here we have to distinguish daylight, incandescent illumination, and fluorescent lamps. All of these sources of visible light may generate a current in the photodiode of the receiver. Incandescent light contains a great deal of infrared light. Therefore, this type of illumination is particularly prone to interference. Daylight which enters a room (i.e not the direct sunlight) contains less infrared radiation. Fluorescent light, on the other hand, includes only a small amount of infrared radiation. However, during the turnon of fluorescent lamp some frequency may interfere with the carrier frequency.

TABLE I

LIST OF INTERFERENCE TYPES PERTINENT TO DIRECT SEQUENCE SYSTEMS

	Radio Communication	IR Diffuse Channel Communication
Narrowband or Partial Band	• CW Tone • Partial-band noise • Multitones	• Thermal noise, moving objects • Light peaks (transients) • Unisotropic distribution of light intensity
Wideband or Full Band	• Wideband noise • Another direct sequency code • Repeat back • Fading	• Constant background light (sunlight, fluorescent, incandencent) • Ray multipath • Monochromatic radiation due to gas discharge in special lamps • Light shadows

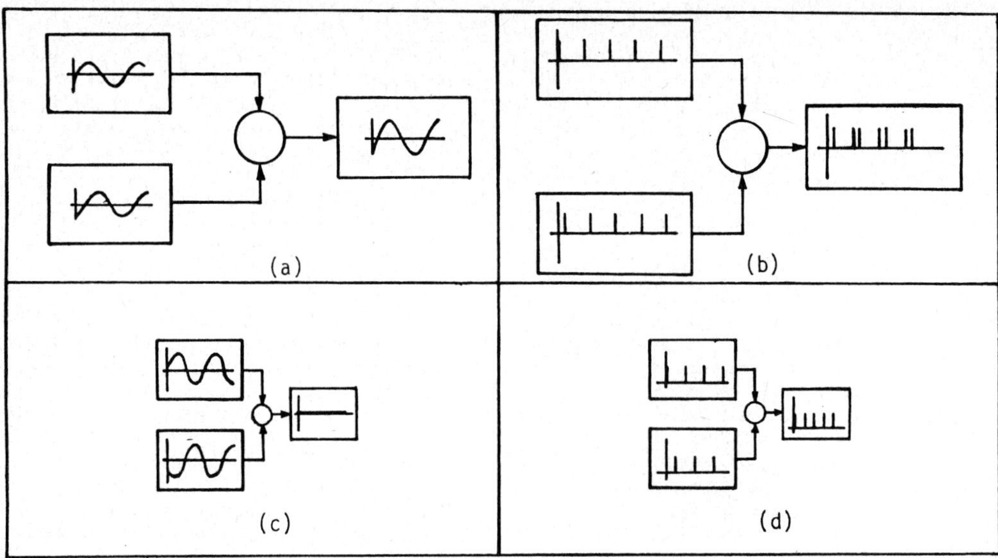

Figure 2 : Basic differences between RF and light pulsed waveform behavior from interference standpoint. Combined RF signals are shown in (a) and (c), whereas combined light pulses are shown in (b) and (d).

During the starting of a gas discharge free electrons in the gas collide with atoms in the gas, exciting or ionizing them. If the applied voltage across the gas exceeds the minimum excitation potential, the exited atom will probably soon return spontaneously to the ground state and emit monochromatic radiation of the frequnecy

$$\omega = \frac{2\pi e V_1}{h} \qquad (4)$$

where e = the charge on the electron and h=Plank's constant, corresponding to a wavelength $\lambda = (1.24/eV)$ μm.

At these low energies only a few quantized energy levels are involved in excitation, and the resulting atomic spectral lines are discrete and weak. As an excited state typically lasts about 10^{-8} s, the natural line width is ~10^8 Hz.

3.3. Rejecting the Additionals from Adjacent Channels.

In an RF channel a simple LC network will resonate at, and pass, only frequencies that are in a narrow range about the tuned frequency of the network. All frequencies outside the narrow band are rejected, including harmonics and subharmonics. There is no such circuit element that can act in a similar fashion when transmitting light pulses over an IR channel in the PRI domain. The discontinuous nature of the PRI's time domain leads to significant anomalies in the behavior of PRI filter elements.

One obvious approach to constructing a pulse-repetition interval filter element would be to use a multivibrator or clock element to generate a tunable time interval against which to sort or select incoming pulses. A given light pulse train (actually, the equivalent electrical pulse train) would then be admitted only if the pulse arrival times coincided with the activation of the multivibrator. Another pulse train at the same PRI but at different phase would not be admitted by such a circuit. Also, the multivibrator exhibits zero bandwidth, that is, however closely it might be tuned to the incoming PRI, it would gradually drift out of synchronization. Additionally, the multivibrator has no tolerance for PRI jitterlike pulse spreading which might be described as a broadening of the PRI spectral line due to multipath of IR reflected sinals in a room with relatively small dimensions. Jitter tolerance could be removed by generating an admittance gate with a selected width. Obtaining bandwidth is more difficult. It might be possible to synchronize the multivibrator to the incoming light pulse train, but when several light pulse trains are present at the same PRI, or two light pulse trains drift through each other and the synchronization circuitry slips from one to the other, there will be a problem.

The phase problem inherent in a fixed-time gate can be solved by utilizing a rotating shift register. In this configuration, a light pulse train that hits at the same location on subsequent rotations of the shift register at the receiver will be passed through, and all other trains will be rejected. The shift register is thus the "tuned circuit", and the rotation period defines the "resonant" PRI.

3.4. Multipath Problems.

In the case of RF communication, fading will occur when the desired signal arrives at the receiver by more than one propagation path. Multiple transmission paths may be due to reflections from walls, ceiling, objects, etc., in an office environment. At some frequencies, the relative time delay between these paths may the signal components to cancel one another at the receiver, while the components may reinforce one another at other frequencies as explained previously (in subsection 3.2). These will result to selective fading and intersymbol interference.(6)

It appears that reflected signal cause a ripple form of envelope delay distortion (EDD) which may be approximated be the well-known formula :

$$\tau_E = r\tau_0 \sin\left[\Delta\omega\tau_o + \varphi\right] \tag{5}$$

where

τ_E = envelope delay distortion (EDD) caused by reflection.

τ_o = time delay of reflection with respect to main signal.

r = relative reflection amplitude with respect to main signal amplitude.

$\Delta\omega$ = angular frequency deviation of carrier with respect to its center frequency.

φ = relative phase angle of main signal and reflection when they combine.

Considering an IR system, we can say that IR communication in the office environment is performed through many different paths.(7) Therefore, the IR channel is a multipath channel (Fig.3). In this type of channel, there is no fading problem. The problem here is the broadening of the receiver light pulses due to multipath propagation which prevents the system from operating at high bit rates and some "shadowed" corners. The most direct way of determining the presence of reflections over an IR path is to transmit a sequence of IR pulses in one direction and observe the reflections trailing each pulse at the receive site after they have been converted into electrical signals.

The techniques mentioned previously will yield satisfactory results when applied to IR communication channel.

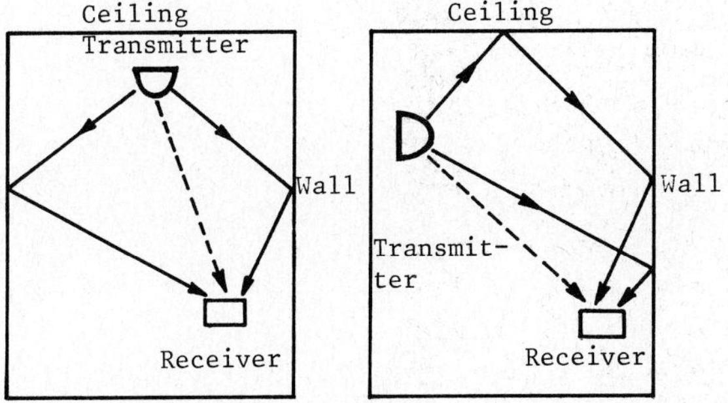

Figure 3 : Multipath propagation in an in-house IR communication system.

4. USING THE SPREAD-SPECTRUM APPROACH

Here, spread spectrum can be used not only for the reduction of required power, but also for the implementation of Code Division Multiple Access (CDMA).

4.1. Code Division Multiple Access (CDMA)

Interest to CDMA is relative to random access communication systems where the number of potential users (subscribers, terminals, etc) is much larger than the maximum number of users simultaneously active in the channel. The identification of the spread spectrum signal is implicit in a receiver being able to correlate and extract data, i.e. the signal is identified by its PN code.

A pure CDMA approach is not capable of accommodating signals with large power differentials which, is termed the "near-far" problem since it typically arises from the large variation in ranges between users in a dispersed network.(8) In other words, the processing gain of the receiver determines, the tolerable total interference, and it does not matter whether there are one thousand signals at the same power level, one hundred signals each at ten times the power level, or ten signals each at hundred times the power level as the desired signal. The alternate is then to provide orthogonal slots, in frequency and/or time such that multiple users can be simultaneously active in the channel even with a large near-far ratio. The extremes are : (1) time slotting leading to time division modes of operation, and (2) frequency slotting leading to frequency division operation.

For signals accessing through a common point, in a way similar to the CDMA communication operation of satellite-repeater, can in principle be closely coordinated with respect to equalization of signal power levels at the common point of reception. Assuming all terminals are equal and that uplink noise is negligible, we can express the total multiple access system data rate, in bits per second, as :(8)

$$R_T = \left(\frac{B_{RF}}{E_b/N_o}\right)\left(\frac{LP_R}{N_oB_{RF}+\lambda P_R}\right) = \left(\frac{B_{RF}}{E_b/N_o}\right)\left(\frac{LQ}{1+\lambda Q}\right), \tag{6}$$

where :

R_T = total data rate

L = useful fraction of relay power, P_R (transponder in case of IR System)

N_o = receiver noise density

B_{RF} = channel bandwidth

λ = fraction of relay power which is intermodulation noise.

$$Q = P_R/N_oB_{IF}$$

The condition $Q < 1$ is called the "power-starved" condition, while $Q > 1$ is "bandwidth-starved". It is then obvious that CDMA in the "power starved" condition can, with control of power levels, closely approach the best possible multiple access performance in that clutter is unimportant, while L can be close to unity. On the other hand, CDMA is rather inefficient in the bandwidth starved condition due to clutter. In the latter case other techniques may be used. Such techniques involve time division multiple access (TDMA) and/or frequency division multiple access (FDMA).

4.2. A Hybrid Approach for the IR System.

Looking into the two-way indoor IR communication system we see that we can use a hybrid approach based on Shannon's theorem, as explained below.

1) Since a zone or office transponder (tranceiver) is fixed and can be powered by the building power, its transmitter for the down-link channel can be made to transmit a relatively high peak power (which of course will be within the safety limits). This means that the factor $\log_2(1+\frac{P}{N})$ will be large, which has the following advantages :

   - It overcomes the background noise (i.e, the signal can be made stronger than any background light noise, etc.).
   - It can afford the use of optical filters with higher atenuation at the receiving end which are less costly.
   - The messages for a peer-to-peer communication can easily be relayed by the central transponder and the regenerated signals can be of high intensity too.

2) Since there is not much power available on each handheld telset, the up-link channel will have to use a spread spectrum technique, i.e an increased "W" (bandwidth) to transmit signal of relatively low power. This means that the down-link may use not only different modulating frequency than the upper-link, but also different type of transmitting technique (modulation and/or coding). For example, the regenerative section of the central transponder could use PN spread spectrum in the receiver of up-link and a normal modulation scheme in the transmitter of down-link, thus simplifying somewhat the overall system.

5. CONCLUSION

In an office environment, interferences and noise are not easily predictable and avoidable, especially due to various objects and the walls where multiple signal reflections occur. Another reason is the change of positions of handheld wireless telsets and the switching of various devices creating transient phenomena. Spread spectrum techniques, which require no knowledge of interference and noise conditions, can be used to suppress noise and interference of various forms which may have the same frequency, same polarization, and same direction of arrival as that of the desired signal.

REFERENCES

[1] Georgopoulos, C.J., Alternative communications techniques in the office of the future, HETELCON'83 (1983).

[2] Dixon, P.C., Spread Spectrum Systems (John Wiley and Sons, New York 1976).

[3] Scales, W.C., Potential Use of Spread Spectrum Techniques in Non-Government Applications, NTIS :FCC -0320 (Dec.1980).

[4] Scholtz, R.A., The origins of spread-spectrum communications, IEEE Transactions on Communications, Vol.Com.30, No.5 (1982) 822.

[5] Colvin, R.D., Spread-spectrum devices cater to new systems, Microwaves(Feb.1981)65.

[6] Henaff, J., Applications of Surface-Acoustic-Wave devices in satellite communication system, 10th European Microwave Conference (1980).

[7] Georgopoulos, C.J.,PABX-Infrared network interfaces, proceedings of fiber optics and communications Local Area Networks : FOC/LAN (1983).

[8] NTIS, Spread Spectrum Communications, Advisory Group for Aerospace Research and Development Sequences," U.S. Department of Commerce (July 1973).

DIGITAL TECHNIQUES in Simulation, Communication and Control
Spyros G. Tzafestas (editor)
Elsevier Science Publishers B.V. (North-Holland) © IMACS, 1985

SAW DEVICES FOR DIGITAL PROCESSING IN ELECTRONIC OFFICE COMMUNICATIONS

Voula C. Georgopoulos

Dept. of Electrical Engineering
University of Thrace
Xanthi, Greece

This paper deals with the application of Surface Acoustic Wave (SAW) devices in digital processing for electronic office communications. It discusses their advantages, their requirements and their limitations in the electronic office environment. One of the major applications of SAW devices in digital processing is to successfully perform real-time correlation of spread-spectrum signals.
A design of an RF 125 MHz transmitter with the use of SAW devices for use in cordless phones is described.

1. INTRODUCTION

Surface Acoustic Wave (SAW) devices are passive electroacoustic devices that allow acoustic energy to be generated, modulated and detected on a piezoelectric substrate.(1) The three basic parts of a SAW device are: a) the piezoelectric substrate, b) the interdigital transducers (IDTs) and c) the package. Other parts of the SAW device are the input and output matching circuits and the damping material.

The basic functions of these devices are: a)delay line, b) bandpass filter, c) convolver, d) dispersive delay-line, e) resonator and f) oscillator. In conjunction with digital devices they can be used to perform the following complex functions: pulse expansion and compression for spread spectrum communications, spectrum analysis, cross correlation and autocorrelation, frequency division multiplexing (FDM) and time division multiplexing (TDM) and many others.

Although SAW device technology first appeared around the middle of the 1960s and their uses have multiplied, a mystery still exists concerning these devices. For example, when something is wrong with a system that uses a SAW device, the first device to be blamed is the SAW. What most people don't realize is the fact that SAW devices are unique devices that need special care as most digital integrated circuits do. However, sensible handling, good RF matching practice and prevention of overstressing allows these devices to be valuable and frequently essential components in the success of a system.

2. GENERAL CHARACTERISTICS OF SAW DEVICES

2.1 Comparison of SAW Devices with Digital ICs

Many present-day digital telecommunications systems and many more future ones will require very high speed and multiple access for their users. These digital systems can include, apart from common devices used, high speed digital devices and surface acoustic wave devices. The digital devices commonly used are mainly sampling circuits and A/D converters, memories, multipliers, correlators and Fast Fourier Transformers (FFTs). However, multipliers, correlators and FFTs are a physical limit to the high speed needed in telecommunications. Consequently, these operations could be performed by SAW devices that can be coupled directly to I/O and storage digital components.(2)

The superiority and the capabilities of SAW devices over commonly used digital devices can be illustrated by the following example: Using SAW devices a signal of bandwidth B=500 MHz and period T=20μs can be directly correlated to a reference signal. A digital correlating device for the same operation would have to perform T*B multiplications in parallel with a pulse frequency of 2B. The fact that a 8*8 bits multiplication needs about 1000 gates gives a Functional Throughput Rate $FTR=2TB^2G=10^{16}$ Gate·Hz.

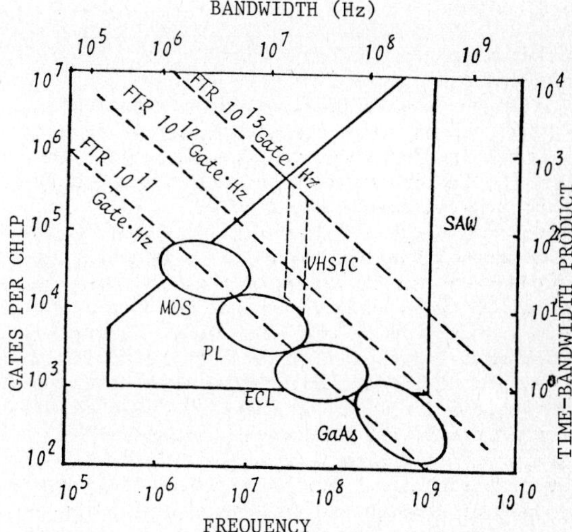

Figure 1 : Comparison of the efficiency of SAW devices and digital ICs in signal processing.

Currently available digital integrated circuits can achieve an FTR in the range of 10^4 up to 10^{12} Gate·Hz as shown in Figure 1. The VHSIC (Very High Speed Integrated Circuit) program of U.S.A. is aiming at an FTR of 10^{13} Gate·Hz reaching a practical limit for digital integrated circuits.(3)

2.2 Advantages of SAW Devices

Apart from the advantages of SAW devices over digital integrated circuits, as described above, the advantages of SAW devices over other commonly used devices are the following:

- **Signal Accessibility:** The signal (wave) is accessible in all its travel giving entirely new possibilities in signal processing.
- **Compactness:** Due to the fact that surface acoustic waves travel with a speed 10^5 times less than electromagnetic waves, large signal delays can be achieved in small physical dimensions.
- **High Reliability:** This can be achieved due fewer connections, less wiring and fewer components needed for complex functions. Thus a lower mean-time before failure can be achieved.
- **Stability:** With a proper selection of the piezoelectric substrate an excellent temperature stability can be achieved making the device very advantageous in military applications.
- **Package:** These devices are in a flat package and consequently, they are directly compatible to integrated circuits for the development of advanced systems.
- **Reproducibility:** They are highly reproducible in manufacturing due to the fact that all critical dimensions and specifications are established by photolithography.

Other advantages include linear phase response and ruggedness.

2.3 Requirements and Limitations

In order for the SAW devices and conventional digital devices to be compatible, it is essential that their performance bands overlap. This applies to signal bandwidth and duration, accuracy, access speed and number of bits.(2)

The region of application of SAW technology is limited by physical, technological and sometimes economical factors. With present day structural analysis waves of up to 1 GHz can be generated, modulated and detected on the substrate with a wavelength of about 3 μm. Above this frequency the insertion loss of the materials used as piezoelectric substrates increase drastically. Therefore, it is almost impossible to achieve higher frequencies. The lower limit of frequencies and of the desired delays depend on the economically allowable size of the piezoelectric substrate. Table I summarizes the practical limits of operation for SAW devices.

TABLE I

PRACTICAL LIMITS IN SAW DEVICE APPLICATIONS

	MINIMUM VALUE	MAXIMUM VALUE
FREQUENCY	10 MHz	1 GHz
BANDWIDTH	10 KHz	500 MHz
DELAY	100 ns	50 μs

3. APPLICATIONS OF SAW DEVICES IN MODERN ELECTRONIC OFFICE DIGITAL PROCESSING

3.1 Spread-Spectrum Communications

Many signal processing problems in the electronic office of the future would have remained unsolved if SAW devicies had not been studied more extensively in relation to advances in communications techniques.

One of the major applications of SAW devices in digital processing is to successfully perform real-time correlation of spread-spectrum signals. Spread-spectrum is a technique where the transmitted signals are spread over a frequency band that is much larger than necessary for the information being transmitted. At the receiver a correlation demodulation process "collapses" the excess bandwidth, obtaining the improved performance of the system.(4) The reasons for using spread-spectrum techniques in radio communications for the electronic office is to reduce multipath interference from the walls, the ceiling and floor and to avoid unauthorized eavesdropping.

Digital processors, as mentioned earlier, are too limited in bandwidth to successfully perform real-time correlation of these spread signals. Although analog processors can process long duration wide-band signals, they cannot simultaneously perform the correlation of signals over a range of relative time delays. Therefore, signal acquisition and identification are complexified. SAW matched filters, convolvers and correlators along with other helpful SAW devices have the ability to process long-duration signals over a range of relative time delays.

Figure 2 is a functional diagram of coherent PSK spread-spectrum by passive correlation. The PN (pseudonoise) sequence generator of the transmitter serially encodes the input data stream, spreading the spectrum of the baseband signal by producing in each data bit interval a sequence of narrow pulses of changing polarity. After a few other functions are performed to complete the spreading of the signal, the spread signal is transmitted. In the receiver, the spread- spectrum signal is first processed by a matched filter and a periodic sequence of correlation peaks results. The repetition rate of the correlation peaks correspond to the repe-

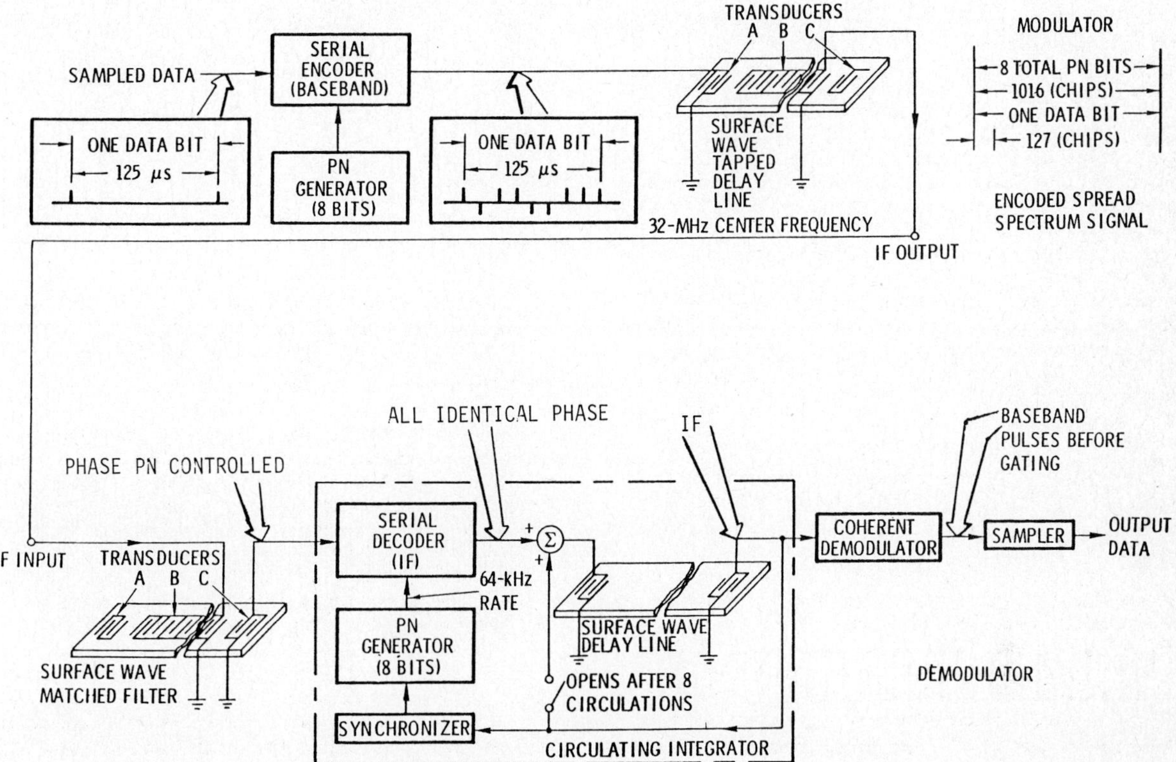

Figure 2 : Functional diagram of coherent PSK spread-spectrum by passive correlation.(5)

tition rate of the pulse generator used in the transmitter, and the phase depends on the signal from the PN generator and the data signal. Further processing yields the original input data stream.(5)

3.2 Other Applications

Other applications of SAW devices in modern electronic office digital processing may include the following:

- Data-Voice Distribution
- TV (cable, pay, security)
- Cordless phones
- PABXs
- LAN (local area network) Data Systems
- Teleconferencing - Image Processing

In the following section the design of an RF 125 MHz transmitter with the use of SAW devices for cordless phones is described.

3.3 Design of an RF 125 MHz transmitter

The design of an RF 125 MHz transmitter was decided to be used for communication in corridors of buildings, between floors of high buildings, in underground tunnels, on university campuses and on company plants.

From the block diagram of Figure 3 we can see five basic parts of the transmitting circuit. They are: a) modulator, b) 1st mixer, c) SAW filter - 60 MHz, d) 2nd mixer (double balanced) and e) SAW filter - 125 MHz.(6)

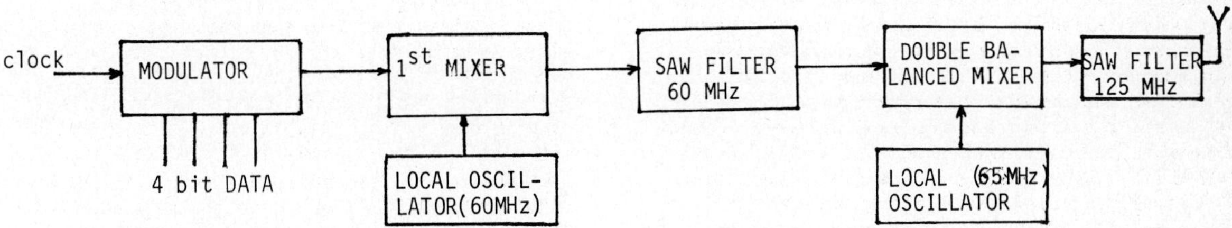

Figure 3 : Block diagram of an RF 125 MHz transitter.(6)

The modulation technique used in this transmitter is a 16-phase digital PSK modulating circuit. The inputs to the modulating circuit are 4 bits of data which are modulated to give the 16-phase PSK. The output of the modulator is a carrier frequency of 1 MHz. This output is mixed with a sinusoidal 60 MHz signal in the first mixer. The output of the mixer is then forwarded to a SAW bandpass filter of center frequency 60 MHz which supresses any harmonics and noise present at the output of the mixer. The output of the SAW filter is connected to the first input of a double balanced mixer. The other input of the double balanced mixer is connected to a local oscillator that produces a sinusoidal signal of frequency 65 MHz. The output of the mixer is a mixed signal which is the sum and the difference of the inputs, i.e. 125 MHz and 5 MHz. The 125 MHz signal can be separated from the 5 MHz signal with another SAW filter of center frequency 125 MHz. The expected waveforms of the modulator and the first mixer for a data input of 0011 along with the clock signal are shown in Figure 4.

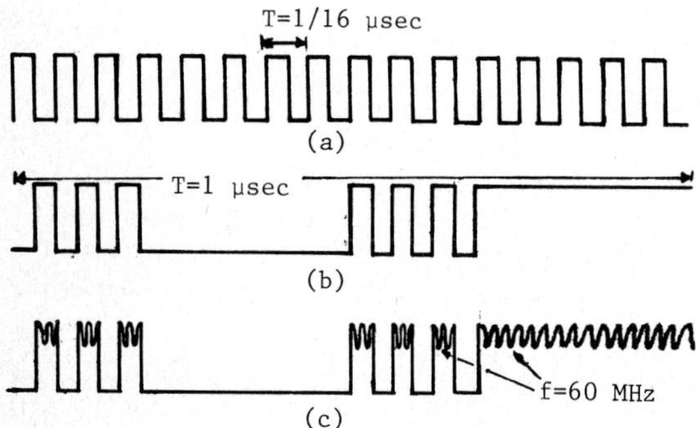

Figure 4 : Waveforms of the modulator and the first mixer for a data input of 0011. (a) clock input, (b) output of modulator, (c) output of first mixer.

In order to understand the operation of the double balanced mixer we can apply a sinusoidal waveform of 60 MHz to the input of the SAW bandpass filter and a sinusoidal 65 MHz signal to the other input of the mixer. The output is as shown in Figure 5. The reason the 60 MHz signal has a much higher peak-to-peak value than the 65 MHz signal is the fact that the first signal passes through the SAW filter which in this case has an insertion loss of about 24dB. If the signal from the local oscillator was stronger than the output of the SAW bandpass filter, then the 65 MHz signal would feedthrough to the output of the mixer and then no mixing would occur. Therefore, a drawback when using SAW filters is their high insertion loss. However, this can be easily remedied using amplifying circuits. In this case, the double balanced mixer used has the ability to amplify weak signals connected to its first input.

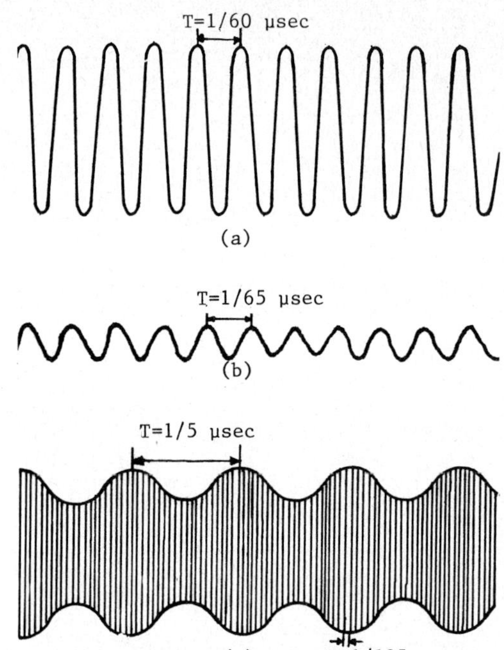

Figure 5 : Waveforms of the double balanced mixer: (a) SAW filter input, (b) output of 65 MHz local oscillator, (c) output of mixer.

4. CONCLUSIONS

SAW devices are valuable and frequently essential components in the success of a digital processing system in electronic office communications. The two examples of the use of SAW devices described in this paper prove the importance of these devices.

REFERENCES

|1| Erikson, C.A.,Jr., SAW prosperity depends on production readiness, Microwaves&RF, Vol.11(1983) 75-83.

|2| Gautier, H. and Tournois, P., Very fast signal processors as a result of the coupling of SAW and digital technologies, IEEE Trans. VOL. SU-28, No.3(1981) 126-131.

|3| Nyffeler, F., Leistungsfahige Signalverarbeiten mit hilfe von SAW Baulementen, Bul. Schweizer Electrotech. Vereins, STEN 1982.

|4| Casseday, M.,et al., Wide-Band Signal Proc. using two-beam SAW Acoustooptic Time Integrating Correlator, IEEE Trans., Vol.SU-28, No.3(1981) 205-212.

|5| Cahn, C., Spread Spectrum Applications and State-of-the-Art Equip., AGARD-766914(1973)

|6| Georgopoulos, V.C., Multiple IR/RF Com. Transmission System with SAWs, Diploma Thesis, EE Dept., U. of Thrace (June 1984).

DIGITAL TECHNIQUES in Simulation, Communication and Control
Spyros G. Tzafestas (editor)
Elsevier Science Publishers B.V. (North-Holland) © IMACS, 1985

64 KBIT/S IR LINK FOR IN-HOUSE COMMUNICATIONS

M.K. Papamiltiadis

Civil Aviation of Greece
Kavala , Greece

C.J. Georgopoulos

Dept. of Electrical Engineering
University of Thrace
Xanthi , Greece

This paper deals with the design of a two-way voice-communications system that has the ability to operate at 64 Kbit/s and 128 Kbit/s, using infrared diffuse light channel, with emphasis on the last stage of the transmitter (LED array driver) and the front-end of the receiver (p-i-n photodiode section). The advantages of infrared technology for wireless telephone and terminal communications in an office over other conventional means include : no interference with spaces outside an office, no allocation of frequencies and simplicity of telsets since it is easy to modulate the light sources in the transmitter.

1. INTRODUCTION

Various office automation systems based on local-area networks or local computer networks have been successfully applied to automated offices. All these systems, however, are based on copper wire (twisted pairs and coaxial) or fiber optics cable interconnections and suffer, to a small or high degree, from the disadvantages of cable connections.(1) In particular, they lack the flexibility of moving terminals around or expanding an existing system. Ideally one would like to operate individual telephones, key-sets, terminals and other related equipment in the office in any location in a room and communicate through one or more wireless channels (Fig.1).

One of the most promising wireless techniques is the method of infrared technology, which has the following advantages over other wireless techniques including ultrasonic and radio :

a) Infrared radiation does not disturb anything outside the room.

b) There is no problem with frequency allocation and eavesdropping.

c) The telsets can be relatively simple because it is easy to modulate the LEDs that will be required in the transmitting section.

d) The telsets will be light in weight and economical in power consumption.

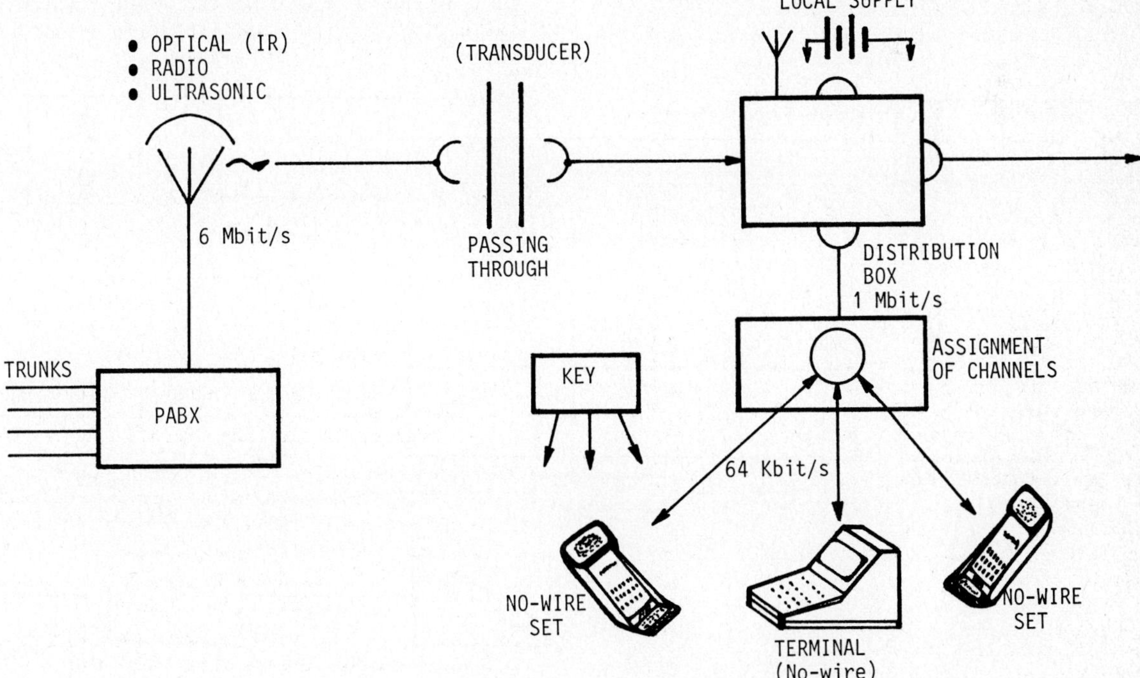

Figure 1 : PABX - User Wireless Telephone and Data Communications.

Preliminary investigations and tests have shown that infrared diffuse light can be used for information transmission (data or voice) in closed areas as is the case of an automated office room. An infrared link with average rate per connection 64Kbit/s and 128Kbit/s has the ability to service that segment of office communications which includes speech, high speed facsimile and slow scan video.

In the infrared telephone link described in this paper, the signals are transmitted between the handset and the stationary section, a ceiling mounded transponder, by means of diffuse infrared light. Light-emitting diodes (LEDs) transmit modulated information in the form of light pulses (in the near infrared region). These light pulses are reflected by the walls, ceiling and furniture of the room and reach the photodiodes (p-i-n) in the receiver as diffused light.

The communications system includes the wireless telephone sets (hand-sets) and a stationary section, the ceiling mounted transponder, wich functions as a remote station that can communicate with a PABX. The handset contains the electronic circuitry, the microphone, the receiver, rechargeable batteries, a set of keys, LED and p-i-n arrays. The transponder like the handset, contains transmit and receive electronic circuitry, matching circuits for the actual telephone set and the ringer. The electronic components are supplied with current via a plug-in ac power supply for the transponder. Data transmission may be either baseband PCM or by modulated carrier methods such as FSK or PSK. The carrier method offers the possibility of having several separate optical channels. For the system presented here the PCM method was chosen. Similar work is being done on other modulation techniques.

2. SOME FUNCTIONS OF THE WIRELESS INFRARED TELEPHONES

The no-wire infrared telephone offers the user the convenience of being able to move about the room freely. This convenience is further increased if the handset has keys allowing the most important functions of the telephone to be controlled. The infrared telephone can be used in combination with an executive telephone to enable the caller to comfortably phone at his desk or can be used to call from any other place in the room. With built-in keys for remote control of various functions the handset can be used for:

- accepting incoming calls,
- calling the secretary,
- checking back,
- allowing others in the room to listen-in to calls over the loudspeaker,
- disconnection function.

There are also numerous other applications where the no-wire telephone with control and dialing functions can be useful.

3. THE OVERALL SYSTEM CONCEPT

3.1. Uplink and Downlink Frequencies.

To realize the full-duplex mode of operation, different subcarrier frequencies are used for the up-link (terminal to transponder) and down-link (transponder to terminal). The subcarrier frequencies are chosen according to the following considerations. If the subcarrier frequency of the down-link is f_1, the transmitted optical pulses from the transponder are reflected from various surfaces, such as floors, walls, and desks. The reflected light pulses come back into the transponder and they reach the p-i-n diodes;

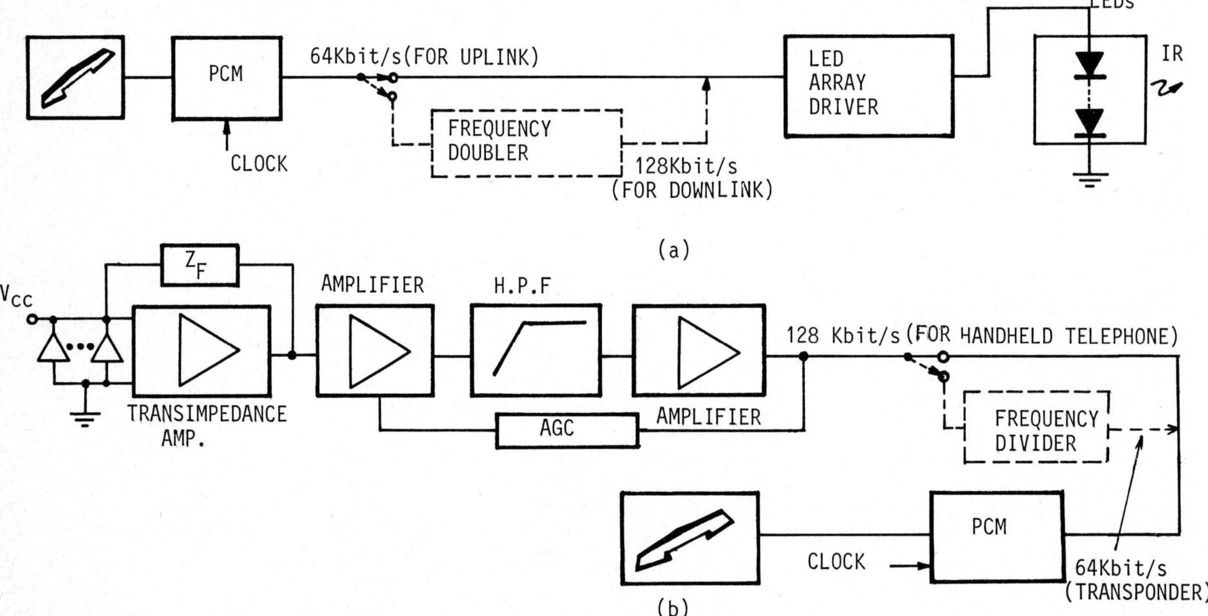

Figure 2 : IR Block diagram of IR communication system. a) Transmitter section and b) Receiver section.

therefore the transponder receives the reflected down-link pulses as well as the up-link pulses. The level of the reflected pulses varies considerably, depending on such conditions as the hight of the ceiling. Another problem here is the nonlinearity of the LEDs, due to which higher-order harmonics of f_1 also enter the transponder receiver.(2) These reflected signals should be filtered out by an electrical filter.

In the system under consideration, PCM baseband transmission is used as shown in the block diagram of Fig.2. The uplink and downlink frequencies are 64Kbit/s and 128Kbit/s, respectively.

3.2. The transmitter Section

The transmitter section of a handheld telset consists of the microphone/receiver set, the PCM circuitry which converts the analog signal into 64 Kbit/s pulses, the LED array driver and the LED array. By adding a frequency doubler this transmitter can be used in the ceiling transponder.

Two types of optical-wave propagation can be achieved with this circuitry. One is direct line-of-sight transmission and the other is diffuse optical propagation. Here, the latter method is used. As mentioned previously, diffuse optical propagation is a type of optical-wave propagation by which the optical waves are spread as uniformly as possible in the room, making use of the reflections of walls and ceilings. In this way, neither a direct line-of-sight nor alignment between the optical transmitter and receiver is required. Various types of LED IR antenna fixtures for uniform optical power distribution in the room have been studied and successfully contructed in our laboratory. Guidelines for proper LED array driver design are given in subsection 4.2.

3.3. The Receiver Section

In the case of an optical transmission system, the overall receiver input-to-output transfer function can be defined at a given signal level by the ratio of its output voltage to its input current from the detector which is called transimpedance.(3) The detector current produces a voltage across a load resistor to ground or across a feedback resistor in the front-end. Additional voltage gain must be provided by the receiver to bring this signal to a usable output voltage. The additional voltage gain is normally accomplished using several amplifying stages that have automatic or manual gain control to adjust level. The gain control must be able to vary the overall transimpedance by an amount sufficient to convert both the maximum and minimum anticipated input signal to the desired output voltage. For PCM, the receiver must also include additional electronic signal processing circuits which restore the output pulse height and shape to its original state.

The total noise increases as receiver bandwidth is increased. For optimum performance, a receiver front-end should be designed for the specific bandwidth at which it will be used. In a well-designed receiver, sensitivity is set by input stage noise. Wideband, high gain, low noise transistors are used in the front-end to minimize noise. Due to the very weak signals applied to the input, electrical shielding and careful power supply decoupling are often required to achieve good sensitivity.(4)

In Summary the receiver must be designed to ensure three basic requirements : a) a good low-noise performance; b) immunity to EMI; c) capability of handling a large D.C. stray illumination without saturation. The receiver of the present system consists of a number of p-i-n photodiodes connected in parallel to form an array, a transimpedance preamplifier, a compensating section (AGC, H.P.F, amplifiers), frequency divider as needed, the PCM unit and the microphone/receiver set. The emphasis, however, as stated previously, is on the front-end of the receiver which is treated in subsection 4.4. The other components can be usual items that are employed in any conventional wire or fiber optic connected system.

4. CONSIDERATIONS OF KEY CIRCUITRY DESIGN

4.1. Light Sources

To date only the light emitting diode (LED) and the semiconductor laser have proven to be suitable as emitters for communication purposes. This is due to the fact that they can be directly modulated at high bit rates with low drive and high output power. Table I shows LEDs and lasers trade-offs.(5)

T A B L E I

LEDs AND LASERS TRADE-OFFS

Laser Advantages

- Directional emmission
- Outputs from milliwatts to as high as 10W
- High response speed (rise time)-typically 1 nanosecond

Laser Disadvantages

- Expensive
- Extremely temperature sensitive
- Relatively short-lived. Although extrapolated lives may be 100 000 hours, most manufactures do not provide guarantees at this level

LED Advantages

- Longevity - 10^6 hours
- Low power consumption
- Simplicity of construction
- Relative cheapness

LED Disadvantages

- Deliver low power - in the microwatt to milliwatt range
- Have slower response time - multiple nanoseconds at best

The choice between the two types of optical sources will be determined by overall system requirements. With respect to fiber-optic system applications, lasers are favoured for wideband long haul communication links on account of their higher performance, and LEDs are advantageous in short haul narrowband systems because of the relative simplicity of their drive and control circuitry. In the case of free-air communications, lasers are used for line-of-sight links, whereas LEDs are suitable for diffuse IR light links, as is the system described in this paper.

High radiant LEDs of 15 milliwatt output power are used in the optical transmitters of both the transponder (ceiling mounted) and handheld terminals. The number of LEDs required depends on the transmission distance. Another factor is the type of the receiver and the background light level it can tolerate.

4.2. LED Array Driver

LED drivers can be either voltage or current types. The voltage drivers apply a voltage to the LEDs through a current limiting resistor. In current drivers, the input signal controls a current source which in turn drives the LEDs.

For our system we developed a simple driver with current limiting capabilities as shown in fig.3. The LED array consists of 12 LD271 LEDs (λ= 950 nm) conected in series between the power supply and the collector of transistor Q_1. When a drive voltage is applied to the driver, transistor Q_1 conducts and causes a current through the diodes and resistor R_1. Transistor Q_2 controls the base current of Q_1 so that the voltage drop across R_1 remains approximately equal to 0.6 at normal operation. Since a current of approximately 100 mA is required through the LEDs to maintain a proper optical power level, resistor R_1 was set at R_1= 0.6V/I = 0.6V/0.1A=6Ω. It should be noted here, however, that this driver although suitable for bit rates up to 128 Kbit/s, it may have to be improved, if higher bit rates are anticipated.

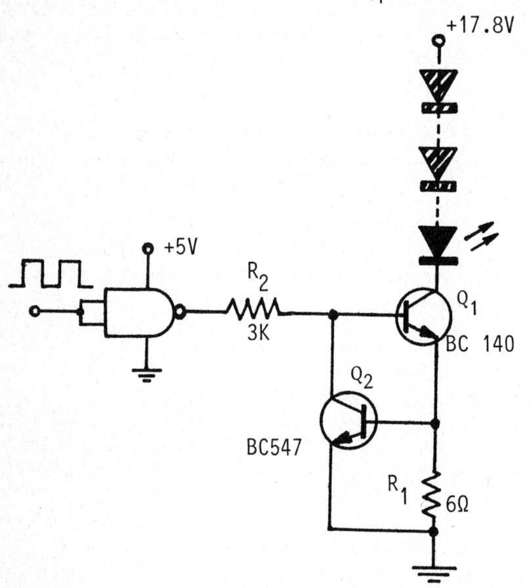

Figure 3 : Simple driver of 12 LEDs.

4.3. Photodetector Array Considerations of IR Receiver

There are many different considerations before picking a detector for free IR channel communication, which, among other things can help in the direction of background and other noise reduction. Here are some guidelines, based on literature and our work so far, for selecting these detectors.

1. Use photodiodes in a proper array form with the largest possible ratio of active area divided by the noise equivalent power (NEP). The NEP is equivalent to the incident radiation in $W\sqrt{Hz}$ necessary to produce on output equal to the detector noise. If possible, intensify the optical power with a lens to get best efficiency.
2. If no NEP value is specified, select a device with the largest ratio of active area x area -independent spectral sensitivity, to the square-root of dark current.
3. Take the highest reverse-voltage for the selected photodiode (for relatively high frequencies).
4. Select a compatible amplifier with a small value of input capacitance.
5. Choose the load resistance for the detector as close as possible to the permissible maximum bandwidth needed. If necessary, allow for a decrease in frequency response at the input and compensate for it in the amplifier.
6. Apply a feedback signal to the low end of the load resistor so that its load resistance is effectively reduced or better still, compensate for the capacitance of the photodetector and amplifier.

In the case of p-i-n photodiodes, the detector noise is manifested as the familiar short noise, due to random arrivals of photons which in turn give rise to individual free carriers. The noise spectral density of short noise is given by

$$2eI_s(A^2Hz^{-1}) , \tag{1}$$

where : e = the electronic charge
I_s= the signal current
A = the detector active area

In an optical receiver, this short noise is small and other sources of noise, such as from the amplifier and resistors, are dominant.

4.4. p-i-n Photodiode Receiver Front-End

Receiver circuitry usually is more complex than transmitter circuitry. The output from photodiodes is usually in the low millivolt or micro-

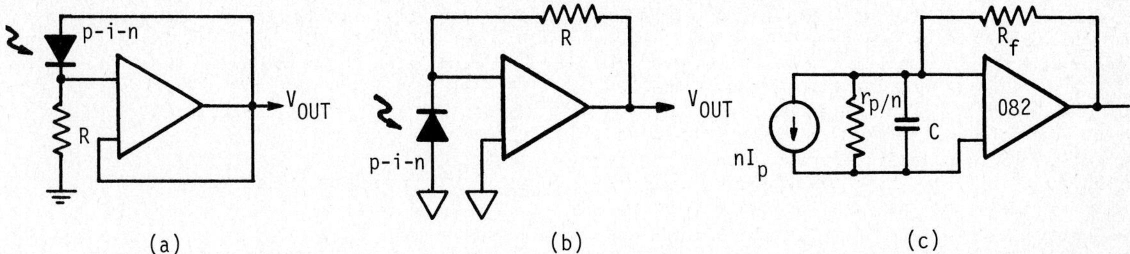

Figure 4 : Receiver amplifier circuitry. a) Bootstrap configuration, b) Transimpedance configuration, and c) Equivalent receiver front-end circuit with n p-i-n diodes connected in parallel.

volt range, requiring high amplification to raise it to logic or analog levels. But this amplification must be provided while minimizing the detector's internal capacitance to achieve the maximum response speed the detector can deliver. Two receiver amplifier configurations-a bootstrap (Fig.4a) or a more popular transimpedance circuit (Fig.4b)-can be used. The latter combines a large dynamic range and low noise.

It is also possible to use integrated detectors. Integrated detectors as an alternative to p-i-n detectors, as the ones used in fiber optic receivers, can offer the systems designer several advantages over conventional circuitry that uses p-i-n plus transimpedance amplifier. The integrated detector/preamplifier (IDP) provides the functions of the photosensitive diode and the transimpedance amplifier in the same package, so that the output of IDP is a voltage from a low impedance (emitter follower) source.

However, in this design a discrete version of a transimpedance amplifier was used in the receiver front-end as shown in Fig.4c. In this figure n p-i-n photodiodes have been replaced by an equivalent circuit, where nI_p is the total current of the diodes, r_p/n is their total parallel internal resistance and C is the total capacitance consisting of nC_p (p-i-n diode capacitance), C_s stray capacitance, and C_{in} the amplifier input capacitance.

A significant factor in this circuit is the amplifier rise time which depends on the time constant $\tau = R_f C$ and the $t_A = 1/GBW$, i.e., the inverse of the gain-bandwidth product. Therefore, the rise time of the amplifier voltage output is given by :

$$t_R = \pi \sqrt{\tau . t_A} \qquad (2)$$

In this design an 082 op amp was used with four BP104 (λ= 950 nm) p-i-n photodiodes which gave very satisfactory results. With a resistor of 10 KΩ in the feedback loop, the rise time was approximately 0.15 μs.

5. CONCLUSION

A 64 Kbit/s IR link for in-house communications has been described. The emphasis was placed on two key circuits :the driving section of the LED array and the p-i-n photodiode receiving section. To make the infrared link an effective full-duplex communication channel, using baseband PCM technique, two different rates 64Kbit/s and 128 Kbit//s, for the uplink and downlink must be used, respectively.

REFERENCES

[1] Georgopoulos, C.J., PABX-Infrared network interfaces, proceedings of fiber optics and communications Local Area Networks : FOC/LAN (1983).

[2] Minami, T., et al., Optical wireless modem for office communications, National Computer Conference (1983) 721-728.

[3] Muoi, T.V., Receiver design for digital fiber optic transmission systems using Manchester (Biphase) Coding, IEEE Trans. on Communications, Vol. COM-3, No.5(1983) 608-619.

[4] Personick, S.D., Receiver design for optical fiber systems, Proceedings of IEEE, Vol.66, No. 12 (1977) 1670-1678.

[5] Williamson, J., Optical comms make rapid progress, Communications Engineering International, Vol.6, No.3(1984) 39.

4. CONTROL SYSTEMS

DIGITAL TECHNIQUES in Simulation, Communication and Control
Spyros G. Tzafestas (editor)
Elsevier Science Publishers B.V. (North-Holland) © IMACS, 1985

ADAPTIVE CONTROL WITH VARIABLE DEAD-ZONE NONLINEARITIES*

David Orlicki, Lena Valavani, Michael Athans and Gunter Stein

Laboratory for Information and Decision Systems
Massachusetts Institute of Technology
Cambridge, Massachusetts 02139

It has been found that fixed error dead-zones as defined in the existing literature result in serious degradation of performance, due to the conservativeness which characterizes the determination of their width. In the present paper, variable width dead-zones are derived for the adaptive control of plants with unmodeled dynamics. The derivation makes use of information available about the unmodeled dynamics both a priori as well as during the adaptation process, so as to stabilize the adaptive loop and at the same time overcome the conservativeness and performance limitations of fixed-dead zone adaptive or fixed gain controllers.

1. INTRODUCTION

Research in recent years has shown that adaptive control algorithms which, under ideas assumptions, have been proven globally asymptotically stable, indeed exhibit unstable behavior in circumstances under which those assumptions are even slightly violated. Of the two instability mechanisms identified for these algorithms, -commonly referred to as "gain" and "phase" instability mechanisms [1],- the former is more unavoidable and is triggered by the controller parameter drift which occurs as a result of nonzero output errors. These are a consequence of the fact that, in the presence of unmodeled dynamics and/or (persistent) disturbances there can be no perfect (transfer function matching between the compensated plant and the reference model over all frequencies, even if "sufficiency of excitation" for the "nominal" model order is guaranteed.

Perfect matching, on the other hand, translates into zero output (tracking) error, under ideal assumptions, and has been the basis for the parameter adjustment laws; only when the output error is zero does adaptation stop. Clearly, then, by design, any nonzero output error is instantaneously attributed to parameter errors. Furthermore, there is nothing in the mathematics of the adjustment mechanisms, as they currently stand, to prevent gain drift due to error sources other than parameters, as for example happens even in cases of "exact modeling," with "sufficiency of excitation," where convergence to the "desired" parameter values has been achieved momentarily; extraneous disturbances entering at that point can cause the parameters to drift from their "desired" values.

Consequently then, the zero tracking error requirement must be suitably relaxed. The rationale is that no parameter adjustment should take place when the output error(s) are due to disturbances and/or unmodeled dynamics. This can be achieved on an existing algorithm by a dead-zone nonlinearity, in the parameter adjustment law, whose width depends on the contribution of the disturbances and/or unmodeled dynamics to the output error.

The idea of a dead-zone nonlinearity in the parameter update law to avoid the effect of disturbances on adaptation was first introduced for indirect adaptive algorithms by Egardt in 1980 [2] and was later amplified by Samson [3]. Also, in 1982 Peterson and Narendra used a dead-zone nonlinearity to prove stability for a class of direct algorithms in the presence of bounded disturbances with no unmodeled dynamics [4]. However, the width of the dead zone was chosen to be constant and had to be based on a very conservative bound so that it yielded only marginally stable systems with extremely poor model tracking as the examples in [4] seem to suggest.

Consequently, obtaining non-fixed accurate bounds for the disturbance and high-frequency dynamics contributions to the output error is crucial to overcoming the conservativeness of the dead-zone width which they define. This depends on the ability to translate frequency domain magnitude bounds, most naturally expressed by L^2-norms into time-domain magnitude bounds of instantaneously measured quantities, most naturally expressed by L^∞- or, for our purposes, L^1- norms which are much less conservative than L^∞- norms.

This paper discusses the use of a deadzone, whose width is adjustable on line, to adaptively control a plant with unmodeled dynamics, with the objective of maintaining its stability and minimizing the adverse effects of a conservative dead-zone width to its performance. Due to space considerations we do not treat the case of output disturbances here; also, the topic of disturbances additionally includes a fixed disturbances rejection mechanism that introduces a modification in the basic structure of the MRAC system so as to merit separate attention.

Section 2 of this paper contains a generic norm translation problem and develops a set of tools required for its solution. Section 3 applies the results of the previous section to the familiar NLV algorithm of the Model Reference type. Other algorithms can be treated similarly. Section 4 discusses the stability of the variable width dead-zone adaptive system and, finally, Section 5 contains the concluding remarks.

2. MATHEMATICAL PRELIMINARIES

In this section we develop the necessary tools for the definition of the variable width dead zone. As was already pointed out in the introduction, the objective is to find satisfactory bounds for the contribution of the unmodeled dynamics to the output of the adaptively controlled process, so that an "accurate" error dead-zone can be defined.

The process, complete with unmodeled dynamics is assumed to be of the Doyle-Stein type, with the high frequency dynamics entering multiplicatively; i.e.

$$g(s) = g_p(s)(1+\ell(s))$$

where $g(s)$ is the actual plant transfer function, $g_p(s)$ its modeled part and $\ell(s)$ the unmodeled dynamics. Typically, a bound on the magnitude of $\ell(s)$ is assumed to be negligible for frequencies below crossover, becoming only appreciable for higher frequencies; no phase information can be assumed. The problem is then to find a bound for the output of the adaptively controlled process due to $\ell(s)$. This is achieved in two stages, as the following subsections indicate. We further remark here that, due to feedback in the adaptive loop, the unmodeled dynamics indirectly influence all the state variables of the nominal adaptive loop, with the magnitude of their contribution depending on the nature of the inputs to the plant.

2.1 Transfer Function Magnitude Bounding

In this subsection we will derive a bound $\Phi(\omega)$ on the magnitude of the frequency response of a special class of transfer functions, that typically arise in MRAC systems. Consider an LTI transfer function $G(\underline{\theta},s)$ of the form

$$G(\underline{\theta},s) = M(s)\left\{\frac{\ell(s)}{1+A(\underline{\theta},s)[1+\ell(s)]}\right\} \tag{2a}$$

where

$M(s)$ is a completely known stable LTI transfer function

$$1+A(\underline{\theta},s) = \prod_{i=1}^{n}(s+p_i(\underline{\theta})) \tag{2b}$$

$\underline{\theta}_\ell \le \underline{\theta} \le \underline{\theta}_u$

$\underline{\theta}$ unknown constant parameter vector with specified bounds (2c)

$$\underline{p}_i(\underline{\theta}) \le 0 \qquad i=1,\dots,n \tag{2d}$$

$$||\ell(j\omega)|| \le \ell_o(\omega) \quad \text{for known } \ell_o(\omega) > 0 \tag{2e}$$

Note that when $\ell(s)=0$, $G(\underline{\theta},s)=M(s)$, and therefore stable. In the context of MRAS, $G(\underline{\theta},s)$ represents the actual transfer function of a plant with feedback, designed to follow a reference model which is prescribed by the transfer function $M(s)$. In the absence of unmodeled dynamics, $\ell(s)$, perfect matching is possible.

When $\ell(s)\neq 0$, the stability of $\underline{G}(\underline{\theta},s)$ can be ensured by (requiring) enforcing the condition

$$1+A(\underline{\theta},j\omega)(1+\ell(j\omega)]\neq 0 \tag{3}$$

This condition is satisfied if, for all θ in the space of admissible parameters, the following is true:

$$||\ell(j\omega)|| \le \ell_o(\omega) \le 1+||A^{-1}(\underline{\theta},j\omega)|| \tag{4}$$

Assuming this condition is true, we proceed to derive an upper bound on $||G(\underline{\theta},j\omega)||$, parametrized by $||M(j\omega)||$. From eqn. (2),

$$G(\underline{\theta},j\omega)=M(j\omega)\left\{\frac{\ell(j\omega)}{D(\underline{\theta},j\omega)+\ell(j\omega)A(\underline{\theta},j\omega)}\right\} \tag{5}$$

where $D(\underline{\theta},j\omega)\equiv 1+A(\underline{\theta},j\omega)$

Next, representing $\ell(j\omega)$, $D(\underline{\theta},j\omega)$ and $A(\underline{\theta},j\omega)$ in polar form,

$$||G(\underline{\theta},j\omega)|| \le ||M(j\omega)|| \left\| \frac{||\ell(j\omega)||e^{j\phi_\ell}}{||D(\underline{\theta},j\omega)||e^{j\phi_D(\underline{\theta})}+||\ell(j\omega)A(\underline{\theta},j\omega)||e^{j(\phi_A(\underline{\theta})+\phi_\ell)}} \right\| \tag{6}$$

An upper bound for $||G(\underline{\theta},j\omega)||$ can be found by maximizing and minimizing respectively the values of the numerator and denominator terms in (6). The denominator achieves its smallest value if the vectors $\ell(j\omega)A(\underline{\theta},j\omega)$ and $\underline{D}(\underline{\theta},j\omega)$ are oppositely aligned and, in addition, $||\ell(j\omega)||$ achieves its maximum allowable value for the $\underline{\theta}$-interval of interest. The above two conditions are satisfied if the phase angles are such that $\phi_\ell+\phi_A(\underline{\theta})=\phi_D(\underline{\theta})+\pi$ and $||\ell(j\omega)||=\ell_o(\omega)$. Note that condition (4) for the stability of $G(\underline{\theta},s)$ ensures that $||\ell_o(j\omega)A(\underline{\theta},j\omega)||<||D(\underline{\theta},j\omega)||$ and, indeed, the choice $||\ell(j\omega)|| = \ell_o(\omega)$ guarantees minimization of the denominator of $G(\underline{\theta},j\omega)$ with stability maintained.

Unlike the denominator, the numerator magnitude is independent of ϕ_ℓ, and is directly maximized by choosing $||\ell(j\omega)||=\ell_o(\omega)$ and ϕ_ℓ appropriately to satisfy the denominator phase angle condition. Consequently, from eqn. (6) we can now write an upper bound for $G(\underline{\theta},j\omega)$ as follows:

$$||\overline{G(\underline{\theta},j\omega)}|| = ||M(j\omega)||\frac{\ell_o(\omega)}{||D(\underline{\theta},j\omega)||-\ell_o(\omega)||A(\underline{\theta},j\omega)||} \tag{7}$$

Finally, we may search the space of allowable values of $\underline{\theta}$ to determine the desired transfer function bound

$$\Phi(\omega) \overset{\Delta}{=} \max_{\underline{\theta}} ||G(\underline{\theta},j\omega)|| \tag{8}$$

In the following subsection we will use $\phi(\omega)$ in order to bound the output of $G(\underline{\theta},j\omega)$, in an absolute value sense, given an input x(t).

2.2 Absolute Value Output Bounding

Consider the system shown in figure 1 with input x(t), output y(t) and $G(\underline{\theta},s)$ as defined before. By taking the inverse Laplace transform of $G(\underline{\theta},s)$, we obtain

$$L^{-1}\{G(\underline{\theta},s)\} = g(\underline{\theta},t) \tag{9}$$

Furthermore, since $g(\underline{\theta},t)$ represents a linear-time-invariant system, by definition of $G(\underline{\theta},s)$, the output y(t) is given by

$$y(t) = g(\underline{\theta},t) * x(t) = \int_{-\infty}^{t} d\tau\ g(\underline{\theta},t-\tau)x(\tau) \tag{10}$$

Substituting now in (10) for $g(\underline{\theta},t-\tau)$ the expression for the inverse Laplace transform of $G(\underline{\theta},s)$ and recalling, further, that $G(\underline{\theta},s)$ is a stable transfer function, we can write

$$y(t) = \int_{-\infty}^{t} d\tau \frac{1}{2\pi j}\int_{-j\infty}^{j\infty} ds\ G(\underline{\theta},s)e^{s(t-\tau)}\ x(\tau) = \frac{1}{2\pi}\int_{-\infty}^{\infty} d\omega\ G(\underline{\theta},j\omega)e^{j_\omega t}\int_{-\infty}^{t} d\tau\ x(\tau)e^{-j\omega\tau} \tag{11}$$

Next, with $\mu(t)$ representing the unit step function we have

$$F\{x(t)\mu(-t)\} = \int_{-\infty}^{\infty} d\tau\ x(\tau)\mu(-\tau)e^{-j\omega\tau} = \int_{-\infty}^{t} d\tau x(\tau)e^{-j\omega\tau} \tag{12}$$

Define $F\{x(t)\mu(-\tau)\}$ with the symbol $\overline{X}(j\omega)$ and substitute in (11). Then

$$y(t) = \frac{1}{2\pi}\int_{-\infty}^{\infty} d\omega\ G(\underline{\theta},j\omega)\overline{X}(j\omega)e^{j\omega t} \tag{13}$$

By the Cauchy-Schwartz inequality it follows from (13) that

$$|y(t)| \leq \frac{1}{2\pi}\int_{-\infty}^{\infty} d\omega\ ||G(\underline{\theta},j\omega)||\ ||\overline{X}(j\omega)|| \tag{14}$$

But from the previous subsection $\Phi(\omega)$ was determined such that

$$\Phi(\omega) \geq ||G(\underline{\theta},j\omega)|| \tag{15}$$

Hence, (14) becomes,

$$|y(t)| \leq \frac{1}{2\pi}\int_{-\infty}^{\infty} d\omega\ \underline{\Phi}(\omega)||\overline{X}(j\omega)|| \equiv \overline{y}(t) \tag{16}$$

which admittedly represents a looser bound on the absolute value of $\overline{y}(t)$ than eqn. (14). However, the bound y(t) can be calculated more readily. The inequality (16) has the following interpretation. Given a bound on the frequency response of a system, a bound on the magnitude of its output due to an input x(t) can be calculated at any instant of time by using the time history of the system input up to and including that instant of time. We note here again the time dependence of $X(j\omega)$ according to eqn. (12).

3. MRAC WITH RELAXED TRACKING ERROR CRITERION

In this section we employ the results of section 2 to derive a variable dead-zone width for the parameter update of the N-L-V algorithm, which overcomes the conservativeness of the fixed width Peterson-Narendra scheme [4]. Before we proceed, we briefly review the concept of parameter update using a dead-zone nonlinearity.

In [4] the authors have shown stability of the system depicted in figure 2.

In fig. 2 the standard notation is used, with $\underline{k}$ representing parameter errors, $\underline{\zeta}$ filtered (auxiliary) state variables, v(t) output deterministic disturbances of bounded magnitude, differentiable and uniformly continuous, ϵ the output error with disturbances; η represents the (part of the) error actually used in the parameter adaptive law and is obtained by ϵ passed through the dead-zone of width E.

It is not our purpose here to present the details of how the above error system as shown in fig. 2, is arrived at. The reader is instead referred to [4] for those as well as the stability proof of that modified algorithm. We simply present here the parameter adaptive laws, with the dead-zone nonlinearity in their simplest form, for the sake of completing the problem description which forms the basis for the developments in the present paper. The paramerer adjustment is as described by eqns. (17) below.

$$\dot{\underline{k}}(t) = \dot{\tilde{k}}(t) = \frac{-\zeta(t)\eta(t)}{1+\alpha\zeta^T(t)\zeta(t)} \quad \alpha>0 \tag{17a}$$

$$\text{with}\quad \eta(t) = \begin{cases} \epsilon(t) & |\epsilon(t)|>E \\ 0 & |\epsilon(t)|<E \end{cases} \tag{17b}$$

where E represents the width of the dead-zone.

Although in [4] the discussion is not particularly enlightening as to how exactly the magnitude E is decided upon, it is the present authors' opinion that

$$E \geq ||v(t)||_\infty = \max_t|v(t)| \tag{18}$$

and, therefore, is very conservative as the same authors have pointed out in [5]. We next proceed to analyze the original NLV Model Reference algorithm, as represented in Fig. 3, with the plant dynamics now replaced by the actual plant $P(\underline{\theta},s)[1+\ell(s)]$.

The component $P(\underline{\theta},s)$ incorporates the designer's knowledge of the dominant, low frequency response of the plant, including a vector $\underline{\theta}$ of uncertain parameters, known only within precomputable bounds. The standard MRAC assumptions about the plant hold for $P(\underline{\theta},s)$. That is, the designer knows

(i) an upper bound on the relative degree n^* of $P(\underline{\theta},s)$

(ii) an upper bound on the degree n of $P(\underline{\theta},s)$

(iii) that $P(\underline{\theta},s)$ is minimum phase

(iv) the sign of the high frequency gain of $P(\underline{\theta},s)$.

The $\ell(s)$ part of the plant represents the (multiplicative) uncertainty associated with the nominal plant $P(\underline{\theta},s)$. This uncertainty is due to high frequency dynamics, which are assumed of unspecified structure but satisfy a magnitude constraint $||\ell(j\omega)|| \leq \ell_o(\omega)$, as already mentioned. Further, we note that the "actual" plant representation $P(\underline{\theta},s)[1+\ell(s)]$ will not in general satisfy any of the four standard assumptions listed above. This fact becomes pivotal in the inability of the adaptive controller to achieve transfer function matching between the compensated plant and the reference model. As a result, it becomes impossible for general inputs to drive the tracking (output) error to zero. However, one may expect the tracking error to be small, if the plant is excited by signals with dominant low frequency content over the range where $P(\underline{\theta},s)$ is a good approximation to the actual plant transfer function.

In what follows we will next show that the error system underlying the structure in figure 3 differs from that of the same structure, as shown in fig. 2, where $\ell(s)=0$, only by an additive perturbation term in the output. This term can be bounded using the results of Section 2 and a variable width dead-zone can be defined for the adaptation mechanism. Stability of the scheme is subsequently discussed in Section 5.

We start by considering first the case where $\ell(s)=0$ in Figure 3. In this case the standard MRAC assumptions about the plant are true. There exists a vector $\underline{k}^*(\underline{\theta})$ of fixed gains which, when applied to the system, results in matching of the compensated plant transfer function with that of the model. We adopt the shorthand notation $C_1(\underline{\theta})$ and $C_2(\underline{\theta})$ to indicate the LTI transfer functions $C_1(\underline{k}_1^*(\underline{\theta}))$ and $C_2(\underline{k}_2^*(\underline{\theta}),\underline{k}_3^*(\theta))$ respectively. Now assuming $\ell(s)\neq 0$ but maintaining the same definitions of $C_1(k_1^*(\underline{\theta}) = C_1(\theta)$ and $C_2(k_2^*(\theta),k_3^*(\theta)), = C_2(\underline{\theta})$ based on the reduced model, we may derive an expression for the error system as follows, where for convenience, the argument's' has been suppressed throughout.

$$\frac{y_p}{R} = \frac{C_1(\underline{\theta})P(\underline{\theta})[1+\ell]}{1+C_1(\underline{\theta})C_2(\underline{\theta})P(\underline{\theta})[1+\ell]} = \frac{C_1(\underline{\theta})P(\underline{\theta})}{1+C_1(\underline{\theta})C_2(\underline{\theta})P(\underline{\theta})} + \frac{C_1(\underline{\theta})P(\theta)}{1+C_1(\underline{\theta})C_2(\underline{\theta})P(\underline{\theta})} \cdot \frac{\ell}{1+C_1(\underline{\theta})C_2(\underline{\theta})P(\theta)[1+\ell]} \tag{19}$$

By definition of $C_1(\underline{\theta})$ and $C_2(\underline{\theta})$ we have

$$\frac{C_1(\underline{\theta})P(\underline{\theta})}{1+C_1(\underline{\theta})C_2(\underline{\theta})P(\underline{\theta})} = M \tag{20}$$

Using this fact and introducing the notation $A(\underline{\theta}) \equiv C_1(\theta)C_2(\underline{\theta})P(\underline{\theta})$ we can write eqn. (19) in a more compact form as

$$\frac{y_p}{R} = M+M \cdot \frac{\ell}{1+A(\underline{\theta})[1+\ell]} \tag{21}$$

Next, defining $\underline{\tilde{k}}(t) = \underline{k}(t)-\underline{k}^*$, referring to fig. 3 and interchanging time domain and transformed quantities, we derive an expression for ϵ as given in eqn. (22).

$$\begin{aligned} \epsilon &= \bar{\epsilon} + \frac{y_p}{R} \cdot R + \frac{y_p}{R} \cdot \tilde{k}^T \underline{w} - \frac{y_m}{R} \cdot R \\ &= \underline{\tilde{k}}^T \zeta + M \cdot \frac{\ell}{1+A(\underline{\theta})[1+\ell)} \cdot (\tilde{k}^T w+r) \end{aligned} \tag{22}$$

For the case where $\ell(s)=0$, this result reduces to the standard augmented MRAC error system of Narendra, Lin and Valavani with $L^{-1}=M$. The new error system is shown in Figure (4) with a variable dead zone non-linearity added to the output signal path.

We observe that the system is of the form shown in fig. 2. In order to specify a stable adaptive law, we need to find a bounding signal $E(t) \geq |v(t)|\ \forall t$.

We may redraw the error system using the fact that $\underline{\tilde{k}}=\underline{k}^*-\underline{k}$ and the input to the plant in Figure 5 is $u=\underline{k}^T w+r$. The resulting representation is shown in Figure 5 below. From precomputed bounds on θ, bounds on k^* can be precomputed also. We now make the definition

$$\underline{\hat{k}}^* = |\max_{\underline{\theta}} \underline{k}^*| \tag{23}$$

where the maximization over $\underline{\theta}$ is carried out individually over every component of $\underline{k}^*$. Using (23) in conjunction with the results of Section 2 it readily follows that an upper bound $E(t)$ for $v(t)$ can be computed. More specifically, we can write

$$E(t) \equiv \int_{-\infty}^{\infty} \Phi(\omega) \Big\{ |\bar{U}(j\omega)| + \sum_{i=1}^{2n-1} |W_i(j\omega)| \hat{k}_i^* \ d\omega \Big] \tag{24}$$

where eqn. (12) has been used for calculation of the transforms $U(j\omega)$ and $W_i(j\omega)$ for the input u(t) and signals $\omega_i(t)$ respectively. An adaptation law of the form described in eqn. (17) can then be employed with the width of the dead zone defined by eqn. (24). The resulting scheme is stable and an outline of its stability proof is given in the following section.

5. STABILITY

The stability proof of the proposed algorithm with variale dead-zone follows along very similar lines for the most part with that in [4]. However, in the present case it is additionally conditioned on the reference model definition and the admissible parameter set, as eqn. (4) of section 2.1 implies. More specifically, the space of admissible parameters is implicitly defined through the reference model by eqn. (4), in conjunction with condition (2c) and is such that the desired (class of) reference model(s) remains stable in the presence of the unmodeled dynamics $\ell(s)$ of the plant. This is a standard and reasonable assumption made in the design of all fixed parameter controllers as well. Due to space considerations we will not elaborate on this further but will instead refer the reader to [6] for more details.

Consequently, given eqn. (4), which is fundamental even for a non-adaptive design, the effect of unmodeled dynamics can be represented as an output perturbation v(t) as suggested in eqn. (22) and depicted in fig. 4. v(t) is the output of a stable linear system which is bounded for bounded inputs. We next proceed to outline the steps for proving boundedness of $\tilde{k},\tilde{u},\zeta,w$ and the output error ϵ.

The boundedness of k follows directly from the standard Lyapunov function definition $(V(\underline{\tilde{k}}) = \frac{1}{2}(\underline{\tilde{k}}^T\underline{\tilde{k}})$ and the adaptation law (17a) in conjunction with eqn. (22) where E(t) is defined. Also, from the definition of the dead-zone, the term $\underline{\tilde{k}}^T\underline{k}$ can be bounded above and below by bounds of the form

$$f_1[E(t)]\,|\underline{\tilde{k}}^T\underline{\zeta}+v(t)| \leq |\underline{k}^T\underline{\zeta}| \leq f_2[E(t)]\cdot|\underline{\tilde{k}}^T\underline{\zeta}+v(t)| \quad (25)$$

where $f_1(\cdot)$ and $f_2(\cdot)$ are continuous functions of E(t).

Next, by the definition of the Lyapunov function, its time derivative, in conjunction with the adaptation law given by eqn. (12a), can be written as

$$\dot{V} = \underline{\tilde{k}}^T\dot{\underline{\tilde{k}}} = -\frac{\underline{\tilde{k}}^T\underline{\zeta}_\eta}{1+\underline{\zeta}^T\underline{\zeta}} \quad (26)$$

From the fact that

$$\int_{t_0}^{\infty} \dot{V}(\tau)d\tau < \infty$$

and eqns. (25) and (26), it is straightforward to conclude that

$$\dot{\underline{\tilde{k}}}(t) \in L^2 \quad (27)$$

From this point on, the proof uses standard arguments, for the boundedness of u,w,ζ, as they first appeared in [7] and outlined in [4]. We only remark here that, in our case $|v(t)|<|E(t)|$ and furthermore, $v(t)=O[\sup_{t\geq\tau}||w(\tau)||]$, as follows from eqn. (22) and fig. 4. The reader is again referred to [6] for all the details of the stability arguments.

6. CONCLUSIONS

A variable dead-zone nonlinearity was introduced in a standard model reference adaptive control algorithm to maintain its stability in the presence of unmodeled dynamics. The variable width dead-zone is determined on-line on the basis of prior information about plant parameter bounds and unmodeled dynamics as well as about information obtained during adaptation. Besides maintaining stability, the algorithm is able to overcome the conservativeness of fixed dead-zone on exponential forgetting factor adaptation mechanisms [4],[8], as simulation results show. Due to space limitations those are deferred until the conference presentation of the paper.

REFERENCES

1. C.E. Rohrs, L. Valavani, M. Athans and G. Stein, "Robustness of Adaptive Control Algorithms in the Presence of Unmodeled Dynamics," Proc. 21st. IEEE Conf. on Dec. and Control, Orlando, Fla., Dec. 1982, pp. 3-11.
2. B. Egardt, "Stability Analysis of Adaptive Control Systems with Disturbances," Proc. Joint Automatic Control Conference, San Francisco, CA. Aug. 1980.
3. C. Samson, "Stability Analysis of Adaptively Controlled Systems Subject to Bounded Disturbances," Automatica , Vol. 19, No. 1, pp. 81-86,1983.
4. B.B. Peterson and K.S. Narendra, "Bounded Error Adaptive Control," IEEE Trans. on Aut. Control, Vol. AC-27, No. 6, Dec. 1982, pp. 1161-1168.
5. D. Orlicki, L. Valavani, and M. Athans, "Comments on Bounded Error Adaptive Control," to appear in IEEE Trans. on Autom. Control, Oct. 1984.
6. D. Orlicki, Model Reference Adaptive Control Systems Using a Dead-Zone Nonlinearity, Ph.D. Dissertation, Dept. of EECS, Laborat Laboratory for Information and Decision Systems, M.I.T., Cambridge, MA, May 1984.
7. K.S. Narendra, Y.H. Lin, and L.S Valavani, "Stable Adaptive Controller Design, Part II: Proof of Stability," IEEE Trans. Automatic Control, Vol. AC-25, pp. 440-448, June 1980.

8. P.A. Ioannou and P.V. Kokotovic, Adaptive Systems with Reduced Models, Springer-Verlag Series, Lecture Notes in Control and Information Sciences, 1983.

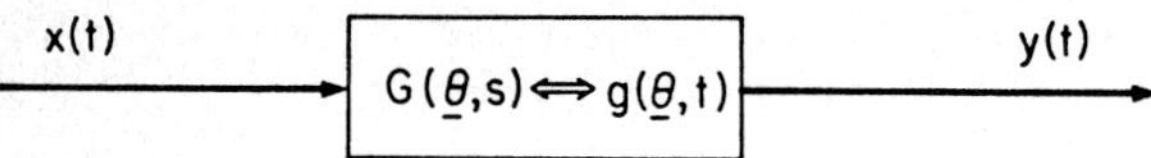

Figure 1:

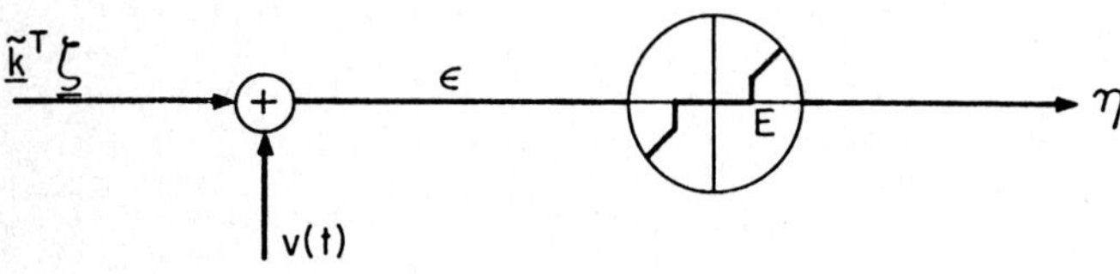

Figure 2:

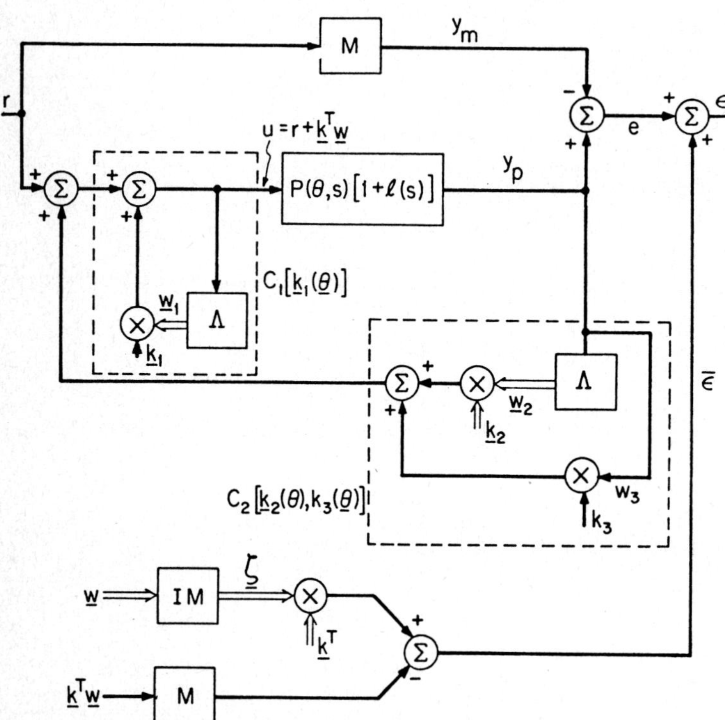

Figure 3:

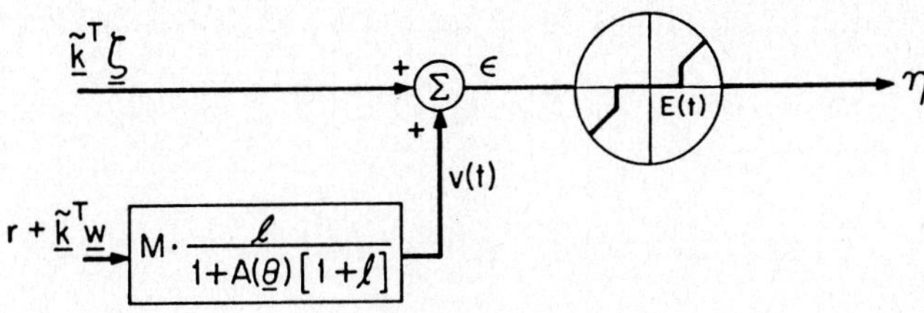

Figure 4:

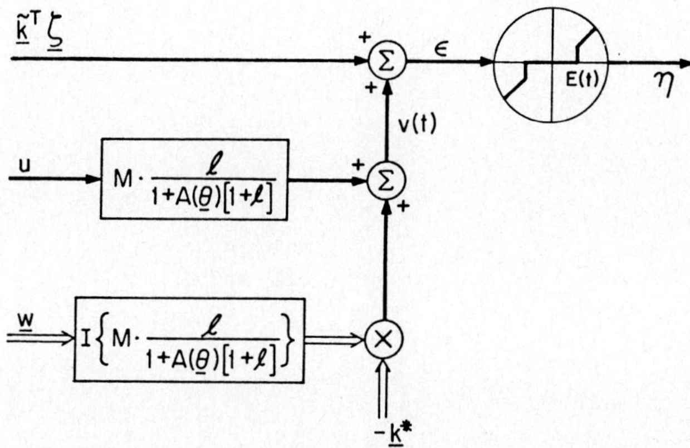

Figure 5:

*Research supported by ONR/N00014-82-K-0582 (NR 606-003). NSF/ECS-8210960 and NASA Ames and Langley Research Centers under grant NASA/NGL-22-009-124.

DIGITAL TECHNIQUES in Simulation, Communication and Control
Spyros G. Tzafestas (editor)
Elsevier Science Publishers B.V. (North-Holland) © IMACS, 1985

A Scheme for Digital Control and Application of a Continuous-Time Adaptive Control with Exponential Rate of Convergence

Zenta Iwai[*1], Akira Inoue[*2], Mitsuaki Ishitobi[*1] and Hidekatsu Tokumaru[*3]

*1) Department of Mechanical Engineering, Kumamoto University, Kumamoto, Japan 860
*2) Department of Basic Engineering, Kumamoto University, Kumamoto, Japan 860
*3) Department of Applied Physics and Mathematics, Kyoto University, Kyoto, Japan 606

This paper proposes a design scheme of an indirect model reference adaptive control system with a desired rate of exponential convergence for continuous-time single-input single-output linear systems. The system designed by the scheme includes less integrators than the system by a scheme proposed by Kreisselmeier and Joos. The reduction of the number of integrators is essential in implementing a control scheme on digital computer since numerical integration replacing the integrators should be executed within sampling time. The exponential convergence is also necessary to be tolerant of modelling errors and noise. The reduction of the number of integrators is obtained by a newly derived adaptive law and an indirect MRACS scheme. The stability of the closed-loop control system and the exponential convergence of the control error are proved. This scheme is applied to a laboratory scale thermal system using a real-time digital computer.

1. Introduction

The problem of controlling a plant with completely unknown parameters to follow a desired model is considered by many authors as a problem of designing a control scheme of a model reference adaptive control system (MRACS) and they have proposed schemes of the MRACS (Monopoli [1], Narendra and Valavani [2], Feuer and Morse [3] and Egardt [4]). In applying these MRACS schemes to a practical control problem, it is desirable that control errors in the control system have exponential convergence onto zero with a fast rate. This property is necessary for the system to be tolerant of modelling errors, noise and deviations of the plant parameters (Anderson and Johnson [5] and Anderson and Johnstone [6]). Johnstone and Anderson [7] showed exponential convergence of discrete-time MRACS with least square adaptive law.

For continuous-time systems, Kreisselmeier [8], [9] proposed state regulators for unknown plants with errors decreasing exponentially with a desired rate. Also, Kreisselmeier and Joos [10] gave an MRACS scheme having such property. State regulators use an estimate of all state-variables of the unknown plant and to get the estimate, the regulators require many integrators. In Kreisselmeier and Joos' MRACS scheme, in order to obtain exponential convergence, their scheme uses an adaptive law derived from least square method and the law includes integration of a covariance matrix and a covariance vector between filtered signals. It also includes filters for generating signals used in an error model and filters for signals in an augmented error model, identifiers of unknown parameters and the desired model.
These facts mean that the system requires many integrators. To implement the system in a real-time digital computer, these integrators have to be replaced by numerical integration in a software program and the integration should be executed within a short sampling interval. Hence, from the practical point the number of integrators needs to be reduced.

This paper proposes a new scheme to reduce the number of integrators used in continuous-time MRACS with exponentially converging characteristics. The reduction is attained in two ways ; the introduction of a new adaptive algorithm and the use of an indirect design method of MRACS. The adaptive algorithm which identifies the unknown parameters is derived from the weighted least square method for continuous-time systems, which is used in Johnstone and Anderson [7] for discrete-time systems. This algorithm does not need the covariance vector which is required in Kreisselmeier and Joos' algorithm. The control algorithm of the indirect MRACS is proposed by Åstrom and Wittenmark [11] and Elliott and Wolovich [12] and it consists of three steps : an adaptive observer identifies unknown parameters of the plant, then parameters in a control law are calculated and, finally, manipulating inputs are generated. Whereas in the direct MRACS scheme parameters in control law are directly identified, the indirect scheme identifies the minimum number of the plant parameters so that the number of parameters to be identified is reduced. This means the reduction of the size of the covariance matrix and the number of filters and identifiers. Since indirect scheme only requires the error model for identifying the parameters and does not need the construction of the augmented error model, we can also save the filters for signals in the augmented error model. These facts give a reduction of the number of integrators.

The stability of the closed-loop MRACS and the exponential convergence of the control error are mathematically proved.

The indirect MRACS scheme proposed in this paper is applied to a laboratory scale thermal system. The plant is a heated tank with second order and its water temperature is controlled by a real-time digital mini-computer. By using the scheme of this paper, the order of the MRACS controller is reduced to 20 from 41 of Kreisselmeier and Joos' scheme.

2. Problem Statement

Consider a plant to be controlled with single-input u(t) and single-output y(t). The plant is supposed to be linear, time-invariant and be described by a transfer function with term $X_0(s)$ representing initial condition ;

$$A(s)y(t)=B(s)u(t)+X_0(s), \tag{1}$$

where A(s), B(s) and $X_0(s)$ are polynomials with degree of n, n-d and n-1. Using

operator vector : $\underline{p}_m^T=[s^{m-1},s^{m-2},\ldots,1]$, (2)
coefficient vectors : $\underline{a}^T=[a_1,a_2,\ldots,a_n]$,
$\underline{b}^T=[b_1,b_2,\ldots,b_{n-d+1}]$ & $\underline{x}_0^T=[x_{01},x_{02},\ldots,x_{0n}]$, (3)

these polynomials are described as

$$A(s)=s^n+\underline{p}_n^T\underline{a},\quad B(s)=\underline{p}_{n-d+1}^T\underline{b},\quad X_0(s)=\underline{p}_n^T\underline{x}_0. \tag{4}$$

A reference model with reference input r(t) and reference output $y_M(t)$ is given by the transfer function :

$$A_M(s)y_M(t)=B_M(s)r(t). \tag{5}$$

The following assumption are made regarding (1) and (5).
(1) The plant is minimum phase, i.e., the numerator B(s) is strictly stable.
(2) The order n of the plant and the difference d of the degrees of denominator A(s) and numerator B(s) are known.
(3) Parameters $\underline{a}$, $\underline{b}$ and $\underline{x}_0$ are unknown. First coefficient b_1 of B(s) is not zero.
(4) The reference model is stable and the difference degree d_M of the transfer function of the model is greater than d.

Then the design problem of MRACS is to determine manipulating input u(t) in such a fashion that the output error between the plant and the model error $e(t)=y(t)-y_M(t)$ tends to zero with exponential rate of decreasing.

3. Adaptive Observer

The indirect MRACS consists of three parts ; an adaptive observer to identify the unknown plant parameters $\underline{a}$ and $\underline{b}$, calculating scheme of parameters in the control law and a control law to generate the input u(t). This section gives the adaptive observer.

First, an output model is obtained, which is used in the identification. Consider an r-th order stable polynomial $K(s)=s^n+\underline{p}_n^T\underline{k}$, where $\underline{k}$ is an n-dimensional coefficient vector, and define n-th order filters ;

$$K(s)\underline{z}_1(t)=\underline{p}_n y(t),\qquad K(s)\underline{z}_2(t)=\underline{p}_n u(t), \tag{6}$$

where
$$\underline{z}_1^T(t)=[z_{11}(t),\ldots,z_{1n}(t)],$$
$$\underline{z}_2^T(t)=[z_{21}(t),\ldots,z_{2n}(t)] \tag{7}$$

are n-dimensional filtered signals. By removing first (d-1) elements $z_{21}(t),\ldots,z_{2d-1}(t)$ of vector $\underline{z}_2(t)$ from 2n-dimensional vector $[\underline{z}_1^T(t)\ \underline{z}_2^T(t)]$, we have (2n-d+1)-dimensional vector $\underline{z}(t)$:

$$\underline{z}_\delta^T(t)=[z_{11}(t),\ldots,z_{1n}(t),z_{2d}(t),\ldots,z_{2n}(t)]. \tag{8}$$

Using (2n-d+1) dimensional parameter vector ;

$$\underline{\delta}=[\underline{a}^T,\underline{b}^T]^T \tag{9}$$

the output y(t) can be written in the form of output model (Kreisselmeier [13]) ;

$$y(t)=\underline{\delta}^T\underline{z}_\delta(t)+\varepsilon_0(t). \tag{10}$$

where $\varepsilon_0(t)$ represents the initial transient status and will decrease exponentially with rate $\lambda[K]$, which is the minimum absolute value of real part of zeros of K(s) (Lukes [14]).

The adaptive law to obtain the identified value $\hat{\underline{\delta}}^T=[\hat{\underline{a}}^T,\hat{\underline{b}}^T]$ is determined from minimizing the weighted square error ;

$$J(t)=\int_0^t\{\hat{y}(t,\tau)-y(t)\}^2e^{-\psi(t-\tau)}d\tau, \tag{11}$$

$$\hat{y}(t,\tau)=\hat{\underline{\delta}}^T(t)\underline{z}_\delta(\tau), \tag{12}$$

where $\psi>0$ is a forgetting factor. At the minimizing value $\hat{\underline{\delta}}(t)$, $\partial J/\partial\hat{\underline{\delta}}=\underline{0}$ holds and this implies normal equation ;

$$R(t)\hat{\underline{\delta}}(t)=\underline{r}(t), \tag{13}$$

$$\dot{R}(t)=-\psi R(t)+\underline{z}_\delta(t)\underline{z}_\delta^T(t), \tag{14}$$

$$\dot{\underline{r}}(t)=-\psi\underline{r}(t)+\underline{z}_\delta(t)y(t), \tag{15}$$

where R(t) is (2n-d+1)x(2n-d+1) symmetric matrix and $\underline{r}(t)$ is (2n-d+1)-dimensional vector (Kreisselmeier [13]). If $R^{-1}(t)$ exists, from (13)-(15) the following adaptive law is derived. See appendix.

$$\dot{\hat{\underline{\delta}}}(t)=-R^{-1}(t)\underline{z}_\delta(t)(\hat{y}(t)-y(t)), \tag{16}$$

$$\hat{y}(t)=\hat{\underline{\delta}}^T(t)\underline{z}_\delta(t). \tag{17}$$

Hence, the identified value is obtained by filters (6), covariance matrix (14) and adaptive law (16) and (17).

4. Model Following Control Law

In this section, a control law which attains the model following and a scheme for calculating parameters in the control law are derived.

To obtain the control law, we derive an error model in the following. First, consider a stable d-th order polynomial $D(s)=s^d+\underline{p}_n^T\underline{d}$. And consider polynomials $R(s)=\underline{p}_n^T\underline{r}$, $S(s)=s^d+\underline{p}_d^T\underline{s}$ and $T(s)=\underline{p}_n^T\underline{t}$ having degrees of n-1, d and n-1 and coefficient vectors ;

$$\underline{r}^T=[r_1,..,r_n],\ \underline{s}^T=[s_1,..,s_d]\ \&\ \underline{t}^T=[t_1,..,t_n], \quad (18)$$

respectively. Above polynomials are chosen so as to satisfy the equations ;

$$D(s)K(s)=A(s)S(s)+R(s), \quad (19)$$
$$S(s)B(s)=b_1K(s)+T(s). \quad (20)$$

Then, using these equations and notations of (2n+1)-dimensional vectors ;

$$\underline{z}^T(t)=[u(t),\underline{z}_1^T(t),\underline{z}_2^T(t)],\ \underline{\theta}^T=[b_1,\underline{r}^T,\underline{t}^T], \quad (21)$$

relation (22) and error model (23) are obtained;

$$K(s)D(s)e(t) =K(s)\{\underline{\theta}^T\underline{z}(t)+S(s)\varepsilon_0(t)-D(s)y_M(t)\}, \quad (22)$$
$$D(s)e(t)=\underline{\theta}^T\underline{z}(t)-D(s)y_M(t)+\varepsilon_1(t), \quad (23)$$

where $\varepsilon_1(t)$ satisfies

$$K(s)\{\varepsilon_1(t)-S(s)\varepsilon_0(t)\}=0, \quad (24)$$

and it also decreases exponentially with rate $\lambda[K]$ as $\varepsilon_0(t)$ does.

If control input u(t) could be determined to satisfy the relation

$$\underline{\theta}^T\underline{z}(t)-D(s)y_M(t)=0, \quad (25)$$

then, from error model (23), e(t) decreases and the output y(t) follows the reference output $y_M(t)$. Since parameters $\underline{\theta}$ are unknown, they need to be replaced by calculated value $\hat{\underline{\theta}}(t)$ which satisfies the relations (19)-(20) with the identified value $\hat{\underline{a}}(t)$ and $\hat{\underline{b}}(t)$ obtained from the adaptive observer. Actually, the value $\hat{\underline{\theta}}(t)$ is straightforwardly calculated by substituting $\hat{\underline{a}}(t)$ and $\hat{\underline{b}}(t)$ into the following equations ;

$$\hat{s}_i(t)=\sum_{j=1}^{i}d_jk_{i-j}-\sum_{j=0}^{i-1}\hat{s}_j(t)\hat{a}_{i-j}(t), i=1,..,d \quad (26)$$

$$\hat{r}_i(t)=\sum_{j=0}^{d}d_jk_{d+i-j}-\sum_{j=0}^{d}\hat{s}_j(t)\hat{a}_{d+i-j}(t), i=1,..,n \quad (27)$$

$$\hat{t}_i(t)=\sum_{j=0}^{d}\hat{s}_j(t)\hat{b}_{i-j}(t)-\hat{b}_1(t)k_i, \ i=1,..,n \quad (28)$$

$$\hat{s}_0(t)=1,\ d_0=1,\ k_0=1,$$
$$\hat{a}_i(t)=0 \text{ for } i>n \text{ and } i<1, \quad (29)$$
$$\hat{b}_i(t)=0 \text{ for } i>n-d+1 \text{ and } i<1.$$

In (25), in order to avoid a division by zero, b_1 is also replaced by $b_u(t)$ given by

$$b_u(t)=\begin{cases}\hat{b}_1(t), & \text{if } \hat{b}_1(t)>b_0, \\ b_0\mathrm{sgn}[\hat{b}_1(t)], & \text{if } \hat{b}_1(t)<b_0. \end{cases} \quad (30)$$

where b_0 is a small positive number. Then replacing $\underline{\theta}$ and b_1 by $\hat{\underline{\theta}}(t)$ of (26)-(29) and $b_u(t)$ of (30), the control law becomes

$$u(t)=-\frac{1}{b_u(t)}\{\hat{\underline{r}}^T(t)\underline{z}_1(t)+\hat{\underline{t}}^T(t)\underline{z}_1(t) -D(s)A_M^{-1}(s)B_M(s)r(t)\}. \quad (31)$$

The above-stated indirect MRACS scheme is schematically shown in Fig. 1.

<u>Remark.</u> Whereas indirect method identifies (2n-d+1) parameters $\underline{\delta}$, direct MRACS identifies 2n+1 parameters $\underline{\theta}^T=[b_1,\underline{r}^T,\underline{t}^T]$ in control law (31) directly using an augmented error model and additional filters ;

$$e(t)=\underline{\theta}_{-1}^T\tilde{\underline{z}}(t) \text{ and } D(s)\tilde{\underline{z}}(t)=\underline{z}(t). \quad (32)$$

5. Exponential Convergence and Stability of Closed-Loop MRACS

Exponential convergence and stability of the control system are assured under the condition of sufficient richness of the filtered signals.

<u>Sufficient richness of filtered signals.</u> Filtered signal $\underline{z}_\delta(t)$ is sufficiently rich if there exist a finite time T>0 and a positive number $\rho>0$ such that for all t>T, the next inequality holds

$$\int_{t-T}^{t}\underline{z}_\delta(t)\underline{z}_\delta^T(t)dt>\rho I_{2n-d+1}. \quad (33)$$

<u>Existence and boundedness of the inverse of matrix R(t).</u> For t>T, $R^{-1}(t)$ exists and its norm is bounded ;

$$\|R^{-1}(t)\|<1/\rho e^{-\psi T}. \quad (34)$$

<u>Exponential convergence of identification.</u> Identified value $\hat{\underline{\delta}}(t)$ and calculated value $\hat{\underline{\theta}}(t)$ converge onto true value $\underline{\delta}$ and $\underline{\theta}$ with the rate $\lambda_0=\min\{\psi/2,\lambda[K]\}$ exponentially, i.e. there exist positive constants M_1 and M_2, the errors decrease faster than an exponential function with exponent λ_0 ;

$$\|\hat{\underline{\delta}}(t)-\underline{\delta}\|<M_1e^{-\lambda_0 t}, \quad (35)$$

$$\|\hat{\underline{\theta}}(t)-\underline{\theta}\|<M_2e^{-\lambda_0 t}. \quad (36)$$

<u>Boundedness of signals and exponential convergence of output error.</u> Signals $\underline{z}_1(t)$, $\underline{z}_2(t)$ and control input u(t) are bounded and output error $e(t)=y(t)-y_M(t)$ converges exponentially with rate $\min\{\psi/2,\lambda[K],\lambda[D]\}$, where $\lambda[K]$ and $\lambda[D]$ are the minimum absolute values of real part of zeros of K(s) and D(s).

Proofs of these statements are given in appendix.

6. Application to a Thermal System

The scheme of indirect MRACS is evaluated by experimentally implementing it on a mini-computer for a heated tank with a water jacket.

Experimental plant, The plant is the same one used in Inoue and Iwai [15] and is shown schematically in Fig.2. It has two tanks. The outer tank water flows in through valve A and goes out through valve B with flow rate Q_0. The water is heated by an electric heater placed at the bottom of the outer tank. The heat from the heater (maximun 1.9kW) is the manipulating input. A software program calculates the adaptive observer (14) and (16) with numerical integration and gives calculated value $\hat{\theta}(t)$ of (26)-(29) and input value u(t) of (31). Then the computer controls the heater through triac controller to output a mount of heat proportional to value u(t). Output y(t) is the measured temperature of the outer tank and is fed into the computer to be used in the calculation of the adaptive observer and the control law. The output is controlled to follow the reference output of a reference model.

Transfer function of the plant. The plant is described approximately by a transfer function of 2nd-order ;

$$y(t)=\frac{b_1 s+b_2}{s^2+a_1 s+a_2}u(t), \tag{37}$$

where parameters a_1, a_2, b_1 and b_2 are unknown and are to be identified by the adaptive observer.

Reference model. The model is selected by the following steps ; first, a 1st-order approximate model of the plant is obtained from a step response experimentally ;

$$\dot{x}_1=\lambda_1 x_1+\lambda_2 u, \quad y(t)=x_1. \tag{38}$$

Then a PI feedback controller for this reduced-order model is considered ;

$$e=x_1-r,$$
$$\tilde{u}=F_1 e+F_2 x_2=u+\lambda_1 r/b \tag{39}$$
$$\dot{e}=\lambda_1 e+\lambda_2 \tilde{u}, \quad \dot{x}_2=e$$

Finally, feedback gains F_1 and F_2 are determined so as to minimize

$$J=\int_0^\infty (Q_1 e^2+Q_2 x_2^2+R\tilde{u}^2)dt \tag{40}$$

and the closed-loop system with the PI feedback having gains F_1 and F_2 ;

$$\begin{bmatrix}\dot{x}_1\\ \dot{x}_2\end{bmatrix}=\begin{bmatrix}\lambda_1+\lambda_2 F_1 & \lambda_2 F_2\\ 1 & 0\end{bmatrix}\begin{bmatrix}x_1\\ x_2\end{bmatrix} \tag{41}$$

gives the reference model.

Experimental result. Table 1 gives experimental conditions and parameters chosen for adaptive observer and reference model. Also are given the calculating equations of parameters $\hat{r},\hat{s},\hat{t}$ in control law from identified plant parameter values $\hat{a}_1,\hat{a}_2,\hat{b}_1,\hat{b}_2$, and it can be seen that the calculation is simple. Reference input r(t) is rectangular wave switching between two values 4.8°C and 7.8°C with period 80 min. Fig.3 shows plant output y(t) and model output $y_M(t)$ and it is shown that output y(t) follows model output $y_M(t)$ well. In Fig.4, manipulating output is depicted.

7. Conclusion

We have proposed a design scheme of a model reference adaptive control system for single-input single-output continuous-time linear systems. The scheme uses an adaptive law derived from least square scheme with a forgetting factor and its control law is based on an indirect MRACS method. A reduction of the number of integrators included in the MRACS is attained. The reduction is due to the omission of a covariance vector in the adaptive law and the use of the indirect method in the control law which identifies the minimum number of parameters. It is noted that the scheme does not require filters to generate an augmented error. It has been also proved that the MRACS in this paper controls the output of a plant to follow the reference output with errors decreasing exponentially and all signals in the MRACS is bounded.

The effectiveness of the MRACS scheme have been confirmed by applying it to a laboratory scale experimental plant. The number of integrators is reduced to 20 from 41 in an other MRACS method and the computing time required to get numerical integration for these integrators is shortened.

The stability of the closed-loop MRACS is proved under the condition of sufficient richness of filtered signals. To find a sufficient condition for sufficient richness of these signals is still an open problem.

References

[1] Monopoli, R. V. : Model reference adaptive control with an augmented error signal, IEEE Trans. on AC, AC-19, 474/484 (1974)

[2] Narendra, K. S. and Valavani, L. S. : Stable adaptive controller design-direct control, IEEE Trans. on AC, AC-23, 557/569 (1978)

[3] Feuer, A. and Morse, A. S. : Adaptive control of single-input single-output linear systems, IEEE Trans. on AC, AC-23, 557/569 (1978)

[4] Egardt, B. : Stability of adaptive controllers, Springer-Verlag (1979)

[5] Anderson, B. D. O. : and Johnson, Jr. C. R.: Exponential convergence of adaptive identification and control algorithms, Automatica, 18, 1/13 (1982)

[6] Anderson, B. D. O. : Johnstone, R. M. :

Adaptive systems and time varying plants, Int. J. Control, 37, 367/377 (1983)

[7] Johnstone, R. M. and Anderson, B. D. O. : Exponential convergence of recursive least squares with exponential forgetting factor-adaptive control, Systems and Control Letters, 2, 69/76, (1982)

[8] Kreisselmeier, G. : Adaptive control via adaptive observation and asymptotic feedback matrix synthesis, IEEE Trans. on AC, AC-25, 717/722 (1980)

[9] Kreisselmeier, G. : On adaptive state regulation, IEEE Trans. on AC, AC-27, 3/17 (1982)

[10] Kreisselmeier, G. and Joos, D. : Rate of convergence in model reference adaptive control, IEEE Trans. on AC, AC-27, 710/713 (1982)

[11] Åström, K. J. : and Wittenmark, B. : Self-tuning controllers based on pole-zero placement, IEE Proc. 127, Pt.D. 120/130, (1980)

[12] Elliott, H. and Wolovich, W. A. : Parameter adaptive identification and control, IEEE Trans. on AC, AC-24, 592/599 (1979)

[13] Kreisselmeier, G. : Adaptive observers with exponential rate of convergence, IEEE Trans. on AC, AC-22, 2/8 (1977)

[14] Lukes, D. H. : Differential equations : Classical to controlled, Academic Press (1982)

[15] Inoue, A. and Iwai, Z. : Design and application of reduced-order adaptive observer with exponential rate of convergence for single-input single-output linear systems, Int. J. Control, 39, 375/393 (1984)

[16] Inoue, A., Iwai, Z. and Sato, M. : An adaptive observer with variable rate of convergence, Trans. SICE, 18, 1159/1164 (1982) (in Japanese)

Appendix

Derivation of adaptive law (16). If $R^{-1}(t)$ exists, differentiating both sides of $R(t)R^{-1}(t) = I_{2n-d+1}$, we obtain

$$\dot{R}(t)^{-1}=\psi R^{-1}(t)-R^{-1}(t)\underline{z}_\delta(t)\underline{z}_\delta^T(t)R^{-1}(t). \tag{42}$$

Substituting this relation into the differentiated equation of $\underline{\hat{\delta}}(t)=R^{-1}(t)\underline{r}(t)$ obtained from (13), adaptive law (16) is derived.

Proof of boundedness of $R^{-1}(t)$. If we denote the minimum eigenvalue of $R(t)$ as $\lambda_{min}[R(t)]$, then norm of $R^{-1}(t)$ is evaluated as follows :

$$\|R^{-1}(t)\|=1/\lambda_{min}[R(t)]=1/\rho e^{-\psi T}. \tag{43}$$

Proof of exponential convergence of identification. First, exponential convergence of $\underline{\hat{\delta}}(t)$ onto $\underline{\delta}$ will be proved. Consider positive function :

$$V(t)=\frac{1}{2}(\underline{\hat{\delta}}(t)-\underline{\delta})^T R(t)(\underline{\hat{\delta}}(t)-\underline{\delta})+\frac{1}{2}\int_t^\infty \varepsilon_0^2(\tau)d\tau. \tag{44}$$

Using (10), (14) and (16), it is shown that, along the trajectory of the adaptive observer, $V(t)$ satisfies inequality

$$\dot{V}(t)=-\frac{1}{2}((\underline{\hat{\delta}}(t)-\underline{\delta})^T\underline{z}_\delta(t)-\varepsilon_0(t))^2 -\frac{\psi}{2}(\underline{\hat{\delta}}(t)-\underline{\delta})^T R(t)(\underline{\hat{\delta}}(t)-\underline{\delta}) \tag{45}$$

$$\leq -\psi V(t)+\frac{1}{2}\psi\int_t^\infty \varepsilon_0(\tau)^2 d\tau. \tag{46}$$

From (45), $\dot{V}(t)$ is negative for all t and $V(t)$ converges a positive number. This fact and exponential convergence of $\varepsilon_0(t)$ with rate $\lambda[K]$ give exponential convergence of $V(t)$ with rate $\min(\psi,2\lambda[K])$ in inequality (46). Using inequality :

$$R(t)>\rho e^{\psi T} I_{2n-d+1}, \tag{47}$$

and

$$V(t)>\rho e^{\psi T}\|\underline{\hat{\delta}}(t)-\underline{\delta}\|^2, \tag{48}$$

derived from sufficient richness (33), convergence of $V(t)$ implies convergence of $\underline{\hat{\delta}}(t)-\underline{\delta}$ with rate $\min(\psi/2,\lambda[K])$.
Exponential convergence of $\underline{\hat{\theta}}(t)-\underline{\theta}$ is shown from convergence of $\underline{\hat{\delta}}(t)-\underline{\delta}$ in the following way. From (26), $\hat{s}_1(t)$ is shown to be linear to $\hat{a}_1(t)$, then convergence of $\hat{a}_1(t)$ gives convergence of $\hat{s}_1(t)$ with the same exponential rate. Also, from (26), $\hat{s}_2$ is linear to $\hat{a}_2$, $\hat{a}_1(\hat{s}_1-s_1)$ and $(\hat{a}_1-a_1)s_1$ and this linear relation gives convergence of $\hat{s}_2(t)$. With repeating these, convergence of all parameters in control law with rate $\min(\psi/2,\lambda[K])$ is shown.

Proof of boundedness of signals $\underline{z}(t)$. Let $\tilde{y}(t)$ be

$$\tilde{y}(t)=D(s)y(t). \tag{49}$$

Then, from (2), (23) and (31)

$$\tilde{y}(t)=-(\underline{\hat{\theta}}(t)-\underline{\theta})^T\underline{z}(t)+D(s)A_M(s)^{-1}B_M(s)r(t) +\varepsilon_1(t). \tag{50}$$

Boundedness of $r(t)$ and exponential convergence of $\underline{\hat{\theta}}(t)-\underline{\theta}$ and $\varepsilon_1(t)$ give

$$|\tilde{y}(t)|\leq M_3 e^{-\lambda_0 t}\|\underline{z}(t)\|+M_4, \tag{51}$$

where M_3 and M_4 are positive constants and $\lambda_0=\min(\psi/2,\lambda[K])$. Using $\tilde{y}(t)$ of (49), components $u(t)$, $\underline{z}_1(t)$, $\underline{z}_2(t)$ of $\underline{z}(t)$ are given by

$$u(t)=A(s)B^{-1}(s)D^{-1}(s)\tilde{y}(t)-B^{-1}(t)X_0(s), \tag{52}$$

$$\underline{z}_1(t)=K^{-1}(s)\underline{p}_n D^{-1}(s)\tilde{y}(t), \tag{53}$$

$$\underline{z}_2(t)=K^{-1}(s)\underline{p}_n A(s)B^{-1}(s)D^{-1}(s)\tilde{y}(t) -K^{-1}(s)\underline{p}_n B^{-1}(s)X_0(s). \tag{54}$$

These relations are described by a state-space equation with matrices $\bar{A}$, $\bar{B}$, $\bar{C}$, $\bar{D}$ and state-variable $\underline{x}(t)$,

$$\dot{\underline{x}}(t)=\bar{A}\underline{x}(t)+\bar{B}\tilde{y}(t), \quad \underline{z}(t)=\bar{C}\underline{x}(t)+\bar{D}\tilde{y}(t), \tag{55}$$

and the solution is

$$\underline{z}(t)=\bar{C}e^{\bar{A}t}\underline{x}(0)+\int_0^t \bar{C}e^{\bar{A}(t-\tau)}\bar{B}\tilde{y}(\tau)d\tau+\bar{D}\tilde{y}(t). \quad (56)$$

Substituting inequality (51) and

$$\|e^{\bar{A}t}\|<M_5 e^{-\lambda_1 t}, \quad (57)$$

into (56), boundedness of $\|\underline{z}(t)\|$ is shown, where λ_1 is minimum real part of eigenvalues of $\bar{A}$.

Proof of exponential convergence of e(t). Using equations (23) and (31), exponential convergence of $\hat{\underline{\theta}}(t)$ onto $\underline{\theta}$ and boundedness of $\underline{z}(t)$ imply exponential convergence of e(t) onto zero with rate $\min(\psi/2,\lambda[K],\lambda[D])$.

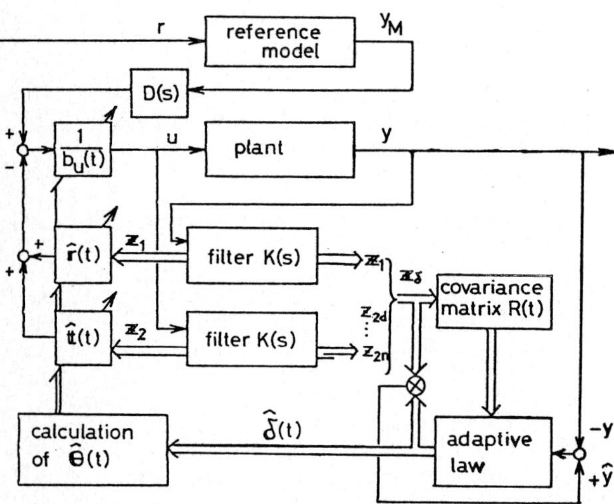

Fig.1. Indirect MRACS scheme.

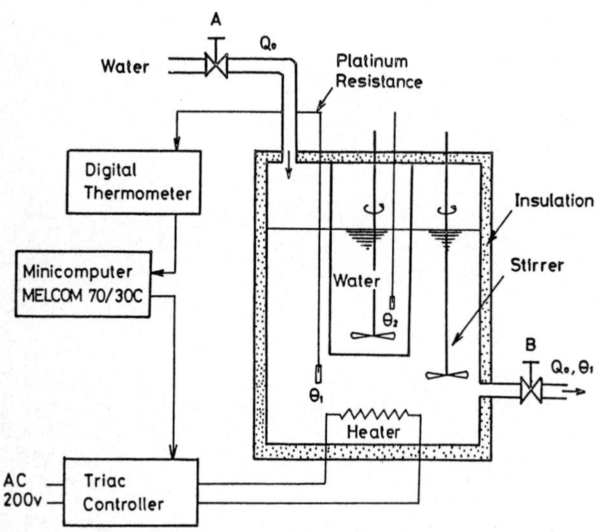

Fig.2. Experimental heated tank plant.

Table 1. Experimental Conditions and Parameters

experimental condition	water capacity of outer tank 17.96 liter inner tank 2.376 liter flow rate Q_0 2.151 liter/min water level of outer tank 30.0 cm inner tank 14.0 cm sampling time 3.0 sec computing time per one sampling 0.29 sec
parameters to determine reference model	performance index $Q_1=1.0,\ Q_2=1.0,\ R=1.0$ PI feedback gain $F_1=-9.134,\ F_2=-1.0$ reduced order model with 1st order reference model $\lambda_1=-0.0582,\ \lambda_2=0.01135$°C/kJ $a_{M1}=-0.01620,\ a_{M2}=-0.01136$ $b_{M1}=0.1620,\ b_{M2}=0.01136$
reference input	rectangular wave with values 4.8°C and 7.8°C, period 80 min.
parameters of adaptive observer	$\psi_0(t)=0.01+0.19\exp(-0.07t)$ * $K(s)=(s+0.01)(s+0.02)$
parameters of control law	$D(s)=s+0.2$
calculating equations of $\hat{\underline{r}},\hat{\underline{s}},\hat{\underline{t}}$	$\hat{s}_1=d_1+k_1-\hat{a}_1$ $\hat{r}_1=d_1k_1+k_2-\hat{a}_1\hat{s}_1-\hat{a}_2,\ \hat{r}_2=d_1k_2-\hat{a}_2\hat{s}_1$ $\hat{t}_1=(\hat{s}_1-k_1)\hat{b}_1+\hat{b}_2,\ \hat{t}_2=-k_2\hat{b}_1+\hat{s}_1\hat{b}_2$

*)Variable gain $\psi_0(t)$ was used here. Note that ψ in the text is evaluated from $\psi=\min\psi_0(t)=0.01$ [16].

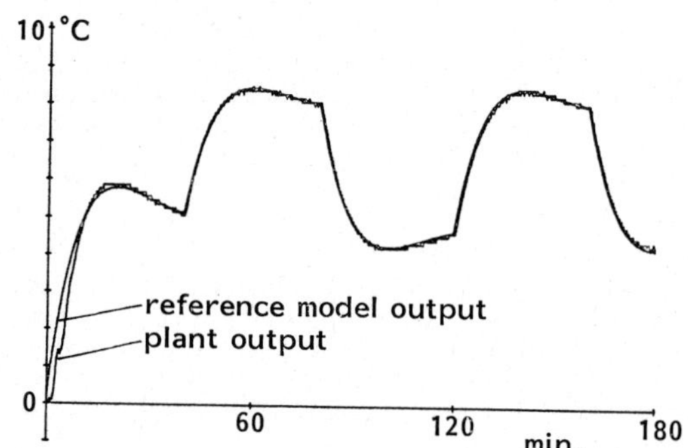

Fig.3. Plant output and reference model output.

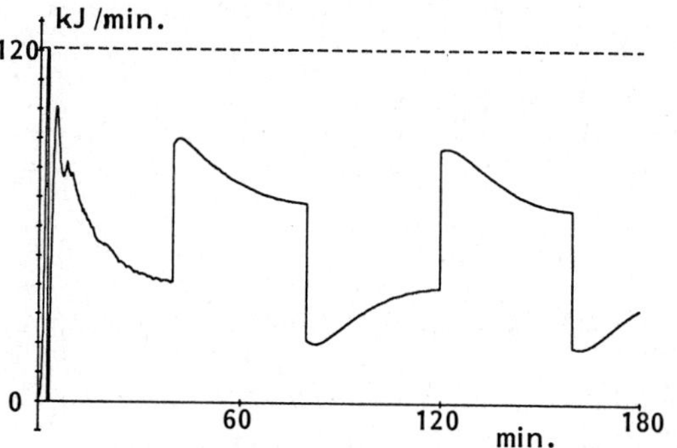

Fig.4. Manipulating input.

DIGITAL TECHNIQUES in Simulation, Communication and Control
Spyros G. Tzafestas (editor)
Elsevier Science Publishers B.V. (North-Holland) © IMACS, 1985

ON MODEL REFERENCE ADAPTIVE CONTROL

F. Fnaiech* and R. R. Mohler**

*Laboratoire d' automatique, E.N.S.E.T.
5 Ave. Taha Hussein 1008 Tunis-TUNISIA

**Naval Postgraduate School
Department of Electrical and
and Computer Engineering
Monterey, California 93943 U.S.A.
(on leave from Oregon State University)
Corvallis, Oregon 97331)

Model reference adaptive control (MRAC) techniques are used for identification and control of nonlinear discrete system. The Hammerstein model contains a nonlinear (NL) characteristic at its input in cascade with a linear dynamic block. Here identification uses the recursive least-square algorithm in either deterministic or stochastic settings. The identification step encompasses both the linear and nonlinear parts of the system. Decomposition of the nonlinear characteristic in a Volterra series is discussed. The nonlinear-characteristic estimation depends mostly upon the linear part of the Volterra-series expansion.

The adaptive-control law is derived from the minimization of a quadratic error criterion. And, the solution of an algebraic nonlinear equation provides the control-law algorithm.

Bilinear systems, their identification and control are presented. Appropriate nonlinear applications are indicated.

1. INTRODUCTION

Most physical systems are nonlinear in nature, and overall system performance is enhanced by making use of these nonlinear dynamics rather than to force small perturbations and linear behavior. In other cases, adaptive nonlinear control may be synthesized to improve system performance. System performance depends on model accuracy which may be estimated by means of physical principles in conjunction with identification methodology.

The parameter-estimation process, in the identification step, can be used to modify the adaptive-control law of a time-varying parametric process. And, the identification problem for linear processes is widely treated in the literature. E.g., see Iserman [1], Strejc [2], Dugard and Landau [3], [4].

The model reference adaptive control and self-tuning regulator is treated by Landau [5], [6] and Kurz [7].

The target of this paper is the application of linear MRAC techniques to nonlinear systems. This application is suggested by Aguilar-Martin [8] who indicates that, under some hypothesis, nonlinear identification can be treated as a linear identification problem.

To synthesize the self-tuning regulator for the Hammerstein model, the work of Goodwin [9, 10] is utilized. And the identification problem of the Hammerstein model was developed by Yoshimura and Tomizuka [11].

+Sponsored in part by the NAVELEX Chair at the Naval Postgraduate School and ONR Contract No. N00014-81-K-0814.

2. THE HAMMERSTEIN MODEL

The Hammerstein model of a linear system, with additive output noise preceded by a lumped zero-memory nonlinearity, can be represented by

$$y(k) = \sum_{i=1}^{n} - a_i y(k - i) + \sum_{j=1}^{m} b_j f_e[u(k - j)] + w'(k), \tag{1}$$

where

$$w'(k) = w(k) + \sum_{i=1}^{n} a_i w(k - i) \tag{2}$$

which is assumed as an additional output noise for convenience.

It is impossible to identify directly the linear dynamic part and the nonlinear characteristic from (1). Therefore correlation exists between linear parameters b_j and the nonlinear characteristic.

To overcome this problem the nonlinearity is decomposed in a Volterra-like series. In general, suppose that $f_e[u(k)]$ can be written as

$$f_e[u(k)] = \sum_{\ell=1}^{N} \alpha_\ell g_\ell[u(k)] + \Delta f_e[u(k)], \quad (3)$$

where $g_\ell[\cdot]$ are known functions, and N is an a'priori chosen integer; α_ℓ are the kernels, and $\Delta f_e[u(k)]$ is an approximation error which might be treated as an additional input noise for convenience.

2.1 Introduction of a New Parameter for the Identification

Substituting (3) into (1) yields

$$y(k) = \sum_{i=1}^{n} - a_i y(k - i)$$

$$+ \sum_{j=1}^{m} \sum_{\ell=1}^{N} \beta_{j\ell} g_\ell[u(k - j)] \quad (4)$$

$$+ \sum_{j=1}^{m} b_j \Delta f_e[u(k - j)] + w'(k),$$

where $\beta_{j\ell} = b_j\alpha_\ell$ (new parameters to be identified);

$$\sum_{j=1}^{m} b_j \Delta f_e[u(k - j)]$$

may sometimes be neglected or approximated by a new noise term. $w'(k)$ is an additional output noise. Equation (4) can be written as

$$y(k) = \theta^T \phi(k - 1) + w(k), \quad (5)$$

where

$$w(k) = w'(k) + \sum_{j=1}^{m} b_j \Delta f_e[u(k - j)], \quad (6)$$

$$\theta^T = [-a_1, -a_2, \dots -a_n, \beta_{11}, \dots, \beta_{1N}, \beta_{2N}, \dots, \beta_{mN}], \quad (7)$$

a parameter vector, and

$$\phi^T(k - 1) = [y(k - 1, \dots, y(k - n), g_1(u(k - 1)), \dots, g_1(u(k - m)), \dots g_N(u(k - m))], \quad (8)$$

an information vector.

2.2 Series Parallel Identifier

To identify the parameters a_i and $\beta_{j\ell}$, it is necessary to define the following terms:

i) The estimated output, $y(k) = \hat{\phi}^T(k)\phi(k - 1)$, where

$$\hat{\theta}^T(k) = [\hat{a}_1(k), \dots, \hat{a}_n(k), \hat{\beta}_{11}(k), \dots, \hat{\beta}_{1N}(k), \dots, \hat{\beta}_{mN}(k)]. \quad (9)$$

and

ii) The a'posteriori prediction error,

$$e(k) = y(k) - \hat{\theta}^T(k)\phi(k - 1). \quad (10)$$

iii) The a'priori prediction error,

$$e^0(k) = y(k) - \hat{\theta}^T(k - 1)\phi(k - 1). \quad (11)$$

The identification algorithm used for the parametric estimation of the Hammerstein model is given by

$$\hat{\theta}(k + 1) = \hat{\theta}(k) + F(k)\phi(k)e(k)$$

with

$$F(k + 1) = \frac{1}{\lambda(k)}\left[F(k) - \frac{F(k)\phi(k)\phi^T(k)F(k)}{\lambda(k) + \phi^T(k)F(k)\phi(k)}\right] \quad (12)$$

and

$$e(k) = \frac{e^0(k)}{\lambda(k) + \phi^T(k)F(k)\phi(k)},$$

where $F(k)$ is a gain matrix, $F(0) > 0$, and $\lambda(k)$ is a "forgetting" factor: $\lambda(k) = \lambda(0)$ with $0.99 < \lambda(0) < 1$.

The procedure is applied successfully to a hyberbolic tangent nonlinearity in [12].

3. ADAPTIVE CONTROL

The application of the self-tuning regulator, realizing the minimum-variance law relative to a multivariable nonlinear Hammerstein system is treated in [13], although the general techniques, for the synthesis of the nonlinear controller are missing due to the diversity of the NL structures and their complexity. In fact, there exist several NL control algorithms based on dynamic optimization methods.

Landau [5],[6] proposed and developed many adaptive control methods used for linear systems in a stochastic and a deterministic environment.

The adaptive control of some classes of bilinear observable systems characterized by an ARMA NL model was proposed and discussed by Goodwin [9], [10] in related applications for waste-water treatment and PH regulations.

For the estimation of the system to be controlled, the RLS algorithm is given by

$$\hat{\theta}(k+1)=\hat{\theta}(k)+\sigma(k)F(k)\phi(k)(y(k+1)-\hat{y}(k+1)), \tag{13}$$

$$y(k+1) = \phi^T(k)\hat{\theta}(k), \tag{14}$$

and

$$F(k) = F(k-1)\left[I - \frac{\phi(k)\phi^T(k)F(k-1)\sigma(k)}{1+\sigma(k)\phi^T(k)F(k-1)\phi(k)}\right] \tag{15}$$

with

$$\sigma(k) = 1 \qquad \text{if } \frac{|y(k+1) - \hat{y}(k+1)|^2}{1+\phi^T(k)F(k-1)\phi(k)} > \Delta^2 \tag{16}$$

$$= 0 \qquad \text{otherwise.}$$

The convergence condition of this algorithm is given in [10]. Here $\Delta > 0$ is limited by sup $|w(k)| = \Delta$, where $w(k)$ characterizes the output noise and discretization errors. The adaptive control law, completing the estimation phase, can be found from

$$\hat{y}(k+1) \doteq \phi^T(k)\hat{\theta}(k) \triangleq y_d(k+1) \tag{17}$$

where $y_d(k+1)$ is the desired output and assumed physically realizable; then, the solution of Equation (17) provides the requested control law $u(k)$.

Goodwin proved in [10] that if $u(k)$ and $y_d(k)$ are bounded, then the output $y(k)$ is bounded and the following relation is verified:

$$\lim_{k\to 0} \sup |y(k) - y_d(k)| \leq K\Delta, \tag{18}$$

where K is a constant.

If the second-order Hammerstein model is controlled, the observation vector $\phi(k-1)$ is nonlinear in control $u(k)$. To compute the control law from Equation (17), the numeric algorithm of Lobatchevski-Graeffe [14] is used for solving the nonlinear algebraic equation. Then, the adaptive control law for the Hammerstein model is given as

$$u(k) = \frac{y_d(k) + \hat{\theta}_1(k)y(k-1) + \theta_2(k)y(k-2)}{\hat{\theta}_3(k)}. \tag{19}$$

4. DISCRETE BILINEAR SYSTEMS

Similar to the above models, a single-input, single-output (SISO), bilinear system (BLS) may be represented by

$$y(k) = \sum_{i=1}^{n} a_i y(k-i) + \sum_{j=1}^{m} b_j u(k-j)y(k-i) + c_j u(k-j). \tag{20}$$

If $y(k)$ is expanded in terms of its Volterra series with y_ℓ designating the ℓth-order term, the solution may be obtained as a summation of the following solutions:

$$y_1(k) = \sum_{i=1}^{n} y_1(k-i) + \sum_{j=1}^{m} c_j u(k-j),$$

$$y_2(k) = \sum_{i=1}^{n} y_2(k-i) + \sum_{j=1}^{m} b_j u(k-j)y_1(k-j) + c_j u(k-j)$$

$$\vdots$$

$$y_\ell(k) = \sum_{i=1}^{n} y_\ell(k-i) + \sum_{j=1}^{m} b_j u(k-i)y_{\ell-1}(k-j) + c_j u(k-j)$$

$$\vdots$$

These terms, $y_1(\bullet)$, ..., y_ℓ, ..., result in the linear portion and successively higher-order polynomial terms of the Volterra series.

In most cases the BLS may be approximated by a finite number of terms, and in certain cases may be described exactly by a finite number of terms. The latter are referred to as weakly BLS.

In general, the state formulation of the discrete BLS is given by

$$x(k+1) = Ax(k) + Bx(k) \otimes u(k) + cu(k), \qquad y(k) = Dx(k), \tag{21}$$

where

$$Bx(k) \otimes u(k) = \sum_{k=1}^{m} B_k u_k x, \tag{22}$$

and $x(\bullet)$, $u(\bullet)$, $y(\bullet)$, A, C and B_k are of appropriate dimensions. Again, for the SISO BLS,

$$y(k) = \sum_{j=1}^{k} w_1(k,j)u_j + \sum\sum_{j_1,j_2=1}^{k} w_2(k,j_1,j_2) \cdot$$

$$\cdot \; u_{j1}u_{j2} + \ldots \qquad (23)$$

Then, the Volterra kernels, $w_j(\cdot)$, may be identified by cross-correlation of output and pseudorandom and tenary or binary input sequences. Certain unknown parameters, such as elements taken from A, B_k, C or D, may be computed indirectly from the kernels. E.g., such computations are presented for BLS, nuclear-fission kinetics in a thermal reactor by Baheti, Mohler and Spang [15]. Also, Walsh-function sequences may be used to approximate the input-output sequences and then to identify certain unknown parameters for the discrete as well as continuous case [16]. The method has been applied successfully to continuous BLS in immunology and nuclear fission [17]. Further work is planned for discrete BLS and online adaptive digital control using these methods.

If noise is added to the system, a stochastic BLS ensues. The control, u(k), is a function (possibly nonlinear) of the output or observation, y(k), the BLS (21) becomes conditionally linear. Further, if the noise inputs to the state and the observation are white Gaussian sequences and the states are initially conditionally Gaussian with respect to the observations, then they are conditionally Gaussian for all time. Hence, a finite-dimensional mean-square-error, filter may be derived which is an extension of the classical linear state estimator [18], [19]. Again, a separation principle has been developed under certain assumptions, to allow synthesis of the conditionally-linear (bilinear feedback system), optimal quadratic performance control based on optimal state estimation [19]. While these results, have been derived rigorously for the continuous case only, the discrete results seem to follow in a logical manner.

This methodology has been applied successfully to more highly nonlinear systems by local and global bilinear approximations - showing not only improvement of linear filtering but also over extended linear filters such as extended Kalman filter and truncated, second-order filter [20], [21].

REFERENCES:

[1] Iserman, R., Practical Aspects of Process Identification, Automatica Vol. 16 (1980) 575-587.

[2] Strejc, V., Least-Squares Parameter Estimation, Automatica 16 (1980) 535-550.

[3] Dugard, L. and Landau, I.D., Stabilite' des algorithmes recursifs d'adaptation, Annales de Telecommunications, tome 36 N°-11-12, (Novembre-Decembre 1981) 626-633.

[4] Dugard, L. and Landau, I.D., Recursive Output Error Identification Algorithms Theory and Evaluation, Automatica 16 (1980) 443-462.

[5] Landau, I.D., Adaptive Control, The Model Reference Approach, Marcel Dekker, Inc., New York (1979).

[6] Landau, I.D., Dualite' asymptotique entre les systemes de commande adaptative avec modele et les regulateurs a variance-minimale auto-ajustables, RIRO auto/sys. ana, cont 14, No. 2 (1980) 189-204.

[7] Kurz, H., Iserman, R. and Schuman, R., Experimental Comparison and Application of Various Parameter Adaptive Control Algorithms, 7th IFAC Helsinki, Finland, (June 1978).

[8] Aguilar-Martin, J., Linear Estimation of Linear Mappings for the Identification of Nonlinear Dynamic Systems, Int. J. Systems Sci. 7 No. 8 (1975) 949-952.

[9] Goodwin, G.C., Long, R.S. and McInnis, B.C., Adaptive Control of Bilinear Systems, Technical report EE 8017 (University of Newcastle, Australia, August 1980).

[10] Goodwin, G.C. and Long, R.S., Adaptive Control Algorithms for Waste-Water Treatment and PH Neutralization, Technical report EE 8112, (University of Newcastle, Australia, November 1981).

[11] Yoshimura, T. and Tomizuka, M., Application of Model Reference Adaptive Techniques to a Class of Nonlinear Systems, Transactions of the ASME 102 (1981) 158-163.

[12] Fnaiech, F., Application of Model Reference Adaptive Techniques to Some Classes of Nonlinear Systems, to appear.

[13] Anbumani, K., Patnaik, L.M. and Sarma, I.G., Self-Tuning Control of a Class Multivariable Nonlinear Systems, Int. J. Systems Sci. 12 No. 11 (1981) 1273- 1285.

[14] Demidovitch, B. and Maron, I., Elements de Calcul Numerique, Edition Mir-Moscou (1979).

[15] Baheti, R.O., Mohler, R.R. and Spang, A., A New Cross Correlation Algorithm for Volterra Kernel Estimation of Bilinear Systems, IEEE Trans. Auto. Cont. AC 24 (1979) 661-664.

[16] Karanam, V.R., Frick, P.A. and Mohler, R.R., Bilinear System Identification by Walsh Functions, IEEE Trans. Vol. AC-23 (1978).

[17] Mohler, R.R., Karanam, V.R. and Hsu, C.S., BLS Identification by Orthogonal Functions with Application to Immunology, Proc. 1976 CDC Conf. (Clearwater, FL, 1976).

[18] Lipster, R.S. and Shiryayev, A.N., Statistics of Random Processes II - Applications, (Springer-Verlag, New York, 1978).

[19] Mohler, R.R. and Kolodziej, Optimal Control of a Class of Nonlinear Stochastic Systems, IEEE Trans. Auto. Cont. AC 26 (1981) 1048-1053.

[20] Halawani, T.U., Mohler, R.R. and Kolodziej, W.J., A Two-Step Bilinear Filtering Approximation, IEEE Trans. Acous., Sp., S.P., ASSP 32 (1984) 344-352.

[21] Kolodziej, W.J. and Mohler, R.R., Analysis of a New Nonlinear Filter and Tracking Methodology, IEEE Trans. Info The. IT 29 (1984) to appear.

DIGITAL TECHNIQUES in Simulation, Communication and Control
Spyros G. Tzafestas (editor)
Elsevier Science Publishers B.V. (North-Holland) © IMACS, 1985

UNIFICATION OF WIENER HOPF AND STATE SPACE APPROACHES TO QUADRATIC OPTIMAL CONTROL

Michael G. Safonov and Athanasios Sideris

Department of Electrical Engineering Systems,
University of Southern California,
Los Angeles, CA 90089-0781 U.S.A.

ABSTRACT
A simple and concise solution of the Wiener-Hopf optimal control problem is given, which allows to bring under a common framework all major existing solutions. It is shown how the Riccati equations of the state-space LQG theory can be used to generate the matrix fraction descriptions, and spectral factors employed in the Wiener-Hopf solution.

1. INTRODUCTION

The design of optimal control systems in the frequency domain based on the minimization of a quadratic performance index has been the subject of various publications in the last fifteen years ([1],[2],[3],[4],[5],[6],[7],[8],[9],[10]).

The first solutions are severely limited, mainly by assuming that the plant is stable. Otherwise the stability of the closed loop system cannot be guaranteed. The design for unstable plants was first treated successfully by Youla et al ([4],[5]). The discrete-time case was treated independently by Kucera (see [8]) using similar methods to those of [5]. Youla recognised the need for carrying out the optimization process over a parametrized set of stabilizing controllers. To derive this parametrization he uses polynomial matrix fraction description (MFD) of systems.

Shaked originated a different approach for solving the general Wiener-Hopf problem by introducing a generalized spectral factorization (GSF), in which the usual stable and minimum phase spectral factors are replaced by ones which have exactly the poles of the plant as poles and are minimum phase ([6],[7]). Though the concept of GSF's proves to be of fundamental importance in any Wiener-Hopf approach, Shaked's derivation is not flawless (see section 5). Grimble also presents a solution which uses these generalized spectral factors, but from a point of view his solution is not really a frequency-domain approach. Grimble derives a time-domain optimality condition, which he next solves using Laplace transforms for the Optimal controller [9].

Youla's parametrization result is generalized in [11] and [12], in the sense that systems are represented by MFD's involving matrices whose elements belong to a ring having properties desired for the closed-loop system. Safonov [13] and Francis [10] give solutions of the Wiener-Hopf problem using this parametrization, where the underlying ring is taken to be the set of proper and stable transfer functions.

In this paper we aim at a unification of the various solutions, and at establishing clear connections between MFD and state-space solutions, a point which has not previously been addressed. We use the results in [11] and [12] to solve the general multivariable problem. The solution we present in section 4 has the merit of clearly identifying all the steps involved, and retaining a generality which allows it to encompass, and in this sense unify, all major Wiener-Hopf approaches. This unification is the subject of section 5. The links between Wiener-Hopf and state-space LQG results are established in section 6, where the familiar Riccati equations of the state-space theory are related to the concept of generalized spectral factors. We also demonstrate explicitly that Wiener-Hopf and time-domain LQG approaches produce identical controllers.

2. PROBLEM FORMULATION AND BASIC RELATIONSHIPS

The basic system configuration is depicted in figure 2.1. The plant, sensor and controller are modelled by linear, time-invariant, finite-dimensional systems, and represented in the frequency domain by the rational transfer function matrices: $G(s)$ $(m\times l)$, $H(s)$ $(k\times m)$, and $C(s)$ $(l\times k)$ respectively, with number of outputs and inputs given in parentheses. The system is driven by the plant noise $d(t)$, and the measurement noise $n(t)$, modelled as uncorrelated, zero-mean, stationary processes with spectral density matrices $\Phi_d(s)$ and $\Phi_n(s)$ respectively.

The objective is to select the controller $C(s)$ so that the closed loop system is asymptotically stable, and the output is optimally regulated in the sense that the performance index (P.I)

$$J = E\{x^T R_x x + u^T R_u u\} \qquad (2.1)$$

is minimized, where the expectation is taken over the noise processes $d(t)$ and $n(t)$. Relation (2.1) can be written as

$$J = \frac{1}{2\pi}\int_{-\infty}^{\infty} \mathrm{tr}[R_x\Phi_x(s)+R_u\Phi_u(s)]\,d\omega \qquad (2.2)$$

where $\Phi_x(s)$ and $\Phi_u(s)$ are the spectral density matrices of the signals x(t) and u(t), and R_x, R_u are weighting matrices.

The following assumptions are made concerning our systems and signals:

(i) H(s) is asymptotically stable - not a very unrealistic assumption for sensing devices. Note however, that G(s) can be open loop unstable and both G(s) and H(s) nonminimum phase.

(ii) There are no unstable pole-zero cancellations in the product: $P(s) = H(s)G(s)$.

(iii) $H(s), \Phi_n(s)$ are proper (i.e. tend to a constant matrix as $s \to \infty$), and $G(s), \Phi_d(s)$ are strictly proper (i.e. tend to the zero matrix as $s \to \infty$).

(iv) $G(s)$, $\Phi_d(s)$, $\Phi_n(s)$ do not have any poles on the imaginary axis.

(v) $R_x = R_x^T \geq 0$ and $R_u = R_u^T > 0$

From figure 2.1 we easily derive the formulae.

$$x(t) = (I-GQH)d(t) - GQn(t) \qquad (2.3)$$

$$u(t) = -Q[Hd(t)+n(t)] \qquad (2.4)$$

where we define

$$Q \triangleq C(I+PC)^{-1} \qquad (2.5)$$

$$P(s) \triangleq H(s)G(s) \qquad (2.6)$$

The quantity Q(s) embodies all of our design freedom, and has often been used in the literature as the design parameter (e.g.[1-3]). Note that equation (2.5) can be solved for the controller:

$$C = Q(I-PQ)^{-1} \qquad (2.7)$$

and since we assumed P(s) to be strictly proper, C(s) is proper if and only if Q(s) is proper. Using (2.3) and (2.4) we express

$$\Phi_x(s) = (I-GQH)\Phi_d(s)(I-GQH)^* + (GQ)\Phi_n(s)(GQ)^* \qquad (2.8)$$

$$\Phi_u(s) = (QH)\Phi_d(s)(QH)^* + Q\Phi_n Q^* \qquad (2.9)$$

By definition : $G^*(s) \triangleq G^T(-s)$ for any rational matrix. Then expression (2.2) for the P.I. transforms as follows:

$$J = \frac{1}{2\pi}\int_{-\infty}^{\infty} tr[R_x(I-GQH)\Phi_d(I-GQH)^* + R_x GQ\Phi_n(GQ)^* + R_u QH\Phi_d(QH)^* + R_u Q\Phi_n Q^*]d\omega \qquad (2.10)$$

3. THE STABILITY OF THE CLOSED LOOP SYSTEM

The space $\mathcal{L}$ of strictly proper rational matrices which have no poles on the imaginary axis can be viewed as an inner-product space by defining:

$$< G, K > \triangleq \frac{1}{2\pi}\int_{-\infty}^{\infty} tr(G^*K)d\omega \qquad (3.1),$$
for $G, K \in \mathcal{L}$.

The inner product induces the two-norm on the elements of $\mathcal{L}$ defined more explicitly by:

$$||G||_2 = \left(\frac{1}{2\pi}\int_{-\infty}^{\infty} tr(G^*G)d\omega\right)^{\frac{1}{2}} \qquad (3.2),$$
for $G \in \mathcal{L}$.

Let us also define by $\mathcal{L}_+$ the subspace of asymptotically stable elements of $\mathcal{L}$, and by $\mathcal{L}_\oplus$ the space of proper and stable rational matrices. Using these definitions we can write (2.10) as:

$$J = ||R_x^{\frac{1}{2}}(I-GQH)\Phi_d^{\frac{1}{2}}||_2^2 + ||R_x^{\frac{1}{2}}GQ\Phi_n^{\frac{1}{2}}||_2^2 + ||R_u^{\frac{1}{2}}QH\Phi_d^{\frac{1}{2}}||_2^2 + ||R_u^{\frac{1}{2}}Q\Phi_n^{\frac{1}{2}}||_2^2 \qquad (3.3)$$

where $R_x^{\frac{1}{2}}, R_u^{\frac{1}{2}}, \Phi_d^{\frac{1}{2}}, \Phi_n^{\frac{1}{2}}$ are such that $R_x = (R_x^{\frac{1}{2}})^*(R_x^{\frac{1}{2}})$ etc. Our assumptions on G, H, Φ_d, and Φ_n guarantee the finiteness of each term in (3.3), and hence of the P.I., given that $Q \in \mathcal{L}_\oplus$. Thus we remark that the finiteness of the PI does not imply (nor is implied by) the asymptotic stability of the closed loop system. The later must be ascertained by additional conditions given in the following lemma.

Consider the MFD's for our "extended" plant P(s) defined by (2.6): (for supporting material and definitions see [11],[12])

$$P(s) = N_r(s)D_r^{-1}(s) = D_\ell^{-1}(s)N_\ell(s) \qquad (3.4),$$

where all numerators and denoninators belong to $\mathcal{L}_\oplus$.

Factorizations (3.4) are called coprime if and only if the Bézout identities

$$U_r N_r + V_r D_r = I \qquad (3.5a)$$

and

$$N_\ell U_\ell + D_\ell V_\ell = I \qquad (3.5b)$$

are satisfied for some $U_r, V_r, U_\ell, V_\ell \in \mathcal{L}_\oplus$. Such coprime factorizations are easily shown to exist for any P(s) [12].

<u>Lemma 3.1</u> ([11]-[12])

The closed loop system of figure 2.1 (under assumptions (i) and (ii) of section 2) is asymptotically stable if and only if the controller C(s) is given by:

$$C(s) = (U_\ell + D_r W)(V_\ell - N_r W)^{-1} \qquad (3.6a) \text{ or}$$

$$C(s) = (V_r - WN_\ell)^{-1}(U_r + WD_\ell) \qquad (3.6b)$$

for some $W \in \mathcal{L}_\oplus$.

Using expressions (3.6) for the controller, every system transfer function can be parametrized in terms of W(s). For example, the closed loop system is stable if and only if the parameter Q(s) has the form:

$$Q(s) = (U_\ell - D_r W)D_\ell \qquad (3.7a) \text{or}$$

$$Q(s) = D_r(-WD_\ell + U_r) \qquad (3.7b)$$

for some $W \in \mathcal{S}_{\oplus}$.

4. DERIVATION OF THE OPTIMAL SYSTEM

In the following we derive the optimal Q(s) or equivalently in view of relations (3.7) the optimal W(s), which minimizes expression (2.10). The derivation is divided in four steps:

(a) Rearrange (2.10), collecting terms with respect to the parameter Q to get:

$$J = \frac{1}{2\pi} \operatorname{tr} \int_{-\infty}^{\infty} [\tilde{R}Q\tilde{\Phi}Q^* - 2Q^*(G^*R_x\Phi_d H^*) + R_x\Phi_d]d\omega \tag{4.1}$$

where: $\tilde{R}(s) \triangleq G^*(s)R_xG(s) + R_u$ (4.2)

and : $\tilde{\Phi}(s) \triangleq H(s)\Phi_d(s)H^*(s) + \Phi_n(s)$ (4.3)

(b) Perform the spectral factorizations $\tilde{R} = R^*R$ and $\tilde{\Phi} = \Phi\Phi^*$. The choice of R(s) and Φ(s) among all possible factors is discussed below while their existence is guaranteed by the assumptions (iv) and (v) of section 2.[14]

(c) Complete the squares in (4.1) to get

$$J = \frac{1}{2\pi} \operatorname{tr} \int_{-\infty}^{\infty} (RQ\Phi - \Sigma)^*(RQ\Phi - \Sigma)d\omega + J_o \tag{4.4}$$

where we define $\Sigma \triangleq (R^*)^{-1}G^*R_x\Phi_d H^*(\Phi^*)^{-1}$ (4.5)

and

$$J_o \triangleq \frac{1}{2\pi} \operatorname{tr} \int_{-\infty}^{\infty} (R_x\Phi_d - \Sigma^*\Sigma)d\omega \tag{4.6}$$

Thus in terms of the notation of section 3, the problem is transformed to:

$$\min_{Q \in \mathcal{V}} \| RQ\Phi - \Sigma \|_2 \tag{4.7}$$

where $\mathcal{V}$ is the set of Q's which make the closed loop system stable and which are described in lemma 3.1. Expressing Q in terms of W by relation (3.7a), we can equivalently solve:

$$\min_{W \in \mathcal{S}_{\oplus}} \| (RD_r)W(D_\ell\Phi) - \Sigma_1 \|_2 \tag{4.8}$$

where we define

$$\Sigma_1 \triangleq RU_\ell D_\ell\Phi - \Sigma \tag{4.9}$$

At this point we observe that problem (4.8) can be considerably simplified by selecting appropriately the spectral factors and the plant MFD's. Consider the factorizations

$$D_r^*\tilde{R}D_r = A^*A \tag{4.10a}$$

and

$$D_\ell\tilde{\Phi}D_\ell^* = BB^* \tag{4.10b}$$

where A and B are stable and minimum phase. Here we make the extra assumption that Φ(∞) is invertible, which is true if the measurement noise covariance matrix $\Phi_n(s)$ is nonsingular at s=∞. Note that R(∞) is invertible because of assumption (v) in section 2. Therefore the factors A and B are biproper and we can take as new MFD's for the plant

$$P(s) = \tilde{N}_r(s)\tilde{D}_r^{-1}(s) = \tilde{D}_\ell^{-1}(s)\tilde{N}_\ell(s) \tag{4.11}$$

where: $\tilde{N}_r \hat{=} N_rA^{-1}$, $\tilde{D}_r \hat{=} D_rA^{-1}$, $\tilde{N}_\ell \hat{=} B^{-1}N_\ell$, and

$$\tilde{D}_\ell \hat{=} B^{-1}D_\ell \tag{4.12}$$

Also by inspection of (3.5) and (4.12), the new Bézout coefficients can be found to be:

$$\tilde{U}_r = AU_r,\ \tilde{V}_r = AV_r,\ \tilde{U}_\ell = U_\ell B, \text{ and } \tilde{V}_\ell = V_\ell B \tag{4.13}$$

Next, from (4.10) we have $\tilde{R} = (AD_r^{-1})^*(AD_r^{-1})$ and $\tilde{\Phi} = (D_\ell^{-1}B)(D_\ell^{-1}B)^*$, which suggests that we can take as spectral factors

$$R_g = \tilde{D}_r^{-1} = AD_r^{-1} \tag{4.14}$$

and

$$\Phi_g = \tilde{D}_\ell^{-1} = D_\ell^{-1}B \tag{4.15}$$

Using (4.14), (4.15), our problem is simplified to:

$$\min_{W \in \mathcal{S}_{\oplus}} \| W - \tilde{\Sigma}_1 \|_2 \tag{4.16}$$

where $\tilde{\Sigma}_1$ is defined by:

$$\begin{aligned}\tilde{\Sigma}_1 &\triangleq R_g\tilde{U}_\ell\tilde{D}_\ell\Phi_g - (R_g^*)^{-1}G^*R_x\Phi_d H^*(\Phi_g^*)^{-1} \\ &= AD_r^{-1}U_\ell B - (A^*)^{-1}D_r^*G^*R_x\Phi_d H^*D_\ell^*(B^*)^{-1} \\ &= \tilde{D}_r^{-1}\tilde{U}_\ell - \tilde{D}_r^*G^*R_x\Phi_d H^*\tilde{D}_\ell^*\end{aligned} \tag{4.17}$$

(d) Projection step. Let us write

$$\tilde{\Sigma}_1 = \tilde{\Sigma}_o + \tilde{\Sigma}_+ + \tilde{\Sigma}_- \tag{4.18}$$

where $\tilde{\Sigma}_o$ is a constant matrix, $\tilde{\Sigma}_+ \in \mathcal{S}_+$ and $\tilde{\Sigma}_- \in \mathcal{S}_+^{\perp}$. Such decomposition is known to exist and be unique [14]. Also let us write in a similar fashion:

$$W = W_o + W_+ \tag{4.19}$$

In order that the minimum in (4.16) is finite, we require

$$W_o = \tilde{\Sigma}_o \tag{4.20}$$

Thus problem (4.16) is finally transformed to:

$$\min_{W_+ \in \mathcal{S}_+} \| W_+ - (\tilde{\Sigma}_+ + \tilde{\Sigma}_-) \|_2 = \min_{W_+ \in \mathcal{S}_+} \| W_+ - \tilde{\Sigma}_+ \|_2 + \| \tilde{\Sigma}_- \|_2,$$

which yields

$$W_{+,opt} = \tilde{\Sigma}_+ \tag{4.21}$$

Thus the optimal value of the parameter W is given from expressions (4.19)-(4.21) as

$$W_{opt} = \tilde{\Sigma}_o + \tilde{\Sigma}_+ \equiv \tilde{\Sigma}_{\oplus}$$

or making use of (4.17):

$$W_{opt} = [\tilde{D}_r^{-1}\tilde{U}_\ell - \tilde{D}_r{*}G{*}R_x\Phi_d H{*}\tilde{D}_\ell^*]_\oplus \tag{4.22}$$

The above solution is unique [15]. Our results are summarized in the form of a theorem:

Theorem 4.1

Under the assumptions of section (2), the unique controller C(s) which minimizes the performance index $J = E\{x^T R_x x + u^T R_u u\}$

while stabilizing the closed-loop system of figure 2.1 is given by:

$$C(s) = (\tilde{U}_\ell + \tilde{D}_r W_{opt})(\tilde{V}_\ell - \tilde{N}_r W_{opt})^{-1}$$

for the value of the parameter W given by expression (4.22). The optimal controller is proper. The plant MFD's and Bezout coefficients are defined in relations (3.4),(3.5),(4.10)-(4.13).

Proof: The proof is clear in view of lemma 3.2 of section 3 and the previous derivation.

5. UNIFICATION OF WIENER-HOPF LITERATURE

In this section all major approaches in the Wiener-Hopf literature are shown to be equivalent with solving an optimization problem of the form (4.7)(or(4.8)) for different choices of the spectral factors R and Φ, and of the rational matrix Σ. However before doing this, we single out another concept which can serve as a unification pole. In section 4, we observe that selecting the spectral factors R and Φ in a certain special way is rather natural in our derivation framework. These factors have the properties that are minimum phase and contain all plant unstable poles. Note that Shaked's GSF's ([7],[8]) have these properties and we will use his terminology for refering to all such spectral factors. We see subsequently that these factors appear explicitly or not in all other approaches that successfully treat the unstable plant case.

Almost all approaches employ a variational argument on relation (2.10) to conclude in an optimality condition of the form:

$T(s) \hat{=} \tilde{R}(s)Q_o(s)\tilde{\Phi}(s) - \tilde{\Sigma}(s)$ has no left half plane poles. (5.1)

Note that this condition is only necessary, thus optimality must be established after the solution is at hand.

Condition (5.1) in view of the inner product structure of the space of strictly proper rational matrices (see section 3) can be interpreted as an orthogonality condition. By the following lemma we can identify the optimization problem whose solution is given by (5.1) to be of the form (4.7) (or (4.8)).

Lemma 5.1

Let $\mathcal{T}$ be a subspace in a Hilbert space H, and A be a linear bounded operator which is invertible. Then if $\omega \in H$ is orthogonal to $\mathcal{T}$ (i.e. $\omega \in \mathcal{T}^\perp$), $A\omega$ is orthogonal to $(A^*)^{-1}\mathcal{T}$, where A^* is the adjoint operator of A. (for definitions see [15]).

Proof: Let $\omega \in H$ be orthogonal to $\mathcal{T}$. Then $\omega \in \mathcal{T}^\perp \Leftrightarrow \ <\omega, s> = 0 \ \forall s \in \mathcal{T} \Leftrightarrow <A^{-1}A\omega, s> = 0 \ \forall s \in \mathcal{T} \Leftrightarrow <A\omega, (A^{-1})^* s> = 0 \ \forall s \in \mathcal{T} \Leftrightarrow A\omega \in [(A^*)^{-1}\mathcal{T}]^\perp$ □

Assuming that T(s) in (5.1) is strictly proper (which is necessary for the finiteness of the PI), condition (5.1) can be written as

$$T \in \mathcal{S}_+^\perp \tag{5.2}$$

Let R and Φ be some spectral factors of R and Φ, i.e. they satisfy $\tilde{R} = R^*R$ and $\tilde{\Phi} = \Phi\Phi^*$. Then by lemma 5.1, (5.2) yields

$$(R^*)^{-1}T(\Phi^*)^{-1} \in [R\mathcal{S}_+\Phi]^\perp \tag{5.3}$$

or equivalently, $(RQ_o\Phi - \Sigma) \in [R\mathcal{S}_+\Phi]^\perp$, where $\Sigma \hat{=} (R^*)^{-1}\tilde{\Sigma}(\Phi)^{-1}$. Thus if some $Q_o(s)$ satisfies condition (5.1), it can be found uniquely from

$$\min_{Q \in \mathcal{S}_\oplus} \|RQ\Phi - \Sigma\|_2 \tag{5.4}$$

In the approaches of [1],[2],[3], the factors R and Φ are taken to be stable and minimum phase. Hence the solution comes to be :

$Q_o = R^{-1}[\Sigma]_\oplus \Phi^{-1}$ using the same reasoning as in the derivation of section 4. This solution does not always satisfy the stability requirements of lemma 3.1, unless the plant is open-loop stable.

(i.e $W = [D_r^{-1}Q + U_r]D_\ell^{-1}$ is not always in $\mathcal{S}_\oplus$, when D_r^{-1} and D_ℓ^{-1} contain unstable poles).

In Shaked's approach [7], the factors R and Φ are taken to be the so-called generalized spectral factors. (i.e. minimum-phase and with poles exactly the plant poles). Then Shaked proceeds by requiring:

$$[R_g Q_o \Phi_g]_+ = [\Sigma_g]_\oplus \tag{5.5}$$

while $Q_o \in \mathcal{S}_\oplus$.

Note that this argument does not produce the solution of (5.4) (The mistake is that (4.16) and (4.17) in [7] are not equivalent). However Shaked proves in his setting that the LQG solution is among the solutions of (5.5).

Youla et al [5] effectively express Q(s) in terms of W(s) using (3.7). Note that in their derivation polynomial MFD's for the plant are used (i.e. D_r, D_ℓ, U_ℓ are polynomial matrices). They factorize $\tilde{R}' \equiv D_r^* \tilde{R} D_r$ and $\tilde{\Phi}' \equiv D_\ell \tilde{\Phi} D_\ell^*$ for the minimum phase and stable spectral factors R' and Φ' respectively. Comparing with (4.10) and (4.14), (4.15), it is clear that they compute essentially GSF's for $\tilde{R}$ and $\tilde{\Phi}$.

Also in this case $\Sigma' \equiv R'U_\ell D_\ell \Phi - (R'^*)^{-1} G^* R_x \Phi_d H^* (\Phi'^*)^{-1}$. Thus their approach is equivalent with solving:

$$\min_{W \in \mathcal{J}_\oplus} \|R'W\Phi' - \Sigma'\|_2 \qquad (5.6)$$

But because they use polynomial MFD's, the solution of (5.6) becomes intricate, since $R'W\Phi'$ is not proper (and thus (5.6) is not finite) for all proper W. However the final result in [5] is identical with expression (4.22).

Finally Francis [10] follows the procedure described in section 4, but solves (4.8) using the inner-outer factorizations $RD_r = U_r M_r$ and $D_\ell \Phi = M_\ell U_\ell$, where R and Φ are the minimum phase, stable spectral factors of $\tilde{R}$ and $\tilde{\Phi}$, U_r, U_ℓ are inner (i.e. $U_r^* U_r = U_\ell U_\ell^* = I$), and M_r, M_ℓ are outer (i.e. stable and minimum phase). Note that in this procedure too we can identify the GSF's as $R_g \equiv U_r^{-1} R = M_r D_r^{-1}$ and $\Phi_g \equiv \Phi U_\ell^{-1} = D_\ell^{-1} M_\ell$.

6. CONNECTIONS WITH LQG RESULTS

In figure 2.1 we make the following identifications:

$$G(s) = (sI-A)^{-1}B, \; H(s) = C,$$
$$\Phi_d(s) = (sI-A)^{-1} BMB^T(-sI-A^T)^{-1}, \Phi_n(s) = N \qquad (6.1)$$

with M, N the state and measurement white noise covariance matrices, and where we assume that (A,B) is stabilizable and (A,C) is detectable. This brings us to the familiar LQG case.

It is a well known fact [17], that the controller which minimizes the performance index (2.1) and stabilizes the closed loop system is given by the expression:

$$C(s) = F(sI-A+KC+BF)^{-1}K \qquad (6.2),$$

where F,K are the full-state feedback and the Kalman-Bucy filter gains respectively. The gains F and K are computed from:

$$F = R_u^{-1} B^T \bar{F} \qquad (6.3)$$

and

$$K = \bar{K} C^T N^{-1} \qquad (6.4),$$

where $\bar{F}$ and $\bar{K}$ solve the control and the filter Riccati equations, respectively:

$$\bar{F}A + A^T\bar{F} - \bar{F}BR_u^{-1}B^T\bar{F} + R_x = 0 \qquad (6.5)$$

$$\text{and } A\bar{K} + \bar{K}A^T - \bar{K}C^TN^{-1}C\bar{K} + M = 0 \qquad (6.6).$$

Equations (6.5), (6.6) have the following well-known frequency domain formulations [17].

$$B^T(-sI-A^T)^{-1}R_x(sI-A)^{-1}B + R_u = F^*(s)R_uF(s) \qquad (6.7)$$

and

$$C(sI-A)^{-1}M(-sI-A^T)^{-1}C^T + N = K(s)NK^*(s) \qquad (6.8)$$

where

$$F(s) \triangleq I + F(sI-A)^{-1}B \qquad (6.9)$$

$$K(s) \triangleq I + C(sI-A)^{-1}K \qquad (6.10)$$

the optimal full-state feedback and optimal Kalman-Bucy filter return difference matrices respectively.

Note that the right-hand side members of (6.7) and (6.8) are $\tilde{R}(s)$ and $\tilde{\Phi}(s)$ respectively, as defined by (4.2) and (4.3) for the particular case of (6.1). Thus from (6.7) and (6.8) $R_g \triangleq R_u^{\frac{1}{2}} F(s)$ and $\Phi_g \triangleq K(s)N^{\frac{1}{2}}$ are spectral factors of $\tilde{R}$ and $\tilde{\Phi}$ and indeed GSF's in view of the properties of stabilizing return difference matrices.

Expressions (4.14) and (4.15) suggest that GSF's can be exploited in computing MFD's for a given plant. (e.g. take $D_r = R_g^{-1}$, $N_r = GR_g$ etc). In particular we prove the following proposition, which was discovered also, independently by Nett et al [18].

<u>Proposition 6.1</u>

Let $P(s) = C(sI-A)^{-1}B$, where the pair (A,B) is stabilizable and the pair (A,C) is detectable. Then P(s) has the following right coprime MFD:

$$N_r(s) = C(sI-A)^{-1}B[I+F(sI-A)^{-1}B]^{-1}R_u^{-\frac{1}{2}} \qquad (6.11)$$

$$D_r(s) = [I+F(sI-A)^{-1}B]^{-1}R_u^{-\frac{1}{2}} \qquad (6.12)$$

and the following left coprime MFD:

$$N_\ell(s) = N^{-\frac{1}{2}}[I+C(sI-A)^{-1}K]^{-1}C(sI-A)^{-1}B \qquad (6.13)$$

$$D_\ell(s) = N^{-\frac{1}{2}}[I+C(sI-A)^{-1}K]^{-1} \qquad (6.14)$$

where F is a stabilizing feedback gain for $(sI-A)^{-1}B$, K is an observer gain for $C(sI-A)^{-1}$, and $R_u^{\frac{1}{2}}$, $N^{\frac{1}{2}}$ are any symmetric, positive definite matrices.

<u>Proof</u>

By the definition of F and K, all quantities defined by (6.7)-(6.10), are stable and it obviously holds:

$P(s) = N_r D_r^{-1} = D_\ell^{-1} N_\ell$ The right coprimeness of (6.11) and (6.12) and the left coprimeness of (6.13) and (6.14) is established by verifying that:

$$U_r N_r + V_r D_r = I \qquad (6.15),$$

$$\text{and} \quad N_\ell U_\ell + D_\ell V_\ell = I \qquad (6.16)$$

respectively, where we define:

$$U_r = R_u^{\frac{1}{2}} F(sI-A+FC)^{-1}K \qquad (6.17),$$

$$V_r = R_u^{\frac{1}{2}}[I+F(sI-A+KC)^{-1}B] \qquad (6.18)$$

$$U_\ell = F(sI-A+BF)^{-1}KN^{\frac{1}{2}} \qquad (6.19)$$

$$V_\ell = [I+C(sI-A+BF)^{-1}K]N^{\frac{1}{2}} \quad (6.20)$$

Note that $U_r, V_r U_\ell, V_\ell$ are stable, by the definition of the gains F and K, and moreover constitute particular solutions of the Bezout identities (6.15) and (6.16) □

Thus, as it remarked in [18], proposition 6.1 offers a procedure for computing MFD's based on state-space methods.

Next as a corollary of theorem 4.1 we prove the generally known fact.

Corollary 6.1

For the LQG case specified by (6.1), the Wiener-Hopf optimal controller determined by theorem 4.1 is given by (6.2)-(6.6).

Proof

First we compute the optimal value of the parameter W(s), given by formula (4.22), using definitions (6.1) and the MFD's of proposition 6.1. More specifically:

$$W_{opt} = [D_r^{-1}U_\ell]_\oplus - [D_r{*}G{*}R_x\Phi_d H{*}D_\ell^{*}]_\oplus ,$$

and $:[D_r^{-1}U_\ell]_\oplus = [R_u^{\frac{1}{2}}(I+F(sI-A)^{-1}B)F(sI-A+BF)^{-1}KN^{\frac{1}{2}}]_+ =$

$$= [R_u^{\frac{1}{2}}F(sI-A)^{-1}KN^{\frac{1}{2}}]_+ .$$

Also:

$$[D_r{*}G{*}R_x\Phi_d H{*}D_\ell{*}]_\oplus = [(R_g^{*})^{-1}B^T(-sI-A^T)^{-1}R_x(sI-A)^{-1} BM(-sI-A^T)^{-1}C^T(\Phi_g^{*})^{-1}]_+$$

$$= [R_u^{\frac{1}{2}}F(sI-A)^{-1}KN^{\frac{1}{2}}]_+ ,$$

as it can be shown by using equations (6.5) and (6.6) and straightforward algebra. (see also the proof of theorem 1 in [7]). Therefore $W_{opt}(s) \equiv 0$, and by theorem 4.1 the Wiener-Hopf optimal controller is given by:

$$C(s) = U_\ell V_\ell^{-1} = [F(sI-A+BF)^{-1}KN^{\frac{1}{2}}] [(I+C(sI-A+BF)^{-1}K)N^{\frac{1}{2}}]^{-1} =$$

$$= F(sI-A+KC+BF)^{-1}K \quad □$$

7 . REFERENCES

[1] Newton, G.C., Gould, L.A. and Kaiser,J.F. (1957), Analytical Design of Linear Feedback Controls. Wiley, New York.

[2] Bongiorno,J.J.(1969),IEEE trans. AC-14, pp.665-673.

[3] Weston, J.E. & Bongiorno, J.J.(1972),IEEE trans. AC-17, pp. 613-620.

[4] Youla, D.C., Bongiorno, J.J.and Jabr, H.A. (1976), IEEE trans. AC-21,pp.3-13.

[5] Youla,D.C., Jabr,H.A. and Bonjiorno,J.J. (1976),IEEE trans AC-21 pp.319-338.

[6] Shaked, U.(1976), Int. J. Control,24, pp.741-770.

[7] Shaked, U. (1976),Int. J. Control,24,pp. 771-800.

[8] Kucera, V.(1979),Discrete linear control, The polynomial Equation Approach. Wiley, New York.

[9] Grimble, M.J.(1978),Proc IEE,Vol 125,No.11, pp.1275-1284.

[10] Francis, B.A (1982),Sys. & Control letters, 2, pp.197-201.

[11] Desoer,C.A.,Liu,R.W., Murray,J, & Saeks,R. (1980),IEEE trans.AC-25,pp.339-412.

[12] Vidyasagar, M., Schneider, H. & Francis, B.A (1982), IEEE trans.AC-27,pp.800-893.

[13] Safonov, M.G.(1981),Fractional representation approach to robust feedback synthesis, Internal Report, Honeywell Systems & Research Centre, Minneapolis, MN, U.S.A.

[14] Youla, D.C(1961), IRE trans. IT-7,pp.172-189.

[15] Luenberger, D.G.(1969),Optimization by vector space methods., Wiley, New York.

[16] Zames, G., and Francis, B.A.(1983),IEEE trans AC-28, pp. 589-600.

[17] Kwakernaak, H. and Sivan, R.(1972),Linear optimal control systems, Wiley, New York.

[18] Nett, K.N., Jacobson, C.A., & Balas, M.J. (1983) A connection between state-space & doubly coprime fractional representations. submitted IEEE, trans.AC.

Research supported in part by AFOSR Grant 80-0013, in part by NSF Grant INT-8302754, and in part by Honeywell Systems and Research Center, Minneapolis, MN. This work was completed while Dr. Safonov was an SERC Senior Visiting Fellow & Mr. Sideris was a visiting research student at University Engineering Dept., Control & Management Systems Division, Mill Lane, Cambridge CB2 1RX, United Kingdom.

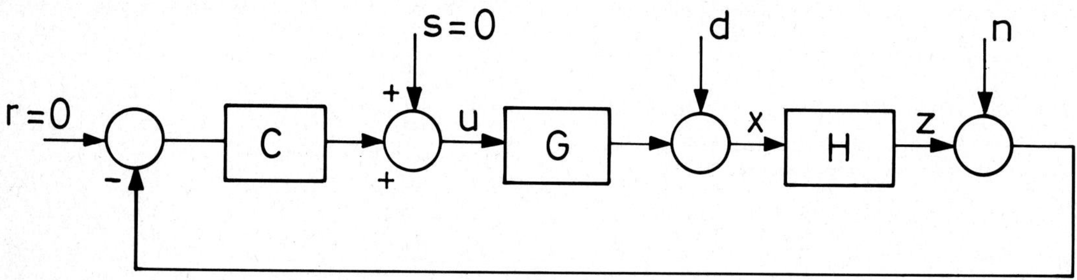

Figure 2.1

DIGITAL TECHNIQUES in Simulation, Communication and Control
Spyros G. Tzafestas (editor)
Elsevier Science Publishers B.V. (North-Holland) © IMACS, 1985

SISO DIGITAL CONTROL SYSTEM ROBUSTNESS VIA OUTPUT FEEDBACK: A DESIGN PROCEDURE

C. H. Houpis

Department of Electrical Engineering
Air Force Institute of Technology
Wright-Patterson Air Force Base, Ohio 45433, USA

The output of a state-feedback SISO control system, under high-forward-gain (h.f.g.) operation, can be designed to be insensitive to parameter variation. The resulting analog feedback unit may not be physically realizable. When this situation arises it may be possible to achieve the desired degree of insensitivity or robustness, with an acceptable loop transmission frequency, of the output to parameter variation by transforming the designed state-feedback continuous-time system to a physically realizable nonunity feedback digital control system. A straight-forward and simple design method is presented, using known concepts, to facilitate the design of a robust digital SISO control system. Unmodeled plant dynamics and the associated stability considerations of the system are not considered.

1. INTRODUCTION

The output Y(s) of the SISO control system of Fig. 1-a is affected by the variation of the plant parameters. To make the output as insensitive as possible to plant parameter variations, one approach is to design [1] a h.f.g. state-feedback system, as shown in Fig. 1-b. This design is based upon satisfying the system performance specifications using the nominal values of the plant parameters. By means of block diagram manipulations, as shown in Fig. 1-c, Fig. 1-b is transformed to its equivalent output feedback representation of Fig. 1-d. The feedback compensator, $H_{eq}(s)$ of Fig. 1-d, is referred to as the state feedback <u>H-equivalent</u> of Fig. 1-b. This compensator may not be physically realizable when it is used in a continuous-time control system. When this situation arises it may be possible, as shown in this paper, to achieve the desired degree of insensitivity (robustness) of the output to parameter variation by transforming the designed state-feedback continuous-time system to an equivalent physically realizable nonunity feedback digital control system. Unmodeled plant dynamics and the associated stability considerations of the system are not considered in this paper. The main emphasis of this paper is to convey a technique, when applicable, for converting an unrealizable s-domain compensator into a realizable one in the z-domain. Also, to illustrate that the Tustin transformation is a "good design tool" for "low" frequency (with respect to f_s) plants.

2. STATE-FEEDBACK CONTINUOUS-TIME CONTROL SYSTEM DESIGN [1]

The configuration of Fig. 1-d is now shown to have the property of minimizing the sensitivity of the output response with respect to a parameter variation between x_n and y. Physical state-variables are indicated in Fig. 1 which require that the transfer functions $G_1(s)$, $G_2(s), \ldots, G_{n-1}(s)$ have the form

$$\frac{A_i}{s}, \quad \frac{A_i}{s+a}, \quad \text{or} \quad \frac{A_i(s+b)}{s+a}$$

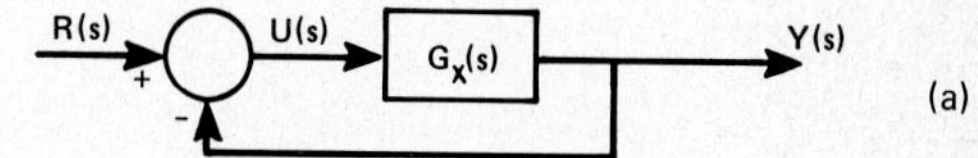

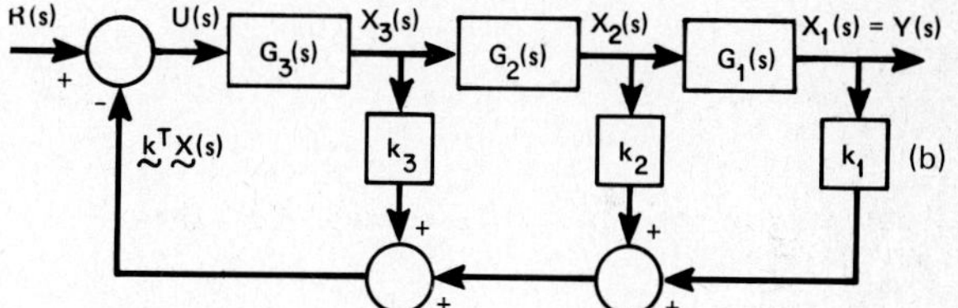

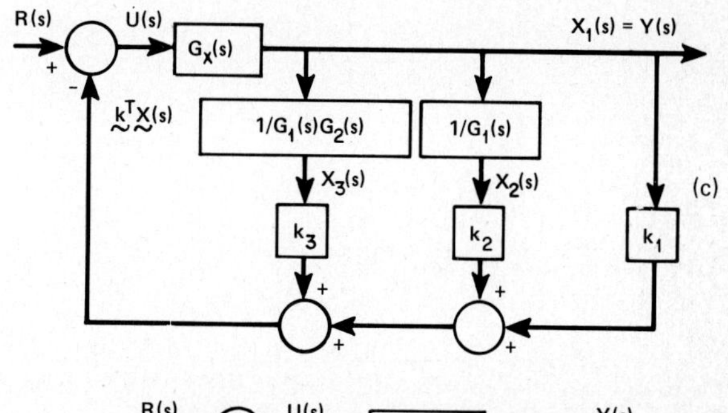

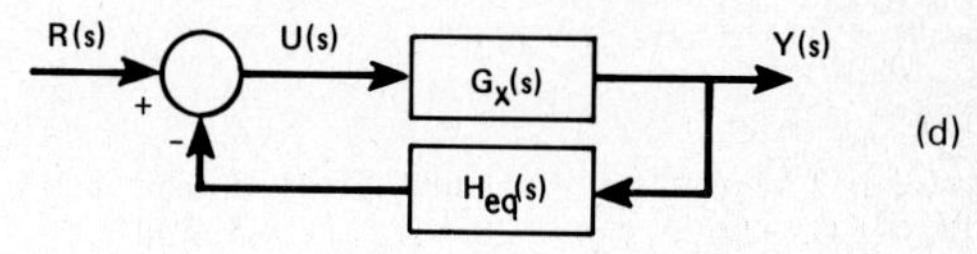

Figure 1. Control Systems:
(a) Unity Feedback; (b) State Feedback;
(c) Output Feedback; (d) H-equivalent

and $G_n(s)$, whose input is U(s), must have the form

$$\frac{A_i}{s} \quad \text{or} \quad \frac{A_i}{s + a}$$

In order to illustrate the design method, in the system of Fig. 1 let

$$G_x(s) = G_1(s)G_2(s)G_3(s) = \frac{10A}{s(s - p_2)(p - p_3)} \tag{1}$$

where

$$G_1(s) = \frac{1}{s}, \; G_2(s) = \frac{5}{s - p_2}, \; G_3(s) = \frac{2A}{s - p_3} \tag{2}$$

and

$$H_{eq}(s) = \frac{\underset{\sim}{k}'\underset{\sim}{X}(s)}{Y(s)} = \frac{\underset{\sim}{k}'\underset{\sim}{X}(s)}{Y(s)} = \frac{\underset{\sim}{k}'\underset{\sim}{X}(s)}{\underset{\sim}{c}'\underset{\sim}{X}(s)} \tag{3}$$

where

$$\underset{\sim}{k}' = [k_1 \; k_2 \; k_3] \tag{4}$$

$$Y(s) = \underset{\sim}{c}'\underset{\sim}{X}(s) = [1 \; 0 \; 0]\underset{\sim}{X}(s) \tag{5}$$

$$\underset{\sim}{c}' = [1 \; 0 \; 0] \tag{6}$$

$$\frac{X_3(s)}{X_1(s)} = \frac{1}{G_1(s)G_2(s)} \tag{7}$$

$$\frac{X_2(s)}{X_1(s)} = \frac{1}{G_1(s)} \tag{8}$$

Substituting from Eqs. (4) through (8) into Eq. (3) yields

$$H_{eq}(s) = [k_3/G_1(s)G_2(s)] + [k_2/G_1(s)] + k_1$$

$$= \frac{k_3 s^2 + 5(k_2 + k_3 p_2)s + 5k_1}{5} \tag{9}$$

and

$$\left[\frac{Y(s)}{R(s)}\right]_A = \frac{G_x(s)}{1 + G_x(s)H_{eq}(s)}$$

$$= \frac{10A}{s^3 + (2Ak_3 - p_2 - p_3)s^2 + [p_2p_3 + 2A(5k_2 - k_3p_2]s + 10Ak_1} \tag{10}$$

Assume the nominal values for this control system to have the values $p_2 = -5$ and $p_3 = -1$ and that the desired control ratio, based upon a set of desired conventional control figures of merit, is

$$[M(s)]_D = \frac{Y(s)}{R(s)} = \frac{100}{s^3 + 101\,s^2 + 142.7s + 100}$$

$$= \frac{100}{(s + 0.70659 \pm j0.70771)(s + 99.987)} \tag{11}$$

Achieving a satisfactory degree of output insensitivity or robustness to parameter variation requires that $[M(s)]_D$ must contain at least one nondominant real pole σ_{ND}, as illustrated by Eq. (11). A pole is nondominant if $|\sigma_{ND}| \geq 6|\sigma_D|$ where σ_D is the real part of the dominant poles $p_{1,2}$ of $[M(s)]_D$. Making this pole more nondominant increases the value of 10A in (10), where $k_1 = 1$ is required to maintain zero steady-state error for a step input which in turn increases the value of gain A. Thus, the requirement of h.f.g. operation is satisfied and the system becomes more insensitive to gain variation. The dominant poles of $[M(s)]_D$ are determined from the system specifications [1]. Equating the corresponding coefficients in Eqs. (10) and (11) yields the nominal values $A = 10$, $k_1 = 1$, $k_2 = -3.393$, and $k_3 = 4.77$. These values are used to plot the root-locus of

$$G(s)H_{eq}(s) = \frac{95.4(s + 0.721698 \pm j0.726202)}{s(s + 1)(s + 5)} = -1 \tag{12}$$

in Fig. 2. Note that the zeros of Eq. (12) are the zeros of $H_{eq}(s)$ which are determined by the nominal values of the plant and $[M(s)]_D$. As illustrated by the root-locus, the state-variable feedback system is stable for all $A > 0$. Since the roots are very close to the zeros of $G(s)H_{eq}(s)$, any increase in gain from the value $A = 10$ produces negligible changes in the location of the dominant closed-loop roots. In other words, for h.f.g. operation, $A > 10$, the system's response is essentially unaffected by variations in A, provided that the feedback

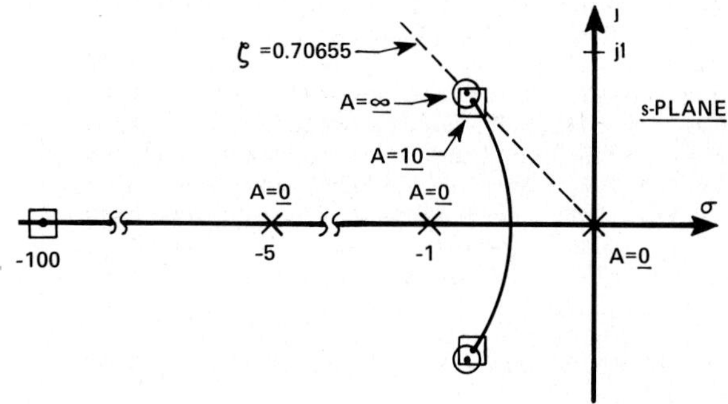

Figure 2. Root-locus diagram for state-variable feedback control system; Eq (12).

coefficients remain fixed. The same effect is noted, with h.f.g. operation, when the parameters p_2 or p_3 vary, provided that $H_{eq}(s)$ is invariant, and the control system configuration of Fig. 1-d is used to implement the system design. Thus, to achieve a high degree of insensitivity to a plant parameter variation, the $H_{eq}(s)$ unit of Fig. 1-d is built using the design obtained based on the nominal plant parameters, $[M(s)]_D$, and Fig. 1-b. Thus, the system is less sensitive to parameter variation when $H_{eq}(s)$ is used that when actual state feedback $\underset{\sim}{k}'\underset{\sim}{x}(s)$ is utilized. Therefore for this example

$$H_{eq}(s) = (4.77s^2 + 6.885s + 5)/5 \tag{13}$$

To illustrate the insensitivity of the control system to plant parameter variations, the values of k_1, k_2, and k_3 determined on the basis of the nominal parameter values are inserted into Eq. (10) to yield

$$\left[\frac{Y(s)}{R(s)}\right]_A = \frac{10A}{s^3 + (9.54A - p_2 - p_3)s^2 + [p_2p_3 + 2A(6.885)]s + 10A} \tag{14}$$

Table 1 presents the figures of merit for the control system represented by Fig. 1-d and Eq. (14) for the cases: (1) nominal values; (2) $A = 20$, $p_2 = -5$, and $p_3 = -1$; (3) $A = 10$, $p_2 = -10$, and $p_3 = -1$; and (4) $A = 10$, $p_2 = -5$, and $p_3 = -2$. Note that the response for the state feedback H-equivalent system is essentially unaffected by plant parameter variation. The 0-dB crossing frequency of Lm $\underset{\sim}{G}_x(j\omega)\underset{\sim}{H}_{eq}(j\omega)$ is 95.2 rad/s. When the components of the feedback unit are selected so that the transfer function $H_{eq}(s)$ is invariant, the implementation of the control system of Fig. 1-c uses the minor-loop compensator $H_c(s) = [(k_3/5)s^2 + (k_3 + k_2)s]$. This compensator requires both first- and second-order derivative action in the minor loop. In many applications, this type of continuous-time active compensator is not feasible because of noise and implementation problems. It may be possible to add poles to $H_{eq}(s)$ that are "far out" in the left-half s-plane in order to implement $H_{eq}(s)$ with R and C components along with Op amps [4]. When this is not feasible then the next section indicates how this active compensator requirement may be satisfied by transforming the continuous controller into a digital controller. Another approach to achieving the desired robustness is by the use of an observer [5,6]. Other definitions of robustness, such as minimizing the effect of unmodeled dynamics, result in different design techniques.

3. STATE FEEDBACK H-EQUIVALENT DIGITAL CONTROL SYSTEM

When the dominant poles and zeros of $[M(s)]_D$ and $G_x(s)$ lie in the shaded area of Fig. 3 [2], then the continuous-time control system of Fig. 1-d may be converted into a digital control system as shown in Fig. 4. For a unit-step input,

Table 1 Time Response Data: Continuous-Time Control System

Case	$M_p(t)$	t_p,sec	t_s,sec	Parameter change
1 (nominal)	1.043^-	4.46^-	5.968	-------
2	1.043^+	4.39^+	5.899	$A = 20$
3	1.04^-	4.62	6.09	$P_2 = -10$
4	1.035^-	4.63^-	5.92	$P_3 = -2$

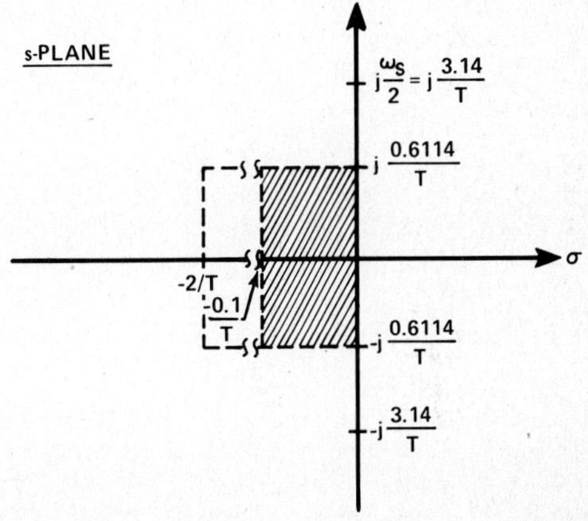

Figure 3. Allowable location (shaded area) of dominant poles and zeros in s-plane for a good Tustin approximation.

$$Y(z) = \frac{G_xR(z)}{1 + H_{z0}G_x(z)H_{eq}(z)} \tag{15}$$

where

$$G_xR(z) = \mathcal{Z}\left[\frac{10A}{s^2(s - p_2)(s - p_3)}\right] = \frac{K_xz(z + a)(z + b)}{(z - 1)^2(z - c)(z - d)} \tag{16}$$

$$H_{z0}G_x(z) = (1-z^{-1})\,\mathcal{Z}\left[\frac{10A}{s^2(s - p_2)(s - p_3)}\right] = \frac{K_x(z + a)(z + b)}{(z - 1)(z - c)(z - d)} \tag{17}$$

$$H_{eq}(z) = \left[H_{eq}(z)\right]_{TU} = \text{Tustin transformation of } H_{eq}(s) \tag{18}$$

For the control system of Sec. 2, a value of T = 10 msec is chosen to ensure that the dominant poles lie in the shaded region of Fig. 3. Thus, Eq. 18

$$\left[H_{eq}(z)\right]_{TU} = \frac{K_{TU}(z - p \pm jq)}{(z + 1)^2} \tag{19}$$

The root-locus plot of $H_{z0}G_x(z)\left[H_{eq}(z)\right]_{TU} = -1$ reveals that the digital control system is

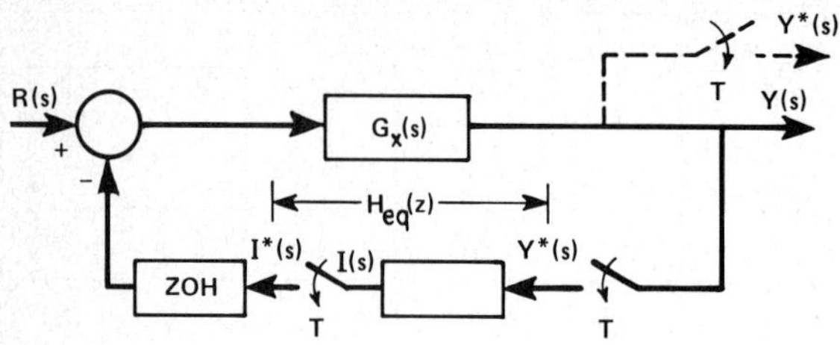

Figure 4. Conversion of the continuous-time control system of Figure 1(d) into a Digital Control System.

completely unstable due to the two poles at -1 contributed by $\left[H_{eq}(z)\right]_{TU}$, i.e., two branches are outside the unit circle. Based upon the Tustin transformation characteristic [2] that the dc gain level is maintained, that is,

$$\left[F(s)\right]_{s=0} = \left[F(z)_{TU}\right]_{z=1}$$

then a good first "engineering" modification to Eq. (19), in order to ensure a conditionally stable system, the factor $(z + 1)^2$ is replaced by $\alpha(z + \delta)^2$ [2,3], where α is the dc gain factor, i.e.,

$$\left[(z + 1)^2\right]_{z=1} = \left[\alpha(z + \delta)^2\right]_{z=1} \tag{20}$$

$\varepsilon > \delta > -1$, and $\varepsilon > 0$ (a very small positive number to ensure that the poles, δ, are non-dominant). Note that the converted control system is a 5th-order system.

Cases (1) and (4) of Sec. 2 are used to illustrate how the conversion of the continuous-time control system into a digital control system, by use of $\left[H_{eq}(s)\right]_{TU}$ maintains the desired parameter insensitivity with a physically realizable digital feedback compensator. The arbitrary choice of $\delta = 0.5$ is made in order that the $H_{eq}(z)$ poles are nondominant and yield a conditionally stable system. For this value of δ results in $\alpha = 16/9$, so that

$$H_{eq}(z) = \frac{K_{zc}(z - p \pm jq)}{(z + 0.5)^2} \tag{21}$$

and $K_{zc} = 9K_{TU}/16$. Thus, for T = 0.01 sec the parameters of Eqs. (17) and (19) are given in Table 2.

Table 3 presents the figures of merit of the continuous-time and digital control systems for Cases (1) and (4) with the configurations of Figs. 1-d and 4, respectively. The results in

Table 2. The parameters of Eqs. (17) and (21)

	Case (1)	Case (4)
a	3.676668598	3.667485636
b	0.2639470221	0.2632881595
c	0.9900498337	0.9801986733
d	0.9512294245	0.9512294245
p	0.9927828829	
q	0.007209801628	
K_x	$1.641922848733 \times 10^{-5}$	1.637822×10^{-5}
K_T	21,620.475	
K_xK_T	$3.549915189 \times 10^{-1}$	$3.541049393 \times 10^{-1}$

Table 3 indicate that the "converted continuous-time control system" of Fig. 4 maintains the desired degree of parameter insensitivity, i.e., the desired performance specifications with a realizable digital feedback controller $H_{eq}(z)$. A root locus of

$$H_{z0}G_x(z)H_{eq}(z) = -1 \tag{22}$$

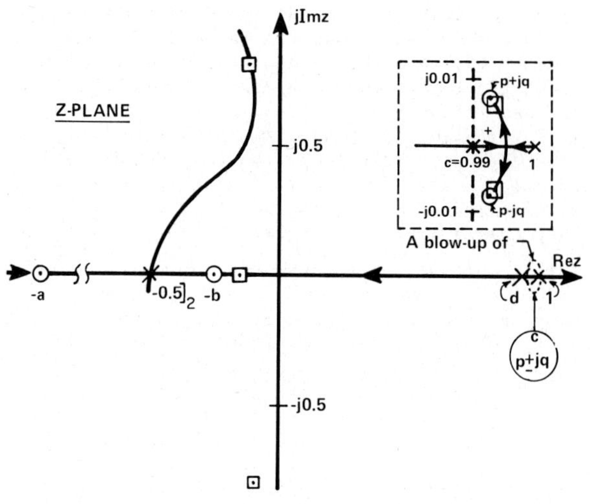

Figure 5. The root-locus plot of Eq (22).

is shown in Fig. 5 for Case (1). It is seen from this figure that this root-locus has equivalent characteristics as the root-locus of Fig. 2 for the continuous-time system, i.e., the dominant roots are very close to the "fixed zeros" of $H_{eq}(z)$ and $H_{eq}(s)$, respectively. It is this characteristic that achieves the degree of parameter insensitivity that is desired for the system design. The additional two poles, of the digital control system, due to

Table 3. Time Response Data

	M_p	t_p,sec	t_s,sec
Case (1)			
Fig. 1	1.043^-	4.46	5.968
Fig. 4	1.043	4.45^+	5.94
Case (4)			
Fig. 1	1.035^-	4.63^-	5.92
Fig. 4	1.035	4.63	5.88

$\left[H_{eq}(z)\right]_{TU}$, are nondominant and thus do not appreciably affect the time response characteristics.

A continuous-time controller, H(s), equivalent to Eq. (13) can yield results similar to those in Table 3. The feasibility of using H(s) in a continuous-time control system lies in its implementation.

4. DESIGN PROCEDURE

The implementation of the state feedback H-equivalent, Fig. 1-d, does not require that the design of $H_{eq}(s)$ be obtained from the physical-variable representation. The design, whether it is modeled by a physical, phase, or canonical state-variable representations results in the same $H_{eq}(s)$. This can be shown as follows: since Eq. (2) is expressed in terms of physical-variables, then in order to express it in terms of phase-variables, consider the transformation

$$\underset{\sim}{X}(s) = \underset{\sim}{T}\underset{\sim}{X}_c(s) \tag{23}$$

where $\underset{\sim}{T}$ is the transformation matrix that transforms the physical-variables, $\underset{\sim}{X}(s)$, into phase-variables, $\underset{\sim}{X}_c(s)$[1]. Thus, substituting from Eq. (23) into Eq. (3) yields

$$\underset{\sim}{H}_{eq}(s) = \frac{\underset{\sim}{k}'\underset{\sim}{X}(s)}{\underset{\sim}{c}'\underset{\sim}{X}(s)} = \frac{\underset{\sim}{k}'\underset{\sim}{T}\underset{\sim}{X}_c(s)}{\underset{\sim}{c}'\underset{\sim}{T}\underset{\sim}{X}_c(s)} = \frac{\underset{\sim}{k}_c'\underset{\sim}{X}_c(s)}{\underset{\sim}{c}_c'\underset{\sim}{X}_c(s)} \tag{24}$$

where $\underset{\sim}{k}_c' = \underset{\sim}{k}'\underset{\sim}{T}$ and $\underset{\sim}{c}_c' = \underset{\sim}{c}'\underset{\sim}{T}$. Using the nominal values for the system of Fig. 1 yields

$$\underset{\sim}{T} = \begin{bmatrix} 1 & 0 & 0 \\ 0 & 1 & 0 \\ 0 & 1 & 0.2 \end{bmatrix} \tag{25}$$

$$\underset{\sim}{k}' = \underset{\sim}{k}'\underset{\sim}{T} = [1 \quad 1.377 \quad 0.954] \tag{26}$$

$$\underset{\sim}{c} = \underset{\sim}{c}'\underset{\sim}{T} = [1 \quad 0 \quad 0] \tag{27}$$

Since $X_i(s) = sX_{i-1}(s)$ for the phase variable representation, then from Eq. (24)

$$H_{eq}(s) = [1 \quad 1.377 \quad 0.954]\begin{bmatrix} X_1(s) \\ sX_1(s) \\ s^2X_1(s) \end{bmatrix}\frac{1}{X_1(s)} = \frac{4.77s^2 + 6.885s + 5}{5} \tag{28}$$

which is identical to Eq. (13). The specific design procedure is as follows:

Step 1 The plant transfer function is expressed in polynomial format:

$$G_x(s) = \frac{Y(s)}{U(s)} = \frac{K_G(s^w + c_{w-1}s^{w-1} + \ldots + c_1s + c_0}{s^n + a_{n-1}s^{n-1} + \ldots + a_1s + a_0} \tag{29}$$

This yields the state and output equations in terms of phase variables as follows:

$$\dot{\underset{\sim}{x}} = \underset{\sim}{A}_c\underset{\sim}{x} + \underset{\sim}{b}_c u \tag{30}$$

$$y = \underset{\sim}{c}_c'\underset{\sim}{x} \tag{31}$$

where

$$\underset{\sim}{A}_c = \begin{bmatrix} 0 & 1 & 0 & \ldots & 0 \\ 0 & 0 & 1 & \ldots & 0 \\ \hline & & & \ldots & 1 \\ -a_0 & -a_1 & -a_2 & \ldots & -a_{n-1} \end{bmatrix} \tag{32}$$

$$\underset{\sim}{b}_c = \begin{bmatrix} 0 \\ 0 \\ \cdot \\ \cdot \\ \cdot \\ K_G \end{bmatrix} \tag{33}$$

$$\underset{\sim}{c}_c' = [c_0 \; c_1 \; \ldots \; c_{w-1} \; 1 \; 0 \; \ldots \; 0] \tag{34}$$

Thus Eqs. (24) and (34) yield

$$\left[H_{eq}(s)\right]_c = \frac{k_n s^{n-1} + k_{n-1}s^{n-2} + \ldots + k_2 s + k_1}{s^w + c_{w-1}s^{w-1} + \ldots + c_1 s + c_0} \tag{35}$$

From Fig. 1-d and substituting from Eqs. (29) and (35) into

$$\left[\frac{Y(s)}{R(s)}\right]_A = \frac{G_x(s)}{1 + G_x(s)H_{eq}(s)} \tag{36}$$

where $H_{eq}(s) = [H_{eq}(s)]_c$ yields

$$\left[\frac{Y(s)}{R(s)}\right]_A = \frac{K_G(s^w + c_{w-1}s^{w-1} + \ldots + c_0)}{s^n + (a_{n-1} + K_G k_n)s^{n-1} + \ldots + (a_0 + K_G k_1)} \quad (37)$$

which is the closed-loop system control ratio.

Step 2 Based upon the system's performance specifications [1] obtain $[M(s)]_D$ which contains at least one non-dominant pole in order to achieve h.f.g. operation. The minimum value of T, T_{min}, allowable should be considered when synthesizing $[M(s)]_D$. That is, the dominant poles and zeros of the plant and $[M(s)]_D$ should be in the shaded area of Fig. 3 and Path A of Fig 6 applies [1]. If this condition cannot be satisfied, a satisfactory design may still be achievable. For this situation, Path B, $[M(s)]_D$ is synthesized, using T_{min}, based only upon the performance specifications.

Step 3 Set Eq. (37) equal to $[M(s)]_D$ and equate the corresponding coefficients to obtain K_G and k_i.

Step 4 By use of the Tustin transformation obtain $[H_{eq}(z)]_{TU}$.

Step 5 Replace $(z+1)^{n-w-1}$ poles of $[H_{eq}(z)]_{TU}$ by the dc equivalent poles $\alpha(z + \delta)^{n-w-1}$ to to obtain the modified feedback controller $H_{eq} = K_{zc}H'_{eq}(z)$. The desired system performance may be met via Path A of Fig. 6 or by adjusting K_{zc}, via Path B of Fig. 6, may yield the desired performance. If the loop transmission frequency is considered to be too large, for example due to noise, then repeat Step 2 with a new $[M(s)]_D$ that may yield a lower value for ω_ϕ or use another design technique.

5. SUMMARY

This paper has illustrated how a physically unrealizable $H_{eq}(s)$ controller can be transformed to an equivalent physically realizable digital controller, $H_{eq}(z)$, which may be easily implemented, that maintains the desired insensitivity of the system output to plant parameter variations. The approach of this paper of implementing an improper H_{eq} may not be feasible when unmodelled system dynamics are present and when the dominant poles and zeros of $G_x(s)$ and $[M(s)]_D$ do not lie in the Tustin region of Fig. 3.

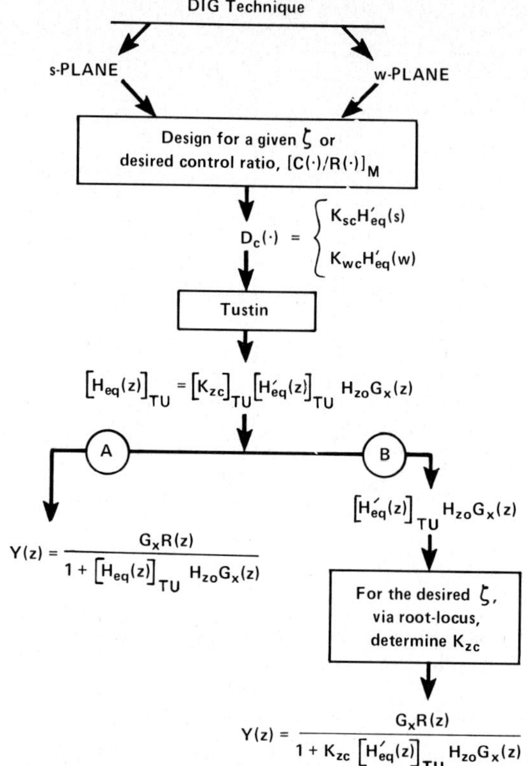

Figure 6. DIG design philosophy for Figure 4.

References

1. D'Azzo, J. J. and C. H. Houpis. Linear Control System Analysis and Design: Conventional and Modern. New York: McGraw-Hill, 2nd Edition, 1981.

2. Houpis, C. H. and G. B. Lamont. Digital Control Systems (Theory, Hardware, Software). New York: McGraw-Hill, to be published in the fall of 1984.

3. Houpis, C. H. "A Refined Design Method for Sampled-Data Control Systems: The Pseudo-Continuous-Time (PCT) Control System Design. An unpublished paper (has been submitted for publication).

4. D'Azzo, J. J. and C. H. Houpis. Feedback Control System Analysis and Synthesis, 2nd Ed. New York: McGraw-Hill Book Co., 1966.

5. Maybeck, P. Stochastic Models, Estimation and Control. New York: Academic Press, Vol. 1, 1979, Vols. 2 and 3, 1982.

6. Jacquot, R. Modern Digital Control Systems. New York: Dekker, 1981.

DIGITAL TECHNIQUES in Simulation, Communication and Control
Spyros G. Tzafestas (editor)
Elsevier Science Publishers B.V. (North-Holland) © IMACS, 1985

GENERIC SYSTEM TYPE FOR DISCRETE-TIME LINEAR MULTIVARIABLE CONTROL SYSTEMS

Shinji Hara

Department of Control Engineering,
Tokyo Institute of Technology,
Meguro-ku, Tokyo, Japan

The system type plays an important role of servo systems for step or ramp type reference commands. This note investigates the multi-input, multi-output system type, named $[l_1, \cdots, l_p]$-type, for discrete-time linear systems with partial parameter perturbations in the sense of genericity. Methods with generic rank conditions are proposed for determining the generic system type of a given plant. A necessary and sufficient condition for the existence of a servo compensator which realizes a prescribed system type is derived. This condition represents the possibility of the system type. A synthesis algorithm for the servo compensators of minimal order is also presented using simple matrix operations.

1. INTRODUCTION

In classical control theory, the steady-state characteristics of single-input, single-output unity feedback systems has been throughly investigated using the concept of system type. The utility of this concept in servo problem is that the steady-state characteristics of a feedback system to a particular polynomial-type reference command, such as a step function, ramp function, etc., can be easily seen from its system type. The extension of this concept of classical control theory to multiple-input and output systems has been made by many researchers [1]-[6]. An $[l_1, \cdots, l_p]$-type feedback system introduced by Hosoe and Ito [3] implies that the i-th output of the system may track a polynomial type reference input of degree l_i-1 without steady-state error.

Many researches on system type except [5] and [6] have not taken account of the parameter perturbations in the plant model, which should be considered in the control system design. In, practice, we often encounter the case where some of the plant parameters are fixed at zero, one, etc. and others are unknown or perturbed. This feature depends on the structure of the plant. We therefore consider discrete-time systems with partial parameter perturbations and discuss the system type in the sense of genericity in this note. Genericity implies that the property holds almost every parameter. The approach taken here is different from that for continuous-time systems investigated by means of structured matrices and graph theory [5], [6]. The structured system approach can not be applied to discrete-time systems, since the corresponding eigen values in polynomial type functions are not zero but one which can not be described by structured matrices. The following example on D.C. motor reveals the importance of the approach with generic rank of matrices whose elements are functions of some non-fixed parameters.

A simplest continuous time model of a D.C. motor is represented by

$$\dot{x}(t) = \begin{pmatrix} 0 & 1 \\ 0 & \theta_1 \end{pmatrix} x(t) + \begin{pmatrix} 0 \\ \theta_2 \end{pmatrix} u(t) , \tag{1.a}$$

$$y(t) = (1 \quad 0)\, x(t) , \tag{1.b}$$

where $x_1(t)$, $x_2(t)$ and $u(t)$ are the angular rotation, the angular velocity and the armature voltage, respectively, and θ_1 and θ_2 are scalar variables determined by the system parameters of the armature circuit, the D.C. motor and the load. It is easily seen that the transfer function of this system is written by

$$Y(s)/U(s) = \theta_2/\{s(s+\theta_1)\} . \tag{2}$$

This implies the system (1) is a type-1 system for almost all θ_1 and θ_2, since the transfer function contains 1/s except for θ_2=0.

Discritizing the system (1) with an appropriate sampling time under the assumption such that the control input maintains some constant value over the sampling period, the discrete-time model of the D.C. motor can be represented by

$$x[k+1] = \begin{pmatrix} 1 & q_3 \\ 0 & q_1 \end{pmatrix} x[k] + \begin{pmatrix} q_4 \\ q_2 \end{pmatrix} u[k] , \tag{3.a}$$

$$y[k] = (1 \quad 0)\, x[k] , \tag{3.b}$$

where q_i(i=1,2,3,4) are scalar variables determined by the sampling time as well as the system parameters. It is also found that the pulse transfer function of the discretized system is expressed as

$$Y(z)/U(z) = \{q_2q_3+q_4(z-q_1)\}/\{(z-1)(z-q_1)\} , \tag{4}$$

which includes 1/(z-1) regardress of the system

parameters and the sampling time. Last equation means that the system (3) is also a type-1 system for almost all q_i. It is useful for the continuous-time case to use the structured matrices by replacing the fixed element 1 with a variable element. This, however, is imvalid for the discrete-time case, since the fixed element 1 has an essential meaning, the mode of a polynomial type function.

The organization of this note is as follows: We define the generic system type for discrete-time linear multivariable systems with partial parameter perturbations in Section 2. Section 3 gives methods with generic system type of a prescribed plant. The possibility of the system type by connecting pre-compensators is discussed in Section 4. A synthesis algorithm for the servo compensators of minimal order is also presented by means of simple matrix operations.

The notation used here is as follows: C^- represents the open left half complex plane. $\sigma(A)$ and $\rho_g[A(q)]$ denote the set of the eigenvalues of A and the generic rank of A(q), respectively. The generic rank is the rank for almost all the parameters q. For example, $\rho_g[A(q)]=2$ and $\rho_g[A(q)-I_2]=1$, where $A(q) = \begin{pmatrix} 1 & q_1 \\ 0 & q_2 \end{pmatrix}$.

2. DEFINITION OF GENERIC SYSTEM TYPE

In this section, we define a generic system type for a discrete-time linear multivariable system $S_p(A(q), B(q), C)$ described by

$$x[k+1] = A(q)x[k] + B(q)u[k] \quad , \tag{5.a}$$

$$y[k] = Cx[k] \quad , \tag{5.b}$$

where $x[k]\varepsilon R^n$, $u[k]\varepsilon R^m$ and $y[k]\varepsilon R^p$, which is extended to a well-known system type for single-input, single-output linear continuous systems. Here, C is a p×n matrix with only fixed elements such as 0 or 1 and the matrices A(q) and B(q) consist of independent variable elements q_i as well as fixed elements, where $q = [q_1, \text{---}, q_r]^T \varepsilon R^r$ denotes a non-fixed parameter vector. Without loss of generality, we assume that (A(q), B(q)) and (C, A(q)) are controllable and observable for almost all q, respectively.

The concept of the system type in classical control theory is closely related to the steady-state characteristics of a unity feedback system for polynomial type reference commands, such as step or ramp functions. Consequently, we shall restrict the control system and the reference input to a system depicted in Figure 1 and functions of polynomial type with respect to time, respectively, so as to define the system type for discrete-time linear multivariable systems. It is well known that any polynomial type reference input r[k] may be generated by a linear free system $S_r(A_r, C_r)$ represented by

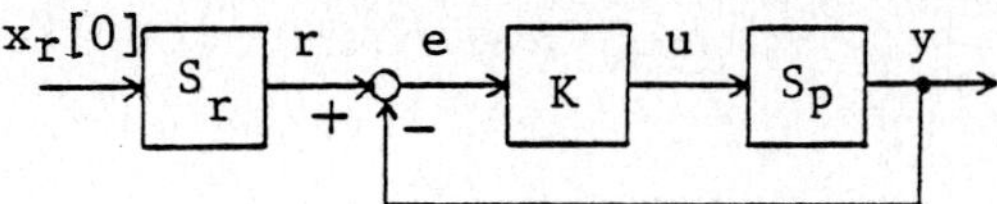

Figure 1 : Feedback system

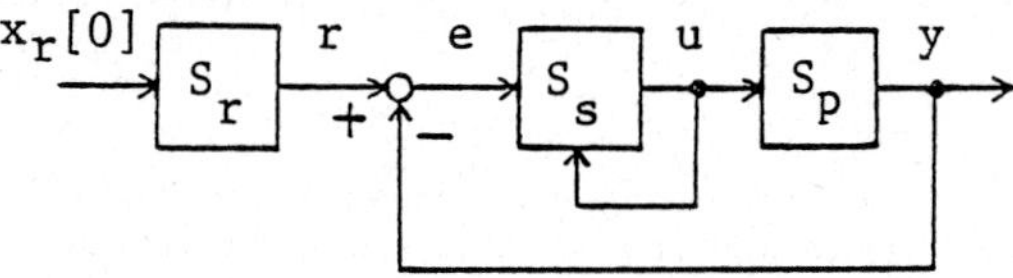

Figure 2 : Feedback system with stabilizer

$$x_r[k+1] = A_r x_r[k] \quad , \tag{6.a}$$

$$r[k] = C_r x_r[k] \quad , \tag{6.b}$$

where $x_r[k]\varepsilon R^{n_r}$, $r[k]\varepsilon R^p$, and

$$A_r = \text{diag}\,[A_{r1}, \text{---}, A_{rp}] \quad , \tag{7.a}$$

$$C_r = \text{diag}\,[C_{r1}, \text{---}, C_{rp}] \quad . \tag{7.b}$$

Here, for i with an integer $h_i \geq 1$,

$$A_{ri} = \left.\begin{pmatrix} 1 & 1 & & 0 \\ & \ddots & \ddots & \\ & & \ddots & 1 \\ 0 & & & 1 \end{pmatrix}\right\} h_i \quad , \tag{8.a}$$

$$C_{ri} = \underbrace{(1\ 0\ \text{--}\ 0)}_{h_i} \quad , \tag{8.b}$$

and there exists no row and column corresponding to A_{ri} and no column corresponding to C_{ri} for i with $h_i=0$. Under this description h_i are equal to 0, 1 and 2 imply the i-th reference commands are zero, step and ramp signals, respectively.

<u>Definition 1</u> :
Consider a stable control system shown in Figure 1, i.e., the control input u[k] is given by

$$u[k] = K(q)e[k] = K(q)(r[k]-y[k]) \quad , \tag{9}$$

where K(q) is an m×p matrix, and the stability condition

$$\sigma(A(q)-B(q)K(q)C) \subset C^- \tag{10}$$

holds. A system $S_p(A(q), B(q), C)$ is called a generical $[l_1, \text{---}, l_p]$-type system, denoted by $[l_1, \text{---}, l_p]_g$-type, if

$$\lim_{k\to\infty} e[k] = 0, \text{ when } 0 \leq h_i \leq l_i \text{ for all i} \quad , \tag{11.a}$$

and

$$\lim_{k\to\infty} e[k] \neq 0, \text{ when } h_i > l_i \text{ for some i} \quad , \tag{11.b}$$

hold for almost all q.

<u>Remark 1</u> : Stabilization of the control system can be achieved by means of a stabilizer S_s,

shown in Figure 2, instead of the control law (9), since S_p is generically controllable and observable. In this case, the composite system made up of S_p and S_s is at least an $[l_1, \text{---}, l_p]_g$-type system.

3. DETERMINATION OF GENERIC SYSTEM TYPE

Determination methods of generic system type are investigated in this section. We need two lemmas to derive these methods.

Lemma 1 :
$S_p(A(q)\,, B(q)\,, C)$ is an $[l_1, \text{---}, l_p]_g$-type system, if and only if the following two conditions hold for almost all q :

i) There exists an $n\times n_r$ matrix $T(q)$ such that

$$\begin{pmatrix} A(q) \\ C \end{pmatrix} T(q) = \begin{pmatrix} T(q)A_r \\ C_r \end{pmatrix} \tag{12}$$

for any h_i $(0\leq h_i\leq l_i)$,

ii) For some integer i such that $h_i > l_i$, there exists no matrix $T(q)$ satisfying (12) when $h_j=0$ for $j\neq i$.

(proof) Eq.(12), which implies an output regulation or internal model condition, is easily derived from the result of Francis and Wonham [7] (Lemma 1). Q.E.D.

A necessary and sufficient condition for the existence of $T(q)$ satisfying (12) is as follows.

Lemma 2 :
Suppose that the minimal polynomial of A_r is given by $(A_r-I)^h=0$, i.e., $h=\max\{h_i\}$. There exists an $n\times n_r$ matrix $T(q)$ satisfying (12) for almost all q, if and only if

$$\rho_g\begin{pmatrix} A_h(q) & 0 \\ C_h & N_h \end{pmatrix} = \rho_g\begin{pmatrix} A_h(q) \\ C_h \end{pmatrix} = nh\ , \tag{13}$$

where

$$A_h(q)=\begin{pmatrix} A(q)-I & -I & & 0 \\ & \ddots & \ddots & \\ & & \ddots & -I \\ 0 & & & A(q)-I \end{pmatrix} : nh\times nh \text{ matrix}\ , \tag{14}$$

$$C_h=\begin{pmatrix} C & & 0 \\ & \ddots & \\ 0 & & C \end{pmatrix} : ph\times nh \text{ matrix}\ , \tag{15}$$

and

$$N_h = \begin{pmatrix} C_r \\ C_r(A_r-I) \\ \vdots \\ C_r(A_r-I)^{h-1} \end{pmatrix} : ph\times n_r \text{ matrix}\ . \tag{16}$$

(proof) Necessity: Eq.(12) can be rewritten by

$$\begin{pmatrix} 0 \\ N_h \end{pmatrix} = \begin{pmatrix} A_h(q) \\ C_h \end{pmatrix}\begin{pmatrix} T(q) \\ T(q)(A_r-I) \\ \vdots \\ T(q)(A_r-I)^{h-1} \end{pmatrix}\ . \tag{17}$$

This equation and assumption of the generical observability of $(C\,, A(q))$ lead to (13).
Sufficiency: If (13) holds, then there exists an $n\times n_r$ matrix $T'(q)$ such that

$$0 = (A(q)-I)^h T'(q) \tag{18.a}$$

and

$$N_h = \begin{pmatrix} C \\ C(A(q)-I) \\ \vdots \\ C(A(q)-I)^{h-1} \end{pmatrix} T'(q) \tag{18.b}$$

for almost all q. Postmultiplying (18.b) by (A_r-I), we get

$$\begin{aligned} N_h(A_r-I) &= \begin{pmatrix} C(A(q)-I) \\ \vdots \\ C(A(q)-I)^{h-1} \\ 0 \end{pmatrix} T'(q) \\ &= N'_h(q)(A(q)-I)T'(q)\ , \end{aligned} \tag{19}$$

where

$$N'_h(q) = \begin{pmatrix} C \\ \vdots \\ C(A(q)-I)^{h-2} \\ C(A(q)-I)^{h-1} \end{pmatrix}\ , \tag{20}$$

since $(A_r-I)^h=0$ and $(A(q)-I)^hT'(q)=0$. Eq.(12) is obtained from (18) and (19) by setting $T(q)=T'(q)$, since the generical observability condition, $\rho_g[N'_h(q)]=n$, is satisfied. Q.E.D.

Two algorithms with generic rank conditions for determining the generic system type are easily derived from Lemmas 1 and 2.

Theorem 1 :
$S_p(A(q)\,, B(q)\,, C)$ is an $[l_1, \text{---}, l_p]_g$-type system, if and only if

$$\rho_g\begin{pmatrix} A_{\ell i}(q) \\ C'_{i,\ell i} \end{pmatrix} = (n-1)l_i \tag{21.a}$$

and

$$\rho_g\begin{pmatrix} A_{\ell i+1}(q) \\ C'_{i,\ell i+1} \end{pmatrix} = (n-1)l_i+n \tag{21.b}$$

hold. Here, a $(p-1)h\times nh$ matrix $C'_{i,h}$ is defined by

$$C'_{i,h}=\begin{pmatrix} C'_i & & 0 \\ & \ddots & \\ 0 & & C'_i \end{pmatrix} \tag{22}$$

where C'_i is a $(p-1)\times n$ matrix generated by removing the i-th row from C.
(proof) Lemmas 1 and 2 directly leads to Theorem 1. Q.E.D.

Theorem 2 :
$S_p(A(q), B(q), C)$ is an $[l_1, ---, l_p]_g$-type system, where

$$l_i = n^2 - \rho_g\begin{pmatrix} A_n(q) \\ C'_{i,n} \end{pmatrix} \; ; \; i=1,---,p . \tag{23}$$

(proof) If (21) holds, then we have

$$\rho_g\begin{pmatrix} A_{hi}(q) \\ C'_{i,hi} \end{pmatrix} = (n-1)l_i + n(h_i - l_i) \tag{24}$$

for $h_i \geq l_i$ (i=1,---,p). Eq.(23) is then obtained by setting h_i=n since $l_i \leq n$ for all i.
Q.E.D.

Note that if only (21.a) holds S_p is at least an $[l_1, ---, l_p]_g$-type system.

Example(D.C. Motor) :
Applying Theorem 2 to a discretized D.C. motor model given by (3), we get

$$l_1 = n^2 - \rho_g[A_2(q)]$$

$$= 2^2 - \rho_g\left(\begin{array}{cc|cc} 0 & q_3 & -1 & \\ & q_1-1 & & -1 \\ \hline & & 0 & q_3 \\ & & & q_1-1 \end{array}\right) = 4-3 = 1 , \tag{25}$$

since $C'_{1,2}$ is a null matrix in the single output case. This result coincidents that stated in Introduction.

4. POSSIBILITY OF GENERIC SYSTEM TYPE

In the previous section, we have discussed the generic system type for a given plant. This section investigates the possibility of generic system type by connecting an appropriate pre-compensator to a given plant. We, now, introduce a pre-compensator $S_c(A_c, B_c, C_c, D_c)$ expressed as

$$x_c[k+1] = A_c x_c[k] + B_c u_c[k] , \tag{26.a}$$

$$u[k] = C_c x_c[k] + D_c u_c[k] , \tag{26.b}$$

where $x_c[k] \varepsilon R^{n_c}$ and $u_c[k] \varepsilon R^{m_c}$, then the composite system made up S_p and S_c, denoted by $\bar{S}(\bar{A}(q), \bar{B}(q), \bar{C})$, is written by

$$\bar{x}[k+1] = \bar{A}(q)\bar{x}[k] + \bar{B}(q)u_c[k] , \tag{27.a}$$

$$y[k] = \bar{C}\bar{x}[k] , \tag{27.b}$$

where $\bar{x}[k] = (x[k]^T, x_c[k]^T)^T$,

$$\bar{A}(q) = \begin{pmatrix} A(q) & B(q)C_c \\ 0 & A_c \end{pmatrix} , \; \bar{B}(q) = \begin{pmatrix} B(q)D_c \\ B_c \end{pmatrix} ,$$

$$\bar{C} = (C \quad 0) .$$

It is required for the composite system $\bar{S}$ to have a prescribed generic system type and to be generically observable, which guarantees the internal stability of the closed loop system shown in Figure 3 [8]. These two requirements only depend on A_c and B_c. If there exist such matrices A_c and C_c we may construct a stable feedback system with desired generic system type by using a stabilizer S_s, since $\bar{S}$ is generically controllable with

$$B_c = (0 , I_{n_c}) \; , \; D_c = (I_m , 0) . \; [8] \tag{28}$$

The purpose of the pre-compensator (also said to be servo compensator) design is, therefore, to determine matrices A_c and C_c of minimal order satisfying the two requirements.

We need the following lemma to derive a necessary and sufficient condition for the existence of such matrices A_c and C_c, which also represents the possibility of the generic system type.

Lemma 3 :
Suppose that the minimal polynomial of A_r is represented by $(A_r - I)^h = 0$. If there exists an $(n+n_c)\times n_r$ matrix $\bar{T}(q)$ such that

$$\begin{pmatrix} \bar{A}(q) \\ \bar{C} \end{pmatrix} \bar{T}(q) = \begin{pmatrix} \bar{T}(q)A_r \\ C_r \end{pmatrix} \tag{29}$$

for almost all q, then

$$\rho_g\begin{pmatrix} A_h(q) & B_h(q) & 0 \\ C_h & 0 & N_h \end{pmatrix} = \rho_g\begin{pmatrix} A_h(q) & B_h(q) \\ C_h & 0 \end{pmatrix}$$

where (30)

$$B_h(q) = \begin{pmatrix} B(q) & & 0 \\ & \ddots & \\ 0 & & B(q) \end{pmatrix} : \text{nh}\times\text{mh matrix.} \tag{31}$$

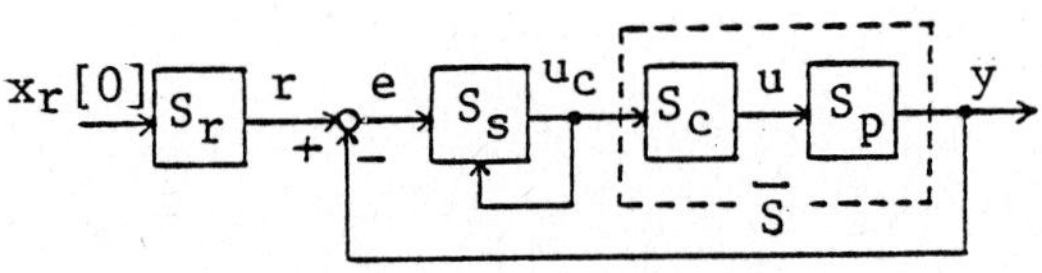

Figure 3 : Feedback system with pre-compensator and stabilizer

(proof) If (29) holds, then

$$\begin{pmatrix} A(q)-I & B(q) \\ C & 0 \end{pmatrix}\begin{pmatrix} T(q) \\ S(q) \end{pmatrix} = \begin{pmatrix} T(q)(A_r-I) \\ C_r \end{pmatrix}, \quad (32)$$

where

$$T(q) = (I_n , 0)\bar{T}(q) \quad , \quad (33.a)$$

$$S(q) = (0 , I_m)\bar{T}(q) \quad . \quad (33.b)$$

In this case, we get

$$\begin{pmatrix} 0 \\ N_h \end{pmatrix} = \begin{pmatrix} A_h(q) & B_h(q) \\ C_h & 0 \end{pmatrix}\begin{pmatrix} \mathcal{T}(q) \\ \mathcal{S}(q) \end{pmatrix} \quad , \quad (34)$$

where

$$\mathcal{T}(q) = \begin{pmatrix} T(q) \\ T(q)(A_r-I) \\ \vdots \\ T(q)(A_r-I)^{h-1} \end{pmatrix}, \mathcal{S}(q) = \begin{pmatrix} S(q) \\ S(q)(A_r-I) \\ \vdots \\ S(q)(A_r-I)^{h-1} \end{pmatrix}. \quad (35)$$

Eq.(34) leads to (30). Q.E.D.

Remark 2 :
The condition in Lemma 3 is the necessary and sufficient condition, when h=1 or the right hand side of (30) has column full rank.

Theorem 3 :
Suppose that

$$\rho_g \begin{pmatrix} A(q)-I & B(q) \\ C & 0 \end{pmatrix} = n+m \quad (36)$$

holds for $S_p(A(q), B(q), C)$. There exists a $S_c(A_c, B_c, C_c, D_c)$ such that the composite system $\underline{S}(\underline{A}(q), \underline{B}(q), \underline{C})$ made up of S_p and S_c is at least $[l_1, \text{---}, l_p]_g$-type and generically observable, if and only if

$$\rho_g \begin{pmatrix} A_{\ell i}(q) & B_{\ell i}(q) \\ C'_{\ell,\ell i} & 0 \end{pmatrix} = \rho_g \begin{pmatrix} A_{\ell i}(q) & B_{\ell i}(q) \\ C_{\ell i} & 0 \end{pmatrix} - l_i = (n+m-1)l_i \quad (37)$$

holds for all i (=1,---,p) .
(proof) The necessity is clear from Lemma 3. The sufficiency is proved by proposing a design procedure of A_c and C_c satisfying the requirements. If (37) holds, then there exist nl_i vectors $t_i(q)$ and ml_i vectors $s_i(q)$ satisfying

$$\begin{pmatrix} 0 \\ e_{i,\ell i} \end{pmatrix} = \begin{pmatrix} A_{\ell i}(q) & B_{\ell i}(q) \\ C_{\ell i} & 0 \end{pmatrix}\begin{pmatrix} t_i(q) \\ s_i(q) \end{pmatrix}, \quad (38)$$

where $e_{i,j}$ is a pj vector whose elements are all 0 except that the i+p(j-1)-th element is equal to 1. In this case, we get

$$\begin{pmatrix} 0 \\ e_{i,1} \end{pmatrix} = \begin{pmatrix} A(q)-I & B(q) \\ C & 0 \end{pmatrix}\begin{pmatrix} t_{i,1}(q) \\ s_{i,1}(q) \end{pmatrix} \quad (39)$$

and

$$\begin{pmatrix} t_{i,j}(q) \\ 0 \end{pmatrix} = \begin{pmatrix} A(q)-I & B(q) \\ C & 0 \end{pmatrix}\begin{pmatrix} t_{i,j+1}(q) \\ s_{i,j+1}(q) \end{pmatrix}, \quad (40)$$

for $j=1,\text{---},l_i-1$, where

$$t_i(q) = (t_{i,l_i}(q)^T, \text{---} , t_{i,1}(q)^T)^T \quad , \quad (41.a)$$

$$s_i(q) = (s_{i,l_i}(q)^T, \text{---} , s_{i,1}(q)^T)^T \quad , \quad (41.b)$$

then it is easily found that (32) holds. Now, we define $ml\times n_r$ matrices S_j (j=1,---,ν) as

$$\mathcal{S}(q) = \begin{pmatrix} S(q) \\ S(q)(A_r-I) \\ \vdots \\ S(q)(A_r-I)^l \end{pmatrix} \overset{d}{=} \sum_{j=1}^{\nu} f_j(q)S_j \quad , \quad (42)$$

where $l = \max\{l_i\}$ and $f_j(q)$;j=1,---,ν are relatively independent scalar functions of q_i.

It is, thus, shown that the following is a minimal order pre-compensator satisfying the prescribed conditions (the proof is omitted, the analogous proof is seen in [8]) :

$$n_c = n_c^* \overset{d}{=} \rho[S_1, \text{---} , S_\nu] \quad , \quad (43)$$

$$A_c = A_c^* = (I_{n_c^*} , 0)P\begin{pmatrix} I_m & I_m & & 0 \\ & \ddots & \ddots & \\ & & & I_m \\ 0 & & & I_m \end{pmatrix}P^{-1}\begin{pmatrix} I_{n_c^*} \\ 0 \end{pmatrix}, \quad (44.a)$$

$$C_c = C_c^* = (I_m , 0)P^{-1}\begin{pmatrix} I_{n_c^*} \\ 0 \end{pmatrix} \quad , \quad (44.b)$$

where P is an $lm\times lm$ non-singular matrix satisfying

$$P\mathcal{S}(q) = \begin{pmatrix} \overset{*}{\mathcal{S}}(q) \\ 0 \end{pmatrix}\begin{matrix} \}n_c^* \\ \}lm-n_c^* \end{matrix} \quad . \quad (45)$$

Q.E.D.

Remark 3 :
Theorem 3 may be applied for the case where (36) does not hold by choosing an m×m' matrix G such that

$$\rho_g \begin{pmatrix} A(q)-I & B(q)G \\ C & 0 \end{pmatrix} = \rho_g \begin{pmatrix} A(q)-I & B(q) \\ C & 0 \end{pmatrix} = n+m' \quad (46)$$

and replacing B(q) with B(q)G. In this case, however, the minimal order of the pre-compensator depends on the choice of the matrix G.

The above remark leads to the following result.

Corollary :
There exists a pre-compensator $S_c(A_c, B_c, C_c, D_c)$ such that the composite system $\bar{S}$ made up of $S_p(A(q), B(q), C)$ and S_c is generically observable and $[l_1, ---, l_p]_g$-type for any $l_i \geq 0$;i=1,---,p, if and only if

$$\rho_g \begin{pmatrix} A(q)-I & B(q) \\ C & 0 \end{pmatrix} = n+p \tag{47}$$

holds.
(proof) Necessity: It is seen from Lemma 3 that the condition

$$\rho_g \begin{pmatrix} A(q)-I & B(q) & 0 \\ C & 0 & I_p \end{pmatrix} = \rho_g \begin{pmatrix} A(q)-I & B(q) \\ C & 0 \end{pmatrix} \tag{48}$$

is required for $\bar{S}$ being $[1, ---, 1]_g$-type. On the other hand, $(A(q), B(q))$ is a generically controllable pair, i.e., $\rho_g(A(q)-I, B(Q)) = n$. This and (48) lead to (47), since the left hand side of (48) is equal to $\rho_g((A(q)-I, B(q)) + p = n+p$.
Sufficiency: If (47) holds, then there exists an m×p matrix G satisfying

$$\rho_g \begin{pmatrix} A(q)-I & B(q)G \\ C & 0 \end{pmatrix} = n+p . \tag{49}$$

We, therefore, have (37) for any $l_i \geq 0$ by replacing B(q) with B(q)G in Theorem 3.

Q.E.D.

5. CONCLUSION

We have discussed the generic system type for discrete-time linear multivariable systems with partial parameter perturbations in this note. Methods of determining the generic system type of the given plant and the possibility for the generic system type using pre-compensators or servo compensators have been proposed. A simple synthesis algorithm for a minimal order pre-compensator such that the compensated system is generically observable and of the prescribed generic system type has been developed. Although only the system type for reference coomands has been treated, the analogous results with respect to the generic system type for disturbance inputs may be easily derived by means of the same technique.

The author wishes to thank Prof. K.Furuta of Tokyo Institute of Technology for his constant encouragement during this work.

REFERENCES

[1] Wiberg, P.M., State Space and Linear Systems (McGraw-Hill, 1971).
[2] Sandell, N. and Athans, M., On "Type L" Multivariable Linear Systems, Automatica 9 (1973) 131-136.
[3] Hosoe, S. and Ito, M., On Steady-State Characteristics of Linear Multivariable Systems, Memories of the Faculty of Engineering, Nagoya Univ. 26 (1974) 54-85.
[4] Wolfe, C.A. and Meditch, J.S., Theory of System Type for Linear Multivariable Servomechanisms, IEEE Trans. on Automt. Contr. AC-22 (1977) 36-46.
[5] Mayeda, H. and Miyoshi, S., Robust Control of Tracking Problem with Internal Stability for Structured System, Proc. 8th IFAC Congress VIII (1981) 97-102.
[6] Hosoe, S., Hayato, H. and Ito, Y., Robust Synthesis of Linear Servomechanisms, Proc. 8th IFAC Congress VIII (1981) 103-108.
[7] Francis, B.A. and Wonham, W.M., The Internal Model Principle for Linear Multivariable Regulators, J. Appl. Math. and Opt. 2 (1975) 170-194.
[8] Hara, S., A Synthesis of Servo Controller for Linear Multivariable Systems with Parameter Perturbations, Ph.D. Thesis, Dept. of Control Engineering, Tokyo Institute of Technology (March 1981).

DIGITAL TECHNIQUES in Simulation, Communication and Control
Spyros G. Tzafestas (editor)
Elsevier Science Publishers B.V. (North-Holland) © IMACS, 1985

SYNTHESIS OF AN ADAPTIVE ALGORITHM FOR THE PROCESS CONTROL

Ljubiša Draganović

Institute for Control and Computer Sciences
P.O. Box 158, Tvornička 3, Stup
71 000 Sarajevo, Yugoslavia

The paper describes the synthesis of a self-adaptive algorithm for the process control. Information employed here to realize adaptive control is on the state of controlled process and on the first derivative of that state only. It is assumed that the controlled process is described by a linear differential equation with non-stationary gain and non-stationary dominant time constant. An adaptive algorithm of control structure (controller) gain variation is suggested, a corresponding expression for that gain is derived, and a proof of gain convergence is presented. Finally, simulation results are given.

1. PROBLEM STATEMENT

A control process is considered the motion of which can be described by the equation

$$\frac{dx^n}{dt^n} + \sum_{i=o}^{n-1} a_i \frac{dx^i}{dt^i} = k_o(t)\{u(t)+f(t)\} \qquad (1)$$

where

x - state variable of the controlled process, $x \in R^1$,

$a_i \cong$ const. $(i=0,1,\dots,n-1)$ - parameters of the controlled process, $a_i \in P^{n-1}$

$k_o(t)$ - non-stationary process gain, $k_o(t) \in K^1$,

$f(t)$ - disturbance, $f(t) \in F^1$

$u(t)$ - control, $u(t) \in R^1$

$R^1, P^{n-1}, K_o{}^1, F^1$ - are spaces of state/ /control, parameters and disturbances respectively.

The disturbance $f(t)$ fulfills the following assumptions [1].

Assumption 1. External disturbance $f(t)$ is of Gauss type.

Assumption 2. For any $\eta > 0$ there exist such values of $t_o, T_o, c(s)$ that for any values of $t > t_o$, $T > T_o$, s there holds the inequality

$$\{\frac{1}{T}\int_o^t e^{\frac{\tau-t}{T}} f(\tau)f(\tau+s)d\tau - c(s)\} < \eta \qquad (2)$$

Open system gain is defined as

$$k(t) = k_r(t)k_o(t) \qquad (3)$$

and satisfies the following assumption.

Assumption 3. Gain coefficient of the process varies within the limits of $k_{o\,min} \le k_o(t) \le k_{o\,max}$, $k_{o\,min} > 0$, and $k_r(t)$ can be varied within the limits of $k_{r\,min} \le k_r \le k_{r\,max}$, $k_{r\,min} > 0$, accordingly. In addition to the above it is supposed the existence of a non-emply single-dimensional set of permissible open system gain values $k(t)$, which permit the existence of minimum permissible system stability margin $r_1 \neq 0$ defined by the relation

$$\max\{(a_o+k)\int_o^\infty |g_k(s)|ds\} \le r_1^{-1} \qquad (4)$$

where

$g_k(s)$ - system weight function (1) taking into account the system feedback via the control $u(t) = u(x)$ at $k(t)$=const=$k \in K^1$ and $k_o(t) = 1$.

2. THE SYNTHESIS OF CONTROL ALGORITHM

Assumption 4. Control $u(t) = U(x)$ is chosen in the form of

$$u(t)=U(x)=(k_2+\frac{1}{T_I p})\{k_r(t)(k_1\varepsilon+T_D p\varepsilon)\} \qquad (5)$$

where

ε - control deviation, error; $\varepsilon = x_z - x$,

x_z - set-point value, where

k_2, T_I, k_1, T_D - constants, positive,

$p \equiv \frac{d}{dt}$ - differentiation operator.

Controller gain is chosen according to the expression, [1], [2]

$$k_r(t) = \frac{L_1 - cL_2}{L_2 + \beta} k \qquad (6)$$

where

$$L_1 = L_1(t, |\varepsilon|) = \begin{cases} |\hat{\varepsilon}| = \frac{1}{T_1} \int_0^t \exp\left(\frac{\tau - t}{T_1}\right) \bar{k}_1 |\varepsilon| d\tau \; \forall |\varepsilon| < \bar{k}_1 |\varepsilon| \\ |\hat{\varepsilon}| = |\hat{\varepsilon}(t_1)| \exp(-t/T_2) \; \forall |\hat{\varepsilon}| > |\varepsilon|, T_2 \gg T_1 \end{cases} \qquad (7)$$

and the time t_1 is obtained from the equation $|\hat{\varepsilon}(t_1)| = \bar{k}_1 |\varepsilon(t_1)|$,

where $|\hat{\varepsilon}(t)|$ - is estimated absolute error magnitude on the given period.

$$L_2 = L_2(t_1, |\dot{x}|) = \begin{cases} |\hat{\dot{x}}| = \frac{1}{T_1} \int_0^t \exp\left(\frac{\tau - t}{T_1}\right) k_2 |\dot{x}(\tau)| d\tau, \forall |\hat{\dot{x}}| < \bar{k}_2 |\dot{x}| \\ |\hat{\dot{x}}| = |\hat{\dot{x}}(t_2 \cdot \exp(-t/T_2), \forall |\hat{\dot{x}}| > \bar{k}_2 |\dot{x}|, T_2 \gg T_1 \end{cases} \qquad (8)$$

and the time t_2 is obtained from the relation $\bar{k}_2 |\dot{x}(t_2)| = |\hat{\dot{x}}(t_2)|$.

where $|\hat{\dot{x}}|$ - is estimated absolute magnitude of the process state first derivative.

The estimation of ε and $\dot{x}$ are made by first order filters with the time constants T_1 and T_2. The constants k, k_1 and $\bar{k}_2$ are positive.

Let us further accept, that the quality criterion of system motion described by the relation (1) is the functional $J = J(k(t))$ continuous on $k \in K^1$ and optimal on a subset of the set K^1 for $k = k_e$, where k_e gain value for which J has an extremum. Consequently, one way of determining the controller gain $k_r(t)$ is the minimization of difference $k_r(t) - k_e(t)$.

3. THE CONVERGENCE PROOF OF ADAPTATION ALGORITHM

Let γ be the maximum permissible variation of controller gain $k_r(t)$ (5), and μ the maximum variation of plant gain $k_o(t)$. Also, take that $|\Delta k(t)| > r_o, r_o > 0$.

By introducing the function of Liapunov in the form of

$$V = (k - k_e)^2 = (\Delta k_e)^2 \qquad (9)$$

then, assuming that $|\Delta k(t)| > r_o$

$$\frac{dV}{dt} = 2\Delta k_e \Delta k_e \{k_o(t)k_r(t) + k_r(t)\dot{k}_o(t)\} < -2r_o\{k_{o\,min}\gamma - \mu k_{r\,max}\} \qquad (10)$$

In order to have $\dot{V}$ as negative-definite function limited from the top side by a negative figure ν_1, it is necessary that

$$\mu = \frac{c_1 k_{o\,min}\,je}{k_{r\,max}} \quad (0 < c_1 < 1) \qquad (11)$$

Herby, it is

$$\frac{dV}{dt} < -2r_o(1 - c_1)k_{o\,min}\gamma = \nu_1 < 0 \qquad (12)$$

On the basis of (12), the finite time interval t_o does not exceed the amount

$$t_o = \max_{K^1} \{\Delta t + \frac{\Delta k(t)}{|\nu_1|}\}, \qquad (13)$$

and from that and the negative-definite function V it is

$$\{\Delta k(t + k_o)\} < r_o \qquad (14)$$

what was necessary to proove.

On the other hand, to make the expression (10) negative-definite, there has to be

$$k_o(t)\dot{k}_r(t) + k_r(t)\dot{k}_o(t) < 0 \qquad (15)$$

and this can be reduced to

$$\gamma \leqslant \frac{k_{r\,max}\,\mu}{k_{o\,min}} \qquad (16)$$

This prooves the control algorithm convergence.

4. SIMULATION RESULTS

The control process was of the fourth order having the transfer operator $G(p) = k_o/(T_o p + 1)^4$. Gain k_o varied within the range of $0 < k_o < 10$. The tests were performed at $x_z = 0$ and disturbance $f(t) = \pm 20$, $\omega = 2\pi \cdot 0{,}05\ 5^{-1}$, square-wave pulses. The quality criterion was $J = |\bar{x}|/k_o$.

Figs. 1, 2 and 3 contain the graphs $J = J(k_o)$ for various magnitudes of T_o as the parameter.

Algorithm parameters (5) were $k_2 = 1{,}0$, $T_I = 0{,}01$ s, $k_1 = 1{,}75$, $T_D = 0{,}04$s.

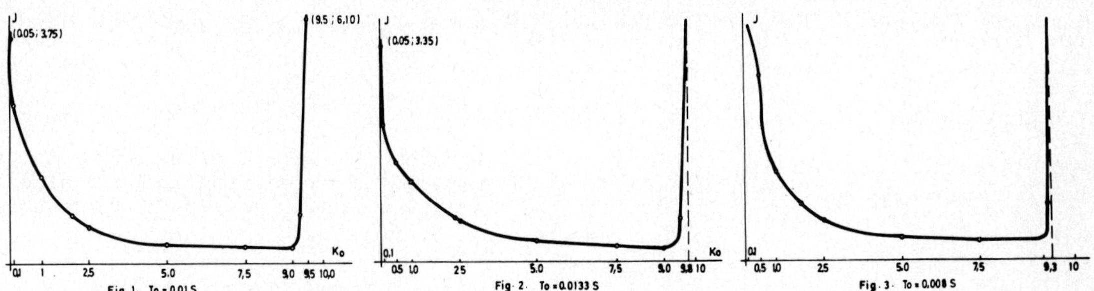

Fig. 1. To = 0,01 S

Fig. 2. To = 0,0133 S

Fig. 3. To = 0,008 S

Time constants in (7) and (8) T_1=0,01 s, T_2=100 T_1=1 s, and the parameters in (6) c=0,80, β=0,1, k = 20 with 0,1 at low and 1,0 at high limit.

5. CONCLUSION

The paper presents the synthesis of a self-adaptive algorithm for the process control. The control law employed is PID with variable gain which is determined only on the basis of controlled process and its first derivative. The control algorithm convergence has been verified from the aspect of controller variable gain. The simulation results show that such an algorithm permits the compensation of plant gain of up to 1:5 what satisfies a wide class of plants.

Key Word Index - Adaptive control; process control; self-adjusting systems; parametar estimation; simulation.

REFERENCES

[1] Ljubiša, S. Draganović: A contribution to the syntesis of adaptive control algorithms of deterministic systems, Ph.D. Thesis, University of Sarajevo, Department of electrical engeenering, 1979.

[2] Техническая кибернетика, № 2, 1979. стр. 167-171. Москва.

[3] Ляпунов А.М. Общая задача об устойчивости движения. Гостехиздат, 1950. Москва.

[4] Автоматика и телемеханика, № 4, 1975. стр. 66-77. Москва.

DIGITAL TECHNIQUES in Simulation, Communication and Control
Spyros G. Tzafestas (editor)
Elsevier Science Publishers B.V. (North-Holland) © IMACS, 1985

ON THE DECENTRALIZED CONTROL OF BILINEAR DYNAMICAL SYSTEMS

Georges Bitsoris

Systems and Measurements Laboratory
University of Patras
Patras - Greece

This paper deals with the design of decentralized control laws for the local stabilization of continuous-time bilinear dynamical systems. By applying aggregation technics conditions for the existence of decentralized linear feedback control laws garanteeing the exponential stability in a prespecified stability region and with a given transient rate are established. The analysis for the determination of these conditions provides in addition an approach for the design of such decentralized control laws.

1. INTRODUCTION

In the last decade, the stabilization problem of bilinear dynamical systems has been extendedly studied, |2|,|4|,|5|,|6|,|7|. From these studies, it is well known that if the linear part of a bilinear dynamical system is controllable, then the bilinear system can be stabilized by a control law linear in the state. However, only local stability is possible when a linear feedback control is applied. 2 .

The control problem of bilinear systems becomes more complicated when constraints on the structure of the gain matrix of the linear feedback control law are imposed. This is the case of decentralized stabilization by linear feedback control. In this case the controlability of the linear part of the bilinear system does not garantee the existence of stabilizing control laws linear in the state.

The object of this paper is to establish sufficient conditions for the existence of decentralized linear feedback control laws garanteeing the exponential stability in a prespecified stability region and with a given transient rate. The paper is organised as follows: In the first part of the paper the system to be studied and the decentralized control problem are presented. In the second part of the paper an aggregation approach is developed which reduces the control problem of the bilinear system to a stability analysis problem of a lower order P-invariant dynamical system. Finally, in the last part of the paper, conditions for the existence of linear decentralized control laws for the bilinear system are obtained.

2. PROBLEM STATEMENT

We consider time-invariant dynamical systems $\tilde{S}$ composed of s linearly interconnected bilinear systems S_i described by the equations

$$S_i:\ \dot{x}_i = \sum_{k=1}^{s} A_{ik}x_k + \sum_{l=1}^{m_i} (\hat{C}_{il}x_i + b_{il})u_{il} \qquad i=1,\ldots,s$$

where $x_i \in R^{n_i}$, $u_{il} \in R$, $A_{ik} \in R^{n_i x n_k}$, $b_{il} \in R^{n_i}$ and and $\hat{C}_{il} \in R^{n_i x n_i}$.

An equivalent description of this system is given by the equations

$$S_i:\ \dot{x}_i = \sum_{k=1}^{s} A_{ik}x_k + \sum_{j=1}^{n_i} (x_{ij}C_{ij} + B_i)u_i \qquad i=1,\ldots,s$$

where $x_i = [x_{i1}\ \ x_{i2}\ \cdots\ x_{in_i}]^T$, $u_i = [u_{i1}\ \cdots\ u_{im_i}]^T$, $B_i = [b_{i1} \mid b_{i2} \mid \cdots \mid b_{im_i}]$ and $C_{ij} = [\hat{c}_{i1j} \mid \hat{c}_{i2j} \mid \cdots \mid \hat{c}_{im_ij}]^T$ $\hat{c}_{ilj}$ being the j-th column of the matrix $\hat{C}_{il}$.

It is a simple task to show that if the couple (A,B) is controllable, where

$$A = \begin{bmatrix} A_{11} & A_{12} & \cdots & A_{1s} \\ A_{21} & A_{22} & \cdots & A_{2s} \\ \vdots & \vdots & & \vdots \\ A_{s1} & A_{s2} & \cdots & A_{ss} \end{bmatrix} \qquad B = \begin{bmatrix} B_1 & 0 & \cdots & 0 \\ 0 & B_2 & \cdots & 0 \\ \vdots & \vdots & & \vdots \\ 0 & 0 & \cdots & B_s \end{bmatrix}$$

then there exists a matrix $\hat{K} = [\hat{K}_1 \mid \hat{K}_2 \mid \ \mid \hat{K}_s]$ $\hat{K}_i \in R^{m_i x n}$ such that with the centralized linear control $\hat{u} = \hat{K}x$ $\hat{u} = [\hat{u}_1 \mid \hat{u}_2 \mid \cdots \mid \hat{u}_s]$ $\hat{u}_i = \hat{K}_i x$ the equilibrium x=0 of the closed loop system

$$\dot{x}_i = \sum_{k=1}^{s} A_{ik} + \sum_{j=1}^{n_i} (x_{ij}C_{ij} + B_i)\hat{K}_i x \qquad i=1,\ldots,s$$

is exponentially stable in a region R(x) of the state space R^n [2]. However, it is not always possible to determine a linear stabilizing control if constraints on the structure of the gain matrix K are imposed. For completely decentralized control laws the matrix K must have the form

$$K=\begin{bmatrix} K_1 & 0 & \cdots & 0 \\ 0 & K_2 & \cdots & 0 \\ \vdots & \vdots & & \vdots \\ 0 & 0 & \cdots & K_s \end{bmatrix}$$

where $K_i \in R^{m_i}$. In this case even if, in addition the couples (A_{ii}, B_i) are controllable, there do not always exist linear control laws $u_i = K_i x_i$ for which the equilibrium of the closed loop system

$$\dot{x}_i = \sum_{k=1}^{s} A_{ik} x_k + \sum_{j=1}^{n_i} (x_{ij} C_{ij} + B_i) K_i x_i \qquad (S)$$

$i=1,2,\ldots,s$ is exponentially stable.

On the other hand, it is well known that it is not always possible to globally stabilize a bilinear system by a feedback control linear in the state. Taking into account this facts the following problem can be stated:

" Given system S, a positive real number β and a region

$$R(x)=\{x \in R^n : \; \|x_i\| \leq d_i \quad i=1,\ldots,s\}$$

d_i being positive real numbers, establish conditions garanteeing the existence of local linear control laws $u_i = K_i x_i$, $K_i \in R^{m_i \times m_i}$ so that

$$\|x(t,t_o,x_o)\| < \alpha \|x_o\| \exp[-\beta(t-t_o)]$$

for all $x_o \in R(x)$, $t_o \in T$, $t \geq t_o$ and for some positive real number α , $x(t,t_o,x_o)$ being the trajectory of the closed loop system (S), $T=[0,\infty)$ and $\|x\|=(x^T x)^{1/2}$."

3. STATE AGGREGATION

Let

$$\dot{\hat{x}}_i = A_{ii}\hat{x}_i + B_i u_i + \sum_{j=1}^{n_i} \hat{x}_{ij} C_{ij} u_i \qquad (\hat{S}_i)$$

be the equations describing the behaviour of the isolated bilinear systems and assume that the couples (A_{ii}, B_i) are controlable. Then for any real number $a_i > 0$ and any matrix $D_i \in R^{n_i}$ such that the couple (A_{ii}, D_i) is observable, there exists a symmetric positive definite matrix $P_i \in R^{n_i \times n_i}$ which satisfies the Riccati equation

$$P_i(A_{ii}+a_i\mathbb{1})+(A_{ii}^T+a_i\mathbb{1})P_i-2P_iB_iB_i^TP_i+D_iD_i^T=0 \quad (1)$$

Let us now associate with each isolated subsystem S_i a candidate Lyapunov function

$$v_i(\hat{x}_i)=\|P_i^{-1}\|\hat{x}_i^T P_i \hat{x}_i$$

where P_i is the positive definite matrix satisfying the Riccati equation (1). Then

$$\dot{v}_{i(\hat{S}_i)}=\|P_i^{-1}\|\hat{x}_i^T(P_iA_{ii}+A_{ii}^TP_i)\hat{x}_i+2\|P_i^{-1}\|\hat{x}_i^TP_iB_iu_i+$$

$$+2\|P_i^{-1}\|\hat{x}_i^TP_i \sum_{j=1}^{n_i}\hat{x}_{ij}C_{ij}u_i$$

where $\dot{v}_{i(\hat{S}_i)}$ denotes the total time derivative of $v_i(\hat{x}_i)$ with respect to the isolated subsystem $\hat{S}_i$.

Consider now the control laws

$$u_i=-B_i^TP_ix_i$$

Then from (1) it follows that

$$\dot{v}_{i(\hat{S}_i)}=-2a_i\|P^{-1}\|\hat{x}_i^TP_i\hat{x}_i+2\|P^{-1}\|\hat{x}_i^TP_iB_iB_i^TP_i\hat{x}_i-$$

$$-\|P_i^{-1}\|x_i^TD_iD_i^T\hat{x}_i-2\|P_i^{-1}\|\hat{x}_i^TP_iB_iB_i^TP_i\hat{x}_1+$$

$$+2\|P_i^{-1}\|\hat{x}_i^TP_i\sum_{j=1}^{n_i}\hat{x}_{ij}C_{ij}B_i^TP_i\hat{x}_i$$

or

$$\dot{v}_{i(\hat{S}_i)}=-2a_iv_i+2\|P_i^{-1}\|\hat{x}_i^TP_i\sum_{j=1}^{n_i}\hat{x}_{ij}C_{ij}P_i\hat{x}_i-$$

$$-2\|P_i^{-1}\|\hat{x}_i^TD_iD_i^T\hat{x}_i$$

$$\leq -2a_iv_i+\frac{1}{\|P_i^{-1}\|}\theta_i\mu_iv_i^{3/2}-\|P_i^{-1}\|\hat{x}_i^TD_iD_i^T\hat{x}_i$$

because as it is proved in Appendix

$$\|P_i^{-1}\|^2 x_i^TP_i\sum_{j=1}^{n_i}x_{ij}C_{ij}B_i^TP_ix_i \leq \theta_i\mu_i(x_i^TP_ix_i)^{3/2}$$

where θ_i is the condition number of the matrix P_i and

$$\mu_i=\left[\sum_{j=1}^{n_i}\max_k\left[\lambda_k\left(\frac{C_{ij}B_i^T+B_iC_{ij}^T}{2}\right)\right]^2\right]^{1/2} \qquad (2)$$

$\lambda_k(\cdot)$ being the eigenvalues of the matrix $\cdot$. For the total time derivative of $v_i(x_i)$ with respect to the interconnected system S we get

$$\dot{v}_{i(S)}=\dot{v}_{i(\hat{S})}+2\|P_i^{-1}\|x_i^TP_i\sum_{j=1}^{s}A_{ij}x_j$$

$$\leq\dot{v}_{i(\hat{S}_i)}+2\|P_i^{-1}\|\,\|x_i^TP_i\|\sum_{\substack{j=1\\ j\neq i}}^{s}\|A_{ij}\|\,\|x_j\|$$

$$\leq -2a_iv_i+2\frac{1}{\|P^{-1}\|}\theta_i\mu_iv_i^{3/2}-\|P_i^{-1}\|x_i^TD_iD_i^Tx_i+$$

$$+2\theta_iv_i^{1/2}\sum_{\substack{j=1\\ j\neq i}}^{s}a_{ij}v_j^{1/2} \qquad (3)$$

with $a_{ij}=\|A_{ij}\|$. If ρ_i denotes the maximal positive real number such that the matrix

$$\rho_i\|P_i^{-1}\|P_i-D_iD_i^T$$

is negative semidefinite, then

$$-2\|P_i^{-1}\|x_i^TD_iD_i^Tx_i \leq -2\rho_iv_i$$

and inequality (3) becomes

$$v_{i(S)}\leq -2(a_i+\rho_i)v_i+2\frac{1}{\|P_i^{-1}\|}\mu_i\theta_iv_i+2\theta_iv_i^{1/2}\sum_{\substack{j=1\\ j\neq i}}^{s}a_{ij}v_j^{1/2}$$

These inequalities may be written in the form

$$\dot{v}_{(S)} \leq h(v)$$

where

$$h(v)=\mathrm{diag}(\theta_i v_i^{1/2})\left[H+\mathrm{diag}\left(\frac{\mu_i}{\|P_i^{-1}\|}v_i^{1/2}\right)\right]\begin{bmatrix} v_1^{1/2} \\ \vdots \\ v_s^{1/2}\end{bmatrix}$$

with

$$H = \begin{bmatrix} -\dfrac{a_1+\rho_1}{\theta_1} & a_{12} & \cdots & a_{1s} \\ a_{21} & -\dfrac{a_2+\rho_2}{\theta_2} & \cdots & a_{2s} \\ \vdots & \vdots & & \vdots \\ a_{s1} & a_{s2} & \cdots & -\dfrac{a_s+\rho_s}{\theta_s} \end{bmatrix}$$

Consider now the dynamical system

$$\dot{w} = h(w) \qquad \text{(CS)}$$

The function $h(w)=[h_1(w) \;\; h_2(w) \; \ldots \; h_s(w)]^T$ is nondecreasing with respect to its off-diagonal variables, that is the functions $h_i(w_1, w_2, .., w_s)$ are nondecreasing with respect to w_j $j\neq i$. Therefore, if

$$v(x_0) \leq w_0 \qquad (4)$$

then

$$v[x(t,t_o,x_o)] \leq w(t,t_o,x_o) \qquad (5)$$

for all $t_o \in T$ and $t \geq t_o$, $w(t,t_o,x_o)$ being the solution of the comparison system CS [7]. In addition, R_+^s is an invariant set of system CS, that is $w(t,t_o,w_o) \geq 0$ for all $w_o \geq 0$, $t_o \in T$ and $t \geq t_o$ [1].

Let us assume that the equilibrium w=0 of system CS is locally exponentially stable, that is

$$\|w(t,t_o,w_o)\|_1 \leq a^* \|w_o\|_1 \exp[-\beta^*(t-t_o)] \qquad (6)$$

for all $t_o \in T$, $t \geq t_o$ and $w_o \in R(w)$,

$$R(w) = \{w \in R_+^s: \; w_i \leq w_i^* \;\; i=1,2,\ldots,s\} \qquad (7)$$

where a^* and β^* are positive real numbers and $w^* \in R_+^s$ is a vector with positive components and $\|w\|_1 = |w_1|+|w_2|+\ldots+|w_s|$. Then from (4)-(7) it follows that

$$\|v[x(t,t_o,x_o)]\|_1 \leq a^* \|v(x_o)\|_1 \exp[-\beta^*(t-t_o)] \quad (8)$$

for all $t_o \in T$, $t \geq t_o$ and $v(x_o) \in R(w)$.
Finally, since

$$\|x_i\|^2 \leq \|P_i^{-1}\| x_i^T P_i x_i \leq \theta_i^2 \|x_i\|^2$$

$\|x\|$ being the Euclidean norm, from (7) and (8) it follows that

$$\|x(t,t_o,x_o)\| \leq a\|x_o\| \exp[-\frac{\beta^*}{2}(t-t_o)]$$

for all $t_o \in T$, $t \geq t_o$ and $x_o \in R(x)$ where

$$R(x)=\{x \in R^n: \|x_i\| \leq \frac{w_i^{*\frac{1}{2}}}{\theta_i} \quad i=1,2,\ldots,s\}$$

and

$$\alpha = \alpha^{*1/2} \max_i(\theta_i)$$

From these results we conclude that the stability analysis problem of the closed loop bilinear system is reduced to an analogous problem of the aggregated dynamical system CS. Therefore setting

$$w_i^* = \theta_i^2 d_i^2 \quad i=1,2,\ldots,s$$

the initial problem is reduced to the determination of conditions of exponential stability of the equilibrium w=0 of system CS in the region

$$R(w)=\{w \in R_+^s: \; w_i \leq \theta_i^2 d_i^2 \quad i=1,2,\ldots,s\}$$

and with exponential stability degree $\beta^*=2\beta$.

4. CONDITIONS OF DECENTRALIZED STABILIZATION

As it has been noted the function h(w) of system CS is non decreasing with respect to its off-diagonal variables. So R_+^s is an invariant set of system CS. Therefore, we shall be interested in the stability properties of the equilibrium w 0 of system CS in R_+^s. A condition of exponential stability for this class of systems is given in the following theorem:

Theorem 1

If there exist a vector $w^* \in R_+^s$ with positive components and two positive real numbers β^* and r^* such that

$$h(rw^*) \leq -r\beta^* w^* \qquad (10)$$

for all $r \in [0,r^*)$, then the equilibrium w=0 of system CS is exponentially stable in R_+^s and

$$\|w(t,t_o,x_o)\|_1 \leq \|w_o\|_1 \exp[-\beta^*(t-t_o)]$$

for all $t_o \in T$, $t \geq t_o$ and $w_o \in R$ (w) where

$$R\,(w)=\{w \in R_+^s: \quad w \leq r^* w^*\}$$

Let us apply this stability condition to system CS. For system CS condition (10) becomes

$$2r\,\mathrm{diag}(\theta_i w_i^{*1/2})\left[H+r^{1/2}\mathrm{diag}\left(\frac{\mu_i}{\|P_i^{-1}\|}w_i^{*1/2}\right)\right]\begin{bmatrix} w_1^{*1/2} \\ \vdots \\ w_s^{*1/2}\end{bmatrix} \leq -r\beta^* \begin{bmatrix} w_1^* \\ \vdots \\ w_s^* \end{bmatrix} \qquad (11)$$

or equivalently

$$2\,\mathrm{diag}(\theta_i)\left[H+r^{1/2}\mathrm{diag}\left(\frac{\mu_i}{\|P_i^{-1}\|}w_i^{*1/2}\right)\right]\begin{bmatrix} w_1^{*1/2} \\ \vdots \\ w_s^{*1/2}\end{bmatrix} \leq -\beta^* \begin{bmatrix} w_1^{*1/2} \\ \vdots \\ w_s^{*1/2}\end{bmatrix}$$

where

$$\mathrm{diag}\left(\frac{\mu_i}{\|P_i^{-1}\|}w_i^*\right) \triangleq \mathrm{diag}\left(\frac{\mu_1}{\|P_1^{-1}\|}w_1^*, \ldots, \frac{\mu_s}{\|P_s^{-1}\|}w_s^*\right)$$

$$\mathrm{diag}(\theta_i) \triangleq \mathrm{diag}(\theta_1, \ldots, \theta_s)$$

and

$$H=\begin{bmatrix} -\frac{a_1+\rho_1}{\theta_1} & a_{12} & \cdots & a_{1s} \\ a_{21} & -\frac{a_2+\rho_2}{\theta_2} & \cdots & a_{2s} \\ \vdots & \vdots & & \vdots \\ a_{s1} & a_{s2} & \cdots & -\frac{a_s+\rho_s}{\theta_s} \end{bmatrix}$$

It is obvious that for the existence of a $\beta^*>0$ and a vector $w^*\in R_+^s$ with positive components satisfying inequality (11) for r belonging to an interval $[0,r^*]$, $r^*>0$, it is necessary and sufficient that there exist a vector $w^*\in R_+^s$ with positive components such that

$$H\begin{bmatrix} w_1^{*1/2} \\ \vdots \\ w_s^{*1/2} \end{bmatrix} < 0 \tag{12}$$

Since the off-diagonal elements of the matrix H are non negative, condition (12) is equivalent to Kotelyanski-Sevastianov conditions:

$$h_{11}<0,\ \det\begin{bmatrix} h_{11} & h_{12} \\ h_{21} & h_{22} \end{bmatrix} > 0, \ldots, (-1)^s \det H < 0$$

Therefore

Theorem 2.

If there exist matrices $D_i\in R^{n_i\times n_i}$ and positive real numbers a_i $i=1,2,\ldots,s$ such that (A_{ii},D_i) are observable and

$$-\frac{a_1+\rho_1}{\theta_1}<0,\ \det\begin{bmatrix} -\frac{a_1+\rho_1}{\theta_1} & a_{12} \\ a_{21} & -\frac{a_2+\rho_2}{\theta_2} \end{bmatrix} > 0, \ldots, (-1)^s \det H< 0$$

where $a_{ij}=\|A_{ij}\|_2$, ρ_i are the maximal positive real numbers for which the matrices

$$\rho_i^2\|P_i^{-1}\|P_i - D_iD_i^T \tag{13}$$

are negative semidefinite and θ_i are the condition numbers of the positive definite matrices P_i satisfying the Riccati equations

$$P_i(A_{ii}+a_i\mathbb{1})+(A_{ii}^T+a_i\mathbb{1})P_i-2P_iB_iB_i^TP_i+D_iD_i^T=0 \tag{14}$$

then the bilinear system S is decentraly stabized with the linear feedback controls

$$u_i=-B_i^TP_ix_i \tag{15}$$

The conditions of this theorem garantee the existence of a region of exponential stability of system S with the controls given by (15). We shall establish a condition for

$$R(x)=\{x\in R^n:\ \|x_i\|\leq d_i \quad i=1,2,\ldots,s\}$$

to be a region of exponential stability with exponential stability degree equal to β . As it has been proved in section 3 this is garanteed if the equilibrium w=0 of system CS is exponentially stable in the region

$$R(w)=\{w\in R_+^s:\ w_i\leq \theta_i^{-2}d_i^2 \quad i=1,2,\ldots,s\}$$

and with exponential stability degree $\beta = 2\beta$. According to Theorem this is true if

$$h(r\theta_1^2d_1^2,\ldots,r\theta_s^2d_s^2)\leq -2r\beta\begin{bmatrix}\theta_1^2d_1^2\\ \vdots \\ \theta_s^2d_s^2\end{bmatrix}$$

for all $r\in[0,1]$, or equivalently, if

$$\mathrm{diag}(\theta_i^2d_i)\left[H+\mathrm{diag}\left(\frac{\mu_i}{\|P_i^{-1}\|}\theta_id_i\right)\right]\begin{bmatrix}\theta_1d_1\\ \vdots \\ \theta_sd_s\end{bmatrix}\leq -\beta\begin{bmatrix}\theta_1^2d_1^2\\ \\ \theta_s^2d_s^2\end{bmatrix}$$

This condition is equivalent to the inequalities

$$-(a_i+\rho_i)\theta_id_i+\mu_i\|P_i\|\theta_id_i^2+\sum_{\substack{j=1\\ j\neq i}}^{s} a_{ij}\theta_jd_j\leq -\beta d_i \tag{16}$$

$i=1,2,\ldots,s$. Therefore

Theorem 3

If there exist matrices $D_i\in R^{n_i\times n_i}$ and positive real numbers a_i $i=1,2,\ldots,s$ such that (A_{ii},D_i) are observable and

$$-(a_i+\rho_i)\theta_id_i+\mu_i\|P_i\|\theta_id_i^2+\sum_{\substack{j=1\\ j\neq i}}^{s} a_{ij}\theta_jd_j\leq -\beta d_i$$

where μ_i are given by (2), ρ_i are given by (13) and θ_i are the condition numbers of the positive definite matrices satisfying the Riccati equations (14), then with the local control laws given by (15) the equilibrium x=0 of the bilinear system S is exponentially stable and

$$\|x(t,t_o,x_o)\|\leq\alpha\|x_o\|\exp[-\beta(t-t_o)]$$

for all $t_o \in T$, $t > t_o$ and $x_o \in R(x)$ where

$$R(x) = \{ x \in R^n : \ \|x_i\| < d_i \quad i=1,2,\dots,s \}$$

and

$$\alpha = \max_i (\theta_i)$$

Based on the results stated in Theorems 1, 2 and 3 we can develop the following approach for the decentralized stabilization and the estimation of the stability region of bilinear dynamical systems.

First, by applying the result stated in Theorem 2 we examine whether the system is stabilizable by local feedback controls linear in state. The problem consists in the determination of matrices D_i and positive real numbers a_i for the matrix H^1 to satisfy the Kotelyansky-Sevastinov conditions. Since the off-diagonal elements of the matrix H are nonnegative and do not depent on the choice of D_i and a_i we must choose D_i and a_i for $\frac{a_i+\rho_i}{\theta_i}$ to be minimized. An approach for solving this matrix minimization problem has been developed by J. C. Geromel [3]. If for the parameters a_i, ρ_i and θ_i determined in this way the matrix H^1 satisfies the Kotelyansky-Sevastianov conditions, then the bilinear system is decentrally stabilizable with the control laws given by (15).

For the estimation of the stability region we apply the criterion established in Theorem 1: The problem consists in the determination of positive real numbers $d_1, d_2, \dots, d_s$ and r^* for

$$h_i(r\theta_1^2 d_1^2,\ r\theta_2^2 d_2^2, \dots, r\theta_s^2 d_s^2) \quad i=1,2,\dots,s \qquad (17)$$

to be negative definite in r in the interval $[0,r^*)$. It can be easily proved that if d_i are chosen so $[\theta_1^2 d_1^2 \ \ \theta_2^2 d_2^2 \ \dots \ \theta_s^2 d_s^2]^T$ to be the eigenvector of the matrix H associated with the maximal eigenvalue of H, then there always exist a $r^*>0$ such that (17) are negative definite in $[0,r^*)$. The stability region is given by the following expression:

$$R(x) = \{ x \in R^n : \ \|x_i\| \leqslant r^{*\frac{1}{2}} d_i \quad i=1,\dots,s \}$$

5. CONCLUSION

The problem of designing decentrally stabilizing control of bilinear dynamical systems has been studied. First, conditions garanteeing the existence of decentrally stabilizing feedback controls linear in state have been established. These conditions have been obtained by using quadratic aggregation function for the construction of a lower order nonlinear dynamical system the stability properties of which imply analogous stability properties for the bilinear system. The stability of this auxiliary dynamical system provides, in addition, sufficient conditions for the existence of local controls linear in state garanteeing the exponential stability in a prespecified stability region and with a given stability degree. Finally, the approach used for the determination of these conditions provides in addition the gain matrices of the controls satisfying the requirements of the coresponding problems.

6. REFERENCES

1 Bitsoris, G., Stability analysis of nonlinear systems, Int. J. Control, 3 (1983), 699-711.

2 Derese, I. and Noldus, E., Design of feedback laws for bilinear systems, Int. J. Control, 2(1980), 219-237.

3. Geromel, J.C., Sur un problême d'optimisation paramétrique de l'équation matricielle de Lyapunov, C. R. Acad. Sciences, 286(1978), 843-846.

4. Gutman, P., Stabilizing controllers for bilinear systems, IEEE Trans. Aut. Control, 4(1981), 917-922.

5. Longchamp, R., Stable feedback control of bilinear systems, IEEE Trans. Aut. Control, 2(1980), 302-306.

6. Longchamp, R., Controller design for bilinear systems, IEEE trans. Aut. Control, 3(1980), 547-549.

7. Slemrod, M., Stabilization of bilinear control systems with applications to nonconservative problems in elasticity, SIAM J. Control and Optim., 16(1978), 131-141.

8. Wazewskii, T., Systêmes des équations te ees inégalités differentielles ordinaires aux deuxiêmes membres monotones et leurs applications, Ann. Soc. Polon. Math., 23(1950), 112-166.

APPENDIX

<u>Proposition:</u>

Let $x \in R^n$, $x\ [x_1 \ x_2 \ \dots \ x_n]^T$, $B \in R^{nxm}$, $C_j \in R^{nxm}$ $j=1,2,\dots,n$ and P a positive definite symmetric matrix $P \in R^{nxn}$. Then

$$\left|\|P^{-1}\|^2 x^T P \cdot \sum_{j=1} x_j C_j B^T P x\right| \leqslant \theta\mu (x^T P x)^{3/2} \qquad (18)$$

where θ is the condition number of the marrix P and

$$\mu = \left[\sum_{j=1}^{n} \max_k \left[\lambda_k \left(\frac{C_j B^T + B C_J^T}{2} \right) \right]^2 \right]^{1/2} \qquad (19)$$

λ_k being the aigenvalues of the matrix in parantheses.

Proof:

$$\|P^{-1}\|^2 x^T P \sum_{j=1}^{n} x_j C_j B^T P x = \|P^{-1}\|^2 \sum_{j=1}^{n} x_j x^T P C_j B^T P x =$$

$$\|P^{-1}\|^{2}\begin{bmatrix}x_1 & x_2 \dots & x_n\end{bmatrix}\begin{bmatrix}x^TPC_1B^TPx\\ x^TPC_2B^TPx\\ \vdots\\ x^TPC_nB^TPx\end{bmatrix} \tag{20}$$

Therefore

$$\left|x^TP\sum_{j=1}^{n}x_jC_jB^TPx\right|\leqslant\|x\|\left[\sum_{j=1}^{n}(x^TPC_jB^TPx)^2\right]^{1/2} \tag{21}$$

Since

$$(x^TPC_jB^TPx)^2<\|Px\|^4\max\left[\lambda_k\left(\frac{C_jB^T+BC_j}{2}\right)\right]^2$$

from (20) and (21) it follows that

$$\|P^{-1}\|^2x^TP\sum_{j=1}^{n}x_jC_jB^TPx<\|P^{-1}\|^2\|Px\|^2\|x\|\,\mu \tag{22}$$

where μ is given by (19).

On the other hand

$$\|Px\|\leqslant\|P\|^{\frac{1}{2}}(x^TPx)^{\frac{1}{2}} \tag{23}$$

$$\|x\|^2\leqslant\|P^{-1}\|x^TPx\leqslant\theta\|x\|^2 \tag{24}$$

By combining inequalities (23), (24) with (22) we obtain relation (18).

DIGITAL TECHNIQUES in Simulation, Communication and Control
Spyros G. Tzafestas (editor)
Elsevier Science Publishers B.V. (North-Holland) © IMACS, 1985

REAL-TIME MULTITASK SYSTEMS AND COORDINATED CONTROL

Michel MARITON, Michel DROUIN

Laboratoire des Signaux et Systèmes
C.N.R.S. - E.S.E.
Plateau du Moulon
91190 Gif sur Yvette, France.

Abstract : Though decomposition coordination techniques appeared in the context of complex systems, it can be said now that they have not solved the problem for on-line control. A new method is presented here that was designed with real time applications in mind. One of these applications is studied in this communication : centralized-hierarchical control of a synchronous machine. It is shown how hierarchical concepts correspond to the structure of modern real-time multitask software.

INTRODUCTION

From a theoretical research point of view, the control of technological processes has been a quickly changing and improving subject for years. Starting from the now classical LQG regulator, techniques evolved to cope with more difficult processes, the so-called "complex processes". For these systems the basic optimization problem is difficult to solve. The reason can be non-linearity of the equations, or their dimensionality, as for large-scale models. A new hierarchical method was proposed recently [1] to design controller for "complex problems". Though it is based on decomposition coordination ideas, the approach is distinct from the techniques that followed the work of Mesarovic [2]. The main advantage of this new method is its suitability for on-line implementation.

The purpose of this communication is to study such an implementation, and, in particular, to emphasize the similarity between hierarchy and coordination concepts and the structure of modern multitask microprocessor systems.

In the first section, the principle of the method will be outlined for linear and non-linear problems. The second section will explain the use of real time software tools to organize a hierarchical calculus. The control of a synchronous machine will illustrate these results in the last section.

I. A HIERARCHICAL CONTROL METHOD

In this communication, attention is restricted to processes with limited spatial extansion, ie where all the available information can be processed by a single computer, without long communication channels. The complementary case, when the process is geographically distributed, will be treated in a companion communication [3].

For the sake of clarity, we first recall the principle of the method for the linear problem, and then turn to the nonlinear case.

1.1 Linear Problem

The idea used here is that to solve a complex problem, a possible scheme is to decompose the optimization in two parts. The first one will consist of a closed loop feedback and the second one of a coordination parameter. The feedback is crucial for on-line applications since it ensures that the process will be controlled, should it be suboptimally, even if the coordination term is not available.

Consider a linear discrete time process :

$$x_{k+1} = Ax_k + Bu_k \tag{1}$$

and a quadratic criterion

$$J = \frac{1}{2} \sum_{k=o}^{K} x_{k+1}^T Qx_{k+1} + u_k^T Ru_k \tag{2}$$

with usual assumptions $\begin{cases} Q \geq 0, \ R>0 \\ (\bar{A},B) \text{ commandable} \end{cases}$

The method considers (K+1) fictituous agents, acting at each instant k, on the instantaneous part of the criterion J_k :

$$J_k = \frac{1}{2} x_{k+1}^T Qx_{k+1} + \frac{1}{2} u_k^T Ru_k \tag{3}$$

The complement $\bar{J}_k$ is affected to the coordinator

$$\bar{J}_k = \frac{1}{2} \sum_{\ell \neq k} x_{k+1}^T Qx_{k+1} + u_k^T Ru_k \tag{4}$$

The subcriterion J_k defines the task of the lower level of the hierarchy at instant k, to achieve optimality a coordinating parameter must be added to minimize the future cost function $\bar{J}_k$.

The optimal control

$$u_k^* = \text{Arg} \min_{u_k} J \tag{5}$$

thus satisfies

$$\frac{\partial J_k}{\partial u_k} + \frac{\partial \bar{J}_k}{\partial u_k} = 0 \tag{6}$$

The parameterization of the second term gives the coordination ρ_k

$$\rho_k = \frac{\partial \bar{J}_k}{\partial u_k} \tag{7}$$

A direct derivation [1] then gives the optimal control

$$u_k^* = \Gamma\, x_k^* + \theta_k^* \tag{8}$$

$$\text{with } \Gamma = -\,(R+B^T QB)^{-1}\, B^T QA \tag{9}$$

$$\theta_k^* = -\,(R+B^T QB)^{-1}\, \rho_k^* \tag{10}$$

The key point is the structure of the law (8) : it includes a feedback (Γx) and a vector of coordinating parameters. Such a structure is said composite, one part being closed-loop (Γx), the other open-loop (θ). This is an advantage of the method compared with other approaches, where the control is in a closed loop form only under severe limitations (linear problems), and is totally in a open-loop form in the general case.

It can be shown [1] that the coordination vector θ_k satisfies the recurrence equations (11). From these expressions it will be actualized on-line from the real process measurements.

$$\rho_k^* = B^T w_k^*$$

$$\text{with } \begin{cases} w_{k-1} = \tilde{A}^T w_k + \Gamma^T R\, u_k + \tilde{A}^T Qx_{k+1} \\ x_{k+1} = \tilde{A}\, x_k + B\theta_k \end{cases} \tag{11}$$

for $\tilde{A} = A + B\Gamma$ and $w_K = 0,\ x_{k=o} = x_o$

1.2 Non-linear problem

Most results for the nonlinear problem [4,5] require computations that are difficult off-line and cannot be applied on-line even for small systems. Here the decomposition $J_k/\bar{J}_k$ is slightly modified to obtain two level solutions adapted for on-line implementation. Once again linear stationary feedbacks are sought at the first level.

Consider a nonlinear discrete time process

$$x_{k+1} = f(x_k,\ u_k) \tag{12}$$

with cost function (2).

The instantaneous criterion J_k is modified in

$$J_k = x_{k+1}^T\, Qx_k + 1/2\ u_k^T\, Ru_k \tag{13}$$

The optimality condition (6) then becomes

$$Ru_k + \frac{\partial x_{k+1}^T}{\partial u_k}\, Qx_k + \rho_k = 0 \tag{14}$$

In the linear case, the expression $\frac{\partial x_{k+1}}{\partial u_k}$, that will be referred to as the "influence matrix", was directly computed from (1)

$$\frac{\partial x_{k+1}}{\partial u_k} = B \tag{15}$$

If the process is linear in u, it will now depend on x

$$\frac{\partial x_{k+1}}{\partial u_k} = G(x_k) \tag{16}$$

Substituting (17) in (14) gives a law of the form

$$u_k = \Gamma(x_k).x_k + \theta_k \tag{17}$$

The feedback matrix Γ is dependant on x. As it is usual in the state space approach, one would prefer a constant feedback. It can be obtained by splitting the influence matrix G in two parts

$$G = G_d + G_i(x_k) \tag{18}$$

The first part G_d, independant on x, will be termed the direct influence, where $G_i(x_k)$ contains the indirect influence of non-linearities.

The control (17) is then rewritten as

$$u_k = \Gamma\, x_k + \varphi k$$

The lower level task will be to compute the feedback Γx_k and the upper level will take charge of the modified coordination φ_k. The expressions are :

$$\Gamma = -R^{-1}\, G_d^T\, Q$$

$$\varphi_k = \theta_k - R^{-1}\, G_i^T(x_k)Q$$

The burden of nonlinear calculus ($G_i = G_i(x_k)$) is reported at the upper level and the lower level consists of the desired constant feedback. Procedures have been developped to shape arbitrary structures to this law (for example output feedback) and to minimize the overall importance of the coordinating term φ_k [6]

II. REAL TIME MULTITASK SOFTWARES

In this section, vocabulary will be the technical vacabulary of the software used on the application (see Section III), though comments clearly apply to other softwares.

2.1 Process control requirements :

The characteristic of process control applications, as opposed to off-line computing, is the occurence of asynchronous events in the real world. This is for example the case in digital control when the digitalizer generates an interrupt, at every discrete time control interval, whatever may be the current state of the processor.

In this context real time softwares provide an efficient tool to easily write down applications. For the control algorithm described in Section I, two tasks were defined. The lower level task, that computes the feedback, is to be activated immediatly after the digitalizer interrupt, just to keep the process under control. It will be shown in 2.4 how real time software can do this with "interrupt processing". A second bridge between decomposition-coordination concepts and real time programming, is then the notion of preemptive priority based scheduling. Paragraph 2.4 will explain how this allows the user to organize its computing power in a hierarchy that reproduces the control hierarchy.

Before these specific features of real-time softwares are described, it is needed to introduce a few basic notions, this is done in paragraphs 2.2 and 2.3.

2.2 Task concept

A task is the fundamental entity of any application. It consists of a set of machine code, it is characterized by its state (active, suspended, asleep) and a descriptor vector (status, processor state ...). Real time programming encounters specific difficulties that are briefly summerized here. The first difference with other types of programming is the necessity to detect events that occur outside the computer, in the real world. These events are asynchronous, and, from the computer point of view, occur at random intervals. Given its limited computing power, the system must react to this events by scheduling its actions to process first the tasks that are most important. This introduces the necessity of some priority concept and measure.

The interest of multitasking is then clear : instead of writing a single program to react to N purposes, one will prefer to write N programs in charge of a single purpose.

The use of tasks thus reduces the complexity of the generated code. This is not negligible for a real time application that is bound to be complex. Moreover tasks will induce very naturally a modular up-building of the application, so that future maintenance of the modular structure will be much easier.

At this point the first bridge with decomposition-coordination control concepts becomes obvious. Two tasks will be generated, one for each level of the hierarchical structure. The lower task, at each control period, computes the feedback loop and the control actually applied to the process, in our application it was activated by the digitalizer interrupt. The upper task iteratively approximates the optimal coordinating parameter.

2.3. System primitives :

For a given set of tasks, it is the real time monitor function to manage them. To do this, the software provides tools that are named system primitives. To gain access to these primitives, the application will include system calls that connect it with the software nucleus. Figure 1 illustrates the layered structure of the operating system

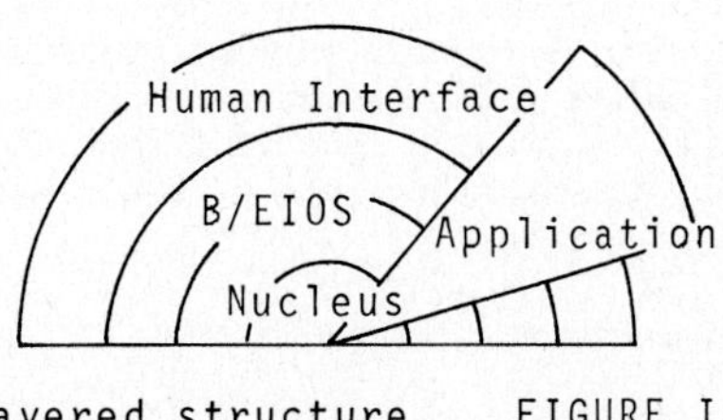

Layered structure FIGURE I

and Figure 2 a typical application buildup.

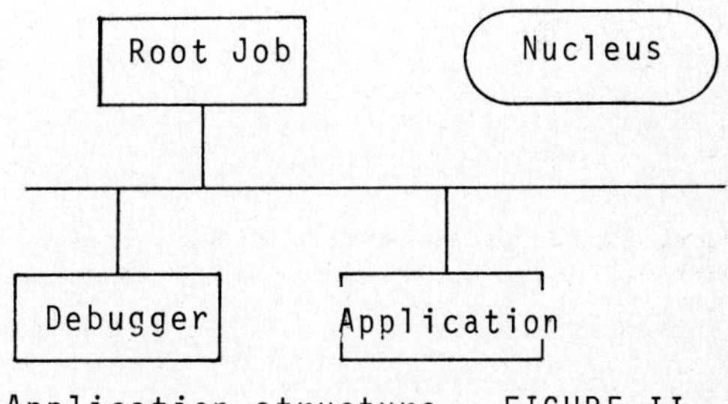

Application structure FIGURE II

For example the task state will be transformed by nucleus calls, as illustrated an Figure 3.

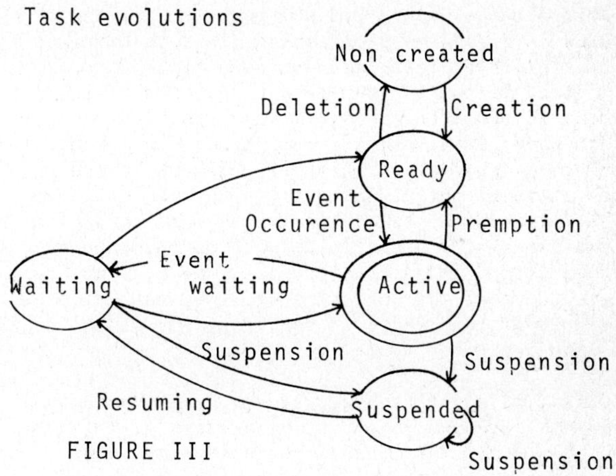

FIGURE III

2.4 Communications and synchronization

The two main problems to solve in a process control application are the communication between tasks,and the synchronisation with respect to the real world time scale.

The first problem is solved by segments and semaphores. A segment is a memory area where tasks can exchange information. This information can either be data, either service messages. Semaphores provide a mutual exclusion function, or elementary synchronisation, that avoid the use of invalid data by a task. The semaphore is a signalling object that must be turned on by the sending task, before the receiving task can read the corresponding exchange area. Figure 4 illustrates this sequence.

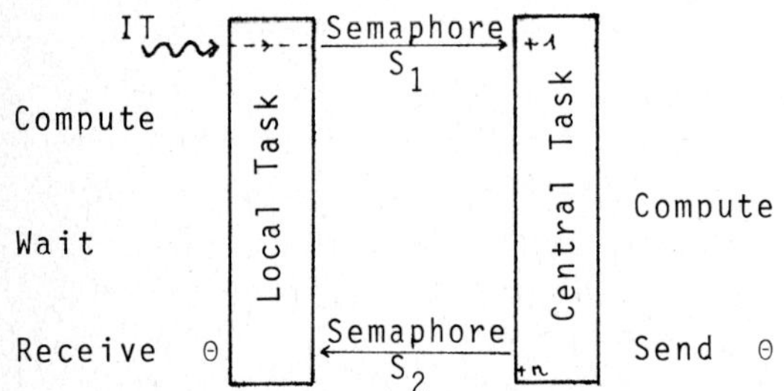

Tasks synchronization FIGURE IV

In general the upper level task will require several periods. So that when θ^*_k is available, the process state is x_{k+n} with $n \geq 0$. The first value of the coordination trajectory (θ^*_k, θ^*_{k+1}, ..., θ^*_{k+n-1}) must therefore be given up, and only θ^*_{k+n}, θ^*_{k+n+1} ... applied. Semaphores S_1 and S_2 keep this count, and transfer it, in order to calculate the shift on θ trajectory.

It was explained in 2.2 why tasks are asynchronous in real time programming. This is crucial to exploit at best, without dead times caused by polling loops ..., the computing power of the machine. Nonetheless synchronisation can be needed under particular circumstances. In a process control application this will clearly be the case at each control interval, since it was shown in 2.1 that the lower level task must be activated immediatly. This is done by defining this task as an "interrupt processed" task, where the occurence of the real time clock pulse activates the lower task whatever the processor state might be.

Premptive priority-based sheduling gives the means to realize the control hierarchy. This facility activates a higher priority task when it becomes ready to run, even if a lower priority task is currently running. Of course the context is saved, and the suspended task will be resumed later, according to the priority hierarchy. As opposed to time sharing systems where the CPU time is sliced between users, this preemptive scheduling characterizes real-time systems.

III. APPLICATION

To describe the application built in our laboratory, it becomes necessary to name the material used. However it is believed that results could be obtained in a similar way with other machines.

The results reported here were tested on a 86/3XX system under iRMX86 operating system (trade marks of Intel Corporation).

The process to be controlled was a synchronous machine connected to an infinite bus. Short circuits on the bus provided transient excitations and the controller was designed to take back the output voltage and frequency to their nominal values. Figure 5 illustrates the studied problem

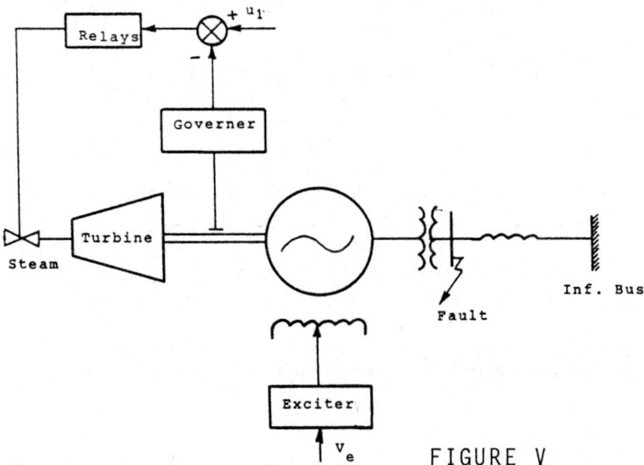

FIGURE V

The nonlinear model of the machine was taken from Singh [7]

$$(S)\quad \begin{aligned} \dot{x}_1 &= x_2 \\ \dot{x}_2 &= B_1 - A_1x_2 - A_2x_3\sin x_1 - B_2/2 \sin 2 x_1 \\ \dot{x}_3 &= u - c_1 x_3 + c_2 \cos x_1 \end{aligned}$$

with x_1 the rotor angle
x_2 the speed deviation
x_3 the field flux linkage

In a first series of measures, (S) was linearized around its steady state regime, and discretized to get the usual recurrence equation

$$x_{k+1} = F x_k + H u_k$$

with $x_k \in \mathbb{R}^3$, $u_k \in \mathbb{R}$ and F, H matrices of suitable dimensions.

Figure 6 presents the principle of the application on a 86/3XX target system.

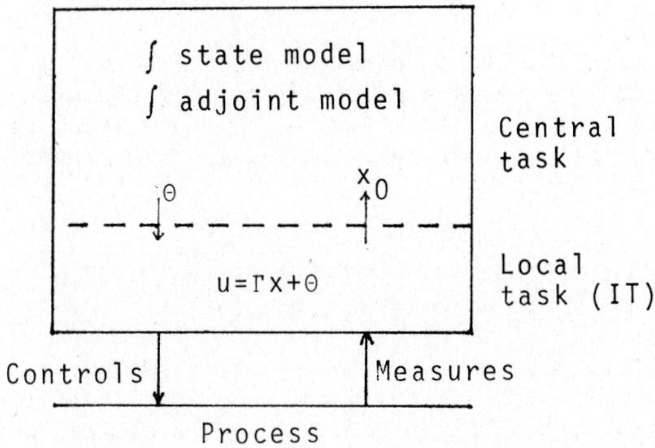

FIGURE VI

A more complete account of the obtained results is given in [8]. Figure 7 shows the influence of the upper level on the process behavior and compares it with the open-loop trajectory.

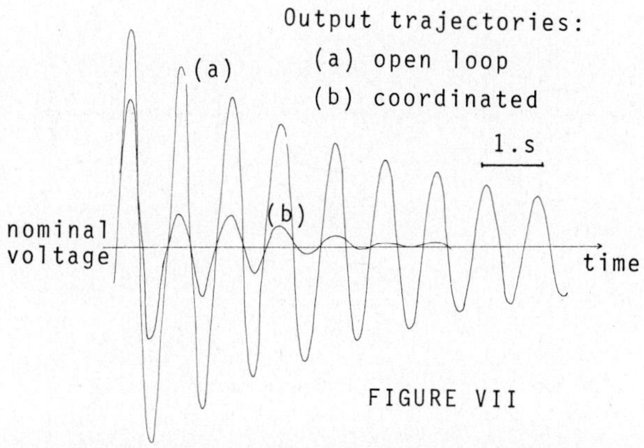

FIGURE VII

Though convergence of the upper level problem required eight iterations, it was possible to complete it in one control interval (250 ms). This prove that the optimal control can be computed in one period even for fast processes. However the process was here simple (the state dimension was 3 and the time span 20), to confirm this conclusion, larger applications will be reported soon. It must be noted anyway that a few control periods delay can be tolerated if it is considered in the control computation. It was shown how semaphores can do this.

CONCLUSION

This communication has outlined the principle of a new hierarchical control method. From a practical point of view, it was striking to note that hierarchy and coordination concepts come very close to the structure of real-time multitask operating systems.

It is this similarity that facilitates the implementation of the algorithm on a realistic problem : the on-line control of a synchronous machine excited by transient short-circuits on its bus line.

For this application, the dynamic of the process induced a control period of 250 ms. Only a fraction of this interval was used by the described control tasks. Building up on the functionning tasks, it is thus possible to define new hierarchical levels, organizing them on the basis of their task-priorities. The next step will be to add first an initial state observer (initial state was supposed measurable in Section 3) and second an adaptation level to react to structural perturbations of the system, or functionning point variations of a non-linear process. Figure 8 gives the principle of this prospective scheme.

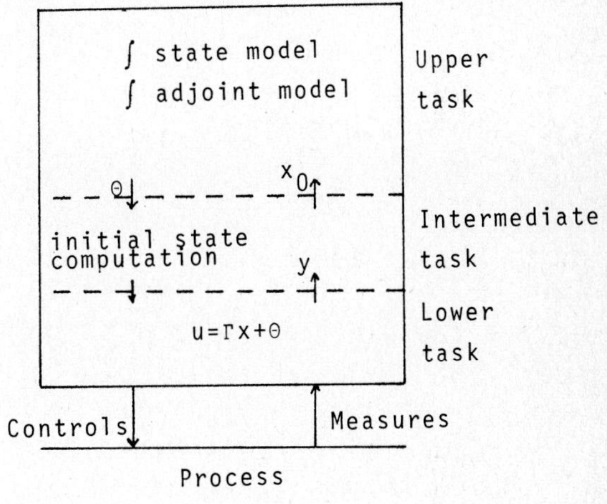

REFERENCES

[1] M. DROUIN, P. BERTRAND, "A new coordination structure for on-line control of complex process", Large Scale Systems 3, 1982, pp.147-157.

[2] M.D. MESAROVIC, D. MACKO, Y. TAKAHARA, "Theory of hierarchical multilevel systems", Academic Press, New York, 1970.

[3] M. MARITON, M. DROUIN, G. DIB, "On the use of a local area network in a microprocessor control structure", these Proceedings.

[4] E.G. AL'BREKHT, "On the optimal stabilization of non-linear systems", J. of Applied Math. and Mech., Vol. 25, N° 5, 1962, pp. 1254-1266.

[5] D.L. LUKES, "Optimal regulation of non-linear dynamical systems", SIAM J. Control, Vol. 7, N° 1, 1969, pp. 75-100.

[6] M. DROUIN, "Elaboration de nouvelles structures de commande des processus complexes", Thèse d'Etat, Université de Paris-Sud, Orsay 1981.

[7] M.G. SINGH, A. TITLI, "Systems : decomposition, optimisation and control", Pergamon Press, London, 1978.

[8] M. MARITON, "Contribution à la commande hiérarchisée des processus complexes. Coordination et contraintes de structure", Thèse 3ème Cycle, Université de Paris-Sud, Orsay 1984.

DIGITAL TECHNIQUES in Simulation, Communication and Control
Spyros G. Tzafestas (editor)
Elsevier Science Publishers B.V. (North-Holland) © IMACS, 1985

OPEN LOOP DEADBEAT CONTROL OF MULTIDIMENSIONAL SYSTEMS

S.G.Tzafestas
Control Systems Laboratory
Electrical Engineering Dept.
University of Patras
Patras, Greece

N. J. Theodorou
Hellenic Air Force Technology
Research Center (KETA)
Delta Falirou, Paleo Faliro
Athens, Greece

For a given linear, shift-invariant, single-input single-output (SISO), m-D discrete system, with real constant coefficients, an input sequence is specified such that the system achieves deadbeat behaviour. This means that the system output reaches a steady value after a minimum number of steps in the space domain and remains at that value thereafter. In the present paper this steady value is chosen to be zero. No feedback control is applied and the appropriate input sequence, leading to deadbeat response is found by pure algebraic methodology.

1. INTRODUCTION

In the present paper linear, shift invariant, SISO, m-Dimensional (m-D), discrete systems, with real constant coefficients are examined. Although some work has been done concerning the deadbeat control of 1-D systems, there are very few results for the case of multidimensional systems. Kaczorek [1] has examined a kind of deadbeat behaviour in 2-D systems, in the sense that the output deviation from a reference input and the input vanish after a minimal 2-D space interval. Tzafestas and Theodorou [2] developed a deadbeat controller using output (for m-D systems) and state feedback (for 2-D systems), which results in a steady output, after a minimal space interval, and for an appropriate input sequence. A comparison of the above multidimensional feedback control methods may be found in [2].

The present work involves an open loop deadbeat control method for m-D systems which may be viewed as an extension of the work of Rao and Janakiraman [3] for 1-D systems. Here, the deadbeat behaviour of a given system has the following meaning: Specify an input sequence, that vanishes after a minimum number of steps in the space domain, such that the system output also vanishes after a minimum-but possibly different from the previous-number of steps in the space domain.

The paper is organized as follows: in Sec. II the minimum space interval of the unknown input sequence is specified (beyond this space interval the input is zero), in Sec. III an appropriate input sequence is found within the above mentioned space interval, such that the output reaches zero within a possibly different but minimum space interval, and in Sec. IV an example illustrates the validity of the proposed method.

2. MINIMUM INPUT SPACE INTERVAL

A linear, shift-invariant, SISO, m-D, discrete system, with real constant coefficients can be represented by its difference equation:

$$\sum_{i_1=0}^{N_1}\cdots\sum_{i_m=0}^{N_m} a_{i_1,\ldots,i_m} y(n_1-i_1,\ldots,n_m-i_m) = \sum_{i_1=0}^{K_1}\cdots\sum_{i_m=0}^{K_m} b_{i_1,\ldots,i_m} u(n_1-i_1,\ldots,n_m-i_m) \tag{1}$$

$$a_{0,\ldots,0}=1,\quad (K_1,\ldots,K_m)\le(N_1,\ldots,N_m) \tag{1a}$$

where u is the input and y is the output of the system. The deadbeat control problem to be examined in the present paper is the following: Specify an input sequence $u(n_1,\ldots,n_m)$ of minimum duration, that is

$$u(n_1,\ldots,n_m) \text{ for } (0,\ldots,0)\le(n_1,\ldots,n_m) < (\ell_1,\ldots,\ell_m)$$

$$u(n_1,\ldots,n_m)=0 \text{ for } (n_1,\ldots,n_m)\ge(\ell_1,\ldots,\ell_m) \tag{2}$$

such that the output $y(n_1,\ldots,n_m)$ of this system reaches zero after a minimum number of steps in the space domain and remains zero thereafter.

According to (1), the output $y(n_1,\ldots,n_m)$ depends on previous output $y(n_1-i_1,\ldots,n_m-i_m)$ and inputs $u(n_1-i_1,\ldots,n_m-i_m)$ which cover an m-D space interval $(N_1,\ldots,N_m)$. Hence, if one starts with an input sequence (2) and some initial conditions, say

$y(-j_1,...,-j_m)$
for $(0,...,0)<(j_1,...,j_m)\leq(N_1,...,N_m)$ (3)

then he may calculate $y(0,...,0)$, $y(1,0,...,0)$, etc., successively. In this way the initial conditions (3) are taken into account when the output reaches the point $(N_1,...,N_m)$, but not before that. Now, if the output $y(n_1,...,n_m)$ is restricted to be zero in the following interval:

$$y(n_1,...,n_m)=0 \text{ for } (\ell_1,...,\ell_m)\leq(n_1,...,n_m)<(N_1\ell_1,...,N_m+\ell_m) \quad (4)$$

Then all the next outputs $y(n_1,...,n_m)$ will be

$$y(n_1,...,n_m)=0 \text{ for } (N_1\ell_1,...,N_m+\ell_1,...,N_m+\ell_m)\leq(n_1,...,n_m) \quad (5)$$

This is because of the recurrence formula (1). Hence the problem is to specify an input sequence $u(n_1,...,n_m)$, as in (2), of minimum duration (i.e. the interval in (2) has to be minimum) such that (4) hold. The interval in (2) is the minimum interval for which both the input and output reach zero and remain zero thereafter. This is so because if one restricts y to be equal to zero before $(\ell_1,...,\ell_m)$, say from $(\ell_1',...,\ell_m')<(\ell_1,...,\ell_m)$ then in order to have y=0 at the successive points, beginning from $(\ell_1',...,\ell_m')$ and going on, it would be necessary to set

$$u(n_1,...,n_m)=0 \quad \text{for}$$

$$(\ell_1',...,\ell_n')<(n_1,...,n_m)<(\ell_1,...,\ell_m) \quad (6)$$

which contradicts with (2). So, both the input and output must reach zero simultaneously.

In conclusion, be deadbeat control problem can now be stated as: Specify an input sequence in (2), such that (4) hold for a minimum space interval T:

$$T=[(0,...,0),(\ell_1,...,\ell_m)[\quad (7)$$

The notation above means that the interval T is closed on the left and open on the right. This simply means that T involves m-D points $(n_1,...,n_m)$, such that

$$(0,...,0)\leq(n_1,...,n_m)<(\ell_1,...,\ell_m) \quad (8)$$

In order to solve the above problem, one expresses $y(n_1,...,n_m)$, according to (1), as a linear combination of past outputs, present and past inputs, and initial conditions, for $(n_1,...,n_m)$ as in (4), and sets y equal to zero. In this way a linear system of A equation in B unknowns $u(n_1,...,n_m)$ as in (2), is formulated, where

$$A=(N_1+\ell_1+1)...(N_m+\ell_m+1)-(\ell_1+1)...(\ell_m+1) \quad (9)$$

$$B=(\ell_1+1)...(\ell_m+1)-1 \quad (10)$$

A necessary condition for the existence of solution, in general, is

$$A\leq B \quad (11)$$
or

$$(N_1+\ell_1+1)...(N_m+\ell_m+1)<2(\ell_1+1)...(\ell_m+1) \quad (12)$$

Thus, the deadbeat control problem was reduced to: Formulate the linear system of A equations in B unknown $u(n_1,...,n_m)$, by expressing y as a linear combination of inputs u and initial conditions and by setting all these y equal to zero. The numbers A and B must obey (12), and the right-hand side of (12) must be minimum. Finally solve this system and possibly find necessary and sufficient conditions for the existence of a solution. The formulation of this system is done in Sec. III. It remains to be seen here, that an m-triple integer set $(\ell_1,...,\ell_m)$ satisfying (12) always exists. For this reason one searches for a solution of the following form:

$$(\ell_1,...,\ell_m)=k(N_1,...,N_m)-(1,...,1) \quad (13)$$

where k is a positive integer. If such a solution exists, it means that (12) has one solution $(\ell_1,...,\ell_m)$, and by solving (12) with respect to one ℓ_i, say ℓ_m, one ends up with the inequality:

$$\ell_m > \frac{N_m(N_1+\ell_1+1)\cdots(N_{m-1}+\ell_{m-1}+1)}{2(\ell_1+1)\cdots(\ell_{m-1}+1)-(N_1+\ell_1+1)\cdots(N_{m-1}+\ell_{m-1}+1)}+1 \quad (14)$$

By the same reasoning of (12) for an (m-1)-D system, the denominator of the right-hand side is positive. So one positive integer and hence an infinite number of positive integers-ℓ_m, satisfying (14) exists. This means that an infinite number of solutions of (12) exists. By making the right-hand side of (12) the minimum interval T is specified. Returning to (13), in order to show that a k satisfying (13) exists, one substitutes (13) into (12) to obtain

$(k+1)N_1 \dots (k+1)N_m < 2kN_1 \dots kN_m$ or

$(k+1)^m N_1 \dots N_m < 2k^m N_1 \dots N_m$

whence

$(k+1)^m < 2k^m$ or $(1+\frac{1}{k})^m < 2 \quad 1+\frac{1}{k} < 2^{\frac{1}{m}}$

Thus finally

$$k > \frac{1}{2^{1/m}-1} \tag{15}$$

There is one, and hence infinite in number, positive integers k, satisfying the above relation,because $2^{1/m}-1>0$, and the conjecture that a solution of the type (13), exists, has been proved.

Special case 1:2-D systems:

Input sequence to be specified:

$$u(n_1,n_2) \text{ for } (0,0) < (n_1,n_2) < (\ell_1,\ell_2) \tag{16}$$

Output sequence to be set equal to zero:

$y(n_1,n_2)=0$ for

$$(\ell_1,\ell_2) \leq (n_1,n_2) < (N_1+\ell_1, N_2+\ell_2) \tag{17}$$

Here

$$A=(N_1+\ell_1+1)(N_2+\ell_2+1)-(\ell_1+1)(\ell_2+1) \tag{18}$$

$$B=(\ell_1+1)(\ell_2+1)-1 \tag{19}$$

Thus $A \leq B$ implies

$$(N_1+\ell_1)(N_2+\ell_2+1) < 2(\ell_1+1)(\ell_2+1) \tag{20}$$

Special case 2:1-D systems

$$\text{Input sequence } u(n) \text{ for } 0 \leq n < \ell \tag{21}$$

$$\text{Output sequence } y(n)=0 \text{ for } \ell < n < N+\ell \tag{22}$$

Here

$$A=B=N=\ell \tag{23}$$

3. FORMULATION OF THE PROBLEM

In order to express the output $y(n_1, \dots, n_m)$ at the points

$$(\ell_1,\dots,\ell_m) \leq (n_1,\dots,n_m) < (N_1+\ell_1,\dots,N_m+\ell_m)$$

use of the m-D Z transform is made The Z transform of an m-D sequence $x(n_1, \dots, n_m)$ is, by definition:

$$Z\{x(n_1,\dots,n_m) = \sum_{n_1=0}^{\infty} \sum_{n_m=0}^{\infty} x(n_1,\dots,n_m) z_1^{-n_1} \dots z_m^{-n_m}\} \tag{24}$$

The Z transform of a delayed sequence $x(n_1-i_1,\dots,n_m-i_m)$ is

$$Z\{x(n_1-i_1,\dots,n_m-i_m)\} = X(z_1,\dots,z_m) z_1^{-i_1} \dots z_m^{-i_m} + \sum_{i=1}^{m} \sum_{1 \leq k_1,\dots k_i,\lambda_1,\dots,\lambda_{m-i} \leq m} \sum_{j_{k_1}=1}^{i_{k_1}} \dots \sum_{jk_i=1}^{i_{k_i}} X(\dots,-j_k,\dots,z_\lambda,\dots) z_{k_1}^{j_{k_1}} \dots z_{k_i}^{j_{k_i}} z_1^{-i_1} \dots z_m^{-i_m} \tag{25}$$

where $k=k_1,\dots,k_i$, $\lambda=\lambda_1,\dots,\lambda_{m-i}$, $i=1,\dots,m$

$X'(\dots,-j_k,\dots,z_\lambda,\dots)$ is the (m-i)-D Z transform of the sequence $x(\dots,-j_k,\dots,j_\lambda,\dots)$, i.e.

$$X'(\dots,-j_k,\dots,j_\lambda,\dots) = \sum_{j_{\lambda_1}=0}^{\infty} \dots \sum_{j_{\lambda_{m-1}}=0} x(\dots,-j_k,\dots,j_\lambda,\dots\} z_\lambda^{-j\lambda_1} \dots z_{m-i}^{-j_{\lambda_{m-i}}} \tag{26}$$

and in the above notation $k<\lambda$ implies $k_1<\lambda_1$, etc., otherwise, if $k>\lambda$, the notation should be, changed to $x(\dots,j_\lambda,\dots,-j_k,\dots)$, $X'(\dots,z_\lambda,\dots,-j_k,\dots)$,etc. Equation (25) is shown in the Appendix.

Applying the Z transform on both siedes of (1), one finds:

$$Y(z_1,\dots,z_m) \sum_{i=0}^{N_1} \dots \sum_{i_m=0}^{N_m} a_{i_1,\dots,i_m} z_1^{-i_1} \dots z_m^{-i_m} + \sum_{i_1=0}^{N_1} \dots \sum_{i_m=0}^{N_m} \sum_{i=1}^{m} \sum_{1 \leq k_1,\dots,k_i,\lambda_1,\dots,\lambda_{m-i} \leq m} \sum_{j_{k_1}=1}^{i_{k_1}} \dots \sum_{j_{k_i}=1}^{i_{k_i}} a_{i_1,\dots,i_m} Y'(\dots,-j_k,\dots,z_\lambda\dots) z_{k_1}^{j_{k_1}} \dots z_{k_i}^{j_{k_i}} z_1^{-i_1} \dots z_m^{-i_m}$$
$$= U(z_1,\dots,z_m) \sum_{i=0}^{K_1} \dots \sum_{i_m=0}^{K_m} b_{i_1,\dots,i_m} z_1^{-i_1} \dots z_m^{-i_m} \tag{27}$$

The second term of the left hand side is written as:

$$\sum_{i=1}^{m} \sum_{1\le k_1,\dots,k_i,\lambda_1,\dots,\lambda_{m-i}\le m} \sum_{i_1=0}^{N_1}\cdots\sum_{i_m=0}^{N_m} \sum_{j_{k_1}=1}^{i_{k_1}}\cdots\sum_{j_{k_i}=1}^{i_{k_i}} a_{i_1,\dots,i_m} Y'(\dots,-j_k,\dots,z_\lambda,\dots)\, z_{k_1}^{j_{k_1}}\cdots z_{k_i}^{j_{k_i}} z_1^{-i_1}\cdots z_m^{-i_m}$$

$$= \sum_{i=1}^{m} \cdots \sum_{1\le k_1,\dots,k_i\lambda_1,\dots,\lambda_{m-i}<m} \sum_{i_{k_1}=0}^{N_{k_1}}\cdots\sum_{i_{k_i}=0}^{N_{k_i}} \sum_{i_{\lambda_1}=0}^{N_{\lambda_1}}\cdots\sum_{i_{\lambda_{m-i}}=0}^{N_{\lambda_{m-i}}} \sum_{j_{k_1}=1}^{i_{k_1}}\cdots\sum_{j_{k_i}=1}^{i_{k_i}} a_{i,\dots,i_m} Y'(\dots,-j_k,\dots,z_\lambda,\dots)\, z_{k_1}^{j_{k_1}}\cdots z_{k_i}^{j_{k_i}} z_{k_1}^{-i_{k_1}}\cdots z_{k_i}^{-i_{k_i}} z_{\lambda_1}^{-i_{\lambda_1}}\cdots z_{\lambda_{m-i}}^{-i_{\lambda_{m-i}}}$$

$$= \sum_{i=1}^{m} \sum_{1\le k_1,\dots,k_i,\lambda_1,\dots,\lambda_{m-i}\le m} \sum_{i_{k_1}=0}^{N_{k_1}} \sum_{j_{k_1}=1}^{i_{k_1}}\cdots\sum_{i_{k_i}=0}^{N_{k_i}} \sum_{j_{k_i}=1}^{i_{k_i}} \sum_{i_{\lambda_1}=0}^{N_{\lambda_1}}\cdots\sum_{i_{\lambda_{m-i}}=0}^{N_{\lambda_{m-i}}} a_{i,\dots,i_m} Y'(\dots,-j_k,\dots,z_\lambda,\dots)\, z_{k_1}^{j_{k_1}-i_{k_1}}\cdots z_{k_i}^{j_{k_i}-i_{k_i}} z_{\lambda_1}^{-i_{\lambda_1}}\cdots z_{\lambda_{m-i}}^{-i_{\lambda_{m-i}}}$$

$$= \sum_{i=1}^{m} \sum_{1\le k_1,\dots,k_i,\lambda_1,\dots,\lambda_{m-i}\le m} \sum_{j_{k_1}=1}^{N_{k_1}} \sum_{i_{k_1}=j_{k_1}}^{N_{k_1}}\cdots \sum_{j_{k_i}=1}^{N_{k_i}} \sum_{i_{k_i}=j_{k_i}}^{N_{k_i}} \sum_{i_{\lambda_1}=0}^{N_{\lambda_1}} \sum_{i_{\lambda_{m-i}}=0}^{N_{\lambda_{m-i}}} a_{i_1,\dots,i_m} Y'(\dots,-j_k,\dots,z_\lambda,\dots)\, z_{k_1}^{j_{k_1}-i_{k_1}}\cdots z_{k_i}^{j_{k_i}-i_{k_i}} z_{\lambda_1}^{-i_{\lambda_1}}\cdots z_{\lambda_{m-i}}^{-i_{\lambda_{m-i}}} \qquad (28)$$

Introducing (28) into (27) and solving for Y, yields:

$$Y(z_1,\dots,z_m) = \Big[U(z_1,\dots,z_m) \sum_{i_1=0}^{K_1}\cdots\sum_{i_m=0}^{K_m} b_{i_1,\dots,i_m} z_1^{-i_1}\cdots z_m^{-i_m} - \sum_{i=1}^{m} \sum_{1\le k_1,\dots,k_i,\lambda_1,\dots,\lambda_{m-i}\le m} \sum_{j_{k_1}=1}^{N_{k_1}} \sum_{i_{k_1}=j_{k_1}}^{N_{k_1}}\cdots \sum_{j_{k_i}=1}^{N_{k_i}} \sum_{i_{k_i}=j_{k_i}}^{N_{k_i}} \sum_{i_{\lambda_1}=0}^{N_{\lambda_1}}\cdots \sum_{i_{\lambda_{m-i}}=0}^{N_{\lambda_{m-i}}} a_{i_1,\dots,i_m} Y'(\dots,-j_k,\dots,z\ ,\dots)\, z_{k_1}^{j_{k_1}-i_{k_1}} z_{k_i}^{j_{k_i}-i_{k_i}} z_{\lambda_1}^{-i_{\lambda_1}}\cdots z_{\lambda_{m-i}}^{-i_{\lambda_{m-i}}}\Big]$$

$$\times \frac{1}{\sum_{i_1=0}^{N_1}\sum_{i_m=0}^{N_m} a_{i_1,\dots,i_m} z_1^{-i_1}\cdots z_m^{-i_m}} \qquad (29)$$

Expanding the m-D Z transform of U and considering (2), the first term of the right-hand side of (29) is written as:

$$U(z_1,\dots,z_m) \sum_{i_1=0}^{K_1} \sum_{i_m=0}^{K_m} b_{i_1,\dots,i_m} z_1^{-i_1}\cdots z_m^{-i_m}$$

$(j_1,\dots,j_m) \neq (\ell_1,\dots,\ell_n)$

$$= \sum_{j_1=0}^{\ell_1}\cdots\sum_{j_m=0}^{\ell_m} \sum_{i_1=0}^{K_1}\cdots\sum_{i_m=0}^{K_m} b_{i_1,\dots,i_m} u(j_1,\dots j_m)\, z_1^{-i_1-j_1}\cdots z_m^{-i_m-j_m} \qquad (30)$$

Similarly, expanding the (m-i)-D Z transforms of Y'and considering (4) and (5), the second term of the right-hand side of (29) is written as:

$$\sum_{i_1=1}^{m} \sum_{1\le k_1,\dots,k_i,\lambda_1,\dots,\lambda_{m-i}\le m} \sum_{j_{k_1}=1}^{N_{k_1}} \sum_{i_{k_1}=j_{k_1}}^{N_{k_1}} \cdots \sum_{j_{k_i}=1}^{N_{k_i}} \sum_{i_{k_i}=j_{k_i}}^{N_{k_i}} \sum_{i_{\lambda_1}=0}^{N_{\lambda_1}} \cdots \sum_{i_{\lambda_{m-i}}=0}^{N_{\lambda_{m-i}}} a_{i_1,\dots,i_m} Y'(\dots,-j_k,\dots,z_\lambda,\dots)\, z_{k_1}^{j_{k_1}-i_{k_1}}\cdots z_{k_i}^{j_{k_i}-i_{k_i}} z_{\lambda_1}^{-i_{\lambda_1}}\cdots z_{\lambda_{m-i}}^{-i_{\lambda_{m-i}}}$$

$$= \sum_{i=1}^{m} \sum_{1\le k_1,\dots,k_i,\lambda_1,\dots,\lambda_{m-i}\le m} \sum_{j_{k_1}=1}^{N_{k_1}}$$

$$\sum_{i_{k_1}=j_{k_1}}^{N_{k_1}} \cdots \sum_{j_{k_i}=1}^{N_{k_i}} \sum_{i_{k_i}=j_{k_i}}^{N_{k_i}} \sum_{i_{\lambda_1}=0}^{N_{\lambda_1}} \cdots \sum_{i_{\lambda_{m-i}}=0}^{N_{\lambda_{m-i}}} \sum_{j_{\lambda_1}=0}^{\ell_{\lambda_1}} \sum_{j_{\lambda_{m-i}}=0}^{\ell_{\lambda_{m-i}}} a_{i_1,\ldots,i_m} y(\ldots,-j_k,\ldots,j_\lambda,\ldots,) z_{k_1}^{j_{k_1}-i_{k_1}} \cdots z_{k_i}^{j_{k_i}-i_{k_i}} z_{\lambda_1}^{-j_{\lambda_1}-i_{\lambda_1}} \cdots z_{\lambda_{m-i}}^{-j_{\lambda_{m-i}}-i_{\lambda_{m-i}}} \quad (31)$$

Finally, by carrying out m-D long division, one obtains:

$$\frac{1}{\sum_{i_1=0}^{N_1} \sum_{i_m=0}^{N_m} a_{i_1,\ldots,i_m} z_1^{-i_1} \cdots z_m^{-i_m}} = \sum_{q_1=0}^{\infty} \cdots \sum_{q_m=0}^{\infty} h_{q_1,\ldots,q_m} z_1^{-q_1} \cdots z_m^{-q_m} \quad (32)$$

Substituting (30),31) and (32) into (29), yields:

$$Y(z_1,\ldots,z_m) = \Big[\sum_{\substack{j_1=0 \\ (j_1,\ldots,j_m)\neq(\ell_1,\ldots,\ell_m)}}^{\ell_1} \sum_{j_m=0}^{\ell_m} \sum_{i_1=0}^{K_1} \sum_{i_m=0}^{K_m} b_{i_1,\ldots,i_m} u(j_1,\ldots,j_m) \sum_{q_1=0}^{\infty} \sum_{q_m=0}^{\infty} h_{q_1,\ldots,q_m} z_1^{-j_1-i_1-q_1} \cdots z_m^{-j_m-i_m-q_m} \Big]$$

$$- \sum_{i=1} \sum_{1\le k_1,\ldots,k_i,\lambda_1,\ldots,\lambda_{m-i}\le m} \sum_{j_{k_1}=1}^{N_{k_1}} \sum_{i_{k_1}=j_{k_1}}^{N_{k_1}} \cdots \sum_{j_{k_i}=1}^{N_{k_i}} \sum_{i_{k_i}=j_{k_i}}^{N_{k_i}} \sum_{i_{\lambda_1}=0}^{N_{\lambda_1}} \sum_{j_{\lambda_1}=0}^{\ell_{\lambda_1}} \cdots \sum_{i_{\lambda_{m-i}}=0}^{N_{\lambda_{m-i}}} \sum_{j_{\lambda_{m-i}}=0}^{\ell_{\lambda_{m-i}}} a_{i_1,\ldots,i_m} y(\ldots,-j_k,\ldots,j_\lambda,\ldots)$$

$$\sum_{q_{k_1}=0}^{\infty} \cdots \sum_{q_{k_i}=0}^{\infty} \sum_{q_{\lambda_1}=0}^{\infty} \cdots \sum_{q_{\lambda_{m-i}}=0}^{\infty} h_{\ldots,q_k,\ldots,q_\lambda,\ldots} z_{k_1}^{j_{k_1}-i_{k_1}-q_{k_1}} \cdots z_{k_i}^{j_{k_i}-i_{k_i}-q_{k_i}} z_{\lambda_1}^{-j_{\lambda_1}-i_{\lambda_1}-q_{\lambda_1}} \cdots z_{\lambda_{m-i}}^{-j_{\lambda_{m-i}}-i_{\lambda_{m-i}}-q_{\lambda_{m-i}}} \quad (33)$$

Now consider the m-D Z transform of y:

$$Y(z_1,\ldots,z_m) = \sum_{n_1=0}^{\infty} \cdots \sum_{n_m=0}^{\infty} y(n_1,\ldots,n_m) z_1^{-n_1} \cdots z_m^{-n_m} \quad (34)$$

Comparing (33) and (34) and equating the coefficients of equal powers of $z_1,\ldots,z_m$ of their right hand sides, the following expressions for the required outputs y at the points $(n_1,\ldots,n_m)$ belonging to the interval in (4), are found:

$$y(n_1,\ldots,n_m) = \sum_{\substack{j_1=0 \\ (j_1,\ldots,j_m)\neq(\ell_1,\ldots,\ell_m)}}^{\ell_1} \cdots \sum_{j_m=0}^{\ell_m} \sum_{i_1=0}^{K_1} \sum_{i_m=0}^{K_m} b_{i_1,\ldots,i_m} u(j_1,\ldots,j_m) h_{n_1-j_1-i_1,\ldots,n_m-j_m-i_m}$$

$$- \sum_{i=1} \sum_{1\le k_1,\ldots,k_i,\lambda_1,\ldots,\lambda_{m-i}\le m} \sum_{j_{k_1}=1}^{N_{k_1}} \sum_{i_{k_1}=j_{k_1}}^{N_{k_1}} \cdots \sum_{j_{k_i}=1}^{N_{k_i}} \sum_{i_{k_i}=j_{k_i}}^{N_{k_i}} \sum_{i_{\lambda_1}=0}^{N_{\lambda_1}} \sum_{j_{\lambda_1}=0}^{\ell_{\lambda_1}} \cdots \sum_{i_{\lambda_{m-i}}=0}^{N_{\lambda_{m-i}}} \sum_{j_{\lambda_{m-i}}=0}^{\ell_{\lambda_{m-i}}} a_{i_1,\ldots,i_m} y(\ldots,-j_k,\ldots,j_\lambda,\ldots) h_{\ldots,n_k+j_k-i_k,\ldots,n_\lambda-j_\lambda-i_\lambda,\ldots} \quad (35)$$

where

$k=k_1,\ldots,k_i,\ \lambda=\lambda_1,\ldots,\lambda_{m-i},\ i=1,\ldots,m$

$(\ell_1,\ldots,\ell_m)\le(n_1,\ldots,n_m)\le(N_1+\ell_1,\ldots,N_m+\ell_m)$

In more compact form the above is written as

$$y(n_1,\ldots,n_m) = \sum_{\substack{i_1=0 \\ (i_1,\ldots,i_m)\neq(\ell_1,\ldots,\ell_m)}}^{\ell_1} \cdots \sum_{i_m=0}^{\ell_m} c_{i_1,\ldots,i_m} u(i_1,\ldots,i_m) - \sum_{i_1=-N_1}^{\ell_1} \sum_{i_m=-N_m}^{\ell_m} d_{i_1,\ldots,i_m} y(i_1,\ldots,i_m) + \sum_{i_1=0}^{\ell_1} \cdots \sum_{i_m=0}^{\ell_m} f_{i_1,\ldots,i_m} y(i_1,\ldots,i_m) \quad (36)$$

The second and third term of the above show that $y(n_1,\ldots,n_m)$ is a linear combination of the initial conditions (3) and the outputs y at points $(i_1,\dots,i_m)$, always involving at least one negative index, $i_p, p=1,\dots,m$ (this is why the third term, involving only positive indices i_p, is excluded from the whole expression for $y(n_1,\dots,n_m)$. The outputs at these points $(i_1,\dots,i_m)$, involving negative indices, have to be calculated separately and substituted in the final expression (35) or (36). The above set of expressions of $y(n_1,\dots,n_m)$ for $(\ell_1,\dots,\ell_m)\le(n_1,\dots,n_m)<(N_1+\ell_1,\dots,N_m+\ell_m)$ can be further written in the form

$$\bar{y}=C.V - D.\Psi \tag{37}$$

where $\bar{y}$, V and Ψ are column vectors having the outputs $y(n_1,\dots,n_m)$. the inputs $u(i_1,\dots,i_m)$ and outputs $y(i_1,\dots,i_m)$ as their elements, according to (36) and C and D are rectangular matrices involving the coefficients $c_{i_1,\dots,i_m}$, $d_{i_1,\dots i_m}$ and $f_{i_1,\dots,i_m}$. By setting $\bar{y}=0$ it is found that:

$$C.V-D.\Psi=0 \text{ whence } C.V=D.\Psi \tag{38}$$

This is a system of A equations in B unknowns $V_1,\dots,V_B$ in matrix form. Necessary and sufficient conditions for the existence of a solution of the deadbeat problem is

$$\text{rank}(C)=A \tag{39}$$

In this case B-A unknown inputs $u(n_1,\dots,n_m)$, for $(0,\dots,0)\le(n_1,\dots,n_m)<(\ell_1,\dots,\ell_m)$, may be given arbitrary values, (say zero, and the rest may be found by solving (38). This set of inputs $u(n_1,\dots,n_m)$, together with the initial conditions drive the system into deadbeat behaviour, i.e. both the input and output become zero after a minimum space interval $[(0,\dots,0),\dots(\ell_1,\dots,\ell_m)[$.

Special case 1:2-D systems

For 2-D systems the expression of the output corresponding to (36) is:

$$y(n_1,n_2)=\sum_{\substack{j_1=0\\(j_1,j_2)\neq(\ell_1,\ell_2)}}^{\ell_1}\sum_{j_2=0}^{\ell_2}\sum_{i_1=0}^{K_1}\sum_{i_2=0}^{K_2} b_{i_1,i_2}u(j_1,j_2)\,h_{n_1-j_1-i_1,n_2-j_2-i_2}$$

$$-\sum_{j_1=1}^{N_1}\sum_{i_1=j_1}^{N_1}\sum_{j_2=0}^{\ell_2}\sum_{i_2=0}^{N_2} a_{i_1,i_2}y(-j_1,j_2)\,h_{n_1+j_1-i_1,n_2-j_2-i_2}$$

$$-\sum_{j_1=0}^{\ell_1}\sum_{i_2=0}^{N_2}\sum_{j_2=1}^{N_2}\sum_{i_2=j_2}^{N_2} a_{i_1,i_2}y(j_1,-j_2)\,h_{n_1-j_1-i_1,n_2+j_2-i_2}$$

$$-\sum_{j_1=1}^{N_1}\sum_{i_1=j_1}^{N_1}\sum_{j_2=1}^{N_2}\sum_{i_2=j_2}^{N_2} a_{i_1,i_2}y(-j_1-j_2)\,h_{n_1+j_1-i_1,n_2+j_2-i_2} \tag{40}$$

for $(\ell_1,\ell_2)\le(n_1,n_2)<(N_1+\ell_1,N_2+\ell_2)$

Special case 2:1-D systems A=B=N=ℓ

Here

$$y(n)=\sum_{j=0}^{N-1}\sum_{i=0}^{K} b_i u(j)h_{n-j-i} - \sum_{j=1}^{N}\sum_{i=j}^{N} a_i y(-j)h_{n+j-i} \tag{41}$$

for $N\le n<2N$.

This is the result obtained in [3].

4. EXAMPLE

Consider the following 2-D system described by its difference equation:

$$y(n_1,n_2)=a_1y(n_1-1,n_2)+a_1y(n_1,n_2-1)+a_2y(n_1-1,n_2-1)$$
$$=b_0u(n_1,n_2)+b_1u(n_1-1,n_2)+b_1u(n_1,n_2-1) \tag{42}$$

From previous analysis it follows that

$$N_1=N_2=K_1=K_2=1 \tag{43a}$$

$$a_{0,0}=1,\ a_{1,0}=a_{0,1}=a_1,\ a_{1,1}=a_2 \tag{43b}$$

$$b_{0,0}=b_0, b_{1,0}=b_{0,1}=b_1,\ b_{1,1}=0 \tag{43c}$$

According to (20) are obtains

$$(\ell_1+2)(\ell_2+2)<2(\ell_1+1)(\ell_2+1) \tag{44}$$

The solution of the above, for which the

right-hand side is minimum, is $\ell_1=2, \ell_1=2$.

Hence

$$A=7, \quad B=8 \tag{45}$$

Thus the required output sequence is

$$u(0,0), u(1,0), u(0,1), u(1,1), u(2,0), u(0,2),$$

$$u(2,1), u(1,2) \tag{46}$$

One of the above may be set equal to zero and the rest may be specified, by solving the linear system (38) of seven equations is seven unknowns.

But the system at hand has a symmetry and not all of the above input values must be specified. Indeed, if the unknown input sequence is only:

$$u(0,0)=u_0, \quad u(1,0)=u(0,1)=u_1, \quad u(1,1)=u_2 \tag{47}$$

and the following output expressions are equated to zero:

$$y(1,1)=0, \quad y(2,0)=0, \quad y(2,1)=0 \tag{48}$$

then, because of symmetry, it will also be true that

$$y(0,2)=0, \quad y(1,2)=0, \quad \text{etc.} \tag{49}$$

and all the rest outputs $y(n_1,n_2)$ for $(n_1,n_2)\geq(2,2)$ will be zero. That is the system's output will vanish

$$y(n_1,n_2)=0 \quad \text{for } (n_1,n_2)\geq(1,1) \tag{50}$$

and the system will obtain deadbeat behaviour. In this case, because of the symmetry of the system, there are only three equations, namely (48), to be solved with respect to three unknown, u_0, u_1, u_2, as in (46). So, instead of (45), one has

$$A=B=3 \tag{51}$$

Assuming zero initial conditions, (36) gives:

$$y(n_1,n_2)=\sum_{j_1=0}^{\ell_1}\sum_{j_2=0}^{\ell_2}\sum_{i_1=0}^{K_1}\sum_{i_2=0}^{K_2} b_{i_1,i_2} u(j_1,j_2) h_{n_1-j_1-i_1,n_2-j_2-i_2}$$

whence

$$y(n_1,n_2)=\sum_{j_1=0}^{1}\sum_{j_2=0}^{1}\sum_{i_1=0}^{1}\sum_{i_2=0}^{1} b_{i_1,i_2} u(j_1,j_2) h_{n_1-j_1-i_1,n_2-j_2-i_2} \tag{52}$$

for $(n_1,n_2)=(1,1),(2,0),(2,1)$.

In order to find the coefficients $h_{1-j_1-i_1,1-j_2-i_2}$, long division is applied, resulting in

$$\frac{1}{\sum_{i_1=0}^{N_1}\sum_{i_2=0}^{N_2} a_{i_1,i_2} z_1^{-i_1} z_2^{-i_2}} = \frac{1}{1+a_1z_1^{-1}+a_1z_2^{-1}+a_2z_1^{-1}z_2^{-1}}$$

$$=1-a_1z_1^{-1}-a_1z_2^{-1}+(2a_1^2-a_2)z_1^{-1}z_2^{-1}+a_1^2z_1^{-2}+a_1^2z_2^{-2}$$

$$+(2a_1a_2-3a_1^3)z_1^{-2}z_2^{-1}+(2a_1a_2-3a_1^3)z_1^{-1}z_2^{-2}+\ldots \tag{53}$$

Hence

$$h_{0,0}=1, \quad h_{1,0}=h_{0,1}=-a_1, \quad h_{1,1}=(2a_1^2-a_2) \tag{54a}$$

$$h_{2,0}=h_{0,2}=a_1^2, \quad h_{2,1}=h_{1,2}=2a_1a_2-3a_1^3 \tag{54b}$$

From (52) for $(n_1,n_2)=(1,1)$, it is found that

$$\begin{aligned} y(1,1)=&(b_{0,0}h_{1,1}+b_{1,0}h_{0,1}+b_{0,1}h_{1,0}\\ &+b_{1,1}h_{0,0})u(0,0)+(b_{0,0}h_{0,1}\\ &+b_{0,1}h_{0,0})u(1,0)+(b_{0,0}h_{1,0}\\ &+b_{1,0}h_{0,0})u(0,1)+b_{0,0}h_{0,0}u(1,1)\end{aligned}$$

Thus, by (43),(47),(48) and (54):

$$\begin{aligned} y(1,1)=&-[a_2b_0+2a_1(b_1-a_1b_0)]u_0\\ &+2(b_1-a_1b_0)u_1+b_0u_2=0\end{aligned} \tag{55}$$

From (52) for $(n_1,n_2)=(2,0)$, it is found that

$$\begin{aligned} y(2,0)=&(b_{0,0}h_{2,0}+b_{1,0}h_{1,0})u(0,0)\\ &+(b_{0,0}h_{1,0}+b_{1,0}h_{0,0})u(1,0)\end{aligned}$$

Thus by (43),(47), (48) and (54):

$$y(2,0)=(b_1-a_1b_0)(-a_1u_0+u_1)=0 \tag{56}$$

From (52) for $(n_1,n_2)=(2,1)$, it is found:

$$\begin{aligned} y(2,1)=&(b_{0,0}h_{2,1}+b_{1,0}h_{1,1}+b_{0,1}h_{2,0}\\ &+b_{1,1}h_{1,0})u(0,0)+(b_{0,0}h_{1,1}\\ &+b_{1,0}h_{0,1}+b_{0,1}h_{1,0}+b_{1,1}h_{0,0})u(1,0)\end{aligned}$$

$$+(b_{0,0}h_{2,0}+b_{1,0}h_{1,0})u(0,1)+(b_{0,0}h_{1,0}+b_{1,0}h_{0,0})u(1,1)$$

Thus again by (43),(47),(48) and (54):

$$y(2,1)=[3a_1^2(b_1-a_1b_0)+2a_1a_2b_0-a_2b_1]u_0+[3a_1(b_1-a_1b_0)+a_2b_0]u_1+(b_1-a_1b_0)u_2=0 \quad (57)$$

Equations (55), (56) and (57) constitute a linear system of three equations in three u_0, u_1, u_2. If

$$b_1=a_1b_0 \quad (58)$$

then, by substitution of the above into (55) and (57), it is found that:

$$u_0 \text{ arbitrary},\ u_2=a_2u_0,\ u_1=a_1u_0 \quad (59)$$

Now provided that

$$b_1\neq a_1b_0 \quad (60)$$

eq. (56) gives

$$u_1=a_1u_0 \quad (61)$$

and by substitution of the above into (55) and (57), one obtains:

$$u_2=a_2u_0 \quad (62)$$

Hence, again an infinite number of solutions exists, but with only one degree of freedom, u_0:

$$u_0\varepsilon R,\ u_1=a_1u_0,\ u_2=a_2u_0 \quad (63)$$

Indeed, substituting the above values of the input sequence in (42), one finds that

$$y(0,0)=b_0u_0,\ y(1,0)=y(0,1)=b_1u_0, \quad (64)$$

and

$$y(n_1,n_2)=0 \text{ for all } (n_1,n_2) \text{ different from } (0,0),(1,0),(0,1) \quad (65)$$

Thus deadbeat response has been achieved.

5. CONCLUSION

It is clear that several alternative definitions of the term deadbeat behaviour of a linear system exist. In this paper an input sequence is calculated, driving the system into the zero steady state after minimum steps in the space domain. If, instead, the system output y is required to coincide with a prespecified output sequence y_p, after a minimum number of steps, then one may consider $y-y_p$ as another system output, and apply the deadbeat control technique on this new system to make the output $y-y_p$ vanish after a minimum space interval.

In [1] and [2] different definitions of the deadbeat behaviour were considered and feedback control was used to obtain deadbeat characteristics. It is really interesting to derive results by using open loop techniques, with different deadbeat definitions, as well by feedback control techniques applied to obtain deadbeat response according to the definition of the present paper.

APPENDIX: PROOF OF (25)

$$Z\{x(n_1-i_1,\dots,n_m-i_m)\}=\sum_{n_1=0}^{\infty}\dots\sum_{n_m=0}^{\infty}x(n_1-i_1,\dots,n_m-i_m)z_1^{-n_1}\dots z_m^{-n_m}$$

$$=\sum_{j_1=-i_1}^{\infty}\dots\sum_{j_m=-i_m}^{\infty}x(j_1,\dots,j_m)z_1^{-j_1-i_1}\dots z_m^{-j_m-i_m}$$

$$=\Big(\sum_{j_1=-i_1}^{-1}+\sum_{j_1=0}^{\infty}\Big)\dots\Big(\sum_{j_m=-i_m}^{-1}+\sum_{j_m=0}^{\infty}\Big)x(j_1,\dots,j_m)z_1^{-j_1}\dots z_m^{-j_m}(z_1^{-i_1}\dots z_m^{-i_m}) \quad (66)$$

The operators $\sum_{j=a}^{\beta}$ obey an algebra, i.e. the rules of addition, multiplication, etc. hold, e.g.

$$\Big(\sum_{j_1=-i_1}^{-1}\ \sum_{j_1=0}^{\infty}\Big)\Big(\sum_{j_2=-i_2}^{-1}+\sum_{j_2=0}^{\infty}\Big)f(j_1,j_2)$$

$$=\Big(\sum_{j_1=-i_1}^{-1}\sum_{j_2=-i_2}^{-1}+\sum_{j_1=-i_1}^{-1}\sum_{j_2=0}^{\infty}+\sum_{j_1=0}^{\infty}\sum_{j_2=-i_2}^{-1}+\sum_{j_1=0}^{\infty}\sum_{j_2=0}^{\infty}\Big)f(j_1,j_2) \quad (67)$$

In order to express (66) in a closed form, the following algebraic relation, between the number $a_i, b_i, i=1,\dots,m$, belonging to a given field (e.g. the real field) is used:

$$(a_1+b_1)\dots(a_m+b_m)=\sum_{i+j=m}\ \sum_{1\le k_1,\dots,k_i,\lambda_1,\dots,\lambda_{m-i}\le m}a_{k_1}\dots a_{k_i}b_{\lambda_1}\dots b_{\lambda_j} \quad (68)$$

The meaning of the above notation is that the sum of the products $\alpha_{k_1},\dots,\alpha_{k_i}\beta_{\lambda_1}\dots\beta_{\lambda_j}$ involves all possible combinations of the 2m numbers α_i,β_i, $i=1,\dots,m$, taken m at a time. There are 2^m such products. The above may be written in a more compact form.

$$\prod_{i=1}^{m}(\alpha_i+\beta_i)=\sum_{i=0}^{m}\sum_{1\le k_1,\dots,k_i,\lambda_1,\dots,\lambda_{m-i}\le m}\alpha_{k_1}\dots\alpha_{k_i}\beta_{\lambda_1}\dots\beta_{\lambda_{m-i}} \qquad (69)$$

where k_i,λ_i, for $i=1,\dots,m$ are all distinct integers and $k_0=\lambda_0=0$ (i.e. the respective terms including k_0 or λ_0 do not exist). Applying the algebraic relation (69) to (66) yields:

$$Z\{x(n_1-i_1,\dots,n_m-i_m)\}$$

$$=\sum_{i=0}\sum_{1\le k_1,\dots,k_i,\lambda_1,\dots,\lambda_{m-i}\le m}\sum_{j_{k_1}=-i_{k_1}}^{-1}\dots\sum_{j_{k_i}=-i_{k_i}}^{-1}\sum_{j_{\lambda_1}=0}^{\infty}\sum_{j_{\lambda_{m-i}}=0}^{\infty}$$

$$x(\dots,j_k,\dots,j_\lambda,\dots)z_{k_1}^{-j_{k_1}}\dots z_{k_i}^{-j_{k_i}}z_{\lambda_1}^{-j_{\lambda_1}}\dots z_{\lambda_{m-i}}^{-j_{\lambda_{m-i}}}z_1^{-i_1}\dots z_m^{-i_m} \qquad (70)$$

for $k=k_1,\dots,k_i$, $\lambda=\lambda_1,\dots,\lambda_{m-i}$, $i=1,\dots,m$.

According to (26) the above is written as:

$$Z\{x(n_1-i_1,\dots,n_{m-im})\}=$$

$$=\sum_{i=0}\sum_{1\le k_1,\dots,k_i,\lambda_1,\dots,\lambda_{m-i}\le m}\sum_{j_{k_1}=-i_{k_1}}^{-1}\sum_{j_{k_i}=i_{k_i}}^{-1}X'(\dots,j_k,\dots,z_\lambda,\dots)z_{k_1}^{-j_{k_1}}\dots z_{k_i}^{-j_{k_i}}z_1^{-i_1}\dots z_m^{-i_m}$$

$$=\sum_{1\le\lambda_1,\dots,\lambda_m\le m}X(z_1,\dots,z_m)z_1^{-i_1}\dots z_m^{-i_m}$$

$$+\sum_{i=1}^{m}\sum_{1\le k_1,\dots,k_i,\lambda_1,\dots,\lambda_{m-i}\le m}\sum_{j_{k_1}=-i_{k_1}}^{-1}\dots\sum_{j_{k_i}=-i_{k_i}}^{-1}X'(\dots,j_k,\dots,z_\lambda,\dots)$$

$$z_{k_1}^{-j_{k_1}}\dots z_{k_i}^{-j_{k_i}}z_1^{-i_1}\dots z_m^{-i_m} \qquad (71)$$

But in the second summation the distinct numbers $\lambda_1,\dots,\lambda_m$, satysfying $1\le\lambda_1,\dots,\lambda_m<m$ are $\lambda_i=i$, $i=1,\dots,m$ and hence only one term in this summation exists. Finally, by making the change of summation integers namely $j_{k_i}=-j'_{k_i}$, $i=1,\dots,m$, the above results in (25). Q.E.D.

Special case 1:2-D systems

$$Z\{x(n_1-i_1,n_2-i_2)\}=X(z_1,z_2)z_1^{-i_1}z_2^{-i_2}+\sum_{j_1=1}^{i_1}X'(-j_1,z_2)z_1^{j_1-i_1}z_2^{-i_2}+\sum_{j_2=1}^{i_2}X'(z_1,-j_2)z_1^{-i_1}z_2^{j_2-i_2}+\sum_{j_1=1}^{i_1}\sum_{j_2=1}^{i_2}x(-j_1,-j_2)z_1^{j_1-i_1}z_2^{j_2-i_2} \qquad (72)$$

Special case 2:1-D systems

$$Z\{x(n-i)\}=X(z)z^{-i}+\sum_{j=1}^{i}x(-j)z^{j-i} \qquad (73)$$

REFERENCES

1. T. Kaczorek, "Dead-beat servo problem for 2-dimensional linear systems", Int.J.Control, Vol. 37, pp. 1349-1353, 1983.
2. S.G.Tzafestas, and N.J.Theodorou, "Feedback Dead-Beat Control of 2-Dimensional Systems", in Multivariable Control:Concepts and Tools (S.Tzafestas, Editor) D. Reidel, Holland,1984.
3. P.V.Rao and P.A.Janakiraman, "Time Optimal Design of Discrete Data Systems in the Frequency Domain", Automatica, Vol.10,pp.539-543, 1974.

DIGITAL TECHNIQUES in Simulation, Communication and Control
Spyros G. Tzafestas (editor)
Elsevier Science Publishers B.V. (North-Holland) © IMACS, 1985

MICROCOMPUTER SEQUENTIAL CONTROLLERS A LOOK - UP TABLE TECHNIQUE APPLICATION

Roman Świniarski

Institute of Control and Industrial
Electronics, Warsaw Technical University
Warsaw, Poland

The paper deals with the problem of designing of microcomputer based sequential controllers. The proposal of application of look-up table technique to the designing of fast sequential controllers is presented

INTRODUCTION

Industrial processes often consist of several discrete subprocesses which can be characterized by the binary control and the output signals. For this kind of processes usually a control algorithms have a logical sequential features. We can find a sequential control algorithms for numerical machine control, assembly lines control, diagnostic of industrial installations, controllers of computer peripherals, controllers of power electronics equipment and others.

A sequential control algorithm generally describes generation of binary control signals as a specific function of binary process outputs and time.

Rapid growth of microprocessor techniques creates possibility of designing of programmable inteligent sequential controllers competetive from the economic point of view to classical "hard wired logic" sequential devices.

A sequential control algorithms are usually implemented in microcomputer real-time systems as a programmes written either in assembly languages [1] ar in a special problem ariented languages [3].

These programmes are constructed [1,3] usually based on interpretation of boolean function describing of sequential algorithms. This technique requires a substantial memory size for interpreting routines and are relative slow due to necessity of executing of interpreting procedure in each control step.

In the paper the alternative attitude

to desiqning of sequential control software is proposed which based on look--up table concept which guarantee the fast execution of control programmes.

DESCRIPTION OF SEQUENTIAL CONTROL ALGORITHMS

Generally a sequential control algorithm ought to guarantee a proper (rcutine) realisation of discrete process which is sequence of elementary operations (i.e. assembly operation) ; before each operation the sets of logical conditions are evaluated which testify a finishing of preceding operation and starting of next one (Figure 1).
The elementary operations can be realized in sequential mode as well.

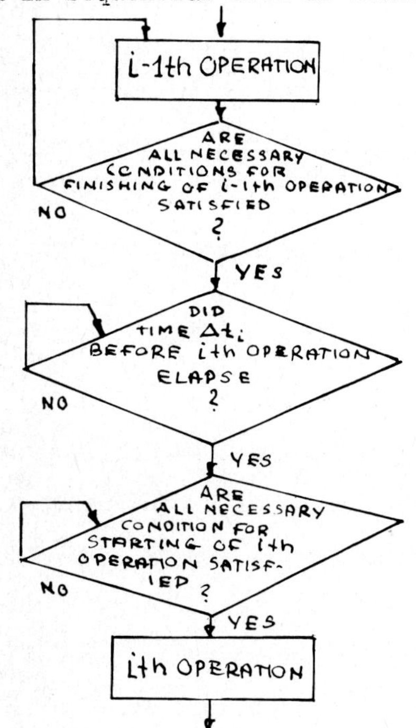

Figure 1 : The flow-chart of sequential control

There are different ways of describing of sequential logic algoritms [3] : verbal description of schedulling opetarions, operational flow-chart (fig.1) Petri nets, automata theory formalisms etc.
Refering to the operational flow-chart depicted in Figure 1 a decision concerning with an intialization of the next kth process operation can be established after the positive testing of the condition [3]

$$(S^P(t) \in S_k^P) \wedge WL(y(t)) \wedge (\Delta t_k > t - t_{k-1})$$

where S_k^P is the set of the process states $S^P(t)$ which is characteristic for finishing of the (k-1)th operation. The $WL(y(t))$ denotes the Boolean function of the binary process outputs $y(t)$ which is taken into consideration for decision about finishing of the (k-1)th operation and begining of kth operation.
The term Δt denotes the time period which from the technological point of view has to elapse before operation kth can be bigining (counting from the time t_{k-1} of finishing (k-1)th operation).
In cases when an elementary operations has a logical character one can applied the automata formalism for their description [3]

$$A=\langle y(t),u(t),s(t),f,g,SI,SF\rangle \qquad (2)$$

where

$y(t)$ - is the m dimensional vector representing the binary process outputs (the automata inputs); $y_i(t)\in\{0,1\}$, $y(t)\in Y$, $Y=2^m$

$u(t)$ - is the n dimensional vector of automata binary outputs (control siqnals, input to the process); $u_i(t)\in\{0,1\}$, $u(t)\in U$, $U=2^n$

$s(t)$ - is the r dimensional automata binary internal state; $s_i(t)\in\{0,1\}$, $s(t)\in S$, $S=2^r$

f - is the transient function of automata; $YxS \to S$

SI - is the set of possible (sensible) states of automata; $SI\subset S$

SF - is the set of desired final states of automata; $SF\subset S$

Refering to the formula (1) which describes a interoperation situation in sequentially controlled discrete process, the process states $S^P(t)$ can be modelled by the automata states $s(t)$. The process states trajectory $S^P = (S_0^P, S_1^P, \ldots, S_f^P)$ will follows to automata states trajectory $s=(s_0,s_1,\ldots s_f)$. In various industrial situation the control algorithms of certain operations has memory - less property and can be modelled by a com binatorial automata

$$u(t) = F\,(y(t)) \qquad (3)$$

where $F(.)$ is the boolean, generally multidimensional function, commonly written using "or", "and", "not" elementary logic operators.

In the cases when the elementary operation of the discrete process can by controlled either by automata (2) ar by combinatorial automata (3) the sequential control algorithm can be written as follows

⋮

i. realisation of sequential control algorithm desribed by (2) or (3) for operation i

i+1 testing of condition (1) for ith operation, if "true" go to next step, else go to i.

i+2 realization of sequential control algorithm described by (2) or (3) for operation i+1

⋮

For combinatiorial control in condition (1) the term $S^P(t)\in S_K^P$ can be neglected.

HARDWARE OF SEQUENTIAL CONTROLLERS

Begining from a relay realization actually we have various microcomputer based implementation of industrial sequential controllers for

discrete processes. These controllers can be easy programmed and a control algorithms (or their parameters) can be flexible change often without necessary hardware reconstructions.
For interfacing of microprocessor with a process binary inputs and outputs a simple imput-ouput parallel ports can be used (For example for the INTEL 8080 family; 8212 elements). The more flexible applications guarantee using of programmable parallel peripheral interface. For example the elements 8255 from the INTEL 8080 family can be easy programmed as a interface between microprocessor and 24 process binary signals (inputs or outputs).

SOFTWARE OF SEQUENTIAL CONTROLLERS

A real-time programme for a microcomputer sequential controllers usually consist of

1. real-time monitor (supervisor)
2. subroutines for initialisation and realisation of binary measurements (eventually with measurements validations)
3. subroutine for clock interrupts service
4. ubroutine for actuating of control signals
5. subroutine for basic control algorithm realisation
6. optionally subroutine for linking with the supervisory level of control

The sequential controllers software can be written either in assembly (or hexadecimal notation) language or in problem orinted language [1, 3].
When we use the programme written in problem orinted language with interpreting technique of translation, the interpreter ouqht to reside in ROM memory during a programme real-time execution.
The subroutines 1 ÷ 4 in above software classification occupy usually 0.5 - 1.5 k bytes of memory and this size de not much depend on designer invention (exept monitor concept).
Also a time of execution of these subroutines could not be decrease substantially by special designing technique.
However, the subroutine for basic control can be designed in diferent ways and the proper construction can decrease substantially for example execution time without unreasonable memory size requirement.
A commen practice in designing the sequential control programmes in problem oriented languages [3] is to use a logical assignment statements

$$R = WL \tag{4}$$

where R is the logical variable and WL is the logical expression. The sequence of this kind of statements can desribe either of combinatorial or sequential algorithm (when R represents for example the state and WL depend on process output and automata states [3]). A interpreting of logical expression requires the appriopriate memory size and relative large number of microprocessor instruction cycles during execution.

In an alternative approach we can apply a look-up table as a base for designing of subroutine for basic control.

LOOK-UP TABLE APPROACH

The look-up table as a representation of the sequential control algorithms can be written for a combinatorial algorithms as

$$LU_1 = \langle Y, U, R_1 \rangle \qquad (5)$$

where $R_1 : Y \rightarrow U$, and for sequential algorithms as

$$LU_2 = \langle \{ YxS \}, U, S, R_2, R_3 \rangle \qquad (6)$$

where

$R_2: \{ YxS \} \rightarrow U, R_3: \{ YxS \} \rightarrow S$

In the above formulas R denotes the rule of selecting the value of control u(t) from the set of U for the given process situation (y(t)) or (y(t), s(t)).

We will propose the organization of look-up table for sequential control (computed off-line) which guarantees the small memory requirements and fast execution of basic control algorithm.

Let us consider at the begiming the combinatorial control algorithm (eqns (3) and (5)).

Assume that a number of process outputs (automata inputs) m is less than 17 and that after measurement the elements of vector y(t) are adjusted to the "right" side of bytes pair (I,J) (Figure 2).

Possible $M = 2^m$ binary realisation of the vector y(t) stored according to the structure given in Figure 2 can be used as a base for relative adressing of look-up table which consist of relevant to the each realisation y(t) the values of n dimensional vector u(t) ($nx2^m$ binary elements).

For microcomputers with 8 bit words memory organization a eight realisation of control elements $u_2(t)$ can be stored in a one adressed memory word thus we can first select the word of eight realisation u(t) by calculating value of (I,J) module

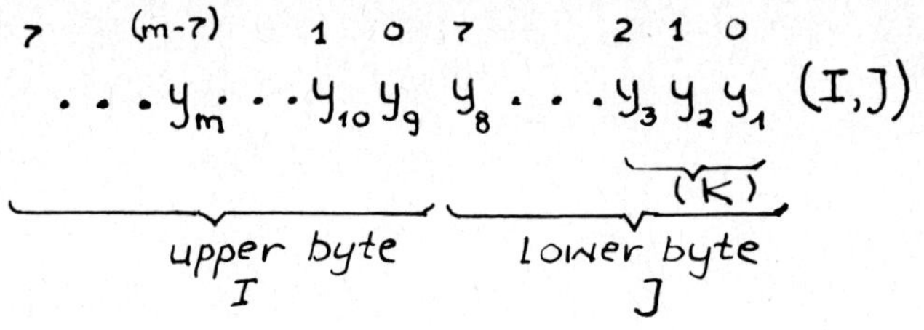

$$\underbrace{\overset{7}{\ldots} \overset{(m-7)}{y_m} \ldots \overset{1}{y_{10}} \overset{0}{y_9}}_{\text{upper byte } I} \; \underbrace{\overset{7}{y_8} \ldots \overset{2}{y_3} \overset{1}{y_2} \overset{0}{y_1}}_{\text{lower byte } J} \quad (I,J)$$

$(K) = y_3 y_2 y_1$

Figure 2: The structure of pair (I,J) conteins y(t)

eight and then select the specific value of u(t) from this word.

The structure of look-up table accor-

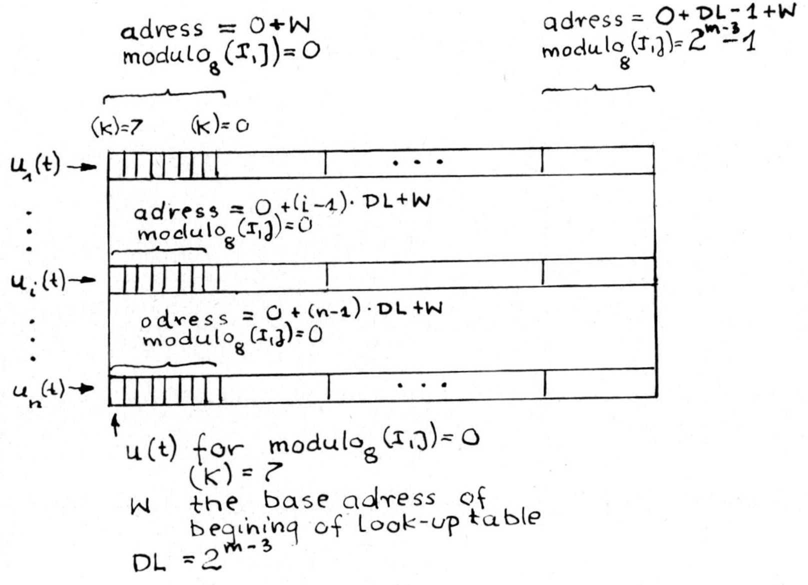

Figure 3: The structure and adressing of look-up table for combinatiorial control

ding to the proposed concept is depicted in Figure 3.

From the Figure 3 we can observe that calculating of adress of the memory word which contein a element $u_i(t)$ for the given value of vector y(t) st red in the pair (I,J) can by realized by the using of formula

adress $u_i(t)$ = modulo_8 (I,J) + W

(K) = three last bit (I,J)

Then from the already read word one can easy select the proper value of element $u_i(t)$ according to the value of (K).

The subroutine for INTEL 8080 microcomputer for selecting of $u(t)$ from the look-up table for given $y(t)$ is given in the appendix. In these programme we assume that $N \leqslant 8$.

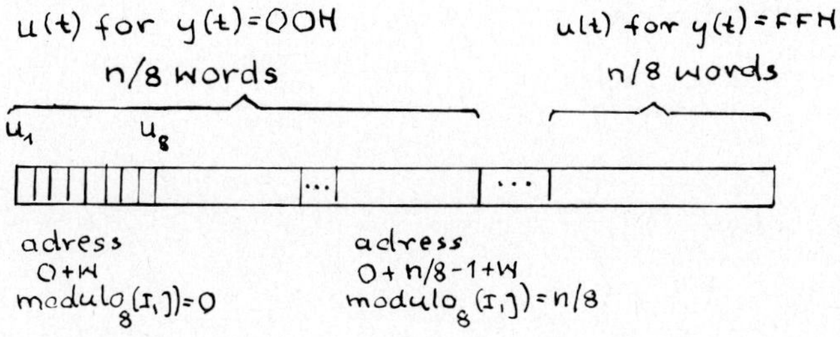

u(t) for y(t)=00H
n/8 words
u(t) for y(t)=FFH
n/8 words
u_1 u_8
adress
0+W
$modulo_8(I,J)=0$
adress
0+n/8-1+W
$modulo_8(I,J)=n/8$

Figure 4: The look-up table for case $n = i \cdot 8$

But extension required only slight change of programme.

In the case when the order of $u(t)$ is $i \cdot 8$ (when i integer) the continquous look-up table can be simplyfy from the adressing point of view (Figure 4).

For sequential control the look-up table have to be modyfied. For example for order of vector $y(t)$ equal to 8 and the 8 state vector elements, we can modify the pair (I,J) when I represent $y(t)$ and J represent $s(t)$. Then for the pair (I,J) we can buid the look-up table for $u(t)$ and next states $s(t)$ using proposed concept.

CONCLUSIONS

The look-up tables for combinatorial control for dimension of $y(t)$ equal to m and demension of $u(t)$ equal to n requires $NM=2^{m-3}.n$ memory bytes. For example for $m=16$ and $n=1$ we have $NM=2^{13}$ = 8K bytes of memory. For $m=8$ and $n=8$ we have $NM=256$ words. The look-up table technique substantially decrese the exectution time of basic control algorithm. Considering the presented programme, we can show that only few dozens of instruction execution is necessary for complete the control vector $u(t)$ for given $y(t)$. The classical algorithms which has been described at the begining requires a hundreds of instructions for the same problem solution [3] .

The look-up table gives promissing possibility to build fast and simple small size sequential controllers implemented for example in single-chip microcomputers.

REFERENCES

[1] Biehl, G., and Pitzinger, A., Computer aided design microprocessor based digital controllers. Microprocessing and Microprogramming. The Euromicro Journal, vol.24, (1981), 326-337.

[2] Niederliński, A., Systemy cyfrowe automatyki przemysłowej (WNT, Warszawa, 1977).

[3] Świniarski, R., Optimal control and microcomputer systems (Warsaw Technical University Press, Warsaw 1980).

[4] Świniarski, R., Programmable inteligent sequential controllers and real-time languages. Proceedings of IX World IFAC Congres, Budapest 3-6 July (1984).

APPENDIX

```
;BASC
;BASIC CONTROL ALGORITHM
;SELECTION OF VECTOR U FROM Y
;INPUT Y IN H,L ADJUSTED TO THE RIGHT
;INPUT W BASE ADRESS FOR DECISION TABLE
;INPUT DL=2**(M-3)
;INPUT N ORDER OF U IN REG.C
;OUTPUT VECTOR U IN REVERSE ORDER IN E
BASC: CALL SELA
DOC:  MOV M,A ; U TO A
;SELECTION OF UI FROM U FOR K IN B
R2:   MOV C,A
      MOV A,B
      ORA A
      JZ R3
      MOV A,C
      RAR
      DCR B
      JMP R2;BIT UI IN AO POSITION
      ANI H
      ADD E
      RAL
      MOV A,E
      DCR C
      JZ KON
; ADRESS FOR THE NEXT ELEMENT U I+1
      LXI D,DL
      DAD D
      JMP POC
KON:  RET
;SELA
; SELECTION OF K AND ADRESS MODULO 8
;INPUT Y IN H,L ,W BASE ADRESS,K IN B
;OUTPUTS K IN B, ABSOLUTE ADRESS IN H,L
SELA: MOV A,L
      ANI 7H
      MOV B,A
;RELATIVE ADRESS CALCULATION
      MOV A,L
      ANI OF8H
      MOV L,A
      MOV A,H
      ANI 7H
      ADD L
      MVI D,3H
R1:   MOV A,H
      RAR
      MOV H,A
      MOV A,L
      RRC
      MOV L,A
      DCR D
      JNZ R1
      LXI D,W
      DAD D
      RET; ABSOLUTE ADRESS IN H.L
```

5. APPLICATIONS

5.1 ROBOTICS
5.2 INDUSTRIAL APPLICATIONS
5.3 MISCELLANEOUS APPLICATIONS

DIGITAL TECHNIQUES in Simulation, Communication and Control
Spyros G. Tzafestas (editor)
Elsevier Science Publishers B.V. (North-Holland) © IMACS, 1985

ON THE REAL-TIME CONTROL OF AN INTELLIGENT ROBOTIC SYSTEM

G.N. Saridis and K.P. Valavanis

Department of Electrical, Computer and Systems Engineering

Rensselaer Polytechnic Institute, Troy, New York 12181

The high level decision making of the digital computer and the advanced mathematical modeling and synthesis techniques of system theory, provide the tools towards the realization of an Intelligent Robotic System, capable for performing complex and various but specific tasks. A unified approach of the different steps needed for the utilization of such a system is presented and the real-time problems are discussed. As an application of the approach suggested, a Unimation PUMA-600 series robot arm is used.

1. INTRODUCTION

Robotic systems demonstrate nonlinear variations of their dynamics which are almost impossible to model. Based on the fact that the dynamic performance of such a system is directly associated with the dynamic models derived for them, it is apparent that the result are imprecise control laws or strategies to achieve the desired response. This desired response of an arm is to maintain a prescribed motion along a prespecified time-based trajectory by applying corrective compensation torques to the actuators for adjustment of possible deviations of the arm from the trajectory.

The industrial approach for the control of such a robot arm is inadequate, since each joint of the arm is treated as a simple servomechanism, neglecting the possible changes of the motion and configuration of the whole arm mechanism. In order to improve the performance of such a system, sophisticated controllers and utilization of the power of the digital computer is needed. In the following sections two different configurations with the digital computer on-line will be presented.

2. THE CONTROLLER OF THE UNIMATION PUMA ROBOT ARM

The PUMA-600 has six revolute joints as shown in Figure 1 (shown on next page) along with the axes and degrees of joint rotation. The most important component of the whole robot system is the controller whose components are: DEC LSI-11 computer, digital and analog servoboards, interface boards, clock/terminator board, power supplies, power amplifier assembly, high power discharge board and arm cable board.

The LSI-11 system contains the LSI-11/02 processor, memory and communication boards. System software resides in EPROM and user program information is stored in RAM. Communication between the processor and the other components of the PUMA system is accomplished via a four-part asynchronous serial I/O board, the DLV 11-J, and via a DRV 11 that provides parallel-line communication to and from the digital servoboards and links the processor to the interface board. The interface board connects the LSI-11 computer system of the controller with the servoboards that control the six joints of the arm. The behavior of the arm is thus controlled by the digital and analog servoboards as dictated by the LSI-11 commands [1], [2].

Given the structure of the controller, observe that it can be considered as "hierarchically arranged" and as the series connection through an interface board of a higher level - the computer level - and a lower level - the joint control level - whose performance is dominated by the six joint microprocessors, the 6503s, attached on the digital servoboards [3], [4].

The purpose of the LSI-11/02 computer is to perform two major tasks:

i) on-liner user interaction and subtask scheduling from the user's VAL (the language used by the PUMA robot arm) and commands, and

ii) subtask coordination with the six joint microprocessors to carry out the command.

The on-line interaction with the user includes parsing, interpreting and decoding the VAL commands and also report error messages to the user. Once a VAL command has been decoded, internal routines residing in the EPROM of the LSI-11/20 computer are activated to perform functions like coordinate systems transformations, joint-interpolated trajectory planning, that involves sending of incremental location updates every 28 ms to each joint, acknowledging from the joint microprocessors that each joint has completed its required incremental motion and

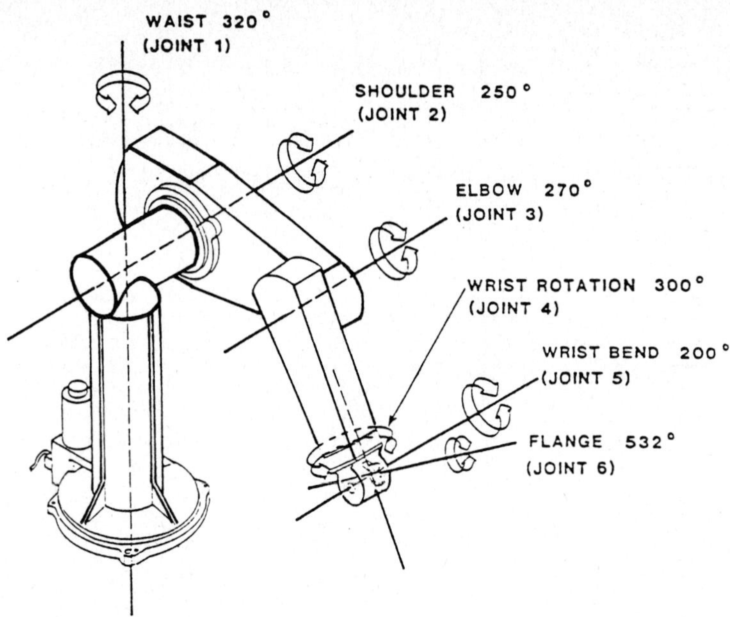

Figure 1 Robot Arm: Degrees of Joint Rotation

two instructions look ahead to perform the continuous path interpolating if the robot is in the continuous path mode.

At the lower level, the joint control level, the components consist of the digital and analog servoboards and the power amplifiers. Each joint microprocessor directly controls each axis of motion of the arm joints and performs the following functions:

i) Every 28 ms, receive and acknowledge set-points from the LSI-11/02 computer and perform interpolation between the current joint value and the desired joint value.
ii) Every 0.875 ms, read the register value which stores the incremental values from the encoder mounted on each axis of rotation.
iii) Update the error actuating signals derived from the joint-interpolated set-points and the valves from the axis encoders.
iv) Convert the error actuating signal to voltage using the DAC's and send the voltage to the analog servoboard which move the joint.

Note that since the joint microprocessors expect new set-points every 28 ms and read the value from the optical encoders every 0.875 ms, they devide the angle to be travelled into 32 equal increments and each time they servo the joints they add the increment and servo the joint to the updated angle value. The performance of the microprocessors is based on the set-points every 28 ms, meaning that any other rate different than that causes problems. If the set-points are acknowledged by the joint micros in time intervals less than 28 ms, then the joint microprocessors will not have time to complete their 32 servoings and a large step in position error will be the result when the new set-point is issued. If the set-points are acknowledged in time intervals greater than 28 ms., then the joint will reach the set point, stop and then start again when the new set-point is issued. The overall control scheme is shown in Figure 2 on the following page.

From Figure 2 see that there are two servo-loops for each joint control, the outer being the one providing the error information updated by the joint microprocessors every 0.875 ms and the inner consisting of analog devices and a compensator with derivative feedback to put damping on the velocity variable. The gains of the servo-loops are constants and tuned to perform as a "critically-damped" joint system.

Concluding the description of the controller, it is repeated that position and velocity are interpolated linearly over 32 servo cycles, the commanded velocity is the difference between successive VAL set-points and that the acceleration is constant over a VAL cycle and is the difference between successive commanded velocities.

3. DISADVANTAGES OF THE PUMA ROBOT ARM CONTROLLER

The disadvantages of such a control scheme are summarized below:

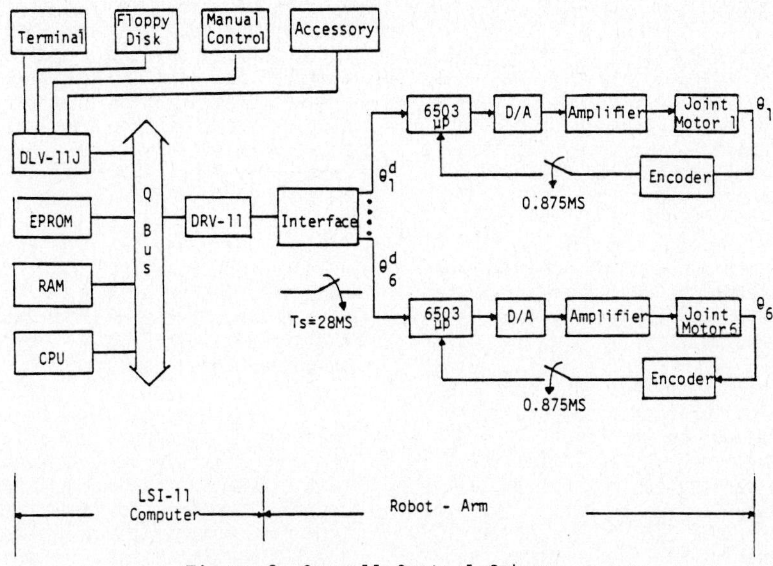

Figure 2 Overall Control Scheme

i) All VAL commands are "open-loop" commands that send set-points to the joint microprocessors every 28 ms and LSI-11/02 computer of the controller is not a part of the joint control servo-loops.

ii) VAL is almost exclusively Kinematic, while in order to apply modern control theories the dynamics of the arm must be derived and the modeling of the arm be based on them.

iii) The feedback gains are constant and prespecified and there is no flexibility of updating them under varying payloads.

iv) Position, velocity and/or acceleration data are not fed back to the computer level.

v) Because such a robot is a highly non-linear system with much coupling between the joints, such a control scheme is inadequate even for simple tasks under varying speeds and payloads.

In order to improve the performance of the arm, first of all, an accurate mathematical model must be derived based on the dynamic equations of the arm and proper modifications in the controller be performed. The modifications include both modifications in the computer level and also in the joint control level.

4. DERIVATION OF THE NEW CONTROLLER

For the PUMA system, the problem to be solved is the smooth and anthropomorphic motion of the arm from an initial position in the three-dimensional space to a prespecified one (end-point) with certain velocity and/or acceleration, based on modern control theories.

It has been shown above that neither the existing controller nor VAL are so powerful for such a complicated purpose. Additionally, VAL is not so flexible for such applications and the solution of disconnecting VAL and connecting the arm to a new controlling computer is adapted.

Such a new controlling computer will have many advantages over the existing one, summarized in that it may be quicker, especially if the host computer has a floating-point processor which the LSI-11/02 does not, more sophisticated and most important of all, it is possible to derive a new language, very flexible, to control the arm rather than restricting to the VAL operating system.

In order to control the PUMA robot system without VAL the LSI-11 computer that includes the LSI-11/02 processor the EPROM, the RAM, the DVL 11-J and the parallel board, the DRV 11, is disconnected from the joint control level. The new host computer is connected to the joint control level through the arm interface board via a new parallel board. The first computer controlled scheme is presented in the sequel.

4.1 A VAX-11/750 Computer-Controlled PUMA Robot Arm

The host computer is the DEC VAX-11/750, that represents the "higher-level" of the hierarchy, and communicates with the joint control level via a new parallel board, the DR 11-W. This means that the VAX computer can communicate directly with the joint microprocessors that control each joint of the arm.

The above is not an easy task because of

the following two reasons:

i) Disconnecting the LSI-11 computer including the VAL operating system, we lose access to all the safety routines, initialization and calibration procedures that VAL runs in order to avoid situations that have to do with the hardware limits of the arm.

ii) The DRV 11 and the DR 11-W, though both are parallel boards, are not exactly compatible and a number of modifications must be done on the DR 11-W in order to interface the joint control level with the VAX computer.

Considering the safety routines, the initialization and the calibration procedures, the appropriate software must be written on the VAX and the same tests must be run every time the arm is initialized, exactly in the same way as with the old system.

Considering the interfacing problems, the situation is much more complicated.

The DRV 11 is a general purpose interface unit used for connecting parallel line TTL or DTL devices to the LSI-11 bus. It permits program-controlled data transfers at rates up to 40K words per second and provides LSI-11 bus interface and control logic for interrupt processing and vector generation. Data is handled by 16 diode-clamped input lines and 16 latched output lines. The unimation interface board transmits data from the joint microprocessors through the DRV 11 to the LSI-11 system and data from the LSI-11 system to the joint microprocessors. On the 16 I/O lines of the DRV 11, two have to be mentioned for their importance. The Request A line that is used from the joint microprocessors to indicate "ready" situations so that data can be sent to or received from the joint microprocessors and the Request B line that is used to indicate error conditions. [5].

The DR 11-W is a general purpose, UNIBUS, direct memory access (DMA) device that provides the means to connect a user device to the UNIBUS of a VAX computer in either single or multiple DR 11-W system configurations. It can be operated in either a programmed I/O or DMA mode. In programmed I/O, data is moved to or from the user device under CPU program control. When operated in DMA mode, the DR 11-W becomes bus master via an NPR request and operates directly on the memory to satisfy requests originated at the user device [6].

Replacing the DRV 11 with the DR 11-W, one needs a cross-connector interface box that matches the output lines of the unimation interface board to those of the DR 11-W and also modification for the Request B line that must be checked periodically for error conditions.

Since the timing and in general, the overall operation of the joint control level components is very difficult to change, it is obvious that the joint microprocessors expect new set points every 28 ms. This operation was controlled in the old configuration of the system by an event signal line that connected the clock/terminator board with the LSI-11/02 and generated an interrupt every 7 ms. Every fourth generated interrupt an error indication was sent from the joint microprocessors if a new set point was not received. With the new host computer, this problem can be solved by either using a software generated interrupt every 28 ms. or by using the ATTN H line of the DR 11-W that will connect the signal line from the clock/terminator board to the new host computer CPU. (See Figure 3).

The advantage of such a configuration is that the host computer is a very powerful one and very flexible for any kind of complicated task. Despite the communication with the joint control level of the robot arm, the VAX computer can also communicate with other systems like the vision system that can provide "visual" information about the location of objects that are in the environment of the robot arm.

The disadvantage of such a configuration is that since the VAX computer is a time-shared machine every time a task has to be executed it is necessary to be performed on a "single user" basis. In addition to that, the VAX computer does all the computations and "grubby details" that need to be done before and during the execution of specific tasks, besides the interpretation of higher level commands and communication with other systems. For this reason an alternative approach is suggested.

4.2 A VAX-11/750, LSI-11/23 Computer Controlled PUMA Robot Arm

According to this configuration, the LSI-11/02 processor is replaced with an LSI-11/23 one that is faster and also has the option of floating point arithmetic that improves the accuracy in the calculations. The existing RAM card is replaced with a new 128K word memory card more than enough to store the user's programs. The EPROM card that had the VAL code is replaced with a new general purpose 64K card in which the new software resides, more flexible than VAL. The DRV 11 doesn't change. The LSI-11/23 automatically generates the 7 ms interrupt signal exactly in the same way as in the old configuration with the LSI-11/02. This "update" of the LSI-11/02 to an LSI-11/23 system is only the first step. The second is the communication between the VAX-11/750 and the LSI-11/23 via a DR 11-W board that interfaces the UNIBUS to the LSI-11/23 Q-BUS. Such a scheme has two parallel interface boards. The DRV 11 that interfaces the LSI-11/23 with the joint control level and the DR 11-W that interfaces the VAX with the LSI-11/23.

The advantage of this scheme is that all

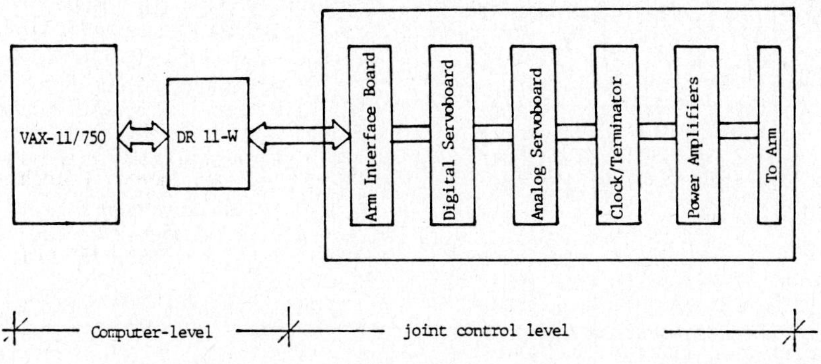

Figure 3

the calculations for the control of the arm are performed in the LSI-11/23 level and not on the VAX level. The VAX computer communicating with the LSI-11/23 computer only to report updating information from the vision system on other high level commands. The flexibility of the system is that programs can be also down loaded from the VAX to the LSI 11/23 and then the LSI-11/23 can take over to control the arm. In such a system the VAX is the "organizor" the LSI-11/23 the "coordinator" and the joint-control level the "hardware control" level according to the hierarchical control theory [7],[8].

The disadvantage of this scheme is that the connection between the VAX and the LSI-11/23 is very complicated and can be performed with either a DECNET or with the installation of a new operating system in the LSI-11/23, most likely the RT-11 one, and a number of protocol oriented communicating routines for the VAX LSI-11/23 connection. The configuration of the scheme is shown in Figure 4.

4.3 MODIFICATIONS IN THE JOINT-CONTROL LEVEL

Based on the fact that the control loops are closed only in the joint microprocessors level and no information is fed back to the host computer - either LSI-11/23 or VAX- and in order to apply modern control theories the host computer must be always on the line, modifications must be performed in the joint control level.

The modifications are summarized on a new card where using position information, differentiate twice it to obtain velocity and acceleration data that are fed back to the computer every .875 ms., each time the joint microprocessors servo the six joints of the arm.

Also due to the nonlinearities, the consideration of the member masses as point masses and the assumption that some system parameters are constant, though highly dependent on the relative position of the arm instead of trying to find a complicated mathematical model to improve the performance of the arm, a minor loop

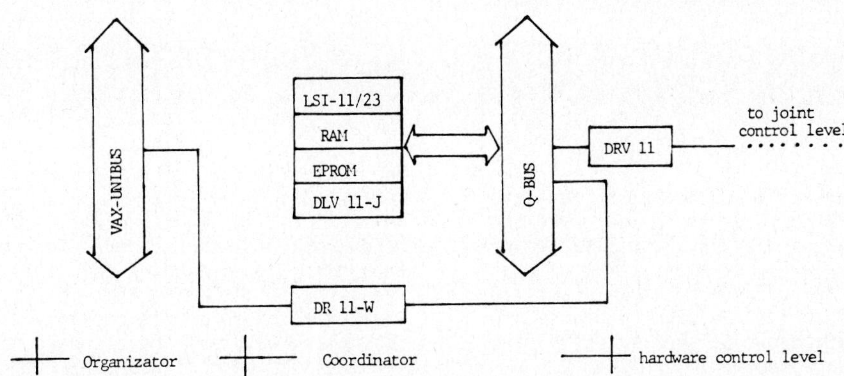

Figure 4

The above two schemes conclude the modification in the computer level.

with a compensator built in to increase the robustness of the system is designed around each of the DC motors obtaining measurements through torque sensors. The torque servo is based on the joint torque sensor and is closed around the motor and gear reduction being independent of the configuration of the manipulator. The joint torque control loop has two servo-loops. The inner is a velocity servo whose purpose is to provide damping and the outer is a torque servo whose purpose is to provide a critically damped second order system such that the sensor output will track the desired torque.

A similar minor compensating loop based on measurement of joint accelerations rather two joint torques can be also designed compensating all nonlinear torques and ending up on simpler controller which can be very easily realized with analog circuits [9]. The overall controller configuration is shown in figure 5.

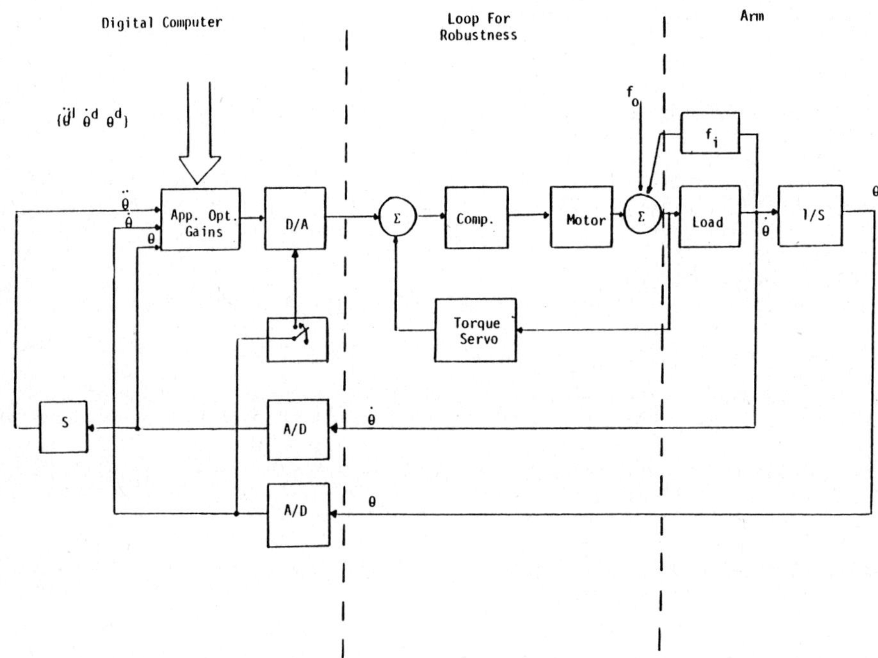

Figure 5 Suboptimal Arm Control with Minor Torque Compensating Loops

5. ADVANTAGES OF THE DERIVED CONTROLLER

i) The superiority of the VAX-750 and/or LSI-11/23 computer is obvious over the LSI-11/02 used by VAL. Utilization of the high-level decision making of the digital computer is applicable and flexibility in the language to be used for the applications of the various control methods available.
ii) The new software is based on the dynamics of the arm, resulting in a more accurate and more advanced mathematical model.
iii) The control loops are closed back to the computer level giving the capability to control the arm movement from the host-computer and the minor derivative loops guarantee the robustness of the arm.
iv) The gains are not constant and prespecified but adjustable according to the movements to be done.
v) Optimal and/or suboptimal control theories are applicable and comparison of the results obtained capable.

The above advantages prove the superiority of the derived computer-controlled system over the existing controller for the PUMA.

6. DISADVANTAGES AND ADVANTAGES OF THE REAL-CONTROL

There are certain time constraints that have to be met in every real-time based system. In this system the time limitations are due to the fact that the joint microprocessors expect new set points every 28 ms. Since their timing is very critical and no modification is encouraged, all real-time control methods must update the joint angle values within the interval of the 28 ms. This means that control laws and strategies based on the complete dynamic model of the arm with all the off-diagonal acceleration related and the nonlinear Coriolis and Centrifugal terms cannot be applied. In return, control laws based on simplified efficient models that update their data within 28 ms. must be derived and applied.

There is not a certain and clear method to overcome the above problem. It is the authors' intention that research in the area of parallel concurrent programming techniques will decrease the computation time to such a point so that one would be able to test almost all of the control methods based on the complete models.

The big advantages of the real-time control are that it can give definite answers for the potential of the various methods that have been tested so far only by simulation, and also about the overall performance of the arm.

7. SUMMARY AND CONCLUSIONS

The control scheme of the PUMA robot arm has been described and explained why it is inadequate for application of modern control theory. The new proposed controller is shown to be superior over the old one and its advantages are presented. It is believed that such a system will greatly improve the performance of the arm.

REFERENCES

[1] Valavanis, K., "Unimate PUMA Manipulator Manual", Technical Report, RAL 3, March 1982, RPI, Troy, New York.

[2] UNIMATE PUMA™, Robot Manual 398H.

[3] Short Publications from Unimation.

[4] Valavanis, K., "Controlling the PUMA with and/or without Using VAL", Technical Report, RAL 16, 5/83, RPI, Troy, New York.

[5] PDP-11 Microcomputer Interfaces Handbook by DEC.

[6] DR 11-W Direct Memory Interface Module by DEC.

[7] Saridis, G.N., "Intelligent Robotic Control", Technical Report RAL 2, February 1982, RPI, Troy, New York.

[8] Saridis, G.N., "Intelligent Robotic Control", IEEE Transactions on Automatic Control, vol. AC-28, No. 5, May 1983.

[9] Saridis, G.N. and Valavanis, K.P., "Application of Optimal Control Theory" to the Unimation PUMA arm. SMC, Seattle, Washington, October, 1982.

DIGITAL TECHNIQUES in Simulation, Communication and Control
Spyros G. Tzafestas (editor)
Elsevier Science Publishers B.V. (North-Holland) © IMACS, 1985

PERFORMANCE ANALYSIS OF CONTROL ALGORITHMS FOR SENSOR BASED OBJECT RECOGNITION

Ludvik Gyergyek**, Saša Prešern*

*Jožef Stefan Institute, Jamova 39, Ljubljana
**Faculty of Electrical Engineering, Edvard Kardelj University, Tržaška 25, Ljubljana
Yugoslavia

Robotic systems are nowadays equipped with a number of sensors. Different methods of AI (artificial intelligence) are used to organise and process data from sensors in order to identify an object or analyse a scene. The impact of the search strategy is studied in order to find the optimal algorithm by which the smallest average number of measurements have to be made for object identification. This paper deals with failure probability and performance analysis during the object identification process. This approach allows the development of an optimal search strategy and also results in a model for object identification by a computer supported sensing system. Applications of the method are discussed and examples given.

1. INTRODUCTION

Industrial robots are equipped with different sensors for object recognition or automated inspection nowadays. [1], [2]. Computer vision [3] and tactile sensing [4] appears to be the most attractive sensing systems in robotics. A number of sensing systems have been implemented and different techniques known from signal processing and also from artificial intelligence have been developed and applied in industry. Microcomputer technology enabled a powerfull tool for control of sensing systems and effective analysis of sensor data.

Sensing includes performing a sequence of measurements in order to analyse some feature of an object. Sensor data is compared to world model and depending on a result of comparison, a decision is made in an object recognition process.

In each measurement some probability of failure exsists, depending on the quality of the equipment which is used as the sensing system, and on noise from the environment. If different objects have similar physical properties which are measured by sensors, a failure in measurement might cause pruning of a wrong branch in the identification tree, and have as a consequence, a wrong identification. The question is, whether the structure of the identification tree or choice of different search algorithms has any effect on the reliability of the clasification and if so, how much.

2. PROBABILITY OF FAILURE IN MEASUREMENT

Insufficient light, poor contrast between an object and the background, and dust polluted air cause noise in optical sensing systems. All sensors have only a limited accuracy.

The object identification process consists of a set of measurements M. A set of measurements M consists of h measurements

$$M = (m_1, m_2, \dots, m_j, m_{j+1}, \dots, m_h) \qquad (1)$$

In a single measurement m_j, one of the possible results A_i ($1 =< i =< n$) is expected. We say that a measurement m_j consists of n elements A_i

$$m_j = (A_1, A_2, \dots, A_i, \dots, A_n) \qquad (2)$$

The probability of obtaining the value A_i by measurement m equals p_i. All probabilities p_i ($1 =< i =< n$) for realisation of an event $A_i \in m_j$ form a set P

$$P = (p_1, p_2, \dots, p_i, \dots, p_n) \qquad (3)$$

with the property

$$\sum_{i=1}^{n} p_i = 1 \qquad (4)$$

A different measurement m_{j+1} consists of g different elements A_i

$$m_{j+1} = (A_2, \dots, A_i, \dots, A_g)$$

with probabilities p_i for realisation of an event $A_i \in m_{j+1}$

$$P = (p_2, \dots, p_i, \dots, p_g) .$$

All objects o_i $(1 =< i =< s)$ which are treated by a computer supported sensing system form a set N, a so-called sensor world

$$N = (o_1, o_2, ..., o_i, ..., o_s) \quad (5)$$

Mean values of physical properties $u(A_k)$, $(1 =< k =< l)$ of each object o_i $(1 =< i =< s)$

$$o_i = (u(A_1), u(A_2), ..., u(A_k), ..., u(A_l))$$

are stored in a permanent data base, known as the symbolic description of the object.

Mean values of h physical properties of all s objects o_i ϵ N are represented in a matrix form

	m_1 ...	m_h
o_1	$u(A_i)$ ...	$u(A_j)$
.	. ...	.
.	. ...	.
.	. ...	.
o_s	$u(A_k)$ ...	$u(A_l)$

where each row represents a symbolic description of an object $o_i \in N$ and each column represents possible outcomes of each measurement $m_j \in M$.

The problem of object identification is solved when an unknown object o_j is identified as one element of the set N

$$o_j \in N .$$

A measurement of some physical property is called a trial. The outcome of repeated trials does have different values because of noise, and they are given by normal distribution [5], [6].

A measurement is regular if

$$u(A_i) - j =< A_i =< u(A_i) + j \qquad 1 =< i =< 9 \quad (6)$$

otherwise it is unregular.

A problem arises if two or more results A_i have similar values so that (Fig. 1)

$$u(A_i) + j > u(A_j) - j \quad (7)$$

In this case a measurement with a result

$$A_i = u(A_i) + e \qquad e < j \quad (8)$$

cannot be identified as nonregular, but is wrongly considered to be a regular measurement A_j. We call this situation a similarity effect and it occurs in a critical sector of a measurement

$$A_j =< u(A_j) - e \quad (9)$$

A failure which is caused by this effect is denoted as P_g.

3. TREE STRUCTURES BY DIFFERENT SEARCH ALGORITHMS

We are going to consider three search algorithms which are used by the identification process [7]:

- depth search: in this algorithm all available measurements are performed first before pruning;
- breadth search: in this algorithm pruning is performed after each measurement;
- beam search: in this algorithm only a beam of near miss alternatives is kept in the three, while all other branches are pruned.

Other search techniques (alpha–beta search, minimax search, etc.), are only improved versions of the basic

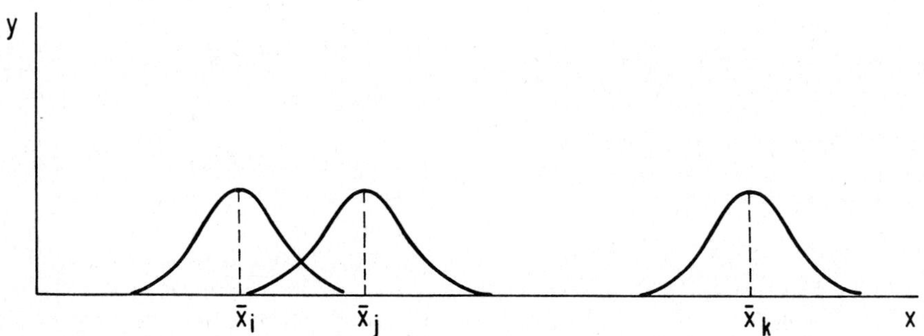

Fig. 1: Mean values $u(A_i)$ and $u(A_j)$ being close together (as given by relation (7)).

three search techniques mentioned above.

The heuristic power of a search technique depends heavily on the particular factors specific to a given problem. Estimating heuristic power involves judgements, based on experience rather than calculations. Certain measurements of performance can be calculated, however, and though they do not completely determine heuristic power, they are useful in comparing various search techniques.

Let us look at the reliability in object identification of each search algorithm in an example, considering a set of 5 objects

$$N = (o_1, o_2, o_3, o_4, o_5) . \qquad (10)$$

The identification process consists of a set of 4 measurements

$$M = (m_1, m_2, m_3, m_4) . \qquad (11)$$

Possible results of each measurement are

$$\begin{aligned} m_1 &= (u(A_1), u(A_6), u(A_9)) \\ m_2 &= (u(A_2), u(A_4)) \\ m_3 &= (u(A_3), u(A_5)) \\ m_4 &= (u(A_7), u(A_8)) . \end{aligned} \qquad (12)$$

The task of the identification system is to identify which one of the possible 5 objects is treated.

Let us construct a search tree for each algorithm and determine the probability of a failure in each step in the tree and on each leaf node.

4. PERFORMANCE ANALYSIS

In this section we are going to analyse:

1. the reliability of object identification with different search algorithms;
2. compare the speed of identification;
3. select an optimal search algorithm for object identification of a set of objects (10).

(1, 2, and 3 correspond to sections 4.1, 4.2 and 4.3).

4.1. Reliability analysis of search algorithms

The probability of a failure in identification of five objects $o_i \in N$ $(i = 1,2, ..., 5)$ with a set of measurements M, using different search algorithms is given in Table 1. A non regular result is a consequence of too much noise present during a particular measurement, while a wrong result is a consequence of the similarity effect.

	o_1	o_2	o_3	o_4	o_5	probability
breadth	0.16	0.16	0.16	0.0	0.16	wrong id.
search	0.06	0.10	0.10	0.05	0.02	non regular id.
	0.22	0.26	0.26	0.05	0.18	together
depth	0.0	0.0	0.0	0.0	0.0	wrong id.
search	0.014	0.014	0.014	0.014	0.014	non regular id.
	0.014	0.014	0.014	0.014	0.014	together
beam	0.0	0.0	0.0	0.0	0.0	wrong id.
search	0.14	0.14	0.14	0.05	0.14	non regular id.
	0.14	0.14	0.14	0.05	0.14	together

Table 1: Probability of a failure (because of wrong or non regular result) by different search algorithms.

It is interesting to see that the probability of a failure due to non regular identification is greater by the beam search than by the breadth search. This is understandable, because in a beam search more measurements have to be performed in order to identify an object, and each measurement is non regular with a certain probability. Another interesting fact is the comparison of the depth search with other two. The number of measurements is the highest in depth search algorithm. In spite of this fact, the probability for a failure because of non regular identification is minimal. This is so because an object can be correctly identified even if one measurement failed. The probability for more than one measurement to be non–regular is so small, that this algorithm is the most reliable for identification (Fig. 2).

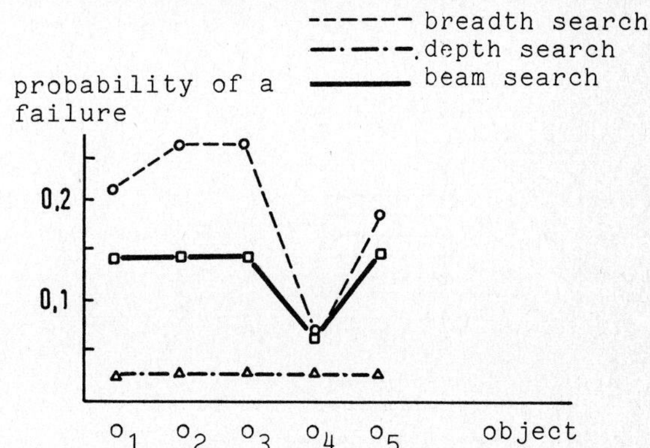

Fig. 2: Probability of a failure in identification of an object o_i $(i = 1,...,5)$ with different search algorithms.

4.2. Comparison of speed of identification

To identify an object o_i, k_i number of measurements have to be performed. A detailed study showed that the number of measurements k_i = 10, 20 and 13 measurements for breadth, depth and beam search respectly.

Arrival frequency equal the probability that an unknown object is the object $o_i \in N$. This is the percentage $p(o_i)$ of objects o_i in a set of all objects N. The number of objects $o_i \in N$ is denoted with $n(o_i)$. Therefore $p(o_i)$ equals

$$p(o_i) = \frac{n(o_i)}{\sum_{i=1}^{s} n(o_i)} \quad (13)$$

The average number of measurements N' for identification of an object equals

$$N' = \sum_{i=1}^{s} p(o_i)\, k_i \ . \quad (14)$$

where k_i equals a total number of measurements which are required to identify all objects.

Let us find the average number of measurements N' by the three search algorithms for a set of 5 test objects. Let $p(o_i) = 0.2$ for i = 1,2, ..., 5. So N' for different search strategies equals:

- breadth search: $N' = p(o_i) \sum_{i=1}^{s} k_i = 0.2 \ \ 10 = 2$ meas./obj.
- depth search: $N' = p(o_i) \sum_{i=1}^{s} k_i = 0.2 \ \ 20 = 4$ meas./obj.
- beam search: $N' = p(o_i) \sum_{i=1}^{s} k_i = 0.2 \ \ 13 = 2.6$ meas./obj.

Fig. 3 shows the relation between N' and the choice of the search algorithm.

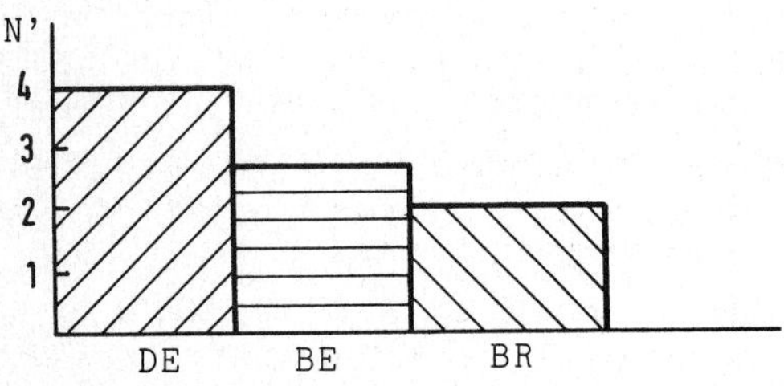

Fig. 3: Comparison of the average number of measurements N' by different search algorithms.

If each measurement m_i requires an equal processing time, then the relation in Fig. 3 indicates the speed of the three search algorithms in object identification in our example.

4.3. Selection of an optimal search algorithm

In selecting an optimal search algorithm, two parameters have to be taken into account:

- the probability for a failure of classification of objects with a given algorithm, and
- the cost of identification c (this is proportional to the average number of measurements N' which are required for object identification).

$$c = s\,N' \quad (15)$$

where

c = cost of identification
s = cost of one measurement
N'= average number of measurements to identify an object.

The relation between costs is equal to the relation between N' for different algorithms. Let us denote the average number of measurements for a depth search by N' and set

$$N'd = 1 \ . \quad (16)$$

Therefore N' beam for a beam search equals

$$N'beam = 0.65\ N'd \quad (17)$$

and N'b for a breadth search equals

$$N'b = 0.5\ N'd \ . \quad (18)$$

A solution for the optimal value is obtained from Fig. 4 where two curves are plotted:

- the cost of identification c of an unknown object by different search algorithms and,
- the probability of a failure by each object $o_i \in N$ where different search algorithms are used.

We see that curve c crosses most of the curves p on Fig. 4 close to the beam search algorithm. This is the optimal value. So, the beam search algorithm is the optimal algorithm for object recognition in our example.

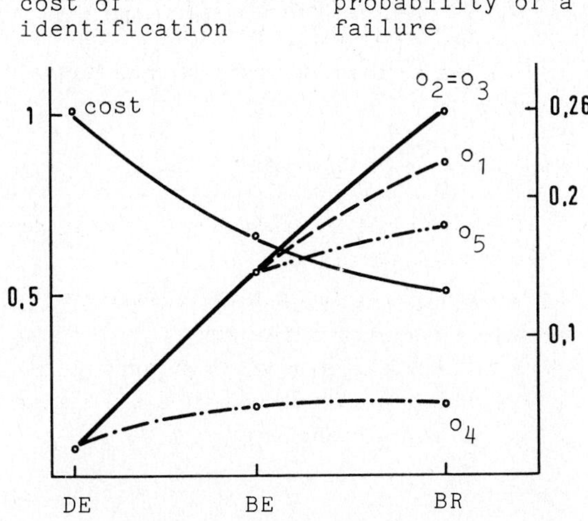

Fig. 4. Cost of identification for different search algorithms and probability of a failure.

We should be aware of the meaning of the plotted curves in Fig. 4. On the abscissa, only discrete points can be chosen, this is any one of the three algorithms. In spite of this fact, curves for p and c are plotted continuously for the purpose of a better visual comparison of costs for identification, and probability of a failure by different search algorithms.

We see that for all test objects, the optimal algorithm for identification is a beam search algorithm. Only for identification of object o_4 is the optimal algorithm the breadth first algorithm.

If we have a set N of objects $o_i \in N$ where

$$n(o_4) < n(o_1) + n(o_2) + n(o_3) + n(o_5) \quad (19)$$

then a beam search algorithm is selected for object identification. If

$$n(o_4) > n(o_1) + n(o_2) + n(o_3) + n(o_5) \quad (20)$$

then object identification should be performed by a breadth search algorithm. This conclusion was expected because a beam search is redundant if objects are very different from one another, so that no similarity effect occurs, and on the other hand, it is required if objects are similar so that a similarity effect does occur.

5. CONCLUSION

The design evaluation and performance analysis of control algorithms for sensor based object recognition technique require understanding of tree structure and the influence of search technique and tree prunning during the object recognition process. This paper integrates a variaty of analytical and simulation results into a survey discussion which suggests a minimal overage time for object recognition in robotics. We first present three most commonly used search algorithms which are used for object recognition in robotics: breadth search, depth search and beam search. Comparison of simulation data for case study enables us to determine an overage object recognition time in order to recognize any unknown object. Price of an object identification is proportional to time required to recognize that object. Computer supported sensing system is tuned so that an optimal search strategy is selected.

It was shown that the depth search is the most reliable in the identification process, but requires the most computation. On the other hand, the breadth search is the most unreliable, but the fastest. The advantages of both, reliability (especially in critical sectors) and a reduced amount of computation, are used in the beam search. Therefore beam search algorithms are the most suitable for robotic applications which have to be performed rapidly (operations in real time) and at the same time reliably.

The implementation of concepts discussed in the paper in industry promise to promote progress due to increased speed of object recognition.

6. REFERENCES

[1] Warnecke, H.J. et al., An adaptive programmable assembly system using compliance and visual feedback, Proc. 10th Int. Symp. on Industrial Robots and 5th Int. Conf. on Industrial Robot Technology, Milan, Italy, Mar. 5–7 (1980) 481–490.

[2] Prešern, S., Gyergyek, L., An intelligent tactile sensor — an on–line hierarchical object and seam analyser, IEEE, Vol. PAMI 5, No. 2 (1983).

[3] Coleman, E.N. et al., Shape from shading for surfaces with texture and specularity, Proc. 7th Int. Joint Conf. on Artificial Intelligence, Vol. II, (Aug. 1982) 652–657.

[4] Nevin, J.L. et al., Programmable assembly system research and its application — A status report, RI — SME Tech. Paper (MS82–125), 1982.

DIGITAL TECHNIQUES in Simulation, Communication and Control
Spyros G. Tzafestas (editor)
Elsevier Science Publishers B.V. (North-Holland) © IMACS, 1985

A VERSATILE μ-COMPUTER BASED EQUIPMENT FOR ROBOTIC LABORATORY EXPERIMENTS

Jules O'Shea, Pierre-Marie Clivio, Charles Capaday
Automatic Control Division
Electrical Engineering Department
Ecole Polytechnique
Montréal, Canada

In this paper, a robotic system consisting of two AIM-65 μ-computers operating in parallel and a Rhino XR-1 manipulator is described. The system was developed and tested for the purpose of laboratory experimentation.
The first μ-computer serves as "guidance unit" transforming coordinates and generating trajectories. The second μ-computer acts as a "control unit" implementing either adaptive or conventional DDC algorithms for servoing the motors.
This paper covers the design of the interfaces, of the guidance, control and communication systems. The performances show that it is reasonnable to propose the equipment that was built as a means for controlling small industrial type robots as well.

1. INTRODUCTION

After a lengthy search for adequate off-the-shelf equipment which would permit our electrical engineering students to get a better understanding of manipulator dynamics and control besides improving their knowledge of real-time μ-computer hardware and software, it appeared that none of the robot demonstration systems available on the market could meet our requirements. Therefore, it was decided to design one: the main components or sub-systems to chose were obviously the μ-computer and the manipulator. For pedagogical reasons, single board μ-computers were preferred over PCs althought both types are used in our laboratories. In particular, the AIM-65 was chosen since the 6502 processor coupled to the 6522 VIA are well-adapted for real-time applications and, for a small investment, it includes the key-board, the display, the printer, an assembler, a Basic interpreter, a cassette interface, two 8-bit bidirectionnal ports and two programmable real-time clocks. The manipulator was the other important unit requiring careful considerations. To keep the cost down, industrial manipulators were eliminated at once. Among the numerous educative types, the Rhino XR-1 seemed the best suited. The justification for that choice comes mostly from the following characteristics of the XR-1: it can reach objects sufficiently far (0,7 metre) to allow for realistic manipulations, it can carry loads heavy enough (450 gr) to permit many assembly operations, it is moved by DC motors which give more flexibility than stepping motors for testing various control strategies, it can be easily modified for mounting sensors or other special purpose mechanical components.

The main units of the system were thus chosen. However, most of the study remained to be done. For the control system, the general configuration proposed in [1] was adopted. It comprises two blocks: the guidance block which performs the coordinates transformation and the optimal trajectory computation; and the control block which performs the servoing of the axis motors. The guidance block is purely software while the control block also incorporates the interfaces, the actuators, the sensors and the robot dynamics. Therefore it must be studied first for determining the hard constraints.

2. THE CONTROL STRUCTURE

In order to move the effector along the trajectory generated by the guidance block each axis-motor is servoed by a position feedback DDC loop.

2.1 The manipulator characteristics

For determining the sampling period of these loops, the step response of each axis-motor was measured. The time constants were roughly the same for the three principal joints. The minimum value being 35 msec when there was no load in the effector. That the base axis has a time constant as short as those of the second and third joints, results from modification of its drive: the small Pittman motor (model GM9413C540) of the original design was replaced by a much bigger Electro-craft motor (model E650) which was nevertheless limited by the power (180 watt-peak) supplied by a Kepco amplifier type BOP-36-5. Picture no. 1 shows that the Electro-craft motor lays horizontally and is coupled to a reducer (80:1) which is coupled in its turn to a right angle drive, with a 4:1 ratio (not visible on the picture) that transmits the torque to the first axis. The reason for this modification was to make more evident the effects of the Coriolis and centrifugal forces.

Since the generalized coordinates for a revolute-type manipulator are the angles that the links make with each other, it is much more convenient that these variables be fedback for control purposes. Unfortunately, the encoders installed on the XR-1 manipulator measure the angular position of the motors and it is only throught calculations that the angle between two links can be derived. This calls for frequently bringing the arm back to its mechanical zero-reference position in order to correct errors due to slippage in the cable - and - pulleys transmission (notwithstanding all other sources of errors). Therefore, it was decided to mount servo-potentiometers directly on each joint as shown on picture no. 1. Potentiometers with an infinite resolution and an accuracy of 0.1% were preferred to resolvers or encoders of equal performances because they are less expensive, light weight, small in size and reliable in the hands of the students.

2.2 The A/D converter

The resolution of the converter requires some considerations. Since they are inexpensive, one is tempted to favor 8-bit converters. But 12-bit converters are still affordable. Besides there is no incentive to choose converters with resolution between 8 to 12 bits. One is therefore left with those two alternatives. Because standard servo-pots are one-turn potentiometers, the full range of the associated converters normally corresponds to 360 degrees. Therefore the overall resolution is either 360/256 or 360/4096 degree. Thus seen, the 8-bit converter is not acceptable. There remained to choose specific 12-bit A/D and D/A converter systems. Most of the commercially available systems are intended for large scale applications, are costly and often require additional purchases of hardware, such as motherboards (STD-BUS, MULTIBUS,...) for interfacing to a micro-computer. It was thus decided to design and build our own 12-bit A/D and D/A converter system using commercially available I.C's. The costs and the implementation time to produce a complete system compare favourably with purchasing commercially available systems.

The description of this A/D and D/A converter system was published in [2]. They are mounted on two separate printed-circuit cards. They are connected "in parallel" to the J-1 connector of the AIM-65: the 12 pins which correspond to the data word are shared by the two converters. In order to prevent interference, the design of the A/D card is based on the AD-574 IC which permits to turn the output to the third state (high impedance).

2.3 The actuators interface

The use of DC motors for moving the manipulator links, allows for easy interchangeability of the type of drive. Industrially, the PWM (Pulse Width Modulation) type is prefered because the power linear amplifier is much more expensive and because the Bang-Bang type could excite resonant modes of the links specially for small robots. Nevertheless, for the sake of comparison, a D/A converter card was built as well as a PWM card. Therefore, the students can compare the performances of both. Since there is no appreciable increase in technical intricacy while yielding a nice cost reduction, these cards were both designed with a demultiplexer that allows for a multi-axis output. The A/D converter system without the demultiplexer, as mentionned previously, has been described in [2]. Figure 1 shows the wiring diagram of the associated demultiplexer. The PWM modulator has been described in [3]; figure 2 reproduces, for convenience, its wiring diagram. The A/D converter system has so far been tested for driving nothing but the three principal axes so that the wrist center of rotation follows the optimal trajectory generated by the guidance block. The PWM system also includes the pitch-axis of the wrist (its roll axis and the gripper are operated according to an on-off mode from a

Photo no. 1

simple interface which is plugged into the J-3 connector of the G-computer.

2.4 Control algorithms

The first strategy, that was tested, implemented a decoupling and recursive compensation algorithm published in [1]. Figure 3 shows a block diagram illustrating its principles. As a brief explanation, one has to recall the vector-form of the Lagrange equation applied to a manipulator:

$$\Gamma(t) = A(\theta)\ddot{\theta}(t) + G(\theta) + \dot{\theta}C\dot{\theta}^T + Tf \quad (1)$$

where

- $\Gamma(t)$ = vector of the motor torques;
- $A(\theta)$ = inertia matrix;
- $\theta(t)$ = vector of the generalized coordinates;
- $G(\theta)$ = vector of the torques due to gravity;
- $\dot{\theta}C\dot{\theta}^T$ = abuse of notation standing for the Coriolis and centrifugal torques;
- Tf = vector of friction torques.

Which can be rewritten thus:

$$\ddot{\theta}(t) = A^{-1}(\theta)\,[\Gamma(t) - G(\theta) - \dot{\theta}C\dot{\theta}^T - T_f] \quad (2)$$

Let, $u(t)$ = control signal

and assume that the acceleration is to be controlled:

$$\ddot{\theta}(t) = u(t)$$

Hence, $$u(t) = A^{-1}(\theta)[\Gamma(t) - T_c(t)]$$

where, $Tc(t) = G(\theta) + \dot{\theta}C\dot{\theta}^T + Tf$. Then, premultiplying $u(t)$ by $D = A(\theta)$ (for decoupling) and adding $Tc(t)$ (a compensation signal that linearizes the term due to non-linear forces) one gets the signals for the torques that the axis-motors must generate. The execution time for this algorithm when run in assembly language and using single precision for the multiplications and double precision for the additions, totaled 5.315 milliseconds for the three axes.

Later on, simple PI controllers, without decoupling, were implemented instead of the adaptative algorithm described above. The performances were quite comparable: the load as seen by the motors is practically constant because it is mostly made-up of Coulomb friction in the transmission mechanisms. Moreover, the gear ratios being of the order of 300:1 to 500:1, mean that the moment of inertias as seen by the motors are at least 90,000 times smaller than the actual values. Therefore their variations and the variations of forces due to Coriollis and centrifugal effects are not significant. Only the extreme variations of the gravitational term has some influences on the top speed of the motors. But, if the trajectory is such that the links are never required to move at speeds above 20 deg/sec (saturation level when going up at full load with full extension of the arm), high gain feedback loops can easily equalized the effects due to loading variations.

The execution time for the PI control algorithm when run in assembly language and using double precision arithmetic totaled 2.76 milliseconds per axis.

3. THE GUIDANCE STRUCTURE

It is recalled that the guidance block besides generating reference signals that serve as inputs to the servo-loops of the axis-motors, has to transform the cartesian coordinates, entered by the operator, into joint angles.

3.1 Coordinates Transformation

In order to move the end effector from one point to another in the working space of the robot, the operator needs only enter the cartesian coordinates of the point to be reached (destination) assuming the starting point is the actual position. Since the transformation is done off-line, it was coded in Basic. It takes roughly one second to calculate the joint angles that correspond to the cartesian coordinates based on simple trigonometric relationships.

3.2 The Reference-Trajectory Computation

For the new values of the joint angles not to be applied as big step functions at the input of the servo-loops, first order filters are sometimes used [4]. But there is no rigourous criteria to choose their time constant. Instead, a law that minimizes or maximizes a performance criteria has more merit, at least for teaching purposes. The minimum acceleration trajectory, for instance, offers the advantage of minimizing vibrations. The execution time for the minimum acceleration algorithm derived in [1], when run in assembly language and using double precision arithmetic, was 5.3 milliseconds per axis.

4. THE COMPUTER SYSTEM CONFIGURATION

The shortest time constant being 35 milliseconds while the execution time of the control algorithm for the three principal axes varying between 5 and 9 milliseconds and the execution time for the guidance algorithm being 5.3 milliseconds per axis, it comes that the throughput of the AIM-65 would not allow for an acceptable sampling period.

4.1 A Distributed Architecture

The sampling period could be reduced considerably by using one µ-computer per axis providing that each one has its own A/D converter and its own analog output plus good communication capability. But, for cost considerations, no communication network could be used also the number of µ-computers and the number of interfaces had to be minimized. Therefore, efforts were done to limit the size of the system to two AIM-65s. Since the servo-loops require A/D and either D/A converters or PWM modulators, the number of interfaces are minimized by partitionning the system so that one µ-computer acts as the control block (called C-computer) leaving the functions of the guidance block to another µ-computer (called G-computer).

4.2 The Interconnections

4.2.1 The D/A Case

The A/D and D/A converters require that, many pins of the J1 connector (the I/O ports) be dedicated for their control signals (see table 1) or for data bits (PB0 to PB7 and PA0 to PA2 and PA7).

TABLE 1

PIN #	FUNCTION	PIN #	FUNCTION
CA-1	A/D STS	CB-2	D/A CK
CA-2	A/D R/C	PA-4	ADRESS OF
PA-3	A/D CE	PA-5	A/D MUX AND
		PA-6	D/A DMUX

Therefore, for hand-shaking purposes, it seems that only the CB-1 pin remains available. But CB-2 can serve for hand-shaking if used in conjonction with PA4 to PA6 (when PA4, PA5, PA6 are all low, signals from CB-2 are not intended for the D/A converter). Thus, pins CB-1 and CB-2 of the C-computer were respectively connected to pins CA-1 and CA-2 of the G-computer. Besides the PA and PB pins of both computers where connected in parallel. In this manner, providing PA-4 to PA-6 are low, the G-computer puts an interrupt request on its CA-1 pin when ready to transmit new reference inputs. Then the C-computer acknowledges, after the cycle of the servoing action is over, by sending on CB-2 a "start transmission" signal. Following the transmission of a data word for one axis by the G-computer, CB-2 goes low as a "data read" signal. This permits to synchronise both computers for data transmission. Photo no. 2 shows the µ-computer system built for the DDC-loop type of applications.

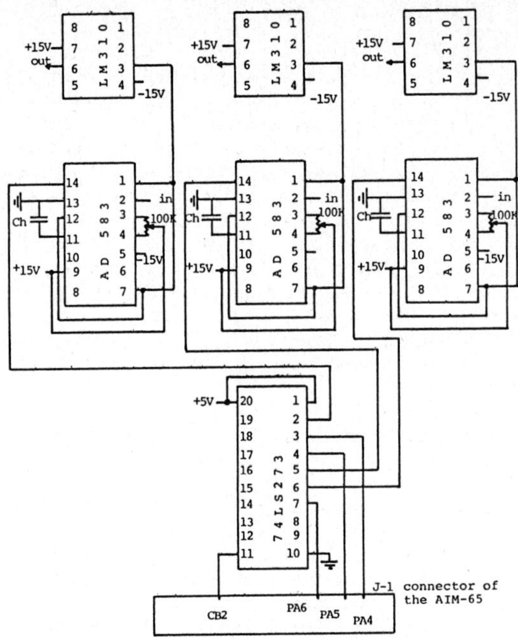

FIGURE 1: WIRING DIAGRAM OF THE THREE-AXIS DEMULTIPLEXER.

4.2.2 The PWM Case

The desire to improve the error prone protocol just described, led to an up-graded hand-shaking version at the time the more recent design of the PWM interface took place. The major difference consists in using the expension connector J-3 of the C-computer for pluging-in the PWM interface. The D/A converter being removed, pins PA-4 to PA-6 and CB-2 become available solely for communication purposes between the computers.

In this case, the C-computer leads the dialogue by sending a request for interruption on CB-2 and by indicating on PA-4 to PA-6 the nature of the data to be transferred. An acknowledge signal is returned by the G-computer on its CA-2 pin. The C-computer transforms its PA and PB pins into inputs and sends a pulse on CB-1 to ask for data. The G-computer transforms its PA and PB pins into outputs and sends a pulse on CA-2 as a "data ready" signal. After the data is read by the C-computer, it sends a pulse on CB-1 as a "completion" signal. Then the G-computer transforms its PA and PB pins to inputs. The whole system is then ready for the next step.

5. CONCLUSIONS

The PWM version has been tested extensively. After many weeks of uses, it has proven to be reliable. Its positionning accuracy (measured as ±1mm at a distance of 30 cm from the base with the wrist centre of rotation at a height of 15 cm from the table top) permits many interesting experiments and even non-critical assembly operations can be done. The maximum tracking error of the D/A version with a PI controller never exceeded 0.9 degree per axis during the performance tests. The final positionning accuracy was within the resolution limits of the A/D converter due to the integral action.

Therefore, for non critical industrial applications, the hardware and the software developed in this project can well serve to control small industrial manipulator. From a teaching point of view, the only drawback, which is due to the manipulator, comes from the fact that the high gear ratios mask the effects of the changing moment of inertias as well as the effects of the Coriolis and centrifugal forces. Thus, conventional high gain position servos give results as good as those of complex adaptive control system.

Based on the observed performances, the main objective of building a low-cost robotic system for laboratory experiments which has a high pedagogical value for electrical engineering students has been attained.

ACKNOWLEDGEMENTS

The work reported in this paper has been carried out with the help of our technicians R. Grenier and Y. Léonard.

REFERENCES

[1] Chaudet R., O'Shea J., Validation of an Adaptive Robot Control Structure by Means of Simulation, Proc. of the IMACS Symposium on Simulation in Engineering Sciences, (Elsevier, 1983), 411-416.

[2] Capaday C., O'Shea J., A/D and D/A 12-bit Interfaces for Direct Digital Control Using the AIM-65 microcomputer, Interfaces in Computing, Vol. 2, No. 3, (Elsevier, 1984), 249-258.

[3] Clivio P.-M., O'Shea J., Interface de commande tri-axiale avec le micro- ordinateur AIM-65, Paper no. 88, Proc. of the 1984 Canadian Conf. on Industrial Computer Systems (C.I.C.S., Ottawa, 1984).

[4] Sahba M., Mayne D.Q., Computer-aided Design of Nonlinear Controllers for Torque Controlled Robot Arms, IEE Proc. Vol. 131, Pt.D., No. 1 (1984) 8-14.

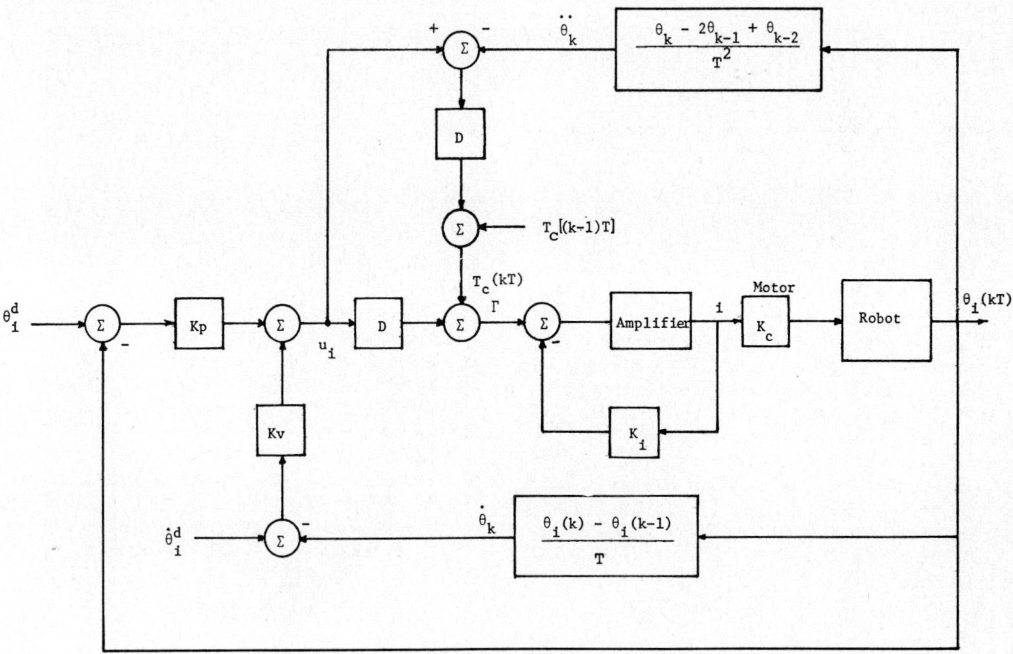

FIGURE 3: THE ROBOT CONTROL STRUCTURE WITH RECURSIVE COMPENSATION

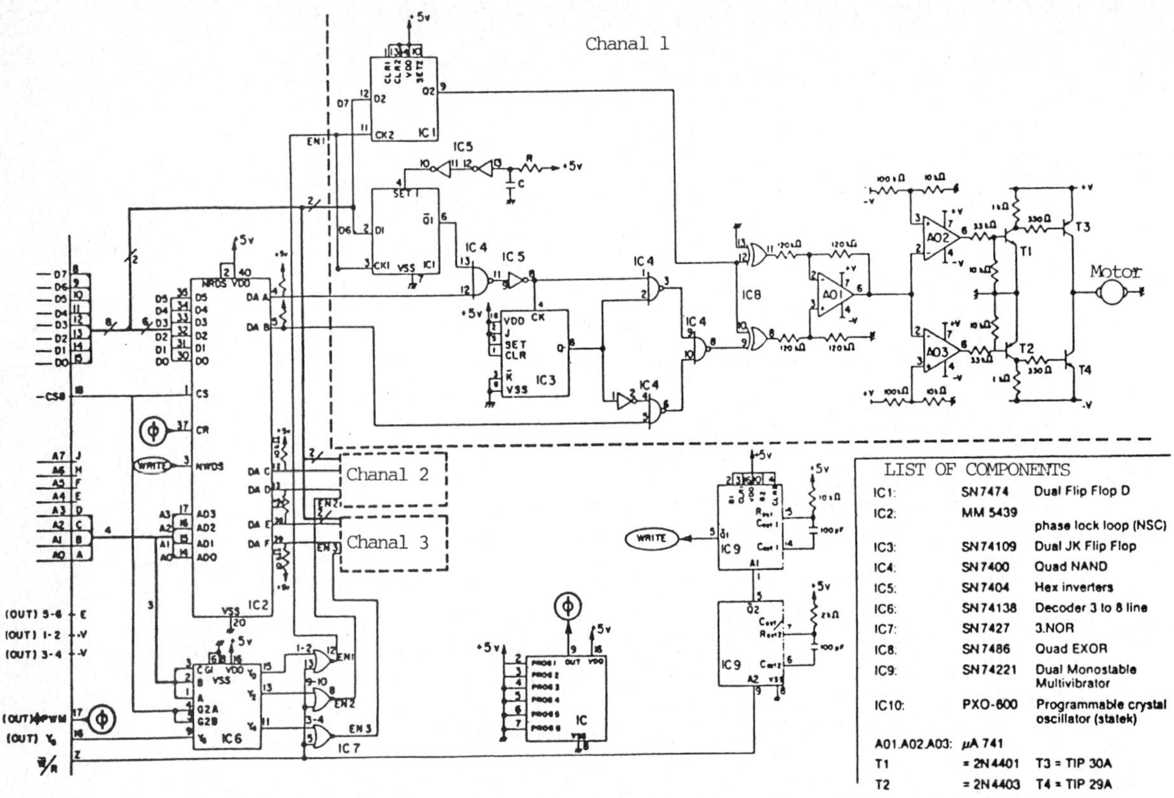

FIGURE 2: SCHEMATIC OF THE PWM MULTI-AXIS MODULATOR.

Photo no. 2

DIGITAL TECHNIQUES in Simulation, Communication and Control
Spyros G. Tzafestas (editor)
Elsevier Science Publishers B.V. (North-Holland) © IMACS, 1985

A MULTI-MICROPROCESSOR TREE NETWORK CONFIGURATION USED ON ROBOT VISION SYSTEMS

BOURBAKIS N. AND VAITSOS C.

DEPARTMENT OF COMPUTER ENGINEERING AND INFORMATICS
UNIVERSITY OF PATRAS
26 500 PATRAS, GREECE

This paper presents the detailed design of a Multi-microprocessor Tree Network (MTN) Configuration, used as the basic part of a real-time Robot Vision System. The MTN consists of 21 μPs R-6502 in complete quad-tree mode. The 16 leave-μPs accept the original nXn image data in parallel mode.
Primary, each leaf-μP processes its data, trying to infer the information that its data include. Whether the individual perception of a leaf-μP is complete or incomplete, then this leaf-μP communicates with its master-slave μP and transmittes to it all the required information. The master-slave μP accumulates the required information given from its four slave μPs and tries to resolve the existing problem by using the memories of the slave μPs.
Secondary, if the master-slave μPs can not perceive the existing information, they communicate with their master μP,which undertakes the control of the whole system and all the information given.
The MTN input and output procedure takes place in the quad-tree leaves by an I/O processor.
The MTN system works in a parallel-serial mode.

1. INTRODUCTION.

The robot installation into the industrial environment is a fact [21]. The first robots were automatic branches, which realized a small number of operations. Nowadays, a vision system is added on these branches and the robots acquired the ability to "see". The installation of the vision systems in the robots increases their flexibility and effectiveness [21, 22,23].
A robot vision system is a system of automatic analysis of the visual objects, so that to recognize an object or a set of objects and to determine their features [1].
A great part of the today robot vision systems in industry is able to recognize separate objects of two dimensions, which are lain on a production line.
Many researchers have proposed or designed various robot vision systems [2,3,4, 5,6,7,8]. These systems are divided in two basic categories :(i) In the systems that implement the visual perception with a different way than the human perception does, and (ii) in the systems that their design and operation approaches to the behaviour of the human vision. Both system categories have the same input and output, but they differ on the way that the perception is implemented.
In the first vision systems category belong the systems that are based on general purpose mini-computer systems [6,9]. These systems arise difficulties while responsing in real-time processes, but their implementation is a simple one.
In the second vision systems category the visual perception is a parallel-serial process [10] and an appropriate way to describe them is by using hierarchical structures [3,10,11]. It is obvious, that both the support and the development of this category systems require the development of real-time microprocessor systems in parallel-serial mode [2,3,4,5,12]. Under this requirement the robot vision systems could have the ability of fast and complete perception of the moving objects in real-time.
This paper presents a Multi-microprocessors Tree Network (MTN) Configuration, which is applied on robot vision systems [3,13]. The MTN consists of 21 μPs R-6502 in complete quad-tree mode and realizes the image processing in a parallel-serial manner.

2. THE MULTI-MICROPROCESSOR TREE NETWORK

The presentation of the MTN consists of three main parts. In the first part basic concepts are discussed, in the second part the internal structure is described and in the third part the function of the internal communication of the MTN is presented.

2.1. BASIC CONCEPTS.

The presented MTN is of a complete quad-tree mode, as shown in Fig. 1.
A MTN, in its general mode, consists of $((n^2/4)-1)/3$ μP nodes, which $n^2/16$ nodes are leaf-nodes [3,13,14] and accept the image data.
The choise of the tree structure of the MTN based on fundamental observations of the human visual system [3,10,11,13] and on the hierarchical structures (pyramids, quad-trees), which can implement this behaviour [10,13,15,16,17].
One of these observations, that have already been proved, is that:"the original image information, which the human system receives, is transferred, by reducing it, into a set of cerebral cortex cells [10, 18,19].
An additional important observation, due to [11], is that the human visual system has the possibility to perceive, with a general view, its visual area and if it is desired to "see" something more specific, concentrate its attention on the desired object [11,20].
In this way, it becomes obvious that the above observations lead to the hierarchical structured processings.
A significant feature of the discussed MTN is the way of conjuction the image areas to the leaf-nodes, Fig. 1 .
The above correspondence gives a lot of advantages in image processing in parallel-serial mode [3,13, 14, 15]
One of these is [3] :If AII is the area of intergrated information, then the area of an image in a row mode of k elements is AII_r, in orthogonal mode of k elements is AII_{re} and in square mode of k elements is AII_s, fig. 2 . Then we have

$$AII_s > AII_{re} > AII_r$$

which says that the area of an image in a square mode of k elements has the possibility of implementing the most of intergrated information [13].
Finally, the above tree mode of the MTN gives the possibility of neighboring areas, creating continuously greater square areas of image, including more and more intergrated information [13,15,20] .

2.2. THE INTERNAL STRUCTURE.

In this section the detailed design of the MTN is presented.
The MTN consists of 21 nodes in complete quad-tree mode. The input and output procedure takes place in the 16 leaves and is undertaken by an I/O processor. The root of the quad-tree has the control of the whole system and all the information the MTN processes.

2.2.1. DESCRIPTION OF THE NODES.

The MTN, which is a complete quad-tree, has one root, four nodes and sixteen leaves called the full master, the master slaves and the slaves respectively, all in three levels Fig. 1.
The M/S node is the most completed mode of a MTN node, as regards the communication in the network and, furthermore, the M/S node is going to be presented in detail. After this, the structure of the Full Master node and of the slave node results easily.
In the places of the CPU's, the R-6502 are used, because they were available in the Digital Systems Laboratory in the Department of Computer Science and Informatics, where the implementation of the MTN is in progress.
To solve the arising problems of the connection and of the communication of the nodes in the MTN the below architecture was followed,Fig. 3,4,5 .
Each node is composed of a R-6502 CPU, 8k memory, three devices T.S.D.1, T.S.D.2 and T.S.D.3 and four 2X4 decoders.
The structure of the R-6502, which is an 8-bits per byte, memory mapped I/O CPU, is widely known. The 8k memory is divided into two main parts. The one is approachable by the CPU and the four slave processors and the other only by the CPU, where there is operating system.
The T.S.D.1 is a selection device, which receives seletion signals from the R-6502 and directs its data channel either to its memory or to the T.S.D.1 of the master node, or even connects the data channels of the slave nodes from their T.S.D.1's to its memory in a specific position each one [Table 1] , Fig. 6a.
The T.S.D.2 is a similar selection device, which receives selection signals from the R-6502 and directs its address channel either to its memory or to the T.S.D.2 of the master node, or even connects the address channels of the slave nodes from their T.S.D.2 to its memory in a specific position each one [Table 1] , Fig. 6b.
Also, the T.S.D.2 directs the address channel signals as an input in T.S.D.3.
The T.S.D.3 is a device, which receives signals from the T.S.D.2 and gives as an output operation signals or special commands which are directed either to its CPU or to the CPU of the master node or to the CPU's of its slave nodes. Fig. 6c.
The above three Target Selecting Devices composed only of logic gates.
Each node communicates with its Master node and with its slave nodes using address and data channels or with signals from the T.S.D.3.

2.2.2. INTERNAL CONNECTION OF THE NODES.

The main problem arising was, that the CPU is not able by itself to send selection signals and special commands, since the only available pins, sending signals of any kind, are the Address Bus pins.
The problem was solved as follows : The AB pins AB15 and AB14 are free from addressing operations and send now selection signals to the T.S.D.1 and T.S.D.2. Also the AB13 is connected with the S.O. pin of the slave nodes, which function is explained in paragraph 2.3.3. The rest AB pins are directed to the T.S.D.2 and from there they have double task, depending on the selection signals that the T.S.D.2 receives from the CPU's A_{15} and A_{14}, see Table 1.
So a great deal of control signals and special commands are able to be "sent out" from the AB channel with the disadvantage of 8K available memory than 64K in ordinary connection.
Another significant problem arised in the communication with the slave nodes regarding the distribution of the memory.
The problem solved with the selection signals from the AB15 and AB14 and with the devices T.S.D.1 and T.S.D.2 as follows :
The CPU can approach the whole 8K memory with the proper selection signals and the four slave processors can with the proper selection signals approach distinguished positions simultaneously.
In this way there is communication between the M/S and the slave processors, by the M/S memory, and so on between the full master and the M/S processors, by the full master memory.
The differences between the full master node and the master-slave node as well as between the master-slave and the slave node are limited.
The full master node has no upper level to communicate with, so there is no need for the T.S.D. to direct the address channel, the data channel or the signals of the special commands to an upper level. It can be easily done by disconnecting the "01" input of the T.S.D.1 and T.S.D.2 as well as the "00" input of the target selection of the T.S.D.3 ,Table 2.
The slave node has no lower level to communicate with, but there is the I/O processor, which does the address and the data channel to a lower level needed, but there is no need of connecting the "01" input of the target selection and all the slave selection inputs in T.S.D.3.
Now, its obvious that the hardware of the system has parallel-serial mode as regards and communication.

2.3. THE FUNCTION MTN PARTS.

As it has been discussed the microprocessor tree network (MTN) has as the main task the hierarchical processing of a two-dimension data array.
In this section specific priority will be given on the communication among the processors in the quad-tree network.

2.3.1. INITIAL STAGE

It is assummed that the original image is stored into the slave-Processors memory in spatial mode, like the figure shows. This proper storage has been undertaken by an I/O processor after the image digitization. Each slave-processor memory contains a multiple amount of the basic area, 4X4 pixels. The picture processing begins at the slave-processors level simultaneously.

2.3.2. PHILOSOPHY OF COMMUNICATION.

The fundamental principle of the hierarchical communication is the "bottom-up" transmission of information, so that, the recognition of an integrated amount of information is realized at a level, where the processor has the ability to do it.
Another important factor in the hierarchical communication is the "top-down" procedure of the integrated decision at a proper tree level.
The above factor indicates that in the lower levels some tree-nodes have the ability to recognize pieces of information, so that, some father-nodes to compose those pieces.
Priorities among the processors communication have not been determined, because the system design does not require them for the parallel communication of the nodes with their father.
Finally, the tree root recognizes the whole picture and the partial recognitions at each tree level.
It must be noted that, although the recognition task takes place in several levels of the tree, the picture information remains at the slave-processors memory, so that, the memories of the rest procesors are available only for communication and recognition subroutines.
In this way,the picture recognition (in upper levels) is realized by using the memories of the leaves. This feature means memory saving and speeded-up processing.
After the end of the recognition process, the root-processor, which has the general control of the MTN, undertakes to give out the required information about the picture objects that have been recognized. Sometimes, if it is necessary a master-slave processor, under the control of the full master, realizes the information output.

It is obvious that the MTN can be the basic part of real-time robot vision systems.

2.3.3. PROCESS OF COMMUNICATION.

According to the previous network design, a leaf-processor communicates with its father - processor, by setting the required information into its father's memory. Also, a father-processor communicates with its son-processors, by setting its information into predetermined locations of its memory and informing proper son-processor to take it.
In more details, when the recognition processing, which takes place at a leaf-processor memory, has been completed, then the leaf-processor "asks"to communicate with its father-processor (slave to master/slave communication).
Initially, the slave-processor, through the T.S.D.2 and T.S.D.3 devices, see figure 6 , sends a signal to the master-slave processor, into S.O. pin, and askes for communication.
The slave-processor does not send its code number, thus, the master-slave can not recognize, which processor askes for communication. The master-slave processor checks its S.O. bit, in microprogramming mode, and realizes when that bit has been set. Then the master-slave processor carries out its processing, that it is executing, disconnects its memory from itself and connects its slave-processors with the proper locations of its memory. This procedure is realized by the proper signals to the T.S.D.2 device. Sometimes it is not necessary to be the master-slave processing completed, when this processing does not require some memory accessing, thus, the master-slave processor has the ability to connect its slave-processor with its memory.
It is important to note that the slave-processor does not need to send its code number to its master-slave. This is obvious from the following observation that, there is the possibility of four slave-processors to ask for communication simultaneously, with the master-slave processor's S.O. bit, through an OR gate. Then the master-slave processor repeats the same procedure, less than four processors cases,by connecting its memory with its slave-processors. This feature gives the MTN the ability of parallel communication among its processors.
After the proper master-slave memory connection with the slave processors is done each available slave-processor stores into the proper memory location a specific byte, which indicates its "status". After that each slave processor resets the S.O. bit of the master-slave.
The term "status" means that the slave-processor informs its master-slave in which stage of the following is found : (i) It has recognized an integrated information in its area, see figure 4,5 . (ii) It has not recognized an integrated information in its area. (iii) It is empty of information and (iv) It has not carried out the recognition processing yet.
The (iv) stage indicates that the corresponding processor has not completed the processing of its data yet and does not ask for communication. At this case this processor does not send the specific byte of its status to its master-slave processor. However,the master-slave processor recognizes the (iv) stage of this slave-processor, because the proper memory location of the specific byte contains the special value 0 (zero).
Now, after the slave-processors communication demand with its master-slave, the slaves reset the S.O. bit of its master-slave. Then the master-slave researches the slaves' specific bytes and recognizes which stage each slave-processor is found in, and knows the required duration that the slave processor needs to send to it the processed information from its picture part.
The way by which the master-slave processor inform its slave-processors that "is ready" to send him their information, is by setting their S.O. bit. When the S.O. bit is "set" the slave-processors (which have asked for communication) send their data to their master-slave. When the S.O. bit is "reset" the slaves can not send information to their master processor.
Now, the communication among the slave-processors and its master-slave, while the S.O. bit is "set", is not allowed.
In some cases when the master-slave processor "wishes" to send information or askes for something from its slave-processors, it informs them through the special commands to read the contents of the specific memory locations.
It is noted that the communication among the master-slave processors and the full master appears to have the same characteristics to that of the slave-processors and the master-slave one.
It is perceptible that the "bottom-up" and the "top-down" communication presented has a parallel-serial mode, similar to the human vision perception.

3. CONCLUSIONS.

In this paper the Microprocessor Tree Network (MTN) Configuration applied on robot vision systems is presented. The MTN consists of 21 R-6502 μPs in a complete quad-tree mode. The MTN appears to have a behavior similar to the human vision system.

The partial and parallel-serial mode of picture processing gives the MTN the ability to stand among the most efficient, real-time robot vision system. The implementation of the MTN is in progress in the Digital Systems Laboratory in the Department of Computer Science and Informatics and the general form of it, is the next research step of the authors.

REFERENCES.

1.- E. Lerner/APPLICATIONS:COMPUTERS THAT SEE/IEEE Spectrum, Oct. 1980, pp.89-93

2.- M. Duff,D. Watson, T. Fountain and G. Shaw/A CERCULAR LOGIC ARRAY FOR IMAGE PROCESSING/Journal of Pattern Recognition, Pergamon Press, 1973, Vol. 5, No. 3, pp. 229-247.

3.- N. Bourbakis and D. Panagiotopoulos/ /A PROPOSAL FOR THE DESIGN OF A ROBOT EYE/Proc. of the IASTED Int. Symp. on ROBOTICS, March 1982, Davos,Switzerland, pp. 20-23.

4.- A. Shackil/SPECIAL REPORT XI:AN ELECTRONIC HUMAN EYE/IEEE Spectrum, Sept. 1980, pp. 89-93.

5.- G. Bylinsky/AND NOW, CHIPS THAT CAN SEE/Fortune, Aug. 1981, pp. 161-169.

6.- R. Jarvis/A COMPUTER VISION AND ROBOTICS LABORATORY/Computer, June 1982, pp. 8-22.

7.- W. Perkins/A MODEL-BASED VISION SYSTEM FOR INDUSTRIAL PARTS/IEEE Trans. on Computers, Febr. 1978, Vol.C-27, No.2, pp. 247-253.

8.- S. Tanimoto and A. Klinger/STRUCTURED COMPUTER VISION/ Academic Press, N.Y. 1980.

9.- C.Vaitsos / A MICROPROCESSOR TREE NETWORK FOR REAL-TIME DATA PROCESSING OF A TWO-DIMENSIONAL ARRAY/ Technical Report, Dept. of Computer Engineering, University of Patras, Patras Greece.

10.- L. Uhr/PSYCHOLOGICAL MOTIVATION AND UNDERLYING CONCEPTS/Academic Press, N.Y. 1980,(editors:S. Tanimoto and A. Klinger / STRUCTURES COMPUTER VISION).

11.- R. Bajcsy and D. Rosenthal/VISUAL AND CONCEPTUAL FOCUS OF ATTENTION/Academic Press, N.Y. 1980, (editors:S. Tanimoto and A. Klinger/STRUCTURED COMPUTER VISION).

12.- B. Kruse/SYSTEM ARCHITECTURE FOR IMAGE ANALYSIS/Academic Press,N.Y. 1980,(editors:S.Tanimoto and A.Klinger/SRUCTURED COMPUTER VISION).

13.- N. Bourbakis/NEW, REAL-TIME PROCESSING METHODS OF STRUCTURED IMAGES/ PhD thesis 1982, Dept. Of Computer Engineering, University of Patras, Patras Greece.

14. - N.Bourbakis/ON MICROCOMPUTERS BASED PARALLEL IMAGE PROCESSING MACHINE/ 4th IASTED International Symposium and Course MECO- 81, Sept.1-3, 1981, Cairo, Egypt, pp. 204-207.

15.- A. Klinger/REGULAR DECOMPOSITION AND PICTURE STRUCTURE/ Proc. 1974 International Conference IEEE on S. M. C., Dallas Texas, N. Y. 1974, pp. 307 - 310.

16.- M. Levine/REGION ANALYSIS USING A PYRAMID DATA STRUCTURE/ Structured Computer Vision (S. Tanimoto and A. Klinger eds.) Academic Press, New York 1980, pp. 57-100.

17.- S. Tanimoto and T. Pavlidis/A HIERARCHICAL DATA STRUCTURE FOR PICTURE PROCESSING/Computer Graphics and Image Processing 4, 1975, pp. 104 119.

18.- D. Hubel and T. Wiesel/BRAIN MECHANISMS OF VISION/Scientific American, 1979, pp. 150-162.

19.- D. Hubel/THE VISUAL CORTEX OF THE BRAIN/Sensory Processes and Perception Nov. 1963, pp. 253-261.

20.- N. Bourbakis/IMAGE SCANNING ALGORITHMS USED BY A ROBOT VISION SYSTEM/ /Proc. of the IASTED Int. Symp. on APPLIED INFORMATICS, March 1983, Lille France, Vol. 1, pp. 193-196.

21.- R. Allan/APPLICATIONS:BUSY ROBOTS SPUR PRODUCTIVITY/IEEE Spectrum, Sept. 1979, pp. 31-36.

22.- J. Ferreira/THE STATUS OF ROBOTICS/ 46th Int. Conf.:"UPDATE ON DATABASES /ROBOTICS", April 1981, Athens Greece.

23.- A.Nicola/IMPLEMENTED ROBOTICS SYSTEMS IN FIAT AND ASSEMBLY DIVISION/46thInt. Conf.:"UPDATE ON DATABASES/ROBOTICS", April 1981, Athens Greece.

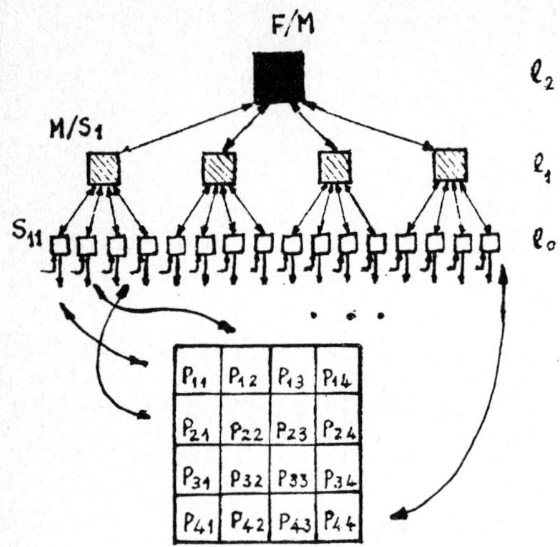

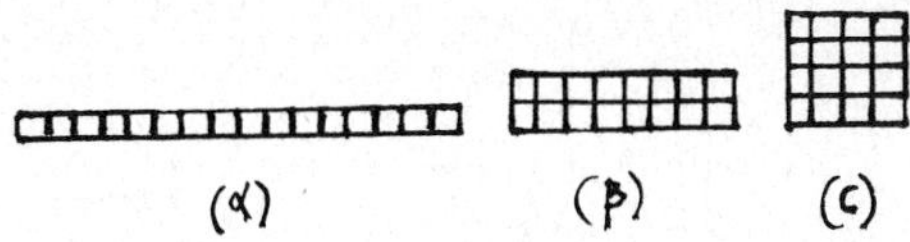

Fig. 2: It shows three forms of pixels areas a) row-area, b) rectagular-area and c) square-area.

Fig. 1: It shows the quad-tree mode of the MTN and the picture quadrants that correspond to the slave-processor nodes.

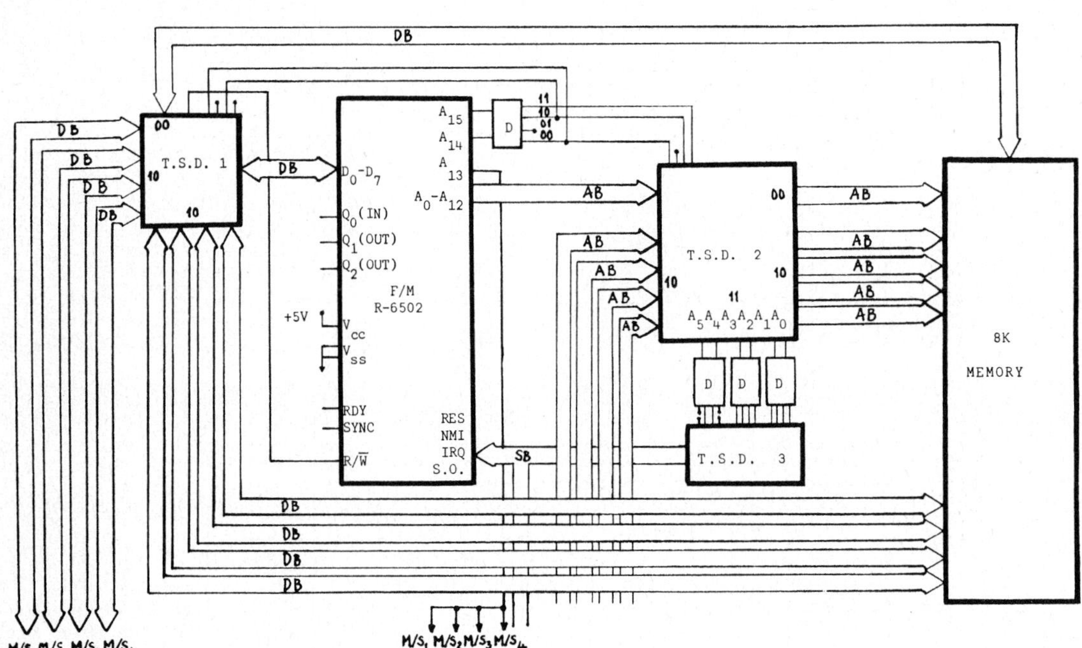

Fig. 3: It shows the internal structure of the Full/Master processor(F/M) of the MTN.

TABLE 1

A_{15}	A_{14}	
0	0	AB and DB "to" its memory
0	1	AB and DB "to" master's memory
1	0	AB and DB "to" slaves' memories
1	1	AB "to" T.S.D. 3

TABLE 2

A_5	A_4	A_3	A_2	A_1	A_0	
				0	0	"to" slave 1
				0	1	"to" slave 2
				1	0	"to" slave 3
				1	1	"to" slave 4
		0	0			RES
		0	1			NMI :Special Commands
		1	0			IRQ
		1	1			S.O.
0	0					"to" master
0	1					"to" slaves
1	0					"to" its processor
1	1					N.C.

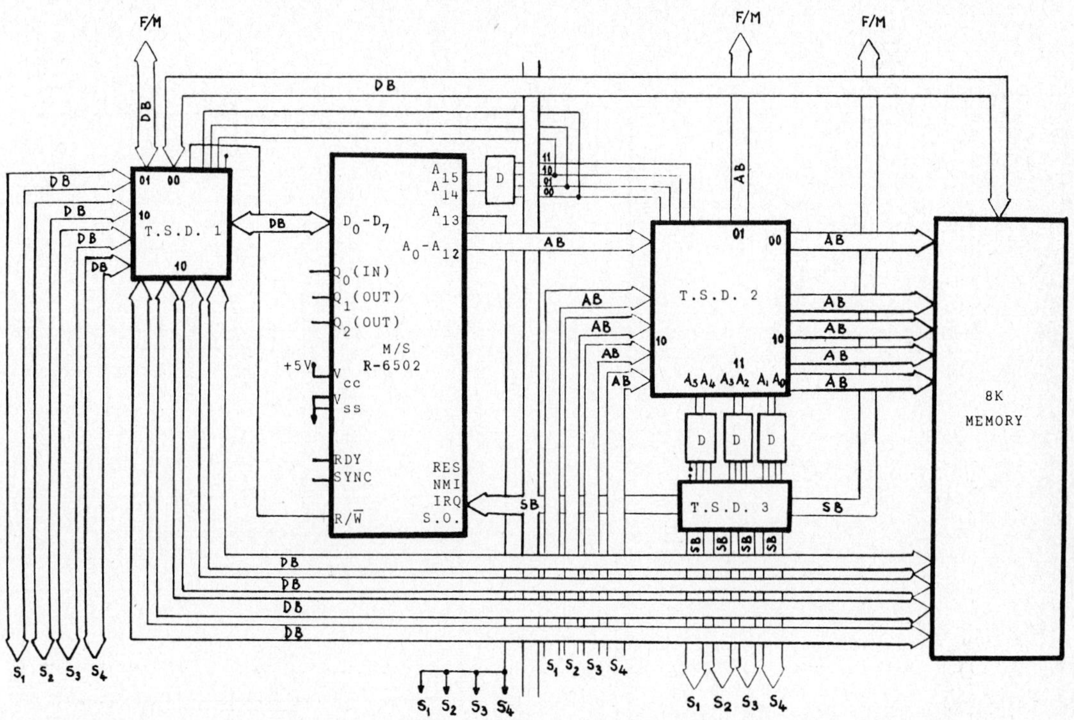

Fig. 4: It shows the internal structure of the Master/ Slave processor(M/S) of the MTN.

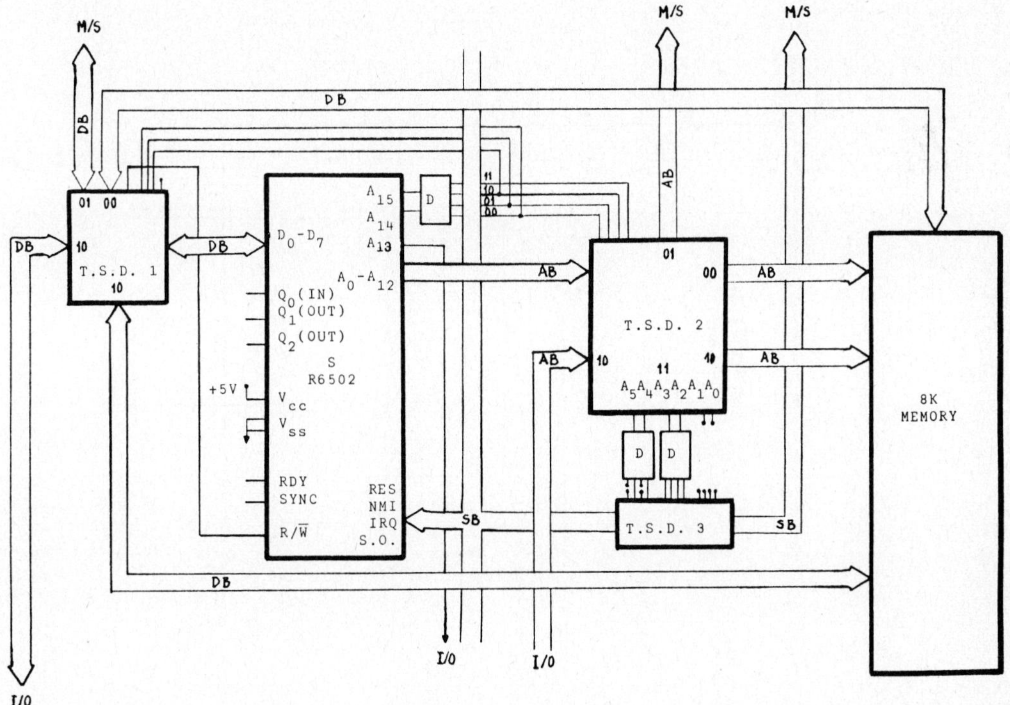

Fig. 5: It shows the internal structure of the Slave-processor (S) of the MTN.

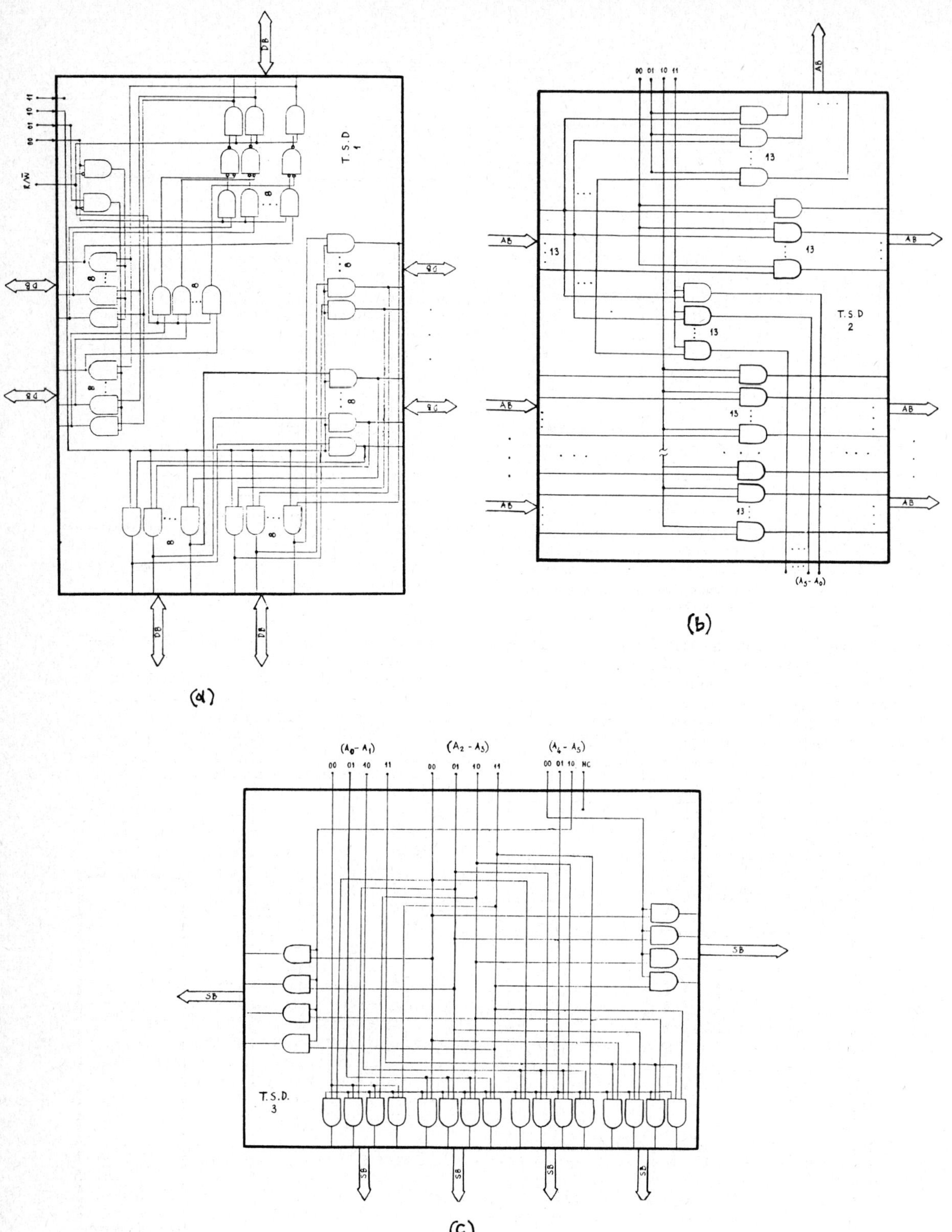

Fig. 6: It shows the internal structure of the Target Selscting Devices (T.S.D. 1, T.S.D. 2, and T.S.D. 3).

DIGITAL TECHNIQUES in Simulation, Communication and Control
Spyros G. Tzafestas (editor)
Elsevier Science Publishers B.V. (North-Holland) © IMACS, 1985

AN ANALYSIS AND DESIGN APPROACH FOR STATIC POWER CONVERTERS BASED ON DIGITAL SIMULATION

P.D. Ziogas E.P. Wiechmann

Concordia University
Department of Electrical Engineering
Montreal, Quebec, Canada H3G 1M8

The relative success of the "cut and try" method has made the design of static power converters more of an 'art' than a 'science'. As a result, no comprehensive analysis approach is available today that can be used to design static converters with a good degree of confidence. Some important aspects of this problem -concerning mainly static voltage source inverters- are treated in this paper within the framework of a generalized analysis and design method. The subject approach utilizes the switching function concept to derive relevant analytical expressions, and digital simulation to obtain relevant design data.

I. INTRODUCTION

Despite the ongoing intensive research activity in the area of static power converters there is no comprehensive analysis method available today that can be used to obtain relevant design information for these converters.

Proper converter design requires that maximum rms, peak and average current and voltage ratings are known so that components with adequate safety margins can be selected. The same information is also essential to the potential user who wants an in depth evaluation of a converter under consideration.

The task of finding the maximum component ratings requires that:

(a) The load is adequately modelled.
(b) Worst operating conditions are specified or identified.
(c) The static converter is adequately modelled.
(d) A suitable analysis method is established.

Continuing research in modelling of active converter loads, such as electric motors, has resulted in several models of varying degrees of accuracy and complexity [1],[2],[3]. Less complex loads, such as office and emergency type of equipment can be modelled by a combination of passive elements and voltage and/or current sources.

Identifying worst operating conditions requires careful consideration of operating characteristics and requirements of both load and converter components. For example, typical worst case operating conditions for a thyristor inverter occur while supplying maximum load with minimum DC bus voltage. The respective conditions for a transistor inverter, however, occur while the inverter is supplying maximum load with maximum dc bus voltage. The reason is that transistors (especially bipolars) are much more sensitive to over voltage than over current stresses [4].

With a load model available and worst operating conditions identified, the next step, in obtaining the required component ratings, is to develop an adequate converter model. Experience with static converts [5],[6] has shown that the most useful analytical information is obtained when the converter is viewed by the input and output terminals as a multi-frequency ac current and/or voltage source.

Consequently the converter can be modelled as a black box whose transfer characteristics are analytically described by the Fourier series expansion of its respective set of switching functions [5], [6], [7]. By multiplying converter switching functions with expressions describing respective input voltages, analytical expressions for the converter output voltages are obtained. Line current components are derived next as ratios of voltages and respective impedances. Finally, the required component ratings are calculated from the products of line currents and voltages with the appropriate switching functions. These are the basics of converter method of analysis presented in this paper.

The remaining part focusses, for brevity, on an important class of dc to ac converters known as voltage source inverters. However, the analysis method developed can be applied with minor modifications, to any other class of static converters, such as, current source inverters, rectifiers, cycloconverters, etc.

II. SWITCHING FUNCTIONS AND INVERTER MODELLING

As mentioned in Section I, a converter model as a multi-frequency ac generator is based on the particular switching function employed. For each converter configuration however, there are several switching functions that yield identical output results. Such a case is shown in Fig. 2, where two inverter switching functions $S_1(\omega t)$ and $S_2(\omega t)$ (obtained with the sine PWM control scheme [8], [9], Fig. 2.a) are presented. Multiplication of the inverter input voltage E (Fig. 1) with either of the two functions yields, after phase voltage subtraction, the same line to line voltage waveforms (e.g. V_{ab} Fig. 2.c). Specifically, function $S_1(\omega t)$ represents the switching function of one of the three inverter legs (i.e. leg comprised of S_{w_1} and S_{w_2}, Fig. 1) while $S_2(\omega t)$ is the switching function of one of the six inverter switches (i.e. S_{w_1}). Consequently $S_1(\omega t)$ type of functions have the advantage of simplifying the analysis, evaluation and selection of PWM schemes, while $S_2(\omega t)$ type of functions are more effective with the computation of current ratings of inverter components.

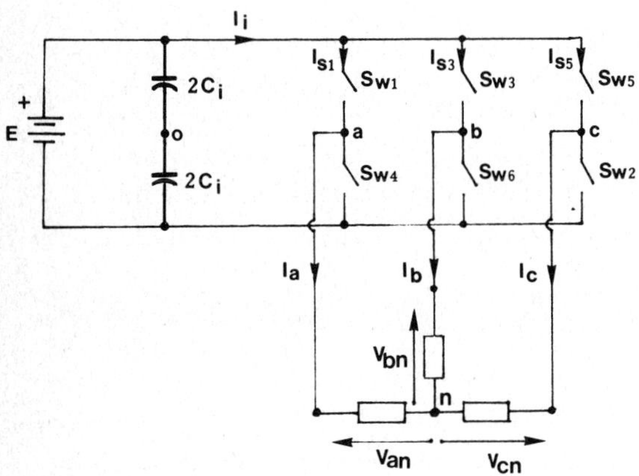

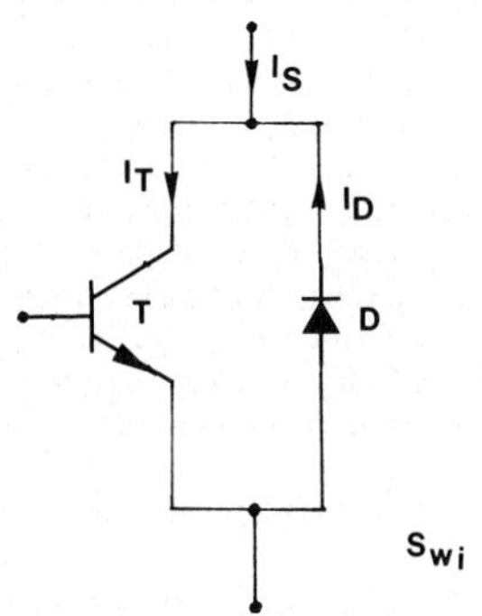

Fig. 1: (a) simplified Voltage Source (V.S.) inverter circuit diagram
(b) actual configuration of $S_{w_1}, S_{w_2}, \ldots, S_{w_6}$

Although switching function patterns (e.g. as in Figs. 2.b and 2.d) help to visualize the generated inverter voltage and current waveforms, they are not suitable for further analytical work. Effective inverter analysis requires that suitable mathematical expressions are found for $S_1(\omega t)$ and $S_2(\omega t)$ functions.

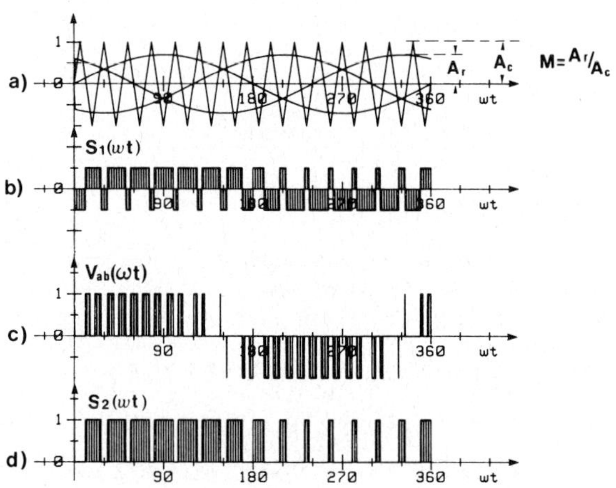

Fig. 2: The sine PWM inverter control scheme
(a) method of obtaining inverter switching points
(b) inverter phase, $S_1(\omega t)$ type of switching function
(c) respective inverter line-line voltage waveform
(d) inverter phase, $S_2(\omega t)$ type of switching function

Such expressions can be obtained by deriving the respective Fourier series expansions, as shown next with eqns. (1) and (2).

$$S_1(\omega t) = \sum_{\substack{n=1 \\ n \text{ odd}}}^{\infty} A_n \sin(n\omega t) \qquad (1)$$

$$S_2(\omega t) = B_o + \sum_{\substack{n=1 \\ n \text{ odd}}}^{\infty} B_n \cos(n\omega t) \qquad (2)$$

It is noted that the only difference between $S_1(\omega t)$ and $S_2(\omega t)$ is that $S_2(\omega t)$ has a dc component not present in $S_1(\omega t)$.

III. ANALYSIS METHOD

With the inverter switching functions $S_1(\omega t)$ and $S_2(\omega t)$ identified (as in Fig. 2) and analytically specified (as with eqns. (1) and (2)), the inverter phase voltages $V_{ao}(\omega t)$, $V_{bo}(\omega t)$ and $V_{co}(\omega t)$ (Fig. 1) are given by;

$$V_{ao}(\omega t)=E\ S_1(\omega t)=\frac{E}{2}\sum_{\substack{n=1\\ n\ \text{odd}}}^{\infty} A_n \sin(n\omega t) \quad (3a)$$

$$V_{bo}(\omega t)=V_{ao}(\omega t-120°) \quad (3b)$$

$$V_{co}(\omega t)=V_{ao}(\omega t+120°) \quad (3c)$$

Similarly, the respective line to line voltages $V_{ab}(\omega t)$, $V_{bc}(\omega t)$ and $V_{ca}(\omega t)$ are given by;

$$V_{ab}(\omega t)=V_{ao}(\omega t)-V_{bo}(\omega t)=\sqrt{3}\,\frac{E}{2}\sum_{\substack{n=1\\ n\ \text{odd}\\ n\neq \text{triplen}}}^{\infty} A_n \sin[n(\omega t+30°)] \quad (4a)$$

$$V_{bc}(\omega t)=V_{ab}(\omega t-120°) \quad (4b)$$

$$V_{ca}(\omega t)=V_{ab}(\omega t+120°) \quad (4c)$$

and assuming a 3-ϕ balanced load, the inverter line currents are given by:

$$I_a(\omega t) = \frac{\sqrt{3}\ V_{ab}\ (\omega t-30-\phi)}{Z(\omega t)} = \frac{3E}{Z(\omega t)}\ S_1(\omega t) \quad (5a)$$

$$I_b(\omega t) = I_a(\omega t-120°) \quad (5b)$$

$$I_c(\omega t) = I_a(\omega t+120°) \quad (5c)$$

where: $Z(\omega t)$ is the impedance of the equivalent delta connected phase load.

A simulated $I_a(\omega t)$ waveform obtained with eqn. (5a), load power factor angle ϕ = 60°, and the PWM scheme shown in Fig. 2, is presented in Fig. 3.b.

Next, the portion of line current conducted by each of the six ideal inverter switches of Fig. 1 $I_{s_i}(\omega t)$, is obtained from the product of the line current waveform with the respective switching function (e.g. $I_a(\omega t)$ and $S_2(\omega t)$), as follows:

$$I_{s_1}(\omega t) = I_a(\omega t) \cdot S_2(\omega t) \quad (6)$$

A simulated $I_{s_1}(\omega t)$ waveform obtained with eqn. (6), for the above example, is shown in Fig. 3.d. Furthermore, each of the six ideal inverter switches shown in Fig. 1, consists of an unidirectional controlled switch (e.g. thyristor, transistor, etc.) with an anti-parallel diode (Fig. 1.b). Therefore, the ideal switch current $I_{s_i}(\omega t)$ can be analytically decomposed into its unidirectional controlled switch and diode components, $I_{T_i}(\omega t)$ and $I_{D_i}(\omega t)$ respectively, according to:

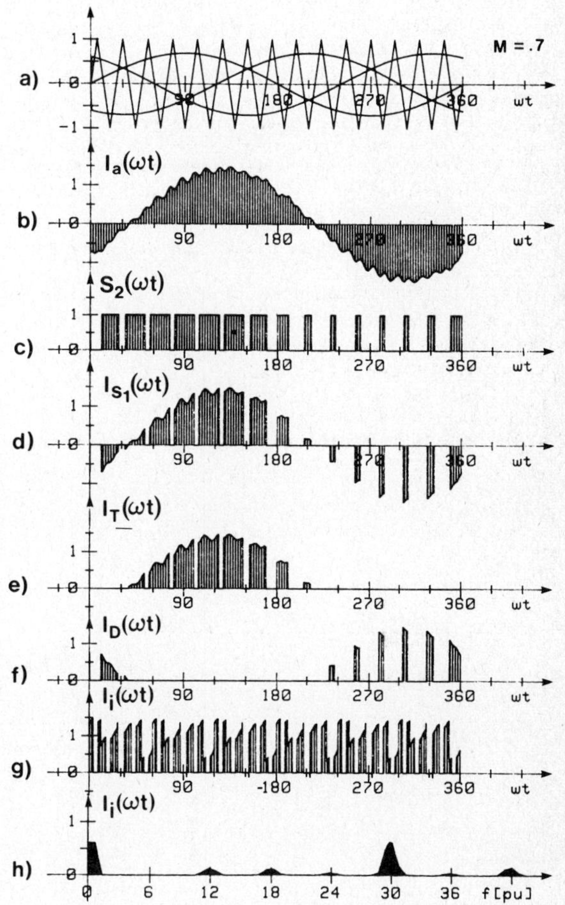

Fig. 3: Inverter generated current waveforms with the SPWM control scheme and load p.f. = .8 lagging
(a) method of obtaining inverter switching points
(b) inverter line current $I_a(\omega t)$ waveform
(c) $S_2(\omega t)$ type of switching function
(d) ideal switch current $I_{s1}(\omega t)$ waveform
(e) controlled switch current $I_T(\omega t)$ waveform
(f) diode current $I_D(\omega t)$ waveform
(g) inverter input current $I_i(\omega t)$ waveform
(h) inverter input current spectrum

$$I_{s_i}(\omega t) = I_{T_i}(\omega t) + I_{D_i}(\omega t) \qquad (7)$$

Now, since this kind of analysis is typically performed with a digital computer, the numerical values of the current waveform $I_{s_i}(\omega t)$ (obtained with eqn. (6)) are assumed to be stored into an n-dimensional array ($\vec{I}_{s_i}(n)$). Consequently, eqn. (7) can be readily implemented by subjecting each array vector to the conditional statements:

$$\text{IF: } \vec{I}_{s_i}(n) > 0 \text{ then } \vec{I}_{T_i}(n) = \vec{I}_{s_i}(n) \qquad (8)$$

$$\text{IF: } \vec{I}_{s_i}(n) < 0 \text{ then } \vec{I}_{D_i}(n) = \vec{I}_{s_i}(n) \qquad (9)$$

Simulated $I_T(\omega t)$ and $I_D(\omega t)$ waveforms obtained with expressions (8) and (9) are shown in Figs. 3.e and 3.f respectively.

The average and rms values of $I_T(\omega t)$ and $I_D(\omega t)$ are computed next through numerical integration of respective vectors $\vec{I}_T(n)$ and $\vec{I}_D(n)$, as follows:

$$\bar{I}_T = \frac{1}{2n}\sum_{k=1}^{n}(\vec{I}_T(k) + \vec{I}_T(k-1)) \qquad (10)$$

and

$$I_{TR} = \sqrt{\frac{1}{2n}\sum_{k=1}^{n}(\vec{I}_T^{\,2}(k) + \vec{I}_T^{\,2}(k-1))} \qquad (11)$$

The same formulae can also be employed to obtain $\bar{I}_D$ and I_{DR} ratings. Relevant simulated results for $\bar{I}_T$, I_{TR}, $\bar{I}_D$ and I_{DR}, obtained with the SPWM control scheme, are shown in Figs. 4.a,b,d and 4.e respectively. Moreover, peak I_T and I_D values can be easily identified by successively examining respective array vectors $\vec{I}_T(n)$ and $\vec{I}_D(n)$. Again, relevant results for $\hat{I}_T$ and $\hat{I}_D$ are shown in Figs. 4.c and 4.f respectively.

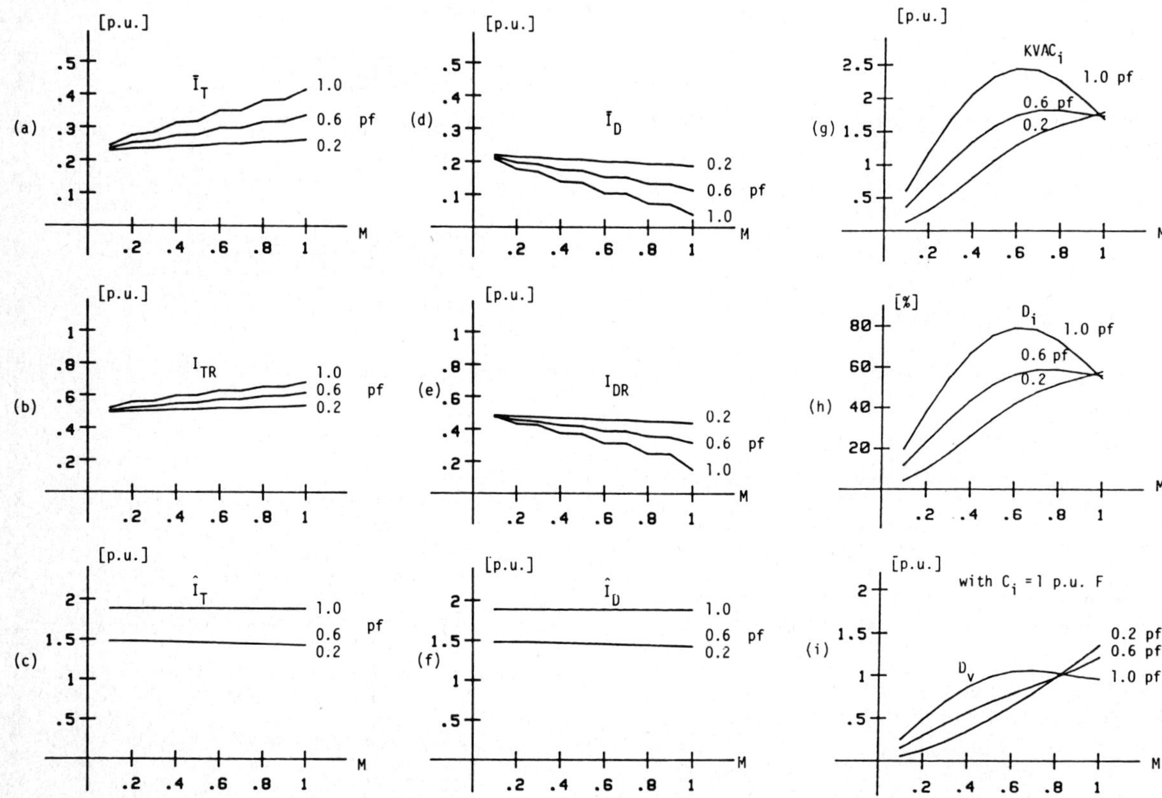

Fig. 4: Normalized inverter component ratings with the sine PWM control scheme.

(a) controlled switch (transistor) average current ratings, $\bar{I}_T$
(b) controlled switch rms current ratings, I_{TR}
(c) controlled switch peak current ratings, $\hat{I}_T$
(d) diode average current ratings, $\bar{I}_D$
(e) diode rms current ratings, I_{DR}
(f) diode peak current ratings, $\hat{I}_D$
(g) input filter capacitor KVA ratings, $KVAC_i$ (eqn. 16)
(h) inverter input current distortion ratings, D_i (eqn. 15)
(i) inverter input voltage distortion ratings, D_v (eqn. 14)

To complete the inverter modelling as multi-frequency ac current generator the analysis method is extended to include the inverter input current $I_i(\omega t)$ and its spectra.

From Fig. 1.

$$I_i(\omega t) = I_{s_1}(\omega t) + I_{s_3}(\omega t) + I_{s_5}(\omega t) \quad (12)$$

and by using eqn. (6)

$$I_i(\omega t)=I_a(\omega t)\cdot S_2(\omega t)+I_a(\omega t-120)\cdot S_2(\omega t-120) + I_a(\omega t+120) \cdot S_2(\omega t+120) \quad (13)$$

A simulated $I_i(\omega t)$ waveform and its respective spectrum, obtained with eqn. (13), is shown in Figs. 3.g, and 3.h. It is obvious that in addition to its dc component, $I_i(\omega t)$, contains a large number of undesired harmonics which must be supplied from the input filter capacitor C_i without causing serious voltage distortion D_v to the dc input bus. For a given $I_i(\omega t)$ spectrum (e.g. Fig. 3.h) and assuming; C_i = 1 p.u. capacitor, the amount of inverter input dc voltage distortion D_v is given by;

$$D_v = \frac{100}{E} \left[\sum_{n=2}^{\infty} \left(\frac{I_{in}}{n}\right)^2 \right]^{\frac{1}{2}} [\%] \quad (14)$$

While the respective inverter input current distortion, D_i, and normalized input (filter) capacitor kVA, $kVAC_i$, are given by;

$$D_i = \frac{100}{I_{i1}} \left(\sum_{n=2}^{\infty} I_{in}^2 \right)^{\frac{1}{2}} [\%] \quad (15)$$

$$kVAC_i = E \times \left(\sum_{n=2}^{\infty} I_{in}^2 \right)^{\frac{1}{2}} (p.u.) \quad (16)$$

<u>where</u>: I_{in} is the nth harmonic component of the inverter input current I_i, and E is the inverter input dc voltage (being $E = 2\sqrt{2}$ p.u. with the SPWM scheme).

I_{in} is the nth harmonic component of $I_i(\omega t)$

E is the rated value of dc bus voltage.

D_v, D_i and $kVAC_i$ curves obtained with eqns. (14), (15) and (16) for various operating conditions are shown in Figs. 4.i, h and g respectively.

IV. EVALUATION OF PREDICTED RESULTS

Generalized results for inverter component ratings obtained with the analysis method discussed in Section III are presented in Fig. 4. For maximum applicability these results are expressed in per unit (p.u.), where; the rated rms value of the fundamental component V_{ao1} of the inverter load (line to neutral) voltage V_{ao} (Fig. 1) has been taken as one p.u. volts, and the respective rms value of the fundamental load current I_{a_1} as one p.u. Amps. Moreover, the results have been obtained with the assumption that the load is balanced and that line currents I_{a_1}, I_{b_1} and I_{c_1} remain constant and equal to one p.u. Amps. while inverter output voltage V_{ao} varies from one p.u. to zero volts. The purpose of this assumption is the simulation of ac motor type of loads in their constant torque variable speed region of operation (i.e. Volts/Herz ratio approx. constant).

More specifically, Figs. 4.a and b show that $\bar{I}_T$ and I_{TR} ratings of the unidirectional controlled switches increase as load power factor and modulation index M increases. The opposite is true with respective diode ratings $\bar{I}_D$ and I_{DR}, as shown in Figs. 4.d and 4.e. The explanation is that conduction intervals of unidirectional controlled switches decrease with M and reactive currents flowing through feedback diodes increase.

Other results of interest are the D_v (eqn. (14)), D_i (eqn. (15)), and $kVAC_i$ (eqn. (16)) curves shown in Figs. 4.i, h and g. These results reveal that inverter input current distortion D_i and associated input capacitor kVA increase as load power factor increases and become worst around the M = 0.6 point. The opposite is true with the worst input voltage distortion D_v. It is also noted that D_i and $kVAC_i$ values shown in Figs. 4.h and g are independent of carrier frequency f_c while D_v values decrease as f_c increases.

<u>Discussion</u>: It is noted that the analytical results presented and discussed in this section have been obtained assuming circuit components with ideal switching characteristics. Therefore, the effect on inverter component ratings of factors such as; finite switching times and snubber and/or commutation circuits have not been included in these results. The reason is that such effects cannot be properly assessed before converter topology, type of switches, switching frequencies, snubber configuration and component values, etc. are known. Moreover, present design and manufacturing trends, for obvious reasons, favor the complete elimination of all auxiliary components. Consequently, the omission of the aforementioned deviations from the proposed design approach does not present a serious problem. Also, one could simply perform the first converter design iteration by using results obtained as shown in this section and then include, on subsequent iterations, all relevant secondary factors not previously included.

V. A DESIGN EXAMPLE

In order to illustrate the significance and facilitate understanding of predicted results discussed in Section IV, the following design example is presented.

Example: With the three phase system shown in Fig. 1, it is assumed that:

- rated output power : 30 kVA (17)
- rated phase load voltage: 100 V_{rms} (18)
- expected load p.f. variation: $0.2 < p.f. < 1.0$ lagging (19)

With the inverter employing the sine PWM scheme (Fig. 2), find the maximum: peak, average and rms current values for the inverter components, as well as, input filter capacitor kVA.

Solution: From eqns. (17) and (18),

$$1 \text{ p.u. power} = \frac{30{,}000}{3} = 10{,}000 \text{ VA} \quad (20)$$

and

$$1 \text{ p.u. voltage, rms} = 100 \text{ Volts} \quad (21)$$

Therefore:

$$1 \text{ p.u. current, rms} = \frac{10{,}000}{100} = 100 \text{ Amps} \quad (22)$$

Furthermore, from Fig. 4 the required maximum current values are found to be:

$\hat{I}_T$ =1.9 p.u. (Fig. 4.c, with: p.f.=1.0, M=1.0)
$\bar{I}_T$ =0.41p.u. (Fig. 4.a, with: p.f.=1.0, M=1.0)
I_{TR}=0.67p.u. (Fig. 4.b, with: p.f.=1.0, M=1.0)
$\hat{I}_D$ =1.6 p.u. (Fig. 4.f, with: p.f.=0.2, M=0.0)
$\bar{I}_D$= 0.23p.u. (Fig. 4.d, with: p.f.=0.2, M=0.0)
I_{DR}=0.5 p.u. (Fig. 4.e, with: p.f.=0.2, M=0.0)

Moreover, maximum input filter kVA;

$kVAC_i$=2.4p.u.(Fig. 4.g, with: p.f.=0.6, M=1.0)

And, conversion of in p.u. values into actual Amps. and kVA values, yield:

$\hat{I}_T$ = 100 × 1.9 p.u. = 190 Amps
$\bar{I}_T$ = 100 × 0.41 p.u. = 41 Amps
I_{TR} = 100 × 0.67 p.u. = 67 Amps
$\hat{I}_D$ = 100 × 1.6 p.u. = 160 Amps
$\bar{I}_D$ = 100 × 0.23 p.u. = 23 Amps
I_{DR} = 100 × 0.50 p.u. = 50 Amps

And;

$kVAC_i$ = 10.0 × 2.4 p.u. = 24.0 kVA

Experimental Results

To check the validity of the proposed analysis and design method, selected theoretical results were verified with an experimental 2 kVA unit. In particular Figs. 5.a and b illustrate experimental inverter output line to line voltage $V_{ab}(\omega t)$ and line current $I_a(\omega t)$ waveforms, obtained with the sine PWM control scheme, while Figs. 5.d and c show the respective switch current $I_{s_1}(\omega t)$ and inverter input current $I_i(\omega t)$ waveforms. The frequency spectrum for $I_i(\omega t)$ is shown in Fig. 5.e. Comparison with results shown in Figs. 2.c, 3.b, c, g and h, reveals a close agreement between predicted and experimental current/voltage waveforms and values. Moreover, agreement in waveforms implies agreement in respective peak, average rms current/voltage values.

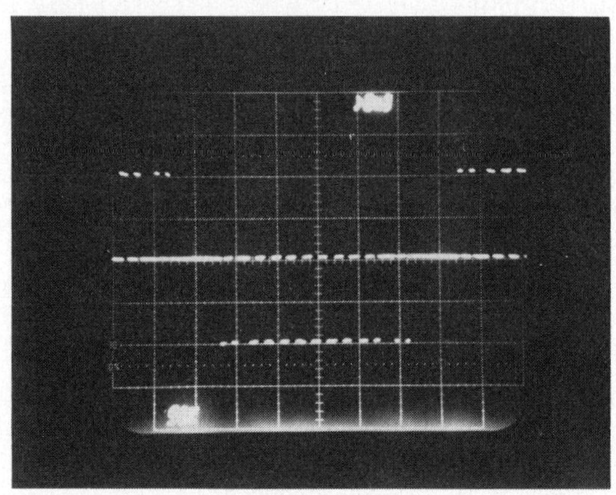

50 Volts/div.
f_o = 60 Hz
(a) Inverter output line-line voltage, V_{ab}

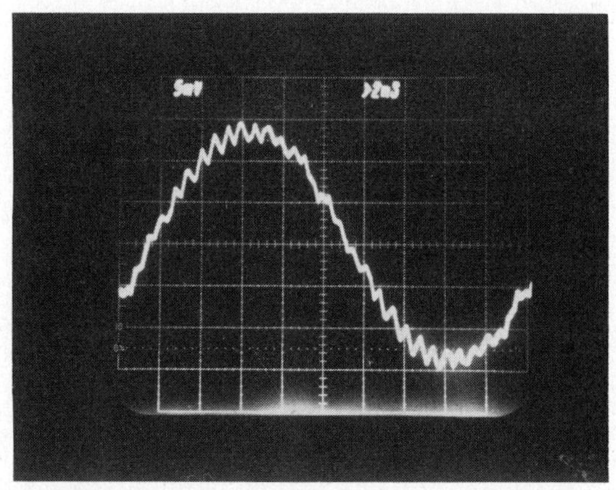

4 Amps/div.
f_o = 60 Hz
(b) Inverter output line current, I_a

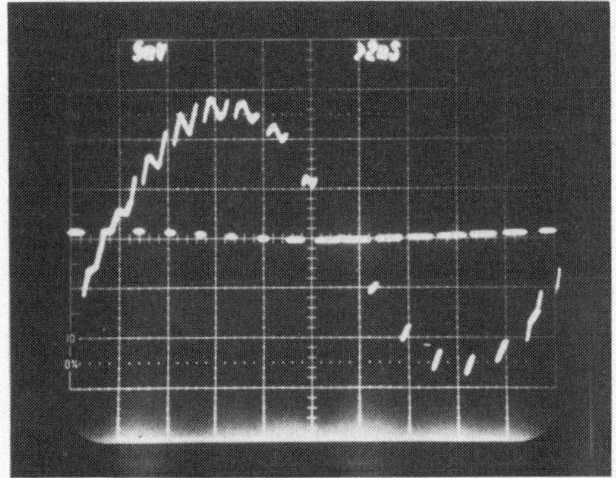

4 Amps/div.
f_o = 60 Hz
(c) Inverter input current, I_i

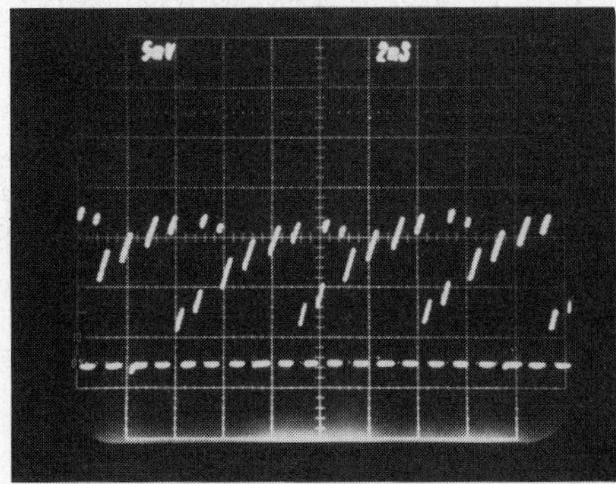

4 Amps/div.
f_o = 60 Hz
(d) Inverter switch current, I_s

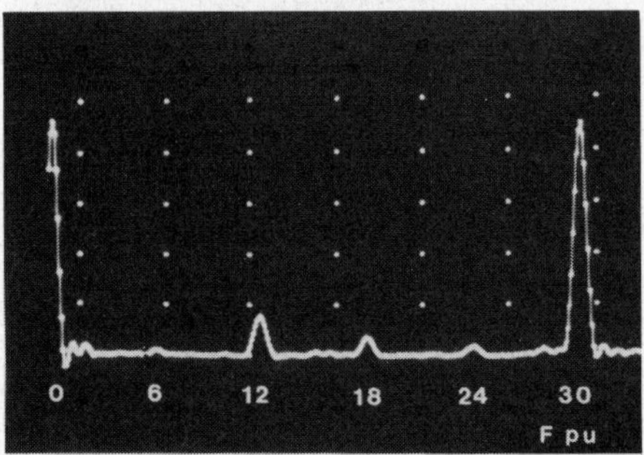

(e) Frequency spectrum of the inverter input current, I_i

Fig. 5: Experimental inverter voltage and current waveforms with the SPWM scheme and load pf = .8 lagging

Further experimental results, regarding worst case average, peak and rms inverter switch current ratings, are shown in Fig. 6. To facilitate comparison, respective predicted results have been plotted on the same set of axes. Close agreement between experimental and predicted results is again evident.

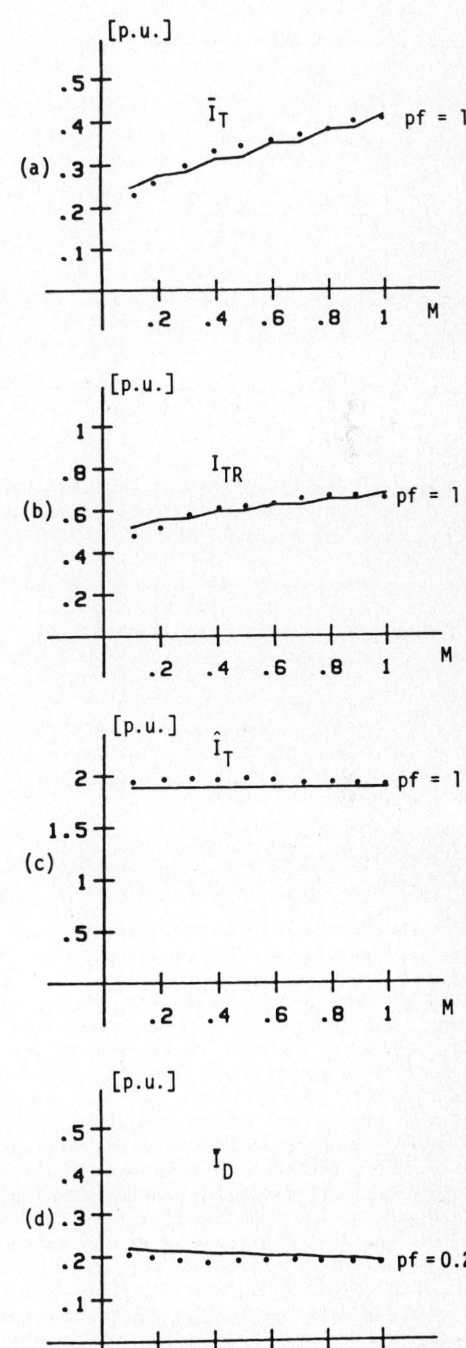

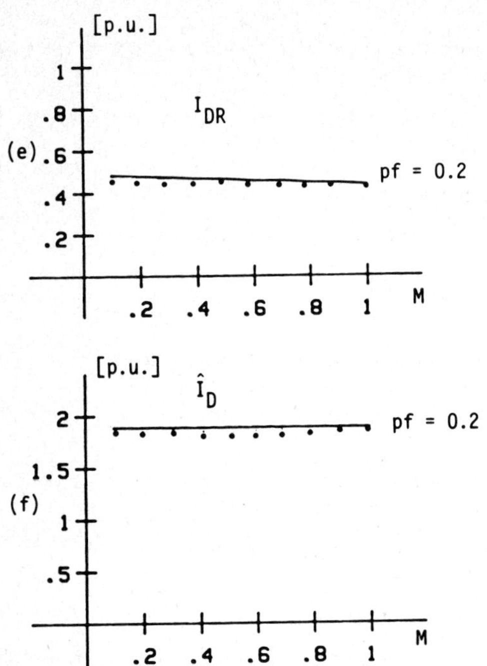

Fig. 6: Worst case experimental (dotted lines) and predicted (solid lines) inverter component current ratings with the SPWM scheme

(a) controlled switch (transistor) average current ratings, $\bar{I}_T$

(b) controlled switch rms current ratings, I_{TR}

(c) controlled switch peak current ratings, I_T

(d) diode average current ratings, $\bar{I}_D$

(e) diode rms current ratings, I_{DR}

(f) diode peak current ratings, I_D

CONCLUSIONS

A generalized analysis and design approach for forced commutated static converters has been presented in this paper. The approach is analytically based on the switching function [10] concept and employs digital simulation to obtain relevant design data. Although it requires a considerable amount of number 'crunching' the subject approach is conceptually very simple and can be easily implemented on todays personal computers. The particular application considered in this paper is static voltage source inverters. Component ratings for the well known SPWM inverter structure have been obtained by using the proposed approach. Results have been expressed in per unit form for maximum applicability. Finally, selected predicted results have been verified experimentally on a two kVA laboratory prototype unit.

REFERENCES

[1] Bimal K. Bose, "Adjustable Speed AC Drives Systems," IEEE Press, 1981.

[2] Paul C. Krause and Thomas A. Lipo, "Analysis and Simplified Representations of Rectifier-Inverter Induction Motor Drive," IEEE Trans. Power App. Syst., Vol. PAS-88, pp. 588-596, May 1969.

[3] John M.D. Murphy and Michael G. Egan, "A Comparison of PWM Strategies for Inverter-Fed Induction Motors," IEEE Trans. on Industry Appl., Vol. IA-19, No. 3, May/June 1983.

[4] Warren J. Schultz, "Power Transistors Safe Operating Area," Power Conversion International, pp. 62-66, July/Aug. 1982.

[5] P.D. Ziogas, "Synthesis of Optimum Gain Functions for Static Power Converters," IEEE Trans. Ind. Appl., Vol. IA-19, No. 3, pp. 401-408, May/June 1983.

[6] P.D. Ziogas and P.N.D. Photiadis, "An Exact Input Current Analysis of Ideal Static PW Inverters", IEEE Trans. Ind. Appl., Vol. IA-19, No. 2, March/April 1983.

[7] P.D. Ziogas, S. Manias and E. Wiechmann, "Application of Current Source Inverters in UPS Systems," IEEE-IAS-1983 Conference Record, pp. 949-957.

[8] A. Shonung and H. Stemmler, "Static frequency changers with subharmonic control in conjunction with reversible speed ac drives," Brown Boveri Review, pp. 555-577, Aug./Sept. 1964.

[9] K. Heintze et al., "Pulse width modulating static inverters for the speed control of induction motors," Siemens-Z, Vol. 45 (3), pp. 154-161, 1971.

[10] I.J. Pitel, S.N. Talukdar and P. Wood, "Characterization of Programmed-Waveform Pulse Width Modulation," IEEE Trans. Ind. Appl., pp. 707-715, Sept./Oct. 1980.

DIGITAL TECHNIQUES in Simulation, Communication and Control
Spyros G. Tzafestas (editor)
Elsevier Science Publishers B.V. (North-Holland) © IMACS, 1985

SUPERVISORY CONTROL OF CEMENT MILLS

Robert E. King & John G. Gatopoulos

Process Management Systems
AMBER Computer Systems S.A.
POB 3500, Athens, Greece

ABSTRACT

The paper outlines certain features of a subsystem of a hierarchical distributed control system involving a network of microcomputers linked to a central mini-computer. Product specifications and production data are maintained in the data base of the highest level of the hierarchical system. Process status and report generation are integral functions of the subsystem whose primary functions are maintaining product quality through accurate materials proportioning and optimum control of the closed grinding circuit by means of an 'expert system'. Continuous fault diagnosis is also an essential function of the subsystem which is currently in operation at a 'Heracles' General Cement plant in Greece.

INTRODUCTION

Manufacturing consistently and efficiently high quality cement from varying raw materials is a formidable task and taxes the best in operations and management capabilities. Plant economics depend largely on production rates, fuel efficiency and equipment uptime, all of which can vary widely on a day-to-day basis. In a highly competitive world cement market it has become almost mandatory to make extensive and intelligent use of efficient digital computers both for plant management as well as for control. The advent of digital computers in the 1950's had a profound effect on industry and progressive manufacturers were quick to recognize the potential of this important tool which today forms a integral part of many large scale plants.

THE CEMENT CONTROL PROCESS

The principal control over cement composition is in proportioning of the raw materials to ensure the proper relative amounts of the various oxides in the materials fed to a rotary kiln. Proper burning in the rotary kiln to control the extent of the various reactions in turn ensures a proper clinker composition. Finally, finish grinding of the clinker, which is blended with a retardant and other additives to the proper physical characteristics, ensures high quality cement.

These three stages - proportioning, burning and grinding are the basis of the cement manufacturing process. Accuracy and consistency in each of these operations is critical where economy, quality and productivity are to be maximized.

FINISH GRINDING

The finish grinding operation comprises three principal components : the ball mill itself (which reduces the size of the raw materials entering it), an elevator (which transports the mill product upto a separator) and a separator (which splits the ground material according to size). Oversize material is recycled to the mill for further grinding whilst the remainder is the desired finely ground product output of the mill, i.e. cement. The figure shows a flow sheet of a ball ball mill fed with materials stored in three silos (each of which may contain a binary or ternary blend, preblended by a separate computer controlled proportioning subsystem) in addition to the fundamental component, clinker. The closed nature of the system is clearly evident.

All but a small portion of the power consumed in grinding is converted into heat and less than 10% of the energy is consumed by size reduction. It is obvious that to minimize power comsumption per unit of production, the mill must be operated at its full capacity

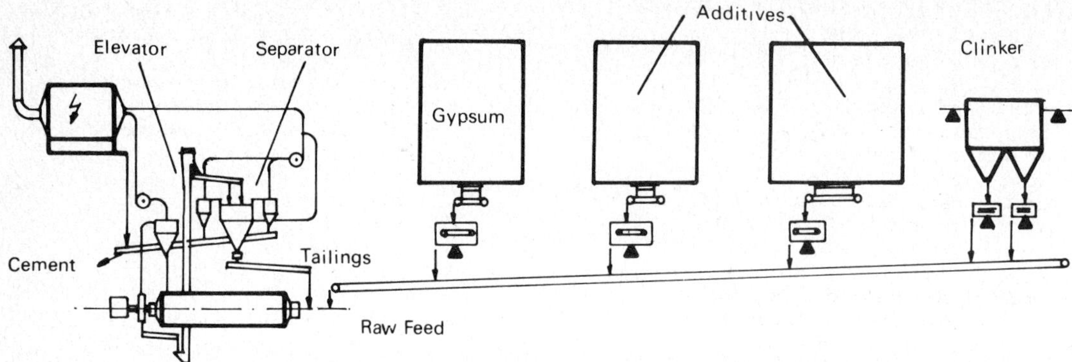

and under optimum conditions. The major control variables in the closed mill circuit are the fresh feed rate to the mill and the separator speed both of which directly influence the properties of the final product.

The chemical properties of cement, are critically dependent on the precision of proportioning of the clinker and the other components added during the finish grinding stage. The complexity of the proportioning problem depends directly on how many materials are blended together as well as the variability of the chemical properties of the raw components which constitute the blend. The basic components of original Portland cement are a binary blend of clinker and gypsum and clearly computer control is not called for and would be uneconomical. More complex cements, however, involve a muliplicity of components, making manual proportioning very difficult if not impossible. Computer-controlled proportioning under these circumstances is essential.

Computer controlled blending was used as early as 1959 in the Riverside Cement Company's Oro Grande plant in California. Since then much progress has been made in computer control in the cement industry, an industry which is one of the leaders and innovators in the application of computers. This is not surprizing since the cement manufacturing process is plagued with some of the most difficult and complex control problems to be found in any industrial environment, problems that have consistently defied solution through conventional and modern control techniques.

In this brief paper we outline a supervisory mill control subsystem which has been designed and implemented at 'Heracles' General Cement Co. The subsystem has been in operation at the 'Heracles II' plant of 'Heracles' General Cement Co. in Aliveri, Greece for the past eighteen months and is part of an integrated large scale hierarchical process management system which includes data-acquisition and logging, computer-assisted design and analysis of cement and optimum real-time weigh feeder control and fault diagnosis as well as expert knowledge-based subsystems for the control of essential variables associated with the cement production process.

MAIN FUNCTIONS OF THE SUB-SYSTEM

The main functions of the supervisory mill proportioning control subsystem are as follows:

1. Cement specification subsystem which includes computer-assisted design of cements having specific properties. Cement formulas, which are interactively designed with economic criteria, are coded according to cement type and stored (in dry component form) in the data base. Any formula, which is protected and can only be accessed by special password may be recalled for review or modification only by the quality control department. The data base is augmented with information supplied by the laboratory on component humidities, test results etc.

2. The data base is accessed by the mill operator who follows a production schedule on keying the formula number to be milled on his console terminal. The mill proportioning subsystem corrects the desired (dry) formula for humidity and computes the desired weigh-feeder setpoints which are then transmitted to the lower layer of the hierarchy to effect the servomechanisms.

3. Data acquisition and logging of the principal variables of the mill is performed every 5 minutes. Data so gathered is stored for two days for daily report generation. Simultaneously continuous weigh feeder diagnosis is performed. A warning alarm is sounded at the control panel terminal whenever any weigh feeder malfunctions or shows unacceptable deviations from the desired values. Process data may also be accessed from the lower layer by the supervisor at a higher rate when continuous information is sought. The mill operator has the ability to recall and display present and past production trends as well as latest laboratory analyses.

4. At intervals of a 4-8 hours, cement samples are chemically analysed for loss on ignition, sulphur content and insoluble residues. These quantities, which constitute the observed system output variables, are entered and compared to their nominal values stored in the data base. A linguistic algorithm then computes the corrections necessary to the setpoints which are subsequently transmitted to the weigh feeders. The controller also calls attention to possible errors in preblending and forms the closure of the basic quality control loop of the subsystem.

5. At regular intervals of two hours cement samples are analysed chemically for their fineness (Blaine). This information is entered in the laboratory and transmitted to the mill operator who takes corrective actions by altering the speed of the separator as well as the raw feed rate. An 'expert system' using Fuzzy Logic has been implemented to advise the operator on the necessary changes to these settings based on information on the circulating load, feed rate and Blaine.

6. Daily production reports are automatically generated by the system as are those for productivity, malfunction and quality control.

The mill proportioning control subsystem is implemented on a PDP 11/44 having 256 KB of random access memory, two 10MB disks and includes terminals located in the production department, laboratory, quality control department and the mill operator's console.
The minicomputer, which forms the third and uppermost layer of the hierarchical system, uses the RSX11M real-time operating system and communicates to a host of Z80-based microcomputers which form the second and first layers of the three layer hierachical system. Communication to the microcomputers is performed at 1200 baud, a rate which is satisfactory for the sampling rates used.

At the 'Heracles II' plant the mill supervisory subsystem controls proportioning for two 140 t/h ball mills which are in continuous operation and subject to frequent cement type changes. The mill supervisory subsystem, is a module of an extensive integrated process management system which includes proportioning for a 400 t/h raw mill as well as 'expert' control of the kiln.

CONCLUSION

Whether a computer system is useful or required in a particular plant for this purpose depends to a great extent on the plant's difficulty in correctly and economically proportioning the available materials making up the final blend.

Computer controlled proportioning was considered essential in the particular manufacturing environment and two such subsystems have been implemented. These have been in continuous operation at 'Heracles' General Cement Company's plants in Greece, controlling the weigh feeders of 5 large ball mills. The subsystems are characterized by their reliability and versatility, factors which have impoved productivity and quality significantly and reduced down time through prompt fault diagnosis.

BIBLIOGRAPHY

Bristol E. 'Process Control: An application theorist's view of control', IEEE Control Systems Magazine, Mar 1982.

Haimes Y.Y. (Ed) 'Large Scale Systems', North-Holland, NY, 1982.

Kaiser V.A. 'Computer Control in the Cement Industry', Proc. IEEE, Vol 58, No 1, Jan 1970.

Williams T.J. 'Control Theory and Applications in Chemical Process Control', Proc. IBM Scientific Computing Symposium on Control Theory & Applications, IBM NY, 1964.

Williams T.J. 'Minicomputers and microprocessors in industrial process control systems: present and future applications', Arabian Journal for Science & Engineering, Vol 7, No 4, Oct 1982.

--,'Le Teil : a fully automated cement plant', World Cement Technology, Dec 1980.

DIGITAL TECHNIQUES in Simulation, Communication and Control
Spyros G. Tzafestas (editor)
Elsevier Science Publishers B.V. (North-Holland) © IMACS, 1985

A FAULT TOLERANT LIQUID MIXING MACHINE MICROCOMPUTER CONTROLLER

C.C. LEFAS P.P. NIKOLAOU

Ministry of Physical Planning, Housing and the Environment, GREECE

The present paper describes the controller of a liquid mixing machine. The machine mixes ten liquid substances by controlling the flow rate of each substance through separate control loops. The controller is a multiprocessor system where each processor controls the flow rate of one substance. However there are routes for any controller to take over the control functions of another loop in the event of a component failure. The controller provides access to the analog and digital iput buses, the analog and digital output buses and the common memory bus.

1. INTRODUCTION

The present paper describes the controller of a liquid mixing machine. The machine consists of ten individual liquid flow rate control loops, all ending up in a common tug where the final substance is accumulated. The quality of the final product depends sharply on the accuracy with which the flow rate of each individual liquid substance is controlled and therefore the control function is of significance. Each substance flow regulation forms a separate control loop and therefore this application is suited for implementation of a multiprocessor controller. One processor is dedicated to each control loop so that a smaller sampling interval may be achieved or more complicated control algorithms may be implemented. Since however multiple controllers are used the system posses a significant degree of redundancy so that if it is carefully designed it can provide a very reliable service. The redundancy exists in the sense that there are components in the system that may take over the functions of other components that may fail. By no means there is duplication of any function in the system since every processor carries out the control functions of its own control loop.

2. THE SYSTEM AND THE CONTROLLER

The system configuration is shown in figure 1. It may be seen that the machine consists of virtually independent control loops to control each liquid substance flow rate. The usual approach is in this case the selection of a sufficiently powerful CPU to perform the necessary calculations for all loops within an acceptably small time interval, which will then be the sampling interval. Data acquisition is performed by a single, fast Analog to Digital Converter (ADC) with an analog multiplexer in its front end to scan all plant outputs. For driving multiple output points several Digital to Analog Converters (DAC) are used. In a less common approach a single DAC may be used followed by several Sample and Hold Amplifiers but this approach has the disadvantage that Sample and Hold Amplifiers suffer from drifts and therefore the output cannot be held constant for very long. The architecture of these controllers is shown in fig 2.

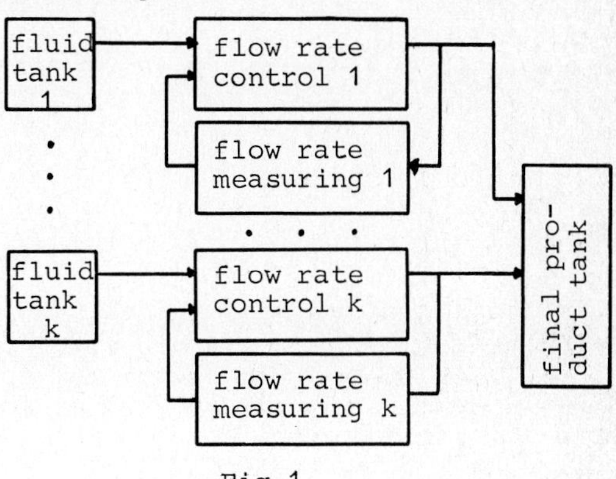

Fig 1

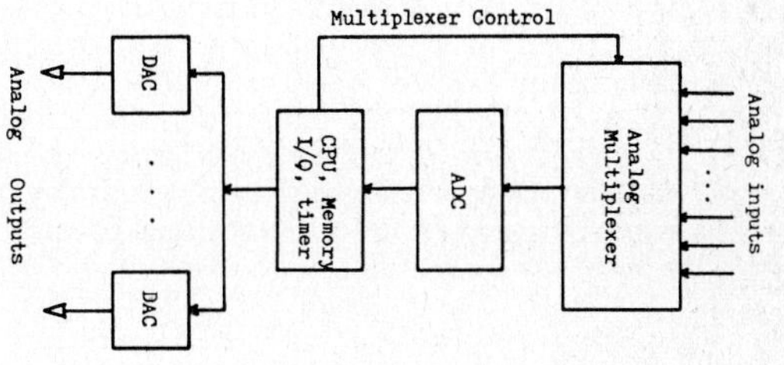

Fig 2

VLSI developments however have brought component prices down so that it is perfectly feasible today to employ one processor for each individual loop. In this case each loop controller contains a dedicated CPU, a dedicated ADC and a dedicated DAC. The configuration of this system is shown in fig 3

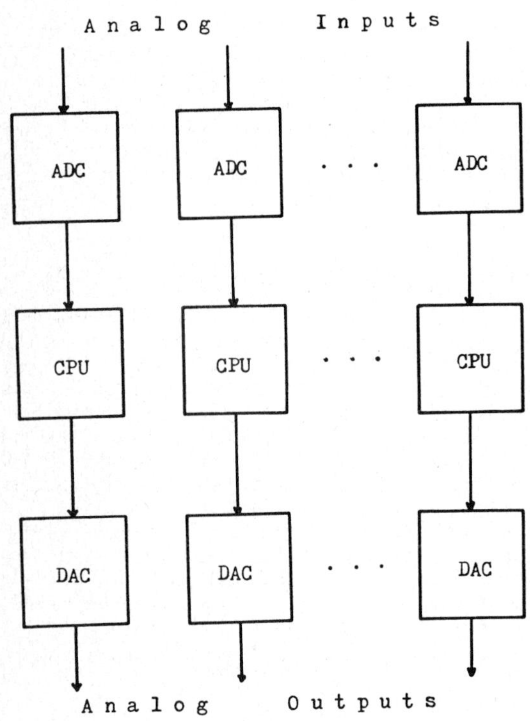

Fig 3

Such a configuration has several advantages over the one shown in fig 2. The most significant is that processing may now be done in parallel at a much greater speed. Thus lower speed components may be used so that the total cost of a system with this configuration may compare favourably to the cost of a system with the former configuration. This configuration however does not offer any redundancy although similar components are used in the loops. The reason for that is that no interconnection between the loop controllers so that a failed component may be replaced by a similar one operating in another control loop.

The above disadvantage is overcome by the inclusion of interconnection buses between individual controllers at several points in the circuit as is shown in fig 4. The philosophy behind this architecture is that faults are detected in real time at a major component level, major components being considered the ADC, the CPU, the memory and the DAC. Therefore interconnection is provided at the analog input level, the digital input level, the memory bus level, the gigital output level and the linear output level. It should also be noted that communication buses are meant to be used in a failure event only and not during normal operation. Separate connections are therefore foreseen so that during normal operation components in the same loop can communicate without the use of the common buses.

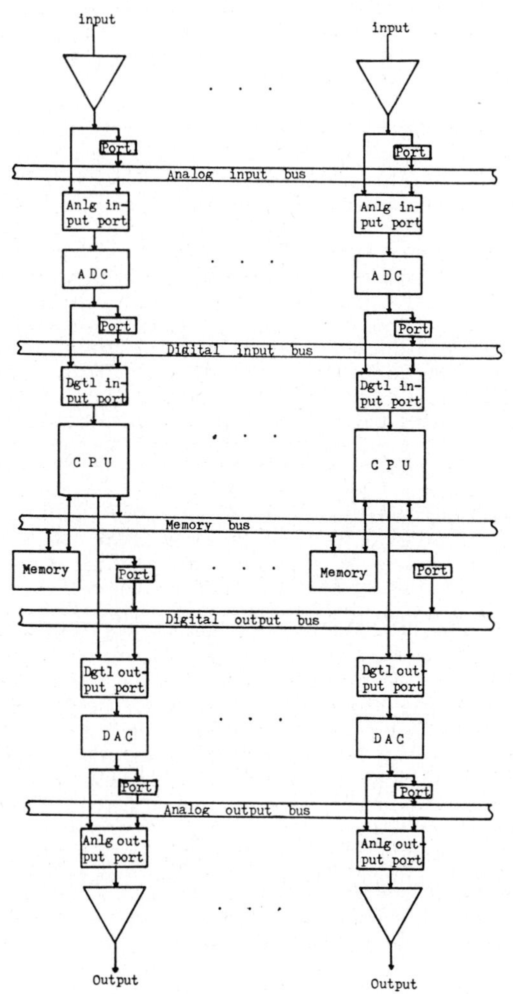

Fig 4

Common buses communicate with the major controller components via "ports" which are inserted between the component and the bus. If the ports are inactive then the controller reduces to the configura-

tion shown in fig 3. Ports are practically analog and digital switches. Every common bus has associated with it a control register that controls the opening and closing of the switches. The configuration is such that the upper half of the register controls the input switches and the lower half controls the output switches (input and output are here referred to the bus). This control register contains also a flag bit indicating that the bus is being used. The set of five registers that are required appears to the CPUs as a set of output ports that may be accessed by all CPUs.
To avoid conflict during bus operation no CPU not being in control of that bus can write its control register unless the bus is idle. The disadvantage of this configuration is that it allows the communication of only two components through the same bus at the same time. In the event of a double failure the two failed components cannot be replaced by others in parallel even though there are idle components, because of bus conflict problems. This is however an unlikely situation in the present application since the failure of the first component will attract service attention.

For this application Motorola's 68701 single chip computer has been selected as the single loop controller because of the high degree of integration that it offers. The only difference between the architecture adopted and that shown on fig 4 is that no common memory bus in included since RAM is contained in the 68701 wafer and it is considered a single module. The 68701 chip operates in the single chip mode.
Common bus requests are handled via ports 1 and 2. With every common bus there is a bus request priority encoder associated to which the CPUs make requests by setting bit 0 of their port 1. These pins are connected as input to the priority encoder whose output is read by all CPUs. A CPU gains acces to the bus only when its code appears on the encoder output. Fig 5 shows the whole arrangement. This arrangement implies that there is a constant priority level assigned to each CPU. The switches on each bus are controlled by a 24 bit wide bus configuration register which is written by the CPU having access to the bus. This register appears as three locations to each CPU. Requests are made asynchronously so that independent CPU operation is possible. To prevent a higher priority CPU to gain access to the bus whilst it is being used by another CPU, a bus in use flag is associated with every bus and is set by the CPU currently using the bus. This is tested by any CPU wanting to write the bus configuration register and no CPU may gain access to the bus as long as this flag is set. The master of the bus releases the bus when it is no longer required. This procedure is encoded in every CPU ROM as part of the routines for failure recovery. Note that under normal circumstances no CPU will make bus use requests. The main disadvantage of this approach is that it may result in long delays in the event of multiple failures. This however is an unlikely situation since the first failure will attract service attention.

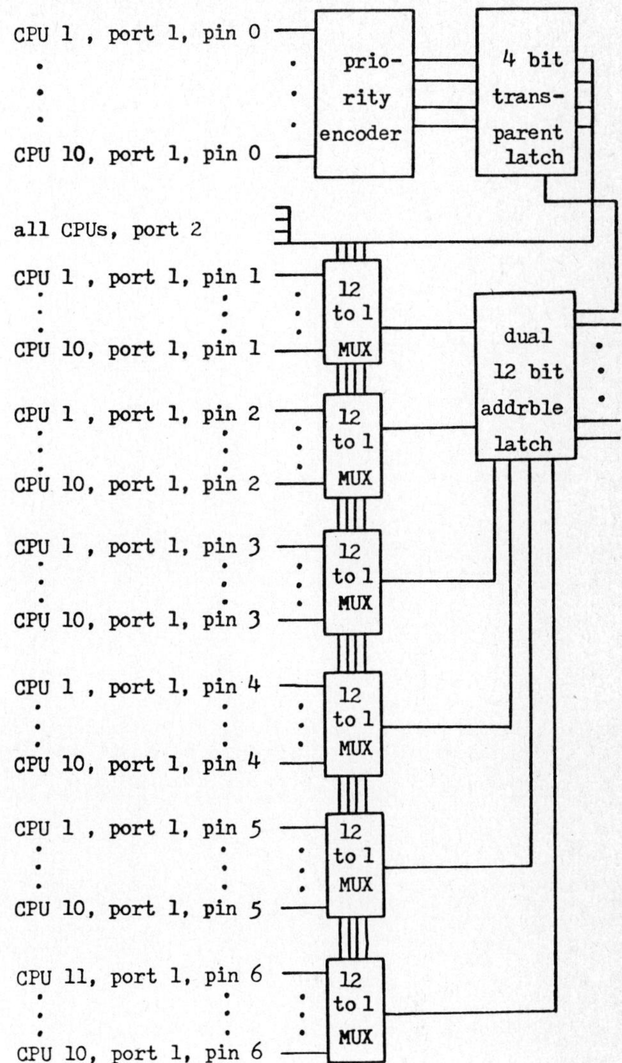

Fig 5

3. CONCLUSIONS

A parallel processor controller has been presented providing a high degree of fault tolerance. This scheme has been used in a fluid mixing machine but is suitable for any multiloop control situation.

DIGITAL TECHNIQUES in Simulation, Communication and Control
Spyros G. Tzafestas (editor)
Elsevier Science Publishers B.V. (North-Holland) © IMACS, 1985

MICROCOMPUTER CONTROL OF HYDROGENERATORS

C.C. LEFAS

Ministry of Physical Planning,
Housing and the Environment
GREECE

N.D. HATZIARGYRIOU

Power system laboratory
National Technical University
of Athens, GREECE

The present paper describes the basic control loops of hydrogenerators and the implementation of the control functions in a microcomputer controller. In particualar the hardware implementation problems are discussed. The design aims to serve as a feasibility study for the development of a high quality single chip integrated controller.

1. INTRODUCTION

The control mechanism of hydrogenerators is of great importance and much effort has been devoted in the design of stable and reliable control systems. Initially purely mechanical systems have been used. In later years several mechanical parts have been replaced by analog electronic circuits. This paper investigates the possibility of introducing microprocessors for the control of hydrogenerators.

Microprocessors offer a significant degree of flexibility and quite complicated control algorithms can be employed (including nonlinear and adaptive control algorithms e.g. refs 1,2) In addition to that microprocessor controllers can communicate with each other through suitable communication buses (including serial communication) so that larger control networks can be built. In this case each generator has its own controller, so that each generator is optimally controlled, whereas the network can be managed remotely by a control facility issuing commands to local controllers.

Apart from the above advantages microprocessor controllers suffer from several disadvantages. Being discrete state machines microprocessor controllers have a finite resolution and therefore quantization errors exists which do not occur in analog circuits. Also a nonzero computation time is required which might be significant if too complicated control algorithms are employed (ref 1). It can be finally argued that microprocessors, being far more complicated devices than conventional analog circuits, are more easily damaged by strong electric fields spikes and other types of noise present near generators. This latter argument however can be alleviated by careful controller design.

2. SPEED GOVERNING SYSTEMS

2.1 Mechanical hydraulic systems

The mechanical-hydraulic speed governing system for a hydroturbine consists of a speed governor, a pilot valve and servomotor, a distributor valve and gate servomotor, and governor controlled gates. The block diagram of fig 1 is an approximate nonlinear model for the speed governing system (ref 3).

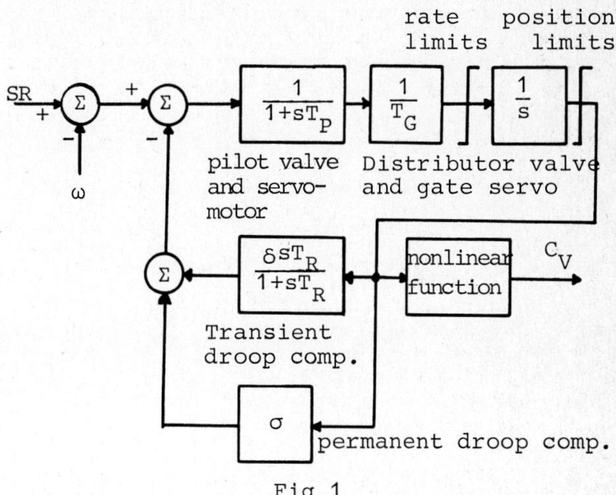

Fig 1

Typical parameters for this model are shown in table 1 (ref 3).

Table 1

Parameter	Typical value	Range
T_R	5.0	2.5-25.0
T_G	0.2	0.2-0.4
T_P	0.04	0.03-0.05
δ	0.3	0.2-1.0
σ	0.05	0.03-0.06

2.2 Electric Hydraulic control systems

Modern speed governing systems for hydroturbines may involve electronic apparatus to perform low power functions associated with speed sensing and droop compensation. It is widely accepted today that electronic apparatus provides greater flexibility and improved performance in both dead band and dead time. Within an appropriate parameter selection the system can be represented by the simplified diagram of fig 2.

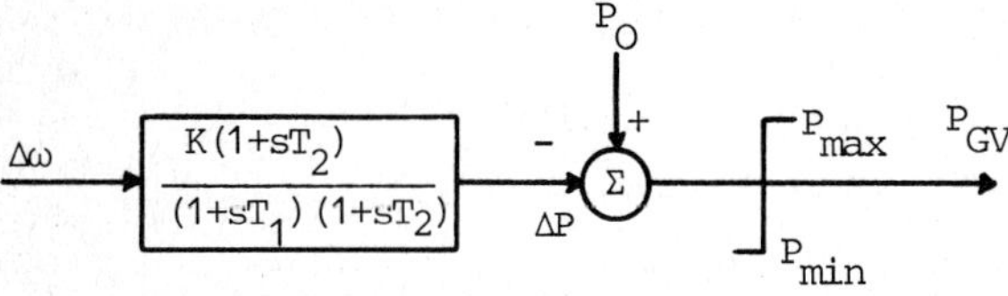

Fig 2

Obviously the servomotor and valves cannot be replaced but the rest of the circuit can be replaced by a microprocessor controller. The only difficulty is that now the system is a sampled data system and therefore the z transform is used rather than the Laplace transform to represent the entire control system. In this case the system is represented as in fig 3.

$$B=(1-T_2/T_3)e^{-T/T_1} - (1-T_2/T_1)e^{-T/T_2}$$

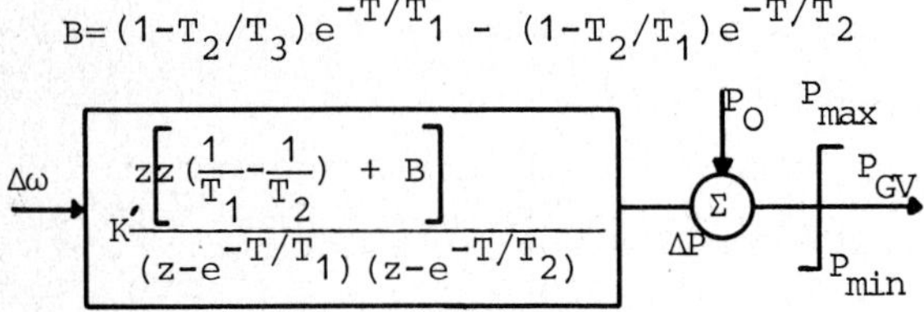

Fig 3

3. EXCITATION SYSTEMS

Fig 4 shows the block diagram used to represent most current excitation systems (ref 4) in a simplified form.

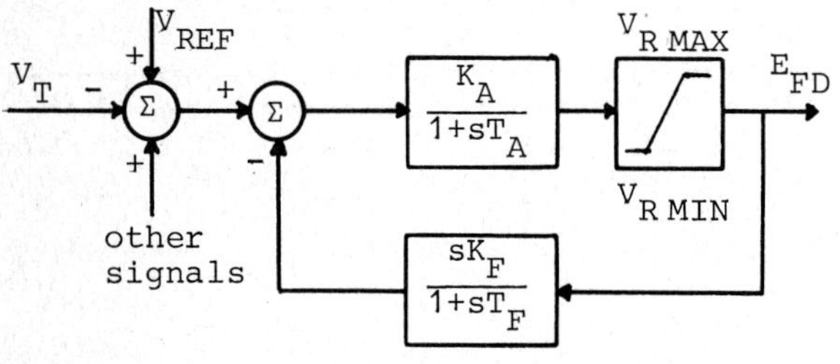

Fig 4

V_T is the generator terminal voltage applied to the regulator onput. The first summing point compares the regulator reference with V_T to determine the voltage error input to the regulator amplifier. The second summing point combines voltage error input with the excitation major damping loop signal. The main regulator transfer function is represented as a gain K_A and a time constant T_A. Following this, the maximum and minimum limits of the regulator are imposed so that large input error signals cannot produce regulator output which exceeds practical limits. Major loop damping is provided by the feedback transfer function from exciter output E_{FD} to the first summing point $sK_F/(1 + sT_F)$. Table 2 gives typical excitation system constants (ref 4).

Table 2

parameter	range
K_A	25-400
T_A	0.05-0.20
K_F	0.01-0.08
T_F	0.35-1.0

4. MICROPROCESSOR IMPLEMENTATION OF THE CONTROL FUNCTIONS

Microprocessor controllers may be used to implement the low power control functions on both the speed regulation and excitation regulation loops. Microprocessors offer a good deal more flexibility than current hardwired controllers and it is in this sense that their possible implementation is viewed in the present paper. However microprocessors are relatively sensitive to spikes and strong electromagnetic fields so that careful design is of utmost importance for a reliable microprocessor controller. The present paper concentrates from now on on these hardware design aspects. The fist thing to establish is the maximum sampling interval in which all calculations should be performed. Tables 1,2 give typical time constants and a reasonable sampling interval is set to be equal to the smallest time constant. This is in the order of 30 ms. The next thing to consider is the computation power required. It may be seen that the control algorithms currently being implemented are not very complicated so that the computation requirements can be satisfied by a fast 8 bit processor. INTEL's 8051 has been selected because of its high speed clock (12 MHz), its enhanced instruction set which includes powerful instructions such as multiply and divide, and its high degree of integration. On a single wafer the 8051 contains 4K ROM, 128 bytes RAM, 12 registers, two 16 bit timer counters, a serial line interface and 32 I/O lines, i.e. all necessary logic. In this case the controller can be realized by a single chip computer, providing a higher degree of reliability than multiple component controllers. The only difficulty in this case remains the isolation of the controller from the power network. The speed transducer is simply a dented wheel mounted on the rotor shaft. A magnetic switch is used to sense dent proximity. In this way a series of pulses is created whose frequency is a direct multiple of the rotor angular velocity. To avoid EMI the circuit output drives a LED and the pulses are transferred to the controller via a low cost fiber link. It is expected that the distance between the measuring point and the controller will not be greater than 20m so that low cost components may be easily used. Fig 5 shows the transducer configuration.

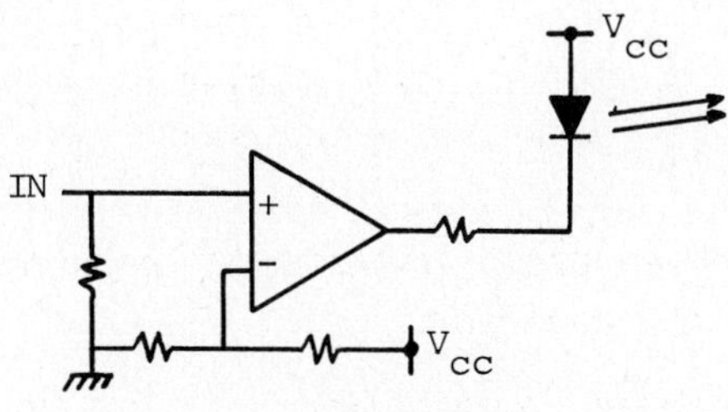

Fig 5

Generator output voltage is measured via an optical linear coupler (fig 6).

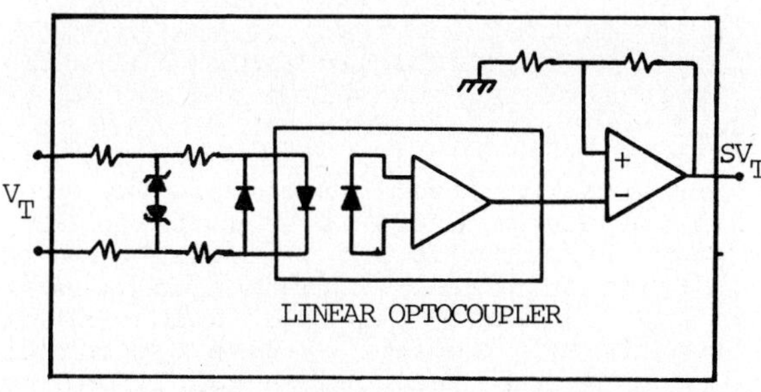

Fig 6

Transient suppressor diodes are used for additional device protection. The coupler acts as a half wave rectifier, so that total power dissipation of the device is reduced. The coupler output is amplified by a single op-amp and is fed into an Analog to Digital Converter (ADC) in the controller module shown in fig 7. This arrangement offers better isolation and device protection than the use of a step down transformer. Fig 7 shows the block diagram of the microcomputer controller.

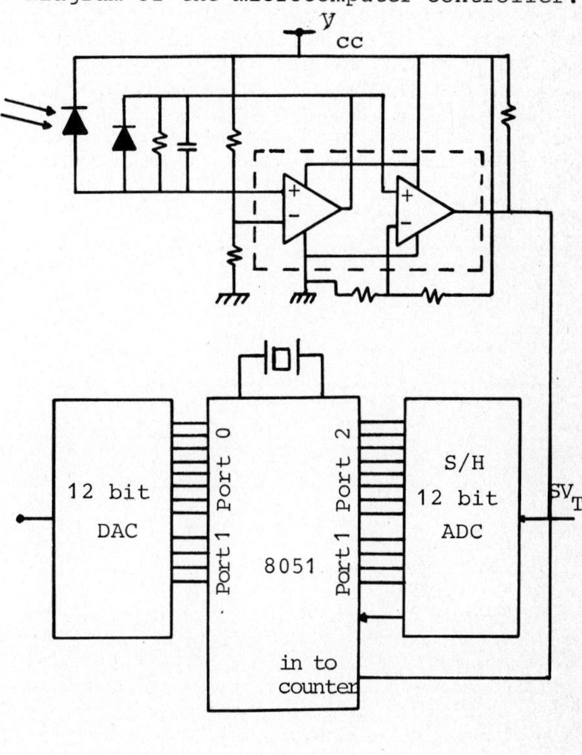

Fig 7

5. CONCLUSIONS

Modern single chip microcomputers offer a sufficient degree of integration and computing power to implement control strategies similar to the ones used in linear harwired controllers. In addition they offer the capability of implementing far more sophisticated control strategies, such as self tuning regulators, which result in a superior system performance.

REFERENCES

1. J. Kanniah, O.P. Malik, G.S. Hope "Excitation control of synchronous generators using adaptive regulators,Part1: Theory and simulation results" IEEE trans. PAS-103 No 5, May 1984

2. J. Kanniah, O.P. Malik, G.S. Hope "Excitation control of synchronous generators using adaptive regulators, Part 2: implementation and test results" IEEE trans. PAS-103, No 5, May 1984

3. IEEE Committee report "Dynamic models for steam and hydroturbines in power system studies" IEEE trans. PAS Nov-Dec 1973

4. IEEE Committee report "Computer representation of Excitation Systems", IEEE trans, PAS, June 1968.

DIGITAL TECHNIQUES in Simulation, Communication and Control
Spyros G. Tzafestas (editor)
Elsevier Science Publishers B.V. (North-Holland) © IMACS, 1985

A COMPLEX GEOMETRY SIMULATION FOR HEAT TRANSFER CALCULATIONS: THE GREEK RESEARCH REACTOR CASE

John G. Bartzis

Nuclear Research Center "Democritos"
Aghia Paraskevi, Attiki
Athens-Greece

In the present paper the thermal hydraulic analysis of a thermally interacting heated channel bundle of complex geometry is presented. The bundle is completely or partially immersed into the cooling medium. Forced or natural convection can be allowed through each channel. Heat is transferred by conduction, convection and radiation. The analytical tool used is the ThEAP-I Code, a transient three dimensional heat transfer computer code which is under development in NRC "Democritos". Results are presented for the 5 MW open pool Greek Research Reactor (GRR-1).

1. INTRODUCTION

The heating or cooling of a thermally interacting channel system of complex or simple geometry has several applications in energy problems (e.g. nuclear reactors, solar systems). The present work is part of a task which is under way in NRC "Democritos" dealing with the thermal hydraulic analysis of such channel system The analytical tool used is the ThEAP-I code (1,2) a transient three dimensional heat transfer computer code.

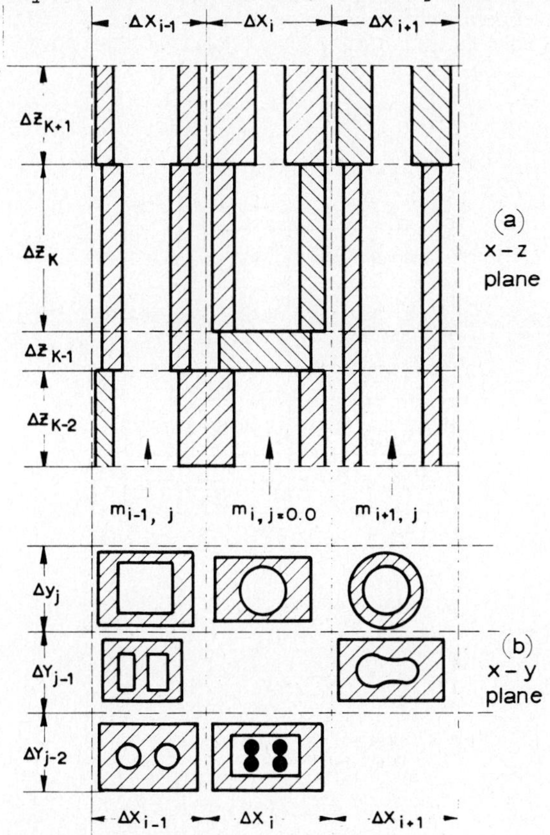

Fig. 1 Geometry Simulation.

The overall effort consists of the following main steps:

(a) real geometry simulation to a set of discrete nodes as shown in Fig. 1.
(b) heat transfer phenomena modeling.

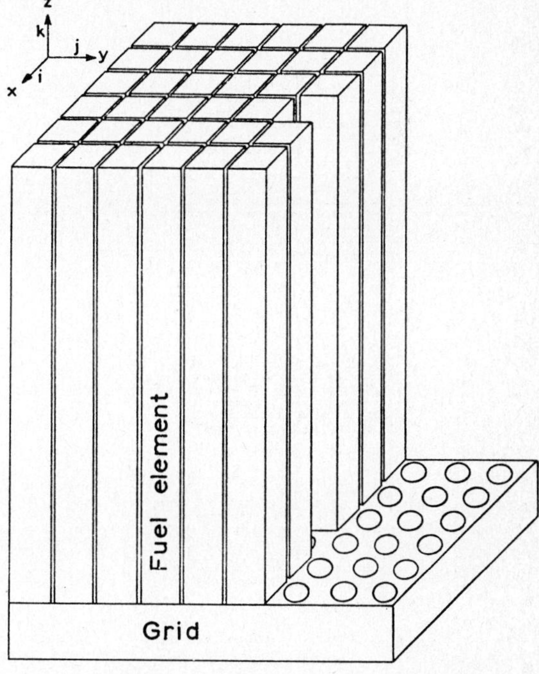

Fig. 2. Idealized GRR–1 core configuration.

and (c) temperature field prediction using finite difference techiques.

The particular geometry that will be analyzed in the present paper, is the core of the 5 MW open pool Greek Research Reactor (GRR-1) with the geometry configuration shown in Fig. 2 (1,4).

2. THE MODEL

The main objective of the present work is to be able to analyze the channel bundle shown in Fig. 1. Each channel can be of complex geometry. The material in each sector is variable. Support structure also can exist but it is represented by a single temperature. The whole bundle is partially or fully immersed into the cooling medium (e.g. water, air) . Internal cooling is allowed where this is possible, in a natural or forced convection mode. Each channel can be partially or totally heated internally or externally. Each channel exchanges heat with the neighboring channels and neighboring structures. The mechanisms of heat transfer considered is conduction, natural convection and heat radiation. The heat interchange between channel wall and internal flow is natural or forced convection.

The results of the analysis are expressed as temperature field distribution as a function of time for the channel structure, the internal flow and the support plate. In the natural convection mode the flow rate per channel is another output parameter.

The above results are obtained by solving the energy equations for the channel, internal flow and support plate. The natural convection flow is calculated from the momentum equation along the channel axis. The above equations are given in Table I.

The above differential equations are transformed into finite difference ones and are solved numerically using Gauss iteration method (5).

More details for the numerical analysis and heat transfer modeling are given in Ref. (1).

3. APPLICATION: THE GREEK RESEARCH REACTOR CASE

Present calculations have been performed to establish specification for the 5 MW open pool type research reactor operating in NRC "Democritos".

The reactor core configuration, the fuel element geomtry and the power distribution are shown in Fig. 2,3 and 4 (3). The fuel is UAl Alloy whereas the rest

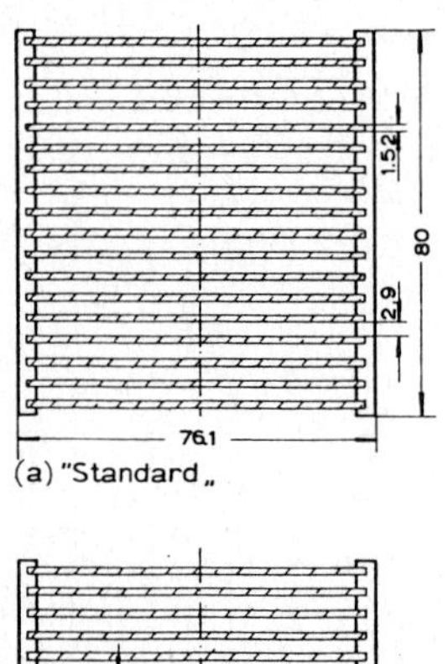

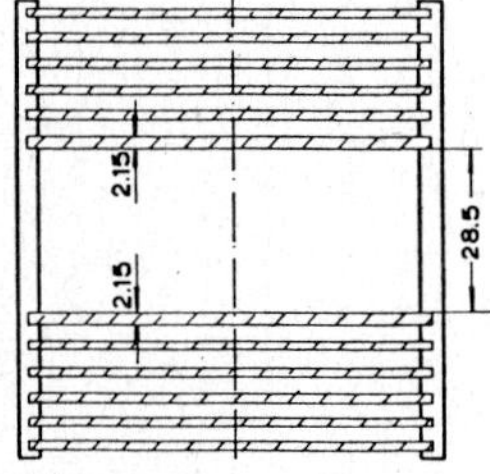

Fig. 3. GRR-1 Fuel Element Cross Section.

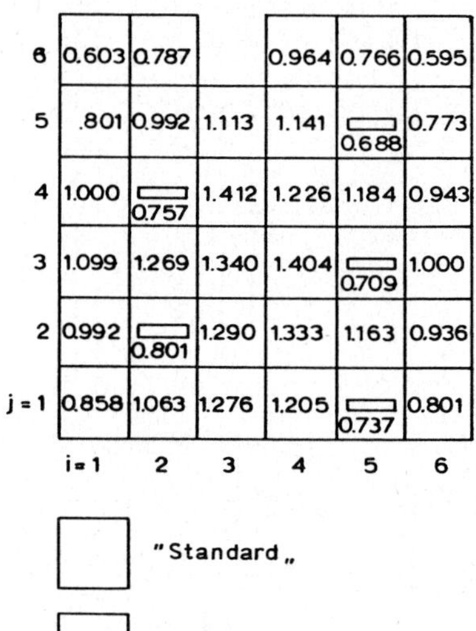

Fig. 4 GRR-1 Core Power Distribution.

of the core structure is Aluminum. The core is immersed to a water tank 8.5 to 8.8 meters deep.

3.1 Operation in Forced Convection Mode

The hot channel temperature distribution is shown in Fig. 5. The hot spot occurs about 6/10 downstream the fuel plate region and is estimated to be 31.3 K above the inlet temprature.

Another important feature for the reactor operation is the operation region with respect to power, flow and temperature limitations.

The constraints applied to establish safety limits is that in no case the maximum wall temperature will exceed water saturation temperature. Taking as limitation the 6.5 MW reactor power, 329 K exit temperature and assuming reading errors as shown in Fig. 6, the operation region can be estimated and is shown in Fig. 6. The minimum flow rate is around 47 kg/s whereas the maximum water tank temperature for normal flow (126 kg/s) cannot be higher than 314 K.

3.2. Operation in Natural Convection Mode

Detailed calculation have been performed in various power levels. In Fig. 7 the maximum clad temperature is given as a function of the power elevation. Fig. 8 shows the corresponding flow rates. The estimated maximum power level for steady state operation in natural convection mode provided that the water tank temperature does not exceed the 330 K, is of the order of 780 KW.

Fig. 9 shows the temperature distribution along the hot channel axis in the power level of 500 KW. The hot spot occurs about 2/3 downstream the fuel plate region and it is of the order of 42 K above the water tank temperature level.

4. CONCLUSIONS

The following conclusions can be drawn from the discussion in the present paper.

a. The ThEAP-I code has sufficient capability to analyze the temperature field in a thermally interacting channel system in a forced convection and natural convection mode.

b. The application to GRR-1 reactor core with the power distribution shown in Fig. 4, shows:

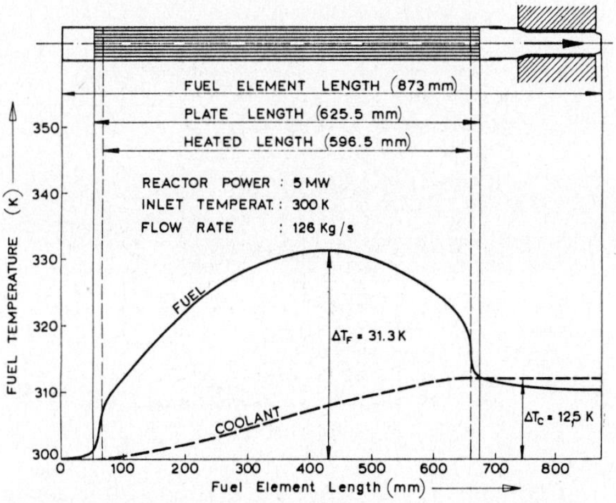

Fig. 5. Fuel Element Temperature Distribution at the position (i=3, j=4) in Forced Convection Mode.

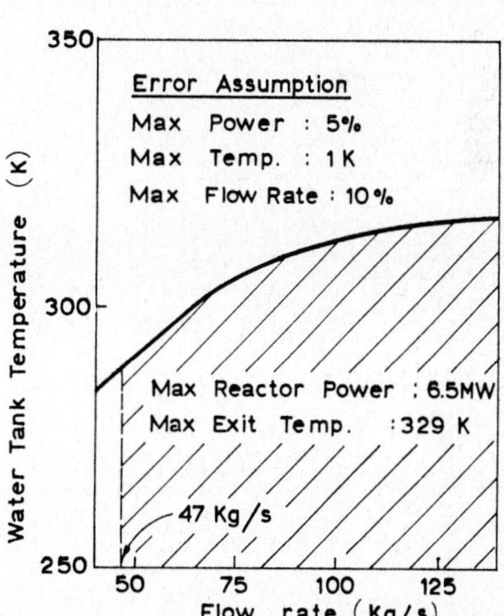

Fig. 6. GRR-1 Operation Region in Forced Convection Mode

(i) The hot spot occurs in the channel (i = 3, j = 4) 60-70% downstream the fuel plate region.

(ii) Given the limitations tabulated in Fig. 6, the minimum flow rate is of the order of 47 kg/s i.e. 40% the nominal value.

(iii) The estimated maximum power level for steady state reactor operation in natural convection mode is of the order of 780 KW.

5. REFERENCES

1. Bartzis J.G.,"Temperature Estimations in Air Cooled Fuel Elements on an Open Pool Research Reactor Core after Loss of Coolant", DEMO Report 83/17 November 1983.

2. Bartzis J.G.,"Thermal Behavior of the Air Cooled Fuel Elements in an Open Pool Reactor after Loss of Coolant Accident". Proceedings of the International Symposium on the Use and Development of the Low and Medium Flux Research Reactors, October 17-19, MIT 1983.

3. Safety Analysis Report of the Greek Research Reactor-1 (GRR-1), Vol. I. Department of Reactors, Nuclear Center "Democritos", Athens (1981).

4. Papastergiou C.N. and Deen J.R., "Neutronic Calculations for the Conversion of the GRR-1 Reactpr from HEU fuel to LEU fuel "Argonne National Laboratory, November 1981.

5. Clark J.M., Hansen, K.F, <u>Numerical Methods of Reactor Analysis</u> p.p 121-125, Academic Press 1964.

Table I. The Constitutive Equations.

Component	Equations
Channel Structure	$(\rho c_p \gamma_v A_z)_{i,j} \frac{\partial T_{w,i,j}}{\partial t} - (\kappa \gamma_z A_z)_{i,j} \frac{\partial^2 T_{w,i,j}}{\partial z^2}$ $+(h\delta_y)_{i+\frac{1}{2},j}(T_{w,i+1,j})+(h\delta_y)_{i-\frac{1}{2},j}(T_{w,i,j}-T_{w,i-1,j})$ $+(h\delta_x)_{i,j+\frac{1}{2}}(T_{w,i,j}-T_{w,i,j+1})+(h\delta_x)_{i,j-\frac{1}{2}}(T_{w,i,j}-T_{w,i,j-1})$ $+(h_f P_{wf})_{i,j}(T_{w,i,j}-T_{f,i,j})+(h\delta_c)_{pl}(T_{w,i,j}-T_{pl}) = q_{i,j}$
Fluid	$(\rho_f c_{pf} A_f)_{i,j} \frac{\partial T_{f,i,j}}{\partial t} + \dot{m} c_p \frac{\partial T_{f,i,j}}{\partial z} = (h_f P_{wf})_{i,j}(T_{w,i,j}-T_{f,i,j})$
Support Plate	$(mc_p)_{pl} \frac{\partial T_{pl}}{\partial t} = \sum_{i,j} (h_c A_c)_{pl}(T^{av}_{w,i,j}-T_{pl})-(hA)_{pl}(T_{pl}-T_a)$
Channel Flow	$\sum_{\ell}(\frac{H}{A_f} \frac{\partial \dot{m}}{\partial t} + m^2(\frac{1}{(\rho_f A_f^2)_{ex}} - \frac{1}{(\rho_f A_f^2)_{in}}) + \frac{C_\ell \dot{m}}{2D_H^2 A_f} \int_\ell \frac{\mu_f dz}{\rho_f}$ $+ \sum_n \zeta_n \frac{\dot{m}^2}{2\rho_f A_f^2} + g \int_0^{H_T} \rho_f dz = \rho_a g H_T$

A area (m^2)
C_ℓ friction coefficient constant
c_p specific heat (J/kg/K)
D_H hydraulic diameter (m)
$h\delta$ equivalent heat transfer coefficient (W/m/k)
H height (m)
H_T total height of the channel (m)
P_w channel wetted perimeter (m)
q heat source (W/m)
γ_v, γ_z structure volume and surface porosity
κ thermal conductivity (W/m/K)
μ viscosity (Pas)
ρ density (kg/m^3)

Subscripts/Superscripts

a	ambient	f	internal stream
av	average	in	inlet
c	contact	pl	support plate
ex	exit		

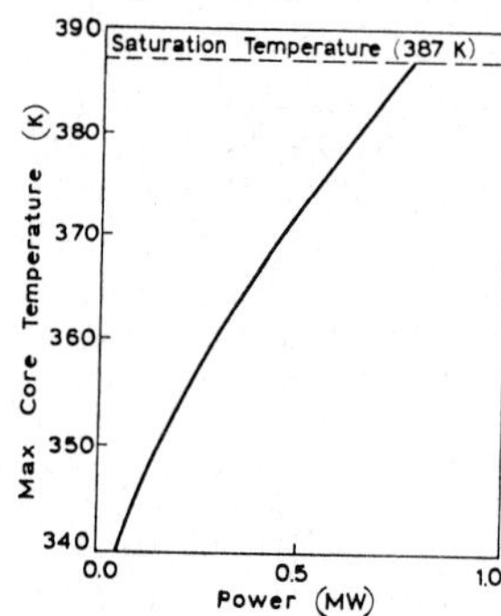

Fig. 7. Natural Convection Mode. Maximum Core Temperature vs Power.

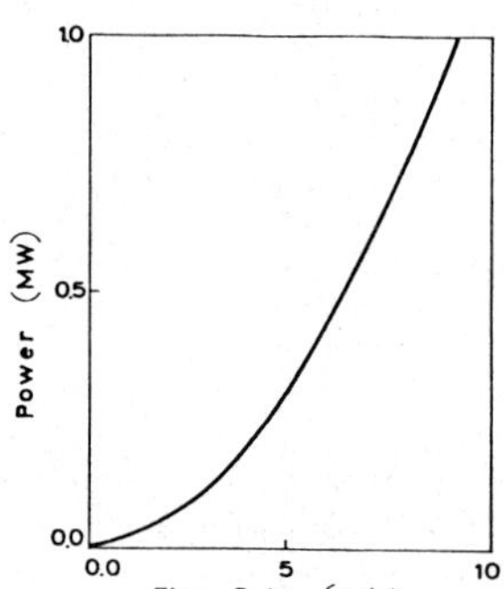

Fig. 8. Natural Convection Mode. Flow Rate vs. Power.

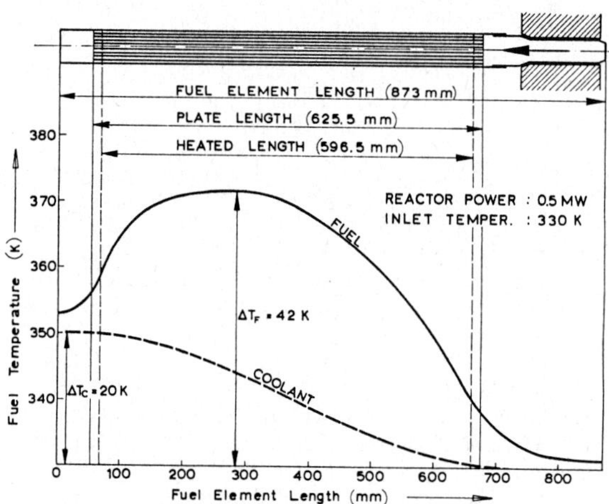

Fig. 9. Fuel Element Temperature Distribution at the position (i=3, j=4) in Natural Convection Mode.

DIGITAL TECHNIQUES in Simulation, Communication and Control
Spyros G. Tzafestas (editor)
Elsevier Science Publishers B.V. (North-Holland) © IMACS, 1985

ADAPTATIVE PETRI NETS FOR REAL TIME APPLICATIONS

Didier Corbeel, Christian Vercauter and Jean-Claude Gentina

Laboratoire d'Automatique et d'Informatique Industrielle
Institut Industriel du Nord, B.P. 48
59651 Villeneuve d'Ascq Cédex - France

We present, in this paper, an overview of the applications of a model, the Adaptative Petri-Nets. This model takes account of several sides of the specification of real-time applications :

- the command representation level,
- the handling and control representation level.

INTRODUCTION

This article presents a methodology and tools allowing to solve in a structural way the definition of a software for real-time application processing a large project. The application field of this method is mainly the process control. Starting from the specification of the functions and the needs of a project, we propose a first overall level of description using the Adaptative Petri-Nets. This tool allows both a high level representation and a confrontation to the initial specifications on the structural and semantic point of view.

This first part of the article defines briefly this tool, then in a second part we present several applications of Adaptative Petri-Nets concerned with applications in the field of process control. The last part of this paper presents three illustrative examples of the Adaptative Petri-Nets : the solving of indeterminism in parallelism, the parametrization of links between tasks and the study of the degradate mode of a process control.

1. ADAPTATIVE PETRI-NETS [1] [2] [3] [4]

1.1. Definitions

An adaptative Petri net (A P-Net), $R = (P,T,pre,post,M_o)$ is defined by :

- a set of places $P = \{p_1, p_2, \ldots, p_q\} \cup V$, where V is a set of special places,
- a set of transitions $T = \{t_1, t_2, \ldots, t_r\}$, disjoint with P,
- a $\mathbb{N}$-subset* M_o of P, called initial marking of R and two $\mathbb{N}$-subsets pre and post of $T \times P \times P$.

In the set V, let us characterize the places : $one_1, one_2, \ldots, one_s$ such as $M_o(one_i) = 1$, $i \in 1, \ldots, s$.

1.2. Graphical representation

A graphical representation of R as a bipartite multigraph is obtained by representing each $(p,q,t) \in P \times P \times T$ such that $pre(p,q,t) = n \neq 0$ by n copies of an edge :

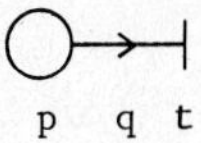

Figure 1.1

and each such tuple with $post(p,q,t) = m \neq 0$ by m copies of an edge :

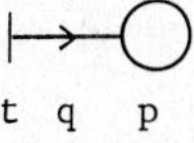

Figure 1.2

A label $q = one_i$, $one_i \in V$ such as $M(one_i) = 1$, may be omitted.

An example of an Adaptative Petri-Net is given in Figure 1.3.

$$R_1 = \{P,T,pre,post,M_o\}$$

with :

$$P = \{a,b,c,d,r,q,one_1\} \qquad V = \{one_1,q\}$$

$$T = \{1,2,3,4\}$$

$$M_o = \{1,0,1,0,1,1,1\}$$

---

* $\mathbb{N}$ denotes the set of non negative integers. A $\mathbb{N}$-subset of a set X is a function $f : X \to \mathbb{N}$.

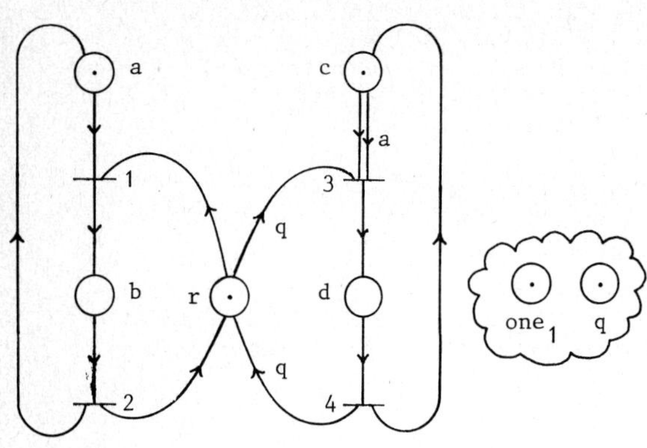

Figure 1.3

For this net, and for t = 3, we have :

pre(3,.,.)

	a	b	c	d	r	q	one_1
a	0	0	0	0	0	0	0
b							
c	1						1
d							
r						1	
q							
one_1							

post(3,.,.)

	a	b	c	d	r	q	one_1
a							
b							
c							
d							1
r							
q							
one_1							

1.3. Dynamic evolution of the marking

A marking of an A P-Net R is a $\mathbb{N}$-subset of P.

1.3.1. Conditions for firing of a transition

A transition t can be fired for a given marking M, (M(t>), if for all $p \in P$:

(i) $M(p) \geq \sum_{q \in P} pre(t,p,q).M(q)$,

(ii) $\sum_{q \in P} pre(t,p,q).M(q) > 0$

which we denote :

(1) $M(t> \Longrightarrow M \geq pre(t,.,.) * M > 0$

where $*$ représents the generalized scalar product :

$$(pre(t,p,.) * M = \sum_{q \in P} pre(t,p,q).M(q))$$

1.3.2. Firing of a transition : dynamic evolution of a marking net M

The firing of a transition $t \in T$, will change a marking M in a marking M' :

$M(t>M'$: $\Longleftrightarrow$ (i) firing conditions (1) are satisfied for M

(ii) $\forall p \in P : M'(p) = M(p) - \sum_{q \in P} pre(t,p,q).M(q) + \sum_{q \in P} post(t,p,q).M(q)$

which we denote :

$$M(t>M' \Longleftrightarrow M' = M - pre(t,.,.) * M + post(t,.,.) * M$$

or :

$$M(t>M' \Longleftrightarrow M' = (U - pre(t,.,.) + post(t,.,.)) * M$$

where U is an identity matrix.

1.4. Expression of invariant marking set of an Adaptative Petri-Net

The A P-N, like Petri-Nets, enable to study the structural properties. It is possible to find, for these nets, invariants (5).

For the example of the Figure 1.3, the following equations hold for all marking M :

(1) $M(one_1).M(a) + M(one_1).M(b) = M_o(one_1).M_o(a) + M_o(one_1).M_o(b)$

but $M(one_1) = 1$, $\forall$ M, $M_o(b) = 0$, $M_o(a) = 1$

then, (1) becomes : $\underline{M(a) + M(b) = M_o(a)}$ (1')

(2) $M(one_1).M(c) + M(one_1).M(d) = M_o(one_1).M_o(c) + M_o(one_1).M(d)$

then : $\underline{M(c) + M(d) = M_o(c)}$ (2')

(3) $M(one_1).M(b) + M(one_1).M(r) + M(q).M(d) =$

$M_o(one_1).M_o(b) + M_o(one_1).M_o(r) + M_o(q).M_o(d)$

then $\underline{M(b) + M(r) + M(q).M(d) = M_o(r)}$ (3')

These equations are called bilinear invariants and can be written as (n,n)-matrices I over $\mathbb{Z}$ such that :

$$M^{tr}.I.M = M_o^{tr}.I.M_o \quad \forall M$$

2. THE PARAMETRIZATION

An adaptative Petri-Net can be seen as a Petri-Net for which it is possible to ensure a dynamicaly change of the net structure. Hence, adaptative Petri-nets enable the parametrization of the representation of a model of process control command.

The adaptative Petri-nets enable to reduce the interpretation of the net :

(i) they enable the representation of test to zero (inhibition edge)

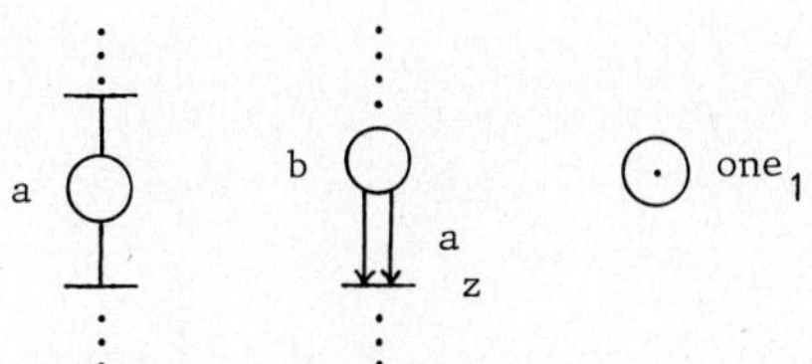

Figure 2.1

If we assume that the places a and b are 1-bounded, the condition of firing of the transition z can be stated as follows :

$$1 \geq M(b) \geq M(one_1) + M(a) \Rightarrow M(a) = 0$$

Hence firing of transition z is allowed only if the place a is empty.

(ii) Representation of reset nets

Firing of the transition t can reset the place a to zero and will disconnect the place a from the transition t :

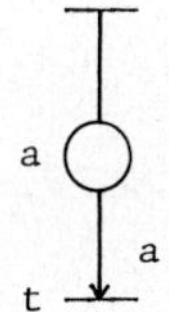

Figure 2.2

(iii) Representation of hold condition of a net or of a subnet

If we consider the place one_i of V, we can consider that the net of the higher hierarchical level will mark these places. It gives a token at the place "one_i" and then activates the tasks P_i. Otherwise it takes a token of the place "one_j" to inhibate the task P_j.

3. SOLUTION BASED ON ADAPTATIVE PETRI-NET TO WORK OUT THE INDETERMINISM OF PARALLELISM (6)

In this chapter, we study the problem of the exclusive resource shared between two task P_1 and P_2. As an example, Figure 3.1, contains a low level representation of this mutual exclusion between two processes.

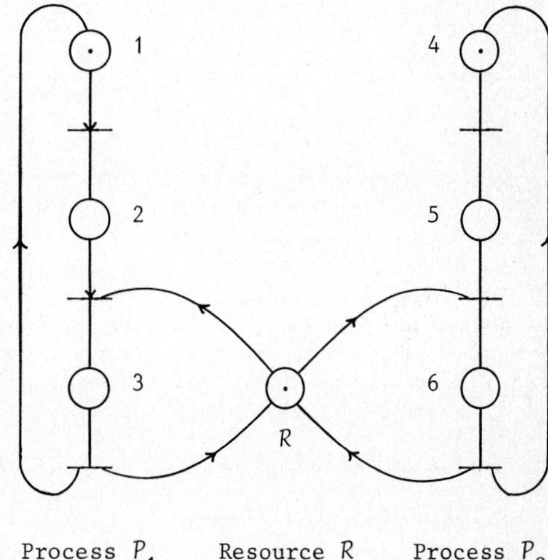

Figure 3.1

This system owns an anomaly, when the two processes will simulteneously request the resource R, the choice of the selected process is undetermined.

In the next part of this chapter, we present several possible solutions to remove this fault.

3.1. Static priority using for solving the undeterminism in parallelism

In order to resolve this difficulty, it is possible to introduce a static priority between the two processes. For example, let us assume that the process P_1 will have priority on P_2. As a first solution, let us consider the Petri-net of the Figure 3.2, the transition t_5 is firing if the three next conditions are satisfied :

(i) The process P_2 is in the state p_5

(ii) The process P_1 is not in the state p_2 (request of the resource R)

(iii) The resource R is free (place R owns a token)

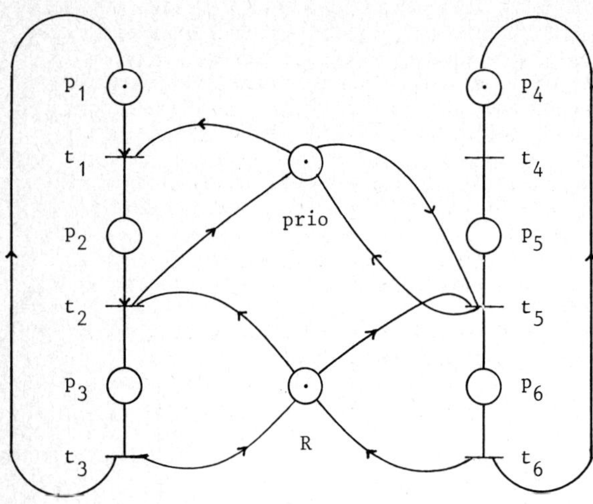

Figure 3.2

But if we study carefully this net, we remark the places p_1 and p_5 are, now, in structural conflict and the same problem of undeterminism will appear again. Then we can consider that ordinary Petri-nets are inefficient to solve this problem.

The static priority can be seen as special case of adaptative Petri-net. We pretend to describe a solution by means of the net of Figure 3.3, for which the above restrictions do not exist. When p_2 is marked, then transition t_5 can't be actived since process P_2 is one-marked. Then P_1 will have definitely priority on P_2 when places p_2 and p_5 are simultaneously marked.

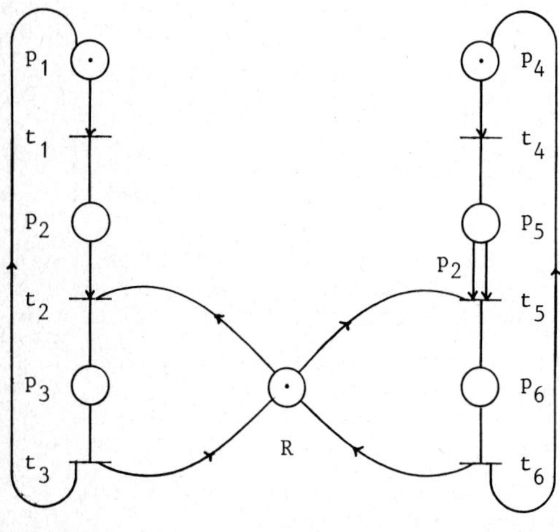

Figure 3.3

Adaptative Petri-net are really efficient to describe more sophistiqued solution. Let us now first present two criticisms of the above solution in order to present after this a solution using dynamical priority

(i) the priority is fixed in the conception phase of the process control,

(ii) it will exist a risk of famine : the process P_2 may be permanently blocked.

As example of the notion of equitable sharing of resource R, we may now introduce a dynamic priority.

3.2. Example of dynamic priority

The access conflict between the two processes for the exclusive resource, may be solved by a dynamic priority. After each access of one process P_i (i = 1 or 2), the other process $P_{(i+1) \bmod 2}$ will have priority for the next access.

Let us consider the adaptative Petri-net of the Figure 3.4, this net represents a solution of the dynamic parametrization.

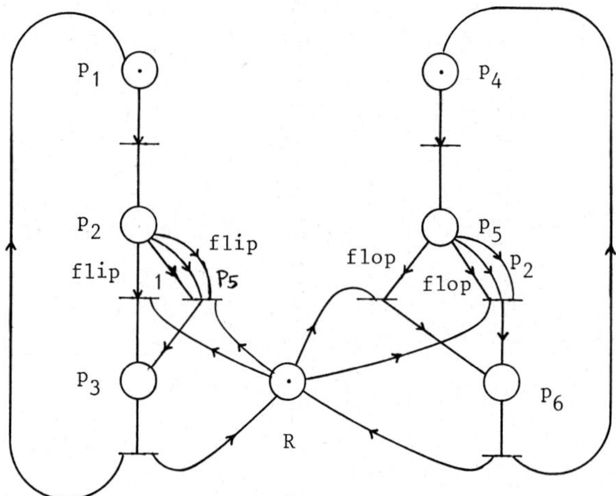

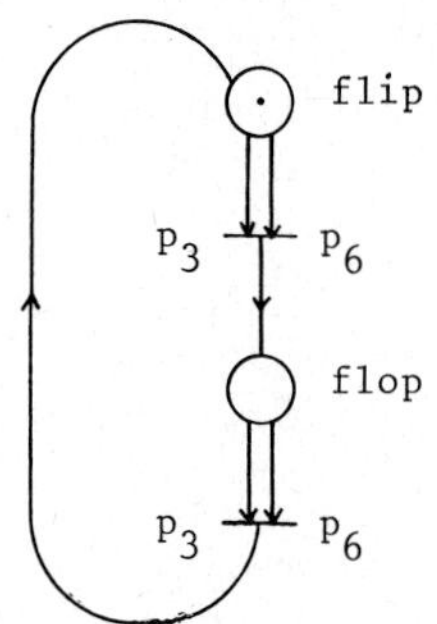

Figure 3.4

4. DYNAMIC EVOLUTION OF A CONTROL SYSTEM MODEL

In this chapter, we are studying a set of m processes which share n copies of one resource. Such a procedure can be used only by one user with the additional condition $m > n$. The number of resources is now variable and evolve under the control of a high level system. Others resources could be added to reduce access conflicts, or also could be deleted when exceptions or failures are detected.

The adaptative net of Figure 4.1. represents an example of three processes sharing n resources (with $n = 1$ or 2). The Figure 4.2 corresponds to the modelisation of the high level control system which drives the system described Figure 4.1.

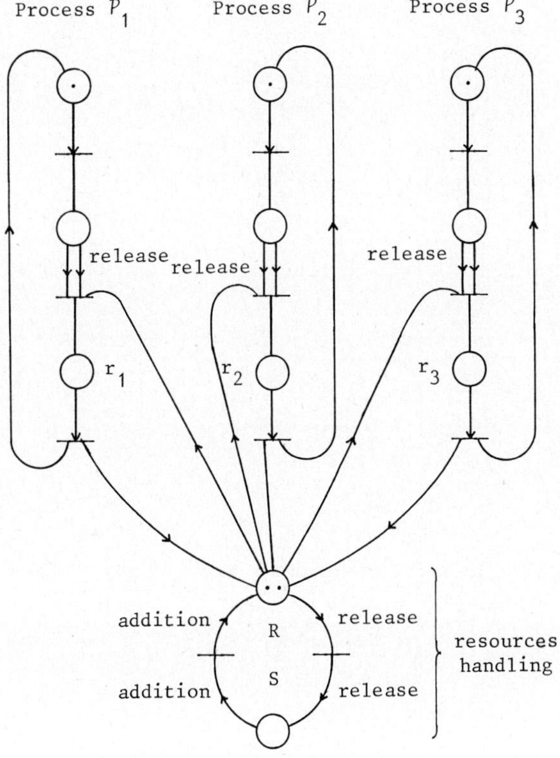

Figure 4.1

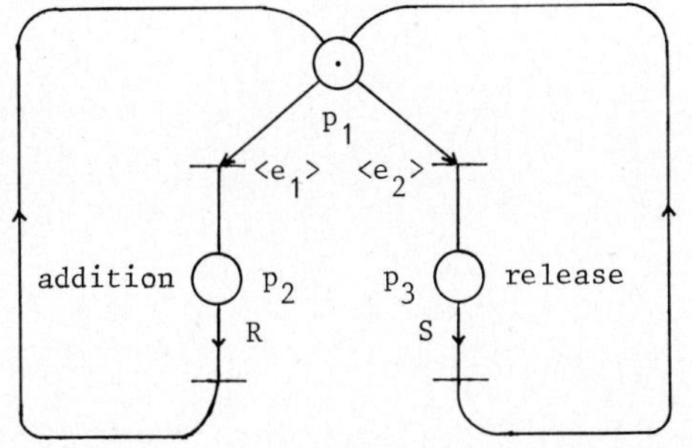

Figure 4.2 : Representation of the high level system

The net of Figure 4.2 is an interpreted net for which events e_1 and e_2 correspond to an addition request or a release request of an unit of resource. The place p_1 represents the wait state of the process ; the self modifying interpreted edges named by the places R and S of Figure 4.1 represents the acknowledge of the addition and release operations of one resource.

Release condition from hierarchical level Figure 4.2 will hold the whole low level processes P_1, P_2 and P_3 when place p_3 (release) is marked.

5. REPRESENTATION OF THE ALTERED MODES OF A PROCESS CONTROL SYSTEM

In this section, we'll study a parallel process control system with two levels of hierarchy :

(i) the first level supervision will ensure the parametrization of the second one. More precisely the hierarchical level will define the operate or hold mode of the low level process, it will also generate control for addition or deletion of resources used by the low level processes, and the reconfiguration of the control system in case of functional failure.

We'll not discuss here of failure detection and we make the hypothesis that the high level process is able to detect all misfunctions provided by user.

5.1. Activation / Desactivation of how level process

Each process is presented by a self-modifying net, RAM = {P,T,pre,post,M}, when P contains a distinguished place one_i. The activation of process P_1 consists to put a token into the place one_i and the hold state to take back this token. If we suppose that each process is controlled by such a place, activation and holding are then selectives operations under control of the high level process.

5.2. Parametrization of resources

In Section 4, we illustrated how it is possible to add or delete one resource : these operations are one of the functions of the high level system.

5.3. Anomaly recovering of a process

This operation consists first to recover all the resources used by this process and then to put it in a hold state. So, we have only to combine the solutions presented in the last two chapters.

CONCLUSION

In this article we have presented a tool, the adaptative Petri-Nets, which allows the description of parallel process control system with different hierarchical levels. The property is very useful to take account of :

(i) the parametrization of the number of available resources,

(ii) the parametrization of the stream of tokens through the edges of the net, under the control of a high level system.

This allows the representation of :

- test to zero (inhibition edge),

- reset nets,

- hold condition of a net ou a subnet,

- disconnection and connection of a subnet, which is very important to describe the degradate mode of a system.

The resolution of the problems of indeterminism is now possible with this tool by means of dynamic priority assumed to different processes.

Finally what appears very important here is the fact to be able to represent with a same model different levels for the handling and the control of real-time applications.

REFERENCES

(1) Valk, R., "Self-modifying nets, a natural extension of Petri-nets", ICALP 1978, Lect. Notes in Computer Sc., n° 62, Springer, Berlin, 1978.

(2) Valk, R., "On the computational power of extended Petri-nets", MFCS 1978, Lect. Notes in Computer Sc., n° 64, Springer, Berlin, 1978.

(3) Valk, R., "Generalizations of Petri-nets", MFCS 1981, Lect. Notes in Computer Sc., n° 118, Springer, Berlin, 1981.

(4) Corbeel, D., Gentina, J.C. and Vercauter, C., "Généralisation des réseaux de Pétri", AI'83 IASTED Symposium, Lille, March 1983.

(5) Lautenbach, K. and Schmid, H.A., "Use of Petri nets for proving correctness of concurrent process systems", Information Processing 74, North-Holland Publishing Company, 1974.

(6) Brams, G.W., "Réseaux de Pétri : théorie et pratique", Masson, 1981.

DIGITAL TECHNIQUES in Simulation, Communication and Control
Spyros G. Tzafestas (editor)
Elsevier Science Publishers B.V. (North-Holland) © IMACS, 1985

A MODEL FOR SIMULATION OF THE RAILWAY TRAFFIC IN THE PORT AREA

Eduard Rădăceanu
Academia "Stefan Gheorghiu" Bucureşti, R.S.România

The paper presents the concept of the railway traffic simulation model concerning the seaport operation for a better management of this activity. The model can be used as a part of the seaport management system by using real time computation capabilities.
Many alternatives for priorities, time distributions of arrivals and for train operation times can be run by using this model of more than 1200 GPSS bloks built for the traffic on the railway network at the mole V of the Constanţa seaport.

A seaport is an intermediate node in the world-wide commercial flow of goods. It is an initial node for the importing country economy and a final one for the exporting countries.

The transfer of goods in the seaport involves a set of activities which are , roughly speaking, the same for any seaport, but with some specific aspects of technical or procedural nature depending on the specificity of the economy, geographical configuration and labour conditions in the seaport.
The main specific characteristics of the seaport activities, that influence the management system are:

- The existence of several seaport operating entreprises, whose activities are corelated especialy when a ship is operated by more than one entreprise

- The diversity of goods manipulated and their packing form and the diversity of transportation means
- The loading/unloading techniques and equipments
- The great area of activities
- The existence of perturbation and conjunctural factors as metheorological, economic, a.s.o.
- The great number of working norms and legal regulations with internal or international character

- The great amount of data which are vechiculated through the information system with degree of perishability, many of them with random character.

All these characteristics make the seaport operation very complex, with specific problems for the management system.

The seaport operation activities refer especialy to the ship operation at the berth and the flow of goods in the seaport which leads us to consider the seaport as a complex service system.
The main phases of the service of the transactions in the system are:

- the acceptance of the ship arrival
- the dispatch and mooring of the ship at the berth
- the transportation of goods to and from the ship
- the final operations.

These activities are influenced by conjunctural factors and perturbations, which by their synergical action in the entropic or negentropic way are conditioning the seaport capacities utilization degree.
The main influence on the loading/unloading operations have equipments and transhipment technologies, which can be direct, indirect or of mixted type (fig.1) on wagons, trucks or barges.

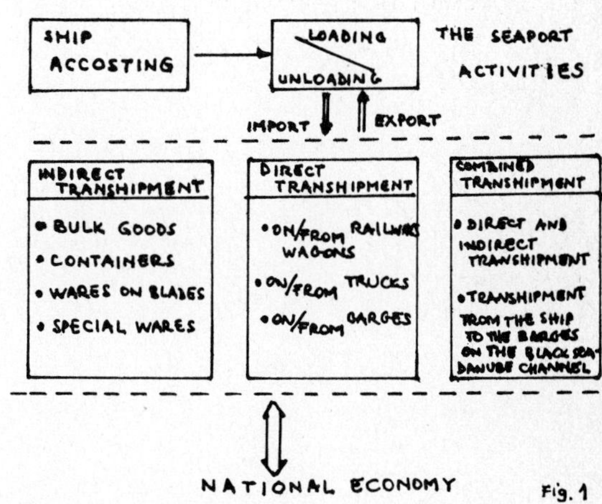

Fig. 1

The transhipment type is chosen according the technological development of the seaport operation and facilities and the types of goods in the flow to ensure the avoidance of the operation overtimes and demurrage, to respect the charter party.
The interdependence of the main indicators for the seaport operation can be made obvious by simulation models, like those made for La Valetta, Carachi, Valparaiso and Los Angeles /1,2/. Another approach can be found in /6/. Such a simulation model represents the main variables and characteristics of the seaport operation concerning equipments and another facilities, their dynamics, labour organisation, berth specialisation , a.s.o.
A special role in this concerto of facts has the railway transportation in the seaport, especialy when there are great amounts of minerals and coal to be transported as in the case of Constanţa seaport.
The management of the seaport operation can be approached as a hierarchical cybernetic system with two levels of control /3,4,5/.
The first level of control (loop), corresponding to the strategic-tactic management level, represented by the seaport headquarter, has especialy coordination tasks in achieving the objectives (the fullfilment of plan indicators), and is operating on longer time-horizons and is using more aggregated data and indicators than at the second control level (loops), corresponding to the operative management of functional compartments, where primitive data,or at a low level of aggregation,are used on shorter time horizons to take operative decisions.
The system is structured as a cybernetic system (fig. 2a).
This structure gives the requirements for the real time computer oriented management system.
Because the seaport operation takes place on a large area the system has also the characteristics of a distributed parameter system (fig. 2b).

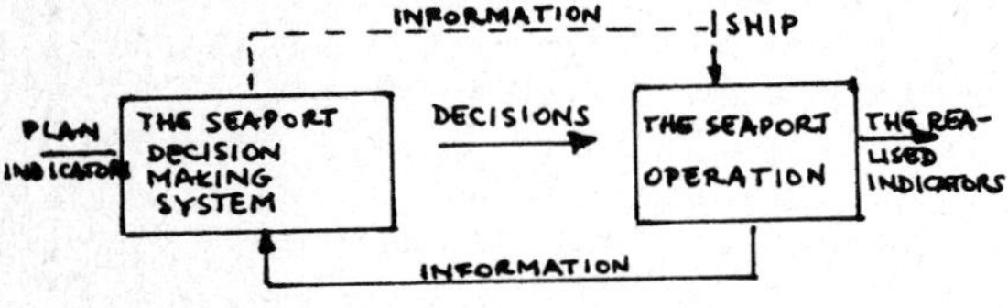

Fig. 2a

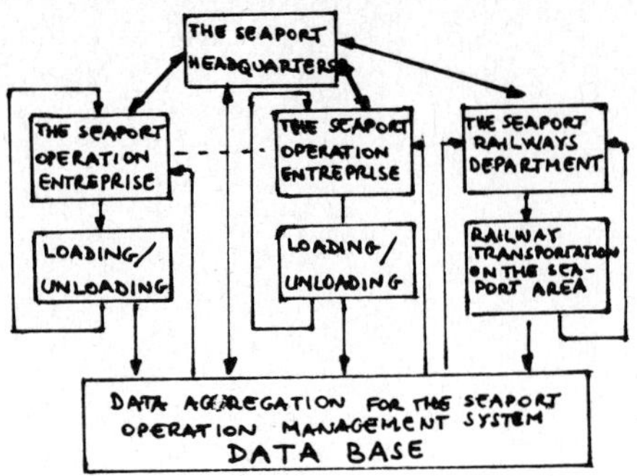

Fig. 2b

The harbour operation entreprises belong to different economic departments and their activities are zoned in the seaport area.
A very important objective in the ship operation is to avoid the overtime operation and the demurrage in consequence.
A schema with main reasons for such demurrage is given in fig. 3.
It shows the action points of the seaport management and of the functional compartments in the systemic approach and suggests the hardware and software requirements (the need for teleprocessing and communications facilities and the network structure) for the real time computer oriented management system to realise a good objectives/resources harmonization by high quality decisions.

The railway traffic in the seaport of Constanţa is very intensive and this fact makes necesary permanent control actions in the seaport railway network and in the national network as well (in the Empty Wagons Division).
These control actions are best implemented only under operation of a real time informatic management system.
Concerning the railway activity in the seaport of Constanţa there are designed and implemented some systems like SITCON-designed at the Computing Centre of the Transportation Ministry - which handle the interface between the railway network, the seaport and the national railway network managing the wagons flow between the two networks, and POSEIDON - designed at the Technological Research Institute of the same ministry (ICPTT) for the seaport operation management.
These systems contain many useful data and information for a real time informatic management system of the railway system of the seaport as well.

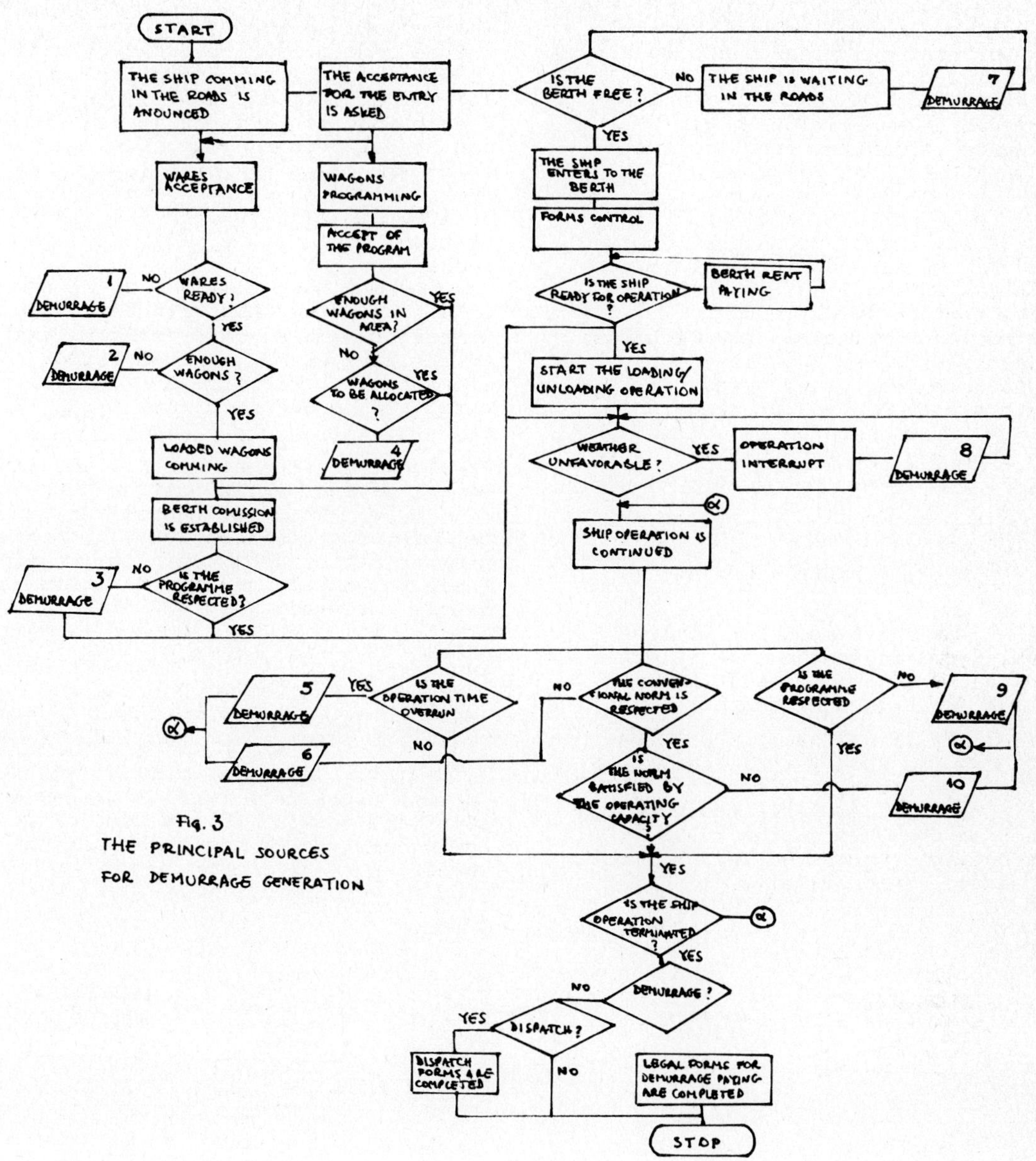

Fig. 3
THE PRINCIPAL SOURCES FOR DEMURRAGE GENERATION

The latter ensures:
- rapid flows of data and information between functional compartments of the harbour operating entreprises,
- data input at the terminals near the place where these data are generated and validated, for teletransmision and teleprocessing,
- good information background for decision making at different management levels, the system being operated by using a data base /4/, dedicated to nonspecialised users in informatics .
The data base is operated under control of the data management system SOCRATE and run on Romanian made computer FELIX C-512 with minicomputer M18 as data concentrator with DAF 2o10 terminals.
POSEIDON applications (fig.4) use some data concerning railway system (some data about wagons) and therefore an extention of this system to include the remaining data concerning railway system operation in the harbour is to be made.

Until such a real time computer management system is ready, a simulation model of the railway traffic was built in GPSS and run on a IBM 360/40 computer.

In the model are represented conditions for trains arrivals, accordingly to the circulation flowchart, the train reception, marshalling, composition and decomposition, train loading or unloading, final control and dispatching, as represented in fig.5

Lines and points are considered in the GPSS program of the simulation model as facilities and conditions for free way in the marshalling, by boolean variables properly defined.

These boolean variables have as terms the states of lines and pines , which can be free or occupied and the operators used, AND and OR, take into account conditions to be fullfiled for a free way for each marshaling to be completed, like in the following formula

$$BV_i = \bigcup \prod_k FNU\$L_k * \prod_p FNU\$M_p$$

where BV_i is the symbol for boolean variable; FNU indicates that is necessary that the facility must be free (unused) and L_k and M_p indicates that the facility is a line or a pin respectively. The sign \$ indicates that the line and the pins are used in the model with names properly chosen , by respecting the GPSS syntax rules, the names beeing represented in the formula by L_k and M_p respectively.

The results for each run give the degree of utilisation for each entity of equipment, lines and pins, warning about the overloaded facilities.

The train evolution through the network can be followed, as well as the dispatching of trains that are terminated.

The simulation run can be made for a desired time interval or for a number of terminated trains, loaded or unloaded.

The model allows to run a great number of alternatives which can differ by different values, or priorities assigned to the activities, arrival time distribution, the rate between trains which are loaded in direct transhipment and trains loaded in indirect mode.

By studying alternatives for the improvement of the quality of the activities especialy when bottlenecks appear because of a too intensive input rate of trains, better decisions are prepared, their potential consequences are more deeply analysed.

The model , which reffers to the most important area of the Constanţa harbour the mole five, where minerals and coal are transhiped in direct and indirect mode, comprises more than 1200 of GPSS bloks.

In this area a number of 27 lines and 47 pines are considered , a part of lines beeing grouped in two zonal marshalling yards.

THE POSEIDON SYSTEM

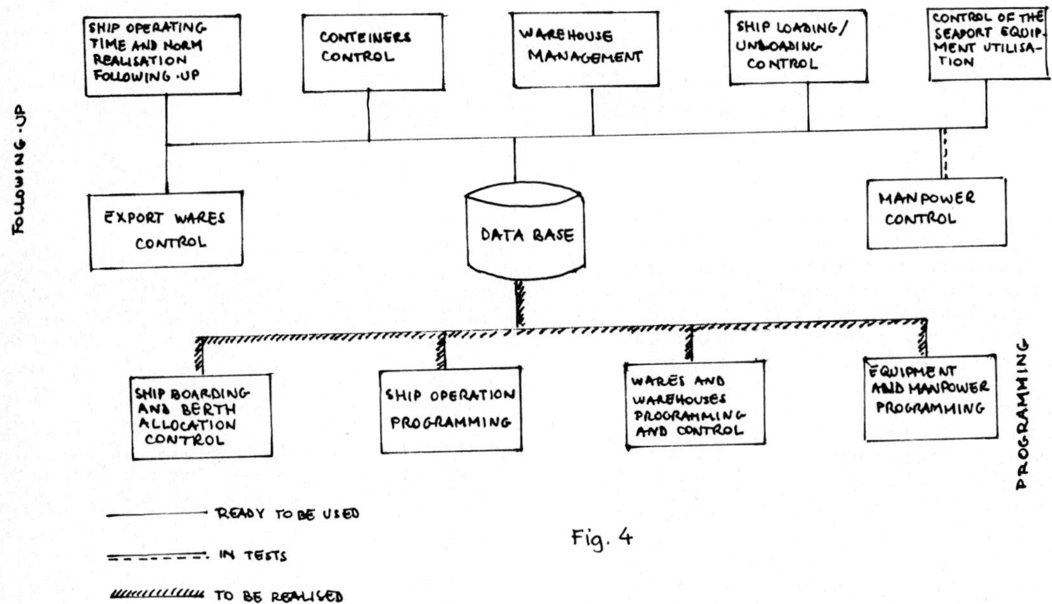

Fig. 4

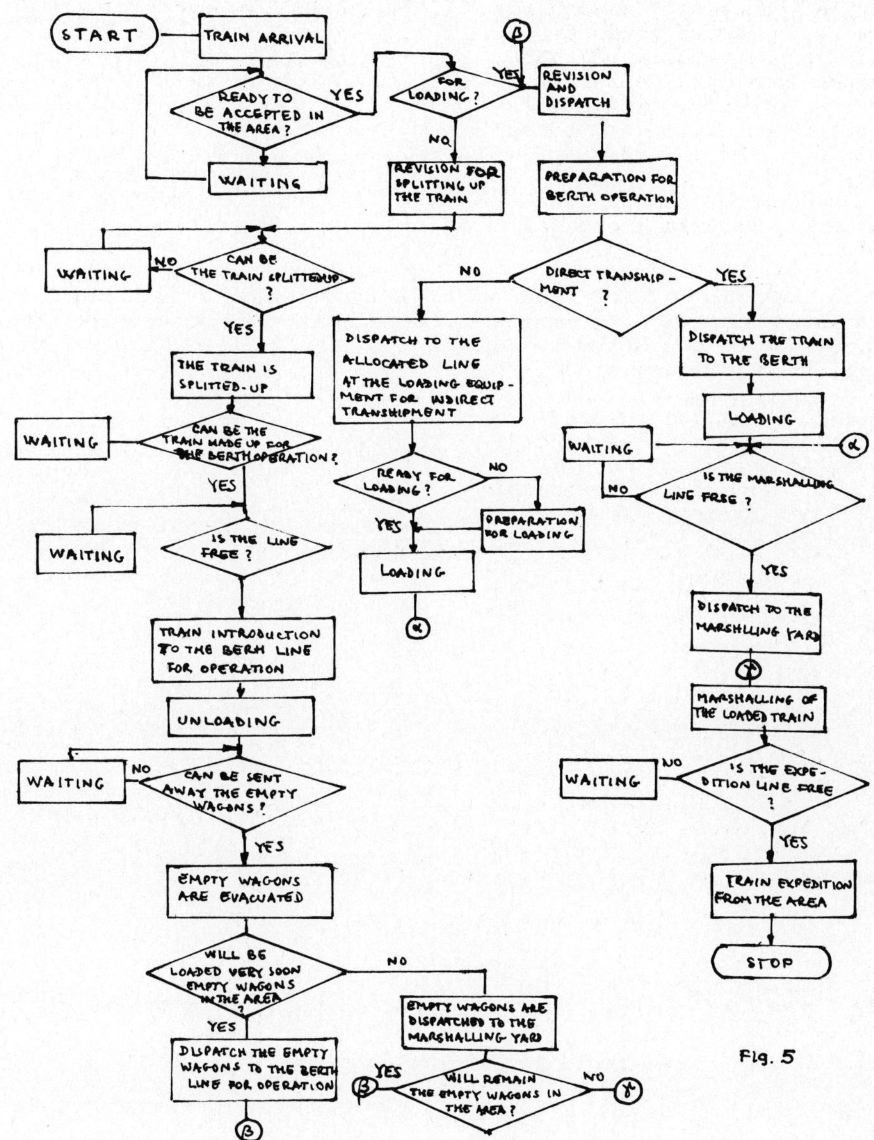

Fig. 5

The model can be used for exemple to study the consequences of the transfer of some activities concerning the trains reception and expedition from the harbour area to a former waiting yard, which increase the operating capacity of the railway network by decreasing waiting times because of conditions to be fullfiled for free ways in marshalling or even by removing the traffic cut-off situation.

The simulation model allows to identify the limits for an efficient utilisation of seaport railway network and can be used as a computer assisted design tool and for operative purposes as well as in case of production flows design and management /7,8/.

REFERENCES

/1/ +++ Berth throughput. Systematic methods for improving general cargo operations. Rep.by the Secretariat of UNCTAD (U.N. New York 1973).

/2/ +++ Port developemnt. A handbook for planners in developing countries Prep.by the Secretariat of UNCTAD (U.N. New York, 1976)

/3/ Constantinescu, P. and Rădăceanu, E. The MIS as a Model of Management and Managed Systems in class S_2. Economic Computation and Economic Cybernetics Studies and Research , 1, (1975), 5-23.

/4/ Rădăceanu, E., Martin, M., Stanciu, V., Bolcu, E. - Asupra conducerii cibernetice a activităţii portuare şi feroviare în portul Constanţa, com.la a 2-a Conferinţă Naţională de Cibernetică şi Sisteme, Bucureşti 5-8 oct.1983

/5/ Rădăceanu, Ed.- Modelarea conducerii intreprinderii, Revista economică, 41 (1975).

/6/ Kauffman, A., Mètodes SIMUPORT pour la simulation des ports de commerce, in Agard, J. (ed.), Les Méthodes de simulation (Dunod, Paris, 1968).

/7/ Rădăceanu, Ed., Simulation used for design and control of production flows, in Tzafestas, S.G., Simulation of Distributed Parameter and Large-Scale Systems (North Holland - Amsterdam, 1980).

/8/ Rădăceanu, Ed., Limbaje de Simulare (Editura Militară , Bucureşti, 1981)

DIGITAL TECHNIQUES in Simulation, Communication and Control
Spyros G. Tzafestas (editor)
Elsevier Science Publishers B.V. (North-Holland) © IMACS, 1985

COMPUTER SIMULATION FOR FINANCIAL PLANNING IN A MANUFACTURING FIRM

Jacek K. Hunek, Kazimierz B. Czechowicz

Institute of Organization and Management
Institute of Control and Systems Engineering
Technical University of Wrocław
Wrocław, Poland

The paper presents a financial model of the company operating on market. The company is treated as a lower level element in the two-level economic system. The higher level of the system is a govermental administration body (control body) affecting the company behaviour with economic parameters. Both the systems elements possess own utility functions and strive after their maximisation.
Discussed is also an applicability of the model for financial planning through the computer simulation method.

1. INTRODUCTION

The presently implemented economic reforms in Poland changes radically the position of state-owned companies in the economic system. The companies have gained lawful and economic independence, whereas governmental administration bodies may influence the behaviour of the companies with lawful and systems regulations and economic parameters. Each company develops independently its own production plans by follwoing the criterion of economic efficiency, whereas economic plans developed by the centre (governmental planning organs) are only an information category. The problem of consistence between goals that comprise all the aspects of economy and company goals is solved by laying down proper values of economic parameters and by making bids for production in the form of governmental orders.

From the viewpoint of a single company we can thus say of the formation of the two-level economic system where the higher level is occupied by the governmental administration body (control body) that represents interests of the state and at the lower level resides the company. Each of the elements of that system has its own utility function and tends to optimize it. The basic decision problem for the company is to find such a production plan, P, that will provide maximisation of its utility function (profit) and such a distribution policy of financial means gained by sales of products and services that will assure the meeting of company needs as well as needs of workers employed in the company.

The general rules for administrating company finances are established by appropriate legal instruments compulsory in the whole economic system. They define principles of the company economics and economic instruments that may be used by governmental administration bodies. These are such instruments of the economic policy as prices, taxes, interest rates, import duties etc.

Under circumstances of the slight stability of economic processes it is particularly desired to make economic analyses for the needs of financial planning in the company. A useful research method in this respect is a computer simulation.

2. FORMULATION OF THE PROBLEM

The subject of this analysis is a two-level economic system whose elements are:

- at the lower level - the production company that operates on market
- at the higher level - the governmental administration body (control body).

The company conducts an economic activity consisting in manufacturing and sales of products as well rendering services and in virtue of that it gains the definite profit P. The amount of the profit depends on the production plan V and on prices π_i; $i = 1,\dots,n$, where n - number of production and services brands. The production plan and the prices are fixed by the company.

The profit P is then divided be into the part for the company and the part for the state, a structure of that division is established by the control body by parameters of the tax system.

The control body also impacts upon the amount of financial means (funds) allocated to the company staff by using definite parameters that fix taxes on salaries. The company is independent in distribution and allocation of a part of profits left in the company (after the deduction of taxes), by setting up funds which are to finance development needs, needs of the company staff and the current operations of the company as well.

Both the components of the economic system strain after maximisation of their own utility functions which for the company is the total amount of funds at disposal, and for the control body is the total amount of taxes paid for a definite production structure.

Striving after reaching the impact on the company behaviour the control body establishes rules of calculating economic indexes and control parameters as well. The control body proceeds with a policy stable over the period of one year but variable over a longer period of time.

The whole of the regulations directing the company behaviour is an economic-financial system. Tending to the best policy the company must have a capability of analyzing financial effects which may arise after particular alternatives of its production plan will be introduced. To do it the most convenient way is to build up a model of the company financial system and then analyze it with a simulation method.

3. FINANCIAL MODEL

The general diagram of the financial model composed of segments is presented in fig.1. The segments refer to elements of the company financial system and are to calculate the following: sales, costs, accumulation for particular products and services, financial outcome, taxes, profit, company funds, balance of financial needs and potentialities as well as a value of a utility function.

Each of these segments is described by one or by a few mathematical or logical formulae.

The segment SALES may be formulated as follows

$$S_i(t) = \sum_{i=1}^{k} P^r_{i'}(t)\cdot \pi_{i'}(t) + \sum_{i=m-k}^{m} \bar{P}^r_{i'}(t)\cdot \bar{\pi}_{i'}(t) \quad (1)$$

where:

$S_i(t)$ - total sales amount for the i-th product over the period of t, $t>0$,

$P^r_{i'}(t)$ - size of the i-th production brand for internal (home) market,

$\pi_{i'}(t)$ - unit price of the i-th product on home market,

$\bar{P}^r_{i'}(t)$ - size of production of the i-th product on exports,

$\bar{\pi}_{i'}(t)$ - unit price of the i-th product on exports,

n - number of production brands,

m - number of the i-th brand products,

$S(t)$ - total sales

$$S(t) = \sum_{i=1}^{n} S_i(t) \quad (2)$$

The segment COSTS is to calculate the unit cost C_i for each brand of products and total costs:

$$C_i(t) = \sum_{j=1}^{k} C^m_j(t) + \sum_{j=l-k}^{l} C^n_j(t) \quad (3)$$

$$C(t) = \sum_{i=1}^{n} C_i(t)\cdot P_i(t) \quad (4)$$

where:

$C_i(t)$ - unit cost of the i-th product,

$C^m_j(t)$ - the j-th component of unit material costs,

$C^n_j(t)$ - the j-ht component of unit non-material costs,

k - number of components of the material costs,

$l-k$ - number of components of the non-material costs,

$C(t)$ - total costs of the company.

The segment ACCUMULATION allows the company not only to compute the accumulation gained on the unit of each product but also to make a choice of the production structure - possibly the best - from the viewpoint of the utility function.

The accumulation A_i on product of the i-th brand is calculated by comparing (1) and (3)

$$A_i(t) = S_i(t) - C_i(t)\cdot P_i(t) \quad (5)$$

$$A(t) = \sum_{i=1}^{n} A_i(t) \quad (6)$$

where:

$A(t)$ - total accumulation.

The segment FINANCIAL OUTCOME may be expressed as follows:

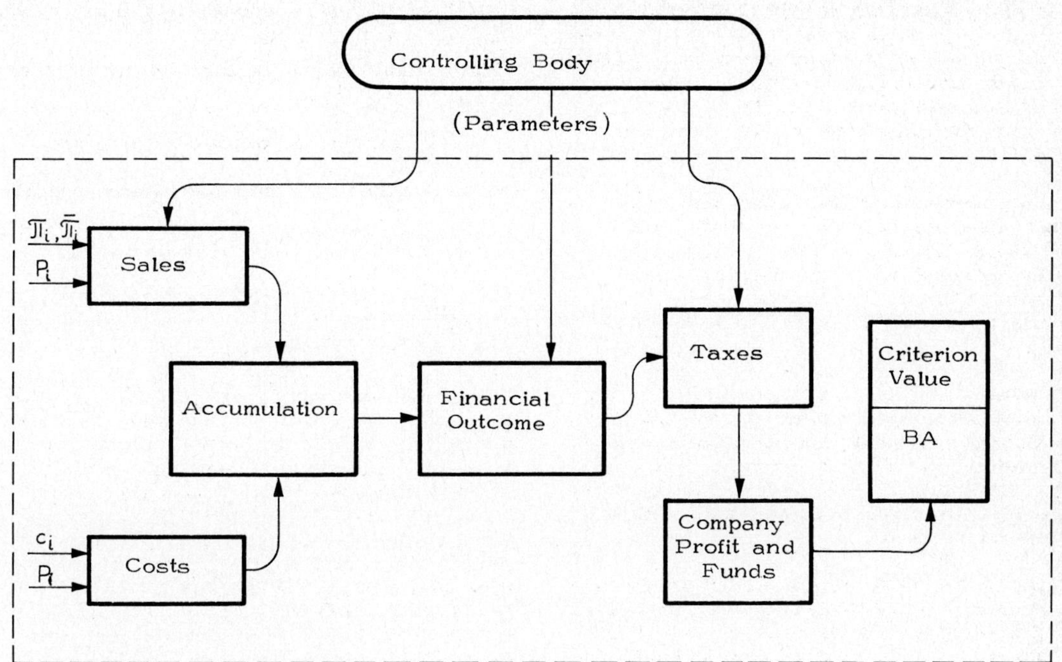

Figure 1: Segments of financial model

$$F(t) = A(t) - T^{O}(t) + D(t) + R(t) \qquad (7)$$

$$T^{O}(t) = \left[\sum_{i=1}^{n} S_i(t) + U(t)\right] \cdot \eta^{O}(t) \qquad (8)$$

$$R(t) = \sum_{p=1}^{q} R_p(t) \qquad (9)$$

where:

$T^{O}(t)$ - amount of the turnover tax,

$\eta^{O}(t)$ - turnover tax rate,

$D(t)$ - state subsidies,

$R(t)$ - balance of extra profits and losses,

$U(t)$ - amount of services.

The segment TAXES serves calculating the taxes that charge the company profit i.e.: income tax, tax on immovables and salary tax. The formulae to compute the taxes can be written as follows:

$$T(t) = T^{(I)}(t) + T^{S}(t) + T^{M}(t) \qquad (10)$$

$$T^{(I)} = \alpha F(t) + \mu(t) \qquad (11)$$

$$T^{(S)} = \beta \cdot \sum_{j=1}^{k} Q^{c}(t) + \beta_1 \cdot \sum_{l=1}^{r} Q^{p}(t) \qquad (12)$$

$$T^{(M)} = \gamma \cdot M \qquad (13)$$

where:

$T(t)$ - amount of taxes charging the company balance profit,

$T^{(I)}(t)$ - income tax,

$T^{(S)}(t)$ - salary tax,

$T^{(M)}(t)$ - tax on immovables,

$Q^{c}(t), Q^{p}(t)$ - salaries

M - sum of immovables,

$\alpha, \beta, \gamma, \beta_1, \mu$ - non-negative parameters.

The segment COMPANY PROFIT and FUNDS is to calculate the amount of the profit $P(t)$ left in the company:

$$P(t) = F(t) - T^{I}(t) \qquad (14)$$

and then deductions to form the company funds:

1) the compulsory funds
   a) the reserve fund

$$\Delta F^R(t) = \alpha^R \cdot P(t) \tag{15}$$

   b) the salary increase liabilities

$$\Delta F^A(t) = \alpha^A \cdot Q(t),$$

$$\alpha^A = \begin{cases} 0, & \text{for } Q \leqslant Q^o \\ 0 \leqslant \alpha^A \leqslant 1 & \text{for } Q > Q^o \end{cases} \tag{16}$$

2) the non-compulsory funds
   - the staff fund (for remunerations and bounties)

$$\Delta F^Z(t) = \alpha^Z \left[P(t) - (\Delta F^R(t) + \Delta F^A(t)) \right] = \alpha^Z \cdot P'(t) \tag{17}$$

   - the development fund

$$\Delta F^D(t) = \alpha^D \cdot P'(t) = (1 - \alpha^Z) \cdot P'(t) \tag{18}$$

where:

$\Delta F^R(t)$ - deduction from the profit on the reserve fund,

$\Delta F^A(t)$ - liability of the profit by the salary increase,

$\Delta F^Z(t)$ - deduction from the profit on the staff fund,

α^D, α^Z - non-negative parameters, $\alpha^D + \alpha^Z = 1$

α^A - parameter related to the profit encumbrance caused by the rise in salaries,

$P'(t)$ - profit lessened by the deductions on the compulsory funds.

The distribution of the profit over the funds is made parametrically on the basis of analysis of the company financial needs and potentialities.

The segment CALCULATION of the CRITERION VALUE serves deriving a value of the function:

$$\phi(t) = Q(t) + P(t) - \Delta F^A(t) \longrightarrow \max \tag{19}$$

after satisfying the following constraints:

a) necessary needs of the company must be fulfilled:

$$F^D(t_o) + F^D(t) + \Delta F^D(t) \geqslant N^D(t) \tag{20}$$

$$F^S(t_o) + F^S(t) + \Delta F^S(t) \geqslant N^S(t) \tag{21}$$

$$F^M(t_o) + F^M(t) + \Delta F^M(t) \geqslant N^M(t) \tag{22}$$

b) the financial outcome must not be lesser than zero:

$$F(t) \geqslant 0 \tag{23}$$

c) sum of expenses laid out of the profit cannot exceed its total amount:

$$\Delta F^R(t) + \Delta F^A(t) + \Delta F^D(t) + \Delta F^S(t) + \Delta F^M(t) + + \Delta F^Z(t) \leqslant P(t) \tag{24}$$

The model segments are mutually interrelated and linked with environment represented by deliverers of production agents, by receivers of products and services and by the state budget.

The whole of these interrelations is not shown here and fig. 2 presents an exemplary network of the segments: FINANCIAL OUTCOME, TAXES and PROFIT. The detailed description of the model as well as its variables can be found in [1].

It can be generally asserted that the model comprises the three groups of quantities:

1) the quantities characterizing external conditions independent of the company:

- parameters generally compulsory in the whole economy e.g. turnower tax rate, income tax rate, interest rates,

- parameters fixed up by the control body e.g. tax rate charging the profit in virtue of the rise in salaries,

2) the quantities characterizing the company internal conditions which are decision variables e.g. production size, prices, indexes of deductions from the profit etc.,

3) the quantities characterizing the company internal conditions which are parameters e.g. amount of instalments for bank credits, social and housing needs, size of production in process etc.

4. APPLICATION OF THE MODEL

The above presented model of the company financial system as well as the computation procedure[1] corresponding to it has been developed in the form of the computer programme FIPLAN in FORTRAN and implemented at the minicomputer MERA 400. It used a method of the discrete-events simulation.

[1] Description of the procedure may be found in paper [2].

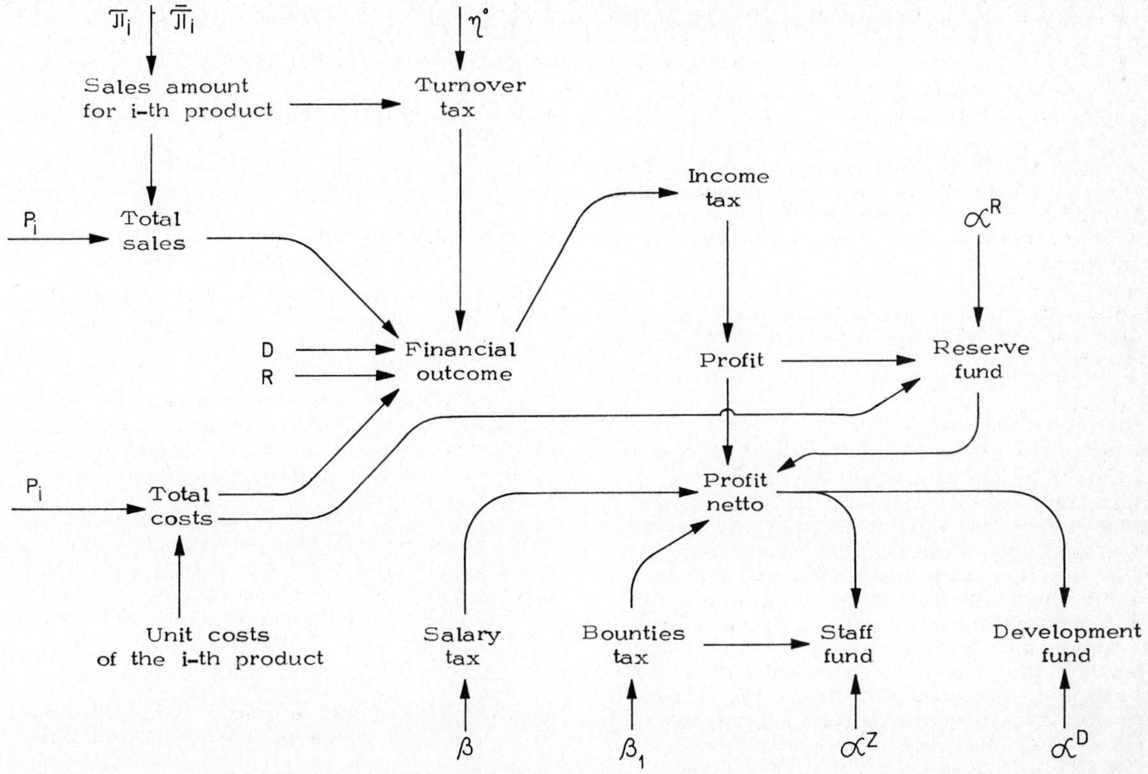

Figure 2: An exemplary network configuration for two segments

The FIPLAN programme is designed to analyze effects of the company financial policy alternatives regarding the choice of its production programme and how to divide the profit and finance the company needs. By the multiple reiteration of computations for various decision policies it is possible to compare as different profits as their distributions and to choose the best policy with regard to the criterion function (the utility function).

It is also possible to perform simulation experiments for needs of one year's planning - the control body realizes a stable control policy or to make long-term plans - the control body changes control parameters for each planning year. The program provides four basic types of simulation experiments:

1) basic variant whereby the company makes changes in a group of decision variables related to the production structure and costs (e.g. number of products, unit prices and costs) while the remaining variables and parameters remain unchanged,

2) "profit distribution" variant in which for a definite production structure changes in parameters related to the profit distribution and formation of funds are performed,

3) "changes in environment" variant which allows the company to analyze effects of changes in financial parameters caused by the control body - while no own reactions to these changes are undertaken,

4) "changes in internal parameters" variant which in the case of the fixed production plan and the fixed profit distribution structure - examines effects of changes in internal parameters of the company assessed on the basis of records from the past.

It is also possible to design much more complex experiments including combinations of the basic types.

The FIPLAN programme is used for carrying out a number of simulation experiments ordered by textile industry companies and by electromachinery industry companies. Results of the simulations were applied to developing and modifying companies' financial plans for the year of 1984. Analyzed were effects of variant decision policies assuming that the control body would not change the fixed control parameters over the year.

On the basis of the experience and companies' opinions the attempt at implementing the model by the Apple II microcomputer with the VISICALC system [3] has been undertaken. It allows users possessing such own microcomputers to use the FIPLAN programme and thus to reduce evidently costs.

Actually the work on developing a dialogue version for the MERA-400 minicomputer is conducted.

5. SUMMARY

The model of the financial system presented in this paper has been developed for requirements of the company top management and may be used for issuing variants of the company financial plan. Its application in practice diminishes planning labouriousness and significantly increases a set of the plan alternatives under investigation. The concept of treating the company as an element of the two-level economy allows for mapping interactions between the company and its environment. The significant constraint of using the presented version of the FIPLAN programme lies in batch-processing. It makes difficulties in designing simulation experiments.

REFERENCES

[1] Brol W.M., Hunek J.K., Kroik J., Procedura planowania finansowego w przedsiębiorstwie "FIPLAN". Res. Report No PRE 77/84, Inst. of Organisation and Mgt., Tech. Univ. of Wrocław (July 1984).

[2] Hunek J.K., Brol W.M., Kroik J., Komputerowe wspomaganie planowania finansowego w przedsiębiorstwie, in: INFOGRYF'84 Proceedings (TNOiK o/Szczecin, Kołobrzeg 1984).

[3] Hunek J.K., Brol W.M., Zastosowanie systemu VISICALC do wspomagania systemu planowania w przedsiębiorstwie., Conf. Proceedings "Microcomputers in automation and system science" (Wrocław 1984).

DIGITAL TECHNIQUES in Simulation, Communication and Control
Spyros G. Tzafestas (editor)
Elsevier Science Publishers B.V. (North-Holland) © IMACS, 1985

OPTIMAL RESOLVING OF THE OVERLOADS IN AN ENERGY SUPPLY SYSTEM

Miroslav Ivantchev, Nicola Janev, Jordan Mitev

University of Sofia, Sofia, Bulgaria

It is well known fact, that every power supply system operates in a balanced state only, i.e. the generated power is equal to the demands. In a case of greater demands, the system enters a state of overload, which remaining unresolved for an appropriate interval of time becomes a destructive factor. The system is balanced through power brake-down which depending on the importance of the consumers (plants, houses etc.) leads to different loss measured in money. In this paper we suggest a 0-1 programming models and algorithms which on the basis of: reaction time, expected loss, current or expected disbalance, consumption rate, produce a recomendation list of consumers, whose disconnection leads to minimal loss.

1. INTRODUCTION

The problem, considered here, is of the following type: given is a set of consumers c_i , $i=\overline{1,n}$ of a product P produced in a source S with production capacity L . The total quantity L is distributed among the consumers, according their needs S_i . Depending on various factors, there could be periods of time in which is reduced to a level L' such that $\sum S_i > L'$, i.e. the system is overloaded. In such situation the unsufficient quantity $L-L'$ (namely deficit) is covered through finding a feasible subset I so that $\sum_{i\in I} S_i \geq L-L'$. That means that some of the consumers are disconnected from the source S . Normaly the disconnection of the consumer i leads to loss $c_i(t)$ - considered here as a increasing function of the time t , $t\in[0,T]$. If T is finite, the problem is to find a feasible subset I^* , which minimizes $\sum c_i(t)$ over the family of all feasible subsets.

2. MODELS

The real life example of the abovementioned system is for instance an electric power supply system. We will ommit the details concerning the terminology, used for describing the object, included in the system and the reasons for arrising of overloads. Further we will distinguish between two types of overloads called here as "unexpected" and "expected" overload.

The unexpected overload is one which arrises instantly and could not be prognosed. It is of limited duration in one unit of time. The problem here is to find the subset of consumers, which beeng disconnected for this unit of time will cover the deficit $L-L'$ with minimal loss.

Obviously, the mathematical model of this problem is the well known knapsack problem with 0-1 variables.

Realy, if $x_j = 1$ means j-th consumer is off, and $x_j = 0$ - otherwise, then for a set of n consumers with the notations from the introduction we obtain:

$$\sum_{j=1}^{n} c_j x_j \rightarrow min$$
$$\sum_{j=1}^{n} s_j x_j \geq L - L'$$
$$x_j \in \{0,1\}, \; j = \overline{1,n}$$

Although this is an NP-hard problem, it could be easily generated and solved (near optimaly) in a time less than a minute even for large n, which is quite satisfactory for the needs of practice.

The second type of overload posses a much more difficulties becous of its nature. In the case of expected overload it is assumed that the quantity $L - L'$ is a known function of time $t \in [0,T]$. Choosing a suitable measure, the period $[0,T]$ could be subdevised in K subperiods. With this discretization the functions $L - L'$ and $c_i(t)$ are converted in vectors in K-dimensional spase: $(l_1, l_2, \ldots, l_K)$, $(c_{i1}, c_{i2}, \ldots, c_{iK})$. Then the problem is to find for every consumer $i, i = \overline{1,n}$ the subset of subperiods in which its supply is suspended. Of course, in every subperiod j the total sum of the demands s_i for the consumers with suspended supply must be not less than l_j. Another natural restriction for that type of overload is: if the supply for a given consumer is restored, then he can not be off more (see restriction (3) below).

The mathematical model in zero-one variables could be easily given but unfortunately rather difficulty solved:

$$(1) \qquad \sum_{i=1}^{n} c_i(y_i) \rightarrow min$$

$$(2) \qquad \sum_{i=1}^{n} s_i x_{ij} \geq l_j, \; j = \overline{1,K}$$

$$(3) \qquad \sum_{j=1}^{K} (x_{ij} - x_{ij+1})^2 \leq 2, \; i = \overline{1,n}, \; j = \overline{1,K}$$

$$(4) \qquad x_{ij} \in \{0,1\}, \; i = \overline{1,n}, \; j = \overline{1,K}$$

To justify this claim it suffices to interpret $c_i(y_i) = c_{iy_i}$ if $y_i \equiv \sum_{j=1}^{K} x_{ij} > 0$

$$x_{ij} = \begin{cases} 1, & \text{as consumer } i \text{ is off in subperiod } j, \\ 0, & \text{otherwise.} \end{cases}$$

For $n > 1000$ the practical implementation of the known exact methods for solving such a problems is unthinkable. The heuristic, given below, is one of the ways for avoiding this obstacle.

3. Heuristic

The heuristic, suggested here, is connected with the following decomposition of the problem:

$$(P_j) \qquad \sum_{i \in I} \bar{c}_i x_i \rightarrow min$$
$$\sum_{i \in I} s_i x_i \geq l_j$$

where
$$x_i \in \{0,1\}, \; i \in I$$
$$t_i = \sum_{j=1}^{K} x_{ij}, \quad \bar{c}_i = c_{it_{i+1}} - c_{it_i}$$
$$I = \{i \,/\, t_i > 0, \; x_{i,j+\varepsilon} = 1 \text{ or } t_i = 0, \varepsilon = \pm 1\}$$

Initialy all $x_{ij} = 0$ and $j = l$. Then we solve K subproblems P_j varying j from l to K ($\varepsilon = 1$), and next from $l-1$ to 1 ($\varepsilon = -1$). If x_i^* is the optimal solution of P_j, the j-th column of the matrix $x_l = \|x_{ij}\|$ is updated to:

$$x_{ij} = x_i^* \qquad \text{for } i \in I \; .$$

If P_j^l is the optimal value of the subproblem P_j with starting period l, then after K subperiods hav e been solved (in the abovementioned order) we obtain an approximate solution, recorded in x_l with objective function value $\sigma_l = \sum_{j=1}^{K} P_j^l$. Varying l from 1 to K we can choose the best one, noted as x_{l*}, $\sigma_{l*} = min\{\sigma_1, \sigma_2, \ldots, \sigma_K\}$, as a solution of (1)-(4).

The strategy, choosen here, is in some sence similar to a "greedy" algorithms with the main advantage - That it is practicaly implementable for large n on computers with moderate possibilities. The main disadvantage is that up to now we were not able to estimate the worst-case behavior of the algorithm.

4. Conclusions

The distribution problem, considered here, is influenced by the real life situation, connected with the operating of the electric energy set of Bulgaria. The computerized version of the system, based on the abovementioned consideration, proved to be highly efficient in practice, where the computerized control of overload eliminates the need of subjective decision of a dispatcher. It seems to us that the future will face us more and more with the problems of distribution of restricted resources (water, fuel, energy ect.). That is why the following generalizations of the problem seems perspective: if in a case of overload the supply for a given consumer could be reduced below his demand s_i down to given level or is suspended, and his loss are function not only of the time but also and of unsufficient quantity. Then we will have a distribution problem, which is much more complicated but in some instances more realistic.

Reference

1. Fayard D., Plateau G., Algorithm 47. An algorithm of the 0-1 knapsack problem, Computing, 1982, 3.

DIGITAL TECHNIQUES in Simulation, Communication and Control
Spyros G. Tzafestas (editor)
Elsevier Science Publishers B.V. (North-Holland) © IMACS, 1985

A NEUTRON AVERAGE ENERGY MEASUREMENT TECHNIQUE THE CASE OF DELAYED NEUTRONS

S. Synetos

N.R.C."Democritos"
Nuclear Technology Department
Aghia Paraskevi, Attiki
Athens-Greece

A method for the determination of the average energy of neutron emitting sources is developed. The neutron detector consists of a long BF_3 counter surrounded in turn by polythene cylinders of various thickness. The polythene thicknesses are chosen on the merit of exhibiting different efficiency versus energy curves. Thus, the ratio of efficiencies for each pair of cylinders would be a function of the energy. The energy of a neutron emitting source is then determined by the ratio of counts obtained with such a pair of cylinders. The efficency curves for each pair of cylinders are obtained using a Monte Carlo simulation and are corrected for real neutron sources by counting sources of known spectra. The method is then used to obtain the average energy of delayed neutrons following thermal neutron induced fission of U-235. Both equilibrium and delayed neutron group average energies are obtained. Finally, the obtained count ratios are used in a consistency check of equilibrium delayed neutron spectra, published in the literature. The observed inconsistencies indicate that further delayed neutron spectrum measurements are needed to provide data to the required accuracy.

1. INTRODUCTION

In addition to the prompt neutrons emitted from each fission event, a small number of delayed neutrons is also emitted. The criterion for classifying a neutron as prompt or delayed is the time scale of the emission. While prompt neutrons are emitted 10^{-14} sec after the fission event, delayed neutrons are associated with the neutron rich fission products and are emitted .2sec to 1 min after fission. It is known that delayed neutrons constitute less than 1% of all neutrons produced in fission. Nevertheless they are of utmost importance in reactor operation. Thus, a lot of effort has being devoted (1,2,3) for the accurate determination of the characteristics of their emission (i.e. delayed neutron precursors, yield, time scale and spectrum of emitted delayed neutrons Especially fast breeder reactors seem to be particularly sensitive to the details of the delayed neutron spectra used for their analysis (4).

In a previous paper (5) we have reported a measurement of delayed neutron yields and decay constants.

In this paper we report on a method developed to measure average energies of neutron emitting sources, and we use this methodology to determine the average energy of delayed neutrons emitted from thermal neutron induced fission of U-235. A count rate ratio technique is employed to measure the average energy of the equilibrium delayed neutron emission, as well as the average energy for each delayed group. The obtained ratios are also used as a means of checking delayed neutron spectra and their uncertainties as published by other authors.

The determination of the average energy of a neutron emitting source gives a useful measure of the spectrum under examination (3) and thus gives a sensitive gauge which can be applied to published spectrum measurements.

The determination of the average energy for each delayed group, which is directly useful for reactor calculations (6), will give an independent check of the average energies and energy spectra of different precursors, as well as reported spectra corresponding to the six delayed neutron groups.

2. THE METHOD

The method employed in this work is based on the ring ratio technique proposed by Reeder et al (7,8).

A long BF_3 counter surrounded in turn by three polythene cylinders of different thicknesses is used to measure ratios of counts, normalized to the same number of neutrons emitted from the sample. If the shape of the efficiency curve for each moderator thickness is different, then the ratio of efficiency for a pair of cylinders would be a function of energy. Thus, the ratio of counts of any neutron emitting source obtained with such a pair of cylinders would be a function of the energy of the neutron emission.

A preliminary calculation showed that polythene cylinders of diameters 9,5 and 2 inches surrounding the BF3 detector, would have quite different efficiency curves.

Calculation curves for two pairs of cylinders were obtained using a Monte Carlo simulation. The energy region of interest (20 KeV to 2 MeV) was divided into 10 intervals, and the efficiency of each cylinder $\varepsilon(E_i)$ was calculated as the number of neutrons absorbed in the detector per source neutron emitted with energy within the boundaries of group i.

The calibration curves based on the above calculation do not accurately represent the calibration curves needed for sources having a broad spectrum of neutron energies (e.g. delayed neutron spectra. In order to take account of spectral sources we proceeded as follows:

The effective efficiency of each cylinder to a calibrated Am-Li source, whose spectrum is known to be similar to the equilibrium d.n. spectrum, was calculated from the relation:

$$\varepsilon_{eff} = \frac{\sum_i N(E_i)\,\varepsilon(E_i)}{\sum_i N(E_i)} \qquad (1)$$

where $\varepsilon(E_i)$ is the efficiency function of each cylinder, and $N(E_i)$ the source spectrum. ε_{eff} was then related to the true average energy of the source, defined as:

$$E_{av} = \frac{\sum_i N(E_i)\,E_i}{\sum_i N(E_i)} \qquad (2)$$

The resulting effective efficiency ratios were then normalized to the measured efficiency ratios (for the Am-Li source) for each pair of cylinders. We thus end up with calibration curves normalized to the Am-Li source counting, and exhibiting one point (Am-Li counting) corrected for spectral sources. Counting of a calibrated Cf source provides a check of the normalization, and a second point in the calibration curves, corrected for spectral sources.

The d.n. average energy can then be deduced from the experimentally obtained count ratios, and the calibration curves obtained from the above analysis.

It should be noted that the technique described above gives correct E_{av} values under certain conditions. The following analysis is performed:
The effective efficiency ratio R_{eff} for a spectrum N(E) is:

$$R_{eff} = \frac{\int N(E)\,\varepsilon_1(E)\,dE}{\int N(E)\,\varepsilon_2(E)\,dE} \qquad (3)$$

where ε_2 refers to the reference, and ε_1 to some other detector. Expanding the efficiency ratio in a power series

$$\frac{\varepsilon_1(E)}{\varepsilon_2(E)} = a + bE + cE^2 + d.. \qquad (4)$$

and inserting (4) in (3) we get: R_{eff} =

$$= a + b\frac{\int N(E)\,\varepsilon_1(E)\,E\,dE}{\int N(E)\,\varepsilon_2(E)\,dE} + c\frac{\int N(E)\,\varepsilon_1(E)\,E^2\,dE}{\int N(E)\,\varepsilon_2(E)\,dE} + d.. \qquad (5)$$

In order for R_{eff} to be a function of E_{av} only it is necessary that:

$$c = 0,\ d = 0 \text{ etc} \qquad (6)$$

and

$$\varepsilon_2 = \text{const.} \qquad (7)$$

In this case equation (5) gives:

$$R_{eff} = a + b\,E_{av} \qquad (8)$$

and R_{eff} is a function of E_{av} only, and does not depend on any other attribute of the spectrum. Thus, for the method to be valid a reference detector exhibiting an efficiency function constant with energy, and a second detector which has an efficiency function having the form a + bE should be employed.

3. CALIBRATION OF THE DETECTORS

3.a Experimental setup

Figure 1 depicts the experimental setup, as it is used for the delayed neutron measurements. The moderator consists of polythene cylinders hollowed around their axis to accomodate the long BF3 counter. The counting end of the flight tube is used for the positioning either of the neutron sources, or the delayed neutron sample.

Scattering has been kept to a minimum by using as little an amount of structral material as possible.

Background was kept at reasonable levels by enclosing the counting end of the system in a Cd sheet (Fig. 1).

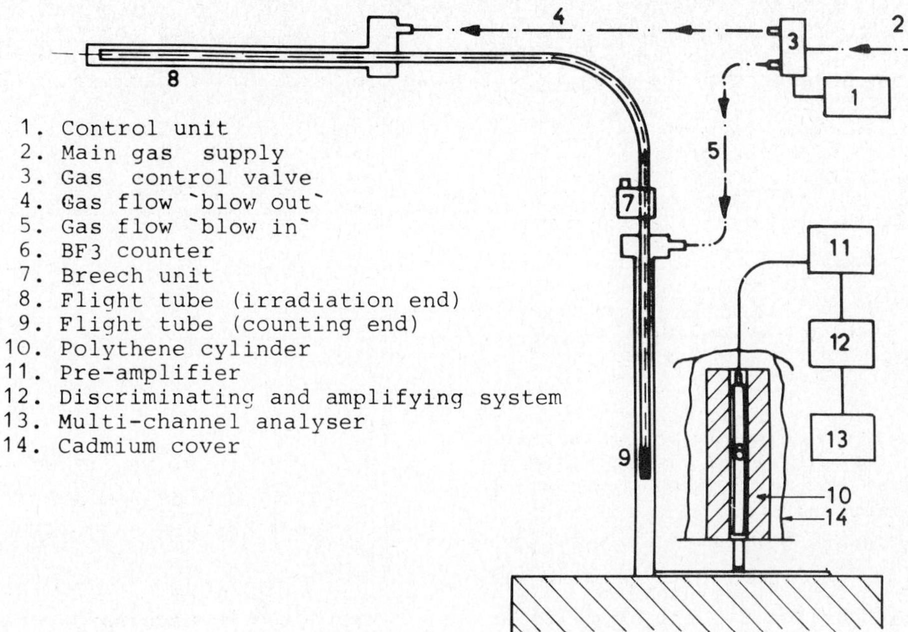

Figure 1: Block diagram of the experimental setup

3.b Determination of the efficiency functions of the detectors

The absolute efficiency of each of the three detectors was determined using calibrated Am-Li and Cf neutron sources. Although the measurement of the neutron sources is straight forward, a number of corrections has to be applied, so that the result is directly comparable to ratios obtained using the U-235 sample. This is done as described in (5), and the results are shown in Table I.

The response of each of the three polythene cylinders to monoenergetic neutron sources was calculated using the code MONK (9). The Monte Carlo technique of using random numbers to sample statistical probability distributions was employed for the investigation of neutron histories in a manner analogous to natural random processes. The geometry routines package is an outstanding feature of MONK, allowing a very accurate representation of the experimental setup into the calculation. Nuclear data for each nuclide involved in the calculation were taken from the MONK Nuclear Data Library, whose ultimate source is the UKNDL. For the response function calculation we assumed a point source located at the same position as the centre of the U-235 foil in the experiment.

To obtain reasonable statistical accuracy, the Monte Carlo technique requires a large number of neutrons to be tracked. In order to make best use of the allocated computer time we took the following two steps: first, we restricted the emission of the source towards the solid angle subtended by each cylinder, so that most of the started neutrons would contribute to the calculated response. The statistical accuracy requirements are mainly imposed by the use of the response functions in the consistency check of delayed neutron spectra. We thus apportioned the total permissible number of starting neutrons, so that to get better statistical accuracy for the groups in which most of the response is.

The response functions as calculated by

Efficiency	Cylinder diameter		
	2inch	5inch	9inch
Experiment	.00033±.6%	.00287±.6%	.00145±.7%
Anisotr corr.	x .970±1.5%	x.982±.9%	x.990±.5%
Volume corr	x1.014±.7%	x.1.014±.7%	x1.014±.7%
Result	.000325±1.8%	.00286±1.3%	.00146±1.1%
Calculated	.00040	.00379	.00241
C/E value	1.231	1.325	1.651

TABLE I. Comparison of the calculated and experimental efficiency for the Am-Li source.

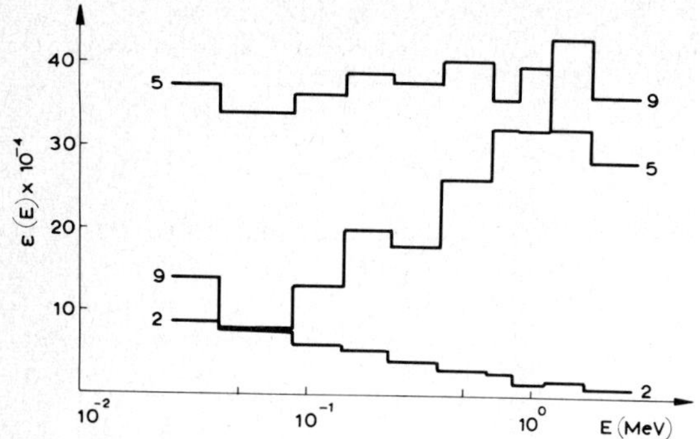

Fig. 2. Efficiency curves for the three cylinders (2,5 and 9 inch respectively)

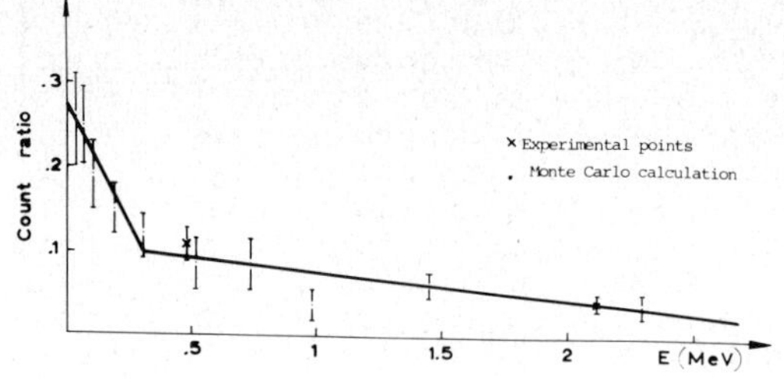

Fig. 4. Count ratio versus neutron energy (2/5" cylinder)

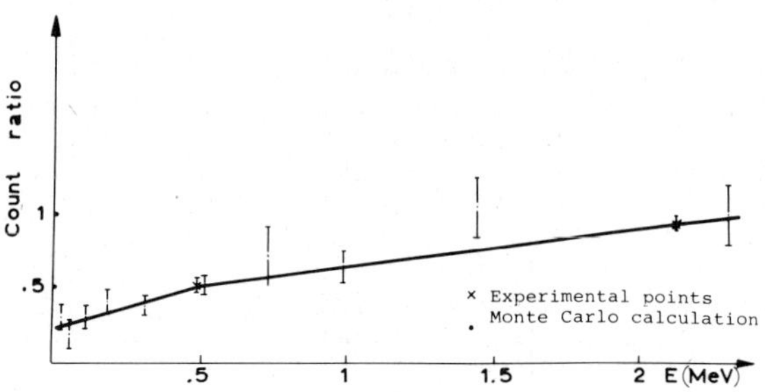

Fig. 3. Count ratio against neutron energy (9/5" cylinders)

MONK are given in Fig. 2. The uncertainties were calculated from the statistics of the program and are expresed as one standard deviation.

The shape of the response functions is generally in agreement with that of polythene spheres of the same diameter (10). The response function for the 5" cylinder is almost constant as a function of energy, while that of the 9" cylinder is a linear function of energy.

3.c Construction of the calibration curves

We are now equipped with enough data to construct the count ratio versus neutron energy curves.

Table I shows the Am-Li source efficiency for each polythene cylinder, first as measured and second as calculated using equation (1). For the Am-Li and Cf sources the spectra given in the references (11) and (12) were used. It is apparent that the calculation overpredicts the efficiency of all detectors. Discrepancies towards the same direction have been reported in (13) and (14). What is disturbing in our case is that the overprediction increases with increasing polythene thickness. One possible explanation is that the thermalization of neutrons in the polythene is underestimated in the MONK calcualtions. This would result in a decrease of the number of neutrons absorbed in the polythene and a hardening of the spectrum of neutrons entering the BF_3 detector region. Thus, the efficiency of the 9 inch cylinder as calculated by MONK would increase, while that of the 2 inch cylinder would decrease.

For the purpose of our analysis we assumed that the shape of the efficiency functions as calculated by the Monte Carlo code was correct, but we multiplied them by a normalizing factor, so that the calculated efficiency for the Am-Li source would agree with the experimental one.

Figures 3 to 4 depict the calibration curves for the two pairs of cylinders. Am-Li and Cf source counting provides two points corrected for spectral sources. The shape of the calibration curves is complemented by the ratios of the normalized efficiency functions.

4. APPLICATION OF THE METHOD

The calibrated detector was used for the determination of the average energy of the delayed neutron emission. For the d.n. measurements the detector-moderator assembly has to be coupled to a sample transfer system (Fig. 1). The mechanical parts of the transfer system consist of a double walled aluminium irradiation flight tube sleeved with cadmium, two heavy polythene tubes (flight tube and gas inlet-outlet tube), tube couplings and a second double walled aluminium tube supplied with a loader at the counting end of the system.

The experimental procedure was very similar to that followed in (5). The sample consisting of a .2g metal foil (95.54% in U-235), is suttled between the irradiation position and the counting end. The irradiation position is at the centre of a shperical cavity in one of the thermal columns of the CONSORT reactor, where the neutron flux is well thermalized.

The cycle times used were 10 min irradiation and 10 min counting.

A LABEN multi-channel analyser was used to register the decay curves in 2048 time channels. The number of runs for each detector was chosen to be inversely proportional to its efficiency, so that the resulting counting statistics would be of the same order for all three detectors. A monitor counter (fission chamber) was operating during the irradiations, giving thus a means of normalizing the total delayed neutron counts obtained with each detector, to the same flux, and therefore to the number of fissions.

4.a Delayed neutron average energies

The average energy for the equilibrium d.n. emission is deduced from the measured count ratios and the curves of figures 3 and 4. From the 9/5 inch curve we get 480 KeV and from the 2/5 inch curve we get 500 KeV. The average for E_{av} is calculated to 490±100 KeV, where the uncertainty includes statistical and systematic errors.

We must qualify the above result with the statement that it is normalized to the Am-Li source counting, and thus depends on the spectrum assumed for the Am-Li source.

The value of E_{av} obtained here can be compared with E_{av} = 540 KeV obtained by Reeder et al (7) using a similar technique. Reeders' et al reviewed measurement (8) gives an even higher value for E_{av}. On the other hand, calculations of E_{av} based on d.n. spectra measured by Saphier et al (15) and Eccleston and Woodruff (16) gave average energies 462 KeV and 405 KeV respectively. This might indicate that the second spectrum is inconsistent with our measurement.

The time dependent decay curves obtained with each cylinder thickness were analysed using the least squares technique. The group half lives were fixed to those found in (5) or to Keepin's (1) values following equation was fitted to the decay curve for each cylinder j:

$$C_j(t) = b y_d \sum_{K=1}^{m} C_{mK} \sum_i P_{ij} e^{-\lambda_i t} + \delta(t) \quad (9)$$

where y_d = absolute delayed neutron yield per fission

b = calibration factor of monitor counts to number of fissions, constant for all three cylinders.

C_{mK} = monitor counts per sec for the kth run

bC_{mK} = n_{FK} = fissions per sec for the kth run

P_{ij} = $\alpha_i \varepsilon_{ij}$ = relative yield x detector efficiency for detector j and delayed group i

λ_i = the group i decay constant (fixed)

$\delta(t)$ the statistical discrepancy of the count ratio from its expectation value.

The problem (9) is a linear one. From the least squares fit we get $b\varepsilon_{ij}\alpha_i$ for the three detectors. Taking into account that b and α_i are the same for each detector, the ratios of efficiencies per group are obtained, and through the calibration curves we get the average energy per group.

The obtained ratios of efficiencies per group and the deduced E_{av} are given in Table II. The uncertainties in the ratios represent the uncertainties in the last squares fir and in the normalization. The uncertainties in E_{av} are then deduced from the calibration curves. A weighted average value for each group is calculated from the results obtained using each of the two ratios. The result is shown

Group	9/5"	E_{av}	2/5"	E_{av}	$\bar{E}_{av}$ (KeV)
λ_i=(5)					
1	.407±5%	290±20	.140±5.5%	235±15	255±12
2	.548±3%	600±60	.081±5.2%	900±110	670±53
3	.425±15%	320±110	.112±17%	280±30	284±29
4	.587±11%	740±250	.083±17%	870±370	781±207
5	.572±28%	660±420	.084±45%	860±500	740±322
λ_i=(1)					
1	.403±5%	285±20	.141±5%	230±15	250±12
2	.547±3%	600±60	.081±5%	900±110	670±53
3	.455±10%	360±70	.108±12%	290±30	300±28
4	.608±11%	810±260	.080±19%	910±400	841±218
5	.547±39%	600±400	.099±53%	320±220	385±193

TABLE II. Group count ratios and average energies.

Ref. \ Group	1	2	3	4	5	6
(14)	300±60	670±10	650±90	910±90	400±70	-
(19)	250±60	560±60	430±60	620±60	420±60	-
(20)	250±20	460±10	410±20	450±20	-	-
(21)	280±30	480±50	450±50	430±40	-	-
(7)	150	460	690	540	520	610
(22)	200	424	390	429	395	539
This work	250±12	670±53	300±28	841±218	385±193	385

TABLE III. Average energies (KeV) of delayed neutron groups in thermal neutron fission of U-235

in table II for both Synetos' and Williams (5) and Keepin's (1) group structures. Average energies for groups 1, 2 and 3 are identical for ours and Keepins' group structures. The differences in E_{av} for the other 2 groups reflect the differences between the two group structures. The higher E_{av} for our group 5 (which includes part of group 6) compared with Keepin's indicates that group 6 has a harder spectrum. This agrees with the result of Reeder et al (7).Our results are consistent with those of Evans and Krick (12), where a trend towards higher average energies for the shorter lived d.n. groups is reported.

Table III presents a comparison of the group E_{av} obtained in this work with previously published data. Our result confirms that group 1 has the softest spectrum. Our result is in good agrrement with that of Hughes et al (19). It disagrees with most of the other measurements, especially for group 3 which appears quite soft in our measurement. The uncertainties associated with group 4 and 5 appear high in our calculation, and this reflects the big uncertainties in the parameters α_i and λ_i fitted to groups 4 and 5. It is suggested that irradiation-counting cycles accentuating the contribution of groups 4 and 5 would improve the accuracy here.

4b Consistency check of d.n.spectra

The obtained ratios of efficiencies are also used as a means of checking d.n. spectra and their uncertainties, as published by other authors. The problem is formulated as follows:

if: $X_d(E)$ = literature spectrum for near equilibrium d.n. emission

$X_{d_i}(E)$ = literature spectrum for delayed group i

$\varepsilon_j(E)$ = efficiency function for the jth detector,

then:

$$\frac{b\varepsilon_{ij}}{b\varepsilon_{iJ}} = \frac{\int_0^\infty X_{d_i}(E)\,\varepsilon_j(E)\,dE}{\int_0^\infty X_{d_i}(E)\,\varepsilon_J(E)\,dE}$$

and

$$\frac{\sum_i \alpha_i\varepsilon_{ij}}{\sum_i \alpha_i\varepsilon_{iJ}} = \frac{\sum_i \int_0^\infty \alpha_i X_{d_i}(E)\,\varepsilon_j(E)\,dE}{\sum_i \int_0^\infty \alpha_i X_{d_i}(E)\,\varepsilon_J(E)\,dE}$$

but:

$$X_d(E) = \sum_i \alpha_i X_{d_i}(E)$$

Cylinder ratio	C/E values		
	Assumed delayed neutron spectrum		
	Saphier et al (15)	Eccleston and Woodruff (16)	Weaver et al (17)
2/5 inch	.885±.073	.779±.076	.801±.072
9/5 inch	.955±.054	.884±.062	.797±.029

TABLE IV. Comparison of experimental and calculated cylinder ratios, used in the delayed neutron spectrum consistency check.

therefore:

$$\frac{\sum_i \alpha_i\varepsilon_{ij}}{\sum_i \alpha_i\varepsilon_{iJ}} = \frac{\int_0^\infty X_d(E)\,\varepsilon_j(E)\,dE}{\int_0^\infty X_d(E)\,\varepsilon_J(E)\,dE}$$

, and by replacing the energy integration by summation over the energy groups g, we get:

$$\frac{\sum_i \alpha_i\varepsilon_{ij}}{\sum_i \alpha_i\varepsilon_{iJ}} = \frac{\sum_g X_{dg}\varepsilon_{jg}}{\sum_g X_{dg}\varepsilon_{Jg}} \qquad (10)$$

Equation (10) relates the experimental ratios of $\sum_i \alpha_i\varepsilon_{ij}$ with the published spectra, folded with the calculated efficiency function. In order to check the consistency of the two parts of equation (10) one has to answer the following question:

Given experimental ratios and $X_d(E)$ with assumed errors, what would the errors on $X_d(E)$ have to be before we could accept the consistency of equation (10)? We have assumed here that the two parts of equation (10) carry identical information, i.e. the experimental conditions under which the d.n. spectra were originally measured are similar to those of our experiment. (that is, the range of time integration and precursors for which data were obtained are similar).

For the purpose of our analysis we have chosen three of the latest published d.n. spectra for U-235. These are the following: Saphier et al (15), Eccleston and Woodruff (16) and Weaver et al (17). The first spectrum is the result of an evaluation based on the measurements of Shalev and Rudstan (18) of d.n. spectra from 20 fission product isotopes. It covers the energy range 50 to 1600 KeV. The second spectrum was obtained using a proton-recoil spectrometer, and covers the energy region 35 to 1500 KeV. The Weaver et al (17) spectrum was measured using a ^{3}He detector and covers the energy range 30 to 2000 KeV. It is believed that these spectra represent the present state of the art in the field of d.n. spectroscopy.

All these spectra were transformed to the 10 group energy structure and subsequently folded with the normalized efficiency functions of the three detectors. The count ratios were then calculated, and compared to the experimental count ratios (Table IV). The errors in the experimental ratios are determined from the counting data. For the calculation of the uncertainties in the calculated ratios, we assumed that the errors in the published spectra are in the order of 20% for all energy groups. This figure is perhaps high compared with what the authors report but we feel that they have not included all sources of possible error in their quoted uncertainties. The uncertainties in the efficiency functions were taken from the MONK calculation. The uncertainties in the spectra and the efficiency functions were then propagated into the calculated count ratios using standard methods.

The results of Table IV show a big discrepancy between the experimental and the calculated ratios, well outside the quoted uncertainties. The smaller value of calculated ratios compared with the experimental ones suggests that all three spectra are too soft. In the case of the Saphier et al (15) spectrum the energy range excludes both low and high energy neutrons.

The observed inconsistency could partly be attributed to the fact that the three spectra do not carry identical information, because the energy of the neutrons inducing fission was different in each case. The Weaver et al (17) spectrum used in our analysis was obtained with incident neutrons of 940 KeV energy. The Eccleston and Woodruff (16) spectrum was obtained with incident neutrons of an approximately prompt fission spectrum. Only the Saphier et al (15) spectrum corresponds to thermal neutron induced fission and it is thus directly comparable with our measument. On the basis of our calculations one can suggest that the error associated with the mean energy of the Saphier et al (15) spectrum is in the order of 20%, although the authors do not quote any erros in their original paper. For the other two spectra the discrepancy cannot be explained as experimental error only. We suggest that the differences in the energies of the incidnet neutrons introduce a bias in the resulting d.n. energy distribution, and this is partly responsible for the discrepancies observed in this work.

REFERENCES

1. Keepin G.R., Physics of Nuclear Kinetics, Addison-Wesley Publishing Co (1963).

2. Tuttle R.J., Nucl. Sc. Eng. 56,p37 (1975).

3. Kratz K.L., in Proceedings of the consultants'meeting on delayed neutron properties, Vienna, March 1979.INDC (NDS)-107/G+Special, p. 103

4. Saphier D. and Yiftah S., Nucl.Sc.Eng.. 42, p. 272 (1970).

5. Synetos S. and Williams J.G.,Nucl. Energy, 22, p. 267 (1983).

6. Hammer Ph., Same as (3), p.1

7. Reeder P.L. et al, Phys.Rev.C 15, p. 2098 (1977).

8. Reeder P.L. and Warner R.A., same as (3), p. 239.

9. Sherriffs V.S.W.SRD R86,UKAEA (1978).

10. Bricka M. et al, IAEA-SM-167/19 (1971)

11. Maerker R.E. et al, ORNL-TM-3451 and 3465 (1971).

12. Evans A.E. and Krick M.S., ANS trans. 23, p. 491 (1976).

13. Lorch E.A., Int.J.Appl. Rad. Isot.,24 p. 590 (1973)

14. Burgy M. et al, Phys. Rev., 70, p. 104 (1946).

15. Saphier D. et al, Nucl. Sc. Eng., 62 p.660 (1977).

16. Eccleston G.W. and Woodruff G.L.,Nucl. Sc. and Eng. 62, p. 636 (1977).

17. Weaver D.R. et al, same as (3)

18. Shalev S. and Rudstam G., Nucl. Sc. and Eng. 51, p. 52 (1973).

19. Hughes D.J. et al, Phys. Rev., 73, p. 111 (1948).

20. Batchelor R. and McHyder H.R., J.Nucl. Eng., 3, p. 7 (1956)

21. Fieg G., J. Nucl. En, 26, p. 585 (1972)

22. England T.R. et al, Nucl. Sc. and Eng. 85, p. 139 (1983).

DIGITAL TECHNIQUES in Simulation, Communication and Control
Spyros G. Tzafestas (editor)
Elsevier Science Publishers B.V. (North-Holland) © IMACS, 1985

A GENERAL PURPOSE INSTRUMENT I/O PHILOSOPHY AND INTERFACE CONFIGURATION

C.C. LEFAS P.P. NIKOLAOU

Ministry of Physical Planning, Housing and the Environment, GREECE

The present paper describes the use of a desktop computer as a data logging or real time control system. This requires the design and construction of dedicated I/O cards which are inserted in the computer's backplane bus. The architecture of this approach is discussed and nonstructured approach is selected

1. INTRODUCTION

The cost of commercially available desktop computers is steadily been driven down in the last few years. In addition increased flexibility and sophistication is being offered. Sophisticated operating systems, several programming languages, graphics utilities are just some of the features offered in modern desktop computers. In several cases (e.g. in laboratories) the need to use them in diverse applications frequently arises but for only a short period. Such applications are data collection and real time control of experimental installations. The use of existing desktop computers is in several cases attractive not just because of reduced total costs but also because data logging in a machine familiar to the end user tends to create a more friendly environment for the processing of the data which may then be performed easily and efficiently. The problem of development overheads may not be accute in experimental setups, as it may look at a first glance, since practically in every experimental setup some time has to be spent to design the measurement system. The additional cost therefore involved in the development of dedicated I/O cards for a destop machine is diluted into the cost of development of proper sensing and signal conditioning equipment.

The present paper describes the problems of using a desktop computer based on the 68000 as a data collection system. The problems analyzed here are that of the architecture of the system. It is assumed that access is provided on the backplane bus of the computer where major control signals are assumed to be available. The physical implications is that the problem reduces to the design of dedicated I/O cards that are inserted in spare slots in the frame of the central computer rather than enclosing the cards in their own case. This has the advantage that the cards can be cooled by the mainframe fan with an increase in reliability and a larger amount of power than can be dissipated. Added to each card may be a metal backplate to reduce EMI and improved safety.

2. SYSTEM I/O ARCHITECTURE

There is a key issue for the design of efficient and reliable I/O at a low cost, i.e. the way in which the CPU (68000) communicates and interacts with the I/O interface electronics. Two basic schemes are examined. The first is microprocessor based where each I/O card contains a standard interface harware and a microprocessor with enough processing power to handle I/O related operations. In this case the communication between the I/O card and the mainframe CPU is on a relatively high level. The machine level I/O code of the mainframe CPU is the same for all I/O cards. The microprocessor on each interface handles the peculiarities associated with each external device.

The second interface method between the mainframe CPU and the I/O interface electronics is nonstructured. In this method the standardization of the I/O interface hardware is kept to a minimum. The I/O hardware is concerned more with the peculiarities of its particular external external device and is designed to provide these functions in an efficient manner. In this case the communication with the mainframe CPU is at a more primitive level. Each signal on the bus has only one meaning . In addition interrupt lines can be used if they are provided on the backplane bus.

The question which of the two approaches to use is answered by looking at the development overheads that each approach implies. In the software area the microprocessor solution appears in the first place to have an edge since the I/O access routines can be standardized for the mainframe CPU. This however is not so in practice. The task of writing I/O dedicated software is simply moved from the mainframe CPU to the peripheral processor. Additional tools are then required to debug and develop this software which are usually different than the ones available for the mainframe CPU which adds to the cost of the total system. On the other hand the nonstructred approach does not prohibit the standardization of the I/O routines, it merely moves them at a higher level in the operating system hierarchy. The driver routines that would be in the I/O processor move to the main CPU and are invoked each time an I/O interaction takes place. Thus the nonstructured approach provides more flexibility because only one set of development tools is required and software is developed in an environment familiar to the user.

On the hardware side there are many dedicated VLSI components available in the market today (e.g. IEEE 488 interfaces) of which a design might take advantage. For the I/O microprocessor approach the question arises on how such a dedicated device and the I/O microprocessor share the I/O tasks. Since the I/O processor is logically placed between the mainframe CPU and the external device, the mainframe CPU should talk to the dedicated device through the I/O processor. Of course the I/O card can be designed so that the mainframe CPU can also talk to a dedicated device directly but this tends to make the I/O processor redundant. Also this tends to make I/O routines specialized, which is a deviation from the standard I/O routine philosophy that is argued for the I/O processor approach. Finally there is also the goal to keep hardware down which favours the nonstructured approach. The I/O cards should take advantage of any available VLSI components dedicated to one job , so that greater reliability and less power dissipation is provided than with MSI discrete components.

Thus considering the advantages and disadvantages of both approaches and the practical problems of cost and board space the nonstructured approach has been chosen as the basic I/O philosophy.

3. INTERFACE DETAILS

Two types of I/O, usually provided on desktop computers, are considered in the present paper: programmed I/O and interrupt I/O. Fig 1 shows the signals on the backplane associated with each type. Most are signals of the 68000 CPU, usually buffered to provide the necessary drive for the bus. It should be noted that the bus is asynchronous, i.e. the system's clock is assumed to be unavailable on the backplane bus.

Therefore device synchronization is performed by I/O control signals. Such a design however is susceptible to skew problems between the information and the control signal caused by differences in capacitive loading and differences in logic path delays of the respective signals. Care therefore should be excercised to determine the worst situation that could arise in the system and cater for it, usually in the I/O driving routine and by selecting appropriate I/O card components.

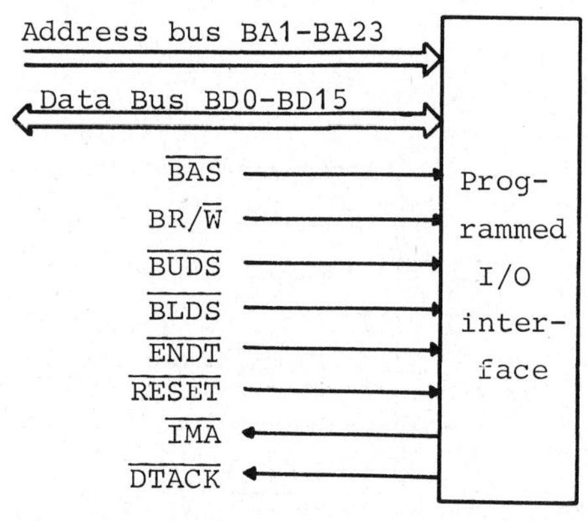

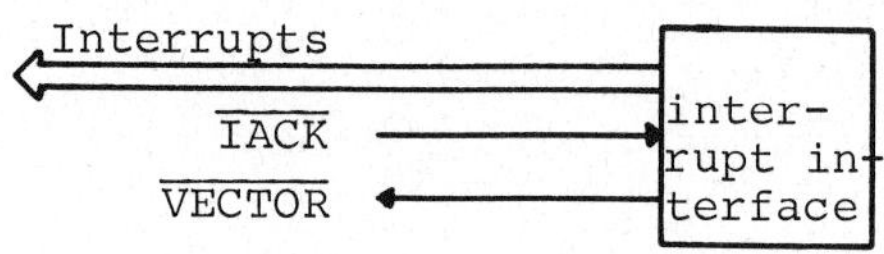

Fig 1

3.1 PROGRAMMED I/O

The programmed I/O interface caters for the basic communication between the main CPU and the external devices. Memory mapped I/O is used conforming with the capabilities of the 68000. Therefore I/O is accessed under program control via memory address mapping. Since memory and I/O are accessed in the same way they have to conform with the same timing specifications. Figs 2,3 show the timing of an I/O Read and I/O Write cycle. Just prior to the beginning of the cycle the buffered Read/Write (BR/$\overline{W}$) signal, the upper/lower data strobes ($\overline{BDS}$), and the data transfer acknowledge ($\overline{DTACK}$) signal are pulled high to ensure the proper data polarity at the

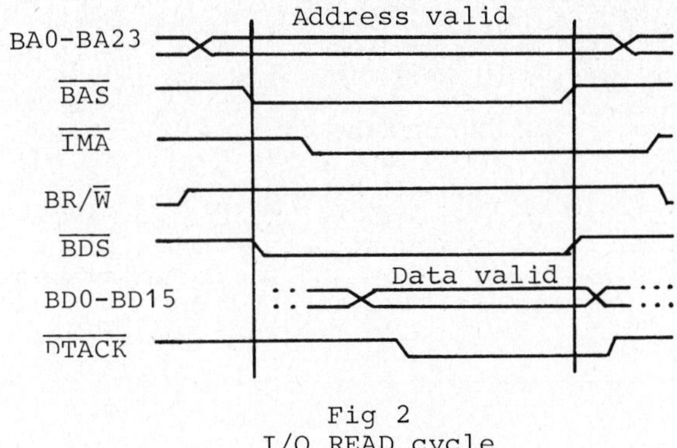

Fig 2
I/O READ cycle

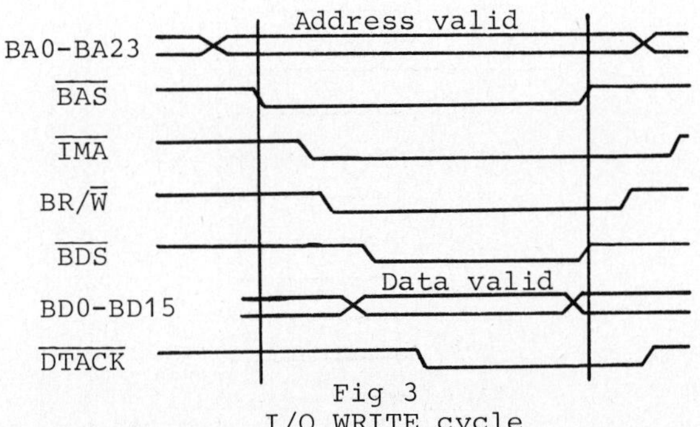

Fig 3
I/O WRITE cycle

beggining of the cycle. The bus master then defines the memory address to be read or written to by driving the address bits BA1-BA23. Note that BA0 is not available as address bus signal but is used only internally by the main CPU. The data bus is 16 bits wide and BA0 determines whether upper or lower byte is requireed in byte-oriented instructions. It appears therefore as upper/lower byte strobe on the backplane bus.

After allowing sufficient setup time for the address, the bus master pulls the $\overline{BAS}$ strobe signal low to indicate that the address is now valid. All cards connected to the bus decode the address using $\overline{BAS}$ as an enable signal to determine whether they contain this memory location or not. The addressed card responds by the $\overline{IMA}$ signal and holds the $\overline{DTACK}$ high while it is being accessed. The $\overline{IMA}$ is used by the logic of the mainframe CPU card to switch ON the appropriate data bus buffers. The main CPU also provides the appropriate $\overline{BDS}$ strobe concurrently with the $\overline{BAS}$ signals. Only now the addressed I/O card may switch its buffers ON since it knows that it is going to be involved in the memory cycle and data direction has been already defined. Note that for the Write cycle the buffered Read/Write signal is not defined properly until the $\overline{IMA}$ is properly produced so that a conflict could arise at the beggining of the Write cycle if the $\overline{BAS}$ signal is used alone to determine buffer switch ON.

Once the addressed card has placed the data on the bus and has allowed sufficient setup time, it pulls $\overline{DTACK}$ low to indicate the availability of valid data on the bus. The bus master detects the $\overline{DTACK}$ and latches the data asynchronously at its convenience. It then ends the cycle by pulling $\overline{BAS}$ and the $\overline{BDS}$ strobes high. This enables the addressed to identify the end of the cycle and releases the data from the data lines and cancels the $\overline{IMA}$ and $\overline{DTACK}$ signals.

The Write cycle is similar. All signals are the same as in the Read cycle up to and including the assertion of the $\overline{IMA}$ signal. The bus master then pulls the BR/$\overline{W}$ strobe low to indicate that this cycle is a Write cycle. Next the bus master places the data on the data lines and after the proper setup time asserts the $\overline{BDS}$ strobes to indicate the availability of the data. The addressed I/O card detects the data strobes and stores the available data. Then it pulls the $\overline{DTACK}$ strobe low to indicate that the cycle can end. The bus master detects the $\overline{DTACK}$ signal and removes the $\overline{BDS}$ and $\overline{BAS}$ strobes. The I/O card then cancels its $\overline{IMA}$ and $\overline{DTACK}$ signals.

The protocol described above is practically an asynchronous handshake scheme. The address and data strobes provide the sourcing information. The $\overline{DTACK}$ signal provides the response of the I/O card. As a last feature the bus cycles should be provided with a time trap to detect the failure of an I/O card to respond within certain time limits.

3.2 INTERRUPT I/O

Interrupt I/O provides the ability to external devices to interrupt the normal instruction execution sequence of the main CPU. The 68000 provides 7 interrupt priority levels of hardware interrupt. External devices are assigned levels higher than internal pripherals for the following reason. The human interface is of secondary importance to external devices in real time control and data logging applications. On the high priority end the highest prioti-ty level should be reserved for the RESET key to provide the user with full control over his equipment. In practice no more than two interrupt levels are required for data logging applications. More may be required for real time control situations.

4. DISCUSSION

A simple hardware expansion scheme for desktop computers has been described so that they may be used for real time data logging and real time control applications

DIGITAL TECHNIQUES in Simulation, Communication and Control
Spyros G. Tzafestas (editor)
Elsevier Science Publishers B.V. (North-Holland) © IMACS, 1985

EXPERIMENT CONTROL: A SYSTEMATIC APPROACH

Miodrag Askrabic*, Genadii P. Maliushonok**, Rajko Milovanovic*

*ENERGOINVEST Institute for Computer and Information Systems (IRIS), Sarajevo, Yugoslavia
**Institute for High Temperature of the Academy of Sciences (IVTAN), Moscow, USSR

This paper presents a systematic approach to the design of the general purpose experiment control system. Both the formulation of experimental set up and the hardware and software structure of the adequate experiment control system are presented. The main features, development and scope of use are also discussed.

1. INTRODUCTION

Increasing intensity and cost of scientific research is a very important motivation for the development of experimental control system. Higher degree of utilisation of the computing equipment and lesser involvement of the experimenter in activities that are not his prime interest are achieved with the aid of the general purpose experimental control system. A very high level formulation of experiment set-up, control and supervision tasks allow the researcher to concentrate on the essence of his problem and experimental research. This paper presents the development of such a system. Its basic hardware and software, as well as its main features and scope of use are discussed.

2. THE EXPERIMENT CONTROL SYSTEM

2.1 Background

The experiment control system (ECOS) presented here includes one or more microcomputers, process interfaces, mostly based on the IEEE-583 standard (CAMAC), experiment control software, human interface devices and other special devices. ECOS has some special features in comparison to standard control systems, namely:

- control of the very fast process,
- more frequent changes,
- acquisition of large data sets,
- communication with highly skilled and demanding operator,
- more complex data processing.

Main features of the ECOS are in particular:

- automated experiment preparation,
- experiment control and supervision,
- stopping the experiment,
- data acquisition according to a given algorithm,
- data processing during and after experiment,
- interpretation analysis at the end of experiment,
- interactive operation,
- data base updating and different and complex data processing after experiment has ended.

2.2 Hardware Structure

Efficient and modular hardware structure is necessary for achieving expected system performances. The system outlined is designed with a number of standard components, used elsewhere for similar systems.

The process interface chosen is CAMAC, specially designed for the experiment automation. The CAMAC is of the modular type and simple for manipulation, reconfiguration, utilization and maintenance by an operator non familiar with electronics. The central intelligence of a high level "experiment control system" is a computer, micro or mini. Our choice was DEC, and DEC compatible computer family, used frequently in similar systems. Fig. 1 presents several possible system configurations. The link between the computer and interface may be either parallel or serial.

2.3 Experiment Control Software

ECOS is a tool rather than an end by itself. It is often necessary to modify it from time to time as the experiment is progressing in order to realize different variants and solutions, or develop new measurement instrumentation. Solutions that can be modified by software without reprogramming are more suitable for the experimenter. In this way, the operator can set up the specifications of a family of experiments, rather than of a single fixed experiment. Setting different parameters (start time, acquisition time, experiment control algorithm etc), and changing structures of ECOS, adding new variables to be scanned, the experimenter has more freedom to experiment realisation and solution work. This requirement for easy modification maintenance, and high level of system abstraction and formalisation leads to the structure shown in fig. 3. ECOS software consists of

* system software (fig. 2)
* special software: an extension of system software, making the experimenter capable of specifying experimental tasks in a very high level, natural-like language, rather than

programming in a lower level language (e.g. assembler language),

* application software (experimental task specification, special data processing, characteristic for particular experiments).

2.4 Software Structure

Both synthetic and analytic methods are used for ECOS development. A synthetic method is concerned with using structured and modular programming, to develop reliable software. Top-down design, step-wise refinement, formal specification and very high level of abstraction are included too.

Analytic methods are primarily used for testing and validating a program after it has been designed and implemented, in order to improve its reliability and correctness. Basic components of ECOS special software are:

*INTERPRETER for experiment control (IRISON, fig. 3),
*LBASE, local data base,
*MONITOR, real-time executive,
*ULIB, library of common data processing functions,
*DIALOG, man-machine communication.

The INTERPRETER supports the operator to specify the actions in a very high level, non-procedural language (what is to be done rather than how to do it). The syntax of INTERPRETER (fig. 4) is of a natural-language-like type. The sentence of the program consists of: verb (function or action), noun (objects and their attributes in data base), conditional clause (whether the action should be performed, event (specific object at data base), computation, and some syntactic action. This subsystem consists of two components: parser and translator to stack machine "code", and "code" interpreter.

The INTERPRETER is suitable for the description of the experimenter's actions, and the referencing of objects of the experiment. To make ECOS more flexible and more modular, action description is separated from objects and data definition.

For data description we use a special data base management system for experiment control (LBASE, fig. 3). LBASE is designed such that the operator knows what an object or attribute of objects means, rather than how it is referenced.

The MONITOR is an event-driven executive that interprets the data from LBASE, the stack-machine code of INTERPRETER and the commands of operator executing tasks of experiments. In ECOS, an event is a significant time instant when something is happening, causing appropriate actions. An event may be deterministic (time-out, absolute or relative) or non-deterministic (interrupt from the process, signal value above the limit, operator command).

DIALOG is man-machine interface for ECOS. It has support for three languages: Serbocroat, Russian, and English. There are two modes of the dialog between the experimenter and system:
a) machine-driven dialog, with three submodes:

- long explanation on what the operator should do and how to do it using the available menu (for beginners),
- short explanation, with menu too,
- expected answer only, without any explanation (for operators well-acquainted with the system).

b) Man-driven dialog, essentially represented by INTERPRETER. Fig. 5 shows the structure of DIALOG.

The experimenter-operator selects the dialog mode at the beginning of communication and can change it during communication.

GEN is a software tool for particular system generation and modification.

3. CONCLUDING REMARKS

This article has outlined a systematic approach for experiment control system design. It has presented a recent development of a system like this including its basic characteristics.

Several important worth-noting features of the system are:

(i) It is easy to learn, manipulate and maintain,
(ii) experiment tasks can be easily specified,
(iii) new experimental input/output points and hardware components can be easily added into the system,
(iv) a minimum of writing is required for experiment specification and programming,
(v) it involves a natural-language-like dialog and subsequent interpretation.

4. REFERENCES

1. H.E. Pike, "Process control software", Proc. IEEE, vol. 58, No. 1, 1970.
2. T.G. Gaspar, "New process language uses English terms", Control Eng. 15, No. 10, 1968.
3. M. Askrabic, "Data Structure at Data Acquisition Systems", M.Sc. Thesis, Belgrade, 1983.
4. M. Askrabic, "Use of Interpreter at SCADA design", Proc. of Jahorina Symp., Sarajevo, 1982.
5. S.E. Madnick, "Operating Systems", New York, 1974.

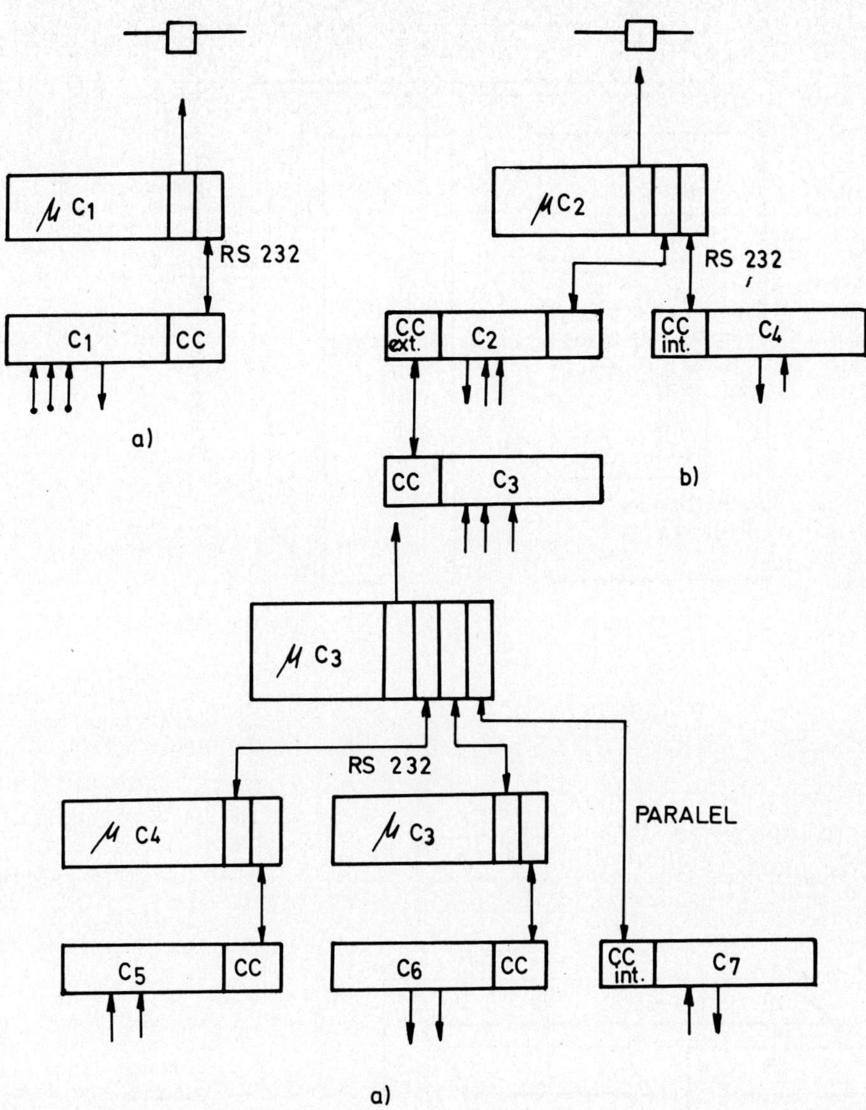
μ C1
RS 232
C1
CC
a)
μC2
RS 232
CC ext.
C2
CC int.
C4
CC
C3
b)
μ C3
RS 232
PARALEL
μ C4
μ C3
C5
CC
C6
CC
CC int.
C7
a)

Fig. 1.

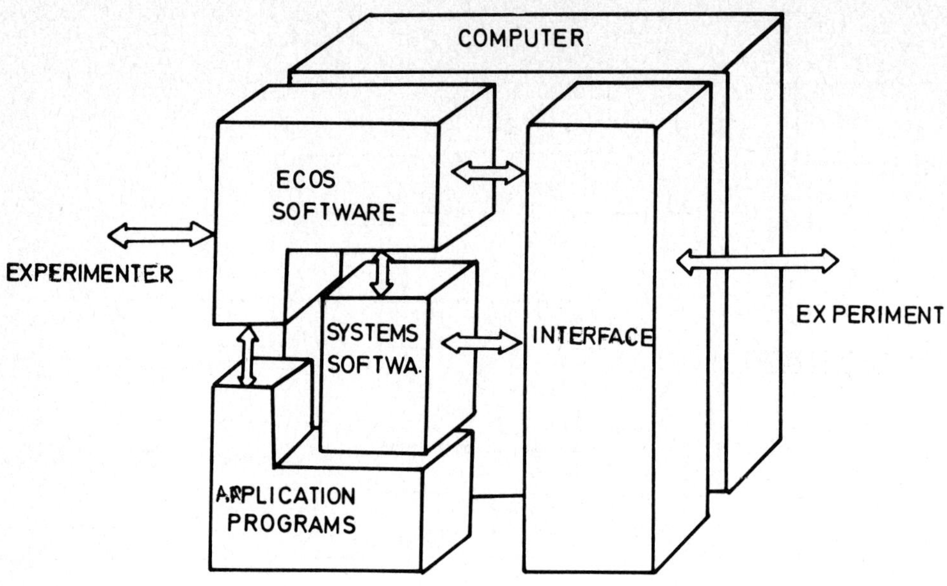

Fig.2.ECOS

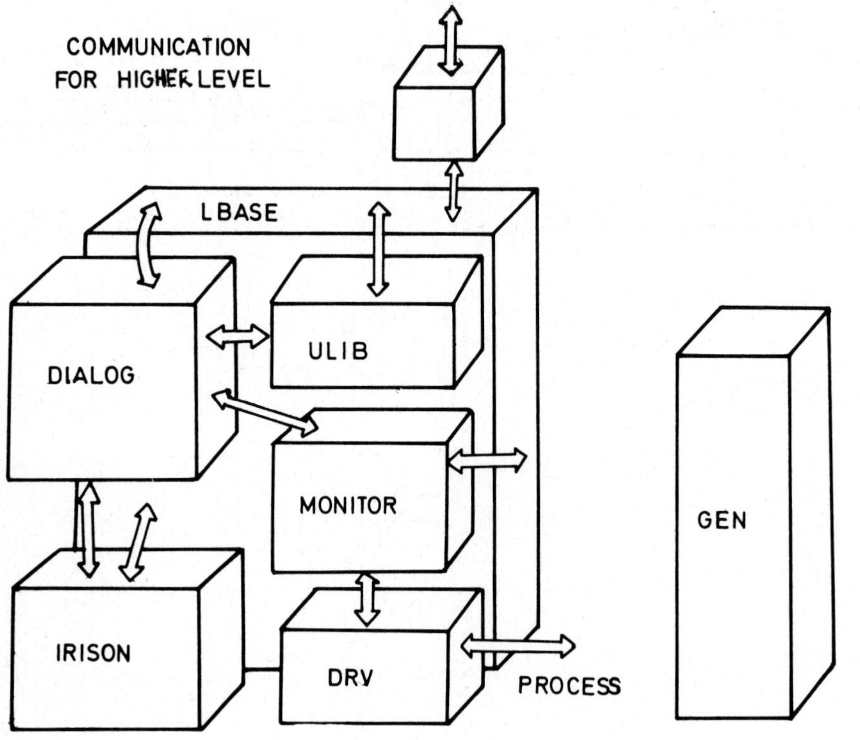

Fig. 3.

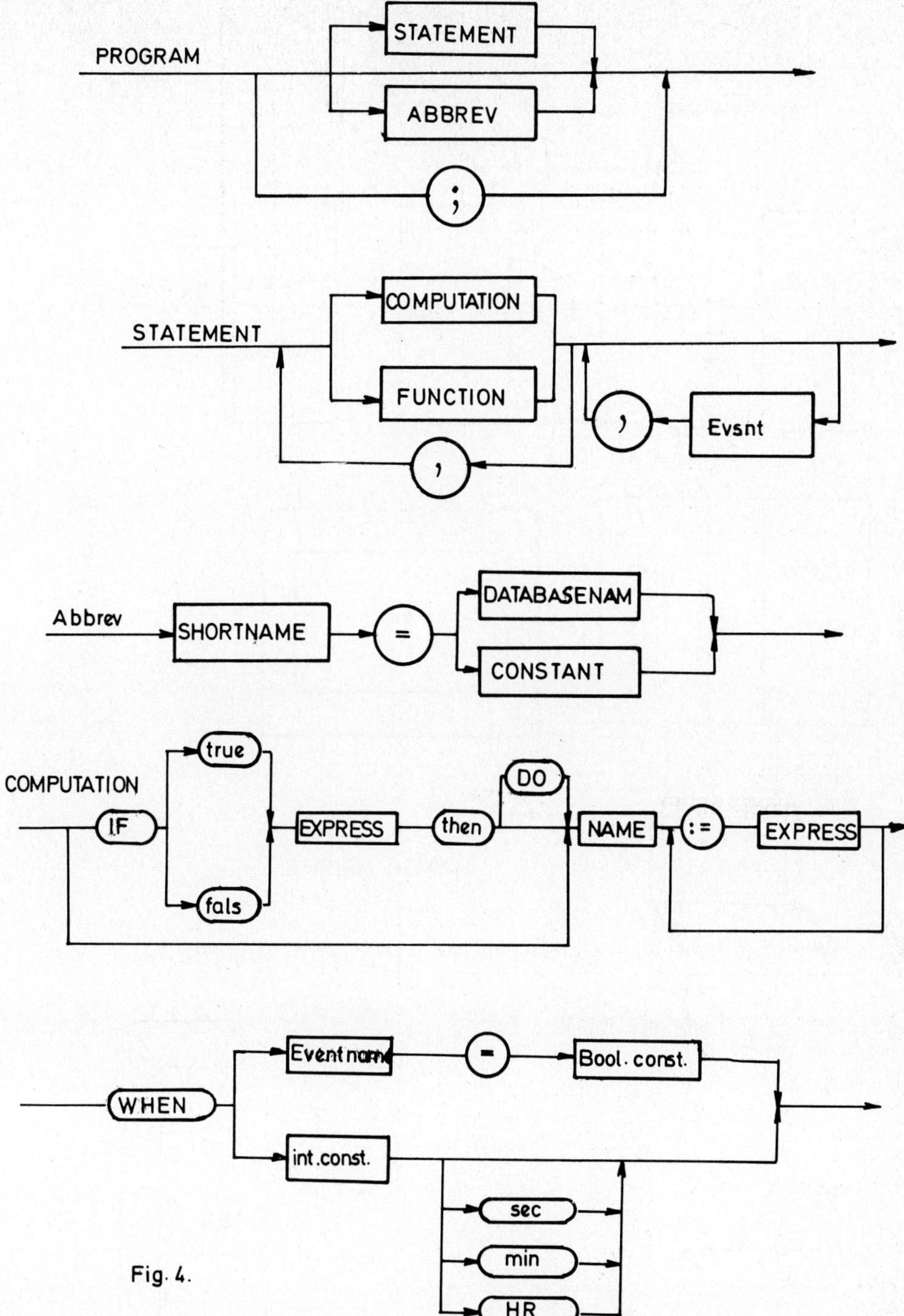
PROGRAM
STATEMENT
ABBREV
;
STATEMENT
COMPUTATION
FUNCTION
,
,
Evsnt
Abbrev
SHORTNAME
=
DATABASENAM
CONSTANT
COMPUTATION
IF
true
fals
EXPRESS
then
DO
NAME
:=
EXPRESS
WHEN
Event name
=
Bool. const.
int.const.
sec
min
HR

Fig. 4.

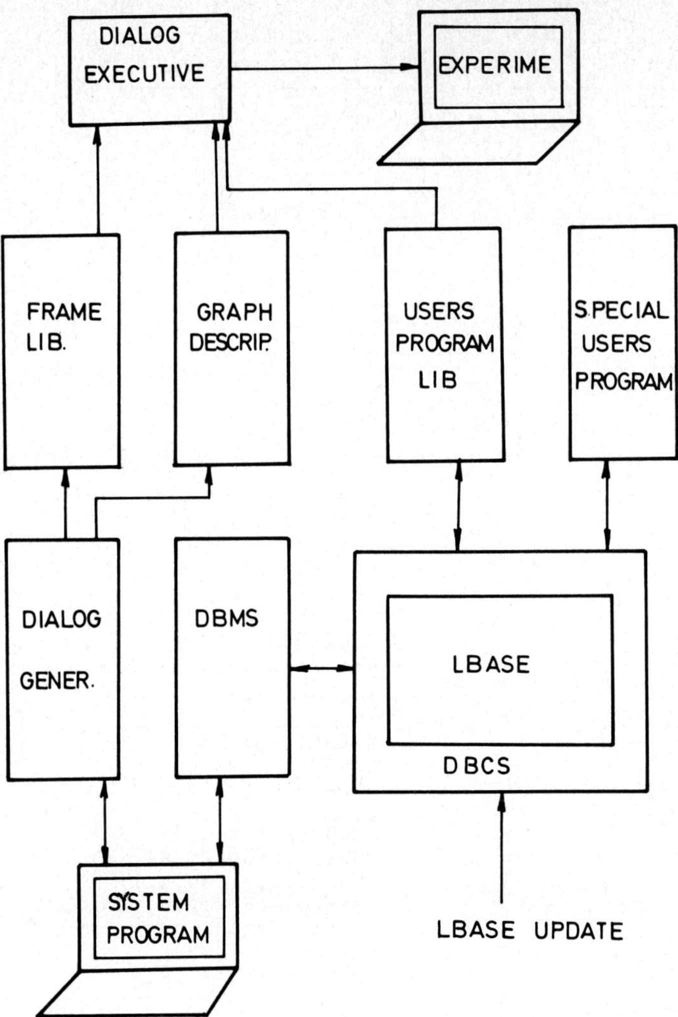
DIALOG
EXECUTIVE
EXPERIME
FRAME
LIB.
GRAPH
DESCRIP.
USERS
PROGRAM
LIB
SPECIAL
USERS
PROGRAM
DIALOG
GENER.
DBMS
LBASE
DBCS
SYSTEM
PROGRAM
LBASE UPDATE

Fig. 5.

AUTHOR INDEX

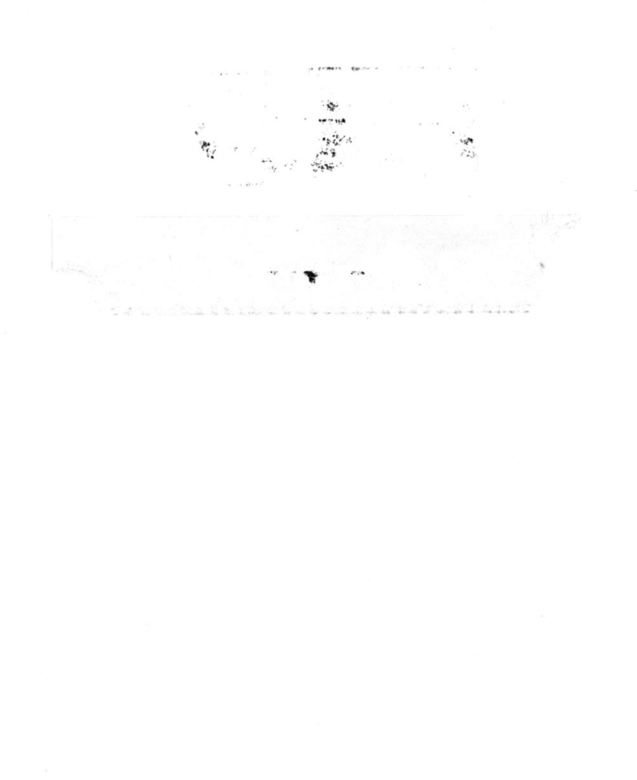